Sloinnte Zaebeal ır Zall
IRISH NAMES AND SURNAMES

COLLECTED AND EDITED
WITH
EXPLANATORY AND HISTORICAL NOTES

BY

REV. PATRICK WOULFE

Priest of the Diocese of Limerick
Member of the Council, National Academy of Ireland

baıle Áta Clıat
m. h. mac an Zoıll ⁊ a mac
DUBLIN
M. H. GILL & SON, LTD

1923

PRINTED AND BOUND BY
JOHN ENGLISH & CO.
WEXFORD

PREFACE

It is now nearly twenty-five years since I began to collect Irish names in one of the large towns of Lancashire. At that time there was still, in most of the industrial districts of England, a good sprinkling of Irish speakers, exiles of the famine years half a century before. Of those I met nearly all were from the West of Ireland. Not one of them, I am sure, is now living. In the course of two or three years I took down from them most of the names westward of a line drawn from Limerick to Sligo.

Those were the early days of the Irish Language Movement, when there was a great demand on the part of students for the Irish forms of their names, and I was urged to bring out in book form the names I had collected. My collection was, however, far too embryonic to admit of publication at that stage, and I decided before going to press to tap such remaining sources of information, oral and written, as were then accessible to me. My position as assistant chaplain to the Limerick Workhouse enabled me to get a good number of names from different parts of Munster, and my annual holidays for some years were spent in the same quest. In the autumn of 1905 I made an excursion to the Highlands of Scotland, where I became acquainted with Scottish Gaelic names. At the same time I sought, and in most instances received, lists of names from Irish scholars living in the various Irish-speaking districts, and the lists sent in for the Oireachtas prize (1901) were placed at my disposal by the Publication Committee of the Gaelic League. The result of seven or eight years' research was published in 1906, and though still far from complete, was exceedingly well received. A new edition was published in the spring of last year, enlarged by about sixty pages.

It was my intention from the beginning to add a second part containing explanatory and historical notes, but pressure of other work and the outbreak of the European

War, coupled with the difficulties of the task itself, delayed its publication until now. That the book has not suffered by the delay, I am confident. Long and patient study was required to strip our present English names of the various corruptions that in course of time had fastened upon them, trace them back to older forms, and bring to light and identify with them their Irish originals. That study I can now claim to have given to the subject. Whether I have been successful or not, it is for others to judge. I do not say that the book is free from error in every detail —that would be a rash thing to say—but I can honestly claim to have left nothing undone to make it as complete and reliable as possible.

On one point alone must I speak with considerable diffidence. Investigation into the meaning of ancient personal names is, in the most favourable circumstances, surrounded with great difficulty, but in the case of Irish names the task is rendered well-nigh impossible for want of a dictionary of Old and Middle Irish. To deal adequately with this portion of the work would require another volume as large as the present, but it cannot be satisfactorily undertaken until the publication of the Royal Irish Academy Dictionary is complete.

To give anything like a detailed history of the various families would be manifestly impossible within the compass of a single volume. Books as bulky as the present have been written on the history of more than one Irish family, and there are hundreds more whose history would supply material for a nice monograph. My aim has been rather to compress within the limits of a single volume such information as would be of interest to the ordinary Irish citizen.

To the gentlemen, clerical and lay, who sent me lists of names, I am deeply indebted, but above all I owe grateful acknowledgments to my friend, Rircéאրդ Ó ꞇoᵹlaᴅa, whose invaluable assistance I had in reading the proofs.

pádraiᵹ ᴅe búlb.

Kilmallock, May 18, 1923.

CONTENTS

ABBREVIATIONS

acc.—accusative.
adj.—adjectival.
angl.—anglice, anglicised.
Ang.-Sax.—Anglo-Saxon.
Celt.—Celtic.
Cf., cf.—compare.
comp.—compound.
dat.—dative.
der., deriv.—derivative.
des.—descendant.
dess.—descendants.
dim.—diminutive.
Eng.—English.
fem.—feminine.
Fr.—French.
Frank.—Frankish.
g., gen.—genitive.
Gen.—Genesis, Genealogies.
Ger.—German.
Gr.—Greek.
Heb.—Hebrew.

ibid.—ibidem, in the same place.
id.—idem, the same.
i.e.—id est, that is.
Ir.—Irish.
Lat.—Latin, latinised.
masc.—masculine.
Mid. Eng.—Middle English.
Mid. Ir.—Middle Irish.
mod. Fr.—modern French.
Nom.—nominative.
Nor.—Norman.
Nor. Fr.—Norman French.
Old Eng.—Old English.
O. Fr., Old Fr.—Old French.
Old Ir.—Old Irish.
q.v.—which see.
Teut.—Teutonic.
V., v.—see.
var.—variant, variants.
voc.—vocative.

N.B.—Special Abbreviations employed in the lists in Part I
are given at pp. 42-5.

INTRODUCTION

In early times, when the population of Ireland was small and scattered, one name generally sufficed to designate each individual, and one name, as a rule, is all that we find. A man was known to his neighbours as Aᴘᴄ, or Conn, or ꞃɪᴀʟʟ, and as long as there was no one else of the same name in the locality nothing more was required to complete the identification. Personal names were, of course, far more numerous then than now, and it was by no means difficult for each individual in an average Irish community to have a distinct name all to himself. But surnames or family names, as we understand them, were unknown. The Irish had, indeed, from a remote period a well-established system of clan-names, formed from the names of distinguished ancestors, as : Uí ꞃéɪʟʟ, descendants of Niall of the Nine Hostages, in Meath and Ulster ; Uí ꞃꞃɪúɪn, descendants of his brother Brian (or Brion), in Connacht and Breifney ; Eoᵹᴀnᴀᴄᴄ and ᴐᴀʟ ᵹᴄᴀɪꞃ, descendants of Eoghan Mor and Cormac Cas respectively, in Munster ; but these names were ordinarily used in the plural and as a common designation of the whole clan. For the individual the single name was the rule.

Nor was this peculiar to Ireland. The Bible is, of course, our oldest record of human nomenclature. There all the names, at least in the earlier books, are single appellations—Abraham, Isaac, Jacob, Joseph, David— given for the most part from some circumstance of birth or as an expression of some religious sentiment. Among the Greeks, too, and the early Romans, the same practice prevailed. The use of the single name was, in fact, universal among the nations of antiquity.

That personal names were originally all significant, there can be no doubt. In the earliest times it must have been so, for without a pre-existing stock to draw from, names, if given at all, could only be given out of the spoken language of the people by whom they were first imposed. The same is true of primitive peoples everywhere. As a matter of fact, the use of proper names only becomes general in a more or less advanced stage of civilisation, when the spoken tongue has drifted away from its primitive form, and intercourse with foreign nations makes possible the use of archaic and exotic words, the meaning of which is commonly unknown. Among the negroes of certain African tribes there are no proper names, nor is the need for them felt, their want being fully supplied by the general use of nicknames. The difference between these two classes of appellations is this : a proper name is given, altogether independently of its meaning, for the sole purpose of distinguishing him on whom it is bestowed from all others ; while a nickname is given precisely because of its signification and as a description of him on whom it is imposed, who is thereby marked off from others by some personal characteristic which distinguishes him being brought into prominence. When, therefore, a name is given because of its signification, it is a nickname ; when given independently of its signification, it is a proper name. All personal names were originally nicknames, in the sense that they were significant and descriptive.

The facility with which nicknames lose their descriptive character tends to convert them rapidly into proper names. Take, for example, the Irish name Oubᵹiolla, meaning ' black youth.' As originally employed, it was without doubt a nickname descriptive of the person on whom it was first imposed. But if Oubᵹiolla lived long enough, there came a time when he was no longer a ' black youth,' but a grey-haired old man. The name had thus already ceased to be descriptive. Suppose Oubᵹiolla had a grandson called after him, but who was not black like his grandfather but fair, here the name would be no longer descriptive, would not even be given because of its signification, but rather quite independently of it—would, in fact, have already become a proper name. And once a name got adopted into a family, the tendency was to perpetuate it and pass it on from one generation to another independently of its original signification.

Few, if any, of our present names have a meaning for the unlearned. Most of them are archaic words which were once part and parcel of the common speech of our ancestors, but now discharge no other function but that of distinguishing between persons. Others are borrowed names that had each a meaning in the original language to which it belonged ; but unlike common words which when translated bring their meaning with them, proper names, having no need of a meaning to serve their purpose, lose whatever meaning they had when taken from their original language. There is scarcely a civilised people but has some names which have no meaning, or of which the meaning has so far remained a mystery. Some of these have come down from ancient languages now lost ; others are exotic words which have undergone such changes that it is impossible to trace their roots. Proper names, too, are in a special way exposed to corrupting influences which tend to disfigure their form and hide their original meaning. Not the least important of these is the practice of forming ' pet ' names, which in turn become the starting point of new names bearing often not the slightest resemblance to the original.

The main sources from which names were originally derived may be enumerated under the following heads : religion and mythology ; circumstances connected with the birth ; physical, mental, or moral qualities or defects ; animal characteristics ; dress ; rank, occupation, office ; trees, fruits, flowers ; weapons ; abstract ideas.

The dithemetic character of the Aryan or Indo-European system of name-giving, which was common to all the Aryan races with the striking exception of the Romans, is well exemplified in the case of many of our Irish names. The Aryan name in full was a compound of two elements placed side by side without anything to show their grammatical relationship. The elements are usually epithets drawn from the strenuous and warlike aspects of life. Animal names may form one of the elements, the wolf and the bear being prominent. Religion naturally enters largely into these compounds. Some nations, like the Greeks and Anglo-Saxons, made the name show descent from father or grandfather, and, according to Professor Weekley, a very common practice was to compound the name from that of the father and mother, somewhat after the practice followed by modern racehorse owners. As a consequence of this genealogical practice, the meanings of dithemetic names are not always consistent, and in interpreting them one can only indicate the general idea which each part expressed.

The single-name system, which, as I have said, was universal in the beginning, after a time broke down. With the growth of population, or as one name outstripped others in popularity, difficulties of identification arose. Namesakes were necessarily multiplied and the single name was no longer sufficient in many cases to particularise the individual, with the result that a further distinction became a necessity.

From an early period we find the patronymic in use for this purpose. Irish patronymics were formed by prefixing ᵐᴀᴄ to the genitive case of the father's name, or uᴀ (or Ó) to that of the grandfather, and the Irish Annals are full of designations of this character. Coᴩᵐᴀc ᵐᴀcᴀᴉᴩᴄ (Cormac, son of Art) and Lᴀoᵹᴀᴉᴩe ᵐᴀcᴨéᴉʟʟ (Leary, son of Niall), among the names of our early kings, are examples. In addition to this there were descriptive epithets of various kinds. Some personal characteristic, physical, mental, or moral, complimentary or the reverse, the trade one followed, or the place where he was born, or was fostered, or lived ; one or other of these—it mattered not which—gave rise to a sobriquet which attached itself to the name and like the patronymic served to give increased individuality to the bearer. Epithets denoting age, size, shape, peculiarities of complexion, existed in endless variety, and instances of their use are to be found in every page of the Annals. This system of distinguishing between namesakes was extremely common at every period of Irish history and still survives in a modified form in Irish-speaking and semi-Irish-speaking districts, especially where the same surname largely prevails.

Nor, any more than in the case of the single name, was it peculiar to Ireland. As long as men are living in small and isolated communities there is little danger of confusion in the use of single names, especially when the stock of names is very large ; but when people congregate together in a town or city, with the same name common to several individuals, difficulties of identification must necessarily at once arise. As Canon Bardsley observes, we cannot imagine to ourselves how such a population as that of Manchester or Birmingham could possibly get on with but single appellations. It is no wonder then that in the later books of Moses we should find the Israelites falling back on the patronymic as a means of identifying the individual. ' Joshua, son of Nun ' is a type of name of frequent occurrence ; and in the New Testament we have not only ' Simon Barjonas,' that is, Simon, son of Jonas, but also ' Simon Zelotes ' and ' Simon the Leper ' and ' Simon of Cyrene.' Among the Greeks and Romans the same custom prevailed, since there was the same need.

Of all ancient peoples, the Roman patricians had the most precise and elaborate system of nomenclature, a system which had already reached its full development at the dawn of history. The few facts which have reached us from times anterior to the taking of Rome by the Gauls are traditional and so far conjectural, but there is every reason to believe that the early Romans, like all other ancient peoples, were called by single names, with the occasional addition of a distinguishing epithet. Within historical times, however, while the slave was still known by a single name indicative of his place of origin or some other characteristic, the freeman had three names, the *praenomen*, or forename, corresponding to our baptismal name, the *nomen*, or name of his *gens*, what we might term his clan-name, and the *cognomen*, or family name, which corresponded to our present surname. ' Marcus Tullius Cicero ' and ' Caius Julius Caesar ' are examples of the type of name ordinarily borne by a Roman citizen. In addition to these, some persons had what was called an *agnomen*, or an appendage to the name proper, as Publius Cornelius Scipio Africanus. With the overthrow of the Empire this system was lost ; the patricians who bore these names fled or were exterminated ; and there remained only the common people who, like the barbarians themselves, had been content with single names.

The Celts of Gaul, before the conquest of their country by the Romans, were called each by a proper name, to which was added, when there was need to avoid confusion, either an epithet implying personal description or the name of the father in the genitive case followed by the word *cnos* (son), as Atengnatos Druti-cnos (Atengnatos, son of Drutos), Andecamulos Toutissi-cnos (Andecamulos, son of Toutissus).* Similarly, the Anglo-Saxons used *ing* as a termination to express sonship, as Baducing (son of Baduc), Cidding (son of Cidda or Cydda).

After the fall of the Western Empire the loss of hereditary names was in part supplied by the use of patronymics. These, which were general among all the Latin peoples, were formed from the genitive case of the father's name preceded by the word *filius* (son), expressed or understood, as Petrus filius Martini, or simply Petrus Martini (Peter, son of Martin). Among the Normans, who borrowed it from the French, *filius* was represented by the corrupt form *fitz*, as fitzGerald, fitzSimon. But in the spoken language everywhere the prefix was soon dropped ; among the French, even the genitive termination fell off and the patronymic finally came to be merely the father's name in its simple and unaltered form such as we now see it in so many surnames of Norman origin. Among the Spaniards, filiation was shown by the ending -ez, as in Rodriguez (son of Rodrigo or Roderick), Gonzalez (son of

*This word, *cnos*, is now represented by the diminutive termination -án, found in so many Irish names, as Conán, Dallán, &c.

Gonzalo), Fernandez (son of Fernando).* The Basques employed for the same purpose the ending -ana or -ena, as Lorenzana (son of Lorenzo or Laurence), Juanena (son of Juan or John), Michelena (son of Michael).

Welsh patronymics were formed by prefixing Mab or Map (son), shortened to ab or ap, as ab Evan, now Bevan, ab Owen, now Bowen, ap Howel, now Howel and Powell.

Among the Teutonic races the patronymic ending was -son, or its cognates -shon, -sen, -zon, as English : William-son, Richardson ; German : Mendelsshon, Davidshon ; Danish : Andersen, Jansen ; Dutch : Janzon or Jantzon ; Swedish and Norwegian : Olsen, Petersen, Magnussen ; and among the Slavonic races, -vich, -evich, -wicz, -ich, -vitch, -evitch, -itch, -off and -eff, so common in Russian and Polish names. The Polish -ski is an adjectival suffix, like the Irish -ᴀċ, which is added to place-names to form surnames ; with names of women it becomes -ska.

In the early Middle Ages the use of epithets or nick-names for the purpose of distinguishing individuals of the same name was also very common throughout Western Europe. As in the case of the patronymic, it was probably a result of the loss of hereditary names in the barbarian invasions. Many of these epithets have come down to our own time in the form of surnames. Thus arose in France such surnames as ' le Grand,' ' le Fort,' ' le Bon,' and in Germany ' Roth,' ' Weiss,' ' Schwarz,' ' Schneider,' &c. Designations derived from place of birth or residence were very frequent. In France and Spain these were characterised by the use of the preposition ' de ' ; in Italy, of ' di ' and ' da ' ; in Germany, of ' von ' ; in Holland, of ' van,' corresponding to the English ' of.'

*The origin of this Spanish name-genitive in -ez has been much discussed. Harrison does not think there is any doubt that it is the old Teutonic genitive suffix -es (Gothic -is), though he quotes a German writer on nomenclature who affirmed that it represented the Latin -icius. Letelier, the Spanish writer, also says it was a Latin ending. In documents of date prior to the 10th century it was written -izi, as Federnandizi, Roderizi, &c. ; in those im-mediately after, Federnandiz, Roderiz, &c. ; while from the 11th century onwards, the modern form -ez was gradually substituted.

These second designations were not, however, surnames in the modern sense of that term. They were not fixed or hereditary, nor common to all the members of a family. The adjunct, whether descriptive or patronymic, was purely personal and ceased with him whom it described and to whose name it was attached. The son in due course got a designation of his own, but this again was no more hereditary than his father's before him. And so things went on for several centuries, only as population grew and the number of namesakes increased the difficulties of identification became every day greater, until at length individuals could only be described by a complete string of patronymics or by a number of epithets and patronymics combined.*

Surnames in the modern sense are the growth of the 10th and three succeeding centuries. During that period the patronymic, which before was purely personal and changed with each generation, gradually became fixed, like the clan-names centuries before, and began to assume the permanent and hereditary character of a family name. Canon Bardsley writes : " By a silent and unpremeditated movement over the whole of the more populated and civilised European societies, nomenclature began to assume a solid lasting basis. It was the result, in fact, of an insensibly growing necessity. Population was on the increase, commerce was spreading, and society was fast becoming corporate. With all this arose difficulties of individualisation. Is was impossible, without some further distinction, to maintain the current identity. Hence what had been but an occasional and irregular custom became a fixed and general practice—the distin guishing sobriquet, not, as I say of premeditation, but by a silent compact, became part and parcel of a man's pro-

*The father of Saul is described in the First Book of Kings (IX, 1) as " Cis, son of Abiel, son of Seror, son of Bechorath, son of Aphia, son of a man of Jemini." As an example of a Welsh patronymic, the following has often been quoted : " Jenkin ap Griffith ap Robin ap William ap Rees ap Evan." With these we may compare many entries in the Irish Annals of the 9th and 10th century.

perty, and passed on with his other possessions to his direct descendants."*

The period at which this change began can only be determined approximately. It is stated by Keating and others, and the statement has been adopted by O'Curry, that surnames first became fixed in the reign of Brian Boru (A.D. 1002-1014) and in obedience to an ordinance of that monarch. O'Curry's words are :—

" Previous to the time of Brian Boroimhe (about the year 1000), there was no general system of family names in Erinn ; but every man took the name either of his father or his grandfather for a surname. Brian, however, established a new and most convenient arrangement, namely, that families in the future should take permanent names, either those of their immediate fathers, or of any person more remote in their line of pedigree."†

Now, if this were true, Brian himself, as the originator of the system, should have been the first to set the example of obedience to his own laws. But Brian never adopted a hereditary surname. Nor did his sons. It was only in the time of his grandsons that the surname Ó Bριαιη (O'Brien) first came into existence. It is clear that the new system was of gradual growth and that it arose, as Bardsley remarks, out of the necessity of the time, rather than as part of a settled policy or according to any pre-arranged plan. Apart from the fact that royal ordinances of the kind described by O'Curry were unknown in Ireland before the Anglo-Norman invasion, and in the best of times would be difficult, if not impossible, to enforce, it can be shown from the Irish Annals that fixed surnames were already in process of formation before Brian was born and that the process was not complete until nearly two centuries after his death.

Ó Cléιρισ (O'Clery) was probably a fixed surname as early as the beginning of the 10th century, for we find the death of Τιξεαριας Uα Cléιρισ, lord of Aidhne, recorded in the Annals of the Four Masters at the year 916, and that of his brother ꝼLⱥnn Uⱥ CLéiꝑiᵹ, lord of South Connacht, who was slain by the men of Munster, at the year 950. I doubt if we have any older surname in Europe. Ó Cⱥnⱥnn-áin of Tirconaill is mentioned at 941; ᴅoṁnⱥLL Uⱥ ṅéiLL, the first of the O'Neills of Ulster, at 943; Uⱥ Ruⱥiꝑc of Breifney and Uⱥ Ciⱥꝑᴅⱥ (O'Keary) of Cairbre, at 952; mⱥᵹ ᴀonᵹuꝑⱥ (Maguiness) at 956; while Ó mⱥoLᴅoꝑⱥiᴅ (O'Muldory) of Tirconaill, Ó ᴅuᴅᴅⱥ (O'Dowd) of Tireragh, Ó CeⱥLLⱥiᵹ (O'Kelly) of Ui Maine, and many others were firmly established as surnames before the end of the century.

With a view to showing that the statement of Keating and others just referred to was more rhetorical than correct, Dr. O'Donovan drew up a list of the progenitors of various important Irish families, showing the periods at which, according to the Irish Annals, they flourished or died, the dates being taken for the most part from the Annals of Ulster or the Four Masters. This list, which cannot fail to be of interest to Irish readers, is here subjoined :

Fox (Sionnach) of Teffia, slain 1084.
MacCarthy of Desmond, slain 1043.
MacEgan of Ui Maine, flourished 940.
MacEochy, or Keogh, of Ui Maine, 1290.
MacGillapatrick of Ossory, slain 995.
MacMurrough of Leinster, died 1070.
MacNamara of Thomond, flourished 1074.
O'Boyle of Tirconnell, flourished 900.
O'Brien of Thomond, died 1014.
O'Byrne of Leinster, died 1050.
O'Cahill of Ui Fiachrach, flourished 900.
O'Callaghan of Desmond, flourished 1092.
O'Canannan of Tirconnell, flourished 950.
O'Clery of South Ui Fiachrach, flourished 850.
O'Conor of Connacht, died 974.
O'Connor of Corcomruadh, died 1002.
O'Connor of Offaly, died 977.
O'Dea of Thomond, flourished 1014.
O'Doherty of Tirconnell, flourished 901.

O'Donnell of Corca Bhaiscinn, slain 1014.
O'Donnell of Ui Maine, flourished 960.
O'Donnell of Tirconnell, flourished 950.
O'Donoghue of Desmond, flourished 1030.
O'Donovan, slain 976.
O'Dowda of Tireragh, flourished 876.
O'Dugan of Fermoy, flourished 1050.
O'Faelain of Decies, flourished 970.
O'Flaherty of Iar-Connacht, flourished 970.
O'Gallagher of Tirconnell, flourished 950.
O'Heyne of Ui Fiachrach, flourished 950.
O'Keeffe of Desmond, flourished 950.
O'Kelly of Ui Maine, flourished 874.
O'Kevan of Ui Fiachrach, flourished 876.
O'Loughlin of Burren, died 983.
O'Madden of Ui Maine, flourished 1009.
O'Mahony of Desmond, slain 1014.
O'Melaghlen of Meath, died 1022.
O'Molloy of Feara Ceall, slain 1019.
O'Muldory of Tirconnell, flourished 870.
O'Neill of Ulster, slain 919.
O'Quin of Thomond, flourished 970
O'Ruairc of Breifny, died 893.
O'Scanlan of Ui Fiachrach, flourished 946.
O'Shaughnessy of Ui Fiachrach, flourished 1100
O'Sullivan of Desmond, flourished 950.
O'Tuathail or O'Toole of Leinster, died 950.

From this list it will be seen that the ancestors of the most distinguished Irish families, whose names have been preserved in the surnames of their descendants, flourished at some period between the middle of the 9th and the end of the 13th century. In the case of families whose eponymous ancestor flourished in the 9th century, as O'Clery, O'Dowd, O'Kelly of Ui Maine, O'Kevan of Ui Fiachrach, O'Muldory of Tirconaill and O Ruairc of Breifney, the date when the surname became fixed cannot have been much later than the beginning of the 10th century, though it may not appear in the Annals until a considerable time after.

The date, at most, cannot have been more than sixty years from the period when the ancestor flourished or died ; but, indeed, there is no reason why the surname might not have become fixed even in his lifetime, as seems to have happened in the case of the family of Ó Canannáin of Tirconaill, where the surname is mentioned in the Annals at the year 941, while the *floruit* of the ancestor is set down at 950. The surname O'Neill of Ulster, which was taken from Niall Glundubh, Monarch of Ireland, slain in 919, appears in the Annals at the year 943. Instances where the ancestor flourished or died in the first half of the 10th century are numerous, as, besides those just mentioned, MacEgan, O'Cahill of Ui Fiachrach, O'Doherty, O'Donnell of Tirconaill, O'Gallagher, O'Heyne, O'Keeffe, O'Scanlan of Ui Fiachrach, O'Sullivan and O'Toole. All these must have been fixed surnames before Brian Boru began his reign and became such independently of any royal ordinance.

On the other hand, many surnames only came into existence long after Brian's time. Surnames like Mac-Giollapatrick (Fitzpatrick) of Ossory, O'Connor of Connacht, O'Connor of Offaly, O'Donovan, O'Phelan of Decies, O'Flaherty of Connacht, O'Loughlin of Burren, and O'Quin of Thomond, must have been already fixed in the early part of the 11th century ; but many others, as MacCarthy of Desmond, MacMurrough of Leinster, Mac-Namara of Thomond, O'Byrne, O'Callaghan, O'Dea, O'Donoghue of Desmond, O'Dugan of Fermoy, O'Melaghlen of Meath, O'Molloy of Feara Ceall and O'Shaughnessy, cannot have become fixed until long after Brian had been laid to rest at Armagh.

But while it cannot be admitted that our surnames owe their existence to any ordinance of Brian Boru, still many of them arose in his time. The 11th and 12th centuries must, however, be assigned as the period within which the great bulk of our Irish patronymics became fixed and began to assume the hereditary character of family names. The practice of forming surnames with Ua (or Ó) had almost certainly ceased before the coming of the English,

and I doubt if we have any Ó-surname that can be shown
to have arisen at a later date. Mac-surnames are,
generally speaking, of later date than Ó-surnames ; still
I think it must be admitted that by the end of the 12th
century surnames were universal among Irish families. It
is true, indeed, that they were not all at first of a lasting
character, and in some instances were laid aside after a
generation or two in favour of new surnames taken from
less remote ancestors. Thus Ó Roḃuiḃ was replaced by
Maɜ Oipeaċtaiɜ (Mageraghty), Ó Maolpuanaiḃ (O'Mulrooney), originally a branch of the O'Connors, by Mac
Oiapmaḋa (MacDermott), Ó ḧeoċaḋa (O'Heochy) by
Mac Ouinnpléiḃe (MacDunlevy), Ó ɜéapaḃáin (O'Geran)
by Maɜ Fionnḃaipp (Gaynor). It is also true that many
Mac-surnames of purely Irish origin are of later date than
the Anglo-Norman invasion, but this was due to the
breaking up of the old surnames into septs and the assumption of new surnames in Mac by branches that had
separated from the parent stock. After the Anglo-Norman
invasion, many of the great families began to split up into
septs, some of which took distinct surnames from the names
of their founders, even at a comparatively late period.
The instances are numerous. Thus the MacSweenys are,
according to MacFirbis, a branch of the O'Neills of Ulster ;
the MacMahons of Thomond, the MacConsidines and the
MacLysaghts, of the O'Briens ; the MacGoldricks of the
O'Rourkes ; the MacAuliffes of the MacCarthys ; the Mac-
Crohans and MacGillicudys, of the O'Sullivans ; the Mac-
Eochys, or Keoghs, of Connacht, of the O'Kellys of Ui
Maine ; the MacDermotts and MacManuses of Connacht,
of the O'Connors ; the MacDonoughs of Sligo, of the Mac-
Dermotts ; the MacGillykellys, or Kilkellys, of the O'Clerys ;
the MacDunlevys, of the O'Heochys of Ulidia ; the Mac-
Gilhoolys, of the O'Mulveys ; the MacSheedys and Mac-
Clancys of Thomond, of the MacNamaras ; the MacClos-
keys and MacAvenues, of the O'Kanes ; the MacDevitts
and MacConnellogues, of the O'Dohertys ; the MacCaffreys,
MacAwleys and MacManuses of Fermanagh, of the Maguires ; and so on. At what period this practice ceased

it is impossible to say with any degree of certainty, but it is well known that some of the foregoing surnames cannot be allowed a higher antiquity than the 13th or 14th century. I think we have a few surnames that originated only in the 16th.

It is a remarkable fact, though so far as I am aware hitherto unnoticed, that Ireland was the first country after the fall of the Western Empire to adopt hereditary surnames. I have already mentioned Ó Cléiμιζ as our oldest Irish surname ; and several others, as I have shown, were already fixed by the end of the 10th century. All these must be older than any other existing surnames in Europe. The oldest surnames on the Continent are those of France and Italy, especially the Province of Venice, but the earliest date assigned to them is the 11th century. Among the common people hereditary surnames were not universal until more than two or three centuries later.

Of surnames in England, William Camden, the oldest authority on the subject, in his ' Remaines concerning Britaine,' writes :

" As for my self, I never hitherto found any hereditary surname before the Conquest (1066), neither any that I know ; and yet both I my self and divers whom I know, have pored and pusled upon many an old Record and evidence to satisfie our selves herein ; and for my part I will acknowledge my self greatly indebted to them that will clear this doubt."

Freeman, in his History of the Norman Conquest of England, states that " in England before the Conquest there is no ascertained case of a strictly hereditary surname." " If the Norman Conquest had never happened," he writes, " it is almost certain we should have formed for ourselves a system of hereditary surnames. Still, as a matter of fact, the use of hereditary surnames begins in England with the Conquest, and it may be set down as one of its results."

The late Isaac Taylor, author of the celebrated ' Words and Places ' and ' Names and their Histories,' in a contribution to ' Notes and Queries ' (2nd Feb., 1901), writes :

"Surnames grew out of descriptive appellations, and the date at which they originated varied according to the locality and the person's rank in life. In the South we find them at the beginning of the 12th century. In the Northern counties they were not universal at the end of the 14th; and in remote parts of Wales, in the mining districts, and in the slums of Glasgow they are still unknown. They were first used by the barons and franklins, then by the tradesmen and artisans, and lastly by the labourers."*

The approximate date of the introduction of surnames in France is given by Camden as 1000, and that he was not much out in his calculation appears when comparison is made with the investigations of modern scholars. Monsieur H. de Gallier, in an essay on the origin of proper names in ' La Revue,' Paris, 1901, shows that the heredity of names was not evident in France before the 11th century, and then was confined to the nobility.†

Freeman writes : " At the time of the Norman invasion of England, the practice of hereditary surnames seems still to have been a novelty in Normandy, but a novelty that was fast taking root. The members of the great Norman houses already bore surnames, sometimes territorial, sometimes patronymic, of which the former class easily became hereditary."‡

In the Lowland Scottish towns the use of surnames began in the 12th century. The oldest Highland surnames, Mac Oubʒaill and Mac Oomnaill (MacDougall and MacDonald), only date from the 13th century. Oubʒaill, who was son of Somerled, flourished about 1200 ; Oomnaill, who was grandson of Somerled, about 1250. The surname Campbell is recorded somewhat later in the same century. Surnames were rare in the Highlands until the 16th and 17th centuries. Manx Gaelic surnames appear to have been formed about the same time as Scottish Gaelic surnames.

---

*Quoted by Harrison, Surnames of the United Kingdom, II, p. ii.
†Ibid. p. iii.
‡History of the Norman Conquest of England.

In regard to Wales, it is stated in the 16th Annual Report of the Registrar-General for England and Wales (1853) that " hereditary surnames were not in use even among the gentry of Wales until the time of Henry VIII, nor were they generally established until a much later period ; indeed, at the present day they can scarcely be said to be adopted among the lower classes in the wilder districts, where, as the marriage registers show, the Christian name of the father still frequently becomes the patronymic of the son."

In Scandinavian countries, as in Wales, surnames were of comparatively late introduction. Of Iceland, Baring-Gould, in his ' Family Names and their Story ' (1910) says that " to this day there does not exist a family name in the island pertaining to a native. Every man is known by his personal designation, and as the son of his father."[*]

Of surnames in Germany it has been said : " Family names did not come into general employ until late in the Middle Ages. First of all, the nobility in the 12th century called themselves after their ancestral seats, as Conrad von Wettin, Rudolf von Hapsburg ; then among the citizens they were adopted in the 14th century, but did not become general until the 16th century."[†]

Surnames were not general in Spain at the time of the discovery of the New World.

So tenaciously did the Jews stick to their single Hebrew names that it was only in the 18th and 19th century that they were forced by governmental action in Austria, Germany and France to adopt hereditary surnames.

Strictly speaking, all our Irish surnames are of patronymic origin, that is to say, formed from the names or other designations of ancestors by prefixing ṁac or Ó, and in that respect they differ most from English surnames in which the descriptive and local elements predominate. There are, however, some apparent exceptions. In districts where the same surname largely prevailed, epithets,

or, as we should now call them, nicknames, continued to
be used, as indeed they do to the present day, for the
purpose of distinguishing persons of the same name and
surname, and in some instances these in course of time
supplanted the real surnames. Strangers, too, were often
called by names indicative of their place of origin, as in
the case of the celebrated family of MacDunlevy, members
of which were known all over Ireland by the sobriquet of
ulⱦⱥᴄ in reference to their Ulidian origin. Similarly we
had muimneⱥᴄ (Munsterman), Lⱥⱶneⱥᴄ (Leinsterman),
ⱱéireⱥᴄ (Decian, native of the Decies of Waterford), &c.
All these families had, however, originally distinct surnames in mⱥᴄ or ó, but owing to constant disuse these
were in course of time forgotten and the epithet had
thenceforward to do duty instead. The distinctive mark,
therefore, of a real Irish surname is mⱥᴄ or ó, according
to the well-known lines :

> Per Mac atque O, tu veros cognoscis Hibernos ;
> His duobus demptis, nullus Hibernus adest ;

which have been translated :

> By Mac and O
> You'll always know
>   True Irishmen, they say ;
> But if they lack
> Both O and Mac,
>   No Irishmen are they.

But as we shall see in a moment, many surnames in ó and
mⱥᴄ are of foreign origin.

The only difference between a surname commencing
with mⱥᴄ and one commencing with ó is that the former
was taken from the name of the father and the latter from
that of the grandfather of the first person who bore the
surname. Dr. O'Donovan thought it " perhaps not improbable " that at the period when surnames first became
hereditary some families went back several generations to
select an illustrious ancestor from whom to take a surname,

but though his conjecture is supported by O'Curry, it seems to me altogether groundless, for the simple reason that surnames arose naturally without premeditation, and were given rather than taken. The idea certainly was that all the members of a family derived their origin from the ancestor whose name they bore in their surname ; but not all families of the same name are of the same origin. Every Murphy, for instance, is proclaimed by his surname to be descended from an ancestor named Muṙċaḋ, but not all the Murphys are descended from one original Muṙċaḋ, nor all the Caseys from one original Caṫaṙaċ.

Instead of Ó or Mac, ní, a contraction of ingean, daughter, was used in the surnames of women, as Máire ní Ḃriain (Mary O'Brien), and this is still the practice when speaking Irish. (See p. 27).

Let us now consider the effect of the invasions of the Norsemen and Anglo-Normans on our name-system.

It may be stated at once that we have no distinct class of surnames that can properly be termed Norse or Danish,* and that beyond the introduction of a certain number of new names the Norse invasions do not seem to have materially influenced our nomenclature. At the period of the Norse invasions, hereditary surnames, it will be remembered, were not yet in vogue, and whatever surnames were adopted at a later period by the Norsemen who settled down in Ireland were formed after the Irish fashion by prefixing Ó or Mac to the names or other designations of their ancestors. Meanwhile through intermarriages and other alliances of friendship with the Irish, they had been adopting Irish personal names. The

*The viking-settlements in Ireland, and particularly the kingdom of Dublin, were Norwegian, not Danish. This, of course, does not exclude the possibility that many Danes also lived in Ireland, just as in the Danish settlement Danelage in England, there was a considerable number of Norwegians. But the bulk of the people was Norwegian, and likewise the royal race of Dublin came from Norway.—Contributions to the History of the Norsemen in Ireland, by Dr. Alexander Bugge, 1900.

Landnámabók, which contain an account of the settlements
in Iceland from the 9th century to the middle of the 13th,
has a good number of Irish names which the invaders who
returned took back with them to their homes in the North ;
and even within the last century Finn Magnussen, or, as
we should call him in Irish, ᵽionn MacMaᵹnuiᵱ, a native
of Iceland, was the chief authority for Scandinavian
antiquities. Moreover, some of the Norsemen had, in
addition to their native names, names of a descriptive
character bestowed on them by the Irish, and were thus
known to the Irish by Irish names. Ouḃċeann and
Cúallaiḋ, the names of two of the sons of Ivar of Limerick,
were not Norse, but Irish, meaning respectively ' black-
head ' and ' wild-dog ' or ' wolf.' The Irish, in like manner,
borrowed names from the Norsemen, and some of the
names thus introduced have been popular ever since. As
a consequence of this interchange of names between the
two nations, a name, whether Norse or Irish, was, at the
period when surnames were being formed, no sure indication of nationality, and for the same reason it is now
impossible to say, judging merely from the surname,
whether a family is of Irish or Norse descent. A Norse
eponym, generally speaking, merely indicates a Norse
strain in the family, Norse names having been adopted by
the Irish mostly through intermarriages.

It is not, at the same time, an improbable conjecture
that Ó Ouḃᵹaill (O'Doyle), Ó hAᵱailc (O'Harold), Ó
hEanᵱaic (O'Henrick), Ó hÍomaiᵱ (O'Hure or Howard),
Mac Oiciᵱ (MacCotter), and some few other surnames
represent Norse or Danish families. The Irish distinguished between two nations of the Northmen, the Fionn-
Ghaill, or fair strangers, and the Dubhghaill, or black
strangers, Norwegians and Danes respectively. The individual of the latter nation was known as Ouḃᵹall, the
black-stranger, or Dane. This in course of time became
a personal name ; Ouḃᵹall, for instance, was the name of
one of the Danish leaders who fell at Clontarf. Ó Ouḃᵹaill (O'Doyle) is ' grandson of Ouḃᵹaill,' the black
stranger. The family, as I have said, is probably of

Danish or Norse race, for while there are O'Doyles in all
parts of Ireland, it will be remarked that they are most
numerous in the maritime counties of Leinster and Munster, and in the neighbourhood of the old Norse or Danish
settlements. Ó hᴀᴘᴀɪʟʟ (O'Harold) is a surname that
almost certainly originated at Limerick, and Aᴘᴀɪʟ, as
we know, was one of the sons of Ivar, king of the Norsemen
of Limerick. Ivar himself has left us his name in the
Thomond surname Ó hɪoṁᴀɪᴘ, now generally anglicised
Howard. Ó hEᴀnᴘᴀɪc (O'Henrick) is a surname of Norse
origin in Waterford or Wexford. Mᴀc Oɪcɪᴘ (MacCotter,
Cotter) is an unmistakably Norse surname and the family is
almost certainly of Norse descent. More than one leader
named Oɪcɪᴘ is mentioned among the invaders. In 916,
the Earl, Oɪcɪᴘ ᴅuʙ, or Oitir the Black, arrived at Waterford in one hundred ships and plundered all Munster.
Another Oɪcɪᴘ ᴅuʙ, probably his grandson, is mentioned
among the leaders of the Norsemen at Clontarf.

On the other hand, many families bearing surnames
formed from a Norse eponym are of purely Irish descent.
The MacDugalds of Scotland, for instance, are of the same
stock as the MacDonalds, who claim to be Gaels and
descendants of Colla Uais, King of Ireland. So also are
the MacSorleys, from the Norse Soṁᴀɪᴘʟe (or Somerled),
and some of the MacRorys. The MacAuliffes and Mac-
Awleys, the MacManuses and MacCaffreys, are, as we have
seen, branches of some of our chief Irish families. Ó
Sɪocᴘᴘᴀᴅᴀ (Segrue) comes from a famous Norse name,
Sigefrid, but the family so called is said to be a branch of
the O'Sullivans. ʙᴘuᴀᴅᴀᴘ, whence the well-known surname Ó ʙᴘuᴀᴅᴀɪᴘ, is commonly regarded as Danish and
identical with the name of the Dane who slew King Brian
at Clontarf. The difficulty is that it seems to occur too
early. The Norse invasions began in 795, but for many
years after the inland parts of the country were unmolested.
The Annals of the Four Masters, however, record under
the year 809 (*recte* 814) the death of ʙᴘuᴀᴅᴀᴘ, lord of Ui
Fidhgheinte, the present Co. Limerick, who must have
got his name some considerable time previous to the

first appearance of the invaders. But though this seems to prove that Ḃṗuaḋaṗ is not of Norse origin, yet it is just possible that a Norse name may have been introduced through commercial intercourse with that people prior to the period of the warlike invasions. Ḃṗuaḋaṗ certainly became common as a personal name only during the period of the Norse invasions, and this seems to lend colour to the theory of its Norse origin. There is no reason, however, for thinking that any of the several families of Ó Ḃṗuaḋaṗ in Ireland is of Norse descent. Coiṗḋeaṫḃaċ, anglice Turlough, was a famous name among the O'Briens, who got it from their ancestor, Coiṗḋeaṫḃaċ, who was son of Caṫaḋ, King of Munster in the early part of the 7th century. It occurs too early to be Norse ; Caṫaḋ, the father of Coiṗḋeaṫḃaċ, died in 620. Still, it appears to have its root in a Norse word. Thor was the Jupiter of the North. We have his name in the word Thursday, and it is the root of many personal names. Coiṗḋeaṫḃaċ is ' Thor-shaped,' shaped like the god Thor. Oiṗḋeaṫḃaċ, whence the surname Mac Oiṗḋeaṫḃaiġ (Costelloe), is of exactly similar formation and import, meaning ' god-shaped,' or shaped like the god Os. I have already mentioned MacManus as the name of two families of Irish descent. Maġnuṗ was the Latin Magnus borne by a son of St. Olave of Norway and introduced by the Norsemen into Ireland. Ó Comnaiṗ (O'Toner) comes from a famous Norse name, but the family is a branch of Cineal Eoghain. The Annals of Ulster, under the year 874, record the slaying of Oiṗcín, son of Aṁlaoiḃ, king of the Norsemen. Oiṗcín is the source of the surname Ó hOiṗcín, borne by a Connacht family who were followers of the MacDermotts of Moylurg and apparently of purely Irish descent.

The Anglo-Norman invasion, unlike that of the Norsemen, profoundly influenced our Irish system of momenclature. Not only was an entirely new set of Christian names introduced, and a type of surname previously unknown, but the continuous existence side by side for centuries of two peoples speaking different languages

necessitated a bilingual nomenclature, to meet the needs
of which each name and surname had to appear in both
a native and a foreign dress.

The old Irish system of nomenclature was a very marked
one. Down to the Anglo-Norman invasion, the personal
names in use in Ireland were almost purely Celtic. The
Irish had been very slow in adopting either Scriptural
names or the Latin and Greek names of saints. The few
Norse names that had come in as a result of the invasions
of the Northmen scarcely affected the Celtic character of
our nomenclature. The nomenclature of the Anglo-
Normans, on the other hand, was partly Teutonic, partly
Scriptural and saintly. The most popular names were
those Germanic names which the Franks had brought
across the Rhine and which ultimately found their way
into every corner of Europe. Of names common to the
Irish and Anglo-Normans, there were none. To take a
name that afterwards found favour with both peoples, we
had no Patricks except among the Norsemen in the cities.
So that at the period of the invasion and for several centuries after a man's name was an absolute guide to his
nationality. Every Donald, every Dermott, was an Irishman ; every Robert, every William, a Norman or Englishman. In England after the Conquest it was different.
There the use of Norman names at once became the fashion.
In a short time the great mass of Anglo-Saxon names were
driven out, a few only excepted which were favoured by
special circumstances. " The Englishman," says Freeman,
" whose child was held at the font by a Norman gossip,
the Englishman who lived on friendly terms with his
Norman lord or his Norman neighbour, nay the Englishman who simply thought it fine to call his children after
the reigning king or queen, cast aside his own name and
the names of his parents, to give his sons and daughters
names after the new foreign pattern. . . . In every
list of names throughout the 11th and 12th centuries we
find the habit spreading. The name of the father is
English ; the name of the son is Norman. This is a point
of far more importance than anything in the mere history

of nomenclature. It helps to disguise one side of the fusion between Normans and Englishmen. Many a man who bears a Norman name, many a Richard or Gilbert whose parentage does not happen to be recorded, must have been as good an Englishman as if he had been called Ealdred or Æthelwulf. No one would have dreamed that Robert, the most daring of knights, was of other than of Norman descent, if the English name of his father had not by good luck been preserved."* But unlike the English, the Irish for centuries clung to their ancient names. Here and there, indeed, a Norman name was borrowed, but down to the end of the reign of Elizabeth, in every Irish family without exception, the bulk of the names were Celtic ; and in those cases where the surname left it doubtful, it was possible to judge, with tolerable accuracy, a man's nationality from the name he bore. But ever since the Irish power was broken at Kinsale, Irish names have been falling into decay and their places taken by names of Norman origin. In the long run, what happened in England after the Conquest was sure, unless arrested, to happen in Ireland. Already eighty per cent of the names borne by Irishmen and ninety per cent. of those borne by Irishwomen are of foreign origin. The rarer names were the first to die out. Those which still survive are names which were too frequent and too widespread to be killed off in the space that has elapsed since the fashion of taking foreign names began.

Besides the introduction of a new set of Christian names, the Anglo-Norman invasion brought with it also a new type of surname. Irish surnames were, as I have said, all patronymic, the only exceptions being those descriptive epithets which at a later period supplanted the real surnames. At the time of the Norman Conquest, hereditary surnames had not yet arisen in England. Even in Normandy they were still a novelty, but, as Freeman says, a novelty which was fast taking root. Members of the great Norman houses already bore surnames, sometimes patronymic, sometimes territorial. Many of these were

*The History of the Norman Conquest of England, Chap. XXV.

brought into England by the Conqueror and his followers, thus setting the example of hereditary surnames. And besides patronymics and local surnames, those distinctive epithets indicative of the bearer's calling or descriptive of his person, which were already common everywhere on the Continent, also came in and took root in England as hereditary surnames. Englishmen took surnames after the Norman fashion, patronymic, local, occupative and descriptive ; and surnames of all these types were introduced into Ireland by the Anglo-Normans, and all except the first were new.

The character of the surnames borne by the Anglo-Norman invaders will be best illustrated by examples taken from our oldest Anglo-Irish records : (1) patronymics, with fitz, as Maurice fitz Gerald, Meiler fitz Henry, Adam fitz Simon ; or the ancestor's name appears in its simple and unaltered form, without any prefix, as : John Jordan, Robert Wallerond, Adam Fraunceis, William Matheu, John Herberd, Robert Bryan ; (2) local, with de, as Richard de Burgo, William de Barri, William de Freynes, John de Hynteberge, Henry de Maundeville, Philip de Stauntoun, Adam de Keusaac, Roger de Hyda, Hugh de Lacy, John de Verdune, John de Cogan, John de Kent, John de Andoun, Walter de Lecton, Robert de Stapiltoun, Maurice de Rochfort, David de Cauntetoun, Richard de Val ; (3) occupative, with le, as : Thomas le Clerc, Philip le Harpur, Michael le Fireter, Henry le Marescal, Richard le Archer ; (4) descriptive, with le (sometimes corrupted to de), as : Fromund le Brun, Richard le Blake, Geoffrey le Hore, John de Long, William le Graunt, John le Fort, Maurice le Wolf, William le Poer, Thomas le Engleys, Rys le Waleys, Milo de Bret, Adam le Flemyng, Robert le Deveneys.

At the period of the invasion, surnames were still far from universal in England, and many of the first settlers came to this country with only single names. Some of these took surnames on Irish soil, after the Norman fashion, from the places where they settled, as : John de Athy, Richard de Fineglas, Adam de Trim. Others were surnamed from the places abroad whence they set forth, or from the trades they followed, as : Jordan de Anglia (England), Peter de Birmegham, William de London, Walter le Tailur ; but these, except the first, cannot be distinguished from other Anglo-Norman surnames of the same period.

A further effect of the Anglo-Norman invasion on our name-system was the introduction of bilingualism, as a result of which most of our names and surnames have two forms, one Irish and the other English. Ever since the coming of the Anglo-Normans, a contest for supremacy has been going on between the two races that inhabit this island ; and English policy once deemed it of such political importance to force Irishmen to conform to English ways and adopt English surnames, that the matter was thought worthy of special legislation. Accordingly it was enacted by the Statute of 5 Edward IV (1465), that every Irishman dwelling within the Pale, which then comprised the counties of Dublin, Meath, Louth and Kildare, should take an English surname. This Act which curiously illustrates the history of Irish family names contained the following provision, namely : that every Irishman dwelling among the English in the counties mentioned shall " take to him an English surname of one towne, as Sutton, Chester, Trym, Skryne, Corke, Kinsale ; or colour, as white, blacke, browne ; or art or science, as smith or carpenter ; or office, as cooke, butler ; and that he and his issue shall use this name under payne of forfeyting of his goods yearely till the premises be done, to be levied two times by the yeare to the king's warres, according to the discretion of the lieutenant of the king or his deputy."* This Statute, though it did not, to any great extent, produce the desired effect, caused some of the Irish families of the Pale to translate their surnames or assimilate them to English ones. They must, however, have been very few ; for about a century later, we find the poet Spenser

---

*5 Edward IV, c, 3. Statutes at Large, Ireland, vol. I, p. 29, quoted by O'Donovan, Top. Poems, Introduction, p. 26.

recommending a revival of the Statute, inasmuch as the Irish were then as Irish as ever.*

Meanwhile, the descendants of the Anglo-Norman invaders were being gradually absorbed into the Irish nation. They had in many places laid aside entirely their Norman-French dialect and were speaking the Irish language. This necessitated an Irish form of their names. The Norman Fitz was replaced by mᴀc. Other forms of surname were either hibernicised or the families who bore them took patronymic surnames after the Irish fashion by prefixing mᴀc to the Christian names of their ancestors. Thus the Birminghams took the surname of mᴀc ꝑeóᴘᴀıᴘ, from an ancestor named Piers or Peter de Bermingham ; the Stauntons, that of mᴀc ᴀn ṁıᴌeᴀᴅᴀ (MacEvilly), from an ancestor named Milo de Staunton ; the de Exeters, that of mᴀc Sıúᴘᴄᴀın, from Jordan de Exeter, the founder of the family.

Like the great Irish families, some of the Anglo-Norman families also split up into septs which adopted distinct surnames of their own. Thus the MacDavids, the Mac-Philbins, the MacKeoneens, the MacGibbons, the Mac-Walters and MacRedmonds of Connacht are all said to be branches of the great Anglo-Irish family of de Burgo or Burke.

It was only after the defeat of the Irish at Kinsale that what the Statute of 5 Edward IV aimed at really began to be accomplished. Then set in the fashion of changing Irish into English surnames ; and it continued all through the century, until, after the fall of Limerick, the Irish people were brought completely into subjection. Thenceforward an Ó or mᴀc to a man's name was no recommendation in the eyes of the powers that ruled the country. The people were taught or forced to believe that they

*The following appeared in the *Cork Examiner* of 2nd Feb., 1921 : " Miss Abina Corkery, MacCurtain St., Macroom, trading in the name of her deceased father, was obliged to remove from the facia board over the shop window the Gaelic characters ' Séᴀmuᴘ Ó Coᴘcoᴘᴀ.' She was informed by the authorities that failure to comply with the order within seven days would result in the burning down of the premises. The Irish inscription has been painted over."

must have an English surname, or at least an English version of their Irish surname. Hence the almost wholesale rejection of the Ó and mᴀc during the long night of slavery and oppression through which Ireland passed in the century of the penal laws. To reduce one's name as much as possible to the level of English pronunciation, to give it an English appearance, to modify it in some way and to some degree, was almost a condition of life. Fortunately, however, the original surname continued to live on, unaffected by any changes in the English form, wherever the Irish language continued to be spoken, and thus we are able to recover the Irish form of many surnames that otherwise would have long since disappeared for ever.

BIBLIOGRAPHY

Barber H. *British Family Names*. London, 1894.

Bardsley, C. W. *A Dictionary of English and Welsh Surnames*. London, 1901.

——*English Surnames*. London, 1906.

Baring-Gould, S. *Family Names and their Story*. London, 1910.

Camden, W. *Remaines concerning Britaine*. London, 1605.

Foerstemann, E. W. *Altdeutsches Namenbuch*. Bonn, 1900.

Fumagalli, G. *Piccolo Dizionario dei nomi italiani di persone*. Genova, 1901.

Harrison, H. *Surnames of the United Kingdom*. London, 1912-1918. 2 vols.

Heintze, A. *Die deutschen Familiennamen*. Halle, 1903.

Kleinpaul, R. *Die deutschen Personennamen*. Leipsig, 1909.

Letelier, V. *Ensayo de Onomatologia ó estudio de los Nombres Propios y Hereditarios*. Madrid, 1906.

Long, H. A. *The Names we Bear*. Glasgow. n.d.

Lower, M. A. *English Surnames*. London, 1849. 2 vols.

Macbain, A. *Personal Names and Surnames of the Town of Inverness*. Inverness, 1895.

Moody, S. *What is Your Name?* London, 1863.

Moore, A. W. *Manx Names*. London, 1903.

Pianigiani, O. *Che cosa significa il mio nome?* Lucca, 1911.

Poma, C. *Saggio di onomastica italiana*. Torino, 1911.

Stolfi, N. *I Segni di distinzione personali*. Napoli, 1905.

Toro y Gisbert, M. de. *Ortologia castellana des nombres propios*. 1911.

Trauzzi, A. *Attraverso l'onomastica del medio evo in Italia*. Rocca S. Casciano, 1911.

Weekley, E. *The Romance of Names*. London, 1914.

——*Surnames*. London, 1916.

Weidenhan, J. L. *Baptismal Names*. Washington, D.C. 1919.

Yonge, Charlotte M. *History of Christian Names*. London, 1884.

Brash, R. R. *The Ogam Inscribed Monuments of the Gaedhil*. London, 1879.

Colgan, John. *Acta Sanctorum Hiberniae*. Louvain. 1645.

Dunn, Joseph. *The Ancient Irish Epic Tale Táin Bó Cúalnge*. London, 1914.

Ellis, H. *General Introduction to Domesday Book*. London, 1833. 2 vols.

Farley, A. *Domesday Book.* London, 1783. 2 vols.

Giles, J. A. *The Venerable Bede's Ecclesiastical History of England.* London, 1859.

Hennessy, W. H. *Chronicum Scotorum—A Chronicle of Irish Affairs.* London, 1866.

——*The Annals of Loch Cé. A Chronicle of Irish Affairs from A.D. 1014 to A.D. 1590.* London, 1871. 2 vols.

—— & MacCarthy, B. *Annals of Ulster.* Dublin, 1887-1901. 4 vols.

Hogan, E. *Cath Ruis na Rig for Bóinn.* Dublin, 1892.

——*Onomasticon Goedelicum Locorum et Tribuum Hiberniae et Scotiae.* Dublin, 1910.

Jónsson, Finnur. *Landnámabók.* Kobenhavn, 1900.

Joyce, P. W. *Irish Names of Places.* Dublin, 1883-1913. 3 vols.

Kelly, M. *The Martyrology of Tallaght.* Dublin, 1857.

MacAlister, R. A. S. *Studies in Irish Epigraphy.* London, 1897-1907.

Mac Firbhisigh, Dubhaltach. *Genealogical Manuscript in the Royal Irish Academy.*

——*Annals of Ireland. Three Fragments* (edited by O'Donovan). Dublin, 1860

MacNeill, John. *Notes on the Distribution, History, Grammar, and Import of the Irish Ogham Inscriptions* (R.I.A. Proc., vol. XXVII, Sect. C).

——*Early Irish Population Groups : Their Nomenclature, Classification and Chronology* (R.I.A. Proc., vol. XXIX, Sect, C).

Moran, P. F. *Irish Saints in Great Britain.* Dublin, 1879.

Murphy, D. *The Annals of Clonmacnoise.* Dublin, 1896.

Ó Cléıꝛış, Luᵹᴀıᴆ. ḃeᴀᴄᴀ Ꭿoᴆᴀ Ruᴀıᴆ uí Ꭰoṁnᴀıll. Dublin, 1893.

O'Conor, C. *Annales Buellani (in Rerum Hibernicarum Scriptores,* Tom. II). Buckinghamiae, 1825.

——*Annales Inisfalenses (in Rerum Hibernicarum Scriptores,* Tom. II). Buckinghamiae, 1825.

——*Annales Tigernachi abbatis Cluanensis (in Rerum Hibernicarum Scriptores, Tom. II).* Buckinghamiae 1825.

O'Curry, E. *Lectures on the Manuscript Materials of Ancient Irish History.* Dublin, 1878.

O'Donovan, John. *The Circuit of Ireland by Muircheartach Mac Neill.* Dublin, 1841.

——*The Banquet of Dun na n-Gedh and the Battle of Magh Rath.* Dublin, 1842.

——*The Tribes and Customs of Hy-Many.* Dublin, 1843.

——*The Genealogies, Tribes, and Customs of Hy-Fiachrach.* Dublin, 1844.

——*Leabhar na gCeart or the Book of Rights.* Dublin, 1847.

——*Miscellany of the Celtic Society.* Dublin, 1849.

——*Annals of the Kingdom of Ireland by the Four Masters.* Dublin, 1851. 7 vols.

——*The Tribes of Ireland by Aenghus O'Daly*. Dublin, 1852.

——*The Topographical Poems of John O'Dubhagain and Giolla na Naomh O'Huidhrin*. Dublin, 1862.

O'Donnell, Manus. *Betha Colaim Chille—Life of Columcille* (edited by A. O'Kelleher and G. Schoepperle). Chicago, 1918.

O'Hanlon, John. *Lives of the Irish Saints*. Dublin. 9 vols.

Plummer, C. *Bethada Naem nErenn : Lives of Irish Saints*. Oxford, 1922. 2 vols.

Petrie, George. *Christian Inscriptions in the Irish Language*. Dublin, 1872.

Power, P. *The Place-Names of Decies*. London, 1907.

Reeves, W. *Vita Sancti Columbae, auctore Adamnano*. Dublin, 1857.

Searle, W. G. *Onomasticon Anglo-Saxonicum*. Cambridge, 1897.

Todd, J. H. *Cogadh Gaedhel re Gallaibh—The War of the Gaedhil with the Gaill*. London, 1867.

Thorpe, B. *The Anglo-Saxon Chronicle*. London, 1861. 2 vols.

Uᴀ ᴅuinnín, ᴘ. ᴍe ʒuiᴅiᴘ ᵹeᴀᴘᵯᴀnᴀċ : *The Maguires of Fermanagh*. Ꝺᴀile Áċᴀ Cliᴀċ, 1917.

Walsh, Paul. *The Place-Names of Westmeath*. Dublin, 1915.

——*The Flight of the Earls*. Dublin. 1916.

Williams Ab Ithel, John. *Brut y Tywysogion ; or The Chronicle of the Princes*. London, 1860.

Bibliography of Irish Philology and of Printed Irish Literature. Dublin, 1913.

Islands Landnamabok, Hoc est : Liber Originum Islandiae. Havniae, 1774.

Martyrologium Romanum. Romae. MDCCCCXIII.

The Martyrology of Donegal. Dublin, 1864.

The Miscellany of the Irish Archaelogical Society. Vol. I. Dublin, 1846.

Conán ᴍᴀol. ᴍᴀc ᵹinʒín ᴅuḃ. Ꝺᴀile Áċᴀ Cliᴀċ. 1903.

Hyde, D. *The Religious Songs of Connacht*. Dublin and London. 2 vols.

MacNeill, John. *Clare Island Survey : Place-Names and Family Names* (R.I.A. Proc., Vol. XXXI).

Meehan, C. P. *The Poets and Poetry of Munster*. Fourth Edition.

O Flannghaile, Tomas. *For the Tongue of the Gael*. London, 1896.

Ó Siocᵹᴘᴀᴅᴀ, ᴘᴀᴅᴘᴀiʒ. ᴀn Ꝺᴀile Seo 'ᵹᴀinne. Ꝺᴀile Áċᴀ Cliᴀċ. 1916.

Uᴀ ᴅuḃᵹᴀill, Séᴀmuᴘ. ḃeiᴘᴄ ᵹeᴀᴘ ó'n ᴏᴄuᴀiċ. Ꝺᴀile Áċᴀ Cliᴀċ. 1903.

——ᴘᴘáᴄᴀí ᵯiċíl ᴄᴀiᴏʒ. Ꝺᴀile Áċᴀ Cliᴀċ. 1904.

——ᴍuinnᴄeᴀᴘ nᴀ ᴄuᴀċᴀ. Ꝺᴀile Áċᴀ Cliᴀċ. 1921.

Uᴀ ᴅuinnín, ᴘ. ᴀᵯᴘáin Seᴀʒáin Clÿᴘᴀiʒ ᵯic ᴏoᵯnᴀill Ꝺᴀile Áċᴀ Cliᴀċ. 1902.

——ᴅánᴄᴀ Séᴀᵹᴘᴀiᴏ uí ᴅonn ċᴀᴏᴀ ᴀn ʒleᴀnnᴀ. Ꝺᴀile Áċᴀ Cliᴀċ. 1902.

——Aṁráin Eoġain Ruaiḋ Uí Śúilleaḃáin. baile Áta Cliaṫ. 1901.

——Filiḋe na Máiġe. baile Áta Cliaṫ. 1906.

Ua Laoġaire, peaḋar. mo Sġéal féin. baile Áta Cliaṫ. 1915.

——Suaire. baile Áta Cliaṫ. 1915.

The Gaelic Journal. Dublin, 1882-1909. 19 vols.

Proceedings of the Oireachtas, 1899-1901.

Bosworth, Rev. Joseph. A Compendious Anglo-Saxon and English Dictionary. London, 1887.

Dinneen, P. S. Foclóir Gaeḋilge aġur béarla, an Irish-English Dictionary. Dublin and London, 1904.

Halliwell, J. O. Dictionary of Archaic and Provincial Words. London, 1847. 2 vols.

Kelham, R. A Dictionary of the Norman or Old French Language. London, 17 . . (date obliterated).

Liddell & Scott. Greek-English Lexicon.

Macbain, Alexander. An Etymological Dictionary of the Gaelic Language. Stirling, 1911.

——Etymology of the Principal Gaelic National Names, Personal Names and Surnames. Stirling, 1911.

mac Giolla Eáin, E. C. Ḋánta Aṁráin ir Caointe Śeaṫrúin Céitinn. baile Áta Cliaṫ. 1900.

Marstrander, Carl J. S. Dictionary of the Irish Language Dublin, 1913.

Meyer, Kuno. Contributions to Irish Lexicography. Halle a S., 1906.

O'Brien, J. Focalóir Gaoidhilge-Sax-Bhéarla or an Irish-English Dictionary. Paris, 1768.

O'Connell, F. W. A Grammar of Old Irish. Belfast and London, 1912.

Ó Ḋonnċaḋa, Taḋġ. Ḋánta Śeáin Uí Ṁuirċaḋa na Ráitíneaċ. Dublin, 1907.

——Saoṫar filiḋeaċta an Aṫar páoraiġín haicéaḋ. baile Áta Cliaṫ. 1916.

O'Donovan, John. A Grammar of the Irish Language. Dublin, 1845.

Ó flannġaile, Tomár. Eaċtra Giolla an Amaráin: The Adventures of a Luckless Fellow. Dublin, 1897.

Ó foġluḋa, R. Aṁráin piarair Ṁic Ġearailt. Dublin, 1905.

——Cúirt an Ṁeaḋon Oiḋċe. Dublin, 1912.

O'Kelly, J. J. Leaḃar na Laoiteaḋ: A Collection of Ossianic Poems. Dublin, 1911.

O'Rahilly, T. F. Gadelica. Dublin, 1912-1913.

O'Reilly, Edward. Irish-English Dictionary. Dublin, 1817.

Pokorny, J. A Concise Old Irish Grammar and Reader. Halle a S. and Dublin, 1914.

Stokes, W. Three Irish Glossaries. London, 1862.

——On the Calendar of Oengus. Dublin, 1880.

——Saltair na Rann. Oxford, 1883.

——The Old-Irish Glosses at

Wurzburg and Carlsruhe.
Hertford, 1887.
——*Urkeltischer Sprachschatz.*
Gottingen, 1894.
——and Meyer, K. *Archiv für
Celtische Lexikographie.*
Halle a S. and London, 1907.
——and Strachan, J. *The-
saurus Palaeohibernicus.*
Cambridge, 1901-1903. 2
vols.

Uᴀ Ꝺu1nn1n, ꝑ. Ꝺánꞇᴀ ꝑ1ᴀꝑᴀ1ꝛ
ꝼe1ꝑꞇéꝛ. Dublin, 1900.
Uᴀ Lᴀoᵹᴀ1ꝛe, ꝑeᴀꝺᴀꝛ. Luᵹᴀ1ꝺ
mᴀc Con. ᴅᴀ1le Áꞇᴀ
Cl1ᴀꞇ. 1914.
——Ꝺꝛ1cꝛ1ú. ᴅᴀ1le Áꞇᴀ Cl1ᴀꞇ
1915.
Windisch, E. *A Concise Irish
Grammar.* Cambridge,
1882.
——*Compendium of Irish
Grammar.* Dublin, 1883.
Wright, Thomas. *Dictionary of
Obsolete and Provincial
English.* London, 1857.
2 vols.
Zeuss, J. C. *Grammatica Celtica.*
Lipsiae, 1853. 2 vols.
Eriu. *Dublin.* Dublin, 1904.
Irish Texts Society Publications.
London, 1898-1920. 22
vols.
Revue Celtique. Paris, 1870-.
Welsh Dictionary.

Begley, J. *The Diocese of
Limerick, Ancient and
Mediaeval.* Dublin, 1905.
Berry, H. F. *Ancient Charters
in the Liber Albus Ossor-
iensis* (R.I.A. Proc., vol.
XXVII, Sect. C).
Brady, W. Maziere. *The Epis-
copal Succession in England,
Scotland and Ireland,
A.D. 1400 to 1875.* Rome,
1876.

Burke, W. P. *Irish Priests in
the Penal Times.* Water-
ford, 1914.
Butler, R. *Registrum Prioratus
Omnium Sanctorum juxta
Dublin.* Dublin, 1845.
Costello, A. *De Annatis
Hiberniae* (A.D. 1400-
1535). Vol. I. Dublin, 1912.
Gilbert, John T. *Historic and
Municipal Documents of
Ireland,* A.D. 1172-1320.
London, 1870.
——*A Contemporary History of
Affairs in Ireland from
1641 to 1652.* Dublin, 1879-
1880. 6 vols.
——*History of the Irish Con-
federation and War in Ire-
land,* 1641-1649. Dublin,
1882-1891. 7 vols.
——*" Crede Mihi."—The Most
Ancient Register Book of the
Archbishops of Dublin before
the Reformation.* Dublin,
1897.
Grace, James. *Annales Hiber-
niae.* Dublin, 1842.
Hogan, E. *Description of Ire-
land in* 1598. Dublin, 1878.
Laffan, T. *Tipperary Hearth
Records.*
Lawlor, H. J. *A Calendar of the
Liber Niger and Liber Albus
of Christ Church, Dublin*
(R.I.A., Proc., Vol. XXVII,
Sect. C).
——*Calendar of the Liber Ruber
of the Diocese of Ossory*
(R.I.A. Proc., Vol. XXVII,
Sect. C).
——*A Calendar of the Register
of Archbishop Sweteman*
(R.I.A. Proc., Vol. XXIX,
Sect. C).
MacCaffrey, J. *The Black
Book of Limerick.* Dublin,
1907.

Matheson, R. E. *Varieties and Synonymes of Surnames and Christian Names in Ireland.* Dublin, 1901.

——*Special Report on Surnames in Ireland.* Dublin, 1909.

Meillet, A. *Introduction a l'Étude Comparative des Langues Indo-Européennes.* Paris, 1912.

Mills, James. *Calendar of Justiciary Rolls, Ireland, temp. Edward I.* Part I, Dublin, 1905 ; Part II, London, 1914.

——*Justiciary Rolls, Ireland,* 1295-1303. London, 1906.

Morrin J. *Calendar of the Patent and Close Rolls of Chancery in Ireland, of the reigns of Henry VIII, Edward VI, Mary, and Elizabeth.* Dublin, 1861-1862. 2 vols.

——*Calendar of the Patent and Close Rolls of Chancery in Ireland, of the reign of Charles I.* London, 1863.

Murphy, D. *Triumphalia Chronologica Monasterii Sanctae Crucis in Hibernia.* Dublin, 1891.

O'Grady, S. *Pacata Hibernia.* London, 1896. 2 vols.

Reeves, W. *Ecclesiastical Antiquities of Down, Connor, and Dromore.* Dublin, 1847.

Sweetman, H. S. *Calendar of Documents relating to Ireland* (A.D. 1171-1307). London, 1875-1886. 5 vols.

Calendar of State Papers, Ireland. Herry VIII Edward VI, Mary, Elizabeth, and James I. 1860-1912. 16 vols.

Calendar of Papal Registers, 1198—1435. London, 1894-1915. 10 vols.

Irish Patent Rolls of James I.

Reports of the Deputy Keeper of the Public Records in Ireland (1 to 47).

Report of the Franciscan Manuscripts. Dublin, 1906.

Rotuli Hundredorum temp. Henry III & Edward I (1273). Vol. I (1812). Vol. II (1818).

Rotuloroum Patentium et Clausorum Cancellariae Hiberniae Calendarium. Vol. I, Part I, Henry II—Henry VII. 1828.

Transactions of the Ossory Archaeological Society. Kilkenny, 1879.

Bugge, A. *Contributions to the History of the Norsemen in Ireland.* Christiania, 1900.

——*On the Fomorians and Norsemen by Duald Mac Firbis.* Christiania, 1905.

Connellan, Owen. *The Annals of Ireland by the Four Masters.* Dublin, 1847.

D'Alton, John. *Illustrations, Historical and Genealogical, of King James' Irish Army List.* Dublin, 1855.

Frost, J. *The History and Topography of the County of Clare.* Dublin, 1893.

Haliday, C. *The Scandinavian Kingdom of Dublin.* Dublin, 1884.

Hardiman, James. *The History of Town and County of the Town of Galway.* Dublin, 1820.

Harris, Walter. *The Works of Sir James Ware concerning*

Ireland. Dublin, 1739-1746. 4 vols.

Healy, W. *History and Antiquities of Kilkenny.* Kilkenny, 1893.

Hogan, E. *Distinguished Irishmen of the Sixteenth century.* London, 1894.

Hyde, D. *A Literary History of Ireland.* London, 1906.

Johnston, W. & A. K. *The Scottish Clans and Their Tartans.* 5th edition. Edinburgh & London.

Kelly, M. *Cambrensis Eversus.* Dublin, 1848-1852. 3 vols.

Lenihan, M. *Limerick; its History and Antiquities.* Dublin, 1866.

Mageoghegan, Abbe. *History of Ireland.*

Meehan, C. P. *The Rise, Increase, and Exit of the Geraldines.* Dublin. Third Edition.

Mitchell, Dugald. *A Popular History of the Highlands and Gaelic Scotland.* Paisley, 1900.

Morley, H. *Ireland under Elizabeth and James I.* London, 1890.

O'Callaghan, J. C. *History of the Irish Brigades in the Service of France.* Glasgow, 1870.

O'Connell, Mrs. M. J. *The Last Colonel of the Irish Brigade.* London, 1892. 2 vols.

O'Conor Don, C. O. *The O'Conors of Connaught.* Dublin, 1891.

O'Flaherty, R. *Ogygia.*
——*A Chronological Description of West or H-Iar-Connaught.* Dublin, 1846.

O'Hanlon & O'Leary. *History of the Queen's County.* Dublin, 1907.

O'Laverty, J. *An Historical Account of the Diocese of Down and Connor.* Dublin, 1880. 2 vols.

O'Mahony, John. *History of Ireland by Geoffrey Keating.*

O'Rorke, T. *The History of Sligo.* Dublin. 2 vols.

O'Sullevan, Philip. *Historiae Catholicae Iberniae Compendium.* Dublinii, 1850.

O'Toole, P. L. *History of the Clan O'Toole and other Leinster Septs.* Dublin, 1890

Prendergast, J. P. *The Cromwellian Settlement of Ireland.* London, 1870.

Skene, W. F. *The Highlanders of Scotland.* Stirling, 1902.

Stuart, James. *Historical Memoirs of the City of Armagh.* Dublin, 1900.

Webb, Alfred. *A Compendium of Irish Biography.* Dublin, 1878.

White, P. *History of Clare and the Dalcassian Clans.* Dublin, 1893.

Archivium Hibernicum. Dublin, 1912-1916. 5 vols.

Proceedings and Transactions of the Kilkenny and South-East of Ireland Archaeological Society. 10 vols.

The Celtic Review. Edinburgh, 1904-1914. 10 vols.

The Irish Ecclesiastical Record (1864-1916).

Bourke, U. J. *The Aryan Origin of the Gaelic Race and Language.* London, 1875.

Freeman, Edward A. *The History of the Norman Conquest of England.*

Gougaud, Louis. *Les Chrétientes Celtiques.* Paris, 1911.

Green, Alice Stopford. *The Making of Ireland and its Undoing.* London, 1908.

Healy, J. *Insula Sanctorum et Doctorum; or Ireland's Ancient Schools and Scholars.* Dublin, 1893.

Hull, E. *A Text Book of Irish Literature.* Dublin and London, 1906.

Johnson, A. H. *The Normans in Europe.* London, 1877.

Joyce, P. W. *Old Celtic Romances.* London, 1907.

Lanigan, John. *An Ecclesiastical History of Ireland.* Dublin, 1829. 4 vols.

MacNeill, Eoin. *Phases of Irish History.* Dublin, 1919.

——*Celtic Ireland.* Dublin and London, 1921.

Perry, Walter C. *The Franks.* London, 1857.

Taylor, Isaac. *Words and Places.* London, n.d.

Baudrand, Michel-Antoine. *Dictionaire Geographique et Historique.* Paris, 1705.

Biblia Sacra.

Butler, Alban. *Lives of the Saints.* Dublin, 1872. 12 vols.

Gazetteer of the United Kingdom.

General Topographical Index of Ireland. Dublin, 1904.

Journal of the Ivernian Society. 7 vols.

Proceedings of the Royal Irish Academy. Vol. XXVII-XXXI.

The Catholic Encyclopedia.

The New Ireland Review.

TABLE OF THE VALUES OF IRISH LETTERS

(For the use of readers unacquainted with Irish.)

The vowels in Irish are of two kinds, *broad* and *slender*. The broad vowels are ᴀ, o, u ; and the slender e, ı. Each vowel, whether broad or slender, has two sounds, a *long* sound and a *short* sound. Long vowels are marked by an acute accent, as á, é, í, ó, ú ; short vowels have no mark. After accented syllables the short vowels have an obscure sound, like *a* in the word *tolerable*. Final vowels are usually pronounced with a short or obscure sound. The consonants are also divided into *broad* and *slender*. A consonant is said to be broad when the vowel next to it in the same word is broad ; and slender when the vowel next to it is slender. Most of the consonants, whether broad or slender, are subject to 'aspiration,' which changes their radical sound. Aspiration is shown by a dot placed over the consonant, as ᵬ, ċ, ḋ, &c. When Roman type is used in the printing of Irish the aspiration is shown by inserting an h after the aspirated consonant. The following Table shows approximately the values of the Irish letters and the various combinations of vowels and consonants :—

A.—SINGLE LETTERS.

Irish Letters			Equivalent in Roman Letters		sounds like	in the word
ᴀ́	á		{ A	a }	a	call, or mar
ᴀ	ᴀ				a	that, or fat
ᵬ	b	broad	{ B	b }	b	bad, been
ᵬ	b	slender				
ᵬ̇	ᵬ̇	broad	{ Bh	bh }	v	vote,
ᵬ̇	ᵬ̇	slender		*or* w	wool, power
					v	van
c	c	broad	{ C	c }	c	cool
c	c	slender			k	king
ċ	ċ	broad	{ Ch	ch }	gh	lough
ċ	ċ	slender			h	hill
ᴅ	ᴅ	broad	{ D	d }	th	though
ᴅ	ᴅ	slender			d	duke, radiant
ᴅ̇	ᴅ̇	broad	{ Dh	dh }	gh	lough
ᴅ̇	ᴅ̇	slender			y	year

Irish Letters			Equivalent in Roman Letters			sounds like	in the word
é	é		{ E	e	}	e	where, there
e	e					e	met
f	f	broad	{ F	f	}	f	fall
f	f	slender				f	fill
ḟ	ḟ	broad	{ Fh	fh	}		silent
ḟ	ḟ	slender					
ʒ	ʒ	broad	{ G	g	}	g	gall
ʒ	ʒ	slender				g	give
ʒ̇	ʒ̇	broad	{ Gh	gh	}	gh	lough, sight
ʒ̇	ʒ̇	slender				y	year
h	h		H	h		h	hat, hit
í	í		{ I	i	}	ee	feel
ı	ı					i	mill
l	l	broad	{ L	l	}	l	law
l	l	slender				ll	million
m	m	broad	{ M	m	}	m	man, mill
m	m	slender					
ṁ	ṁ	broad	{ Mh	mh	}	v, or w	vain, or win
ṁ	ṁ	slender				v	vile
n	n	broad	{ N	n	}	nh	
n	n	slender				n	new
ó	ó		{ O	o	}	o	more, or lord. or
o	o					o	other, or lot [move
p	p	broad	{ P	p	}	p	past
p	p	slender				p	pet
ṗ	ṗ	broad	{ Ph	ph	}	ph or f	
ṗ	ṗ	slender				in English	
ʀ	ʀ	broad	{ R	r	}	r	raw
ʀ	ʀ	slender				rr	carrion
s	s	broad	{ S	s	}	s	son
s	s	slender				sh	shun
ṡ	ṡ	broad	{ Sh	sh	}	h	hall, hill
ṡ	ṡ	slender					
c	c	broad	{ T	t	}	th	thaw
c	c	slender				t	tune
ċ	ċ	broad	{ Th	th	}	h	hall, hill
ċ	ċ	slender					
ú	ú		{ U	u	}	u	rule
u	u					u	full

B.—DIPHTHONGS AND TRIPHTHONGS.

		sounds like	in the word
ᴀe		ay	mayor
Áı		awi	drawing
ᴀı	{	a	art. plaid
	or	i	king
	in Munster	ay	mayor
ᴀo	in Connacht	uee	queen
	in Ulster	ooi	wooing
ᴀoı		uee	queen
éᴀ		ea	swear, or fear
eᴀ		ea	heart
eÁ		a	father
eÁı		awi	gnawing
éı		ei	reign
eı		e	ferry
eó	{	oa	shoal
	in Ulster	aw	shawl
eo	{	u	just
	in Ulster	o	mock
eóı	{	owi	owing
	in Ulster	awi	gnawing
ıᴀ		ea	fear
ıᴀı		ei	being
ío		ee	see
ıo		io	motion
ıú		ew	few
ıúı		ewi	chewing
ıu		oo	good
óı	{	oi	going
	in Ulster	awi	drawing
	{	u	shut
oı	or	e	let
	or	i	hit
uᴀ		ooe	wooer
uᴀı		ooi	wooing
úı		ui	ruin
uı		ui	guilt

C.—COMBINATIONS OF CONSONANTS.

	sounds like			sounds like
ḃf	f	ʟp	sometimes	rr
ḃḟ	f	ṁṫ		f or v
bp	b	nᴅ		nn
ḃṫ	f or v	nʟ		ll
cṁ	f	ṫḃ		f or v
ᴅl	ll	ṫṁ		f or v
ʒc	g	ᴅS		t

D.—COMBINATIONS OF VOWELS AND CONSONANTS.

	in final syllable of a name			sounds like	in the word
ᴀɪḃ, ᴀɪᵹ	,,	,,	,,	y	trusty
ᴀɪḃe, ᴀɪᵹe	,,	,,	,,	ee	trustee
ᴀɪḃín	,,	,,	,,	ueen	queen
ᴀoɪḃ	first	,,	,,	uee	queen
eᴀḃ, eᴀᵹ	,,	,,	,,	a	father
eoḃ, eoᵹ	,,	,,	,,	oa	shoal
ɪᴀḃ	,,	,,	,,	ea	fear
ɪḃ, ɪᵹ	first	,,	,,	ee	feel
	final	,,	,,	y	trusty
ɪḃe, ɪᵹe	first	,,	,,	ee	feel
	final	,,	,,	ee	trustee
ɪoḃ, ɪoᵹ	first	,,	,,	ee	feel
oɪḃe	,,	,,	,,	ee	feel
uᴀɪḃ	any	,,	,,	ooi	wooing
uɪḃ	first	,,	,,	uee	queen
uɪḃe, uɪᵹe	final	,,	,,	uee	queen

E.—IRREGULAR SOUNDS OF VOWELS AND CONSONANTS

ᴀḃ, in the combinations ᴀḃᴀ, ᴀḃl ᴀḃn, forming the first syllable of a name, is pronounced in Munster and Connacht like *ou* in *ounce*, but in Ulster like ó. In any other syllable it is pronounced like ú, or *oo* in *tool*.

ᴀḋ and ᴀᵹ in an accented syllable, when followed immediately by a broad vowel or one of the consonants c, ᵹ, are generally pronounced like *i* in *high*, but in North Ulster like *uee* in *queen*, and in South Ulster and parts of Connacht and Thomond like *ay* in *mayor*. When followed by l, m, n, or r, they are generally pronounced like *i* in *high*, but in Connacht generally like á, or *aw* in *saw*. ᴀḋ, final, is sounded like *a* in *tolerable*.

ᴀḋᴀ, in the termination of surnames sounds like ú.

ᴀɪḋ and ᴀɪᵹ in an accented syllable, when followed by a vowel or one of the consonants l, m, n, r, ᵹ, ṡ, ċ, are pronounced in Munster and Connacht like *oi* in *toil*, but in Ulster like *ai* in *main*.

ᴀɪḃ and ᴀɪṁ in an accented syllable, when followed by a vowel, or l, n, or r, are pronounced in Munster like *oi* in *toil*.

ᴀɪ in monosyllabic names ending in ll, m, nn, nc, and in the accented syllable of dissyllabic names when followed by ll, m, nn, and another consonant, is pronounced in Munster like *oi* in *toil* or like *uee* in *queen*.

ᴀ in similar circumstances is pronounced in Munster like *ou* in *ounce*.

ᴀṁ, in the combinations ᴀṁᴀ, ᴀṁl, ᴀṁn, ᴀṁr, forming the first syllable of a name, is pronounced in Munster and Connacht like *ou* in *ounce*, but in any other syllable like *oo* in *tool*.

ᴀoḃ and ᴀoᵹ are sometimes pronounced like *oo* in *tool*, sometimes like *oi* in *toil*.

ḃ, in the combinations lḃᴀ, nḃᴀ, ɼḃᴀ, generally sounds like ú. ḃ, final, after l and ɼ is sometimes pronounced ú. -ıḃe in the termination of surnames in Ulster is sometimes pronounced ıú.

ċ, broad, is sometimes pronounced like c, sometimes like ᵹ, frequently like f, and in the combination -ᴀċċ in South Ulster is silent.

ḋᴀ, in the termination of names, is generally pronounced like ᴀ, but sometimes like ᵹᴀ.

ᴀḃᴀċ, in the termination of names, is pronounced like ıᴀċ.

ᴀḃᴀıᵹ, in the termination of names, is generally pronounced like ᴀıḃe, or *ee* in *trustee*, sometimes corrupted to uıᵹċe, sometimes to ᴀċᴀıᵹ, ᴀᵹᴀıᵹ. Similarly, eᴀḃᴀıᵹ is pronounced like ıḃe, or *ee* in *trustee*, sometimes corrupted to ıᵹċe.

ᴀḃ, medial, is sometimes pronounced like ᴀċ.

ḋ, broad and slender, is sometimes pronounced like ḃ ; as also ᵹ, broad.

eᴀḃᴀ, in the termination of surnames, is sounded like í, oı *ee* in *trustee*.

eᴀḃ, in the termination of surnames, is pronounced in Ulster like ıu.

eᴀ, in the combinations eᴀḃᴀ, eᴀṁ, is pronounced like ᴀḃ above.

eᴀnnɼ is pronounced like *our*.

eıḃ, in an accented syllable, followed by a vowel or l, m, n, or ɼ, is pronounced in Munster like *ei* in *height*. eıṁ in similar circumstances is pronounced sometimes like *ei* in *height*, sometimes *ee* in *feel*.

eıḋ and eıᵹ, in an accented syllable, are pronounced like *ei* in *height*.

ᵹ, final, is sometimes pronounced in Munster like ᵹ.

ᵹᴀıl and ᵹᴀıle, in the final syllable of surnames, are pronounced respectively ᴀoıl, úıl, and ᴀoıle, úıle.

ᵹuıɼ and ᵹuɼᴀ, in the same position, are pronounced ᴀoıɼ and ᴀoɼᴀ.

ı, followed by ll or nn, in monosyllabic names, is pronounced in Munster sometimes like *ee* in *feel*, sometimes like *i* in *high*.

ıo, in similar circumstances, is pronounced like ıú.

ṁ, in the combinations lṁᴀ, nṁᴀ, ɼṁᴀ, generally sounds like ú.

nn, slender, sometimes sounds like nᵹ.

o in the combinations oḃ and oṁ sounds like ó.

oḃ and oᵹ, in names of two syllables, are pronounced in Munster like *ou* in *ounce*, but in Connacht and Ulster like ó.

oı, followed by ll or nn, in monosyllabic names, is pronounced in Munster sometimes like *uee* in *queen*, sometimes like *oi* in *toil*.

ċ, broad, in the middle of a name is sometimes pronounced like ċ, and sometimes is silent.

u, followed by ḃ or ᵹ is pronounced ú.

uı, followed by ll or nn, in monosyllabic names, is pronounced in Munster like *uee* in *queen* or like *oi* in *toil*.

uıḃ, uıḋ, uıᵹ and uıṁ, in an accented syllable, when followed by a vowel, or n, are similarly pronounced.

I

THE IRISH NAME--SYSTEM

CHAPTER I—PERSONAL NAMES

§ 1—NATIVE NAMES

The Ancient Irish, like the Greeks and Hebrews, were called by only one name, as Ɑonᵹuſ, Ɗıɑſmɑıɔ, Ɗoṁnɑll, &c. ; but, for the sake of distinction, a cognomen derived from some personal peculiarity, or a patronymic formed by prefixing mɑc to the genitive case of the father's name, or ó to that of the grandfather, was sometimes added. Surnames in the modern sense were unknown in Ireland before the tenth century.

This usage necessitated a large number of names and led to the formation of a very varied and interesting Gaelic personal nomenclature. The Annals of the Four Masters alone contain nearly two thousand names, and perhaps as many more might be collected from genealogical books and other sources.

Some of these names, no doubt, lived only for a short time and have long since entirely disappeared ; but we have names, like Ɑoɔ, Ɑſτ, Cıɑn, Concoƀɑſ, Ɗıɑſmɑıɔ, Ɗoṁnɑll, Ɗonncɑɔ, Θoċɑıɔ, Θoᵹɑn, &c., which have been in uninterrupted use from the earliest period of which we have any record down to the present day ; while many others, though long obsolete as Christian names, are still preserved in our surnames.

§ 2—Classification of Irish Names

Irish personal names may be divided according to form into several classes :

1. The first and oldest class consists of names formed by the union of two independent elements or themes,* both nouns and generally monosyllables, as :

Aon-ṡuṟ †(one-choice).	Maon-ṡal (gift-valour),
bláṫ-ṁac (blossom-son).	Muṡ-ṟón (slave-seal).
bṟan-ṡal (raven-valour),	Muiṟ-ṡeaṟ (sea-choice).
Caiṫ-nia (battle-hero),	Muṟ-caḃ (sea-warrior),
Caṫ-al (battle-ruler).	Muṟ-ṡal (sea-valour),
faol-caḃ (wolf-warrior),	Niall-ṡuṟ (champion-choice).
flaiṫ-ṡeaṟ (dominion-choice).	Tuaṫ-al (people-ruler),
leaṟ-ṡuṟ (sea-choice),	Tuaṫ-ṡal (people-valour).

2. The second class comprises names formed by the union of two nouns, the first of which governs the second in the genitive case, as :

Cú-caṫa (hound of battle),
Cú-maṟa (hound of the sea).
Ḋonnṟléiḃe (Brown-man‡ of the mountain).
Ḋuḃ-eaṁna (Black-man of Eaṁain),
Ḋuḃ-ṟíte (Black-man of peace),
Maol-anṟaiḃ (chief of the storm).

The second noun sometimes takes the article, **as** .

Cú-an-aonaiṡ (hound of the fair),
Ṡiolla na naoṁ (servant of the saints).

A large number of names of this class are compounds of Maol, or Ṡiolla, and the name of God or a saint, as :

Maolḃṟíṡve (servant of St. Brigid),
Maolṟáḃṟaiṡ (servant of St. Patrick).
Ṡiolla Ċṟíoṟc (servant of Christ)
Ṡiolla Ḋé (servant of God).

---

*Such names are termed dithematic. The first element is called the prototheme, the second the deuterotheme. Some themes are exclusively protothemes, others exclusively deuterothemes; while others can be either protothemes or deuterothemes, Names containing only one element are termed monothematic.

† In order to show more clearly the composition of the names, the themes are separated by a hyphen.

‡Or Lord of the mountain.

Céile was used in the same way, as :

Céile Críost (spouse of Christ),
Céile Peadair (spouse of Peter).

Oub is frequently compounded with a word, or place-name, preceded by the numeral Oá, two, as :

Oub-Oá-boipeann (Black of the two Burrens),
Oub-Oá-críoċ (Black of the two territories),
Oub-Oá-inbeap (Black of the two river mouths),
Oub-Oá-leite (Black of the two sides, or halves).

Peap was similarly used, as :

Peap-Oá-críoċ (man of the two territories),

Cú, a hound, and figuratively a warrior or chieftain, enters largely into the composition of names of this class.

3. The third class, which comprises only a few names, consists of names formed from two nouns connected by a conjunctive particle, as :

Cú-ġan-máċaip (motherless hound),
Oál-pe-Oocaip (difficult division).
Peap-ġan-ainm (nameless).

4. The fourth class, which is very numerous, comprises names formed by the union of a noun and a qualifying adjective, as :

Ápo-ġal (high valour),   Oub-cú (black hound),
Ciap-ṁac (black son),   Oub-ġiolla (black lad),
Oonn-ceann (brown head),   Pionn-bapp (fair head),
Oub-ceann (black head),   Plann-caḃ (ruddy warrior),

Or the adjective may follow the noun, as :

Oaipp-pionn (fair head),   Cú-Oub (black hound),
Opan-Oub (black raven),   Ġiolla-Oub (black lad),
Ceann-Oub (black head),   Maol-caoin (gentle chief).

5. The fifth class comprises " pet" names,* or shortened forms of the dithematic names already described, as :

Oaippe, Oaipe, Oappa for Oaipppionn or Pionnbapp :
Pionna, Pionnu, Pinnia for Pionnbapp, or some other name commencing with Pionn-.

---

* Ordinary " pet " names are : Pat and Paddy for Patrick, Tom and Tommy for Thomas, Will and Willie for William.

Sometimes no trace of the second element remains, and the "pet" name is then undistinguishable from a monothematic name (next class below). Thus, for instance, ᏧᎾᏌ may be a shortened form of ᎠᎡᎤᏣᎥᏁ, ᎠᎤᏴᎦᎦᎡ, or ᎠᎤᏴᎷᎤᏳ, or it may be a monothematic name and originally bestowed directly. Besides, the "pet" name may be either the prototheme or the deuterotheme. ᎥᎢᎦᎾ, for instance, may be short for ᎥᎢᎦᎾᏧᎤ or ᎥᎢᎦᎾᏃᎡᎦ, or for ᎠᎢᏣᎥᎢᎦᎾ or ᏌᎠᎤᎷᎥᎢᎦᎾ or ᏁᎡᎷᎷᎥᎢᎦᎾ; or it may be a monothematic name. "Pet" names are usually found with a diminutive termination, especially -áꞃ. (See below, Class 8).

6. The sixth class consists of monothematic names, that is, names which contain only a single element and at the same time are not reduced forms of dithematic names, as:

ᏙꞃeᎾᏟ (speckled, spotted),	ᏔuᎾꞃꞃe (noble, generous),
ᏙꞃoᏟ (a badger),	ᏒeᎾᏁᏁ (a spear),
ᏟᎾᏴᏞᎾ (fair, beautiful),	ᏚeᎾꞃꞃᎾᏟ (a foal, flighty),
ᏟᎾᎧᏁᎻ (gentle, loveable),	ᏚᎥoᏴᎾ (silk, silken),
ᏟᎧᏞᎷ (a dove),	ᏓᎡᏁᎻeᎾᏁ (dark, grey).

7. The seventh class comprises derivatives, that is, names formed from other names, and from nouns and adjectives, by the aid of prefixes and suffixes, as:

Prefixes:	Suffixes:
ᎠᎢᏁ-éᎢꞃᎢꞃ	ᏟᎾᏟ-ᎾᏟ
ᎠᎢᏁ-ᏳeᎢᏁ	ᎠᏉᏁᎾᏴ-ᎾᏟ,
ᎠᎢᏁ-ᎻᎢꞃe,	ᎥᏞoꞃᏟ-ᎾᏉ,
ᎠᎢᏟ-ᏳeᎢᏁ,	ᏞᎾᏴꞃ-ᎾᎥᏉ*,
ᎠᏁ-ᏳᎾᏞ,	ᎠᎧꞃᏟ-ᎾᎥᎧe,
ᎠᏁ-ᏞᏻᎾᏁ,	ᏚᏟoᏞ-ᎾᎢᏳe,
ᏟᎧᎻ-ᏳᎾᏁ,	ᏞᎾᎧᏳ-ᎾᎢꞃe,
ᏟᎧᎻ-ᏳᎾᏞᏞ,	ᏟᎢᎾꞃ-ᏴᎾ,
ᎠᎥᎧ-ᏟᏳ,	ᎠᏌᏴ-ᏴᎾ,
ᎠᎥᎧ-ᎻᎾꞃᎾᏟ,	ᎥꞃuᎾᎥᏉ-eᎾᏉ,
ᎠᏉ-ᏟᎾꞃᏟᎾᏟ,	ᏒᎢᎻ-eᎾᏉ,
éᎢᏳ-ᏟeᎾꞃᏟᎾᏟ,	ᏳᎾᎢꞃ-ne,
eᎧ-ᏳᎾᏁ,	ᏟᎧᎢᏁ-neᎾᏟ,
ᏌᎾᎢꞃ-ᏟeᎾᏞᏞᎾᏟ,	ᏟᏁᎾᎻᎻ-ꞃeᎾᏟ,
ᏒᏲ-ᏴᎾꞃᏟᎾᏟ,	ᏟᎧᏞꞃ-ᏟᎾ,
ᏚᎧ-ᏟᎾꞃᏟᎾᏟ,	ᎠᏌᏴ-ᏟᎾᏟ,
Ꮪu-ᎢᏴne,	ᏓꞃᎧᎢᏳ-ᏟeᎾᏟ.

*When the suffix is added to a dissyllabic name or word, contraction usually takes place.

8. The eighth class consists of diminutives. These are formed by the addition of the following terminations, viz. : -án* (eán), -agán† (-eagán), -éin, -ín, and -óg(-eóg), as :

Ailġeanán,	Bradagán,	Cróinín,	Maoḋóg,
Ceallaċán,	Eoċagán,	Duiḃín,	Gormóg,
Ionṁaineán,	Muireagán,	Finnéin,	Muineóg.

The same root word, or "pet" or monothematic name, has often several diminutive forms. Thus many have diminutives in -án and -agán, as :

Art ,	Artán,‡	Artagán,
Bran,	Branán,	Branagán,
Fionn,	Fionnán,	Fionnagán,
Flann,	Flannán,	Flannagán,
Niall,	Niallán,	Niallagán ;

some in -án and -ín as :

Cas,	Casán,	Caisín,
Crón,	Crónán,	Cróinín,
Glas,	Glasán,	Glaisín,
Os,	Osán,	Oisín ;

and a few in -án and -óg as :

Caoṁ,	Caoṁán,	Caoṁóg,
Colm,	Colmán,	Moċolmóg.

A large number have three forms of diminutive, viz. : in -án, -ín, and -agán, as :

Ciar,	Ciarán,	Céirín,	Ciaragán,
Donn,	Donnán,	Duinnín,	Donnagán,
Duḃ,	Duḃán,	Duiḃín,	Duḃagán,
Odar,	Oḋrán,	Uiḋrín,	Oḋragán ;

---

*-án had originally the force of a patronymic, like the Greek *-ides*, and meant " son of."

† -agán is a double diminutive from -óg and -án.

‡Many of these diminutives are "pet" names. Thus Anfaḋán (little storm) is best explained as a pet diminutive of Maolanfaiḋ (chief of the storm) ; Gaoiṫín of Maolġaoiṫe (chief of the wind) ; Sléiḃín of Donnḟléiḃe (Lord of the mountain) ; Cogaḋán of Cú ċogaiḋ (hound of war) ; Naoṁán (little saint) of Giolla na Naoṁ (servant of the saints).

also in -án, -óg, and -agán, as :

Aod,	Aodán,	Maoóg,*	Aodagán,
Sopm,	Sopmán,	Sopmóg,	Sopmagán ;

and in -án, -ín, and -óg, as :

eapna,	eapnán,	eipnín,	meapnóg.

There is also a diminutive form in -nat (modern -nait) used in the names of females and corresponding to -án in names of males.

Examples :

Male.	Female.
Aodán,	Aodnat,
Cianán,	Ciannat,
Damán,	Damnat,
Soban,	Sobnat,
Odpán,	Odapnat,
Opán,	Opnat,
Rónán,	Rónnat.

Some names take the article, as : An Calbac, An Cornamac, An Dubaltac, An Feapoopca, An Siolla Dub, &c.

§ 3—Foreign Names in Ireland

Probably all the names in use in Ireland before the fifth century were of Gaelic, or at least Celtic, origin ; but from that period onwards foreign names have been borrowed from time to time from the various nations with which Ireland was brought into contact, directly or indirectly, in the course of her history.

A number of names of Latin, Greek, and Hebrew origin came in with Christianity. They were almost exclusively Biblical names and the Greek and Latin

---

*The names of saints are sometimes preceded by mo, my, a term of endearment, and at the same time take the diminutive termination -óg as : mocaomóg moceallóg, mocolmóg. When the name begins with a vowel, the o of mo is elided and the m incorporated with the name, as maoóg, foe, &c.

names of saints; but, strange to say, they were not
adopted, to any considerable extent, as Christian
names by our Gaelic ancestors. The few instances of
their use recorded in the Annals and elsewhere show
that they were, for the most part, borne only by monks
and ecclesiastics, who had, we may not doubt, taken
them at their monastic profession or ordination.

Adam must have been in use and, in its diminutive form,
Adamnan, was borne by the celebrated Abbot of Iona.
Abel was somewhat of a favourite, and we have several
instances of its use in the Annals. Noe gave name to
two Irish saints. Joseph occurs once, as do Aaron
and David. Of the names of the prophets, Daniel
is of rather frequent occurrence; and we had also
Abdias and Habacuc.*

New Testament names are represented by John, for
John the Baptist, always a favourite baptismal name
among Christian nations, and an occasional Philip
and Thomas. Of saintly names, we had Augustine,
Donat, Hilary, Januarius, Liber, Martin, Natal, &c.,
all exceedingly rare.

John (Eóin) is apparently the only one of all these
names that attained permanency. Patrick, the name
of the national apostle, came into general use only at
a comparatively late period, and its adoption even
then was due to Danish and English influence. It
is only in the thirteenth century that we first find
it in use among Irishmen. Michael, another name
of the same class, which now bids fair to rival in
popularity the name of the national saint, was until
a few centuries ago extremely rare in Ireland. Mary,
the name of the Blessed Virgin, was not used at all
until long after the Anglo-Norman invasion. Martha
occurs once, in the eighth century, as the name of an
Abbess of Kildare.

---

*See Annals of the Four Masters at the year 539 where a
strange story is told of an Irishman of this name, which is
scarcely surpassed by the adventure of his Hebrew namesake,
as related in Daniel, XIV., 32 et seqq.

Strange as it may appear, it was the very reverence
in which these names were held that prevented their
more widespread adoption, our ancestors preferring to
be known as the servants, rather than the namesakes,
of the saintly men and women who bore them. Hence,
instead of directly adopting the name of the saint,
they formed from it a new name by prefixing to it the
word maol* or ʒiollaț signifying servant or devotee,
and names so formed were common in Ireland—those
formed with maol from early Christian times. The
following is a list of such names: ‡

maol beanóin (servant of Benignus),
maol eóin (servant of John),
maol íora (servant of Jesus),
maol ʒiṗic (servant of Cyriacus),
maol máṗcain (servant of Martin),
maol miċíl (servant of Michael),
maol muiṗe (servant of Mary),
maol páoṗaiʒ (servant of Patrick),
maol peaoaiṗ (servant of Peter),
maol póil (servant of Paul),
maol Seaċlainn (servant of Secundinus),
ʒiolla aoamnáin (servant of Adamnan),
ʒiolla eóin (servant of John),
ʒiolla íora (servant of Jesus),
ʒiolla Steaṗáin (servant of Stephen),
ʒiolla máṗcain (servant of Martin),
ʒiolla miċíl (servant of Michael),
ʒiolla muiṗe (servant of Mary),
ʒiolla páoṗaiʒ (servant of Patrick),
ʒiolla peaoaiṗ (servant of Peter),
ʒiolla póil (servant of Paul),
ʒiolla Seaċlainn (servant of Secundinus),

*maol originally meant bald, hence tonsured, and when pre-
fixed to the name of a saint, the tonsured servant or devotee
of that saint. It is now confused with the old word mál
(Old Celtic maglos), a chief, and consequently has sometimes
also that meaning, as in maolanṗaio, chief of the storm,
maolcaoin, gentle chief &c.

† ʒiolla is probably derived from the Norse " gisl," a pledge
or hostage. It only became common during the Danish period
when it was largely used by the Northmen, on their conver-
sion to Christianity, to form Christian names. In this connection it signifies servant or devotee. At other times it has

Many of these scriptural and saintly names, and others of the same origin, were again introduced as a later period by the Normans, when they passed into more general use. Hence, names of this class have sometimes two forms in Irish, according to the date and channel of introduction, the older form being used exclusively for the saint, and the more modern one for ordinary individuals of the name. Examples:

	Older Form.	Later Form.
Adam,	Áoám,	Áoam,
Mary,	muine,	máine,
John,	eóin,	Seán, Seón,
Andrew,	Ainoméar,	Ainoniú,
Stephen,	Steapán,	Sciabna,
Martin,	mántan,	máintín, &c.

The British missionaries who accompanied St. Patrick to Ireland, and the Saxon saints and students who frequented the Irish schools, have left us a few names; but probably the only one that still survives as a Christian name is that of St. Beircheart (anglice Benjamin) of Tullylease.

Owing to intermarriage, and other alliances of friendship, many Danish and Norse names passed into Irish families during the ninth, tenth and eleventh centuries, and some of them became very popular. A few still survive as Christian names, and they have left us

---

to be translated youth, boy, lad, &c., as: Siollaoub, the black youth, Siollanuao, the red-haired lad, Siolla na neac, the horse-boy, &c.

‡ In the case of names like the present, in which the second element is a proper name, the initial letter of the second part may be a capital, or it may be written small and the second part itself joined on to the first, as Siolla páonaig or Siollapáonaig, maol muine or maolmuine. After Siolla it is better to separate the second part when it commences with a vowel, as Siolla íona, Siolla iaracta. Similarly cú ulao, but genitive Conulao.

several important surnames. The following are the
principal names of this class :

Aṁlaoiḃ,	Maġnup,
Apalt	Oipᴄín.
Ḃpuaḋap,	Oiᴄip,
Caplup,	Raġnall,
Ḋuḃġall,	Ruaiḋpí,
eanpac,	Ruaḋpac,
Ꝫoᴄpaiḋ,	Siocppaiḋ,
Íoṁap,	Siᴄpeac,
Loċlaınn,	Somaiple, &c.

In the same manner Norman and English names
became current in Irish families during the thirteenth
and subsequent centuries. These have now almost
completely supplanted the old Gaelic names.

The names borne by the Normans and by them
introduced into Ireland were of three kinds : (1) names
of Scandinavian origin which their ancestors had
carried with them to Normandy ; (2) names of Germanic
origin which the Frankish conquerors had brought
across the Rhine and which had ousted the old Celtic
and Latin names from France ; and (3) Biblical names
and Latin and Greek names of saints, which the Normans
began to adopt about the beginning of the eleventh
century.

Together with these came in a few Celtic names from
Brittany, a small number of Anglo-Saxon names, some
Danish and Norse names from England, and one or
two British or Welsh names. These were nearly all
very rare and most of them soon died out. Of the
Anglo-Saxon names, only two, Edmund and Edward,
and these owing to special circumstances, survived.
Alfred has been revived in recent times.

At the period of the Invasion, Frankish names were
by far the most popular among the Normans, but
Biblical and saintly names were coming rapidly into
favour. The following is a list, in order of frequency,

of the more common names borne by the early Anglo-Norman invaders, the Biblical and saintly names of Latin and Greek origin being printed in italics :

William, Robert, Richard, *John*, Walter, Roger, Ralph, *Adam*, Hugh, Henry, *Thomas*, *Nicholas*, Gilbert, Geoffrey, *Elias*, *Peter* (*Piers*), Osbert, Reginald, *Jordan*, *Simon*, Alan, *Stephen*, *Philip*, *David*, Arnold, *Alexander*, *Laurence*, Baldwin, Herbert, *Martin*, *Maurice*, Godfrey, *Andrew*, Alfred, *James*, *Samson*, Turstein, Warin, Ailward, *Daniel*, Edward, *Gregory*, Bernard, *Benedict*, Hamon, *Matthias*, *Michael*, Gerard, Gervase, Lambert, Wilkin, *Patrick*, Edmund, Edwin, Hubert, Ivor, *Joseph*, Oliver, *Mark*.

The following in alphabetical order were all very rare : *Abraham*, Adelard, Ailmer, *Antony*, *Augustine*, Brian, *Clement*, *Constantine*, Estmund, *Eustace*, Everard, Gocelin, *Isaac*, Leonard, *Luke*, *Matthew*, *Miles*, *Milo*, Odo, Osbern, Osmund, Pagan, *Ponce*, Randulf, Redmund Rodulf, *Silvester*, Turold, Ulf, *Vincent*.

The following names only came in, or at least became popular, at a later period : *Bartholomew*, *Christopher*, *Francis*, Gerald, *George*, *Paul*, Roland, Theobald.

Women's names among the Normans were all, or nearly all, of the Biblical or saintly class, as :

Agnes, Alice, Amelina, Anastasia, Annabella, Catherine, Cecily, Christina, Dorothy, Egidia, Eleanor, Evelyn, Frances, Honora, Isabella, Johanna, Matilda, Margaret, Susanna. The name Mary does not seem to have come into use in Ireland before the end of the 16th century. Brigid only began to be used about the same period.

The Anglo-Normans had several diminutive suffixes, viz. : -el, -et, -ot, (-at), -in, -on, (-en), -oc, -uc, -kin, and -cock. These were generally added to the shortened or " pet" form of the name, as : Martel, dim. of Martin ; Benet, dim. of Benedict ; Davet, dim. of David ; Adamot, dim. of Adam ; Milot, dim. of Miles ; Baldin, dim. of Baldwin ; Dobin, dim. of Dob (Robert) ;

Baldon, dim .of Baldwin ; Gibbon, dim. of Gilbert ;
Paton, dim. of Patrick ; Davoc, dim. of David ; Jonoc,
dim. of John ; Mayoc, dim. of Matthew ; Aduc, dim. of
Adam ; Hobuc, dim. of Hob (Robert) ; Philbuc, dim.
of Philip ; Robuc, dim. of Robert ; Tomuc, dim. of
Thomas ; Adkin, dim. of Adam ; Baldkin, dim. of
Baldwin ; Hobkin, dim. of Hob ; Hodgkin, dim. of
Hodge, Roger ; Tomkin, dim. of Thomas ; Alcoc, dim.
of Alan ; Simcoc, dim. of Simon, &c.

Not infrequently we find a double diminutive suffix,
as :—-elin, -elet, -inet, -elot, sometimes contracted
to -lin, -let, -net, -lot, &c.   Examples :—Gocelin,
Hughelin,   Hughelet,   Hughelot, Hamelin, Hamelet,
Hamlet, Robinet, Robnet, Tomelin, Tomlin, &c.

Religious motives have frequently led to the introduction of names of foreign saints.   The Spanish
name Iago (James) was brought to Ireland in the thirteenth or fourteenth century by pilgrims from the
shrine of St. James at Compostella, and other names
of foreign saints, as Aloysius, Alphonsus, Dominic,
Agatha, Monica, Teresa, &c., have been adopted from
time to time from similar motives.   In England, a
large number of new names from Holy Scripture was
introduced by the Puritans, and some of these have
found their way into Ireland.

It may be remarked that many foreign names found
at present in Ireland are merely modern substitutes
for Irish names which they are supposed to translate,
but with which they have often little or no connection,
as Cornelius for Conócóbap, Denis for Donncaó, Daniel
for Domnall, Eneas for Aongup, Eugene for Eogan,
Hugh for Aoó, Humphrey for Amlaoib, Jeremiah and
Jerome for Diapmaió, Malachy for Maol Seaclainn,
Justin for Saepbpeacac, Mortimer for Muipceapcac,
Moses for Maoóóg, Myles for Maolmuipe and Maolmópóa, Roger for Ruaiópí, Terence for Coipóealbac,
Timothy for Caóg and Comalcac, etc.   Charles was

an extremely rare name in Ireland until the early part
of the 17th century when it began to be substituted
in honour of Charles I., for several Irish names, such as
Catal, Cataoin, Conmac, etc. Similarly, in the case
of women's names, we have Abigail and Deborah for
Gobnait, Agnes for Mór and Úna, Dorothy for Doineann,
Gertrude and Grace for Gráinne, Mabel for Meadb,
Penelope for Fionnguala, Sarah for Sorca and Sadb,
Winefred for Úna, etc.

§ 4—Cognomina

A cognomen, or epithet, was frequently added to a
name to distinguish different individuals of the same
name. These cognomina were of three kinds :—

1. An adjective conveying personal description,
   as Cormac Cas, Domnall Bán, Eogan Ruad.

2. A substantive in -ac, denoting place of birth,
   residence, fosterage, etc., Aod Muimneac,
   Domnall Caománac, Eóin Catánac.

3. A noun in the genitive case, usually with the
   article, signifying place of origin, residence,
   or some other connection, as Brian an Doire,
   Tadg an Tsléibe, Conn na mbocc.

§ 5—Interchange of Names

A marked feature of our Irish name-system was the
frequent interchange of names of the same or similar
meaning. This was doubtless due to the fact that our
ancestors paid attention to the meaning no less than
to the form of their names.

The following classes of names are to a greater or less extent interchangeable :—

(1) Variants of the same name, as Aoḃán and Maoḋóg, Colmán and Moċolmóg, foe and Míḋe
(2) A name and its diminutives, and the various diminutive forms among themselves, as : Fionnḃarr and Fionntán, Fiaċán and Feiċín.
(3) Names of the same signification, though differing in form, as : Dairḟḟionn and Fionnḃarr.
(4) Different names used for the same individual, as : Cárṫaċ and Moċuḋa.

§ 6—DECLENSION OF NAMES

The declension of names follows the ordinary rules for common nouns. The following points may, however, be noted :—

1. Many names belong to more than one declension.
2. A few names have in the course of time changed their declension.
3. Names of the fifth declension which form their genitive case by adding ċ or n, generally drop these letters in the spoken language.
4. Diminutives in -óg are masculine and invariable.
5. In the case of compound names, the part to be inflected depends on the nature of the compound. Sometimes both parts are inflected, as Cú ḋuḃ, gen. Conḋuiḃ ; sometimes the second only, as Ḋuḃċú, gen. Ḋuḃċon. When the second part is already in the genitive case the first alone changes, as Cú Ulaḋ, gen. Con Ulaḋ, Conulaḋ.
6. The nominative case is sometimes used for the genitive, and *vice versa*.

A perusal of the list of surnames will show the genitive form of most names.

CHAPTER II—SURNAMES

§ 1—GAELIC SURNAMES

Gaelic surnames comprise surnames of Irish, Scottish-Gaelic, and Manx origin.

Irish surnames came into use gradually from about the middle of the tenth to the end of the thirteenth century, and were formed from the genitive case of the names of ancestors who flourished within that period, by prefixing Ó (also written Ua) or Mac (sometimes written Mag*), as :

Ó Bριαιn,	Mac Λοὐαჳάιn,
Ó hΛοὐα,	Mac Cάρταιჳ,
Ó néιll,	Mag uιὀιρ.

Ó literally signifies *a grandson*, and Mac *a son* : but in the wider sense which they have acquired in surnames both now mean any male descendant. The only difference between a surname commencing with Mac and one commencing with Ó is that the former was taken from the name of the father and the latter from that of the grandfather of the first person who bore the surname. Mac-surnames are, generally speaking, of later formation than Ó-surnames.

Surnames were frequently formed, not from the real name of the ancestor, but from some other designation, as rank, trade, occupation, etc., as :

Ó ჳoბαnn (descendant of the smith),
Ó hιceαὐα (descendant of the healer),
Mac αn ὐάιρο (son of the bard),
Mac αn τSαοιρ (son of the craftsman).

The Gaels of Scotland belonged by race and language to the Irish nation, bore the same or similar personal names, and formed their surnames in the same manner as the Irish from the names or designations of their

---

*Mag is used before vowels, the consonants C, ჳ, l, n, and R, and the aspirated consonants ბ, ὀ, ρ, ṁ, Ś, and τ, but not always even before these.

ancestors. Scottish-Gaelic surnames are, however,
of much later date than Irish surnames. The instances
of the use of Ó are very rare.*

The Manx language is closely allied to the Irish and
Scottish-Gaelic. Manx surnames were formed in the
same manner as Irish surnames, by prefixing ṁ⒜c.
Ó, however, was not used. The modern spelling is
very corrupt, ṁ⒜c being generally represented by an
initial C or K.

The Danes and Norsemen who settled in Ireland in
the ninth and tenth centuries took surnames after the
Irish fashion, by prefixing Ó or ṁ⒜c to the genitive
case of the names of their ancestors; but the surnames
so formed are in nowise distinguishable from the surnames adopted about the same time by Irish families.
What are called Danish surnames are merely surnames
formed from a Danish eponym, which, however, owing
to the interchange of names, was, at the period when
surnames were formed, no longer a sure indication of
nationality. The following are examples of this class
of surname :

Ó hⒶᖇⒶⒾⒸⒸ,	ṁⒶⒸ ⒶṁⓁⒶⓄⒾb,
Ó ⒷᖇⓊⒶⒹⒶⒾᖇ,	ṁⒶⒸ ⒾⓄṁⒶⒾᖇ,
Ó ⒹⓊbᵹⒶⒾⓁⓁ,	ṁⒶⒸ ⓄⒾⒸⒾᖇ.

Many Scottish and Manx surnames are of this hybrid
class.

---

*Down to the eighteenth century, the Irish and the Scot-
tish Gaels had a common literary language, though the spoken
tongues had diverged considerably. In that century Scottish
Gaelic broke completely with the Irish and began a literary
career of its own. The spelling of surnames in modern Scottish Gaelic is consequently somewhat different from what it
would be in Irish. The Scottish surnames included in this
book are given in the Irish spelling.

§ 2—Surnames of the Sean-Gaill

The surnames brought into Ireland by the Anglo-Normans were of four kinds :—

1. Patronymic.   3. Occupative.
2. Local.   4. Descriptive.

1. The Norman patronymic was formed by prefixing Fitz (a corruption of the French " fils," Latin " filius"), denoting " son of," as Fitz-Gerald, Fitz-Gibbon, Fitz-Herbert, Fitz-Simon. The English added " -son," as Richardson, Williamson ; or merely the genitive suffix " -s," as Richards, Williams. Welsh patronymics were formed by prefixing " ap" or " ab," from older " Map," cognate with the Irish ᴍᴀc, which, when it came before a name beginning with a vowel or h, was in many instances incorporated with it, as Ab Evan, now Bevan ; Ab Owen, now Bowen ; Ap Howel, now Howell and Powell.

English surnames in " -s" and " -son," and Welsh surnames in " Ap" were, however, at first extremely rare ; they became common only at a much later date.* The type of patronymic most common among the Anglo-Normans was that in which the father's name appears in its simple and unaltered form, without prefix or desinence. Fitz seems to have been dropped early.† The great bulk of Anglo-Norman patronymic surnames are of this type.

---

*The early Anglo-Norman invaders, coming as they did from Wales, were called ᴃpᴇᴀċnᴀɩ̇ᵹ, or Welshmen, by the Irish ; but Welshmen they certainly were not, at least to any appreciable extent, as the almost complete absence of Welsh Christian names from among them amply proves. English surnames in " s " and " son " were peculiar to the Danish districts in the North of England, from which few, if any, of the early invaders came.

† Nothing is more common at the present day in certain parts of the country than to hear a man designated. no matter what his surname, as Maurice William or John James, meaning Maurice, son of William, or John, son of James. This is but a survival of the Norman practice.

The names from which these patronymic surnames were formed were of Norman, Anglo-Saxon, Norse, Danish, Flemish, Breton, Welsh, and even Irish origin.*

2. Local surnames were taken either from specific place names, or common local designations, or some local landmark; and the language in which they occur may be either Norman-French or English. If the surname was from a specific place name and the language Norman-French, the local element was preceded by " de"; if English, by " of," familiarly pronounced " a," as : Robert de Arcy, David de Barri, Torkaill of Kardif, Samsun of Stanlega. The local element may be the name of a country, province, county, city, town, village, or even farmstead. Surnames derived from places in Normandy alone denote Norman origin.

When the source of the surname was a common local designation, or mere landmark, the Normans prefixed " de la," " del," or " du"; the English " atte," which became " atten" before a vowel, as Henry de la Chapelle, Richard de la Felda, John de la Hyde. Robert del Bois (du Bois), Robert atte Brigge, Gilbert atte Wode, Walter atten Angle, Simon atten Ashe. The local element may be either Norman-French or English or Welsh. †

3. Occupative surnames are those derived from office, profession, trade, or occupation generally. They were originally all common nouns, and usually Norman-French. The definite article " le," the English " the," was generally, but not always, prefixed, as : le Archer, le Baillif, le Botiller, le Boucher, le Erchedecne, le Marescall, the Miller.

4. Descriptive surnames are those which convey

* The name Colman which occurs in Domesday Book is an instance.

†A small number of surnames—perhaps not more than thirty—are formed after the Norman fashion from Irish place-names. These, however, were not brought in by the invaders, but taken by them from places where they settled in Ireland.

personal description, and they are of various kinds according to the different ways in which a person can be described. They are generally Norman-French or English, but we have a few surnames formed from Welsh and Anglo-Saxon nouns and adjectives.

Physical peculiarities are represented by " le Gras," " le Grant," " le Petit," " le Brun," " le White," " the Black" ; mental and moral by " le Prut," " le Curteis," " le Salvage," " l'Enfant," " the Babe" ; animal characteristics by " le Bacoun," le Veel," " le Wolf," " the Fox" ; nationality by " l'Engleys," " le Fleming," " le Lombard," le Waleys."

Many of the early Anglo-Norman families assumed surnames after the Irish fashion by prefixing mac to the names or other designations of their ancestors, as :

mac Ceóṗaıṗ,   mac an ṁíleaḋa
mac Seóınín,   mac an Rıoṗṗe ;

but most of them retained their original surname in an hibernicised form, as : Oalacún for Dalton, Réamonn for Redmond, Hoıṗeaḃáṗo for Herbert, etc. The Norman Fitz was replaced by mac, as mac Ȝeaṗaılc, mac Sıomúın for FitzGerald, FitzSimon. English surnames ending in -s and son are similarly hibernicised ; but Anglo-Norman patronymic surnames which had neither prefix nor filial desinence have the same form in Irish as the Christian name. The diminutive suffixes -el, -et, -ot, -in, -on, -oc, -uc, -kin, and -cock are represented in Irish by -éıl,* -éıo, -óıo, -ín, -ún, -oc (óȝ), -uc (ac), -cín, and -cóc respectively.

The prefix " de" of Norman surnames is represented in Irish by " oe," as oe Búṗc for de Burgh, oe Léıṗ for de Laci, etc. oe is sometimes incorporated with the local part of the surname, as Oácún for de Autun, Oéaḃṗúṗ for d'Evereux, etc. oe also sometimes stands for " de la," as oe Múṗa for " de la Mor ; or perhaps its English equivalent " atte Mor." " de la"

---

* Or éal. The usage is not uniform.

itself, in the few instances in which it survives, is in-corporated with the second part of the surname, as 𐌃ᴀᴌᴀɪᴄᴏ for " de la Hyde," ᴅᴀᴌᴀᴍᴀᴘᴀ for " de la Mare." ᴏe, pronounced ᴏᴏ, is possibly for the Norman " du," the equivalent before masculine nouns of " de la." The English " of" is, of course, represented by " ᴀ" in Irish, but " ᴀ" is sometimes a worn down " ᴏe," as in ᴀ ᴃᴌᴀᴄ, ᴀ �. The English " atte," or " at the," is also represented in Irish by ᴏe, as ᴏe ᴃᴏ� for " atte Wode," at the wood. The n of the extended form, " atten," is attracted over to the second part of the name, as ᴏe ᴍᴏᴚᴌᴀ for " atten Angle," at the corner ; ᴏe ᴍᴀɪᴘ for " atten Ashe," at the ash.

The Norman definite article " le" and the English " the," used with occupative and descriptive surnames, are both represented in Irish by ᴏe, " le" having ap-parently been translated into its English equivalent " the" before the surname was hibernicised, as ᴏe ᴘᴀᴏɪᴄ for " le Whyte," the White, ᴏe ᴃᴌᴀᴄᴀ for " the Blake," the Black, ᴏe ᴃᴏᴘᴄ for " the Fox," ᴏe ᴃᴜᴌᴃ for " le Wolf," the wolf, ᴏe ᴃᴀɪᴌéɪᴘ, ᴏe ᴃᴀɪᴌɪᴘ for, " le Waleys," the Welshman, etc.

There was, almost from the first, a strong tendency to drop all these enclitic particles, and in many instances they had actually been dropped before the surnames to which they had been attached attained an Irish form ; hence many of these surnames have no prefix in Irish.* Norman diminutives, it should be remarked, like Blanchet, Porcel, Russel, never took the article and consequently never take " ᴏe" in Irish.

---

*This is true of nearly all English surnames which came in after the fifteenth century. In my list I have inserted ᴏe in every instance where I had the authority of old Anglo-Irish records or the present spoken language for its use. ᴏe should not be used before surnames derived from personal names. Norman diminutives, or Anglo-Saxon or Welsh nouns or ad-jectives.

§ 3—Cognomina used as Surnames

A small number of surnames are substantives in -ᴀċ, -eᴀċ, indicative of nationality, place of origin, fosterage, etc., as ḃpeᴀċnᴀċ, Cᴀoṁánᴀċ, Ɗéipeᴀċ, Muiṁneᴀċ, Ultᴀċ.

A few are descriptive adjectives, as ḃán, ḃeᴀ5, 5lᴀp, liᴀt, Uᴀiċne, etc.

We have also a few surnames derived from place of residence, as ᴀn Ṁᴀċᴀipe, nᴀ ḃpí5ḋe.

These three classes of surnames are merely cognomina substituted for the real surnames which are now lost or forgotten. Families bearing these surnames may be of either Irish or English origin.

§ 4—Alternative Form of Surnames

Most of the patronymic surnames given above (§§ 1-2) have a second form obtained by dropping Ó or mᴀc and postfixing -ᴀċ (-eᴀċ) to the nominative case of the name of the ancestor,* as Ó ḃpiᴀin or ḃpiᴀnᴀċ, Ó ḃpoin or ḃpᴀnᴀċ, Ó Nuᴀlláin or Nuᴀllánᴀċ, mᴀc Suiḃne or Suiḃneᴀċ.

This form is also used in the case of surnames of foreign origin, as Céicinn or Céicinneᴀċ (Céicneᴀċ), Ɗᴀippi5 or Ɗᴀippi5eᴀċ, Ɗᴀlᴀcún or Ɗᴀlᴀcúnᴀċ, peicíḋ or peicíḋeᴀċ. The prefix ḋe is dropped when -ᴀċ is postfixed, as ḋe ḃúpc or ḃúpcᴀċ, ḋe Róipce or Róipceᴀċ. Surnames ending in -éil and éip change these terminations into -éᴀl and -éᴀp before -ᴀċ is added.

The foregoing forms when standing alone have an indefinite signification and cannot, unless defined by

---

*When the name of the ancestor already ends in -ᴀċ (-eᴀċ) the termination is not repeated, as Ó Ceᴀllᴀi5; or Ceᴀllᴀċ, Ó Cinnpeᴀlᴀ5 or Cinnpeᴀlᴀċ.

the context, be used to indicate a particular individual.*
To make them definite they must be preceded by the
Christian name or a title, or turned into one of the
forms mentioned in the remaining paragraphs of this
section, as: Oomnall Ó Ópiain, Copmac Mac Cáptaig,
páopaig Condún, Éamonn de Oúpc, Ualtap Caománac,
an teappcg Ó Oomnaill, an Ooctúip Ó Loingpig

The forms in -ac may also be made definite by prefixing the article and can then be used for a particular
individual without the Christian name or title.† The
form has then the force of the English Mr. when the
Christian name is not expressed, as an Oappac, Mr.
Barry ; an Oúpcac, Mr. Burke ; an Opianac, Mr.
O'Brien ; an Suioneac, Mr. MacSweeny.

Another way of indicating a particular individual,
without using the Christian name, is to prefix Mac
to the genitive case of the surname, as Mac Uí Ópiain,
Mr. O'Brien, Mac Uí Caoim, Mr. O'Keeffe, Mac mic
an Oáipd, Mr. Ward. In this construction surnames
commencing with Mac are sometimes treated as if
they commenced with Ó, as : Mac Uí geapailt, Mr.
Fitzgerald, Mac Uí Suione, Mr. MacSweeny.

We have also corresponding forms of -ac-surnames
with the article, as : Mac an Ópeatnaig, Mr Walsh,
Mac an Oúpcaig, Mr. Burke ; Mac an Róiptig, Mr.
Roche.

---

*In the case of surnames in Ó and Mac, the name alone was
formerly used as the title of the chief of the name, as Ó néill,
(The) O'Neill, Ó Oomnaill, (The) O Donnell ; and it is still
used as an honorary title in some families, as Ó Concobaip
Oonn, The O'Conor Don, Mac Oiapmada, The MacDermott.

†This -ac form with the article was formerly used, in the case
of surnames of foreign origin, to signify the chief of an Anglo-
Irish family, and corresponded to the use of the surname alone
in the case of native Irish chiefs.

§ 5—Synopsis of Types of Surnames

It will be convenient to summarize here under different types the surnames of which we have so far treated.

Type I.	Ó Briain. Ó hAoḋa. Ó Néill.		XI.	De Bál. De Búrc. Céitinn. Conḋún.
II.	Ó Bruaḋair. Ó Duḃġaill. Ó hAṁailt.			
III.	Ó Goḃann. Ó hIceaḋa.		XII.	De Bailéir. De Borc. De Faoit. Aingléir. Airféir. Laiġléir.
IV.	Mac Aoḋaġáin. Mac Cárṫaiġ. Maġ Uiḋir.			
V.	Mac Ioṁair. Mac Maġnuir. Mac Feórair. Mac Seóinín.		XIII.	an Ṁácaire. na Bríġde.
VI.	a Paol. a Prír.		XIV.	Brianaċ. Búrcaċ. Róirteaċ.
VII.	Mac an Báird. Mac an tSaoir. Mac an Ṁíleaḋa. Mac an Rioṁe.		XV.	an Brianaċ. an Búrcaċ. an Róirteaċ.
VIII.	Báróid. Mirtéil. Réamonn.		XVI.	Mac uí Briain. Mac uí Caoiṁ. Mac mic an Báirn Mac uí Gearailt. Mac uí Suiḃne. Mac an Breatnaiġ Mac an Búrcaiġ Mac an Róirtiġ.
IX.	Bán. Beaġ. Liaċ.			
X.	Breatnaċ. Caoṁánaċ. Ultaċ.			

§ 6—Declension of Surnames

In surnames of Types I, II, III, IV, V, and VII, the name or designation of the ancestor is in the genitive case and remains unchanged in the declension of the surname, except that its initial letter is sometimes aspirated or eclipsed, if a consonant, or has h or n prefixed, if a vowel. With this exception ᵯac and Ó alone change.

Ó, or Uᴀ, and ᵯac are thus declined :—

	Singular.		Plural.	
Nom. and acc.	Ó	Uᴀ	í	Uí
gen.	í	Uí	Ó	Uᴀ
dat.	Ó	Uᴀ	íb	Uíb
voc.	ᴀ	Uí	ᴀ	Uí.
Nom. and acc.	ᵯac		ᵯic, ᵯeic, ᵯᴀcᴀ	
gen.	ᵯic, ᵯeic		ᵯac	
dat.	ᵯac		ᵯᴀcᴀıb	
voc.	ᴀ ᵯic		ᴀ ṁᴀcᴀ.	

Ó, is the usual form in the nominative case, Uí in the genitive. When the name of the ancestor begins with a vowel, ṅ is prefixed after Ó in the nominative case singular,* and n in the genitive plural. Ó sometimes aspirates ꝑ in the nominative case singular, and always eclipses in the gen. plural, if the name commences with an eclipsable consonant. Uí causes aspiration in the singular. ᵯac sometimes aspirates the initial consonant of the name in the nominative case singular. The ᵯ of ᵯac is itself frequently aspirated in the nom. case singular after the Christian name ; always in the genitive case, and sometimes in the dative,

---

*There are a few exceptions.

EXAMPLES :

(a) Brian Ó hAirt

Nom. and acc.		Brian Ó hAirt
gen.	ainm	Briain Uí Airt
dat.	ag	Brian { Ó hAirt / Ó Airt
Voc.	a	Briain Uí Airt.

(b) Brian Ó Domnaill.

Nom. and acc.		Brian Ó Domnaill
gen.	ainm	Briain Uí Domnaill
dat.	ag	Brian Ó Domnaill
voc.	a	Briain Uí Domnaill.

(c) Brian Mac Domnaill.

Nom. and acc.		Brian Mac Domnaill
gen.	ainm	Briain Mic Domnaill
dat.	ag	Brian Mac Domnaill
voc.	a	Briain Mic Domnaill.

The plural forms of Ó and Mac are now met with only in place-names derived from clan or family names, as : Uí Cinnrealaig, Uí Dróna, Cúil Ó bFinn, Mainirtir Ó dTórna, i nUib Laogaire. The modern collective plural of surnames of these types is formed by prefixing Muinnteap, Clann, or Síol* to the genitive case of the name of the ancestor, as :

Muinnteap Baoigill, the O'Boyles ;
Muinnteap Éilide, the O'Healys ;
Muinnteap Ragallaig, the O'Reillys ;
Muinnteap Ruairc, the O'Rourkes ;
Clann Amlaoib, the MacAuliffes ;
Clann an Báird, the MacWards ;
Clann Diarmada, the MacDermotts ;
Clann tSíčig, the MacSheehys ;
Síol mBriain, the O'Briens ;
Síol gCeallaig, the O'Kellys ;
Síol Móroa, the O'Mores ;
Síol Uidir, the Maguires.

Muinnteap is used in the case of Ó-surnames ; Clann, with a few exceptions, is confined to Mac-surnames.

---

*Muinnteap and Clann cause aspiration, Síol eclipsis.

Síol is now used only in literature. muinnᴄeaṗ and
Clann are sometimes prefixed to the gen. case of the
surname, as: muinnᴄeaṗ Uı Ċeallaċáin, the
O'Callaghans; Clann ṁıc Conmaṗa, the MacNamaras.

The following examples show the declension of surnames in -aċ (Types X, XIV, XV):—

(a) An Caoṁánaċ.

	Singular.	Plural.
Nom. and acc.	an Caoṁánaċ	na Caoṁánaıġ
gen.	an Caoṁánaıġ	na ᵹCaoṁánaċ
dat.	leıṗ an ᵹCaoṁánaċ	leıṗ na Caoṁánċaıḃ
voc.	a Ċaoṁánaıġ	a Ċaoṁánċa.

(b) An ᴄlúṗᴄáṗaċ.

Nom. and acc.	an ᴄlúṗᴄáṗaċ	na hlúṗᴄáṗaıġ
gen.	an lúṗᴄáṗaıġ	na nlúṗᴄáṗaċ
dat.	leıṗ an lúṗᴄáṗaċ	leıṗ na hlúṗᴄáṗċaıḃ
voc.	a lúṗᴄáṗaıġ	a lúṗᴄáṗċa.

(c) An Sáḃaoıṗeaċ.

Nom. and acc.	an Sáḃaoıṗeaċ	na Sáḃaoıṗıġ
gen.	an ᴄSáḃaoıṗıġ	na Sáḃaoıṗeaċ
dat.	ᴅo'n ᴄSáḃaoıṗeaċ / leıṗ an Sáḃaoıṗeaċ	leıṗ na Sáḃaoıṗeaċaıḃ,
voc.	a Sáḃaoıṗıġ	a Sáḃao ṗeaċa

Surnames of Types VI, VIII, XI, XII are not declined. All these surnames form their collective
plurals like surnames in -aċ, as: na Ḃaṗóıᴠıᵹ, the
Barretts; ᴄeaċ na mḂúṗcaċ, the house of the Burkes.

Surnames of Type IX follow the rule of adjectives.
They form their plural like surnames in -aċ.

Surnames of Type XIII are invariable. The plural
is formed by prefixing muinnᴄeaṗ.

In surnames of Type XVI., mac alone changes.

A personal epithet, or cognomen, comes between the Christian name and the surname, and, if an adjective, agrees in case with the Christian name, as: Doṁnall Bán Ó Briain, bó Ḋoṁnaill Ḃáin Uí Ḃriain.

Sometimes the father's name, in the genitive case with Mac prefixed, is inserted in the same position to distinguish persons of the same name and surname, as: Doṁnall mac Ḋonnċaḋa Ó Briain; or the patronymic may follow the surname, as: Doṁnall Ó Briain mac Ḋonnċaḋa. Mac always aspirates in this case. The mac is now usually dropped, but the aspiration remains, as: Pádraig Ṫaiḋg Óig Ó Conaill.

When two Christian names are used, the second is put in the gen. case, with its initial letter aspirated, —mac being understood if the father's name, and giolla if the name of a saint, as: Seán Ṗeadair Ó Néill, John Peter O'Neill.*

In the case of a double surname in English, as Patrick Sarsfield O'Donnell, Hugh O'Neill Flanagan, the first surname assumes the -aċ termination, thus: Pádraig Sáirséalaċ Ó Doṁnaill, Aoḋ Niallaċ Ó Flannagáin.

When a personal cognomen of the ancestor appears in the surname, it agrees in case with the name of the ancestor, as: Seán Mac Ṁuiris Ruaiḋ, Taḋg Mac Conaill Óig.

An agnomen used to distinguish different branches of the same family agrees in case with the surname; in other words, it is in the same case as Mac or Ó, as: Magnus Mac Diarmada Ruaḋ, Ó Conċobair Donn.

§ 7—Surnames of Females

Instead of Ó and Mac, Ní and Nic respectively are used after names of females in surnames of Types I, II, III, IV, V and VII. Ní is an abbreviation of ní

---

* This rule is not always observed by present-day Irish speakers.

(from ıngeαn, a daughter) and í or Uí (genitive case of Ó or Uα) ; and ᵁic of ᵁí ᵐᵘic.

Examples :—

{ Pádpaıg Ó 'Domnaıll, Patrick O'Donnell
{ máıne ᵁí 'Domnaıll, Mary O'Donnell

{ Seán Ó hÓgáın, John Hogan
{ eıblín ᵁí Ógáın, Ellen Hogan.

{ Séamuᵖ Mac Seóınín, James Jennings
{ Cáıc ᵁic Seóınín, Kate Jennings.

{ Pádpaıg Mac an Goıll, Patrick Gill
{ máıne ᵁic an Goıll, Mary Gill.

{ eogan Mac Aovágáın, Owen Egan
{ máıne ᵁic Aovágáın, Mary Egan.

The unabbreviated form ᵁí ᵐᵘic is used in some places, as :

{ Seán Mac an Báıp'o, John Ward
{ máıne ᵁí ᵐᵘic an Báıp'o, Mary Ward.

ᵁig is the form corresponding to Mag, as :

{ Conĉobaᵖ Mag Uıᵒıᵖ, Connor Maguire
{ Soᵖĉa ᵁig Uıᵒıᵖ, Sarah Maguire.

Surnames of females are sometimes, like those of males, formed directly from the name of the ancestor, as :

Cáıc ᵁí cSeóınín, Kate Jennings
Bᵖígıᵒ ᵁí cSuıbne, Brigid MacSweeny
máıne ᵁí Paᵖĉaláın, Mary MacPartland.

It will be seen from the foregoing examples that in the surnames of females, except those formed directly from the name of the ancestor, the part of the surname following ᵁí or ᵁic is in all cases the same as that after Uí or ᵐᵘic in the surnames of males. The reason of this is obvious, ᵁí and ᵁic being contractions of ᵁí Uí and ᵁí ᵐᵘic respectively.*

---

*Hence eıblín ᵁí Ógáın, not eıblín ᵁí hÓgáın, is the correct form.

In surnames of Types VI, VIII, XI, XII and XIII.,
the form of the surname after names of females is the
same as after those of males, as :

{ Seán Báróiv, John Barrett
{ peiʒ Báróiv, Peg Barrett.
{ Seán Dṗún, John Brown
{ Máiṗe Dṗún, Mary Brown.
{ Réamonn ve Róiṗce, Redmund Roche.
{ Máiṗe ve Róiṗce, Mary Roche.
{ Éamonn na Dṗíʒve, Edmond Bride
{ Eibłín na Dṗíʒve, Ellen Bride.

Surnames of Type IX, being adjectives, are aspirated
in the nominative case, as : Máiṗe Ʒlaṗ, Mary Green.

Surnames of Types X and XIV, that is, all surnames
ending in -ać, may be either substantives or adjectives,
When the surname is an adjective, its initial letter is
aspirated in the nominative case after names of females,
as :

{ Seán Dṗeaċnać, John Walsh
{ Cáic Dṗeaċnać, Kate Walsh.
{ Seán Cáṗċać, John MacCarthy
{ Siobán Cáṗċać, Joan MacCarthy.*

The following forms corresponding to Type XVI may
be used as equivalent to the English *Miss* when the
Christian name is omitted :—

Inʒean Uí Dṗiain, Miss O'Brien.
Inʒean an Cáṗċaiʒ, Miss MacCarthy.
Inʒean Ṁic an Dáiṗv, Miss Ward.
Inʒean an Ʒeaṗalcaiʒ, Miss Fitzgerald.
Inʒean an Dúṗcaiʒ, Miss Burke.
Inʒean an Róiṗciʒ, Miss Roche.†

*This was first pointed out to me by the late Canon O'Leary
(An cÁċaiṗ peavaṗ), who, when the first edition of this book
was passing through the press, kindly sent me the following
note on the Introductory Chapters which he had read :
" I have just one remark to make. In the case of women's
names I have heard ' Siobán Cáṗċać, not ' Siobán Cáṗċać,' and
' Cáic Dṗeaċnać,' not 'Cáic Dṗeaċnać.' That is to say,
when the surname is an *adjective* it agrees with the noun like any
adjective. When the surname is not an adjective I have heard
exactly what you say, *i.e.*, ' peiʒ Báróiv,' not ' peiʒ Báróiv.'
Instead of ' Máiṗe Dṗeaċnać' I have heard ' Máiṗe an Dṗeaċ-
naiʒ,' where the surname is treated as a definite noun."
†But not Inʒean ve Dúṗc, Inʒean ve Róiṗce, &c.

The same construction may be used to express *Miss* with the Christian name, as :

> máιρe, ιnɣeaɴ uí Óρυaιn, Miss Mary O'Brien.
> eιblín, ιnɣeaɴ aɴ Óúρcaιɣ, Miss Eileen Burke.

Mrs. may be similarly expressed, as :

> beaɴ uí Óρυaιn, Mrs. O'Brien.
> beaɴ aɴ Óúρcaιɣ, Mrs. Burke.
> beaɴ mιc aɴ Óáιρο, Mrs. Ward.
> beaɴ Seáιn uí Óρυaιn, Mrs. John O'Brien.
> beaɴ Caιóɣ mιc aɴ Óáιρο, Mrs. T. Ward.
> beaɴ Éaᴍuιɴɴ οe Róιρce, Mrs. Edmund Roche.
> máιρe, beaɴ mιc aɴ Óáιρο, Mrs. Mary Ward.
> Cáιc, beaɴ Seáιn οe Óúρc, Mrs. Kate Burke, or
> Mrs. John Burke.*

In the case of a widow, baιɴcρeaċ (baιɴcρeaбaċ) is to be used instead of beaɴ, as :

> baιɴcρeaċ Seáιn uí Óρυaιn, Mrs. John O'Brien.
> baιɴcρeaċ Éaᴍuιɴɴ οe Óúρc, Mrs. Edmund Burke.
> baιɴcρeaċ aɴ Óρeaċɴaιɣ, Mrs. Walsh.
> máιρe, baιɴcρeaċ aɴ Róιρcιɣ, Mrs. Mary Roche.

Married women retain their maiden name in Irish. We may therefore say : máιρe ɴí Óρυaιn, beaɴ Seáιn οe Óúρc, Mrs. John Burke, née Mary O'Brien.

ɴí and ɴιc do not change in the genitive case.

§ 8—Surnames in the Spoken Language

Surnames are variously corrupted in the spoken language, and deviate in many important respects from the standard or literary form, but it would be impossible within the limits of a short introduction to deal with this aspect of the subject in detail. The corruptions and variations of Ó and mac, as they affect

---

*But not beaɴ Óρeaċɴaċ, beaɴ οe Óúρc, beaɴ οe Róιρce, &c. which are incorrect.

a large number of surnames, may however be briefly
noted.

Ó, or Ua, is corrupted as follows :

1. Sometimes shortened to A, as : A Deóráin for
   Ó Deóráin, A Ȝním for Ó Ȝním.
2. Sometimes altogether dropped, as : Caomáin
   for Ó Caomáin, Cataraiȝ for Ó Cataraiȝ.
3. Sometimes replaced by the gen. case Uí, as : Uí
   Floinn for Ó Floinn, Uí Laoȝaire for Ó
   Laoȝaire.
4. Sometimes prefixed to surnames to which it
   does not properly belong, as: Ó Diolúin for
   Diolúin, Ó Ȝoȝáin for Ȝoȝán, Ó Róirte for
   De Róirte.

The following are the corruptions and variations of
Mac and Maȝ :—

1. c or Ȝ attracted over to the name of the ancestor.
   This happens when the name of the ancestor
   commences with a vowel or H or with L, N,
   or R, or with a consonant aspirated after Mac
   or Maȝ. The name of the ancestor is then
   treated in all the forms of the surname as if it
   commenced with C or Ȝ. Examples:—

   > Mac Captáin for Mac Aptáin
   > Mac Ceoȝain for Mac Eoȝain
   > Mac Coitir for Mac Oitir
   > Mac Ȝraic for Maȝ Raic.

   Hence such forms as : Bár an Coitiriȝ for
   bár an Oitriȝ ; an Ceoȝnac for an teoȝnac ;
   na Ceoȝnaiȝ for na heoȝnaiȝ.

2. m in some places always aspirated after the
   Christian name, as : Eoȝan Maȝ Aoḋa,
   Séamur Maȝ Floinn, Domnall Mac Suiḃne ;
   and sometimes entirely dropped, as : Séamur
   'ac Conraoi. The c of Mac is also very
   frequently aspirated, as Eamonn 'ac Síṫiȝ.

3. Sometimes takes the form ṁა, ṁა, ṁé, the
   c or ჳ being attracted over as above, as : ṁა
   ჳloınn for ṁაჳ floınn, ṁა ჳıonnáın for
   ṁაჳ fıonnáın, ṁა ჳuıḃır for ṁაჳ uıḃır,
   ṁა ჳრაıċ for ṁაჳ Raıċ, ṁé ჳuḃáın for ṁაჳ
   Ďuḃáın.

4. Takes the form ა when ṁ is dropped and c or
   ჳ attracted over, as : Cაḋჳ ა Cıonnრაċċაıჳ
   for Cაḋჳ ṁაc ıonnრაċċაıჳ.

5. Sometimes c or ჳ alone retained, as Cაıḃıრċín
   for ṁაc Aıḃıრċín, Cuılcín for ṁაc Uılcín,
   ჳıonnჳაıle for ṁაჳ fıonnჳაıle.

6. Sometimes made ṁáჳ, ṁáჳ, as : ṁáჳ Coċláın,
   ṁáჳ ჳაffაıḋ.

7. Sometimes ṁóc, ṁóჳ, and then, by the dropping of the initial ṁ, óc, óჳ, uაc, uაჳ. When
   in this case c or ჳ is attracted over, the final
   form is the same as ın Ó surnames. Examples :—

   Ó Cაċṁაoıl for ṁაc Cაċṁაoıl.
   Ó Ceაċṁარcაıჳ for ṁაc eაċṁარcაıჳ
   Ó Ceóınín for ṁაc Seóınín.
   Ó Cıúრċáın for ṁაc Sıúრċáın.
   Ó Coṁnაıll for ṁაc Ďoṁnაıll
   Ó Connċაḃა for ṁაc Ďonnċაḃა.
   Ó Cuრċáın for ṁაc Cuრċáın.
   Ó ჳრıაḋა for ṁაჳ Rıაḋა.
   Ó ჳრuაırc for ṁაჳ Ruაırc.
   Ó ჳuḃáın for ṁაჳ Ďuḃáın.
   Uა Coıbıcín for ṁაc hoıbıcín.
   Uა ჳoıრeაċċაıჳ for ṁაჳ Oıრeაċċაıჳ.

8. In a few instances simply replaced by Ó, as :
   Ó fılıbín for ṁაc fılıbín, Ó Sıúრċáın for
   ṁაc Sıúრċáın, Ó Suıḃne for ṁაc Suıḃne.

9. Frequently replaced by the genitive case ṁıc
   or 'ıc, as : Séამuრ ṁıc Seóınín for Séამuრ
   ṁაc Seóınín, Séამuრ 'ıc ან fრაnncაıჳ for
   Séამuრ ṁაc ან fრაnncაıჳ.

10. In Omeath, ṁაc ჳıolla is corrupted to ṁა'l,
    as ṁა'l რáḋრაıჳ for ṁაc ჳıolla რáḋრაıჳ,
    ṁა'l Coılle for ṁაc ჳıolla ċoılle.

Corruptions and variations of individual surnames, especially when they are reflected in the anglicised form, are noted as they occur in the lists.

§ 9.—Interchange of Surnames.

1. Some Irish families have two surnames, each derived from a different ancestor, or one derived from the name and another from a designation of the same ancestor, as :—

> Ó maoᴌpuᴀnᴀóᴀ and mᴀc ᴅᴀpmᴀóᴀ,
> mᴀc Conmᴀpᴀ and mᴀc Síoóᴀ,
> mᴀc ᴣᴎoᴌᴌᴀ pᴀópᴀᴎᴣ and mᴀc Séᴀpcᴀ,
> mᴀc Síomoᴎnn and mᴀc ᴀn Rᴎᴅᴎpe.

2. Some families of foreign origin have two Irish surnames, one an hibernicised form of the foreign name and the other a patronymic formed from the name or a designation of the ancestor, as :—

> Conóún and mᴀc mᴀᴎᵹeóc,
> ᴅᴀᴌᴀmᴀpᴀ and mᴀc hoᴎpeᴀbᴀᴎpo,
> ᴅe búpc and mᴀc Uᴎᴌᴌᴎᴀm,
> Sconóún and mᴀc ᴀn mᴎᴌeᴀóᴀ.

3. Nearly a dozen families have two surnames one commencing with Ó and another with mᴀc, followed by the same ancestral name ; but whether both surnames are derived from the same ancestor, or from two different ancestors of the same name, it is impossible to say. Examples :—

> Ó Cᴀoᴄᴀᴎn and mᴀc Cᴀoᴄᴀᴎn,
> Ó Coᴅᴌᴀcᴀᴎn and mᴀc Coᴅᴌᴀcᴀᴎn,
> Ó ᴣeᴀpᵹᴀᴎn and mᴀc ᴣeᴀpᵹᴀᴎn.

4. A few families have besides their surname a cognomen which is sometimes used instead, as :—

> Ó ᴅuᴎnnpᴌéᴎbe and Uᴌcᴀᴄ.

All these double surnames were used interchangeably, so that the same person might be called indifferently by one or the other, irrespective of the anglicised form. In the majority of cases only one surname is now retained ; but as the anglicised form is, in many instances, derived from the one that has become obselete, there is often apparently no connection between the anglicised form and its present Irish equivalent. Thus the surname Fitzpatrick is derived from mac ʒiolla pádraiʒ, but the present Irish equivalent of Fitzpatrick in many parts of the South of Ireland is mac Séartá or mac Séatra, a new surname which the Fitzpatricks took from an ancestor named Geoffrey or Séartá mac ʒiolla pádraiʒ. Similarly the Birminghams are called in Irish mac Feórair from an ancestor named Piers de Bermingham.

Besides the interchange of totally distinct surnames, our Irish name-system admitted, with considerable latitude, of the substitution one for another of different forms of the same surname, and even of different surnames of the same or somewhat similar meaning. Hence we find the following classes and variants of surnames sometimes interchanged :—

1. Surnames of the same signification though differing in form, as :

mac Capluir and mac Catail (Caplur and Catal, each = Charles).
mac an mavaid and Ó mavaidín (both from mavad, a dog).

2. A surname and its diminutive, as :

mac Bruaideada and mac Bruaidín.
Ó Lactna and Ó Lactnáin.
Ó Scannail and Ó Scannláin.

3. Surnames derived from different diminutives of the same root, as :

Ó Branáin and Ó Branaʒáin,
Ó Ciapáin and Ó Ciapaʒáin,
Ó Dubáin and Ó Duibín,
Ó Fiacáin and Ó Feicín.

4. Surnames derived from different genitive forms
of the same name, as :

Ó ₥eaɲꜱuɲa and Ó ₥eaɲꜱuiɲ.
Ó ₥iaic and Ó ₥éic.
₥ac an Ѣɲeiceaṁan and ₥ac an Ѣɲeicṁ.

5. Variants of the same surname owing to aspiration, attenuation, and interchange of letters, as :

₥ac Ꝺoṁnaill and ₥ac Ꝺoṁnaill.
Ó Ѣɲoilcáin and Ó Ѣɲoileacáin.
Ó Ꝺeaɲáin and Ó Ꝺioɲáin.
Ó ₥acáin and Ó ₥ocáin.

6. A standard or literary form and a corrupt or
spoken form, as

Ó ₥uiɲꜱeaɲáin and Ó Ѣɲíoɲáin.
Ó Caoinꝺealƀáin and Ó Caoinlioƀáin.
Ó heiꝺiɲɲceóil and Ó Ꝺiɲɲceóil.

7. An older form and a more modern one, as :—

₥ac an Aiɲcinniꝁ and ₥ac an Oiɲcinniꝁ.
₥aꝁ Aiɲeacꞇaiꝁ and ₥aꝁ Oiɲeacꞇaiꝁ.

A discrepancy (similar to that mentioned above)
between the anglicised form and its present-day Irish
equivalent often results from the interchange of these
forms

§ 10.—ANGLICISATION OF SURNAMES

The various ways in which Irish surnames have been
anglicised may be enumerated under the following
heads :

1. Phonetically.
2. By translation.
3. By attraction.
4. By assimilation.
5. By substitution.

1. *Phonetically.*—This was the method almost exclusively adopted when surnames were first anglicised.* The surname was written down more or less as it was pronounced, but without any regard to the Irish spelling, as :

O'Brien for Ó bⱭⱭin,
O'Callaghan for Ó CeⱭⱭⱭcáin,
O'Donoghue for Ó ⱅonncⱭvⱭ,
O'Flanagan for Ó ⱅⱭnnⱭⱲáin,
O'Neill for Ó néill.†

The same Irish surname often gives several very different anglicised forms owing to dialectical variations and the vagaries of the phonetic system employed to represent them, as :

Ó CobⱅⱭⱲ, Coffey, Cowie, Cowhey, Cowhig, &c.,
Ó ⱅubⱅⱭⱲ, Duffy, Dowie, Dooey, Duhig, &c.

On the other hand, very different Irish surnames have sometimes the same anglicised form, as :

Coffey for Ó CobⱅⱭⱲ, Ó CⱭⱅbⱭvⱭ, Ó CⱭⱅbuⱭvⱭⱲ, Ó CⱭⱅmoⱲⱭ.

In many instances the anglicised form has in course of time been contracted, as: O'Hare for O'Hehir, O'Kane for O'Cahan ; and not unfrequently only a part of the original form is retained, as Ryan for O'Mulryan. Most surnames have been mutilated by dropping Mac or O', and Mac when retained in usually, but improperly, written Mc or M'.

---

*Most Irish surnames were anglicised during the second half of the 16th century (1550-1600), and appear for the first time in in an English dress in the State documents of that period. The anglicisation seems to have been the work of Anglo-Irish government officials possessing, in some instances at least, a knowledge of the Irish language. The present anglicised forms, generally speaking, date from that period.

† It may be remarked that the anglicised form was in most instances originally much nearer the Irish pronounciation than at present, owing partly to a change in the sound of the English letters, and partly to the corruption of the Irish forms. Thus O'Brien and O'Neill were originally pronounced O'Breen and O'Nail

2. *Translation.*—During the last and the preceding century, many families rejected the old phonetic rendering of their surnames and adopted instead an English surname which was supposed to be a translation of the Irish surname. These "translations" are, in most instances, incorrect. The following are examples of translated surnames :—

Ó Ḃruic	translated	Badger,
Ó Ḃruacáin	,,	Banks,
Ó Caḃáin	,,	Barnacle,
Ó Maoilḃeannacta	,,	Blessing,
Ó Marcaiġ	,,	Ryder,
Ó Ḃraḋáin	,,	Salmon and Fisher,
Mac an tSaoir	,,	Carpenter, Freeman
Mac Conraoi	,,	King,
Mac Confnáṁa	,,	Forde,
Mac Seáin	,,	Johnson.

The translated form sometimes takes an English termination, as :

Ó Oraiġneáin	translated	Thornton,
Ó Ġaoiṫín	,,	Wyndham.

3. *Attraction.*—A surname of comparatively rare occurrence is often attracted to, and confounded with, a better known surname of somewhat similar sound existing in the same locality, and instead of its proper anglicised form assumes that of the better known or more numerous surname. The following are examples :

	Anglicised	attracted to
Ó Ḃláṫṁaic,	Blawick, Blowick,	Blake,
Ó Ḃraoin,	O'Breen, Breen,	O'Brien,
Ó Ouiḃḋíorma,	O'Dughierma, Dooyearma,	MacDermott,
Ó heocaġáin,	O'Hoghegan,	Mageoghegan,
Ó Maoil Seaċlainn,	O'Melaghlin,	MacLoughlin.

It must be remembered that a surname of comparatively rare occurrence in one district may be quite common in another, and *vice versa*, and that consequently the attracting surname in one locality may be itself attracted in another.

4. The custom of assimilating Irish to foreign names is old in Ireland. During the Middle Ages Irish scholars writing in Latin, instead of latinising the Irish names with which they had to deal, often simply substituted for them well-known Latin names of somewhat similar sound or meaning. Hence we find such substitution as Cornelius for Conćobap, Eugenius for eoġan, Thaddaeus for Caóg, Virgilius for feapġal, etc. This practice was well known in the sixteenth century, and was frequently followed in the anglicisation of Irish Christian names. Nearly all the anglicised forms of this kind existing at present were already in use in the time of Elizabeth, the only important exceptions being Jeremiah for Diapmaio, and Timothy for Caóg, which only came into use about half a century later.

The extension of the practice to surnames is of still later date, few traces of such anglicisation being found earlier than the middle of the seventeenth century. The principal cause of the change of these names, according to O'Donovan, was the ridicule thrown upon them by English magistrates and lawyers, who were ignorant of the Irish language; but an anxiety on the part of the people themselves to get rid of uneuphonious or otherwise undesirable surnames doubtless operated in the same direction. The following are examples of surnames anglicised in this way :

> Broderick for Ó Opuaoaip,
> Carleton for Ó Caipealláin,
> Harrington for Ó háppaććáin and Ó hiongapoail,
> Reddington for Ó Roioeaćáin,
> Summerville for Ó Somaćáin.

In a few instances the assimilation is to a French surname, as :

> De Lapp for Ó Lapáin,
> De Moleyns for Ó maoláin,
> D'Ermott for Ó Duibóiopma.

5. *Substitution.*—Substitution differs from assimilation only in degree. The similarity between the Irish surname and its English equivalent is in this case much more remote ; very often there is no connection whatsoever. The following are examples :

> Clifford for Ó Clúmáin,
> Fenton for Ó Fiannachta,
> Loftus for Ó Lachtnáin,
> Neville for Ó Niadh,
> Newcombe for Ó Niadhóg.

It sometimes happens that the natural phonetic rendering of an Irish surname has, when Ó or Mac is dropped, the same form as an English surname, as : Ó Beargha, Barry ; Mac an Báird, Ward ; Ó Buachalla, Buckley.

EXPLANATORY NOTE.

Lists of Christian Names.—The names contained in these lists are of three kinds, viz. : (1) names at present in use, of whatever origin, but well-known abbreviations and pet names are not always included ; (2) names which, though now obsolete, were at one time in use under an anglicised form and which it may be considered well to revive ; and (3) names of Irish saints taken from the Martyrology of Donegal. These have not been in use as Christian names within English-speaking times, but they might now under the influence of the Gaelic revival very appropriately be given as baptismal names to Irish children. Every name on these lists is, therefore, a genuine Christian name, either in use at the present time or at some period in the past.

List of Surnames.—We have unfortunately no complete list of Irish surnames. The present one is compiled from two imperfect lists published by the late Registrar-General, supplemented from such addtional sources as newspaper reports, personal observation, lists received from different parts of the country, the writings of Dr. O'Donovan and Father O'Growney, etc. All the more common varieties of the anglicised forms are included. Mac is written—as it should be—in full, not contracted to M' or Mc.

The Irish Forms.—The arrangement is the same for both Christian names and surnames. The English or anglicised name or surname is followed by the Irish form. Variants of the latter are separated only by commas, as :

Andrew, ᴀɪnᴅʀéᴀʀ, ᴀɪnᴅʀɪᴀʀ, ᴀɪnᴅʀɪú.
O'Brallaghan, ó ḃʀoɬċáɪn, ó ḃʀoɬᴀċáɪn, ó ḃʀoɪɬeᴀċáɪn.

Distinct names or surnames, when there are two or more corresponding to the same English or anglicised name or surname, are separated by semicolons, as :

Ferdinand, ꝼeᴀʀᴅoopéᴀ ; ꝼeᴀʀᴅᴀnᴀɪnm ; ꝼeᴀʀᴀḃᴀċ ; ꝼeᴀʀᴅ̊ʀ.

The locality in which each of the Irish forms is found is usually indicated by a number placed after the name or surname, as:

Barry*, bappa 7 ; beapac 9.
O'Brien, Ó Ópiain 12 ; Ó Ópaoin 15.

Single forms are marked only for some special reason. In the case of names and surnames used everywhere interchangeably there is no need of localisation ; but variants, or distinct forms, used interchangeably only in certain places are localised. It is not necessary in every case, nor is it possible, to localise the Christian names.

In some cases the different forms can be distinguished, if at all, only by reference to origin or nationality. This is indicated by the letters I, E, or S placed after the name or surname, and meaning respectively Irish, English, and Scottish. When in the case of foreign surnames no Irish form has been ascertained to exist, the letter E or S is inserted instead.

The relation between different Irish names or surnames having the same English or anglicised form, that is, whether they are synonyms, or distinct names used interchangeably, or the one an older form, or a spoken form, of the other, is indicated by letters placed in brackets between the two forms. In order to avoid confusion it will often be necessary to use the spoken form in preference to the literary or standard form. Hence the spoken form is frequently the one given, the literary form being generally placed after it with the letters (o.f.) prefixed.

The initials of authorities quoted are placed in brackets after the name.

When two or more surnames have the same anglicised form in the same locality, whether owing to attraction or otherwise, local knowledge is necessary to determine the correct Irish form in each case. The older spelling of the anglicised form will ofter throw light on it, or recourse may be had to the local peancaiöe. In cities and large towns it will generally have to be determined by the part of the country from which the family originally came. Thus in the City of Limerick the name Mannix is both Ó muineóz and Ó maincín, the former family coming from Co. Clare and the latter from Co. Limerick.

In case of doubt the form phonetically nearest the anglicised form is the one to be used.

* Christian name.

LIST OF ABBREVIATIONS

(a) LOCATION.

1—Usual form in any part of Ireland.
2—Some parts of Ireland.
3—Leaᴄ Cuınn—the northern half of Ireland.
4—Leaᴄ ṁoᴈ̲a—the southern half of Ireland.
5—The Midland Counties.
6—Ulster.
7—Munster.
8—Leinster.
9—Connacht.
10—Usual form, except in the district or districts to which another name is assigned.
11—Usual form, including places to which other forms are assigned. There are in this case two or more names or surnames similarly anglicised in the same locality.
12—Usual form, but only rarely met with in the district or districts in which another name or surname is stated to be similarly anglicised.
13—Armagh.
14—Kildare.
15—Westmeath.
16—Donegal.
17—Limerick.
18—Co. Dublin.
19—Mayo.
20—Some parts of Ireland, but not met with in the district or districts for which another name is given as similarly anglicised.
21—Some parts of Ireland, including places to which other forms are assigned.
22—Some parts of Ireland, but only rarely met with in those places to which other forms are assigned.
23—Fermanagh.
24—Kilkenny.
25—Offaly—King's County.
26—Derry.
27—Tipperary.
28—Wexford.
29—Sligo.

30—Leaṫ Cuinn, but not those parts of it for which other forms
are given.

31—Usual form in Leaṫ Cuinn, including the parts of it to
which other names or surnames are assigned.

32—Some parts of Leaṫ Cuinn.

33—Tyrone.

34—Roscommon.

35—Monaghan.

36—Antrim.

37—Louth.

38—Down.

39 —Leitrim.

40—Leaṫ Moġa, but not those parts of it for which other forms
are given.

41—Usual form in Leaṫ Moġa, including the parts of it to
which other names or surnames are assigned.

42—Some parts of Leaṫ Moġa.

43—Meath.

44—Carlow.

45—Leix—Queen's County.

46—Clare.

47—Waterford.

48—Wicklow.

49—Kerry.

50—The Midland Counties, but not in the district or districts
for which other forms are given.

51—Usual form in the Midland Counties, including the district
or districts to which other names or surnames are assigned.

52—Some of the Midland Counties.

53—North Longford, North Westmeath, South Leitrim, and
West Cavan.

54—South Longford, West Westmeath, and East Roscommon.

55—Longford.

56—Leitrim and Cavan.

57—Westmeath and Roscommon.

58—Westmeath and Cavan.

59—Roscommon and Longford.

60—Ulster, but not those parts of it for which other forms are
given.

61—Usual form in Ulster, including the parts of it to which
other names or surnames are assigned.

62—Some parts of Ulster.

63—Donegal, Derry, Tyrone, and Antrim.

64—Louth, Armagh, Monaghan, and Fermanagh.

65—Tyrone, Armagh, Monaghan, and Fermanagh.

66—Donegal, Derry and Antrim.

67—Cavan.

68—Antrim and Down.

69—Donegal, Tyrone, and Fermanagh.
70—Munster, but not those parts of it for which other forms are given.
71—Usual form in Munster, including the parts of it to which other names or surnames are assigned.
72—Some parts of Munster.
73—Clare, Limerick, North Kerry, and North Tipperary.
74—Cork, Waterford, South Kerry, and South Tipperary.
75—East Limerick, North East Cork, and South West Tipperary.
76—Clare, North East Limerick, and North Tipperary.
77—Cork.
78—Tipperary, Kilkenny, and Waterford.
79—Kerry, West Limerick, and West Cork.
79a—Kerry, Cork, and Limerick.
80—Leinster, but not those parts of it for which other forms are given.
81—Usual form in Leinster, including the parts of it to which other names or surnames are assigned.
82—Some parts of Leinster.
83—Meath, Louth, and Co. Dublin.
84—Wicklow, Wexford, and Carlow.
85—Kildare, Leix, and Offaly.
86—Meath and Louth.
87—Carlow and Wexford.
88—Co. Dublin and Wicklow.
89—Longford, Westmeath and Offaly.
90—Connacht, but not those parts of it for which other forms are given.
91—Usual form in Connacht, including the parts of it to which other names or surnames are assigned.
93—Mayo, Sligo, and Leitrim.
94—Galway and Roscommon.
95—North Galway, East Mayo, and West Roscommon.
96—Sligo, Mayo, North Leitrim, and North Roscommon.
97—Galway.
98—Roscommon and South Leitrim.
99—West Mayo and West Galway.
 When the location mark consists of three figures, the first two have the same signification as above. The third varies or modifies the meaning as in the following examples :
191—Usual form in Mayo, including the parts of it to which other names or surnames are assigned.
192—Some parts of Mayo.
273—The northern half of Tipperary.
274—The southern half of Tipperary.
775—Mid-Cork.
976—North Galway.
977—South Galway.

978—East Galway.
979—West Galway.
N.B.—A location mark refers not only to the form immediately preceding it, but to all the forms preceding it, back to the last one numbered or to the last semicolon.

(b) RELATION.

The relation between different names or surnames having the same anglicised form is sometimes indicated by the following letters placed in brackets between the different forms :—

(s.)—Synonym, that is, the second name or surname has the same signification as the one immediately preceding and is on that account sometimes used interchangeably with it ;

(s.s.)—Second surname, that is, there are two surnames in the same family.

(G.p.)—Gaelic patronymic surname taken by a family of foreign origin ;

(o.s.)—Older surname, now obsolete ;

(o.f.)—Older form of the present surname ;

(s.l.)—Form in the spoken language of the name or surname immediately preceding.

N.B.—A relation mark refers not only to the name or surname immediately following, but to all the forms following it, on to the next one *similarly* marked, or to the next semicolon.

(c) AUTHORITIES QUOTED.

The intials of authorities quoted are placed in brackets after the name, thus :—

(G.J.)—The Gaelic Journal.

(K.)—Keating.

(O'C.)—O'Curry.

(O'D.)—O'Donovan.

(O'G.)—O'Growney.

(O'M.)—O'Mahony in his Edition of Keating's History.

(S.L.)—Spoken Language.   The spoken language is in this case the only authority for the name.   The spelling, therefore, may not always be etymologically correct.

(d) OTHER ABBREVIATIONS.

I.—Irish origin.

E.—English or foreign origin.

S.—Scottish origin.

NAMES OF MEN

ENGLISH—IRISH

Abban, Abbán.
Abraham, Ábraham.
Adam, Áḋaṁ, Adam.
Aedan, Aoḋán.
Aeneas, Aonġus 1; Éigneaċán Eigneaċán, 16.
Affy, Aiḃistín.
Aghy, Eaċaiḋ.
Aidan, Aoḋán 11, (s.) Maoḋóg 28.
Alban, Albán.
Albert, Alby, Ailbe.
Alex, Alexander, Alsandar, Alastrann, Alastrom, Alastar.
Alfons, v. Alphonsus.
Alfred, Ailfrid.
Alick, v. Alexander.
Allen, Ailín.
Allister, Alastar.
Aloysius, Alabaois; Luġaiḋ.
Alphonsus, Alḟonsus, Alfonsus 1; Annluan 49.
Alvy, Ailbe.
Ambrose, Ambrós, Ambrus 1; Anmċaḋ 978.
Andrew, Aindréas, Aindrias, Aindriú.
Aneslis, Ainéislis.
Angus, Aonġus.
Anlon, Annluan.
Anthin, Anntoin.
Anthony, Antony, Antoine, Antoin, Anntoin 1; Uaiṫne 8, 72.
Archibald, Giolla Easpuig.
Ardal, Arnold, Árdġal.
Art, Art.
Arthur, Artúr; Art.
Augustin, Augustine, Águistín, Áġuistín, Aḃuistín, Aiḃistín.
Auliffe, Aṁlaoiḃ.
Austin, Aiḃistín, Oistín. V. Augustine.
Avvy, Aiḃistín.

Barclay, Barkley, Parṫlón. V. Bartholomew.
Barnaby, Barney, Brian.
Barry, Barra 7; Bearaċ 9.
Bartel, v. Bartley and Bartholomew.
Bartholomew, Parṫalán, Párṫalán, 11, Párṫlán 72, Parṫlón 26, 62, Pártlán 92, Pártnán 72.
Bartlemy, Pártnán. V. Bartholomew.
Bartley, Beartlaiḋ. V. Bartholomew.
Basil, Breasal.
Bat, Batt, Parṫalán, Párṫlán.
Becan, Beacán.
Ben, Beirċeart.
Benedict, Maolbeannaċta.
Benen, Benignus, Beineán, Beineón, Beanón, Bineán.
Benjamin, Beirċeart.
Bercan, Bearċán.

Berkley, ρ∧ρċlóη. V. Bartholomew.

Bernard, ḃe∧ρήάρṽ ; ḃρι∧η 11 ;
ḃeιρċe∧ρċ 272.

Bertie, ḃeιρċe∧ρċ ; ∧ιlḃe.

Boetius, ḃ∧oċʒ∧l∧ċ ; ḃu∧ṽ∧ċ
49.

Bowes, ḃ∧oċʒ∧l∧ċ.

Bran, ḃρ∧η.

Brasil, ḃρe∧ρ∧l.

Brendan, ḃρé∧η∧ιηη, ḃρe∧η-
ṽáη, ḃρe∧ηηṽáη.

Brian, Brien, Brine, Bryan,
ḃρι∧η.

Buagh, ḃu∧ṽ∧ċ.

Caffar, c∧ṫḃ∧ρρ.

Cahal, c∧ṫ∧l.

Cahir, c∧ṫ∧oιρ, c∧ṫ∧ιρ.

Cain, cι∧η.

Callaghan, ce∧ll∧ċáη.

Calvagh, ∧η c∧lḃ∧ċ, c∧lḃ∧ċ.

Canice, c∧ιηηe∧ċ, coιηηe∧ċ.

Carbry, c∧ιρḃρe.

Carroll, ce∧ρḃ∧ll.

Cartagh, Cartage, c∧ρṫ∧ċ.

Celsus, ce∧ll∧ċ.

Charles, Sé∧ρl∧ρ, Sé∧ρluρ,
c∧ρluρ ; c∧ṫ∧l 7, 9 ; coρm∧c
7, 64 ; ce∧ρḃ∧ll 72 ; c∧ṫ∧oιρ
8, 72 ; ∧η c∧lḃ∧ċ, c∧lḃ∧ċ, 8,
9 ; s∧m∧ιρle, Soṁ∧ιρle 36 ;
coιρṽe∧lḃ∧ċ 16.

Christian, ʒιoll∧ cρίoρc.

Christopher, Christy, cρίoρcóιρ
1, cρίoρc∧l 33.

Cole, coṁʒ∧ll.

Colin, coιlíη, coιle∧η 1 ;
c∧ιle∧η S.

Colla, coll∧.

Colm, colm.

Colman, colmáη 11, cóιlíη 99.

Colum, Columba, colm, colum.

Columban, colmáη.

Coman, comáη.

Comyn, cuιmíη.

Con, Conn 1 ; coηċoḃ∧ρ 7,

Conall, con∧ll.

Conan, conáη.

Conary, con∧ιρe.

Conleth, Conley, connl∧oṽ,
connl∧oċ.

Conn, conn.

Connell, con∧ll.

Connor, Conor, conċoḃ∧ρ.

Constantine, conρ∧ṽóíη 7 ; Conn
26, 33 ; cú éonn∧ċc 23.

Cooey, cúṁ∧ιʒe.

Cooley, cú ul∧ṽ.

Cormac, coρm∧c.

Cornelius, Corney, conċoḃ∧ρ.

Covey, cúṁe∧ṽ∧.

Cowan, coṁṽ∧η, coṁʒ∧η.

Crevan, cριoṁṫ∧ηη.

Crohan, cρóċáη.

Cronan, cρóηáη.

Cuan, cu∧η.

Cullo, cú ul∧ṽ.

Cumin, cuιmíη.

Cyril, coιρe∧ll.

Dahy, ṽáṫι.

Daniel, ṽoṁη∧ll.

Darby, ṽι∧ρm∧ιṽ.

Dary, ṽáιρe.

David, ṽáιḃιṽ, ṽáιḃιṽ, ṽ∧ιḃéιṽ,
ṽáιṫί.

Davy, ṽáιṫί, ṽáċ, ṽáιċ, ṽáιṫíη.

Declan, ṽé∧ʒláη.

Denis, Denny, ṽonnċ∧ṽ.

Dermod, Dermot, ṽι∧ρm∧ιṽ.

Desmond, ṽe∧ρṁuṁn∧ċ.

Dominic, Dominick, ṽoιmιηιc
1, ṽ∧ṁn∧ιc, ṽ∧ṁl∧ιc 26.

Donaghy, ṽonnċ∧ṽ.

Donall, Donald, ṽoṁn∧ll.

Donat, ṽonnċ∧ṽ.

Donn, ṽonn.

Donnan, ṽonnáη.

Donogh, Donough, ṽonnċ∧ṽ.

Douglas, ṽuḃʒl∧ρ.

Dowan, ṽuḃáη.

Duald, Dualtagh, ṽuḃ∧lc∧ċ.

Dudley, ṽuḃṽáleιce, 34 ; ṽuḃ-
∧lc∧ċ 3 ; ṽuḃṽ∧ρ∧ċ, ṽuḃ-
ṽ∧ρ∧ 99.

Dugald, Duḃġall.
Duncan, Donnċaḋ.

Ea, Aoḋ.
Eamon, Éamonn.
Eber, Éiḃear.
Edan, Aoḋán.
Eddie, Edmond, Edmund, Éamonn.
Edward, Éadḃárd; Éamonn.
Egan, Aoḋagán.
Enan, Éanán.
Enda, Éanna.
Eneas, Aonġus 1; Éigneaċán, Eigneaċán, 16.
Eny, Éanna.
Eoghan, Eoġan.
Eoin, Eóin.
Ercan, Erkan, Earcán.
Erevan, Eireaṁón.
Ernan, Ernest, Earnán.
Ernin, Eirnín.
Eugene, Eoġan.
Eunan, Aḋaṁnán.
Eustace, Iústás.
Euston, Úistean.
Eveny, Aiḃne.
Ever, Éiḃear, Éiṁear.
Evin, Éiṁín.

Fachnan, Faċtna.
Falvy, Fáilḃe.
Farrell, Fearġal.
Farry, Fearaḋaċ.
Feagh, Fiaċa.
Feary, Fiaċra.
Fehin, Feiċín
Felan, Faolán
Felimy, Feiḋlimiḋ.
Felix, Feiḋlimiḋ, Feiḋlim.
Ferdinand, Feardorċa; Fear-ganainm; Fearaḋaċ; Fear-ġus.
Fergal, Fearġal.
Fergus, Fearġus.
Festus, Feiċín 11; Faċtna 97.
Fiachra, Fiaċra.
Finan, Fionnán.

Fineen, Finġin.
Finian, Finnian; Finġin.
Finn, Fionn.
Finbar, Fionnḃarr.
Finneen, Finnin, Finġin.
Fionan, Fionnán, Fionán.
Fintan, Fionntán.
Flan, Flann.
Flannan, Flannán.
Florence, Florry, Flaiṫrí 9; Finġin 7; Flann 92; Fiṫeal 92.
Foulk, Folc.
Francis, Próinsias, Proinnsias, Proinnseas.
Frank, Frainc 7; Preanndaiġ 64.
Frederick, Feardorċa.
Fursey, Fursa.

Garrett, Gearóid, Gioróid.
Garvan, Garḃán.
Geoffrey, Seafraiḋ, Siofraiḋ, Séafra, Séaṫra, Séarṫa, Séaṫrún, Seaṫrún, Searṫún, &c.
George, Seóirse.
Gerald, Gearalt, Gearóid.
Gerard, Gearárd, Giorárd, Gearóid, Gioróid.
Gibbon, Giobún.
Gilbert, Gilibeart.
Gilbride, Giolla Ḃríġde.
Gildea, Giolla Ḋé.
Gill, Gillesa, Gillisa, Giolla Íosa.
Gilvarry, Giolla Ḃearaiġ.
Glasny, Glaisne.
Godfrey, Goṫfraiḋ, Goṫraiḋ.
Gordon, Gordan.
Gorry, Goṫraiḋ.
Gregory, Gréagóir.

Harold, Aralt.
Harry, v. Henry.
Heber, Éiḃear, Éiṁear.
Hector, Eaċtair; Eaċann 68.

Henry, Éinrí, ᴀnnᴘᴀoi,
  ḃᴀnᴘᴀoi.
Herbert, ḃoiᴘeᴀḃᴀᴘᴠ.
Heremon, Hermon, eiᴘeᴀṁón.
Hewney, Uᴀiċne.
Hubert, ḃoiḃeᴀᴘᴠ.
Hugh, ᴀoᴠ́ 11 ; ḃoiḃeᴀᴘᴠ.
  92.
Hughey, Hughie, ᴀoᴠ́ᴀiᴣ 26 ;
  Cúṁᴀiᴣe 64.
Hugony, úᴣᴀine.
Humphrey, Unᴘᴘᴀiᴠ́ ; ᴀṁᴌᴀoiḃ
  79.

Ignatius, Ꞓiᴣneᴀċán, Éiᴣneᴀċán.
Irial, 1ᴘiᴀᴌ.
Irving, eiᴘeᴀṁón.
Isaac, ioᴘᴀc, ioᴘóc, ioᴘóᴣ.
Ivor, ioṁᴀᴘ 1 ; Ꞓiḃeᴀᴘ, Éiṁeᴀᴘ
  64.

James, Séᴀmuᴘ.
Jarlath, 1ᴀᴘᴘᴌᴀiċ.
Jarmy, ᴠiᴀᴘmᴀiᴠ.
Jasper, ᴣeᴀᴘᴘᴀᴘ.
Jeffrey, v. Geoffrey.
Jeremiah, Jerome, Jerry, ᴠiᴀᴘ-
  mᴀiᴠ.
Jimmy, Simiᴠ́, Siomᴀiᴠ́,
  Séᴀmuiᴘín.
John, Eóin, Seᴀᴣán, Seán,
  Seón.
John Baptist, Eóin ḃᴀiᴘᴛe.
Joseph, 1óᴘeᴘ, 1óᴘeᴘ. Seóᴘᴀᴘ,
  Seóᴘᴀᴘ, Seóᴘᴀṁ
Justin, Sᴀeᴘḃᴘeᴀċᴀċ 7.

Kealan, Kelan, Cᴀolán.
Kean, Ciᴀn.
Kellagh, Ceᴀᴌᴌᴀċ.
Kenan, Ciᴀnán
Kennedy, Cinnéiᴠiᴠ́, Cinnéiᴠiᴣ
Kenny, Coinneᴀċ.
Kerill, Coiᴘeᴀᴌᴌ.
Kevan, Cᴀomán.
Kevin, Cᴀoiṁᴣin.
Kian, Ciᴀn,
Kienan, Ciᴀnán.

Kieran, Ciᴀᴘán.
Killian, Ciᴌᴌín, Ciᴌᴌiᴀn.

Laserian, ᴌᴀiᴘᴘiᴀn.
Laughlin, ᴌeᴀċᴌᴀinn, (o.f.)
  mᴀeᴌ Seᴀċᴌᴀinn ; ᴌoċᴌᴀinn,
  ᴌoċᴌᴀnn.
Laurence, ᴌᴀḃᴘáᴘ ; ᴌoᴘcán.
Leo, ᴌeón.
Lewis, Lewy, ᴌuᴣᴀiᴠ́ 1 ;
  ᴌᴀoiᴣᴘeᴀċ, ᴌᴀoiᴘeᴀċ 2.
Loman, ᴌomán.
Lonan, ᴌonán.
Lorcan, ᴌoᴘcán.
Loughlin, ᴌoċᴌᴀinn, ᴌoċᴌᴀnn.
  V. Laughlin.
Louis, ᴌᴀoiᴣᴘeᴀċ, ᴌᴀoiᴘeᴀċ ;
  ᴌuᴣᴀiᴠ́.
Lucan, ᴌúcán.
Lucius, ᴌᴀoiᴣᴘeᴀċ, ᴌᴀoiᴘeᴀċ ;
  ᴌᴀċᴛnᴀ.
Luke, ᴌúcáᴘ, 1, ᴌᴀḃcáᴘ 9.
Lysagh, ᴌᴀoiᴣeᴀċ, ᴌᴀoiᴘeᴀċ.

Maelisa, mᴀeᴌ ioᴘᴀ.
Mahon, mᴀċᴣᴀṁᴀin.
Malachy, mᴀeᴌ Seᴀċᴌᴀinn ;
  mᴀoᴌ ṁᴀoᴠ́óᴣ*.
Malcolm, mᴀeᴌ Coᴌuim, mᴀeᴌ
  Coᴌm.
Manasses, mᴀᴣnuᴘ.
Mantan, mᴀnnᴛán.
Manus, mᴀᴣnuᴘ, máᴣnuᴘ.
Marcus, Mark, mᴀᴘcuᴘ.
Martin, máᴘᴛᴀn, máᴘᴛᴀin,
  máiᴘᴛín.
Mat, mᴀiᴛ, mᴀiᴛín.
Matthew, mᴀᴛᴀ, mᴀiᴛiú ;
  mᴀċᴣᴀṁᴀin.
Matthias, mᴀiᴛiᴀᴘ, mᴀiᴛiᴀᴘ.
Maurice, muiᴘiᴘ ; muiᴘᴣeᴀᴘ.
Melaghlin, mᴀeᴌ Seᴀċᴌᴀinn.
Melchor, meiᴌᴘeóiᴘ.
Meldan, Mellan, meᴀᴌᴌán.
Melrone, mᴀoᴌ Ruᴀᴠ́áin.
Meyler, mᴀoiᴌiᴘ ; mᴀoᴌ ṁuiᴘe.
Michael, míċeáᴌ, miċeáᴌ.

* The name of St. Malachy of Armagh.

Miles, Milo, maol muipe; maolmóṙḋa: mael Seaċlainn 26
Mogue, maoḃóg.
Morgan, muiṙċaḃ 1. (s.l.) ḃroċaḃ 99.
Mortimer, muiṙċeaptaċ.
Moses, maoḃóg.
Munchin, maincín.
Mundy, Réamonn.
Murrough, muiṙċaḃ.
Murry, muiṙeaḃaċ.
Murtough, Murty, muiṙċeaptaċ
Myles, maol muipe; maolmóṙḋa.

Naugher, Noghor, Nohor, Conċoḃap.
Neal, Neale, niall 11, néill 62.
Neece, Neese, naop. (o.f.) aonġup.
Nehemiah, ġiolla na naoṁ.
Neil, néill, 6; Conċoḃap 7.
Nessan, neaṙán.
Nevan, naoṁán.
Niall, niall
Niallan, niallán
Nicholas, nioclár 11; naop 62,
Nicol, niocol
Niece, naop, (o.f.) aonġup.

Oghie, eoċaiḃ.
Oisin, Oiṙín.
Clave, aṁlaoiḃ.
Oliver, Oiliḃéap.
Oney, Uaiṫne.
Oran, Oḋrán.
Oscar, Orcap.
Ossian, Oiṙín.
Owen, eoġan 1; eóin 99.
Owney, Uaiṫne.
Oynie, eoġainín; Uaiṫne.

Padden, páiḋín.
Paddy, páiḋín, paiḋi, paḋṙa, paṙṙa.
Parlan, paṙtalán, páṙtalán, páṙtlán.

Pat, páḋ.
Patrick, páḋraig, páḋraic, páḋnaig, páḋraic. &c.
Paul, pól.
Peregrine, cúċoigcríḋe, cúcríḋe.
Peter, peaḋap, peaḋaiṙ.
Phelim, Phelimy, feiḋlimiḋ, feiḋlim.
Philip, pilib, filib 11; feiḋlimiḋ, feiḋlim 62.
Pierce, piapap, feópap.
Pius, píup.

Quintin, Quinton, Cúṁaiġe.

Ralph, Ráḃulḃ; Roḃulḃ.
Randal, Raġnall, Ráġnall.
Randulph, Rannulḃ; Raġnall.
Raymond, Redmond, Réamonn.
Reginald, Raġnall.
Revelin, Raiḃilín, Roiḃilín, Ruiḃilín.
Richard, Rickard, Riṙteáṙḃ, Riocáṙḃ, Riocaṙḃ.
Robert, Rioḃaṙḃ, Rioḃaṙc, Roiḃeáṙḃ, Roiḃeaṙḃ, Riḃeaṙḃ, Riḃeaṙc, Riḃiṙc.
Robin, Roiḃín, Roiḃean.
Roddy, v. Rory.
Roderick, Roger, Ruaiḋrí 1, (s.l.) Raiḋrí 2, Reiḋrí 7.
Roland, Roḃlann 1, Roḃlaiḋe 2
Ronald, Raġnall.
Ronan, Rónán.
Rory, Ruaiḋrí 1, (s.l.) Raiḋrí 2. Reiḋrí 7.
Ross, Rop.
Rowan, Ruaḋán.
Rowland, Roḃlann 1, Roḃlaiḋe 2; Roiḃilín, Ruiḃilín 64.

Samuel, Soṁaiṙle.
Senan, Seanán.
Shane, Seaġán, Seán.
Sheary, Séaṙpa, Séa.
Geoffrey
Shemus, Séamup

Sheron, Seáċpún, Séáṫpún.
Shiel, Siaḋal, Siaġal.
Sidney, Séaṿna.
Simon, Síomonn, Síomón,
Síomún ; Suiḃne 2.
Sinan, Sinon, Sionán, Seanán.
Sivney, Suiḃne.
Solomon, Solaṁ.
Sorlev, Soṁaiple.
Standish, Stanislaus, Ainéirlir.
Stephen, Steaṗán, Stioṗán,
Staḃán, Staḃna, Stiana,
Stiḃin, Steiṁin.
Sylvester, Sailḃeaṗtaṗ.
Synan, Seanán, Sionán.

Teague, Teige, Taḋg.
Terence, Terry, Coiṗvealḃaċ.
Thaddaeus, Thaddeus, Thady,
Taḋg.
Theobald, Tioḃóiṫ, Teaḃóiṫ.
Theodore, Téaṫóiṗ.
Thomas, Tomáṗ.
Tibbot, Tioḃóiṫ, Teaḃóiṫ.
Tiernan, Tiġeapnán.
Tierney, Tiġeapnaċ.

Tim, Taḋg, Taiḋgín.
Timothy, Tiomóiṫ 19; Taḋg 1 ;
Tomaltaċ 34.
Toal, Tuaċal.
Tobias, Tioḃóiṫ, Teaḃóiṫ.
Tomaltagh, Tomaltaċ.
Tommy, Tomáiṗín.
Tully, Tuaċal.
Tumelty, Tomaltaċ.
Turlough, Toiṗvealḃaċ, (s.l.)
Tpaelaċ, Tapla.

Ulick, Uillioc, Uileóg.
Ultan, Ultán.
Ulysses, Uillioc, Uilleac,
Uileóg.

Val, Ḃail.
Valentine, Ḃailintín.
Victor, Ḃuaḋaċ.
Vincent, Uinṗionn, Uinṗeann.

Walter, Ualtaṗ, Uaiċéiṗ.
Wilfrid, Uilfṗiv.
William, Willie, Uilliam, Liam.

NAMES OF WOMEN

ENGLISH—IRISH

Abbie, Abby, v. Abigail.

Abigail, Abaigeal, Abaig 26, 64 ; Gobnaic 7, 9.

Abina, Gobnaic.

Afric, Africa, Aiffic.

Agatha, Agata.

Agnes, Aignóip : úna ; Móp 92.

Aileen, Aibilín, Eiblín.

Alastrina, Alexandra, Alaptpíona.

Alice, Alicia, Ailip, Ailíp, Ailípe, Ailpe, Eilíp, Eilípe.

Alley, Ailiú, Alaiú.

Allison, Allpún.

Alvy, Ailbe

Amelina, Aimilíona

Anastasia, Annptáp, Stéipe.

Angela, Aingeal.

Anna, Ánna, Anna ; Áine.

Annabel, Annabella, Annábla, Náible ; Ipibéal, Sibéal 26.

Anne, Áine ; Ánna, Anna ; Neanp, Náinpeaú.

Annie, Eitne. V. Anne.

Aphria, Aiffic.

Arabella, v. Annabella.

Attracta, Atpact.

Atty, Aitce.

Aylce, v. Alice.

Bab, Baibín.

Babe, Báb.

Barbara, Barbary, Baipbpe, Báipbpe 1, Baibín 99 ; Goppmflaic 2.

Beesy, Bpígiú, Bpígóín.

Bella, v. Annabella.

Benvon, Bean Muman.

Benvy, Bean Miúe.

Bessie, Betsey, Betty, v. Elizabeth.

Bevin, Bébinn.

Bidelia, Bidina, Birdie, Bpígiú, Bpígóín.

Blanche, Bluinpe ; Blinne 64.

Breeda, Bride, Bridget, Brigid, Bpígiú 1, Bpígúe 2.

Catherine, Caitpíona, Catpaoine, Caitpín, Caitlín.

Cecelia, Cecily, Celia, Sipile, Síle.

Charlotte, Séaplaic.

Christina, Cuiptíona. Cuiptín.

Daisey, Nóipín Nóinín

Debby, Deborah Gobnaic

Delia, Bpígiú Bpígóín.

Derval, Dervilia Deapbail.

Devnet, Daimnaic.

Dillie, Dina, Bpígiú, Bpígóín.

Dolly, Dorothy, Dorren, Doipeann.

Downet, Dymphna, Daimnaic.

Eavan, Aoibeann.

Edwina, Éaúaoin.

Eileen, Eiblín.

Eithne, Eitne.

Eleanor, Eleanora, Eilíonóip, Eileanópa 1, Léan 49.

Eliza, Elizabeth, Eilíp, Eilípe 1 ; Ipeabal, Ipibéal, Sibéal 2.

Ellen, Ellie, Ciḃlín.
Elsha, Ailṗe.
Elva, Ailḃe, Oilḃe.
Emily, eimíle.
Enat, Ena, Eny, Aoúnaic.
Ernet, eaṗnaic.
Esther, eiṗciṗ; Airlinn,
   Airling 64.
Ethna, Etney, eicne.
Eva, Aoiṗe.
Eveleen, Evelyn, Aiḃilín,
   eiḃilín, eiḃlín.

Fanny, Painċe; ppoinnṗéaṗ.
Feena, Feenat, Piaúnaic.
Finola, Pionnġuala.
Flora, ḃláċ; Pionnġuala.
Florence, bláċnaiv.
Frances, ppoinnṗéaṗ, ppóin-
   ṗéaṗ.

Gertrude, Gertie, Ʒṗáinne.
Gobinet, Gobnet, Ʒobnaic.
Gormlaith, Gormley, Ʒoṗm-
   ṗlaiċ.
Grace, Ʒṗáinne.
Gubby, Ʒobnaic.

Hannah, Sioḃán, Siuḃán, Sioḃ-
   áinín, Siuḃáinín 1; Onóṗa,
   Nóṗa 16, 26.
Helen, eiḃlín.
Hilda, Hildy, hilve.
Honor, Honora, Onóṗa, huṗa

Ida, íve.
Ina, Aʒna.
Ita, íve.
Isabella, Iṗiḃéal, Iṗeabal,
   Siḃéal.

Jane, Jannet, Jenny, Sinéav l.
   Sineaiv, Sine 26.
Joan, Johanna, Sioḃán, Siuḃán.
Josephine, Seóṗaiṁcín; Sio-
   ḃáinín, Siuḃáinín.
Jude, Judith, Judy, Síle 11;
   Sioḃán, Siuḃán. 3.

Julia, July, Síle 1; Siuḃán,
   Sioḃán 9.

Kate, Cáic.
Kathleen, Caicilín, Caiclín.
Katie, Cáicín, Tṗíona, Tṗaoine.
Katty, Caici, Cáicín.
Keavy, Caoiṁe.
Keelin, Caoilṗionn.
Keenet, Kinnat, Ciannaic.

Lassarina, Laṗaiṗṗíona.
Lelia, Líle.
Lena, eiḃlín.
Lily, Lil, Líle.
Lizzie, eilíṗ. V. Elizabeth.
Louisa, Laḃaoiṗc.
Lucy, Luiʒṗeaċ.

Mabbina, meaóḃ, meiṗḃín.
Mabel, máiḃle; náḃla; meaóḃ
Madeline, máiʒolín, mavail-
   éin.
Madge, meaóḃ 6; maiʒṗéav
   70; Muṗainn 499.
Marcella, maiṗṗíl, maiṗṗíle.
Maggie, v. Margaret.
Margaret, máiṗʒṗéav, maiṗ-
   ʒṗéav, muiṗʒéav, maiʒṗéav,
   máiṗéav, maiṗéav, muiṗ-
   éav, máṗaov, muṗáiv.
Margery, meaóḃ; máille,
   máilṗe, máilci.
Maria, máiṗe.
Marjory, v. Margery.
Marion, muiṗeann, muiṗinn,
   muṗainn.
Martha, maṗca; móṗ.
Mary, muiṗe*, máiṗe; móṗ 2;
   méaṗṗ 492.
Matilda, maicilve.
Matty, maici.
Maud, máva; meaóḃ.
Maureen, Mav, máiṗín.
Meave, meaóḃ.
Meeda, míve.
Mella, mealla.
Moira, máiṗe.

* The name of the Blessed Virgin Mary.

Molly, máiṗín; mallaıḋ, máılle, máılṗe, máıltı.
Mona, Monat, muaṪnaıc.
Monica, monca.
More, móp.
Moreen, móıṗín.
Morrin, muıṗeann, muıpınn, muṗaınn.
Murel, muıṗġeal.

Nabla, náḃla, náıḃle.
Nan, Nance, Nancy, neanp, naınpeaḋ.
Nanno, nópa.
Nappy, nuala, ᵽıonnġuala.
Nell, Nellie, neıll, neıllı, eıḃlín.
Nessa, neapa.
Nonie, nóıṗín 1; Sıoḃán 499.
Nora, Norah, Onópa, nópa.
Nuala, nuala.

Olive, oılḃe.
Orlaith, Ópᵽlaıċ.
Orna, Ornat, OṪapnaıc.

Peg, Peggy, peıġ, peıġí.
Penelope, Penny, ᵽıonnġuala, nuala.
Poll, Polly, pal, paılp, paılı.

Regina, Ríoġnaċ.
Renny, Raċnaıc.

Richella, Rıċeal.
Rose, Róıp, Róıpe, Róıpín.

Sabia, Saḋḃ.
Sabina, Saıḋḃín 1 : Síle 19, 97.
Sally, Sopċa 1; Saḋḃ (Saḃa) 99; Síle 192.
Sarah, Sopċa 1; Saḋḃ 16, 64.
Selia, Sheela, Sheila, Síle.
Sibby, Síle; Sıḃéal, Sıbı, S'obaıġ.
Sive, Saḋḃ.
Slany, Sláıne.
Sophia, Sophy, Saḋḃ, Saḋḃa 16, 26.
Susan, Susanna, Sópanna, Sópaıḋ, Sıúı; Sıoḃán, Sıuḃán 3, 469.
Sybil, Sıḃéal.

Teresa, Tessie, toıṗéapa, Tpeapa, Tpeıpe.
Tilda, Tılḋe.
Trina, Tpıona, Tpaoıne.

Una, Unity, Uny, úna.
Ursula, Uppula.

Vivian, béḃınn.

Webbie, ġobnaıc.
Whiltierna, ᵽaoıltıġeapna.
Winefred, Winifred, Winnie, Winny, úna.

SURNAMES

ENGLISH—IRISH

Abbott, Abbóro.
Abraham, Abpaham.
Adair, Ó Dáipe.
Adams, Mac Ádaim, Mac Adaim 1 ; Mac Adamóro 99 ; Mac Conpnáma 197.
Adamson, Mac Ádaim, Mac Adaim.
Addley, Addly, Ó hÁolaiġ.
Addy, Mac Ádaiṫ.
Adkins, Adkinson, Adkisson, Mac Aroicín.
Adorian, Ó Deópaóáin, Ó Deópáin.
Adrian, Adrien, Ó Dpeáin.
Agar, Éigeap.
Agarty, Ó hÁgaptaiġ.
Aghoon, Ó heaċṫubáin.
Agnew, Ó Ġnim.
Ahearn, Ahearne, v. Ahern.
Aher, Ó hAiċip.
Aheran, Aherin, Ahern, Aherne, Aheron, Ó heaċṫiġeipin, Ó eaċṫiġeipin, &c.
Ahessy, Ó hAiċeapa.
Aiken, v. Eakin.
Ailward, v. Aylward.
Airey, Áipiġ.
Aison, Mac Aoóa.
Alcock, Alcóc.
Alexander, Alpanoaip 1 ; Mac Alpanoaip 2, Mac Alaptpainn 2, Mac Alaptpuim 2.
Allan, Ó hAllaṁain 197. V. Allen.

Allen, Ó hAilín, Ó hAillín 4 ; Mac Ailín 8 ; Ailín 2 ; Ailéin 82 ; Ó hAllaṁain 197.
Alleine, Alleyne, Ailéin.
Allin v. Allen.
Allman, Alamán.
Alton, Altún.
Alyward, v. Aylward.
Ambrose, Ambpóp, Ampóp, Ampup.
Anbora, Anborough, v. Hanbury.
Anders, Mac Ainopiú.
Anderson, Mac Ainopiú 11 ; Mac Ġiolla Ainopéip 36 ; Anopaopán 192.
Andrew, Ainopiú.
Andrews, Andrewson, Mac Ainopiú.
Angland, Aingleont.
Anglim, Ó hAngluinn, (s.l.) Ó hAngluim 179.
Anglin, Ó hAngluinn.
Angus, Mac Aonġuip.
Anketell, Ankethill, Ancoitil.
Ankland, v. England.
Ankle, v. Anketell.
Ansberry, Ansboro, Ó hAinṁipeaċ, (s.l.) Ó hAinmnneaċ, Ó Ainmneaċ 97.
Anthony, Antony, Antóin, Antoine 2 ; Mac Antoine 2.
Archabald, Archbald, Archbold, Áippeabóro 1 ; Áippibéal 19.
Archdeacon, Áippoéicin, Áiptéicin ; (G.p.) Mac Óoa.

Archer, Áirréir, áiréir 4;
mac Apcail 83.
Archfield, Áirréil:
Archibald Archibold Áirrea-
bóir l, Áirríbéal 6
Ardagh Áruaca.
Arkins Ó hOpcáin.
Armstrong, Cpéanlámac l;
Ó Labpaóa Cpéan 68.
Arnold, Arnott, Apnóiv.
Arthur, Arthurs, mac Apcúir
2; Apcúr 2.
Ashe, Áir, l, Áȝap, Ácapác
172, 499.
Asken, Askin, v. Heskin.
Aspel, Aspell, Áireabóiv.
Aspig, eappoȝ 2; mac ȝiolla
eappuiȝ 2; mac an eappuiȝ 2.
Aspill, v. Aspell.
Asping v. Aspig.
Aspol, v. Aspell.
Atamney, mac an Ciompánaiȝ.
Atasney, mac an tSapanaiȝ.
Athy, Átaoi.
Atkins, Atkinson, mac Aivicín.
Aughney, mac fácrna.
Auher, Áiréir.
Aungier, Dóinréir.
Aurachaun Ó hAnnpacáin.
Austen, Austin, Oirtín l; mac
Aibirtín 9.
Aylmar, Aylmer, Aiȝlmeap.
Aylward, Aiȝleapc.
Ayres, Ó hiappac (S.L.) 469.

Babe, Báb.
Bacon, ve bacún, bacún.
Badger, Ó bpuic.
Bagley, v. Begley.
Bagnall, Bagnell, baȝnal 11;
Ó beiȝléiȝinn 43.
Baggot, Baggott, Bagot,
Bagott, baȝóiv.
Bailey, Bailie, Baillie, Baily,
báille.
Bain, bán.
Baird, mac an báipv.
Baith, v. Bath.

Baker, báicéir, bácaeir.
Bakey, Ó béice.
Baldin, Baldoon, bálvún.
Baldwin, bálvún, bálvuinȝ l:
Ó maolaȝáin 16 (O'D).
Balfe, balb.
Ball, bál.
Ballantine, bailintín.
Ballard, ballápv.
Ballesty, bailirce.
Ballevan, Ó balbáin.
Ballinger, bailinréir.
Ballon, bálvún.
Banan, v. Bannon.
Banane, Ó banáin l; buinneán
49.
Banahan, Ó beannacáin.
Bane, bán.
Banfell, Banfield, v. Bonfield.
Banigan, Ó banaȝáin.
Banim, Banin, Ó banáin.
Banks, Ó bpuacóȝ 19, Ó
bpuacáin 45.
Bannan, Bannen, Bannin, Ó
banáin.
Bannigan, Ó banaȝáin.
Bannon, Banon, Ó banáin 11,
(s.l.) Ó bionáin 2.
Banvill, Banville, v. Bonfield.
Baragrey, v. Barragry.
Bardan, Barden, Bardon, Ó
bápváin.
Bargrey, v. Barragry.
Barker, bapcap.
Barnacle, Ó caváin.
Barnane, Ó beapnáin.
Barnard, beapnápv 11; Ó
beapnáin 779.
Barnavill, v. Barnwell.
Barnes, beapnair l; Ó beapáin
92, Ó biopáin 19.
Barnewall, Barnwell, ve
beapnabál, beapnabál.
Baron, bapún.
Barr, Ó bairir.
Barragry, mac beapcaȝra
Barratt, Barrett, bápóiv,
bapóiv 7; bairéiv 9.

Barrie, v. Barry.
Barrington, E. Í ; Ó beapáin 46.
Barron, bapún 78 ; Ó beapáin 16, 46.
Barry, ve bappa 11 ; Ó báipe 772, 492 ; Ó beapxa 172.
Bartholomew, Bartley, mac papcaláin.
Barton, ve bapcún, bapcún.
Baskin, Ó baircinn.
Basnet, bairnéiv.
Bass, ve bap.
Bassett, bairéiv.
Bastable, Bastible, ve bapcábla.
Baston, beapcún.
Bates, Bath, ve bác, bác.
Battle, Battles, mac concaca.
Baun, bán.
Baun-Lavery, Ó labpava bán.
Bawn, bán.
Bayley, Bayly, báille.
Bayne, Baynes, bán.
Beaghan, Beahan, Ó beacáin.
Beaky, Ó béice.
Bean Beane, Ó beacáin.
Bearkery, v. Berkery.
Bearnes, v. Barnes.
Beary, Ó béapa.
Beasley, béaplaiz béaplaoi.
Beasty, Ó biapca.
Beatagh, Beattie, Beatty, biavcac, (s.l.) Óbiava 979
Beaumont, ve buamonn, bua monn.
Beausang, ppanncac.
Beck, ve beic 11 ; Ó béice 2 (O'D).
Beegan, Ó beacáin.
Begane, Ó beagáin.
Begg, Ó beiz 2 ; beag 2
Beggan, Ó beagáin.
Beggs, Ó beiz 2 ; beag 2.
Beglan, Ó beizléizinn, Ó bizléizinn.
Begley, Ó beaglaoic.
Beglin, v. Beglan.
Behan, Behane, Ó beacáin.

Beirne, Beirnes, Ó beipn, Ó bipn.
Bell, ve beil 1 ; mac ziolla an cloiz 19.
Bellew, beilliú, beille.
Bellingham, beilleagam.
Belton, ve béalacún, béalacún.
Benan, v. Bannon.
Bennett, beinéiv, binéiv, bionóiv 1 ; buinneán 496.
Benson mac binéiv 11 ; mac ziollavé 39; Ó manacáin 19.
Bera, Ó béapa.
Berachry, v. Berkerry.
Beresford, vúinppméapac.
Bergan, Bergen, Bergin, Berigin, Ó háimipzin, Ó háimeipzin, (s.l.) Ó beipzin.
Berkerry, Berkery, mac biop- caspa, mac beapcaspa.
Bermingham, mac peópair, mac peópuir, maz peópair, maz peópuir, (s.l.) a ceópair, &c.
Bernard, beapnápv 1 ; Ó beapnáin 779.
Berne, v. Beirne.
Berney, v. Birney.
Bernwell, v. Barnwell.
Berocry, v. Berkerry.
Berrall, v. Berrill.
Berrane, Ó beapáin, Ó biopáin.
Berreen, Ó bipín.
Berrigan v. Bergan.
Berrill, boipéil.
Berry, Ó béapa.
Berth, beipc.
Bertram, beapcpam.
Beston, beapcún.
Betagh, Betty, biavcac.
Bex, ve beic.
Biern, Bierne, v. Beirne.
Bigam, Biggam, v. Bingham.
Biggane, Ó bizeáin, Ó beagáin.
Biggar, Bigger, bizeap.
Biggin, Biggins, Ó bizín, Ó beizín.
Biggs, v. Beggs.

Biggy, Ó biʒiʒ.
Bigham, v. Bingham.
Bigly, v. Begley
Bignel, v. Bagnall.
Binchy, binnre.
Binane, buinneán.
Bingham, bionʒam, binʒeam.
Biracrea, Biracree, v. Berkerry.
Bird, E. 1; Ó héanna, Ó héinne 19; Ó héiniʒ 2; Ó héanacáin, Ó héineacáin 19, 97; mac Conaonaiʒ, (s.l.) mac an éanaiʒ 35, 43.
Birmingham, v. Bermingham.
Birne, Birues, v. Byrne.
Birney, mac biopna.
Birrane, Ó biopáin.
Birrell, boipéil.
Bishop, eappoʒ 1 ; mac an eappuic 2 ; mac ʒiolla eppuiʒ 2.
Bissett, bipéiv ; (G.p) mac eóin.
Blacagh, blácać.
Black, Ó Ouib 2 ; mac Ouib 2 ; mac ʒiolla Ouib 2; Ó Oubéaiʒ 62.
Blackhall, ve blácál 1 ; Ó Oubʒaill 469.
Blackam, ve blácain.
Blackwood, Coilloub.
Blake, ve bláca, ve blác 11 ; Ó blácṁaic 192.
Blanchfield, Blanchville, ve bluinnpíol, (s.l.) bluinnpín.
Blaney, bléine.
Blawick, Ó blácṁaic.
Blayney, bléine.
Bleheen, Ó blicín.
Blessing, Ó maoilbeannacta.
Blewett, blaov, bliúit.
Bligh, Blighe, Ó bliʒe.
Bloomer, Ó ʒoippmpleaʒaiʒ, 6.
Blouk, Blowick, Ó blácṁaic.
Bluett, Blute, blaov, bliúit.
Bly, v. Blighe.
Blythe, ve blaʒv.
Boag, v. Bogue.
Boal, Boale, Boales, v. Bole, Boles
Bockley, Ó baclaiʒ.

Bodan, Boden, bóvún 14, bóivín 82 ; Ó buaváin 24, 45.
Bodkin, bóivicín.
Bogan, Boggan, Ó boʒáin.
Bogue, Ó buaváiʒ.
Bohan, Ó buaváćáin.
Bohanan, Ó buaváćáin 469.
Bohane,* Ó buaváćáin.
Bohig, Ó buaváiʒ.
Bohill, Ó baoéʒalaiʒ 6.
Boice, v. Boyce.
Boil, Boile, v. Boyle.
Bolan, Boland, Ó beólláin 11; Ó bpeólláin 192.
Bole, Boles, (?) Ó baoiʒill.
Bolger, Ó bolʒuivip.
Bollard, ballápv.
Bolton, ve bolltún, bóltún.
Bonar, Ó Cnáiṁpiʒe, (s.l.) Ó Cráiṁpiʒe.
Bond, Bonde, ve bonv.
Bone, ve botún.
Boner, v. Bonar.
Bones, mac Cnáiṁ 19, mac Cnáṁaiʒ 192.
Bonfield, ve buinbíol.
Bonin, buinneán.
Bonner, v. Bonar.
Boohan, Ó buaváćáin.
Boran, Ó boúpáin.
Borris, v. Burris.
Borroughs, Borrowes,ve bpuʒa.
Borthwick, bóptuic.
Bosher, v. Busher.
Bostick, Bostock, ve boptóc.
Boucher, Bouchier, búipéip.
Boughan, Ó buaváćáin.
Boughla, Ó buaćalla.
Bouhan, Ó buaváćáin.
Boulger, v. Bolger.
Bourke, ve búpc, ve búpca.
Bowden, v. Boden.
Bowdren, búvpán.
Bowe, Ó buaváiʒ.
Bowen, ve botún, bóinn, 45, 72 ; Ó buaváćáin 77; Ó Cnáiṁín 46.

* Bohane, in the neighbourhood of Skibbereen, is generally used as a nickname for a branch of the O'Sullivans (? na mbotán).

Bowes, Ó ḃuaḋaiġ 11; Ó
    ḃaoċġalaiġ 62.
Bowie, Ó ḃuaḋaiġ.
Bowland, v. Boland.
Bowle, v. Bole.
Bowler, ḃóiléir, ḃoḃléir.
Bowles, v. Boles.
Bowman, buaman.
Bownes, v. Bones.
Bowsher, v. Busher.
Boyan, v. Boyhan.
Boyce, ṿe ḃúp 10; Ó ḃuaḋaiġ 16.
Boyd, ṿe ḃúit, a ḃúit,
    ḃúiteaċ.
Boyes, v. Boyce.
Boyhan, (?) Ó ḃuaḋaċáin 77.
Boylan, Boyland, Ó ḃaoiġeall-
    áin.
Boyle, Ó ḃaoiġill.
Boyne, Ó ḃaoiċín 2; mac
    ḃaoiċín 2.
Boyse, v. Boyce.
Boyton, ṿe ḃaṿtún, ḃaiṿtiún.
Brabazon, ḃpabapún 11; Ó
    ḃpoiċáin 67.
Bracken, Ó ḃpeacáin.
Bradagan, Ó ḃpaṿaġáin, Ó
    ḃpaṿaċáin.
Bradan, Ó ḃpaṿáin.
Braddell, Ó ḃpaṿġail, Ó
    ḃpaṿġaile.
Bradden, Ó ḃpaṿáin.
Braddigan, Ó ḃpaṿaġáin.
Bradacan, Ó ḃpatacáin, Ó
    ḃpaṿaċáin, Ó ḃpaṿaġáin.
Bradigan, Ó ḃpaṿaġáin.
Bradley, Bradly, Ó ḃpolċáin,
    Ó ḃpolaċáin, (s.l.) Ó ḃpoileaċ-
    áin 19.
Brady, mac ḃpáṿaiġ 6, 8; Ó
    ḃpáṿaiġ 2; Ó ḃpaṿaċáin, Ó
    ḃpaṿaġáin 19.
Bragan, Ó ḃpaġáin.
Brahan, Ó ḃpaċáin.
Braidon, v. Breadon.
Bran, ḃpan.
Branagan, Ó ḃpanaġáin.
Branagh, ḃpeatnaċ.

Branan, v. Brannan.
Brand, ḃpant.
Brandon, mac ḃpeanṿáin 49 :
    ṿe ḃpanṿún, ḃpanṿúň 37.
Brangan, v. Branagan.
Braniff, Ó ḃpanṿuiḃ.
Branigan, Brankin, Ó ḃpanaġáin.
Brannagh, ḃpeatnaċ.
Brannan, Ó ḃpanáin 11; mac
    ḃpanáin 34.
Branne, ḃpan.
Brannick, ṿe ḃpeannóc,
    ḃpeannóc, ḃpannóc.
Brannigan, Ó ḃpanaġáin.
Brannock, v. Brannick.
Brannon, Branon, v. Brannan.
Bransfield, ṿe ḃpionnḃíol,
    ḃpionnḃíol.
Brant, ḃpant.
Brassill, Ó ḃpeapail.
Brauders, Ó ḃpuaṿaip.
Brawley, Ó ḃpólaiġ.
Brawn, Ó ḃpoṗáin.
Brawnick, v. Brannick.
Bray, ṿe ḃpí 1; Ó ḃpeaġaiġ,
    Ó ḃpeaġóa 71; Ó ḃpóiṫ 772.
Brayden, v. Breadon.
Brazel, Brazil, Ó ḃpeapail.
Breadon, ṿe ḃpéaṿún.
Bready, v. Brady.
Breanon, v. Brennan.
Brearton, v. Brereton.
Breckley, v. Brickley.
Bredin, Bredon, ṿe ḃpéaṿún.
Bree, v. Bray.
Breedeth, mac ġiolla ḃpíġṿe.
Breen, Ó ḃpaoin 1; mac
    ḃpaoin 24.
Breheny, Brehony, mac an
    ḃpeiṫeaṁan, mac an
    ḃpeiṫeaṁnaiġ 11, mac an
    ḃpoiṫiṁ 19.
Brenan, v. Brennan.
Brendon, v. Brandon.
Brennagh, ḃpeatnaċ.
Brennan, Ó ḃpanáin 11, (s.l.)
    Ó ḃpanáin 192; Ó ḃpanáin
    6, 91; mac ḃpanáin 34.

Brennigan, Ó bpanagáin.
Brennock, ve bpeannóc,
bpeannóc.
Brennon, Brenon, v. Brennan.
Brereton, Brerton, bpéaptún
Bresland, Breslane, Breslaun,
Breslawn, Breslin, Ó bpeap-
láin, Ó bpeipleáin, Ó bpeip-
lein, (s.l.) Ó bpiopláin, Ó
bpipleáin, &c.
Bresnahan, Bresnane, Bresne-
han, Bresnihan, Ó bpop-
nacáin, Ó bpoipneacáin.
Brett, ve bpic, ve bpeic, bpic.
Bretton, ve bpeacún, ve
bpiocún.
Brew, Ó bpugavá.
Breydon, ve bpéavún.
Brian, v. Bryan.
Briceson, Ó bpíopáin. (o.f.) Ó
muipgeapáin.
Brick, Ó bpuic 49; Ó bpic 47.
Brickley, bpuicléig, bpuicléic.
Bride, bpíve, bpíveac 2; na
bpígve 77.
Bridge, ve bpig, bpigeac.
Bridgeman, Ó Opoiciv.
Bridson, mac giolla bpígve.
Brie, ve bpí.
Brien, Briens, v. O'Brien, Mac
Brien, & Bryan.
Brigg, Briggs, ve bpig, bpigeac.
brinan, Brinane, v. Brennan.
Briody, Ó bpuaivevavá.
Brisco, Briscoe, bpiopcú.
Brislan, Brislane, Brislaun,
Brislawn, Brislin, v. Bresland,
Breslane, &c.
Briton, v. Britton.
Britt, ve bpic, bpic.
Brittan, Britten, Britton, ve
bpiocún.
Brock, bpoc.
Brodders, Broder, Broderick, Ó
bpuavaip.
Brodie, v. Brody.
Brodigan, v. Bradigan.
Brodrick, v. Broderick.

Brody, mac bpuaiveavá.
Broe, Ó bpugavá.
Brofie, v. Brophy.
Brogan, Ó bpógáin.
Broggy, Ó bpogaiv.
Brohan, Ó bpuacáin.
Brohoon, mac an bpeiceaman.
Brolan, Ó bpeólláin.
Brollaghan, Ó bpolcáin, Ó
bpolacáin.
Brolly, Broly, Ó bpólaig.
Brooder, Ó bpuavaip.
Broone, v. Bruen.
Broothers, v. Brothers.
Brophy, Ó bpóice 11, (s.l.) Ó
bpóic 772.
Broslin, v. Breslin.
Brosnahan, Brosnahen, Bros-
nahin, Brosnan, Brosnihan,
Ó bpopnacáin.
Brother, Brothers, Brouder, Ó
bpuavaip.
Broudin, mac bpuaivín.
Broughan, Ó bpuacáin.
Broughton, ve bpoctún.
Browder, v. Brouder.
Browe, Ó bpugavá.
Brown, Browne, ve bpún, bpún
Bruce, ve bpúp, ve bpúp.
Bruder, Brudher, v. Brouder.
Bruen, Bruin, Ó bpaoin, (s.l.)
Ó bpúin.
Brunnock, bpannóc.
Brunty, v. Prunty.
Bruodin, mac bpuaivín.
Brusnahan, Brusnehan, Brus-
nihan, v. Brosnahan.
Bruton, v. Britton.
Bryan, Bryans, Bryen, Bryne,
Brynes, bpian 24, 28; Ó
bpiain 2; mac bpiain 2.
Bryson, Ó bpíopáin, (o.f.) Ó
muipgeapáin.
Buckley, Ó buacalla 1; Ó
baclaig 19.
Bueg, beag.
Buggy, Ó bogaig.
Buhilly, Ó buacalla.

Buie, Ó buaóaiġ 16; mac
Ġiollabuióe 68.
Bulfin, bulpin.
Bulger, Ó bolġuióip.
Bunfield, Bunfill, ve buinbfol.
Bunyan, buinneán.
Burbage, búpbaċ.
Burchell, buippéil.
Burdon, ve bupoún.
Burges, Burgess, Burgiss, buip-
ġéip, buipġéip 1 ; ve bpuġa,
bpuġa 2.
Burke, ve búpc, ve búpca.
Buru, v. Byrne.
Burney, v. Birney.
Burns, Ó bpoin 6, 8, 71; Ó
beipn, Ó bipn 91; Ó
biopáin 75, 97; Ó biopainn
499; Ó boipne 192, mac
Conboipne 192; bpan 469.
Burrell, boipéil.
Burris, buipġéip 1 ; ve bpuġa 2,
Burrowes, Burrows, ve bpuġa,
bpuġa.
Burton, ve bupcún.
Bury, ve bpuġa.
Busher, búipéip.
Buskin, Ó baipcinn.
Bussher, v. Busher.
Bustard, bupcápo.
Butler, ve buic1léip, ve
buicléip, buic1léip, buicléip,
builcéip, builcéip.
Butt, ve boc.
Butterly, buvapláiġ.
Buttimer, buiciméip.
Bwee, Ó buaóaiġ 16; mac
Ġiollabuióe 68.
Byran, Byrane, Ó biopáin.
Byrne, Byrnes, Ó bpoin 11;
Ó beipn, Ó bipn 91; Ó
biopáin 75, 97; mac bpoin
62; Ó boipne 192.
Byron, Ó biopáin 75; Ó bipn
2; Ó bpoin 2.
Byrrane, Ó biopáin.
Bywater, Ó Spucáin, Ó
Spuiceáin.

Cadagan, v. Cadigan.
Cadan, Ó Caváin.
Caddell, Caval.
Cadden, Ó Caváin 6; mac
Áivín, (s.l.) Ó Cáivín 9.
Caddle, Cadell, v. Caddell.
Caden, v. Cadden.
Cadigan, Cadogan, Ó Cévoaġáin
77, Ó Cévoaċáin 49.
Caddow, v. MacCaddo.
Cafferky, Cafferty, mac
eaċṁapcaiġ 11, (s.l.) Ó
Ceapapcaiġ 19.
Caffery, Caffrey, mac ġappaió,
mac Cappaió, maġ Cappaió,
&c.
Cagney, Ó Caingne.
Cahalan, Cahalane, Cahalin,
Cahallane, Ó Caċaláin.
Cahan, Cahane, Ó Caċáin 1;
mac eaċáin 62.
Caheerin, mac eaċċiġeipin.
Cahelan, Cahelin, v. Cahalan.
Caheny, Ó Caicniaó.
Cahill, Ó Caċail.
Cahillane, Ó Caċaláin.
Cahir, Ó Caċaoip 76; mac
Caċaoip 2.
Cahy, mac eaċaió 1 ; Ó Caċaiġ
25.
Cain, Caine, Ó Caċáin.
Cairn, Cairnes, Cairns, Ó Céipín
1, Ó eiapáin. 2.
Calaghan, Calahan, v. Callaghan.
Caldwell, Ó hUapuipce 63 ; mac
Conluain 93 ; mac Caċṁaoil
62.
Calhoun, Ó Caċluain.
Calinan, v. Callinan.
Callaghan, Ó Cealláċáin 11;
Ó Céileáċáin 64 ; Ó Cloċáċáin
469.
Callagy, Ó Calġaiġ.
Callahan, v. Callaghan.
Callaly, mac Ailġile.
Callan, Ó Caċláin, Ó Caċaláin.
Callanan, Callanane, Ó Callan-
áin 11; Ó Cuileannáin 779.

Callaughan, Calleghan, v. Callaghan.

Callen, v. Callan.

Callender, Cuileanṿaṛ.

Callery, mac Ṡiollaṃaḃaiṡ 5; (?) mac Ṡiolla aṗṗaiṫ 2.

Calligan, Callighan, v. Callaghan.

Callily, mac Aiḷṡile.

Callin, v. Callan.

Callina, (?) mac an Laiṡniṡ.

Callinan, Ó Callanáin 11; Ó Cuileannáin 779.

Calliry, v. Callery.

Callister, mac Alaṛṫaiṛ.

Callnan, v. Callanan.

Callwell, v. Caldwell.

Calnan, v. Callanan.

Calvey, mac an Ċalḃaiṡ, mac Calḃaiṡ.

Cambell, v. Campbell.

Cambridge, mac Amḃṛóiṛ.

Cameron, Camṛṛón 1; Ó Cumṗáin, (s.l.) Ó Cumaṛán 19.

Campbell, Caimḃéal S; mac Cailín 66; mac Caṫṁaoil 19, 61; mac Callanáin 132.

Campion, Caimpion.

Canally, mac an ḟailṡiṡ. V. MacNally.

Canavan, Ó Ceannṿuḃáin.

Canaway, v. Conway.

Candless, Candlish, v. MacCandlish and Quinlish.

Cane, Ó Caċáin.

Cangney, Ó Caingne.

Caning, v. Canning.

Cannan, v. Cannon.

Cannavan, v. Canavan.

Canniff, Canniffe, Ó Ceannṿuiḃ.

Canning, Ó Cainín, 52, Ó Canáin 97; MacCoinín 2; ÓCanann 16.

Cannon, Ó Canann 16; Ó Canáin, Ó Conáin, Ó Cuineáin, 9.

Canny, Ó Caiṫniaṿ 19; mac Annaiṿ, (s.l.) mac Cannaiṿ, Ó Cannaiṿ 46.

Canon v. Cannon.

Cantillon, Cantlin, Cantlon, ṿe Cannṫalún, Cannṫalún.

Canton, ṿe Cannṫún, Cannṫún, Canṫún.

Cantwell, ṿe Cannṫual, ṿe Canṫual, Canṫual, Canṫual.

Canty, Ó an Ċáince, Ó Cáince 11, (s.l.) Ó Cannṫaṿa, Ó Cannṫaiṿ 72.

Caorish, mac ḟeóṛaiṛ, mac ḟeóṛuiṛ.

Capeless, Caples, Caplice Cáplaiṛ.

Cappack, v. Cappock.

Capples, Capplis, Cáplaiṛ.

Cappock, Cappuck, ṿe Ceaṛóc, ṿe Ceaṛóṡ.

Carabine, v. Coribeen.

Caragher, Caraher, mac ḟeaṛċaiṛ.

Carberry, Carbery, Carbry, Ó Caiṛḃṛe 8; mac Caiṛḃṛe 2.

Cardell, mac Aṛṿṡail.

Carden, Cáiṛṿín.

Cardiff, ṿe Caṗuiṿ.

Cardin, Cáiṛṿín.

Cardle, mac Aṛṿṡail.

Cardwell, mac Aṛṿṡail 62; mac Ceaṛḃaill 62.

Carellan, Ó Caiṛealláin.

Caren, Ó Caṛṛaiṿín.

Carew, ṿe Caṛṛún, Caṛṛún.

Carey, Ó Ciaṛṿa 14, 15, 43, 46, 75, 979; mac ḟiaċṛa, mac ḟiaċṛaċ 972; Caṛṛún 71; Ó Caṛṛáin, Ó Coṛṛáin 72; Ó Ciaṛáin, Ó Ceaṛáin, Ó Cioṛáin, 197, 199, Ó Céiṛín 2; Ó Ciaṛṁaċáin, 779.

Cargill, mac ḟeaṛṡail.

Carha, mac Cáṛṫaiṡ.

Carigan, v. Carrigan.

Carkill, mac ḟeaṛṡail.

Carlan, Carland, Ó Caiṛealláin, Ó Coiṛealláin 11; Ó Ceaṛḃalláin 62.

Carleton, ṿe Caṛlṫún 2; Ó Caiṛealláin 6.

Caulin, Ó Cacaláin.
Cavan, Ó Caomáin, Ó Caoimín.
Cavanagh, v. Kavanagh.
Cave, Mac Dáibíd.
Cavendish, Ó Caomáin 19.
Cavey, Mac Dáibíd.
Cavish, Mac Támair.
Caviston, Mac Aibirtín.
Cawley, Mac Amalgaḋa, Mac Amalgaiḋ 5; Mac Amlaoiḃ 8.
Cawlin, Ó Cacaláin, Ó Caclám.
Chaff, Ó Lócáin.
Chamberlain, Chambers, Seambap, Seambapp, Seambpac.
Charles, Séaplup E. 2; Mac Séaplup, Mac Séaplaip 1; Mac Cacail 19.
Charleson, Mac Séaplup, Mac Séaplap.
Cheasty, Ó Seapta, Ó Siopta.
Cheevers, Chevers, Síḃeap.
Cheyne, Chine, Mac Seáin, Mac Seagáin.
Chisholm, Chissell, Sipeal.
Chivers, Síḃeap.
Christian, Mac Cpirtín.
Christie, Mac Cpíopta.
Christopher, Cpíoptóip.
Christopherson, Mac Cpíoptópa.
Christy, Chrystie, Chrysty, Mac
Chute, Siúit.   (Cpíopta.
Clabby, Ó Clabaiġ.
Claffey, Claffy, Mac Flaicím, Mac Laitim, Mac Lacaiġ.
Clahane, Ó Clacáin, (o.f.) Ó Cacláin, Ó Cacaláin.
Clair, v. Clare.
Clanchy, Clancy, Mac Flann-caḋa, Mac Flanncaiḋ.
Clandillon, Clannoiolúin.
Clare, De Cláp, Cláp.
Clarey, v. Cleary.
Clark, Clarke, Cléipeac E 2; Ó Cléipiġ 11; Mac an Cléipiġ, Mac Cléipiġ 32; Ó Cléipcín 64, Ó Cléipeacáin 56, 192; Mac Giolla appaic 29.

Clarkins, Ó Cléipeacáin, Ó Cléipcín.
Clarkson, Clarson, Mac an Cléipiġ.
Classon, Clausson, Mac Niocláip
Clavan, Ó Clamáin.
Claveen, Clavin, Ó Claimín.
Clay, Mac an Leaġa.
Clayton, De Cléatún.
Clear, De Cléip.
Cleary, Ó Cléipiġ 11; Mac an Cléipiġ, Mac Cléipiġ 67; Mac Giolla appaic 29.
Cleeland, Mac Giolla Faoláin.
Cleere, De Cléip.
Cleery, v. Cleary.
Clehane, Ó Clacáin (o.f.), Ó Cacláin, Ó Cacaláin.
Cleland, Clelland, Clellond, Mac Giolla Faoláin.
Clemens, Clement, Clements, Climéip, Climéipeac 2; Mac Laġmainn 2.
Clenaghan, Mac Leannacáin.
Clerihan, Ó Cléipeacáin.
Clerkan, Ó Cléipeacáin, Ó Cléipcín.
Clerke, v. Clarke.
Clerkin, Ó Cléipcín, Ó Cléipeacáin.
Clery, Ó Cléipiġ 11; Mac an Cléipiġ, Mac Cléipiġ 67.
Clifford, De Cliofopc, Cliofopc E 2; Ó Clúmáin 79a, 93.
Climents, Climons, v. Clemens
Clinane, Ó Claonáin.
Clinch, Clinpe, Clinpeac.
Clinchy, Mac Loinġriġ.
Cline, Mac Giollactaoin.
Clinton, De Cliontún, Cliontún 2; Gleantún 2.
Clisham, Mac Clipeam (S.L.) 19.
Clogan, Ó Clocacáin.
Clogherty, Ó Clocapcaiġ.
Cloghery, Mac Clocaipe.
Cloghessy, Ó Clocapaiġ.
Cloherty, Ó Clocapcaiġ.

Clohessy, Ó Cloċaraiġ.
Cloney, v. Clooney.
Cloonan, Ó Cluanáin.
Clooney, Cloony, Ó Cluanaiġ 1; mac Cluanaiġ 2.
Cloran, mac Labráin.
Close, Ó Cluaraiġ.
Closkey, mac Bloscaiḋ.
Cloughry, mac Cloċaire.
Clovan, Cloven, Ó Clúmáin.
Clowney, Clowny, v. Clooney.
Clowry, mac Labraḋa.
Cloyen, mac Giollaċiaoin.
Clucas, mac Lúcáir.
Clunan, Ó Cluanáin.
Clune, Ó Cluain 87; mac Glúin 76.
Cluney, v. Clooney.
Clusby, mac Giolla earpuiġ.
Clusker, mac Bloscaire.
Cluskey, mac Bloscaiḋ.
Cluvane, Ó Clúmáin.
Clymens, v. Clemens.
Clymonds, mac Laġmainn.
Clynch, Clinċe, Clinreaċ.
Clyne, Clynes, mac Giolla-ċiaoin.
Coady, mac Óda.
Coakley, mac Caoċlaoiċ, mac Claoċlaoiċ 77.
Coall, v. Cole.
Coalter, Ó Coltair, Ó Coltaráin.
Coan, v. Coen.
Coates, Cat.
Cochrane, Cockrane, Ó Cogaráin, mac Cogaráin 46, 97.
Codd, Coda.
Cody, mac Óda 11; Ó Cuidiġtiġ 782.
Coe, Ó Coḃċaiġ.
Coen, Ó Comḋain, Ó Comġain 11; mac Eoġain 2.
Coey, Ó Coḃċaiġ.
Coffee, Coffey, Ó Coḃċaiġ 11; Ó Caċḃuaḋaiġ 49; Ó Caċḃaḋa 27; Ó Caṫṁoġa 97.

Cogan, Ó Cuagáin 1; mac Cogáin 43, 58; mac Eoċagáin 62; De Cogán, Gogán 77.
Cogavin, Cogeen, mac Cogaiḋín.
Coggan, Coggins, mac Cogáin.
Coghlan, Coghlen, Coghlin, Ó Coċláin 1, mac Coċláin, maġ Coċláin 25.
Coghran, Ó Cogaráin, mac Cogaráin.
Cogley, Ó Coigliġ.
Cogran, v. Coghran.
Cohalan, Cohalane, Ó Caċaláin.
Cohane, Ó Caċáin 1; Ó Ceoċáin 779.
Cohen, v. Coen.
Coholane, v. Cohalane.
Coid, mac Uaiḋ.
Coiles, v. Coyle.
Cokely, v. Coakley.
Colahan, mac Uallaċáin.
Colavin, mac Conluain.
Colbert, a Colbáro, Colbárd.
Colclogh, Colclough, Colcloċ.
Coldrick, mac Ualġairg.
Coldwell, Ó hUapuirce 63; mac Conluain 93.
Cole, cól E 2; mac Giolla Comġaill 16; mac Duḃġaill 2
Coleman, Ó Colmáin 11: mac Colmáin 2; Colmán E 2; Ó Clúmáin 17, 19, 49, 87, &c.
Coles, v. Cole.
Colgan, Ó Colgan 8, 9; mac Colgan 6.
Colhoon, Colhoun, Colċún 1; Ó Caċluain 6; Ó Cuileaṁain 87.
Coligan, v. Colgan.
Colin, Ó Coċláin 2; Ó Caċaláin 2.
Colins, v. Collins.
Coll, mac Colla 2; Ó Colla 2; Col 17.
Collagan, v. Colligan.
Collatan, Ó Coolaċáin, mac Coolaċáin.

Collen, v. Cullen.
Collender, Cuileanuaṗ.
Colleran, Ó Callaṗáin í, mac
Allṁuṗáin 2.
Collery, mac Ṡiolla aṗṗaiċ.
Colleton, Ó Couladáin. mac
Couladáin
Collier, Ccléiṗ.
Colligan, Ó Colṡan 8. 9 : mac
Colṡan 6.
Collina, Colliney (?), mac an
Laiṡniṡ.
Collins, Ó Coileáin, Ó Cuileáin
1 ; mac Coilín 6.
Collopy, Ó Colpċa, Ó Colpa.
Colloton, v. Collatan.
Collum, Collumb, mac Coluim
Collwell, v. Coldwell.
Colman, v Coleman.
Colohan, mac Uallaċáin
Colomb, mac Coluim.
Colovin, mac Conluain.
Colquhoun, Colquohoun, Colċún.
Colreavy, mac Cúilṗiaḃaiṡ.
Colter, Ó Coltaiṗ, Ó Coltaṗáin.
Colthurst, Colltiṗ.
Colton, Coltún 1 ; Ó Comaltáin 2.
Colum, Columb, mac Coluim
Colvan, mac Conluain
Colville, v. Coldwell.
Colvin, v. Colvan.
Colwell, v. Coldwell.
Coman, Ó Comáin.
Comaskey, mac Cumarcaiṡ.
Comba, v. Conba.
Comber, ve Cómaṗ, Cómaṗ 99 ; Ó
Ciaṗáin 976 ; Ó Ciaṗaṡáin 19, 94.
Combes, mac Cómaiṗ.
Comer, v. Comber.
Comerford, Comaṗtún 1 ; mac
Cumarcaiṡ 53.
Comerton, Comaṗtún.
Comesky, v. Comaskey.
Comey, mac Ṡiolla Cóimṁeaḃ.
Comford, Comfort, v. Comerford
Comish, mac Cómaiṗ.
Comiskey, mac Cumarcaiṡ.

Commane, Ó Comáin.
Commaskey, v. Comiskey.
Commerford, Commerfort, v.
Comerford.
Commins, Ó Comáin 11 ; mac
Coimín 62.
Common, Commons, Ó Comáin.
Comyn, Comyns, Coimín,
Cuimín 46, 57, 77, 78 ; mac
Coimín, mac Cuimín 6, 42 ;
Ó Coimín, Ó Cuimín 29, 72.
Conaboy, v. Conboy.
Conacher mac Conċoḃaiṗ.
Conaghan, Ó Connaċáin.
Conaghty, Ó Connaċtaiṡ.
Conallan, Ó Conalláin. V.
Conlon.
Conally, v. Connelly.
Conalty, Ó Conalltა.
Conan, Ó Conáin 1 ; Ó Cuanáin 29.
Conarchy, Ó Conaiṗce.
Conary, Ó Conaiṗe.
Conaty, Ó Connaċtaiṡ.
Conba, Conbay, Ó Conḃáṡa, Ó
Conḃáiḋ,
Conboy, Ó Conburḋe 9 ; Ó
Conḃáṡa, Ó Conḃáiḋ 99.
Concannen, Concannon, Ó Con-
ċeannainn, Ó Conċeanainn.
Conderick, v. Condrick.
Condon, Connṿún, Conṿún 1 ;
Ó Conṿuḃáin 23, 33.
Condrick, mac Annṗaic, mac
eanṗaic, mac eanṗaic.
Condrin, Condron, Ó Conaṗáin.
Coneely, Ó Conṡaile 11 ; mac
Conṡaile 92.
Conefry, mac Conṗṗaoiċ.
Conelly, v. Connelly.
Coner, v. Connor.
Coney, v. Cooney.
Conheeny, mac Conaonaiṡ.
Conify, mac Ṿonnċaiḋ.
Conlan, Conland, v. Conlon.
Conley, mac Connla, mac
Connlaoḋა. V. Connelly.
Conliffe, Ó Conṿuiḃ.

Conlogue, mac Conaill Óig.
Conlon, Ó Conalláin 11; Ó Caoinvealbáin 43; Ó Claonáin 19.
Conly, v. Conley.
Conmee, Conmey, Conmy, mac Conmeava 5; mac Conmive 6.
Connaghton, Ó Connactáin.
Connaghty, Ó Connactaig.
Connally, Connaly, Ó Congalaig
Connaughton, Ó Connactáin.
Conneally, Connealy, Conneely, Ó Congaile 11; mac Congaile 92; mac Congaola 972.
Conneff, Conneffe, mac Convuib
Connell, Ó Conaill.
Connellan, Ó Conalláin 11; Ó Caoinvealbáin 43.
Connelly, Connely, Ó Congalaig 12; Ó Congaile 91; mac Congaile 197; Ó Coingeallaig, mac Coingeallaig 77, 78.
Conner, v. Connor.
Connerney, mac an Oircinnig, mac an Aircinnig.
Connerton, Ó Connactáin.
Connery, Ó Conaire.
Conney, Ó Coinne 6; mac Connaib 2.
Connick, mac Conmaic.
Conniff, Conniffe, mac Convuib 9; Ó Convuib 46.
Connigan, Ó Connagáin.
Connington, Ó Connactáin.
Connison, mac Coinnig.
Connole, Ó Coineóil.
Connollan, v. Connellan.
Connolly, Connoly, Ó Congalaig 12; Ó Congaile 91; mac Congaile 197; Ó Coingeallaig, mac Coingeallaig 77, 78.
Connor, Connors, Ó Concobair 11; mac Concobair 66.
Connorton, Ó Connactáin.
Connoway, v. Conway.
Conole, Ó Coineóil.

Conolly, Conoly, v. Connolly.
Conoo, Ó Conmaig.
Conor, Conors, v. Connor.
Conotty, Ó Connactaig.
Conrahy, Ó Conrata, mac Conrata.
Conran, Ó Conapáin.
Conree, mac Conraoi.
Conrick, mac Annraic.
Conron, Ó Conapáin.
Conroy, mac Conraoi 73, 97; Ó Conraoi 62, 92; Ó Conaire 99; Ó Conrata, mac Conrata 25, 45; Ó Maolconaire 92, 462.
Conry, mac Conraoi 197; Ó Conrac, Ó Conra 92; Ó Conaire 7; Ó Maolconaire 29, 34, 46.
Considine, mac Conraroin.
Convery, mac Ainmire.
Convey, v. Conway.
Conway, Ó Connmaig 7, 8, 34, 67; mac Connmaig 252, 462; Ó Conbuive 92; Ó Conmeava 2; mac Conmeava 2; Ó Connmacáin 91; mac Nuavav, mac Nuavat 252.
Conwell, mac Conmaoil.
Conwy, v. Conway.
Conyeen, Ó Coinín 5; mac Coinín 2.
Conyngham, v. Cunningham.
Cooey, Ó Cobtaig.
Coogan, Ó Cuagáin 1; mac eocagáin 62.
Cooke, Cúc 1; mac Vabóc, mac Vabóg, (s.l.) mac Cuag, mac Guag, Guag 97.
Cooken, v. Coogan.
Coolahan, Ó Cúlacáin 17, 19, 27; mac Uallacáin 97.
Coole, mac Vubgaill.
Cooley, Ó Cúile 77; mac Giolla Cúile 46, 97.
Coolican, Coolihan, Ó Cúlacáin 11; Ó Ciobhlacáin 92.
Coomey, Ó Camta.

Coonaghan, Coonahan, Ó
Cuᴀnᴀċáin.

Coonan, Ó Cuᴀnáin.

Coonerty, Ó Cuᴀnᴀpᴛᴀiṡ.

Cooney, Ó Cuᴀnᴀċ, Ó Cuᴀnᴀ
11 ; Ó Cuᴀnᴀċáin 72.

Coonihan, Ó Cuᴀnᴀċáin.

Cooper, Cúipéip.

Coote, Cúᴛ.

Copinger, Coipinṡéip.

Copley, Cóipliḋe.

Coppinger, Coipinṡéip.

Corbally, ᴅe Copḃᴀile.

Corban, Corbane, Ó Copḃáin.

Corbett, Copḃᴀiᴅ 25, 43, 99 ;
Ó Copḃáin 1, Ó Coipḃín 2 ;
Ó Conḃáṡᴀ, Ó Conḃáiᴅ, 179.

Corbin, Ó Coipḃín.

Corbitt, v. Corbett.

Corboy, Corby, Ó Copḃuiḋe
77 ; Mᴀc Copḃuiḋe 27, 45.

Corcoran, Corcorin, Ó Copcpáin
7, 91 ; Mᴀc Copcpáin 25 ;
Ó Copcáin 19, 52, 97.

Cordan, Ó Coppᴀᴅáin.

Corduff, Copᴅuḃ.

Corey, Ó Coṁpᴀiḋe.

Coribeen, Ó Coipḃín.

Corish, Mᴀc Ƒeópᴀip, Mᴀc
Ƒeópuip.

Corken, Ó Copcáin 1 ; Mᴀc
Copcáin 48.

Corkeran v. Corcoran.

Corkerry, Corkery, Ó Copcpᴀ.

Corkhill, Mᴀc Ƈopcᴀill.

Corkin, Ó Copcáin 1 ; Mᴀc
Copcáin 48.

Corkoran, Corkran, v. Corcoran.

Corless, Mᴀc Cᴀpluip 11 ; Mᴀc
Cᴀṫᴀil 197.

Corley, Mᴀc Ƈoipᴅeᴀlḃᴀiṡ.

Cormac, Cormack, Ó Copmᴀic
1 ; Ó Copmᴀcáin 2 ; Mᴀc
Copmᴀic 2.

Cormican, Ó Copmᴀcáin.

Cormick, v. Cormack.

Cormocan, v. Cormican.

Corneen, Ó Cuipnín.

Corr, Corra, Ó Copppᴀ 1 ; Mᴀc
Coppᴀ 2.

Corran, Ó Coppáin.

Corree v. Corry.

Corridon, Ó Coppᴀᴅáin.

Corrie, v. Corry.

Corrigan, Ó Coppᴀṡáin.

Corry, Ó Coppᴀ, Ó Coppᴀiᴅ 1 ;
Mᴀc Coppᴀ, Mᴀc Coppᴀiᴅ
2 ; Ó Coṁpᴀiḋe 15, 46, 77 ;
Mᴀc Ṡoṫpᴀiᴅ 23, 67.

Coscor, Ó Copcᴀip 4; Mᴀc Opcᴀip
3 ; Mᴀc Ṡiollᴀ ċopcᴀip 32.

Cosgrave, Cosgreave, Cosgreve,
Cosgriff, Cosgrive, Cosgrove,
Cosgry, Ó Copcpᴀiṡ 11 ; Mᴀc
Copcpᴀiṡ 35 ; Ó Copcpᴀċáin
62 ; Mᴀc Copcpᴀċáin 38 ;
Mᴀc Opcᴀip 62 ; Mᴀc Ṡiollᴀ
ċopcᴀip 32 ; Mᴀc Ṡiollᴀ
ċoipcle 32 ; Mᴀc Ḃlopcᴀipe
132.

Cosker, v. Coscor.

Coskeran, Coskerin, Ó Copcpᴀċáin 1 ; Mᴀc Copcpᴀċáin 38.

Coskerry, Coskery, Ó Copcpᴀiṡ,
Costello, Costelloe, Mᴀc Coip-
ᴅeᴀlḃ, Mᴀc Coipᴛeᴀlḃᴀiṡ,
(o.f.) Mᴀc Oipᴅeᴀlḃ 11 ;
Mᴀc Ṡiollᴀ ċoipcle 62, (s.l.)
Mᴀ'l ċuipleᴀċ 37.

Costen, Mᴀc Oipᴛín, (s.l.) Ó
Coipᴛín.

Costigan, Mᴀc Oipᴛicín, Mᴀc
Oipᴛiṡín, (s.l.) Mᴀc Cop-
ᴛᴀṡáin, Ó Copᴛᴀṡáin.

Costillo, Costily, v. Costelloe.

Costin, Costine, Mᴀc Oipᴛín,
(s.l.) Ó Coipᴛín.

Costolloe, Costoloe, Costley, v.
Costelloe.

Costum, Costune, Copᴛún.

Cotter, Cottier, Cottiers, Mᴀc
Oiᴛip, (s.l.) Mᴀc Coiᴛip.

Cottle, Ó Coiᴛil.

Cotton, ᴅe Coᴛún.

Coughlan, Coughlen, Coughlin, Ó Coċláin 1; mac Coċláin, maᵹ Coċláin 25.

Coulahan, Coulihan, Ó Cúlaċáin 17, 19, 27; mac Uallaċáin 97.

Coulter, Ó Colꞇair, Ó Colꞇapáin.

Coulton, v. Colton.

Coumey, v. Coomey.

Counihan, Ó Cuanaċáin.

County, v. Canty.

Courcey, ꝺe Cúrra, Cúrraċ.

Courigan, Ó Corraᵹáin.

Courn, Ó Corráin.

Cournane, Ó Cúrnáin, Ó Curnáin.

Courneen, Ó Cúirnín, Ó Cuirnín.

Coursey, ꝺe Cúrra, Cúrraċ.

Courtayne, mac Cuirꞇáin.

Courtney, Ó Cúrnáin, Ó Curnáin 17, 25, 46, 49; Ó Cúirnín, Ó Cuirnín, 93, 462; mac Cuarꞇa, mac Cuairꞇ 37, 99.

Cousin, Cousine, Cousins, Cúirín.

Covaddy, mac an maꝺaiꝺ.

Coveney, Ó Coiḃḟeanaiᵹ 24, 45; mac Coiḃḟeanaiᵹ 2.

Cowan, Cowen, Ó Comḋain, Ó Comᵹain 11; mac ᵹiolla Comḋain, mac ᵹiolla Comᵹain 62; mac Eoᵹain 2.

Cowey, Cowhey, Cowhig, Cowie, Ó Coḃꞇaiᵹ.

Cowin, v. Cowen.

Cowley, mac amalᵹaiꝺ, mac amalᵹaꝺa 5, 9; mac amlaoiḃ 2; E 2.

Cowman, Ó Comáin.

Cowmey, Ó Camꞇa.

Cowper, Cúipéir.

Cowran, Ó Cuḃráin.

Cox, Coxe, Cocr, Cocraċ 34; mac an Coiliᵹ, mac Coiliᵹ, mac Coiliꞃ 34; Ó Coiliᵹ 16, 92; mac Coiliᵹin 77; mac Conċoille, mac Conċoilleaꝺ 17, 63, 79a, 84.

Coy, v. MacCoy.

Coyd, mac Uaiꝺ.

Coyle, mac ꝺuḃᵹaill.

Coyne, Ó Caḋáin 91; Ó Cuinn (Ó Cuinn) 81; Ó Cuain 93; Ó Comḋain, Ó Comᵹain 92; mac ᵹiollaċaoin 39, 82; mac Eoᵹain 92.

Craan, Ó Corráin.

Craddock, Creaꝺóc, Creaꝺóᵹ.

Craford, v. Crawfor⸱

Crage, v. Craig.

Crahan, Ó Carráin, Ó Corráin.

Craig, ꝺe Carraiᵹ, ꝺe Craiᵹ, ꝺe Creaᵹ, Creaᵹ, Creoᵹ.

Craigan, v. Cregan.

Crain, Ó Carráin, Ó Corráin.

Crampsey, Crampsie, Crampsy, Cramsie, Ó Cráiṁṫiᵹe, (o.f.) Ó Cnáiṁṫiᵹe.

Crane, Ó Carráin, Ó Corráin.

Cranley, Ó Crónᵹaile.

Crangle, Ó Crónᵹail.

Cranny, Crany ,(?) mac Ḃranaiᵹ

Crauford, v. Crawford.

Craughwell, Ó Creaċṁaoil (S.L.)

Cravane, Ó Cráḃáin.

Craven, Cravin, Ó Cráḃáin, Ó Cráiḃín 1; mac Cráḃáin 64.

Crawford, ꝺe Cráꞃorꞇ, Cráꞃoirꞇ 1; mac Cráḃaᵹáin 64.

Crawley, mac Ráᵹallaiᵹ. V. Crowley.

Crayford, v. Crawford.

Creagh, Craoḃaċ.

Creaghan, Ó Créaċáin 1; Ó Carráin 2.

Crean, Creane, Ó Croiḃeáin 16, 19, 29; Ó Créaċáin 72, 97; Ó Carráin, Ó Corráin, Ó Corraiḃín, Ó Cuirín 77, 87.

Creaton, Ó Créaċáin, Ó Críoċáin.

Creaven, Creavin, Ó Cʀábáin,
Ó Cʀáibín 1 ; Ó Cʀaobáin 29 ;
Mac Cʀábáin 64.

Creed, Creedon, Ó Cʀíováin,
(o.f.) Mac Cʀíováin.

Creegan, v. Cregan.

Creehan, v. Crehan.

Creely, Mac Raʒailliʒ.

Creen, v. Crean.

Creevey, Creevy, Ó Cʀaoibe.

Cregan, Ó Cʀiaʒáin, (o.f.) Mac
Riaʒáin.

Cregg, ve Cʀaiʒ, Cʀeaʒ, Cʀeoʒ.

Creghan, Crehan, Ó Cʀéacáin,
Ó Cʀiocáin, Ó Cʀíocáin 1 ;,
Ó Cappáin, Ó Coppáin 2.

Creigan, v. Cregan.

Creighan, Creighton, Ó Cʀéacáin, Ó Cʀíocáin.

Creilly, Crelly, Mac Raʒailliʒ.

Cremeen, Cremen, Cremin, Ó
Cʀoimín, Ó Cʀuimín.

Crenegan, Ó Cʀuonaʒáin.

Crennan, Ó Cʀíonáin, Mac
Cʀíonáin.

Cribbin, Cribbins, Cribbon, Ó
Cʀoibín.

Crickard, Mac Riocaiʀv.

Cricket, Mac Ricéiv.

Crigley, Mac Raiʒilliʒ.

Crilly, Mac Raʒailliʒ.

Crimmeen, Crimmins, Ó Cʀuimín.

Crinigan, Ó Cʀuonaʒáin.

Crinion, Crinneen, Ó Cʀíonáin,
Mac Cʀíonáin.

Cristy, Mac Cʀíoʀʒa.

Croake, Cʀóc.

Croan, v. Crohan.

Crofton, ve Cʀoccún.

Crofts, ve Cʀoccaʀ.

Croghan, Crohan, Mac Con-
cʀuacán.

Croke, Cʀóc.

Crolly, Croly, Mac Roʒallaiʒ ;
(s.l.), Ó Cʀovlaoic, Ó Cʀuavlaoic.

Crombie, Cromie, Crommie,
Cʀomca.

Cromwell, Cʀomail.

Cronan, Ó Cʀónáin, Ó Cʀóinín

Crone, Cʀón 2; Ó Cʀóin 2.

Cronekan, Ó Cʀónaʒáin.

Cronelly, Ó Cʀónʒaile 1; Mac
Cʀónʒaile 2.

Croniken, Ó Cʀónaʒáin.

Cronin, Ó Cʀóinín.

Cronley, v. Cronelly.

Cronyn, v. Cronin.

Crook, Crooke, Crookes, Crooks,
Cʀóc, Cʀúc.

Crosbie, E 1 ; Mac an Cʀoʀáin 2.

Cross, ve Cʀúiʀ, Cʀúiʀ 2 ; Mac
an Cʀoʀáin 2.

Crossan, Crossen, Crossin,
Crosson, Mac an Cʀoʀáin.

Crotty, Ó Cʀoccaiʒ.

Crough, v. Crowe.

Croughan, Mac Concʀuacán.

Crowe, Mac Concʀava.

Crowley, Ó Cʀuavlaoic 9 ; Mac
Roʒallaiʒ, (s.l.) Ó Cʀo-
ʒallaiʒ, Ó Cʀovlaoic, Ó
Cʀuavlaoic 7.

Crozier, Cʀúiʀéiʀ.

Crudden, Mac Rováin.

Cruice, Cruise, ve Cʀúiʀ,
Cʀúiʀ.

Crumley, *Ó Cʀomlaoic.

Crumlish, (?) Ó Cʀompuiʀc.

Crummell, Cʀomail.

Crummy, Ó Cʀomca.

Cryan, Ó Cʀaiveáin.

Cudahy, Cuddehy, Cuddihy,
Cuddy, Cudihy, Ó Cuiviʒéiʒ.

Cudden, v. Cadden.

Cuffe, Mac Ðuib 1 ; Ó Cobcaiʒ
469 ; Ó Ðoipnín, Ó Ðuipnín
19, 62.

Cuhy, Mac Eocaiv.

Cuinane, Ó Cuineáin.

Culgan, Culgin, Ó Colʒan.

Culhane, Ó Cacláin, Ó Cacaláin,
(s.l.) Ó Calcáin.

Culhoun, Colcún l ; Ó Catluáin,
6 ; Ó Cuileamáin 87.
Culkeen, Culkin, Mac Uilcín.
Cull, v. Coll.
Cullan, Ó Cuileáin.
Cullanan, Ó Cuileannáin.
Cullane, Ó Cuileáin.
Cullen, Ó Cuilinn 81 ; Mac
Cuilinn 64 ; Ó Cuileáin, Ó
Cuilín 777 ; Mae Coilín, 16,
39, 68 ; Ó Catluain 62 · Ó
Cuileamáin 87.
Culleton, Ó Coolatáin 11,
Mac Coolatáin 87.
Cullian, v. Cullen.
Culligan, Ó Colgán 4 ; Mac
Colgán 6.
Cullin, v. Cullen.
Cullinan, Cullinane, Ó Cuileann-
áin.
Culliney, (?) Mac an Laignig.
Cullington, Ó Coolatáin, Mac
Coolatáin.
Cullins, v. Cullen.
Culliton, v. Culleton.
Cullity, Ó Coolata, (s l.) Ó
Collata.
Cullivan, Mac Conluain.
Culloo, Mac Conulaó.
Culloon v. Culhoun.
Culloty v. Cullity.
Cully, Ó Colla.
Culnane, v. Cullinane.
Culreavy, Mac Cúilriabaig.
Cumaskey, Mac Cumarcaig.
Cumbaw, v. Conba.
Cumberford, v. Comerford.
Cumesky, Mac Cumarcaig.
Cumin, Cuming, Cumings,
Cumins, v. Cummings.
Cumisk, Cumiskey, Cumisky,
Mac Cumarcaig.
Cummane, Ó Comáin.
Cummens, v. Cummins.
Cummerford, v. Comerford.

Cummin, Cumming, Cummings,
Cummins, Ó Comáin 71, 81,
91, Ó Cuimín 72, 82, 92'; Mac
Cuimín 6, 72 ; Cuimín 46, 57'
77, 78.
Cummiskey, v. Cumiskey.
Cunagum, v. Cunningham.
Cundlish, Ó Cuinolir.
Cuneen, v. Cunneen.
Cunhane, Ó Conáin 976.
Cunif, Cuniff, v. Cunniffe.
Cunihan, v. Cunnahan.
Cunion, v. Cunneen.
Cunlish, Ó Cuinolir.
Cunlisk, Ó Coinlirc, Ó Coin-
leirc.
Cunnahan, Ó Cuinneacáin.
Cunnane, Ó Cuineáin 11, Ó
Conáin 92.
Cunnea, Ó Coinne.
Cunnean, v. Cunneen.
Cunneely, v. Conneely.
Cunneen, Ó Coinín 5 ; Mac
Coinín 9.
Cunneeny, Mac Conaonaig.
Cunniam, Cunnien, v. Cunneen.
Cunniffe, Mac Conouib 9 ; Ó
Conouib 46, 92.
Cunning, Ó Conaing.
Cunningan, Ó Cuinneagáin, Mac
Cuinneagáin.
Cunningham, Ó Cuinneagáin 11,
Ó Connagáin 2, Mac Cuinne-
agáin 2. Ó Cuinneacáin 2,
Ó Connacáin 2.
Cunnion, v. Cunneen.
Cunnoo, Ó Connmaig.
Cunny, Ó Coinne.
Cunree, Mac Conraoi.
Cunreen, Mac Conruain.
Cunvane, Ó Conbáin.
Cuolahan, Cuolohan, v. Coula-
han.
Curby, v. Corby.
Curland, Ó Coirealláin.
Curley, Mac Toirroealbaig.
Curnane, Ó Curnáin, Ó Cúrnáin.

Curneen, Curneene, Curnin, Ó
Cuirnín, Ó Cúirnín.
Curoe, (?) mac Ꝃotpaⱱa.
Curran, Currain, Currane, Ó
Corráin, Ó Curráin 11,
Ó Corraiⱱín (Ó Coirín,
Ó Cuirín), 19, 77, 87, 97.
Curreen, Curren, Ó Corraiⱱín
(Ó Cuirín) 1 ; mac Corraiⱱín
(mac Corraoin) 29, 39.
Currid, Ó Coрѐaⱱ (S.L.).
Currie, v. Curry.
Currigan, Ó Corragáin.
Currin, Ó Corraiⱱín 1 ; mac
Corraiⱱín 29, 39. V. Curreen.
Curry, Ó Corra, Ó Corraiⱱ 1 ;
mac Corra, mac Corraiⱱ 2 ;
Ó Coṁraiⱱe 15, 46, 77 ; mac
Ꝃotpaiⱱ 23, 67 ; mac
muireaⱱaiẛ 62.
Curtain, Curtan, Curtayne, mac
Cuirtáin 1, mac Cairteáin 2.
Curteis, v. Curtis.
Curten, v. Curtin.
Curties, v. Curtis.
Curtin, mac Cuirtín, (o.f.) mac
Cpuirtín 46, 178 ; mac Cuirtáin
79a, mac Cairteáin 772, Ó
Cuirtáin 49, 179.
Curtis, ⱱe Cuirtéir, Cuirtéir
1 ; mac Cpuirtín 64.
Cusack, ⱱe Cíoṁróg, ⱱe
Ciúṁróg, Cíoṁróg, Ciúṁróg,
Cíoróg 1 ; mac Íoróg, mac
Íoróg 16, 46, 94, mac Íreóg
972, (s.l.) Círeóg 976.
Cushanan, Ó Cornacáin.
Cushen,Cushing, Cushion, Cúirn.
Cushlane, Ó Cairealáin.
Cushley, mac Ꝃiolla ċoircle.
Cushnahan, Ó Cornacáin.
Cusick, v. Cusack.
Cuskelly, v Cuskley.
Cusker, Ó Corcair 4 ; mac
Oрcair 3 ; mac Ꝃiolla
ċorcair 32.
Cuskern, Ó Corcracáin 1 ; mac
Corcracáin 38.

Cuskery, Ó Corcraiẛ.
Cuskley, mac Ꝃiolla ċoircle.
Cuskor, v. Cusker.
Cusnahan, Ó Cornacáin.
Cussack, v. Cusack.
Cussane, Ó Copáin (o.f.) Ó Caráin, (s.s.), mac Páⱱín 197,
976
Cussen, Cúirín.
Cussick, v. Cusack.
Cuthbert, Cuthbertson, mac
Cúiѐṗeiѐ.

Dade, mac ⱱaiⱱéiⱱ.
Daffy, Ó ⱱeaṁѐaiẛ.
Dahill, Ó ⱱaѐail, Ó ⱱaiѐẛil.
Dahony, Ó ⱱuṁċonna.
Daid, mac ⱱaiⱱéiⱱ.
Daily, v. Daly.
Dallaghan, Ó ⱱalaċáin.
Dallagher, Ó ⱱalaċair.
Dallon, Ó ⱱalláin.
Dalton, D'Alton, ⱱalaѐún 11,
ⱱalѐún 72; ⱱáѐún 24.
Daly, Ó ⱱálaiẛ.
Danagher, Danaher, Ó ⱱuineaċair.
Danahy, Ó ⱱuineaċⱱa.
Dane, v, Dean.
Danger, ⱱáinréir.
Daniel, Daniels, Ó ⱱoṁnaill
7 ; mac ⱱoṁnaill 2.
Daniher, Ó ⱱuineaċair.
Danihy, Ó ⱱuineaċⱱa.
Dannaher, Ó ⱱuineaċair.
Dannahy, Ó ⱱuineaċⱱa.
Daragh, v. Darragh.
Darby, Ó ⱱiarmaⱱa, 2 ; mac
ⱱiarmaⱱa 2.
Darcy, D'Arcy, ⱱairriẛ,
ⱱairriẛeaċ 15, 83, 97 ; Ó
ⱱorċaiⱱe 1, 84, 97.
Dardis, ⱱairⱱir.
Dargan, Ó ⱱeargáin.
Darkey, Ó ⱱorcaiⱱe.
Darmody, Ó ⱱiarmaⱱa 4, (s.l.)
Ó ⱱearmaⱱa 979 ; mac
ⱱiarmaⱱa 2.

Darney, Ó Ꝺoꞃꞃнnne.

Darra, Darragh, Darrah, mac Ꝺaꝛa, mac Ꝺaꝛaċ, (o.f.) mac Ꝺuḃꝺaꝛaċ 2; Ó Ꝺaꝛa, Ó Ꝺaꝛaċ, (o.f.) Ó Ꝺuḃꝺaꝛaċ 62.

Darrick, Ó Ꝺuḃꝛaic.

Darrock, v. Darragh.

Daton, Ꝺáꞇún.

Daugherty, v. Dogherty.

Daughton, v. Daton.

Davane, Ó Ꝺaṁáin.

Davenny, Ó Ꝺuiḃeannaiġ.

Davenport, Ó Ꝺonnꝺuḃaꝛꞇaiġ 46.

Davern, Ó Ꝺáḃoiꝛeann, (o.f.) Ó Ꝺuḃꝺáḃoiꝛeann 1; Ó Ꝺoḃaꝛáin 197.

Daveson, Davey, Davidson, Davies, mac Ꝺáiḃiꝺ.

Davin, Davine, Ó Ꝺaiṁín.

Davis, Ꝺáiḃiꞃ 1; mac Ꝺáiḃiꝺ 6; mac Ꝺáiḃiꝺ móꝛ 28; Ó Ꝺaiṁín 972.

Davison, Davisson, mac Ꝺáiḃiꝺ.

Davitt, Davits, mac Ꝺáiḃiꝺ 10, mac Ꝺaiḃéiꝺ 19.

Davoran, Davoren, Ó Ꝺáḃoiꝛeann 1; Ó Ꝺoḃaꝛáin 197.

Davy, Davys, mac Ꝺáiḃiꝺ 1; Ó Ꝺaiṁín 972.

Daw, Ó Ꝺeaġaiꝺ, Ó Ꝺeaꝺaiꝺ.

Dawley, Dawly, Ó Ꝺálaiġ.

Dawney, v. Dahony and Downey.

Dawson, mac Ꝺáiḃiꝺ, Ꝺáꞃon Ꝺáꝛan.

Dawtin, Ꝺáꞇún.

Day, Ó Ꝺeaġaiꝺ, Ó Ꝺeaꝺaiꝺ.

Dayly, v. Daly.

D'Aylmer, v. Aylmer.

Dea, Ó Ꝺeaġaiꝺ, Ó Ꝺeaꝺaiꝺ 1, (s.l.) Ó Ꝺiaġaiꝺ, Ó Ꝺiġe 74, 79, 99.

Deacon, Ó Ꝺeocáin.

Deady, Ó Ꝺéaꝺaiġ 1, Ó Ꝺaoꝺa 17, 49.

Deakin, Ó Ꝺuiḃcinn.

Dealy, Ó Ꝺuiḃġiolla.

Dean, Deane, Ó Ꝺéaġáin 42, 16; mac an Ꝺeaġánaiġ 31, mac an Ꝺeaġáin 16, 19, 28; Ó Ꝺuiḃne 49.

Deanie, Ó Ꝺuiḃne.

Dearan, Ó Ꝺeaꝛáin.

Dease, Ꝺéiꞃe.

Deasey, Deasy, Ꝺéiꝛeaċ 1; mac an Ꝺéiꝛiġ 29.

De Burgh, ꝺe Búꝛc, ꝺe Búꝛca.

De Courcey, De Courcy, ꝺe Cúꝛꝛa, Cúꝛꝛaċ, Cúꝛꝛeaċ.

Dee, v. Dea.

Deegan, Deegin, Ó Ꝺuiḃġinn, Ó Ꝺuiḃcinn.

Deehan, Ó Ꝺíoċon.

Deely, Ó Ꝺuiḃġiolla.

Deen, v. Dean.

Deeney, Ó Ꝺuiḃne.

Deenihan, Ó Ꝺuinneaċáin.

Deeny, Ó Ꝺuiḃne.

Deere, Ó Ꝺuiḃóiꝛ.

Deering, Ꝺíꝛinġ.

De Ermott, v. Dermott.

Deery, Ó Ꝺaiġꝛe, Ó Ꝺoiġꝛe.

Deevey, Deevy, O Ꝺuiḃiꝺe, Ó Ꝺuḃuiꝺe.

Deffely, Ó Ꝺuiḃġiolla.

Degidan, Ó Ꝺuiḃġeaꝺáin.

Dehan, Ó Ꝺíoċon.

Deharty, Ó Ꝺoiċeaꝛꞇaiġ.

Deheny, Ó Ꝺuḃċonna.

Deherty, Dehorty, Ó Ꝺoiċeaꝛꞇaiġ.

Deighan, Ó Ꝺíoċon 2; Ó Ꝺuiḃġinn 2.

Deignan, Ó Ꝺuiḃġeannáin.

Delacour, Ó Ꝺuḃluaċꝛa.

De Lacy, ꝺe Léiꞃ, Léiꝛeaċ. V. Lacy.

Delahan, Ó Ꝺuiḃleaċáin.

Delahide, Delahoyde, Ꝺalaiċíꝺ 8; Ó Scinġín 6.

Delahunt, Delahunty, Ó Oul-
ċaoinnċiᵹ, Ó Oulċonca.
Delamar, Delamere, Oalamaṗa.
Delane, Ó Oalláin.
Delaney, Delany, Ó Oubḟláine,
Ó Oubḟláinᵹe 1 ; Ó Oalláin
91 ; Ó Oubláin 976.
Delap, De Lapp, Ó Lapáin.
Delargey, De Largey, Delargy,
Ó Ouibleaᵹᵹa.
Delaroe, Ó Oalaṗuaiḃ (S.L.).
Delay, Delea, Ó Ouinnḟléiḃe.
Deleacy, v. De Lacy.
Deleany, v. Delaney.
Delee, v. Delea.
Delemar, Oalamaṗa.
Deleney, v. Delaney.
Delhunty, Dellunty, Ó Oul-
ċaoinnċiᵹ, Ó Oulċonca.
Delmar, Oalamaṗa.
Delohery, Delooghery, Deloorey,
Deloughery, Delouhery, De-
lury, Ó Ouibluaċṗa, Ó Oub-
luaċṗa.
De Moleyns, Ó maoláin.
Dempsey, Ó Oíomaṗaiᵹ.
Denahy, v. Dennehy.
Denanny, Ó Ooineannaiᵹ.
Denegan, Ó Ouinneaᵹáin.
Denehan, Ó Ouinneaċáin.
Deneher, Ó Ouineaċaiṗ.
Denehy, v. Dennehy.
Deney, v. Deeney and Dennehy.
Denigan, Ó Ouinneaᵹáin.
Denis, Denison, Ó Oonnᵹuṗa
2 ; mac Oonnċaiḃ 2.
Denn, Oenn.
Dennahy, v. Dennehy.
Dennan, Dennany, Ó Ooineann-
aiᵹ.
Dennehy, Ó Ouineaċḃa.
Denning, Ó Ouinnín.
Dennis, Dennison, Ó Oonnᵹuṗa
2 ; mac Oonnċaiḃ 2.
Dennivan, Ó Ouinneaḃáin.
Denny, Ó Ouiḃne 11 ; Ó
Ouineaċḃa 77.

Denroche, Ó Ouiḃinnṗeaċcaiᵹ.
Denson, v. Dennison.
Dergan, Ó Ooṗᵹáin.
Derham, v. Durham.
Derivan, Derivin, Ó Ooṗḃáin.
Dermid, v. Dermott.
Dermody, Ó Oiaṗmaoa 4 ; mac
Oiaṗmaoa 2.
Dermond, v. Dermott.
Dermoody, v. Dermody.
Dermott, D'Ermott, Ó Oiaṗ-
maoa 1 ; mac Oiaṗmaoa 2 ;
Ó Ouibḃíoṗmaiᵹ 32, (s.l.) Ó
Oíoṗma 16.
Dermoty, v. Dermody.
Deroe, Derow, Ó Oaiṗḃṗe.
Derrane, Ó Oeaṗáin.
Derrick, Derrig, Ó Oeiṗᵹ.
Derry, Ó Ooiṗeiḃ, Ó Ooiṗuḃ
62 ; Ó Oaiᵹṗe, Ó Ooiᵹṗe 62.
Derwin, Ó Ooiṗḃín.
Desmond, Ó Oeaṗṁuṁnaiᵹ.
de Valera, oe Ḃailéaṗa.
Devane, Ó Oubáin 7, 9 ; Ó
Oaṁáin 6.
Devaney, Devanny, Devany,
Ó Ouibeannaiᵹ 16, 68 ; Ó
Ouibeaṁna 65 ; Ó Oubán-
aiᵹ 16, 29 ; Ó Oubáin 19,
97, Ó Ouibín 192, 972.
Deveen, Ó Ouibín.
Develin, D'Evelyn, v. Devlin.
Deven, Ó Oaiṁín, Ó Ooiṁín.
Devenish, Oeiḃniṗ.
Devenny, Deveny, v. Devanny.
Dever, Ó Ouibḃíṗ.
De Vere, oe Ḃéiṗ.
Devereux, Oéaḃṗúṗ 2, 28 ; Ó
Ouibṗic 276 ; Ó Oeiṗḃṗeó 25.
Devers, Ó Ouibḃíṗ.
Devery, v. Devereux.
Devett, mac Oaiḃéiḃ.
Devilly, Devily, Ó Ouibᵹiolla
Devin, Devine, Ó Oaiṁín, Ó
Ooiṁín 6, 37 ; Ó Ouibín 71,
91, Ó Oubáin 72, 92.
Devinney, v. Devanny.

Devins, Ó ·Uaiṁín, Ó Doiṁín.
Devitt, Mac Daiḃéiv.
Devlin, Ó Doḃailein, Ó Doiḃilein, Ó Doiḃilín.
Devon, Ó Daiṁín 6 ; Ó Duiḃín 9.
Devoy, Ó Duḃuiḋe.
Dewane, Ó Duḃáin.
DeYermond, Deyermott, Ó Duiḃ-ṿíoṗmaiʒ, Ó Duiḃṿíoṗma.
Diaman, Diamon, Diamond, Ó Diamáin, Ó Díomáin, Ó Déamáin 6 ; Ó Maoileacáin 97.
Diarmid, Diarmod, Diarmond, v. Dermott.
Dicksoᴙ, Mac Riocaiṙo.
Diermott, v. Dermott.
Diffely, Diffily, Ó Duiḃʒiolla.
Diffin, Ó Duiḃṗinn.
Diffley, Ó Duiḃʒiolla.
Digan, Ó Duiḃʒinn.
Digany, Mac an Deaʒánaiʒ.
Diggin, Ó Duiḃʒinn.
Dignam, Dignan, Ó Duiḃ-ʒeannáin.
Dillahan, Ó Duiḃleacáin.
Dillane, Ó Duilleáin.
Dilleen, Ó Duillín.
Dillon, Díolún, Díolṁain 1 ; Ó Duilleáin 73, 97 ; Ó Duiḃleacáin 2.
Dilloughery, Dillury, Dillworth, Dilworth, Ó Duḃluaċṙa, Ó Duiḃluaċṙa.
Dimond, v. Diamond.
Dinahan, Ó Duinneacáin.
Dinan, Ó Daʒnáin.
Dineen, Ó Duinnín.
Dingavan, Ó Duinneaḃáin.
Dinihan, Ó Duinneacáin.
Dinkin, Ó Duinnċinn.
Dinneen, Ó Duinnín.
Dinnegan, Ó Duinneaʒáin.
Direen, Ó Diṙín.
Dirrane, Ó Díoṙáin, Ó Deaṙáin.
Diskin, Ó Díṙcín.
Diurmagh, Ó Díoṙmaiʒ, Ó Díoṙma.

Divan, Divane, Ó Duḃáin.
Diveen, Ó Duiḃín.
Divenney, Divenny, Ó Duiḃ-eannaiʒ. V. Devanny.
Diver, Ó Duiḃiḋiṙ.
Diviney, Ó Duiḃeannaiʒ. V. Devanny.
Divitt, Mac Daiḃéiv.
Divver, Ó Duiḃiḋiṙ.
Dixon, Mac Riocaiṙo 1 ; Ó Duiḃʒeaḃáin 469.
Doag, Doake, Mac Daḃóc, Mac Daḃóʒ.
Doane, Ó Duḃáin.
Dobbin, Dobbins, Doiḃín 1 ; Biḃíne, Biḃíneać 376.
Dobbs, Doḃ.
Dobbyn, Dobbyns, Dobin, v. Dobbin.
Dockeray, Dockery, Dockrey, Dockry, Ó Docṙaiḋ, Ó Docṙaiʒ.
Dodd, Dova.
Dodding, Doiṿín.
Dodds, Dova.
Doey, Ó Duḃċaiʒ.
Dogheny, v. Doheny.
Dogherty, v. Doherty.
Dohenny, Doheny, Ó Duḃċonna.
Doherty, Ó Doċaṙtaiʒ 11, Ó Doiċeaṙtaiʒ 72 ; Ó Duḃaṙtaiʒ 17.
Dohony, v. Doheny.
Dohorty v. Doherty.
Doig v. Doag.
Dolaghan, Ó Dalacáin 5 ; Ó Duḃlacáin 6.
Dolaher, Ó Dalacaiṙ.
Dolan, Ó Duḃláin.
Dolfin, Doilṗín.
Dollard, Dollaṙo, Dollaṙt.
Dollery, Ó Dailḃṙe, Ó Dalaṙuaiḋ.
Dolly, Ó Daċlaoiċ.
Dologhan, v. Dolaghan.
Dolohunty v. Delahunty.
Dolphin, Doilṗín.

Domegan, Ó Domaġáin.
Donagan, v. Donegan.
Donagh, Donaghey, mac Donncaiḋ 1; Ó Donncaiḋ 2.
Donaghoe, Ó Donncaḋa.
Donaghy, mac Donncaiḋ 1; Ó Donncaiḋ 2.
Donaher, Ó Duineaċair.
Donahoe, Ó Donncaḋa.
Donahy, v. Donaghy.
Donald, Donaldson, mac Domnaill.
Donarty, Ó Donnḋuḃairtaiġ.
Dondon, Donḋún, Donnḋún.
Donegan, Ó Donnagáin 11; Ó hOnéon 44.
Donelan, Donellan, Ó Domnalláin.
Donely, v. Donnelly.
Doney, v. Downey.
Dongan, Ó Donnagáin 11; Donġán 14, 18.
Donigan, v. Donegan.
Donlan, Donlon, Ó Domnalláin.
Donly, Donnally, v. Donnelly.
Donnan, Ó Donnáin, Ó Dúnáin.
Donneely, Ó Donnġaile.
Donnegan, v. Donegan.
Donnell, Ó Domnaill 1; mac Domnaill 2.
Donnellan, Ó Domnalláin.
Donnelly, Ó Donnġaile 11; Ó Donnġalaiġ, Ó Dúnġalaiġ 72, 97.
Donney, v. Downey.
Donnolly, v. Donnelly.
Donogh, mac Donncaḋa.
Donogher, Ó Duineaċair.
Donoghue, Donohoe, Donohue, Ó Donncaḋa 11; mac Donncaḋa 976.
Donor, Ó Donnaḃair.
Donoughoo, v. Donoghue.
Donovan, Ó Donnaḃáin 11; Ó Donnamáin 777.
Donworth, Ó Donnḋuḃairtaiġ.
Dooal, Ó Duḃġaill.
Dooan, Ó Duḃáin.

Doocey, Doocie, Doocy, Ó Duḃġusa, Ó Duḃaṗa.
Doody, Ó Duḃḋa.
Dooey, Ó Duḃċaiġ.
Doogan, Ó Duḃagáin.
Doohan, Ó Duḃċon,
Doohane, Ó Duaċáin.
Dooher, Ó Duḃċair.
Dooherty, Ó Duḃairtaiġ. V. Doherty.
Dooladdy, Doolady, Ó Duḃlaḋaiġ.
Doolaghan, Ó Duḃlaċáin.
Doolaghty, Ó Duḃlaċta, Ó Duḃlaċtna.
Doolan, Ó Duḃlainn, 2; Ó Duḃláin 2; Ó Dúnlaing 2.
Doole, v. Doyle.
Doolen, v. Doolan.
Dooler, Ó Dalaċair.
Dooley, Ó Duḃlaoiċ, Ó Duḃluiġe.
Doolin, v. Doolan.
Dooling, v. Dowling.
Dooloughty, Ó Duḃlaċta, Ó Duḃlaċtna.
Dooly, v. Dooley.
Doon, Ó Duḃáin.
Doona, A' Dúna.
Doonan, Ó Dúnáin.
Dooner, Ó Donnaḃair.
Dooney, Ó Dúnaḃaiġ 11, mac Dúnaḃaiġ 97.
Doonican, Ó Donnacáin, Ó Dúnacáin.
Doordan, mac Duḃraḋáin.
Doorigan, (?) Ó Dorċáin.
Dooris, Ó Duḃrora.
Doorley, Doorly, Ó Duḃurtuile
Doorty, Ó Duḃairtaiġ.
Dooyearma, Ó Duiḃḋíorma.
Doran, Ó Deóráin.
Dorcey, Ó Dorċaiḋe.
Dordan, mac Duḃraḋáin.
Dore, Ó Doġair.
Dorgan, Ó Dorċáin 77; Ó Deargáin 772.

Dorian, Ó Deóṗáin, Ó Deóp-aḃáin, Ó Deóṗaiḃín.
Doris, Ó Duḃṗora.
Dornan, Ó Doṗnáin, 1, Ó Duiṗnín 2.
Dorney, Ó Doiṗinne.
Dornin, Ó Doiṗnín, Ó Duiṗnín
Dorran, Dorrian, Ó Deóṗ in, Ó Deóṗaḃám, Ó Deóṗaiḃín.
Dorr, (?) Ó Doṗaiḋ.
Dorrigan, v. Dorgan.
Doud, v. Dowd.
Doudall, v. Dowdall.
Douey, v. Dowey.
Dougall, Mac Duḃġaill.
Dougan, Ó Duḃagáin.
Doughan, Ó Duaċáin 16; Ó Duḃċon 42.
Doughar, Ó Duḃċaiṗ.
Dougheny, Ó Duḃċonna.
Dougher, Ó Duḃċaiṗ.
Dougherty, Ó Doċaṗtaiġ.
Doughney, v. Dougheny.
Douglas, Duḃġlaṗ.
Dougle, v. Dougall.
Douie, v. Dowey.
Dowd, Dowda, Ó Duḃḋa.
Dowdall, Dowdell, Duḃḋal.
Dowdican, Ó Duḃḋacáin, Ó Duḃḋagáin.
Dowdie, Dowds, Ó Duḃḋa.
Dowell, Mac Duḃġaill 2; Ó Duḃġaill 2.
Dower, Ó Doġaiṗ.
Dowey, Dowie, Ó Duḃċaiġ.
Dowlan, v. Doolan.
Dowler, Ó Dalaċaiṗ.
Dowley, Ó Duḃlaoiċ, Ó Duḃluiġe.
Dowlin, Dowling, Ó Dúnlaing 1 ; Ó Duḃlainn 2.
Down, Downes, Ó Duḃáin.
Downey, Ó Dúnaḋaiġ 4, 9, Mac Dúnaḋaiġ 97 ; Ó Maoldoṁn-aiġ 62; Mac Giollaḋoṁnaiġ62
Downing, Ó Duinín, Ó Duinnín 77 ; Ó Dúnaḋaiġ 499.

Doyle, Ó Duḃġaill 1 ; Mac Duḃġaill 34 ; Ó Duḃġaile 2.
Doyne, Ó Duinn.
Draddy, Ó Dreaḋa 7 ; Ó Draoḋa 9.
Drain, Draine, Ó Dṗeáin.
Drake, Dṗac.
Draper, Dṗaoṗaṗ.
Drea, Ó Dṗae 49, 179, Ó Dṗaoi 46.
Dreelan (?) Ó Dṗaoileáin.
Dreinan, Drennan, Ó Dṗaġnáin, Ó Dṗaiġneáin.
Drew, Ó Dṗaoi, Ó Dṗae, Ó Dṗuaiḋ 73 ; Mac an Dṗuaiḋ 34, 35 ; Dṗoġ, Dṗú, Dṗiú, 15, 25.
Drewry, v. Drury.
Drinan, Drinane, Ó Dṗaiġneáin, Ó Dṗaġnáin.
Driscall, Driscoll, Driskell, Driskill, Ó Dṗiṗceóil, (o.f.) Ó heiṗoiṗceóil.
Drislane, Ó Dṗiṗleáin.
Drohan, Drohane, Ó Dṗuaċáin.
Droman, Ó Dṗomáin.
Dromey, Ó Dṗoma.
Dromgoole, De Dṗomġúl, Dṗomġúl.
Droney, Ó Dṗóna.
Droody, Ó Dṗaoḋa.
Droohan, Ó Dṗuaċáin.
Drough, Dṗoġ.
Drought, Ó Dṗoċtaiġ.
Drudy, Ó Dṗaoḋa.
Drum, Ó Dṗoma.
Drumgoold, Drumgoole, De Dṗomġúl, Dṗomġúl.
Drumm, Ó Dṗoma.
Drummin, Ó Dṗuimín.
Drummond, Drummy, Ó Dṗoma
Drury, Dṗúiṗiḋe E 2; Ó Dṗuaiḋ, Ó Dṗaoi, Ó Dṗae 73 ; Mac an Dṗuaiḋ 34.
Duan, Duane, Ó Duḃáin.
Duany, Ó Duḃánaiġ.
Duarty, Ó Duḃaṗtaiġ.

Ducey, Ó Ouḃġusa, Ó Ouḃaṡa.
Duck, Ó Lacáin, Ó Leocáin 43 (O'D.).
Duddie, Duddy, Ó Ouḃṫa.
Dudican, Ó Ouḃḋacáin, Ó Ouḃḋaġáin.
Dudley, Ó Ouḃḋáleiṫe, 777.
Duff, Ouḃ 2 ; Ó Ouiḃ 36, 45, 92 ; Mac Ġiollaḋuiḃ 62.
Dufferly, Ó Ouḃuirṫuile.
Duffin, Ó Ouiḃḟinn.
Duffley, Ó Ouiḃġiolla.
Duffy, Ó Ouḃṫaiġ 11, (s.l.) Oúiṫċe 62, 92 ; Ó Ooiṫe 99.
Dugald, Mac Ouḃġaill.
Dugan, Duggan, Duggen, Ó Ouḃaġáin 11 ; Ó Ouiḃġinn 2 ; (?) Ó Ouḃḋúin 2.
Dugidan, Ó Ouiḃġeaḋáin.
Duhig, Duhy, Ó Ouḃṫaiġ.
Duigan, Ó Ouiḃġinn.
Duigenan, Duignam, Duignan, Ó Ouiḃġeannáin.
Dulanty, Dulinty, Ó Oulcaoinṫiġ, Ó Oulconṫa.
Dullaghan, Ó Ḋalacáin 5 ; Ó Ouḃlacáin 6.
Dullard, Oollarḋ, Oollairṫ.
Dullea, Ó Ouinnṡléiḃe.
Dullenty, Ó Oulcaoinṫiġ.
Dumegan, Ó Oomaġáin.
Dun, Ó Ouinn.
Duncahy, Ó Oonncaṫaiġ, Ó Ouinncaṫaiġ.
Duncan, Mac Oonncaiḋ S 6 ; Ó Oonnacáin, Ó Oonnaġáin 5 ; Ó Ouinncinn 29, 82 ; Oonġán 14, 18.
Dundas, Ó nára (S.L.) 979.
Dundon, Oonnḋún, Oonḋún.
Dune, Ó Ouḃáin.
Dunford, Dunfort, Ó Oonnḋuḃairtaiġ.
Dunfy, v. Dunphy.
Dungan, Oonġán 14, 18 ; Ó Oonnaġáin 2.
Dunican, ÓOúnacáin, Ó Oonnacáin.

Dunigan, v. Donegan.
Dunion, Ó Oúinín, Ó Ouinnín.
Dunkin, Ó Ouinncinn.
Dunlavy, Dunlea, Dunleavy, Dunleevy, Dunlevy, Ó Ouinnṡléiḃe ; (s.s.) Ultaċ, Ultacán.
Dunlief, Dunlop, Mac Ouinnṡléiḃe.
Dunn, Dunne, Ó Ouinn 1 ; Mac Ġiollaḋuinn 29.
Dunnegan, Ó Oonnaġáin.
Dunner, Ó Oonnaḃair.
Dunnigan, v. Dunnegan.
Dunning, Ó Oúinín, Ó Ouinnín.
Dunny, Ó Oúnaḋaiġ.
Dunphy, Ó Oonnċaḋa, Ó Oonnċaiḋ.
Dunroche, Ó Ouiḃinnreaċtaiġ.
Dunworth, Ó Oonnḋuḃairtaiġ.
Durack, Ó Ouḃraic.
Durcan, Mac Ouarcáin.
Durham, De Ouram.
Durick, Ó Ouḃraic.
Durkan, Durkin, Mac Ouarcáin.
Durmody, v. Dermody.
Durnan, Ó Ooirnáin.
Durnian, Durnin, Durnion, Ó Ouirnín.
Durr, (?) Ó Ooraiḋ.
Durrane, Ó Oioráin.
Durrian, v. Dorrian.
Durrig, Ó Oeiriġ.
Durry, Ó Ooraiḋ.
Dwain, Dwan, Dwane, Ó Ouḃáin.
Dwire, Dwyer, Ó Ouḃuiḋir, Ó Ouiḃiḋir.
Dyer, Ó Ouiḃiḋir, 6, 8 ; Mac Ouiḃiḋir 29.
Dyermott, Ó Ouiḃḋíorma, Ó Ouiḃḋiormaiġ.
Dygnam, v. Dignam.
Dyle, v. Doyle.
Dynan, Ó Oaġnáin.
Dyne, Ó Ouinn.

Eagan, v. Egan.
Eagar, éiȝear.

Eagleton, mac 1oιpacáιn, Ó
hιoιpacáιn.

Eakin, Eakins, Ó hᴀoᴠᴀѕáιn.

Earl, Earle, Earls, mac ᴀn
ιᴀpιᴀ 2 ; ιᴀpιᴀιᴠe 979.

Early, Ó mᴀoιṁoιceιpѕe, (s.l.)
Ó mᴀoιṁocóιpѕe 1, Ó mᴀoι-
ṁocóιp 192, Ó mocóιpѕe 95,
Ó mocóιp 192.

Earner, Earnor, Ó Sᴀopᴀιᴠe,
Ó Sᴀocpᴀιᴠe.

Eason, mac ᴀoᴠᴀ.

Eaton, Éacún.

Edmonds, Edmondson, Ed-
munds, Edmundson, mac
Éamoιnn, mac Éamuιnn.

Edwards, mac Éᴀoᴠáιpᴠ.

Egan, mac ᴀoᴠᴀѕáιn 11 ; Ó
hᴀoᴠᴀѕáιn 2.

Egar, Éιѕeᴀp.

Eggleton, v. Eagleton.

Egnew, Ó ѕníṁ.

Eivers, Ó híoṁᴀιp 76, 93 ; mac
íoṁᴀιp 19.

Elfred, Oιιeᴀᴠápᴠ.

Ellard, ᴀιᴠ́ιeᴀpc, ᴀιápᴠ, Oιápᴠ.

Ellison, Ó heιιѕeᴀpáιn 62,

Ellmore, Ó hιomnᴀ (G. J.).

Ellwood, Oιιeᴀᴠápᴠ, Oιιeᴀᴠᴀpᴠ

Elmer, v. Aylmar.

Elshander, Elshinder, v. Alexander.

Elward, v. Aylward & Ellard.

Elwood, v. Ellwood.

England, ᴀιnѕιeᴀnᴠ, ᴀιnѕιeonc.

English, ᴀιnѕιéιp, ιnѕιéιp,
ιnѕιιp 1 ; mac ᴀn ѕᴀιιóѕ-
ιᴀιѕ 15, 86.

Englishby, mac ᴀn ѕᴀιιóѕιᴀιѕ.

Englishe, v. English.

Ennes, Ennis, Ó hᴀonѕuιp 1 ;
mac ᴀonѕuιp 2.

Enraght, Enright, mac ιonnpᴀct-
ᴀιѕ 11, mac ιnnpeᴀctᴀιѕ 2.

Enroe, mac Conpuᴠᴀ.

Erke, Ó heιpc.

Erksine, ᴀpᴀpcᴀιn.

Erought, Erraght, Erraught
Ó hOιpeᴀctᴀιѕ.

Errington, Ó hᴀppᴀctáιn.

Ervine, Erwin, Ó heιpeᴀṁóιn
1 ; Ó Cιᴀpṁᴀcáιn 772.

Esbald, Esball, ᴀιpeᴀᴠóιᴠ.

Esmond, Esmonde, eᴀpmonn.

Etchingham, eιcιnѕeᴀm.

Eurell, ᴠe Oιpѕιᴀιι.

Eustace, Eustice, ιúpcáp.

Evans, Evens, ᴀoιᴠιn, ᴀoιᴠιnn
47, 49 ; Ó héιṁín, Ó héᴀṁáιn
73.

Everard, éιᴠeᴀpápᴠ, Éᴀᴠpápᴠ.
Éᴀᴠpóιᴠ.

Everett, Everitt, Éᴀᴠpóιᴠ.

Evers, v. Eivers.

Evins, v. Evans.

Evoy, v. MacEvoy.

Eyre, Eyres, ιᴀppᴀc.

Fadden, Faddin, mac páιᴠín.

Fade, mac páιᴠ.

Fadian, mac páιᴠín.

Fagan, fáѕán 15, 18, 43 ; Ó
fáѕáιn 65 ; Ó fᴀoᴠᴀѕáιn 37,
38 ; Ó fιᴀcáιn 2 ; mac páιᴠín
16.

Faggy, mac páιᴠín (mac páιᴠι)

Faghy, Ó fᴀtᴀιѕ.

Fagin, v. Fagan.

Faheney, Ó fιᴀcnᴀ.

Faherty, Ó fᴀcᴀpcᴀιѕ.

Fahey, Fahy, Ó fᴀtᴀιѕ 11,
(s.l.) Ó fᴀιc 92.

Fair, fιonn.

Falahee, Falahy, Ó fᴀιcᴀιᴠ,
(o.f.) Ó fᴀoιcᴀιᴠ.

Falconer, Falkner, fácnᴀp 11 ;
Ó fᴀcnᴀ 9.

Fallaher, Ó fᴀιcᴀιp ,(o.f.) Ó
fᴀoιcᴀιp.

Fallen, Fallin, Fallon, Falloon,
Faloon, Faloona, Ó fᴀιιᴀṁ-
ᴀιn, Ó foιιᴀṁᴀιn.

Falsey, Ó fᴀιcᴀιᴠ

Falvey, Ó fáιιᴠe

Fanagan, Ó fιonnᴀѕáιn.

Fane, Ó Fiacáin, Ó Féicín.
Fannerty, Ó Fionnactaig.
Fannin, Fanning, Fainín, (o.f.)
  painín 7, 8; Ó Fionnáin, Ó
  Fionáin 9; Ó Finngin 87.
Fannon, Ó Fionnáin.
Fant, Fannt.
Faragher, Faraher, Ó Fearcair.
Faran, v. Farren.
Farelly, v. Farrelly.
Faren, v. Farren.
Farghur, Mac Fearcair.
Farguson, v. Ferguson.
Farin, v. Farren.
Faris, v. Farris.
Farker, Mac Fearcair.
Farley, Ó Fairceallaig.
Farmer, Mac an Scolóige, Mac
  Scolóige.
Farnan, Farnand, Farnham,
  Farnon, Ó Farannáin, Ó
  Forannáin.
Farquehar, Farquer, Farquhar-
  son, Farquher, Mac Fearcair.
Farragher, Farraher, Ó Fear-
  cair.
Farrahill, Ó Feargail.
Farrally, v. Farrelly.
Farran, v. Farren.
Farrell, Ó Feargail 11, Ó
  Feargaile 2.
Farrelly, Farrely, Ó Fair-
  ceallaig 1; Ó Feargaile 2.
Farren, Ó Fearáin 26, 33; Ó
  Faracáin 16.
Farris, Farrissy, Ó Fearguir,
  Ó Feargura.
Farron, v. Farren.
Farry, Ó Fearavaig 6; Ó
  Farraig 9.
Farshin, Fairfring.
Faughnan, Ó Factnáin.
Faughy, Ó Fataig.
Faulkner, v. Falconer.
Faulkney, Ó Factna.
Fausset, Faussette, Fawcett,
  Fóiféiv.

Fay, Ó Féic, Ó Fiaic 1, 91; Ó
  Fait 97; ve Fae, a Fae,
  Faeveac 15.
Feagan, Ó Faovágáin. V.
  Fagan.
Fealan, Ó Faoláin.
Fealey, Fealy, Ó Fióigeallaig
  1; Ó Fáile (Ó Fáilbe) 496.
Feane, Ó Fiacáin, Ó Féicín.
Fearen, Fearn, Fearon, Ó
  Fearáin.
Feary, Ó Fiacra, Ó Fiacrac.
Fedigan, Ó Féavagáin.
Fee, Ó Fiaic 11; Ó Fiaca 35.
Feehan, Ó Fiacáin.
Feeharry, Mac Annriaoi, Mac
  hannriaoi.
Feehely, Ó Fitceallaig.
Feeheny, Ó Fiacna.
Feehery, Ó Fiacra.
Feehily, Ó Fitceallaig.
Feehin, Ó Féicín.
Feeley, Feely, Ó Fitceallaig,
  Ó Fióigeallaig, (s.l.) Ó Fitille
  976.
Feen, Ó Féicín.
Feenaghty, Feenaghy, Ó
  Fiannacta, Ó Fionnactaig.
Feeney, Feeny, Ó Féinneaóa,
  (s.l.) Ó Fiannaióe, Ó Fianna
  93; Ó Fióne, (s.l.) Ó Fínne,
  Ó Fíne 94.
Feerey, Ó Fiacra.
Feerick, Mac Piaruic, Mac
  Piaraic, (s.l.) Ó Fiaraic,
  Fiaraic.
Fegan, Ó Faovágáin 1; Ó
  Fiacáin 2. V. Fagan.
Feghany, Ó Fiacna.
Fehan, Fehane, Ó Fiacáin.
Fehely, v. Fehily.
Fehen, Ó Féicín.
Fehill, Ó Fitcill.
Fehilly, Fehily, Ó Fitceallaig.
Feighan, Ó Fiacáin.
Feighery, Ó Fiacra.
Feighney, Ó Fiacna.

Feighry, Ó Fiacra.
Felan, Ó Faoláin 7. V. Phelan.
Feley, mac Seappaig.
Fenaghty, Fenaughty, Ó Fionn-
    acta, Ó Fionnactaig, Ó
    Finneacta, &c.
Fendlon, v. Fenlon.
Feneily, v. Fennelly.
Fenelon, Ó Fionnalláin.
Fenihan, Ó Fionnacáin.
Fenley, v. Fennelly.
Fenlon, Ó Fionnalláin.
Fennell, Ó Fionngail, Ó Fionn-
    gaile.
Fennelly, Ó Fionngalaig.
Fennerty, Ó Fionnacta, Ó
    Finneactaig, &c.
Fennessy, Ó Fionngura.
Fennors, Fionúip, Fionnúip.
Fenton, Ó Fiannacta 71; Ó
    Fiacna 72.
Feoghney, Ó Fiacna.
Feore, Ó Fioóábaip.
Feran, Ó Feapáin.
Fergison, Ferguison, v. Fergu-
    son.
Fergus, Ó Feapguip, Ó Feap-
    gura 9; mac Feapguip 6.
Ferguson, Fergusson, mac Feap-
    gura, mac Feapguip.
Feris, v. Ferris.
Ferley, Ferly, v. Farrelly.
Fern, Ó Feapáin. V. Ferns.
Fernan, Fernane, Ó Feapnáin.
Ferns, Ó Reannacáin.
Feron, v. Fern.
Ferrall, Ó Feapgail.
Ferran, Ó Feapáin.
Ferreter, v. Ferriter.
Ferris, Ó Feapguip, Ó Feapgura
    7, 9.
Ferriter, Feipitéip, Feiptéip,
    Fipitéip, Fiptéip.
Ferrons, Ó Reannacáin.
Ferry, Ó Feapaóáig 6; (?) Ó
    Foippeió 62.
Fetton, Fiotún, Piotún.

Fettridge, mac Peaopuip.
Fey, Ó Féic, Ó Fiaic.
Fidgeon, v. Pidgeon.
Fie, v. Fye.
Field, ve Fítoe 18; Ó Fit-
    ceallaig 4, Ó Frógeallaig 2, Ó
    Fitcill 2.
Fielding, Fihelly, Fihily, Ó
    Fitceallaig.
Filan, v. Phelan.
Filbin, mac pilibín, mac
    pilbín, mac Filibín, (s.l.) Ó
    Filibín.
Finaghty, Ó Fionnacta.
Finalay, v. Finlay.
Finamore, Fionamúp.
Finan, Ó Fionáin, Ó Fionnáin
Finch, Fúinpe.
Findlay, Findley, v. Finlay.
Finegan, Ó Fionnagáin.
Finelly, v. Finnelly.
Finerty, Ó Finneacta, Ó Fionn-
    acta, &c.
Finglas, ve Fionnglap, Fionglap.
Finigan, v. Finegan.
Finlay, Finley, Ó Fionngalaig
    1, Ó Fiangalaig 2.
Finn, Ó Finn.
Finnaghty, Ó Finneacta, Ó
    Finneactaig, &c.
Finnally, v. Finnelly.
Finnamore, Finnamure, Fiona-
    múp.
Finnan, Ó Fionnáin.
Finne, Ó Finn.
Finnegan, Ó Fionnagáin.
Finnell, Ó Fionngail, Ó Fionn-
    gaile.
Finnelly, Ó Fionngalaig, Ó
    Fiangalaig.
Finnemor, Fionamúp.
Finneran, Ó Finntigeapín.
Finnerell (?) Ó Fiongapvail,
Finnerty, Ó Fionnacta, Ó
    Fionnactaig, Ó Finneacta,
    Ó Finneactaig, Ó Fiannact-
    aig, Ó Fiannacta, &c.

Finnessy, Ó Fionnġuṙa.
Finney, v. Feeney.
Finnigan, Ó Fionnaġáin.
Finning, Ó Finġin.
Finnucane, Ó Fionnṁacáin.
Finny, v. Feeny.
Finucane, Ó Fionnṁacáin.
Fisher, mac an tapcaiṗe 1 ; Ó
    Ḃpaḋáin 16.
Fitton, Piotún, Piotún.
Fitsimmons, Fitsimons, v. Fitz-
    simons.
Fitzgerald, FitzGerald, mac
    ᵹeaṗailt.
Fitzgibbon, mac ᵹiobúin.
Fitzharris, Fitzhenry, mac Ann-
    ṗaoi, mac hanṗaoi, mac Éinṙí.
Fitzherbert, mac hoiṗeaḃaiṙo.
Fitzmartin, mac máiṙtín.
Fitzmaurice, Fitzmorice, Fitz-
    morris, mac muiṗiṙ, mac
    ṁuiṗiṙ.
Fitzpatrick, mac ᵹiolla
    ṗáoṗaiᵹ 11 ; (s.s.) mac
    Séaṗca, mac Séaṗtaiḃ 75,
    78 ; mac ṗáoṗaiᵹín 2.
Fitzsimmons, Fitzsimon, Fitz-
    simons, Fitzsummons, mac
    Síomóin, mac Síomoinn 11 ;
    (s.s.) mac an Rioiṗe 15.
Fitzstephen, Fitzstephens, mac
    Steaṗáin, mac Stioṗáin, &c
    V. Stephens.
Flagherty, v. Flaherty.
Flahavan, Ó Flaiteaṁáin, Ó
    Flataṁáin.
Flahavin, Ó Flaitiṁín, Ó
    Flaiteaṁáin, Ó Flataṁáin.
Flaherty, Ó Flaitḃeaṗtaiᵹ 11 ;
    Ó Fataṗtaiᵹ 972.
Flahevan, v. Flahavan.
Flahive, Flahy, Ó Flaitiṁ, (s.l.)
    Ó Flataiᵹ.
Flanagan, Ó Flannaġáin.
Flanaghan, Ó Flannaċáin.
Flanahy, Ó Flannċaḋa, Ó
    Flannċaiḋ.

Flang, Ó Flainn.
Flanigan, Flannagan, Ó Flann-
    aġáin.
Flannelly, Ó Flannġaile.
Flannery, Ó Flannaḃṗa 11 ; Ó
    Flannġaile 19, 29.
Flannigan, Ó Flannaġáin.
Flatley, v. Flattley.
Flattery, Ó Flaitiṗe, (o.f.) Ó
    Flaitile, (o.f.) Ó Flaitṗileaḋ
Flattley, Ó Flaitile, (o.f.) Ó
    Flaitṗileaḋ.
Flavahan, Ó Flaiteaṁáin.
Flavell, Ó Flannġail.
Flaverty, Ó Flaitḃeaṗtaiᵹ.
Flavin, Ó Flaitiṁín, Ó Flait-
    eaṁáin.
Fleming, Flemming, Flemon,
    Flemyng, pléamonn, pléim-
    eann.
Fletcher, mac an Fleaṗtaiṗ.
Fleury, v. Fury.
Flinn, Ó Floinn.
Flint, Flint.
Flood, Flóiḋ 62, 82; Ó maol-
    tuile 11, mac maoltuile,
    mac ṁaoltuile 9, (s.l.) mac
    an tuile, mac tuile, Ó
    tuile, Ó tuine 192, 972.
Floyd, Flóiḋ. V. Flood.
Flyng, Flynn, Ó Floinn, Ó
    Flainn.
Fodaghan, Ó Fuaḋaċáin.
Foddy, Ó Fuaḋa.
Fodha, Faḋa.
Fogarty, Fogerty, Ó Fóᵹaṗtaiᵹ 1,
    (s.l.) Ó Fóᵹaṗtá 499.
Folan, mac Fualáin, (o.f.) mac
    Faoláin, (s.l.) Ó Cualáin
    99.
Foley, Ó Foᵹlaḋa, Ó Foḋlaḋa
    7, 8 ; mac Seaṗṗaiᵹ, 6, 9 ;
    Ó Seaṗṗaiᵹ 64.
Foody, Ó Fuaḋa.
Foohy, Ó Fuataiᵹ.
Fooley, Ó Fuallaiᵹ.
Foorde, Furd, Fúṙoaċ.

Foote, Ó τροιξτιξ 2 (O'D);
mac Coιre 2 (O'D.).

Foran, Ó ξυαρτάιn, Ó ξυαρράιn,
Ó ξυαράιn.

Forbes, Forbis, Forbish, mac
ξιρβιριξ ,(s.l.) mac ξοιρβιρ,
Coιρβιρ 19, 29 ; ξοιρβιρ,
ξοιρβιρεαč S. 2.

Ford, Forde, ξόιτ, ξόρτ, ξύρτ
86 ; mac αn άτα, (o.f.) mac
Conξnάιha 96, 976 ; mac
ξιολλα na naoṁ, (s.l.) mac
ξιολλαρnάč, Ó ξιολλαρnάč 97,
197; Ó ξυαράιn, Ó ξυαράιn 7.

Forehan, Forehane, Ó ξυαρτάιn,
Ó ξυαρράιn, Ó ξυαράιn.

Forestall, ξυιρεαρταl 11 ; mac
αn Čoιll (S.L.) 197.

Forhan, Ó ξυαρτάιn.

Forkan, Ó ξαβλάιn.

Forke, Ó ξαβαλαιξ.

Forker, mac ξεαρčαιρ.

Forkin, Ó ξαβλάιn.

Forran, Ó ξαραčάιn 16.

Forrest, ξοιρέιρ, ξυιρέαρτ.

Forrestal, Forrester, ξυιρεαρταl

Forry, Ó ξαρραιτ 19.

Forstall, Forster, Foster, ξυιρεαρταl.

Fortin, Ó ξοιρτčειρn.

Fortune, Ó ξοιρτčειρn 1 ; ξαιρ-
ριnξ 779.

Fottrell, ξυτραιl.

Foudy, Ó ξυατα.

Fouhy, Ó ξυαčαιξ.

Fourhane, Ó ξυαρτάιn.

Fourker, v. Forker.

Fowcett, ξόιρέιτ.

Fowhey, Ó ξυαčαιξ.

Fox, Foxe, τe βορc, βορcαč
17 ; Sιοnnαč, (o.s.) Ó
Cαčαρnαιξ 25, 55 ; Ó Sιοn-
nαιξ, Ó Sιοnαιξ 19, 29, 37,
77 ; mac αn τSιοnnαιξ 2 ; Ó
Sιοnαčάιn 58 ; mac Seαnčα,
mac Seαnčαιτe 39.

Foy, Ó ξιαιč 11 ; Ó ξαιč 976.

Foynes, ξαξαn, ξαξαn.

Fraher, Ó ξρεαčαιρ, Ó ξεαρčαιρ.

Frahill, Ó ξρεαčαιl, (o.f.) Ó
ξεαρξαιl.

Frain, Frainey, Frainy, τe
ξρέιn, τe ξρέιne, α ξρέιn 8,
78 ; mac αn ξραnncαιξ 9.

Francey, Francis, ρρόιnρέιρ.

Frane, Franey, v. Frain.

Franklin, ξραιnclίn.

Fraser, ξρίρεαl ; (G.p.) mac
sιmιτ.

Fraul, Ó ξρεαčαιl, (o.f.) Ó
ξεαρξαιl.

Frawley, Ó ξρεαξαιle, Ó ξεαρ-
ξαιle.

Frayne, v. Frain.

Frazer, ξρίρεαl, ξρίρεαlαč.

Freal, v. Freel.

Free, Ó sαορατte.

Freehill, Ó ξριčιl, (o.f.) Ó
ξιηξιl.

Freehily, Ó ξριčιle.

Freel, Ó ξριξιl, Ó ξιρξιl.

Freely, Ó ξριξιle, Ó ξιηξιle

Freeman, Ó sαορατte 9 ; mac
αn τSαοιη 67.

Freeney, Freeny, τe ξρέιne 8 ;
mac αn ξραnncαιξ 9.

Frehen, Ó ξραοιčίn.

Frehill, Ó ξριčιl.

Frehilly, Ó ξριčιle.

Frein, τe ξρέιn, α ξρέιn.   V.
Frain.

French, τe ξρέιnρ 28, 97 ;
ξυιnρe, ξυιnρεαč 19 ; ρριοnn-
ρα, ρριοnnραč 34 ; Ó ξραοč-
άιn 92.

Freney, Freny, τe ξρέιne, α
ξρέιne 8 ; mac αn ξραnnc-
αιξ 9.

Frewen, Frewin, ξρυύιn.

Freyne, τe ξρέιn, α ξρέιn 8,
78 ; mac αn ξραnncαιξ 9.

Friar, Friary, mac αn ρρίρ,
mac αn ρίορα.

Friel, Ó ξριξιl, Ó ξιρξιl.

Frier, v, Friar.
Frisell, Frizell, Frizzle, ꝼuıpeal.
Frost, an tSeaca 76 ; ꝼuıpéapt 77.
Frvar, Frver. mac an pꝛíp, mac an pꝛíopa.
Fulten, v. Fallon.
Fullarton, ꝼulaptún.
Fuller, mac an úcaıpe.
Fullerton, ꝼulaptún.
Fuohy, Ó ꝼuatáıᵹ.
Furey, Fury, Ó ꝼíoḋaḃpa.
Furlong, ꝼuplonᵹ.
Fyans, ꝼaᵹan, paᵹan.
Fye, Ó ꝼıaıċ 11 ; Ó ꝼıaca 35.
Fyfee, Ó ꝼıaca.
Fylan, Fyland, v. Phelan.
Fynn, Ó ꝼınn.

Gabbett, Gabbott, ᵹaḃóıṽ.
Gaff, maᵹ eaċaċ.
Gaffeney, v. Gaffney.
Gaffey, maᵹ eaċaıṽ.
Gaffikan, Gaffikin, maᵹ eaċaᵹáın.
Gaffiney, Gaffney, Gafiney, Gafney, Ó ᵹamna 78, 87, 96 ; mac ᵹamna 18, 55, 67 ; mac comᵹamna 19, 55, 77, 97 ; maᵹ paċtna 52 ; mac Cappᵹamna 152.
Gagan, Gahagan, maᵹ eaċaᵹáın.
Gahan, Ó ᵹaoıtín 84 ; mac ᵹaoıtín, (s.l.) maᵹ ᵹatan 64; Ó ᵹáċáın(o.f) Ó ᵹáıḃteaċáın 19.
Gahey, maᵹ eaċaıṽ.
Gaine, Ó ᵹéıḃınn.
Gainer, Gainor, maᵹ ꝼıonnḃaıpp.
Gairlan, v. Garlan.
Galagher, v. Gallagher.
Galavan, Galavin, v. Gallivan.
Galbally, ṽe ᵹallḃaıle.
Galbraith, Galbreath, ᵹallḃpeatnaċ.
Galespy, mac ᵹıolla eappuıᵹ.

GaH, ᵹall.
Gallagher, Gallaher, Gallaugher, Ó ᵹallċoḃaıp, Ó ᵹallċuḃaıp.
Gallahue, Ó ᵹallċuḃa, (o.f.) Ó ᵹallċuḃaıp.
Gallen, Ó ᵹaláın, Ó ᵹalláın 1 ; Ó ᵹaıllín 62.
Gallery, mac ᵹıollapuaḃaıᵹ.
Galligan, Ó ᵹealaᵹáın.
Galliher, Gallihur, v. Gallaher.
Gallin, v. Gallen.
Gallinagh, Ó ᵹaılıneaċ (S.L.) 16.
Gallivan, Ó ᵹealḃáın.
Gallogher, Ó ᵹallċoḃaıp.
Gallogly, mac an ᵹallóᵹlaıᵹ.
Gallon, Ó ᵹaláın, Ó ᵹalláın.
Galloway, Gallway, ṽe ᵹallıṽe, ᵹaıllıṽe.
Galt, ᵹallṽa.
Galvan, Galven, Galvin, Ó ᵹealḃáın.
Galway, Galwey, ṽe ᵹaıllıṽe, ᵹaıllıṽe.
Gambell, Gamble, ᵹamal.
Gambling, ᵹaımlín.
Gambon, ᵹambún.
Gamel, ᵹamal.
Gamlin, ᵹaımlín.
Gammel, ᵹamal.
Gammon, ᵹambún.
Ganagher, maᵹ ṽuıneaċaıp.
Ganley, Ganly, maᵹ Seanlaoıċ.
Gannissy, maᵹ aonᵹupa.
Gannon, maᵹ ꝼıonnáın, (s.l.) Ó ᵹıonnáın, Ó ᵹeannáın 19, 97.
Gantly, maᵹ Seanlaoıċ.
Gara, Ó ᵹaṽpa.
Garagan, v. Gargan.
Garahan, maᵹ ᵹapaċáın, maᵹ apaċáın.
Garahy, maᵹ ꝼeapaṽaıᵹ, (s.l.) maᵹ ᵹeapaċaıᵹ.
Garavin, v. Garvin.
Garde, ṽe ᵹéapṽ, ᵹeápṽ.
Garden, Gardin, ᵹáıpṽín.
Gardiner, Gardner, ᵹáıpnéıp.

Gargan, Ó Ṡeaṉġáin, (s.s.) Mac
Ṡeaṉġáin.
Garity, Maṡ Aiṟeaċtaiṡ.
Garlan, Garland, Garlin, Ṡeaṉ-
lann (o.f.) Ṡeaṉlún, (o.f.)
Ṡeaṉṉún
Garner, v Gardner
Garraghan, Maṡ Ṡaṉaċáin, Maṡ
Aṉaċáin.
Garratt, Garrett, Ṡeaṉóiṫ,
Ṡioṉóiṫ.
Garrigan, v Gargan.
Garrihy, v Garahy.
Garrity, v Garity.
Garron, Maṡ Ṡaṉaċáin.
Garry, Maṡ Ḟeaṉaḋaiṡ 1; Ó
Ṡaoṉa 2
Gartlan, Gartland, Gartlin,
Ṡeaṉtlan,Ṡeaṉlann.V.Garlan
Garvan, Ó Ṡaṉḃáin.
Garveagh, Ó Ṡaiṉḃṟéiċ, Ó
Ṡaiṉḃṟaiċ.
Garven, v Garvin.
Garvey, Ó Ṡaiṉḃiċ, Ó Ṡaiṉḃeiċ
1; Mac Ṡaiṉḃiċ, Mac Ṡaiṉ-
ḃeiċ 16, 64, 67, 192; Ó
Ṡaiṉḃṟéiċ, Ó Ṡaiṉḃṟaiċ 49;
Ó Ṡaiṉḃín 94, 191.
Garvin, Garwin, Ó Ṡaiṉḃín 1,
Ó Ṡaṉḃáin 2.
Gascoigne, Gascoyne, Gaskin,
ṽe Ṡaṉcún.
Gasson, Ó Ṡuṟáin.
Gaston, Ṡaṟcún.
Gately, Ó Ṡatlaoiċ.
Gaughan, Ó Ṡáiḃṫeaċáin, (s l)
Ó Ṡáċáin 19; Maṡ eaċáin 2.
Gaughney, Maṡ Ḟaċtṉa.
Gaughran, Maṡ eaċṟáin.
Gaughy, Gaugy, Maṡ eaċaiṽ.
Gaul, Gaule, Ṡall.
Gault, Ṡallṽa.
Gaussen, Ó Ṡuṟáin.
Gausslin, Ṡéiṟlín.
Gavacan, Gavagan, Gavaghan,
Gavahan, Ó Ṡáiḃṫeaċáin 9;
Maṡ eaċáin 6.

Gavan, Gaven, Ó Ṡáḃáin.
Gavigan, v Gavagan
Gavin, Ó Ṡáiḃín, Ó Ṡáḃáin.
Gaw, Maṡ Áṽaiṁ.
Gawley, Maṡ Aṁalġaṽa, Maṡ
Aṁalġaiṽ.
Gay, Mac Ṡiolla Ṽé.
Gayer, Ṡéaṉ 1; Mac an Ṡéaiṟṟ
2.
Gaynard, Ó Ṡánaiṟṽ (S L) 976.
Gaynor, Maṡ Ḟionnḃaiṟṟ, 1,
Maṡ Ḟionnḃaṟṟa 2; Ó
Ṡánaiṟṽ (S L) 976.
Gcagan, Maṡ eoċaṡáin.
Gealon, Ó Ṡialláin.
Geane, Ó Ṡéiḃinn.
Geaney, Ó Ṡéiḃeannaiṡ.
Geanor, v Gaynor.
Geany, v Geaney.
Gearn, Gearns, Gearon, Ó
Ṡéaṉáin.
Gearty, Maṡ Oiṟeaċtaiṡ.
Geary, Ó Ṡaoṉa 11; Mac
Ṡaoṉa, (s.l.) Maṡ Ṡaoṉa 97;
Maṡ Ḟeaṉaḋaiṡ 2.
Geaveney, Geaveny, Mac Ṡéiḃ-
eannaiṡ 6; Ó Ṡéiḃeannaiṡ 9.
Gee, Maṡ Aoiṽ.
Geehan, Ó Ṡaoiċín
Geelan, Ó Ṡialláin.
Geffeken, v Gaffikin.
Gegan, Maṡ eoċaṡáin.
Geghan, Maṡ eaċáin, Maṡ eoċ-
aṡáin.
Gehagan, Gehegan, Maṡ
eoċaṡáin.
Gelaspy, Mac Ṡiolla eaṟṟuiṡ.
Gellan, Gelland, Ó Ṡealáin 9;
Mac Ṡiolla Ḟaoláin 6.
Gellen, Ó Ṡealáin, Ó Ṡilín.
Gellespey, v. Gelaspy.
Gelshinan, v. Gilshenan.
Gelvarry, Mac Ṡiolla Ḃeaṟaiṡ.
Gennagh, Maṡ Cineáiċ.
Gennell, Maṡ Ḟionnġail.
Geogan, Geoghegan, Maṡ eoċ-
aṡáin.

Geoghery, Ó ʒoċṁaıṁ. 4.
Geon, mаʒ eoʒaın.
George, ѕeóır̃ѕe.
Geraghty, mаʒ Oır̃eаċтаıʒ 11 ;
Ó hOır̃eаċтаıʒ 16, 29, 99.
Geran, Ó ʒéаr̃áın.
Gerard, ʒeаr̃ár̃ᴅ 1, ʒeаr̃óıᴅ 2.
Gerarty, Geraty, Geraughty,
Gerity, v. Gerraghty.
German, ʒeаr̃mán.
Germon, ʒeаr̃monn.
Gernon, ʒeаr̃nún.
Gerraghty, mаʒ Oır̃eаċтаıʒ 11,
(s.l.) Ó ʒoır̃eаċта 92 ; Ó
hOır̃eаċтаıʒ 16, 29, 99.
Gerrard, v. Gerard.
Gerret, v. Garrett.
Gertey, Gerty, mаʒ Oır̃eаċтаıʒ.
Gervase, Gervis, ʒeаr̃ḃár̃.
Gery, mаʒ r̃eаr̃аṁаıʒ.
Getty, mаʒ eıтıʒ.
Ghagan, mаʒ eаċаʒáın.
Ghee, mаʒ аoıṁ.
Ghegan, mаʒ eoċаʒáın.
Gheraty, v. Gerraghty.
Gibb, ʒıb.
Gibben, Gibbin, mаʒ r̃ıbín.
Gibbings, Gibbins, mаc ʒıob-
úın 2 ; mаʒ r̃ıbín 2.
Gibbon, Gibbons, Gibbonson,
mаc ʒıobúın.
Giblin, Ó ʒıbeаlláın, Ó ʒıob-
аlláın.
Gibney, Giboney, Ó ʒıbne.
Gibsey, Ó ʒıbeаlláın, Ó ʒıob-
аlláın.
Gibson, mаc ʒıb, ʒıobr̃on,
ʒıobr̃аn 1 ; Ó ʒıbeаlláın, Ó
ʒıobаlláın 197, 976.
Gibulawn, Ó ʒıbeаlláın, Ó
ʒıobаlláın.
Giffen, mаʒ ᴅuıbr̃ınn.
Gihon, Ó ʒаoıċín.
Gilberson, v. Gilbertson.
Gilbert, ʒılbeаr̃т.
Gilbertson, mаc ʒılbeır̃т, mаc
ʒıllıbeır̃т.

Gilbey, Gilboy, mаc ʒıollа-
ḃuıṁe 16, 93, Ó ʒıollаḃuıṁe
16.
Gilbride, mаc ʒıollа Ḃr̃íʒᴅe.
Gilchreest, Gilchriest, Gilchrist,
Gilcrest, Gilcriest, Gilcrist,
mаc ʒıollа Cr̃íoѕт.
Gildea, mаc ʒıollа Ṁé.
Gildowney, mаc ʒıollа ᴅoṁ-
nаıʒ.
Gilduff, mаc ʒıollаṁuıḃ.
Giles, Ó ʒlаıѕne 376.
Gilfeather, Gilfedder, mаc
ʒıollа Peаᴅаır̃.
Gilfillan, Gilfilland, mаc ʒıollа
Fаoláın.
Gilfoyle, mаc ʒıollа Póıl.
Gilgan, v. Gilligan.
Gilgar, mаc ʒıollаʒéаır̃r̃.
Gilgrinn, mаc ʒıollаʒr̃ınn.
Gilgunn, mаc ʒıollаṁuınn.
Gilheany, mаc ʒıollа Cаınnıʒ.
Gilhool, mаc ʒıollа Coṁʒаıll.
Gilhooly, mаc ʒıollаʒuаlа,
mаc ʒıollаr̃úılıʒ.
Gilkelly, mаc ʒıollа Ceаllаıʒ.
Gilkeson, Gilkinson. Gilkison
mаc uılcín.
Gill, mаc аn ʒoıll 11 ; mаʒ
ʒıollа 64.
Gillan, Gilland, Gillane, Ó
ʒıolláın.
Gillanders, mаc ʒıollа Aın-
ᴅr̃éır̃.
Gillaspy, mаc ʒıollа eаѕr̃uıʒ.
Gillbee, v. Gilbey.
Gilleece, mаc ʒıollа íoѕа.
Gilleen, Ó ʒılín.
Gilleland, mаc ʒıollа Fаoláın.
Gillen, Ó ʒılín 9 ; Ó ʒıolláın 6.
Gilleran, mаc ʒıollаr̃áın, (o.f.)
mаc ʒıollа Éаnáın, (s.l.) Ó
ʒıollаr̃áın 92.
Gillesby, Gillespie, mаc ʒıollа
eаѕr̃uıʒ.
Gillick, mаʒ uılıc, mаʒ uıllıc.

Gilligan, Ó Ʒiollaʒáin 1 ; mac
Ʒiollaʒáin 66.
Gillilan, Gilliland, mac Ʒiolla
ꝼaoláin.
Gillinan, mac Ʒiolla ꝼionnáin.
Gillinnion, mac Ʒiolla ꝼinnéin
Gillis, mac Ʒiolla íora.
Gillispie, mac Ʒiolla earpuiʒ.
Gillivan, mac Ʒiollabáin.
Gillon, Ó Ʒilín 9 ; Ó Ʒiolláin 6.
Gillooly, mac Ʒiollaʒuala.
Gilloon, mac Ʒiolla eóin.
Cilloway, mac Ʒiollabuiðe.
Gillowly, mac Ʒiollaʒuala.
Gilmartin, mac Ʒiolla máptain
Gilmary, mac Ʒiolla muipe.
Gilmer, Gilmor, mac Ʒiollamipi
29 ; mac Ʒiolla muipe 68, 92.
Gilmore, Gilmour, mac Ʒiolla
muipe.
Gilpatrick, mac Ʒiolla páv-
paiʒ.
Gilpin, mac Ʒiollapinn.
Gilrain, Gilrane, mac Ʒiollapáin.
Gilroy, mac Ʒiollapuaið.
Gilsenan, Gilshenan, Gilshenon,
Gilson, mac Ʒiolla Seanáin,
mac Ʒiolla Sionáin 11, (s.l.)
maʒ uinnpeannáin, maʒ
uinnpionnáin, Ó Cuinpioʒán,
67, 86.
Giltenan, Giltenane, Giltinane,
mac Ʒiolla tSeanáin.
Gilvanny, Gilvany, mac Ʒiolla
meana.
Gilvarry, mac Ʒiolla beapaiʒ.
Gilvoy, Gilwee, mac Ʒiolla-
buiðe.
Ginaty, Ginity, maʒ ꝼinneact-
aiʒ, maʒ ꝼionnactaiʒ, &c;
Ginivan, maʒ ðuinneabain.
Ginley, maʒ ꝼionnʒaile.
Ginn, maʒ ꝼinn.
Ginna, maʒ Cineáit.
Ginnane, Ó Cuineáin, Ó Cuinn-
eáin 76 ; maʒ Cineáit 762.
Ginnaw, maʒ Cineáit.

Ginnell, maʒ ꝼionnʒail.
Ginnelly, maʒ ꝼionnʒaile.
Ginnity, Ginty, maʒ ꝼinneact-
aiʒ, maʒ ꝼionnactaiʒ, &c.
Gipsey, Ó Ʒioballáin, Ó
Ʒibealláin.
Girvan, Girvin, (?) Ó Ʒapbáin,
Ó Ʒaipbín.
Givan, Giveen, Given, Givin,
maʒ ðuibín.
Glackan, Ó Ʒlacáin.
Gladdery, Gladdry, Ó Ʒleavpa
9 ; mac Ʒleavpa 6.
Glaffey, maʒ ꝼlaitim, maʒ
Laitim, maʒ Lataiʒ.
Glakan, Ó Ʒlacáin.
Glancy, maʒ ꝼlanncaða, maʒ
ꝼlanncaið.
Glanders, mac Ʒiolla ainvpéip.
Glanfield, ve Ʒlainbíol.
Glanny, a' Ʒleanna.
Glanton, a' Ʒleanntáin.
Glanville, ve Ʒlainbíol.
Glashby, Glaspy, mac Ʒiolla
earpuiʒ.
Glasheen, Ó Ʒlaipín.
Glass, Ʒlap.
Glassett. Ʒlaipéiv.
Glavey, maʒ ꝼlaitim, maʒ
Laitim, maʒ Lataiʒ.
Glavin, Ó Ʒláimín.
Gleasure, Ʒléapúp.
Gleeson, Ó Ʒliapáin, (o.f.) Ó
Ʒlapáin.
Glenane, maʒ Leannáin.
Glenn, ve Ʒlin 2 ; a' Ʒleanna 2
Glennon, maʒ Leannáin.
Glenny, a' Ʒleanna.
Glessane, Ó Ʒlapáin.
Glinn, ve Ʒlin. V. Glynn, Glenn.
Glissane, Glissawn, Ó Ʒlapáin,
Ó Ʒliapáin.
Gloon, mac Ʒiolla eóin.
Glorney, (?) Ó Ʒlóiaipn.
Glynn, maʒ ꝼloinn 11 ; ve
Ʒlinn 2.
Gna, maʒ Cineáit.

Goan, v. Gowan.

Gobin, Ó Ɣobáin, Ó Ɣuibín.

Goddan, Ó Ɣováin.

Godfrey, mac Ɣoᵹpaıᵭ 1 ; Ó
Ɣoᵹpaıᵭ 17, 27 ; Ɣoᵹpaıᵭ 2.

Godrick, maᵹ ualᵹaıpᵹ.

Godwin, Ɣoıᵭín E 1 ; Ó Ɣoıᵭín
192, Ó Ɣováin 2 (O'D.) ; Ó
ᵭeaᵹaıᵭ, Ó ᵭıaᵹaıᵭ 91.

Goff, Ɣoᵭ 7, 8 ; maᵹ eoᵭaᵭ,
maᵹ eoᵭava 6, 9.

Goran mac eoᵭaᵭáin 1 ; Ɣoᵹán,
Ɣóᵹan, Ɣaᵹaın, 2.

Gogarty, Gogarty, maᵹ póᵹapᵗaıᵹ.

Goggan, Goggin, Goggins, ᵭe
coᵹán, Ɣoᵹán.

Gogin, v. Gogan, Goggin.

Gohary, v. Godfrey.

Going, mac an Ɣovann.

Golagley, Golagly, mac an
Ɣallóᵹlaıᵹ.

Golden, Ɣuılín 8, 72 ; Ó Ɣoıll-
ıᵭe, (o.f.) Ó Ɣoıllín 49, 77 ;
mac cuallaᵭᵗa, (s.l.) Ó
Ɣuallaᵭᵗa 19, 29 ; maᵹ ualᵹaıpᵹ 91 ; Ó Ɣabláın 976.

Goldie, Ɣuılıᵭe.

Golding, v. Golden.

Goldrick, maᵹ ualᵹaıpᵹ, (s.l.)
mac Ɣualpaıᵹ, mac Ɣual-
paıc.

Goligher, Gollagher, Golligher,
Golliher, Gollogher, Golloher.
Ó Ɣallᵭováıp, Ó Ɣallᵭubaıp,

Gollan, Ó Ɣaláin, Ó Ɣalláin,

Gologly, mac an Ɣallóᵹlaıᵹ.

Golrick, maᵹ ualᵹaıpᵹ.

Gomory, mac ıomaıpe.

Gonn, Ɣunna.

Gonoude, maᵹ nuaᵭaᵭ, maᵹ
nuaᵭaᵗ.

Good, Ɣuᵭ.

Goodman, Ɣoᵗmonn E 1 ; mac
Ɣıollamaıᵗ 64.

Goodwin, v. Godwin.

Googan, maᵹ eoᵭaᵹáin.

Googarty, maᵹ puaᵹapᵗaıᵹ,
maᵹ póᵹapᵗaıᵹ.

Goold, Goolde, Ɣul.

Goolden, v. Golden.

Gooley, Ɣuılıᵭe l ; Ó Ɣabalaıᵹ
15.

Goonan, Goonane, Ó Ɣamnáin.

Goonery, Goonry, Ó Ɣamnaıpe.

Gooney, Ó Ɣamna.

Gooravan, maᵹ Sampaváin,

Goorey, Ó Ɣuaıpe.

Gordon, ᵭe Ɣópᵭún, Ɣópᵭún,
Ɣópᵭan 1 ; maᵹ muıpneaᵭ-
áin 19, 38, (s.l.) maᵹ Ɣuap-
naᵭáin 19 ; mópᵭoıpneaᵭ
19.

Gore, ᵭe Ɣaop.

Gorevan, maᵹ Sampaváin.

Gorey, Ó Ɣuaıpe.

Gorham, ᵭe Ɣupam, (s.l.) Ó
Ɣuaıpım 97.

Gorish, maᵹ peópaıp.

Gormagan, Ó Ɣopmaᵹáin.

Gormally, Gormaly, v. Gormley.

Gorman, Ó Ɣopmáin 11 ; mac
Ɣopmáin 35, 76 ; Ó Ɣopmóᵹ
192 (O'D.) ; Ó Ɣopmᵹaıl,
(s.l.) Ó Ɣopmpúıl 19, 97, Ó
Ɣopmᵹaıle, (s.l.) Ó Ɣopm-
púılıᵹ 192.

Gormican, Ó copmacáin.

Gormilly, Gormley, Ó Ɣoıpm-
pleaᵹaıᵹ, Ó Ɣoıpmleaᵹaıᵹ 6 ;
Ó Ɣopmᵹaıle, (s.l.) Ó Ɣopm-
púılıᵹ 91, Ó Ɣopmᵹaıl, (s.l.)
Ó Ɣopmpúıl 192 ; mac
Ɣopmᵹaıle 2.

Gorry, mac Ɣoᵹpaıᵭ.

Goslin, Gosling, Ɣóıplín.

Gosnall, Gosnell, Ɣóıréıp.

Gossan, Ó Ɣupáin.

Gosselin, Ɣóıplín.

Gosson, Ó Ɣupáin.

Gostlin, Ɣóıplín.

Gough, Ɣoᵭ 7, 8 ; maᵹ eoᵭaᵭ
6, 9 ; Ó cuaᵭáin 192 (O'D.)

Gould, Ɣul.

Goulding, Ḟúilín 8. 72 ; Ó
Ḟoillíḋe, (o.f.) Ó Ḟoillín 49
77 ; Ó Ḃabláin 976 ; mag
Ualġaiŋg 91; mac Cuallaċta,
(s.l.) Ó Ḟuallaċta. 19, 29

Gouldrick, Goulrick, mag Ualġaiŋg.

Gouldy, Ḟúilíḋe.

Gourley, mag Ċoiṗḋealḃaig.

Governey, (?) mac Coiḃḋeanaig.

Gow, Ḟoḃa 2 ; mac an Ḟoḃa 2.

Gowan, Gowen, Gowing, mac
an Ḟoḃann, mac an Ḟaḃann
1 ; Ó Ḟoḃann, Ó Ḟaḃann 67.

Gowran, Ó Ḟaḃráin.

Grace, Ḟráṡ.

Graddy, Ó Ḟreaḋa.

Graden, mag Ḃraḋáin.

Grady, Ó Ḟráḋa 11 ; Ó Ḟreaḋa
72 ; mag Riaḋa, (s.l.) Ó
Ḟriaḋa 19, 97.

Graeme, Graham, Ó Ḟréaċáin
11, (s.l.) Ó Ḟreiṫim 72.

Grainger, Ḟráinréiṁ.

Grame, v. Graham.

Grandan, Grandon, ḋe Ḟranḋún, Ḟranḋún.

Grange, Ḟráinṡeaċ.

Granger, Ḟráinṡéiṁ.

Grannell, mag Raġnaill.

Grannon, Ó Ḟrianáin.

Granny, mag Ráiġne, mag
Ḟráinne, mag Ḟránna 2 ;
Ḟránna, Ḟránḋa 2.

Grant, ḋe Ḟrannṫ, Ḟrannṫ 11 ;
mag Ḟránna 64 ; Ḟránḋa 2.

Grattan, (?) mag Reaċṫáin,
(o.f.) mag neaċṫain. Cf.
Natton.

Graves, v. Greaves.

Gray, ḋe Ḟrae, Ḟrae E 1 ; liaṫ
976 ; mac Ḟiollariaḃaig 5.

Grayhan, Ó Ḟréaċáin.

Gready, v. Grady.

Greaghan, Greaham, Greahan,
Ó Ḟréaċáin.

Grealish, Ó Ḟrialluiṗ, mag
Riallġuiṗ, (o.f.) mag niallġuiṗ.

Greally, Grealy, mag Raġall
aig, (s.l.) Ó Ḟrálaig, Ó
Ḟraolaig 19 ; Ó Ḟriallluiṗ,
mag Riallluiṗ, (o.f.) mag
niallġuiṗ 972.

Greame, Greames, Ó Ḟréaċáin.

Greaney, Greany, Ó Ḟráinne.

Grear, v. Greer.

Greaven, Ó Ḟríoḃṫáin, (s.l.) Ó
Ḟriaḃáin.

Greaves, ḋe Ḟréiḃ E 1 ; Ó
Ḟríoḃṫáin, (s.l.) Ó Ḟriaḃáin
976.

Greehy, Ó Ḟríoċa, (o.f.) Ó
Ḟríoḃṫa.

Greely, v. Grealy.

Green, ḋe Ḟraoin 17, 18, 47;
Ó huaiṫne, Ó huainíḋe 779,
Ó huaiṫnín 19, 27, 46 ; mac
Ḟlaráin, mac Ḟlairín 26, 64 ;
mac Ḟiollaġlair 16 ; uaiṫne,
2 ; Ḟlar 2 ; Ó huróṗín 992 ;
Ó raċaig 972 (O'D.)

Greenan, Ó Ḟrianáin, (o.f.) mag
Ḃraonáin 29.

Greene, v. Green.

Greer, mac Ḟríoġair 1 (s.i.)
Ḟraḃar. 19.

Gregan, Ó Ḟréaċáin.

Gregory, Ḟréaġóiṗ 1 ; mac
Ḟréaġaiṗ, mac Ḟríoġaiṗ 2.

Greham, Grehan, Ó Ḟréaċáin.

Greir, v. Greer.

Grene, v. Green.

Grennan, Ó Ḟrianáin.

Grevin, v. Greaven.

Grey, v. Gray.

Greyhan, Ó Ḟréaċáin.

Gribben, Gribbin, Gribbon, mag
Roiḃín 1 ; Ó Ḟuiḃín 16.

Grier, v. Greer.

Grieves, v. Greaves.

Griffey, Ó Ḟríoḃṫa.

Griffin, ႸႰႨႰႨ́ᘉ 47 ; Ó ႸႰႨ́ᘉႨᘉ, Ó
ႸႰႨ́ბ̇ᴄ́ɪᴎ 79 ; Ó ႸႰႨ́ᴏ̇ბ̇ᴄᴀ 71,
91 ; Ó ႸႰႨ́ᴏ̇ბ̇ᴄᴀ́ɪᴎ 27, 972 ;
mᴀᵹ ᴎɪᴀᴌᴌᵹᴜɪႰ, (s.l.) mᴀᵹ
RɪᴀᴌᴌᵹᴜɪႰ, Ó ᵹႰᴜᴀᴌᴌᴜɪႰ 192,
972.
Griffith, Griffiths, Ó ᵹႰɪ́ᴏ̇ბ̇ᴄᴀ
91, Ó ᵹႰɪ́ᴏ̇ბ̇ᴄᴀ́ɪᴎ 976.
Griffy, Ó ᵹႰɪ́ᴏ̇ბ̇ᴄᴀ.
Grimes, Ó ᵹႰᴇɪᴏ̇m (S.L.) 7 ;
Ó ᵹႰᴇᴀᴄ́ᴀ́ɪᴎ 62, 91 ; Ó ᵹᴏႰm-
ᵹᴀɪᴌᴇ 192 ; Ó ᴄᴏɪᴎᴌᴇɪႰᴄ, Ó
ᴄᴏɪᴎᴌɪႰᴄ 199.
Grimley, v. Gormley, Grumley.
Groarke, mᴀᵹ RᴜᴀɪႰᴄ.
Groden, mᴀᵹ Rᴏᴏ̇ᴀ́ɪᴎ 29 ; mᴀᵹ
ᴜ̇Ⴐᴀᴏ̇ᴀ́ɪᴎ 38.
Grogan, Groggan, Ó ᵹႰᴜᴀᵹᴀ́ɪᴎ,
Ó ᵹႰᴜ́ᵹᴀ́ɪᴎ.
Gronel, mᴀᵹ Rᴀᵹᴎᴀɪᴌᴌ.
Groogan, v. Grogan.
Grosby, mᴀᴄ ᴀᴎ ᴄ̇ႰᴏႰᴀ́ɪᴎ.
Grourke, mᴀᵹ RᴜᴀɪႰᴄ.
Grubb, mᴀᵹ Rᴏb.
Grumley, Ó ᵹᴏɪႰmᴌᴇᴀᵹᴀɪᵹ̇.
Grummell, ᵹႰᴏmᴀɪᴌ.
Gubbins, Ó ᵹᴜɪbɪ́ᴎ, Ó ᵹᴏɪbɪ́ᴎ.
Guckeane, Gucken, Guckian,
mᴀᵹ ᴇᴏᴄ́ᴀɪᴏ̇ɪ́ᴎ.
Guerin, Ó ᵹᴇ́ᴀႰᴀ́ɪᴎ 7 ; mᴀᵹ
ᴜɪᴏ̇Ⴐɪ́ᴎ 38.
Guigan, mᴀᵹ ᴇᴏᴄ́ᴀɪᴏ̇ɪ́ᴎ, mᴀᵹ
ᴇᴏᴄ́ᴀ́ɪᴎ.
Guighan, Guihan, Guiheen,
Guihen, Ó ᵹᴀᴏɪᴄ́ɪ́ᴎ 2 ; mᴀᴄ
ᵹᴀᴏɪᴄ́ɪ́ᴎ 2.
Guiken, mᴀᵹ ᴇᴏᴄ́ᴀɪᴏ̇ɪ́ᴎ.
Guilchrist, mᴀᴄ ᵹɪᴏᴌᴌᴀ ᴄ̇Ⴐɪ́ᴏႰᴄ.
Guilfoyle, mᴀᴄ ᵹɪᴏᴌᴌᴀ ᴘ̇ᴏ́ɪᴌ.
Guilliland, mᴀᴄ ᵹɪᴏᴌᴌᴀ ᴘ̇ᴀᴏᴌᴀ́ɪᴎ.
Guilmartin, mᴀᴄ ᵹɪᴏᴌᴌᴀ ṁᴀ́Ⴐ-
ᴄᴀɪᴎ.
Guina, mᴀᵹ ᴄɪᴎᴇᴀ́ɪᴄ̇.
Guinan, Guinane, Ó ᴄᴜɪᴎᴇᴀ́ɪᴎ, Ó
ᴄᴜɪᴎᴎᴇᴀ́ɪᴎ 1 ; Ó ᵹᴀɪbᴎᴇᴀ́ɪᴎ 778.
Guinea, Guinee, Ó ᵹᴜɪᴎɪᴏ̇ᴇ(S.L.).
Guinevan, mᴀᵹ ᴏ̇ᴜɪᴎᴎᴇᴀბ̇ᴀ́ɪᴎ.

Guiney, Ó ᵹᴇɪბᴇᴀᴎᴎᴀɪᵹ̇ 7 ; Ó
ᵹᴜɪᴎɪᴏ̇ᴇ. Ó ᵹɪᴎɪᴏ̇ᴇ 49, 776.
Guinna, mᴀᵹ ᴄɪᴎᴇᴀ́ɪᴄ̇.
Guinnane, Ó ᴄᴜɪᴎᴎᴇᴀ́ɪᴎ.
Guinnaty, mᴀᵹ ᴘɪᴏᴎᴎᴀᴄ́ᴛᴀ, mᴀᵹ
ᴘɪᴏᴎᴎᴀᴄ́ᴛᴀɪᵹ̇, &c.
Guinness, mᴀᵹ ᴀᴏᴎᵹᴜɪႰ, mᴀᵹ
ᴀᴏᴎᵹᴜႰᴀ.
Guiny, v. Guiney.
Guiry, Ó ᵹᴀᴏ̇Ⴐᴀ.
Gulan, Gullan, Ó ᵹᴏᴌᴌᴀ́ɪᴎ.
Gullion, ᵹɪᴌᴌᴇᴀ́ᴎ.
Gully, v. Gooley.
Gumbleton, ᵹᴜmᴀႰᴄᴜ́ᴎ.
Gunn, ᵹᴜᴎᴎᴀ 1 ; mᴀᴄ ᵹɪᴏᴌᴌᴀ-
ᴏ̇ᴜɪᴎᴎ 29.
Gunnell, mᴀᵹ ᴄᴏᴎᵹᴀɪᴌ.
Gunner, ᵹᴜᴎᴎᴀႰ.
Gunnigan, mᴀᵹ ᴏ̇ᴏᴎᴎᴀᵹᴀ́ɪᴎ.
Gunnigle, mᴀᵹ ᴄᴏᴎᵹᴀɪᴌ.
Gunning, Ó ᴄᴏᴎᴀɪᴎᵹ 76 (O'D.) ;
Ó ᵹᴀṁᴎᴀ́ɪᴎ 46, 87.
Gunshinan, mᴀᵹ ᴜɪᴎᴎႰᴇᴀᴎᴎᴀ́ɪᴎ,
mᴀᵹ ᴜɪᴎᴎႰɪᴏᴎᴎᴀ́ɪᴎ, Ó ᴄᴜɪᴎ-
Ⴐɪᴏᵹᴀ́ᴎ, (o.f.) mᴀᴄ ᵹɪᴏᴌᴌᴀ
ᴄᴇᴀᴎᴀ́ɪᴎ.
Gurrin, mᴀᵹ ᴄᴏႰႰᴀ́ɪᴎ, mᴀᵹ
ᴄᴏႰႰᴀɪᴏ̇ɪ́ᴎ.
Gurdan, v. Jordan.
Gurry, mᴀᴄ ᵹᴏᴄ̇Ⴐᴀɪᴏ̇.
Gutherie, Guthrie, Guttery, Ó
ᴌᴀɪᴄ̇ɪ́m, Ó ᴌᴀᴄ́ᴀɪᵹ̇.
Guy, ᵹᴜɪᴏ̇.
Gware, ᴏᴇ ᵹᴀᴏႰ.
Gweehin, Ó ᵹᴀᴏɪᴄ́ɪ́ᴎ.
Gwyn, Gwynn, Gwynne, ᵹᴜɪᴎ.
Gyles, Ó ᵹᴌᴀɪႰᴎᴇ 64.

Habbagan, ᴎᴏbᴀᴄ́ᴀ́ᴎ.
Habbert, ᴎᴏɪbᴇᴀ́Ⴐᴏ̇.
Hackett, ᴎᴀɪᴄᴇ́ɪᴏ̇ 1 : ᴎᴀᴄᴀᴇᴏ̇,
ᴀɪᴄᴇ́ɪᴏ̇, ᴀᴄᴀᴏᴏ̇ 2 ; mᴀᴄ ᴎᴀɪᴄ-
ᴇ́ɪᴏ̇ 972 ; mᴀᴄ ᴇᴀᴄ́ᴀɪᴏ̇, mᴀᵹ
ᴇᴀᴄ́ᴀɪᴏ̇ 23, 35.
Hadden, v. Haddon.
Haddigan, Ó ᴎᴇɪᴏ̇ᴇᴀᵹᴀ́ɪᴎ.
Haddon, Haden, Hadian, Ó ᴎᴀɪᴏ̇-
ɪ́ᴎ, Ó ᴎᴇɪᴏ̇ɪ́ᴎ, Ó ᴎᴇɪᴏ̇ᴇᴀɪᴎ.

Hadnet, v. Hodnett.
Hafferon, Haffron, Ó háṁṗáir.
Haffy, Ó heaċaṁ.
Hagan, Hagans, Ó háżáin
(o.f.) Ó hóżáin 61; Ó haoṁ-
Ażáin 8, 62; mac aoṁażáin
2.
Hagarty, Hagerty, Ó héiżceaṗt-
Aiż, Ó héiżeaṗtaiż 19, 46,
63, 77; Ó háżaṗtaiż, Ó
háżaṗtaiż 64, 82.
Haggan, Haggans, v. Hagan.
Haggarty, v. Hagarty.
Haggens, v. Hagans.
Haggerty, v. Hagerty.
Haghan, Haghen, Ó heaċáin.
Haghey, Ó heaċaṁ.
Hagin, v. Hagan.
Hahasy, Hahessy, Ó haiċeaṗa.
Hahee, Ó heaċaṁ.
Haidee, Haidy, Ó haiṁiċ, Ó
haiṁiṁe, Ó haiṁeiċ, Ó
héiṁiṁ, Ó héiṁeaṁá.
Haier, Ó hoiċiṗ.
Haigney, v. Heagney.
Hainen, v. Heanen.
Haines, Ó héiṁín.
Hainey, v. Heaney.
Hair, Haire, Ó híṗ 3; Ó haiċiṗ,
Ó hoiċiṗ 4; Ó żioṗṗaiṁe,
(o.f.) mAż ṗeaṗaṁaiż 976.
Hale, Hales, mac haol.
Halferty, Ó háilbeaṗtaiż.
Halfpenny, Ó háilpín, (o.f.) Ó
háilpene, (s.l.) Ó hálpan
376.
Hall, ṽe hál.
Hallaghan, Hallahan, Ó hallaċ-
áin, Ó hailleaċáin.
Hallan, Ó hallaṁain, (o.f.) Ó
ṗallaṁain.
Hallanan, Ó háilżeanáin.
Halleran, Ó hallṁuṗáin.
Hallessy, Ó háilżeaṗa.
Halley, v. Hally.
Halligan, Ó hallażáin, Ó
hailleażáin.

Hallihan, Hallihane, Ó hailleaċ-
áin.
Hallin, Ó háilín, Ó háillín.
Hallinan, Ó háilżeanáin.
Hallion, Ó háilín, Ó háillín.
Hallissey, Hallissy, Ó háil-
żeaṗa.
Halloran, Ó hallṁuṗáin.
Hally, Ó háilċe 17, 27; Ó
háille 46; Ó hallaiṁe 47.
Halpeny, Halpin, Ó háilpín.
Haltigan, Ó hultaċáin.
Halton, ṽe háltún.
Halvey, ṽe halbuiṁe, hal-
buiṁe, haluiṁe 1; Ó háil-
ṁic 19, 97.
Hamell, Hamill, Ó háṁmaill,
Hamilton, ṽe hamaltún,
hamaltún 1, (s.l.) Ó ham-
áilltín 469; Ó huṗmoltaiż
7779.
Hamlen, Hamlin, Hamlyn,
haimlín.
Hammell, Hammill, Ó háṁ-
maill, Ó háżmaill.
Hammon, Hammond, hámonn
1; hamon 2; mac ámoinn
2.
Hamondson, mac ámoinn.
Hampton, ṽe hamtún.
Hamrock, Hamrogue, hamṗóc,
hamṗóż 1; seamṗóż 976.
Hanafey, v. Hanify.
Hanafin, Ó háinṗeáin, Ó háin-
ṗín, Ó háiniṗeáin, Ó háini-
ṗin, (o.f.) Ó háinḃteáin, Ó
hainḃtín.
Hanafy, v. Hanify.
Hanan, Ó hannáin.
Hanaty, Ó hionnaċtaiż, (o.f.)
Ó ṗionnaċtaiż.
Hanberry, Hanbery Hanbury
ṽe hanbṗuża 2; Ó háin-
ṁiṗe, Ó háinṁiṗeaċ, (s.l.) Ó
hainṁneaċ, Ó áinṁneaċ 97.
Hancock, hancóc.

Hand, Ⓜ️as Laitim (s.l.) Ⓜ️as
Láim 29, 39, 55; Ⓜ️as Laié-
imín, (o.f.) Ⓜ️as ꝼlaitimín,
(s.l.) Ⓜ️as Láimín 19, 34.
Handbury, v. Hanbury.
Handcock, Ⓗ️ancóc.
Handlon, v. Hanlon.
Handly, v. Hanly.
Handrahan, v. Hanrahan.
Handrick, v. Hanrick.
Hands, v. Hand.
Haneen, v. Hanneen.
Hanefan, v. Hanifan.
Hanephy, v. Hanify.
Hanheen, v. Hanneen.
Hanick v. Hanwick.
Hanifan, Hanifin, Ó hainꝼeáin,
Ó hainꝼín, Ó hainiꝼeáin, Ó
hainiꝼín, (o.f.) Ó hainb-
teáin, Ó hainbtín.
Hanify, Ó hainꝼit, Ó hainꝼit,
(o.f.) Ó hainbeit, Ó hainbit,
(s l.) Ó hainte, Ó hanaite
972.
Hanihan, Ó hannacáin.
Hankard, Ⓗ️ancáꝛo.
Hanlan, v. Hanlon.
Hanley, Ó hainlige, Ó háin-
lige, Ó hainle, Ó háinle.
Hanlin, Hanlon, Ó hannluain,
Ó hanluain 1, (s.l.) Ó hann-
láin 2.
Hanly, v. Hanley.
Hanna, *Ó hannaio.
Hannafy, v. Hanify.
Hannahan, Ó hannacáin.
Hannan, Ó hainnín, Ó haintín
11; Ó hannáin 17, 75; Ó
hannacáin 2;.
Hannaway, v. Hanway.
Hanneen, Ó hainnín, Ó hain-
tín.
Hannell, Ó hionngail, (o.t.) Ó
ꝼionngail.
Hannen, v Hannan.
Hannerty, Ó hionnactaig.
Hannify v. Hanify

Hannigan, Ó hannacáin
Hannin, Hannon Hanon
Hannan.
Hanrahan, Ó hanꝛacáin.
Hanratty, Ó hanꝛactaig.
Hanrick, Ó hannꝛaic, Ó heᴀ
ꝛaic.
Hanvey, Hanvy, Hanway,
hainbit, Ó hainbeit.
Hanwick, (?) Ó hailmic.
Hara, Ó heagꝛa, Ó heaúꝛa.
Haraghy, Ó heaꝛcaóa, Ó heaꝛ
caió.
Harald, v. Harold.
Haran, Ó heaꝛáin 6; Ó heag-
ꝛáin 97, Ó heacꝛáin 2; Ó
haꝛꝛacáin 27, 45; Ó hann
ꝛáin 732.
Harberd, Harbert, Ⓗ️oiꝛeabáꝛꝟ
Ⓗ️oiꝛeabaꝛo.
Harbin, Ⓗ️oiꝛbín.
Harbinson, Harbison, Ⓗ️ ꝯ
Ⓗ️oiꝛbín.
Harden, Ⓜ️ac giolla oeacaiꝛ
Hardford, oe heaꝛꝼoꝛt.
Hardiman, Ó haꝛgaoáin, Ó
haiꝛgeaoáin.
Harding, Hardinge, Ⓗ️áiꝛoín
Hardman, Ⓗ️eaꝛman.
Hardwood, Ⓗ️aꝛóꝟo.
Hardy, Ⓜ️ac giolla oeacaiꝛ.
Hare, Ó híꝛ 3; Ó haicíꝛ, Ó
hOicíꝛ 4; Ó gioꝛꝛaióe, (o ꝛ.)
Ⓜ️as ꝼeaꝛaóaig 976.
Harel, v. Harrell.
Haren, v Haran
Harford, oe heaꝛꝼoꝛt.
Hargadan, Hargaden, Harga-
don, Ó haꝛgaoáin, Ó haiꝛ-
geaoáin.
Hargan, v. Horgan.
Harhan, Harhen, v. Haran.
Harkan, Ó heaꝛcáin 6; Ó
hOꝛcáin 19, 46.
Harkey, Ó heaꝛcaió.
Harkin, Harkins, Harkon, v
Harkan.

Harney, Ó heaᴘᵹaile.

Harman, Harmon, heaᴘman 1 ;
Ó haᴘᵹaváin 97 ; macᵹiolla
veacaiᴘ 37.

Harnedy, Harnett, Ó haiᴘᴄnéava.

Harney, Ó hácaiᴘne, (s.l.) Ó
háiᴘne.

Harnon, Ó heaᴘnáin.

Harold, haᴘóiv, aᴘóiv, aᴘalᴄ
1 ; Ó haᴘailᴄ 17.

Haroughten, Haroughton, Ó
haᴘᴘacᴄáin.

Harper, Harpur, ve haᴘᴘúᴘ,
haᴘᴘúᴘ.

Harragher, Harraher, Ó heaᴘ-
ċaiᴘ, (o.f.) Ó ᶂeaᴘċaiᴘ.

Harren, v. Haran.

Harrel, Harrell, Ó heaᴘᵹail,
(o.f.) Ó ᶂeaᴘᵹail.

Harren, v. Haran.

Harrett, v. Harrot.

Harricks, Ó heiᴘᴄ.

Harries, v. Harris.

Harrigan, Ó haᴘᴘaᵹáin.

Harrihy, Ó heaᴘċaiv.

Harrington, Ó haᴘᴘacᴄáin 73,
95 ; Ó haiᴘeaᴄᴄaiᵹ 16, 29,
55, 462, 498 ; Ó hionᵹaᴘvail,
(s.l.) Ó húᴘvail 77, 277, 497.

Harris, haiᴘiᴘ E 1 ; mac
hannᴘaoi, mac annᴘaoi 2 ;
mac eannᴘaic 47 ; Ó heaᴘ-
ċava, Ó heaᴘċaiv 19.

Harrison, mac annᴘaoi, mac
hannᴘaoi 1 ; Ó heaᴘċava, Ó
heaᴘċaiv 19.

Harrity, Ó haiᴘeaᴄᴄaiᵹ.

Harroe, Ó heaᴘċava.

Harrold, v. Harold.

Horron, v. Haran.

Harroughton, Ó haᴘᴘacᴄáin.

Harrot, haᴘóiv.

Hart, Harte, Ó háiᴘᴄ 11 ; mac
áiᴘᴄ 2 ; haᴘᴄ E 62.

Hartan, Harten, Ó haᴘᴄáin.

Hartery, Ó haiᴘᴄᴘí.

Hartford, ve heaᴘᶂoᴘᴄ.

Hartican, Hartigan, Ó haᴘᴄ-
aᵹáin.

Hartin, Ó haᴘᴄáin.

Hartley, Ó haᴘᴄᵹaile.

Hartnane, Ó heaᴘnáin.

Hartnett, Ó haiᴘᴄnéava.

Hartney, Ó hácaiᴘne.

Harton, Ó haᴘᴄáin.

Hartry, Ó haiᴘᴄᴘí.

Harty, Ó hácaᴘᴄaiᵹ, (s.l.) Ó
háᴘᴄaiᵹ, Ó háᴘᴄa 4 ; mac
áᴘᴄa 197 ; Ó haiᴘeaᴄᴄaiᵹ 52.

Harvey, Ó haiᴘiṁeavaiᵹ 1 ;
E 28.

Harwood, haᴘóiv.

Hasken, Haskin, Ó hoiᴘcín.

Hassan, Ó hoᴘáin.

Hassett, Hassey, Ó haiᴘeava.

Hassin, Hasson, Ó hoᴘáin.

Hastie, mac hoiᴘᴄe, mac oiᴘᴄe

Hasting, Hastings, Ó hoiᴘᴄín.

Hasty, mac hoiᴘᴄe, mac oiᴘᴄe.

Hatton, mac ᵹiolla ċaᴄáin
26, 62.

Haugh, Ó heaċaċ.

Haughan, Ó heaċáin.

Haughean, Ó heaċaivín.

Haughey, Ó heaċaiv, Ó heaċava.

Haughian, Ó heaċaivín.

Haughran, Ó heaċᴘáin.

Haughton, ve hoċᴄún 11 ; Ó
heaċáin 38.

Haveran, Havern, Haveron, v.
Heveran.

Haverty, Ó háváᴘᴄaiᵹ.

Havey, v. Heavey.

Havron, v. Heveran.

Havy, v. Heavey.

Hawe, Hawes, Hawey, Ó
heaċaċ, Ó heaċava, Ó heaċaiv.

Hawkins, háicín E 1 ; Ó heaċáin, Ó heaċaivín 38.

Hay, ve hae 28 ; Ó haova 2.

Hayden, Haydin, Haydon, Ó
heɩveáɩn, Ó heɩveáɩn, Ó
heɩvóɩn, Ó heɩvóɩn 11; ve
héavúɩn 18.

Hayes, Ó haová 11; mac aová
197; ve hae 28.

Hayfron, v. Haffron and
Heveran.

Hayles, mac haol 2; Ó healaɩve 37.

Haynan, v. Heenan.

Haynes, Ó heɩvɩn.

Hays, v. Hayes.

Hayward, héɩbeaɩpc.

Hazel, Hazelton, Hazleton.
Hazelwood mac concoll-
coɩlle.

Headen, Headon, v. Hayden.

Heafy, v. Heaphy.

Heagan,Ó haovaɜáɩn.V.Hagan.

Heagney, Ó heɩɜnɩɜ, Ó héɩɜnɩɜ.

Healion, Ó haoláɩn.

Heally, Healy, Ó héɩlɩve, Ó
héɩlɩɜe 11, Ó healaɩve 2, Ó
hᴅaluɩɜce 77, Ó healuɩɜce
2, (o.f.) Ó healavaɩɜ; Ó
haɩlle 762; Ó ceɩpɩpc 498.

Heanaghan, Heanahan, Ó
héɩneacáɩn, Ó héanacáɩn.

Heanen, v. Heenan.

Heaney, Ó héanna 7, 91, (s.l.)
Ó héanaɩɜ 2, Ó héɩnne 2; Ó
héɩnɩɜ 6, 92; Ó héanavá
972; mac ɜɩolla coɩnnɩɜ
(s.l.) ma'l ceanac 376.

Heanue, Ó hcanavá, Ó héɩn-
eavá.

Heany, v. Heaney.

Heaphy, Ó héamcaɩɜ, (s.l.) Ó
héapa, (o.f.) Ó héamaɩɜ.

Hear, Ó híp.

Hearaghty, Ó hoɩpeaccaɩɜ.

Heare, Ó híp.

Hearn, Hearne, Ó heaccɩɜeɩpn
7; Ó heapáɩn 6; Ó huɩvpín
85; héapún 87.

Hearnon, Ó hɩapnáɩn.

Hearon, v. Hearn.

Hearty, Ó haɜapcaɩɜ, (s.l.) Ó
haopcaɩɜ 1; mac apca 197.

Heary, Ó híopuaɩv.

Heavern, v. Heveran.

Heavey, Heavy, Ó héamaɩɜ, Ó
héɩmɩɜ.

Hedderman, Ó héavpomáɩn.

Hedegan, Ó heɩveaɜáɩn.

Heden, Ó heɩvóɩn, Ó héɩvóɩn.
V. Hayden.

Hedigan, Ó heɩveaɜáɩn 1; Ó
haoɩlleacáɩn 469.

Hedivan, Heduvan, Ó heav-
amáɩn.

Heelan, Ó haoláɩn, (o.f.) Ó
faoláɩn.

Heenan, Ó héanáɩn 11; Ó
héɩneacáɩn, Ó héanacáɩn 192.

Heeney, Heeny, v. Heaney.

Heery, Ó híopuaɩv.

Heever, Ó hɩomaɩp.

Hefferan, Hefferin, v. Heffron.

Heffernan, Heffernin, Heffernon,
Ó hɩpeapnáɩn 11, Ó heapnáɩn
72, 82.

Heffron, Ó héɩmpín 19; Ó
hámpáɩn 68; Ó huɩvpín 85;
Ó hɩpeapnáɩn 7, 78.

Hegan, Hegans, Ó haovaɜáɩn.
V. Hagan.

Hegarty, Hegerty, Heggarty,
Ó héɩɜceapcaɩɜ, Ó héɩɜeapc-
aɩɜ 19, 46, 63, 77; Ó haɜapcaɩɜ, Ó haɜapcaɩɜ 64, 82.

Heggert, Ó haɜaɩpc.

Heggerty, v. Hegarty.

Hegher, Ó hoɩcɩp, Ó haɩcɩp.

Hegney, Ó heɩɜnɩɜ, Ó héɩɜnɩɜ.

Hehir, Ó haɩcɩp, Ó hoɩcɩp.

Heify, v. Heaphy.

Heins, Ó heɩvɩn.

Helbert, Helbet, hoɩleabapv.

Helehan, Ó haoɩlleacáɩn.

Helen, v. Heelan.

Helihan, Hellican, Ó haoɩlleacáɩn.

Hely, v. Healy.

Henaghan, Henahan, Ó héineacáin, Ó héanacáin.

Henan, v. Heenan.

Henchy, Ó háonġuṛa 2; mac Aonġuṛa 2.

Henderson, mac Ainoṛéiṛ, mac Ainoṁaṛa, mac Ainoṁú.

Hendrick, Ó héanṛaic.

Hendry v. Henry.

Heneberry, Henebery, Henebry, ᴅe hionbuṛġa, (ᴅe hinᴅebeṛġ).

Heneghan, Henehan, Ó héineacáin, Ó héanacáin.

Henekan, Ó héanaġáin, Ó héanacáin.

Henery, Ó hinneiṛġe. V. Henry.

Henesy, v. Hennessy.

Heney, v. Heaney.

Henihan, v. Henehan.

Henissy, v. Hennessy.

Henley, v. Hanley.

Hennan, v. Heenan.

Henneberry, Hennebry, ᴅe hionbuṛġa.

Hennelly, Ó hionnġaile.

Hennerty, Ó hionnactaiġ, Ó hinneactaiġ.

Hennessy, Ó háonġuṛa.

Hennigan, Ó héanaġáin.

Henrick, Ó héanṛaic, Ó héannṛaic.

Henright, v. Enright.

Henrion, Ó hionṛáin, Ó hionnṛáin, (o.f.) Ó hionṛaváin, Ó hanṛaváin.

Henry, mac Éinṛí, mac Annṛaoi, mac hannṛaoi 11; Ó hinneiṛġe 6.

Hensy, Ó háonġuṛa.

Heraghty, Ó hoiṛeactaiġ.

Herald, Ó heaṛġail, (o.f.) Ó ṛeaṛġail.

Heran, v. Hearn.

Heraty, Ó hoiṛeactaiġ.

Herbert, hoiṛeabáṛᴅ, hoiṛeabaiṛᴅ 11, hoibeáṛᴅ 17, 77.

Herbertson, Herbison, mac hoiṛeabáiṛᴅ, mac hoiṛeabaiṛᴅ.

Herdman, heaṛman.

Hereward, hoiṛeabáṛᴅ.

Herford, ᴅe heaṛṛoic.

Herguson, mac ṛeaṛġuṛa.

Herley, Herly, Ó heaṛġaile, Ó hiṛġile 10; Ó hiaṛṛlata 79.

Herlihy, Ó hiaṛlata, Ó hiaṛṛlata

Herne, v. Hearne.

Hernon, Ó hiaṛnáin 9, Ó heaṛnáin 2.

Heron, v. Hearn.

Herr, Ó hoiciṛ.

Herran, Ó heaṛáin. V. Hearn.

Herreran, Herrerin, Ó heaṛaṛáin, Ó heaṛaiṛín.

Herrick, Herricks, Ó heiṛc.

Herrigan, Ó háṛṛaġáin.

Herron, v. Hearn.

Hertnan, Hertnon, Ó heaṛnáin.

Hervy, v. Harvey.

Herward, hoiṛeabáṛᴅ.

Heskin, Ó hoiṛcín, Ó huiṛcín.

Heslin, Ó heiṛlin, Ó heiṛleanáin.

Hessian, Hession, Ó hoiṛín.

Hester, Ó hoiṛciṛ.

Hestin, Hestings, Hestion, Ó hoiṛcín.

Heuson, mac aoḃa.

Hevaghan, Ó héaṁacáin, Ó héiṁeacáin.

Hever, Ó hioṁaiṛ.

Heveran, Heverine, Heveron, Ó héiṁṛín 9; Ó huiᴅṛín 8. Cf. Heffron.

Hevey, Ó héiṁiġ, Ó héaṁaiġ.

Hewett, Hewitt, húiġéiᴅ.

Hewlett, Hewlitt, húiléiᴅ.

Hews, v. Hughes.

Hewson, mac aoḃa.

Heydon, v. Hayden.

Heyfron, v. Heffron.

Heyland Ó háoláin.
Hibbard, híbeáꞃⱱ, híobáꞃⱱ.
Hickey Hickie, Ó híceáⱱa, Ó híciⱱe.
Hiffernan, Ó híꞃeaꞃnáin.
Higerty, Ó héiɠeaꞃtaiɠ.
Higgans, Ó háoⱱaɠáin.
Higgens v. Higgans and Higgins
Higgins, Ó huiɠinn, Ó huiɠín.
1 ; Ó huiɠe 778.
Higginson, mac huiɠín.
Highland, Hiland, Ó háoláin.
V. Hyland.
Hilbert, hoileabaꞃⱱ.
Hilferty, Ó háilbeaꞃtaiɠ.
Hill, a' Ċnuic.
Hillan, Hilland, Hillane, Ó hioláin, Ó háoláin.   V.
Hyland.
Hillee, Ó híċċeallaiɠ, (o.f.) Ó ꝼiċċeallaiɠ.
Hillen, v. Hillan.
Hilligan, Ó háilleaɠáin.
Hillind, v. Hilland.
Hilly, v. Hillee.
Hinan, Ó heiⱱoneáin.
Hinchey, Hinchy, Ó háonɠuꞃa, (s.l.) Ó hinꞃe 2 ; mac aonɠuꞃa 2.
Hinds, Hines, v. Hynes.
Hiney,Ó háúnaiⱱ,Ó háiⱱne &c
Hingerty, Hinnerty,Ó hinneáċaiɠ, Ó hionnáċtaiɠ, &c., (o.f.) Ó ꝼinneáċtaiɠ, Ó ꝼionnáċtaiɠ, &c.
Hinsy, v. Hennessy.
Hiraghy, Ó heaꞃċaiⱱ.
Hirl, Ó híꞃɠil.
Hishon, Ó huiꞃeáin, Ó hoiꞃeáin, Ó hoiꞃín.
Hiskey, Ó huiꞃce.
Histion, Histon, Ó hoiꞃtín.
Hoad, Hoade, hóⱱ, hóⱱaċ.
Hoar, Hoare, ⱱe hóꞃ, ⱱe hóꞃa, a hóꞃa, 17, 18, 74, 84 ; Ó huiⱱíꞃ 772 ; Ó heaꞃċaⱱa 29 ; Ó hiomaiꞃ 762.

Hoban, Ó húbáin.
Hobart, Hobard, hoibeáꞃⱱ, hiobáꞃⱱ.
Hobbagan, hobacán.
Hobbard, Hobbart, v. Hobart.
Hobbikin, mac hoibicín, mac Oibicín. V. Hopkins.
Hobbs, hob.
Hobert, v. Hobart.
Hobson, mac hob.
Hoctor, Ó heaċtaiꞃ.
Hodge, hoiꞃce.
Hodgkin, hoiꞃticín.
Hodgkins, Hodgkinson, mac hoiꞃticín.
Hodnett, hoⱱnae ; (G.p.) mac Séaꝼta.
Hoey, Ó heoċaiⱱ, Ó heaċaiⱱ.
Hogan, Ó hÓɠáin11 ; Ó heoċaɠáin 977 ; Ó háoⱱaɠáin 2.
Hogart, Ó hÓɠaiꞃc.
Hogarty, Hogerty, Ó hÓɠaꞃtaiɠ (o.f.) Ó ꝼóɠaꞃtaiɠ.
Hogg, Hogge, hoiꞃce.
Hoins, Ó heoɠain.
Holahan, Ó huallaċáin.
Holey, Ó hoɠlaⱱa, (o.f.) Ó ꝼoɠlaⱱa.
Holian, Ó hÓileáin, (o.f.) Ó ꝼaoláin.
Holland, Ó háoláin 8, 9, 61, (o.f.) Ó ꝼaoláin, (s.l.) Ó hualáin 6, 82, Ó holáin 19, Ó hioláin 97 ; Ó huallaċáin 77 ; Ó maol Ċallann 63.
Holleran, Holloran, Ó hallmuꞃáin.
Holloway, Hollway, ⱱe halbuiⱱe.
Holly, Ó Cuilinn 2 ; mac Cuilinn 2.
Hollywood, ⱱe halabóiⱱ, halabóiⱱ 86 ; Ó Cuileannáin 2.
Holmes, mac Ċómaiꞃ, mac Támaiꞃ, mac Ċomáiꞃ.

Holohan, Holoughan, Ó huallaċ-
áin.
Holoway, ꝺe halḃuiꝺe.
Holt, Holte, hólc.
Holywood, halaḃóiꝺ.
Homes, v. Holmes.
Honahan, Ó huaṁnaċáin.
Honan, Ó heoᵹanáin.
Hone, Ó heoᵹain.
Honeen, Ó huaiċnín.
Hooban, Ó húḃáin.
Hood, Ó huiꝺ.
Hoolaghan, Hoolahan, Hooli-
han, Hoologhan, Ó huallaċ-
áin.
Hooney, Ó huaiċne, Ó huainiꝺe
Ó huaiċniᵹ.
Hop, Hope, hob.
Hopkin, Hopkins, Hopkinson,
mac hoibicín, mac Oibicín,
(s.l.) Ó hoibicín, Ó coibicín,
&c., 19.
Hopps, Hopson, mac hob.
Horogan, v. Horrigan.
Horahan, Ó háppaċáin.
Horaho, Horahoe, Ó heapċaꝺa.
Horan, Ó hóꝺpáin 1 ; Ó hoᵹ-
páin, (o.f.) Ó huᵹpóin 19, 97 ;
Ó hannpáin 73, 85, Ó hápp-
aċáin 27, 45.
Hore, v. Hoare.
Horgan, Ó hapᵹain, Ó hApp-
aᵹáin.
Horish, Ó huapᵹuip.
Horisky, Ó huapuipce.
Horkan, Horkin, Ó hopcáin.
Horoho, Horohoe, Ó heapċaꝺa.
Horrigan, Ó hAppaᵹáin, (o.f.)
Ó hAnpaꝺáin.
Horsey, ꝺe hóppaiᵹ.
Hosey, Hosie, Ó heoꝺapa, Ó
heoꝺupa, Ó heoᵹapa.
Hoskins, Ó huipcín, Ó hoipcín.
Hosty, mac hoipce, mac
Oipce.
Hotchkin, hoipcicín.
Hough, Ó heoċaċ.

Houghegan, Ó heoċaᵹáin.
Houghney, v. Hooney.
Houghton, ꝺe hoċtún.
Houghy, Ó heoċaiꝺ.
Houlaghan, Houlehan, Houli-
han, Ó huallaċáin.
Houneen, Ó huaiċnín.
Hourahan, Hourican, Ó hAnn-
paċáin.
Hourigan, Ó hAnnpaᵹáin 17,
27 ; Ó hóúpaᵹáin 779.
Hourihan, Hourihane, Ó hAnn-
paċáin.
Hourisky, Ó huapuipce.
Houstin, Houston, mac úipcin.
Hoverty, Ó hóᵹapcaiᵹ 1 ; Ó
héiᵹeapcaiᵹ 198.
Howard, hioḃápꝺ 48, 49 ; héi-
ḃeapc 19 ; Ó hioṁaip 76 ;
Ó hoᵹaipc 2.
Howay, Ó heoċaiꝺ.
Howe, Ó heoċaꝺa.
Howel, Howell, Howells, haol,
mac haol.
Howen, Ó heoᵹain.
Howes, Ó heoċaꝺa.
Howett, húiᵹéiꝺ.
Howey, Howie, Ó heoċaiꝺ.
Howitt, húiᵹéiꝺ.
Howlen, v. Howlin.
Howlet, Howlett, húiᵹléiꝺ,
húiléiꝺ.
Howley, Ó huallaiᵹ.
Howlin, Howling, huiᵹlín,
húilín.
Hoy, Hoye, Ó heoċaiꝺ, Ó
heoċaꝺa.
Hoyle, Hoyles, (?) mac ᵹiolla-
ċoille.
Hoyne, Hoynes, Ó heoᵹain.
Huban, Ó húḃáin.
Hubbard, Hubbart, Hubbert,
hobápꝺ, hoibeápꝺ, hiobápꝺ,
hibeápꝺ.
Hubbock, hubuc, hobac.
Huddy, Ó huaꝺa, (s.l.) Ó
huꝺaiᵹ 976.

Hue, Hueson, Mac Aoḋa.
Huett, Húiġéid.
Huey, Ó hEoċaiḋ.
Huggins, Ó hAoḋagáin.
Hugginson, Mac Huigín.
Hughes, Ó hAoḋa 11; Mac Aoḋa 192.
Hughey, Mac Eoċaiḋ.
Hughs, v. Hughes.
Hughston, Mac Úistín.
Huleat, Huiġléid, Húiléid.
Hulihan, Ó hUallaċáin.
Hultaghan, Hultahan, Ó hUltaċáin.
Humfrey, Humphrey, Unfraiḋ.
Humphreys, Humphries, Mac Unfraiḋ, Mac Hunfraiḋ.
Huneen, Ó hUaiṫnín.
Hunt, Ó Fiaiċ 11, Ó Féiċ 2; Ó Fiaċa, Ó Fiaċaċ 47, 72; Ó Fiaċna, Ó Fiaċnaċ 29, 34, 172, 192, 272, 772; Ó Fiaċra, Ó Fiaċraċ 25, 33, 48; Hunt E 2.
Hunter, (?) Ó Fiaċa, Ó Fiaċaċ 7.
Hurley, Ó hUrṫuile, Ó hUirṫuile 11; Ó Comáin 197, 462 772; Ó hIarflaṫa 7792; Ó Murṫuile 7792.
Hurney, Ó hUrnaiḋe.
Hurroe, Ó hEarċaḋa.
Hurst, de Hórsaiġ, (s.l.) Ó hOrsaiġ 47.
Hussey, de Hosae, de Húsae, Húsae, Hiosae 17, 18, 43, 49; Ó hEoḋusa 6, 9. 72, 82.
Hussian, Ó hOisín.
Huston, Mac Úistín.
Hutch, Huiste
Hutchinson, Huisteaċáin 979.
Hyde, de Híde 1; Ó Seiṫeaċáin 779.
Hylan, Hyland, Ó hAoláin, 1, (o.f.) Ó Faoláin, (s.l.) Ó hAoileáin 72, Ó hOileáin 82, 191, Ó hOláin 192, Ó hIoláin 97.
Hyle, Hyles, v. Hoyle, Hoyles.
Hynan, Ó hEiḋneáin.
Hyndes, Hynds, v. Hynes.
Hynes, Ó hEiḋin 11, Ó hÉiḋin 2; Ó hEoġain 6, 24, 44.
Hyney, Ó hAḋnaiḋ, Ó hAḋnaiġ, Ó hAiḋne, Ó hEiḋniġ.

Iago, Iagó 1; Mac Iagó 9.
Igo, Igoe, Mac Iagó 11, Mac Iagóg 92.
Ildowney, Mac Giolla Doṁnaiġ.
Ilhinney, Mac Giolla Ċoinniġ.
Ilroy, Mac Giollaruaiḋ.
Ilwee, Mac Giollaḃuiḋe.
Inglesby, v. Ingoldsby.
Inglis, Ingléis, Inglis. V. English.
Ingoldsby, Mac an Ġallóglaiġ.
Ingram, Iongram.
Innes, Innis, Mac Aonġuis.
Inright, v. Enright.
Insgelby v. Ingoldsby.
Ireland, de Írleont, Írleont.
Irish, de Iréis, Iréis.
Irrington, Ó hArraċtáin.
Irvine, Irving, Irwin, Ó hEireaṁóin 1; Ó Ciarṁacáin 772
Ivers, Ivor, Ivors, Ó hÍoṁair 76, 93; Mac Íoṁair 19.

Jack, Jacke, Jackman, Seac.
Jackson, Mac Siacais, Mac Siacuis.
Jacob, Iacob.
Jacques, Siacus.
Jaffery, Jaffrey, Seafraiḋ.
Jago, Jagoe, Iagó.
James, Séamus.
Jameson, Jamieson, Jamison, Mac Séamuis.
Jarman, Iarmyn, Gearmán.
Jarrett, Gearóid.
Jarvis, Gearḃás
Jeffers. Jefferson, Jeffreson, Mac Seafraiḋ.
Jeffery, Jeffrey, Seafraiḋ.

Jeffries, mac Seaṗṁaiṫ.

Jemison, mac Séamuir.

Jenkin, Seinicín.

Jenkins, Jenkinson, Jenkison, mac Seinicín.

Jennens, Jennings, mac Seinín 10 ; mac Seóinín 9, (s.l.) Ó Ceóinín 19.

Jerety, maż Oiṗeaċtaiż.

Jerman, Jermyn, Żeaṗmán.

Jerrett, Żeaṗóiṫ.

Jervaise, Jervis, Żeaṗḃáṗ.

Jimison, mac Séamuir.

Jinkins, mac Seinicín.

Johnson, Johnston, Johnstone, mac Seáin, mac Seaġáin 1, mac Seóin 2, mac eóin 2.

Joie, Seóiż.

Jones, mac Seóin, Seónṗ.

Jordan, Jorden, Jordon, Jourdan, Siúṗṫán, Siúṗtán 10 ; mac Siúṗtáin 9.

Joy, Seoż, Seóiż, Seożaċ, Seoiżeaċ.

Joyce, Seożaṗ, Seóṗaċ 24, 77 ; Seoż, Seóiż, Seożaċ, Seoiżeaċ 1, Seoiżeaċ 2.

Joyner, Siúinéiṗ.

Joynt, ṫe Siúnta.

Judge, mac an Ḃṗeiteaṁan, mac an Ḃṗeiteaṁnaiż, mac an Ḃṗeitiṁ.

Julian, Julien, żilleán.

Jurdan, v. Jordan.

Kadell, Kadle, Caṫal.

Kain, Kaine, v. Kane.

Kairns, v. Kearns.

Kanavaghan, Ó Connṁaċáin.

Kane, Ó Catáin 11 ; mac Aoṫáin, (s.l.) Ó Caoṫáin 92.

Kangley, Ó Coinżeallaiż, mac Coinżeallaiż 78, 779 ; mac Ceanżlaiż 53, 67.

Kappock, ṫe Ceaṗóc, ṫe Ceaṗóż.

Karey, v. Carey.

Karr, v. Carr.

Kavanagh, Kavenagh, Caoṁánaċ, (o.s) mac Muṗċaṫa Caoṁánaċ 81 ; Ó Caoṁáin, Ó Caoṁánaiż 7, 9, 15, 24, 25.

Keady, Ó Céaṫaiż, mac Céaṫaiż 9 ; mac Céṫoiż, (o.f.) Ó meicéṫoiż 77.

Keag, mac taiḋż

Keaghery, mac ṗiaċṗa, mac ṗiaċṗaċ

Keague, mac taiḋż .

Keahan, Ó Caoċáin, mac Caoċáin.

Keahery, mac ṗiaċṗa, mac ṗiaċṗaċ

Kealahan, Ó Céileaċáin

Kealy, Ó Caollaiṫe, Ó Caollaiże 45, 78, 87 ; Ó Caṫla 9 ; Ó Céile 86.

Kean, Keane, Ó Catáin 11 ; Ó Céin 47 ; mac Aoṫáin, (s.l.) Ó Caoṫáin 92.

Keaney, Keany, Ó Cianaiż (S.L.) 97.

Keappock, ṫe Ceaṗóc, ṫe Ceaṗóż.

Kearin, Kearn, Kearnes, v. Kearns.

Kearney, Ó Ceaṗnaiż 11 ; mac Ceaṗnaiż 13, 16, 38, 43 ; Ó Cataṗnaiż 172, 192 ; Ó Ceiteaṗnaiż 192.

Kearns, Kearon, Kearons, Ó Céiṗín, Ó Ciaṗáin 11, (s.l.) Ó Ceaṗáin, Ó Cioṗáin 19 ; Ó Ceiteaṗnaiż 2.

Kearsey, ṫe Céaṗṗaiż, (s.l.) Ciaṗaṗaċ.

Kearson, mac ṗiaṗair.

Keary, Ó Ciaṗṫa 8 ; mac ṗiaċṗa, mac ṗiaċṗaċ 9 ; (?) mac żiolla Céiṗe 2.

Kearse, mac ṗiaṗair.

Keating, Keatinge, Céitinn 11 ; Ó Céatṗaṫa 462.

Keatley, Ó żatlaoiċ.

Keaty, Ó Céatfaóa.

Keaveney, Keaveny, Ó ʒéiḃeannaiʒ 94; mac ʒéiḃeann-aiʒ 6, 93; Ó coiḃḋeanaiʒ 8; Ó caománaiʒ 2.

Keavy, Ó Ciaḃaiʒ.

Keawell, mac Caṫṁaoil

Kedney, v Kidney.

Kee, mac aoió

Keefe, Keeffe, Ó caoiṁ.

Keegan, mac aoóaʒáin, 1 (s.l.) Ó caoʒáin 9.

Keehan, Ó caoċáin, mac caoċáin.

Keelaghan, Ó Céileaċáin.

Keelan, Ó caoláin.

Keeley, v. Kealy.

Keelighan, Ó Cóileaċáin.

Keelin, Keeling, v. Keelan.

Keelty, Ó caoilte, Ó caoiltiʒ.

Keely, v. Kealy.

Keena, v. Keeny.

Keenaghan, Ó coinneaċáin, Ó cuinneaċáin.

Keenan, Ó cianáin 1; mac finʒin, (s.l.) mac cinín 34; Ó cuinneaċáin 2.

Keene, v. Keane.

Keeney, Keeny, Ó cianaiʒ.

Keerawin, Ó ciarrouḃáin, Ó ciorrouḃáin.

Keerivick, Ó ciarṁaic, Ó cíuṁic.

Keern, v. Kieran.

Keesack, v. Cusack.

Keeshan, Ó cireáin.

Keevan, Keevane, o caoṁáin 11; Ó ciaḃáin 779.

Keevers, mac íomair.

Keevey, Ó ciaḃaiʒ.

Keevlin, Ó ciḃlín 1, Ó ciḃleaċáin 976.

Kegley, Ó coiʒealaiʒ, Ó coiʒliʒ.

Keheerin, mac eiċtiʒeirín.

Kehelly, mac caoċlaoiċ, (o.f.) (?) mac caoċfile, (s.l,) mac claoċlaoiċ.

Kehering, v. Keᵖeerin.

Keherny, Ó ceitearnaiʒ, mac ceitearnaiʒ.

Kehigan, mac eoċaʒáin.

Kehilly, v. Kehelly.

Kehoe, mac eoċaóa

Keighron, Ó cíocaráin.

Keighry, mac fiacra, mac fiaċraċ.

Keightley, Ó ʒatlaoiċ.

Keilly, v. Keily.

Keiltagh, Ó caoilte, Ó caoiltiʒ.

Keily, Ó caóla 11; mac caoċlaoiċ 779.

Keiran, Keirans, Ó ciaráin.

Keitley, Ó ʒatlaoiċ.

Kelaghan, Keleghan, Kelihan, Kellaghan, Ó Céileaċáin.

Kellard, v. Keller.

Kelledy, Ó callaóa.

Kellegher, Ó céileaċair.

Kellegy, Ó calʒaiʒ.

Kelleher, Keller, Ó céileaċair

Kelley v. Kelly.

Kelliher, Ó céileaċair.

Kellops, mac filib.

Kelrick, (?) mac ʒiollaḃṁic.

Kelly, Ó ceallaiʒ (s.l.) Ó cealla 11; mac ceallaiʒ 2; Ó caollaióe, Ó caollaiʒe 17, 24, 49; mac ʒiolla ċeallaiʒ 972; Ó caóla 492; mac caoċlaoiċ 7792.

Kenah, v. Kenna.

Kenchyla, v. Kinsella.

Kendellan, Ó caoinoealḃáin.

Kendrick, mac eanraic, mac eanrpaic.

Kenealy, Kenelly, v. Kenneally.

Kenerney, mac an Oirċinniʒ.

Kenlan, v. Kennellan.

Kenna, Kennah, Ó cionaoiċ 4, (s.l.) Ó cionáiċ, Ó cineáiċ, Ó cnáċ.

Kennane, Ó Coineáin, Ó Cuineáin.
Kenneally, Kennealy, Ó Cinnḟaolaiḋ 11 ; Ó Coingeallaiġ, Mac Coingeallaiġ 24, 779. V. Kennelly.
Kennedy, Ó Cinnéide, Ó Cinnéidiḋ, Ó Cinnéidiġ.
Kennefeck, de Cinipéic, Cinipéic.
Kennellan, Ó Caoinḋealḃáin.
Kennelly, Ó Cinnḟaolaiḋ 71 ; Ó Coingeallaiġ, Mac Coingeallaiġ 24, 779 ; Ó Congáile, Mac Congáile 19, 97.
Kennifeck, de Cinipéic, Cinipéic.
Kenning, Kennon, Mac Coinín 2 ; Mac ḟingin 2.
Kenny, Ó Cionaoḋa, Ó Cionaoiṫ 11 ; Mac Cionaoḋa, Mac Cionaoiṫ 2 ; Ó Coinne 38, Ó Coinniġ 32 ; Mac Giolla Coinniġ 2.
Kennyon, Kenyon Mac Coinín 2 ; Mac ḟingin 2.
Kenrick, Mac eanraic, Mac eanraic.
Kent, de Ceannt, Ceannt, Cint.
Kenure, Mac ḟionnḃairr.
Keogan, Mac eoċagáin, (s.l.) Ó Ceogáin.
Keogh, Mac eoċaḋa, Mac eoċaċ, (s.l.) Mac Ceoċ, Mac Ceoċaċ.
Keoghane, Mac eoċáin, (s.l.) Ó Ceoċáin.
Keoghoe, Keoghy, Mac eoċaḋa, Mac eoċaiḋ.
Keohane, Mac eoċáin, (s.l.) Ó Ceoċáin.
Keon, Mac eóin 2 ; Mac eogáin 2.
Keoneen, Mac Seóinín, (s.l.) Ó Ceóinín.
Keough, v. Keogh.
Keown, Mac eogáin 2 ; Mac eóin 2.

Keppock, de Ceapóc, de Ceapóg.
Kerans, Ó Ciaráin.
Kerbin, Ó Coirbín.
Kerby, v. Kirby.
Kerdiffe, de Carduiḃ.
Kereen, Ó Céirín.
Kerevan, Ó Ciarduḃáin.
Kergan, Kerigan, Ó Ciaragáin.
Kerin, Kerins, Ó Céirín.
Kerisey, v. Kearsey.
Kerivan, Kerivin, Ó Ciarduḃáin, Ó Cíorduḃáin.
Kerley, Mac ḟeargaile 2 ; Mac Ṫoirḃealḃaiġ 2.
Kerlin, Ó Coirealláin.
Kerly, v. Kerley.
Kermode, Mac Ḋiarmada.
Kermody, Ó Cearmada.
Kernaghan, Kernahan, Ó Cearnaċáin.
Kernan, Ó Cearnaċáin 16, 29 ; Mac Ṫiġearnáin 67.
Kerney, Ó Ceiṫearnaiġ, Mac Ceiṫearnaiġ.
Kernohan, v. Kernahan.
Kernon, v. Kernan.
Kerns, Kerons, v. Kearns.
Kerr, v. Carr.
Kerragher, Mac ḟearċair.
Kerragy, v. Carrigy.
Kerraher, Mac ḟearċair.
Kerrane, Ó Cearáin, Ó Cioráin.
Kerrigan, Ó Ciaragáin 11 ; Ó Cíocaráin 972.
Kerrin, Kerrins, Ó Céirín 1, Ó Ciaráin 2.
Kerris, Kerrish, Kerrisk, Kerrison, Mac ḟiarair 1, (s.l.) Ó Ceirisc 498.
Kervan, Ó Cearḃáin.
Kerwick, Ó Ciarṁaic, Ó Cirṁic.
Kerwin, Ó Ciarduḃáin.
Keshin, v. Cashin.
Kessidy, v. Cassidy.
Kett, Ó Ceit, Ceaṫaċ.
Kettle, Kettyle, Mac Coitil.

Kevane, Kevans, Ó Caomháin.
Kevany, Kevanny, Keveney, Keveny, Kevney, Ó Géibeannaig 94; mac Géibeannaig 6, 93; Ó Coibdeanaig 8; Ó Caománaig 2.
Keverney, (?) Ó Coibdeanaig.
Keville, Ó Cibil 1, Ó Ciblín 192.
Kevin, Ó Caoimhín.
Kevlean, Ó Ciblín 1, Ó Cibleacáin 92.
Kevlihan, Ó Cibleacáin.
Keyes, Keys, mac Aoid, mac Aoda 979; (?) mac an Caoic 58, 73.
Kickham, Ciceam.
Kidney, Ó Dubáin 77.
Kielly, Ó Caóla.
Kielt, Kielty, Ó Caoilte, Ó Caoiltig.
Kiely, Ó Caóla.
Kieran, Ó Ciaráin.
Kiernan, mac Tigearnáin 11; Ó Cearnacáin 62.
Kiervan, Ó Ciardubáin, Ó Cíorrubáin.
Kierce, mac Fiarair.
Kilahy, mac Giolla acaid (O'G.).
Kilamartin, mac Giolla Mártain.
Kilbane, mac Giollabáin.
Kilbeg, mac Giollabig.
Kilboy, mac Giollabuide.
Kilbride, mac Giolla Brígde.
Kilby, mac Giollabuide.
Kilcar, Kilcarr, mac Giolla Catair.
Kilcash, mac Giollacair.
Kilchreest, Kilchriest, Kilchrist, mac Giolla Críost.
Kilcline, mac Giollaclaoin.
Kilcommons, mac Giolla Comáin.
Kilcooley, mac Giolla Cúille.
Kilcourse, (?) mac Giollagairb.

Kilcoyne, mac Giollacaoin, mac Giolla Cáoine.
Kilcrow, mac Giollagairb.
Kilcullen, mac Giolla Coillin, mac Giolla Caillin.
Kilday, Kildea, mac Giolla Dé.
Kilduff, mac Giolladuib.
Kildunn, mac Giolladuinn.
Kilfedder, Kilfeder, mac Giolla Peadair.
Kilfillan, mac Giolla Faoláin.
Kilfoyle, mac Giolla Póil.
Kilgallen, Kilgallon, mac Giolla Caillin.
Kilgannon, mac Giolla Gannáin.
Kilgar, mac Giollagéairr.
Kilgarriff, mac Giollagairb.
Kilgray, mac Giollariabaig.
Kilgrew, mac Giollagairb.
Kilgrist, mac Giolla Críort.
Kilgunn, mac Giolladuinn.
Kilkeary, mac Giolla Céire.
Kilkelly, mac Giolla Ceallaig.
Kilken, mac Uilcín.
Kilkenny, mac Giolla Coinnig.
Kilker, mac Giollagéir.
Kilkey, mac Giollacaoic.
Kilkison, Kilkisson, mac Uilcín.
Killackey, mac Giolla acaid (O'G.).
Killan, Killane, Ó Cilleáin.
Killby, mac Giollabuide 11; Ó Giollabuide 62.
Killeavy, mac Duinnfléibe.
Killeen, Ó Cillín.
Killelea, mac Giollaléit.
Killemeade, Killemet, mac Uilliméid.
Killen, Ó Cillín.
Killeran, mac Giollaráin, (o.f.) mac Giolla Éanáin.
Killerlean, mac an Firléiginn.
Killery, mac Giollariabaig.
Killevy, mac Duinnfléibe.
Killgore (?) mac Giollagairb,
Killian, Ó Cillín, Ó Cilleáin.

Killiger, a Cligeóiṗ (S.L.) 77.
Killimith, mac Uilliméiv.
Killin, Killion, Ó Cillín, Ó Cilleáin.
Killips, mac Ḟilib.
Killkelly, mac Ġiolla Ċeallaiġ.
Killooley, mac Ġiollaġuala.
Killops, mac Ḟilib.
Killoran, mac Ġiolla Luaiċ-ṗinn.
Kilmartin, mac Ġiolla Ṁáṗ-ṫain.
Kilmary, mac Ġiolla Ṁuiṗe.
Kilmet, mac Uilliméiv.
Kilmore, Kilmurry, mac Ġiolla Ṁuiṗe.
Kiloughry, Kiloury, mac Con-luaċṗa.
Kilpatrick, mac Ġiolla Páv-ṗaiġ.
Kilrain, Kilrane, mac Ġiolla-ṗáin, (o.f.) mac Ġiolla Éanáin.
Kilroe, mac Ġiollaṗuaiṿ.
Kilronan, mac Ġiolla Rónáin.
Kilroy, mac Ġiollaṗuaiṿ.
Kilty, Ó Caoilte, Ó Caoiltiġ.
Kilvey, mac Ġiollaḃuiṿe.
Kimins, Kimmings, Kimmins, mac Coimín, mac Cuimín.
Kinaghan, Kinahan, Ó Coinneaċáin, Ó Cuinneaċáin.
Kinane, Ó Cuinneáin.
Kinarney, mac an Aiṗċinniġ.
Kinavan, Ó Ceannvuḃáin.
Kincaid, Cinnicéiv.
Kincart, mac an Ċeaiṗt (S.L.) 19.
Kinchela, Kinchella, Kinchley Cinnṗealaċ 1; Ó Cinnṗealaiġ 2.
Kindellan, Ó Caoinvealḃáin.
Kindregan, Ó Cinnveaṗġáin.
Kine, Ó Caṿain.
Kinealy, v. Kenneally.
Kineavy, Ó Cinnċnáṁa nó mac Conṗnáṁa.

Kinerney, mac an Oiṗċinniġ.
King, Ó Cingeav, Ó Cionġa 88, 89, 97, 199, 462; mac Con-ṗaoi 17, 19, 49, 64, 97; mac Ḟeaṗavaiġ 2; mac Conṗuain 2; mac Ġiollaṗuaiṿ 2.
Kingarty, Kingerty, mac Ḟinn-eaċta, mac Ḟinneaċtaiġ.
Kinghan, Ó Cuinneáin.
Kingsley, Ó Cinnṗealaiġ (O'D.)
Kingston, Kingstone, mac Cloċ-aiṗe 55; mac Oinṗeamáin, (s.l.) Ó Cinnṗeamáin, Cinn-ṗeamáin 779.
Kinighan, Kinihan, Ó Coinneaċ-áin, Ó Cuinneaċáin.
Kiniry, mac Inneiṗġe.
Kinlan, Kinlen, Ó Caoinleáin, (o.f.) Ó Caoinvealḃáin.
Kinlough, mac Conloċa.
Kinna, v. Kenna.
Kinnan, Ó Cianáin 62; mac Ḟionnáin 2; Ó Cuinneaċáin 2.
Kinnane, Ó Cuinneáin, Ó Cuin-eáin.
Kinnavane, Ó Ceannvuḃáin.
Kinnavy, v. Kineavy.
Kinneally, Kinnealy, v. Kenneally.
Kinnear, mac an Ḟiṗ.
Kinneen, mac Coinín.
Kinneevy, v. Kineavy.
Kinnegan, Ó Cuinneaġáin, mac Cuinneaġáin.
Kinner, mac an Ḟiṗ.
Kinnerk, mac an Aiṗċinn, mac an Oiṗċinn 1; mac Eanṗaic 469.
Kinnevane, Ó Ceannvuḃáin.
Kinney, v. Kenny.
Kinnian, Ó Coinín, Ó Cuinín.
Kinnier, mac an Ḟiṗ.
Kinnighan, Ó Cuinneaċáin, Ó Cuinneaġáin.
Kinnock, Ó Cuineóg.
Kinregan, Ó Cinnveaṗġáin.
Kinrock, mac Eanṗaic.

Kinsela, Kinsella, Kinshela, Kinsley, CınnﬁeaLaċ 1, Ó CınnﬁeaLaıġ 2.
Kinucane, mac Fıonnṁacáın.
Kirby, Ó Cıaﬁṁaıc 1, (s.l.) Ó Cıaﬁba 17, 46, 49 ; Ó Coıﬁbín 92 ; mac Ġeıﬁble 192.
Kirivan, Ó Cıaﬁ˜ḃuḃáın, Ó Cíoﬁ˜ḃáın.
Kirk, Ó Cuıﬁc.
Kirkpatrick, mac ĠıoLLa Ṗáoﬁaıġ.
Kirland, Ó CoıﬁeaLLáın.
Kirley, v. Kerley.
Kirlin, Ó CoıﬁeaLLáın.
Kiroy, mac Cıoṫnuaıḋ.
Kirrane, Ó Cıoﬁáın, (o.f.) Ó Cıaﬁáın.
Kirrell, Ó CoıﬁıLL.
Kirvan, Kirwan, Kirwen, Kirwin, Ó Cıaﬁ˜ḃuḃáın, Ó Cíoﬁ˜ḃáın 11 ; Ó Ceaﬁḃáın 82 ; Ó Cıaﬁaġáın 972.
Kissack, v. Cusack.
Kissane, Ó Cıoﬁáın, (o.f.) Ó Caﬁáın.
Kissick, Kissock, v. Cusack.
Kitson, mac Ceıt 469.
Kitterick, Kittrick, mac Śıtﬁıc.
Kiville, Ó CıḃıL 1. Ó Cıḃlín 192.
Klyne, v. Cline.
Klisham, mac Clıﬁeam (S.L.) 19.
Kneafsey, Ó Cnáıṁﬁıġe.
Knee, Ó nıaḋ.
Kneeland, Ó nıaLLáın.
Knight, mac an Rıoıﬁe 2 ; mac neaċtaın 62.
Kniland, Knilans, Ó nıaLLáın.
Knowd, Ó nuaḋat.
Knowels, Knowles, Ó CnúċaıL, Ó CnúṫġaıL.
Knox, ve Cnoc.
Koen, Ó Comḋáın, Ó Comġaın 11 ; mac Eoġaın 2.
Korish, mac Feóﬁaıﬁ, mac Feóﬁuıﬁ.

Kough, mac Eoċaḋa.
Kulkeen, Kulkin, mac Uılcín.
Kyley, Ó Caola.
Kyne, Ó Caḋáın.

Lacey, v. Lacy.
Lachlin, Ó LaċLaınn.
Lacy, ve Léıﬁ, léıﬁeaċ 1 ; Ó Laıteaﬁa, Ó Laıtġeaﬁa, (o.f.) Ó Flaıteaﬁa, Ó Flaıtġeaﬁa 87.
Ladden, Ó Laıveáın, Ó Loıveáın.
Ladrigan, v. Landregan.
Laffan, Laffen, Lapán.
Lafferty, Ó Laıtḃeaﬁtaıġ, (o.f.) Ó Flaıtḃeaﬁtaıġ.
Laffey, Laffy, Ó Laıtıṁ, (s.l.) Ó Laıtṁe, Ó Lataıġ, (o.f.) Ó Flaıtıṁ.
Lagan, Ó Leoġáın.
Laghlen, Laghlin, Ó LaċLaınn.
Lahan, Ó Laċáın 2 ; Ó Leaċáın 976.
Laheen, (?) O Laıtín, (o.f.) Ó Laıtıṁín, Ó Flaıtıṁín.
Laherty, Ó Laıtḃeaﬁtaıġ, (o.f.) Ó Flaıtḃeaﬁtaıġ.
Lahey, Lahiff, Lahiffe, Lahive, Lahy, Ó Laıtıṁ, Ó Lataıġ, (o.f.) Ó Flaıtıṁ.
Laine, Ó Leaċáın 976.
Laing, Ó Laınn, (o.f.) Ó Flaınn.
Laird, v. Lord.
Lally, Ó maoLaLaıḋ, (o.f.) Ó maoL Falaıḋ.
Lalor, Ó LeaċLoḃaıﬁ.
Laman, v. Lammon.
Lamb, v. Lambe.
Lambart, v. Lambert.
Lambe, Ó Luaın 11 ; Ó Luanáın 16 ; Ó nuaḋan, Ó nuaḋáın 5, 9.
Lambert, Laımbeaﬁt 1 ; Lampoﬁt 28.
Lambin, Lambyn, Laımbín.

Lammon, Lamon, Lamond, Lamont, mac laṡmainn, mac laṁmainn.

Lampart, Lampert, v. Lambert.

Landers, ve lonoṗar, ve lunoṗar, lomoṗaraċ, lunoṗaraċ 1, ve lonoṗa, lonoṗaċ 79 ; leainoi (S.L.) 47.

Landon, ve lonoún.

Landregan, Ó lonġarġáin.

Landrey, ve lonoṗa. V. Landers.

Landy, leainoi.

Lane, Ó laiġin, Ó laioín 1, (s.l.) Ó liaġain, Ó liaváin, Ó liġin, Ó lioín 47, 79, Ó leiġin, Ó leioín 772 ; Ó leaċáin 976 ; ve léiġinn, ve léin, léiġinn E 2.

Laney, Ó 'Duḃḟláine, Ó 'Duḃḟláinġe.

Lang, Ó lainn, (o.f.) Ó ḟlainn.

Langan, Ó lonġáin.

Langford, lanġṗorc, lonġṗorc·

Langin, Ó lonġáin.

Langton, ve lanġcún, lanġcún.

Lanigan, Ó lonaġáin, Ó luineaġáin.

Lannan, Lannen, Ó leannáin 1 ; Ó lonáin, (s.l.) Ó lionáin 779·

Lannigan, v. Lanigan.

Lannin, Lannon, Lanon, v. Lannan.

Lant, lannc.

Laphin, Ó laṗáin 3 ; laṗán 4.

Lapin, Lappin, Ó laṗáin.

Laracy, Ó learġura.

Lardner, Ó lorġnáin, Ó loirġneáin.

Larens, laḃranc, laḃṗár.

Largan, Ó lorġnáin, Ó loirġneáin.

Larken, Larkin, Larkins, Ó lorcáin.

Larney, Ó maoil earna 89, (s.l.) Ó leáṗnaċ 64.

Larrissy, Ó learġura.

Latten, laicín.

Lauder, láioiṗ.

Laugheran, v. Lougheran.

Laughlin, v. Loughlin.

Laughnan, Ó laċcnáin.

Launders, v. Landers.

Laurence, laḃranc, laḃṗár.

Laurison, mac laḃṗainn, mac laḃṗáir.

Lavallen, Lavallin, leaḃailin.

Lavan, Ó láiṁín 91, Ó láṁáin 92, (o.f.) Ó ḟlaiciṁín, Ó ḟlaiceaṁáin.

Lavelle, Ó maolḟáḃail.

Laven, v. Lavan.

Laverty, Ó laicḃearcaiġ, (o.f) Ó ḟlaicḃearcaiġ.

Lavery, Ó laḃraóa.

Lavin, v. Lavan.

Lavins, v. Levins.

Lawder, láioiṗ.

Lawell, Ó maolḟáḃail.

Lawlee, láLaióe.

Lawler, Ó leaċloḃaiṗ.

Lawless, laiġléir 11 (s.l.) laiġṗéir 972.

Lawlor, Ó leaċloḃaiṗ.

Lawrance, Lawrence, laḃranc, laḃṗár.

Lawrenson, Lawrinson, Lawrison, Lawson, mac laḃṗainn, mac laḃṗáir.

Lawton, Ó laċcnáin.

Layne, Ó laiġin, Ó laioín. V. Lane.

Layng, Ó lainn, (o.f.) Ó ḟlainn.

Lea, v. Lee.

Leach, Leache, v. Leech.

Leacy, v. Lacy.

Leader, léavaṗ.

League, v. Leeogue.

Leahey, Leahy, Ó laoċóa 11, (s.l.) Ó laoċṗa 469 ; Ó Laċaiġ, (o.f.) Ó laicíṁ, Ó ḟlaicíṁ 782.

Leamy, Ó Laomḋa, Ó Léime (K.).

Lean, Leane, Ó Liaġáin, Ó Liaḋáin, Ó Liġin, Ó Liḋín, (o.f.) Ó Laiḋín, Ó Laiġín.

Learhinan, Ó Loiṗġneáin.

Leary, Ó Laoġaire.

Leavy, mac Ḋuinnṡléiḃe.

Leddan, Ó Loiḋeáin, Ó Luiḋeáin 11 (o.f.) Ó Loḋáin, (s.l.) Ó Lioḋáin 92.

Leddy, Ó Liḋeaḋa.

Ledger, ⅁e Sailiġéiṗ, Sailiġéiṗ Sailinġéiṗ, Sailinéiṗ, Saileaṗcaṗ.

Ledwich, Ledwidge, Ledwitch Ledwith, ⅁e Léaḃúṗ, Léaḃúṗ.

Lee, Ó Laiḋiġ 9, Ó Laoiḋiġ 7; mac Laiḋiġ, mac Laoiḋiġ 45; mac an Leaġa 3; Liac 2; ⅁e Léiġ 14, 24, 43, &c.

Leeane, Ó Liacáin.

Leech, Liaiġ 1; Ó Laoġós, Ó Laoḃós 94.

Leehan, Leehane, Ó Liacáin.

Leehy, v. Leahy.

Leeman, Leemon, v. Lemon.

Leen, v. Lean.

Leeney, Ó Laiġniġ.

Leeogue, Ó Laoġós, Ó Laoḃós.

Leery, v. Leary.

Lees, v. Lee

Leeson, * Ó Liṗeáin.

Leetch, v. Leech.

Legge, ⅁e Léiġ; mac Coire (O'D.).

Lehane, Ó Liacáin.

Lehy, v. Leahy.

Leicester, ⅁e Leaṗcaṗ.

Leigh, ⅁e Léiġ 1; mac Laiḋiġ 82; mac an Leaġa 62.

Leland, mac Ġiolla Ṗaoláin.

Lemmon, Lemon, mac Laġmainn 6; Ó Lomáin 4.

Lenagan, Ó Luineaġáin.

Lenaghan, Lenahan, Ó Léanacáin, Ó Líonacáin 9.

Lenane, Ó Lonáin, (s.l.) Ó Lionáin 779; Ó Luingeáin, (o.f.) Ó Longáin 47. V. Lennon.

Lenard, v. Leonard.

Lenden, Ó Leanḋáin, Ó Leannáin.

Leneghan, Lenehan, Ó Léanacáin, Ó Líonacáin 9.

Lenigan, Ó Luineacáin.

Lenihan, Ó Léanacáin, Ó Líonacáin 9; Ó Luingeacáin 71, (s.l.) Ó Luineacáin, Ó Laoineacáin 72.

Lennard, v. Leonard.

Lennihan, v. Lenihan.

Lennon, Ó Leannáin, Ó Lionnáin 1; Ó Lonáin 77,82, Ó Luinín,23.

Lennox, Lenox, Loaṁnac.

Lenord, v. Leonard.

Lenton, v. Linton.

Leo, ⅁e Liac.

Leogue, Ó Laoġós, Ó Laoḃóg.

Leonard, Lionárⅾ E 2; Ó Lionnáin, Ó Leannáin 61, 91; Ó Lonáin 77, 78, (s.l.) Ó Lionáin 779; Ó Luingeáin, (o.f.) Ó Longáin 79a; Ó Luinín 23, 34, 35; mac Loineáin 976; mac Ġiolla Ṗinnéin 23, mac Ġiolla Ṗionnáin 2; mac Ġiolla Seanáin. mac Ġiolla Síonáin, (s l.), maġ Uinnṗeannáin, maġ Uinnṗionnáin 33, 43, 67.

Lerhinan, Lerkinan, Ó Loiṗġneáin.

Leslie, ⅁e Lioṗla, Leaṗlaoi.

Lester, ⅁e Leaṗcaṗ, Leaṗcaṗ 2; mac Alaṗcaiṗ 62.

L'Estrange, Scṗáinṗe 1; mac Concoiġcṗíce 15, 25.

Letter, Letters, (?) mac Conleicṗeac.

Levenston, v. Levinston.

Leveson, Levey, mac Ḋuinnṡléiḃe.

Levinge, Levins, Levinson, Levinston, Levingston, Levingstone, Leviston, Mac Ḋuinnf́léiḃín.

Levett, Luiḃéiṿ.

Lewis, Loḃaoir.

Leycester, ṽe Leartar.

Leyden, Ó Loiṽeáin, Ó Luiṽeáin 11, (o.f.) Ó Loṽáin, (s.l.) Ó Lioṽáin 92, Ó Liaṽráin 469.

Leyhane, Ó Liaċáin.

Leyne, Ó Laiġin, Ó Laiḃín, (s.l.) Ó Leiġin, Ó Leiḃin.

Liddane, Ó Loiṽeáin, Ó Luiṽeáin. V. Leyden.

Liddy, Ó Liṽeaṽá.

Lidwich, ṽe Léaṽúr, Léaṽúr.

Lihane, Ó Liaċáin.

Lilley, v. Lilly.

Lillis, Laiġléir, (s.l.) Laoiġléir 462, Lílear 17, 77.

Lilly, Mac Ailġile.

Liman, Mac Laġmainn.

Limerick, Ó Luimḃric.

Linagh, v. Lynagh.

Linahan, v. Linehan.

Linane, v. Linnane.

Linchey, Linchy, Ó Loinṡriġ.

Lincoln, ṽe Lioncól.

Lind, Ó Loinn, (o.f.) Ó F́loinn.

Linden, Lindin, Lindon, Ó Lionṽáin, Ó Leanṽáin 1; Mac Ġiolla F́inṽéin 62.

Lindsay, Lindsy, Ó Loinṡriġ 38; Ó Loinn, (o.f.) Ó F́loinn 68 (O'D.); Mac Ġiolla F́ionntóġ 62.

Line, v. Lyne.

Lineen, Ó Luinín.

Lineham, v. Lynam.

Linehan, Ó Líonaċáin 9; Ó Luinṡeaċáin 7. V. Lenihan.

Lines, v. Lyons.

Lingane, Ó Luinṡeáin.

Lingard, Líonṡárṽ.

Linham, v. Lynam.

Linighan, v. Linehan.

Linn, Ó Loinn, (o.f.) Ó F́loinn.

Linnagar, Ó Luinín.

Linnahan, v. Linehan.

Linnane, Ó Lionnáin 9, 46; Ó Luinṡeáin 79a.

Linneen, Ó Luinín.

Linnegar, Ó Luinín.

Linnehan, v. Linehan.

Linnen, Ó Luinín.

Linnox, Leaṁnaċ.

Linskey, Ó Loinrciġ.

Linton, ṽe Liontún 1; Mac Ġiolla F́ionntáin 62.

Lion, Lions, v. Lyons.

Lister, ṽe Leartar, Leartar 2; Sailartar 2.

Liston, ṽe Liortún, Liortún.

Little, ḃeaġ 2; Ó ḃeiġ 2; Ó ḃeaġáin 2; ṕeitív 28.

Littleton, Ó ḃeaġáin 1, Ó ḃiṡeáin 17, 46.

Livingston, Livingstone, Mac Ḋuinnf́léiḃín.

Livott, Lioḃóiṽ.

Lloyd, Laoiṽe, Lóiṽ, Luíṽ.

Loag, Loague, v. Logue.

Loane, Ó Luain.

Lochlin, Ó Loċlainn.

Lochrane, Ó Luċairṕeáin, Ó Luċṕáin.

Lockard, Lockart, Locárṽ.

Lockery, v. Loughrey.

Lockhart, Locárṽ.

Loftus, Loftus, ṽe Loctúr 20, 23, 28; Ó Laċtnáin 19, 97, (s.l.) Ó Loċláin 192; Mac Loċlainn 192.

Logan, Ó Lóġáin, Ó Leoġáin.

Loghan, Ó Lóċáin, (o.f.) Ó Lotċáin, Ó Leoċáin.

Loghlin, Ó Loċlainn.

Logue, Ó Laoġóġ 11; Ó Maol Aoṽóġ 16, 19.

Lohan, Ó Lóċáin. V. Loghan.

Loman, Lomand, Ó Lomáin 4; Mac Laġmainn 6.

Lombard, Lombárd.
Lomond, v. Lomand.
Lomosney, Ó Lomarna, Ó
Lomarnaiġ.
Lomdergan, v. Londregan.
London, ve Lonvún.
Londregan, Londrigan, Loner-
gan, Ó Longarġáin, (s.l.) Ó
Lonnarġáin, Ó Lonnraġáin.
Loney, Ó Luiniġ.
Long, ve Lonġ 2; Ó Longaiġ
79a ; Ó Longáin 2 ; ɼava 2.
Longan, Ó Longáin.
Lonican, Ó Luinġeaċáin.
Lonney, Ó Luiniġ.
Looby, Ó Lúḃaiġ.
Looney, Loony, Ó Luanaiġ 7 ;
Ó Luiniġ 6.
Loran, Ó Laḃráin.
Lord, Ó Tiġearnaiġ 97 ; mac
Tiġearnáin 67.
Lordan, Ó Lórváin.
Lorkan, Lorkin, Ó Lorcáin.
Lorrigan, v. Lonergan.
Lough, (?) mac Conloċa.
Loughan, Ó Lóċáin. V. Loghan.
Lougheran, Ó Luċairneáin.
Loughlan, Loughlen, Loughlin,
Ó Loċlainn 41 ; mac Loċ-
lainn 6 ; Ó Loċláin, (o.f.) Ó
Laċtnáin 19, 24 ; Ó maoil
Seaċlainn 2.
Loughnan, Loughnane, Ó Laċt-
náin.
Loughney, Ó Laċtna.
Loughran, Loughrane, Ó Lu-
ċairneáin, Ó Luċráin 3 ; Ó
Loċráin, (o.f.) Ó Laċtnáin 46.
Loughrey, Loughry, Ó Luaċra
19 ; (?) mac Conluaċra 46.
Louney, v. Looney.
Lovat, v. Lovett.
Love, mac Ionṁain.
Lovell, Luiḃéil.
Lovett, Lovitt, Luiḃéiv 1,
Liḃéiv 499.

Lowe, mac Luġava.
Lowery v. Lowry.
Lowney, Ó Luanaiġ. V. Looney
Lowroo, Ó Laḃrava.
Lowry, Ó Laḃrava, Ó Laḃraiv
1 ; (?) mac Conluaċra 462.
V. Loughry, Kiloughry.
Luby, Ó Lúbaiġ.
Lucas, Lúcár.
Lucet, Lúipéiv.
Lucey, Ó Luaraiġ.
Lucid, Lúipéiv.
Lucy, Ó Luaraiġ.
Ludden, Ó Lováin, Ó Loiveáin,
Ó Luiveáin.
Luddy, Ó Loiviv.
Ludwig, ve Léavúp, Léavúp.
Luke, Lúcár.
Lumbard, Lombárv.
Lundergan, v. Lonergan.
Lundon, ve Lonvún.
Lunican, Ó Luinġeaċáin.
Lunneen, Ó Luinín.
Lunney, Lunny, Luny, Ó
Luiniġ.
Luogue, v. Logue.
Lupane, Ó Lapáin.
Lutterel, Luttrell, Lotairéil,
Lotrail.
Lydden, Lyden, Lydon, Ó Lio-
váin, Ó Loiveáin, &c. V.
Leyden.
Lyhan, Lyhane, Ó Liaċáin.
Lyle, Ó Laoiġill.
Lynagh, Laiġneaċ.
Lynam, Ó Laivġeanáin 1 ; Laiġ-
neaċ 25.
Lynan, Ó Laivġeanáin, Ó Laiv-
eanáin, Ó Laiġeanáin, Ó Laiv-
ġneáin, Ó Laivneáin, Ó Laiġ-
neáin.
Lynane, v. Linnane.
Lynch, Ó Loingriġ 11, Ó Loing-
reaċáin 16, 93 ; ve Línre, a
Línre 43, 97.

Lynchahan, Lynchahaun, Lynchehan, Ó Loinʓpeacáin 11, (o.f.) Mac Loinʓpeacáin 16.

Lynchy, Ó Loinʓpiʓ.

Lyne, Ó Laiʓin, Ó Laiⴂín, 10, (sl.) Ó Leiʓin, Ó Leiⴂín 17, 49..

Lynegan, Ó Luineaʓáin.

Lynegar, Ó Luinín 23.

Lyneham, v. Lynam.

Lynes, v. Lyons.

Lynham, v. Lynam.

Lynn, Ó Loinn, (o.f.) Ó Floinn.

Lynott, Lionóiⴂ.

Lynskey, Ó Loinpciʓ.

Lynton, ⴂe Liontún 1; Mac Ʒiolla Fionntáin 2.

Lyon, ⴂe Líon.

Lyons, ⴂe Líon 86; Ó Laiʓin, Ó Laiⴂín 1, (sl.) Ó Leiʓin, Ó Leiⴂín 17, 49; Ó Laiʓniʓ 19; Laiʓneac 19; Ó Liatáin 16, 772.

Lysaght, Lysatt, Mac Ʒiolla iapacta.

Lyster, ⴂe Leaptap, Leaptap 2; Saileaptap 2.

Lyttle, v. Little.

Lyttleton, v. Littleton.

Lyvott, v. Livott.

Mabe, máb.

Macabe, Mac Cába.

MacAbee, Mac an Beaca (O'G).

MacAboy, v. MacAvoy.

MacAdam, MacAdams, Mac Áⴂaim, Mac Aⴂain.

MacAdarra, MacAdarrah, Mac Dubⴂapa, Mac Duibⴂapa, (o.f.) Mac Dubⴂapac, (s.l.) Mac Dapa, Mac Dapac.

MacAdo, MacAdoo, Mac Con-ⴂuib.

MacAdorey, Mac an Deópaiⴂ.

MacAfee, MacAffee, Mac Duib-ṡíⴂe.

MacAfferty, Mac Eacṁapcaiʓ.

MacAffie, Mac Duibṡíte.

MacAghy, Mac Eacaiⴂ.

MacAimon, Mac Éamoinn, Mac Éamuinn.

MacAlarry, MacAlary, Mac Ʒiolla appaic 2; Mac Ʒiolla Cappaiʓ 2.

MacAldin, Mac Ailín.

MacAlea, Mac an Leaʓa 2; Mac Duinnṡléibe 2.

MacAlean, Mac Aileáin 9 Mac Ʒiolla Eáin 6.

MacAlearney, Mac Ʒiolla Eapna.

MacAleavy, Mac Duinnṡléibe.

MacAlee, Mac an Leaʓa 2; Mac Duinnṡléibe 2.

MacAleece, Mac Ʒiolla Íopa.

MacAleenan, Mac Ʒiolla Finnéin.

MacAleer, Mac Ʒiolla uiⴂip.

MacAleery, Mac Ʒiolla appaic.

MacAleese, Mac Ʒiolla Íopa.

MacAlen, Mac Ailín.

MacAleney, Mac Ʒiolla Coinniʓ.

MacAlernon, Mac Ʒiolla Eapnáin.

MacAlery, Mac Ʒiolla appaic.

MacAlester, Mac Alaptaip.

MacAlilly, Mac Ailʓile.

MacAlin, Mac Ailín.

MacAlinda, (?) Mac Ʒiolla Fionⴂa.

MacAlinden, Mac Ʒiolla Finⴂéin, Mac Ʒiolla Finnéin.

MacAlindon, Mac Ʒiolla Fionntáin.

MacAlingen, MacAlinion, Mac Ʒiolla Finnéin, Mac Ʒiolla Finⴂéin.

MacAlinney, Mac Ʒiolla Coinniʓ

MacAlinon, Mac Ʒiolla Finnéin.

MacAlish, Mac Ʒiolla Íopa.

MacAlister, Mac Alaptaip.

MacAlivery, Mac Ʒiolla ʓeimⴂiⴂ.

MacAll, v. MacCall.

MacAlleaon, MacAllen, Mac-Allion, mac Ailín.

MacAllester, MacAllister, mac Alapcaip.

MacAllon, Macallon, mac Ailín.

MacAlonan, mac Giolla Aḋaṁnáin.

MacAloney, mac Giolla Coinniġ.

MacAloon, MacAloone, mac Giolla Eóin.

MacAlpin, MacAlpine, mac Ailpin.

MacAlroy, mac Giollapuaiḋ.

MacAlshander, MacAlshender, MacAlshinder, mac Alpanvaip.

MacAlunney, MacAlunny, mac Giolla Coinniġ.

MacAmbrose, mac Amḃróir.

Macan, v. MacCann.

MacAnabb, mac an Abbaḋ 11 ; mac Anabaḋa 62.

MacAnallan, MacAnallen, mac an Ailín (S.L.).

MacAnally, mac an Failġiġ. V. MacNally.

MacAnalty, mac Conallta.

MacAnanama (?),

MacAnaspie, mac an Earpuiġ.

MacAnaul, mac Conulaḋ, mac Con Ulaḋ.

MacAnave, mac Giolla na naoṁ.

MacAnawe, mac Confnáṁa, (s.l.) mac an Áṫa.

MacAndless, mac Cuinvlip.

MacAndrew, mac Ainvuiṁ 11 ; mac Ainvuéip, mac Ainvuiapa 2.

MacAneany, mac Conaonaiġ, (s.l.) mac an Éanaiġ.

MacAneave, mac Giolla na naoṁ.

MacAneeny, MacAneny, mac Conaonaiġ, (s.l.) mac an Éanaiġ.

MacAnern, mac an Aipċinn, (o.f.) mac an Aipċinniġ.

MacAnerney, mac an Aipċinniġ, mac an Oipċinniġ.

MacAniff, mac Conḋuiḃ.

MacAnilly, mac an Fileaḋ, mac an Filiḋ.

MacAnliss, mac Cuinvlip.

MacAnn, v. MacCann.

MacAnnally, mac an Failġiġ. V. MacNally.

Mac-an-Ree, mac Connaoi, (s.l.) mac an Raoi.

MacAnspie, mac an Earpuiġ.

MacAntire, MacAntyre, mac an tSaoip.

MacAnuff, mac Conḋuiḃ.

MacAnulla, mac Con Ulaḋ, mac Conulaḋ.

MacAnulty, mac an Ultaiġ.

MacArchey, MacArchy, mac Ḋoirċaiḋ.

MacArdell, MacArdle, mac Áṗoġail.

MacAready, mac Conpaḋa.

MacAreavy, mac Giollapiaḃaiġ

MacAree, mac Connaoi, (s.l.) mac a' Raoi 2 ; mac Fearaḋaiġ, (s.l.) mac a' Ríoġ 2.

MacArevy, mac Giollapiaḃaiġ.

MacArgle, mac Fearġail.

Macarha, mac Cárṫaiġ.

MacArory, mac Ruaiḋrí.

MacArt, mac Aipt.

Mac Artarsney, mac an tSarainaiġ.

MacArthur, mac Aptúip.

MacArthy, mac Cárṫaiġ 11 ; mac Aipt 192.

MacArtie, mac Cárṫaiġ.

Macartney, v. MacCartney.

MacAsey, Macasey, mac Caṫaraiġ.

MacAshinah, mac an tSionnaiġ.

MacAskie, mac Arcaiḋ.

MacAskill, mac Arcaill.

MacAsparan, mac an Spapáin.

MacAssie, Macassy, Ó macapa 4; mac Catapaiġ 6.
MacAstocker, mac an Stocaipe
Mac A'Taghlin, mac ġiolla tSeaclainn, (s.l.) mac 'a tSeaclainn.
MacAtaminey, Mac Atamney, mac an Tiompánaiġ.
MacAtasney, mac an tSapanaiġ
MacAtear, mac an tSaoip.
MacAtee, mac an tSaoi.
MacAteer, mac an tSaoip.
MacAteggart, mac an tSagaipt.
MacAtier, v. MacAteer.
MacAtilla, mac an Tuile, (o.f.) mac maoltuile.
MacAtimeny, MacAtimney, mac an Tiompánaiġ.
MacAulay, Macaulay, Mac Auley, MacAuly, mac Amalġaóa 5; mac Amlaoib 6.
MacAuliffe, mac Amlaoib.
MacAvaddy, MacAvady, mac an maóaió.
MacAveely, mac an míleaóa.
MacAveigh, mac an ḃeaca, mac an ḃeacaó.
MacAvenue, mac Aióne.
MacAvey, mac an ḃeaca, mac an ḃeacaó l; mac ġiolla-ḃuióe, (s.l.) mac 'a ḃuióe 38.
MacAvin, mac ḋuiḃín.
MacAvinchy, mac ḋuiḃinpe.
MacAvinue, mac Aiḃne 26; mac ḋuiḃne 67.
MacAvish, mac an ḃáipo.
MacAvock, mac ḋaḃuc.
MacAvoy, mac ġiollaḃuióe, (s.l.) mac 'a ḃuióe 2; mac Aoóa ḃuióe 2; mac ḟíoóḃuióe, (o.f.) mac ḟíoóḃaóaiġ 45; mac an ḃeaca, mac an ḃeacaó 2.
MacAward, mac an ḃáipo.
MacAweeny, mac maonaiġ.
MacAwley, MacAwly, mac Amalġaóa 5; mac Amlaoib 6.

MacBain, mac beatan.
MacBarron, mac an ḃapúin.
MacBay, mac beaca, mac beacaó.
MacBean, mac beacan.
MacBeath, MacBeith, mac beaca, mac beacaó.
MacBennett, mac beinéió, mac ḃinéió.
MacBeth, MacBey, mac beaca, mac beacaó.
MacBirne, mac ḃpoin.
MacBirney, mac ḃiopna.
MacBrairty, mac ḃpiaptaiġ, (o.f.) mac muipceaptaiġ.
MacBratney, mac ḃpeatnaiġ.
MacBrearty, mac ḃpiaptaiġ, (o.f.) mac muipceaptaiġ.
MacBreatney, mac ḃpeatnaiġ.
MacBreen, mac ḃpaoin.
MacBretney, mac ḃpeatnaiġ.
MacBride, mac ġiolla ḃpíġoe, (s.l.) mac 'a ḃpíġoe l, ma'l ḃpíġoe 376.
MacBrien, mac ḃpiain.
MacBrin, MacBrinn, mac ḃpoin
MacBrody, mac ḃpuaioeaóa.
MacBroudin, MacBruodin, mac ḃpuaioín.
MacBryan, MacBryen, mac ḃpiain.
MacBurney, mac ḃiopna.
MacByrne, mác ḃpoin.
MacCabe, mac Cába.
MacCadam, MacCaddam, mac Aóaim, mac Aóaim.
MacCadden, mac Caóáin, mac Aóáin.
MacCaddo, MacCadoo, mac Conouib.
MacCady, mac Aóa, mac Aóaió.
MacCaet, mac ḋaiḃéió.
MacCaffaley, mac eacmílió, mac eacmíleaóa.
MacCaffarky, mac eacmapcaiġ.
MacCaffely, mac eacmílió, mac eacmíleaóa.

MacCafferty, mac eAċṁArcAiġ.

MacCaffery, MacCaffray, Mac
Caffrey, MacCaffry, Mac
Cafry, mac ʒAppAiú, mac
CAppAiú, mac ʒoppAiú, mac
ʒoppAúA, mAʒ CAppAiú, mAʒ
ʒAppAiú.

MacCagheron, mac eAċpáin.

MacCagherty, mac eAċṁArcAiġ.

MacCaghey, MacCaghy, mac
eAċAiú.

MacCague, mac ṫAiúʒ.

MacCahan, mac CAċáin 21;
mac eAċáin 68.

MacCaharty, mac eAċṁArcAiġ.

MacCahern, mac eAċpáin 2;
mac eAċṫiʒeipn 2.

MacCaherty, mac eAċṁArcAiġ.

MacCahon, v. MacCahan.

MacCahugh, mac eAċAúA, mac
eoċAúA.

MacCahy, mac eoċAiú.

MacCaig, MacCaigue, mac
ṫAiúʒ.

MacCain, mac eáin 1; mac
CAċáin 2.

MacCalden, mac Ailín.

MacCall, mac CAċṁAoil 1; mac
CAċAil 62.

MacCalla, v. MacCauley.

MacCallan, MacCallen, Mac
Callion, mac CAilín.

MacCalliskey, MacCallisky, (?)
mac Conuipce.

MacCallister, mac AlArcAip.

MacCallnon, mac CAllAnáin.

MacCallum, mac CAluim.

MacCally, mac eAċṁíliú.

MacCalman, MacCalmont, mac
CAlmáin, mac ColmáIn.

MacCalpin, mac Ailpín.

MacCalslander, MacCalshender,
MacCalshinder, mac AlpAn-
úAip.

MacCalum, mac CAluim.

MacCalvey, mac An ĊAlbAiġ,
mac CAlbAiġ.

MacCalvin, mac ConluAin.

MacCambridge, mac Ambpóip.

MacCamley, (?) mac CAmlAoiċ.

MacCammon, MacCammond,
mac Ámoinn.

MacCance, (?) mac AonʒuIp.

MacCandlass, MacCandleish,
MacCandless, MacCandlis,
MacCandliss, MacCanlis, mac
CuinúilIp, mac CuinúlIp.

MacCann, mac AnnA, mac
CAnnA, mac CAnA 11; mac
CAnAnn 192.

MacCanuff, mac Conúuiḃ.

MacCardle, mac ÁpúʒAil.

MacCarha, mac CápċAiġ.

MacCarney, mac CeApnAiġ.

MacCarnon, mac ṫiʒeApnáin.

MacCaron, mac CAppʒAṁnA.

MacCarragher, mac peApċAip.

MacCarrell, mac peApʒAil.

MacCarrick, mac ConċAippʒe,
mac ConċAppAiʒe 1; mac
ConċAċpAċ 93.

MacCarrie, v. MacCarry.

MacCarrogher, mac peApċAip.

MacCarroll, mac CeApḃAill 2;
mac peApʒAil 2.

MacCarron, mac CeApáin, (o.f.)
mac CiApáin.

MacCarroon, mac CAppʒAṁnA.

MacCarry, mac peApAúAiġ 2;
mac An CAppAiġ 2.

MacCart, mac AIpc.

MacCartan, MacCarten, mac
ApcáIn, (s.l.) mac CApcáIn.

MacCarter, MacCarthur, mac
Apcúip.

MacCarthy, mac CápċAiġ 1;
mac eAċṁArcAiġ 692.

MacCartie, mac CápċAiġ.

Mac Cartin, mac ApcáIn, (s.l.)
mac CApcáIn.

MacCartiney, MacCartney, mac
CApcAine

MacCarton, mac ApcáIn, (s.l.)
mac CApcáIn.

MacCarty, mac CápċAiġ.

MacCarvill, MacCarville, mac
Ceaṅḃaill.
MacCasey, mac Caṫaṛaiġ.
MacCassarly, mac Caṛaṛlaiġ.
MacCashin, mac Caiṛín.
MacCaskie, mac Aṛcaiḋ.
MacCaslan, (?) mac Caiṛealáin,
MacCateer, mac an tSaoiṛ.
MacCaufield, mac Caṫṁaoil.
MacCaughan, mac Eaċáin.
MacCaugherty, mac Eaċṁaṛc-
aiġ.
MacCaughey, mac Eaċaiḋ.
MacCaughin, mac Eaċáin.
MacCaughley, mac Eaċṁíliḋ,
mac Eaċṁíleaḋa.
MacCaul, mac Caṫṁaoil 1 ;
mac Caṫail 62.
MacCaulay, MacCauley, mac
Aṁalġaḋa, mac Aṁalġaiḋ
5 ; mac Aṁlaoiḃ 6.
MacCaulfield, mac Caṫṁaoil.
MacCauliffe, mac Aṁlaoiḃ.
MacCausland v. Mac Caslan
MacCavanagh, (?) mac Caoṁ-
ánaiġ.
MacCave, mac Ḋáiḃiḋ.
MacCaverty, mac Eaċṁaṛcaiġ.
MacCavey, mac Ḋáiḃiḋ 1.   V.
MacAvey.
MacCavill, mac Caṫṁaoil.
MacCavish, mac Ṫáṁaiṛ.
MacCavitt, mac Ḋaiḃéiḋ.
MacCavock, mac Ḋaḃuc.
MacCaw, mac Áḋaiṁ.
MacCawel, MacCawell, mac
Caṫṁaoil.
MacCawl, mac Caṫṁaoil 1 ;
mac Caṫail 62.
MacCawley, MacCawly, mac
Aṁalġaḋa, mac Aṁalġaiḋ
5 ; mac Aṁlaoiḃ 6.
MacCay, mac Aoḋa.
MacCeig, mac Ṫaiḋg.
MacCheyne, mac Seáin, mac
Seaġáin.
MacChrystall, mac Cṛioṛtail.

MacClachlin, mac Laċlainn 6 ;
mac Ġiolla Seaċlainn 86.
MacClafferty, mac Laiṫḃeaṛt-
aiġ, (o.f.) mac Ḟlaiṫḃeaṛt-
aiġ.
Mac Clafflin, v. Mac Clachlin.
MacClain, v. MacClean.
MacClamon, mac Laġmainn,
mac Laḋmainn.
MacClancy, mac Ḟlannċaḋa,
mac Ḟlannċaiḋ.
MacClane, v. MacClean.
MacClarnon, mac Ġiolla Eaṛ-
náin.
MacClary, v. MacCleary
MacClatton, mac Ġiolla Caṫáin
MacClave, mac Laiṫiṁ, (o.f.)
mac Ḟlaiṫiṁ, (s.l.) mac Láiṁ.
MacClaverty, mac Laiṫḃeaṛt-
aiġ.
MacClavish, mac Ġiolla ṗáṁaiṛ
MacClay, mac an Leaġa 2 ; mac
Ḋuinnṗléiḃe 2.
MacClean, mac Ġiolla Eáin 1 ;
mac Aileáin 9, 62 ; mac an
Leaġa 192.
MacClearnon, mac Ġiolla Eaṛ-
náin.
MacCleary, MacCleery, mac an
Cléiṛiġ, mac Cléiṛiġ 11 ;
mac Ġiolla aṛṛaiṫ 29, 36.
MacCleish, mac Ġiolla Íoṛa.
MacClellan, MacClelland, mac
Ġiolla Ḟaoláin.
MacClement, MacClements, Mac
Clemonts, mac Laġmainn,
MacClenaghan, MacClenahan,
MacCleneghan, MacClenighan,
MacClennon, mac Leannaċáin.
MacCleod, mac Leóiḋ.
MacClernand, MacClernon, mac
Ġiolla Eaṛnáin.
MacClery, v. MacCleary.
MacClester, mac Alaṛtaiṛ.
MacCleverty, mac Laiṫḃeaṛt-
aiġ, (o.f.) mac Ḟlaiṫḃeaṛt-
aiġ.
MacClew, mac Ḋuinnṗléiḃe.

MacCliment, MacClimond, Mac Climont, mac Laʒmainn, mac Laómainn.

MacClinchy, mac Loinʒriʒ.

MacClintock, mac ʒiolla fionntóʒ.

MacClinton, mac ʒiolla fionntáin

MacCloghery, mac Cloċaire.

MacClory, mac Labraḋa.

MacCloskey, mac blorcaiḋ.

MacCloud, mac Leóiḋ.

MacCloughery, MacCloughry mac Cloċaire.

MacCloy, mac Ḋuinnfléibe.

MacCluggage, (?) mac Lúcáir.

MacClughan, (?) mac Clúċáin.

MacClune, mac ʒiolla eóin.

MacClung, mac Luinʒe.

MacClure, mac ʒiolla uiḋir.

MacClurg, mac Luirʒ.

MacClusker, mac blorcaire.

MacCluskey, mac blorcaiḋ.

MacClymon, mac Laʒmainn, mac Laómainn.

MacClyntock, mac ʒiolla fionntóʒ.

MacCobrie, mac Cúiṫbréiṫ.

MacCogan, MacCoggan, mac Coʒáin, (o.f.) mac Coʒaḋáin 1 ; mac eoċaʒáin 62.

MacCoghlan, mac Coċláin.

MacCole, mac ʒiolla Comʒaill 16 ; mac Comʒaill 2 ; mac Ḋubʒaill 2.

MacColgan, mac Colʒan.

MacColl, mac Colla.

MacCollom, mac Coluim.

MacCollough, mac Colla, (s.l.) mac Collaċ.

MacCollum, mac Coluim.

MacCollyams, mac Uilliam.

MacColman, mac Colmáin.

MacColum, mac Coluim.

MacComb, MacCombes, Mac- Combs, mac Cóm, mac Cómair.

MacComick, mac Cómuic.

MacComish, mac Cómair.

MacComiskey, mac Cumarcaiʒ.

MacComley, (?) mac Camlaoiċ.

MacComming, mac Coimín.

MacComoskey, mac Cumarcaiʒ.

MacCona, mac Ḋonnċaḋa.

MacConachie, Mac Conaghy, mac Ḋonnċaiḋ.

MacConamy, MacConaway, mac Conmeaḋa, mac Conṁeaḋa 5 ; mac Conṁiḋe 6.

MacConchie, mac Ḋonnċaiḋ.

MacCone, mac eoʒáin 1 ; mac Comḋáin, mac Comʒáin 62.

MacConell, mac Ḋoṁnaill.

MacCongail, MacConigly, mac Conʒail, mac Conʒaile.

MacConkey, mac Ḋonnċaiḋ.

MacConloy, mac Ḋuinnfléibe.

MacConn, mac ṁíolċon.

MacConnachie, MacConnaghy, Mac Connaughey, mac Ḋonn- ċaiḋ.

MacConnaughty, mac Connaċt- aiʒ.

MacConnell, mac Ḋoṁnaill 1 ; mac Conaill 2.

MacConnellogue, macConaillóiʒ

MacConnerty, mac Connaċtaiʒ.

MacConnon, mac Canann.

MacConohy, mac Ḋonnċaiḋ.

MacConol, mac Ḋoṁnaill.

MacConomy, mac Conmiḋe.

MacConready, mac Conriaḋa.

MacConvery, mac Ainṁire.

MacConville, mac Conṁaoil.

MacConway, mac Conṁeaḋa.

MacCoo, mac Aoḋa.

MacCooey, mac Coḃṫaiʒ.

MacCoog, MacCook, mac Ḋabuc (s.l.) mac Cuaʒ.

MacCool, v. MacCole.

MacCorcadale, mac Corcaḋail.

MacCord, mac Cuairt.

MacCordick, (?)

MacCorkell, MacCorkill, Mac- Corkle, mac Corcaill, mac Curcaill.

MacCorley, mac Coirvealbaiġ.

MacCormac, MacCormack, Mac Cormick, mac Cormaic, 11 ; mac Cormacáin 197 ; Ó Cormacáin 462.

MacCormicken, macCormacáin.

MacCormilla, mac ġormġaile.

MacCorquodale, mac Corcavail.

MacCorrikle, mac Corcaill, mac Curcaill.

MacCorry, mac Corraiv 2 ; mac ġotraiv 2.

MacCosh, mac Coire.

MacCoskar, MacCosker, mac Orcair..

MacCosbey, mac Orraic.

MacCottar, MacCotter, Mac Cottier, mac Oitir, (s.l.) mac Coitir.

MacCoubrey, mac Cúiċbréiċ.

MacCoughey, mac eoċaiv.

MacCoughlan, MacCoughlin, mac Coċláin.

MacCoughy, mac eoċaiv.

MacCoulaghan, mac Uallacáin.

MacCourt, MacCourtney, mac Cuarta, mac Cuairt.

MacCovera, mac Cúiċbréiċ.

MacCovey, mac Cobċaiġ.

MacCowan, mac Comváin, mac Comġain 1 ; mac eoġain 2 ; mac ġiolla Comváin, mac ġiolla Comġain 62.

MacCowell, MacCowhill, mac Caṫṁaoil.

MacCowley, mac Aṁalġava, mac Aṁalġaiv 5 ; mac Aṁlaoib 6.

MacCownley, mac Annlaoib.

MacCoy, mac Aova.

MacCracken, mac Reaċtain, (o.f.) mac neaċtain.

MacCrail, mac Réill, (o.f.) mac néill.

MacCrainor, mac Créinfir.

MacCraith, mac Craiċ, (o.f.) mac Raiċ.

MacCrann, mac Vrain.

MacCranor, mac Créinfir.

MacCray, MacCrea, mac Raiċ, mac Craiċ.

MacCready, mac Riava 11 ; mac Conriava 62.

MacCreanor, mac Créinfir.

MacCreary, mac Ruivrí (mac Ruaivrí).

MacCreavy, mac Riabaiġ.

MacCreech, mac Raoir, (o.f.) mac Aonġuir.

MacCreedy, v. MacCready.

MacCreery, v. MacCreary.

MacCreesh, mac Raoir, (o.f.) mac Aonġuir.

MacCreevy, MacCrevey, mac Riabaiġ.

MacCrifferty, mac Riċbeartaiġ.

MacCrilly, mac Raġailliġ.

MacCrindle, mac Raġnaill.

MacCrink, (?) mac frainnc.

MacCroberts, mac Roibeáirv, mac Roibeairv.

MacCroghan, mac Conċruaċan 9.

MacCrohan, mac Cruoṁtainn 49, (s.l.) mac Cruoċan.

MacCrorken (?) mac Ruarcáin.

MacCrory, mac Ruaivrí.

MacCrossan, mac an Croráin. mac Croráin.

MacCrub, mac Rob.

MacCrudden, mac Rováin.

MacCrum, MacCrumb, (?) mac Cruim.

MacCrystall, mac Criortail.

MacCubrae, mac Cúiċbréiċ.

MacCudden, mac Caváin, (s.l.) ma' Cuvan.

MacCudy, mac Óva.

MacCue, mac Aova.

MacCull, MacCulla, MacCullagh, MacCullah, mac Colla, (s.l) mac Collaċ.

MacCullen, MacCullion, mac Coilín 68, 69 ; mac Cuilinn 64.

MacCulloch, MacCullogh, mac Colla, (s.l.) mac Collac.

MacCullough, MacCullow, mac Colla, (s.l.) mac Collac 1; mac Con ulaó 2.

MacCullum, mac Coluim.

MacCully, mac Colla.

MacCullyam, mac uilliam.

MacCumesky, Mac Cumisky, mac Cumarcaig.

MacCumming, MacCummings, mac Cuimín.

MacCune, mac eogain.

MacCunneela, mac Congaola.

MacCunnigan, mac Cuinneagáin.

MacCunny, mac Connaió.

MacCurdy, mac muircéarpaig, (s.l.) mac Cuirrig.

MacCure, mac íomair.

MacCurry, mac Corraió 2; mac Joirraió 2.

Mac Curtain, mac Curtáin.

MacCurtin, mac Cuirtín, (o.f.) mac Cruitín 76.

Mac Cushen, mac Oirín.

MacCusker, mac Orcair.

MacCuskern, mac Corcrácáin.

MacCuskin, (?) mac uircín.

MacDacker, mac Jiolla veacair.

MacDade, MacDaid, mac Oaibéió, (s.l.) mac Oaéió.

MacDaniall, MacDaniel, mac Oómnaill.

MacDara, mac Oara, mac Oarac, (o.f.) mac Ouibvarac.

MacDarby, mac Oiarmava.

MacDary, mac Oáire.

MacDavid, MacDavitt, mac Oáibió, mac Oaibéió.

MacDermott, mac Oiarmava 1, mac Oiarmava 97; Ó Ouibvíorma, Ó Ouibvíormaig 16, 26.

MacDermott Gall, mac Oiarmava Jall mac Oiarmava Jallva.

MacDermottroe, mac Oiarmava Ruaó.

MacDevitt, mac Oaibéió.

MacDiarmod, v. MacDermott.

MacDigany, mac an Oeagánaig.

MacDire, mac Ouibióir.

MacDivitt, mac Oaibéió.

MacDole, mac Oubgaill.

MacDona, MacDonagh, mac Oonncava 1, mac Oonncava, (s.l.) Ó Conncava 192.

MacDonald, mac Oómnaill.

MacDonnagh, v. MacDonagh.

MacDonnell, mac Oomnaill 1, mac Oomnaill, (s.l.) Ó Comnaill 19.

MacDonogh, MacDonough, v. MacDonagh.

MacDool, MacDougal, Mac Dougald, MacDougall, Mac Dowall, MacDowell, mac Oubgaill.

MacDorcy, mac Oorcaió (O'D.)

MacDowney, mac Jiolla Oómnaig 6.

MacDrury, mac an Oruaió.

MacDuff, mac Ouib.

MacDugal, MacDugald, mac Oubgaill.

MacDunn, mac Ouinn.

MacDunphy, mac Oonncaió.

MacDwyer, mac Oubuióir, mac Ouibióir.

MacEchern, mac eicticeirin.

MacEgan, mac Aovagáin.

MacElany, v. MacElhenny.

MacElcuddy, mac Jiolla Cuva, mac Jiolla mocuva.

MacElderry, (?) mac Jiolla Oorca.

MacEldowney, mac Jiolla Oómnaig.

MacEldrew, (?) mac Jiolla Oorca.

MacElduff, mac Jiollavuib.

MacEleary, mac Jiolla arraic.

MacEleavy, mac Ouinnrléibe.

MacElerney, mac Jiolla earna.

MacElestrim, mac Alaptpuim.
MacElfatrick, MacElfedrick,
mac giolla páopaig.
MacElgan, mac giollagáin.
MacElgun, MacElgunn, mac
giolla óuinn.
MacElhair, MacElhar, mac
giolla Catáip.
MacElharry, mac giolla
cappaig.
MacElhatton, mac giolla
Catáin.
MacElhenny, MacElheny, mac
giolla Coinnig.
MacElhill, mac giolla coille.
MacElhinney, mac giolla
Coinnig.
MacElholm, mac giolla Colm,
mac giolla Coluim.
MacElhone, mac giolla Com-
gáin, mac giolla Comóain.
MacElhoney, mac giolla Coin-
nig.
MacElhoyle, mac giolla coille.
MacElhuddy, mac giolla Cuóa,
(o.f.) mac giolla mocuóa.
MacElistrum, mac Alaptpuim.
MacElkenny, mac giolla Coin-
nig.
MacEllen, mac Ailín.
MacElligott, mac uileagóio.
MacElin, mac Ailín.
MacEllister, mac Alaptaip.
MacEllistrim, MacEllistrum,
mac Alaptpuim.
MacElmeel, mac giolla micil
1 ; mac giolla maoil 2.
MacElmoyle, mac giolla maoil
MacElmurray, mac giolla
muipe.
MacElnea, mac giolla na
naom.
MacElrath, MacElreath, Mac
Elreavy, mac giollapiaóaig.
MacElroe, mac giollapuaió.
MacElrone, mac giolla Ruaó
áin.
MacElroy, mac giollapuaió.

MacElshander, Mac Elshender,
mac Alpanoaip.
MacElsinan, mac giolla Sion-
áin.
MacElvaine, mac giollabáin.
MacElvee, mac giollabuióe.
MacElveen, mac giollamín.
MacElvenna, MacElvenny, mac
giolla meana.
MacElvie, mac giollabuióe.
MacElvogue, mac giolla maoó-
óg.
MacElwain, MacElwane, Mac-
Elwean, mac giollabáin.
MacElwee, mac giollabuióe.
MacElwreath, mac giollapiaó-
aig.
MacEnally, mac an pailgig.
V. MacNally.
MacEnchroe, MacEncroe, mac
Concpaóa.
MacEndoo, mac Conouió.
MacEndry, mac Cinpí, mac
Annpaoi.
MacEneaney, MacEneany, mac
Conaonaig, (s.l.) mac an
éanaig.
MacEneilis, mac niallguip.
MacEnerney, MacEnerny, mac
an Oipcinnig, mac an Aip-
cinnig.
MacEnery, mac Cinpí, mac
Annpaoi 10 ; mac inneipge
7.
MacEniff, mac Conouió.
MacEniry, mac inneipge.
MacEnnis, mac Aonguip.
MacEnright, mac ionnpactaig,
mac inpeactaig.
MacEnroe, mac Conpuóa.
MacEnry, v. MacEnery.
MacEntagert, MacEntaggart,
MacEntaggert, mac an tSag-
aipt.
MacEntee, mac an tSaoi.
MacEnteer, mac an tSaoip.
MacEntegart, mac an tSagaipt.
MacEntire, mac an tSaoip.

MacEntosh, mac an ⱅaoiⱃiᵹ.

MacEoin, MacEown, mac eóin 2 ; mac eoᵹain 2.

MacErchar, mac ⱔeaⱃⱅaiⱃ.

MacErlain, MacErlane, MacErlean, MacErleen, mac ⱔiⱃ-léiᵹinn.

MacErrigle, mac ⱔeaⱃᵹail.

MacErrilly, mac ⱔeaⱃᵹaile.

MacErvel, mac ⱅeaⱃⱃaill.

MacEtavey, mac an ⱅsámaiᵹ.

MacEvaddy, MacEvady, mac an maⱃaiⱃ.

MacEvanny, MacEvany, mac an manaiᵹ.

MacEvely, mac an miliⱃ, mac an mileaⱃa.

MacEver, mac éimiⱃ 2 ; mac íomaiⱃ 2.

MacEvilly, mac an miliⱃ, mac an mileaⱃa.

MacEvin, mac ⱅⱃuiⱃín.

MacEvinie, MacEvinney, mac ⱅⱃuiⱃne 67 ; mac aiⱅne 26.

MacEvoy, mac ᵹiollaⱅuiⱃe, (s.l.) mac 'a ⱅuiⱃe 2 ; mac aoⱃa ⱅuiⱃe 2 ; mac ⱔíoⱃ-ⱅuiⱃe, (o.f.) mac ⱔíoⱃⱅaⱃaiᵹ, 45 ; mac an ⱅeaⱅa, mac an ⱅeaⱅaⱃ 2.

MacEwan, MacEwen, mac eoᵹain.

MacFaal, Ó maolⱔáⱃail.

MacFadden, MacFaddin, MacFaddon, MacFaden, MacFadian, MacFadyen, MacFadzen, mac ⱔáiⱃín.

Mac Fall, MacFalls, mac ⱔáil 1 ; Ó maolⱔáⱃail 62.

MacFarlaine, MacFarland, MacFarlane, mac ⱔaⱃⱅaláin, mac ⱔáⱃⱅaláin.

MacFarson, mac an ⱔeaⱃⱃúin, mac an ⱔeaⱃⱃain.

MacFate, mac ⱔáiⱃ.

MacFatridge, mac ⱔeaⱃoⱃuiⱃ.

MacFattrick, mac ⱔáⱅⱃaic.

MacFattridge, mac ⱔeaⱃoⱃuiⱃ.

MacFeat, mac ⱔáiⱃ.

MacFeddan, mac ⱔáiⱃín.

MacFee, mac ⱅⱃuiⱔⱔíⱅe.

MacFeeley. MacFeely, (?) mac ⱔiⱅⱅeallaiᵹ.

MacFeerish, mac ⱔiaⱃaiⱃ.

MacFeeters, mac ⱔeaⱃaiⱃ.

MacFerran, mac meaⱃáin.

MacFerson, mac an ⱔeaⱃⱃúin, mac an ⱔeaⱃⱃain.

MacFetridge, MacFetrish, mac ⱔeaⱃoⱃuiⱃ.

MacFettrick, mac ⱔáⱅⱃaic.

MacFettridge, mac ⱔeaⱃoⱃuiⱃ.

MacFie, mac ⱅⱃuiⱔⱔíⱅe.

MacFirbis, mac ⱔiⱃⱃiⱃiᵹ.

MacFlinn, MacFlynn, mac ⱔloinn.

MacGaffigan, maᵹ eaⱅaᵹáin.

MacGaffin, maᵹ ⱅⱃuiⱃⱔinn.

MacGaffrey, mac ᵹaⱃⱃaiⱃ, maᵹ caⱃⱃaiⱃ, maᵹ ᵹaⱃⱃaiⱃ.

MacGaggy, maᵹ eaⱅaiⱃ.

MacGagh, maᵹ eaⱅaⱅ, maᵹ eaⱅaⱃa.

MacGahan, mac ᵹaoiⱅín 1, (s.l.) maᵹ ᵹaⱅan 64 ; maᵹ eaⱅáin 52.

MacGaheran, maᵹ eaⱅⱃáin.

MacGahey, maᵹ eaⱅaiⱃ.

MacGahran, maᵹ eaⱅⱃáin

MacGahy, maᵹ eaⱅaiⱃ.

MacGale v. Mac Call.

MacGaley, v. Mac Gawley.

MacGall, v. MacCall.

MacGalliogly, mac an ᵹallóᵹ-laiᵹ.

MacGan, MacGann, maᵹ canna, maᵹ cana 1, maᵹ annaiⱃ 34 maᵹ eaⱅáin 52 ; maᵹ canann 46.

MacGannon, maᵹ ⱔionnáin 9 ; maᵹ canann 46.

MacGaraghan, MacGarahan, maᵹ aⱃaⱅáin, maᵹ ᵹaⱃaⱅáin mac ᵹaⱃaⱅáin.

MacGarahy, mᴀᵹ ꝼeᴀꞃᴀⱱᴀıᵹ, (s.l.) mᴀᵹ ᵹeᴀꞃᴀċᴀıᵹ.
MacGaraty, MacGarity, mᴀᵹ ᴀıꞃeᴀċᴛᴀıᵹ.
MacGarr, mᴀc ᴀn ᵹeáıꞃꞃ.
MacGarran, mᴀᵹ ᴀꞃᴀċáın, mᴀᵹ ᵹᴀꞃᴀċáın, mᴀc ᵹᴀꞃᴀċáın 23 ; (?) mᴀᵹ eᴀċꞃáın 692.
MacGarrell, mᴀᵹ ꝼeᴀꞃᵹᴀıl.
MacGarrett, mᴀc ᵹeᴀꞃóıⱱ.
MacGarrigal, mᴀᵹ ꝼeᴀꞃᵹᴀıl.
MacGarrigan, mᴀc ᵹeᴀꞃᵹáın.
MacGarrigle, mᴀᵹ ꝼeᴀꞃᵹᴀıl.
MacGarrity, mᴀᵹ ᴀıꞃeᴀċᴛᴀıᵹ, mᴀᵹ Oıꞃeᴀċᴛᴀıᵹ.
MacGarroll, mᴀᵹ ꝼeᴀꞃᵹᴀıl.
MacGarry, mᴀᵹ ꝼeᴀꞃᴀⱱᴀıᵹ 1, (s.l.) mᴀᵹ ᵹᴀꞃᴀıⱱ 34, mᴀc ᵹéᴀꞃᴀıⱱ 197.
MacGartlan, mᴀc ᵹᴀꞃᴛlᴀn, uᴀ ᵹᴀꞃᴛlᴀn (S.L.). V. Garlan.
MacGarty, v. MacGaraty.
MacGarvey, mᴀc ᵹᴀıꞃⱱeıċ, mᴀc ᵹᴀıꞃⱱıċ.
MacGaskell, mᴀᵹ ᴀꞃcᴀıll.
MacGaugh, mᴀᵹ eᴀċᴀċ, mᴀᵹ eᴀċᴀⱱᴀ.
MacGaughey, mᴀᵹ eᴀċᴀıⱱ.
MacGaughran, mᴀᵹ eᴀċꞃáın.
MacGaughy, MacGaugie, mᴀᵹ eᴀċᴀıⱱ.
MacGaulay, MacGauley, mᴀᵹ ᴀṁᴀlᵹᴀⱱᴀ, mᴀᵹ ᴀṁᴀlᵹᴀıⱱ.
MacGauran, MacGaurn, Mac-Gavern, mᴀᵹ ꞅᴀṁꞃáın, (o.f.) mᴀᵹ ꞅᴀṁꞃᴀⱱáın.
MacGaver, mᴀᵹ éıṁıꞃ 2 ; mᴀᵹ íoṁᴀıꞃ 2.
MacGavick, MacGavock, mᴀᵹ ⱱᴀⱱuıc, mᴀᵹ ⱱᴀⱱuc.
MacGaw, mᴀc ᴀⱱᴀıṁ.
MacGawlay, MacGawley, mᴀᵹ ᴀṁᴀlᵹᴀⱱᴀ, mᴀᵹ ᴀṁᴀlᵹᴀıⱱ.
MacGawran, mᴀᵹ ꞅᴀṁꞃáın 1 ; (?) mᴀᵹ eᴀċꞃáın 62.
MacGeady, (?) mᴀc céᴀⱱᴀıᵹ.
MacGeagh, mᴀᵹ eᴀċᴀċ, mᴀᵹ eᴀċᴀⱱᴀ.

MacGean, mᴀc ᵹᴀoıċín.
MacGeany, (?) mᴀᵹ éᴀnnᴀ.
MacGeary, mᴀc ᵹᴀⱱꞃᴀ 91, (.l.s) mᴀc ᵹᴀoꞃᴀ 97 ; mᴀᵹ ꝼeᴀꞃᴀⱱᴀıᵹ 6, 92.
MacGee, mᴀᵹ ᴀoⱱᴀ, mᴀᵹ ᴀoıⱱ 11, (s.l.) Ó ᵹᴀoıⱱ 976 ; mᴀc ᵹᴀoıċe 16 ; Ó mᴀoılᵹᴀoıċe 16, 19.
MacGeehan, mᴀc ᵹᴀoıċín.
MacGeehee, mᴀc ᵹᴀoıċe.
MacGeehin, mᴀc ᵹᴀoıċín.
MacGeever, MacGeevor, mᴀᵹ íoṁᴀıꞃ.
MacGehan, mᴀc ᵹᴀoıċín.
MacGellan, mᴀc ᵹeᴀláın.
MacGellick, mᴀᵹ uılıc.
MacGennis, MacGenniss, mᴀᵹ ᴀonᵹuıꞅ, mᴀᵹ ᴀonᵹuꞅᴀ.
MacGeoghegan, mᴀᵹ eoċᴀᵹáın.
MacGeough, mᴀᵹ eoċᴀċ, mᴀᵹ eoċᴀⱱᴀ.
MacGeown, mᴀᵹ eoᵹᴀın 2 ; mᴀᵹ eóın 2.
MacGeraghty, MacGerety, mᴀᵹ Oıꞃeᴀċᴛᴀıᵹ.
MacGerr, mᴀc ᴀn ᵹıꞃꞃ.
MacGerraghty, mᴀᵹ Oıꞃeᴀċᴛᴀıᵹ.
MacGerrigan, mᴀc ᵹeᴀꞃᵹáın.
MacGerrity, mᴀᵹ Oıꞃeᴀċᴛᴀıᵹ.
MacGerry, mᴀᵹ ꝼeᴀꞃᴀⱱᴀıᵹ.
MacGetrick, MacGetterick, mᴀᵹ ꞅıᴛꞃıc.
MacGettigan, mᴀᵹ eıᴛeᴀᵹáın, mᴀᵹ eıᴛıᵹeın.
MacGhee, v. MacGee.
MacGherry, mᴀᵹ ꝼeᴀꞃᴀⱱᴀıᵹ.
MacGhie, v. MacGee.
MacGhoon, v. MacGowan.
MacGibben, MacGibbin, mᴀᵹ ꞅıⱱín 2 ; mᴀc ᵹıoⱱúın 2.
MacGibbon, mᴀc ᵹıoⱱúın.
MacGibney, mᴀc ᵹıⱱne.
MacGiff, mᴀᵹ ⱱuıⱱ.
MacGiffen, mᴀᵹ ⱱuıⱱꝼınn.
MacGihan, MacGihen, mᴀc ᵹᴀoıċín.

MacGilduff, mac ᵹiollaᵈuiḃ.
MacGilfoyle, mac ᵹiolla póil.
MacGilharry, mac ᵹiollaċarpaiᵹ.
MacGill, mac an ᵹoill 11 ; mac ᵹiolla 62.
MacGillacowan, mac ᵹiolla Comᵹain, mac ᵹiolla Comᵈáin.
MacGillacuddy, mac ᵹiolla Cuᵈa, mac ᵹiolla Moċuᵈa.
MacGillan, mac ᵹileáin.
MacGillbride, mac ᵹiolla Uríᵹᵈe.
MacGilldowie, mac ᵹiolla ᵈuḃṫaiᵹ.
MacGilldowney, mac ᵹiolla ᵈomnaiᵹ.
MacGillecuddy, mac ᵹiolla Cuᵈa.
MacGillen, mac ᵹileáin.
MacGilleroy, mac ᵹiollaruaiᵈ.
MacGillespie, mac ᵹiolla easpuiᵹ.
MacGillick, maᵹ uillic, maᵹ uilic.
MacGillicuddy, mac ᵹiolla Cuᵈa, mac ᵹiolla Moċuᵈa.
MacGilligan, mac ᵹiollaᵹáin.
MacGillivray, mac ᵹiolla Uráṫa.
MacGilloway, MacGillowy, mac ᵹiollaᵇuiᵈe.
MacGill Patrick, MacGillpatrick, mac ᵹiolla páᵈraiᵹ.
MacGillreavy, mac ᵹiollariaḃaiᵹ.
MacGillroy, mac ᵹiollaruaiᵈ.
MacGillshenan, mac ᵹiolla Seanáin.
MacGilly, maᵹ Coiliᵈ.
MacGillycuddy, mac ᵹiolla Cuᵈa, mac ᵹiolla Moċuᵈa.
MacGilpatrick, mac ᵹiolla páᵈraiᵹ.
MacGilpin, mac ᵹiollaᵖinn.
MacGilrea, mac ᵹiollariaḃaiᵹ.
MacGilroy, mac ᵹiollaruaiᵈ.

MacGilvane, mac ᵹiollaᵇáin.
MacGilvie, MacGilway, Mac Gilwee, mac ᵹiollaᵇuiᵈe.
MacGimpsey, mac ᵈíomaraiᵹ.
MacGin, maᵹ ᵖinn.
MacGindle, maᵹ ᵖionnᵹail.
MacGinety, maᵹ ᵖionnaċtaiᵹ, maᵹ ᵖinneaċtaiᵹ, &c.
MacGing, maᵹ ᵖinn.
MacGiniss, maᵹ aonᵹuiᵖ.
MacGinity, maᵹ ᵖionnaċtaiᵹ, maᵹ ᵖinneaċtaiᵹ, &c.
MacGinley, MacGinly, mac ᵖionnᵹaile.
MacGinn, maᵹ ᵖinn.
MacGinness, maᵹ aonᵹuiᵖ, mac aonᵹuᵖa.
MacGinnety, v. MacGinety.
MacGinnis, maᵹ aonᵹuiᵖ, maᵹ aonᵹuᵖa.
MacGinnitty, MacGinty, maᵹ ᵖionnaċtaiᵹ, maᵹ ᵖinneaċtaiᵹ 11 ; mac an tSaoi 352,
MacGirl, maᵹ ᵖearᵹail.
MacGirr, mac an ᵹiᵖᵖ.
MacGivena, maᵹ ᵈuiḃne.
MacGiver, maᵹ uiᵈiᵖ.
MacGiveran, MacGiverin, Mac Givern, maᵹ uiᵈᵖín.
MacGivney, maᵹ ᵈuiḃne.
MacGladdery, mac ᵹleaᵈra.
MacGlade, maᵹ léiᵈ.
MacGladery, mac ᵹleaᵈra.
MacGlan, (?) maᵹ ᵖlainn.
MacGlancy, maᵹ ᵖlannċaᵈa, maᵹ ᵖlannċaiᵈ.
MacGlare (?) mac ᵹiolla Cáᵈaiᵖ
MacGlashan, MacGlashin, mac ᵹlaᵖáin, mac ᵹlaiᵖín.
MacGlathery, mac ᵹleaᵈra.
MacGlaughlin, maᵹ loċlainn 11 ; mac ᵹiolla Seaċlainn 25, 37, 97.
MacGlave, maᵹ laiṫim, (o.f.) maᵹ ᵖlaiṫim, (s.l.) maᵹ láim.
MacGleish, mac ᵹiolla íoᵖa.
MacGlew, (?) mac ᵈuinnᵖléiḃe.

MacGlin, Mag Ḟloinn.
MacGlinchey, MacGlinchy, Mag Loingriġ.
MacGloin, MacGlone, Mac Giolla Eóin.
MacGlory, Mag Labraḋa.
MacGloughlin, Mag Loċlainn.
MacGlue (?) Mac Duinnṡléiḃe.
MacGlynn, Mag Ḟloinn.
MacGoey, Mag Eóċaiḋ.
MacGoff, Mag Eoṫaċ, Mag Eoċaḋa.
MacGoggy, Mag Eoċaiḋ.
MacGoldrick, MacGolrick, Mag Ualġairg (s.l.) Mag Gualraic.
MacGonagle, MacGonegal, Mac Gonegle, MacGonigal, Mac Gonigle, Mac Congail.
MacGonnell, v. MacConnell.
MacGonnigle, Mac Congail.
MacGoogan, Mag Guagáin, (o.f.) Mag Eoċagáin.
MacGoohan, Mac Cuaċáin 39; Mag Eoċáin 2.
MacGookin, Mac Guaicín, (o.f.) Mag Eoċaiḋín.
MacGoorty, Mag Dorċaiḋ, Mag Dorċaiḋe.
MacGorish, MacGorisk, Mag Ḟeórais, Mag Ḟeóruis.
MacGorl, Mag Ḟearġail.
MacGorley, Mag Ṫoirdealḃaiġ.
MacGorlic, MacGorlick, Mag Ualġairg.
MacGorman, Mac Gormáin.
MacGorrian, MacGorrin, Mag Corraiḋín.
MacGorry, Mac Goṫraiḋ.
MacGorty, Mag Dorċaiḋ, Mag Dorċaiḋe.
MacGough, Mag Eoṫaċ, Mag Eoċaḋa.
MacGouldrick, Mag Ualġairg, (s.l.) Mag Gualraic.
MacGouran, Mag Ṡaṁráin.
MacGourkey, MacGourty, Mag Dorċaiḋ, Mag Dorċaiḋe.
MacGovern, MacGovran, Mag Ṡaṁráin, (o.f.) Mag Ṡaṁraḋáin.
MacGoverney, (?) Mac Coiḃḋeanaiġ.
MacGowan, MacGowen, MacGown, Mac an Ġoḃann, Mac an Ġaḃann, Mac Goḃann, Mac Gaḃann 1; Mac Gaṁna, 2; Mag Duḃáin 19.
MacGowran, Mag Ṡaṁráin.
MacGra, Mag Raiṫ, Mag Craiṫ.
MacGrade, MacGrady, Mag Ḃrádaiġ.
MacGragh, Mag Raiṫ, Mag Craiṫ.
MacGranahan, Mag Reannaċáin.
MacGrane, Mag Ráiġne, (s.l.) Ma Gráine, Ma Grána 64.
MacGranell, Mag Raġnaill.
MacGrann, Mag Ḃrain.
MacGrath, Mag Raiṫ, Mac Craiṫ, Mag Craiṫ.
MacGrattan, (?) Mag Reaċtain, (o.f.) Mag Neaċtain. Cf. MacCracken.
MacGraun, v. MacGrann.
MacGraw, v. MacGrath.
MacGreal, Mag Réill, (o.f.) Mag Néill.
MacGrean, Mag Raiġne.
MacGreen, Mag Raiġne 2; Mac Glasáin 2.
MacGreer, Mac Grioġair.
MacGreevy, Mag Riaḃaiġ.
MacGregan, Mag Riagáin.
MacGregar, MacGregor, MacGregory, Mac Gréagóir, Mac Greagair, Mac Griogair.
MacGrenahan, MacGrenehan, Mag Reannaċáin.
MacGrenor, Mag Ṫréinḟir.
MacGrievy, Mag Riaḃaiġ.
MacGriffin, Mac Gríḟín.
MacGrillan, (?) Mag Rialláin, (o.f.) Mag Nialláin.

MacGrillish, mᴀ ʒ Riaℓℓʒuip, (o.f.) mᴀʒ niaℓℓʒuip, (s.l.) mᴀʒ ʒpiaℓℓuip.

MacGriskin, mᴀc Cpipⲧín.

MacGroany, mᴀʒ Cappʒᴀmnᴀ,

MacGronan, mᴀʒ Raʒnᴀinn, (o.f.) mᴀʒ Raʒnᴀiℓℓ.

MacGrory, mᴀʒ Ruᴀiópí.

MacGrotty, (?) mᴀʒ Raⳣᴀ.

MacGrudder, mᴀʒ Úpuᴀⱱᴀip.

MacGuane, mᴀʒ Úubáin.

MacGuckian, MacGuckin, mᴀʒ eoⳣᴀióín, (s.l.) mᴀc ʒuᴀicín.

MacGueran, (?) mᴀc ʒéᴀpáin 46.

MacGuff, mᴀʒ Úuiⱱ.

MacGuffin, mᴀʒ Úuiⱱpinn.

MacGughian, MacGuickian, mᴀʒ eoⳣᴀióín.

MacGuiehan, mᴀc ʒᴀoiⳤín.

MacGuigan, MacGuiggan, mᴀʒ eoⳣᴀʒáin, (s.l.) mᴀc ʒuᴀʒáin, mᴀc ʒúiʒeᴀn.

MacGuighan, mᴀʒ eoⳣáin.

MacGuill, mᴀc Cuiℓℓ.

MacGuillan, mᴀc Coiℓín.

MacGuinn, mᴀc Cuinn.

MacGuinness, MacGuinnessy, mᴀʒ ᴀonʒuip, mᴀʒ ᴀonʒupᴀ.

MacGuire, mᴀʒ uióip.

MacGuirk, mᴀʒ Cuipc, mᴀc Cuipc.

MacGullian, MacGullion, mᴀc Coiℓín.

MacGuone, MacGuown, v. Mac Gowan.

MacGurgan, (?) mᴀc Úuᴀpcáin.

MacGurk, MacGurke, mᴀc Cuipc, mᴀʒ Cuipc.

MacGurkin, (?) mᴀc Úuᴀpcáin.

MacGurl, v. MacGorl.

MacGurn, MacGurran, MacGurrin mᴀʒ Coppáin, mᴀʒ Coppᴀióín.

MacGurrell, v. MacGarrell.

MacGurry, mᴀc ʒoⳤpᴀió.

MacGushion, mᴀʒ Oipín.

MacGuskin, mᴀʒ uipcín.

MacGusty, mᴀc Oipⲧe, mᴀʒ Oipⲧe.

MacHaffie, MacHaffy, mᴀc Úuibpíⳤe.

MacHaig, mᴀc ⳤaióʒ.

MacHale, mᴀc hᴀoℓ, mᴀc hᴀeℓ, mᴀc héiℓ.

MacHall, mᴀc Cᴀⳣᴀiℓ 2 ; mᴀc Cᴀⳣmᴀoiℓ 62.

MacHanfry, Machanfry, mᴀc hunppᴀió.

MacHarnon, mᴀc Ⲧiʒeᴀpnáin.

MacHarroll, mᴀc ɸeᴀpʒᴀiℓ 2 ; mᴀc Ceᴀpbᴀiℓℓ 2.

MacHarry, mᴀc Ꭺmppᴀoi 2 ; mᴀc ɸeᴀpᴀóᴀiʒ 2 ; mᴀc ʒioℓℓᴀcᴀppᴀiʒ 29.

MacHay, mᴀc ᴀoⱱᴀ.

MacHeath, mᴀc Síⳤiʒ.

MacHeffey, mᴀc eᴀⳤᴀió.

MacHendrie, MacHendry, v. MacHenry.

MacHenery, v. MacEnery.

MacHenry, mᴀc éippí, mᴀc ᴀnppᴀoi, mᴀc hᴀnppᴀoi.

MacHinch, mᴀc ᴀonʒuip.

MacKinny, v. MacKinny.

MacHue, MacHugh, mᴀc ᴀoⱱᴀ 1, mᴀc ᴀoió 2.

MacIlboy, macIlbwee, mᴀc ʒioℓℓᴀbuióe.

MacIlchon, mᴀc ⱦíoℓⳤon.

MacIlderry, (?) mᴀc ʒioℓℓᴀ ⱱopⳣᴀ.

MacIldoon, mᴀc ⱦᴀoiℓⱱúin.

MacIldowie, mᴀc ʒioℓℓᴀ Úubpᴀiʒ.

MacIldowney, mᴀc ʒioℓℓᴀ Úomnᴀiʒ.

MacIlduff, mᴀc ʒioℓℓᴀóuiⱱ.

MacIleboy, mᴀc ʒioℓℓᴀbuióe.

MacIleese, mᴀc ʒioℓℓᴀ íopᴀ.

MacIlfatrick, MacIlfederick, mᴀc ʒioℓℓᴀ pápᴀiʒ.

MacIlgorm, mᴀc ʒioℓℓᴀʒuipm.

MacIlhair, mᴀc ʒioℓℓᴀ Cᴀⳤᴀip.

MacIlhaney, mᴀc ʒioℓℓᴀ Cᴀinniʒ.

MacIlhar, mac ʒiolla Catair.

MacIlhargy, mac ʒiolla feaṙʒ.

MacIlharry, mac ʒiollacarraiʒ

MacIlhatton, mac ʒiolla Cataín.

MacIlhenny, mac ʒiolla Coinniʒ.

MacIlherron, mac ʒiolla Ciaráin.

MacIlhone, mac ʒiolla Comʒáin, mac ʒiolla Comṗáin.

MacIlhoney, mac ʒiolla Coinniʒ.

MacIlhoyle, mac ʒiolla coille.

MacIlhun, mac ṁioltcon.

MacIllhatton, mac ʒiolla Cataín.

MacIllicuddy, mac ʒiolla Cuva

MacIllwain, mac ʒiollabáin.

MacIlmoil, MacIlmoyle, mac ʒiollamaoil.

MacIlmurray, mac ʒiolla muire.

MacIlpatrick, mac ʒiolla Pároiʒ.

MacIlravy, MacIlrea, mac ʒiollaruaṫaiʒ.

MacIlroy, mac ʒiollaruaiṫ.

MacIlvany, mac ʒiolla ṁeana.

MacIlveen, mac ʒiollamín.

MacIlwaine, mac ʒiollabáin.

MacIlwee, mac ʒiollabuiṫe.

MacIlwraith, MacIlwrath, mac ʒiollaruabaiʒ.

MacInally, mac an failʒiʒ. V. MacNally.

MacInch, mac Aonʒuir.

MacIndoo, mac Convuib.

MacIneely, mac Conʒáile.

MacInerney, MacInerny, Mac Innerney, mac an Airċinniʒ, mac an Oirċinniʒ.

MacInnes, mac Aonʒuir.

MacIntagert, MacIntaggart, mac an tSaʒairt.

MacIntee, mac an tSaoi.

MacInteer, mac an tSaoir.

MacInteggart, mac an tSaʒairt

MacIntire, mac an tSaoir.

MacIntosh, mac an Taoiriʒ.

MacIntyre, mac an tSaoir.

MacIveagh, mac an Veaṫa, mac an Veaṫaṫ.

MacIver, MacIvers, MacIvor, mac íoṁair.

MacJimpsey, mac Víomaraiʒ.

MacKage, MacKague, Mac Kaige, mac Caiʒ.

MacKain, mac eáin 1; mac Cataín 2.

MacKalshander, mac Alranvair.

MacKane, mac eáin 1; mac Cataín 2.

MacKann, v. MacCann.

MacKaree, mac fearavaiʒ.

MacKarel, mac fearʒail.

MacKay, Mackay, mac Aoṫa.

MacKeady, mac Céavaiʒ 5; mac Céiviʒ, mac Éiviʒ 779.

MacKeag, MacKeague, mac Caiʒ.

MacKean, mac eáin, mac iain 1; Ó Moċaiṫein 64.

MacKeane, mac Aoṫáin, 19, 97.

MacKeany, mac Éanna 4; mac Cionaoiċ 6.

MacKearney, mac Cearnaiʒ.

MacKeary, mac fiaċra, mac fiaċraċ 1; mac fearavaiʒ 2.

MacKeating, (?) mac Céitín.

MacKeaveney, MacKeaveny, mac ʒéibeannaiʒ.

MacKeaver, mac íoṁair.

MacKee, mac Aoiṫ 11; mac an Caoiċ 67, 82.

MacKeefrey, mac fiaċra, mac fiaċraċ.

MacKeegan, mac Aoṫaʒáin.

MacKeeman, MacKeemon, mac Síomóin, mac Síomoinn.

MacKeen, mac Cataín 46.

MacKeeney, MacKeeny, v. MacKeany.

MacKeever, MacKeevor, mac
ıoṁaıp.

MacKeighry, mac ꝼıaċṗa, mac
ꝼıaċṗaċ.

MacKeigue, mac caıóg.

MacKeith, mac Síċıg.

MacKeiver, mac ıoṁaıp.

Mackel, v. Magill.

MacKeleghan, mac ceallaċáın

MacKellan, MacKellen, mac
aıleáın, mac coılín.

MacKellop, mac ꝼılıb.

MacKelly, mac ceallaıg.

MacKelshenter, mac alpan-
óaıp.

MacKelvey, mac ꝣıollabuıóe.

MacKemmin, mac áṁoınn.

Mackelwaine, mac ꝣıollabáın.

Macken, Ó maıcín 1, Ó macáın,
2 ; mac maıcín 16.

MacKendrick, mac annpaıc,
mac eanpaıc.

MacKendry, v. MacHenry.

MacKenery, v. MacEnery.

MacKeniry, mac ınneıpġe.

MacKenna, mac cıonaóóa, mac
cıonaoıt 1, (s.l.) maꝣ cıneáıt
7 ; mac éanna 2.

MacKennery, v. MacEnery.

MacKenny, mac cıonaoıt.

MacKensie, v. MacKenzie.

MacKenty, mac an tSaoı.

MacKenzie, Mackenzie, mac
coınmıġ.

MacKeo, mac eoċaóa.

MacKeoan, mac eoġaın.

MacKeogh, mac eoċaóa, mac
eoċaċ, (s.l) mac ceotaċ, mac
ceóċ.

MacKeon, MacKeone, mac éoın
2 ; mac eoġaın 2.

MacKeough, mac eoċaóa.

MacKeowen, MacKeown, mac
éoın 2 ; mac eoġaın 2.

MacKerel, mac ꝼeanꝣaıl.

MacKerley, MacKerlie, mac
ꝼeanꝣaıle 2 ; mac coıpóealb-
aıġ 2.

MacKernan, mac cıġeapnáın.

MacKerr, (?) mac coppa, mac
cappa.

MacKerrall, MacKerrell, mac
ꝼeanꝣaıl.

MacKerrigan, mac cıapaꝣáın.

MacKerrow, mac cıoċpuaóa.

MacKervel, mac ceapbaıll.

Mackessy, Ó macapa.

MacKetian, (?) mac céıtín.

MacKetterick, MacKettrick,
mac Sítpıc.

MacKevin, mac óuıbín.

MacKevitt, mac óaıbéıo.

MacKevor, mac ıoṁaıp.

MacKew, mac aoóa.

MacKewen, mac eoġaın 2 ;
mac éoın 2.

MacKey, mac aoóa, mac aoıó.

Mackey, mac aoóa, mac aoıó
1 ; Ó macóa 17, 27, 77.

MacKibben, MacKibbin, mac
ꝼıbín.

MacKibbon, mac ꝣıobúın.

MacKie, mac aoıó.

MacKiernan, mac cıġeapnáın.

MacKiever, mac ıoṁaıp.

MacKilbouy, mac ꝣıollabuıóe.

MacKilbride, mac ꝣıolla
bpíġóe.

MacKilkelly, mac ꝣıolla ċeall-
aıġ.

MacKillen, MacKillian, Mac
Killion, mac coılín, mac
aıleáın.

MacKillip, MacKillop, Mac
Killops, mac ꝼılıb.

MacKilmurray, mac ꝣıolla
ṁuıpe.

MacKilveen, mac ꝣıollaṁín.

MacKilvie, mac ꝣıollabuıóe.

MacKilwane, mac ꝣıollabáın.

MacKim, mac Sım.

MacKimmie, mac Sımıó.

MacKimmon, Mackimmon, mac
Síomóın, mac Síomoınn.

Mackin, Ó maıcín 1, Ó macáın
2 ; mac maıcín 16.

MacKinaul, Mackinaul, mᴀc Con ulᴀḃ.

MacKinch, mᴀc ᴀonġuiṟ.

MacKinerkin, MacKinerking, mᴀc ᴀn ᴀiṟċinn, mᴀc ᴀn Oiṟċinn.

MacKinestry, mᴀc ᴀn ᴀiṟtṟiġ.

MacKing, mᴀc ḟinn.

MacKiniff, mᴀc Conḋuiḃ.

MacKinirking, v. Mac Kinerking.

MacKinlay, MacKinley, mᴀc ḟionnlᴀoiċ S 2, (o.f.) mᴀc ḟionnloġᴀ, (s.l.) mᴀc Ciúllᴀ; mᴀc Conleᴀġᴀ, (o.f.) mᴀc ᴀn leᴀġᴀ 2.

MacKinn, mᴀc ḟinn.

MacKinnawe, mᴀc Conḟnᴀṁᴀ.

MacKinney, MacKinnie, mᴀc Cionᴀoiċ 2; mᴀc Coinniġ 2.

MacKinnon, mᴀc ḟionġuine. (s.l.) mᴀc ḟionúin.

MacKinny, v. MacKinney.

MacKinstry, mᴀc ᴀn ᴀiṟtṟiġ.

MacKintosh, Mackintosh, mᴀc ᴀn Tᴀoiṟiġ.

MacKinty, mᴀc ᴀn tSᴀoi.

MacKinzie, v. MacKenzie.

MacKirdy, mᴀc Muiṟċeᴀṟtᴀiġ.

MacKirtrick, mᴀc Sitṟic.

MacKissock, mᴀc Ioṟóc, mᴀc Ioṟóg.

MacKitterick, MacKittrick, mᴀc Sitṟic 1; mᴀc Cioctᴀḋᴀ 376.

MacKiver, Mackiver, mᴀc Ioṁᴀiṟ.

Mackle, v. Magill.

Macklebreed, mᴀc Ṡiollᴀ Ḃríġḋe.

Macklehattan, mᴀc Ṡiollᴀ Ċᴀtᴀin.

Macklemoyle, mᴀc Ṡiollᴀ-ṁᴀoil.

MacKlern, mᴀc Ṡiollᴀ Ċiᴀṟᴀin.

Macklewaine, mᴀc Ṡiollᴀḃᴀin.

Macklewraith, mᴀc Ṡiollᴀṟiᴀḃᴀiġ.

MacKneight, v. MacKnight.

MacKniff, mᴀc Conḋuiḃ.

MacKnight, mᴀc ᴀn Riḋiṟe 2; mᴀc Eᴀċᴀḋ 35; mᴀc Neᴀċtᴀin 62.

MacKnulty, mᴀc ᴀn Ultᴀiġ.

MacKoen, MacKone, mᴀc Eoġᴀin 2; mᴀc Comġᴀin, mᴀc Coṁḃᴀin 2.

MacKonkey, mᴀc Ḋonnċᴀḋ.

MacKonnigham, mᴀc Coinneᴀġᴀin.

MacKough, mᴀc Eoċᴀḋᴀ, mᴀc Eotᴀċ.

MacKoy, mᴀc ᴀoḋᴀ.

MacKrann, mᴀc Ḃṟᴀin.

MacKrell, mᴀc ḟeᴀṟġᴀil.

MacKurdy, mᴀc Muiṟċeᴀṟtᴀiġ.

MacKuscar, MacKusker, mᴀc Oṟcᴀiṟ.

MacKussack, mᴀc Ioṟóc, mᴀc Ioṟóg, mᴀc Iṟeóc.

MacLachlan, MacLachlin, mᴀc Lᴀċlᴀinn.

MacLagan, mᴀc Ṡiollᴀ Aḋᴀṁᴀġᴀin.

MacLaghlan, mᴀc Lᴀċlᴀinn.

MacLain, MacLaine, v. Mac Lean.

MacLamond, mᴀc Lᴀġmᴀinn, mᴀc Lᴀḋṁᴀinn.

MacLandrish, mᴀc Ṡiollᴀ Ainḋṟéiṟ.

MacLane, v. MacLean.

MacLaren, mᴀc Lᴀḃṟᴀinn.

MacLarenon, MacLarinon, mᴀc Ṡiollᴀ Eᴀṟnᴀin.

MacLarney, Ó Mᴀoil Eᴀṟnᴀ 89. V. MacLerney.

MacLarnon, mᴀc Ṡiollᴀ Eᴀṟnᴀin

MacLary, mᴀc Ṡiollᴀ ᴀṟṟᴀiċ.

MacLauchlin, mᴀc Lᴀċlᴀinn, mᴀc Loċlᴀinn.

MacLaughlin, mᴀc Lᴀċlᴀinn, mᴀc Loċlᴀinn 11; Ó Mᴀoil-eᴀċlᴀinn, Ó Mᴀoil Seᴀċlᴀinn 8, 9; Ó Lᴀċtnᴀin 99.

MacLauren, MacLaurin, mᴀc Lᴀḃṟᴀinn.

MacLave, mac Laıċıṁ, (o.f.)
mac Flaıċıṁ, (s.l.) mac Láıṁ.
MacLaverty, mac Laıċḃeaptaıʒ,
(o.f.) mac Flaıċḃeaptaıʒ.
MacLavery, mac Laḃṁaḋa.
M'Lavin, ó maoıl Éıṁín.
MacLean, mac ʒıolla eáın 1 ;
mac Aıleáın 9, 62 ; mac an
leaʒa 192.
MacLear, mac ʒıolla uıḋıp.
MacLearey, MacLeary, mac
ʒıolla appaıċ.
Macleav, mac an leaʒa 2 ; mac
Ðuınnpléıḃe 2.
MacLee, mac an leaʒa 1 ; mac
Laoıḃıʒ 45.
MacLeery, mac ʒıolla appaıċ.
MacLees, MacLeese, Macleese,
MacLeesh, mac ʒıolla íopa.
Maclehatton, mac ʒıolla
Catáın.
MacLehenny, MacLehinney,
MacLehinny, mac ʒıolla
Coınnıʒ.
MacLeise, MacLeish, Macleish,
mac ʒıolla íopa.
MacLeister, mac Alaptaıp.
MacLeland, MacLellan, Mac
Lelland, mac ʒıolla Faoláın
MacLement, mac Laʒmaınn.
MacLenaghan, MacLenahan,
MacLeneghan, MacLenihan,
mac Leannaċáın.
MacLennan, MacLennon, mac
ʒıolla Fınnéın 23 ; mac
ʒıolla Aḋaṁnáın 68 ; mac
Loıneáın 976 ; mac Leannaċ-
áın 2.
MacLeod, mac Leóıv.
MacLerney, mac ʒıolla eapna
9. V. MacLarney.
MacLernon, mac ʒıolla eap-
náın.
Macleroi, MacLeroy, mac
ʒıollapuaıḋ.
MacLester, mac Alaptaıp.
MacLhinney, mac ʒıolla Coın-
nıʒ.

MacLice, mac ʒıolla íopa.
MacLimont, mac Laʒmaınn.
MacLinden, MacLindon, maċ
ʒıolla Fınvéın, mac ʒıolla
Fıonntáın.
MacLinney, mac ʒıolla Coın-
nıʒ.
MacLintock, mac ʒıolla Fıonn-
tóʒ.
MacLinton, mac ʒıolla Fıonn-
táın.
Maclise, mac ʒıolla íopa.
MacLister, mac Alaptaıp.
MacLochlin, MacLoghlen, Mac
Loghlin, mac Loċlaınn. V.
MacLoughlin.
MacLoon, MacLoone, mac
ʒıolla eóın.
MacLoonie, (?) mac Cluanaıʒ.
MacLorinan, mac ʒıolla eap-
náın.
MacLoskey, MacLosky, mac
Ḃlopcaıḋ.
MacLoughlan, MacLoughlen,
MacLoughlin, mac Loċlaınn
11 ; ó maoıl Seaċlaınn, ó
maoıleaċlaınn 8, 9 ; ó Laċt-
náın 992.
MacLouᵹhrey, (?) mac Con-
luaċpa.
MacLroy, mac ʒıollapuaıḋ.
MacLucas, mac Lúcáıp.
MacLune, mac ʒıolla eóın.
MacLuney, mac ʒıolla Coın-
nıʒ.
MacLung, mac Luınʒe.
MacLure, mac ʒıolla uıḋıp.
MacLurg, mac Luıpʒ.
MacLuskey, MacLusky, mac
Ḃlopcaıḋ.
MacLynn, mac Loınn, (o.f.)
mac Floınn.
MacMa, mac Conmeaḋa 5; mac
maċa 6.
MacMachan, v. MacMahon and
MacMeechan.
MacMachon, v. MacMahon.
MacMackin, mac maıcín.

MacMagh, mac máċa.
MacMaghen, MacMaghon, Mac
Maghone, MacMahan, Mac
Mahon, mac maṫġaṁna 11;
Ó maṫġaṁna 37, 38.
MacManaman, MacManamon,
mac meanman.
MacManamy, mac meanma.
MacManis, v. MacManus.
MacMann, v. MacMahon.
MacMannion, MacMannon, mac
manainn.
MacMannus, MacManus, mac
maġnuir, mac máġnura.
MacMaster, mac an máiġirtir.
MacMath, mac máċa.
MacMay, mac máiġe, (s.) mac
máiġeóc, mac máiġeóg.
MacMearty, mac muirċeartaiġ
MacMechan, MacMeckan, Mac
Meckin, MacMeechan, Mac
Meekan, MacMeeken, Mac
Meekin, (?) mac miaḋaċáin.
MacMeel, mac ġiolla ṁiċil 1,
mac miċil 2; mac ġiolla-
ṁaoil 2.
MacMeenamon, v. MacMenamin.
MacMeichan, v. MacMechan.
MacMenamen, MacMenamin,
MacMenamon, mac mean-
man.
MacMenamy, mac meanma.
MacMenemen, mac meanman
MacMenemy, mac meanma.
MacMenim, mac meanman.
MacMenimey, mac meanma.
MacMenimin, mac meanman.
MacMerty, mac muirċeartaiġ.
MacMey, v. MacMay.
MacMichael, mac ġiolla ṁiċil,
mac miċil.
MacMichalin, mac miċilín.
MacMichall, v. MacMichael.
MacMichan, v. MacMechan.
MacMighall, v. MacMichael.
MacMillan, mac maoláin.
MacMillen, MacMillin, mac
maoláin, mac maoilín.

MacMinamy, mac meanma.
MacMinimin, mac meanman.
MacMinn, (?)
MacMonagle, MacMonegal, Mac
Monigal, MacMonigle, mac
maongail.
MacMoran, mac muġróin, (s.l.)
mac moġráin 39, 97; mac
muirċáin 2.
MacMordie, mac muirċeartaiġ.
MacMorin, MacMorns, Mac
Morran, v. MacMoran.
MacMorray, v. MacMurray.
MacMorris, mac muirir, mac
ṁuirir 2; mac muirġuir,
mac muirġeara 2.
MacMorrow, mac muirċaḋa 1;
mac muireaḋaiġ 67.
MacMorry, mac muireaḋaiġ.
MacMouran, v. MacMoran
MacMoyler, mac maoilir.
MacMrearty, mac muirċeart-
aiġ.
MacMullan, MacMullen, Mac
Mullin, MacMullon, mac
maoláin.
MacMunaway, (?)
MacMunigal, mac maongail.
MacMurdy, mac muirċeartaiġ.
MacMurlan, MacMurland, mac
muirġaláin.
MacMurran v MacMoran.
MacMurray mac muireaḋaiġ
1; mae muirċaḋa 33 (O'D);
mac ġiolla ṁuire 2.
MacMuren, MacMurrin, v. Mac
Moran.
MacMurrough, mac muirċaḋa.
MacMurrough Kavanagh, mac
muirċaḋa caoṁánaċ.
MacMurry, mac muireaḋaiġ.
MacMurtery, MacMurthry, Mac
Murtie, MacMurtry, mac
muirċeartaiġ.
MacNabb, mac an abbaḋ 11
mac anabaḋa 62.
MacNabo, MacNaboe, Mac
Nabow, mac anabaḋa.

MacNaboola, mac Con na buaile
MacNaghten, MacNaghton, mac neaċtain.
MacNail, mac néill.
MacNair, mac an maoiṗ.
MacNairn, mac an aiṗċinn.
MacNale, mac néill.
MacNally, mac an ḟailġiġ 11 ; mac Con ulaḋ 62.
MacNalty, mac Conallta.
MacNama, mac Conmeaḋa.
MacNamanamee, (?)
MacNamara, MacNamarra, Mac Namarrow, mac Conmara.
MacNamee, mac Conmíḋe.
MacNarry, mac náraḋaiġ.
MacNaugher, mac Conċoḃaiṗ.
MacNaught, MacNaughten, Mac Naughton, mac neaċtain.
MacNay, MacNea, MacNeagh, mac niaḋ, mac néiḋe.
MacNeal, mac néill.
MacNealey, MacNeally, Mac Nealy, mac Conġaile 91 ; mac Conġaola 92 ; mac an ḟileaḋ, mac an ḟiliḋ 6.
MacNearney, mac an Oiṗċinn-iġ.
MacNeary, mac náraḋaiġ.
MacNee, mac niaḋ, mac néiḋe.
MacNeece, mac naoiṗ, mac naora, (o.f.) mac Aonġuiṗ, mac Aonġura.
MacNeel, mac néill.
MacNeela, v. MacNealy.
MacNeeld, MacNeele, mac néill.
MacNeely, v. MacNealy.
MacNeeny, mac Conaonaiġ.
MacNeese, mac naoiṗ, mac naora (o.f.) mac Aonġuiṗ, mac Aonġura.
MacNeffe, mac Conḋuiḃ.
MacNeice, mac naoiṗ, mac naora (o.f.) mac Aonġuiṗ, mac Aonġura.
MacNeigh, mac néiḋe, mac niaḋ.

MacNeight, mac neaċtain.
MacNeilage, mac niallġuiṗ.
MacNeile, MacNeill, mac néill.
MacNeilly, v. MacNealy.
MacNeiry, mac inneiṗġe.
MacNelis, mac niallġuiṗ.
MacNella, MacNello, v. Mac Nealy.
MacNeney, mac Conaonaiġ, (s.l.) mac an Éanaiġ.
MacNerhenny, mac an aiṗ-cinniġ, mac an Oiṗċinniġ.
MacNerland, MacNerlin, mac an ḟiṗléiġinn.
MacNern, mac an Oiṗċinn.
MacNerney, MacNertney, mac an aiṗċinniġ, mac an Oiṗ-cinniġ.
MacNestry, mac an aiṗtṗiġ.
MacNevin, mac Cnáimín.
MacNicholas, mac niocláiṗ.
MacNickle, MacNicol, mac niocoil, mac niocóil.
MacNiece, mac naoiṗ, mac naora, (o.f.) mac Aonġuiṗ, mac Aonġura.
MacNielly, v. MacNealy.
MacNiff, mac Conḋuiḃ.
MacNight, mac neaċtain.
MacNilly, mac an ḟileaḋ, mac an ḟiliḋ.
MacNinch, mac Aonġuiṗ.
MacNirny, MacNirney, mac an Oiṗċinniġ, mac an aiṗċinniġ.
MacNish, mac naoiṗ, (o.f.) mac Aonġuiṗ.
MacNite, v. MacNight.
MacNiven, mac naoimín.
MacNoger, MacNogher, Mac Noher, mac Conċoḃaiṗ.
MacNuff, mac Conḋuiḃ.
MacNulty, mac an ultaiġ.
MacNutt, mac nuaḋaḋ, mac nuaḋat.
MacOscar, mac Oṗcaiṗ.
MacOstrich, (?) mac Oṗṗaic.
MacOubery, MacOubery, mac Cúiṫḃṗéiṫ.

MacOwen, mac eoġain 1 ; mac
eóın 2.
MacPadden, MacPadden, Mac
Paden, MacPadgen, Mac
Padian, mac páıvín.
MacPake, mac péıce.
MacParland, MacParlin, Mac
Partlan, MacPartland, Mac
Partlin, mac paptaláın, mac
páptaláın, mac páptláın,
mac papláın.
MacPaul, mac póıl 62 ; ó
maoılṗáḃaıl 66.
MacPeake, mac péıce.
MacPhadden, mac páıvín.
MacPhail, mac póıl, mac póıl,
mac páıl.
MacPharland, mac paptaláın,
mac páptaláın.
MacPhatrick, mac pátpaıc.
MacPhee, mac ḋuıḃṗíċe.
MacPhelan, mac faoláın.
MacPhelimy, Mac Phellimy,
mac feıḋlımıḋ.
MacPherson, mac an ṗeappúın.
MacPhettridge, mac ṗeaṫoṁuıp.
MacPhilbin, mac pılıbín.
MacPhillemy mac feıḋlımıḋ..
MacPhillips, mac pılıb.
MacPhilpin, mac pılıbín, mac
pılbín, mac fılıbín.
MacPhun, mac ṁunna.
MacPolin, mac póılín.
MacQuade, MacQuaid, Mac
Quaide, mac uaıv.
MacQualter, mac ualtaıp.
MacQuarrie, mac guaıpe.
MacQuatters, mac uaıtéıp.
MacQuay, mac aoḋa.
MacQueen, Macqueen, mac
Suıḃne.
MacQuestion, MacQueston, mac
úıptın.
MacQuey, mac aoḋa.
Macquien, v. MacQueen.
MacQuiggan, mac guaıgín, mac
guıgean, (o.f.) mac eoċaıḋín.
MacQuilin, v. MacQuillin.

MacQuilkan, MacQuilkin, mac
uılcín.
MacQuill, mac cuıll.
MacQuillan, MacQuillen, mac
coılín 69 ; mac cuılınn 64 ;
mac uıṙılín, mac uıṙlín,
mac uıġılín 36.
MacQuilliams, mac uıllıam.
MacQuillian, MacQuillin, Mac
Quillion, MacQuillon, v. Mac
Quillan.
MacQuilly, mac an ċoılıġ, mac
coılıġ, mac coılıḋ 2 ; mac
uıḋlıḋ 36.
MacQuilquane, mac uılcín.
MacQuin, mac cuınn.
MacQuiney, (?) mac Suıḃne.
MacQuinn, mac cuınn.
MacQuinney, (?) mac Suıḃne.
MacQuirk, MacQuirke, mac
cuıpc.
MacQuish, mac coıpe.
MacQuiston, mac úıptın.
MacQuoid, mac uaıv.
MacQuorcodale, mac ṫopcav-
aıl, mac ṫupcavaıl.
MacRae, mac Raıċ.
MacRanald, MacRandell, mac
Raġnaıll.
MacRann, mac Ḃpaın.
MacRannal, MacRannall, mac
Raġnaıll.
MacRay, MacRea, mac Raıċ.
MacReady, mac Rıava.
MacReavy, mac Rıaḃaıġ.
MacRedmond, mac Réamoınn.
MacReedy, mac Rıava.
MacReery, mac Ruıḋpí.
MacRenn, mac Ḃpoın.
MacReynold, MacReynolds,
mac Raġnaıll.
MacRichard, mac Rıocáıpv,
mac Rıocaıpv, mac Rıp-
teáıpv, mac Rıpteaıpv.
MacRoarty, mac Roḃaptaıġ.
MacRoary, mac Ruaıṙpí.
MacRoberts, mac Roıbeáıpv,
mac Roıbeaıpv.

MacRobin, mac Roibín.
MacRory, mac Ruaidrí.
MacRub, MacRubs, mac Rob.
MacRuddery, mac an Rioire.
MacRum, mac Cruim.
MacRynn, mac Broin.
MacScollog, mac an Scolóige, mac Scolóige.
MacSeveney, mac Suibne.
MacShaffrey, MacShafrey, mac Seaffraid.
MacShan, mac Seáin, mac Seagáin.
MacShanaghy, mac Seanca, mac Seancaide.
MacShane, mac Seáin, mac Seagáin.
MacShanley, mac Seanlaoic.
MacShannon, mac Seanáin 2 ; mac Seanacáin 2.
MacSharry, mac Searraig.
MacSheehy, mac Síthig.
Mac Sheffrey, mac Seaffraid.
MacSherry, mac Searraig.
MacShufrey, mac Sioffraid, mac Seaffraid.
MacSkeaghan, MacSkean, mac Sceacáin.
MacSkimmins, (?), mac Cuimín.
MacSliney, MacSliny, mac Sleimhne.
MacSlowey, MacSloy, mac Sluagadaig.
MacSoley, MacSolly, mac Soillig.
MacSoreley, MacSorely, Mac Sorley, mac Somairle.
MacSpaddin, mac Spáidín.
MacSparran, mac an Sparáin.
MacSpeddin, mac Spáidín.
MacStay, M'Stay, Ó Maoilsteighe.
MacSteen, mac Stibín, mac Stín.
Mac Stocker, mac an Stocaire.
MacStravick, (?)
MacSurley, mac Somairle.

MacSwan, mac Suain.
MacSween, MacSweeney, Mac Sweeny, MacSweney, mac Suibne.
MacSwiggan, MacSwiggin, Mac Swigin, (?) mac Suigin.
MacSwine, MacSwiney, mac Suibne.
MacTaggart, mac an tSagairt.
MacTaghlan, MacTaghlin, mac Giolla tSeaclainn.
MacTague, mac Taidg.
MacTamney, mac an Tiompánaig.
MacTavish, mac Támair.
MacTeague, mac Taidg.
MacTeer, mac an tSaoir.
MacTeggart, mac an tSagairt.
MacTegue, MacTeigue, mac Taidg.
MacTernan, mac Tigearnáin.
MacTier, mac an tSaoir.
MacTiernan, mac Tigearnáin.
MacTierney, mac Tigearnaig.
MacTigue, mac Taidg.
MacTimney, mac an Tiompánaig.
MacToole, mac Tuatail.
MacTucker, mac Tuaccair.
MacTurk, mac Tuirc,
MacUsker, mac Orcair.
MacVady, mac an Mhadaid.
MacVail, mac Páil, mac Póil.
MacVanamy, mac Meanma.
MacVann, mac Beatán.
MacVany, mac an Mhanaig.
MacVarry, mac Fearadaig.
MacVay, MacVea, MacVeagh, mac an Beata, mac an Beatad.
MacVean, mac Beatán.
MacVeigh, mac an Beata, mac an Beatad.
MacVeety, MacVeity, mac an Biadtaig.
MacVerran, mac Mearáin.
MacVerry, mac Fearadaig.

MacVey, мас ан Ѵеаċа, мас
ан Ѵеаċаѵ.

MacVicar, MacVickar, Mac
Vicker, мас ан Ѵіосáіре,
мас ан Ѵіосара.

MacVitty, MacVity, мас ан
Ѵіаѵċаіż.

MacVoy, v. MacAvoy.

MacWade, мас uаіѵ.

MacWalter, мас uаlcаір.

MacWard, мас ан Ѵáірѵ.

MacWatters, мас uаісéір.

MacWeeney, MacWeeny, мас
ṁаонаіż 9; мас Ѕuіѵне б.

MacWherter, мас Арсаір.

MacWhinney, MacWhinny, (?)
мас Ѕuіѵне.

MacWhirter, мас Арсаір.

MacWhiston, мас Úірсін.

Mac White, MacWhitty, мас
раоісіż.

MacWhorter, мас Арсаір.

MacWiggan, MacWiggin, мас
żuаіżін, мас żuіżеан, (о.f.)
мас Еоċаіѵін.

MacWilkin, мас uіlсín.

MacWilliam, MacWilliams, мас
uіllіам.

MacWillie, мас uіѵlіѵ.

MacWiney, MacWinney, Mac
Winny, (?) мас Ѕuіѵне.

MacWray, мас Rаіċ.

Madden, Ó маѵáін 1, Ó маѵаіѵ-
ín, Ó маѵоín, 19, 97, (s.)
мас ан ṁаѵаіѵ 192.

Maddigan, Ó маѵаżáін.

Maddock, Maddocks, Maddox,
Maddux, маѵóс, маѵóż.

Maddy, Ó маѵаіѵ.

Madigan, Ó ṁаѵаżáін.

Madole, Madowell, мас Ѵuѵ-
żаіll.

Madox, маѵóс.

Magahan, мас żаоісín 1, (s.l.)
маż żаċан 64; маżЕаċáін 52

Magaharan, Magaheran, Magahern, маż Еаċráін.

Magall, v. MacCall.

Magan, Magann, маż Саnnа,
маż Саnа 1, маż Аnnаіѵ
34; маż Саnаnn 46. ; маż
Еаċáін 52.

Magarry, маż ѓеараѵаіż.

Magauran, Magaurn, маż Ѕаṁráін, (о.f.) маż Ѕаṁраѵáін.

Magaw, маż Áѵаіṁ.

Magawley, маż Аṁаlżаѵа,
маż Аṁаlżаіѵ.

Magawran, маż Ѕаṁráін, (о.f.)
маż Ѕаṁраѵáін.

Magee, маż Аоѵа, маż Аоіѵ
11 ; мас żаоісе 16 ; Ó маоl-
żаоісе 16, 19.

Mageehan, Magean, Mageen,
мас żаоісín.

Magenis, Magennis, маż Аон-
żuір, маż Аоnżура.

Mageogh, маż Еоċаѵа, маż
Еоċаċ.

Mageoghegan, маż Еоċażáін.

Mageown, маż Еоżáін 2 ; маż
Еóін 2.

Mageraghty, маż Оіреаċсаіż.

Magettigan, маż Еісеażáін,
маż Еісіżеін.

Magetty, маż Еісіż.

Maghan, Ó маċáін.

Magher, Ó меаċаір.

Maghery, ан ṁаċаіре.

Magill, мас ан żоіll 11 ; мас
żіоllа 62.

Magillowy, мас żіоllаѵuіѵе.

Magilly, маż Соіlіѵ.

Maginess, маż Аоnżuір.

Maginley, маż ѓіоnnżаіlе.

Maginn, маż ѓінn.

Maginness, маż Аоnżuір.

Maginnetty, маż ѓіоnnаċсаіż,
маż ѓіnnеаċсаіż, &c.

Maginnis, маż Аоnżuір.

Maginty, маż ѓіоnnаċсаіż,
маż ѓіnnеаċсаіż, &c.

Magiveran, Magiverin, Magivern
маż uіѵrín.

Maglade, маż léіѵ.

Maglamery, (?) маż lаѵраіѵ.

Maglanchy, mᴀᵹ ꜰlᴀɴɴċᴀᴅᴀ, mᴀᵹ ꜰlᴀɴɴċᴀɪᴅ.
Maglennon, mᴀᵹ leᴀɴɴᴀ́ɪɴ.
Magloin, Maglone, mᴀc ᵹɪollᴀ eóɪɴ.
Magner, Magnier, Magnir, Magnor, mᴀɪɴᵹɴéɪɾ.
Magolrick, mᴀᵹ uᴀlᵹᴀɪɾᵹ, (s.l.) mᴀᵹ ᵹuᴀlᴘᴀɪc.
Magone, mᴀᵹ eoᵹᴀɪɴ.
Magonigle, mᴀᵹ coɴᵹᴀɪl.
Magorish, Magorisk, mᴀᵹ ꝼeóɾᴀɪɾ, mᴀᵹ ꝼeóɾuɪɾ.
Magorlick, mᴀᵹ uᴀlᵹᴀɪɾᵹ, (s.l.) mᴀᵹ ᵹuᴀɾlᴀɪc.
Magough, mᴀᵹ eoċᴀċ, mᴀᵹ eoċᴀᴅᴀ.
Magournahan, mᴀᵹ ᵹuᴀɾɴᴀċᴀ́ɪɴ.
Magoveran, Magoverin, Magovern, mᴀᵹ Sᴀ́mᴘᴀ́ɪɴ, (o.f.) mᴀᵹ Sᴀ́mɾᴀᴅᴀ́ɪɴ 11 ; mᴀᵹ uɾᴅɾ́ɪɴ 62.
Magowan, Magowen, mᴀc ᴀɴ ᵹoḃᴀɴɴ, mᴀc ᴀɴ ᵹᴀḃᴀɴɴ mᴀc ᵹoḃᴀɴɴ, mᴀc ᵹᴀḃᴀɴɴ l ; mᴀc ᵹᴀ́mɴᴀ 2 ; mᴀᵹ ᴅuḃᴀ́ɪɴ 19.
Magra, Magragh, mᴀᵹ Rᴀɪċ, mᴀᵹ Cᴘᴀɪċ.
Magrane, mᴀᵹ Rᴀɪᵹɴe, (s.l.) mᴀ ᵹɾᴀ́ɪɴe, mᴀ ᵹɾᴀ́ɴᴀ 64.
Magrannell, mᴀᵹ Rᴀᵹɴᴀɪll.
Magrath, Magraw, mᴀᵹ Rᴀɪċ, mᴀᵹ Cᴘᴀɪċ.
Magrean, mᴀᵹ Rᴀɪᵹɴe.
Magreavy, mᴀᵹ Rɪᴀḃᴀɪᵹ.
Magreece, mᴀᵹ Rᴀoɪꝼ, mᴀᵹ Rᴀoꝼᴀ, (o.f.) mᴀᵹ ᴀoɴᵹuɪꝼ, mᴀᵹ ᴀoɴᵹuꝼᴀ.
Magreely, mᴀᵹ Rᴀᵹᴀllᴀɪᵹ, (s.l.) mᴀᵹ Rᴀoᵹᴀllᴀɪᵹ.
Magreevy, mᴀᵹ Rɪᴀḃᴀɪᵹ.
Magrery, mᴀᵹ Ruɪᴅɾ́ɪ.
Magrillan, (?) mᴀᵹ Rɪᴀllᴀ́ɪɴ, (o.f.) mᴀᵹ ɴɪᴀllᴀ́ɪɴ.
Magroarty, mᴀᵹ Roḃᴀɾcᴀɪᵹ.
Magroder, mᴀᵹ Uꝼuᴀᴅᴀɪɾ.

Magrory, mᴀᵹ Ruᴀɪᴅɾ́ɪ.
Magrudden, mᴀᵹ Roᴅᴀ́ɪɴ.
Maguane, mᴀᵹ ᴅuḃᴀ́ɪɴ.
Maguigan, mᴀᵹ eoċᴀᵹᴀ́ɪɴ, (s.l.) mᴀᵹ ᵹuᴀᵹᴀ́ɪɴ, mᴀᵹ ᵹuɪᵹeᴀɴ.
Maguil, mᴀc ᴀɴ ᵹoɪll.
Maguiness, Maguinis, Maguinness, mᴀᵹ ᴀoɴᵹuɪꝼ, mᴀᵹ ᴀoɴᵹuꝼᴀ.
Maguire, mᴀᵹ uɪᴅɪɾ.
Maguirke, mᴀᵹ cuɪɾc.
Magullion, mᴀc coɪlɪɴ.
Maguran, Magurn, mᴀᵹ coɾɾᴀ́ɪɴ 9 ; mᴀᵹ Sᴀ́mɾᴀ́ɪɴ 6.
Mahady, ó moɪċɪᴅe.
Mahaffy, mᴀc ᴅuɪḃꝼɪ́ċe.
Maharry, mᴀc ꝼeᴀɾᴀᴅᴀɪᵹ.
Mahedy, ó moɪċɪᴅe.
Maher, ó meᴀċᴀɪɾ.
Mahew, mᴀɪᵹɪú l ; mᴀc mᴀɪᵹɪú 19.
Maholland, ó mᴀolċᴀllᴀɴɴ.
Mahollum, Maholm, ó mᴀol ċoluɪm, ó mᴀol ċolm.
Mahon, ó mᴀċᴀ́ɪɴ 61, ó moċᴀ́ɪɴ 91 ; ó mᴀcᵹᴀ́mɴᴀ 68 ; mᴀc mᴀcᵹᴀ́mɴᴀ 92.
Mahoney, Mahony, ó mᴀcᵹᴀ́mɴᴀ.
Mailey, v. Malley.
Main, v. Mayne.
Mainey, v. Meany.
Maires, v. Mears.
Makenry, v. MacEnery.
Makeon, v. MacKeon.
Malady, ó mᴀoɪlᴇ́ɪɴᴅɪᵹ.
Malarky, ó mᴀoɪl eᴀɾcᴀ.
Malcolm, ó mᴀol ċolm 2 ; mᴀc mᴀol ċoluɪm 2.
Malcolmson, Malcomson, mᴀc mᴀol ċolm, mᴀc mᴀol ċoluɪm.
Maley, v. Malley.
Malia, v. Melia.
Malick, v. Mallick.
Malie, v. Malley.
Maliffe, ó mᴀolᴅuɪḃ.
Malise, mᴀc mᴀoɪl ɪoɾᴀ.

Mallagh, Ó máille, máilleác.
Mallaghan, Ó maolácáin.
Mallan, Ó mealláin.
Mallavin, Ó maoiléimín.
Mallen, Ó mealláin.
Mallew, Ó maol aoúa.
Malley, Ó máille 76, 91; Ó meallaig 99; Ó maol aoúa 6, 78, Ó maoil aoúa 47.
Mallia, v. Malley.
Mallick, mac míoluic.
Mallin, Mallon, Ó mealláin.
Malloney, Mallowny, Ó maol 'oomnaig.
Mallyn, v. Mallin.
Malmona, Ó maolmóna.
Malone, Ó maoil eóin 11; mac giolla eóin 64; Ó maolblogáin 73.
Malony, Malowny, Ó maol 'oomnaig.
Maloy, v. Molloy.
Manachan, Manahan, Ó manacáin, Ó mancáin 1, Ó maincín 7.
Manally, mac an pailgig.
Manary, mac nápaváig.
Manasses, mac magnupa.
Mandevile, 'oe móinbíol, móinbíol, múinbíol.
Maneely, Maneilly, mac an pileaú, maac an piliú.
Manelis, mac niallguip.
Mangan, Manghan, Manghen, Mangin, Ó mongáin 1, Ó muingeáin 2; Ó mancáin 2, Ó managáin 49; Ó mainnín 972.
Mangner, maingnéip.
Manice, mac naoip. (o.f.) mac aonguip.
Manihan, Manihin, Ó maincín.
Manion, Ó mainnín.
Manley, Ó maongaile.
Mann, Ó macáin.
Mannering, Ó manapáin.
Mannice, mac naoip, (o.f.) mac aonguip.

Mannight, mac neactain.
Mannin, Ó mainnín.
Manning, Ó mainnín 11; Ó mongáin 779.
Mannion, Ó mainnín 11; Ó mongáin 192.
Mannix, Ó maincín 79a, Ó manóg, Ó muineóg 25, 46, 97; mac naoip, (o.f.) mac aonguip 6.
Manogue, Ó manóg, Ó muineóg.
Manron, Ó manapáin.
Mansell, móinréil.
Mansfield, móinréil 1; 'oe móinbíol, móinbíol 47, 772.
Mansill, móinréil.
Manus, mac magnuip.
Many, Ó maine.
Mape, máp.
Maqueen, mac Suibne.
Mara, Ó meaúpa, Ó meápa.
Maragan, Ó muipeagáin.
Marchal, v. Marshall.
Marcom, Marcum, v. Markham.
Maree, Mariga, Ó meapaváig, Ó meapúa.
Marinane, Ó mapannáin, Ó mapnáin.
Mark, mac mapcuip.
Markahan, Markan, Ó mapcacáin.
Markey, Ó mapcaig.
Markham, Ó mapcacáin.
Marks, mac mapcuip.
Marley, Ó mupgaile 16, Ó meaplaig 19.
Marmion, (?) mac meanman.
Marnan, Marnane, Ó mapnáin.
Marren, Ó meapáin.
Marrilly, Ó mupgaile.
Marrinan, Ó mapannáin, Ó mapnáin, (o.f.) Ó manannáin.
Marron, Ó meapáin.
Marsh, 'oe moipéip.
Marshall, mapapcal.

Meghan, Ó miaváċáin.
Meginniss, v. Maginness.
Meglamry, v. Maglamery.
Meglaughlin, v. MacGlaughlin.
Megowan, v. Magowan.
Megrath, Megraw, v. MacGrath.
Meguiggan, v. Maguigan.
Mehaffy, v. Mahaffy.
Mehan, v. Meehan.
Mehigan, Ó maoċaġáin.
Meighan, Ó miaváċáin.
Mekerrell, v. MacKerrell.
Mekill, v. Magill.
Melane, Ó maoláin.
Melanphy, Ó maolanpaiú.
Melarkey, Ó maoil eapca.
Melay, Ó maol aová, Ó maoil
    aová.
Meldon, Ó maolvúin.
Meleady, Meledy, Ó maoiléiviġ.
Melia, Ó máille.
Melican, Ó maoileaċáin, Ó
    maoileaġáin.
Mellan, Ó meall250áin.
Melledy, Ó maoiléiviġ.
Mellet, Mellett, Mellette, míol-
    óiú 11, méalóiú 92.
Mellis, mac maoil íopa.
Mellit, v. Mellet.
Mellon, Ó mealláin.
Mellot, Mellott, míolóiú 11,
    méalóiú 92, máloiú 192.
Mellowes, Ó maoil íopa.
Melly, Ó meallaiġ, 1 ; Ó máille 2
Melody, Ó maoiléivoġ.
Meloy, v. Molloy.
Melroy, Ó maoípuaiú.
Melvenny, Ó maoil meana.
Melville, Ó maoil míċil 46; Ó
    maolpábail 97.
Melvin, Ó maoilmín.
Menaght, mac neaċtain.
Menahan, Ó muineaċáin.
Menary, Menarry, mac nápaú-
    aiġ.
Menautt, v. Menaght.
Meneely, v. Maneely.
Meneese, v. Manice.

Menemin, mac meanman.
Menocher, v. MacNogher.
Menton, Ó manntáin.
Meran, Ó meapáin.
Mergin, Ó meipġín, (o.f.) Ó
    haimeipġín.
Merlehan, Ó méipleaċáin.
Mernin, (Ó) méipnín.
Merrick, meiḃpic, meipic 1,
    mac meiḃpic, mac meipic,
    mac míḃpic 2.
Merrigan, Ó muipeaġáin 1 ; Ó
    meipġín 7.
Merriman, Merryman, mac
    meanman.
Merry, Ó meapaváiġ, Ó
    meapúa.
Merwick, v. Merrick,
Mescall, Mescel, Meskell, Ó
    meipcill.
Meyers, Ó meiúip.
Meyler, mac maoilip 1,
    maoilip 28, miléip 47.
Meyrick, v. Merrick.
Miall, v. Michael.
Michael, miċeál E 2 ; Ó maoil
    míċil 9 ; mac ġiolla míċil 6.
Michell, v. Michael and Mitchell.
Miell, v. Michael.
Miers, Ó miúip, Ó míp.
Mighil, Mihell, v. Michael.
Migrillan, v. Magrillan.
Miland, Ó maoileáin.
Miles, mílip, mílió 2 ; mac
    mílip, mac milió 2 ; Ó maol
    muipe 19.
Miley, Ó maoil aová, Ó maol
    aová, Ó maoil aoiú.
Milford, Ó maolpoġmaip, Ó
    maolpoġmaip.
Miligan, Ó maoileaġáin.
Millan, Millane, Ó maoláin, Ó
    maoileáin.
Millar, muilleóip.
Millbride, Ó maoil Ḃpíġve.
Millea, Ó maoil aová, Ó maol
    aová.
Millen, Ó maoilín.

Miller, muitleóir.
Millerick, ó maoil ξeiric, ó maoil ξiric.
Millet, Millett, míolóro.
Millican, Milligan, Milligen, Millikan, Milliken, Millikin, ó maoileacáin, ó maoileaξáin.
Mills, an muilinn.
Millin, ó maoilín.
Milmo, Milmoe, ó maolmuaro.
Milreavy, ó maoilriabaiξ.
Milroy, ó maolruaro.
Minagh, muimneac.
Minahane, Minahane, ó mionac-áin, (o.f.) ó manacáin 11 ; ó muimneacáin 19.
Mineely, v. Maneely.
Minett, v. Mannight.
Mingane, ó muinξeáin.
Miniece, Miniese, v. Mannice.
Minihane, v. Minahane.
Miniter, minitéir, mintéir.
Minnagh, Minnaugh, muimneac.
Minnis, Minnish, v. Mannice.
Minnitt, v. Mannight.
Minochor, v. MacNogher.
Minnock, ó muineóξ.
Minogher, v. MacNogher.
Minogue, ó muineóξ.
Minoher, v. MacNogher.
Minteer, mac an tSaoir.
Mintin, ó manntáin.
Mirreen, ó mirín.
Miscella, mac scalaiξe.
Miskell, ó meircill.
Miskella, Miskelly, mac scal-aiξe.
Missett, ve miréro, miréro.
Mitchell, mirtéil 1 ; ó maoil micil 92 ; mac ξiolla micil 62.
Moakley, ó motla, ó mottaiξ.
Moan, ó mocáin.
Moany, ó maonaiξ.
Mockler, móicléir.
Moen, ó mocáin.
Moeran, v. Moran.
Moghan, Mohan, ó mocáin.

Moher, ó mocair, ó muitir.
Mohilly, ó motla, ó mottaiξ.
Molamphy, ó maolanraro.
Mollan, ó maoláin.
Mollony, Mollowney, ó maol-ṽomnaiξ 11 ; ó maol ṗactna 27.
Molloy, ó maolmuaro 11 ; ó maol aoṽa, ó maoil aoṽa, ó maoil aoro 91, (s.) ó maol aoṽóξ 19, (s.) ó maol maoṽóξ 16 ; ó laoξóξ, ó laoṽóξ 16, 19 ; ó maolait (o.f.) ó maolaitce, ó maol-aitξein 192; ó sluaξaṽaiξ 62.
Mologhney, ó maol ṗactna.
Molohan, ó maolacáin.
Moloney, Molony, Molowny, ó maolṽomnaiξ 11 ; ó maol ṗactna 27.
Molphy, v. Murphy.
Moloy, v. Molloy.
Molumby, ó maolcomaṽ.
Molvin, ó maoilmín.
Molyneux, ó maol an muaro 49 ; ó maolaξáin 16.
Monaboe, mac anabaṽa.
Monachan, Monaghan, v. Mona-han.
Monagle, mac maonξail.
Monahan, ó manacáin, ó man-cáin 11, ó muineacáin 192, 462, ó mionacáin 497, 779, ó maincín 2, ó muineóξ 342, 462.
Monaher, ó manacair.
Monan, ó maonáin.
Monday, mac ξiolla eóin.
Monegan, ó manaξáin.
Monehan, v. Monahan.
Money, ó maonaiξ.
Mongan, ó monξáin.
Mongavan, ó monξabáin.
Mongey, ó monξaiξ.
Mongon, v. Mongan.
Monk, Monks, mac an manaiξ 1 ; ó manacáin, ó mancáin 2.

Monley, Monnelly, Ó mᴀonᵹᴀιle.
Monohan, v. Monahan.
Monroe, mᴀc ᴀn Róċᴀιċ, S ; Ó mᴀolꞃuᴀιó 19.
Monsell, móιnꞃéιl.
Montague, mᴀc Cᴀιúᵹ.
Montane, Montang, Montangue, Ó mᴀnntáιn 11; ꝺe montáιn, montáιn 77.
Montgomery, mᴀc ιomᴀιꞃe 97, mᴀᵹompᴀċ 469.
Moody, Ó muᴀꝺᴀιᵹ (S.L.).
Moohan, Ó moċáιn.
Moon, Ó moċáιn 1 ; ꝺe moċún 2.
Moonan, Ó mᴀonáιn, (s.l.) Ó muᴀnáιn.
Moone, v. Moon.
Mooney, Ó mᴀonᴀιᵹ 11 ; Ó muιṁnιᵹ 2.
Moore, Ó móꞃꝺᴀ 11 ; ꝺe móꞃᴀ, ꝺe múꞃᴀ 72, 92 ; Ó moċᴀιꞃ, Ó muιċιꞃ 772.
Morahan, Ó muꞃċáιn.
Moran, Ó móꞃáιn 11 ; Ó moᵹꞃáιn, (o.f.) Ó muᵹꞃóιn 94 ; mᴀc moᵹꞃáιn, (o.f.) mᴀc muᵹꞃóιn 92 ; Ó muιꞃeáιn, Ó muιꞃín 2 ; Ó muꞃċáιn 14.
More, Ó móꞃꝺᴀ 11 ; ꝺe múꞃᴀ 72, 92.
Moreen, Ó móιꞃín.
Moreland, mᴀc muꞃᵹᴀláιn.
Morell, Ó muꞃᵹᴀιl.
Moren, Ó móιꞃín.
Moreton, ꝺe móꞃtún, móꞃtún.
Morey, Ó móꞃꝺᴀ.
Morgan, Ó muιꞃeᴀᵹáιn 1 ; Ó muꞃċáιn 2 ; moꞃᵹán 2, 28.
Moriarty, Ó muιꞃċeᴀꞃtᴀιᵹ.
Morice, v. Morris.
Morin, Ó móιꞃín.
Morisey, v. Morrissey.
Morison, v. Morrison
Moriss, v. Morris.
Morisson, v. Morrison.
Morissy, v. Morrissey.

Morkan, Morkin, Ó muꞃċáιn 1 ; mᴀc muꞃċáιn 2.
Morland, mᴀc muꞃᵹᴀláιn.
Morley, Ó muꞃᵹᴀιle, Ó muꞃċuιle.
Mornan, Ó mᴀꞃnáιn, Ó muꞃnáιn.
Morohan, Ó muꞃċáιn.
Moroney, Morooney, Ó mᴀolꞃuᴀnᴀιó, (s.l.) Ó muꞃꞃuᴀnᴀιó.
Morphy, v. Murphy.
Morran, v. Moran.
Morresh, ꝺe moιꞃéιꞃ, moιꞃéιꞃ, muιꞃéιꞃ.
Morriessey, v. Morrissey.
Morrin, Ó muιꞃín, Ó muιꞃeáιn 1 ; Ó muꞃċáιn 2.
Morris, Ó muιꞃᵹιꞃ, Ó muιꞃᵹeᴀꞃᴀ 1 ; mᴀc muιꞃᵹιꞃ, mᴀc muιꞃᵹeᴀꞃᴀ 2 ; mᴀc muιꞃιꞃ, mᴀc muιꞃιꞃ 19 ; ꝺe moιꞃéιꞃ, moιꞃéιꞃ, muιꞃéιꞃ 17, 77, 78, 85.
Morrison, Ó muιꞃᵹeᴀꞃáιn 11 ; Ó muιꞃᵹeᴀꞃᴀ 2 ; ꝺe moιꞃéιꞃ, muιꞃéιꞃ 178.
Morrisroe, mᴀc muιꞃιꞃ Ruᴀιó, mᴀc muιꞃιꞃ Ruᴀιó.
Morrissey, Ó muιꞃᵹeᴀꞃᴀ 11 ; mᴀc muιꞃᵹeᴀꞃᴀ 2 ; moιꞃéιꞃ 47.
Morrisson, v. Morrison.
Morrogh, v. Morrough.
Morrolly, Ó muꞃᵹᴀιle, Ó muꞃċuιle.
Morrough, mᴀc muꞃċᴀóᴀ.
Morrow, mᴀc muꞃċᴀóᴀ 1 ; mᴀc muιꞃeᴀóᴀιᵹ 67.
Morrowson, mᴀc muꞃċᴀóᴀ.
Mortagh, mᴀc muιꞃċeᴀꞃtᴀιᵹ.
Mortell, moιꞃtéιl.
Mortimer, Mortimor, ꝺe moιꞃtιméιꞃ, moιꞃtιméιꞃ 43 ; mᴀc muιꞃċeᴀꞃtᴀιᵹ 192.
Mortland, mᴀc muꞃᵹᴀláιn.
Morton, ꝺe móꞃtún, móꞃtún.
Mortymer, v. Mortimer.
Moss, Ó mᴀolmónᴀ.

Moughan, Ó mocáin.
Moughty, Ó mocca.
Mountain, Ó manntáin 11 ; ve monncáin, monncáin 77.
Mountcashel, Ó maolcairil.
Mowen, Ó mocáin.
Moy, Ó muiġe 16 (G.J.).
Moyers, mac an maoir. V. Myers.
Moylan, Ó maoileáin, Ó maoláin.
Moyles, v. Miles.
Moylin, Ó maoilín, Ó maoileáin.
Mylott, Mylotte, míolóiv 11, méalóiv 99, málóiv 192.
Moynagh, muimneac.
Moynahan, Moynan, v. Moynihan.
Moyney, Ó muimniġ.
Moynihan, Ó muimneacáin 1 ; Ó mionacáin 2.
Mucbrin, mac broin.
Muckady, mac áva, mac ávaiv.
Muckaran, mac eacráin.
Muckedan, mac caváin.
Muckeen, Muckian, v. MacKean.
Muckilbouy, mac ġiollabuive.
Mucklebreed, mac ġiolla bríġve.
Muckler, móicléir.
Muckley, Ó maolcluice.
Mugan, v. Magan.
Muir, ve múra, ve móra.
Muirland, mac muriġaláin.
Mulally, Ó maolalaiv, (o.f.) Ó maol falaiv.
Mulavil, Mulavill, Ó maolfábail.
Mulbrandon, Ó maoil breanndáin.
Mulberry, Ó maoil beariaiġ.
Mulbreedy, Mulbride, Ó maoil bríġve.
Mulcahy, Ó maol cataiġ 11 ; Ó maolcluice 1782.
Mulcair, Ó maoil céire.

Mulcashel, Mulcashell, Ó maoilcairil.
Mulcessor, (?)
Mulchrone, Ó maolcróin.
Mulconry, Ó maol conaire.
Mulcreevy, Ó maolcraoibe.
Mulcroan, Mulcrone, Mulcroon, Ó maolcróin.
Mulcrowney, Ó maol cróine.
Muldarry, Ó maolvoraiv.
Mulderg, Mulderrig, Ó maoilveiriġ.
Mulderry, Ó maolvoraiv.
Muldon, Muldoon, Ó maolvúin.
Muldooney, Muldowney, Ó maolvomnaiġ.
Mulfaal, Ó maolfábail.
Mulgan, Ó maolagáin.
Mulgeehy, Ó maolġaoite.
Mulgrave, Mulgrew, Mulgrievy, Mulgroo, Ó maolcraoibe.
Mulhall, Ó maol catail.
Mulhallen, Ó maolcallann.
Mulhane, Ó maoláin.
Mulhare, Ó maoil céire.
Mulhartagh, Ó maolatartaiġ, (o.f.) Ó maol fatartaiġ.
Mulhatton, Ó maol catáin.
Mulhearn, Mulheeran, Mulheran, Mulherin, Mulhern, Mulherrin, Mulherron, Ó maoil ciaráin.
Mulhollan, Mulholland, Ó maolcallann.
Mulhollum, Mulholm, Ó maol coluim, Ó maol colm.
Mulholn, Ó maolcallann.
Mulhooly, Ó maolġuala.
Mulick, v. Mulleague.
Mulkearn, Mulkearns, Ó maoil ciaráin.
Mulkeen, Ó maolcaoin.
Mulkern, Mulkerns, Mulkerrin, Ó maoil ciaráin.
Mulkerry, Ó maoil céire.
Mulkhearn, Mulkieran, Ó maoil ciaráin.
Mullagan, Ó maolagáin.

Mullahy, Ó mᴀolᴀɪċċe, Ó mᴀol-ᴀɪċ, (o.f.) Ó mᴀolᴀɪċġeɪn.
Mullally, Mullaly, Ó mᴀolᴀlᴀɪ́ᴅ, (o.f.) Ó mᴀol fᴀlᴀɪᴅ.
Mullan, Mullane, Ó mᴀolᴀ́ɪn.
Mullaney, Ó mᴀoɪleᴀnᴀɪġ.
Mullanphy, Ó mᴀolᴀnfᴀɪᴅ.
Mullany, Ó mᴀoɪleᴀnᴀɪġ.
Mullarkey, Ó mᴀoɪl eᴀrcᴀ.
Mullavin, Ó mᴀoɪl éɪmɪ́n.
Mullavogue, Ó mᴀol ṁᴀoᴠóġ.
Mullbride, Ó mᴀoɪl ḃrɪ́ġᴅe.
Mulleady, Ó mᴀoɪléɪᴠɪġ.
Mulleague, mᴀc mɪ́oluɪc.
Mullee, Ó mᴀol ᴅoᴠ́ᴀ, Ó mᴀol ᴀoɪᴠ, Ó mᴀoɪl ᴀoᴠ́ᴀ, Ó mᴀoɪl ᴀoɪᴠ.
Mulleen, Ó mᴀoɪlɪ́n.
Mullen, Ó mᴀolᴀ́ɪn 11, Ó mᴀoɪleᴀ́ɪn 972; mᴀc mᴀolᴀ́ɪn 2; Ó meᴀllᴀ́ɪn 62.
Mullerick, Ó mᴀoɪl ġeɪrɪc, Ó mᴀoɪl ġɪrɪc.
Mullery, Ó mᴀol ṁuɪre.
Mullet, Mullett, mɪ́olóɪᴠ.
Mulligan, Ó mᴀolᴀġᴀ́ɪn 11, Ó mᴀoɪleᴀġᴀ́ɪn 2; Ó mᴀolᴀċᴀ́ɪn, Ó mᴀoɪleᴀċᴀ́ɪn 19, 97.
Mullin, Mullins, Ó mᴀolᴀ́ɪn 1, Ó mᴀoɪlɪ́n 2; Ó mᴀoɪlfɪnn 87; mᴀc mᴀolᴀ́ɪn 2.
Mullock, mᴀc mɪ́oluɪc, mᴀc mɪ́oluc.
Mullogan, Ó mᴀolᴀġᴀ́ɪn.
Mullon, Ó mᴀolᴀ́ɪn.
Mulloney, v. Moloney.
Mulloughney, Ó mᴀol fᴀċᴛnᴀ.
Mullowne, v. Malone.
Mullowney, v. Moloney.
Mulloy, v. Molloy.
Mullpeters, Ó mᴀoɪl peᴀᴠᴀɪr.
Mullreavy, Ó mᴀoɪlrɪᴀḃᴀɪġ.
Mullveen, Ó mᴀoɪlṁɪ́n.
Mullvihill, Ó mᴀoɪl mɪċɪl, Ó mᴀoɪl mɪċɪl.
Mulmona, Ó mᴀolmónᴀ.
Muloney, v. Moloney.
Mulooly, Ó mᴀolġuᴀlᴀ.

Muloy, v. Molloy.
Mulqueen, Ó mᴀolċᴀoɪn 11, Ó mᴀol Cᴀoɪne 462.
Mulqueeny, Ó mᴀol Cᴀoɪne.
Mulquin, Ó mᴀolċᴀoɪn.
Mulrain, Ó mᴀoɪl Rɪᴀġᴀɪn, Ó mᴀoɪl Rɪᴀɪn.
Mulready, Ó mᴀoɪl ḃrɪ́ġᴅe.
Mulreany, Ó mᴀoɪlrɪéᴀnᴀ, (o.f.) Ó mᴀoɪl ḃréᴀnᴀɪnn.
Mulreavy, Ó mᴀoɪlrɪᴀḃᴀɪġ.
Mulrenan, Mulrenin, Mulrennan, Mulrennin, Ó mᴀoɪl ḃréᴀnᴀɪnn, Ó mᴀoɪl ḃreᴀnᴀɪnn.
Mulrine, Ó mᴀoɪl Rɪᴀɪn.
Mulroe, Ó mᴀolruᴀɪᴅ.
Mulrony, Ó mᴀolruᴀnᴀɪᴅ.
Mulroon, Ó mᴀolruᴀɪn, Ó mᴀolruᴀnᴀɪᴅ.
Mulrooney, Ó mᴀolruᴀnᴀɪᴅ.
Mulrow, Mulroy, Ó mᴀolruᴀɪᴅ.
Mulry, Ó mᴀolruᴀɪᴅ 2; Ó mᴀol ṁuɪre 2.
Mulryan, Mulryne, Ó mᴀoɪl Rɪᴀġᴀɪn, Ó mᴀoɪl Rɪᴀɪn.
Mulshinogue, Ó mᴀoɪl Sɪonóġ.
Mulumy, Ó mᴀolċomᴀɪᴅ.
Mulvagh, Ó mᴀoɪlṁeᴀᴠ́ᴀ.
Mulvane, Ó mᴀolḃᴀ́ɪn.
Mulvanerty, Ó mᴀoɪlḃeᴀnnᴀċᴛᴀ.
Mulvanny, Mulvany, Ó mᴀoɪl ṁeᴀnᴀ.
Mulveen, Ó mᴀoɪlṁɪ́n.
Mulvenna, Ó mᴀoɪl ṁeᴀnᴀ.
Mulvennon, Ó mᴀoɪl ḃeᴀnóɪn.
Mulvenny, Ó mᴀoɪl ṁeᴀnᴀ.
Mulverhill, Ó mᴀoɪl mɪċɪl.
Mulvey, Ó mᴀoɪlṁɪᴀᴠ́ᴀɪġ 39; Ó mᴀoɪlṁeᴀᴠ́ᴀ 76.
Mulvihil, Mulvihill, Ó mᴀoɪl mɪċɪl, Ó mᴀoɪl mɪċɪl.
Mulvin, Ó mᴀoɪlṁɪ́n.
Mulvy, v. Mulvey.
Munday, mᴀc ġɪollᴀ eóɪn.
Mungavan, Mungavin, Ó monġᴀḃᴀ́ɪn.
Mungay, Mungey, Ó monġᴀɪġ.

Munkettrick, Munkittrick, mac Śitric.
Munnelly, Ó maongaile.
Munroe, Munrow, v. Monroe.
Munster, Ó muirmneacáin.
Muran, v. Murran.
Murchan, Ó murcáin 1 ; mac murcáin 2.
Murchison, mac murcaiỡ, mac murcáỡa.
Murchoe, Ó murcáỡa.
Murdoch, Murdock, Murdough, Murdow, Murdy, mac muircéartaiż.
Murhilla, Ó murcuile.
Murkin, Ó murcáin 2 ; mac murcáin 2.
Murland, mac murgaláin.
Murley, Ó murcuile.
Murnaghan, Ó muirneacáin.
Murnain, Murnan, Murnane, Ó muirnáin, (o.f.) Ó manannáin.
Murney, mac muirniż.
Murphy, Ó murcáỡa 11 ; mac murcáỡa, mac murcaiỡ 62.
Murran, Murrane, Ó muirneáin.
Murray, Ó muireaỡaiż 1, (s.l.) Ó muiriżte 7, 972 ; mac muireaỡaiż 62 ; mac ġiolla muire 232, 332.
Murready, Ó maoil ỡriżỡe.
Murren, Ó muirreáin, Ó muirín.
Murricane, v. Murrigan.
Murricohu, Ó murcáỡa.
Murrigan, Ó muireagáin.
Murrihy, Ó muiriżte, (o.f.) Ó muireaỡaiż.
Murrin, Ó muirín, Ó muireáin.
Murroney, Ó maolruanaiỡ,(s.l.) Ó murruanaiỡ.
Murrough, mac murcáỡa.
Murrow, mac murcáỡa 1 ; mac muireaỡaiż 67.
Murry, v. Murray.
Murt, Murta, mac muircéartaiż.
Murtagh, Murtaugh, Ó muircéartaiż 1 ; mac muircéartaiż 62.

Murtha, v. Murta.
Murtland, mac murgaláin.
Mustay, Ó maoilrtéiże
Myall, v. Michael,
Myers, Ó meiỡir 1, Ó miỡir, Ó mír 46, 97.
Myhan, Myhane, Ó miaỡacáin.
Myhill v. Michael.
Myler v. Meyler.
Myles v. Miles
Mylett, Mylott, Mylotte, míolóiỡ 11, méalóiỡ 99, málóiỡ 192.
Mynahan, v. Moynihan.
Myniter, v. Miniter.
Myres, v. Myers.

Nagel, v. Nagle.
Naghten, Naghton, Ó neactain.
Nagle, Nagill, ỡe nógla.
Nail, v. Neill.
Naish, v. Nash.
Nale, v. Neill.
Nallen, mac nailín (S.L.).
Nally, mac an ḟailżiż. V. MacNally.
Nalty, mac Conallta.
Nanany, mac Conanaonaiż.
Nangle, ỡe nógla ; (G.p.) mac Oirỡealb, mac Oirỡealbaiż.
Nary, Ó nákaỡaiż.
Nash, ỡe nár 1 ; ỡe nár 2.
Natton, Ó neactain.
Naugher, mac Concobair.
Naughtan, Naighten, Ó neactain.
Naughter, mac Concobair.
Naughton, Ó neactain.
Naulty, v. Nalty and Nulty.
Navan, Navin, mac Cnáimín 46, 99 ; Ó Cnáimín 93.
Nawn, Ó nátan, Ó náan.
Neagle, ỡe nógla.
Neal, Neale, v. Neill.
Nealis, mac niallżuir, mac niallżura.
Nealon, Ó nialláin.
Neaphsey, Ó Cnáimriże.

Neary, Ó náṗaváiġ.

Neavin, mac Cnáiṁín 1 ; mac naoiṁín 87.

Nee, Ó niaṫ.

Neecy, Ó Cnáiṁriġe.

Needham, E 6 ; Ó niaṫ 7, 9.

Neehan, Ó niaṫáin.

Neelan, Neelands, Ó niallain.

Neely, v. MacNealy.

Neenan, Neenin, Ó naoiveanáin.

Neeson, (?) mac niaṫ.

Nehill, Ó neiġill.

Neight, mac neaċtain.

Neilan, Neiland, Neilands, Ó niallain.

Neill, Ó néill 1 ; mac néill 2.

Neilson, mac neiġill.

Nelan, Neland, Nelands, Ó niallain.

Neligan, Ó niallaġáin.

Nelis, mac niallġuir, mac niallġura.

Nelson, mac neiġill.

Nerhenny, Nerney, Nertney, mac an Aiṗċinniġ, mac an Oiṗċinniġ.

Nery, Ó náṗaváiġ.

Nestor, mac an Aġartaiṙ, mac an Aṫartaiṙ, (o.f.) mac ġiṙṙ an Aġartaiṙ.

Netterfield, Netterville, ve neaṫraiḃíol.

Neven, v. Nevin.

Neville, ve nuiḃíol 87 ; ve neaṫ 77 ; Ó niaṫ 17, 46, 49 ; Ó Cnáiṁín 469.

Nevin, Nevins, Ó Cnáiṁín 7 ; mac Cnáiṁín 9 ; mac naoiṁín 8.

Newcombe, E 11 ; Ó niaṫóġ 19.

Newell, Newells, Newill, Ó Cnúċ- ġail, Ó Cnúċail.

Newman, nuaman.

Newnan, Ó nuanáin. V. Noonan.

Newton; Ó núṫáin (S.L.).

Neylan, Neyland, Neylon, Ó niallain.

Nichol, Nichold, Nicholds, Nicholl, Nicholls, Nicholson, Nickle, Nickles, Nickleson, Nicol, Nicoll, Nicolls, Nicols, Nicolson, mac niocoil, mac niocóil.

Niell, v. Neill.

Nielson, mac neiġill.

Night, v. Knight.

Nihill, Ó neiġill.

Nilan, Niland, Nilon, Ó niallain.

Nirney, mac an Aiṗċinniġ, mac an Oiṗċinniġ.

Nivin, v. Nevin.

Nix, mac niocair.

Nixon, mac nic, mac niocláir.

Noakley, Ó neoṫallaiġ (S.L.).

Nocher, mac Conċoḃair.

Nochtin, Nochton, Ó neaċtain.

Nocker, Nocter, mac Conċoḃair.

Nocton, Ó neaċtain.

Noghar, Nogher, mac Conċoḃair.

Nohally, Ó neoṫallaiġ (S.L.).

Noher, mac Conċoḃair.

Nohilly, Ó neoṫallaiġ (S.L.).

Nolan, Ó nuallain 19 ; mac nuallain 19 ; Ó huallaċáin 98, Ó nuallaċáin 19 ; Ó hultaċáin 23, 67.

Noland, Nolans, v. Nolan

Nolty, v. Nulty.

Noonan, Noonane, Ó nuanáin 11, (o.f.) Ó hionṁaineáin 7 ; Ó nuaṫán 19 ; Ó naoiveanáin 172, 492.

Noone, Ó nuaṫán 11, Ó nuanáin 97.

Nooney, Ó hionṁaine.

Normile, Normoyle, mac Con ṫormaoile, (s.l.) mac Conoṙ- ṁaoile,

Norris, Norrish, Norries, ve noiṗéir, noiṗéir, noṗair 1 ; ve noṗaṫ, ve noṗaiṫ 74.

North, Northridge, v. Norris.
Norton, Ó Neaċtain 1; ve
noptún 2.
Norway, ve Nopaú, ve Nopaıú.
Noud, Ó Nuaúat 16; Mac
Nuaúat, Mac Nuaúaú 2.
Noughton, Ó Neaċtain.
Noury, ve Nopaú, ve Nopaıú.
Nowd, v. Noud.
Nowlan, Ó Nualláin. V. Nolan.
Nowry, ve Nopaú, ve Nopaıú.
Nugent, ve Núinnpean, Núinn-
pean 11; Uinnpeaúún, ínn-
peaúún 77; Maʒ Uinnpean-
náin, Maʒ Uinnpıonnáin, Ua
Cuinpıoʒán 43, 64, 67, (o.f.)
Mac ʒıolla Seanáin, Mac
ʒıolla Sıonáin.
Nulty, Mac an Ultaıʒ.
Nunan, Nunun, v. Noonan.
Nyhane, Ó Nıaċáin.
Nyhill, Ó Neıʒıll.
Nynane, Ó Naoıúeanáin.

Oak, Oakes, Oaks, Mac ναpaċ,
(o.f.) Mac Óuıbúναpaċ 1; Ó
ναpaċ, (o.f.) Ó Óuıbúναpaċ 2.
Oates, Mac Cuıpc, (s.l.) Mac
Coıpce.
O'Begley, Ó beaʒlaoıċ.
O'Beirne, O'Bierne, Ó beıpn, Ó
bıpn.
O'Boyce, Ó buaúaıʒ.
O'Boyle, Ó baoıʒıll.
O'Brady, Ó bpáναıʒ 97.
O'Brallaghan, Ó bpolċáin, Ó
bpolaċáin, Ó bpoıleaċáin.
O'Brazil, Ó bpeapaıl.
O'Brennan, Ó bpaonáin. V.
Brennan.
O'Brian, Ó bpıaın.
O'Brick, Ó bpuıc 49; Ó bpuıc 47.
O'Brien, Ó bpıaın 12; Ó bpaoın
15.
O'Brollaghan, v. O'Brallaghan.
O'Bryan, O'Bryen, Ó bpıaın.
O'Byrne, Ó bpoın 11; Ó beıpn,
Ó bıpn 9.

O'Cahan, Ó Caċáin.
O'Caharney, O'Caherney, Ó
Caċapnaıʒ.
O'Callaghan, O'Callahan, Ó
Ceallaċáin 10; Ó Céıleaċ-
áin 64.
O'Carrigan, Ó Cappaʒáin.
O'Carroll, Ó Ceapbaıll.
O'Carthy, Ó Cápċaıʒ
O'Casey, Ó Caċapaıʒ.
O'Caughan, Ó Caċáin.
O'Clery, Ó Cléıpıʒ.
O'Cloghessy, O'Clohessy, Ó
Cloċapaıʒ.
O'Coigley, Ó Coıʒlıʒ.
O'Colohan, Ó Cúlaċáin.
O'Colter, Ó Coltaıp, Ó Col-
tapáin.
O'Concannon, Ó Conċeanainn,
Ó Conċeannainn.
O'Connell, Ó Conaıll.
O'Conner, O'Connor, O'Conor,
Ó Conċoúaıp.
O'Conor Don, Ó Conċoúaıp
 νonn.
O'Corry, Ó Coppa.
O'Crowley, Ó Cpuaúlaoıċ 9; Ó
Cpoúlaoıċ 7. V. Crowley.
O'Cuill, Ó Cuıll.
O'Cullane, Ó Cuıleáin, Ó Coıl-
eáin.
O'Curran, Ó Coppáin, Ó Cuppáin
O'Currobeen, Ó Coıpbín.
O'Curry, Ó Compaıνe 46.
O'Daly, Ó νálaıʒ.
O'Dea, Ó νeaʒaıύ, Ó νeaύaıύ,
(s.l.) Ó Oıaʒaıύ 72, 92.
O'Deere, Ó Ouıbúıp, (s.l.) Ó
Ouıύıp.
O'Dempsey, Ó νíomapaıʒ.
O'Dermott, Ó Oıapmava 1; Ó
νíopma, (o.f.) Ó Ouıbύíopma
16, 26.
O'Devine, Ó Oaımín 6; Ó
Ouıbín 7, 9.
O'Diff, Ó Ouıb 8; Ó Ooıċe 19.
O'Dogherty, O'Doherty, Ó νο-
ċaptaıʒ.

O'Donnell, Ó Domnaill.
O'Donnelly, Ó Donngaile.
O'Donoghue, O'Donohoe,
O'Donohue, Ó Donncúa.
O'Donovan, Ó Donnabáin.
O'Doogan, Ó Dubagáin.
O'Dooghany, Ó Dubconna.
O'Dolan, Ó Dubláin.
O'Doolan, Ó Dubláinn 2; Ó Dubláin 2.
O'Doran, O'Dorian, Ó Deóráin, (o.f.) Ó Deópaváin.
O'Dornan, Ó Dopnáin.
O'Doud, Ó Dubda.
O'Dougherty, Ó Docaptaig.
O'Dowd, O'Dowda, Ó Dubda.
O'Driscoll, Ó Opipceóil, (o.f.) Ó heroippceóil.
O'Duffy, Ó Dubtaig. V. Duffy.
O'Durnin, Ó Duipnín.
O'Dwane, Ó Dubáin.
O'Dwyer, Ó Dubuidip, Ó Duibidip.
O'Falvy, Ó Fáilbe.
O'Farrell, Ó Feapgail.
O'Farrelly, Ó Faipceallaig.
O'Fegan, v. Fegan.
O'Ferrall, Ó Feapgail.
O'Ferry, Ó Feapaváig.
O'Filbin, Ó Filibín, (o.f.) Mac Filibín.
O'Finan, Ó Fionnáin.
O'Flaherty, Ó Flaicbeaptaig.
O'Flanagan, Ó Flannagáin.
O'Flannelly, Ó Flanngaile.
O'Flynn, Ó Floinn, Ó Flainn.
O'Foody, Ó Fuava.
O'Friel, Ó Fipgil.
Ogan, úgán.
O'Gallagher, Ó Gallcóbaip, Ó Gallcúbaip.
O'Gara, Ó Gaúpa.
O'Garriga, Ó Geapaga, (o.f.) Mag Feapaváig.
O'Gilbie, O'Gilvie, Ó Giollabuíde.
O'Gorman, Ó Gopmáin 1; Mac Gopmáin 46.

O'Gormley, Ó Goipmleagaig 6; Ó Gopmgaile 9. V. Gormley.
O'Gowan, Ó Gobann, Ó Gabann.
O'Grady, Ó Gráda 11; Ó Greava 74.
O'Gready, Ó Greava.
O'Growney, Ó Gpamna, (o.f.) Mac Caprgamna.
O'Hagan, Ó hÁgáin, (o.f.) Ó hÓgáin 6; Ó hAováxáin 8.
O'Hahasy, Ó haiteapa.
O'Haire, v. O'Hare.
O'Hallaran, O'Halleran, O'Halleron, Ó hAllmupáin.
O'Hallinan, Ó hAilgeanáin.
O'Halloran, Ó hAllmupáin.
O'Hamill, Ó hÁvmaill, Ó hÁgmaill.
O'Hanlon, Ó hAnnluain, Ó hAnluain.
O'Hanrahan, Ó hAnpacáin.
O'Hara, Ó heagpa, Ó heaúpa.
O'Hare, Ó hípi 3; Ó haicip, Ó hoicip, Ó haiccip 4; Ó Gioppaíde, (o.f.) Mag Feapaváig 976.
O'Harra, v. O'Hara.
O'Harran, Ó heapáin 6; Ó heagpáin 97.
O'Harrigan, Ó happagáin.
O'Hart, O'Harte, Ó haipt.
O'Hartigan, Ó haptagáin.
O'Hea, Ó haová.
O'Hear, Ó hípi.
O'Hegan, Ó hAováxáin 8; Ó hÁgáin 6.
O'Hehir, Ó hoicip, Ó haicip.
O'Herlihy, Ó hiapflata, Ó hiaplata, Ó hiaplaice.
O'Hern, v. Hearn.
O'Heyne, Ó heroín.
O'Hickey, Ó híceava, Ó hícíde.
O'Higgin, O'Higgins, Ó huigín, Ó huiginn 1; Ó haoilleacáin 472.
O'Hood, Ó huiv.
O'Hora, Ó hópa, Ó hoúpa.

O'Houlihan, Ó huallacáin.
O'Hourihane, Ó hannracáin.
O'Huadhaigh, Ó huadaig.
O'Hure, Ó hiomair.
O'Hurley, Ó hurtuile.
O'Kane, O'Keane, Ó catáin.
O'Kearney, Ó Cearnaig.
O'Keeffe, Ó Caoim.
O'Keenan, Ó Cianáin.
O'Keeney, Ó Cianaig.
O'Kelleher, O'Kelliher, Ó Céileacair.
O'Keily, Ó Caóla.
O'Kelly, Ó Ceallaig 1; Ó Caollaide, Ó Caollaige 2. V. Kelly.
O'Kennedy, Ó Cinnéidig, Ó Cinnéidið.
O'Keoneen, Ó Ceóinín, (o.f.) Mac Seóinín.
O'Kerane, Ó Ciaráin.
O'Kermody, Ó Cearmada.
O'Kibbon, Ó Ciobúin, (o.f.) Mac Giobúin.
O'Kielt, O'Kielty, Ó Caoilte, Ó Caoiltig.
O'Kieran, Ó Ciaráin.
O'Kissane, Ó Ciosáin.
O'Knee, Ó tnad.
O'Kirwan, Ó Ciardubáin.
O'Lafferty, Ó Laitbeartaig, (o.f.) Ó Flaitbeartaig.
O'Lalor, Ó Leatlobair.
O'Lane, Ó Laigin, Ó Leigin. V. Lane.
O'Laverty, Ó Laitbeartaig, Ó Flaitbeartaig.
O'Leary, Ó Laogaire.
O'Lee, Ó Laidig, Ó Laoidig.
O'Leery, Ó Laogaire.
O'Lehane, Ó Liatáin.
O'Leyne, Ó Laigin, Ó Leigin, Ó Leidin.
Oliver, Oilibéar.
O'Loan, O'Loane, Ó Luain.
O'Loghlen, Ó Loclainn.
O'Lomasney, Ó Lomarna.

O'Lone, Ó Luain.
O'Looney, Ó Luanaig 7; Ó Luinig 6.
O'Loughlan, O'Loughlin, Ó Loclainn 11; Ó Loclainn, (o.f.) Ó Lactnáin, 19, 24; Ó Maoileaclainn, Ó Maoil Seaclainn 82, 92.
O'Loughran, Ó Lucaireáin, Ó Lucráin 6; Ó Lactráin, (o.f.) Ó Lactnáin 46.
Olus, Ó heólura, Ó heóluir.
O'Lynn, Ó Loinn, Ó Floinn.
O'Lyons, Ó Laigin, Ó Laidín 11; Ó Liatáin 16, 77; Ó hóileáin 19.
O'Madden, Ó Madaidín, Ó Madín.
O'Mahony, Ó Matgamna.
O'Malley, Ó Máille. V. Malley
O'Malone, Ó Maoil eóin.
O'Mara, Ó Meadra.
O'Meagher, Ó Meacair.
O'Meally, Ó Máille.
O'Mealue, Ó Maol aoda.
O'Mealy, Ó Máille.
O'Meara, Ó Meadra.
O'Meehan, O'Meehon, Ó Miadacáin.
O'Mellon, Ó Meallláin.
O'Molloy, Ó Maolmuaid. V. Molloy.
O'Moore, O'More, Ó Mórda.
O'Moran, Ó Móráin, Ó Mográin. V. Moran.
O'Moynan, Ó Muimneacáin; Ó Muineacáin.
O'Mullane, Ó Maoláin.
O'Mulrennin, Ó Maoil Bréanainn
O'Muracha, O'Murphy, Ó Murcada.
O'Naughton, Ó Neactain.
O'Neal, O'Neill, Ó néill.
O'Nial, Ó neigill.
O'Nolan, O'Nowlan, Ó nualláin.
Oogan, úgán.
Oonin, Ó huaicnín.
O'Phelan, Ó Faoláin.

O'Pray, ⱹn ṗréiṫ, (s.l.) Ó ṗréiṫ.
O'Quigley, Ó coiᵹliᵹ.
O'Quin, Ó cuinn.
O'Rafferty, Ó Raḃⱹrⱹaiᵹ, (s.l.)
  Ó Raiṫḃeⱹrⱹaiᵹ.
O'Rahill, Ó Ráᵹaill.
O'Rahilly, Ó Raiṫile.
O'Rawe, (?)
Orchard, áiṗréiṗ.
O'Realley, Ó Raᵹallaiᵹ, Ó
  Raᵹailliᵹ, (s.l.) Ó Raoᵹall-
  aiᵹ.
O'Regan, Ó Riaᵹáin 1, (s.l.) Ó
  Réaᵹáin 2.
O'Reiley, O'Reilly, Ó Raᵹall-
  aiᵹ, Ó Raᵹailliᵹ.   V.
  Reilly.
O'Renehan, Ó Reⱹnnaċáin.
Organ, Ó hAṗᵹáin.
O'Rielly, v. O'Reilly.
O'Riordan, Ó Ríoᵹḃarⱹⱹáin,
  (s.l.) Ó Ríoṗⱹáin.
Ormond, Ó Ruⱹiṫ.
Ormsby, áirⱹar, áirⱹrear.
O'Roarke, O'Rorke, O'Rourke,
  Ó Ruⱹiṗc.
O'Ryan, Ó Riⱹin 8; Ó mⱹoil
  Riⱹin 7; Ó Ruⱹiṫín 9.   V.
  Ryan.
Osborne, Órḃuṗ.
O'Scannell, Ó Scⱹnnⱹil.
O'Sevnagh, Ó Suiḃne.
O'Shannessy,   O Shaughnessy,
  Ó Seⱹċnⱹṗaiᵹ.
O'Shea, O'Shee, Ó Séaᵹṫa.
O'Shiel, Ó Siⱹṫⱹil, Ó Siⱹᵹail.
O'Sullivan, Ó Súileⱹḃáin, Ó
  Súilleⱹḃáin.
O'Summⱹchan,   O'Summahan,
  Ó Somⱹċáin.
Oswald, Oswell, Ó heoṫorⱹ
  23 (O'D.).
O'Thina, Ó cⱹine.
O'Tierney, Ó ciᵹeⱹrnaiᵹ.   V.
  Tierney.
O'Toole, Ó cuⱹṫⱹil, Ó cuⱹṫᵹail.
O'Toomey, Ó cuⱹmⱹ.
Otterson, mⱹc Oiṫiṗ.

O'Twomey, Ó cuⱹmⱹ.
Ougan, úᵹán.
Ounihan, Ó hOnċon.
Owen, Owens, Ó heoᵹain 11 ;
  mⱹc eoᵹain 642.

Padden, Paden, Padian, Padin,
  mⱹc páiṫín 2 ; páiṫín 2.
Paine, paᵹan.
Pallas, Palles, pⱹiliṗ.
Palmer, pámar 1 ; Ó mⱹolṗoᵹ-
  ṁaiṗ, Ó mⱹolṗoᵹṁaiṗ 19
  (O'D.).
Panneen, pⱹinín.
Paragon, v. Parrican.
Paiill, peⱹrⱹil.
Parish, ᵹe páiṗiṗ.
Parker, páiṗcéiṗ, pⱹṗcaṗ.
Parkins, Parkinson, mⱹc peáiṗ-
  cín.
Parle, peⱹrⱹil.
Parlon, mⱹc páṗcⱹláin.   V.
  MacParlan.
Parnell, peáiṗnéil, páṗnⱹil.
Parrican, mⱹc páṫⱹⱹicín, mⱹc
  páṫⱹⱹicín.
Parrott, peⱹṗóiṫ.
Parsons, mⱹc an peⱹṗṗúin.
Partland, mⱹc páṗcⱹláin, mⱹc
  páṗcⱹláin, mⱹc páṗcⱹláin.
Paton, v. Patten.
Pⱹtrician, mⱹc páṫⱹⱹicín, mⱹc
  páṫⱹⱹiᵹín.
Patrick, páṫⱹⱹiᵹ.
Patten, Ó peⱹcáin, Ó piocáin
  16, 91, Ó piceáin 192 ;
  páiṫín E. 2 ; mⱹc páiṫín
  992 ; pⱹcún 2.
Patterson, mⱹc páiṫín, mⱹc
  páiṫín 9 ; (s.s.) Ó Cⱹⱹáin, Ó
  Coⱹáin 197, 976.
Pattin, v. Patten.
Pattinson,   Pattisson,   mⱹc
  páiṫín, mⱹc páiṫín.
Patton, v. Patten.
Paul, Ó mⱹolṗáḃail 66.
Paulett, póiléiṫ.
Paulson, mⱹc póil, mⱹc póil.

Payne, paʓán.
Payton, Ó peatáin 16, 92 ; ve
péatún 2 ; mac páivín 92,
(s.l.) Ó páivín 34.
Peacock, Peacocke, péacóc,
péacóʓ.
Peake, mac péice.
Pearse, piapap 1 ; mac piapaip
2.
Pearson, mac piapaip.
Peck, Ó béice (O'D.).
Peden, Pedian, v. Padden.
Peelan, v. Phelan.
Pegum, péaʓum.
Peirson, mac piapaip.
Pelan, v. Phelan.
Pembroke, ve pionbpóc, ve
piombpóʓ, piombpóʓ.
Pender, pionvap 1 ; pionvap-
ʓáp 2.
Pendergast, Pendergrass, pion-
vapʓáp, pionvapʓpáp, &c.
V. Prendergast.
Penders, v. Pender.
Pendeville, ve ppionnvíol.
Peppard, Pepper, piobap, piob-
apc, piobaipe.
Perkins, mac peáipcín.
Perrott, peapóiv, piopóiv
Perry, ve poipe.
Peters, Peterson, mac peavaip.
Petit, Petite, peicív, peicív.
Peton, v. Payton.
Petters, Petterson, v. Peters.
Pettitt, Petty, peicív, peicív.
Peyton, v. Payton.
Phair, pionn.
Pharis, v. Farris.
Phelan, Phelon, Ó paoláin 1 ;
Ó pialáin 6 ; Ó paoilleacáin.
5. V. Whelan.
Phelim, mac peiólim, mac
peiólimiv.
Pherson, mac an peappúin,
mac an peappain.
Phibbs, mac pib.
Philan, Ó pialáin 3; Ó paoláin 4.

Philban, Philbin, mac pilibín,
mac pilbín, mac pilibín.
Philmey, mac peiólimiv.
Philpin, mac pilibín, mac
pilibín.
Philips, v. Phillips.
Philipson, mac pilib, mac
pilib.
Phillipin, mac pilibín, mac
pilibín.
Phillips, mac pilib 1, mac
pilib 19, 97 ; mac pilibín,
mac pilibín 992.
Philomy, mac peiólimiv.
Philson, mac pilib, mac pilib,
mac pilib.
Phippen, Phippin, mac pibín.
Phipps, Phipson, mac pib.
Phylan, v. Philan.
Pike, píc.
Pickett, piocóiv.
Pidgeon, v. Pigeon.
Pierce, Pierse, piapap 1 ; mac
piapaip 2.
Pierson, mac piapaip.
Pigeon, mac ʓuaiʓín 62 ; mac
Cuilinn 64 ; mac Coluim
2 (O'G.).
Piggott, Pigott, pioʓóiv,
piocóiv.
Pilliu, Pillon, pilin.
Pindar, Pinder, pionvap 1 ;
pionvapʓáp, pionvapʓpáp 2.
Pindergast, pionvapʓáp. V.
Prendergast.
Pinders, v. Pinder.
Piper, Pipper, v. Pepper.
Pirrie, ve poipe.
Plover, mac pilibín, mac
pilibín, mac pilibín 19.
Plunket, Plunkett, pluincéiv,
pluinʓcéiv, pluinʓcéiv.
Poer, ve paop, paop.
Poland, Polin, póilín, mac
póil n.
Pollard, polápv
Pollen, póilín.
Pollett, póiléiv.

Pollick, Pollock, polóc.
Poison, mac póil.
Pomeıoy, Pomroy, ve pompae.
Poor, ve paop, paop.
Portabello, ve poıptıngéıl, poıptıngéıl.
Porter, póıptéıp 18, 28, 43, 47 ; póptúp 2.
Potter, potap.
Powderly, púvaplaış.
Powel, Powell, a paol, paol 2 ; póıl 979 ; mac ȝıolla póıl 25, 27.
Power, ve paop, paop.
Powlett, póıléıv.
Powlson, mac póıl, mac póıl.
Poyne, paȝan.
Prat, Pratt, ve ppát.
Pray, a'ppéıt, (s.l.) ó ppéıt.
Prendergast, ve ppıonvapȝáp, ve ppıonvpaȝáp, ppıonvapȝáp, pıonvapȝáp, pıonvapȝpáp, &c. ; (G.p.) mac Seaptúın.
Prenderville, Prendeville, Prendible, ve ppıonnvíol, ppoınnvíol.
Preston, ve ppeaptún, ppeaptún, ppıoptún.
Prey, v. Pray.
Priall, ppíováıl.
Price, a ppíp, ppíp, ppaıȝeap 1 ; ó ppíopáın, (o.f.) ó muıpȝeapáın 19.
Prichard, Prickard, a ppıpteaıpv, a ppıocaıpv.
Priel, ppíováıl.
Prindergast, v. Prendergast.
Prinderville, Prindeville, Prindiville, v. Prenderville.
Prior, mac an ppíopa, mac an ppíp.
Pritchard, a ppıpteaıpv.
Prout, ppút.
Prunty, ó ppoınntıȝe.
Pryall, ppíováıl.
Pryce, Pryse, a ppíp, ppíp, ppaıȝeap.

Pryle, ppíováıl.
Punch, ponnp, púınpe.
Purcell, Purcill, Pursell, puıpréıl 1, ppuıréıl 2.
Purtell, Purtill, Purtle, ve poptuıl, poptuıl.
Pyke, píc.
Pyne, paȝan.
Pyper, v. Pepper.

Quade, Quaid, Quaide, mac uaıv 1 ; ó Cuaın 17.
Quaine, ó Cuaın.
Qualey, v. Queally.
Qualter, Qualters, mac ualtaıp.
Quan, Quane, Quann, ó Cuaın.
Queally, Queally, ó Caollaıȝe, ó Caollaıve 1 ; ó Caúla 9.
Queelty, ó Caoılte, ó Caoıltıȝ.
Queen, ó Cuınn.
Queenan, Queenane, ó Cuıneáın, ó Cuınneáın.
Queeney, (?) mac maonaıȝ 34.
Quenan, v. Queenan.
Querk, Quick, ó Cuıpc.
Quiddihy, ó Cuıvıȝtıȝ.
Quigley, ó Coıȝlıȝ.
Quiligan, v. Quilligan.
Quilkin, mac uılcín.
Quill, ó Cuıll.
Quillan, Quillen, ó Cuıleáın, ó Cuılín 1 ; mac Coılín 68, 69 ; mac Cuılınn 64 ; mac uıólín 36.
Quillenan, ó Cuıleannáın.
Quilligan, ó Cuıleaȝaın, ó Coılıȝın, (o.f.) ó Colȝan.
Quillinan, Quilnan, ó Cuıleannáın.
Quilter, ve Cuıtléıp, (s.l.) Cuılltéıp.
Quilty, ó Caoılte, ó Caoıltıȝ.
Quin, ó Cuınn 11 ; ó Coınne 62.

Quinane, Ó Cuineáin Ó Cuinn-
eáin.
Quinlan, Ó Caoinleáin, (o.f.)
Ó Caoinvealbáin.
Quinlish, Quinlisk, Ó Cuinolir,
(s.l.) Ó Coinlirc, Ó Cointeirc.
Quinlivan, Ó Caoinvealbáin,
(s.l.) Ó Caoinliobáin.
Quinn, Ó Cuinn 11 ; Mac Cuinn
2 ; Ó Coinne 62.
Quinnell, Ó Coinṡill.
Quinnelly, Ó Coinṡeallaiṡ, (s.)
Mac Coinṡeallaiṡ.
Quinniff, Ó Convuiḃ 2 ; Mac
Convuiḃ 2.
Quinny, Ó Coinne.
Quirk, Quirke, Ó Cuirc.
Quish, Ó Coire.
Quoid, Mac Uaiv.

Rabbett, Rabbit, Rabbitt, Ó
Coinín, Ó Cuinín 11, Ó
Cuineáin 192, 972 ; Mac
Coinín 92 ; Mac Consonaiṡ
972.
Ractigan, Ó Reaċċaṡáin
Rae, v. Rea
Rafe v. Ralph.
Raferty, Rafferty, Ó Raḃarcaiṡ
(s.l.) Ó Raiċḃearcaiṡ.
Rafter, Ó Reaċcaḃair.
Raftery, Ó Reaċcaḃra, Ó Reaċc-
aire.
Raftiss, Ó Reaċcaḃair, (s.l.) Ó
Reaċcaḃair.
Raggett, Raṡav, Raṡac.
Raghneen, Ó Reaċcnín.
Raghtigan, Ó Reaċcaṡáin.
Raheny, (?) Ó Raiċne.
Raher, Ó Reaċair, (o.f.) Ó
Ḟreaċair, Ó Feariċair.
Rahill, Ó Ráṡaill.
Rahilly, Ó Raiċile.
Rail, Rails, Ó Ráṡaill, Ó
Ráiṡill.
Rainey, Ó Raiṡne, Ó Ráiṡne
9 ; Mac Raiṡne 2.

Raleigh, ve Ráiléiṡ, Ráiléiṡ,
Rálaiṡ 14, 17, 27 ; Ó Ráṡall-
aiṡ, Ó Roṡallaiṡ 2.
Rall, Ó Ráṡaill.
Rally, Ó Ráṡallaiṡ.
Ralph, Ráḃulḃ 11, Riap 192.
Ramsay, Ramsey, ve Ramraiṡ,
Ramraiṡ.
Ranaghan, Ranahan, Ó Reann-
aċáin.
Ranaldson, Mac Raṡnaill.
Randall, Randell, Ranval 1 ;
Raṡnall 2 ; Mac Raṡnaill 2.
Randals, Randalson, Randles,
Mac Raṡnaill.
Raney, Ó Ráiṡne 9 ; Mac
Raiṡne 2.
Rankin, Raincín.
Rannals, Mac Raṡnaill 2 ;
Raṡnall 2.
Ranny, v. Raheny.
Ranolds, v. Rannals.
Rashford, Ratchford, v. Roch-
ford.
Ratecan, Ó Reaċcaṡáin.
Rath, ve Ráċ.
Ratican, Ratigan, Rattigan, Ó
Reaċcaṡáin.
Raverty, Ó Raḃarcaiṡ, Ó Raiċ-
ḃearcaiṡ.
Ravery, Ó Raḃarcaiṡ, Ó Raiċ-
ḃearcaiṡ, (s.l.) Ó Raiċḃearcaiṡ
Ravy, Ó Riaḃaiṡ.
Rawleigh, Rawley, v. Raleigh.
Ray, Ó Riaḃaiṡ.
Raymond, Réamonn.
Raynard, Raṡnarv.
Rea, Ó Riaḃaiṡ 1 ; Riaḃaċ 2 ;
Mac Raiċ 62.
Read, Reade, v. Reid.
Readdy, Ready, Ó Riava, Ó
Réava.
Reagh, Riaḃaċ.
Real, Ó Raṡaill, (s.l.) Ó Raoṡaill.
Realy, Ó Raṡailliṡ, (s.l.) Ó
Raoṡallaiṡ.
Reaney, Reany, Ó Raiṡne, Ó
Ráiṡne 1 ; Mac Raiṡne 2.

Reardan, Reardon, Ó Ríorváin, (o.f.) Ó Ríoġḃarváin.
Reaveny,
Reavey, Reay, Ó Riaḃaiġ.
Reckle, Ó Raiġill.
Redahan, Ó Roḋacáin, Ó Roiḋeacáin.
Reddan, Reddin, Redding, Ó Roḋáin.
Reddington, Ó Roḋacáin, Ó Roiḋeacáin 11; Ó Maoilveinṫ 196.
Reddy, Ó Roḋaiġ, Ó Roiḋiġ.
Redehan, Ó Roḋacáin, Ó Roiḋeacáin.
Redington, v. Reddington.
Redmon, Redmond, Redmont, Redmun, Réamonn 1; Mac Réamoinn 9; Roḋmonn 2.
Reed, Reede, v. Reid.
Reel, Ó Raġaill, (s.l.) Ó Raoġaill.
Reely, Ó Raġailliġ, (s.l.) Ó Raoġallaiġ.
Reen, O Rinn.
Reeves, Ó Ríṁeaḋa.
Regan, Ó Riaġáin 1, (s.l.) Ó Réaġáin 2.
Reid, Réiv E 1; ṫiolcaċ 19; Ó Maoilveinṫ 16; Ó Maoil Ḃríġve 92.
Reidy, Ó Riava.
Reigh, Riaḃaċ 1; Ó Riaḃaiġ 2.
Reighill, Reihill, Ó Raġaill, Ó Raiġill.
Reilly, Reily, Ó Raġallaiġ, Ó Raġailliġ, Ó Raiġilliġ, (s.l.) Ó Ráġallaiġ, Ó Raoġallaiġ, &c.
Reiny, Ó Raiġne 2; Mac Raiġne 2.
Reirdan, v. Riordan.
Relehan, Relihan, Ó Roileacáin.
Renaghan, Ranahan, Ó Reannacáin.
Renan, Ó Maoil Ḃreanainn, Ó Maoil Ḃréanainn.
Renard, Raġnarv.

Reneghan, Renehan, Renihan, Ó Reannacáin.
Renken, Renkin, Raincín.
Rennaghan, Ó Reannacáin.
Rennie, Renny, v. Reiny.
Renolds, v. Reynolds.
Reordan, v. Riordan.
Restrick, Ráirtric.
Reville, Roiḃeal.
Rewan, Ó Ruaḋáin.
Reynalds, v. Reynolds.
Reynard, Raġnarv.
Reyney, Mac Raiġne 1; Ó Raiġne 9.
Reynolds, Mac Raġnaill, Mag Raġnaill 11; Raġnall 18, Raġnóiv 2.
Reynoldson, Mac Raġnaill.
Rhategan, Rhatigan, Ó Reácṫaġáin.
Riall, Ó Raġaill, (s.l.) Ó Raoġaill.
Ribbon, Ó Ruibín.
Ricards, v. Rickards.
Rice, Rír, Ríreaċ 1; Ó Maolcruoiḃe 38.
Richards, Richardson, Mac Rirteáirv, Mac Rirteáirv.
Richmond, ve Rireamonn.
Rickard, Riocáirv, Riocarv.
Rickards, Mac Riocáirv, Mac Riocairv.
Rickets, Ricketson, Mac Ricérv.
Riddell, Riddle, ve Riovál, Riveal.
Ridge, Mac Iomaire 97.
Rieley, Rielly, Ó Raġallaiġ, Ó Raġailliġ.
Rierdan, Rierdon, v. Riordan.
Rigley, Ó Raiġilliġ.
Rigney, Ó Raiġne.
Rile, v. Ryle.
Riley, Rilly, v. Reilly.
Rinaghan, Rinahan, Ó Reannacáin.
Ring, Ó Rinn.
Rinihan, Ó Reannacáin.
Rinn, Ó Rinn.

Rior dan, Riorden, Ó Ríoġḃairoáin, (s.l.) Ó Ríorváin.
Roache, ve Róirte, Róirteaċ.
Roa n, Roane, Ó Ruaváin.
Roa ntree, Ó Caoirtannáin.
Roa rke, Ó Ruaiic.
Roa rty, Ó Robairtaiġ.
Robbins, Robbinson, mac Roibín.
Robb, Robbs, mac Rob.
Robert, Riobáirv, Roibeairv.
Roberts, Riobáirv, Roibeairv 2; mac Roibeáirv, mac Roibeairv 2, mac Roibirv 2.
Robertson, mac Roibeáirv, mac Roibeairv 2; Roburtún, Roburún 2; mac Vonnċaiv S. 2.
Robinson, mac Roibín 1; Roburtún, Roburún 2.
Robson, mac Rob.
Roche, ve Róirte, Róirteaċ.
Rochefort, Rochford, Rochfort, *ve Rorroirt, Rortairv 1, Rortún 17; Ó Reaċtnín 19.
Rochneen, Ó Reaċtnín.
Rock, ve Cairraiġ 1; mac Conċairriġe, mac Conċairraiġe 9.
Rodan, v. Rodden.
Rodaughan, Ó Rovaċáin.
Rodden, Roddon, Ó Rováin 10; mac Rováin 13, 16.
Roddy, Ó Rovaiġ.
Roden, v. Rodden.
Rodger, Rodgers, mac Ruaiórí; maġ Ruaiórí 1; Ó Ruaiórí 38, 43, 77, 992, (s.l.) Ó Reiórí 779.
Rodin, v. Rodden.
Rodmont, Rodmund, Rovmonn
Rody, v. Roddy.
Roe, Ruav, 1; Ó Ruaiv, 47; mac Ruaiv 2; mac Conruba 56.
Roe-Lavery, Ó Laḃravá Ruaḃ.
Rogan, Ó Ruavaġáin, Ó Ruaváċáin.
Roger, Rogers, v. Rodgers.

Rogerson, mac Ruaiórí.
Rohan, Ó Roḃaċáin, Ó Reaḃaċáin 4; Ó Ruaváċáin ℓ.
Roland, Ó Roċláin, Ó Roiċleáin 9.
Rolfe, Rolph, Roóulḃ.
Ronaghan, Ó Reannaċáin.
Ronaldson, mac Raġnaill.
Ronan, Ronane, Ronayne, Ó Ronáin 11; Ó Ruanáin, Ó Ruanaváin 29, 92.
Rone, Ó Ruaváin.
Roney, v. Rooney.
Roohan, v. Rohan.
Roon, Ó Ruaváin.
Roonan, Roonane, Ó Ruanáin, (o.f.) Ó Ruanaváin.
Rooneen, Ó Ruanaivín.
Rooney, Ó Ruanavá, Ó Ruanaiv 1; Ó Ruanaivín 93; Ó maoilruanaiv 23, 29, 97, &c.
Roonoo, Ó Ruanavá.
Roorke, Ó Ruaiic.
Roragh, Ó Ruaóraic.
Rorison, mac Ruaiórí.
Rorke, Ó Ruaiic.
Rory, Ó Ruaiórí.
Rose, ve Rúr, Rór.
Ross, ve Ror, Roraċ ; (G.p.) mac Ainvréir, mac Ainvmara.
Rosseter, Rossiter, Rossitor, Roraiteair.
Rossney, Ó Rorna.
Rostig, Róirteaċ.
Roth, Rothe, Rút.
Rouane, Ó Ruaváin.
Roughan, Ó Roḃaċáin, Ó Reaḃaċáin 4; Ó Ruaváċáin ℓ.
Roughasy, (?) Ó Ruóġura.
Roughneen, Ó Reaċtnín.
Rountree, Ó Caoirtannáin.
Rourke, Ó Ruaiic 11, (o.f.) Ó Ruaóraic 2.
Routh, Rút.
Rowan, Ó Roḃaċáin 76; Ó Ruaváin 9.

Rowe, Ruaʋ 1; Ó Ruaıú 47; mac Ruaıʋ 2; mac Conꝛuba 56.

Rowen, Ó Ruaıʋín.

Rowland, Roʋlann 1; Ó Roċláin, Ó Roıċleáın 9.

Rowley, Ó Roġallaıġ 1; Ó Roċláın, Ó Roıċleáın 9.

Rowney, Ó Ruanaʋa, Ó Ruanaıʋ.

Roy, mac Ruaıʋ 2; mac ꝣıollaꝛuaıʋ 62.

Royan, Ó Ruaʋáın, Ó Ruaıʋín.

Royce, v. Rice.

Roynane, Ó Ruanáın, (o.f.) Ó Ruanaʋáın.

Royse, v. Rice.

Ruan, Ruane, Ó Ruaʋáın 11, Ó Ruaıʋín 192.

Ruarke, Ó Ruaıꞃc.

Ruckston, Rucꞃꞇon.

Ruddan, v. Rudden.

Ruddell, v. Ruddle.

Rudden, Ruddin, Ó Roʋáın 1 0; mac Roʋáın 13, 16.

Ruddle, ʋe Rıoʋal, Rıoʋal.

Ruddy, Ó Roʋaıġ 1; mac Roʋaıġ 16.

Rudican, Rudihan, Ó Roʋaċáın, Ó Roıʋeaċáın.

Ruhan, v. Rohan.

Ruineen, Ó Ruanaıʋín.

Ruirk, Ó Ruaıꞃc.

Runey, v. Rooney.

Runian, Ó Ruanaıʋín.

Ruorke, Rurke, Ó Ruaıꞃc.

Rush, Ó Ruıꞃ 43, 88; Ó Luaċaıꞃ, Ó Luaċꞃa 9; Ó ꝼuaʋa 62; ʋe Ruıꞃ 2.

Rushford, v. Rochford.

Russell, Ruıꝛéıl.

Ruth, Rúꞇ.

Ruthledge, Rutledge, Rutlege, Ruıꞇléıꞃ, Ruıꞇlıꞃ 11; Ó maoılʋeıꞃꞅ 19.

Ruttle, v. Ruddle.

Ryall, Ó Raġaıll.

Ryan, Ó Rıaın 8; Ó maoıl Rıaın 7; Ó Ruaıʋín 91, Ó Ruaʋáın 92; Ó Sꝛuıċeáın 192.

Ryder, Ó maꞃcaıġ 3; Ó maꞃcaċáın 4, 9.

Ryely, v. Reilly.

Ryle, Ó Raġaıll, (s.l.) Ó Reıġıll.

Ryley, v. Reilly.

Reynard, Raġnaꝛʋ.

Ryney, Ó Raıġne 2; mac Raıġne 2.

Rynn, Ó Rınn 7; mac Ʋꝛoın 39.

Sall, ʋe Sál, Sál.

Sallanger, Sallenger, Sallinger, Saılınġéıꞃ, Saılıġéıꞃ, Saılınéıꞃ.

Salmon, Sammon, Ó Ʋꝛaʋáın.

Sampson, Samson, Samꞃún.

Samuels, Samuelson, mac Samuel.

Sandall, Sandell, ʋe Sanʋál, Sanʋál.

Sanders, Sanʋaꞃ, Sanʋaıꞃ.

Sanderson, mac Sanʋaıꞃ.

Sanford, ʋe Sanꝼoꞃꞇ.

Santry, ʋe Saınꞇꞃeaʋ, ʋe Seanꞇꞃeaʋ 1; Sıꞇꞃıc 779.

Sargeant, Sargent, Sargint, Sáıꞃꞵeanꞇ.

Sarseil, Sáıꞃꝛéıl.

Sarsfield, Sáıꞃꝛéıl 11, Sáıꞃéıl 19, Saınꝛéıl 192.

Saul, ʋe Sál, Sál.

Saunders, Sanʋaꞃ, Sanʋaıꞃ.

Saunderson, mac Sanʋaıꞃ.

Saurin, ʋe Saʋꞃaınn.

Sausheil, Sáıꞃéıl.

Savage, Sáʋaoıꞃ, Saʋaoıꞃ 1, Saʋáıꞃꞇe 24, 47; Ó Saʋáın 27, 49, 77.

Savin, Ó Saʋáın.

Sayer, Sayers Saoġaꞃ.

Scahill, Ó Scaċġaıl, (o.f.) mac Scaıċġıl.

Scales, ʋe Scéalaꞃ.

Scallan, Ó Sceallái n.
Scally, Ó Scalaiġe, Mac Scalaiġe 11 ; Ó Scolláin 92.
Scamaton, Scampton, Scamtún, Sceaimicín.
Scandlon, Scanlan, Scanlon, Ó Scannláin.
Scannell, Ó Scannail.
Schail, Schaill, Ó Scatġail.
Schofield, Scholefield, Scofield, ve Scoful, Scoful.
Scolard, Scollard, Scoláro.
Scott, Scot 1 ; Albanaċ 2.
Scriven, ve Scribin.
Scuffil, ve Scoful, Scofub.
Scullane, Scullion, Ó Scolláin, (o.f.) Ó Scealláin.
Scully, Ó Scolaiġe, Ó Scolaivे 11 ; Ó Scolláin 92.
Scurlock, Scoplóġ.
Scurry, Ó Scuppa, Ó Scuipe, Ó Scuipiv.
Sdundon, ve Stonnvún, Stonnvún, Stonvún, Stúnvún.
Seagrave, Seagrove, v. Segrave.
Sear, Seares, Sears, Saoġap, Mac Saoġaip, (s.l.) Mac Séappaċ 19.
Searson, Mac Saoġaip.
Seaver, Saoṁap.
Seaward, Saobapo.
Seerey, Seery, Ó Saopaive, (o.f.) Ó Síoġpava, Ó Síoġpaiv.
Segrave, Segre, ve Saoġráब.
Segrue, Ó Siocfpava, Ó Siocpava.
Seix, Saġap.
Selenger, Sellinger, Sailinġéip, Sailiġéip, Sailinéip.
Semore, Semour, Saomap.
Sergeant, Sergent, Saipġeant.
Setright, Mac Sicpic.
Seward, Saobapo 1 ; Ó Suaipo, Ó Suaipt 14 ; Ó Claiṁín 19.
Sewell, Ó Súiliġ 2 ; Saobal 2.
Sexton, Ó Seapnáin, Ó Siopnáin.

Seymore, Seymour, Saomap.
Shaftery, Mac Seappaiv.
Shahan, Ó Séavaċáin.
Shails, Shales, v. Sheils.
Shairp, v. Sharpe.
Shalloe, Shallow, Shally, Shalvey, Ó Sealbaiġ.
Shamrock, Seampóġ.
Shanaghan, Ó Seanaċáin.
Shanagher (?), Ó Seanaċaip.
Shanaghy, Mac Seanċa, Mac Seanċaive.
Shanahan, Shanahen, Ó Seanaċáin, Ó Seanċáin.
Shanahy, v. Shanaghy.
Shanan, v. Shannon.
Shane, Mac Seaġáin, Mac Seáin 1 ; Ó Séavaċáin 2.
Shanessy, v. Shaughnessy.
Shanihan, v. Shanahan.
Shanley, Mac Seanlaoiċ.
Shannagh, Ó Seanaiġ.
Shannahan, v. Shanahan.
Shannessy, v. Shaughnessy.
Shannihan, v. Shanahan.
Shannon, Ó Seanáin 10, 87 ; Ó Seanċáin, Ó Seanaċáin 15, 46, 87 ; Mac ġiolla tSeanáin 46, (s.l.) Ó Cilltpeáin 462.
Shanny, Ó Seanaiġ.
Shanon, v. Shannon.
Sharket, Sharkett, Ó Seapcóiv.
Sharkey, Ó Seapcaiġ.
Sharman, Seapman.
Sharpe, ġéap 1 ; Ó ġéapáin 16.
Sharry, Mac Seappaiġ 13, 16, 29 56 ; Ó Seappaiġ 16, 36, 64, 77.
Sharvin, Ó Seapbáin.
Shasnan, Ó Seapnáin.
Shaughness, Ó Seaċnaip.
Shaughnessy, Ó Seaċnapaiġ 11, (s.l.) Ó Seaċnaip 2.
Shaw, Seavaċ, Seaġaċ.
Shea, Ó Séaġva.
Sheahan, Ó Séavaċáin, Ó Síovaċáin.
Sheales, Sheals, v. Sheils.
Shealy, Ó Sealbaiġ.

153

Shean, Ó Séaváčáin, Ó Síováčáin.
Shearhoon, mac Séaptúin.
Shearlock, v. Sherlock.
Shearman, Seaṗman.
Shee, Ó Séaṡva.
Sheean, Ó Síováčáin, Ó Séaváčáin.
Sheedy, Ó Síova 1 ; mac Síova 76.
Sheehan, Ó Síováčáin, Ó Síveačáin. Ó Síoččáin.
Sheehy, mac Síčiṡ 11, Ó Síčiṡ 72.
Sheen, Ó Síováčáin, Ó Síveačáin.
Sheenan, Ó Sionáin.
Sheera, mac Séaṗča.
Sheeran, Sheeren, Ó Síoṗáin, Ó Síṗín.
Shegrue, Ó Siocṗṗava, Ó Siocṗava.
Shehan, v. Sheehan.
Sheil, Sheilds, Sheils, Ó Siaváil, Ó Siaṡail.
Sheily, Ó Sealváiṡ.
Sheirdan, v. Sheridan.
Sheles, v. Sheils.
Shellew, Shelloe, Shelly, Ó Sealváiṡ.
Shera, mac Séaṗča.
Sherden, Sherdon, Sheredan, Sheridan, Sheriden, Ó Siṗiveáin, Ó Sioṗaváin, Ó Seiṗeaváin.
Sherin, Ó Síṗín.
Sherlock, Scoṗlóṡ 1, Seaṗlóṡ 47.
Sherman, Seaṗman.
Sherodan, v. Sheridan.
Sherra, mac Séaṗča.
Sherridan, v. Sheridan.
Sherry, mac Seaṗṗaiṡ 13, 16, 29, 56 ; Ó Seaṗṗaiṡ 16, 36, 64, 77.
Sherwin, Ó Seaṗváin.
Shevlin, Ó Siṫleáin, Ó Siṫliain, Ó Seiṫleáin, Ó Seiṫlín.
Shiel, Shields, Shiells, Shiels, Shiles, Ó Siaváil, Ó Siaṡail.
Shinagh, v. Shinnagh.

Shine, Ó Seiṡin.
Shinkwin, Simicín.
Shinnagh, Sionnač 2 ; Ó Sionnaiṡ 2.
Shinnahan, Ó Sionačáin.
Shinnan, Ó Sionáin.
Shinnick, Ó Sionnaiṡ, Ó Sionaiṡ.
Shinnock, Sionnač 2 ; Ó Sionnaiṡ 2.
Shinnor, Shinnors, ve Sionúiṗ, Sionúiṗ 11, Soiniúiṗ 92.
Shinny, Shinwick, Ó Sionaiṡ, Ó Sionnaiṡ.
Shirdan, v. Sheridan.
Shirlock, v. Sherlock.
Shirra, mac Séaṗča.
Shonagh, Shonogh, Sionnač.
Short, Ṡeaṗṗ 1 ; mac an Ṡeáiṗṗ, mac an Ṡiṗṗ 6.
Shortall, Shortell, Soiṗtéil, Seaṗtal.
Shorten, Seaṗtáin.
Shorthall, Shortle, v. Shortall.
Shortice, Shortis, Seoṗtúṗ.
Shortt, v. Short.
Shoughnessy, v. Shaughnessy.
Shovelin, Shovlin, v. Shevlin.
Shoye, Seóiṡ.
Shryhane, Ó Sṗuiṫeáin.
Shughrue, Ó Siocṗṗava, Ó Siocṗava.
Shunagh, Sionnač.
Shunny, Ó Sionaiṡ, Ó Sioṗ naiṡ.
Shurdan, Ó Sioṗaváin.
Sigerson, mac Síoṡaiṗ.
Siggins, Siṡín.
Silk, Ó Síova.
Silver (?) Ó háiṗṡeaváin
Simcox, Siomcóc, Siomcóṡ.
Simkin, Simkins, Simicín.
Simmonds, Simmons, Simonds, Simons, Simonson, mac Síomóin, mac Síomoinn.
Simpkin, Simpkins, Simicín.
Simpson, S.ms, Simson, mac Sim.

Sinclair, Sinclare, Sincler, ᴠe Sincléiⱜ, Sincléiⱜ ; (G.p.) mac Riocaiⱜᴠ.

Singen, Singin, ᴠe Suingean, Suingean.

Singleton, ᴠe Sinⱜealⱅún, (s.l.) Ó Sinᴠile, Ó Sionᴠuile 46, 77.

Sinjohn, Sinjun, v. Singen.

Sinnott, Sinott, Sionóiᴠ 1 ; Sionúiⱜ, Soiⱜiúiⱜ 19, 97.

Size, Saⱜaⱜ.

Skahill, Ó Scaⱅⱜail, (o.f.) mac Scaiⱅⱜil.

Skally, Ó Scalaiⱜe, (s.) mac Scalaiⱜe 11 ; Ó Scolláin 92.

Skeahan, Skeane, Ó Scéacáin 4 ; mac Scéacáin 6.

Skeffington, Sceⱜmealⱅún.

Skehan, v. Skeahan.

Skelly, Ó Scalaiⱜe, (s.) mac Scalaiⱜe.

Skelton, ᴠe Scealⱅún.

Skerrett, Sceaⱜaⱅ, Sciⱜéiᴠ.

Skiddy, Sciᴠiⱜ, Sciᴠiⱜeac.

Skiffington, v. Skeffington.

Skillen, Scillinⱜ, Scillinn.

Skinner, Scinéiⱜ.

Skinnion, Ó Scinⱜín.

Skivington, Sceⱜmealⱅún.

Skoolin, Ó Scolláin.

Skryne, ᴠe Scⱜín.

Slamon, (?) Ó Sléiᴠín.

Slane, ᴠe Sláine.

Slattery, Ó Slaⱅaⱜⱜa, Ó Slaⱅⱜa.

Slavin, Sleavin, Sleevin, Slevan, Slevin, Ó Sléiᴠín.

Sleyne, Sliney, Sliny, mac Sleiⱜne.

Sloan, Sloane, Ó Sluaⱜáin, (o.f.) Ó Sluaⱜaᴠáin.

Slocombe, Slócúm, Slócum.

Sloey, v. Slowey.

Slone, v. Sloan.

Slowey, Ó Sluaⱜaᴠaiⱜ.

Slown, v. Sloan.

Sloy, v. Slowey.

Sloyan, Sloyne, Ó Sluaⱜáin, Ó Sluaiⱜín, (o.f.) Ó Sluaⱜaᴠáin, Ó Sluaⱜaiᴠín.

Small, beaⱜ 1 ; Ó Caoilⱅe, Ó Caoilⱅiⱜ 64.

Smallen, Ó Smealáin, (o.f.) Ó Spealáin.

Smallwoods, mac Concoillín.

Smart, Smeaⱜⱅ.

Smeeth, Smíⱜⱅ.

Smiddy, Smiᴠiⱜ, Smiᴠiⱜe 1 ; Smíⱜⱅ 2.

Smith, mac an ⱷobann, mac an ⱷabann 11, mac an ⱷoba 2, mac ⱷobann, mac ⱷabann 2 ; Ó ⱷobann, Ó ⱷabann 35, 38, 58, 67, 86 ; ⱷoba 2.

Smithwick, Smiᴠic 1 ; Smiᴠiⱜ, Smiᴠiⱜe 2 ; Smíⱜⱅ, Smíⱜⱅeac 778.

Smollan, Smollen, Smullen, Ó Smoláin, (o.f.) Ó Smealáin, (o.f.) Ó Spealáin.

Smyth, Smythe, v. Smith.

Smythwick, v. Smithwick.

Snee, Ó Sniaᴠaiⱜ.

Snow, an ⱅSneacⱅa.

Soghlahan, Ó Soclacáin.

Solly, mac Soilliⱜ.

Soloman, Solomon, Solomons, mac Solaiⱜ.

Somahan, Somahaun, Ó Somacáin.

Somers, Ó Saⱜⱜaⱜ 7, 87 ; Ó Somacáin 9 ; maⱜ Saⱜⱜáin 2.

Somerville, Ó Somacáin.

Sommers, v. Somers.

Sommerville, v. Somerville.

Soolivan, Ó Súileaᴠáin.

Soraghan, Sorahan, Soran, Soroghan, Ó Soⱜacáin.

Soughly, Ó Soclaiⱜ.

Soutar, Souter, Súⱅaⱜ.

Spain, ᴠe Spáine, Spáineac.

Spalane, Ó Spealáin.

Spearin, Speariug, Spéiⱜinⱜ.

Speed, Speedy, Ó ⱷuaᴠa 9, Ó ⱷuaᴠacáin 6.

Spelessy, v. Spellessy.

Spellane, Ó Spealáin.

Spellissy, Ó Spealġuṟa, Ó Spil-ġeaṟa.

Spellman, Spelman, Ó Spealáin.

Spencer, Spenser, Mac Speal-áin, Mac Spealláin.

Spilacy, v. Spillessy.

Spilane, Spillane, Ó Spealáin, Ó Spioláin.

Spillessy, Ó Spilġeaṟa, Ó Speal-ġuṟa.

Splaine, v. Spilane.

Spollan, Spollane, Ó Spealáin, (s.l.) Ó Spoláin.

Spratt, Spṟaṫ.

Sreenan * Ó Spianáin.

Sruffaun, Ó Spuṫáin, Ó Spuiṫ-eáin.

Stack, Stac.

Stackpole, Stackpoole, Stacpole, ve Stacabúl, ve Stacapúl ; (s.s.) Ġalloub.

Stafford, ve Staṟoṟt, Staṟoṟt 1 ; Mac an Stocaiṟe 26.

Staines, ve Stáineaṟ.

Stancard, Stanṟaṟo, Stan-caṟo.

Stanford, ve Stanṟoṟt.

Stanley, ve Stainléiġ.

Stanton, ve Stonnoún, Stonn-oún, Stonoún ; (G.p.) Mac an ṁileaṓa, Mac an ṁilio.

Stapleton, Stapleton, ve Stáb-altún ; (s.s.) Ġalloub ; (G.p.) Mac an Ġaill.

Starkey, Starkie, Staṟcaio.

Staunton, v. Stanton.

St. Clair, St. Clare, ve Sincléiṟ, Sincléiṟ ; (G.p.) Mac Rioc-aiṟo.

Stead, Steadman, Steed, Mac Eaċaio 35.

Steen, Stiḃin.

Steenson, Steinson, Stenson, Mac Stiḃin, Mac Stín.

Stephens, Stiḃin 1 ; Mac Stiḃin 81, 91, Mac Steaṟáin. Mac Stioṟáin, Mac Stioṟ-áin, 92 ; Mac Ġiolla Steaṟ-áin 2 ; Ó Steaṟáin 45.

Stephenson, Stevens, Stevenson Stevinson, Mac Stiḃin, Mac Steaṟáin, Mac Steiṁin, Mac Stiaḃna, &c.

Steward, Stewart, Stíoḃaṟo Stíoḃaṟc, Stiuḃaṟo.

Stinson, Mac Stiḃin, Mac Stín

St. John, ve Suinġean, Suin-ġean.

St. Ledger, St. Leger, Sailin-ġéiṟ, Sailiġéiṟ, Sailinéiṟ 11, Saileaṟtaṟ 78.

Stoakes, Stokes, ve Stóc. Stóc.

Stone, Ó Maolċluiċe 1 ; Ó Cloċaṟtaiġ 99.

Storan, Ó Stóiṟín.

Strachan, Straghan, Strahan, Strain, Ó Spaiċeáin, Ó Spuiṫ-eáin, Ó Spuṫáin.

Strange, Stṟáinṟe 1 ; Stṟonnġ, Stṟonġ 78 ; Mac Conċoiġ-cṟíċe 52.

Stritch, Stṟaoit, Stṟaoitṟ, Stṟaoitṟeaċ.

Strohane, Ó Spuiṫeáin, Ó Spuṫ-áin.

Strong, Stronge, Stṟonnġ, Stṟonġ.

Stuart, v. Stewart.

Stubbin, Stubbins, Stóiḃín.

Studdert, Stuoaṟc.

Stundon, ve Stonnoún, Stonn-oún, Stúnoún.

Suche, Súiṟce.

Suckley, Ó Soċlaiġ.

Suel, Ó Súiliġ 2 ; Saoḃal 2.

Sugrew, Sugrue, Ó Siocṟṟaṓa, Ó Sioċṟaṓa.

Sullahan, Sullehan, Ó Súileaċ-áin.

Sullevan, Sullivan, Ó Súileabáin, Ó Súilleabáin 1; Ó Súileacáin 37, 55, 67.
Sumahean, Ó Somacáin.
Summerly, Ó Somacáin 19.
Summers, v. Somers.
Summerville, Ó Somacáin 19, 97.
Suppell, Supple, Suipéil.
Surtill, Soiptéil.
Suter, Sutor, Sutter, Sútap.
Sutton, ve Sucún.
Swaine, Suan.
Swainson, mac Suain.
Swan, Suan.
Swanson, mac Suain.
Swanton, ve Suantún.
Swayne, Suan.
Sweeney, Sweeny, mac Suibne 11, Ó Suibne 772.
Sweetman, Suatman.
Sweney, Sweny, v. Sweeney.
Swift, Ó Fuava 9; Ó Fuavacáin 6.
Swine, Swiney, mac Suibne.
Switzer, Suitréip.
Sword, Swords, Ó Suaipv, Ó Suaipt 8 ; Ó Claimín 9.
Swyne, mac Suibne.
Sylver, v. Silver.
Symmonds, Symmons, Symonds Symondson, Symons, mac Síomóin, mac Síomoinn.
Synan, Ó Sionáin.
Synnott, Synott, Sionóiv 1 ; Sionúip, Soirnúip 19, 97.
Syron, (?) mac Séaptúin.

Taaffe, Taff, Tác.
Tagan, Ó Tavgáin.
Tagart, Tagert, Taggart, Taggert, mac an tSagaipt.
Tagney, Ó Teangana.
Tague, Ó Taivg 2 ; mac Taivg 2.
Talbot, Talbóiv.
Tallant, Tallent, Talant.
Tallon, Talún.

Tally, Ó Taiclig, Ó Taiclig.
Talty, Ó Tailtig.
Tamney, mac an Tiompánaig.
Tangney, Ó Teangana.
Tankard, Tanncápv.
Tannan, v. Tannian.
Tanner, Tanúip.
Tannian, Tannion, Ó Tanaiveáin.
Tansey, Ó bliorcáin (S.L.) 9.
Tarmey, Ó Topmava, Ó Topmaig.
Tarpey, Ó Tappa, Ó Tappaiv, Ó Tappaig.
Tarrant, Tapant. Topanta 77; Ó Tapáin, Ó Topáin 2.
Tarsnane, Ó Taprnáin.
Taugher, Ó Tuaccaip.
Taulty, Ó Tailtig.
Tavey, mac an tSámaig.
Tayler, Taylor, Taylour, Táilliúip.
Teaghan, Ó Téacáin.
Teague, Ó Taivg 2 ; mac Taivg 2.
Teahan, Ó Téacáin, (o.f.) Ó Teiceacáin.
Tee, Ó Taivg.
Teegan, Ó Tavgáin.
Teehan, Ó Téacáin.
Teeling, Taoiling.
Teevan, (?) Ó Teimneáin.
Tegan, Ó Tavgáin.
Tegart, Teggart, Teggarty, mac an tSagaipt.
Tehan, Tehane, Ó Téacáin.
Teigan, Ó Tavgáin.
Teige, Teigue, mac Taivg 1 ; Ó Taivg 4, 9.
Tempany, Tempeny, Tenpeny, mac an Tiompánaig.
Tempest, mac Anpaiv.
Ternan, v. Tiernan.
Terney, Terny, v. Tierney.
Terry, Tuipiv, Toipiv 1 ; Tupaoin 47 ; mac Toipvealbaig 2.

Tevnan, Tevnane, Ó Ceiṁneáin.

Tew, ꞇe Ciú, Ciú.

Thirkell, Mac Copcaill.

Thom, Cóm.

Thomas, Comáp 1; Mac Comáip 2, Mac Cómaip, (s.l.) Ó Cómaip 19, 97.

Thompson, Thomson, Mac Comáip 1, Mac Cómaip, (s.l.) Ó Cómaip 19, 97, Mac Cáṁaip 6.

Thoran, Thorn, Ó Copáin.

Thornhill, Copnuil.

Thornton, Copanca, 47, 77; Ó Copáin, Ó Capáin 2; Ó Opaṡ-náin, Ó Opaiṡneáin 19, 97; muineaꞅ 192; Ó muineaꞅáin 92; Mac SceaꞒáin 64.

Thulis, Ó CuaꞒaláin.

Thunder, Cunꞗap.

Thurkell, Thurkill, Thurkle, Mac Copcaill.

Thynne, Ó Ceiṁin.

Tidins, (?) Ó Cuapuipc.

Tiernan, Mac Ciṡeapnáin 11, Mac Ciṡeapnáin 97; Ó Ciṡeapnáin 16, 91; Ó Ciṡeap-naiṡ 15, 19.

Tierney, Ó Ciṡeapnaiṡ 11; Ó Ciṡeapnáin 91; Mac Ciṡeap-náin 976.

Tighe, Ó Caiꞗṡ 4, 91; Mac Caiꞗṡ 22, 56; Mac Cean-ꞅalaiṡ 43, 67 Ó CeanꞅlaꞒ-áin 19.

Tigue, Mac Caiꞗṡ 19. V. Teigue.

Tilly, Ó CaiꞒliṡ, Ó CaiꞒliṡ.

Timblin, Timlin, Mac Coimilín, Mac Coimilín, (s.l.) Ó Cuim-lin, Ó Cuimlín 19.

Timmin, Timmins, Timmons, Coimín 14, 87; Mac Coimín 19, Ó Coimín 2; Ó Ciomáin 692, 872.

Timony, Ó Ciománaiṡ 69; Mac an Ciompánaiṡ 62.

Timothy, Mac Comalcaiṡ 97

Timpany, Mac an Ciompánaiṡ

Tinan, Ó Ceiṁneáin, Ó Ceiṁnín

Tinckler, Cincléip.

Tinin, Ó Ceiṁnín.

Tinkler, Cincléip.

Tinsley, Ó Ceinnꞅealaiṡ (O'D.).

Tivane, (?) Ó Ceiṁneáin.

Tivnane, Ó Ceiṁneáin.

Toal, Toale, Ó CuaꞒail, Ó CuaꞒṡail.

Tobin, Tobyn, Cóibín.

Togher, Ó CuaꞒaip.

Toghill, Tohall, Ó CuaꞒail, Ó CuaꞒṡail.

Toher, Ó CuaꞒaip.

Tohill, Ó CuaꞒail, Ó CuaꞒṡail.

Toke, Cóc.

Tolan, Toland, Ó CuaꞒaláin.

Toler, Ó CalꞒaip.

Tolin, Ó CuaꞒaláin, (s.l.) Ó Coláin 19.

Tolleran, Ó CalꞒapáin.

Toman, Ó Cuamáin, Ó Comáin.

Tomblin, Tomblinson, Mac Coimilín.

Tomilty, Mac Comalcaiṡ 1; Ó Comalcaiṡ 87, 88.

Tomkin, Tomkins, Cóimicín.

Tomkins, Tomkinson, Mac Cóimicín.

Tomlin, Tomlins, Tomlinson, Comlyn, Mac Coimilín.

Tompkins, Mac Cóimicín.

Toner, Ó Coṁnaip, (o.f.) Ó Coṁpaip.

Tonra, Tonry, Ó Coṁnpa (o.f.) Ó Coṁpaip.

Tooey Ó CuaꞒaiṡ.

Tooher Ó CuaꞒaip.

Toohig, Ó CuaꞒaiṡ.

Toohill, Ó CuaꞒail, Ó CuaꞒṡail.

Toohy, Ó CuaꞒaiṡ.

Took, Tooke, Cóc.

Tooker, Ó CuaꞒaip.

Toolan, Ó CuaꞒaláin.

Toole Ó Ꞇuaꞇail 11 Ó Ꞇuaꞇ-
ᵹail 2 ; Mac Ꞇuaꞇail 92.
Tooley (?) Ó Ꞇuaꞇᵹaile.
Toolis, Ó Ꞇuaꞇaláin.
Tooman, Ó Ꞇuamáin.
Toomey, Ó Ꞇuama.
Toompane, (?) Ó Ꞇuamáin, nó
Mac an Ꞇiompánaiᵹ.
Toorish, Ó Ꞇuaṗuir.
Toran Ó Ꞇoráin Ó Ꞇaráin.
Torley, Mac Ꞇoirⅾealḃaiᵹ.
Tormey, Ó Ꞇormaḋa, Ó Ꞇor-
maiᵹ.
Torney, Ó Ꞇórna.
Torpy, Ó Ꞇórpa, Ó Ꞇórṗaiᵹ.
Torran, Ó Ꞇoráin, Ó Ꞇaráin 2;
Ꞇuraoin 2.
Torrance, Torrans, Torrence,
Torrens, Torrins, Ó Ꞇoráin,
Ó Ꞇaráin 1 ; Ꞇuraoin 47 ;
Mac Ꞇoirⅾealḃaiᵹ 2
Torry, v. Terry.
Tothill, Ó Ꞇuaꞇail (O'M).
Toughall, v. Toughill.
Tougher, Ó Ꞇuaꞇcair.
Toughill, Ó Ꞇuaꞇail, Ó Ꞇuaꞇ-
ᵹail.
Touhig, Ó Ꞇuaꞇaiᵹ.
Touhill v. Toughill.
Touhy Ó Ꞇuaꞇaiᵹ.
Toulhan, Ó Ꞇuaꞇaláin, (s.l.) Ó
Ꞇuaiꞇáin.
Tourisk Ó Ꞇuaruirc.
Towell Ó Ꞇuaꞇail.
Towey Ó Ꞇoᵹḋa 19 34 ; Ó
Ꞇuaꞇaiᵹ 20.
Towhig, Ó Ꞇuaꞇaiᵹ.
Towill. Ó Ꞇuaꞇail.
Towmey, Ó Ꞇuama.
Townley, ⅾe Ꞇúinléiᵹ, Ꞇúin-
léiᵹ, Ꞇúnluiⅾ.
Toy, Toye, Ó Ꞇuaiꞇ (S.L.) 19.
Tracey, Tracy, Ó Ꞇreararaiᵹ.
Trahey, Ó Ꞇraiᵹꞇiᵹ.
Trainor, Tranor, Mac Ꞇréinṗir.
Trant, ⅾe Ꞇreanꞇ, Ꞇreanꞇ,
Ꞇreannꞇ.

Trassy, Ó Ꞇrearaiᵹ.
Travers, Travors, ⅾe Ꞇráiḃearr,
Ꞇráiḃearr 1 ; Ó Ꞇreaḃair 35,
39, 55.
Trayner, Traynor, Mac Ꞇréinṗir.
Treacy, Ó Ꞇrearaiᵹ.
Treanor, Mac Ꞇréinṗir.
Trehy, Ó Ꞇraiᵹꞇiᵹ, Ó Ꞇroiᵹ-
ꞇiᵹ.
Trench, Ꞇrinre, Ꞇrinnre.
Trenor, Mac Ꞇréinṗir.
Tressy, Ó Ꞇrearaiᵹ.
Trevor, Ó Ꞇreaḃair.
Trevors, v. Travers .
Trew, Ꞇriú.
Trim, ⅾe Ꞇruim.
Trim-Lavery, Trin-Lavery Ó
Laḃraḋa Ꞇréan.
Tristan, Tristram, Ꞇrorꞇan.
Trodden, Troddyn, Ó Ꞇreoⅾáin.
Trower, Ó Ꞇreaḃair.
Troy, ⅾe Ꞇreó, Ꞇreó 24, 47 ;
Ó Ꞇraiᵹꞇiᵹ, Ó Ꞇroiᵹꞇiᵹ 2 ;
Ó Ꞇréaṁain 469.
Trueman. Ꞇriúman.
Tryn-Lavery, v. Trin-Lavery.
Tubridy, Tubrit Ó Ꞇioḃraiⅾe.
Tucker, Ó Ꞇuaꞇcair.
Tuffy, Ó Ꞇoᵹḋa.
Tuhill, Ó Ꞇuaꞇail.
Tuhy, Ó Ꞇuaꞇaiᵹ.
Tuite, ⅾe Ꞇiúiꞇ, Ꞇiúiꞇ, (o.í.) ⅾe
Ⅾiúiⅾ, Ⅾiúiⅾ.
Tuke, Ꞇóc.
Tully, Ó Ꞇaiꞇliᵹ, Ó Ꞇaiꞇliᵹ 65 ;
Ó Maolꞇuile 8, 67, 97, (s)
Mac Ṁaolꞇuile, (s l.) Mac
an Ꞇuile, Mac Ꞇuile 16, 95,
Ó Ꞇuile 99.
Tumalty, Tumblety, Tumelty,
Tumilty, Mac Ꞇomalꞇaiᵹ 1 ;
Ó Ꞇomalꞇaiᵹ 87, 88.
Tumman, Tummon, Ó Ꞇuam-
áin, Ó Ꞇomáin.
Tumpane, v. Toompane.
Tumulty, v. Tumalty.
Tunney, Tunny, Ó Ꞇonnaiᵹ 11 ;
Ó Ꞇuine 192.

Tuohig, Ó Cuaċaiġ.
Tuohill, Ó Cuaċail.
Tuohy, Ó Cuaċaiġ.
Tuomy, Ó Cuama.
Turbett, Turbit, Corbóiꝺ.
Turish, Ó Cuaruir.
Turley, mac Coirꝺealḃaiġ.
Turner, Cornóir.
Turney, Ó Córna.
Turnor, Turnour, Cornóir.
Tuthill, Tuttell, Tuttill, Tuttle
    Ó Cuaċail (O'M.).
Tutty, Ó Cuaċaiġ.
Twigley, Ó Coiꝁliġ.
Twohig, Ó Cuaċaiġ.
Twohill, Ó Cuaċail.
Twohy, Ó Cuaċaiġ.
Twomey, Ó Cuama.
Twoohy, v. Twohy.
Twoomy, Ó Cuama.
Tye, Tyghe, v. Tighe.
Tymmany, v. Timony.
Tymmins,   Tymmons,   v.
    Timmins, Timmons.
Tynan, Ó Ceiṁneáin.
Tyne, Ó Ceiṁin.
Tynnan, v. Tynan.
Tynne, v. Tyne.
Tyrrell, Cirial, Crial.

Uiske, mac Conuirce.
Ultagh, Ultaċ.   V. Dunleavy.
Umphrey, Unꝼraiꝺ.
Unehan, Ó hOnċon.
Uniack, Uniacke, Uniake, ꝺoin-
    ꝁeárꝺ, ꝺoinneárꝺ, ꝺuin-
    ꝁeárꝺ, ꝺuinneárꝺ.
Upton, Uptún.
Urrell, ꝺe Oiriġiall.
Usher, Ussher, Uiréir.
Ustace, Iúrtár.

Vaddock, mac ṁaꝺóc, mac
    ṁaꝺóg.
Vadin, mac Páiꝺín.
Vahey, Vahy, mac an ḃeaċa,
    mac an ḃeaċaꝺ.
Vail, mac Páil, mac Póil.

Valentine, ḃailintín.
Vallely, Vallily, (?) mac ꝁiolla
    ṁuire.
Vally, mac an ḃallaiġ.
Varden, ꝺe ḃearoún 1 ; mac
    Páirín 99.
Vargis, Vargus, mac ꝼearꝁura.
Varily, Varley, Varrelly, Var-
    rilly, mac an ḃearꝼúiliġ.
Vaughan, Ó maċáin, Ó moċáin
    1 ; Uaċán 18, 28, 82.
Veale, ꝺe ḃéal, ꝺe ḃial.
Veasy, mac an ḃeaċa, mac an
    ḃeaċaꝺ 19.
Veigh, mac an ḃeaċa, mac an
    ḃeaċaꝺ.
Veldon, ꝺe ḃéalatún, ḃéala-
    tún.
Verdin, Verdon, ꝺe ḃearoún.
Verlin, Verling, ꝼeóirlinꝁ.
Vesey, v. Veasy.
Vicars, Vickers, Vickery, mac
    an ḃiocáire, mac an ḃiocara.
Victory, mac anabaꝺa.
Vikers, v. Vickers.
Vincent, Uinreann.
Vingin, Ó ꝼiaċa, Ó ꝼiaċaċ 47.
Vogan, Úꝁán.

Wadden, Uaiꝺín.
Waddick, mac ṁaꝺóc.
Wadding, Uaiꝺín.
Waddock, mac ṁaꝺóc, mac
    ṁaꝺóg.
Wade, Uaꝺa 1 ; mac Uaiꝺ 6
    mac meaḃaċain (S.L.) 19.
Wadick, Wadock, mac ṁaꝺóc,
    mac ṁaꝺóg.
Waid, Waide, v. Wade.
Waldron, Ualꝺrán 19 ; mac
    Ualꝺráin, mac ḃalꝺráin 92,
    mac Ualronta, mac ḃal-
    ronta 8 ; mac Uailꝺín, mac
    Uailtrín, mac ḃailꝺín, mac
    ḃailtrín 192.
Walker, an tSiuḃail.
Wall, ꝺe ḃál, ꝼáltaċ.

Wallace, Wallice, Wallis, de Ḃailéis, de Ḃailís, de Ḃailis, Ḃailis.

Walsh, Walshe, Breaṫnaċ 11; de Ḃailéis, de Ḃailís, de Ḃailis, Ḃailis 2; Ḃarain, Baranṫaċ 493.

Walter, Walters, Mac Ualtair.

Walton, de Ḃáltún.

Ward, Mac an Ḃáird.

Warnock, Mac Ṁearnóg, (o.f.) Mac Giolla Ṁearnóg.

Warren, Warrin, Ḃarain 11; Ó Murnáin 497.

Waters, Mac Uaitéir 1; Mac Conuisce, (s.l.) Mac an Uisce 19, 35; Ó hUisce, Ó hOisce 92; Ó hUiscín, Ó hOiscín 972; Ó Fuaruisce, Ó hUaruisce 16, 29; Ó Tuaruisc 16, 92.

Waterson Mac Uaitéir.

Watson Mac Uait.

Watters, v. Waters.

Watterson, Mac Uaitéir.

Watts, Mac Uait.

Wayland, (?) Ó Faoláin.

Weadock, Mac Ṁadóc, Mac Ṁadóg.

Wear, Weere, Weir, Mac an Ṁaoir 1; Ó Corra 62.

Welch, v. Walsh.

Weldon, de Béalatún, Béalatún.

Wellesley, Uaisléiġ; (G.p.) Mac Ualronta, Mac Ḃalronta.

Welsh, v. Walsh.

Were, v. Wear.

Welsey, v. Wellesley.

Weston, Uasdún, Uastún.

Whalan Whealan Whealon, v. Whelan.

Whearty, Ó Faġartaiġ.

Wheelahan, Ó Faoilleaċáin.

Wheelan, v. Whelan.

Whelahan Ó Faoilleaċáin.

Whelan, Ó Faoláin 11 (s.l.) Ó Faoileáin, Ó Fualáin 2, Ó Foileáin 92, Ó hAoláin 2, Ó hOileáin, Ó hÓileáin, Ó hOláin 91, Ó hUileáin, Ó hIoláin 99; Ó Faoilleaċáin 52.

Wheleghan, Whelehen Ó Faoilleaċáin.

Whelen, Whelon, v Whelan.

White, de Faoit 1, de Faoite 72; Bán 2; Ó Banáin 23, 29; Ó Gealagáin 2.

Whitehead, Ó Ceannduḃáin.

Whiteley, de Fuitléiġ.

Whitesteed, Ó hEaċḋuḃáin.

Whitley, de Fuitléiġ.

Whitney, de Fuitniġ.

Whitty, de Fuite.

Wholey, Ó hUallaiġ, (s.l.) Ó Fuallaiġ.

Wholihan, Wholihane, Ó hUallaċáin (s l) Ó Fuallaċáin.

Wholy v. Wholey.

Whoolahan, Whoolehan, v. Wholihan.

Whooley, Whooly, v. Wholey.

Whoriskey, Whorriskey, Ó Fuaruisce.

Whyte v. White.

Wier Mac an Ṁaoir.

Wigin, Mac Gúigín, Mac Gúigean.

Wigmore de Uigeamór.

Wilhair, Wilhere, Ó Maoil Ċéire.

Wilkins, Wilkinson, Wilkisson, Mac Uilcín.

Williams, Williamson, Mac Uilliam.

Willis, Uilis.

Willmit, Willmott, v. Wilmot.

Wills Uilis.

Wilmot, Uileamóid, Uilmit.

Wilson, Mac Liam.

Windham, Ó Gaoiṫín 97.

Windle, Uingil.

Wingfield, Uingféil, Uingil.

Wingle, Winkle, Uingil.

Winn, v. Wynne

Winters, Ɐn Ᵹeiṁpiⱅ 1 ; mⱯc ꝽiollⱯ Ᵹeiṁpiⱅ 62.

Wire, mⱯc Ɐn ṁⱯoip.

Wisdom, Ó Céile.

Wise, ⱱe uiⱱeⱯp, uiⱱeⱯp.

Wixted, uicpⱅéiⱱ.

Wogan, Úᵹán.

Wofe, ulⱇ 2; Ó mⱯcⱅípe, Ó mic-ⱅípe 778; ⱱe Ꝃulꝃ, ⱱe Ꝃul 73.

Woodlock, uⱯⱱlóc, uⱯⱱlóᵹ.

Woods, ⱱe Ꝃóiⱱ E 2; mⱯc Conċoille, mⱯc ConċoilleⱯꝃ 26, 33, 72, 82; mⱯc Con-ċoillín 2 ; mⱯc ꝽiollⱯ ċoille 62, 92 (O'D.) ; Ó Ċoilliᵹ 9 (O'D.) ; Ó CⱯoilⱅe 92 ; Ó Cuill 792.

Wooley, ⱱe Ꝃulꝃ, (s.l.) Ɐ ꝂulⱯ 197.

Wooloughan, Ó huⱯllⱯċáin, (s.l.) Ó ⱇuⱯllⱯċáin.

Woulfe, ⱱe Ꝃulꝃ, ⱱe Ꝃul.

Wrafter, Ó ReⱯċⱅⱯꝃⱯip.

Wray, v. Rea.

Wren, Wrenn, Ó Rinn 10 ; mⱯc Ꝃpoin 9.

Wright, RⱯᵹⱯiⱅ 1; mⱯc Ɐn ĊeⱯipⱅ (S.L.) 19 ; Ó ⱱeipeⱯl 97.

Wrynn, Ó Rinn 7 ; mⱯc Ꝃpoin 9.

Wyer, mⱯc Ɐn ṁⱯoip.

Wynne, Ᵹuin 1 ; ⱱe Ꝃuinn 47 ; Ó ꝽⱯoiⱅín 19, 97 ; mⱯc ꝽⱯoiⱅín 39 ; Ó mⱯolᵹⱯoiⱅe 2 ; mⱯc ꝽⱯoiⱅe 2.

Wyse, v. Wise.

York, Yorke, mⱯc Con ĊeⱯpcⱯ, mⱯc ConċeⱯpcⱯ.

Young, Younge, ⱱe Siún.

Yourell, ⱱe OipᵹiⱯll.

Zorkin, mⱯc ꝧuⱯpcáin.

Zouche, Súipⱅe.

SUPPLEMENT

Ashlin, Airlinn.
Auterson, v. Otterson.
Barnidge, beapnair.
Beades, na bparoiir.
Beazley, v. Beasley.
Begaddon, Ó beagacáin.
Biesty, v., Beasty.
Blackwell, ve blácual.
Blood, a blóiv, blóiv.
Branley, Brannelly, Ó bpan-
    ṡaile.
Bratton, ve bpátún.
Brinn, mac bpoin.
Brooke, Brookes, Brooks, ve
    bpóc, ve bpúc.
Brunton, ve bpúntún.
Butcher, búircéir.
Cady, mac ávaiv.
Candon, v. Canton.
Cargin, Ó Cappaṡáin.
Carron, mac Ceapáin.
Clafflin, v. MacClachlin.
Condra, mac Annpaic.
Connon, mac Canann.
Corket, Coircaic.
Cott, Cac.
Cranitch, Cpanuic.
Croarkien, (?) mac Ruaipcín.
Cush, mac Coire.
Dagney, mac an veaṡánaiṡ.
Dergan, Ó veapṡáin.
Digney, mac an veaṡánaiṡ.
Divilly, Ó vuibṡiolla.
Domigan, Ó vomaṡáin.
Doorish, Ó vubpuir.
Emmet, eiméiv.
Fagarthy, Ó faṡaptaiṡ.
Fawsitt, fóiréiv.
Feenan, Ó fionnáin.
Funge, fúinre.
Gaan, mac an ṡobann.
Garrahan, Garrahen, v. Gar-
    raghan.
Gatchell, ṡairceal.
Giles, mac ṡoill 97.
Gilloran, v. Killoran.
Glendon, mac ṡiolla finvéin
Goodbody, mac ṡiolla maic.
Goodfellow, macṡiolla maic.

Gonagle, mac Conṡail.
Green, Ó ṡuiana (S.L.) 16.
Grierson, mac ṡrioṡaip.
Herky, Ó heapca.
Horton, Ó hapcáin.
Houston, mac ṡiolla cseac-
    lainn (s.l.) mac 'a cseac-
    lainn 162
Huggins, huṡúin.
Kennish, mac naoir.
Killyleigh, v. Killelea.
Kinnish, mac naoir.
Law, ve lá.
Leahane, Ó liacáin.
Loran, Loughran, Ó lucaipeáin,
    Ó lucpáin.
MacAnespic, mac an eappuiṡ.
MacBarklie, mac papclóin.
MacBlain, mac maoláin.
MacCaughern, mac eacpáin.
MacCooe, mac cobtaiṡ.
MacEdmond, mac éamoinn.
MacGeaveny, mac ṡéibeannaiṡ.
MacLysaght, mac ṡiolla
    iapacta.
MacMunn, mac munna.
MacNamanamee, mac Conan-
    aonaiṡ.
MacNully, mac Conulav.
MacPoland, mac póilín.
MacQuatt, MacWatt, mac uaic.
Marry, Ó meapavaiṡ.
Meldron, Ó maolpuain.
Mucleen, Mulkeen, Ó maol-
    claoin 19.
Mulroyan, Ó maoilpuain.
O'Loran, Ó lucaipeáin, Ó luc-
    páin.
O'Mullan, Ó maoláin.
O'Prey, Ó ppéic, (o.f.) a'ppéic.
O'Shannon, Ó seanáin.
Proud, pjúc.
Rouine, Ó Ruaivín.
Temple, ciompail.
Tinney, mac an cSionnaiṡ.
Tone cón.
Weddick, v. Waddick.
Yanahan, Ó hannacáin.
Yeats, ve ṡeaca.

II

EXPLANATORY NOTE

Names of Men and Women.—These are given in both the nom. and gen. case (cf. § 6, p. 14). English or angl. forms not derived from the Irish name either phonetically or by translation, but substituted by attraction or assimilation (see p. 38), are enclosed in brackets. Our names are drawn from several different languages. The original form of each name is given, together with its signification, as far as it is possible to ascertain it. The manner in which foreign names found their way into Ireland is indicated. Finally, a Latin form is added which it is hoped will prove useful for purposes of registration.

Surnames.—Each surname is given in the nom. case masculine, but in several classes of surnames the same form is common to males and females. The declension of surnames is explained in § 6, pp. 24-7. The form of the surname to be used with names of females is shown in § 7, pp. 27-9. The class to which a surname belongs is indicated by a Roman numeral immediately following the surname. These numerals (I-XIV) refer to § 5, p. 23, but for the convenience of the reader an amplified table of the different classes of surnames is given below. The older English or angl. forms, now obsolete, are printed in italics. These, which are nearly all taken from the Fiants of Elizabeth and the Patent Rolls of James I, show the different steps in the process of anglicising our surnames and generally supply the links between the Irish surname and its present-day angl. equivalents. The modern angl. forms are printed in Roman characters. These have not always been derived from the Irish surname either phonetically or by translation (see pp. 35-7), but substituted by attraction or assimilation (see pp. 37-9). These substituted forms are generally enclosed in round brackets. In consequence of the interchange of surnames (see § 9, pp. 33-5), there is often apparently no connection between the Irish surname and its present English or angl. equivalents. In this case the English or angl. form is enclosed in square brackets. English surnames which are merely equivalents of Irish surnames are similarly enclosed. The original form of the surname, with its meaning, is given whenever possible. The former and present location of the surname is generally noted, and a short sketch added of the family or families who bore it. I have aimed at giving all the genuine variants of each Irish surname, but in the case of certain classes of variants, where to insert all would greatly increase the size of the book, the uniform use of one of the variants was considered sufficient. Thus, Ó is used instead of uᴀ throughout. The combinations ꞃc, ꞃp, ꞃꞇ are, with a few exceptions which explain themselves, used instead of ꞃᵹ, ꞃb, ꞃꝺ respectively. The uninflected form mᴀoꞁ- is used instead of mᴀoꞁ- when followed by a broad vowel in the next syllable. ꝺub- in similar circumstances is used instead of ꝺuıb-. -éꞁ and -éꞃ are used instead of -éᴀꞁ and -éᴀꞃ respectively in the final syllable of Norman surnames. The alternative forms treated of above (pp. 21, 22) are not included, except in a few instances and for some special reason. See also remarks p. 9, note.

CLASSES OF SURNAMES

I.—Surnames of this class are formed by prefixing Ó or uᴀ, grandson, descendant, to the gen. case of a native Irish personal name, as Ó bꞃıᴀın, des. of bꞃıᴀn ; Ó hᴀoꝺᴀ, des. of ᴀoꝺ ; Ó néꞁꞁ, des. of nıᴀꞁꞁ (see p. 15). This is our oldest and most numerous class of surnames. For declension, see p. 25.

II.—Surnames of this class are formed by prefixing Ó or uᴀ, grandson, descendant, to the gen. case of a name of foreign origin, as Ó bꞃuᴀꝺᴀıꞃ, des. of bꞃuᴀꝺᴀꞃ ; Ó ꝺubᵹᴀꞁꞁ, des. of ꝺubᵹᴀꞁꞁ ; Ó hᴀꞃᴀꞁꞇ, des. of Harald. Surnames of this class are mostly of Norse and Danish origin. See p. 16, and for declension, p. 25.

III.—Surnames of this class are formed by prefixing Ó or uᴀ, grandson, descendant, not to the personal name of the ancestor, but to the gen. case of a word indicative of his trade, profession, rank, or occupation, as Ó ᵹobᴀnn, des. of the smith ; Ó híceᴀꝺᴀ, des. of the healer (see p. 15). Only a comparatively small number of surnames belongs to this class. For declension, see p. 25.

Note.—The above three classes comprise all genuine surnames in Ó or uᴀ. Many apparently Ó-surnames are merely corruptions of surnames in mᴀc- or mᴀᵹ- (see p. 32).

IV.—Surnames of this class are formed by prefixing mᴀc or mᴀᵹ, son, to the gen. case of a native Irish personal name, as mᴀc ᴀoꝺᴀᵹᴀın, son of ᴀoꝺᴀᵹᴀn ; mᴀc Cᴀꞃꞇᴀıᵹ, son of Cᴀꞃꞇᴀċ ; mᴀᵹ uıꝺıꞃ, son of Oꝺᴀꞃ (see p. 15). This is an old and numerous class of surnames. For declension, see p. 25.

V.—Surnames of this class are formed by prefixing mᴀc or mᴀᵹ, son, to the gen. case of a name of foreign origin, as mᴀc Íomᴀıꞃ, son of Ivor ; mᴀc mᴀᵹnuıꞃ, son of Magnus ; mᴀc Féóꞃᴀıꞃ, son of Piers ; mᴀc Seóınín, son of little John. Surnames of this class are mostly of Norse and Norman origin. See pp. 16, 19.

VI.—This class comprises surnames of Welsh origin, formed by prefixing ' ab ' or ' ap ', son, to a Welsh personal name (see p. 17). Only a few surnames belong to this class. For declension, see p. 26.

VII.—Surnames of this class are formed by prefixing mac, son, not to the personal name of the ancestor, but to the gen. case of a word indicative of his trade, profession, rank, or occupation, as mac an báinᴅ, son of the bard ; mac an tsaoiɾ, son of the craftsman ; mac an Rioɾɾe, son of the knight (see p. 15). Families bearing surnames of this class may be of either Irish or foreign origin.

VIII.—This class comprises all patronymic surnames of foreign origin in which the father's name appears in its simple and unaltered form, without prefix or desinence (see pp. 17, 19). The great bulk of Anglo-Norman patronymic surnames belong to this class. For declension, see p. 26.

IX.—This class comprises Irish descriptive adjectives which have supplanted the real surnames (see p. 21). For declension, see p. 26.

X.—This class comprises surnames in -ać, -eać, indicative of nationality, place of origin, fosterage, &c. (see p. 21). They may be either substantives or adjectives. For declension, see p. 26.

XI.—This class comprises foreign surnames of local origin (see pp. 18, 19, 20). This class is very numerous. For declension, see p. 26.

XII.—This class comprises occupative and descriptive surnames of foreign origin (see pp. 18, 19, 20). This class is very numerous. For declension, see p. 26.

XIII.—This class comprises Irish surnames formed from the gen. case of place of residence, or some peculiarity (see p. 21). They were not originally surnames in the strict sense, but took the place of real surnames which are now lost. For declension, see p. 26.

XIV.—This class comprises alternative forms of surnames (see p. 21). For declension, see p. 26.

NAMES OF MEN

IRISH—ENGLISH

ⱥbbⱥn, *g.* -áin, Abban; dim. of ⱥbb, an abbot; the name, of a famous Leinster saint of the 6th century; associated chiefly with Wexford. Lat. Abbanus.

ⱥbrⱥhⱥm, *g.* -ⱥim, Abraham; Heb. Abbrahám, father of a multitude (cf. Gen. XVII, 5); the name of the progenitor of the Jewish nation; propagated in France and the Netherlands through St. Abraham of Auvergne; introduced into Ireland by the Anglo-Normans, but never became common. Lat. Abraham, -ae.

ⱥbuistín, *v.* Áṡuirtín.

Áṫⱥṁ, *g.* -ⱥiṁ, **Áṫⱥm**, *g.* -ⱥim, Adam; Heb. Adám, one made or produced, hence creature; the name of the first man; apparently in use in Ireland and Scotland from early Christian times; one of the most popular names among the Anglo-Normans. Lat. Adam, -ae, Adamus.

Áṫⱥṁnán, *g.* -áin, Adamnan, Eunan; dim. of Áṫⱥṁ (q.v.); the name of a celebrated Abbot of Iona in the 7th century, author of the Life of St. Columba and patron of the Diocese of Raphoe. Lat. Adamnanus, Eunanus.

Áṡuistín, **Áṡuistín**, *g.* id., Augustine, Augustin, Austin, &c.; Lat. Augustinus, dim. of Augustus, venerable; the name of the renowned Bishop of Hippo and Doctor of the Church; also of the Apostle of England. To the latter it was that it owed its popularity in England, where it was formerly common as Austin. It is only in comparatively recent times that it has come much into use in Ireland. Also ⱥbuirtín, Áibirtín and Oirtín.

Aíbistín, *g.* id., Augustine, Augustin, Austin, Avvy, Affy ; a var. in Connacht of Águirtín, q.v. Also Abuirtín.

Aíbne, *g.* id., Eveny ; a Derry name, peculiar to the O'Kanes, MacCloskeys and O'Brallaghans.

Ailbe, *g.* id., Alby, Alvy, (Albert, Bertie) ; the name of the patron of the Diocese of Emly ; revived in recent times, but the angl. form is generally Albert (Bertie), which is incorrect. St. Ailbe died in 541. His feast is kept on 12 September. Lat. Albeus.

Ailfrid, *g.* id., Alfred ; Ang.-Sax. Ælfred, elf-counsel ; the name of a king of the West Saxons, known as Alfred the Great ; came into Ireland at the time of the Anglo-Norman invasion, but did not long survive. Ailfrid is a recent revival. Lat. Alfredus, Aluredus.

Ailín, *g.* id., Allen ; an ancient Irish personal name, probably dim. of some name commencing with Ail-, noble. Lat. Ailenus.

Aindréas, Aindrias, *g.* -réir, -riara, Andrew ; Gr. 'Ανδρέας (Andréas), from 'ανήρ (anér), *g.* 'ανδρός (andrós), man ; the name of one of the Twelve Apostles, the brother of St. Peter. The adoption of St. Andrew as the patron of Scotland made Andrew a national name. It was also one of the commonest names among the Anglo-Norman settlers in Ireland (v. Aindriú). Lat. Andreas, -ae.

Aindriú, *g.* id, Andrew ; a var. of Aindréar (q.v.), through the Norman-French Andreu ; very common among the Anglo-Norman settlers in Ireland.

Aineislis, *g.* id., Aneslis, (Standish ; Stanislaus) ; comp. of ain-, negative, and éislir, neglect, forgetfulness, hence careful, thoughtful ; an Irish name formerly in use among the O'Gradys, O'Donovans, O'Heynes, etc.

Alabaois, *g.* id., *Aloys*, Aloysius ; Teut. Hlúdwig, famous battle, Frank. Hluodowig, Cluodowic, Cludowich (Lat. Chlodovisus and Ludovicus), Clovis, Clouis, Fr. Louis, Provençal Aloys (Lat. Aloysius) ; adopted in Ireland in honour of St. Aloysius Gonzaga.

ⱥLⱥSⱦⱥR, *g.* -ⱥıₚ, Allister, Alexander, &c.; an Irish form of Alexander. V. ⱥⱡₚⱥnⱱⱥₚ.

ⱥLⱥSⱦRⱥnn, *g.* -ⱥınn, *Alestren*, Alexander, &c.; an Irish form of Alexander. V. ⱥⱡₚⱥnⱱⱥₚ.

ⱥLⱥSⱦROm, *g.* -ⱦₚuım, Alexander, &c.; an Irish form of Alexander. V. ⱥⱡₚⱥnⱱⱥₚ.

ⱥLbⱥn, *g.* -ⱥın, Alban; Lat. Albanus, from 'albus,' white; the name of the proto-martyr of England.

ⱥLₚOnSuS, ⱥLₚOnSuS, *g.* -uıₚ, Alphonsus, Alfons; Teut. Adalfuns, noble eagerness; a name adopted in Ireland in honour of St. Alphonsus Liguori, founder of the Congregation of the Most Holy Redeemer and Doctor of the Church. Lat. Alphonsus.

ⱥLSⱥnⱱⱥR, *g.* -ⱥıₚ, Alexander, Alex, Alick; Gr. Ἀλέξανδρος (Aléxandros), defending men; perhaps the most widespread as well as the most famous of all personal names. The conquests of Alexander the Great caused it to become widely diffused among eastern nations, while the large number of saints and martyrs of the name in the early Church—the Roman Martyrology mentions no fewer than thirty-nine—popularised it all over Europe. It was introduced into Scotland by Queen Margaret, where it was borne by three of the Scottish kings and became a national name. It was also very common among the early Anglo-Norman settlers in Ireland. The ordinary Gaelic form of the name in Ireland and Scotland was ⱥLⱥₚⱦⱥₚ or ⱥLⱥₚⱦₚom, q.v. Lat. Alexander, -dri.

ⱥmbRÓS, *g.* -óıₚ, Ambrose; Gr. Ἀυβρόσιος (Ambrósios), immortal, divine; the name of the great Bishop of Milan and Doctor of the Church; never, however, very common in Ireland. Lat. Ambrosius.

ⱥmbRuS, *g.* -uıₚ, Ambrose; an Ulster var. of ⱥmbₚóₚ, q.v.

ⱥmLⱥOıb, *g.* id., Auliffe, Olave, (Humphrey); Norse, Ólafr, ancestral relic; also written Onlaf and Anlaf; a name introduced by the Norsemen and adopted by the Irish; it first occurs in the Annals at the year 851; still common in West Munster, but absurdly angl. Humphrey. St. Olave, King of Norway, who was slain in battle, July 29, 1030, has made it one of the most popular of Scandinavian names. Lat. Olavus.

ᚐn Cᚐlbᚐċ g. ᚐn Cᚐlbᚐıᵹ, Callough, (Charles). V. Cᚐlbᚐċ.

ᚐnluᚐn, g. -ᚐın, Anlon, (Alphonsus) ; comp. of ᚐn, great, and luᚐn, a hero, champion, or warrior ; a rare name, found only among the O'Briens and a few other families ; angl. Alphonsus among the MacEgans of Kerry ; also, but less correctly, written ᚐnnluᚐn. Lat. Anluanus.

ᚐnmċᚐb, g. -ᚐıb and -ᚐbᚐ, (Ambrose) ; a rare name, peculiar to the O'Maddens, among whom it was angl. Ambrose. Lat. Anmchadus and Animosus.

ᚐnnluᚐn, v. ᚐnluᚐn.

ᚐnnrᚐoı, g. id., Henry, Harry. V. Єınrı.

ᚐnnᴄoın, ᚐnᴄoın, ᚐnᴄoıne, g. id., Antony, Anthony, Anthin ; Lat. Antonius, an ancient Roman name, popularised by St. Antony of Egypt and St. Antony of Padua. It was introduced into Ireland by the Anglo-Normans, but never became very common.

ᚐob, g. ᚐobᚐ and ᚐoıb, Ea, (Hugh) ; Celt. *Aidu-s, fire, Old Ir. Aed ; an ancient and very common Irish name ; a favourite name among the O'Connors of Connacht and the ONeills and O'Donnells of Ulster ; now always angl. Hugh. Lat. Aidus, Ædus.

ᚐobᚐᵹᚐn, g. -ᚐın, Egan ; dim. of ᚐob, q.v. ; Old Ir. Aidacan. Lat. *Aidacanus.

ᚐobᚐıᵹ, g. id., Hughey ; a pet form of ᚐob, q.v.

ᚐobᚐn, g. -ᚐın, Aidan, Aedan, Edan ; dim. of ᚐob, q.v. ; fairly common in the 8th and 9th centuries. Twenty-three saints of the name are mentioned in the Martyrology of Donegal. Lat. Aidanus, Edanus.

ᚐonᵹus, g. -ᵹurᚐ and -ᵹuır, Angus, Aeneas, Eneas, Neese, Neece, Niece ; Celt. *Oino-gustu-s (from oinos, one, and gustus, choice), Old Ir. Oingus, g. Oingusso, Mid. Ir. Oengus, Aengus, g. -gusa ; an ancient and once common Irish name, frequent

among the MacDonnells, O'Dalys, O'Leynes, &c.;
sometimes shortened to ⁿᴀₒᵳ, q.v. Five saints of
the name are mentioned in the Martyrology of Donegal.
Lat. Ængussius, Æneas.

ᴀʀᴀᴌᴛ, *g.* -ᴀιᴌᴛ, Harold; Norse, Haraldr, army-might;
a name brought into Ireland by the Norsemen. Lat.
Haraldus.

ᴀʀᴏᵹᴀᴌ, *g.* -ᵹᴀιᴌ. Ardal, (Arnold); comp. of ᴀᵳ, high,
and ᵹᴀᴌ, valour; a favourite name among the Mac
Kennas and MacMahons of Ulster by whom it was
angl. Arnold; still in use. Lat. Ardgalus.

ᴀʀᴛ, *g.* ᴀιᵳᴛ, Art, (Arthur); Celt. *Arto-s, a stone, or
bear; an ancient Irish personal name; common
among the MacMurrough Kavanaghs, O'Connors and
O'Molloys in Leinster, the O'Keeffes and O'Learys
in Munster, the O'Haras and O'Rourkes in Connacht, and the O'Neills in Ulster; now generally
angl. Arthur. Lat. Artus.

ᴀʀᴛúʀ, *g.* -úιᵳ, Arthur; a name of uncertain origin; in
use in Ireland in the 9th century and among the
Scoto-Irish in the time of St. Columcille, in the form
of Artuir, Lat. Arturius by Adamnan. Lat. Arturus,
Arthurus.

ᴃᴀιᴌ, Val; a pet form of ᴃᴀιᴌιⁿᴛíⁿ, q.v.

ᴃᴀιᴌιⁿᴛíⁿ, *g.* id., Valentine; Lat. Valentinus, dim. of
valens, strong, healthy; the name of several martyrs
in the early Church; never common in Ireland.

ᴃᴀₒᴛᵹᴀᴌᴀċ, *g.* -ᴀιᵹ, *Behellagh, Beolagh,* (Boetius,
Bowes); comp. of ᴃᴀₒᴛ, vain, foolish, and ᵹᴀᴌᴀċ,
valorous; a name peculiar to the MacEgans, O'Dalys,
and a few other families. Lat. Boetgalachus, Boetius.

ᴃᴀʀʀᴀ, *g.* id., Barry; a pet form of ᴃᴀιᵳᵳᶠιₒⁿⁿ or ᶠιₒⁿⁿ-
ᴃᴀᵳᵳ, q.v.; the name of the patron of the Diocese of
Cork. Lat. Barreus.

ᴃᴇᴀċáⁿ, *g.* -áιⁿ, Becan; dim. of ᴃᴇᴀᵹ, small; the name
of a celebrated Munster saint of the 6th century.
His feast was kept on 26th May. Lat. Becanus.

ᴃᴇᴀⁿóⁿ, *g.* -óιⁿ, Benen, Benignus. V. ᴃᴇιⁿᴇóⁿ.

beaRac, *g.* -aig, Barry; deriv. of beaṗ, a spear, javelin,
or anything pointed; the name of a celebrated Connacht saint of the 6th century, Abbot of Cluain
Coirpthe, in the present Co. Roscommon, and patron
of the O'Hanlys; explained in the Life of the saint
as signifying "one who takes a direct aim at an
object, or reaches it, as it were, with the point of the
sword." "Rightly has this name been given to
him," said the priest, Froech, by whom he was baptised, "for he shall be a saint and his place shall be in
heaven." beaṗac, angl. Barry, continued in use as a
Christian name among the O'Hanlys down to recent
times. Lat. Berachius.

beaRcán, *g.* -áin, Bercan; dim. of beaṗac, q.v.; the
name of five Irish saints. Lat. Berchanus.

beaRnáRd, *g.* -áiṙd, Bernard; Frank. Bernhard, strong
bear, brave warrior; the name of the celebrated
Abbot of Clairvaux, whose fame made it universal in
Europe; introduced into Ireland by the Anglo-
Normans, among whom it was rather common, and
later adopted as a synonym for the native name
bṗian, q.v. Lat. Bernardus.

beaRtlaid, *g.* id., Bartley; a modern rendering of the
English name Bartley. V. paṗtalán.

beineán, *g.* -áin, Benignus, Benen; a var. of beineón,
q.v.

beineón, *g.* -óin, Benignus, Benen; Lat. Benignus, good,
kind, mild; the name given by St. Patrick to his
favourite disciple and successor in the See of Armagh.

beiRceaRt, *g.* -ceiṗt, (Benjamin, Ben; Bernard;
Bertie); Ang.-Sax. Beorhthere, bright-army; the
name of an Anglo-Saxon saint who settled at Tullylease, Co. Cork, where he died on 6th December,
839; common in many parts of Cork, Kerry and
Limerick under the angl. form of Benjamin; in parts
of Tipperary, it is made Bernard. Lat. Berichertus.

bineán, *g.* -áin, Benignus, Benen; a var. of beineón,
q.v. Lat. Bineanus.

bRan *g.* bṗain and bṗoin Bran; and old and once

common Irish name meaning ' raven ' ; in use in the
family of O'Byrne down to the middle of the 17th
century or later. Lat. Branius.

ḃReaNaiNN, *g.* id., Brendan ; the name of several Irish
saints, of whom the most celebrated were St. Brendan,
Abbot of Clonfert, and St. Brendan of Birr. The
name in modern Irish is ḃreanoán or ḃreannoán.
Lat. Brendanus.

ḃReaNoáN, ḃReaNNoáN, *g.* -áin, Brendan. V.
ḃréanainn.

ḃReasaL, *g.* -aiL, Brasil, (Basil) ; Old Ir. Bressal, from
Celt *brestelo-s, strife, war ; the name of an Irish
saint whose feast-day was 18th May ; common among
the O'Kellys and O'Maddens of Connacht. Lat.
Bressalius.

ḃRiaN, *g.* -ain, Brian, Bryan, (Bernard ; Barnaby, Barney);
a name made famous by King Brian Boru, victor of
Clontarf, and ever since common in most Irish families.
Lat. Brianus.

ḃRoċaO, Morgan ; a corruption in West Connacht of
ṁurċaO, q.v.

ḃuaOaċ, *g.* -aiȝ, Buagh, (Boetius), Victor ; deriv. of
buaiO, victory ; formerly a favourite name among
the O'Sullivans.

caiLeaN, *g.* -ein, Colin ; a Scottish-Gaelic form of the
Irish CoiLeán, q.v. ; more of less peculiar to the
Campbell family. Lat. Colinus.

caiNNeaċ, *g.* aiȝ, Canice ; an older form of CoinneaC,
q.v. ; Lat. Cainnechus in the Book of Armagh.

caiRḃRe, *g.* id., Carbry ; Old Ir. Coirbre, charioteer ;
formerly a common name among the O'Farrells,
O'Beirnes, &c. ; in use in a few families down to
recent times. Four saintly bishops of the name are
mentioned in the Martyrology of Donegal. Lat.
Corbreus.

caLḃaċ, *g.* -aiȝ, Calvagh, Callough, (Charles) ; an Irish
name, meaning ' bald ' ; once common among the
O'Connors of Offaly, O'Carrolls of Ely, O'Molloys,

O'Donnells, O'Reillys, &c.; now generally angl.
Charles. Also **An Calbac**. Lat. Calvachus.

Caoimġin, g. id., Kevin; Old Ir. Coemgen, comely
birth; the name of the celebrated Abbot of Glendalough; fast becoming a popular mane. Lat. Coem-
genus.

Caolán, g. -áin, Kealan, Kelan; dim. of **caol**, slender;
the name of seven Irish saints. Lat. Coelanus.

Caomán, g. -áin, Kevan; dim. of **caom**, comely, mild,
&c.; sometimes Latinised Pulcherius by translation;
the name of no fewer than fifteen Irish saints. Lat.
Coemanus.

Carlus, g. -uir, Charles; the Latin name Carolus which
was adopted by the Norsemen in honour of Charlemagne (Carolus Magnus) and by them introduced into
Ireland.

Cártac, g. -aiġ, Cartagh, Carthage; Old Ir. Carthach,
from Celt. *karatako-s, loving; an ancient Irish name
borne by the celebrated Abbot and Bishop of Lismore
and patron of that diocese. Lat. Carthachus,
Carthagus.

Catair, g. id., Cahir; a Donegal var. of **Cataoir**, q.v.;
found chiefly in the families of O'Doherty and
O'Gallagher. Lat. Cathirius.

Catal, g. -ail, Cahal, (Charles); Celt. *Katu-valo-s,
battle-mighty; an ancient and very common Irish
name, especially among the O'Connors of Connacht,
O'Farrells, O'Reillys, O'Rourkes and Maguires; now
generally angl. Charles. Lat. Cathalus, Cathaldus.

Cataoir, g. id., Cahir, (Charles); Celt. *Katu-viro-s,
Old Ir. Cathfer, Cather, battle-man, warrior; an
ancient Irish name, most frequent amongst Leinster
families, especially the O'Connors of Offaly, the Mac
Coghlans, O'Molloys and O'Byrnes; now always
angl. Charles. In Donegal, **Catair** (q.v.) is a variant.
Lat. Cathirius.

Catbarr, g. -airr, Caffar; comp. of **cat**, battle, and
barr, head, hence a helmet; a name peculiar to the
O'Donnells of Tirconnell. Lat. Caffarrus.

ceallaċ, g. -aiġ, Kellagh, (Celsus) ; an ancient and once very common Irish name, meaning ' war ' or ' strife ' ; borne by at least three saints, of whom one was the celebrated Archbishop of Armagh, better known as St. Celsus, who died at Ardpatrick in Munster, on 1st April, 1129. Lat. Cellachus, Kellachus.

ceallaċán, g. -áin, Callaghan ; the name of two Irish saints in the Martyrology of Donegal ; also that of a celebrated King of Munster in the tenth century, still borne by his descendants, the MacCarthys and O'Callaghans. Lat. Cellachanus, Kellachanus.

cearḃall, g. -aill, Carroll, (Charles) ; a once common Irish name, especially among the O'Dalys, now angl. Charles. Lat. Kervallus.

cian, g. Céin, Kian, Kean, Cain ; an old Irish name, meaning ' ancient ' ; common among the O'Haras and O'Garas of Connacht and the O'Carrolls of Ely, who, no doubt, took it from their great ancestor, Cian, the son of Olioll Olum, King of Munster, and among the O'Mahonys of South Munster, after their great ancestor, Cian, the son-in-law of Brian Boru, who led the forces of Desmond at the battle of Clontarf ; still in use, but sometimes ridiculously angl. Cain. Lat. Cianus, Kianus.

cianán, g. -áin, Kienan, Kenan ; dim. of Cian, q.v. ; the name of three Irish saints, of whom one was the celebrated Bishop of Duleek. Lat. Ciananus, Kenanus.

ciarán, g. -áin, Kieran ; dim. of ciar, black ; the name of no fewer than fifteen Irish saints mentioned in the Martyrology of Donegal, of whom the best known are St. Kieran of Saighir, patron of the Diocese of Ossory, and St. Kieran, Abbot of Clonmacnoise and patron of that diocese. Their feasts occur respectively on 5th March and 9th September. Ciarán is still a common Christian name in Cape Clear and is also in use in parts of Connacht. Lat. Ceranus, Kiranus, Kieranus.

cillian, g. -téin, Killian ; ' pet ' dim. of Ceallaċ, q.v. ;

the name of a celebrated Irish missionary who was martyred at Wurtzburg in Germany, on 8th July, about the year 689. Lat. Chilianus, Kilianus, Killianus.

Cillín, *g.* id., Killian; a var. of Cillian, q.v. Lat. Cillenus, Killinus.

Cinnéroro̅, cinnéroiᵹ, *g.* id., Kennedy; comp. of ceann, a head, and éroe, armour, hence ' helmeted-head '; the name of the father of Brian Boru; still in use among the O'Briens. Lat. Kinnedius.

Coileán, *g.* -áin, Colin; also written Cuileán; an old Irish personal name meaning ' whelp,' the same as the Scottish Cailean or Colin among the Campbells; rather rare and in later times almost peculiar to the family of O'Dempsey. Lat. Culanus, Culenus.

Coilín, *g.* id., Colin; a var. ot Coileán, q.v. Coilín was also in use among Anglo-Irish families as a ' pet ' form of Nicol or Nicholas. Lat. Colinus.

Cóilín, *g.* id., Colman; dim. of Colmán, q.v.; in use in Connemara.

Coinneac, *g.* -niᵹ, Canice, Kenny; older Cainneac, fair one; the name of the patron of Kilkenny. Lat. Cainnechus, Canicius.

Coireall, *g.* -nill, Kerill, (Cyril); the name of a saintly Irish Bishop whose feast was kept on 13th June. Lat. Carellus, Cyrillus.

Colla, *g.* id, Colla; an ancient Irish name, formerly common among the MacDonalds, MacSweenys and MacMahons of Ulster. Lat. Colla.

Colm, *g.* id., Colm, Colum, Columba; also written Colum; an old Irish name, signifying ' dove '; made famous by St. Columcille, Apostle of Scotland, whose name signifies ' dove of the church.' Lat. Columba.

Colmán, *g.* -áin, Colman, Columban; dim. of colm, a dove; formerly one of the commonest of Irish names; borne by nearly one hundred Irish saints, of whom three are patrons of Irish dioceses, namely, Cloyne, Dromore and Kilmacduagh. Lat. Colmanus.

Colum, *g.* -uim, Colum, Columba; a var. of Colm, q.v.

comán, g. -áin, Coman; dim. of cam, bent; the name of twelve Irish saints, from one of whom Roscommon was so called. Lat. Comanus.

comḋan, v. Comġan.

comġall, g. -aill, Cole; Old Ir. Comgell, co-pledge, fellow-hostage; the name of the celebrated Abbot of Bangor and six other saints mentioned in the Martyrology of Donegal. Lat. Comgallus.

comġan, g. -ain, Cowan; also written Comḋan; Old Ir. Comgan, co-birth, perhaps meaning 'twin' (cf. Comár); the name of three Irish saints. Lat. Comganus.

conáire, g. id., Conary; an ancient Irish name. Lat. Conarius.

conall, g. -aill, Conall, Connell; Celt. *Kuno-valo-s, high-mighty; an ancient and once common Irish personal name; still in use among a few families. Eight saints of the name are mentioned in the Martyrology of Donegal. Lat. Conallus.

conán, g. -áin, Conan; the name of at least six Irish saints, of whom one was St. Conan of Assaroei, Co. Donegal, a relative of St. Columcille, who flourshed in the 6th century and was venerated on 8th March. Lat. Conanus.

concoḃar, g. -air, Conor, Connor, Naugher, Noghor, Nohor, Conny, Con, (Cornelius, Corney, Neil); an ancient and very common Irish name, meaning 'high will' or 'desire'; found in most Irish families; still very much in use, but generally angl. Cornelius. Lat. Conchovarius, Conquovarus.

conn, g. Cuinn, Conn, Con, (Constantine); Old Ir. Cond, from Celt. *kondo-s, sense, reason, intelligence; also a freeman; an ancient Irish name, common among the O'Neills, O'Donnells and O'Rourkes. In the 17th century, it was angl. Constantine by the O'Neills. Lat. Connus.

connlaoḋ, g. -aoḋa, connlaoṫ, g. -aoṫa, Conleth, Conley; comp. of connla, prudent, chaste, and aoḋ, fire; written Conlaid in the Book of Armagh; the name of the patron of the Diocese of Kildare. Lat. Con-laethus, Conlethus.

Consaroín, *g.* id., Constantine; Lat. Constantinus, a name which seems to have been adopted by the O'Briens in the 12th century, but never became common.

Cormac, *g.* -aic, Cormac, (Charles); Old Ir. Corbmac, chariot-son, charioteer, or son of Corb; an ancient Irish name, very common among the MacCarthys, MacDermotts, MacDonoughs, Maguires, O'Clerys, O'Connors of Connacht, O'Donnells and O'Farrells; now generally angl. Charles. Eight saints of the name are mentioned in the Martyrology of Donegal. Lat. Cormacus.

Criomtann, *g.* -ainn, Crevan; an old, but rare, name, meaning 'fox'; common among the Kavanaghs of Leinster. It was the first name of St. Columcille. St. Criomhthann was venerated on 23rd May. Lat. Crimthanus.

Criostal, *g.* -ail, Christopher, Christy; a Scottish and North of Ireland form of Críortóir, q.v.

Críostóir, *g.* -óra, Christopher, Christy; Gr.Χριστοφόρος, (Christophoros), Christ-bearing; a name in use from early Christian times and popularised through Europe by the legend of St. Christopher. It does not appear to have been frequent among the first Anglo-Norman settlers in Ireland, but by the end of the 16th century it had become rather common. Lat. Christophorus.

Cróċán, *g.* -áin, Crohan; the name of a Kerry saint, still much venerated in Cahirdaniel and neighbourhood, where Crohan is rather common as a Christian name. Lat. Crocanus.

Crónán, *g.* -áin, Cronan; dim. of crón, dark-brown; the name of the celebrated Abbot of Roscrea and more than twenty other Irish saints. Lat. Cronanus.

Cuan, *g.* -ain, Cuan, the name of four Irish saints. Lat. Cuanus.

Cúċoiġcríċe, *g.* Conċoiġcríċe, Peregrine; an Irish

name meaning ' hound of the border ' ; peculiar to the
Mageoghegans, O'Molloys, and a few other families
in Westmeath and Offaly ; probably now obsolete.
Peregrine was supposed to be a translation. Lat.
Peregrinus.

Cúċonnaċt, *g.* Conċonnaċt, (Constantine) ; a favourite
name among the Maguires, meaning ' hound of Connacht.' Lat. Cuconnactus.

Cúċríċe, *g.* Conċríċe, Peregrine ; the same as Cúċoiʒ-
críċe, q.v.

Cuimín, *g.* id., Cumin, Comyn ; dim. of cam, bent ; the
name of several Irish saints ; still in use. Lat.
Cominus, Cuminus.

Cúṁaiʒe, *g.* Conṁaiʒe, Cooey, Hughey, (Quintin,
Quinton) ; a rare Derry name, meaning ' hound of
the plain ' ; peculiar to the family of O'Kane and
MacCloskey, by whom it is angl. Quintin.

Cúṁeaḃa, *g.* Conṁeaḃa, Covey ; an Irish name signifying ' hound of Ṁeaḃ ' (a place-name) ; peculiar to
the MacNamaras.

Cú ulaḃ, *g.* Conulaḃ, Cullo, Cooley ; an Irish name,
meaning ' hound of Ulidia ' ; formerly in use among
the MacMahons, MacCawels, MacCanns, &c., but
now very rare, if not obsolete.

Daiḃéiḃ, *g.* id., David ; Nor. Davet, dim. of David
(v. Daiḃiḃ).

Daiḃiḃ, Dáiḃiḃ, *g.* id., David ; Heb. Dávídh, beloved,
probably a shortened form of Dōdavahu, beloved of
Jehovah ; the name of the great King of Israel, psal-
mist and prophet ; the national name in Wales, out
of reverence for St. David of Menevia ; rather common
among the Anglo-Normans, who brought it into
Ireland, where it has ever since enjoyed a steady
popularity. In the spoken language it is often
shortened to Dáit and Dáċ, with dim. Dáiċín. Lat.
David, -is.

Dáire, *g.* id., Dary ; an old Irish name. Lat. Darius.

Dáit, *g.* id., Davy ; a pet form of Daiḃiḃ, q.v.

ⱷⱭⁱⱦⁱ, g. id., Dahy, Davy, David; (1) an old Irish name, meaning 'swiftness,' 'nimbleness'; borne by the celebrated King Dahy and retained by his descendants, the O'Dowds, down to recent times; and (2) a form of ⱷⱭⁱⱱⁱⱷ, q.v.

ⱷⱭⁱⱦⁱⁿ, g. id., Davy; dim. of ⱷⱭⁱⱦ or ⱷⱭⁱⱱⁱⱷ, q.v.

ⱷⱭⱜⱡⱭⁱⱯ, g. id., Dominic, Dominick; very common in Derry for ⱷⱺⁱⱯⁱⱯⁱⱯ, q.v.

ⱷⱭⱯⁱⱯⱭⁱⱯ, g. id., Dominic, Dominick; an Irish form of Dominic; in use in Co. Derry.

ⱷⱭⱦ, g. ⱷⱭⁱⱦ, Davy; a pet form of ⱷⱭⁱⱱⁱⱷ, q.v.

ⱷⱸⱭⱬⱡⱭⁿ, g. -Ɑⁱⁿ, Declan; the name of the patron of Ardmore, where his feast is kept on 24 July; a rather common name in Co. Waterford. Lat. Declanus.

ⱷⱸⱭⱾⱜⱳⱜⁿⱭⱦ, g. -Ɑⁱⱬ, Desmond; an old Irish name or designation, meaning native of, or belonging to, Desmond or South Munster. Lat. Desmundus.

ⱷⁱⱭⱤⱜⱭⁱⱷ, g. -ⱭⱷⱭ, Dermod, Dermot, (Darby; Jeremiah, Jarmy, Jerry; Jerome); Old Ir. Diarmait, comp. of di, without, and airmit, injunction, hence a freeman; an ancient and very common name, especially among the MacCarthys, MacDermotts, O'Briens, and O'Connors; still found in every part of Ireland, but generally angl. Jeremiah. Eleven saints of the name are mentioned in the Martyrology of Donegal. Lat. Diermitius, Dermitius.

ⱷⱺⁱⱯⁱⱯⁱⱯ, g. id., Dominic, Dominick; Lat. Dominicus, belonging to the Lord, or born on Sunday; the name of the founder of the Order of Preachers, in whose honour it was adopted in Ireland.

ⱷⱺⱜⱯⱭⱡⱡ, g. -Ɑⁱⱡⱡ, Donall, Donald, (Daniel); Old Ir. Domnall, from Celtic *Dumno-valo-s, world-mighty, *Dubno-valo-s, mighty in the 'deep'; one of the most ancient and popular of Irish names, still in use in every part of the country, but generally angl. Daniel; also one of the most popular names in Scotland, where it is angl. Donald. Only one saint of the name is mentioned in the Irish martyrologies; his feast was kept on 26th April. Lat. Domnaldus, Donaldus.

ᴅoɴɴ, *g.* ᴅuıɴn, Donn ; a rare name, almost peculiar to the family of Maguire. Lat. Donnus.

ᴅoɴɴáɴ, *g.* -áıɴ, Donnan ; dim. of ᴅoɴɴ, brown ; the name of four Irish saints. Lat. Donnanus.

ᴅoɴɴċaᴅ, *g.* -aᴅa, -aıᴅ, Donogh, Donough, Donaghy, (Donat, Denis, Duncan) ; Old Irish Donnchad, Dunchad, from Celt *Donno-catu-s, *Duno-catu-s, brown warrior, or strong warrior ; an ancient and very common Irish name, still found in every part of the country, but generally angl. Denis. The Scots make it Duncan. St. Dunchadh was Abbot of Iona ; his feast was kept on 25th May. Lat. Donnchadus, Donatus.

ᴅuḃaltaċ, *g.* -aıᵹ, Dualtagh, Duald, (Dudley) ; a rare Irish name, meaning ' black-jointed ' ; borne by the celebrated antiquary ᴅuḃaltaċ mac ꝼıꞃḃıꞃıᵹ, called in English Duald or Dudley MacFirbis. Lat. Dubaltachus.

ᴅuḃáɴ, *g.* -áıɴ, Dowan ; dim. of ᴅuḃ, black ; the name of two Irish saints, whose feasts were kept on 11th February and 11th November respectively. Lat. Dubanus.

ᴅuḃᴅáleıte, *g.* ᴅuıḃᴅáleıte, (Dudley) ; an ancient Irish personal name, meaning ' the black-man of the two sides, or halves ' ; now very rare, if not actually obsolete.

ᴅuḃᴅaꞃa, ᴅuḃᴅaꞃaċ, *g.* ᴅuıḃᴅaꞃaċ, (Dudley) ; an old Irish name, meaning ' the black-man of the oak ' ; still in use in West Connacht, angl. Dudley. Lat. Dubdarus.

ᴅuḃᵹall, *g.* -aıll, Dugald ; comp. of ᴅuḃ, black, and ᵹall, a foreigner ; a name given by the Irish to the Danes ; still in use among the Scots, angl. Dugald. Lat. Dugaldus.

ᴅuḃᵹlas, *g.* -aıꞃ, Douglas.

eaċaıᴅ, *g.* id. and -aᴅa, Aghy ; a var. of eoċaıᴅ, q.v.

eaċaɴɴ, *g.* -aıɴɴ, Hector ; older eaċᴅoɴɴ, horse-lord ;

an old Irish name, still in use among the Scots, angl. Hector.

éaoḃáṙo, g. -áiṗo, Edward; Ang.-Sax. Eadweard, blessed-guard; the name of two saintly kings of England, known respectively as Edward the Martyr and Edward the Confessor; introduced into Ireland by the Anglo-Normans, but has been almost completely absorbed by éamonn, q.v. Lat. Eduardus.

éamonn, g. -oinn, -uinn, Eamon, Edmund, Edmond, (Edward); Ang.-Sax. Eadmund, blessed-protection; the name of a saintly King of England, who was martyred on 20th November, 870; introduced into Ireland by the Anglo-Normans, where it has become very popular and has almost completely absorbed the other great Anglo-Saxon name Edward, the Irish éamonn generally standing for both names. Lat. Eadmundus, Edmundus.

éanán, g. -áin, Enan; the name of several Irish saints Lat. Enanus.

éanna, g. id., Enda; an old Irish name, made famous by St. Enda, Abbot of Aran, whose feast is on 21st March. Lat. Endeus.

eaṙcán, g. -áin, Ercan, Erkan; dim. of eaṙc, red, or speckled; the name of several saintly Irish bishops and priests. Lat. Ercanus.

eaṙnán, g. -áin, Ernan, (Ernest); dim. of eaṙna, knowing, experienced; the name of eight Irish saints. Lat Ernanus.

eiḃeaṙ, g. -ḃiṙ, Ever, Heber, (Ivor); a common name among the MacMahons and a few other families in Ulster; also common in Cape Clear Island, angl Heber; in the North, sometimes angl. Ivor. Also written eiṁeaṙ. Lat. Heberus, Eberus, Iberus.

eiġneacán, eiġneacán, g. -áin, (Æneas, Eneas Ignatius); dim. of eiġnac or eiġnac; an old Irish name, peculiar to the O'Donnells, O'Dohertys, and a few other families of Tirconnell, pronounced locally eiġneacán or iġneacán. Lat. *Egnechanus.

Éiṁear, *g.* -ṁir, Ever, Heber, (Ivor); a var. of Éibear, q.v. Lat. Emerus.

Éiṁín, *g.* id., Evin; dim. of eiṁ, swift, active; the name of three Irish saints, one of whom was the founder of Monasterevan and patron of the O'Dempseys. Lat. Eminus.

Éinrí, *g.* id., Henry; Teut. Heimrich or Heinrich, home-ruler; one of the commonest names among the early Anglo-Norman settlers in Ireland; largely adopted by Irish families, especially the O'Neills. Lat. Henricus.

Eireaṁón, *g.* -óin, Erevan, Heremon, Hermon, (Irving); an ancient Irish name, still in use in Cape Clear Island; now pronounced Eireaṁán. Lat. Heremon, Eremon, -onis.

Eirnín, *g.* id., Ernin; dim. of earna, knowing, experienced; the name of no fewer than seventeen Irish saints. Lat. Erninus.

Eoċaiḋ, *g.* id., and -aḋa, Oghie; formerly a very common name, but now almost obsolete. It was a favourite name among the O'Hanlons. Lat. Eochodius

Eóin, g. id., Eoin, John, (Owen); Heb. Jochanan, grace, or gracious gift of Jehovah; the name of the precursor of Our Lord, and of the beloved disciple; common in all Christian countries; in use in Ireland from early Christian times; one of the most frequent names among the Anglo-Norman settlers, and now by far the most popular name in Ireland. V. Seaġán, Seán and Seón. Lat. Joannes, -is.

Eóin Baiste, John Baptist.

Eoġan, g. -ain, Eoghan, Owen, (Eugene); an ancient and rather common Irish name, explained as meaning 'well-born'; still in use, but generally angl. Eugene. Lat, Eoganus, Eugenius.

Eoġainín, g. id., Oynie; a dim. of Eoġan, q.v.

Faċtna, g. id. and -nan, Fachnan, (Festus); the name of four Irish saints, one of whom is patron of the Dioceses of Ross and Kilfenora; formerly in use among the O'Kellys of Connacht by whom it was angl. Festus. Lat. Fachtnanus.

ꝼáⱡⱱe, g. id., Falvy; an ancient Irish name, borne by fourteen Irish saints. Lat. Falbeus.

ꝼáoⱡáп, g. -áιп, Felan; dim. of ꝼáoⱡ, a wolf; the name of fourteen Irish saints, one of whom was a brother of St. Fursey and a famous missionary in Flanders, where he was killed about the year 656. Lat. Foelanus.

ꝼeáрáⱱác, g. -áιʒ, Farry, (Ferdinand); an ancient Irish name, meaning ' manly '; rather common in early times; retained until recently among the O'Maddens and O'Naughtons of Connacht, by whom it was angl. Farry. Finally it was turned into Ferdinand. Lat. Ferdachus.

ꝼeáрⱱoрcá, g. ꝼιрⱱoрcá, Fardoragh, (Frederick; Ferdinand); also áп ꝼeáрⱱoрcá; comp. of ꝼeáр, a man, and ⱱoрcá, dark, hence ' the dark-complexioned man '; a rather common name in the 16th century and in use down to comparatively recent times, but probably now obsolete. Lat. Fardorchus.

ꝼeáрʒáⱡ, g. -ʒáιⱡ and -ʒáιⱡe, Fergal, Farrell; an ancient and once very common name, especially among the MacDonnells, MacDonoughs, Mageoghegans, O'Farrells, O'Neills and O'Rourkes; still in use, but rare. It is supposed to have been the Irish name of the celebrated St. Virgilius, the Irish ꝼeáр- having been equated with the Latin Vir-(man). Lat. Fergalius.

ꝼeáрʒáпáιпm, g. ꝼιрʒáпáιпm, Fergananym, (Ferdinand); comp. of ꝼeáр, a man, ʒáп, without, and áιпп, a name, hence ' anonymous, nameless.' This peculiar name was formerly rather common in Ireland. It is supposed to have been first given to persons who had not been baptised in their childhood.

ꝼeáрʒus, g. -ʒuрá, -ʒuιр, Fergus, (Ferdinand); Celt. *Ver-gustu-s, super-choice, super-selection, Old Ir. Fergus, g. -gosso; formerly a rather common name in Ireland and Scotland. Ten saints of the name are mentioned in the Martyrology of Donegal. Lat. Fergusius.

ꞓeıċín, g. id., Fehin, (Festus) ; dim. of ꞓıaċ, a raven ;
the name of five Irish saints, one of whom was Abbot
of Fore and patron of West Connacht, where the
name is now angl. Festus. St. Feichin's Day is 20
January. Lat. Fechinus.

ꞓeıdlım, g. id., Phelim, (Felix ; Philip) ; a shortened
form of ꞓeıdlımıd, q.v. Lat. Fedelmius, Fedlimius.

ꞓeıdlımıd, g. id., Felimy, Phelimy, Phelim, (Felix ;
Philip) ; an ancient Irish name, explained as meaning
' the ever good ' ; common among the Maguires,
O'Connors, O'Donnells, O'Neills and O'Reillys ; and
borne by six Irish saints, one of whom is patron of
the Diocese of Kilmore. Lat. Fedelmidius, Fed-
limidius.

ꞓeóras, g. -aıꞃ, Pierce ; an Irish form of the Norman
Piers (Fr. Pierre, Lat. Petrus, Peter).

ꞓıaċa, g. -aċ, Feagh ; a name among the O'Byrnes,
borne by the famous Feagh MacHugh. St. Fiacha's
Day was 27 December. Lat. Fiachus.

ꞓıaċꞃa, g. -aċ, Fiachra, Feary ; the name of eight Irish
saints, of whom the most celebrated was St. Fiachra
the Solitary, founder of the monastery of Breuil, in
France, whose shrine is a constant place of pilgrimage,
where innumerable miracles are said to have been
performed. The French form of the name is Fiacre.
Lat. Fiachrius.

ꞓılıb, g. id., Philip ; usually ꞃılıb, q.v.

ꞓınġın, g. id., Fineen, Finneen, Finnin, (Florence, Florry) ;
an ancient Irish name, explained as meaning ' fair
birth ' or ' fair offspring ' ; common among the Mac
Carthys, O'Sullivans, O'Mahonys, O'Driscolls, and
other families in West Munster, by whom it is absurdly angl. Florence. St. Finghin's Day was 5
February. Lat. Fingenus, Finginus.

ꞓınnıan, g. -éın, Finnian, Finian ; dim. of ꞃıonn, fair ;
the name of several Irish saints, of whom the most
celebrated were St. Finnian, Abbot of Moville, and
St. Finnian, Abbot of Clonard and founder of the
famous school of that place. Lat. Finnianus.

ꝼıonáʼn, g. -áın, Fionan, Finan ; also written ꝼıonnáʼn ;
dim. of ꝼıonn, fair ; the name of at least nine Irish
saints, some of whom were very celebrated, as St.
Fionan Cam and St. Fionan, the Leper. Lat.
Fionanus.

ꝼıonn, g. ꝼınn, Finn ; an ancient and once common
name ; made famous by Fionn MacCumhal. It was
borrowed by the Norsemen and is still in use as a
Christian name in Scandinavia and Iceland. Lat.
Finnius.

ꝼıonnáʼn, v. ꝼıonáʼn.

ꝼıonnḃarr, g. -aıꞃꞃ, Finbar ; comp. of ꝼıonn, fair, and
ḃarr, a head ; the name of several Irish saints, of
whom one is patron of the Diocese of Cork ; also
called ḃaıꞃꝼıonn, shortened to ḃarra, q.v. Lat.
Finnbarrus.

ꝼıonntáʼn, g. -áın, Fintan ; dim. of ꝼıonn, fair ; the
name of upwards of twenty Irish saints, of whom one
of the most celebrated was St. Fintan of Clonenagh.
Lat. Fintanus.

ꝼıṫeal, g. -ṫıl, (Florence, Florry) ; a corruption of
ꝼıṫċeallaċ (whence the surname Ó ꝼıṫċeallaıġ) ;
in use among the O'Mulconrys, by whom it was angl.
Florence.

ꝼlann, g. ꝼlaınn and ꝼloınn, Flann, Flan, (Florence,
Florry) ; an ancient and once common Irish name,
meaning 'ruddy.' It survived among the MacEgans
and O'Mulconrys down to comparatively recent
times. Several saints of the name are mentioned in
the Martyrology of Donegal. Lat. Flannus.

ꝼlannáʼn, g. -áın, Flannan ; dim. of ꝼlann, ruddy ; the
name of the patron of the Diocese of Killaloe, whose
feast is kept on 18th December. Lat. Flannanus.

ꝼolc, Foulk ; a Frankish name introduced by the Normans
and still found among a few families. It was generally
pronounced ꝼúc. Lat. Fulcus.

ꝼraınc, g. id., Frank ; a pet form of Francis. V.
Pꞃoınnꞃıaꞃ.

ᵹᴀᴦᴃᴀ́ɴ, g. -ᴀ́ɪɴ, Garvan ; dim. of ᵹᴀᴦᴃ, rough ; the name
of five Irish saints. Lat. Garvanus.

ᵹᴇᴀᴦᴀʟᴄ, g. -ᴀɪʟᴄ, Gerald ; Teut. Gerwald, spear-might ;
a name introduced into Ireland by the Anglo-Normans.
It was rare at first, but by the end of the 16th century
had become very common. Its popularity has again
declined. V. ᵹᴇᴀᴦᴀ́ᴦᴅ and ᵹᴇᴀᴦóɪᴅ. Lat. Giraldus,
Geraldus.

ᵹᴇᴀᴦᴀ́ᴦᴅ, g. -ᴀ́ɪᴦᴅ, Gerard ; Frank. Gerhard, spear-
brave ; a name borne by two saints, one Bishop of
Toul and the other Abbot of Namur, after whom it
became popular among the Normans, who introduced
it into Ireland. It appears, however, to have soon
died out, having been apparently absorbed by Gerald
(v. ᵹᴇᴀᴦᴀʟᴄ). The present popularity of the name
in Ireland is due to St. Gerard Majella. Lat. Gerardus.

ᵹᴇᴀᴦóɪᴅ, g. id., Garrett, Gerald, Gerard ; apparently
not a dim. of Gerald (v. ᵹᴇᴀᴦᴀʟᴄ), but merely the
Norman pronunciation of that name. Lat. Giraldus,
Geraldus.

ᵹᴇᴀsᴩᴀᴦ, g. -ᴀɪᴦ, Jasper ; a fancy name given to one
of the Magi who came from the East to adore the
Infant Saviour. The Magi, according to tradition,
were three kings named Gaspar, Melchior and Balthasar, who afterwards suffered martyrdom. The
translation of their supposed relics from Constan-
tinople to Milan, and thence to Cologne in the 12th
century, made their names known in Europe. Gaspar
became very common in Germany, and was in use in
France as Gaspard and in England as Jasper. All
three names were at one time in use in Ireland, but
none of them ever became common. Gaspar was
represented in the Fiants of Elizabeth by ' Gaspar
Synnott,' ' Jasper Browne,' and ' Jasper Butler,'
and is still in use. Melchior was current in the neighbourhood of Youghal, while Balthasar was a name
among the Nugents. Lat. Caspar.

ᵹɪʟɪᴃᴇɪᴦᴄ, g. id., Gilbert ; Frank. Giselbert, hostage-
bright ; very common as Gilbert among the Normans,

who introduced it into Ireland. Lat. Gilbertus.

ᵹⁱⁱᵒᵇúⁿ, g. -úıⁿ, Gibbon ; a dim. of Gilbert (v. ᵹⁱⁱⁱᵇeⁱⁿᴄ).

ᵹⁱᵒˡˡᴀ ᵇeᴀʀᴀⁱᵹ, g. id., Gilvarry ; an Irish name, meaning ' servant of St. Barry ' (v. ᵇeᴀʀᴀᴄ). Lat. Berachianus.

ᵹⁱᵒˡˡᴀ ᵇʀⁱᵹᵒe, g. id., Gilbride ; an Irish name, meaning ' servant of St. Brigid ' (v. ᵇʀⁱᵹⁱᵒ). Lat. Brigidianus.

ᵹⁱᵒˡˡᴀ ᴄʀⁱᵒsᴄ, g. id., Christian ; an Irish name, meaning ' servant of Christ.' Lat. Christianus.

ᵹⁱᵒˡˡᴀ ᵒé, g. id., Gildea ; an Irish name, meaning ' servant of God.' Lat. *Gildeus.

ᵹⁱᵒˡˡᴀ eᴀsᵖuⁱᵹ, g. id., Archibald ; an Irish name, meaning ' bishop's servant ' ; strangely angl. Archibald in the North of Ireland and in Scotland.

ᵹⁱᵒˡˡᴀ íᵒsᴀ, g. id., Gillisa, Gillesa, Gill ; an Irish name, meaning ' servant of Jesus.' Lat. *Gilisius.

ᵹⁱᵒˡˡᴀ ⁿᴀ ⁿᴀᵒⁱ́, g. id., (Nehemiah) ; an Irish name, meaning ' servant of the saints.' Lat. *Sanctianus.

ᵹⁱᵒʀᴀ́ʀᵒ, g. -ᴀⁱʀᵒ, Gerard ; a var. of ᵹeᴀʀᴀ́ʀᵒ, q.v.

ᵹⁱᵒʀᵒⁱᵒ, g. id., Garrett, Gerald, (Gerard) ; a var. of ᵹeᴀʀóⁱᵒ, q.v.

ᵹˡᴀⁱsⁿe, g. id., Glasny ; formerly a favourite name in several Ulster families ; survived down to recent times. Lat. Glasnaeus.

ᵹᵒʀᵒᴀⁿ, g. -ᴀⁱⁿ, Gordan ; a name among the O'Neills of Ulster, first borne by a son of Sir Phelim O'Neill, who was so called from his grandfather, the Marquis of Huntly in Scotland, whose family name was Gordon. Lat. * Gordanus.

ᵹᵒᴄfʀᴀⁱᵒ, ᵹᵒᴄʀᴀⁱᵒ, g. id. and -ᴀᵒᴀ, Godfrey, Gorry ; Norse Gothfrithr, God-peace ; a Norse name early adopted by the Irish, among whom it was at one time rather common. Lat. Godefridus.

ᵹʀéᴀᵹóⁱʀ, g. -óʀᴀ, Gregory ; Gr. Γρηγόριος (Gregórios), watchman ; a frequent episcopal name in the Eastern Church from early times, and borne by no fewer than sixteen Popes. Although rather common among the early Anglo-Norman settlers, it never became popular in Ireland. Lat. Gregorius.

ᵹᴿⁱᴼᵹᴀᴿ, g. -ᴀⁱᴘ, Gregory ; a var. of ᵹᴘéᴀᵹóⁱᴘ, q.v.

ᴴᴀⁿⁿᴿᴀᴼⁱ, ᴴᴀⁿᴿᴀᴼⁱ, g. id., Henry, Harry ; common var. of éⁱⁿᴘí, q.v.

ᴴᴼⁱᵬᵉᴀᴿᴅ, g. -ᴀⁱᴘᴅ, Hubert, (Hugh) ; Teut. Hugibert, mind-bright ; a common name in France ; introduced into Ireland by the Anglo-Normans, but never became popular. St. Hubert was the patron of hunters. Lat. Hubertus.

ᴴᴼⁱᴿᵉᴀᵬᴀᴿᴅ, g. -ᴀⁱᴘᴅ, Herbert ; Frank. Haribert, Heribert, army-bright ; common as Herbert among the Anglo-Norman settlers in Ireland, but it quickly declined in popularity and for centuries has been very rare. Lat. Heribertus.

ⁱᴀᴿᖴᴸᴀⁱᴛ, g. -ᴀᴛᴀ, Jarlath ; the name of the patron of the Diocese of Tuam. Lat. Iarlathus.

ⁱᴼᵐᴀᴿ, g. -ᴀⁱᴘ, Ivor ; Norse Ivarr ; a name borrowed by the Irish from the Norsemen.

ⁱᴼ⁵ᴀᴄ, g. -ᴀⁱᴄ, Isaac ; Heb. Yitschaq, laughter ; the name of the Jewish patriarch, son of Abraham and father of Esau and Jacob ; probably so called on account of the joy occasioned by his birth (cf. Gen. XVII, 17) ; always exceedingly rare in Ireland. Lat. Isaac.

ⁱóᵚᵉᴘ, ⁱóᵚᵉᴘ̇, g. id., Joseph ; Heb. Yoseph, May God add (cf. Gen. XXX, 23-24) ; the name of one of the sons of Jacob and Rachel, afterwards prime minister of Pharaoh in Egypt, and also of the spouse of the B. V. Mary and foster-father of Jesus Christ ; in use in Ireland from early Christian times and re-introduced by the Anglo-Normans, but it is only within comparatively recent times that it has become really popular. Lat. Josephus.

ⁱᴼ⁵óᴄ, ⁱᴼ⁵óᵹ, g. id., Isaac ; var. of ⁱᴼᵚᴀᴄ, q.v.

ⁱᴿⁱᴀᴸ, g. -ᴀⁱᴸ, Irial ; an ancient Irish name ; formerly in use among the O'Farrells, O'Kennedys and O'Loghlens. Lat. Irialus.

1úsτás, g. -áıτ, Eustace; **Gr.** Εὖστάχυς (Eustachus), fruitful; the name of a Roman martyr whose relics were translated to the Church of St. Denis at Paris in the 12th century, making the name common in France. It was brought into Ireland by the Anglo-Normans, but has always been very rare. Lat. Eustachius, Eustasius.

Laúcás, g. -áıτ, Luke; a var. in parts of Connacht of Lúcáτ, q.v.

Laúrás, g. -áıτ, Laurence; Lat. Laurentius, i.e., belonging to Laurentum, a town in Latium; the name of a celebrated Roman deacon who suffered martyrdom under Valerian, in the 3rd century; popular among the Anglo-Normans, who introduced it into Ireland. Sometimes Laúτaτ and Luúτáτ.

Lacτna, g. id., (Lucius); the name of the great-grandfather of Brian Boru; hence the name Lucius among the O'Briens.

Laisrian, v. Laτaıτıan.

Laoızseac, Laoıseac, g. -ız, Lysagh, (Lucius, Lewis, Louis); deriv. of Laoızıτ, i.e., belonging to Leix; a name in use among the O'Mores and a few other families.

Lasaırıan, g. -éın, Laserian; dim. of Laτaıτ, a flame; the name of four Irish saints, one of whom is patron of the Diocese of Leighlin. Lat. Lassarenus, Laserianus.

Leaclaınn, g. id., Laughlin, Lanty; a shortened form of maeleaclaınn, q.v.

León, g. -óın, Leo; Lat. Leo, g. -onis, lion; a common Latin name, borne by thirteen Popes in honour of the last of whom—the great Pope Leo XIII—it was adopted in Ireland.

Lıam, g. id., William; a pet form of Uıllıam, q.v.

Loclaınn, g. id., Loughlin, Laughlin; a name borrowed from the Northmen. The native home of the northern invaders was known to the Irish as Loclaınn, a name which is supposed to signify 'Lakeland' or 'Fiordland.' This was quickly adopted by the Irish as a personal name and became very popular. Dr. MacBain suggests that it was originally **Macloclainne** ' son of Scandinavia,' hence a Scandinavian. It still survives, angl. Loughlin and Laughlin. Lat. Lochlunius.

Loclann, g. -ainn, Loughlin, Laughlin ; a var. of **Loc-lainn**, q.v.

Lomán, g. -áin, Loman ; dim. of **Lom**, bare ; the name of four Irish saints, one of whom was a disciple of St. Patrick. Lat. Lomanus.

Lonán, g. -áin, Lonan ; dim. of **Lon**, a blackbird ; the name of eight Irish saints. Lat. Lonanus.

Lorcán, g. -áin, Lorcan, (Laurence) ; dim. of **Lorc**, fierce ; the Irish name of St. Laurence O'Toole, patron of the Diocese of Dublin. Lat. Lorcanus.

Lúcán, g. -áin, Lucan ; the name of four Irish saints. Lat. Lucanus.

Lúcás, g. -áis, *Lucas*, Luke ; Gr. Λουκᾶς (Loukas), traced by St. Jerome to the Hebrew and explained by him as meaning ' resurrection,' but generally considered to be a contraction of the Greek form, Λουκανος (Loukanos), of the Latin Lucanus, a Roman forename probably derived from Lucania, a district in Southern Italy ; the name of one of the Four Evangelists, native of Antioch and physician by profession. ' Lucas ' was the old English form of the name, as it is still in Spanish and Portuguese. Lat. Lucas, -ae.

Lugaid, g. -ada, Lewy, (Lewis, Louis, Aloysius) ; an ancient Irish name, borne by ten saints ; a favourite name among the O'Clerys. Lat. Lugadius.

maeleaclainn, **maelseaclainn**, g. **maoileac-lainn**, Melaghlin, Laughlin, Lanty, (Malachy ; Milo ; Miles, Myles) ; an Irish name, meaning ' servant of St. Secundinus,' disciple of St. Patrick and patron of the family of **Ó maoilfeaclainn**, or O'Melaghlen ; rather common in the tenth and succeeding centuries, especially among the O'Melaghlens, O'Farrells, O'Kellys and O'Connors ; still in use, but generally disguised as Malachy. Lat. Malachias.

mꜵelíosꜵ, g. **mꜵoil íorꜵ**, Maelisa ; formerly a not uncommon Irish name signifying ' servant of Jesus.'
Lat. Moelisa.

mꜵᵹnus, g. **-urꜵ** and **-uir**, Manus, (Manasses) ; Lat.
Magnus, great ; a name adopted by the Northmen in
honour of Charlemagne (Carolus Magnus), and by
them introduced into Ireland. It became very
common among some Irish families, especially the
O'Donnells of Tirconnell. Often pronounced **mꜵᵹnur**
or **mꜵonur**. Eight saints of the name are mentioned
in the Roman Martyrology.

mꜵincín, g. id., Munchin ; dim. of **mꜵnꜵc**, a monk ; the
name of several Irish saints, one of whom is patron
of the Diocese of Limerick. Lat. Manchinus,
Munchinus.

mꜵirtín, g. id., Martin ; Lat. Martinus, dim. of Martius
(deriv. of Mars, the Roman god of war) ; the name of
the celebrated St. Martin of Tours, said to have been
a relative of St. Patrick, in whose honour it was
popular in France, whence the Normans brought it
into England and Ireland. Under the form of **mꜵrtꜵn**,
however, it had been already in use in Ireland from
early Christian times.

mꜵit, g. id., Mat ; a pet form of **mꜵitiú**, q.v.

mꜵitín, g. id., Mat ; a dim. of **mꜵitiú**, q.v.

mꜵitiꜵs, g. **-tir**, **mꜵitiꜵs**, g. **-tír**, Matthias ; probably
of same origin as **mꜵitiú**, q.v. ; the name of the Apostle
who supplied the place of Judas ; always rare in
Ireland. Lat. Mathias, -ae.

mꜵitiú, g. id., Matthew ; Heb. Mattattjah, gift of
Jehovah ; the name of one of the Twelve Apostles
and the first of the Four Evangelists ; a rare name
among the early Anglo-Norman settlers in Ireland.
Lat. Mattheus.

mꜵoᵹóᵹ, g. id., Mogue, (Aidan, Moses) ; a var. of **ꜵoᵹán**,
q.v. The initial **m** represents the possessive pronoun
mo, my, prefixed as a term of endearment to the
names of saints, while **-óᵹ** is merely another dim.
termination. Lat. Maidocus.

ⱮⱯⱭⰻⰻⰻⱤ, g. id. Meyler ; Welsh Meilir or Meilyr ; very rare. Lat. Milerus, Mylerus.

ⱮⱭⱭⰝⰤⰵⱭⱀⱀⱭⰸⱭ, g. ⰰⱭⱁⰻⰝⰵⱭⱀⱀⱭⰸⱭ, Benedict ; an ancient Irish name, signifying ' one desirous of the blessing.'

ⱮⱭⱭⰝⰹⱁⰝⰲ, ⰰⱭⱭⰝⰢⱁⰝⱆⰻⰰ, g. ⰰⱭⱁⰻⰈⱁⰝⰲ, Malcolm ; an Irish name signifying ' servant of St. Columcille ' ; a royal name in Scotland, where it is still in use. It does not appear to have been at any time a very common name in Ireland. Lat. Malcolmus.

ⱮⱭⱭⰝⰰⱁⱢⰵⱭ, g. ⰰⱭⱁⰻⰝⰰⱁⱢⰵⱭ, (Miles, Myles) ; an ancient Irish name signifying ' majestic chief ' ; a favourite name among the O'Reillys, by whom it was angl. Miles or Myles. Lat. Maelmorus.

ⱮⱭⱭⰝⰰⱆⰻⱤⰵ, g. ⰰⱭⱁⰻⰝⰰⱆⰻⱤⰵ, (Meyler, Milo, Miles, Myles) ; an Irish name, signifying ' servant of the B. V. Mary ' ; a favourite name among the Mac Sweenys, by whom it was angl. Miles or Myles. Lat. Maelmarius.

ⱮⱭⱭⰝⱤⱆⱭⰲⱭⰻⱀ, g. ⰰⱭⱁⰻⱤⱆⱭⰲⱭⰻⱀ, Melrone an Irish name, meaning ' servant of St. Ruadhan.' Lat. Maelruadanus.

ⰌⱭⱤⰸⱤⰁ, g. -ⱆⰻⱤ, Marcus, Mark ; Lat. Marcus, a common name in ancient Rome and its provinces ; of uncertain origin, but supposed to be a deriv. of Mars, the Roman god of war ; the name of the second of the Four Evangelists. The Anglo-Normans brought it into Ireland, but it never became common.

ⰌⱭⱤⰸⱭⰻⱀ, g. id., Martin ; a var. of ⰰⱭⰻⱤⰸⰻⱀ, q.v.

ⰌⱭⱤⰸⱭⱀ, g. -Ɑⰻⱀ, Martin ; a var. of ⰰⱭⰻⱤⰸⰻⱀ, q.v.

ⰌⱭⰸⱭ, g. id., Matthew ; a var. of ⰰⱭⰻⰸⰻⱆ, q.v.

ⰌⱭⰸⰃⱭⰰⱭⰻⱀ, g. -ⱭⰰⱀⱭ, Mahon, (Matthew) ; a well-known Irish name, signifying ' a bear ' ; borne by the brother of Brian Boru, and common among the O'Briens, O'Connors, O'Farrells, &c., but now disguised under the angl. form of Matthew. Lat. Mathgamanius.

ⰰⰵⱭⰝⰝⱭⱀ, g. -Ɑⰻⱀ, Mellan, Meldan ; dim. of ⰰⰵⱭⰝⰝ, pleasant ; the name of four Irish saints. Lat. Mellanus.

meιlseóιn, g. -ópᴀ, Melchor ; a fancy name given to one of the Magi (v. ʒeᴀnpᴀn) ; still in use in the neighbourhood of Youghal. Lat. Melchior, -oris.

míceᴀl, mίċeᴀl, g. -ċιl, Michael ; Heb. Mikael, Who like God ? ; the name of one of the archangels, chief of the heavenly hosts and conqueror of Satan ; rare until comparatively recent times, but now one of the most popular names in Ireland. Lat. Michael, -is.

muιnċeᴀnᴄᴀċ, g. -ᴀιʒ, Murtaugh, Murty, (Mortimer) ; comp. of muιn, sea, and ceᴀnc, right, meaning ' sea-director,' ' expert at sea,' ' able navigator ' ; an ancient Irish name, common among the O'Briens, O'Connors, &c. ; still in use, but generally angl. Mortimer, with which it has no connection. Lat. Murchertachus.

muιneᴀᴅᴀċ, g. -ᴀιʒ, Murry ; deriv. of muιn, sea, meaning ' seaman ' ; also ' lord ' ; formerly a very common Irish name ; borne by two saints, one of whom is patron of the Diocese of Killala. Lat. Muredachus.

muιnʒeᴀs, g. -ʒeᴀnᴀ and -ʒιn, (Maurice) ; comp. of muιn, sea, and -ʒun, choice ; formerly a common Irish name ; now merged in muιnιn, q.v. Lat. Murgessius.

muιnιs, g. id., Maurice ; Lat. Mauritius, Moorish, a Roman name for a man of Moorish lineage ; borne by the captain of the Thebean legion who was martyred, together with his companions, in Switzerland, by order of Maximian, in the 3rd century ; common among the Anglo-Norman settlers in Ireland.

muncᴀᴅ, g. -ᴀᴅᴀ and -ᴀιᴅ, Murrough, (Morgan) ; Celt. *Mori-catu-s, sea-warrior ; an ancient Irish name, formerly common in most Irish families, especially among the O'Briens, O'Flahertys, &c. ; still in use, but generally angl. Morgan. Lat. Murchadus.

nᴀomán, g. -áιn, Nevan ; dim. of nᴀom, holy ; the name of an Irish saint whose feast was kept on 13 September. Lat. Sanctanus.

nᴀos, g. -nᴀ, Neece, Neese, Niece, (Nicholas) ; a pet

form of Aóngup, q.v. ; formerly common in Ulster and still extant in that province.

neasán, g. -áin, Nessan ; the name of five Irish saints, of whom the best known is St. Nessan, the deacon of Mungret. Lat. Nessanus.

néill, v. niall.

niall, g. néill, Niall, Neal, Neale, Neil ; an ancient Irish name, specially common in Ulster among the O'Neills, O'Donnells, O'Dohertys, O'Boyles, &c. ; still in use, but the gen. néill is sometimes used instead of the nominative. Lat. Niallus, Niellus, Nellus.

niallán, g. -áin, Niallan ; dim. of niall, q.v. Lat. Niallanus.

nioclás, g. -áip, Nicholas ; Gr. Νικόλαος (Nikólaos), victory of the people ; the name of one of the seven first deacons. The legend of St. Nicholas, Bishop of Myra, made it universal. It was one of the commonest names among the early Anglo-Norman settlers in Ireland, and still retains its popularity. Lat. Nicolaus.

niocol, g. -oil, Nicol ; a short form of nioclár, q.v.

oórán, g. -áin, Oran ; dim. of oóap, pale-green ; the name of nine Irish saints, one of whom is patron of Waterford. Lat. Odranus, Otteranus.

oilibéar, g. -éip, Oliver ; almost certainly a Gallicised form of the Norse Ōlafr or Ōleifr, ancestor's relic (v. Amlaoib) ; a name introduced into Ireland by the Anglo-Normans and once fairly common, until its association with Cromwell made it unpopular. With the beatification of Blessed Oliver Plunket it is likely to be revived. Lat. Oliverus, Oliverius.

oisín, g. id., Ossin, Ossian ; dim. of op, a deer ; the name of the Fenian poet, son of Fionn MacCumhail ; also borne by four Irish saints. Lat. Ossenus.

oistín, g. id., Austin ; a Norse form of Augustine. It occurs in the Annals of Ulster, at the year 874, as the name of a son of Aṁlaoiḃ, king of the Norsemen. V. Áġuirtín.

OSCAR, g. -air, Oscar ; Norse Asgeirr, a common Norse name, meaning ' divine spear ' or ' spear of the Anses or gods,' the same as the Ang.-Sax. Osgar (occurring in Domesday Book) ; but ' oscar ' is also an Irish word, meaning ' champion ' or ' combatant ' ; the name of the son of Oisin and grandson of Fionn Mac Cumhail ; also a name among the Maguires in the 14th century. Lat. Osgerus.

paḋra, g. id., Paddy ; a pet form of paoraiġ, q.v.

paḋraic, paḋraic, paḋraiġ, paḋraiġ, g. id., Patrick ; Lat. Patricius, Patritius, patrician, noble ; the name of the National Apostle of Ireland.

paio, g. id., Pat ; a pet form of paoraiġ, q.v.

paioi, g. id., Paddy ; a pet form of paoraiġ, q.v.

paioín, g. id., Padden, Paddy, Pat ; a pet dim. of paoraiġ, q.v.

parra, g. id., Paddy ; a pet form of paoraiġ, q.v.

parṫalán, parṫalán, parṫlán, parṫlán, parṫnán, g. -áin, parṫlón, g. -óin, Bartholomew, Bartlemy, Bartley, Barkley, Berkley, Barclay, Bartel, Parlan, Bat, Batt ; Heb. Bār Talmāi, son of Talmāi ; the name of one of the Twelve Apostles ; fairly common in Ireland. Lat. Bartholomaeus.

peaḋar, g. -air, Peter ; Lat. Petrus, rock ; the name given by Christ to Simon, son of Jonas, whom He made Chief of the Apostles and the foundation-stone of His Church. This form of the name is comparatively recent, piaṁar (q.v.) being the form previously in general use.

peaḋair, g. id., Peter ; a var. of peaḋar, q.v.

piaras, g. -air, Piers, Pierce ; the Norman form of Peter (v. peaḋar), from French Pierre ; a common name among the early Anglo-Norman settlers in Ireland. Lat. Petrus, Piercius, Percius.

pilib, g. id., Philip ; Greek (Ϸιλιππος (Philippos), horse-lover ; the name of one of the Twelve Apostles ; in use in Ireland in early Christian times ; a very common name among the Anglo-Norman settlers. Lat. Philippus.

pius, g. id., Pius ; Lat. Pius, pious ; the name of eleven Popes.

pól, g. póil, Paul ; Lat. Paulus, small ; the name of the Apostle of the Gentiles ; never a common name in Ireland.

pReannoaiʒ, g. id., Frank ; a pet form of pṗoinnpiaṗ ; in use in Omeath.

pRoinnsias, pRoinnséas, pRóinsias, g. -réiṗ, Francis ; Lat. Franciscus, Frenchman, a name given in his youth to St. Francis of Assisi (whose original name was John), from the readiness with which he acquired and spoke the French language, and which from him became a name of world-wide popularity.

Ráóulb, g. -uilb, Ralph ; Teut. Raedwulf, swift-wolf, or counsel-wolf, Frank. Radulf ; one of the most frequent names among the Anglo-Norman settlers in Ireland, but it rapidly declined in popularity, and even in the 16th century was very rare. Lat. Radulfus.

Raʒnall, g. -aill, Reginald, *Reynald*, Ronald, (Randal, Randulph) ; Teut. Raginwald, Reginwald, mighty-power, Norse Rognvaldr, Nor. Ragenald, Regnault, Reynald, Eng. Reynold ; a Teutonic name which reached us by two channels, first through the Norsemen when it was largely borrowed by the Irish and Scottish Gaels, especially the MacDonnells, by whom it was incorrectly angl. Randal, and again through the Anglo-Normans, among whom it was very common. The pronunciation is often Ráʒnall or Raonall. Lat. Raganaldus, Reginaldus.

Raibilín, Revelin. V. Roibilín.

RaióRí, v. RuaióRí.

Rannulb, g. -uilb, Randulph ; Frank. Randulf, shield-wolf ; a name introduced by the Anglo-Normans, but always very rare. Its angl. form, Randal, has been

absorbed by Raṁnaɭɭ, q.v. Lat. Randulfus, Ran-
dulphus.

Réamonn, g. -oinn, Raymond, Redmond, Mundy;
Teut. Raginmund, Reginmund, mighty-protection,
Fr. Raimond, or Ang.-Sax. Raedmund, counsel-
protection ; a name introduced by the Anglo-Normans
and formerly not uncommon in many Irish families.
Lat. Raymundus, Reymundus, Remundus.

Reióri, v. Ruaióṗí.

Ribeard, g. -aiṗo, Ribeart, g. -birṫ, Ribirṫ, g. id.,
Riobáro, g. -áiṗo, Riobart, g. -airṫ, Robert.
V. Roibeáṗo.

Riocáro, g. -áiṗo, Riocaro, g. -aiṗo, Rickard, Richard;
Teut. Rikhard, Richard, powerful-brave, Fr. Ricard,
Ricart, Richard ; one of the most frequent names
among the Anglo-Norman settlers in Ireland. It
owed its popularity to an Anglo-Saxon king of Kent,
who in the 7th century left his throne to become a
monk at Lucca, where he was reputed to have wrought
many miracles. Lat. Richardus.

Risteáro, g. -áiṗo, Richard ; a var. of Riocáṗo, due
to French influence. This is the common form of
the name. Cf. Italian Ricciardo for Riccardo.

Roólaióe, g. id., Roland, Rowland ; a pet form of
Roólann, q.v.

Roólann, g. -ainn, Roland, Rowland ; Teut. Hruodlant,
Hrothland, famous-land, Nor. Rollant, Roland ; a
name introduced by the Anglo-Normans, among whom,
however, it was not of frequent occurrence. Lat.
Rotlandus, Rolandus.

Roóulb, g. -uilb, (Ralph) ; Teut. Hruodwulf, Hroth-
wulf, famous-wolf, Nor. Rodulf (Rolf in Domesday
Book) ; a rare Anglo-Norman name ; absorbed by
Ráóulb, q.v. Lat. Rodulfus, Rodulphus.

Roibean, v. Roibín.

Roibeáro, g. -áiṗo, Roibeáro, g. -aiṗo, Robert ;
Teut. Hruodberht, Hrothberht, fame-bright, Nor.
Rodbert, Fr. Robert ; one of the commonest names
among the early Anglo-Norman settlers in Ireland,

but it has greatly declined in popularity and is now a rather rare name. Roıbín (q.v.) is a diminutive. Lat. Robertus.

Roıbílín, g. id., Revelin, (Roland, Rowland) ; a rare name, peculiar to the MacDonnells and the Savages of the Ards, Co. Down ; perhaps the same as Ravelin of Domesday Book ; also written Raıbılín and Ruıbílín.

Roıbín, g. id., Robin ; dim. of Roıbeápꝺ, q.v. Roıbeán is sometimes a variant.

Rónán, g. -áın, Ronan ; dim. of rón, a seal ; an ancient Irish personal name, borne by twelve saints. Lat. Ronanus.

Ros, g. -ꝛa, Ross ; a rare name, formerly in use among the Mageoghegans, MacMahons, Maguires, O'Loghlens, &c. Lat. Rossius.

Ruaꝺán, g. -áın, Rowan ; dim. of ruaꝺ, red ; the name of the celebrated Abbot of Lorrha, whose feast was kept on 15 April. Lat. Ruadanus.

Ruaıꝺrí, g. id., Rory, Roderick, (Roger, Roddy) ; Teut. Hruodric, Norse Rothrekr, fame-ruler ; a name introduced by the Norsemen and which became very common in many Irish families ; now often incorrectly angl. Roger. Raꝺꝛí and Reıꝺꝛí are dialectical variants. Lat. Rodericus, Rudericus.

Ruıbílín, v. Roıbílín.

Saerbꝛeatac, g. -aıg, Justin ; comp. of ꝛaoꝛ and bꝛeatac, meaning 'noble judge' ; a common name among the MacCarthys, borne by the father of Cáꝛtac, from whom the family name. Lat. Justinus.

Saılbeastar, g. -aıꝛ, Sylvester ; Lat. Silvester, -tri, living in a wood ; the name of two Popes ; brought into Ireland by the Anglo-Normans, but always very rare.

Samaırle, g. id., (Charles) ; a dialectical var. of Somaıꝛle, q.v.

Séaꝺna, g. id., (Sidney) ; an ancient Irish name, borne by four saints. Lat. Sednaeus, Sedonius, Sidonius.

Séᴀꝼꞃᴀ, Seᴀꝼꞃᴀɪꝺ, g. id., Geoffrey ; a var. of Ʒoꞇ-
ꝼꞃᴀɪꝺ (q.v.) owing to French influence ; a common
name among the early Anglo-Norman settlers in
Ireland ; now rare. Lat. Galfridus.

seᴀᵹᴀ́n, g. -ᴀ́ɪn, Shane, John. V. Seᴀ́n.

Séᴀmuꞅ, g. -uɪꞃ, Shemus, James ; Heb. Yākōb, literally
one who takes by the heel (Gen. XXV. 25,
XXVII, 36), from yekeb, a heel, hence to trip up,
defraud, supplant by subtlety ; the name of the
Jewish patriarch (Jacob) and of two of the Twelve
Apostles ; common among the Anglo-Norman
settlers, and ever growing in popularity. It is
in honour of St. James the Greater that the name
is used in Ireland, as in Europe generally. The
angl. form James is derived from the Spanish Jayme.
Lat. Jacobus.

seᴀ́n, g. -ᴀ́ɪn, Sean, Shane, John ; Old Fr. Jehan, Fr.
Jean ; a var. of Eóɪn, q.v. ; one of the commonest
names among the early Anglo-Norman settlers in
Ireland and now by far our most popular man's
name ; also written Seᴀᵹᴀ́n and Seón. Lat. Joannes,
-is.

seᴀnᴀ́n, g. -ᴀ́ɪn, Senan, Sinan, Synan, Sinon ; dim. of
ꞃeᴀn, old, wise ; the name of upwards of twenty Irish
saints, of whom the most celebrated is St. Senan of
Iniscathy ; his feast is kept on 8th March. Lat.
Senanus.

Séᴀꞃʟᴀꞅ, g. -ᴀɪꞃ, Séᴀꞃʟuꞅ, g. -uɪꞃ, Charles ; Teut.
Carl, Karl, man, Fr. Charles ; a rare name in Ireland
until James I called his son and heir Charles as a
lucky royal name. Lat. Carolus.

Séᴀꞃꞇᴀ, g. id., Sheary, Geoffrey, Jeffrey ; a var. of
Seᴀꝼꞃᴀ, q.v.

seᴀꞃꞇún, v. Séᴀꞇꞃún.

Séᴀꞇꞃᴀ, v. Séᴀꞃꞇᴀ.

Séᴀꞇꞃún, seᴀꞇꞃún, g. -úɪn, Sheron, Geoffrey, Jeffrey ;
probably from Fr. dim. of Geoffrey.

seóɪꞃꞅe, g. id., George ; Greek Γεωργος (Georgos), husbandman, rustic ; the name of the patron saint of

England ; rare in Ireland before the advent of the Hanoverian dynasty. Seóṙṙᴀ is sometimes a variant. Lat. Georgius.

seón, g. -óin, John ; a var. of Seáɴ, q.v. ; a late form from the English John.

seórsᴀ, v. Seóiṙṙe.

seósᴀṁ, g. -ᴀiṁ, seósᴀp, seósᴀṗ, Joseph; var. of Ióṙep, q.v.

siᴀ́ᴅᴀl, siᴀᵹᴀl, g. -ᴀil, Shiel ; an old Irish name, borne by two saints, one of whom is said to have been Bishop of Dublin. Lat. Sedulius.

simiᵭ, g. id., Jimmy ; a pet form of Séᴀmuṙ, q.v.

sioᶂrᴀiᵭ, g. id., Geoffrey ; a var. of Seᴀᶂṙᴀiᵭ, q.v.

siomᴀiᵭ, g. id., Jimmy ; a pet form of Séᴀmuṙ, q.v.

siomóɴ, g. -óin, siomonn, g. -oinn, siomúɴ, g. -úin, Simon ; Heb. Shim'ón (Simeon), from the root sháma', to hear (cf. Gen. XXIX 33) ; Greek form Σ ιμόν (Simon), confused with Ang.-Sax. Sigemund, ' victory-protection ' ; the first name of St. Peter and the name of another of the Apostles ; rather common among the early Anglo-Norman settlers in Ireland. Lat. Simon, -onis.

sionᴀ́ɴ, g. -áin, Sinan, Synan, Sinon ; a var. of Seᴀɴáɴ, q.v.

siseᴀl, g. -ṙil, Cecil ; Lat. Caecilius, dim. of caecus, blind.

solᴀṁ, g. -ᴀiṁ, Solomon ; doubtless the Scriptural name ; formerly in use among the MacNamees and O'Mellans of Ulster.

somᴀiRle, g. id., Sorley, (Samuel, Charles) ; Norse Sumerlide, summer-sailor ; a name of Norse origin ; specially common among the MacDonnells, by whom it was angl. Sorley ; now disguised as Samuel and Charles. Lat. Somerledus.

sceᴀᶂᴀ́ɴ, g. -áin, sceiṁin, g. id., sciᴀ́ᴅᴀ́ɴ, g. -áin, sciᴀ́ᴅɴᴀ, sciᴀɴᴀ, scíᴠin, g. id., scioᶂᴀ́ɴ, g. -áin, Stephen ; Greek Στέφανος (Stephanos), crown, or wreath ; the name of the proto-martyr of the Christian faith ; a rather common name among the early Anglo-Norman settlers in Ireland. Lat. Stephanus.

suiḃne, g. id., Sivney, (Simon) ; an old Irish name meaning ' well-going ' ; borne by seven Irish saints. Lat. Suibneus.

τaóᵹ, g. τaıóᵹ, Teige, Teague, (Thaddeaus, Thaddeus, Thady, Thade, Timothy, Tim) ; an ancient and very common Irish name, meaning ' poet ' or ' philosopher' ; still found in every part of Ireland, but now generally angl. Timothy. St. τaóᵹ was martyred at Wurtzburg ; his feast was kept on 8 July. Lat. Thaddaeus.

τaıóᵹín, g. id., Tim ; a dim. of τaóᵹ, q.v.

τaRLa, v. τoıⱃⱱeaLⱱaċ.

τeaⱱóıⱱ, g. id., Tibbot, Theobald, (Tobias, Toby) ; Teut. Theodbald, people-bold, Nor. Thebault, Thebaut, Thibault, Thibaut ; a rare name, introduced by the Anglo-Normans. Lat. Theobaldus.

τéaⱱóıR, g. -óⱃa, Theodore ; Greek θεόδωρος (Theodoros), God-gift. Lat. Theodorus.

τıᵹeaRnaċ, g. -aıᵹ, Tierney ; deriv. of τıᵹeaⱃna, a lord, and meaning ' lordly ' ; an old Irish name, borne by four saints, of whom the best known is St. Tierney of Clones. Lat. Tigernachus.

τıᵹeaRnán, g. -áın, Tiernan ; dim. of τıᵹeaⱃna, a lord ; a common name among the O'Rourkes. St. Tiernan's Day was 8 April. Lat. Tigernanus.

τıoⱱóıⱱ, a var. of τeaⱱóıⱱ, q.v.

τıomóıⱱ, g. id., Timothy ; Greek Τιμόθεος (Timotheos), honouring God ; an ancient name, in use even in pagan times ; borne by the disciple of St. Paul. In Ireland, it appears to be of comparatively recent introduction and is very rare. Timothy as an angl. form of τaóᵹ (q.v.) is, however, very common, but does not appear to have been in use before the Cromwellian period. Lat. Timotheus.

τoıRⱱeaLⱱaċ, g. -aıᵹ, Turlough, (Terence, Terry, Charles) ; an Irish name, meaning ' shaped like Thor,' the Norse Jupiter ; a common name among the O'Briens, O'Neills, O'Donnells, O'Connors of Connacht, MacSweenys, &c. ; now generally angl. Terence. Lat. Tordelvachus.

τomáιsín, g. id., Tommy ; a dim. of τomáp, q.v.

τomaιταċ, -aιʒ, Tomaltagh, Tumelty, (Timothy) ; an old Irish name, formerly rather frequent, especially among the O'Connors of Connacht ; still in use, but disguised under the angl. form of Timothy. Lat. Tomaltachus, Tumultachus.

τomás, g. -áιr, Thomas ; Heb. Tōmā, from tōm, a twin, the same as the Greek δίδυμος (Didymus) ; the name of one of the Twelve Apostles ; very common among the early Anglo-Normans out of devotion to St. Thomas a Becket. Lat. Thomas, -ae.

τráelaċ, a dialectical var. of τoιrroealḃaċ, q.v.

τuaτaι, g. -aιι, Toal, Tully ; Celt. *Touto-valo-s, people-mighty ; an ancient and once rather common name in Ireland ; still in use, but now very rare. Lat. Tuat-halius, Tulius.

uaιτéιr, g. id., Walter ; a var. of uaιταr, q.v.

uaιτne (recte. uaιτne), g. id., Hewney, Oney, Owney, Oynie, (Antony, Anthony) ; an old Irish name, found among the O'Mores, O'Loghlens, &c., by whom it was angl. Antony.

uaιταr, g. -aιr, Walter ; Teut. Waldhar, Walthar, Walther, power-army, Nor. Walter ; one of the commonest names among the early Anglo-Normans in Ireland, but now rather rare. Lat. Valterius.

uιleóʒ, g. id., Ulick, (Ulysses) ; a dim. of uιlliam, q.v. Lat. Ulligus.

uιlfrιo, g. id., Wilfrid ; Ang.-Sax. Wilfrith, will-peace.

uιlleaċ, g. -ιc, Ulick, (Ulysses) ; a var. of uιleóʒ, q.v.

uιlliam, g. id., William ; Teut. Willehelm, Wilhelm, will-protection, Nor. Willaume ; the most common name among the early Anglo-Norman settlers in Ireland. It owed its popularity to William the Conqueror. Lat. Gulielmus.

uιllιoc, v. uιlleaċ and uιleóʒ.

uιnseann, uιnsιonn, g. -rιnn, Vincent ; Lat. Vincentius, conquering ; a name introduced by the Anglo-Normans ; always rare.

úısceán, g. -cın, Euston ; Nor. Hutchen, dim. of Hugh ; a name among the MacDonnells.

ulcán, g. -áın, Ultan ; the name of eighteen Irish saints mentioned in the Martyrology of Donegal. Lat. Ultanus.

unfraıó, g. id., Humphrey ; Teut. Hunfrid, Hunfrith, Hun-peace ; a rare name among the Anglo-Normans. It appears to have gone entirely out of use, except as an angl. form of **áṁláoıó**, q.v. Lat. Hunfridus, Onuphrius.

NAMES OF WOMEN
IRISH—ENGLISH

Abaigeal, g., id., Abigail ; Heb. Abigail father of joy, joyfulness ; the name of the wife of King David, noted for her prudence and beauty ; in use in Derry and Omeath. Lat. Abigail.

Abaig, g. id., Abbey, Abbie ; a pet form of Abaigeal, q.v.

Agata, g. id., Agatha ; Gr. Ἀγαθη (Agathé), good ; the name of a celebrated Sicilian virgin and martyr of the 3rd century. O'Connell's heart rests in her church at Rome. Lat. Agatha.

Agna, g. id., Ina ; the name of two Irish saints ; probably an Irish form of Agnes (v. Aignéir).

Aibilín, g. id., Aileen, Eveleen, Evelyn ; a var. of Eibilín, q.v.

Aifric, g. -ice, Afric, Africa, Aphria ; the name of two abbesses of Kildare, one of whom died in 738 and the other in 833 ; also in use in Scotland and the Isle of Man. It was a lady of this name, Africa, daughter of Godred, King of Man, and wife of John de Courcy, that founded the Cistercian Abbey, known as the Grey Abbey, in the Ards of Co. Down. Now very rare. Lat. Affrica, Africa.

Aignéis, g. id., Agnes ; Gr. Ἀγνη (Agné), sacred, pure ; the name of a Roman virgin, martyred in 304 ; introduced into Ireland by the Anglo-Normans. Lat. Agnes, -etis.

Ailbe, g. id., Alvy, Elva ; also written Oilbe ; formerly common as a woman's name in Ireland. Lat. Albea.

Ailiu, g. id., Alley ; a pet form of Ailir, q.v.

ᴀɪᴌɪꜱ, ᴀɪᴌɪ́ꜱ, ᴀɪᴌɪ́ꜱᴇ, ᴀɪᴌꜱᴇ, g. id., Alicia, Alice, Aylice,
   Elsha ; a pet form of Adelaide (Teut. Adalheid, noble
   rank) ; a name introduced by the Anglo-Normans.
   Lat. Alicia.

ᴀɪᴍɪᴌɪ́ᴏɴᴀ, g. id., Amelina ; a Nor. dim. of Æmilia
   (v. ᴇɪᴍɪ́ᴌᴇ) ; a name introduced by the Anglo-Normans.
   Lat. Æmiliana.

ᴀ́ɪɴᴇ, g. id., Anne, Anna ; an ancient Irish name ; still
   common, but now merged in the Hebrew ᴀ́ɴɴᴀ, q.v.

ᴀɪɴᴈᴇᴀᴌ, g. id., Angela ; Lat. Angela, angel.

ᴀɪꜱᴌɪɴᴈ, ᴀɪꜱᴌɪɴɴ, g. -e, (Esther) ; an Irish name,
   meaning ' a dreamh' ; in use in Derry and Omeath.

ᴀɪᴛᴛᴇ, g. id., Atty ; the name of a holy virgin, patroness
   cf ᴄɪᴌᴌ ᴀɪᴛᴛᴇ in the barony of Kenry, Co. Limerick,
   where her feast-day (Jan. 15) was formerly kept as a
   holiday and a station held.

ᴀᴌᴀɪ́ᴅ, g. id., Alley ; a pet form of ᴀɪᴌɪ́ʀ, q.v.

ᴀᴌᴀꜱᴛʀɪ́ᴏɴᴀ, g. id., Alastrina, Alexandra ; the fem.
   form of ᴀᴌᴀꜱᴛᴀʀ, q.v. Lat. Alexandra.

ᴀᴌᴌꜱᴜ́ɴ, g. id., Allison ; dim. of ᴀɪᴌɪ́ʀ, q.v. ; in use down
   to recent times.

ᴀ́ɴɴᴀ, ᴀɴɴᴀ, g. id., Anna, Anne ; Heb. Hannáh, grace ;
   a Biblical name, borne by the mother of Samuel, the
   wife of Tobias, and the mother of the Blessed Virgin
   Mary. It is to the last of these that the name owes
   its popularity. Very common in Ireland ; confused
   with the native name ᴀ́ɪɴᴇ, q.v. Lat. Anna.

ᴀɴɴᴀ́ʙᴌᴀ, g. id., Annabel, Annabella, Arabella, Bella ;
   a name of uncertain origin ; introduced into Ireland
   by the Anglo-Normans, but never became popular.
   Lat. Annabella.

ᴀɴɴꜱᴛᴀ́ꜱ, g. id., Anastasia ; Gr. Ἀναστάσια (Anastasia), from ἀνάστασις (anástasis), resurrection ; a
   name given by the early Christians to newly baptised,
   to signify that they had arisen to a new life ; introduced into Ireland by the Anglo-Normans. Lat.
   Anastasia.

ᴀᴏᴅɴᴀɪᴛ, g. id. -ᴀᴛᴀ and -ᴀᴛᴀɴ, Enat, Ena, Eny ; fem. dim.
   of ᴀᴏᴅ (q.v.), corresponding to the masc. ᴀᴏᴅᴀ́ɴ (q.v.) ;

the name of an Irish saint whose feast was kept on 9 November. Lat. Aidnata.

ᴀoιƀeᴀnn, g. -ƀne, Eavan ; Old Ir. Aibfinn, Aebfind, fair form ; an ancient Irish name, borne by the mother of St. Enda. Lat. Aibfinnia.

ᴀoιꝼe, g. id., Eva ; an ancient Irish name. Lat. Eva.

ᴀꙅ̇ʀᴀċꙅ̇, g. id. and -ᴀ, Attracta ; the name of an Irish virgin saint, of Ulster origin, who flourished in the 6th century and founded the nunnery of Killaraght, near Lough Gara, Co. Sligo, where her memory is revered on 11 August. Lat. Attracta.

ƀᴀƀ, Babe ; a pet name.

ƀᴀιƀín, g. id., Barbara, Barbary, Bab ; a pet dim. of ƀᴀιꝛƀꝛe, q.v. ; common in West Galway.

ƀᴀιʀƀʀe, ƀᴀιʀƀʀe, g. id., Barbara, Barbary ; Gr. βάρβαρη (Bárbaré), stranger ; a name in use among the ancient Romans ; borne by a holy virgin and martyr of Nicodemia in the 3rd century, who became the patroness of architects and engineers ; common in Connacht. Lat. Barbara.

ƀeᴀn ṁuṁᴀn, Benvon ; an Irish name, meaning ' Lady of Munster ' ; in use down to the beginning of the 17th century.

ƀeᴀn ṁιƀe, Benvy ; an Irish name, meaning ' Lady of Meath ' ; in use down to the beginning of the 17th century.

ƀéƀιnn, g. -ƀιnne, Bevin, (Vivian) ; an ancient Irish name, meaning ' melodious lady ' ; borne by, among others, the mother and a daughter of Brian Boru.

ƀlᴀ̇ꙅ̇, g. -ᴀιꙅ̇e, Flora ; an ancient Irish name, meaning ' blossom,' or ' flower-bud ' ; borne by two virgin saints. Lat. Flora.

ƀlᴀ̇ꙅ̇nᴀιƀ, g. id., Florence ; dim. of ƀlᴀ̇ꙅ̇, q.v. ; an ancient Irish personal name. Lat. Florentia.

ƀlιnne, g. id., Blanche ; a corruption of ṁonιnne ; the name of an Irish virgin, patroness of Killevy, Co. Armagh, whose feast-day is 6 July ; still in use, angl. Blanche. Lat. Moninna.

bluinse, g. id., Blanche ; perhaps a corruption of buinne,
q.v.

briȝoe, v. briȝio.

briȝoín, g. id., Bridie, Breeda, Bidina, Bidelia, Dina,
Delia, Dillie, Beesy, &c. ; dim. of briȝio, q.v.

briȝio, g. -ȝoe, Brigid, Bride, Breeda (Bridget) ; an
ancient Irish name, probably derived from briȝ,
strength ; the name of the goddess of poetry in pagan
Ireland ; sanctified and made for ever illustrious by
St. Brigid of Kildare, patroness of Ireland. It does
not appear to have come into common use as a woman's
name until the 17th or 18th century. In the spoken
language, the gen. case, briȝoe, is sometimes used
for the nominative. The frequent angl. form Bridget
is due to the resemblance of the Irish name to that of
the celebrated Swedish widow, St. Bridget. Lat.
Brigida.

cáic, g. id., Kate ; a pet form of Catherine (v. Caicrín) ;
very common.

caici, g. id., Katty ; a pet form of Caicrín, q.v.

caicilín, g. id., Kathleen, Catherine ; a var. of Caicrín,
q.v. Cf. Spanish Catalina and Hungarian Katalin.

cáicín, g. id., Katie, Katty ; dim. of Cáic, q.v.

caiclín, g. id., Kathleen, Catherine ; a var. of Caicilín,
q.v.

caicrín, caicríona, g. id., Catherine ; Gr. Καθαρινή
(Kathariné), from καθαρός (katharos), pure ; the
name of a celebrated virgin and martyr of Alexandria,
brought into Europe by the crusaders ; but the
popularity of the name is mainly due to St. Catherine
of Sienna. Lat. Catharina.

caoilfionn, g. -finne, Keelin ; comp. of caol, slender,
and fionn, fair ; the name of an Irish virgin saint who
was venerated on 3rd February. Lat. Coelfinnia.

caoime, g. id., Keavy ; an Irish name, signifying 'gentle-
ness,' 'beauty,' 'grace,' 'courtesy' ; borne by a
Scoto-Irish saint whose feast-day is 2 November.
Lat. Pulcheria.

Catraoine, g. id., Catherine ; a var. of Caitrín, q.v.

Ciannait, g. id. -ata and -atan, Kinnat, Keenat ; fem. dim. of Cian (ancient), corresponding to the masc. Cianán, q.v. ; the name of an Irish virgin saint, commemorated on 23 March. Lat. Ciannata.

Cristín, Cristíona, g. id., Christina ; Lat. Christina, deriv. of Christus, a Christian ; the name of a Roman virgin who was martyred at Bolsena in 295 ; brought into Scotland by Queen Margaret, and into Ireland by the Anglo-Normans.

Daṁnait, g. id., -ata, -atan, Devnet, Downet, Dymphna ; fem. dim. of daṁ, a poet, corresponding to the masc. Daṁán ; the name of a celebrated Irish virgin who was martyred at Gheel in Belgium. She is patroness of Gheel where her feast is kept on 15th May. Lat. Dymphna.

Dearḃáil g. *-áile, Derval, Dervilia ; comp. of dearḃ, true, and áil, desire ; an ancient Irish name. Lat. Dervilia.

Doireann, g. -rinne, Dorren, (Dorothy, Dolly) ; an ancient Irish name, meaning 'the sullen.' Lat. Dorinnia.

Éadaoin, g. -ine, Edwina ; the name of a holy virgin of Moylurg (Boyle), Co. Roscommon, whose festival-day was 5 July. Lat. Edwina.

Earnait, g. id. -ata and -atan, Ernet ; fem. dim. of earna, knowing, corresponding to the masc. Earnán, q.v. Lat. Ernata.

Eiḃilín, Eiḃlín, g. id., Eileen, Eveleen, Evelyn, Aileen, Ellen, Helen, Ellie, Eily, Nellie, Nell, Lena ; Gr. 'Ελένη (Elené), from ἑλη (elé), sunlight ; the name of the mother of Constantine ; introduced into Ireland by the Anglo-Normans. Lat. Helena.

Eiléanóir, Eileanóir, Eilíonóra, g. id., Eleanor, Eleanora ; supposed by some to be a distinct name, but really only a Provençal form of Helena (v. Eiḃlín) ; introduced into Ireland by the Anglo-Normans.

eilís, eilíse, g. id. Elizabeth, Eliza, Elsie, Lizzie, Bessie, Betsey, Betty, (Alicia, Alice, Aylice) ; Heb. Eliscéba', from 'el, God, and scéba', an oath, meaning ' God hath sworn,' or ' God is an oath ' ; the name of the wife of Zachary and mother of John the Baptist, and of many other holy women ; Isabella was the form under which it first came into Ireland, where it is very common. Lat. Elisabetha.

eimíle, g. id., Emily ; Lat. Æmilia, the fem. form of Æmilius, the cognomen of one of the most ancient of the patrician gentes of Rome, and the name of several early martyrs.

eistir, g. id., Esther ; Heb. 'Estér, of Persian origin ; the name of the Hebrew lady who was wife of Assuerus, King of Persia ; popularised in France by Racine ; in Ireland, given to children born about Easter. Lat. Esther.

eitne, g. id., Eithne, Ethna, Etney, (Annie) ; an Irish personal name, meaning ' a kernel ' ; borne by three virgin saints. Lat. Ethnea.

fáince, g. id., Fanny ; the name of two saintly Irish virgins, one the sister of St. Enda of Aran and patroness of Rossory, on Lough Erne, whose feast was kept on 1 January ; and the other patroness of Cluain-caoi, in the neighbourhood of Cashel, who was venerated on 21 of same month. Lat. Fanchea.

faoiltiġeaRná, g. id., Whiltierna ; comp. of faol, wolf, and tiġeaṙná, lady ; the name of an Irish virgin saint whose feast-day was 17 March. Lat. Fail-tigerna.

fiáóṅaiṫ, g. id. -áṫá, and -áṫáṅ, Feenat, Feena ; fem. dim. of fiáó, a deer ; the name of a saintly Irish virgin whose festival was celebrated on 4 January. Lat. Fiadnata.

fionnġuáLá, g. id., Finola, Nuala, (Flora, Penelope, Penny, Nappy) ; comp. of fionn, fair, and ġuáLá, a shoulder ; an ancient Irish name, common down to the end of the 17th century and still in use, but often shortened to ⁊uᴀᴌᴀ (q.v.) and generally disguised under the angl. form of Penelope. Lat. Finguala, Finola.

⁊oḃnᴀiṫ, g. id., -ᴀṫᴀ and -ᴀṫᴀn, Gobinet, Gobnet, Gubby, (Abigail, Abbey, Abbie, Abina, Deborah, Debby, Webbie) ; fem. dim. of ⁊oḃ, a mouth, corresponding to the masc. ⁊oḃán ; the name of a celebrated Munster virgin, the patroness of Ballyvourney, whose feast is kept on 11 February ; still common in Cork, Kerry and Limerick, but generally angl. Abbey and Debby. Lat. Gobnata.

⁊oRmḟlᴀiṫ, g. -ᴀṫᴀ, Gormlaith, Gormley, (Barbara, Barbary) ; comp. of ⁊oṟm, blue, and ḟlᴀiṫ, lady ; still in use, but rare. Lat. Gormlata.

⁊RáinnE, g. id., (Grace, Gertrude, Gertie) ; an ancient Irish name, still in use. Lat. Grania.

ḣilóE, g. id., Hilda, Hildy ; the name of a saintly Irish abbess, who was venerated on 18 November. Lat. Hilda.

Íoe, g. id., Ida, Ita ; Old Ir. Itu, thirst ; the name of the celebrated Abbess of Kileedy, in West Limerick, whose feast is kept with great solemnity on 15 January. Lat. Ita.

iseᴀḃᴀl, v. iṟiḃéᴀl.

isiḃéᴀl, g. id., Isabella, Sybil, Sibby, Elizabeth, Eliza, Bessie, (Annabel, Annabella, Bella) ; the French form of Elizabeth (v. ᴀilíṟ) ; apparently the form in which the name first came into Ireland ; still in use, but rare ; also Siḃéᴀl.

lᴀḃᴀoise, g. id., Louisa ; the fem. form of ᴀlᴀḃᴀoiṟ, q.v. Lat. Aloysia, Ludovica.

lᴀsᴀiRḟíonᴀ, g. id., Lassarina ; comp. of lᴀṟᴀiṟ, a flame, and ḟíonᴀ, of wine ; an ancient Irish name, still in use in parts of Connacht. Lat. Lassarina.

léᴀn, g. id., Eleanor, Eleanora ; a pet form of eiléᴀnóiṟ, q.v.

lil, líle, g. id., Lily, Lelia. Lat. Lelia.

luigseac, g. -rige, Lucy ; the fem. form of lugaid, q.v. ; the name of an Irish virgin saint who was venerated on 22 May. Lat. Lugsecha.

máda, g. id., Maud ; a contraction of Matilda (v. maitilde).

madailéin, g. id., Madeline ; a name assumed in honour of St. Mary Magdalen. Lat. Magdalena.

máible, g. id., Mabel ; a shortened form of Amabel, from Lat. Amabilis, loveable.

máigdlin, g. id., Madeline. V. madailéin.

maigréad, g. id., Margaret, Maggie, Madge. V. máirgréad.

máille, máilse, máilti, g. id., Molly, (Margery, Marjory) ; pet form of máire, q.v.

máire, g. id., Mary, Moira, Maria. V. muire.

máiréad, mairéad, v. máirgréad.

máirgréad, mairgréad, g. id., Margaret, Maggie, Madge ; Gr. Μαργαρίτης (Margarítés), a pearl ; the name of a Christian virgin who was martyred at Antioch in the last general persecution ; brought to Europe by the crusaders, when it became very common in France and England ; introduced by the Anglo-Normans into Ireland, where it has ever since been very popular, and is now found under a great variety of forms. Lat. Margarita.

máirín, g. id., Maureen, May, Molly ; a dim. of máire, q.v.

mairsil, mairsile, g. id., Marcella ; Lat. Marcella, a fem. dim. of Marcus (v. marcur) ; the name of a saintly Roman widow ; common in France, whence apparently it came into Ireland.

maiti, g. id., Matty ; a pet form of maitilde, q.v.

maitilde, g. id., Matilda ; Ger. Mahthild, might-heroine ; the name of a royal German saint, the mother of the Emperor Otho I, a lady remarkable for her humility and patience ; formerly very common in France ; brought to England by the wife of William the Conqueror and into Ireland by the Anglo-Normans. The Flemings called the name Mahault, whence the Norman forms, Molde and Maud. Both Matilda and Maud were in use in England, but neither ever became common in Ireland. Lat. Mathildes, -is.

mⱭllⱭⱮ, g. id., Molly ; a pet form of mⱭⱤⱤe, q.v.

muⱤⱭoⱮ, v. mⱭⱮⱤZⱤeⱭⱮ.

mⱭⱤCⱭ, g. id., Martha ; a Biblical name of uncertain origin ; borne by the sister of Lazarus and Mary, and by an Abbess of Kildare, in the 8th century. Lat. Martha.

meⱭⱮⱮ, g. meⱮⱮⱮe, meⱭⱮⱮⱭ, Meave, (Maud, Mabbina, Mabel, Margery, Marjory, Madge) ; the name of the celebrated Queen of Connacht in the first century ; also borne by an Irish saint who was venerated on 22 November. Lat. Meba.

meⱭllⱭ, g. id., Mella ; the name of several holy women in ancient Ireland. Lat. Mella.

meⱭⱤS, g. id., Mary ; a form of mⱭⱮⱤe, q.v. ; in use in Kerry until recent times.

meⱮⱮⱮⱮ, g. id., Meaveen, (Mabbina) ; a dim. of meⱭⱮⱮ, q.v.

mⱮⱮe, g. id., Meeda ; a var. of ⱮⱮe (q.v.) by the prefixing of mⱮ, my, as a term of endearment. Lat. Mita.

mⱮⱮⱤⱮⱮ, g. id., Moreen ; dim. of mⱮⱮ, q.v.

monCⱭ, g. id., Monica ; a name of unknown origin, borne by the mother of St. Augustine. Lat. Monica.

mⱮⱤ, g. mⱮⱮⱮe, More, (Martha, Mary, Agnes) ; an ancient and, until comparatively recent times, very common Irish name, signifying ' great ' ; still in use, but disguised under the angl. forms of Martha, Mary, or Agnes. Lat. *Mora.

muⱭⱮⱮⱭⱮC, g. id., -ⱭCⱭ and -ⱭⱤⱭⱮ, Monat, Mona ; dim. of muⱭⱮ, noble ; the name of an Irish virgin saint, whose festival-day was 6 January. Lat. Muadnata.

muⱮⱤe, g. id., Mary ; Heb. Mrjám, which can be read Mirjám, or better Mariám, a name of difficult interpretation, as are all names which appear in a very contracted form and in which it is difficult to discover

the root-word from which they are derived. About
seventy different meanings are given to Mary, in great
part suggested by devotion to the Mother of God
rather than by solid critical sense. Historically and
grammatically examined, it seems very likely that it
is a Hebrew name signifying ' bitterness,' in the sense
of grief, sorrow, affliction, either in reference to the
pains of childbirth, or to the moral condition of the
mother and family, oppressed by some great mis-
fortune, or perhaps to the sad period of the Egyptian
bondage, to which the Israelites were subject at the
time of the birth of the first Mary, the sister of Moses.
It was afterwards the name of several Jewish women,
including the Blessed Virgin Mary, Mother of Jesus
Christ, but was very slow in creeping in to the Western
Church. It is only about the middle of the 12th
century that we find the first instances of its use in
Europe, whither apparently it had been brought by
the devotion of the crusaders. Even in Ireland,
there were few Marys until comparatively recent
times. I find only a few instances of the use of the
name before the 17th century. At present one-
fourth of the women of Ireland are named Mary.
The ordinary form of the name, however, is máire,
muire being used exclusively for the Blessed Virgin
Mary, and, therefore, the most honoured of all names
of women. Lat. Maria.

muiréad, muirgéad, v. máirgréad.

muireann, muirinn, g. -rinne, Morrin, (Marion,
Madge) ; an ancient Irish name, meaning ' of the long
hair.' Lat. Murinnia.

muirgeal, g. -gile, Murel, Muriel ; comp. of muir,
sea, and geal, bright, meaning ' sea-bright,' or ' fair
one of the sea.' Lat. Murgela.

muráid, v. máirgréad.

murainn, v. muireann, of which it is a variant.

nábla, náible, g. id., Annabel, Annabella, Nabla,
(Mabel), Bella ; a shortened form of Annábla, q.v.

nainseaⱱ, neans, g. id., Nancy, Nance, Nan, Anne;
   popular variants of Ánna, q.v.

neill, neilli, g. id., Nell, Nellie; pet forms of eiblín, q.v.

nóinín, nóirín, Nonie, Daisey; pet form of Nóra, q.v.

nóra, g. id., Nora, Norah, Honor, Honora, Honoria
   Nonie, Nanno, (Hannah); a shortened form of Onóra.
   q.v.

nuala, g. id., Nuala, (Nappy, Penelope, Penny); a shortened form of fionnḃuala, q.v.

oⱱarnait, g. id., -ata, and -atan, Ornat, Orna; fem. dim.
   of oⱱar, pale, olive-colour, corresponding to the masc.
   Oⱱrán, q.v.; the name of an Irish saint, venerated
   on 13 November. Lat. Odarnata.

oilⱱe g. id. Elva; (Olive); a var. of ailⱱe q.v.

onóra g. id., Honor, Honora, Honoria, Nora, Norah,
   (Hannah); Lat. Honoria, fem. dim. of Honorius,
   honourable; a name introduced into Ireland by the
   Anglo-Normans and still very popular under the
   shortened form of Nóra, q.v.

órḟlait, g. -ata, Orlaith; an old Irish name, meaning
   'the golden lady.' Lat. Orlata.

paili, pails, pal, Poll, Polly; var. of mallaⱱ, q.v.

peig, peigi, g. id., Peg, Peggy; rhymed var. of Meg
   and Meggy, for Margaret (v. máirgréaⱱ).

proinnséas, próinséas, g. id., Frances, Fanny;
   Lat. Francisca, fem. form of Franciscus, or Francis;
   a name adopted in honour of St. Francis of Assisi
   and borne by a saintly Roman widow, whose feast-
   day is 9 March.

ratnait, g. id., -ata and -atan, Renny; fem. dim. of rat,
   grace, or prosperity; the name of an Irish saint who is
   patroness of Kilrenny, Co. Kildare. Lat. Ratnata.

riceal, g. -cíle, Richella; the name of a virgin saint
   whose feast-day was 19 May. Lat. Richella.

riognaċ, g. -aige, Regina; the name of a saintly Irish
   virgin, whose feast was kept on 18 December; she was
   the sister of St. Finnian of Clonard. Lat. Regnacia.

róis, róise, g. id., Rose; Teut. Hros, a horse, Nor.

Rohais, Roese, Roesia ; a name introduced, no doubt, by the Anglo-Normans and borne by a lady of the Maguires in the early part of the 16th century. The name of St. Rose of Lima is derived from the Latin rosa, a rose. She was first named Isabella, but was afterwards called Rose from the rose-like appearance of her face in childhood. Róiṗ was, however, a woman's name in Ireland long before the birth of St. Rose. Lat. Rosa.

Róisín, g. id., Rose, Rosie ; a dim. of Róiṗ, q.v.

Saḃa, g. id., Sive, (Sally) ; a var. in West Connacht of Saḋḃ, q.v.

Saḋḃ, g. id., and Saiḋḃe, Sive, (Sabia, Sophia, Sophy, Sarah, Sally) ; an ancient Irish name, meaning ' goodness ' ; still in use, but generally angl. Sally. Lat. Sabia.

Saḋḃa, g. id., Sive, (Sophia, Sophy) ; a var. of Saḋḃ, q.v. ; in use in Donegal and Derry.

Saiḃḃín, g. id., Sabina ; dim. of Saḋḃ, q.v. Lat. Sabina.

Séarlait, g. id., Charlotte ; fem. dim. of Charles ; a name of comparatively recent formation. Lat. Carlotta.

Seósaiṁtín, g. id., Josephine ; fem. dim. of Joseph (v. Ióṗep) ; a name of comparatively recent formation ; borrowed from the French. Lat. Josephina.

Siḃéal, v. Iṗiḃéal.

Siḃi, Sioḃaiġ, g. id., Sibby ; pet forms of Siḃéal or Iṗiḃéal, q.v.

Síle, g. id., Cecelia, Cecily, Celia, Selia, Sheila, Sheela, (Sabina, Sibby, Sally, Julia, July, Judith, Judy, Jude) ; Lat. Caecilia, dim. of caeca, blind ; the name of a celebrated Roman virgin and martyr, the patroness of musicians ; introduced by the Anglo-Normans and ever since common in Ireland, but generally wrongly angl. Julia, &c.

Sine, g. id., Jane, Jannet, Jenny ; a var. of Sinéaḋ, q. v.; in use in Co. Derry.

Sinéaᴅ, g. id., Jane, Jannet, Jenny; a dim. of Fr.
Jeanne, from Johanna (v. Siobán).

Sineaɪᴅ, g. id., Jane, Jannet, Jenny; a var. of Sinéaᴅ,
q.v.; in use in Co. Derry.

Siobáinín, g. id., Hannah, (Josephine); a dim of
Siobán, q.v.

Siobán, g. id., Joan, Johanna, Hannah, (Julia, July,
Judith, Judy, Jude, Susanna, Susan, Nonie); the
fem. form of Joannes, or John (v. Eóin and Seán), which
became common in France in the 12th century
as Jehanne and Jeanne, and in England as Joan;
brought into Ireland by the Anglo-Normans, where
it has ever since been one of the most popular of
women's names. Lat. Joanna.

Sisile, g. id., Cecilia, Cecily; a late form of Síle, q.v.

Siubáinín, a var. of Siobáinín, q.v.

Siubán, a var. of Siobán, q.v.

Siúi, a pet form of Súranna, q.v.

Sláine, g. id., Slany; an old Irish name, meaning
'health'; common among the O'Briens. Lat. Slania.

Sorcᴀ, g. id., Sorcha, (Sarah, Sally); an old Irish name,
signifying 'clear' or 'bright'; still in use, but now
always angl. Sarah or Sally. Lat. Sorcha.

Sósaɪᴅ, g. id., Susie; a pet form of Sóranna or Súranna,
q.v.

Sósanna, g. id., Susanna, Susan; a var. of Súranna, q.v.

Stéise, a pet form of Annrtár, q.v.

Súsanna, g. id., Susanna, Susan; Gr. Ξ ουσανα
(Sousana); the name of a Hebrew maiden who, on
being falsely accused of adultery, was condemned to
death, but saved by Daniel who showed that her
accusers were calumniators; introduced into Ireland
by the Anglo-Normans. Lat. Susanna.

Tilᴅe, g. id., Tilda; a shortened form of Maitilᴅe, q.v.

Toiréasa, g. id., Teresa, Tessie; a name of uncertain
origin; peculiar to Spain until the 16th century,
when the fame of St. Teresa made it world-wide. Lat.
Teresia.

Craoine, Críona, g. id., Trina, Katie, Katty; pet
forms of Catraoine or Caitríona, q.v.

Creasa, Creise, g. id., ; an old Irish name, meaning
'strength'; adopted as the Irish equivalent of Teresa
(v. Toiréara).

Úna, g. id., Una, Uny, (Unity, Winifred, Winefred,
Winnie, Winny, Agnes); an ancient and once common
Irish name; still in use, but generally angl. Winifred.
Lat. Una.

Ursula, g. id., Ursula; Lat. Ursula, little bear; the
name of a Breton maiden who was martyred by the
Huns at Cologne in the 5th century.

SURNAMES

IRISH—ENGLISH

ᴀ ᴅᴀRRᴀ, Barry. V. ᴅe ᴅᴀṗṗᴀ.

ᴀᴅᴅóıᴅ—VIII—*Abbod*, Abbott; 'son of Abbot' (dim. of Abraham); an old Anglo-Irish surname, found at least as early as the beginning of the 14th century.

ᴀ ᴅʟáᴄ, Blake. V. ᴅe ᴅʟáᴄᴀ.

ᴀ ᴅʟóıᴅ—VI—Blood; Welsh 'ab-Lloyd,' i.e., 'son of Lloyd'; a Clare surname. Cf. ꝼʟóıᴅ and ʟóıᴅ.

ᴀᴅRᴀḣᴀm—VIII—Abraham; 'son of Abraham.' This surname in Ireland dates back to the early part of the 13th century.

ᴀ ᴅRıúꞅ, Bruce. V. ᴅe ᴅꞃıúꞃ.

ᴀ ᴅuʟᴀ, Wooley. V. ᴅe ᴅuʟᴅ.

ᴀ ᴅúRᴄ, Burke, Bourke. V. ᴅe ᴅúꞃᴄᴀ.

ᴀᴄᴀoᴅ, Hackett. V. ṅᴀᴄᴀeᴅ, ṅᴀıᴄéıᴅ.

ᴀ ᴄʟıᴈeóıR, Killiger.

ᴀ' Ćnuıᴄ—XIII—Hill; Ir. 'ᴀn Ćnuıᴄ,' i.e., of the hill, from residence thereon.

ᴀ ᴄoʟᴅᴀRᴅ, *Acollobert*, Colbert. V. ᴄoʟᴅáꞃᴅ.

ᴀ' óúnᴀ—XIII—Doona; Ir. 'ᴀn óúnᴀ,' i.e., of the dun or fort, from residence in or thereby; a rare surname, found in parts of Kerry.

ᴀ ꝼᴀe, *Aphaye, Affay, Faie*, Fay. V. ᴅe ꝼᴀe.

ᴀ ꝼRéın, Freyne, Frein, etc. V. ᴅe ꝼꞃéın.

ᴀᴈᴀꞅ—XI—*Aase, Asshe*, Ashe; Mid. Eng. 'atte Asse,' 'atte Ashe,' corrupted to 'de Ass,' 'de Asse,' i.e., at the ash, from residence beside an ash-tree. This form of the surname is common in Kerry and parts of Limerick. V. ᴀıꞃ, ᴅe ṅᴀıꞃ, and ᴅe ṅáꞃ.

ᴀ' ᵹleᴀnnᴀ—XIII—Glanny, Glenny, Glenn; Ir. 'ᴀn ᵹleᴀnnᴀ,' i.e., of the glen, from residence therein.

ᴀ' ᵹleᴀnnᴄáin—XIII—Glanton; Ir. 'ᴀn ᵹleᴀnnᴄáin,' i.e., of the little glen, from residence therein.

ᴀ hóʀᴀ, Hore, Hoare. V. ᴠe hópᴀ.

ᴀicéiᴠ, Hackett. V. hᴀicéiᴠ.

ᴀiᴠleᴀʀᴄ—VIII—*Athelard, Adelard, Ayllard, Eylard,* Ellard; 'son of Adelard' (a Frankish personal name, also written Adelhard and Athelard, the same as the Anglo-Saxon Æthelheard); an old Anglo-Irish surname, dating back at least to the middle of the 13th century. In the time of Edward I, Robert Athelard of Athelardestoun, Co. Louth, was tenant-in-capite of the king.

ᴀiᵹleᴀʀᴄ—VIII—*Aylwert, Eylward, Ayleward,* Ailward, Aylward, Alyward, etc.; 'son of Ailward' (Anglo-Saxon Æthelweard); the name of an Anglo-Norman family who came into Ireland at the time of the invasion and settled at Aylwardstown, Co. Kilkenny, and at Faithleg, near Waterford. The Aylwards were frequently mayors of Waterford. Their castle at Faithleg was besieged and taken by Cromwell in 1649.

ᴀiᵹlmeᴀʀ—VIII—*Ailmar, Eilmer,* Aylmer, Elmer, etc.; 'son of Ailmar' (Anglo-Saxon Æthelmaer); the name of a distinguished Anglo-Irish family who settled in the 13th century in Dublin, Meath and Kildare. In the wars of the 16th century, the Aylmers adhered to the Stuart cause, and many of them were in consequence attainted and lost their property.

ᴀiléin—VIII—*Aleyne, Alleyne, Allaine,* Allan, Allen, etc.; 'son of Alan' (a Breton personal name introduced by the Normans). Families of this name came into Ireland at the time of the invasion and settled in Dublin, Kildare, and other parts of Leinster.

ᴀilín—VIII—*Alwine, Allyne,* Allin, Allen, etc.; 'son of Ailwin' (Anglo-Saxon Æthelwine); the name of an English family who settled in Ireland at or soon after the invasion. It can hardly be now distinguished from ᴀiléin, q.v.

Ⱥⁱⁿⱱⱹⁱú—VIII—*Andreu, Andrewe*, Andrew, Andrews ; ' son of Andrew.'

ȺⁱⁿᵹⱡⰵȺⁿⱱ, Angland, Ankland, England. V. Ⱥⁱⁿᵹⱡⰵⱁⁿⱱ.

Ⱥⁱⁿᵹⱡéⁱꙅ—XII—*Ainglishe*, English, Englishe ; Nor. ' l'Engleys,' i.e., the Englishman ; a descriptive surname evidently applied by Norman-French settlers to their English comrades ; common in many parts of Ireland, but especially in Tipperary where there are still some old and respectable families of the name. Also ⁱⁿᵹⱡéⁱꙛ, q.v.

Ⱥⁱⁿᵹⱡⰵⱁⁿⱱ—XI—*Angylont, Anglant, Englant, Anglound*, Angland, Ankland, England ; Nor. ' de Englond,' Lat. ' de Anglia,' i.e. from England. This surname, strange to say, is very rare. The few families who bear it are located chiefly in Limerick and Cork. Cf. Ⱥⁱⁿᵹⱡéⁱꙛ above.

Ⱥⁱꙛⁱᵹ—XI—Airey ; i.e., ' of Airey ' in Cumberland.

ȺⁱꙛⰿⰵȺꙅ—XI—Ormsby ; i.e., ' of Ormsby ' in England ; a late English surname.

ȺⁱꙛꙅⰵȺⱱóⁱⱱ—VIII—*Archebaud, Archibaud*, Archabold, Archibold, Archbold, etc. ; ' son of Arcenbald' or ' Eorconbeald ' (a Teutonic personal name). This family settled in Ireland at an early period and obtained extensive possessions in Dublin, Wicklow and Kildare. Even as early as 1315, they were in alliance with the O'Byrnes and O'Tooles. They were prominent in the wars of the 17th century, and in 1641 and 1691, several of the name in Dublin, Kildare and Wicklow were indicted of treason and attainted. The name was early corrupted to Ashpole, Ashpool, etc.

Ⱥⁱꙛꙅéⱡ, Archfield.

Ⱥⁱꙛꙅéⁱꙛ—XII—Archer, Orchard ; Nor. ' le Archer,' i.e., the archer or professional bowman ; the name of an Anglo-Norman family who came into Ireland at the time of the invasion and settled in Kilkenny, where they became wealthy and influential. To this family belonged the celebrated Irish Jesuit, Father James Archer.

Ấirsibéẫl—VIII—Archibald; the same origin as Ấippeẫbóiv, q.v.; the name of a Scottish family who settled in the north of Ireland.

Ấirsvéicin—XII—*Arstekin, Archedekyn*, Archdeacon; Nor. ' le Erchedekine,' ' le Ercedekne,' ' le Ercedecne,' i.e., the archdeacon; the name of an Anglo-Norman family who settled soon after the invasion in Co. Kilkenny. They were descended from Odo le Erce-dekne, from whom, when they became Irish, they took the surname of mẫcóvẫ (q.v.), now angl. Cody and Coady. At the beginning of the 17th century, the name was also found in Wexford, Waterford and Cork.

Ấis—XI—*Aysh, Ayshe, Asshe*, Ashe; Mid. Eng., ' atte Ashe,' i.e., at the ash, from residence beside an ash-tree. Families of this name settled soon after the invasion in Meath and Kildare. The following were indicted of treason in the King's Bench and out-lawed in 1641: Thomas Aysh, of Naas, gentleman; Henry Aysh, of same, gentleman; and Walter Aysh, of same, merchant. V. Ấfẫp and ve nẫip.

Ấiseẫbóiv, *Ashbould, Ayshpool, Asbold, Aspoll*, Aspel, Esbald, etc.; a corruption of Ấippeẫbóiv, q.v.

Ấiséip, Archer; a corruption of Ấippéip, q.v.

Ấislinn, Ashlin.

Ấistéicin, *Astekine, Asteken*, Archdeacon; a corruption of Ấippvéicin, q.v.

Ẫlẫmẫn—XI—*Aleman*, Allman; Nor. ' de Alemayne,' i.e., from Alemaigne, or Germany; an old but rare surname in Ireland. It still survives in Kerry.

Ẫlẫrv, Ellard. V. Ấivleẫpt.

Ẫlbẫnẫċ—X—*Albanagh*, Scott; Ir. ' Ẫlbẫnẫċ,' i.e.' the Scot, native of Scotland; a generic name for the Scottish galloglasses, especially the MacDonnells, who came over to Ireland in the 14th, 15th and 16th centuries.

Ẫlcóc—VIII—*Alekoc, Alcoc*, Alcock; ' son of Alcoke ' (a dim. of Alan).

Ẫ linse, Lynch. V. ve linpe.

ᴀlsᴀnᴅᴀıʀ—VIII—*Alesaundre, Alisander, Elysandyr,*
Elshander, Alexander, etc. ; ' son of Alexander.' This
surname is of early record in Ireland, but like
many others of the same class, it doubtless came
in at different periods. It is now found chiefly in
Ulster.

ᴀlᴄún—XI—*Altoun,* Alton ; Nor. ' de Alleton,' 'de
Alton,' i.e., of Alton, the name of more than one place
in England ; an old Anglo-Irish surname.

ᴀmbʀós, ᴀmʀós, ᴀmʀus—VIII—*Ameros,* Ambrose ;
' son of Ambrose ' ; a not uncommon surname in
Limerick and Cork. In Ireland it dates back at least
to the end of the 13th century. In 1601, William
Ambrose of Annagh obtained a grant of pardon from
Queen Elizabeth.

ᴀnᴄoıᴄıl—VIII—*Ankettill,* Anketell, Ankethill, etc. ;
' son of Ancytel,' a Teutonic personal name found in
Domesday Book and early Dublin rolls.

ᴀnᴅʀᴀosán—VIII—Anderson ; a phonetic rendering
of the English surname Anderson.

ᴀn ᴅúnᴀ—XIII—Doona. V. ᴀ'ᴅúnᴀ.

ᴀn ᵹeımʀıᴅ—XIII—Winters ; probably a translation
of the English surname Winters.

ᴀn ᵹleᴀnnᴀ—XIII—Glanny, Glenny, Glenn. V.
ᴀ'ᵹleᴀnnᴀ.

ᴀn ᵹleᴀnnᴄáın—XIII—Glanton. V. ᴀ'ᵹleᴀnnᴄáın.

ᴀn mᴀcᴀıʀe—XIII—Maghery ; Ir. ' ᴀn mᴀcᴀıʀe,' i.e.,
of the field, from residence in or thereby.

ᴀn muılınn—XIII—Mills ; Ir. " ᴀn muılınn,' i.e., of the
mill,' from residence in or thereby.

ᴀn pʀéıᴄ—XIII—'O'Pray, O'Prey, Pray, Prey. V.
ᴀ' pʀéıᴄ.

ᴀnᴄóın, ᴀnᴄoıne—VIII—*Anton,* Antony, Anthony ;
' son of Antony.'

ᴀn ᴄseᴀcᴀ—XIII—Frost ; a translation of the English
surname Frost. The Frosts are a well known family
about Limerick.

ᴀn ᴄsıubᴀıl—XIII—Walker ; Ir. ' ᴀn ᴄʀıubᴀıl,' i.e.,
the pedestrian, one given to walking ; but perhaps a

translation of the English surname Walker, which however has a different meaning.

ⱶn ⱴSⱸⱸⱼⱷⱼⱼⱼⱼ—XIII—Snow ; Ir. ' ⱶn ⱴSⱸⱸⱼⱷⱼⱼ,' i.e., of the snow, perhaps born in time of snow.

ⱶ ⱷⱶoⱡ—VI—*A powell*, Powell ; ' son of Howel ' ; the name of a family of Welsh origin who settled in Ireland some time prior to the beginning of the 17th century.

ⱶ' ⱷⱤⱸⱼⱶ—XIII—*A praye*, O'Pray, O'Prey, Pray, Prey ; Ir. ' ⱶn ⱷⱤⱸⱼⱶ,' i.e., of the cattle-spoil ; a Co. Down surname.

ⱶ ⱷⱤⱼoⱡⱶⱼⱤ'ⱴ—VI—Prickard, Prichard ; ' son of Richard ' ; a Welsh surname, long established in Ireland.

ⱶ ⱷⱤⱼⱼ—VI—*Apprise, Apprice*, Pryse, Price, etc. ; ' son of Rhys ' (a well-known Welsh personal name). This surname, which is the same as the Welsh Ap-Rice or Ap-Rees, is long established in Ireland.

ⱶ ⱷⱤⱼⱴⱸⱶⱼⱤ'ⱴ—VI—Pritchard ; a variant of ⱶ ⱷⱤⱼo-ⱡⱶⱼⱷ'ⱴ, q.v.

ⱶⱤⱶⱡⱶ—VIII—Harald, Harold, Harrold ; ' son of Harald'; the name of a family of Danish origin who settled early in Dublin and Wicklow. In 1315, they were in alliance with the O'Byrnes and O'Tooles, when they plundered the English of Wicklow. V. ⱶⱷⱷⱴ'ⱴ and Ⱶ hⱶⱷⱶⱼⱡⱶ.

ⱶⱤⱶⱴⱡⱶⱼⱼ—XI—Erskine, Erksine ; a well-known Scottish surname.

ⱶⱤ'ⱴⱶⱡⱶ—XI—Ardagh ; Nor. ' de Ardagh,' i.e., of Ardagh in Co. Longford ; the name of an early Anglo-Norman family who settled at, and took its name from, Ardagh. It has always been very rare.

ⱶⱤⱼⱶⱼ, Ormsby. V. ⱶⱼⱷⱼⱸⱶⱤ.

ⱶⱤⱼⱷⱴⱴ'ⱴ—VIII—*Arnolle, Arnoud*, Arnold, Arnott ; ' son of Arnald,' a common Teutonic personal name.

ⱶⱤⱷⱴ'ⱴ—VIII—*Arot, Arrot, Harrod*, Harrot, Harold, etc. ; a var. of ⱶⱷⱶⱼⱡ, (q.v.), of which it is merely the Norman pronunciation.

ⱶⱤⱴⱷⱤ—VIII—*Arthour, Arthure*, Arthur, Arthurs ; ' son

of Arthur.' The Arthurs settled in Ireland soon after the invasion, and were located in Dublin, Meath, Cork and Limerick. They were at one time an influential family in the City of Limerick.

Ꮶꞇᴀᴏⁱ—XI—Athy; Nor. ' de Athi," de Athy,' i.e., of Athy in Co. Kildare; the name of an Anglo-Norman family who first settled at Athy. They removed at an early period to Galway, where tradition relates that one of them erected the first stone house or castle. The surname is now very rare.

Ꮶꞇᴀꞅᴀċ—XIV—Ashe. V. Ꮶᵹᴀꞃ.

ᴃᴀᴃ—XII—Babe; Eng. ' the babe,' i.e., one of guileless disposition, corresponding to the Norman l'Enfant; the name of an old Anglo-Norman family who settled at Ardee and other places in Co. Louth.

ᴃᴀᴄᴀᴇⁱꞃ, Baker. V. ᴃᴀⁱᴄᴇⁱꞃ.

ᴃᴀᴄúɴ—XII—*Bakun, Bacoun*, Bacon. V. ᴅᴇ ᴃᴀᴄúɴ.

ᴃᴀᴅꞇúɴ, Boyton. V. ᴅᴇ ᴃᴀᴅꞇúɴ.

ᴃᴀᵹɴᴀʟ—XI—Bagnall, Bagnell, etc.; i.e., ' of Bagnall,' in Staffordshire.

ᴃᴀᵹóⁱᴅ—VIII—*Bagod, Bagote*, Bagot, Bagott, Baggot, Baggott; ' son of Bagot ' (dim. of a common Anglo-Saxon personal name Baga, Bago, etc.). This family came into Ireland soon after the Anglo-Norman invasion and settled in Dublin, Meath, Kildare, Carlow and Limerick. In 1280, Robert Bagod, chief justiciary of Ireland, obtained a grant of the manor of Rath, near Dublin, since known as Bagot-rath, and of Bonevilstone and Brownstown, in Co. Limerick, since known as Bagottstown. Maurice Baggot of Baggotstown was one of the twenty exempted from pardon by Ireton when he obtained possession of Limerick in 1651.

ᴃᴀⁱᴄᴇⁱꞃ—XII—Baker; Nor. ' le Bakere,' ' de Bakere,' i.e., the baker.

ᴃᴀⁱᴅꞇúɴ. V. ᴅᴇ ᴃᴀᴅꞇúɴ.

ᴃᴀⁱʟⁱɴꞅᴇⁱꞃ—XI or XII—*de Belynger*, Ballinger; Nor. ' de Belynger,' i.e., of Bellinger, probably an English place-name ; or possibly Nor. ' le Bulenger,' i.e., the baker (Fr. boulanger).

ḃáilinċín—XI—Ballentine ; a surname of Scottish origin.

ḃáilinċín—VIII—Valentine ; ' son of Valentine.'

ḃáilís, Wallace, Wallis, Walsh. V. ᴅe ḃáilír.

ḃáilisċe—XII—*Baliste*, Ballesty ; Nor. ' balestier,' Lat. ' balistarius ' i.e., the cross-bowman ; an old, but rare, surname in Ireland. It occurs as ' Baliste ' in Gilbert's Municipal Documents.

ḃáille—XII—Bailie, Bailey, Bayly ; Nor. ' le Baillif,' Eng. ' the Bailie,' i.e., the bailiff ; an old surname in Ireland.

ḃáiréiᴅ—VIII—*Bared, Baret*, Barrett ; ' son of Baret.' Bared, Baret, Boret, Borret, and Borred occur in Domesday Book as names of persons holding land in the time of Edward the Confessor. The name is, therefore, most probably Anglo-Saxon and distinct from ḃápóiᴅ, q.v. The Barretts settled in the 13th century in Tirawley, where they became numerous and powerful. In later times they formed a clan after the Irish fashion, the head of which was known as mac ḃáiċín ḃairéiᴅ ; and there were sub-clans known as Clann Ċóimín and Clann Ainᴅriú.

ḃáiséiᴅ—XII—*Basset*, Bassett ; O. Fr. ' basset,' i.e., the dwarf. In Ireland, this surname is as old at least as the beginning of the 13th century.

ḃáisnéiᴅ—XII—*Basnede*, Basnet ; O. Fr. ' Bassinet,' a double dim. of Bass, low-sized. V. ḃáiréiᴅ above. This family was located in Dublin and Wicklow. There is a Bosnetstown near Kilfinane, Co. Limerick.

ḃál—VIII—Ball ; ' son of Ball,' (very probably a short form of Baldwin) ; the name of an old Anglo-Norman family in Dublin and Meath.

ḃalḃ—IX—Balfe ; Ir. ' ḃalḃ,' Lat. ' balbus,' i.e., the stammerer. Though the name is Irish, the family is of foreign origin. The Balfes came to Ireland at, or soon after, the Anglo-Norman invasion and settled in Dublin and Meath.

bálɒuınᵹ—VIII—Baldwin ; ' son of Baldwin.' This form of the surname, which is found in Co. Cork, is apparently modern. V. bálɒún.

bálɒún—VIII—*Baldone*, Baldoon, Ballon, Baldin, Baldwin ; ' son of Baldon ' (a dim. of Baldwin). Families of this name settled soon after the Anglo-Norman invasion in Dublin, Wexford, Kilkenny, Waterford and Cork. The pronunciation is sometimes bállún or ballún. The town of Cobh stands in the townlond of Ballyvaloon, so called from Baldwin Hodnett, a member of the family who once owned the Great Island.

ballárɒ—XII—Ballard, Bollard ; Mid. Eng. ' the ballard,' i.e., baldheaded ; the name of an Anglo-Norman family who settled in Dublin and Meath soon after the invasion.

bán—IX—Baun, Bawn, Bane, Bayne, Baynes, and sometimes, by translation, White ; Ir. ' bán,' i.e., fair, white ; a descriptive epithet which supplanted the real surname.

baraın—XI—Warren, Warrin, and, in parts of Kerry, Walsh ; Nor. ' de Warenne,' i.e., at the warren, or game-preserve, from residence thereby. This surname came into Ireland at the time of the Anglo-Norman invasion, and was not uncommon in Dublin, Meath, and other parts of Ireland. In East Kerry it has been strangely re-anglicised Walsh. Possibly the Warrens of that locality had two surnames ; but at present they are called only by the one in Irish and the other in English. The adj. form is bapantac (b not aspirated).

barcar—XII—Barker ; Nor. ' le Barker,' Eng. ' the barker,' i.e., one who stripped trees of bark for the tanner. This surname does not appear to be old in Ireland. The Barkers of Waterford were a Cromwellian family.

báróiɒ—VIII—Barrett ; ' son of Baraud ' (a Norman form of the Teutonic Berwald). Families of this name settled in Ireland at the time of the Anglo-Norman

invasion. The Barretts were an influential family
in Cork, and the name is still well known throughout
Munster. Cf. ḃaiṗéⱃo.

ḃaⱃⱅún, Barton. V. ⱁe ḃaⱃⱅún.

ḃaⱃún—XII—*Baroun*, Baron, Barron; Mid. Eng.
'barun,' i.e., the baron, either a real baron, or one
who put on the airs of a baron. Robert Barun was a
member of the Dublin Guild-Merchant in 1226. A
branch of the Fitzgeralds who were barons of Burn-
church, Co. Kilkenny, assumed the surname of
Barron, and were a highly respectable family in
Kilkenny, Tipperary and Waterford.

ḃáⱅ—XI—Bath, Baith, Bates, etc. V. ⱁe ḃáⱅ.

ḃeaᵹ—IX—Bueg, Begg, Begge, and sometimes, by
translation, Little and Small; Ir. ' ḃeaᵹ,' i.e., little,
small; a descriptive epithet which supplanted the real
surname. Cf. ḃán. Note, however, that Bagge,
Bege, and Beg occur frequently as English surnames
in our early Anglo-Irish records.

ḃéaⱡaⱅún, Belton, Weldon, Veldon. V. ⱁe ḃéaⱡaⱅún.

ḃeaⱃnaḃáⱡ, Barnwell, etc. V. ⱁe ḃeaⱃnaḃáⱡ.

ḃeaⱃnaıs, *Barnise*, *Barneis*, *Barnyshe*, Barnidge,
Bearnes, Barnes.

ḃeaⱃnáⱃⱁ—VIII—Barnard, Bernard; ' son of Bernard';
an old surname in Ireland, but always very rare.

ḃeaⱃⱅⱃam—VIII—Bertram; ' son of Bertram,' a
Teutonic personal name.

ḃéaꞅⱡaıᵹ, ḃéaꞅⱡaoı—XI—Beazley, Beasley; i.e.,
' of Beazley,' or ' Beasley,' in England.

ḃeaꞅⱅún—XI—Baston, Beston; probably ' of Beston,'
or ' Baston,' in England, but I can find no instance earlier than the 16th century. The name
was peculiar to Tipperary and Waterford where it
still survives.

ḃeıⱡⱡe, ḃeıⱡⱡıú—XI—*Belewe*, Bellew; Nor. *' de
Belleau,' Lat. ' de Bella Aqua,' i.e., of Belleau (the
fair water), in France; the name of a family of Norman
origin who came into Ireland about the time of the
invasion and settled in Meath and Louth. For much

information about this ancient family, see D'Alton's
' King James' Irish Army List, 1689.'

beilleaᵹam—XI—Bellingham ; i.e., ' of Bellingham,'
in England. The founder of this family came to
Ireland in the 17th century and obtained a grant of
the estate now called Castle Bellingham, in Co. Louth.

beinéiᵭ—VIII—*Benet*, Bennett ; ' son of Benet ' (dim.
of Benedict), formerly one of the most popular names
in England. As a surname, Bennett came into
Ireland at different periods since the invasion, and
is now common in many parts of the country. Also
bionóiᵭ, q.v.

beiRᴄ, Berth ; a var. of ᵭe bᵽeiᴄ, q.v. ; cf. ' le Birt,' for
' le Brit ' ; in use in West Clare.

biaᵭᴄaᴄ—XII—Betagh, Beatagh, Beatty, etc. ; Ir.
' biaᵭᴄaᴄ,' i.e., the hospitaller, public victualler.
This family is said to be of Danish descent, but in the
early Anglo-Irish records the Christian names are
Norman. They were seated in Moynalty, in Co.
Meath, from an early period, and possessed considerable property down to Cromwellian times when, by
fraud and perjury, Francis Betagh was stripped of
his estates. Branches of the family appear to have
settled in Mayo, Galway and Clare.

bibíne, Dobbin, Dobbins

biᵹeaR, Biggar, Bigger ; a surname of doubtful origin,
but probably ' of Biggar ' in Scotland.

binéiᵭ, Bennett. V. beinéiᵭ.

binnse, Binchy.

bionᵹam—XI—Bingham, Bigham ; i.e., ' of Bingham,'
in Nottinghamshire.

bionóiᵭ, Bennett. V. beinéiᵭ, and cf. Fr. Benoit.

biséiᵭ—VIII—*Biset*, Bissett ; ' son of Biset ' (dim. of
an old Teutonic personal name Bis). The Bissetts
were an English family who settled at an early period
in Scotland. In 1242, John Bisset and Walter, his
uncle, were outlawed and fled to Ireland, where they
took refuge in the Glynns of Antrim and effected a
settlement under de Burgo, Earl of Ulster. From

this John the family in after times assumed the Irish patronymic surname of mᴀc eóın. By marriage with an heiress of the Bissetts, the Glynns at a later period came into the possession of the MacDonnells.

blᴀcᴀc—XIV.—Blacagh, Blake. V. ᴅe blᴀcᴀ.

blᴀoᴅ—XII—*Bluet, Bloet, Blowet,* Bluett, Blewett, etc. ; Nor. ' Bluet,' i.e., of blue complexion or dress. This family came into Ireland at the time of the Anglo-Norman invasion. Walter Bloet (circa 1174) was witness to a grant of land to Holy Trinity Church, Dublin. In the 16th century, the name was peculiar to Cork and Limerick, where it still survives. Also bliúıc, q.v.

bléıne, *Bleyne,* Bleney, Bleaney, Blaney, Blainey, Blayney.

bliúıc, Bluett, Blewett. V. blᴀoᴅ.

blóıᴅ, Blood. V. ᴀ blóıᴅ.

bluınnsín, Blanchville, Blanchfield. V. ᴅe bluınnríol.

booléıʀ, Bowler. V. bóıléıʀ.

bóᴅún—VIII—*Boudun, Boudoun, Boudon,* Bowden, Boden, etc. ; ' son of Baldon ' (dim. of Baldwin, sometimes written Bawdewyn in old Anglo-Irish records) ; a var. of bᴀlᴅún, q.v. The family so called came into Ireland about the time of the Anglo-Norman invasion and settled at Bodenstown, in Co. Kildare.

bóıᴅıcín—VIII—*Bawdekyn, Baudekin, Boudekyn, Bodekine,* Bodkin ; ' son of Baldkin ' (dim. of Baldwin). The Bodkins, who are said to be a branch of the Fitzgeralds, appear to have first settled at Athenry and taken an active part in the affairs of that town. Later on, apparently towards the end of the 14th century, they removed to Galway, where they acquired a considerable amount of property and became one of the ' tribes ' of that city, of which many of them were mayors and sheriffs down to the time when it surrendered to Sir Charles Coote in 1652.

bóıᴅín—VIII—*Boydyn, Boydin,* Boden, etc. ; ' son of Baldin ' (dim. of Baldwin). Cf. bóıᴅıcín and bóᴅún.

boiléir—XII—Bowler ; Nor. 'le Boller,' i.e., the bowler, maker of wooden bowls ; an old Kerry surname.

bóinn, Bowen, V. oe botún.

boiréil—XII—*Borel, Burell, Berle,* Burrell, Berrell, Berrall, Berrill, Birrell, etc. ; Nor. ' borel,' ' burel,' i.e., one of reddish-brown complexion. The family so called came into Ireland soon after the Anglo-Norman invasion and settled in Co. Louth.

bóltún, Bolton. V. oe bolttún.

bórtuic—XI—Borthwick ; i.e., ' of Borthwick,' in Scotland.

boscac—XIV.—*Boskagh,* Fox. V. oe borc.

brabasún—XII—*Brabasun,* Brabazon ; Nor. ' le Brabansun,' ' le Brabazoun,' i.e., native of Brabant in Flanders. This surname was not unknown in Ireland as early as the 13th century, but the family to which belongs the Earl of Meath came hither only in the 16th century.

bran, Bran, Branne ; Burns ; a West Clare surname.

branoún—XI—Brandon, etc. ; Nor. ' de Brandon,' i.e., of Brandon (a frequent place-name in England) ; the name of an old Anglo-Norman family who settled in Co. Louth.

brannóc, *Brayhenoc, Braynoc, Bronoke, Bronicke,* Brannock, Brannick, etc. V. oe breannóc.

brant—VIII—Brant, Brand ; ' son of Brand ' (the Norse personal name Brandr) ; an old surname in Ireland.

breannóc, *Brayhnock, Breynoc, Brenoke,* Brennock, etc. V. oe breannóc.

breartún—XI—Brearton, Brerton, Brereton ; i.e., ' of Brereton,' in England.

breatnac—X—*Brathnagh, Brethnagh, Brehnagh,* Brennagh, Brannagh, and by translation Walsh, Walshe, etc. ; Ir. ' breatnac ' (more correctly breatnac), i.e., the Welshman ; a descriptive surname applied generically to the early Anglo-Norman invaders who came hither from Wales ; now one of our most numerous surnames. There are naturally many distinct families so called. See also ᴅe Ḃaıléıṗ, ᴅe Ḃaılíṗ, which is the Norman equivalent.

ḂRıan—VIII—Brian, Bryan, Brien, etc. ; ' son of Brian ' (a common Breton personal name introduced into England at the Conquest). The family so called settled in Kilkenny and Wexford.

ḂRíᴅe—XI—*Bryde*, Bride ; Lat. ' de Sancta Brida,' i.e., of St. Bride's ; an early Anglo-Norman surname in Ireland. ' Henricus de Sancta Brida ' occurs in the Dublin Roll of Names soon after the invasion. But see na Ḃṗıᴣᴅe.

ḂRíᴅeaċ—XIV.—*Bridagh*, Bride. V. Ḃṗíᴅe.

ḂRıᴣeaċ—XIV—*Brigaghe*, Brigg, Bridge. V. ᴅe Ḃṗıᴣ.

ḂRıoscū—XI—*Briskoo*, Briscoe, Brisco ; Eng. ' of Briscoe,' in Cumberland. The family of this name has long been settled in Ireland.

ḂRıṫ, Britt, Brett. V. ᴅe Ḃṗıṫ.

ḂRıṫeaċ—XIV—*Brittagh*, Britt, Brett. V. ᴅe Ḃṗıṫ.

ḂRoc—XII—Brock ; Nor. ' le Broc,' i.e., the badger ; an English surname.

ḂRuᴣa, Burrowes, Burrows ; Burgess. V. ᴅe Ḃṗuᴣa.

ḂRuıcléıᴣ, ḂRuıcléıṫ—XI—*Bricklea*, Brickley ; ' of Brockley ' in Suffolk ; the name of an English family who were seated at Ballycahan in Co. Limerick. About the middle of the 17th century they removed to South Cork, where they still survive.

ḂRún, Brown, Browne. V. ᴅe Ḃṗún.

Ḃuaman—XII—Bowman.

Ḃuamonn, Beaumont. V. ᴅe Ḃuamonn.

ḂuᴅaRlaıᴣ—XI—Butterly ; i.e., of Butterley ; an English place-name.

ḂúᴅRán, *Budran*, *Boudran*, *Bowdran*, Bowdren ; the name of an old Anglo-Irish family in East Cork. I cannot trace its origin.

ḂuıltéıR, ḂuıltéıR, Butler. V. ᴅe Ḃuıctéıṗ.

Ḃuınneán, *Bonane*, *Bonan*, Banane, Binane, Bunyan, and incorrectly Bennett ; the name of an old Kerry family who were seated at, and gave its name to,

Ballybunion in North Kerry. Latterly it is being turned into Bennett, which is altogether wrong and equivalent to the assumption of a new name.

buirséis, buirséis—XII—*Burgeis*, *Burys*, Burgess, Burges, etc. ; Mid. Eng. ' Burgeys,' the burgess, the citizen.

buirséil, Burchell.

buiséir—XII—*Boucher*, *Bossher*, Bowcher, Busher, Bussher, etc. ; Nor. ' le boucher,' i.e., the butcher. Families of this name settled soon after the Anglo-Norman invasion in the counties of Kilkenny, Carlow and Wexford. The name came in again in the 16th century. The older families spell the name with *sh* instead of *ch*. The corresponding English surname is Butcher.

buistéir, Butcher. V. buiréir.

buiteac—XIV—*Bowet*, *Boyt*, *Boyde*, Boyd. V. de búit.

buitiléir, Butler. V. de buitléir.

buitiméir, *Bottymer*, Buttimer ; an old but rare Anglo-Irish surname in Co. Cork, the origin of which I have failed to trace.

buitléir, Butler. V. de buitléir.

bulfin, Bulfin.

búrbac—XI—Burbage ; i.e., ' of Burbach ' or ' Burbage,' an English place-name.

burdún, *Burdun*, Burdon. V. de burdún.

bustárd—XII—*Bostard*, Bustard ; Eng. ' the bustard,' a large bird once common in England. This old surname has long been peculiar to Donegal.

caodal—VIII—Cadell, Caddell, etc. ; ' son of Cadell ' (a Welsh personal name corresponding to the Irish Cathal) ; the name of a family of Welsh origin who came to Ireland in the 13th century and settled in Dublin, Meath and Galway. The Caddells of Galway have long since assumed the surname of Blake. V. de blaca.

caimbéal—XII—Cambell, Campbell, etc. ; Ir. ' cam ' and ' béal,' i.e., wry-mouthed, originally an epithet or nickname which in course of time supplanted the real surname ; not from Norman ' de Campobello,' as some have imagined. The original surname is said to have been Ó Ouibne. Sir Colin Mór Caimbéal, lord of Lochawe, who was knighted by Alexander III, and from whom the Duke of Argyll derives the title of Mac Cailean Mór by which he is known in the Highlands to the present day, was the seventh in descent from Ouibne, the ancestor from whom the family took their original surname of Ó Ouibne. The Campbells were long the most formidable of the Scottish clans, and the name is now one of the most numerous in Scotland.

caimpion—XII—Campion ; Nor. ' le Campion,' i.e., the champion, victor in the village sports.

cáiroín—XI—Cardin, Carden ; i.e., ' of Carden,' a parish in Cheshire.

camsrón—XII—Cameron ; Ir. ' cam ' and ' rpón,' i.e., wry-nosed, an epithet like caimbéal, q.v. ; the name of a distinguished Scottish clan. The Camerons were seated in Inverness and were divided into four septs, of which the best known are the Camerons of Lochiel. In the civil wars of the 17th century, the Camerons were loyal to the Stuart cause, and in 1745 the whole clan was out for Prince Charlie.

canntalún, Cantillon, Cantlon, etc.   V. ve Canntalún.

canntual, cantual, Cantoell, Cantowle, Cantwell. V. ve Canntual.

canntún, cantún, Canton, Candon.   V. ve Canntún.

caománac—X—Cavanagh,   Kavanagh,   etc. ;   Ir. ' Caománac,' i.e., belonging to Caomán. This family derives its name and descent from Domhnall Caomhanach, son of Diarmaid Mac Murchadha who was King of Leinster at the time of the Anglo-Norman invasion. He was so called from having been fostered by the comharb or successor of St. Caomán at Kilcavan, near Gorey ; and the agnomen, contrary to the usual Irish practice, has for many centuries been adopted as a surname by his descendants. Modern

writers sometimes wrongly prefix an Ó to this surname,
making it Ó Caománaiʒ. The patrimony of the
family lay in the present counties of Carlow and
Wexford, where the name is now very common.

cáplais, Capples, Caplis, Caplice ; an hibernicised form
of the English surname Caples.

carrún, *Carrune, Carun,* Carew, Carey. V. ʋe Carrún.

cas—VIII—*Casse,* Cass, Cash ; 'son of Casse' (a common
French name, the same as the Latin Cassius) ; an old
surname in Co. Cork, and other parts of the South of
Ireland.

cat—XI—*Kot, Cote,* Cott, Coates ; Mid. Eng. 'atte cote,'
i.e., at the cot, or cottage, from residence.

ceannt, Kent. V. ʋe Ceannt.

ceárʋ—XII—Caird ; Gaelic 'ceárʋ,' a craftsman ; a
Scottish-Gaelic surname.

ceatac—XIV—Kett. V. Ó Ceit.

céitinn—XI—Keating, Keatinge ; Nor. 'de Ketyng,'
i.e., of Ketyng, a place-name, possibly in England.
I cannot find the spot. The Keatings were among
the earliest of the Anglo-Norman invaders. They
settled first in Wexford, where they obtained large
grants of land, and afterwards spread into Carlow,
Kildare, Tipperary, Waterford and Cork. Dr. Geoffrey Keating has made the name famous in Irish
literary history

ciarasac—XIV—Kearsey. V. ʋe Céarraiʒ.

ciceam—XI—Kickham ; i.e., 'of Kickham,' an English
place-name ; a late English surname, made famous
by Charles J. Kickham.

cinipéic—XI—Kennifeck, Kennefick. V. ʋe Cinipéic.

cinnicéiʋ, Kincaid, Kinkead.

cinnsealac—X—*Kinshellagh, Kinselagh,* Kinshela,
Kinsella, etc. ; Ir. 'Cinnrealac', i.e., belonging to
Ui Cinnsealaigh, in Wexford ; the name of a Wexford
family who are descended from Enna Cinnsealach,
son of Diarmaid Mac Murchadha, King of Leinster at
the time of the Anglo-Norman invasion. Cinnrealac
was, like Caománac (q.v.), an agnomen which sup-

planted the real surname. Ó Cınnɼeᴀlᴀıᵹ is also, though rarely, used.

cınnseᴀmᴀn, Kingston. V. Ó Cınnɼeᴀmᴀın.

cınꞇ, Kent. V. ꝺe Ceᴀnnꞇ.

cíoṁsóᵹ, cíosóᵹ, cıúṁsóᵹ, Cusack, Cussack, etc. V. ꝺe Cıúṁɼóᵹ.

clᴀnnꝺıolúın, Clandillon; probably from an Irish place-name.

clᴀ̄ꞃ, Clare, Clair. V. ꝺe Clᴀ́ꞃ.

cléıꞃeᴀċ—XII—Clarke; Ir. 'Cléıɼeᴀċ,' i.e., the clerk; a very common surname in early Anglo-Irish records. Most of our Irish Clarkes are, however, O'Clerys or MacClerys.

clıméıs—VIII—clıméıseᴀċ—XIV—Clement; 'son of Clement' (Lat. Clemens, Fr. Clemence).

clınse, *Clinshe, Clenche,* Clinch, Clynch. I can discover nothing to throw light on the origin of this surname which was borne by an old Anglo-Irish family of the Pale. The Clinches ranked among the gentry of Dublin and Meath at the end of the 16th century.

clıoꝼoꞃꞇ, Clifford. V. ꝺe Clıoꝼoꞃꞇ.

clıonꞇún, Clinton. V. ꝺe Clıonꞇún.

cocs, Cox; an hibernicised form of the English surname Cox.

coꝺᴀ—VIII—*Cod, Codde,* Codd; 'son of Cod,' (an old Anglo-Saxon personal name; a short form of Cuthbert, Cuthwine, or some other name commencing with Cuth; variously written in Searle's Onomasticon, Coda, Cuda, Cudda, Cudd, Cuta, Cutta, etc. Code appears in Domesday Book as a holder of land in the time of Edward the Confessor). The Codds are an old and respectable family of Co. Wexford, to which county the name is peculiar.

coıléıꞃ—XII—Collier; 'the Coller,' i.e., the collier, or charcoal-burner, a term still used in the north of England.

coıllꝺuꞩ, Blackwood; a translation of the English surname Blackwood.

coımín—XI or VIII—Comin, Comyn, Comyns, Cum-

mins, etc. ; possibly from Fr. ' de Comminges,' i.e., of
Commimges in Gascony, or ' de Comines,' i.e., of
Comines in the north of France bordering on Belgium,
but in old records the prefix ' de ' is never found.
Harrison suggests that it is from a Frankish personal
name, Comin or Cumin. The family in any case
came over to Ireland at the time of the Anglo-Norman
invasion. John Comyn was the first Anglo-Norman
Archbishop of Dublin. The name became very common throughout the southern half of Ireland, and also
in Westmeath and Roscommon, but is now difficult
to distinguish from Mac Cuimín and Ó Cuimín (q.v.),
which are similarly anglicised.

coipingéin—XII—Copinger, Coppinger ; Norse ' Kau-
pungr,' (a nickname) ; the name of a family of Norse
extraction long settled in Cork, where in 1319 Stephen
Coppinger was mayor of the city, as was William
Coppinger in 1535. The Coppingers formed a kind of
clan after the Irish fashion. Many of them were
attained in 1642 and again in 1691. The name is
generally pronounced Coipinéin.

coiplíbe—XI—Copley ; Eng. ' of Copley,' a parish in
the West Riding of Yorkshire ; not an old surname
in Ireland.

cól—VIII—Cole ; ' son of Cole ' (Norse Colr or Kolr, also
in use among the Anglo-Saxons ; Cole, Cola, Colo, etc.
appear in Domesday Book as names of persons holding
land in the time of Edward the Confessor). A family
of this name settled in Fermanagh at the time of the
plantation of Ulster, but most of our Coles are of
Irish origin.

col—VIII—Col, Coll ; ' son of Colle ' (Norse Kollr ; Colle,
Col, etc. among the Anglo-Saxons, but not easily
distinguishable from Cole, Cola, etc.) Colle was the
name of a landholder in the time of Edward the Confessor, and Collo that of an undertenant at the time
of the Domesday survey. The name is of record in
Ireland since the end of the 14th century, and is
chiefly associated with the district around Kilmallock

in Co. Limerick, where the family is of long standing respectability.

Colbárd—VIII—Colbert; 'son of Colbert' (the Anglo-Saxon Colobert or Colbeorht); Colbert and Colibert appear in Domesday Book as the names of land-holders in the time of Edward the Confessor and of undertenants at the time of the survey, an indication that the name is derived from the Anglo-Saxon and not from its Frankish cognate. In Ireland, the Colberts are found chiefly in Cork and Limerick. The Irish form of the name as I have heard it is a Colbárd.

Colcloċ—XI—Colclogh, Colclough; i.e., 'of Colclough' in Staffordshire. A family of this name settled in Wexford in the 16th century.

Colcún—XI—*Colchoun*, Colhoun, Colquhoun, etc.; i.e., 'of Culchone' or Colquhoun, in Dumbartonshire; the name of a Scottish clan, some of whom settled in Ireland.

Colmán—VIII—*Colman*, Coleman; 'son of Colman' (a name in use in England in Anglo-Saxon times, but doubtless borrowed from the Irish. Searle gives it in three forms: Colman, Coloman, and Coleman, under the last of which it appears as the name of a landholder in the time of Edward the Confessor). A family of the name came to Ireland about the period of the Anglo-Norman invasion and settled in Dublin and other places in Leinster.

Colcún—XI—Colton; 'of Colton,' a common place-name in England.

Cómar, Comber. V. ᴠe Cómar.

Comarcún—XI—Comerton, Comerford, etc.; i.e., 'of Comberton,' a parish in Cambridgeshire, if not 'of Comberford,' a village in Staffordshire. The Irish form would seem to point to the former as the origin, but cf. Rorcún for Rochford. The Comerfords, as they are usually called, are an old and respectable family in Kilkenny and Waterford. The head of the family was Baron of Danganmore.

Conᴠún, connᴠún, Condon. V. ᴠe Canncún.

CORḃAIƉ—VIII—Corbett ; ' son of Corbet ' (dim. of French corbeau, a raven, a personal name in Domesday Book). The Corbetts, who are a family of Norman origin, settled in Meath and Offaly, but the name has always been very rare. Nearly all our Corbetts are of Irish origin. V. Ó Corḃáin, Ó Coirḃín and Ó Conḃáġa.

CORCAIƉ, Corket ; a rare Galway surname.

CORRƊUḃ, Corduff ; more correctly Ó Corrḋuiḃ, q.v.

COSƉ⚔ún, Costune, Costume.

CRÁ⚔FORƉ—XI—Craforte, Crawford, etc. V. ƉE Cráꝼorꝉ.

CRAnUIĊ, Cranwich, Cranitch ; i.e., probably ' of Cranwich ' in England.

CRAOḃAĊ—IX—*Creavagh*, Creagh ; Ir. ' craoḃaċ,' branching, or possibly belonging to Craoḃ, a common Irish place-name. The Creaghs are, according to tradition, a branch of the O'Neills of Clare and obtained the cognomen of Craoḃaċ from one of their ancestors who carried a green branch in a battle fought at Limerick with the Danes. They were an ancient and respectable merchant family in Limerick where the name frequently appears in the list of mayors and bailiffs. Many of them, too, attained to high ecclesiastical distinctions. In 1459, William Creagh was Bishop of Limerick ; in 1483 David Creagh was Archbishop of Cashel ; a century later Richard Creagh was appointed by the Pope to the primacy of Armagh ; and at the beginning of the 18th century, Pierce Creagh was Archbishop of Dublin. All these were natives of Limerick. The Creaghs were also an old and wealthy merchant family in Cork.

CREAƉÓC, CREAƉÓɠ—VIII—*Cradok*, *Craddok*, Craddock ; ' son of Caradoc,' (a Welsh personal name, famous in British history as Caractacus) ; not from the place-name Cradoc in Brecnockshire, or Craddock in Devonshire, as in old records it never takes the prefix ' de.' The Craddocks, who are a family of Welsh origin, settled at an early period at Craddockstown in Co. Kildare, whence the name has spread to other parts of Ireland. The Irish form is possibly more correctly Cɼaḃóc.

CReᴀ5, CReo5, Cregg, Craig. V. ᴏe Cɼais.

CRÍOSCÓIR—VIII—*Cristor*, Christopher ; ' son of Christopher.'

CRÓC—VIII—*Croc, Crok*, Croke, Croake ; Crooke, Crooks, etc. ; ' son of Croc ' (old Norse Krokr, a personal name which appears more than once in Domesday Book and was borne by holders of land in the time of Edward the Confessor and by tenants-in-chief and undertenants at the time of the survey). The Crokes settled at an early period in Kilkenny, Tipperary and Cork. Crooke represents a later immigration, and is more widespread.

CROMᴀIL—XI—*Cromall*, Crummell, Grummell, Cromwell ; i.e., ' of Cromwell,' a parish in Nottinghamshire ; the name, strangely enough, of an old Anglo-Irish family in Limerick, where James Cromwell was mayor in 1598. It has now disappeared from Limerick, but is still found in other parts of the country.

CROMCᴀ—IX—Crombie, Cromie, Crommie ; Ir. ' cɼomċᴀ,' i.e., bent, crooked.

CRÓn—IX—Crone ; Ir. ' cɼón,' i.e., brown ; an epithet which supplanted the real surname which is now lost. Cf. ḃán.

CRÚC, Crooke, Crooks, etc. V. Cɼóc.

CRÚIS, Cruice, Cruise, Cross. V. ᴏe Cɼúiɼ.

CRÚISÉIR—XII—Crozier.

CÚC—XII—Cooke ; i.e., ' the cook,' a common name in early Anglo-Irish records.

CUILeᴀnᴏᴀR—XII—Collendar, Callender ; i.e., ' the calender,' one who calenders cloth ; in use in Co. Waterford.

CUILCÉIR, Quilter. V. ᴏe Cuiɟcléiɼ.

CUImín, Comyn, Cumming, Cummins, etc. V. Coimín.

CÚIpÉIR—XII—Cooper, Cowper ; i.e., ' the cooper.'

CUIRCÉIS, Curtis, etc. V. ᴏe Cuiɼɟcéiɼ.

cúisín—XII—*Coushine, Cushine*, Cousin, Cushen, Cussen Cousins, etc. ; Nor. ' le cosyn,' i.e., the cousin, kinsman ; the name of an Anglo-Norman family who settled in Ireland soon after the invasion ; found in nearly all the counties of Munster, and also in Connacht and Westmeath.

cúrsać—XIV—De Courcy, Courcey, Coursey. V. de Cúpṙa.

cúc—XII—Coote ; i.e., ' the coot,' the waterfowl so called.

dáibis, Davis ; an hibernicised form of the English or Welsh surname Davis.

dáinséir—XI—*de Aungers*, Aungier, Danger ; Nor. ' de Aungers,' i.e., of Angers, a city of Anjou ; an old surname of Norman origin.

dáirdis—XI—*de Ardis*, Dardis ; Nor. ' de Ardis,' probably, ' of the Ards ' in Co. Down ; the name of an Anglo-Norman family who settled soon after the invasion in Meath and Westmeath.

dáirsiġ—XI—*de Arcy*, D'Arcy, Darcy ; Nor. ' de Arcy,' i.e. from Arci in Normandy. The D'Arcys were one of the most distinguished of the Norman families who settled in England after the Conquest. The founder of the Irish family of the name was Sir John D'Arcy, chief justiciary of Ireland, in the second quarter of the 14th century. He received large grants of land in Meath, which remained in the possession of his descendants down to the Cromwellian and Williamite confiscations. The first home of the D'Arcys in Ireland, and their chief seat for many centuries, was at Platten, in Co. Meath, from which branched out all the other houses of the name in Ireland. But see Ó Dorċaide, which is also angl. Darcy.

dalaitíd—XI—*de la Hide*, Delahide, Delahoyde ; i.e., ' of the hide,' a measure of land sufficient to support a family (about 120 acres), from residence on or thereby ; an early Anglo-Norman surname. ' Roger de la Hide ' was a member of the Dublin Guild-Merchant in 1226. The family settled in Dublin, Meath and Kildare.

ⱷⱥⱡⱥⰿⱥⱤⱥ—XI—Delamar, Delamere, etc. ; Nor. ' de la Mare,' i.e. of la Mare in Normandy. This family settled in England at the time of the Norman Conquest, and came to Ireland soon after the Anglo-Norman invasion. The Delameres had extensive estates in Co. Westmeath down to the Cromwellian confiscations. They assumed the Irish patronymic surname of MacHerbert.

ⱷⱥⱡⱥⱅⱪⱱ, ⱷⱥⱡⱅⱪⱱ—XI—*de Daltune*, Dalton, D'Alton ; i.e., ' of Dalton,' a common place-name in the north of England ; or it might be from ' de Aletone,' i.e. of Alton. Both forms occur in early Anglo-Irish records. Robert de Daltune and William de Daltune were members of the Dublin Guild-Merchant in 1226. In later times the Daltons were lords of Rathconrath, in Co. Westmeath, but they lost their estates in the Cromwellian and Williamite confiscations.

ⱷⱥⱄⱥⱱ, ⱷⱥⱄⱃⱱ, Dawson ; hibernicised forms of the English surname Dawson.

ⱷⱥⱅⱪⱱ—XI—*de Autun, Dawtone*, Daton, Daughton, Dawtin ; Nor. ' de Autun,' i.e. of Autun in Normandy ; the name of an old Kilkenny family, sometimes incorrectly re-anglicised Dalton.

ⱷⰵⱥⰱⱤⱪⱄ—XI—*de Evereux*, Devereux ; i.e. ' of Evereux' in Normandy. This family came into England at the time of the Norman Conquest, and into Ireland at the time of the Anglo-Norman invasion, when they settled in Co. Wexford. " The Devereuxes," writes Dr. E. Hogan, " were the wealthiest and most powerful of all the Strongbowian race in Wexford."

ⱷⰵ ⰱⱥⱅⱪⱱ—XII—*de Bacoun*, Bacon ; Nor. ' le Bacoun,' i.e. the bacon, the pig, reminiscent of a time when ' the bacon ' meant the live pig ; the name of an English family who came into Ireland soon after the Anglo-Norman invasion and settled in Co. Meath. Cf. ⱣⱸⱪⱤⱤⰵⰰⱡ.

ᴅᴇ ⰁⰀⰊⰕⰤⰐ—XI—*de Boytoun*, Boyton; ' of Boyton,' somewhere in England. The name is in Ireland at least since the 13th century, and was chiefly associated with Cashel.

ᴅᴇ ⰁⰀⰊⰈⰤⰀⰓⰀ—XI—De Valera, de Valera; i.e., ' of Valera,' an ancient city in Spain.

" VALERA, Valeria. C'étoit anciennement une Ville considerable des Celtiberiens, en Espagne. Elle fut ensuite épiscopale, et enfin ruinée. On a bâte de ses rûines trois villages nommez Valera-Quemada, Valera-de-Suso, et Valera-la-Veja, dans la nouvelle Castille, sur le Xucar, à six lieues de Cuença, qui a succedé à l'Episcopat."—*Baudrand, Dictionnaire Geographique et Historique*.

ᴅᴇ ⰁⰀⰊⰈⰤⰊⰔ, ᴅᴇ ⰁⰀⰊⰈⰤⰔ, ᴅᴇ ⰁⰀⰊⰈⰊⰔ—XII—*le Waleys, le Waleis, the Walish*, Wallis, Wallace, Walsh, etc.; i.e. ' the Welshman'; the Norman equivalent of the Irish ⰁⱃⰤⰀⰕⱀⰀⰱ, q.v.

ᴅᴇ ⰁⰀⰊ—XI—*de Val, de Vale, de Vaal, de Wale*, Wall; Nor. ' du Val,' i.e. of the vale, or valley, from residence therein. This surname dates back at least to the 13th century, and is found in many parts of Ireland. In 1335, John de Vale and Walter de Vale were among those summoned to attend Sir John D'Arcy on his expedition to Scotland. In the same century three bishops of the name filled Irish Sees, among whom was Stephen de Wale who became Bishop of Limerick in 1360, and was afterwards translated to Meath and made Lord High Treasurer of Ireland. The Walls were numerous and respectable in the 16th century in Kildare, Carlow, Kilkenny, Tipperary, Cork, Limerick and Galway, and in the last-named county appear to have formed a distinct clan after the Irish fashion, with a chief of the name. In Limerick, the Walls held the manor of Dunmoylan from the 13th century down to 1580 when Ulick de Wale, although blind from his birth, was shamefully put to death by Pelham, and his lands confiscated.

ᴅᴇ ⰁⰀⰊⰕⰤⰐ—XI—*de Waletone, de Walton*, Walton;

i.e., 'of Walton,' a common place-name in England; the name of a family who settled in Dublin in the 13th century.

ᴅe ᴅᴀRRᴀ—XI—*de Barry*, Barry; Nor. 'de Barri,' i.e., of Barri, probably in Normandy; one of the oldest and most illustrious of the Anglo-Norman families in Ireland. The name occurs in the earliest Anglo-Irish records, and has always been specially associated with the County of Cork. In the year 1179, Robert FitzStephen granted to his nephew, Philip de Barry, the three cantreds of Ui Liatháin, Muscraighe-trí-máighe, and Cinel Aodha, now represented respectively by the baronies of Barrymore, Orrery, and Kinelea; and this grant was confirmed by King John in 1207 to William de Barry, son and heir of Philip. In the course of time the Barrys became one of the most numerous and powerful families in Munster. They divided into several branches, the heads of which were known respectively as ᴀn ᴅᴀppᴀċ ᴍóp (the Great Barry), ᴅᴀppᴀċ Ruᴀᴅ (Red Barry), ᴅᴀppᴀċ Óᴈ (Young Barry), ᴅᴀppᴀċ ᴍᴀoᴌ (Bald Barry), ᴅᴀppᴀċ ᴌᴀ́ᴅip (Strong Barry); and one branch adopted the Irish patronymic surname of ᴍᴀc Áᴅᴀim, q.v. The Barrys suffered considerably in the wars of the 17th century, but are still numerous and respectable throughout Munster. There was also a family of the name in Co. Wexford. The Barrys of Co. Limerick, in many instances, belong to the old Irish family of Ó ᴅeᴀpᴈᴀ (q.v.), and not to the Anglo-Norman Barrys.

ᴅe ᴅᴀRᴛûn—XI—*de Bartoun*, *de Barton*, Barton; i.e., 'of Barton' in England. This surname in Ireland dates back to the early part of the 13th century, but in many instances represents more recent immigration.

ᴅe ᴅᴀS—XII—Bass; Nor. 'le Bas,' i.e. of low stature; an old but rare surname in Ireland.

ᴅe ᴅᴀSᴛᴀ́ᴅᴌᴀ—XI—Bastable, Bastible; Nor. 'de Bardastabla,' i.e., of Barnstable, in Devonshire. This surname occurs in old Anglo-Irish records. It appears to be now peculiar to Cork.

ᴅe ᴃᴀᴛ—XI—*de Baa, de Bathe*, Bath, Baith, Bates; i.e., 'of Bath,' in Somerset. This family came into Ireland about the time of the Anglo-Norman invasion and settled in Dublin, Meath and Louth. Many of the name held high offices under the English crown in the 14th and following centuries, until they lost their lands in the Cromwellian and Williamite confiscations.

ᴅe ᴃéᴀʟ—XII—*de Veel*, Veale; Nor. 'le Veel,' i.e., the veal, the calf. Cf. ᴅe ᴅᴀᴄún. This surname, which came into Ireland at the period of the Anglo-Norman invasion, is still well known in Co. Waterford, where it is pronounced ᴅe ᴃıᴀʟ.

ᴅe ᴃéᴀʟᴀᴛún—XI—*de Beletune, de Weleton*, Belton, Veldon, Weldon; i.e., 'of Belton' or 'of Welton,' in England; the name of a family who settled in Dublin in the 13th century.

ᴅe ᴃeᴀʀᴅún—XI—*de Verdoun, de Fardun*, Verdon, Varden, etc.; Nor. 'de Verdun.' i.e., of Verdun, the historic town in the east of France. The de Verduns came to England with William the Conqueror and settled in Leicestershire. Bertram de Verdun, the founder of the Irish branch of the family, came hither at the period of the Anglo-Norman invasion, was made seneschal of Ireland by Henry II and granted the manors of Dundalk and Clonmore, and other estates in Co. Louth. His great-grandson, John de Verdon, by marriage with an heiress of the de Lacys, added to his already extensive patrimony a moiety of Meath, and succeeded to the office of constable of Ireland, which had been originally granted to Hugh de Lacy. He also possessed the castle and manors of Croom and Castle Robert in Co. Limerick. In 1314, Theobald de Verdon became justiciary, but dying in 1317 without heirs male, his estates were divided between four daughters who all married English noblemen. The name however continued to be represented in Louth down to the end of the 17th century, as we find among those attainted in 1642 a John Verdon, and in 1691 another John Verdon, a descendant of the former. Of the Limerick Verdons, William was mayor of the city in 1553 ; and John Verdon, in 1579, was sovereign of Kilmallock, and in 1585 represented that town in parliament. Several of the Verdons of Kilmallock were transplanted to Connacht in 1653.

ᵹe beᴀᴚnᴀbᴀl—XI—*de Bernevale*, Barnewall, Barnavill, Barnwell ; i.e., ' of Bernevale,' probably in Normandy. This family came into Ireland about the time of the Anglo-Norman invasion and settled in Dublin and Meath. They were long one of the most influential families of the Pale, and played an important part in the history of the country.

ᵹe beic—XI—*de Bec*, Beck, Bex ; i.e., ' of Bec,' in Normandy ; the name of a family of Norman origin who came to Ireland about the time of the invasion.

ᵹe beil—XII—*de Bel*, Bell ; Nor. ' le bel,' i.e., the beautiful. This family, which is of Norman origin, first came to Ireland about the time of the invasion.

ᵹe béiᴚ—XI—*de Ver*, De Vere ; i.e., ' of Ver,' in Normandy.

ᵹe biᴀl, Veale. V. ᵹe béᴀl.

ᵹe blᴀcᴀ—XII—*le Blak, le Blake*, Blake ; i.e., ' the black,' from the complexion ; a descriptive epithet which in course of time supplanted the original surname, which was Caddell. Caddel was used as an alias for Blake as late as the 17th century, when it fell into disuse. The Blakes were one of the ' tribes' of Galway. The first of the family to come into prominence was Richard Caddel, or Blake, who was sheriff of Connacht in the early years of the 14th century, and from him are descended the many distinguished families of Blake in Ireland.

ᵹe blᴀcᴀl—XI—Blackhall ; i.e., ' of the black hall,' or ' of Blackhall ' ; a late English surname.

ᵹe blᴀcᴀm—XI—*de Blakeham*, Blackham ; i.e., ' of Blackham ' in England.

ᴅᴇ bláᴄuaᴌ—XI—Blackwell ; i.e., ' of Blackwell,' in England.

ᴅᴇ blaᵹᴅ—XI—*de Blythe*, Blythe ; i.e., ' of Blyth,' in England.

ᴅᴇ bᴌuinnsíoᴌ—XI—*de Blaunchewill, de Blancheville*, Blanchville, Blanchfield ; i.e. ' of Blanchville,' probably somewhere in Normandy. This family, which is of Norman origin, came into Ireland soon after the invasion and settled in Co. Kilkenny, where they held a prominent position down to the Cromwellian confiscations. Sir Edmund Blanchville forfeited his estates by attainder in 1641. The name, in the spoken language, is corrupted to bᴌuinnꞅin, and is even so written by Keating.

ᴅᴇ bóiᴅ—XI—*de Wode, Void, Voide, Woayde*, Wood, Woods ; Mid. Eng. ' atte Wode,' i.e., at the wood, from residence thereby ; a rather common surname in early Anglo-Irish records, but it is now impossible to distinguish it from the many Irish surnames that have been anglicised Wood or Woods.

ᴅᴇ boᴌᴌᴄun—XI—*de Boulton, de Bolton*, Bolton ; i.e., ' of Bolton,' in England.

ᴅᴇ bonᴅ—XII—Bonde, Bond ; Nor. ' le Bonde,' i.e., the bond, householder, husbandman, one who held under the tenure styled bondage. The surname is old in Ireland.

ᴅᴇ bosᴄ—XII—Fox ; i.e., ' the fox,' one of somewhat sly and cunning disposition ; the name of a once respectable old English family in Co. Limerick. Mountfox, near Kilmallock, is called in Irish móin an ᴅoꞃᴄaiᵹ, Fox's bog, from a member of this family.

ᴅᴇ bosᴄóᴄ—XI—*de Bostock, Bostoke*, Bostock ; i.e., ' of Bostock,' in Cheshire ; the name of an old family in Cork and Waterford ; now very rare.

ᴅᴇ boᴄ—XII—*le Bot, le But, But*, Butt ; Nor. ' le bot,' i.e., the short, stumpy person.

ᴅᴇ boᴄún—XI—*de Bohun, de Bohoun, Boone*, Bone, Bowen ; i.e., of Bohun. It occurs as a surname in Domesday Book.

ᵛe ᵛRᴀnᵛúnn—XI—*de Brandon*, Brandon; i.e., 'of Brandon,' a frequent place-name in England; the name of an old English family who settled in Co. Louth.

ᵛe ᵛRᴀᴄúnn—XI—Bratton; i.e., 'of Bratton' in England.

ᵛe ᵛRéᴀᵛúnn—XI—*de Bredun, de Bredone*, Bredon, Breadon, Breydon, etc.; i.e., 'of Bredon' in England.

ᵛe ᵛReᴀnnóc—XI—*de Brechnok, de Braynok*, Brennock, Brannock, Brannick, etc.; i.e., 'of Brechnock' in Wales. Families of this name settled in Ireland at the time of the Anglo-Norman invasion, and in the 16th century were most numerous in Tipperary, Kilkenny and Waterford. Not to be confounded with ᵛpeᴀᴄnᴀċ, q.v.

ᵛe ᵛReᴀᴄúnn, v. ᵛe ᵛpioᴄúnn.

ᵛe ᵛReiᴄ, Brett. V. ᵛe ᵛpiᴄ.

ᵛe ᵛRí—XI—*de Bree, de Bre, de Bray*, Bree, Bray; i.e., 'of Bree,' in England, or 'of Brie,' in Normandy, or possibly 'of Bray' in Co. Wicklow (Irish ᵛpí).

ᵛe ᵛRiᵹ—XI—*de Brugge*, Brigg, Briggs, Bridge; Mid. Eng. 'atte Brigge,' i.e., at the bridge, from residence thereby. Brugge and Brigge were Mid. Eng. forms of Bridge. 'Sibrecht of Brigg' occurs in the Dublin Roll of Names (A.D. 1216).

ᵛe ᵛRioᴄúnn—XII—*de Breton, Britun*, Bretton, Britton, etc.; Nor. 'le Breton,' i.e., the Breton, an immigrant from Brittany. Also ᵛe ᵛpeᴀᴄúnn.

ᵛe ᵛRiᴄ—XII—Britt, Brett; Nor. 'le Brit,' 'le Bret,' i.e., the Breton, native Brittany, the same as ᵛe ᵛpioᴄúnn, q.v. Families of this name came to Ireland at the time of the Anglo-Norman invasion, or soon after, and settled in different parts of the country. ᵛe ᵛpeiᴄ (q.v.) is a variant.

ᵛe ᵛRiúS, Bruce. V. ᵛe ᵛpúp.

ᵛe ᵛRóc—XI—Brooke, Brookes, Brooks; Mid. Eng. 'atte Brok,' i.e., at the brook, from residence thereby.

ᵛe ᵛRocᴄúnn—XI—*de Broghton, de Broughton*, Broughton; i.e., 'of Broughton,' in England.

ᵛe ᵛRúC, Brookes, etc. V. ᵛe ᵛpóc.

ᴅe ⴠⱃⵓⵣⱥ—XI—*de Bury, Burewe, Bru,* Bury, Burrows, Burrowes, etc., and indirectly Burgess ; i.e., ' at the borough,' from residence therein ; the English equivalent of the Norman de Burgo or Burke, being derived from the dative form of the Old English ' burg.'

ᴅe ⴠⱃⵓⵏ—XII—*de Brune,* Brown, Browne ; Nor. ' le Brun,' i.e., the brown, from the complexion ; an old Norman surname, extremely common in England. It came into Ireland at the time of the Anglo-Norman invasion, and is now also very common in this country. The most important families of the name in Ireland in the 16th century were those (1) of Galway, of which the Brownes were one of the ' tribes ' ; (2) of the Neale, Co. Mayo ; (3) of Malrancan, Co. Wexford ; (4) of Hariston, Co. Waterford ; (5) of Aney, Co. Limerick ; (6) of Kilpatrick, Co. Westmeath ; and (7) of Dunbrowne, Co. Kerry. The Brownes of Kenmare came to Ireland only in the reign of Elizabeth, but by purchase and intermarriage succeeded to the vast estates of MacCarthy More, O'Sullivan More, and O'Donoghue of Ross, and as Earls of Kenmare have held an important place in the social and public life of the country.

ᴅe ⴠⱃⵓⵏⱦⵓⵏ—XI—Brunton ; i.e., ' of Brunton,' in England.

ᴅe ⴠⱃⵓⵙ—XI—*de Brus, de Bruis, de Bruce,* Bruce, etc. ; i.e., ' of Brus ' or ' Brousse,' in France. This family came into England with William the Conqueror, and obtained large grants of land in Yorkshire and other places in the north of England. Robert de Bruce, whose father had obtained from David I of Scotland the Lordship of Annandale and other great possessions, was the founder of the royal house of Bruce in Scotland. The name is also old in Ireland, but has always been very rare.

ᴅe ⴠⵓⱥⵎⵐⵐ—XI—Beaumont ; Nor. ' de Beaumont,' Lat. ' de Bello Monte.' i.e., of Beaumont (the fair mount), a frequent place-name in France.

ᴠᴇ Ⴁuinn—XII—Wynne, Winn ; Welsh 'gwyn'; i.e., white, fair.

ᴠᴇ Ⴁuinⴁíoⱡ—XI—*de Boneville*, Banville, Bonfield, Bunfield, etc. ; i.e., ' of Bonville ' in Normandy ; the name of a Norman family who settled in Ireland soon after the invasion. In the early part of the 14th century, John de Boneville was seneschal of the counties of Kildare and Carlow, and the de Bonevilles were among the earliest Anglo-Norman settlers in Co. Limerick. For more than three centuries, the name has been associated chiefly with the district around Killaloe.

ᴠᴇ Ⴁuiⱄ—XI—*Bowet, Boyt, Boyde*, Boyd ; perhaps ' of Bute ' in Scotland ; an old surname in Ireland, still found in Co. Mayo.

ᴠᴇ Ⴁuiⱶiⱡéiⱃ, ᴠᴇ Ⴁuiⱶléiⱃ—XII—Butler ; Nor. ' le Botiller,' ' le Buitiler,' i.e., the butler. This surname originated in the appointment by Henry II of Theobald Walter, the first of the family who settled in this country, to the office of chief butler of Ireland. Theobald, besides being made chief butler, was granted the baronies of Upper and Lower Ormond and other great possessions, and became the founder of one of the most illustrious of the Anglo-Norman families in Ireland.

ᴠᴇ Ⴁuⱡ, ᴠᴇ Ⴁuⱡⴁ—XII—Woulfe, Wolfe ; Nor. ' le Wulf,' ' le Wolf,' i.e., the wolf, one of a rapacious disposition. This family came into Ireland at the time of the Anglo-Norman invasion and settled in Kildare and Limerick. In the former county, they were seated at Baile nuadh, now Newtown, near Athy, and possessed a district, called Cⱃíoċ Ⴁuⱡⴁaċ, or Woulfe's country, on the east side of the Barrow, extending towards Monasterevan. Baile nuadh continued to be the home of the family until forfeited on the attainder of Nicholas Wolfe in 1641. The Woulfes of Limerick, from the 14th to the middle of the 17th century, took an active part in the affairs of the city. Among those exempted from pardon

by Ireton, when he took possession of Limerick in
1651, were Father Francis Woulfe and Captain George
Woulfe. In the county, Ballywilliam and Innis-
couche, the lands of Patrick Woulfe, and Ballywinter-
rourke, the property of John Woulfe, were confiscated
after the Geraldine war in the last quarter of the
16th century; and in 1653, David Wolfe was transplanted to Connacht. Some of the name about the
same time settled in Clare.

ᴅe ᴠúᴿᴄ, ᴠe ᴠúᴿᴄᴀ—XI—*de Burgo*, De Burgh, Burke,
Bourke; i.e., ' of the burgh' or ' borough.' This
family ranks with the Fitzgeralds and Butlers as
among the most illustrious of the Anglo-Norman
settlers in Ireland. They derive their descent from
William Fitz Adelm de Burgo who, in 1171, accompanied Henry II to Ireland, was made governor of
Wexford, and in 1178 succeeded Strongbow as chief
governor of Ireland. In 1179, Fitz Adelm obtained
a grant of a great portion of Connacht. By marriage
with an heiress of the de Lacys, Walter de Burgo
acquired, in addition to his other possessions, the
earldom of Ulster; and the Burkes became the greatest
Anglo-Norman family in Ireland. On the murder,
in 1333, of William, the Brown Earl of Ulster, leaving
only an infant daughter, the leading male representatives of the name adopted the Brehon law, which
provided for a male succession, and dividing the lordship of Connacht between them, proclaimed themselves Irish chiefs under the style of MacWilliam
Uachtar and Mac William Iochtar, that is, the Upper
and Lower MacWilliam, the former seated in Co.
Galway and the latter in Co. Mayo. And so Irish
did the Burkes of Connacht become, that they were at
one time regarded as ' mere Irish.' Minor branches
assumed the surnames of MacDavid, MacPhilpin, Mac
Seoinin, MacGibbon, MacRedmond, etc., from their
respective ancestors. The Burkes were also lords of
the barony of Clanwilliam in Co. Limerick. The name
is now very common all over Ireland.

ᴅe ᴠuʀᴅún—XI—*de Burdune, Burdoun*, Burdon ; i.e., ' of Burdon,' in England. This surname, which is of record in Ireland since the 14th century, has long been peculiar to Co. Cork, but even there is very rare.

ᴅe ᴠuʀᴄún—XI—*de Burtoun, de Burton*, Burton ; i.e., ' of Burton ' in England. This surname came into Ireland at different times since the middle of the 13th century.

ᴅe ᴠús—XI—*de Bois, de Boys*, Boyse, Boyes, Boice, Boyce ; Nor. ' del Bois,' ' de Bois,' i.e., of the wood, from residence by or near a wood ; a surname of Norman origin which has been known in Ireland at least since the early 13th century. Cf. the English ᴅe ᴠóıᴅ above.

ᴅe ᴄᴀıseᴀl—XI—*de Cassell*, Cassell, Cashel, etc. ; Nor. ' de Cassell,' Lat. ' de Castello,' i.e., of Cashel, or at the castle, from residence thereby or therein ; the name of an Anglo-Norman family who settled at Dundalk soon after the invasion.

ᴅe ᴄᴀnnᴄᴀlún—XI—*de Cantelon*, Cantillon, Cantlon, etc. ; Nor. 'de Cauntelowe,' Lat. ' de Cantulupo,' i.e., of Chanteloup in France (Seine-et-Oise) ; the name of an early Anglo-Norman family in Ireland. They were among the first of the invaders, and settled in Limerick and Kerry. In the reign of Edward I, Richard de Cantelupo was sheriff of Kerry, and at the same period Master Thomas de Cantulupo was official of the church of St. Mary at Limerick. The Cantillons were lords of Ballyheigue in Co. Kerry until after the Jacobite wars in the latter part of the 17th century. Many of the name afterwards gained distinction in France where in the last century Antoine Sylvaine de Cantillon was created Baron de Ballyheigue. The name, though never very numerous, still survives in Kerry and Limerick.

ᴅe ᴄᴀnnᴄuᴀl, ᴅe ᴄᴀnᴄuᴀl—XI—de *Cantewell, de Cantwell*, Cantwell ; i.e., ' of Cantwell,' or ' Kentwell,' a spot somewhere in England. This family came to

Ireland at the time of the Anglo-Norman invasion and settled in Kilkenny and Tipperary, where they obtained large grants of land from the Butlers. The original seat of the family was at Cantwell's Court, about four miles to the north-east of Kilkenny. The Cantwells are still a well-known and respectable family in Kilkenny and Tipperary.

ᴅᴇ Cᴀɴɴᴛúɴ—XI—*de Cauntoun, de Caunton, de Canton,* Canton, Candon and Condon ; Nor. ' de Countyntoun,' ' de Cauntyton,' ' de Caunteton,' i.e., of C————, probably the present parish of Canton in Glamorganshire ; an old Norman surname, sometimes angl. Canton and Candon, but generally corrupted to Conɴᴅúɴ (pronounced locally Cúɴúɴ) and anglicised Condon. The Condons are a well-known family in Cork, Waterford and Limerick who formerly possessed considerable property in the neighbourhood of Mitchelstown, from one of whom that town got its name.

ᴅᴇ Cᴀʀᴅᴜɪᴅ—XI—*de Cardif, de Kerdyff,* Cardiff, Kerdiffe ; Nor. ' de Cardif,' i.e., of Cardiff in Wales. Families of this name settled at an early period in Dublin, Meath, Kildare and Wexford. The name, though never very common, still survives in Leinster.

ᴅᴇ Cᴀʀʟᴛúɴ—XI—*de Carletoun, de Carltoun,* Carleton, Carlton ; Nor. ' de Carletoun,' i.e., of Carleton or Carlton, a frequent place-name in England. This surname is old in Ireland. But see Ó Cᴀɪʀᴇᴀʟʟáɪɴ, which has been anglicised Carleton.

ᴅᴇ Cᴀʀʀᴀɪɢ—XI—*de Carricke, de Carrig,* Carrick, Craig, etc., and by translation Rock ; Nor. ' de Carraig,' i.e., of Carrick, a common place-name in Ireland and Scotland, meaning ' the rock ' ; a not uncommon surname in Ireland in the 13th century. But see Mᴀc Conᴄᴀɪɴɴɢᴇ and Mᴀc Conᴄᴀᴛᴘᴀᴄ, which are similarly anglicised.

ᴅᴇ Cᴀʀʀúɴ—XI—*de Carron, de Carrew,* Carew, Carey, etc. ; Nor. ' de Carreu,' i.e., of Carew, a parish in Pembrokeshire ; an Anglo-Norman surname which came into Ireland soon after the invasion and is still common in Munster. V. Cappún.

ᴅᴇ Cᴀᴛᴀɪʀ—XI—*de Cathyr, de Cather, de Caher,* Carr; Nor. ' de Cathyr,' i.e., of Cahir, an Irish place-name, found very frequently all over the country ; the name of an old Co. Limerick family of which we have record since the last quarter of the 13th century and which, though never numerous, is still extant in the county.

ᴅᴇ Cᴇᴀɴɴᴛ—XI—*de Kent,* Kent ; Nor. ' de Kent,' i.e., of Kent in England ; a not uncommon surname in early Anglo-Irish records ; still well known in Co. Cork.

ᴅᴇ Cᴇᴀᴘᴏ́ᴄ—XI—*de Keppoc, de Keppok,* Keappock, Keppock, Cappock, etc. ; Nor. ' de Keppoc,' i.e., of Ceapóᵹ, an Irish place-name signifying a green plot before a house (Dinneen). The ceapóᵹ from which the family took its name was in Co. Louth, where they settled early in the 13th century.

ᴅᴇ Cᴇᴀʀsᴀɪᵹ—XI—*de Kersey,* Kearsey ; Nor. ' de Kersey,' i.e., of Kersey, a parish in Suffolk. This family settled in Ireland in the 13th century. The name still survives in Co. Waterford.

ᴅᴇ Cᴇɪᴛɪɴɴ—XI—*de Ketyng,* Keating. V. Céiᴛɪɴɴ.

ᴅᴇ Cɪɴɴᴘᴇɪᴄ—XI—*de Kenefec, de Kenefeg, Kynnepeke,* Kennifeck, Kennefick, etc. ; Nor. ' de Kenefeg,' i.e., of Kenfig, a parish and ancient town in Glamorganshire. This surname occurs very frequently in the Dublin Roll of Names (A.D. 1216). The family finally settled in Co. Cork where the name, though rare, is still well known.

ᴅᴇ Cɪᴏ́ᴍsᴏ́ᵹ, ᴅᴇ Cɪᴜ́ᴍsᴏ́ᵹ—XI—*de Kisshok, de Keusaac, de Cusaak, de Cusack,* Cusack, etc. ; Nor. ' de Cusak,' i.e., of Cussac in France. This family came to Ireland at the time of the Anglo-Norman invasion and settled in Meath and other parts of Leinster. They were one of the most distinguished families of the Pale and many of them filled high judicial posts under the Anglo-Irish government. In the wars and confiscations of the 17th century they lost their property and were dispersed. The name is now more common in Munster than in Leinster.

ᴅe Cᴌᴀ́ʀ—XI—*de Clare,* Clare ; Nor. ' de Clar,' i.e., of Clare, a parish in Suffolk.

ᴅe Cᴌéᴀᴛúɴ—XI—*de Clayton,* Clayton ; Nor. ' de Clayton,' a parish in Essex, Yorkshire or Lancashire.

ᴅe Cᴌéiʀ—XI—*de Clere,* Cleere, Clear ; Nor. ' de Clere,' from some spot perhaps in Normandy ; the name of an old Anglo-Norman family in Co. Wexford and other parts of the south-east of Ireland.

ᴅe Cᴌioꝑoʀᴛ—XI—*de Clifford,* Clifford ; Nor. ' de Clifford,' i.e., of Clifford, a parish in Herefordshire. The name is old in Ireland, but the vast majority of our Cliffords are of Irish origin. V. Ó Cᴌúṁáin and Ó Coᴌmáin.

ᴅe Cᴌioɴᴛúɴ—XI—*de Clyntoun, de Clynton,* Clinton ; Nor. ' de Clinton.' i.e. of Clinton, some spot in England, if not ' of Glinton,' a parish of Northamptonshire. V. ᴢᴌeᴀɴᴛúɴ. The Clintons were an old family in Co. Louth.

ᴅe Cɴoc—XI—*de Cnocke, Cnok,* Knox ; Nor. ' de Cnocke,' i.e., of the cɴoc (or hill), from residence thereon, a Norman-Irish surname, corresponding to the Irish ᴀ' Cɴuic, the English Hill. Cf. ᴅe Cᴀꝑꝑᴀiᴢ above.

ᴅe Coᴢáɴ—XI—*de Cogan, Cogane,* Cogan, Goggin ; Nor. ' de Cogan,' i.e., of Cogan, a parish in Glamorganshire. This surname came into Ireland at the time of the Anglo-Norman invasion. Milo de Cogan was the first constable of Dublin. He received, jointly with Robert FitzStephen, a grant of the whole of Co. Cork from Henry II. The name is now pronounced ᴢoᴢáɴ, sometimes ᴢóᴢᴀɴ, and is generally anglicised Goggin in Munster.

ᴅe Cómᴀʀ—XII—Comber ; Nor. ' le Comber,' i.e., the (wool-) comber ; an old surname in Ireland. I find it still in this form in Connemara.

ᴅe Coʀᴅᴀiᴌe—XI—*de Corbaly,* Corbally ; Nor. ' de Corbaly,' i.e., of Corbally ; a surname formed after the Norman fashion from an Irish place-name.

ᵈe COCÚⁿ—XI—*de Cotun, de Cottoune,* Cotton; Nor.
‘ de Cotun,’ i.e., of Cotton, the name of several places
in England. Cotton is a Wicklow surname.

ᵈe CRÁꝔORC—XI—*de Crauford,* Crawford, etc.; Nor.
‘ de Crauford,’ i.e., of Crawford, a parish in Lanarkshire. The name is found in Anglo-Irish records as
early as 1218, but, except in Donegal, there is no
old family of Crawfords in Ireland. The Crawfords are for the most part descendants of Scottish
settlers who came over at the time of the plantation
of Ulster.

ᵈe CRAIꝫ, ᵈe CREAꝫ—XI—*de Creck,* Cregg, Craig,
etc.; Nor. ‘ de Creck,’ i.e., of the craig or rock, the same
as ᵈe Cappaiꝫ, q.v. The craig in question must have
been in Scotland or in Wales.

ᵈe CROĊCAS—XI—*de Croftus,* Crofts; i.e., ‘ of the crofts,’
or small farms.

ᵈe CROĊCÚⁿ—XI—*de Croftune,* Crofton; Nor. ‘ de
Croftune,’ i.e., of Crofton in Yorkshire or Hampshire.

ᵈe CRÚIS—XI—*de Cruce, de Crosse,* Cruice, Cruise, Cross;
Nor. ‘ de Cruys,’ Lat. ‘ de Cruce,’ i.e., of the cross,
from residence by the roadside or market cross (Mid.
Eng. crouche, cruche); the name of an Anglo-Norman
family who came to Ireland at the time of the invasion
and obtained lands in Dublin and Meath. The chief
seat of the family was at the Naul, where the ruins of
their castle are still to be seen. In 1653, Peter Cruise
of the Naul was transplanted to Connacht, and in
1691 many of the name were attainted. There was
also an old family of Cruises in Co. Clare.

ᵈe CUIRCÉIS—XII—Curteis, Curties, Curtis; Nor. ‘ le
Curteis,’ i.e., the courteous, one of courtly manners
(Old Fr. curteis). The name is of record in Ireland
since the 13th century.

ᵈe CUICLÉIR—XII—Quilter; Nor. ‘ le Cutiler,’ i.e., the
cutler, maker of knives. This surname had come
into Ireland before the end of the 13th century.
Though always very rare, it still survives, but is now
found chiefly in the neighbourhood of Listowel in Co.

Kerry, where it is pronounced corruptly Cuillcéiji in Irish and made Quilter in English.

ꝺe CÚRSA—XI—De Courcy, Courcey, Coursey ; Nor., ' de Courcy,' i.e., of Courcy in Normandy ; the name of a distinguished Norman family whose ancestors came to England with William the Conqueror. In 1177, Sir John de Courcy came to Ireland and having obtained from Henry II a grant of Ulster, invaded that province, committing dreadful slaughter of the inhabitants. His son, Milo de Courcy, was created Baron of Kinsale by Henry III, since which time the name has been associated chiefly with Co. Cork.

ꝺe ꝺIÚIꝺ, Tuite. V. ꝺe CIúIc.

ꝺe ꝺ́ROMᵹÚL—XI—de Dromgol, Dromgoull, Dromgole. Drumgole, Dromgoole, Drumgoole, Drumgoold ; Nor. ' de Dromgole,' i.e., of ꝺꝛuimᵹ̇aꝺail, a frequent Irish place-name ; the name of an old Co. Louth family. Dromgold of Dromgoldstown was one of the gentlemen of Co. Louth in 1598.

ꝺe ꝺURAM—XI—de Durame, Durham, Derham ; i.e., ' of Durham.'

ꝺe ꝼAe--XI--de Faie, Faie, Fay ; Nor. 'de Faie,' i.e.,of Faie, in Normandy ; the name of an Anglo-Norman family who settled in Co. Westmeath. They were seated at Tromroe and Derrynegarragh, and seem to have been a family of considerable local importance in the 16th and 17th centuries. The name is to be distinguished from the Irish Ó ꝼéic which is also angl. Fay.

ꝺe ꝼAOIC, ꝺe ꝼAOICe—XII—White, Whyte ; Nor. ' le White,' ' le Whyte,' i.e., the white, of fair complexion ; the name of an Anglo-Norman family who came to Ireland at the time of the invasion. There are several respectable families of the name, which is common in all parts of Ireland.

ꝺe ꝼILꝺe—XI—de Felda, Field ; Nor. ' de la Felde,' de Felda,' i.e., at the field, from residence therein or thereby ; the name of an Anglo-Norman family who settled in Co. Dublin soon after the invasion.

ꝺe ꝼIONNᵹLAS—XI—de Fyneglas, Finglas ; Nor. ' de

Fyneglas,' i.e., of Finglas ; the name of an Anglo-Norman family who settled at, and took its name from, the village of Finglas in Co. Dublin.

ᴅe ꝼᴚéιη, ᴅe ꝼᴚéιηe—XI—*de Freyne*, Freyne, Frein, Frayne, Freyne, Freney, Freeney, etc ; Nor. ' de la Freyne,' Lat. ' de Fraxineto,' i.e., of the ash-tree (French frêne), from residence thereby ; the name of an Anglo-Norman family who settled at an early period in Co. Kilkenny. The head of the family lived at Ballyreddy and was usually seneschal of Ormond.

ᴅe ꝼᴚéιη걚—XI—*de Freynes, de Freyns, Freins, Frensh, Freynshe, Frensche,* French ; Nor. ' de Freynes,' Lat. ' de Fraxinis,' i.e., of the ash-trees (cf. ᴅe ꝼᴚéιηe above), from residence thereby ; the name of an Anglo-Norman family in Co. Wexford. A branch of this family settled in Galway in the 15th century and became one of the ' tribes ' ; now represented by Lord ffrench and Lord De Freyne.

ᴅe ꝼᴜιᴄe—XI—*Whittay*, Whitty ; Mid. Eng. ' atte Wytheg,' i.e., at the white hey or enclosure, from residence thereby ; the name of an old Anglo-Norman family in Co. Wexford.

ᴅe ꝼᴜιᴄᴌéιꝪ—XI—Whiteley, Whitley ; Nor. ' de Whitleghe,' i.e., of Whiteley (white meadow), in Northumberland.

ᴅe ꝼᴜιᴄηιꝪ—XI—Whitney ; Nor., ' de Whytene,' i.e., of Whitney in Hereford.

ᴅe Ꝫaιᴌᴌιᴅe—XI—*de Gallweia, de Galloway*, Galloway, Gallway, Galway, etc. ; Nor. ' de Gallweia,' i.e., of Galloway in the S.W. of Scotland ; the name of an Anglo-Norman family who settled in Ireland in the early part of the 13th century. The Galways were wealthy merchant families in Limerick, Cork, Kinsale and Youghal.

ᴅe Ꝫaᴌᴌᴅaιᴌe—XI—*de Galbally*, Galbally ; i.e., ' of Galbally,' one of the small group of surnames formed after the Norman fashion from Irish place-names.

ᴅe Ꝫaoᴚ—XI—*de Guher, de Guer, de Goer, Goer, Gower, Gwerre, Goore*, Gware, Gore ; Nor. ' de Guher,' ' de

Guer,' ' de Goer,' i.e., of Gwyr or Gower, a peninsula in South Wales, projecting into the Bristol Channel, where, since the time of Henry I, there had been a colony of Flemings. This family, which is probably of Flemish origin, came into Ireland about the time of the Anglo-Norman invasion, but has never been very numerous. The name is now found chiefly in Limerick, Kerry and Waterford.

ᴅe ᵹᴀꞄᴄún—XI—*de Gascoyn*, Gascoigne, Gaskin; Nor. ' de Gascoyne,' i.e., of Gascony, Fr. Gascogne, an old province in the S.W. of France; the name of an old Norman family in Dublin. The form ' Gascoigne ' represents a later immigration.

ᴅe ᵹeᴀꞄᴅ—XI—*de Gard*, Garde; probably of same origin as Ꝺoınᵹeᴀꞃᴅ, q.v.; an old surname, still surviving in East Cork.

ᴅe ᵹeᴀᴄᴀ—XI—Yeates; Mid. Eng. ' atte Yate,' ' atte Yeate,' i.e., at the gate (Old Eng. ' geat '), from residence thereby.

ᴅe ᵹᴌᴀınꝎíoᴌ—XI—*de Glanvilla*, Glanville, Glanfield; Nor. ' de Glanville,' i.e., of Glanville in Normandy; an early Norman surname, but always very rare.

ᴅe ᵹᴌınn—XI—*de Glyne*, *de Glen*, Glynn, Glinn, Glenn; Nor. ' de Glyn,' ' del Glyn,' i.e., of Glyn, a parish in Brecknockshire, or of the glyn, or glen. Glyn enters largely into the formation of Welsh place-names. The surname came into Ireland at an early period, but has always been very rare.

ᴅe ᵹóꞄᴅún—XI—*de Gordon*, Gordon; Nor. ' de Gordon,' i.e., of Gordon, a parish in Berwickshire; the name of a celebrated Scottish clan whose history goes back to Richard, lord of Gordon, about the middle of the 12th century. There were Gordons in Ireland as early as the middle of the 14th century, but the name was rare until after the plantation of Ulster. The modern Scottish form of the name is ᵹóꞃᴅon or ᵹóꞃᴅᴀn.

ᴅe ᵹRᴀᴇ—XI and XII—*de Grey*, *de Graye*, Grey, Gray; (1) Nor. ' de Grey,' i.e., of Grey, some spot in England, probably ; (2) Nor. ' le Grey,' i.e., the grey, from the colour of the hair. Both forms occur in early Irish records, but ' de Grey ' was by far the more common.

ᴅᴇ ᵹᴚᴀɴᴅᴜɴ—XI—*de Grendun*, Grandon, Grandan ; Nor. ' de Grendun,' i.e., of Grendon, a parish in Warwickshire, also a parish in Northamptonshire ; an old but extremely rare surname in Ireland.

ᴅᴇ ᵹᴚᴀɴɴᴄ—XII—*de Graunt*, Grant ; Nor. ' le Graunt,' ' le Grant,' i.e., the great, gigantic in size ; the name of a Norman family who came to Ireland some time before the end of the 13th century and settled in Kilkenny, Tipperary, Waterford and Cork. The Grants were also a Scottish clan, some of whom settled in Ulster at the time of the plantation, and are still represented in that province.

ᴅᴇ ᵹᴚᴀᴏɪɴ—XI—*de Grene, Grene*, Greene, Green ; Nor. ' de Grene,' i.e., at the green, or village common, from residence thereby ; the name of an English family who settled in Dublin, Waterford, Limerick, etc. It can hardly now be distinguished from the many Irish surnames that have been anglicised Green.

ᴅᴇ ᵹᴚᴇɪᴅ—XI—*de Greve, Grave*, Graves, Greaves ; Nor. ' de Greve,' i.e., at the grove (Ang.-Sax. graef), from residence thereat.

ᴅᴇ ᵹᴜᴚᴀᴍ—XI—*de Gorham*, Gorham ; Nor. ' de Gorham,' i.e., of Gorham in England. This surname has been in Ireland since the reign of Edward I. It is, no doubt, the origin of the surname which is pronounced Ó ᵹᴜᴀɪᴘɪᴍ in Co. Galway and anglicised Gorham.

ᴅᴇ ʜᴀᴇ—XI—*de Haia, de Haya, de Hay*, Hay, Hays, Hayes ; Nor. ' de la Haye,' Eng. ' atte Haye,' i.e., at the hay, or hedged field, from residence therein ; the name of an Anglo-Norman family who settled about the time of the invasion in Co. Wexford.

ᴅᴇ ʜᴀᴌ—XI—Hall ; Mid. Eng. ' atte Hall,' i.e., at the hall, from residence therein ; an old surname in Cork and Tipperary. It is only in modern times that it has become common in Ireland.

ᴅᴇ ʜᴀᴌᴀᴅᴏɪᴅ—XI—*de Halywode, Holywode, Holywood*,

Hollywood ; Nor. ' de Halywode,' and frequently in early Anglo-Irish records Lat. ' de Sancto Bosco ' and ' de Sacro Bosco,' i.e., of Hollywood (the holy wood), a parish in Co. Dublin. The family so named, which was one of the most distinguished of the Pale, settled about the time of the Anglo-Norman invasion in Dublin and Meath, where they possessed the manors of Artane, Great Holywood, and other estates.

ᴅe **háꞁꞜ uꞜᴅe**—XI—*de Holeweye, de Halee, Halvie,* Halvey, Holloway, Holoway, etc. ; Nor. ' in le Halwye,' ' de Holeweye,' perhaps in the holy, or hollow, way (Mid. Eng. ' halowe,' ' halwe,' ' halghe,' holy) ; apparently an old surname in Ireland ; there is a Ballyhallway in Co. Kildare. The Irish pronunciation is ᴅe **háꞁuiᴅe.**

ᴅe **háꞁꞜꞜ ún**—XI—*de Halton,* Halton ; Nor. ' de Halton,' i.e., of Halton, a parish in Buckinghamshire, a frequent place-name in England. Ballyhalton in Wicklow may have been the original home of the family in Ireland.

ᴅe **hámáꞁꞜ ún**—XI—*de Hameldon, Hamleton,* Hamilton ; Nor. ' de Hambledon,' ' de Hambleton,' i.e., of Hambledon or Hambleton, the name of several parishes in England, or of Hamilton in Scotland. The Hamiltons came over in large numbers from Scotland at the time of the plantation of Ulster.

ᴅe **hámꞜ ún**—XI—*de Hamptun, de Hampton,* Hampton ; Nor. ' de Hamptoun,' i.e., of Hampton in England. V. ᴅonnᴅ ún. This name is of record in Ireland since the reign of Edward I, but has always been extremely rare.

ᴅe **hánꞜuꞜ ꞡá**—XI—*de Haneberge, de Hanburgo, de Haneberwe, de Handbury,* Hanbury, Handbury, Hanbery, Hanberry, Anborough, Anboro, etc ; Nor. ' de Hanburgo,' ' de Haneberge,' etc., i.e., of Hanbury, the name of several places in England. The English -burg and -berg, -bury and -berry, though distinct by origin, have long been confused. The Hanburys in the 14th century were a Co. Louth family.

ᴅe **hᴀꞧpúꞧ**—XII—Harpur, Harper ; Nor. ' le Harpour,' ' le Harpur,' i.e., the harper ; the name of an old Anglo-Norman family who settled, probably in the 13th century, in Co. Wexford, where they are still numerous. The ' Harpers,' as distinct from the ' Harpurs,' are later settlers.

ᴅe **heᴀᴅún**—XI—*de Hedune*, Heden, Headon, Heydon, Haydon, etc. ; Nor. ' de Hedune,' i.e., of Headon or Haydon, the name of several places in England. This surname came into Ireland soon after the Anglo-Norman invasion, but scarcely spread outside Dublin. ' Stephanus de Hedune ' occurs in the Dublin Roll of Names, A.D. 1216.

ᴅe **heᴀꞧꝼoꞃꞇ**—XI—*de Herford, Herford*, Harford, Hartford, etc. ; Nor. ' de Herford,' i.e., of Hereford ; an old surname in Kilkenny.

ᴅe **henebꞃe**, v. ᴅe hıonbuꞃʒᴀ.

ᴅe **híᴅe**—XI—*de Hyda*, Hyde ; Nor. ' de Hyda,' i.e., of Hyde, a market town in Cheshire (other places of the name in Gloucestershire and Hampshire) ; or it may be Eng. ' atte Hide,' i.e., at the hide, a measure of land, from residence therein. The surname is of record in Ireland since the 13th century. Cf. ᴅᴀʟᴀıcío.

ᴅe **hıonbuꞃʒᴀ**—XI—*de Hynteberge, de Hindeberg, de Hyntebrygh, Hynebrye, Henbury*, Henebery, Heneberry, Hennebry, Henebry, etc. ; Nor. ' de Hynteberge, etc.,' i.e., of Hindeberg, the modern Henbury, a parish in Gloucestershire, also a place in Cheshire. The English terminations -burg and -berg, modern -bury and -berry, have been confused. Cf. ᴅe hᴀnbuꞃʒᴀ above. The first of this family of whom we have record was Philip de Hynteberge who, about the middle of the 13th century, was lord of the manor of Rath, near Dublin, and one of the itinerant justices. His grandson, Nicholas de Hynteberge, in 1280, granted this manor to Robert Bagod, and it has since been known as Bagotrath. The family seems to have then settled in Co. Kilkenny, whence they spread into Waterford and Tipperary.

ᴅe **ɦocᴄun**—XI—*de Hochton, de Hoghton, de Houghton,* Houghton, Haughton, etc.; Nor. ' de Hoghton,' i.e., of Houghton, a common place-name in England. This surname came into Ireland in the 13th century, but has always been very rare.

ᴅe **ɦór**, ᴅe **ɦóʀᴀ**—XII—*Horie,* Hore, Hoar, Hoare; Nor. ' le hore,' i.e., the hoary, greyish-white, no doubt from the colour of the hair; the name of an Anglo-Norman family who came to Ireland at the time of the invasion and settled in Dublin, Wicklow, Wexford, Carlow, Waterford, Cork, Kerry, etc. The Hores of Wexford were a distinguished and influential family.

ᴅe **ɦóʀsᴀɪ꜀**—*de Horseye,* Horsey, and incorrectly Hurst; Nor. ' de Horseye,' i.e., of Horsey, a parish in Norfolk. The surname is of record in Ireland since the 13th century, In the reign of Elizabeth, Jasper Horsey was seneschal of Imokilly. It still survives in Co. Waterford, but is corrupted to Ó **ɦóʀʀᴀɪ꜀** and incorrectly re-anglicised Hurst.

ᴅe **ɦosᴀe**, ᴅe **ɦúsᴀe**—XI—*de Hosey, de Husee,* Hussey; Nor. ' de Hosse,' ' de Heose,' etc., i.e. of Houssaye in Normandy. This family came into Ireland at the time of the Anglo-Norman invasion and settled in Dublin, Louth and Meath. In the last-named county the Husseys obtained large possessions, including Galtrim from which they took the title of baron. A branch of the family settled in the 16th century at Dingle, Co. Kerry. The Husseys suffered much in the wars of the 17th century.

ᴅeɪᴅnɪs—XII—Devenish, and incorrectly Devereux; Nor. ' le Deveneis,' i.e., the Devonian, native of Devon; an old surname in Ireland; now wrongly re-anglicised Devereux in Co. Waterford.

ᴅe **íʀeɪs**—XII—*de Ires,* Irish; Nor. ' le Ireis,' i.e., the Irishman, a descriptive name given in England to an early emigrant from Ireland; the Christian names in the Hundred Rolls show, however, that the emigrant was of Norman extraction. The exile, or one of his descendants, brought back the surname to Kilkenny, where, however, it has always been rare.

ᴐe íᴚᴌeonᴄ—XI—*de Yrlond, de Yrlonde, Dirland, de Irland,* Ireland ; Nor. ' de Irland,' i.e., from Ireland, a local descriptive surname given in England to an early emigrant from Ireland. Cf. ᴐe íᴘéíᴚ above The returned exile in this case also settled in Co. Kilkenny. The late Most Rev. John Ireland, D.D., Archbishop of St. Paul's, Min., was the best-known bearer of the name and an illustrious representative of this family.

ᴐéíse—XI—*Deise, Dece,* Dease ; doubtless ' of Deise,' the barony of Deece in Co. Meath ; a Norman surname formed from an Irish place-name. The Annals at the year 1494 record the death of Gerald Deise, ' a good foreign youth of the Baron of Delvin's people.' The Deases resided at Turbotstown, and are one of the few old families who still retain their ancient patrimony.

ᴐéíseᴀᴄ—X—*Deasaghe,* Deasy, Deasey ; Ir. ' ᴐéíᴘeᴀᴄ,' i.e., native of the Decies of Waterford ; a descriptive epithet which supplanted the original surname which is now lost. The Deasys are numerous in Co. Cork.

ᴐe ᴌᴁ—XI—Law ; Mid. Eng. ' atte Lawe,' i.e., at the *law,* or hill, from residence.

ᴐe ᴌᴀnᵹᴄún—XI—*de Langetoun, de Langetone,* Langton ; Nor. ' de Langetoun,' i.e., of Langton, a common place-name in England ; the name of an old Kilkenny family.

ᴐe ᴌéᴀᴐús—XI—*de Ledwich,* Ledwich, Ledwidge, Ledwitch, Ledwith, Lidwich, Ludwig ; Nor. ' de Ledwich,' i.e., of Ledwich, somewhere in England, but I cannot find the spot. This family settled soon after the Anglo-Norman invasion at Ledwichtown in Co. Westmeath.

ᴐe ᴌeᴀsᴄᴀᴚ—XI—*de Leycester, de Lestre,* Leicester, Leycester, Lester, Lister, Lyster ; Nor. ' de Leycester,' i.e., of Leicester, in England.

ᴐe ᴌéíᵹ—XI—*de Lega, de Leye,* Leigh, Legge, Lea, Lee,

etc.; Lat. ' de Lega,' Nor. ' de Leye,' Mid. Eng.
' atte Lea,' i.e., at the legh (ley, lye, lea) or meadow,
from residence therein or thereby. The family so
called came to Ireland about the time of the Anglo-
Norman invasion and settled in Meath, Kildare,
Kilkenny, etc.

ᴐe Léiᵹinn, ᴐe Léin—XI—*de Lane*, Lane; Nor. ' de
Lane,' Mid. Eng. ' atte Lane,' i.e., at the Lane, from
residence thereby; a very rare surname in Ireland,
nearly all our Lanes being of Irish origin.

ᴐe Léis—XI—*de Lesse, de Lease*, De Lacy, Lacy, Lacey;
Nor. ' de Laci,' i.e., of Lacy or Lassy in France. The
de Lacys came over to England with William the
Conqueror, and some of them appear in Domesday
Book as tenants-in-chief. At the time of the Anglo-
Norman invasion, Hugh de Lacy was granted the
whole of the province of Meath, but owing to failure
of male issue this vast territory soon passed away
into other families. A highly distinguished branch
of the de Lacys settled in Co. Limerick where they
had castles at Ballingarry, Bruree, Bruff, etc. Pierce
Lacy of Bruff was a celebrated captain in the wars
against Elizabeth. Several of the de Lacys became
famous in the service of Continental powers, notably
Count Peter de Lacy, born in Co. Limerick in 1678,
who was a celebrated military commander in Russia,
and his son, Maurice, Marshal de Lacy, who was no
less famous in the Austrian service; while another
Maurice de Lacy, also born in Co. Limerick, in 1740,
became a General in the Russian army. The de Lacys
were also distinguished in Spain, where Count de Lacy
was a famous general and diplomat in the 18th century.

ᴐe Liaᴄ—XI—*de Lee, Doleo, Lea*, Leo; of same origin
as ᴐe Léiᵹ above; the name of an old Anglo-Irish
family in East Limerick. In 1600, the castle and
lands of Rathmore were held by James oge Leo, and
about the same time Leo of Tullavin was one of the
chief gentlemen of the county. The name is still
well-known in the neighbourhood of Kilmallock.

ᴅe Linse—XI—*de Lench, Lenche,* Lynch ; Nor. 'de Lench,' i.e., at the linch, or hill, from residence ; the name of a family who soon after the Anglo-Norman invasion settled at Knock in Co. Meath. A branch of this family, about the beginning of the 14th century, removed to Galway where they became one of the leading 'tribes' and occupied a distinguished position down to the end of the Jacobite wars when several of the name were attainted and their property confiscated. There are, however, several respectable families of Lynches still in Connacht. This surname is to be distinguished from the Irish Ó Loingsigh, q.v.

ᴅe Líon—XI—*de Leon, de Lyons,* Lyon, Lyons, etc. ; Nor. 'de Leon,' 'de Lyons,' i.e., of Lyons, the city in France, or possibly of Lyons, a parish in Durham ; the name of an Anglo-Norman family who came to Ireland about the time of the invasion and settled in Meath and other parts of the Pale.

ᴅe Lioncól—XI—*de Lincole, de Lincoll, Lincole,* Lincoln ; Nor. 'de Lincoll,' i.e., of Lincoln, a city in England ; an old but always extremely rare surname in Ireland.

ᴅe Liontún—XI—*de Linton, Lyntoun,* Linton, Lynton, Lenton ; Nor, 'de Linton,' i.e., of Linton, a frequent place-name in England ; an old but always rare surname in Ireland.

ᴅe Liosla—XI—*de l'isula, del Isle, Lisle, Lislie,* Leslie, Lesley ; Nor. 'del Isle,' Lat. 'de Insula,' i.e., of the island, from residence therein. A family of this name came to Ireland about the time of the Anglo-Norman invasion and seem to have settled in Dublin and Meath. Some Scottish Leslies settled in Derry at the time of the plantation of Ulster.

ᴅe Liostún—XI—*de Lextoun, de Lectone, de Lyston, Lystowne,* Liston ; Nor. 'de Lexington,' 'de Lexintoun,' 'de Lessinton,' 'de Lextoun,' 'de Lyston,' i.e., of Lexington, or Laxton, in Nottinghamshire. This family settled in the 13th century at Kilscannell, in Co. Limerick, which they held down to the year

1595, when it was confiscated and granted to Captain Robert Collum. The Listons are still numerous in Co. Limerick.

ᴅe loᴄᴄús—XI—*de Lofthouse,* Loftus, Loftis; Nor. 'de Lofthouse,' i.e., of Loftus in Yorkshire, or of the lofthouse (house with an upper story); a rare surname in Ireland, found chiefly in Wexford. Nearly all our Loftuses are of Irish origin.

ᴅe lonᴅrᴀ, ᴅe lonᴅrᴀs—XI—*de Loundres, Londres, Londra, Londry,* Landrey, Landers, Launders; Nor. 'de Loundres,' i.e., of London. Families of this name came into Ireland soon after the Anglo-Norman invasion and settled in Dublin, Meath, Wexford, Ormond, etc. The form ᴅe lonᴅᴘᴀ is peculiar to West Munster. See also ᴅe lonᴅún.

ᴅe lonᴅún—XI—*de Lundun, de Lundon, de London,* Lundon, London, Landon; a var. of ᴅe lonᴅᴘᴀᴘ, ᴅe lonᴅᴘᴀ, q.v. John de Lundon and Richard de Lundun are mentioned in the Dublin Roll of Names, A.D. 1216. William de London was witness to a grant of land by the dean and chapter of Limerick early in the 13th century, from which period onward the name appears to have been peculiar to the counties of Limerick and Waterford.

ᴅe lonᴤ—XII—Long; Nor. 'le Lung,' 'le Loung,' i.e., the long, one of remarkably tall stature. This surname came into Ireland about the time of the Anglo-Norman invasion, and was not uncommon in many parts of the country. It cannot now be easily distinguished from the many Irish surnames that have been anglicised Long.

ᴅe lunᴅrᴀs, Landers, Launders. V. ᴅe lonᴅᴘᴀᴘ.

ᴅe miséᴅ—XI—*de Miset,* Misset; Nor. 'de Miset,' i.e., of Miset, some spot probably in Normandy; the name of a Norman family who settled with de Lacy in Meath; now very rare, if not obsolete.

ᴅe móinᴅíol—XI—*de Manneville, de Maundeville,* Mandeville, and incorrectly Mansfield in Waterford and parts of Cork; Nor. 'de Magneville,' 'de Man-

deville,' Lat. ' de Magnavilla,' i.e., of Magneville,
corruptly Mandeville, a place-name in Normandy.
Among those who attended William the Conqueror
to England was Sire de Magneville ; and ' de Manneville,' or ' de Monneville ' occurs in Domesday Book.
The name is of record in Ireland since the early part
of the 13th century, but is now very rare, especially
as Mandeville, the form Mansfield having been substituted for it in English. The family settled in
Tipperary and Waterford.

ᵭe moιRéιs—XI—*de Mareys, de Marries, Morreis,*
Morris, and incorrectly Morrison ; Nor. ' de Mareys,'
' de Marreis,' Lat. ' de Marisco,' i.e., of the marsh
(Fr. marais), from residence thereby ; a common
surname in many parts of the south of Ireland, especially in Kilkenny, Tipperary, Offaly, Leix, Cork
and Limerick, where it is now generally anglicised
Morris. In the neighbourhood of Kilmallock, the
angl. form is popularly Morresh, but officially it is
incorrectly turned into Morrison. A family of the
name settled, in 1485, at Galway and became one of
the ' tribes ' of that city.

ᵭe moιRτιméιR—XI—*de Mortimer,* Mortimer, etc.
Nor. ' de Mortemer,' i.e., of Mortemer in Normandy ;
incorrectly Latinised ' de Mortuo Mari ' (of the Dead
Sea), for which reason it was supposed to have arisen
in crusading times. One of the de Mortimers accompanied William the Conqueror to England, and
the name appears in Domesday Book. It came into
Ireland about the time of the Anglo-Norman invasion.
In 1185 Robert de Mortemer was witness to King
John's Dublin Charter. The family settled in Meath,
but was never very numerous.

ᵭe monτáιn—XI—*Montaine, Montayn,* Montane,
Mountain, etc. ; Nor. ' de la Montayne,' i.e., of the
mountain (Old Fr. montaine, mod. Fr. montagne),
from residence thereby ; a rare Norman surname,
found chiefly in Co. Cork. To be distinguished from
Ó mɑnnτáιn q.v.

ᴠe ᵐóʀᴀ—XI—*de Mora*, More, Moore, etc.; Nor. ' de
la More,' Mid. Eng. ' atte Mor,' Lat. ' de Mora,' i.e.,
at the moor or heath, from residence thereby; an old
Anglo-Norman surname in Ireland; still found in
parts of Munster and Connacht. Its angl. forms
cannot be distinguished from those of the Irish Ó
ᵐóʀᴠᴀ, q.v.

ᴠe ᵐóʀᴛún—XI—*de Mortun, de Mortoun, de Morton,*
Moreton, Morton; Nor. ' de Mortun,' i.e., of Morton,
a common place-name in England.

ᴠe ᵐoᴛún—XI—*de Mohun, de Moun*, Moon, Moone;
Nor. ' de Mohun,' i.e., of Mohon or Moon in France.

ᴠe ᵐúʀᴀ, More, Moore; a var. of ᴠe ᵐóʀᴀ, q.v.

ᴠe nᴀıs—XI—*de Nasshe*, Nash, Naish; Mid. Eng.
' atten Ash,' ' atte Nash,' i.e., at the ash, from residence beside an ash-tree; the *n* of the article, having
been attracted over, became the initial of the surname. Etymologically, therefore, Nash is precisely
the same as Ashe (v. ᴀır). This surname appears
in Ireland soon after the Anglo-Norman invasion, and
is now fairly common in Limerick and Kerry. In the
latter county it is sometimes corrupted to ᴠe ʀᴀır.
Cf. ᴠe nᴀr below.

ᴠe nᴀs—XI—*de Naas*, Nash, Naish; Nor. ' de Naas,'
i.e., of Naas in Co. Kildare; a surname taken by an
early Anglo-Norman family from their place of settlement; now confused with, and absorbed by, ᴠe nᴀır,
q.v. It is possible also that, owing to false analogy,
it has, by a process the reverse of that which took
place in the case of ᴠe nᴀır (see above), been corrupted to ' de As,' ' de Asse,' and so may now be
sometimes represented by Ashe. (v. ᴀᴈᴀr).

ᴠe néᴀᴠ—XI—*de Nethe*, now incorrectly Neville; Nor.
' de Nethe,' i.e., of Neath, in Wales. This surname
is in use in Co. Cork, where it is strangely anglicised
Neville.

ᴠe neᴀᴆʀᴀıᴠíoᴌ—XI—*de Netterville, Nettervilde,*
Netterfield, Netterville; Nor. ' de Netterville,' i.e.,
of Netherfield (lower field), name of a parish in

Sussex, and of another in Nottinghamshire. This family came to Ireland about the time of the Anglo-Norman invasion and settled in the counties of Dublin and Meath. Luke Netterville was Archbishop of Armagh in the early part of the 13th century. The Nettervilles were a very distinguished family. They took an active part in public affairs and were prominent in the Confederate and Jacobite wars.

𐌃enn—XI—*de Dene*, Denn ; Mid. Eng. ' atte Dene,' i.e., at the deane, or wooded valley, from residence therein ; an old, but rare, Kilkenny surname.

ᴅe nóꞡlᴀ—XI—*de Nangle, de Nongle, de Nougle, Nogle*, Nangle, Nagle, Neagle, etc. ; Mid. Eng. ' atten Angle,' ' atte Nangle,' Lat. ' de Angulo,' i.e., at the angle or corner, from residence thereat ; the *n* of the article was attracted over, as in the case of ᴅe nᴀiꞃ (q.v.), and thus became the initial of the surname proper. The Nangles or Nagles derive their descent from Gilbert de Angulo, one of the earliest of the Anglo-Norman invaders. They obtained large grants of land in Meath, and were barons of Navan. Branches of the family settled in Westmeath, Kildare, Waterford and Cork. In Munster the name is now always Englished Nagle or Neagle.

ᴅe noiꞃéis—XII—*Norreys*, Norrish, Norris, etc. ; Nor. ' le Norreys,' ' le Noreis,' i.e., the Northman, the Northerner. Families of this name settled in Ireland about the time of the Anglo-Norman invasion.

ᴅe noꞃᴀ𐌃, ᴅe noꞃᴀi𐌃—XI—*de Norragh, de Norroy, de Norwey*, Noury, Nowry, and incorrectly Norris in Waterford, Kerry, etc. ; Nor. ' de Norwey,' i.e., from Norway, Norwegian settler ; synonymous with ᴅe noiꞃéiꞃ, (q.v.) and often similarly anglicised.

ᴅe noꞃᴄún—XI—*de Nortune*, Norton ; Nor. ' de Nortune,' i.e., of Norton, a common place-name in England. This surname came into Ireland soon after the Anglo-Norman invasion, but has always been very rare. Most of our Nortons are really O'Naughtons.

ᴅe ⁿuiбíol—XI—*de Neuville, de Neville,* Neville ; Nor. ' de Neuville,' ' de Neville,' i.e., of Neville or Neuville, a common place-name in France. This family came into Ireland about the time of the Anglo-Norman invasion and settled in Wexford, Carlow and Kilkenny. The Nevilles of Limerick and Cork are of a different origin. See Ó ⁿiaᴅ and ᴅe ⁿéaᴅ. In Co. Clare, Ó Cnáiṁín (q.v.) is sometimes anglicised Neville.

ᴅe ⁿuinnseann—XI—*de Nungent, de Nugent,* Nugent ; Nor. ' de Nugent,' i.e., of Nogent, a common place-name in France. The Nugents came to England with William the Conqueror, and settled in Ireland at the time of the Anglo-Norman invasion. Gilbert de Nugent was made baron of Delvin by Hugh de Lacy, and the title continued in the family down to the year 1621 when Richard Nugent, Baron of Delvin, was created Earl of Westmeath. The Nugents were one of the most illustrious of the Norman families in Ireland. For special reference to the Nugents of Cork, see under Uinnɾeaᴅún.

ᴅe Oiɾ5iall—XI—*de Uriel,* Urrell, Eurell, Yourell ; Nor. ' de Uriel,' i.e., of Oriel ; the name of an old Anglo-Norman family who settled in Co. Louth and afterwards in Westmeath ; now very rare.

ᴅe páiɾis—XI—*de Paris, de Parys,* Parish ; Nor. ' de Paris,' i.e., of Paris. In 1295, Peter de Paris was burgess and merchant of Youghal, and Parish is, or was at the beginning of the 17th century, a Co. Cork surname.

ᴅe páoɾ—XII—Poer, Poor, Power ; Nor. ' le Pover,' ' le Pouer,' ' le Power,' ' le Poer,' ' le Poor,' i.e., the poor (Old Fr. ' povre, paure,' Lat. pauper), a sobriquet hardly bestowed because of ordinary poverty, which must always have been too common to be a mark of distinction, but probably, as Bardsley suggests, of poverty consequent on a vow. The ancestor of this family came to Ireland with Strongbow, from whom he obtained a grant of the territory of Waterford. In 1535, Sir Richard le Poer was created Baron of Curraghmore, but through failure of the male line, at the beginning of the 18th century, the estates of Curraghmore passed by marriage into the family of Beresford. The name is now very common and widespread, especially in Munster and Leinster.

ᐁe ⲡeⲁⲧúⲛ—XI—*de Peton, de Peyton*, Peyton, Payton; Nor. ' de Peton,' i.e., of Peton, Peyton, or Payton in England.

ᐁe ⲡⲓⲟⲙⲃⲣóⳅ, ᐁe ⲡⲓⲟⲛⲃⲣóⲥ—XI—*de Pembrog, de Penbroc*, Pembroke; Nor. ' de Penbroc,' i.e., of Pembroke in Wales; an old, but rare, surname in Ireland. Many of the early Norman invaders came from Pembrokeshire.

ᐁe ⲡⲟⲓⲣe—XI—*de Pirye, Pyrry*, Pirrie, Perry; Nor. ' de la Pirie,' Mid. Eng. ' atte Perye,' i.e., at the perry, or pear-tree (Fr. poire), from residence thereby.

ᐁe ⲡⲟⲓⲣⲧⲓⲛⳅeⲓⳑ—XI—*de Portyngale, Portingale, Portingall*, Portabello; i.e., from Portugal; a rare surname, peculiar to Youghal and district. In 1569, John Portingale was one of the townsmen of Youghal, as was Arthur Portingall thirty years later. The name is now strangely anglicised Portabello.

ᐁe ⲡⲟⲙⲣⲁe—XI—*de Pomeray*, Pomeroy, Pomroy; Nor. ' de Pomeray,' i.e., of the apple-orchard (Fr. pommeraie), from residence thereby; a Co. Cork surname.

ᐁe ⲡⲣⲁⲧ—XI—*Prat*, Pratt; Lat. ' de Prato,' same as the Fr. Duprat, Dupray, i.e., at the meadow (Old Fr. ' prat,' Fr. ' pré,' Lat. pratum), from residence thereby or therein. In early Anglo-Irish records, it generally appears in the Lat. form of ' de Prato.' ' Martinus de Prato ' occurs in the Dublin Roll of Names, A.D. 1216; and Richard Prat was a witness to a document in the Black Book of Limerick.

ᐁe ⲡⲣeⲁⲥⲧúⲛ—XI—*de Preston*, Preston; Nor. ' de Preston,' i.e., of Preston, a common place-name in England. This surname is of record in Ireland since the middle of the 13th century. In 1361, Robert de Preston was knighted by Lionel, Duke of Clarence, and obtained a grant of the manor of Gormanstown; and his great-grandson, another Sir Robert Preston, was, in the year 1478, elevated to the peerage by the title of Viscount Gormanston. It was on the invitation of Nicholas, the sixth Viscount Gormanston, that the noblemen and gentry of the Pale assembled at the historic meeting on the Hill of Crofty in 1641. The Prestons took a prominent part in the Confederate wars, and Viscount Gormanston was exempted by Cromwell from pardon for life and estate. His son and successor, Jenico Preston, was likewise attainted in 1691. It was only in the year 1800 that these outlawries were removed and the family honours restored.

ꝺe ꝑꞃⁱⱺⁿꝺⱭꞃⱬⱭ́ꞅ, ꝺe ꝑꞃⁱⱺⁿꝺꞃⱭⱬⱭ́ꞅ—XI—*de Prendergast*, Prendergast, Prindergast, Pendergast, Pendergrass, Pender, Pinder, etc.; Nor. ' de Prendergast,' i.e., of Prendergast, a parish in Pembrokeshire. Maurice de Prendergast was one of the knights who accompanied Strongbow to Ireland. He and his descendants obtained large grants of land in different parts of the south and west of Ireland. The principal branches of the family were seated in the present counties of Wexford, Kilkenny, Tipperary, Limerick, Mayo and Galway. The surname is variously corrupted in Irish as well as in English.

ꝺe ꝑꞃⁱⱺⁿⁿꝺ́ⁱⱺꞁ—XI—*de Prendeville*, Prendeville, Prindeville, Prendible, Prenderville, Pendiville, etc., and incorrectly Bransfield; Nor. ' de Frendeville,' i.e., of Frendeville, some spot, no doubt, in Normandy; the name of an old Kerry family. Thomas de Frendeville was sheriff of Kerry in 1235. In Co. Cork the name has been strangely changed to Bransfield.

ꝺe ꞃⱭ́ⁱꞁéⁱⱬ—XI—*de Rayleg, de Raleigh, de Raley*, Rally, Rawley, Rawleigh, Raleigh; Nor. ' de Ralegh,' i.e., of Raleigh in England; the name (1) of an old Anglo-Norman family who settled at Rawleystown and other places in Co. Limerick and the adjoining parts of Tipperary, where it is still common; and

(2) of an old Anglo-Norman family in Co. Kildare. This surname appears in old Anglo-Irish records under a great variety of spellings, and the same is true of English records ; Bardsley gives seventeen different forms from the Index to the Register of Oxford University alone. In Co. Limerick 'de Raley' and 'de Roley,' 'Rawlie' and 'Rowlie,' 'Rawley' and 'Rowley,' occur side by side down to the end of the 16th century, when Richard Rowlie, alias Raleigh, of Raleighston (also called Rawleystown, Rolleston, and Ballynrowley), Co. Limerick, gentleman, was the recipient of a pardon from Queen Elizabeth ; and Raleigh, Rowley, Roley, etc., as English place-names, are, or were, similarly interchangeable.

ᴅe ᴚᴀᴍꙅᴀɪᵹ—XI—*de Ramsey, Ramesey,* Ramsey, Ramsay ; Nor. ' de Ramsey,' i.e., of Ramsey, the name of more than one place in England. Though this surname is an old one in Ireland, most of those who now bear it are the descendants of late immigrants, who came hither from Scotland.

ᴅe ᴚᴀᴛ—XI—*de Rath,* Rath ; Nor. ' du Rath,' i.e., of the rath, some spot near Dublin. The surname survives in Co. Louth.

ᴅe ᴚɪoᴅᴀʟ—XI—*de Ridal, de Rydale,* Riddell, Riddle, Ruddell, Ruddle ; Nor. ' de Ridal,' i.e., of Ridal (?), some spot in England. ' de Rydale ' and ' Rydalagh ' occur in old documents relating to Co. Limerick, where Ruddle is a well-known surname. V. ᴚɪoᴅᴀʟ.

ᴅe ᴚɪꙅeᴀᴍoɴɴ—XI—*de Richemond,* Richmond ; Nor. ' de Richemond,' i.e., of Richmond, the well-known town in Surrey.

ᴅe ᴚóɪꙅᴄe—XI—Roche, Roache ; Nor. ' de la Roche,' Lat. ' de Rupe,' i.e., of the rock, from residence beside some prominent rock ; an old Norman surname. Families of this name settled in different parts of Ireland, but the best known were those of Cork, Limerick and Wexford. In the first-named county, the Roches obtained by marriage the district about Fermoy known as Cᴚíoċ ᴚóɪꙅᴄeᴀċ, or Roche's

Country ; the head of this family was Viscount Fermoy.
The Roches of Limerick were a wealthy and respectable merchant family. Among the twenty exempted
from pardon by Ireton when he obtained possession
of the city in 1651, were Alderman Jordan Roche and
Edmund Roche. Roche of Rochesland was one of
the principal gentlemen of Wexford in 1598.

ᴅe ROS—XI—*de Ros*, Ross ; Nor. ' de Ros,' i.e., of Ross,
a Gaelic place-name, probably in Scotland.

*ᴅe ROSFORC—XI—*de Rochefort, de Rocheford, de Rochford*, Rochefort, Rochfort, Rochford, Rushford, etc. ;
Nor. ' de Rochefort,' Lat. ' de Rupe forti,' i.e., of
Rochefort (strong or fortified rock) in France. This
surname came into Ireland at the time of the Anglo-
Norman invasion and soon became very widespread.
In the 16th century, it was found chiefly in Meath,
Westmeath, Kildare, Carlow, Wexford, Waterford
and Limerick. It is now, strange to say, comparatively rare. In Limerick, the Irish forms Rorcanᴅ
and Rorcún (q.v.) are found.

ᴅe RUIS—XI—*de Rush*, Rush ; Nor. ' de Rush,' i.e.,
probably of Rush, Co. Dublin ; a very rare surname.

ᴅe RÚS—XII—*de Rus*, Rose ; Nor. ' le Rus,' ' le Rous,'
Lat. ' Rufus,' i.e., red-haired ; a descriptive surname.
Cf. Ruiréil.

ᴅe SADRAINN—XI—*de Sauverne, Severne, Severn, Saryn*,
Saurin ; Nor. ' de Sauverne,' i.e., of the Severn, from
residence beside the River Severn in England. The
surname is old in Ireland, but has always been very
rare.

ᴅe SAILISéIR—XI—*de Seyntlegger, de St. Ledger*, Sallinger, Sellinger, St. Ledger, etc. ; Nor. ' de St. Ledger,'
Lat. ' de Sancto Leodegario,' i.e., of St. Leger's, a
common place-name in France. This family came
to Ireland probably about the beginning of the 14th
century and settled in different parts of the Pale,
especially in Co. Kilkenny. By the 16th century
they had become so Irish that Stanihurst describes
them as ' mere Irish.' Their chief seat was at Tullagh-

anbroge ; a branch of the family resided at Bally-
fennon. The head of the family was called Baron of
Slieve Margie. V. Saileaṙtaṅ, Sailiʒéiṅ, and Suil-
inʒéiṅ.

ᴠe SⱥⁱⁿⱦⱤⱸⱥᴠ—XI—*de Santry,* Santry ; Nor. ' de
Santry,' i.e., of Santry, Ir. SeaⁿⱦⱤeaᴠ, a village in
Co. Dublin ; the name of an early Anglo-Norman
family. It was never very common, and is now
found chiefly in Co. Cork.

ᴠe Sⱥ́ⁱⱤSéⁱl—XI—*de Sarsefield,* Sarsfield, etc. ; Nor.
' de Sarnesfeld,' ' de Sarnefield,' ' de Chernesfend,'
i.e., of Sarnesfelde (as the name is written in Domesday Book, where it is mentioned as one of the King's
manors) in Herefordshire, the modern name of which
I have failed to discover. This surname came into
Ireland about the time of the Anglo-Norman invasion,
when the family settled in Dublin, Kildare, Cork and
Limerick. There were many distinguished men of
the name, but it is to Patrick Sarsfield, Earl of Lucan,
the celebrated commander in the wars of the Revolution, that it owes its fame in Irish history.

ᴠe Sⱥ́l—XI—*de Salle, Sale, Sawle,* Sall, Saul ; Nor. ' de
la Sale,' i.e., of the hall, from residence therein ; the
name of an Anglo-Norman family who settled early
at Cashel, Co. Tipperary, and at Salestown, Co. Meath.
In 1598, Sale of Saleston was one of the chief gentlemen of Co. Meath. The name is now very rare.

ᴠe Sⱥⁿᴅⱥ́l—XI—*de Sandale, de Sandall,* Sandall, Sandell ; Nor. ' de Sandale,' i.e., of Sandale or Sandal, a
frequent place-name in the north of England ; the
name of an Anglo-Norman family who settled early
in the neighbourhood of Carrickfergus.

ᴠe SⱥⁿꝠⱷⱤⱦ—XI—*de Saunford, de Sanford,* Sanford ;
Nor. ' de Sanford,' i.e., of Sandford, some spot in
England.

ᴠe SⱥⱷʒⱤⱥᴠ—XI—*de Segrave,* Seagrave, Segrave, Seagrove, Segre ; Nor. ' de Segrave,' i.e., of Seagrave
(Ang.-Sax. Saegraf), a parish in Leicestershire. This
family came to Ireland probably in the early part

of the 14th century and settled in Meath and Dublin. Their chief seat was at Killeglan in Co. Meath, with branches at Cabragh and Ballyboghill, in Co. Dublin. In 1322 Stephen Segrave was made Primate of Armagh.

ɴe SCÉAlAS—XI—*de Scales,* Scales ; Nor. ' de Scales,' i.e., of Scales, a common place-name in the north of England ; an old, but extremely rare, surname in Ireland. There are a few families of the name in Limerick.

ɴe SCeAlcúɴ—XI—*de Skelton,* Skelton ; Nor. ' de Skelton,' i.e., of Skelton, the name of a parish in Yorkshire and of another in Cumberland.

ɴe SCOɸul—XI—*de Scoville,* Scuffil, Scofield, Schofield, Scholefield ; Nor, ' de Scoville,' i.e., of Scoville or Escoville in Normandy. This surname is in use in Co. Mayo, but the present angl. forms are incorrect. Scovell or Scovill, as in England, would be better.

ɴe SCRIÐIɴ—XI—*de Screvine, de Skrevyn,* Scriven ; Nor. ' de Screvine,' i.e., of Scriven in Yorkshire ; a rare Cork surname.

ɴe SCRíɴ—XI—*de Scryne, Screne,* Skryne ; Nor. ' de Scryne,' i.e., of Screen, probably in Meath ; an extremely rare surname.

ɴe seAɴcreAð, Santry. V. ɴe SAɴcɾeAð.

ɴe SIɴClÉIR—XI—*de Seynclere, de Sencler,* Sinclare, Sinclair, St. Clair, St. Clare, etc. ; Nor. ' de St. Clair,' Lat. ' de Sancto Claro,' ' de Sancto Clero,' i.e., of St. Clair, a frequent place-name in Normandy. This surname came into England with William the Conqueror, and was borne by an important Scottish clan. In Ireland also it occurs early, but the family was never either numerous or important.

ɴe SIɴ𝔷eAlcúɴ—XI—*de Singleton,* Singleton ; Nor. ' de Singleton,' i.e., of Singleton, the name of a parish in Sussex and of another in Lancashire. This surname in Clare and Cork has been corrupted to Ó Sɪɴðile and Ó Sɪoɴðuile.

ɴe SIOɴúIR—XI—*de Synors, de Sinors, de Sunors,* Shinnor, Shinnors ; Nor. ' de Sinors,' etc., i.e., of

Sinors or Sunors, apparently some spot in England ;
an old, but rare, Anglo-Norman surname found
chiefly in East Limerick and in parts of Connacht.
V. Sionúıꞃ.

ꝺe Sıún—XII—*Yonge*, Younge, Young ; Nor. ' le Jeune,'
' le Jouen,' i.e., the young, in the sense of the younger,
junior, as opposed to senior.   Families of this name
settled about the time of the Anglo-Norman invasion
in Dublin, Kildare, and other parts of Ireland.   Young
of Youngstown was one of the principal gentlemen
of Co. Kildare in 1598, while at the same time Young
of Gareston was one of the ' men of name ' in Co.
Dublin.

ꝺe Sıúnꞇᴀ, Joynt.

ꝺe Sláıne—XI—*de Slane*, Slaan, Slane ; Nor. ' de Slane,'
i.e., of Slane, in Co. Meath ; an early, but always very
rare, Norman surname.

ꝺe Spáıne—XI—*de Spainne*, Spain ; Nor. ' de Spainne,'
i.e., from Spain, an immigrant from Spain.

ꝺe Sꞇábᴀlꞇún—XI—*de Stapeltoun, de Stapulton*,
Stapelton, Stapleton ; Nor. ' de Stapeltoun,' i.e., of
Stapleton, a common English place-name ; the name
of an old and distinguished Anglo-Norman family
who settled, soon after the invasion, in Kilkenny and
Tipperary.   They assumed the Irish surname of Mᴀc
ᴀn Ꞡᴀıll (q.v.), but were also called Ꞡᴀllꝺub, q.v.

ꝺe Sꞇᴀcᴀbúl, ꝺe Sꞇᴀcᴀpúl—XI—*de Stacepole*,
Stacaboll, Stacapoll, Stackpole, Stackpoole ; Nor. ' de
Stacepole,' of Stackpool or Stackpole, a parish in
Pembrokeshire ; also called Ꞡᴀllꝺub, q.v. ; the name
of an early Norman family who settled in Tipperary
and other parts of the south of Ireland. The name is
now very rare.

ꝺe Sꞇᴀꝼoꞃꞇ—XI—*de Stafford*, Stafford ; Nor. ' de
Stafford,' i.e., of Stafford in England ; the name of
an old and distinguished Wexford family ; also found
in Dublin, Louth and Kilkenny.

ꝺe Sꞇáıneᴀs—XI—*de Stanes*, Staines ; Nor. ' de Stanes,'
i.e., of Staines in Middlesex, or Stanes in Lincolnshire.

ᴅe **sᴄᴀɪɴʟéɪ⁊**—XI—*de Stanleye, de Stanley*, Stanley; Nor. ' de Stanley,' i.e., of Stanley, a common English place-name.

ᴅe **sᴄᴀɴꜰoʀᴄ**—XI—*de Stanford*, Stanford, Stancard; Nor. ' de Stanford,' i.e., of Stanford, in England. V. Sᴄᴀɴᴄᴀꝑᴅ.

ᴅe **sᴄóc**—XI—*de Stoke, de Stokes*, Stokes, Stoakes; Nor. ' de Stoke,' i.e., of Stoke, a common English place-name, from Old Eng. ' stoc,' a village. Monosyllabic surnames of local origin often add on the genitive *s* after the manner of patronymics. This surname came into Ireland about the time of the Anglo-Norman invasion, and was common in many parts of the country.

ᴅe **sᴄonnᴅún**—XI—*de Stauntoun, de Stanton*, Staunton, Stanton, Stundon, Sdundon; Nor. ' de Stanton,' i.e., of Stanton, a frequent place-name in England. The Stantons were amongst the earliest of the Anglo-Norman invaders. They settled in Dublin, Kildare, Kilkenny, Cork and Mayo. The Stantons of the last-named county, who were followers of the Burkes, obtained extensive possessions in the barony of Carra, and formed a clan after the Irish fashion. They took the Irish surname of **mᴀc ᴀn ᵯɪʟeᴀᴅᴀ**, i.e., son of the knight, probably from their ancestor, Milo de Stanton, as did also the Stauntons of Cork.

ᴅe **suᴀnᴄún**—XI—*de Swantun*, Swanton; Nor. ' de Swanton,' i.e., of Swanton, in Norfolkshire or Kent.

ᴅe **suɪn⊃eᴀn**—XI—*de St. John*, St. John, Singen, Singin, etc., Nor. ' de St. Jean' ; Lat. ' de Sancto Johanne,' i.e., of St. Jean, a common French place-name. This family settled early in Wexford, Kilkenny and Tipperary. Thomas de St. John was sheriff in Tipperary in 1296.

ᴅe **suᴄún**—XI—*de Suttoun*, Sutton; Nor. ' de Suttoun,' i.e., of Sutton, a common place-name in England. The Suttons are an old and respectable Anglo-Norman family who settled soon after the invasion in Kildare and Wexford.

ᴅe Ⲧⲓⱳ́—XI—*de Tiwe, de Tywe, Tue,* Tew ; Nor. ' de Tiwe,' i.e., of Tew, in Oxfordshire, more anciently Tiwe ; an old, but rare, surname in Kildare, Kilkenny and Waterford.

ᴅe Ⲧⲓⱳ́ⲓⲦ—XI—*de Tuite,* Tuite ; Nor. ' de Tuite,' ' del Tuit,' i.e., of Tuit or Thuit, a frequent place-name in Normandy, of same meaning as the English thwaite, i.e., a woodland clearing. The presence of the article in the old form ' del Tuit ' would seem to show that the surname was taken from the common noun rather than from the place-name. The Tuites were a distinguished Norman family, descended from Richard de Tuite who came over with Strongbow ; and they enjoyed extensive estates in Longford, Meath and Westmeath down to the confiscations of the 17th century. The head of the family was Baron of Moycashel.

ᴅe ⲦⲢⲀⲒⲂⲈⲀⲢⲤ—XI—*de Travers, de Tryveres, de Tryvers, Trevers, Trivers,* Travers, Travors, Trevors, etc. ; Nor. ' de Tryvers,' i.e., of Treviers in Normandy ; a rather old surname in Dublin and many parts of the south of Ireland, especially Kildare, Carlow, Tipperary and Cork.

ᴅe ⲦⲢⲈⲀⲚⲦ—XI—*de Trente,* Trant ; Nor. ' de Trente,' i.e., of Trent, a parish in Somerset, also a place in Dorset ; the name of an old and respectable Kerry family. At the end of the 16th century, the Trants of Dingle were one of the chief families of that county. Sir Patrick Trant was a prominent Jacobite. He was attainted, together with several others of the name, in 1691, and lost extensive estates in Kerry and other parts of Ireland.

ᴅe ⲦⲢⲈⲟ́—XI—*de Troya, de Troie, de Troye,* Troy ; Nor. ' de Troye,' i.e., of Troyes, a city in France, formerly the capital of Champagne ; an old but rare surname in Kilkenny and Waterford. V. Ⲧⲣⲉⲟ́.

ᴅe ⲦⲢⲨⲒⲘ—XI—*de Trim,* Trim ; Nor., ' de Trim,' i.e., of Trim in Co. Meath ; very rare.

ᴅe Ⲧⱳ́ⲓⲚⲖⲈⲒⳌ—XI—*de Townley,* Townley ; Nor. ' de

Townley,' i.e., of Townley, in Lancashire ; a rather old, but extremely rare, surname in Ireland. Richard Townly is mentioned in the Fiants of Elizabeth.

ᴅe ⌶⌶ᴅeᴀꜱ—XII—*de Wees, de Wyz,* Wise, Wyse ; Nor. ' le Wys,' ' le Wise,' i.e., the wise ; hardly from a place-name, the old ' de ' being for the article ' the,' ' le.' The Wyses were an old family in Waterford.

ᴅe ⌶⌶ᴣeᴀᴍóꞃ—XI—*de Wiggemore, de Wigmore,* Wigmore ; Nor. ' de Wigmore,' i.e., of Wigmore in Herefordshire, more anciently Wiggemore, Wigganmor.

ᴅíoʟᵯᴀⵏ, ᴅíoʟúⵏ—VIII—*Dylun, Dilloun,* Dillon ; ' son of Dillon ' (a Norman-French personal name formed from an old Teutonic personal name Dill, Dillo, Dilli, by the addition of the French dim. termination '-on.' Dille appears as a surname in older English records, now written Dill ; and Dilkok, another dim. of the same name, now represented by the surname Dilcock in England, is found in the Patent and Close Rolls of Ireland, Henry II-Henry VII. ᴅíoʟᵯᴀⵏ, the older Irish spelling of the name, may be due to an attempt to assimilate it to the Irish word ᴅíoʟᵯᴀⵏ). The Dillons came to Ireland at the time of the Anglo-Norman invasion. Sir Henry Dillon received from King John large grants of land in Westmeath and Annaly, known in later times as Dillon's Country, and his descendants were barons of Kilkenny West. A branch of the family also settled in Co. Mayo. In the 17th and 18th centuries, the Dillons were distinguished in the service of continental powers.

ᴅíꞃⵏᴣ—VIII—Deering ; ' son of Deoring,' an Anglo-Saxon personal name, given also as Diring and Dyring by Searle.

ᴅoᵬ—VIII—*Dobbe,* Dobbs ; ' son of Dob,' a pet form of the Norman Robert.

ᴅoᴅᴀ—VIII—*Dode,* Dodd, Dodds ; ' son of Doda ' (a common Anglo-Saxon personal name, probably a shortened form of Dodwine ; given by Searle under a great variety of forms, as Dodda, Doddo, Dodd,

Dodo, Duda, Dudda, etc.). It is an old surname in Tipperary.

ꝺoıbín—VIII—*Dobin*, *Dobyn*, Dobbin, Dobbyn, Dobbins, Dobbyns ; ' son of Dobin ' (dim. of Dob, a pet form of Robert) ; the name of an old family in Waterford. Laurence Dobbyn was mayor in 1460, as was Patrick Dobbyn in 1589.

ꝺoıꝺín—VIII—*Dodin*, Dodding ; ' son of Dodwine ' (an Anglo-Saxon personal name) ; formerly a surname in Leix, but probably now obsolete in Ireland.

ꝺoıʟṗín—VIII—*Dolfine*, Dolfin, Dolphin ; ' son of Dolfin,' a common personal name in England even before the Norman conquest. It occurs in Domesday Book as the name of a landholder in the time of Edward the Confessor, and about 1085 was borne by an Earl of Cumberland. In Ireland, the Dolphins settled in Clanrikard, where in the 16th century they formed a distinct clan after the Irish fashion with a chief of the name.

ꝺoınᵹeáꝛꝺ, ꝺoınneáꝛꝺ—XI—*Donnarde*, Uniacke, Uniake, etc. ; Mid. Eng. ' atten yeard,' i.e., at the yard, or enclosure, from residence therein ; the old *n* of the article was attracted over as in the case of ꝺe nóᵹʟa (q.v.), and with the dropping of the preposition ' at ', the form became ' the nyeard.' It was evidently a second surname given to the family of Uniacke from their place of residence. It has now no direct equivalent in English, the family being always called Uniacke in that language. The Uniackes are an old Co. Cork family.

ꝺoʟʟáꝛꝺ, ꝺoʟʟáꝛᴄ—XII—*Dullart*, Dullard, Dollard ; i.e., ' the dullard '; an old surname in Dublin and Meath.

ꝺonꝺún, ꝺonnꝺún—XI—*de Aundon, Daundon, Doundowne*, Dondon, Dundon ; Nor. ' de Anton,' i.e., of Hampton in Middlesex, near which is the old royal palace of Hampton Court. Hampton is sometimes found in Anglo-Saxon charters as ' Heantune,' and was latinised ' Antona '; Antonae Curia was Hampton Court. The Dundons are an old and respectable family in Co. Limerick. At the end of the 16th century, they held the castle of Ballystine, near Askeaton.

ⱃⱁⱀᵹᴀⱀ—VIII—*Dongane*, Dongan, Dungan, Duncan; 'son of Duncan,' (the Irish ⱄⱁⱀⱀᴀᵹᴀⱀ which was adopted by the Anglo-Saxons. Searle gives it in three forms: Duncan, Dunecan, and Dunechan; found along with a few other Irish names in Domesday Book. Cf. Coⱅmᴀⱀ above). The Dongans settled in Dublin and Kildare. Walter Dongan was created a baronet by James I, and after the Restoration his descendant, Sir William Dongan, was advanced to the Earldom of Limerick. His estates, comprising 30,000 acres, were confiscated by the Williamites.

ⱃⱃᴀᴄ—VIII or XII—*Drak*, Drake; 'son of Drake' (old English draca, Lat. draco, meaning 'the dragon,' probably of heraldic origin; or it may be from 'le drake,' i.e., the dragon, though it never takes the French article in Irish, as it does in English, records). The Drakes came to Ireland about the time of the Anglo-Norman invasion and settled in Louth and Meath. 'Herbertus Draco' occurs in the Dublin Roll of Names A.D. 1216, and 'Jordanus Drake' in the list of Free Citizens of Dublin, A.D. 1225-1250. Drake of Drakeston was one of the gentlemen of Co. Louth at the end of the 16th century, as was Drake of Drakerath at the same period in Co. Meath. The name is now very rare.

ⱃⱃᴀⱁⱃᴀⱃ—XII—Draper; Nor. 'le Draper,' i.e., the draper; an old surname in Ireland, but now very rare.

ⱃⱃⰌⱛ, Drew; a late form of ⱃⱃⱛ, q.v.

ⱃⱃⱁᵹ, ⱃⱃⱁᵹᴀ—VIII—*Drogh*, *Drou*, Drough, Drew; 'son of Drogo,' (a personal name of Frankish origin borne, among others, by a son of Charlemagne and brought into England by the Normans, where Drogo of Bevrere, a follower of the Conqueror, obtained a grant of Holderness in Yorkshire); an old surname in Westmeath and Offaly. Later forms are ⱃⱃⱛ and ⱃⱃⱛ, q.v.

ꝺROmᵹúl, Dromgoole, Drumgoole, Drumgoold. V. ꝺe
Oꝛomᵹúl.

ꝺRú—VIII—*Drue*, Drew; 'son of Dru,' a Norman form
of Drogo. V. Oꝛoᵹ.

ꝺRúꝛꝛꝺe—XII—*Druerye, Drurie*, Drury, Drewry; Old
Fr. 'druerie,' i.e., the lover; not an old surname in
Ireland. Drury is often merely an incorrect
anglicisation of the Irish mᴀc ᴀn Oꝛuᴀꝺ and
Ó Oꝛuᴀꝺ, q.v.

ꝺuꝺ—IX—Duff; Ir. 'ꝺuꝺ,' i.e., black; a description
epithet which supplanted the real surname which is
now lost. Cf. ꝺán, ꝺeᴀᵹ, etc.

ꝺuꝺꝺᴀl—XI—*de Duvedale, Dovedale, Dovedall, Dowe-
dale*, Dowdall, Doudall, Dowdell; Nor. 'de Duvedal,'
i.e., of Dove Dale, the upper part of the valley of the
Dove in Derbyshire and Staffordshire; an old and
distinguished family in Dublin, Louth and Meath.

ꝺuꝺᵹlᴀs—XI—*de Douglas*, Douglas; Nor. 'de Douglas,'
i.e., of Douglas, a parish in Lanarkshire; a surname of
Scottish origin.

ꝺuꝛnᵹeáꝛꝺ, ꝺuꝛnneáꝛꝺ, Uniacke. V. Ooꝛnᵹeáꝛꝺ.

ꝺúꝛnsméᴀꝛᴀċ, Beresford; a 'translation' of the
English surname Beresford, as if Berryfort.

éᴀꝺꝛáꝛꝺ, *Evrard*, Everard. V. Éꝛꝺeᴀꝛáꝛꝺ.

éᴀꝺꝛóꝛꝺ—VIII—*Everod*, *Evrett*, Everett, Everitt,
Everard; 'son of Everhault'; a var. of Éꝛꝺeᴀꝛáꝛꝺ,
q.v. Everard and Everhault were probably distinct
names, but they were supposed by the Normans to
be the same. Cf. Gerard and Gerald.

eᴀsmonn—VIII—*Estmund*, *Eetmond*, Esmond, Esmonde; 'son of Eastmund' (an Anglo-Saxon personal
name, written Estmunt in Domesday Book; 'Williel-
mus filius Estmundi' occurs in the Dublin Roll of
Names A.D. 1216). The Esmonds settled at an early
period in Co. Wexford. In 1303, Henry Estmund
was commissioned by Edward I to provide ships at
Wexford and elsewhere for the transporting of his
army to Scotland, and in 1371 Thomas Estmunde was

constable of Wexford castle. The family is at present represented by Sir Thomas H. G. Esmond.

eᴀꙅᴘoᴢ—XII—Aspig; Bishop; a translation, probably, of the English surname Bishop.

éᴀ́ᴛúɴ—XI—Eaton; i.e., 'of Eaton,' a common place-name in England.

éıbeᴀʀᴀ́ʀᴠ—VIII—Everard; 'son of Everard' (a Norman personal name, from the Frankish 'Eberhard,' 'Ebrard,' the same as the Anglo-Saxon 'Eoforheard' or 'Eoferard'). The Everards came to Ireland about the time of the Anglo-Norman invasion and settled in Meath and Tipperary. Both families were highly distinguished.

eıċınᴢeᴀm—XI—*Echingham*, Etchingham; i.e., 'of Etchingham' in England.

éıᴢeᴀʀ—VIII—Agar, Eagar, Egar.

eıméıᴠ—VIII—Emmet; 'son of Emmet' (dim. of Teutonic personal name Emmo); made famous for ever in Ireland by the patriot Robert Emmet.

ꝼᴀ́cnᴀʀ—XII—*Fauconer*, Falconer, Faulkner, etc.; Nor. 'le falconer,' 'le Faukener,' i.e., the falconer, keeper of falcons; a rather common surname in early Anglo-Irish records.

ꝼᴀᴠᴀ—IX—Fodha, Long; Ir. 'ꝼᴀᴠᴀ,' i.e., tall, long; a descriptive epithet which supplanted the real surname; very rare. Cf. bᴀ́n, beᴀᴢ.

ꝼᴀebeᴀċ—XIV—Fay. V. ᴠe ꝼᴀe.

ꝼᴀ́ᴢᴀ́n—VIII—*Fagane*, Fagan, Fagin; 'son of Pagan' (Lat. 'Paganus,' the rustic, the pagan, a personal name introduced into England by the Normans); the name of an old and respectable Anglo-Norman family who settled about the time of the invasion in Meath and Westmeath. To be distinguished from Ó ꝼᴀ́ᴢᴀ́ın and Ó ꝼᴀᴠᴠᴀᴢᴀ́ın, q.v.

ꝼᴀᴢᴀn, *Fyan*, Fyans, Foynes. V. ᴘᴀᴢᴀn and ꝼᴀ́ᴢᴀ́n, of which it is a variant.

ꝼᴀınín—VIII—*Fanyne*, Fannin, Fanning; a variant of ᴘᴀınín (q.v.) by the not uncommon change of ᴘ to

ᵱ; the name of an old Anglo-Norman family who
settled at an early period in many parts of the south
of Ireland. There were influential families of the
name in Limerick, Tipperary and Kilkenny.

ᵱᴀɪRꞅɪnᵹ—IX—*Farshinge*, Farshin, Fortune; Ir. 'ᵱᴀɪᵱ-
ᵱɪnᵹ,' i.e., generous; an epithet applied apparently
to members of the family of MacCarthy in West
Cork; very rare. Not the name of the Fortunes of
Leinster.

ᵱᴀʟᴄᴀċ—XIV—*Faltagh*, Wall; the adjectival form of
ᴅe ʋᴀʟ, q.v.

A.D. 1379—The Bishop of Meath, i.e., ᴀn ᵱᴀʟᴄᴀċ,
died in England—Four Masters.

A.D. 1588—Grant to Oliver Stephenson, of Don
Milline, of the manor of Donmilline, Co. Limerick,
parcel of the possession of Ulick de Wale alias the
Faltagh, of Donmillen, etc.—Fiants Eliz. 5242.

ᵱᴀnnᴄ—XII—*Faunte*, Fant; Nor. ' le Faunt,' a shortened
form of ' l'Enfant,' i.e., the child; a very common
surname in early Anglo-Irish records, but now rare.
A family of the name settled at Fantstown near Kilmallock.

ᵱᴀoɪᴄeᴀċ—XIV—White. V. ᴅe ᵱᴀoɪᴄ.

ᵱeɪRɪᴄéɪR, ᵱeɪRᴄéɪR—XII—*Firiter*, Ferriter; Nor.
' le Fureter,' i.e., the ferreter, probably a dealer in, or
manufacturer of, ferret or silk tape, if not one who
ferrets, or searches out like a ferret. (Cf. Fr. furet,
a ferret). The Ferreters settled in the 13th or 14th
century at Ballyferriter in Co. Kerry, where the name
still survives. Pierce Ferriter was a well-known
Irish poet.

ᵱeóɪRʟɪnᵹ—VIII—*Veerlin*, Verlin, Verling; ' son of
Feorthling' (an Anglo-Saxon personal name, made
Farthing by the Normans. ᵱeóɪᵱʟɪnᵹ is at the present
day the Irish for a farthing). ' Elias filius Rogeri fili
Farthini ' occurs in the Dublin Roll of Names, A.D.
1216; and Warinus Ferthing de Karlel was a member
of the Dublin Guild-Merchant A.D. 1226. The
family must have settled early in Co. Westmeath,

where Farthingstown marks their place of abode ; but for centuries back the name, under the form of Verlin and Verling has been peculiar to Co. Cork.

ꝼꞇꞯꝛꝏ, Feerick.   V. Mꞯc Pꞯꝑꞯꞇc.

ꝼꞇoꞃꞯmúꞯ—VIII—*Finamur*, Finamore, Finnamore, etc. ; 'son of Finamour ' (Fr. fin amour, fair love, perhaps a nickname).   Finamur appears as a surname in the Dublin Roll of Names, A.D. 1212.

ꝼꞇoꞃꞡꞇꞯꞅ, Finglas.   V. ꝺe ꝼꞇoꞃꞃꞡꞇꞯꝑ.

ꝼꞇoꞃꞃ—IX—Fair, Phair ; Ir. ' ꝼꞇoꞃꞃ,' fair ; a descriptive epithet which supplanted the real surname.   Cf. ꝺꞯꞃ, ꝺeꞯꞡ.

ꝼꞇoꞃꞃúꞇꝛ, ꝼꞇoꞃúꞇꝛ—XI—*Fynnor*, Fennors ; probably Nor. ' de Finnure,' i.e., of ꝼꞇoꞃꞃꞯꝺꞯꝑ, a frequent Irish place-name ; one of the small group of Norman surnames formed from Irish place-names.   There can hardly be any doubt about this derivation, but I have not discovered any early forms that would prove it.   The surname is an old one in Tipperary and Kilkenny.

ꝼꞇoꞇúꞃ—VIII—*Fitun*, Fitton, Fetton ; probably ' son of Fitun ' or ' Phitun ' (a Norman personal name). The surname came into Ireland about the time of the Anglo-Norman invasion.   ' Hereuic Fitun' occurs in the Dublin Roll of Names, A.D. 1216.   Sir Edward Fyton of Gawsworth in Cheshire was President of Connacht in the time of Elizabeth, and Sir Alexander Fytton was Lord Chancellor of Ireland in the time of James II.   There are a few families of the name still in Co. Limerick.

ꝼꞇꝛꞇcéꞇꝛ, ꝼꞇꝛcéꞇꝛ, *Firiter*, Ferriter.   V. ꝼeꞇꝑꞇcéꞇꝑ.

ꝼꞇꞇꞃꞇ—VIII—*Flynt*, Flint ; ' son of Flint,' a Teutonic personal name, found as a surname in Domesday Book.   It came into Ireland some time before the end of the 13th century, but has not extended beyond the City of Dublin.

ꝼꞇóꞇꝺ—XII—*Flode*, *Floyde*, Floyd, Flood ; merely the English pronunciation of the Welsh surname Lloyd.   The name is old in Ireland, but has never been very common.

ꝼoiꞃbis—XI—Forbes; i.e., 'of Forbes,' a parish in Aberdeenshire.

ꝼoiꞃéis, Forrest. V. ꝼuiꞃéaꞃꞇ.

ꝼóiséiꝺ, Faussett, Faussette, Fawcett, Fawcitt, Fawsitt, etc.

ꝼóꞃꝺ, ꝼóꞃꞇ—XII—*Forth*, Ford, Forde, etc.; Nor., 'le fort,' i.e., the strong; the name of an Anglo-Norman family who settled in Meath and Louth.

ꝼꞃainclín—XII—Franklin; Nor. 'le frankelein,' i.e., small freeholder. Walter le frankelein was one of the Free Citizens of Dublin, A.D. 1225-1250. The name is not uncommon in north-east Limerick and Tipperary.

ꝼꞃanncaċ—XII—Beausang; Ir. 'ꝼꞃanncaċ,' i.e., the Frenchman; a descriptive name given to the family of Beausang in Co. Cork who are of French origin.

ꝼꞃéine, v. ꝺe ꝼꞃéine.

ꝼꞃiseal—XII—*Fresell*, Frisell, Frizell, Frizzle, Fraser, Frazer, etc.; Nor. 'Frisel,' i.e., the Frisian, native of, or belonging to, Friesland. Simon Fressell came to England with William the Conqueror, and Richard Fresle was one of the tenants-in-chief at the time of the Domesday survey. The name came into Ireland about the time of the invasion. 'Vdardus Fresel' appears in the Dublin Roll of Names, A.D. 1216. Freiselston in Co. Meath was, no doubt, an early home of the family in Ireland. The Frasers were also a distinguished Scottish clan.

ꝼꞃiúin—VIII—Frewin, Frewen; 'son of Freowine,' an Anglo-Saxon personal name, frequent in Domesday Book.

ꝼúinse—VIII—*Founce, Fonce,* Finch, Funge; a variant of ꝼúinꞃe, by change of initial ꝓ to ꝼ; cf. ꝼainín, for ꝓainín, ꝼáꝷán for ꝓáꝷán. There is a possibility that the origin is from the obsolete English word 'fonce,' a knowing, cunning person, but the few instances that we have in Irish records are without the article 'le' or 'the.'

ꝼuiꞃéasꞇ—XI—Forrest, Frost; Eng. 'at the forest,'

from residence thereby. The name is common in Cork. Also ꝼoiṅéiṙ.

ꝼuiṙeᴀsᴄᴀl—XII—*Furestal*, Forestall, Forrestal, Forstall, Forrester, Forster; Lat. 'forestarius,' Eng. 'the forester,' i.e., the forest-keeper, custodian of the forest, very common in early Anglo-Irish records; the name of an Anglo-Norman family long settled in Kilkenny, the head of which held the manors of Kilferagh and Ballyfrunck; also of a family in Co. Wexford.

ꝼulᴀṙᴄún—XI—Fullarton, Fullerton; i.e., 'of Fullarton,' a Scottish place-name, in Lanarkshire or Ayrshire; the name of an old Scottish family who settled in Ireland in the 16th and 17th centuries.

ꝼúṙᴅ, *Foord*, Foorde, Forde, Ford; a variant of ꝼóṙᴅ, ꝼóṙᴄ, q.v. Foord of Foordston was one of the chief gentlemen of Meath in 1598.

ꝼuṙloᵹ—XI—*Forlong*, Furlong; Eng. 'at the furlong,' a division of an unenclosed corn-field, from residence therein or thereby; the name of an old and respectable Anglo-Irish family in Co. Wexford. Their chief seat was at Horestown, but they owned also the manors of Camross, Carrigmanan and Bridestown. The name is still common in Wexford.

ꝼuᴄṙᴀil—XI—Fottrell; i.e., 'of Futterill,' a village in Gloucester; the name of an Anglo-Irish family seated in Co. Dublin.

ᵹᴀᴅóiᴅ—VIII—Gabbott, Gabbett; 'son of Gabbot,' dim. of Gabriel.

ᵹᴀilliᴅe, Galway, Gallway, etc. V. ᴅe ᵹᴀilliᴅe.

ᵹᴀimlín—VIII—Gamlin, Gambling; 'son of Gamelin,' dim. of Gamel (v. ᵹᴀmᴀl). Gamelin occurs as a personal name in Domesday Book.

ᵹáiṙᴅín—XI—Gardin, Garden; i.e., 'at the garden,' from residence thereby.

ᵹáiṙnéiṙ—XII—*Gardener*, Gardiner, Gardner, Garner; Nor. 'le gardiner,' i.e., the gardener; an old surname in Ireland. 'Galfridus le gardiner' occurs in the Dublin Roll of Names A.D. 1216.

ᵹᴀⁱꙅᴛᴇᴀᴌ, Gatchell.

ᵹᴀᴌᴌ—XII—Gall, Gaul, Gaule; Ir. 'ᵹᴀᴌᴌ,' i.e., the foreigner, the Englishman; the designation, and later the name, of a branch of the Burkes, descended from the Red Earl of Ulster, who settled at Gaulstown in Co. Kilkenny. A branch of the family became famous in Austria.

ᵹᴀᴌᴌᴠʀᴇᴀᴛⁿᴀċ—X—Galbraith, Galbreath; i.e., the British or Welsh stranger; a surname of Scottish origin.

ᵹᴀᴌᴌᴠᴀ—IX—*Galdy, Gald, Galte*, Galt, Gault; Ir. 'ᵹᴀᴌᴌᴠᴀ,' i.e., the anglicised; a descriptive epithet which has supplanted the real name of the family, whatever that might have been; now very rare.

ᵹᴀᴌᴌᴠᴜᴠ—XII—*Galduf*, Stackpoole; Stapleton, Stapelton; Ir. 'ᵹᴀᴌᴌᴠᴜᴠ,' i.e., the black foreigner; an Irish designation of members of the family of Stackpoole, and sometimes of Stapleton.

ᵹᴀᴍᴠûⁿ—XII—Gambon, Gammon; Old Fr. 'gambon,' a leg (cf. English name Foote); an old, but rare, surname in Cork and Waterford.

ᵹᴀᴍᴀᴌ—VIII—Gamel, Gammel, Gambell, Gamble; 'son of Gamel,' a personal name of Scandinavian origin, frequent in Domesday Book. Cf. the Irish word ᵹᴀᴍᴀᴌ.

ᵹᴀꙅᴛûⁿ—VIII—*Gastun, Gastoun*, Gaston; 'son of Gaston,' (a Norman personal name apparently). The surname in Ireland dates back to the 13th century.

ᵹéᴀʀ—IX—*Geare*, Gayer; Sharpe; Ir. 'ᵹéᴀʀ,' i.e., sharp, bitter; an epithet which has supplanted the real surname.

ᵹᴇᴀʀᴀʀᴠ—VIII—Gerard, Gerrard; 'son of Gerard' (Teutonic Gerhard, a personal name introduced by the Normans, who regarded it as the same name as Gerald). The Gerrards were a Meath family.

ᵹᴇᴀʀᴠᴀꙅ—VIII—*Gervase, Gervaise*, Gervais, Gervis, Jervaise, Jarvis, Jervis; 'son of Gervase' (a Norman personal name of Teutonic origin). As a surname, it dates back in Ireland to the reign of Edward I.

ʒeᴀᴚᴅ, Garde. V. ᴅe ʒeᴀṗᴅ.

ʒeᴀᴚᴌᴀnn, Gairlan, Gartlan, Garland, Gartland, etc. ;
a corruption of ʒeᴀṗnún, q.v.

ʒeᴀᴚᴌún, *Garlowne, Garlone, Garlon*, Garlan, Garland,
etc. ; a corruption of ʒeᴀṗnún, q.v. ; now further
corrupted to ʒeᴀṗᴌᴀnn, q.v.

ʒeᴀᴚmán—VIII—German, Jarman, etc ; 'son of German,' a Norman personal name which appears oc-
casionally as Germain in early Anglo-Irish records.
V. ʒeᴀṗmonn.

ʒeᴀᴚmonn—VIII—Germon, Jermyn, etc. ; 'son of
Germund,' a Norman personal name. It is now
difficult to distinguish from ʒeᴀṗmán. Both names
appear in early Anglo-Irish records, but Germund
was much more frequent.

ʒeᴀᴚnún—XII—*Gernoun, Gernone, Garnon*, Gernon,
Garlan, Garland, etc. ; Nor. Fr. 'gernon,' 'guernon,'
i.e., a moustache, hence the wearer of a moustache ;
a nickname which became a surname. Robert
Gernon was one of the tenants-in-chief in England at
the time of the Domesday survey. The name came
into Ireland about the time of the invasion, and in
the 16th century was common in Louth, Meath and
Monaghan ; but it has long been corrupted to ʒeᴀṗᴌún
and then to ʒeᴀṗᴌᴀnn, q.v.

ʒeᴀᴚóᴅ—VIII—*Gerot, Garrott*, Garrett, Jerrett, etc. ;
'son of Gerald,' a common personal name among the
Normans, representing two or three distinct Teutonic
names, as Gerwald, Gerhold, and confused with
Gerard. V. ʒeᴀṗáṗᴅ.

ʒeᴀᴚᴚ—IX—Short ; Ir. 'ʒeᴀṗṗ,' i.e., short, low-sized ;
an epithet which took the place of the real surname
which is now lost.

ʒeᴀᴚᴚᴄóiᴚ—XII—Carver ; a translation of the English
surname Carver.

ʒiᴃ—VIII—Gibb ; 'son of Gib,' dim. of Gilbert.

ʒiᴌᴃeᴀᴚᴄ—VIII—Gilbert ; 'son of Gilbert,' a Norman
personal name of Teutonic origin. It appears in
Domesday Book in the Lat. form of 'Gislebertus.'

The dim. Gibbon, in Irish ᵹıobún, was the usual form of the name among the Anglo-Normans in Ireland, where, as a surname, Gilbert is not very old.

ᵹılleán—VIII—*Gillian*, Julian, Julien, and probably Gullion ; ' son of Julian ' (the Lat. Julianus, popularly Gillian), a personal name introduced by the Normans. Julianstown, Co. Meath, was probably the first home of the family in Ireland.

ᵹıobsán, ᵹıobson, Gibson.

ᵹıolcaċ, Reade, Reid, etc. ; a mistranslation of the English surname Reade, or Reid, which means simply ' the red,' from the complexion.

ᵹıoróıᴠ, v. ᵹeapóıᴠ.

ᵹlaıséıᴠ, Glassett.

ᵹlas—IX—Glass, Green ; Ir. ' ᵹlar,' i.e., green, grey from the complexion ; an epithet which supplanted the real surname. Cf. ᴠán, beaᵹ.

ᵹleanτún—XI—*Glanton*, Clinton ; i.e., ' of Glanton,' a parish in Northumberland ; wrongly re-anglicised Clinton.

ᵹléasúr—XII—Gleasure ; i.e., ' the glazier.'

ᵹoba—XII—*Gowe*, Gow, Smith; Ir. ' ᵹoba,' i.e., the smith a trade designation which took the place of the real surname. Cf. Ceápᴠ.

ᵹoċ—XII—*Goch*, Gogh, Gooch, Gough, Goff ; Welsh ' coch,' i.e., the red, from the complexion ; the name of a Welsh family who settled in Dublin and Water-ford.

ᵹoᵹán, ᵹóᵹan, *Gogane*, *Goggane*, Gogan, Goggan Goggin, etc. V. ᴠe Coᵹán.

ᵹoıᴠín—VIII—*Godyn*, *Goodin*, Goodwin, Godwin ; ' son of Godwine,' a very common personal name among the Anglo-Saxons.

ᵹoıséır—XII—Gosnall, Gosnell ; probably Ir. ' ᵹóıréır, a hosier, a dealer in stockings ; the name of a family of late English origin in West Cork who, perhaps first became known to the Irish as hosiers. Henry Gosnell was Queen's attorney in Munster in the reign of Elizabeth.

Góislín—VIII—Gosselin, Goslin, Gauslin, Gosling, Gostlin; 'son of Goscelin' (dim. of Goshelm, a Norman personal name, frequent in Domesday Book). Goslingstown in Co. Kilkenny commemorates the place of abode of the family in Ireland.

Górdún, Gordon. V. de Górdún.

Goṫḟraiḋ—VIII—*Godefraye, Godefrey,* Godfrey; 'son of Godfrey,' a Teutonic personal name, variously written as Gothfrith, Guthfrith, etc.; very common among the Normans, by whom it may be said to have been introduced into England, though as Gothfrith it was sometimes found among the Anglo-Saxons.

Goṫmonn—VIII—*Godmund, Gudmund,* Godman, Goodman; 'son of Godmund,' a Teutonic personal name, not uncommon among the Anglo-Saxons; also written Guthmund. Godman was also a personal name among the Anglo-Saxons, but in early Anglo-Irish records Godmund is the only form found.

Graḋar, Grier, Greir, Greer, etc.; a Mayo surname, doubtless a phonetic representation of the English surname Grier, Greir, etc. V. Mac Grioġair.

Grae, Grey, Gray. V. de Grae.

Gráinseaċ—XI—Grange; i.e., 'at the grange,' (barn, or farm-house) from residence in or thereby.

Gráinséir—XII—*Graunger,* Grainger, Granger; i.e., 'the granger,' the keeper of a grange or granary.

Gránda—IX—*Grany,* Granny, Grant; Ir. 'gránda,' i.e., ugly; an epithet which took the place of the real surname. It is, as might be expected, extremely rare.

Grandún, Grandon, Grandan. V. de Grandún.

Grannt, Grant. V. de Grannt.

Grás—XII—*Graas, Grase,* Grace; Fr. 'le gras,' i.e., the fat; the name of an ancient and distinguished Kilkenny family, said to be descended from Raymond le Gros, one of the companions of Strongbow. The Graces were certainly among the earliest of the Anglo-Norman settlers in Ireland. The head of the family had the title of Baron of Courtstown.

ᵹᴿᴇᴀᵹóıᴿ—VIII—Gregory ; ' son of Gregory.'

ᵹᴿıꝑín—VIII—*Griffine*, Griffin ; ' son of Gruffin ' (a common Welsh personal name, from the Latin ' Rufinus,' dim. of Rufus, i.e., of ruddy complexion. The Welsh equivalent of Rufus is Gruffud, or Gruffydd, whence Griffith, Griffiths. Grifin, son of Mariadoc, evidently a Welshman, was one of the tenants-in-chief in England at the time of the Domesday survey. Griffin is very common in early Anglo-Irish records, but Gruffud hardly occurs). The family settled in Ireland about the time of the Anglo-Norman invasion.

ᵹᴿomaıl, *Gromwell*, Grunnell. V. Cᴿomaıl.

ᵹuᴐ—XII—Good ; i.e., ' the good.'

ᵹuıᴐ—VIII—Guy ; ' son of Guy ' or ' Guido,' a Norman personal name.

ᵹuılıᴐe—VIII—Gooley, Goldie, Gouldy ; ' son of Goldie,' a pet form of Goldwine, an Anglo-Saxon personal name, Gola in Domesday Book.

ᵹuılín—VIII—Golding, Goulding, Golden, Goolden ; ' son of Goldewine,' or ' Goldwine ' (Lat. ' Goldinus') an Anglo-Saxon personal name. Under the form of Golding it came into Ireland soon after the Anglo-Norman invasion when the family settled in Dublin, Meath, Kildare, and parts of Munster.

ᵹuın—XII—Gwyn, Gwynn, Gwynne ; Welsh ' gwyn,' i.e., white, fair.

ᵹúl—VIII—*Gule, Goule, Goole, Gole, Gold*, Gould, Goold ; ' son of Golde,' an Anglo-Saxon personal name, found as Goldus in Domesday Book. The earliest form of the surname in Ireland was Gule : John Gule was a member of the Dublin Guild-Merchant, A.D. 1226 ; and about a century later Maurice Gule was one of the townsmen of Kilmallock. The Goulds appear to have settled at an early period in the city of Cork, where they were wealthy merchants and long one of the most influential families. No fewer than thirty of the name appear in the list of mayors of that city.

ᵹumᴀrᴄún, Gumbleton; probably only a variant of
Comᴀρᴄún, q.v.

ᵹunnᴀ—VIII—*Gunne*, Gunn, Gonne; 'son of Gunna,'
a personal name among the Anglo-Saxons, doubtless
a pet form of Gunnar.

ᵹunnᴀr—VIII—Gunner; 'son of Gunnar,' a very
common personal name among the Anglo-Saxons,
perhaps of Norse origin.

ᓏᴀcᴀeᴅ, ᓏᴀ1céiᴅ—VIII—*Hackede, Haket*, Hackett;
'son of Haket' (a Norman personal name). The
Hacketts came into Ireland at the time of the Anglo-
Norman invasion and settled in Dublin, Wicklow,
Kilkenny, Tipperary, etc. The name occurs frequently
in early Anglo-Irish records.

ᓏᴀ1cín—VIII—*Haukyn*, Hawkins; 'son of Halkin,'
dim. of Harry.

ᓏᴀ1mlín—VIII—*Hamelyn*, Hamlin, Hamlyn, etc.; 'son
of Hamelin' (double dim. of Hamo). This family
came to Ireland in the 13th century and settled in
Dublin and Meath. Hamlen of Smythstown was one
of the chief gentlemen of Meath in 1598.

ᓏᴀirᴅín—VIII—*Hardeyne, Hardyn*, Harding, Hardinge;
'son of Heardwine' (an Anglo-Saxon name; not
from 'Harding,' another Anglo-Saxon name, as the
older forms show); an old surname in Ossory and
Ormond.

ᓏᴀ1r1s—VIII—*Harishe, Harreis*, Harris; a phonetic
rendering of the English surname Harris. There
are, no doubt, many old families of the name in Ireland.

ᓏᴀlᴀᴅóiᴅ, *Holywode, Holywood*, Hollywood. V. ᴅe
ᓏᴀlᴀᴅóiᴅ.

ᓏᴀlᴅuiᴅe, ᓏᴀluiᴅe, Halvey, Holoway, Hollway, etc.
V. ᴅe ᓏᴀlᴅuiᴅe.

ᓏᴀmᴀlᴄún, *Hamleton*, Hamilton. V. ᴅe ᓏᴀmᴀlᴄún.

ᓏᴀmon—VIII—*Hamon, Hammon*, Hammond; 'son of
Hamo,' Norman 'Hamon,' a common personal name
in early Anglo-Irish records. Soon after the invasion
we find the names of 'Adam filius Hamonis' and

'Teboldus filius Haim' in the Dublin Roll. The surname cannot now be distinguished from ḣámonn, q.v.

ḣámonn—VIII—*Hamund, Hammound,* Hammond; 'son of Heahmund' (an Anglo-Saxon personal name, Old Norse Hamundr, a name in use among the Danes of Dublin before the Anglo-Norman invasion). About the year 1174, Hamund, son of Torkill, was granted, on behalf of King Henry II, Censale and adjacent lands, held by him before the arrival of the English in Ireland. Families named Hammond also settled early in Louth, Meath and Limerick. V. ḣamon which is of a distinct origin, but cannot now be distinguished from ḣámonn.

ḣamróc, ḣamróg, Hamrock, Hamrogue; probably 'of Hambrook,' older Hambroke, a hamlet in Gloucestershire. There was a Hamrockstown in Waterford or Cork. V. Seampóg.

ḣancárd, Hankard; an old, but rare, surname in Co. Cork, the origin of which I cannot trace. Perhaps connected with Tankard.

ḣancóc—VIII—*Hancok,* Hancock, Handcock; 'son of Hancok,' i.e., little John, from the short form Han (for Johannes) and the dim. suffix. The Hancocks were a Dublin family.

ḣaol—VIII—*Howel,* Howell, Howels; 'son of Howel' (a Welsh personal name); the name of a Welsh family which came into Ireland as early as the 13th century. V. mac ḣaol.

ḣaróid—VIII—*Haroud,* Harrot, Harwood, Harold, Harrold; 'son of Harold.' V. Áralt and Aróid.

ḣarpúr, Harpur, Harper. V. ṿe ḣarpúr.

ḣart—XII—Hart, Harte; i.e., 'the hart.'

ḣearman—VIII—*Herman,* Harman, Harmon, Hardman, Herdman; 'son of Hereman' (a Teutonic personal name). This surname came into Ireland in the 13th or early 14th century.

ḣearún—XII—*Herun, Heyrun, Heyron,* Heron, Hearon, Herron, Hearn, Hearne, Herne, etc.; Mid. Eng. 'herun,' i.e., the heron, one with long slender legs and

neck like a heron. This surname in Ireland dates
back to the early 13th century, but does nor appear
to have been ever very common, and was confined
to S. Leinster.

ħeiбeᴀʀᴄ—XII—*Heyward, Haward*, Hayward, Howard;
Nor. ' le Hayward,' i.e., keeper of the fences (from
' hay ' a hedge, and ' ward,' a guard) ; an old surname
in Ireland, but very rare, and now disguised as
Howard.

ħiбeᴀʀᴅ, *Hibbard*, Hubbard ; a var. of ħoiбeᴀpᴅ, q.v.

ħioбᴀʀᴅ,*Hibbard*, Hubbard, Hubbert, Hubbart, Hobart,
Hobert, and sometimes incorrectly Howard ; a var.
of ħoбᴀpᴅ or ħoiбeᴀpᴅ, q.v.

ħiosᴀe, Hussey. V. ᴅe ħúpᴀe. The correctness of
this form of the surname, which I got from an old
Irish speaker, is corroborated by the fact that Hissey
is still a var. of Hussey in England.

ħoб—VIII—*Hobbe, Hoppe*, Hop, Hobbs, Hope ; ' son
of Hob,' (a short form of Robert). The Hopes were
once an influential family about Mullingar.

ħoбᴀc, ħoбuc—VIII—*Hobbok, Hobbuge*, Hubbock ;
' son of Hobac ' (dim. of Hob, i.e., Robert). This
surname was formerly in use in Co. Cork, but was
always extremely rare, and is now probably obsolete.

ħoбᴀcán—VIII—*Hobbocane*, Habbagan ; ' son of
ħoбᴀcán ' (double dim. of Hob, i.e., Robert) ;
an old surname in Ireland, but always extremely rare.

ħoбᴀʀᴅ—VIII—*Hobbard*, Hobart, Hubbard ; a var. of
ħoiбeᴀpᴅ, q.v.

ħoᴅ—VIII—*Hod, Hode*, Hoad, Hoade ; probably ' son
of Hod ' or ' Hoda ' (an Anglo-Saxon personal name.
' Hod ' was also an Anglo-Saxon word meaning
a hood, cap, or helmet). John Hod was a member
of the Dublin Guild-Merchant, A.D. 1226. The name,
which was very rare, survives in Co. Mayo.

ħoᴅnᴀe—XI—*Hodney, Hodynet*, Hodnett, Hadnett ;
i.e., ' of Hodnet,' a parish in Shropshire. The Hod-
nets settled at Courtmacsherry, near Timoleague,
in Co. Cork. They assumed the Irish patronymic

298

surname of Mac Séanta (q.v.). Courtmacsherry is still called in Irish Cúinc 'ic Séantaiġ.

hoibeáro—VIII—*Hebbard, Habert,* Habbert, Hobart, Hobert, Hubbert, Hubbard, Herbert ; ' son of Herbert,' not ' son of Hubert,' as one would be inclined to make it. It was a var. of hoineabáno (q.v.), and was formerly common in Limerick and Cork.

hoileabáro—VIII—*Halberd,* Helbert, Hilbert, Helbet ; ' son of Halbert,' (perhaps for Anglo-Saxon Haligbeort, if not a corruption of Heldbeorht or Hildebeorht, names found in Searle). The surname is old in Ireland. Robert Halberd was a member of the Dublin Guild-Merchant in 1226.

hoirbín—VIII—Harbin ; ' son of Harbin,' dim. of Herbert.

hoireabáro, hoireabáro—VIII—*Herbard,* Herbert, Harbert, Harberd ; ' son of Herbert ' (a Norman personal name, already very common among the Anglo-Saxons as Herebeorht). The Herberts came into Ireland about the time of the Anglo-Norman invasion and settled in Kildare, Meath and Limerick. V. hiobáro, hobáro, and hoibeáro, which are variants.

hoireabáro—VIII—Hereward, Herward ; ' son of Hereweard ' (an Anglo-Saxon personal name) ; an old surname in Ireland. ' Adam Hereward ' occurs in the Dublin Roll of Names, A.D. 1216, and somewhat later in the same century Simon Hereward was mayor of Limerick.

hoiste—VIII—Hodge, Hogg, Hogge ; ' son of Hodge,' i.e., Roger. V. Mac hoirte.

hoisticín—VIII—*Hosteken,* Hotchkin, Hodgkin ; ' son of Hodgkin,' i.e., little Roger. Cf. Mac Oirticín.

hólt—VIII—Holt, Holte ; ' son of Holt ' (a personal name, or nickname, apparently of Norse origin, found in Domesday Book) ; an old surname still in use in Kildare and Wicklow. It is to be distinguished from the Anglo-Norman surname ' le Holde,' i.e., the freeholder, which was in use in Ireland in the 13th century when William de Holde was one of the townsmen of Kilmallock.

hubuc, Hubbock. V. hobac.

huʒúin—VIII—Huggins; 'son of Hugin' or 'Hugon' (dim. of Hugh). Huguin and Hugon are still French surnames.

húiʒério—VIII—Hewett, Hewitt, Huet, etc.; 'son of Hughet,' i.e., little Hugh; a surname which first came into Ireland in the 13th century.

húiʒlério, v. húiléro.

húiʒlín, v. húilín.

húiléro—VIII—Hewlett, Hewlitt, Huleat, Howlett, etc.; 'son of Hughelet' (double dim. of Hugh); the name of an Anglo-Norman family who settled in Co. Kildare.

húilín—VIII—Howlen, Howlin, Howling, Holing; 'son of Hughelin' (double dim. of Hugh); the name of an Anglo-Norman family who settled early in Wexford and Kilkenny.

huiste, Hutch; a var. of hoirte, q.v.

huiteacáin, Hutchinson; a phonetic rendering of Hutchinson.

hunfraió—VIII—Humfrey, Humphrey; 'son of Hunfrid' (a Teutonic personal name, long corrupted to Humfrid and Humphrey). This surname came into Ireland soon after the Anglo-Norman invasion. There is a Humphreystown in Co. Wicklow. Also unfraió, q.v.

hunt—XII—Hunt; Nor. 'le Honte,' 'le Hunte,' i.e., the huntsman; the name of an Anglo-Norman family who came to Ireland about the time of the invasion and settled in Dublin and Meath. It was never very common. Nearly all our Hunts are of native origin.

húsae, *Husee*, Hussey. V. de húrae.

iacob—VIII—Jacob; 'son of Jacob.'

iaʒó—VIII—Iago, Jago, Jagoe; 'son of Jago' (a form of Jacob, in use in Britain from ancient times). The surname is found chiefly in Co. Cork. Cf. mac iaʒó.

1ᴀᴦlᴀιᴅe, Earls; a translation of the English 'Earls.'
1ᴀᴦsᴀċ, Eyre, Eyres, Ayres.
1ηɴᴈléιs, 1ηɴᴈlιs, Inglis, English. V. ᴀιηɴᴈléιᴦ.
íηηseᴀᴅún, Nugent. V. uιηηᴦeᴀᴅún.
1oηᴈᴦᴀm—VIII—Ingram; 'son of Ingram.'
íᴦéιs, Irish. V. ᴅe íᴘéιᴦ.
íᴦleoηᴄ, *Irlond*, Ireland. V. ᴅe íᴘleoηᴄ.
1úsᴄás—VIII—Eustace, etc.; 'son of Eustace' (a
common personal name in France, introduced into
England by the Normans). The Eustaces came to
Ireland at the time of the Anglo-Norman invasion,
and obtained large estates in the counties of Kildare
and Carlow. They were one of the leading families
of the Pale, and many of them attained to high distinction. In 1580, James Eustace, Viscount Bal-
tinglas, took up arms in defence of the Catholic faith
and, together with the O'Byrnes and O'Tooles, in-
flicted a crushing defeat on Lord Grey at Glenmalure,
in the autumn of the same year. On the failure of
the rising he, a few years later, fled to Spain. His
estates and those of his followers were confiscated,
and many of them were put to death. The confiscations and attainders of the 17th century completed
the ruin of the family.

lᴀᴅᴦᴀηᴄ, lᴀᴅᴦás—VIII—Larens, Lawrence, etc.; 'son
of Laurence' (Lat. Laurentius), a rather common personal name among the early Anglo-Norman invaders.
lᴀᴦáη—XII—*Lanfant, Lenfaunt, Leffaine, Laffane*,
Laffan, Laffen, Laphin, etc.; Nor. 'l'Enfant,' i.e., the
child, probably applied to a person of guileless disposition; the name of old and respectable families
in Tipperary and Wexford. James Laffan of Grays-
ton was sheriff of Tipperary in the reign of Elizabeth;
and in 1598, Laffan of the Slade (Slade Castle) was
one of the principal gentlemen of Co. Wexford.
lᴀιᴅιᴦ—IX—*Lader, Laudir*, Lauder, Lawder; Ir.
'lᴀιᴅιᴘ,' i.e., strong, powerful; a descriptive epithet
which took the place of the real surname; very rare.

301

Laiġléis—XII—*Lageles, Lagheles, Laweles,* Lawless, Lillis, etc.; Mid. Eng. 'Laghles,' i.e., the lawless, the outlaw; the name of a family who came into Ireland about the time of the Anglo-Norman invasion and ramified through Leinster and Munster. A branch also settled in Tirawley, Co. Mayo. In Connacht it is sometimes corrupted to Laiġnéir, and in Munster to Laoiġléir and Lilear, q.v.

Laiġneaċ—X—*Leynagh,* Lynagh, Linagh, generally, but incorrectly, Lynam in Offaly, and Lyons in Mayo; Ir. 'Laiġneaċ,' i.e., the Leinsterman; a descriptive epithet which has supplanted the real surname.

Laimbeart—VIII—*Lamberde,* Lambart, Lambert; 'son of Lambart' or 'Lambert' (a Teutonic personal name; both forms occur in Domesday Book). The surname is old in Ireland, but apparently confined to Dublin. To be distinguished from Lamport, q.v.

Laimbín—VIII—Lambin, Lambyn; 'son of Lambin,' a dim. of Lambert.

Laitín—VIII—*Latin, Lattine,* Latten; 'son of Latin' (a personal name in Domesday Book). In Ireland, the surname was very rare and peculiar to Co. Kildare. The Rev. J. Latin was a priest of the diocese of Kildare in 1612.

Lálaide—XI—Lawlee; i.e., 'of Lawley,' a parish in Shropshire; a rare West Limerick surname; written Lawley in England where it is not uncommon.

Lamport—XI—*Lamport,* Lampart, Lampert, Lambert; i.e., 'of Lamport,' a parish in Northamptonshire, but confused with Laimbeart, q.v. The Lamports were an old Wexford family.

Langford—XI—Langford; Nor. 'de Langeford,' i.e., of Langford, a common place-name in England. I can find no instance of the surname in Ireland earlier than the 16th century.

Langtún, Langton. V. de Langtún.

Lannt—VIII—*Launt, Launte, Lownt,* Lant; 'son of Lant' (an Anglo-Saxon personal name, found in Domesday Book as the name of a landholder in the time of Edward the Confessor). Lant is an old Kilkenny surname.

Laoide, *Loyde,* Lloyd; a var. of Lóid, q.v.

Laoighléis, Lawless, Lillis. V. Laighléis.

Leabhailin — VIII — Lavallin, Lavallen; 'son of Llywelyn' (a Welsh personal name). The Lavallins have been settled in Cork for more than three centuries.

Léadar, Leader; a late English surname in Co. Cork.

Léadús, Ledwich, Ledwith, etc. V. de Léadús.

Leaindí, Landy.

Leamhnach—X—*Levenach,* Leynox, Lennox, Linnox; Ir. 'Leamhnach,' i.e., a native of, or connected with, Lennox in Scotland; the name of a Scottish family who settled in the north of Ireland, probably at the time of the plantation of Ulster.

Leaslaoi, Leslie, Lesley. V. de Liosla.

Leastar, Lester, Lister, Lyster. V. de Leastar.

Léighinn, Lane. V. de Léighinn.

Léiseach—XIV—Lacy, Lacey. V. de Léis.

Liaigh—XII—*Leche,* Leech, Leach; Mid. Eng. 'leche,' i.e., physician, the same as the Irish liaigh; an old surname in Ireland.

Liath—IX—*Leagh,* Lea, Lee, Gray, Grey; Ir. 'Liath,' i.e., grey, hoary; an epithet which supplanted the real surname. Cf. Bán, Dubh, etc.

Libhéid, Lovett, Lovitt; a var. of Luibhéid, q.v.

Lileas, *Lelasse, Leales, Liales, Lylles,* Lillis; a var. in Limerick and Cork of Laighléis, q.v.

Liobhóid—VIII—Livott, Lyvott; probably 'son of Lovot' (dim. of Love, same as Lovet, a common Norman personal name); an old Mayo surname.

Lionárd—VIII—*Leonarde,* Leonard; 'son of Leonard.' This surname is very rare in Ireland, nearly all our Leonards being of native origin.

Liongárd, Lingard.

Lionóid—VIII—*Lynoid, Lynod,* Lynott; 'son of Lionot' (possibly a dim. of Leonard, certainly from the same root, and meaning 'little lion.' Cf. Lionel which is another diminutive). The Lynotts settled at an early period in Tirawley, Co. Mayo.

Liosⅽúⁿ, *Listowne,* Liston. V. ꝺe Lⁱoⅽⅽúⁿ.

Loꝺaoⁱs—VIII—*Lowyes, Lowes, Lewes,* Lewis; 'son of Lewis' (for Fr. Louis, a common personal name representing the older Clovis, from the latinised form, 'Chlodovisus,' of the old Frankish Hludwig, mod. German Ludwig). This family came into Ireland about the time of the Anglo-Norman invasion and settled in Dublin, Kildare, Wexford, Waterford, Cork, Limerick, etc. 'Lewes of Leweston,' also called 'Lowes of Lowston,' was one of the principal gentlemen of Co. Wexford in 1598.

Locárꝺ—VIII—*Locard, Loccard, Lokard,* Lockard, Lockart, etc.; 'son of Locard' (a French personal name, from Teutonic Lochard). This surname came into Ireland about the time of the Anglo-Norman invasion. About the year 1200, Jordan Loccard was witness to a grant by Philip de Nugent to Holy Trinity Church, Dublin. There is a Ballylockard, or Lockardstown, in Co. Westmeath which was probably the first home of the family in Ireland.

Lóⁱꝺ—XII—*Loyde,* Lloyd; Welsh 'lluyd,' i.e., grey; a well-known surname of Welsh origin. Also Lúⁱꝺ and Laoⁱꝺe, q.v.

Lomɓárꝺ—XII—Lombard, Lumbard; Nor. 'le Lombard,' i.e., native of Lombardy, but later 'lombard' came to mean a banker, money-lender, or pawnbroker. There were old and respectable merchant families of the name in Cork, Waterford and Buttevant. At the beginning of the 17th century, Peter Lombard was Archbishop of Armagh and Primate of Ireland.

Lonꝺrać—XIV—*Londragh,* Landers, Launders. V. ꝺe Lonꝺra.

Lonꝺrasać—XIV—Landers, Launders. V. ꝺe Lonꝺⱥⱥr.

Lonȝꝼorⅽ, Langford.

Loⅽairéⁱl, Loⅽrail—VIII—*Loterell, Luterell,* Lutterell, Lutterel, Luttrell; 'son of Lutherel' (dim. of Lothar or Lothaire, a Frankish personal name). This surname appears in England soon after the Norman Conquest. Sir Geoffrey Lutterell received from King John an estate in the valley of the Liffey which from him took the name of Luttrellstown, and was for centuries the home of his descendants. Branches of the family settled in Meath and Kildare. The Luttrells were one of the chief families of the Pale.

lúcás—VIII—Lucas, Luke; 'son of Luke.' Lucas, not Luke, was the early form of the name.

luibéio—VIII—Lovett, Lovitt, Lovat, Levett; 'son of Lovet' (dim. of Love, a Norman personal name, which came into England with William the Conqueror). As a surname it came into Ireland about the time of the Anglo-Norman invasion.

luibéil—VIII—Lovel; 'son of Lovel' (dim. of Love, a Norman personal name. It occurs in Domesday Book. Cf. Lovet which is another diminutive of the same). As a surname it was rare in Ireland, and found chiefly in Kilkenny.

lúio—XII—Lloyd; Welsh 'lluyd,' i.e., grey; also lóio and laoioe, q.v.

lúiséio—VIII—Lucid, Lucet; probably 'son of Lucet' (dim. of Lucas); an old, but rare, Kerry surname.

lunorasac—XIV—Landers, Launders. V. oe lonorar.

máb—VIII—Mabe; 'son of Mab' (short for Mabel). V. máp.

mac 'a brígoe, MacBride; a shortened form in the spoken language of mac giolla brígoe, q.v.

mac 'a buioe, MacAvoy, MacEvoy, etc.; a shortened form of mac giollabuioe, q.v.

mac áoa, mac áoaio—V—McCada, MacCady, MacCadie, MacKady, Muckady, Cady; [Addy, Addison]; 'son of Addy' (a pet form of Adam); very rare. Addison is the English equivalent.

mac áoaim, mac áoaim—V—MacAdam, MacCadam, MacCaddam, MacAdams, Adams, [Adamson]; 'son of Adam' (one of the commonest names among the early Anglo-Norman settlers in Ireland); an Irish

patronymic surname assumed by the Barrys of Rath-
cormac and Ballynagloch, Co. Cork, and other early
Anglo-Norman settlers.

mac Áoaiṁ—V—MacCaw; 'son of Adam'; the same as
mac Áoaim (q.v.), but from an earlier Gaelic form
of the personal name.

mac Aoáin—V—*M'Caddane, M'Coddan*, MacCadden,
MacCudden, etc.; 'son of Adan' (a dim. of Adam);
a rare and scattered surname. Cf. mac Áioín.

mac Aoamóio—V—Adams; 'son of Adamot' (a dim.
of Adam); a rare Connacht surname.

mac Aibisⴗín—V—Caviston, [Austin, Austen]; 'son
of Augustine' (a name in use among the Anglo-Norman settlers); a rare surname which was, doubtless,
assumed by an offshoot of some Anglo-Irish family.

mac Aiḃne—IV—*M'Aveny, M'Eveny*, MacEvinney,
MacAvinue, MacAvenue; 'son of Aiḃne' (a personal
name peculiar to the families of O'Kane and O'Brallaghan of Derry); the name of a branch of the
O'Kanes.

mac Áioín—V—*M'Adin, M'Aden*, Caden, Cadden; 'son
of Adin' (dim. of Adam); very rare; corrupted in the
spoken language to Ó Cáioín, q.v.

mac Aioicín—V—Adkins, Atkins, Adkinson, Atkinson,
etc.; 'son of Adkin' (a dim. of Adam). Cf. mac
Aiⴗiⴃín.

mac Aileáin—IV—*M'Elean,M'Elane, M'Ilean,M'Ellen,
M'Kilan*, MacAlean, MacClean, MacLean, MacKellan,
MacKellen, MacKillen, etc.; 'son of Aileán'; a var. of
mac Ailín, q.v.; a scattered surname in Ulster and
Connacht. The following entry in the Fiants of Elizabeth throws some light on its origin: A.D. 1602—
Pardon to Elin M'Elane, kern, (in Co. Armagh). The
family is probably an offshoot of the MacDonnells
or Campbells. See also mac Coiteáin and mac Coilín.

mac Ailⴃile—IV—*M'Alylly*, MacAlilly, Callily, Lilly;
'son of Ailⴃil'; the name of a branch of the Maguires
in Co. Fermanagh.

mac Ailín—IV—*M'Aline, M'Alline*, MacAllion, MacAllen,

MacAllon, MacEllin, MacEllen, etc. ; 'son of ᴀɪⱡín ';
the name of a branch of the Campbells of Scotland,
some of whom were brought over by the O'Donnells
as fighting-men, about the middle of the 16th century,
and settled in Tirconnell. This surname easily got
confused with ꝏᴀc Cᴀɪⱡín, q.v.

ꝏᴀc ᴀɪⱡpín—IV—MacAlpine, MacAlpin, MacCalpin ;
'son of ᴀɪⱡpín '; a surname probably of Scottish
origin. The MacAlpins claim to be the most ancient
of the Highland clans.

ꝏᴀc ᴀɪnᴅᴦéɪꞱ, ꝏᴀc ᴀɪnᴅᴦɪᴀꞱᴀ—V—MacAndrew,
[Ross] ; 'son of Andrew' (Lat. Andreas) ; a Gaelic
patronymic surname assumed by the Scottish family
of Ross.

ꝏᴀc ᴀɪnᴅᴦɪú—V—MacAndrew, [Andrewson, Anderson,
Andrews, Anders] ; 'son of Andrew ' ; an Irish patron-
ymic assumed by a branch of the Barretts of Tirawley,
Co. Mayo, who were seated in the district called the
Two Bacs, lying between Lough Conn and the River
Moy. It is now angl. MacAndrew, and is very com-
mon in the district.

ꝏᴀc ᴀɪnꝏíᴦe—IV—M'Anavero, MacConvery, Convery ;
'son of ᴀɪnꝏíᴦe.' Cf. Ó hᴀɪnꝏíᴦe, angl. O'Hanvire.

ꝏᴀc ᴀɪᴦᴄ—IV—M'Art, M'Arte, MacCart, (MacArthy,
Hart, Harte,) ; 'son of ᴀᴦᴄ ' ; very rare.

ꝏᴀc ᴀɪᴦᴄeáɪn—IV—M'Keartan, M'Curtaine, M'Curtayne, Curtayne, Curtain, Curtin, etc. ; 'son of ᴀᴦᴄán '
(dim. of ᴀᴦᴄ) ; an attenuated form of ꝏᴀc ᴀᴦᴄáɪn,
q.v. ; peculiar to Co. Cork. V. also ꝏᴀc Cᴀɪᴦᴄeáɪn.

ꝏᴀc ᴀɪᴄɪʒín—V—Cattigan ; 'son of Atkin' ; a Mayo
surname ; in the spoken language Uᴀ Cᴀɪᴄɪʒín. Cf.
ꝏᴀc ᴀᴅᴏɪcín.

ꝏᴀc ᴀⱡᴀꞱᴄᴀɪᴦ—V—M'Alaster, MacAlister, MacAllister,
MacCallister, MacEllister, MacAlester, M'Closter, Mac-
Clester, MacLester, Callister, Lester, etc. ; 'son of
ᴀⱡᴀꞱᴄáᴦ,' (a Gaelic form of Alexander) ; the name of
a branch of the MacDonalds, long settled in Co.
Antrim.

ꝏᴀc ᴀⱡᴀꞱᴄᴦuɪꝏ—V—M'Alastrom, M'Alastrum, M'El-

listrom, MacElistrum, MacElestrim, MacEllistram, etc. ; ' son of ᴀᴌᴀᴦᴄᴩoᴍ ' (a Gaelic form of Alexander) ; a var. of ᴍᴀᴄ ᴀᴌᴀᴦᴄᴀᴉᴩ, q.v. This form of the surname is peculiar to Kerry, where the family has been settled for centuries.

ᴍᴀᴄ ᴀᴌᴌᴍᴜᴦᴀ́ɴ—IV—Colleran ; ' son of ᴀᴌᴌᴍᴜᴩᴀ́ɴ ' ; found in parts of Connacht ; probably the correct original of Ó Cᴀᴌᴌᴀᴩᴀ́ɴ, q.v.

ᴍᴀᴄ ᴀᴌsᴀɴ'ᴏᴀɪʀ—V—*M'Alexander, M'Alesandre*, Mac-Alshander, MacAlshender, MacAlshinder, MacCalshander, MacElshander, MacKalshander, Alexander, etc. ; ' son of Alexander,' (a not uncommon personal name among the Normans, specially common in Scotland). The surname, which came to us from Scotland, has assumed a great variety of forms. V. ᴍᴀᴄ ᴀᴌᴀᴦᴄᴀᴉᴩ and ᴍᴀᴄ ᴀᴌᴀᴦᴄᴩᴜɪᴍ, which are varients.

ᴍᴀᴄ ᴀ́ᴍoɪɴɴ—V—MacCammon, MacCammond, Mac-Kemman, Hammond, [Hammondson] ; ' son of Amundr ' (a Norse personal name) ; a surname of Norse origin.

ᴍᴀᴄ ᴀᴍᴀᴌᴣᴀᴏ́ᴀ, ᴍᴀᴄ ᴀᴍᴀᴌᴣᴀɪᴏ́—IV—MacAulay, MacAuley, MacCauley, MacCowley, Cawley, etc. ; ' son of ᴀᴍᴀᴌᴣᴀɪᴏ́ ' (an ancient Irish personal name). There are several distinct families of this name, the best known being that of Co. Westmeath, the head of which was formerly lord of Calraighe, comprising the whole of the parish of Ballyloughloe, in the west of that county. It is sometimes impossible to distinguish the angl. forms of this surname from those of ᴍᴀᴄ ᴀᴍᴌᴀoɪᴏ, q.v. V. also ᴍᴀᴣ ᴀᴍᴀᴌᴣᴀᴏ́ᴀ, which is a variant.

ᴍᴀᴄ ᴀᴍᴏ́ʀᴏ́ɪs—V—MacAmbrose, MacCambridge ; ' son of Ambrose ' ; a rare surname of Scottish origin.

ᴍᴀᴄ ᴀɪ́ᴍᴌᴀoɪᴏ—V—MacAuliffe, MacAuley, MacCauliffe, MacCauley, MacCawley, MacCowley, Cawley, Cowley, etc. ; ' son of ᴀɪ́ᴍᴌᴀoɪᴏ ' (an Irish form of the Norse Olaf). There are three well-known families of this name : (1) ᴍᴀᴄ ᴀɪ́ᴍᴌᴀoɪᴏ, angl. MacAuliffe, of Co. Cork, a branch of the MacCarthys. The head of this family resided at Castle MacAuliffe, near Newmarket, and his territory comprised the district lying between Newmarket and the boundaries of the counties of Limerick and Kerry. (2) Mac Amlaoiḃ of Fermanagh, a branch of the Maguires, whose territory comprised the barony of Clanawley. And (3) Mac Amlaoiḃ, angl. MacAulay, of Scotland. The chief seat of this family was at Ardincaple, in Dumbartonshire. A branch of the family settled in Co. Antrim, and many of the Mac-Aulays of the north of Ireland are of this stock. To it belonged also the celebrated Lord Macaulay.

Mac Anaḃáḋa—VII—*M'Anaboy*, *M'Annovoy*, Mac-Naboe, Monaboe, (MacAnabb, MacNabb), and, by 'translation,' Victory; 'son of the premature' (Ir. 'anaḃaiḋ,' unripe); a Breifney surname. It appears to have been early corrupted to Mac na Buaḋa, on the erroneous supposition that it was derived from 'Buaiḋ,' victory, and has been accordingly sometimes 'translated' Victory. It is also apt to be confused with Mac an Aḃḃaḋ, q.v.

Mac an Aḃḃaḋ—VII—*M'an Abba*, *M'Enabb*, Mac-Anabb, MacNabb; 'son of the abbot.' The MacNabbs are mostly of Scottish descent, apparently very few of the name being Irish. They were a branch of the MacKinnons, and at one time a clan of considerable importance.

Mac an Aḋastair, Mac an Aġastair, *M'Innester*, Nestor; a shortened form of Mac Ġiṗṗ an Aḋartair, Mac Ġiṗṗ an Aġartair, q.v.

Mac an Ailín, *M'Enallen*, MacAnallen, Nallen; 'son of——'; a rare surname in Ulster and Connacht, the origin of which I cannot trace. The above represents the pronunciation as I heard it.

Mac an Airċinn, *M'Enarhin*, *M'Enerin*, *M'Kinnertin*, *M'Naryn*, MacAnern, MacNern, MacNairn, MacKinerkin, Kinnerk; a shortened form of Mac an Airċinniġ, q.v.; also Mac an Oirċinn.

Mac an Airċinniġ—VII—MacAnerney, MacEnerney, Mac-Inerney, MacNerhenny, MacNerney, MacNirney, Mac-

Nertney, Connerney, Kenerney, Kinerney, Nerhenny, Nerney, Nertney, Nirney, etc.; 'son of the erenagh' (Ir. 'ᴀɪⱤᴄɪⲛⲛeᴀċ', steward of church lands); the name of several distinct families, each an offshoot of one or other of the great erenagh families. The Roscommon family of the name, who are apparently a branch of the family of Ó ᴠⱤᴀⲛáɪⲛ (q.v.), were erenaghs of St. Patrick's church at Elphin. The Thomond family, who are numerous in Clare and Limerick, formerly held considerable property in the parish of Ballysally, but lost it in the Cromwellian confiscations. The above is the literary form of this surname, but ᵯᴀᴄ ᴀⲛ OɪⱤᴄɪⲛⲛɪᴢ, often shortened to ᵯᴀᴄ ᴀⲛ OɪⱤᴄɪⲛⲛ, has long been the popular form.

ᵯᴀᴄ ᴀⲛ ᴀꙅᴛⱤɪᴢ—VII—MacKinestry, MacKinstry, Mac-Nestry, ; 'son of the traveller' (Ir 'ᴀɪⱤᴛⱤɪᴢᴛeᴀċ'); an Ulster surname, probably of Scottish origin.

ᵯᴀᴄ ᴀⲛ áᴛᴀ, MacAnawe; Ford, Forde; a corruption of ᵯᴀᴄ Coⲛⲋⲛáᵯᴀ, q.v.

ᵯᴀᴄ ᴀⲛ ᴠáɪⱤᴅ—VII—MacAward, MacWard, Ward; 'son of the bard' (Ir. 'ᴠáɪⱤᴅ'); a very common surname; found in every county in Ireland, but especially in Donegal, Galway and Dublin. Three families of the name are known to history: (1) ᵯᴀᴄ ᴀⲛ ᴠáɪⱤᴅ of Tirconnell, who were bards to the O'Donnells; (2) ᵯᴀᴄ ᴀⲛ ᴠáɪⱤᴅ of Ui Maine, who were bards to the O'Kellys, and were seated at Muine Chasain and Ballymacward; and (3) ᵯᴀᴄ ᴀⲛ ᴠáɪⱤᴅ of Oriel.

ᵯᴀᴄ ᴀⲛ ᴠᴀʟʟᴀɪᴢ—VII—*M'Evally*, Vally; 'son of the freckled man' (Ir. 'ᴠᴀʟʟᴀċ'); a rare surname.

ᵯᴀᴄ ᴀⲛ ᴠᴀⱤúⲛ—VII—*M'Baron*, MacBarron; 'son of the baron' (Ir. 'ᴠᴀⱤúⲛ'); the name of an offshoot of the O'Neills; a rather late surname.

ᵯᴀᴄ ᴀⲛ ᴠeᴀⱤꙅúɪʟɪᴢ—VII—*M'Ewaerowly, M'Everrolly,* Varrilly, Varrelly, Varily, Varley; 'son of the sharp-eyed man' (Ir.' ᴠeᴀⱤⱤúɪʟeᴀċ '); a rare Connacht surname.

ᵯᴀᴄ ᴀⲛ ᴠeᴀᴛᴀ, ᵯᴀᴄ ᴀⲛ ᴠeᴀᴛᴀᴅ—IV—*M'Evaghe, M'Eveighe, M'Ivagh, M'Vaghe, M'Veha, M'Vehy,*

MacAbee, MacIveagh, MacAveigh, MacAvey, (Mac-Avoy, MacEvoy, MacVoy), MacVeagh, MacVeigh, MacVey, MacVay, MacVea, Vahy, Veigh, (Veasy, Vesey), etc.; 'son of мас ан beатаb,' (an Irish personal name, meaning 'son of life'); a common surname in many parts of Ulster, found also in some parts of Leinster and Connacht. There is a universal tendency to assimilate its angl. forms to those of мас ꝼíobburbe (q.v.), and consequently it is often disguised as MacAvoy, MacEvoy, etc. In Co. Mayo, it is sometimes strangely anglicised Veasy and Vesey.

мас ан biabtais—VII—MacVeety, MacVity, Mac-Veity, etc.; 'son of the hospitaller' (Ir. 'biabtac'). This surname has apparently come to us from Scotland; at least, I can discover no early instances in Ireland. Cf. biabtac.

мас ан biocáire, мас ан biocara—VII—M'Evicare, M'Ivickaire, M'Vycare, MacVicar, MacVicker, MacVickar, Vickery, Vicars, Vickers, Vickars, etc.; 'son of the vicar' (Ir.. 'biocáipe.') This surname, in the great majority of instances, is of Scottish origin. As an Irish surname, it was exceedingly rare.

мас ан bReiteaman, мас ан bReiteamnais, мас ан bReitim—VII—M'Abreham, M'Ebrehowne, M'Evrehune, M'Evrehoona, M'Evrehon, M'Brehuna M'Brehon, M'Vrehoune, Brehony, Breheny, Brohoon, and, by translation, Judge; 'son of the brehon,' or judge, (Ir. 'bpeiteam', gen. -teaman and -tim, 'bpeiteamnac,' gen. -nais); a common surname in many parts of Ireland, especialy in Connacht and West Ulster. There are, doubtless, several distinct families so called, each an offshoot of one or other of the great brehon families. The surname is now generally angl. Judge, by translation. The form мас ан bpeitim, though common in the spoken language, is apparently modern. This surname is also found in Scotland, where it is angl. Browne.

мас ан Calbais—IV—M'Ecallough, M'Ecallowy, M'Icallowe, MacCalvey, Calvey; 'son of ан Calbac' (an Irish personal name, meaning 'the bald'); a rare surname.

Mac an Caoic—VII—*M'Echey, M'Ekey, M'Keegh*, Mac-Kee, and probably Keyes; 'son of the blind man' (Ir. 'caoc'). This was a designation of a branch of the O'Reillys in Cavan and the neighbouring counties, but was also found in other parts of Ireland, especially in Limerick and Tipperary; hence probably Keyes.

Mac an Carraig—VII—*M'Encarie, M'Incarrie*, Mac-Carrie, MacCarry; 'son of the bald man' (Ir. 'carrac,' bald, scabbed); a rare and scattered surname.

Mac an Ceairt—VII—Kincart, Wright; 'son of the right' (Ir. ceart'); a Co. Mayo surname; evidently an incorrect 'translation' of the English surname Wright.

Mac an Cléirig—VII—*M'Anclery, M'Ecleary, M'Eclery*, MacClery, MacCleary, Clery, Cleary, Clarke, [Clarkson, Clarson]; 'son of the clerk' (Ir. 'cléireac'); a common Cavan surname, probably a var. of Ó Cléirig, q.v. It is now nearly always translated Clarke. Clarkson is the exact English equivalent.

Mac an Coilig—VII—*M'Akolly, M'Anchelly*, MacQuilly, and, by translation, Cox, Coxe; 'son of the cock' (Ir. 'coileac'); the name of a Roscommon family who were coarbs of St. Barry at Kilbarry, in the east of that county, and perhaps of other families in different parts of Ireland. Its angl. forms are difficult to distinguish from those of Mac Concoille, q.v. See also Mac Coilig.

Mac an Coill, Forrestal; a Co. Mayo surname; probably an attempted translation of the English surname Forrestal; or possibly a shortened form of Mac an Coilig above.

Mac an Crosáin—VII—*M'Acrossane, M'Ecrossan*, Mac-Crossan, Crossan, Crossin, Cross, (Crosbie), etc.; 'son of the rhymer' (Ir. 'crosán'); the name (1) of a Tirconnell family, one of whom was Bishop of Raphoe in the 14th century, and who are still numerous in Derry and Tyrone; and (2) of a Leinster family who were bards to the O'Moores and O'Connors, in Leix and Offaly. This family threw in its lot with the English in the 16th century, and assumed the English surname of Crosbie.

Mac an ᴅeaᵹáin, Mac an ᴅeaᵹánaiᵹ—VII—*M'Adegain*, *M'Adegany*, *M'Idegane*, *M'Idigany*, *M'Deane*, MacDigany, Dagney, Digany, Digney, Deane, etc. ; 'son of the dean,' (Ir. 'ᴅeaᵹán,' 'ᴅeaᵹánac,' Lat. 'decanus '). This surname was found in the 16th century in many parts of Ireland, but especially in Donegal, where the families so named seem to have been originally O'Donnells and O'Gallaghers. It is now very often translated Deane.

Mac an ᴅeisiᵹ—VII—*M'Edesey*, Deasy, Deasey ; 'son of the Decian ' (Ir. 'ᴅéireac,' i.e., native of the Decies of Waterford) ; a Co. Sligo surname.

Mac an ᴅeóraiᴅ—VII—*M'Edoire*, MacAdorey ; 'son of the stranger ' (Ir. 'ᴅeóraᴅ ') ; very rare.

Mac an ᴅruaiᴅ—VII—*M'Adrwy*, *M'Edrwe*, Drew, and incorrectly MacDrury, Drewry and Drury ; 'son of the druid,' or ' magician ' (Ir. 'ᴅruaᴅ') ; a rare surname ; formerly peculiar to Monaghan and Roscommon. In the latter county, it is incorrectly angl. Drury.

Mac an éanaiᵹ, MacAneany, MacAneeny, MacEneany, MacAneny, MacNeney, and, by 'translation,' Bird ; a corruption of Mac Conaonaiᵹ, q.v. The ' translated ' form, Bird, is, of course, incorrect, being founded on the erroneous supposition that the surname is derived from 'éan,' a bird.

Mac an easpuic—VII—*M'Enaspicke*, MacAnespic, MacAnaspie, Easping, Aspig, [Bishop] ' son of the bishop ' (Ir. 'earpoc ') ; very rare.

Mac anꝼaiᴅ—IV—Tempest ; 'son of anꝼaᴅ ' (storm).

Mac an ꝼailᵹiᵹ—VII—MacAnally, MacEnally, MacInally, MacNally, Manally, Canally, Nally, etc. ; ' son of the poor man ' (Ir. 'ꝼailᵹeac ') ; cf. ᴅe paop ; a Mayo surname borne by a family of Welsh or Norman origin ; also common, in the 16th century, in many parts of Ulster and Leinster. In the North, it is apt to be confused with Mac Conulaᴅ, q.v.

Mac an ꝼileaᵭ, Mac an ꝼiliᵭ—VII—*M'Anelly,
M'Enelly, M'Enillowe, M'Enilly, M'Inilly,* MacAnilly,
MacNilly, MacNeilly, MacNielly, MacNeely, Mac-
Neally, MacNealey, Maneilly, Maneely, Meneely,
Mineely; 'son of the poet' (Ir. 'ꝼile'); not a very
common surname, and almost peculiar to N.E. Ulster.
To be distinguished from Mac Conᵹaile and Mac
Conᵹaola which are sometimes similarly anglicised.

Mac an ꝼiꝛ—IV—*M'Ener, M'Enir, M'Inner, M'Innier,*
Kinner, Kinnier, etc.; 'son of an ꝼeaꝛ (the man)',
(a short form of ꝼeaꝛᵹanainm, ꝼeaꝛᵭoꝛca, or some
other Irish personal name beginning with ꝼeaꝛ); a
rare and scattered surname. Not the same as the
Scottish Kinnear, Kinneir,

Mac an ꝼiꝛléiᵹinn—VII—*M'Enferline, M'Enyreloyne,*
MacNerlin, MacNerland, Killerlean; 'son of the
lector' (Ir. 'ꝼeaꝛléiᵹinn'); a rare Sligo surname;
also Mac ꝼiꝛléiᵹinn, q.v.

Mac an ꝼleaꞅtaiꝛ—VII—*MacAnaleister,* Fletcher,
'son of the fletcher,' i.e., the arrow-featherer.

Mac an ꝼꝛanncaiᵹ—VII—Frain, Frayne, Freyne,
Frainey, Freney; 'son of the Frenchman' (Ir. 'ꝼꝛannc-
ac'); a Mayo surname. I suspect this surname
is modern; at least, I can discover no early instances.

Mac an ᵹabann, v. Mac an ᵹoбann.

Mac an ᵹallóᵹlaiᵹ—VII—*M'Agaloglie,* MacGallogly,
Gallogly, by 'translation,' English, Englishby, and by
assimilation, Ingoldsby; 'son of the gallowglass' (Ir.
ᵹallóᵹlac'); formerly a Donegal surname; now
found chiefly in Louth and Meath.

Mac an ᵹaill—VII—*M'Agayll, M'Agoyle, M'Egeill,*
MacGill, Gill, [Stapleton]; 'son of the foreigner'
(Ir. 'ᵹall'); a var. of Mac an ᵹoill, q.v. This was
the Irish name assumed by the Stapletons of Co.
Tipperary.

Mac an ᵹeaiꝛꝛ, Mac an ᵹiꝛꝛ—VII—*M'Iyear, M'Eghir,
M'Gayer,* MacGarr, MacGirr, MacGerr, Gayer,
and by translation, Short; 'son of the short,
or low-sized, man' (Ir. 'ᵹeaꝛꝛ' and 'ᵹioꝛꝛ'). Mac

an ᵹeᴀιᵽᵽ, which may be regarded as the Connacht form of this surname, was formerly common in Sligo and Leitrim, and is now well known in Mayo. Mᴀc an ᵹιᵽᵽ is the Ulster form, and was common in Armagh and Tyrone. The family is supposed to be of Scottish origin, but is, more probably, an offshoot of some native family. Both variants were in use in Dublin and Wicklow.

Mᴀc an ᵹobᴀ—VII—*M'Gowe*, Gow, Smith ; a var. of Mᴀc an ᵹobᴀnn, q.v.

Mᴀc an ᵹobᴀnn—VII—*M'Agowne*, *M'Egowne*, *M'Igoine*, *M'Igone*, MacGowan, MacGowen, Magowan, Gowen, Gowing, Goan, etc., and, by translation, Smith, Smyth ; ' son of the smith' (Ir. ' ᵹobᴀ,' gen. ' ᵹobᴀnn ') ; a very common Irish surname. In the South of Ireland, it is now generally translated Smith, but MacGowan and Magowan are common in the North. Clᴀnn ᴀn ᵹobᴀnn of Clare and Tipperary were hereditary historians to the O'Loghlins of Burren and to the O'Kennedys of Ormond respectively.

Mᴀc an ᵹoιll—VII—*Macingill*, *M'Agill*, *M'Egill*, MacGill, Magill, Gill, etc. ; ' son of the foreigner' (Ir. ' ᵹᴀll ') ; an Irish surname given to the descendants of some of the early Anglo-Norman settlers. There were families of the name in every province. V. Mᴀc an ᵹᴀιll, which is a variant.

Mᴀc an ιᴀRlᴀ—VII—*M'Inierligh*, *M'an Erle*, Earl, Earle, Earls ; ' son of the earl' (Ir. ' ιᴀᵽlᴀ ') ; very rare.

Mᴀc an ιᴀscᴀιRe—VII—*M'Inesker*, Fisher ; ' son of the fisherman' (Ir. ' ιᴀᵽcᴀιᵽe ') ; a late importation from Scotland, if not a translation of the English surname Fisher. The Scottish-Gaelic form, as I heard it, is Mᴀc an ιᴀᵽcᴀιᵽ.

Mᴀc an lᴀιᵹnιᵹ—VII—(?) Callina, Collina, Colliney ; ' son of the Leinsterman,' (Ir. lᴀιᵹneᴀc).

Mᴀc an leᴀᵹᴀ—VII—*M'Enlawe*, *M'Enlay*, *M'Enley*, *M'Enlea*, *M'Kinlea*, *M'Elea*, *M'Ellay*, *M'Lea*, MacKinlay, MacKinley, MacAlea, MacAlee, MacClay,

MacLee, Lee, Leigh, and sometimes incorrectly MacLean, MacClean; 'son of the physician' (Ir. 'liaig'). There were several scattered families of this name, each doubtless an offshoot of one or other of great medical families. It seems to have been sometimes used as an *alias* by members of the family of Mac Duinnshléibhe (q.v.), who were famous medical practitioners. See also Mac Conleagha.

Mac an Mhadaidh—VII—MacAvady, MacEvady, MacAvaddy, MacEvaddy, MacVady, Covaddy, (Madden); 'son of the dog' (Ir. 'madadh'); an old Mayo surname; now very often incorrectly angl. Madden, with which it is partly synonymous.

Mac an Mháighistir—VII—*M'Amaster*, *M'Evaster*, *M'Master*, MacMaster, Master, Masterson; 'son of the master' (Ir. máighistir,' Lat. 'magister'). This surname seems to have originated in Co. Cavan, but by the end of the 16th century it had spread into Longford and Roscommon. It is now nearly always angl. Masterson. The Mastersons of Wexford are of English descent.

Mac an Mhanaigh—VII—*M'Ivannagh*, *M'Vany*, MacEvany, MacEvanny, MacVany, [Monk, Monks]; 'son of the monk' (Ir. 'manach'); a rare surname. So far as I know, it survives only in Co. Mayo. The corresponding English surname is Monk or Monks.

Mac an Mhaoir—VII—*M'Ewire, M'Eweir*, Wire, Wyer, Wier, Weir, Wear, Weere, Moyers, and in Scotland MacNair; 'son of the steward' (Ir. 'maor'). There were families of this name in Armagh, Westmeath, Offaly and Roscommon. The head of the Armagh family was hereditary keeper of the Book of Armagh. Mac an Mhaoir is also a Scottish surname, angl. MacNair.

Mac an Mhíleadha, Mac an Mhílidh—VII—*M'Aveely*, *M'Evilee, M'Evelly, M'Ivile, Stanton*, MacEvely, MacEvilly, [Stanton, Staunton]; 'son of the knight' (Ir. 'míleadh'); the Irish surname assumed by the Stauntons (v. de Stondún) of the barony of Carra, Co.

Mayo. Many of the family have resumed the original surname, Staunton or Stanton.

mac anna—IV—*M'Anna*, *M'Canna*, MacAnn, MacCann, etc.; 'son of annaó'; usually written mac canna or mac cana, q.v.

mac annaió—IV—*M'Anna*, *M'Canna*, MacCanny, Canny; 'son of annaó'; the fullest and most correct form of the surname which is usually written mac anna or mac canna, q.v. This form is still in use in Co. Clare, angl. Canny. In the 16th century, the MacCannys were seated in Co. Limerick, and in 1598 one of them held the castle of Drombanny, near the city.

mac annlaoió—V—*M'Awnly*, MacCownley; 'son of Anlaf' (a form of the Norse Olaf); a var. of mac amlaoió, q.v.; very rare.

mac annraic—V—*M'Anrack*, *M'Canricke*, *M'Henricke*, MacKendrick, Kenrick, Conrick, Condrick, Conderick; 'son of annrac' (Norse Heimrekr); a surname of Norse origin, formerly in Cork, Waterford, Wexford and Carlow. Also mac eannraic, q.v.

mac annraoi—V—*M'Hanry*, *M'Harrye*, MacHarry, [Fitzharris, Feeharry, Harris, Harrison]; 'son of Henry'; a var. of mac hannraoi and mac éinrí, q.v.

mac an óglaoic—VII—*M'Nogly*, now probably Nagle; 'son of the soldier' (Ir. 'óglaoc'); the name of a Sligo family who were erenaghs of the church of Killery, near Lough Gill. It is probably still extant under the angl. form of Nagle.

mac an oircinn, a var. of mac an aircinn, q.v.

mac an oircinnig, a var. of mac an aircinnig, q.v.

mac an pearsúin, mac an pearsain—VII—*M'Efarson*, *M'Eparson*, *M'Parson*, MacPharson, Mac-Pherson, MacFarson, MacFerson, Pherson, Parsons; 'son of the parson' (Ir. 'pearsún,' Lat. 'persona'); a scattered surname. Many of the name in Ireland are, no doubt, descended from the famous Highland clan, mac an pearrain.

Mac an Príora, Mac an Prír—VII—*M'Ipriorie,*
M'Eprior, M'Prior, Friary, Prior, Fryer, etc. ; ' son
of the prior ' (Ir. ' ppíoṗ ') ; a scattered surname.

Mac an Raoi, Mac-an-Ree ; King ; a corruption of
Mac Conṗaoi, q.v.

Mac an Ridire—VII—*M'Eridery, M'Iruddery, M'Rud-*
dery, MacRuddery, MacKnight, Knight, [Fitzsimons,
FitzSimons] ; ' son of the knight ' (Ir. ' ṗidire ') ; the
Irish surname assumed by the FitzSimons of Co.
Westmeath, and perhaps also by offshoots of knightly
houses in other parts of Ireland.

Mac an Rótaiċ, Monroe, Munroe ; a Scottish surname.

Mac an Scolóige — VII — *M'Yscollog, M'Scolloige,*
M'Scologe, MacScollog, and, by translation, Farmer ;
' son of the farmer ' (Ir. ' ṡcológ ') ; a rare and scattered surname. In the 16th century, it was most
common in Galway, Tyrone and Fermanagh.

Mac an Sparáin, MacAsparan, MacSparran ; ' son of
the purse ' (Ir. ṡparán).

Mac an Stocaire—VII—MacAstocker, MacStocker,
(Stafford) ; ' son of the trumpeter ' (Ir. ' ṡtocaire).

Mac an Taoisiġ—VII—MacIntosh, MacEntosh, Mac-
Kintosh ; ' son of the chieftain ' (Ir. ' taoireaċ ') ; the
name of a famous Highland clan in Inverness,
some of whom settled in the north of Ireland. The
Scottish Gaelic form of the name is Mac an Tóiṡiċ.

Mac an Tiompánaiġ—VII—*M'Itempany, M'Tympane,*
M'Tempane, MacAtimney, MacAtimeny, MacAtamney,
MacAtaminey, MacTimney, MacTamney, Timpany,
Tymmany, Timony, Tamney, Tempeny, Tenpeny, (?)
Toompane, (?) Tumpane ; ' son of the tympanist ' (Ir.
' tiompánaċ'). This surname was found chiefly in
Down, Tyrone and Sligo, and it still survives, under
a great variety of angl. forms, in the north and west
of Ireland.

Mac Antoine—V—*MacAnthony,* Anthony, Antony ;
' son of Antony.'

Mac an Tṡaġairt—VII—MacEntaggart, MacEntaggert,
MacEntegart, MacIntaggart, MacInteggart, MacTag-

gart, MacTeggart, Taggart, Teggart, Tegart, Tiger, etc.; 'son of the priest' (Ir. 'ᵱᵃᵹᵃᵱᵼ', Lat. 'sacerdos'); an Ulster surname.

mᴀc ᴀn ᴄSᴀ́ṁᴀıᵹ—VII—*M'Etawey*, Tavey; 'son of the mild, or pleasant, man' (Ir. 'ᵱᴀ́ṁᴀᴄ'); a Co. Monaghan surname.

mᴀc ᴀn ᴄSᴀoı—VII—*M'Attye*, *M'Entie*, *M'Inty*, Mac-Atee, MacEntee, MacIntee, MacKenty, MacKinty; 'son of the scholar' (Ir. 'ᵱᴀoı'); a well-known North of Ireland surname. In the 16th century, it was most common in Donegal, Monaghan, Louth and Long-ford.

mᴀc ᴀn ᴄSᴀoıᴚ—VII—MacAntire, MacEntire, MacEnteer, MacInteer, MacIntyre, MacAteer, MacAtear, Mac-Cateer, MacTeer, MacTier, Minteer, Mateer, etc., and, by translation, Carpenter and Freeman; 'son of the craftsman' (Ir. 'ᵱᴀoᵱ,' a mason, carpenter; also a freeman). There are, no doubt, several distinct families so called. About Dublin, this surname has been translated Carpenter. In other places, it has been incorrectly made Freeman, on the erroneous supposition that it is derived from ᵱᴀoᵱ, a freeman. This was also the name of a famous Scottish clan, whose country was Glen O, in Lorn; and many of the MacIntyres of the North of Ireland are, doubtless, of that race.

mᴀc ᴀn ᴄSᴀSᴀnᴀıᵹ—VII—MacAtasney, MacArtarsney, Atasney; 'son of the Englishman' (Ir. 'Sᴀᵱᴀnᴀᴄ'); very rare.

mᴀc ᴀn ᴄSıonnᴀıᵹ—VII—*M'Eteny*, *M'Etanny*, Mac-Ashinah, Tinney, Fox; 'son of the fox' (Ir. 'ᵱıon-nᴀᴄ'); a rare and scattered surname.

mᴀc ᴀn ᴄuıᴌe, *M'Cantully*, *M'Etwille*, MacAtilla, Tully, and by 'translation,' Flood; a corruption of mᴀc ṁᴀoᴌᴄuıᴌe, q.v.; in the spoken language often further corrupted to Ó ᴄuıᴌe, q.v.; a Connacht surname.

mᴀc ᴀn úcᴀıᴚe—VII—*M'Enookery*, *M'Inowkery*, [Fuller]; 'son of the fuller' (Ir. úcᴀıᵱe').

ɱac an uısce, Uiske ; Water, Waters ; a corruption of
ɱac Conuıɼce, q.v.

ɱac an ultaıᵹ—VII—MacAnulty, MacKnulty, Mac-
Nulty, Nulty ; ' son of the Ulidian ' (or native of East
Ulster, Ir. ' ultac ') ; the name of a Donegal family,
who are probably a branch of the O'Dunlevys. (V.
Ó Ɗuınnɼléıɓe and ɱac Ɗuınnɼléıɓe). It is now
common in Mayo and Meath. In the latter county,
it is always angl. Nulty.

ɱac Aoɓa—IV—M'Ea, MacKay, MacKey, MacKee,
MacCoy, MacHugh, Eason, Hughes, Hueson, Hewson,
etc ; ' son of Aoɓ ' (a common Irish personal name,
now angl. Hugh) ; a very common surname, especially
in Ulster and Connacht. There are several distinct
families so called. In the barony of Clare, Co. Galway,
ɱac Aoɓa, of the same stock as the O'Flahertys, was
chief of Clann Choscraigh. The MacKays of Strath-
naver were a well-known Scottish clan, some of whom
are, doubtless, to be found among the MacKays of the
north of Ireland. The angl. form MacCoy is almost
peculiar to Co. Limerick, whither the family migrated
from Ulster more than three centuries ago. V. ɱac
Aoıɓ and ɱaᵹ Aoɓa, which are variants.

ɱac Aoɓa ɓuıɒe—IV—M'Eabuoy, MacEvoy, Mac-
Avoy ; ' son of yellow Aoɓ ' ; very rare.

ɱac Aoɓaᵹáın—IV—M'Egaine, M'Hegane, M'Keagan,
M'Kiegane, MacEgan, MacKeegan, Egan, Heagan,
Keegan, etc. ; ' son of Aoɓaᵹán ' (a dim. of Aoɓ) ;
the name of a distinguished brehon family. They
belonged originally to the district of Ui Maine in
Connacht ; but in the 14th and 15th centuries, branches
of the family settled in Ormond, Desmond, and many
other parts of Ireland. where they became brehons
to the local chieftains. They also kept schools of
law, and many learned men and eminent professors
of the same name are mentioned in the Irish annals.

ɱac Aoɓáın—IV—M'Kiane, M'Kian, MacKeane,
Keane, Kane ; ' son of Aoɓán ' (a dim. of Aoɓ).
This is undoubtedly the correct form of the surname

which, in the spoken language of Connacht, is pronounced Ó Caobáin and anglicised MacKeane, Keane and Kane.

Mac Aoiῦ—IV—*M'Ee*, *M'Eye*, MacKee, MacKie, Kee ; 'son of Aoῦ' ; a var. of Mac Aoῦa, q.v.

Mac Aonguis, Mac Aongusa—IV—*M'Enesse*, *M'Hinchey*, *M'Nisse*, MacEnnis, MacInnes, MacInch, MacKinch, MacHinch, MacNeese, MacNeece, Mac-Niece, MacNish, Mannice, Minnish, Mannix, Kinnish, Ennis, Innes, Hinchey, etc. ; 'son of Aongur' (an ancient Irish personal name) ; a var. of Mag Aonguir, q.v. Also the name of a Scottish clan in Argyleshire.

Mac Arcail—V—Archer ; 'son ot Arkil' (Ang.-Sax. Arcytel).

Mac Árdgail—IV—MacArdel, MacArdle, MacCardle, Cardle, Cardell, Cardwell, ; 'son of Árogal' (high valour) ; a well-known South Ulster surname. The family is probably a branch of the MacMahons.

Mac Artaig—IV—Harty, Hearty ; apparently 'son of Artac,' but probably corrupt ; a rare Co. Mayo surname.

Mac Artáin—IV—*M'Artane*, *M'Artan*, *M'Cartane*, MacCartan, MacCarten, MacCarton, MacCartin, Cartan, Carton, etc. ; 'son of Artán' (a dim. of Art). The head of this family was lord of Cinel Faghartaigh, now the barony of Kinelarty, in Co. Down. At the beginning of the 17th century, the name was common in many parts of Leinster, and it seems to have penetrated into Cork and Kerry. The spelling is often Mac Captáin (q.v.), the c of Mac having been attracted over, and this is further corrupted to Ó Captáin, q.v. See also Mac Airteáin and Mac Cairteáin.

Mac Artúir—V—MacArthur, MacCarthur, MacCarter, Carthurs, Arthurs, etc. ; 'son of Arthur.' This surname is apparently of Scottish origin. The MacArthurs were a branch of the Campbell clan, and at one time a powerful family in Argyleshire ; but early in the 15th century their power was broken, when their chief, John MacArthur, was beheaded by James I and most of their

estates forfeited. The Scottish-Gaelic form of the
name is mac Arꞇaiꞃ.

mac ᴀꞱᴄᴀiꝺ—V—*M'Oskie*, MacAskie, MacCaskie,
Caskey ; 'son of Aꞃᴄᴀiꝺ,' (a pet form of some Norse
or Anglo-Saxon name, perhaps Askell; Searle has
' Asci ') ; a rare North of Ireland surname, probably
of Norse origin.

mac ᴀꞱᴄᴀiꝈꝈ—V—MacAskill ; 'son of AꞃᴄᴀꝈꝈ,' (the
Norse personal name Askell, Ascytel among the Anglo-
Saxons) ; a surname of Scoto-Norse origin.

mac ᴀꞱmuinꞇ—V—Mac*Casmund*, *Casmond*, Casement,
' son of Áꞃmunꝺ ' (the Norse personal name Asmundr,
corresponding to the Anglo-Saxon Osmund) ; an old
Manx surname, made famous in Ireland by Roger
Casement.

mac ꝺᴀiꝈꝺꞃín, mac ꝺᴀiꝈꞇꞃín—V—*M'Waldrin*,
Waldron ; 'son of little Walter' (Ir. ꝺᴀiꝈꞇꞃín ') ; the
name of a Mayo family who are probably a branch of
the Costelloes. Also written mac uᴀiꝈꝺꞃín, mac
uᴀiꝈꞇꞃín.

mac ꝺᴀiꞇín—V—*M'Watten* ; 'son of little Walter'
(Ir. ' ꝺᴀiꞇín ') ; the name or title of the head of the
Barretts of Tirawley, Co. Mayo.

mac ꝺᴀꝈꝺꞃáin—V—Waldron ; a var. of mac ꝺᴀꝈꞃonꞇᴀ,
q.v. ; in use in parts of Connacht. Also written mac
uᴀꝈꝺꞃáin.

mac ꝺᴀꝈꞃonꞇᴀ—V—*M'Falronte*, *M'Valronte*, *Wal-
ronde*, Waldron, [Wesley, Welsley, Wellesley] ; 'son
of Waleran ' (an Anglo-Saxon personal name) ; a
patronymic surname assumed by the family of Wesley
in Leinster among whom Waleran was a favourite
name. Also written mac uᴀꝈꞃonꞇᴀ.

mac ꝺᴀoiꞇín—IV—*M'Boyhin*, Boyne ; 'son of ꝺᴀoiꞇín' ;
formerly a Co. Leitrim surname ; still in use in Connacht, but very rare.

mac ꝺeᴀꞃꞇᴀꝥꞃᴀ, Baragrey, Barragry, Berachry,
Berocry, Bearkery, Berkerry, Berkery ; a var. of mac
ꝺioꞃꞇᴀꝥꞃᴀ, q.v.

mac ꝺeᴀꞇᴀ, mac ꝺeᴀꞇᴀꝺ—IV—*M'Beagh*, Mac-

Beath, MacBeth, MacBeith, MacBey, MacBay; 'son of Macbeth'; a Scottish form of ᵐᴀc ᴀn ᵬᴇᴀᴄᴀ, q.v.; the name of a Scottish family who were hereditary physicians in Islay and Mull, and also historians to the Macleans. Some of them settled in Ulster.

ᵐᴀc ᵬᴇᴀᴄᴀn—IV—MacBean, MacVean; a var. of ᵐᴀc ᵬᴇᴀᴄᴀᵬ (q.v.), but the name of a different family. The MacBeans formed a distinct clan under their own chief.

ᵐᴀc ᵬɪoᴚnᴀ—V—MacBirney, MacBurney, Burney, etc.; 'son of Bjarni' (a Norse personal name); a Scoto-Norse surname.

ᵐᴀc ᵬɪoᴚᴄᴀᴣᴚᴀ—VII—*M'Birehagree*, *M'Birryhaggery*, *M'Birragra*, *M'Birrekry*, *M'Berrickerey*, Biracree, Biracrea, Berachry, Berocry, Berkerry, Berkery; also ᵐᴀc ᵬᴇᴀᴩᴄᴀᴣᴩᴀ, q.v.; 'son of the sharp pleader' (Ir. 'ᵬɪoᴩ' or 'ᵬᴇᴀᴩ,' sharp, and 'ᴄᴀᴣᴩᴀᵬ,' pleading); the name of an Ulster family who were brehons to the O'Neills. They disappeared from Ulster about the middle of the 16th century, and the surname has ever since been peculiar to Tipperary and East Limerick, whither, not improbably, the family migrated in the reign of Elizabeth.

ᵐᴀc ᵬᴌoscᴀɪᵬ—IV—*M'blosgaid*, *M'blosgaigh*, *M'Closkie*, *M'Loskie*, MacCloskey, MacCluskey, MacLoskey, MacLuskey, Closkey, Cluskey; 'son of ᵬᴌoᴚcᴀᵬ' (a personal name among the O'Kanes); the name of a Derry family descended from ᵬᴌoᴚcᴀᵬ Ó Cᴀᴄᴀ́ɪn, who flourished in the 12th century; still common in Derry and other parts of Ulster.

ᵐᴀc ᵬᴌoscᴀɪᴚᴇ—VII—*M'Gloskir*, *M'Gluskir*, MacClusker, Clusker, (Cosgrave); 'son of the public crier' (Ir. 'ᵬᴌoᴚcᴀɪᴩᴇ'); a Co. Armagh surname; perhaps a popular substitution for ᵐᴀc ᵬᴌoᴚcᴀᵬ, q.v.

ᵐᴀc ᵬᴚᴀᵬᴀɪᴣ—IV—*M'Bradie*, *M'Brady*, *M'Brade*, Brady; 'son of ᵬᴚᴀᵬᴀᴄ' (spirited); the name of a great Cavan family. ᵐᴀc ᵬᴚᴀᵬᴀɪᴣ was chief of Cúɪᴌ ᵬᴩɪᴣᵬᴇ, or Cúɪᴌ ᵬᴩɪᴣᵬᴇ́ɪn, comprising the district around Stradone in Co. Cavan. The surname is now very common in Ulster and also in many parts of Leinster.

Mac bᴀ́ᴅᴀıᴈ, *M'Vraddie.* V. Mᴀᴈ bᴀ́ᴅᴀıᴈ.

Mac bᴀᴀın—IV—*M'Bran, M'Bren.* V. Mac bᴘoın.

Mac bᴀᴀın, MacCrann, MacKrann, MacRann; a var. of Mac bᴘoın, q.v.

*Mac bᴀᴀnᴀıᴈ—IV—Cranny, Crany; 'son of bᴘᴀnᴀc.'

Mac bᴀᴀnᴀ́ın—IV—*M'Branane, M'Branon, M'Brenan,* Branan, Branon, Brannan, Brennan, etc.; 'son of bᴘᴀnᴀ́n' (a dim. of bᴘᴀn); the name of a great Roscommon family, the head of which was chief of Corca Achlann, a large district in that county. They are said to be descended from the noble druid, Ona, who granted the site of the church of Elphin to St. Patrick. They appear to have been also called Ó bᴘᴀnᴀ́ın (q.v.), and there is every reason to believe that the Uı bᴘᴀnᴀ́ın who were erenaghs of St. Patrick's church at Elphin are a branch of this family. (V. Mac ᴀn ᴀıᴘcınnıᴈ). Mac bᴘᴀnᴀ́ın is now generally, but not quite correctly, angl. Brennan.

Mac bᴀᴀoın—IV—*M'Brewne, M'Brune, M'Breane,* MacBreen, Breen; 'son of bᴘᴀoın'; the name of a Kilkenny family, formerly seated in the barony of Knocktopher.

Mac bᴀᴇᴀnᴅᴀ́ın—IV—*M'Brandone, M'Brandon,* Brandon; 'son of bᴘᴇᴀnᴅᴀ́n'; a rare Kerry surname. To be distinguished from the English surname Brandon (V. ᴅe bᴘᴀnᴅᴜ́n).

Mac bᴀᴇᴀcnᴀıᴈ—VII—MacBratney, MacBreatney, MacBretney; 'son of the Welshman' (Ir. 'bᴘᴇᴀcnᴀc'); an Ulster surname of Scottish origin.

Mac bᴀıᴀın—IV—*M'Brian,* MacBrien, MacBryan, MacBryen, etc.; 'son of bᴘıᴀn.'

Mac bᴀıᴀᴀcᴀıᴈ, MacBrearty, MacBrairty; a corruption of Mac Mᴜıᴘceᴀᴘcᴀıᴈ, q.v.

Mac bᴀoın—IV—MacBrin, MacBrinn, MacBirne, MacByrne, Brinn, Byrne, etc.; 'son of bᴘᴀn'; a var. of Mac bᴘoın, q.v.; a rare surname.

Mac bᴀoın—IV—Mac Renn, MacRynn, Rynn, Wrynn,

Wrenn, Wren ; a var. of mac bpáin, mac bpáin, and mac bpoin, q.v. ; a rare surname, found chiefly in Co. Leitrim.

mac bruaoair, *M'Broder.* V. maʒ bpuaoaip.

mac bruaioeaoa—IV—*M'Brouddie,* *M'Broudy,* *M'Brodie,* MacBrody, Brody, Brodie ; 'son of bpuaioeaó.' The MacBrodys were hereditary bards and historians to the O'Briens of Thomond from whom they held, in virtue of their office, considerable property at Ballybrody, Kilkeedy and Littermoylan, in Co. Clare. Several distinguished members of the family figure in Irish literary history. Conor MacBrody was one of the learned men whose approbation is prefixed to the Annals of the Four Masters. The family estates were confiscated in Cromwellian times. Also mac bpuaioín, q.v.

mac bruaioín, *M'Bruodyne,* *M'Brodyne,* Mac Broudin, Mac Bruodin, Broudin, Bruodin ; a frequent alias for mac bpuaioeaoa (q.v.), of which it is the diminutive.

mac cába—IV—*M'Caba,* MacCabe, Macabe ; 'son of cába' (probably a nickname ; cf. 'cába,' a cap or hood) ; the name of a military family of Norse origin who came over from the Hebrides, in the 14th century, and settled in Breifney, where they became captains of gallowglasses to the O'Rourkes and O'Reillys. Their pedigree is given by MacFirbis, from which it appears that they are a branch of the Mac Leods (V. mac leóio). The MacCabes are frequently mentioned in the Annals of the Four Masters, the earliest mention being at the year 1358. They are still numerous in Breifney (Leitrim and Cavan), and in the neighbouring counties of Monaghan and Meath.

mac caoáin—IV—*M'Coddane,* *M'Coddan,* MacCadden, MacCudden, Muckedan ; 'son of caoán' (an Irish personal name, Lat. Catanus) ; a rare Ulster surname, peculiar, in the 16th century, to Armagh. It is impossible to distinguish its angl. forms from those of mac aoáin, q.v.

mac cafraio, v. mac ʒaffaio.

Mac Caitín—IV—*M'Calline*, MacCallion, MacCallan, MacCallen, [Campbell] ; 'son of Caitín' (the Scottish Colin) ; also Mac Coitín, q.v. The family of fighting-men brought over from Scotland by the O'Donnells of Tirconnell in the 15th century, were sometimes called Mac Caitín, sometimes Mac Aitín (q.v.), and it is impossible to say which form is correct.

Mac Cairbre—IV—*M'Carbry*, *M'Carbery*, Carbry, Carbery, Carberry ; 'son of Cairbre' (an old Irish personal name). The angl. forms of this surname cannot now be distinguished from those of Ó Cairbre, q.v.

Mac Cairteáin—IV—*M'Keartan*, *M'Curtaine*, *M'Curtayne*, MacCurtain, Curtayne, Curtain, Curtin, &c. ; an attenuated form of Mac Captáin, q.v. This family, which is a branch of that of MacCartan of Co. Down, had settled in Co. of Cork before the end of the 16th century. Father Connor Mac Cairteain (angl. Curtin), P.P. of Glanmire and an Irish poet of no mean order, died in the year 1737.

Mac Caisín—IV—*M'Cashine*, *M'Kasshine*, *M'Cassin*, MacCashin, Casheen, Cashin, Cashen, Cashion, Cassin, Keshin, &c. ; 'son of Cairín' (dim. of cas, bent, curly) ; a well-known family in Leinster and parts of Munster, where they were formerly hereditary medical practitioners ; also an Antrim family.

Mac Calbaig—IV—*M'Callvagh*, MacCalvey, Calvey, &c; a shortened form of Mac an Calbaig, q.v.

Mac Callanáin—IV—*M'Callenan*, MacCallnon, (Campbell) ; 'son of Callanán' ; very rare.

Mac Calmáin—IV—MacCalman, MacCalmont ; 'son of Colmán' ; a var. of Mac Colmáin, q.v.

Mac Caluim—IV—MacCalum, MacCallam ; 'son of Colum' ; a var. of Mac Coluim, q.v.

*Mac Camlaoic—IV—MacCamley ; 'son of Camlaoc' (bent hero). Cf. Mac Caoclaoic.

Mac Cana, v. Mac Canna.

Mac Canann—IV—*M'Cannan*, MacConnon, Connon, (MacCann) ; 'son of Cano' or 'Cana' (whelp, wolf) ;

a rare and scattered surname ; now very often disguised under the angl. form of MacCann.

mac Canna—IV—*M'Canna*, MacCann, MacKann ; 'son of Annaḃ' ; also written mac Cana and, more correctly, mac Anna, q.v. The MacCanns were lords of Cinel Aonghusa, or Clann Breasail, on the south side of Lough Neagh, in Co. Armagh.

mac Cannaiḃ—IV—*M'Canny*, MacCanny, Canny ; a var. of mac Annaiḃ, q.v.

mac Caoċáin—IV—*M'Keaghane*, *M'Keahan*, Keahan, Keehan ; 'son of Caoċán' (the blind man, perhaps a nickname). This surname is found in the neighbourhood of the city of Limerick and in parts of Connacht.

mac Caoċlaoiċ—VII—*M'Keaghlie*, *M'Keighely*, Kehelly, Kehilly, (Coakley, Keily, Kelly) ; 'son of the blind hero' (Ir. Caoċlaoċ), but probably it was originally mac Caoċḟile, 'son of the blind poet' ; an old West Cork surname. V. mac Claoċlaoiċ.

mac Caoilte—IV—MacCaoilte ; 'son of Caoilte.'

*mac Caoṁánaiġ—IV—MacCavanagh, 'son of Caoṁánaċ.'

mac Carluis—V—Corless, Carlos ; 'son of Carlus' (a Norse form of the Lat. 'Carolus,' i.e. Charles) ; a rare surname in Galway and Roscommon. I can find no early angl. form.

mac Carrġaṁna—IV—*M'Carrhon*, MacCarroon, MacCaron, *Carrowny*, *Carony*, *M'Crony*, MacGroaney, Growney, O'Growney, (*M'Gaffney*, Gaffney, Caulfield) ; also written maġ Carrġaṁna, and now corruptly ó Ġraṁna ; 'son of Carrġaṁain' (i.e., spear-calf, an old Irish personal name) ; the name of an ancient family in Co. Westmeath, of the southern Ui Neill race, who derive their descent from Maine, son of Niall of the Nine Hostages. They were at first surnamed mac Ġiolla Ulταin, from Ġiolla Ulταin, one of their ancestors, but afterwards adopted the present surname from Carrġaṁain, the grandson of Ġiolla Ulταin. Their clan-name was Muinntear

ⓂaoilⱤionna, taken from another of their ancestors called ⓂaoilⱤionna, i.e., 'chief of the Shannon,' from the position of his territory near the River Shannon. ⓂaoilⱤionna was the great-grandfather of Ꝫiolla Ultain. The clan-lands of ⓂuinnⱦeaⱤ ⓂaoilⱤionna embraced the district of Cuircne, now the barony of Kilkenny West, which some time after the Anglo-Norman invasion passed into the possession of the Dillons; but that they maintained some shadow of independence as a clan until late in the 16th century is clear from the Fiants of Elizabeth which record that, in the year 1578, 'Hobbert M'Caron, of Killenefaghna, Co. Westmeath, gentleman, was granted the office of chief serjeant of his nation in Co. Westmeath, and certain lands in Kilkeren, Knockan, and the Parke, same co., called the ploughland of Kilmacaron, which of old belonged to the chief of the nation of M'Caron.' This ancient surname has now almost entirely disappeared, being generally disguised under the angl. forms of Caulfield and Gaffney and widely dispersed through Ireland.

Ⓜac CáⱤⱦaiꝫ—IV—*M'Carhig*, *M'Carhie*, MacCarha, MacCarthy, MacCartie, MacCarty, MacArthy, &c.; 'son of CáⱤⱦaċ' (Old Celtic Caratacos, loving, an ancient Irish personal name). The MacCarthys were the chief family of the Eoghanacht, i.e., the descendants of Eoghan Mor, son of Oilioll Olum, King of Munster in the 3rd century. They took their name from CáⱤⱦaċ, lord of the Eoghanacht, whose tragic death, in 1045, is recorded in the Annals. CáⱤⱦaċ was the son of SaeⱤḃⱤeaⱦaċ (a name still in use in the family, angl. Justin), who was the grandson of Ceaillaċán of Cashel, King of Munster in the Danish period. Prior to the Anglo-Norman invasion, the MacCarthys were Kings of Desmond, or South Munster; but shortly after that event they were driven from the plains of Tipperary into the present counties of Cork and Kerry, where, however, they became very numerous and retained considerable

possessions down to the revolution of 1688. They
were divided into three great branches, the heads of
which were known respectively as MacCarthy More
who resided chiefly in Kerry, MacCarthy Reagh, lord
of Carbery in West Cork, and MacCarthy of Muskerry ;
and there were numerous minor branches. In 1565,
Donal MacCarthy, the then MacCarthy More, was
created Earl of Clancar, and other members of the
family were at various periods ennobled as Barons
of Valentia, Earls of Clancarthy, Viscounts Muskerry,
and Lords Mountcashel.

mac CaRτάιn, *M'Cartane*, *M'Cartayne*, *M'Cartyn*,
MacCartan, MacCarten, MacCarton, MacCartin,
Cartan, Carton, &c. ; a var. of mac αρτάιn (q.v.)
owing to the attraction of the c of mac over to the
second part of the surname.

mac CaRτaιne, MacCartney, MacCartiney ; a var. of
macαρτάιn, q.v.

mac Caṡáιn—IV—*M'Chassane*, *M'Cassan*, Cassan,
Cassian ; ' son of Caράn ' (dim. of Cαρ) ; an alias for
mac Caιρίn, q.v.

mac CaṡaRLαιṡ—IV—*M'Cassarlie*, MacCasserly, Cas-
serly, (Cassidy) ; ' son of Caραρlaċ ' (an Irish personal
name, in use as late as the beginning of the 17th
century) ; an old Roscommon surname. Cumumhan
Mac Cassarlaigh was among those who fell at the
battle of Athenry in 1249.

mac CaτaιL—IV—*M'Cahall*, *M'Cahill*, *M'Cale*, MacCall,
MacCaul, MacHall, MacGall ; Charles, Corless ; ' son
of Caταl ' (battle-mighty, a common Irish personal
name, angl. Charles). A family of this name were
followers of O'Kelly of Ui Maine, and the surname
still survives in Co. Galway under the angl. forms of
Charles and Corless. mac CaταιL was, no doubt, also
in use in other parts of Ireland, but its angl. forms,
especially in Ulster, cannot always be distinguished
from those of mac Caτṁαοιl, q.v.

mac Caτάιn—IV—*M'Cahane*, MacCahan, MacKane,
MacKeen, Keane ; ' son of Caτάn ' ; the name of a

Clare family who were formerly coarbs of St. Senan at Iniscattery; still well known about Kilrush, angl. Keane. Also an Ulster surname, but very rare.

Mac Cataoir—IV—*M'Cahire*, *M'Cahir*, *M'Kahir*, Cahir, Carr, Kerr; 'son of Cataoir' (a common Irish personal name); a rare surname.

Mac Catasaig—IV—*M'Casie*, MacCasey, Casey; 'son of Catarac' (vigilant, watchful); an old surname in Monaghan and Armagh. About the middle of the 14th century, Nicholas Mac Cathasaigh was Bishop of Clogher; and several gentlemen of the name in Co. Armagh are mentioned as having received pardon from Queen Elizabeth. The name is now very rare.

Mac Catmaoil—IV—*M'Caughwell*, *M'Cawill*, *M'Kavill*, MacCavill, MacCawell, MacCowell, MacCowhill, MacCawl, MacCaul, MacCall, MacHall, MacCaulfield, Keawell, (Howell, Caulfield, Campbell, Callwell), &c.; 'son of Catmaol' (battle-chief); the name of a family who, says O'Donovan, 'are famous in Irish history for their learning and the many dignitaries they supplied to the church.' They derive their descent from Eoghan, son of Niall of the Nine Hostages, and were for many centuries powerful chiefs in Tyrone. Their patrimony was Kinel Farry, now the barony of Clogher in Co. Tyrone, and other districts in the same county and in Fermanagh. There was amother family of the same name in Co. Down. In the 16th century, the name had spread into Connacht, Westmeath and Carlow. A branch of the family of Tyrone who settled in Co. Wicklow changed the name to Caulfield. This fine old name is now often sadly disguised.

Mac Ceadaig—IV—*M'Keady*, MacKeady, (?) MacGeady, Keady; 'son of Ceadac' (deriv. of cead, a hundred, hundred-possessing, a common personal name among the O'Farrells, O'Mores and Mageoghegans); an old Galway surname.

Mac Ceallacáin—IV—*M'Keallachayn*, *M'Kelleghane*, MacKeleghan; 'son of Ceallacán' (dim. of Ceallac); a rare Westmeath surname.

mac ceaʟʟaɩ̄ᵹ—IV—*M'Kelly*, Kelly; ' son of Ceaʟʟaċ '
(war, contention) ; the name (1) of an Co. Galway
family of the same stock as the O'Maddens, and (2) of
a Co. Leitrim family. There were, no doubt, several
other families of the name in Ireland, but they cannot
now be distinguished from the O'Kellys. mac
Ceaʟʟaɩᵹ is also the name of the Kellys of the Isle
of Man.

mac ceanᵹʟaɩᵹ—IV—Kangley, Tighe ; a rare surname
in Meath and Cavan ; perhaps a corruption of mac
Coɩnᵹeaʟʟaɩᵹ, q.v.

mac ceara, Carr ; in use in Co. Galway.

mac cearáɩn—IV—*M'Carrane*,   *M'Carran*,   Mac-
Carron, MacCarren, Carron ; a var. of mac Cɩapáɩn,
q.v. ; an old surname in Donegal and Derry.

mac cearõaɩʟʟ—IV—*M'Carrowle*, *M'Carvell*, *M'Carwell*, *M'Kerwell*, MacCarroll, MacCarvill, MacCarville,
MacKervel, MacErvel, Carroll, Carvill, (Cardwell) ;
' son of Ceapõaʟʟ ' ; a celebrated family of musicians
in Ulster. In 1594, Ballym'Carroll, parcel of the lands
of Gillekeaghe M'Carroll, of Ballymack-Carroll, was
escheated. There was also a family of the name
in Leix.

mac cearnaɩᵹ—IV—*M'Carny*, *M'Kearnie*, *M'Karney*,
MacKearney, MacCarney, Kearney, Carney ; ' son
of Ceapnaċ ' (victorious). The original home of this
family appears to have been Ballymacarney in Co.
Meath, but in the 16th century the name was found
chiefly in Ulster, in the counties of Down, Armagh
and Donegal.

mac céɩ́oɩᵹ—IV—*M'Keady*, Keady ; a corruption of
Ó meɩcéɩʼoɩᵹ, an old surname in West Cork.

mac céɩʟe—IV—*M'Hely*, *M'Heile*, *M'Heale*, *M'Keale*,
MacHale ; ' son of Céɩʟe ' (companion) ; the name of a
Mayo family who were erenaghs of Killala and coarbs
of St. Caillin at Fenagh, Co. Leitrim. The name has
evidently been confused with mac ɦéɩʟ, q.v.

mac ceɩꞇ—IV—Kitson ; ' son of Ceaꞇ ' ; a rare West
Clare surname.

mac ceiteaꞃnaig—IV—*M'Kehernie*, *M'Keherne*, Keherny, Kerney, (Kearney); 'son of Ceiteaꞃnac'; the name of a Roscommon family who were chiefs of Ciaꞃꞃaiöe, or Kerry, a district in the barony of Castlerea; also Ó Ceiteaꞃnaig (q.v.), which seems to be the only form in which the name has survived.

mac céitín—IV—MacKetian, MacKeating; 'son of *Céitín*' (perhaps dim. of Céatꞃaiö)

mac ceóc, mac ceócac, MacKeogh, Keogh; var. of mac eocaöa and mac eocac (q.v.) owing to the attraction of the c of mac over to the second part of the surname.

mac ciaꞃagáin—IV—MacKerrigan; 'son of Ciaꞃagán' (dim. of ciaꞃ, black); very rare.

mac ciaꞃáin—IV—*M'Kirrane*, *M'Kearrane*, *M'Carrane*, MacCarron; 'son of Ciaꞃán' (dim. of ciaꞃ, black); an old Donegal surname. V. Ó Ceaꞃáin.

mac cinín, Keenan; a rare Roscommon surname; probably a corruption of mac ꞙingin, q.v.

mac cionaoöa, mac cionaoic—IV—*M'Kinna*, *M'Kenay*, *M'Kena*, MacKinney, MacKinny, MacKenny, MacKenna, MacKeany, Kenny, etc.; 'son of Cionaoö'; the name of a family who, though belonging to the southern Ui Neill, were chiefs of the barony of Trough in the north of Co. Monaghan; and also of a family in Co. Roscommon who were followers of the O'Connors. This surname, in Kerry, Cork and Limerick, is corrupted in the spoken language to mag Cineáit (q.v.), but the old angl. forms in these counties show the true origin.

mac ciotꞃuaöa, mac ciotꞃuaiö—V—MacKerrow, Kiroy, (MacKitterick, &c.); 'son of Ciotꞃuaiö' (a name of Norse origin); a rare Midland surname.

mac claoclaoic, Coakley; evidently for mac Caoc-laoic, q.v.; a West Cork surname.

mac cléiꞃig—VII—*M'Clerie*, MacClery, MacCleary, Clarke; a shortened form of mac an Cléiꞃig, q.v.

mac cliseam, Clisham, Klisham; a rare Connacht surname, the origin of which I cannot trace.

Mᴀc Cʟocᴀıʀe—VII—*M'Cloghor*, MacCloughry, Cloughry, and, by 'translation,' Kingstone, Kingston; 'son of the stone-cutter,' or 'mason' (Ir. 'cloċaıpe').

Mᴀc Cʟuᴀnᴀıᵹ—IV—*M'Clonnye*, MacLoonie, Clowney, Clowny, Clooney, Cloney; 'son of Cluᴀnᴀċ' (deceitful, perhaps a nickname).

Mᴀc Cʟúcᴀın—IV—MacClughan, Luccan; 'son of Lúcᴀn' (?)

Mᴀc Cnᴀ́ıṁ—IV—Bones, Bownes; 'son of Cnᴀ́ṁ' (?) (Ir. 'cnᴀ́ṁ,' a bone; probably a nickname). This surname is in use in Co. Mayo, but I have failed to find any early instance. Mᴀc Cnᴀ́mᴀıᵹ (q.v.) is a variant.

Mᴀc Cnᴀ́ıṁín—IV—*M'Cnavin*, *M'Knavin*, MacNevin, Navin, Neavin, Nevin, Neven, Nivin, Nevins; 'son of Cnᴀ́ıṁín' (dim. of cnᴀ́ṁ, a bone); the name of an ancient family in Co. Galway, who were chiefs of a district in Ui Maine and seated at Crannag MacNevin, in the parish of Tynagh. The name is first mentioned in the Annals of the Four Masters at the year 1159. The chief in the time of Elizabeth was Hugh Mac-Knavin. He went out in rebellion, was taken and hanged on the 4th June, 1602, and his lands granted to the Earl of Clanrickard. Other members of the family possessed considerable property at the beginning of the 17th century. The celebrated Dr. MacNevin of the United Irishmen was the last supposed head of the family.

Mᴀc Cnᴀ́mᴀıᵹ—IV—Bones, Bownes; 'son of Cnᴀ́mᴀċ' (bony); a var. of Mᴀc Cnᴀ́ıṁ, q.v. Cf. Mᴀc Cnᴀ́ıṁín.

Mᴀc Coḃtᴀıᵹ—IV—*M'Cooe*, MacCovey, MacCooey, MacCooe; 'son of Coḃtᴀċ' (victorious); a rare Co. Louth surname.

Mᴀc Coċlᴀın—IV—*M'Cochlane*, *M'Coghlane*, **Mac-Coghlan**, MacCoughlan, Coghlan, Coghlen, Coghlin, Coughlan, Coughlen, Coughlin; 'son of Coċlᴀ́n' (dim. of 'coċᴀl,' a cape, cowl or hood). The Mac-Coghlans derive their name from Coċlᴀ́n, lord of Dealbhna Eathra, whose death is recorded in the

Annals at the year 1053 ; and they were for many centuries lords of Dealbhna Eathra, called in later times Delvin MacCoghlane, which comprised almost the entire of the present barony of Garrycastle, in Offaly. They were once a very powerful family, and the name is still common in the midlands. About the middle of the 18th century, a branch of the family settled near Castlebar, Co. Mayo.

mac coolacáin—IV—*M'Colletane, M'Collitan,* Colleton, Collotan, Culleton, Culliton, (Cullington) ; 'son of coolacán' (sleeper) ; the name of an old family in Carlow and Wexford. Also ó coolacáin, q.v.

mac cogadáin, mac cogáin—IV—*M'Cogane,* MacCogan, MacCoggan, Cogan, Coggan ; 'son of cogadán' (a 'pet' form of cúcogaid, an Irish personal name, meaning 'war-hound,' 'warrior ') ; the name of a family in Co. Leitrim who were chiefs of Clann Fearnaighe, now angl. Glanfarne, a district to the east and northeast of Loch Allen. A branch of the family settled in Co. Meath.

mac cogaidín—IV—Cogavin, Cogeen ; a var. of mac cogadáin, q.v.

mac cogaráin—IV—*M'Cogerane,* Coghran, Cochrane, Caughran ; 'son of cogarán' ; the name of an old Thomond family, descendants, no doubt, of cogarán, 'the confidential servant' of Brian Boru. Also ó cogaráin, q.v.

mac coibdeanaig—IV—*M'Cuffeny,* Coveney, (?) MacGoverney, Governey ; 'son of coibdeanac' (trooper) ; a rare surname. We have also ó coibdeanaig, q.v.

mac coilid, mac coilig—VII—*M'Killie,* MacQuilly ; Cox ; a short form of mac an coilig, q.v. Also mag coilig.

mac coiligin, Cox ; a Cork surname ; probably an attenuated form of mac colgan, q.v. Cf. ó cuileagan.

mac coilín—IV—*M'Colline, M'Culline, M'Kellyn,* MacCullion, MacCullen, MacKillen, MacKellen, MacQuillin, MacQuillian, MacQuillion, MacQuillan, Collen,

Cullin, Cullian, Cullen, Quillen, Quillan, Collins, &c.;
'son of Coilín'; a var. of Mac Cailín, q.v. This
form of the surname was very common in Tirconnell,
and in Down and Antrim, at the end of the 16th
century. Its angl. forms cannot always be distinguished from those of Mac Uróilín, q.v.

Mac Coimín—IV—*M'Comin*, *M'Comyn*, MacComming,
MacKimmon, Comyn, Comyns, Commons, Kimmins,
etc.; 'son of Coimín' (dim. of cam, bent). This surname was common in parts of Munster, and in Wexford, Monaghan and Cavan. Its angl. forms cannot
always be distinguished from those of Ó Coimín, Ó
Comáin, nor from the Anglo-Norman Comyn.

Mac Coingeallaig—IV—*M'Cangellye*, *M'Congillye*,
M'Cynelig, *M'Kennella*, *M'Connella*, Quinnelly,
Kennelly, Connelly, Connolly; 'son of Coingeallac'
(faithful to pledges); now always Ó Coingeallaig,
q.v.; the name of a family in West Cork who were
formerly retainers of O'Donovan and at one time
owned seven ploughlands in the parish of Drinagh,
near Drimoleague. Also in use in Ormond.

Mac Coinín—IV—*M'Conine*, *M'Kenyne*, *M'Canine*,
Cuneen, Cunneen, Conyeen, Kinneen, Kenning,
Canning, &c., and, by 'translation,' Rabbit; 'son of
Coinín' (an old Irish personal name); a scattered
surname. There are, no doubt, several distinct
families so called. The Mac Coinins of Mayo, anciently seated in Erris, were noted patrons of learning.

Mac Coinleaga, v. Mac an Leaga.

Mac Coinneagáin—IV—*M'Quenegan*, *M'Konningham*,
Cunningham, &c. V. Mac Cuinneagáin.

Mac Coinnig—IV—*M'Coinny*, MacKinney, MacKenzie,
&c.; 'son of Coinneac' (fair one); the name of a
celebrated Scottish clan. It appears to have been
also an Irish surname, but its angl. forms cannot now
be distinguished from those of Mac Cionaoit, q.v.
The Scottish-Gaelic is Mac Coinnic.

Mac Coirce, Oates; a corruption of Mac Cuirc, q.v.

Mac Coise—VII—*M'Cashie*, *M'Cashy*, MacCosh, Mac-

Quish, Cush ; Legge, Foote ; probably 'son of the courier,' the 'footman.' Erard MacCoise was a celebrated Irish poet and chronicler. The name is found also in Scotland.

Mᴀc COISTEᴀLᴃ, Mᴀc COISTEᴀLᴃᴀIᵹ—IV—Costello, Costelloe ; 'son of OirᴅeᴀLᴃ' ; var. of Mᴀc OirᴅeᴀLᴃ, Mᴀc OirᴅeᴀLᴃᴀIᵹ, owing to the attraction over of the c of Mᴀc to the second part of the surname.

Mᴀc COITIL—V—M'Ketyll, Kettyle, Kettle ; 'son of Ketill ' (a Norse personal name, Ang.-Sax. 'Cytel ') ; a rare, but well-known Irish surname, probably of Norse origin. In the 16th century, it was peculiar to Co. Louth.

Mᴀc COITIR—V—M'Cottir, MacCotter, MacCottier, Mac-Cottar, Cotter, Cottier, Cottiers ; 'son of OITIr' (the Norse Ottar) ; a var. of Mᴀc OITIr (q.v.) by the attraction over of the c of Mᴀc to the second part of the surname.

Mᴀc COLᵹᴀn—IV—M'Collgan, MacColgan, Colgan, Collagan, Colligan, Culligan ; 'son of COLᵹᴀ' ; more anciently Ó COLᵹᴀn ; the name of a sept of the Oirghialla, who were chiefs of Ui MacCarthainn, now the barony of Tirkeevan, Co. Derry, until dispossessed by the Cinel Eoghain, and afterwards erenaghs of Donaghmore, in Inishowen. The celebrated Father John Colgan, the hagiographer, was of this family.

Mᴀc COLLᴀ—IV—M'Colla, M'Collagh, M'Colly, M'Colle, MacCulla, MacCullagh, MacCollough, MacCullough, MacColl, MacCull, &c. ; 'son of Colla' (a common personal name among the MacDonnells and Mac Sweeneys) ; a scattered surname ; in the spoken language, sometimes made Mᴀc COLLᴀc.

Mᴀc COLMᴀIn—IV—M'Collman, MacColman, Coleman ; 'son of COLmᴀn' (dim. of COLm, a dove, a very common Irish personal name).

Mᴀc COLUIm—IV—MacColum, MacCollum, MacCollom, Colum, Collum, &c. ; 'son of COLUm' (dove) ; an Ulster surname, found chiefly in Antrim, Tyrone and

Donegal; also a Scottish surname, written Ɱᴀc Ⲥᴀʟᴜⲓⲙ, q.v.

Ɱᴀc Ⲥⲟⲙ'Ⲃᴀⲓⲛ, Ɱᴀc Ⲥⲟⲙᵹᴀⲓⲛ—IV—*M'Cowane*, *M'Cone*, MacCowan, MacKone, MacKoen; 'son of Ⲥⲟⲙ'Ⲃᴀⲛ,' or 'Ⲥⲟⲙᵹᴀⲛ'; originally a Meath surname but long dispersed through Ulster. It is difficult, if not impossible, to distinguish its angl. forms from those of Ɱᴀc Ⲉⲟᵹᴀⲓⲛ, q.v.

Ɱᴀc Ⲥⲟⲙᵹᴀⲓʟʟ—IV—*M'Cole*, MacCole; 'son of Ⲥⲟⲙᵹᴀʟʟ'; extremely rare.

Ɱᴀc Ⲥⲟⲛᴀⲓʟʟ—IV—MacConnell; 'son of Ⲥⲟⲛᴀʟʟ' (high-ruler); very rare; to be distinguished from Ɱᴀc 'Ⲃⲟⲙⲛᴀⲓʟʟ, which in most instances is the origin of MacConnell.

Ɱᴀc Ⲥⲟⲛᴀⲓʟʟ Óⲓᵹ—IV—*M'Connell oge*, MacConnellogue Conlogue; 'son of young Ⲥⲟⲛᴀʟʟ'; an old Tirconnell surname.

Ɱᴀc Ⲥⲟⲛᴀʟʟⲧᴀ—IV—MacAnalty, MacNalty, Nalty; 'son of Ⲥú-ᴀʟʟᴀⲓ'Ⲃ' (wild-dog, wolf); a Sligo surname to be distinguished from Ɱᴀc ᴀⲛ Uʟⲧᴀⲓᵹ, q.v.

Ɱᴀc Ⲥⲟⲛᴀⲛᴀⲟⲛᴀⲓᵹ—IV—*M'Anonany*, *M'Anenany*, MacNamanamee, Nanany; 'son of Ⲥú-ᴀⲛ-ᴀⲟⲛᴀⲓᵹ (hound of the fair); a var. in Co. Roscommon of Ɱᴀc Ⲥⲟⲛᴀⲟⲛᴀⲓᵹ, q.v.

Ɱᴀc Ⲥⲟⲛᴀⲟⲛᴀⲓᵹ—IV—*M'Enanny*, *M'Nenny*, Mac-Aneany, MacAneeny, MacAneny, MacEneany, Mac-Neney, MacNeeny, Conheeny, Cunneeny, and, by 'translation' Bird in Ulster, and Rabbit in Connacht; 'son of Ⲥú-ᴀⲟⲛᴀⲓᵹ' (hound of the fair); the name of a well-known Monaghan family, who were formerly seated in the neighbourhood of Clones. The surname has been corrupted in Ulster to Ɱᴀc ᴀⲛ Ⲉᴀⲛᴀⲓᵹ and sometimes ridiculously 'translated' Bird. Also the name of a Roscommon family, sometimes called Ɱᴀc Ⲥⲟⲛᴀⲛᴀⲟⲛᴀⲓᵹ (q.v.), who gave its name to the town-land of Kilmacenanny, or Kilmacananneny, in the parish of Lissonuffy, where some of them were still inhabiting at the end of the 16th century. In Connacht, the surname is now generally angl. Rabbit,

owing to its similarity in pronunciation to the word
'coinín,' a rabbit. There was a third family of the
name, apparently a branch of the MacDonnells, in
Co. Antrim, who are now probably represented by
MacAneny in Co. Tyrone.

mac conboirne—IV—*M'Conborney*, Burns; 'son of
Cú-boirne' (hound of Boirean, a place-name); the
name of a family of the Ui Fiachrach race, in Co.
Mayo. O'Donovan found it still extant under the
angl. form of Burns. It was also written Ó
Conboirne.

mac concairrge, mac concarraige—IV—*M'En-
carrigy*, *M'Incargy*, *M'Necargy*, MacCarrick, Carrigy,
Carrigee, Kerragy, Carrick, and, by translation,
Rock; 'son of Cú-carraige' (an Irish personal name
meaning 'hound of the rock'); the name of a Thomond
family who were stewards to the O'Briens in West
Clare. In 1641, they were proprietors of Lisbulligeen,
in the parish of Kilfenora. This surname is also found
in Sligo and Leitrim where, however, it is probably a
substitution for the old surname mac Concatraic, q.v.

mac concata—IV—*M'Conchaa*, *M'Encaha*, Battle,
Battles; 'son of Cú-cata' ('hound of battle,' 'war-
hound'); the name of an old Sligo family who were
living at the end of the 16th century in Coolaney. It
is now always absurdly 'translated' Battle or Battles.
MacConcahy would be the proper angl. form.

mac concatrac—IV—MacCarrick; 'son of Cúcatrac'
('hound of the catair' or fort); the name of a Sligo
family of the Ui Fiachrach race. O'Donovan found
some of the name in the parish of Templeboy in
Tireragh, angl. MacCarrick. V. mac concairrge.

mac concearca—IV—*M'Anyerkaye*, *M'Ingarky*,
M'Egarky, *M'Igarky*, *M'Igarke*, Yorke; 'son of
Cú-Cearca' (hound of Cearc, a place-name); a rare
and scattered surname; in the 16th century, found
chiefly in the midlands, and in Sligo and Galway.

mac concobair—IV—*M'Connogher*, *M'Connoghor*,
M'Conoher, *M'Connor*, MacNogher, MacNaugher, Mac-

Noher, MacNoger, Minogher, Minoher, Connor, Nogher, Noher, Naugher, Naughter, Nocter, &c. ; ' son of Conċoḃaṛ' (an ancient and very common Irish personal name, Lat. ' Cornelius,' and angl. ' Cornelius ' and ' Connor ').

Ṁac conċoṫ̃aiṫ—IV—*M'Enchogy, M'Anhoggy, M'Nagcogy* ; ' son of Cú-ċoṫ̃aiṫ ' (war-hound) ; an old surname in Roscommon and Longford ; now obsolete or, possibly, changed to Ṁac Coṫ̃áin, Ṁac Coṫ̃aiṫín, q.v. O'Donovan gives the angl. form as MacConkey which I have failed to verify.

Ṁac conċoiṫ̃ċríċe—IV—*M'Conchogrye, M'Enkegrie, M'Nikegrie*, and now, by ' translation,' L'Estrange ; ' son of Cú-ċoiṫ̃ċríċe ' (border-hound) ; the name of a family who were anciently chiefs of Muinntear Searcachain in Westmeath or Offaly. It still survives in the midlands under the Frenchified form of L'Estrange.

Ṁac conċoille, Ṁac conċoilleaṫ—IV—*M'Ancoyllew, M'Inchelly, M'Enkelly*, and now, by ' translation,' Woods and Cox ; ' son of Cú-ċoille(aṫ)' (hound of the wood) ; a scattered surname, chiefly in use in Derry and Tyrone, Wicklow and Wexford, Cork and Limerick, but now everywhere disguised under the angl. forms of Woods and Cox, the latter form being due to its similarity to ' coileaċ,' a cock.

Ṁac conċoillín—IV—*M'Necollen*, and now, by translation, Smallwoods, Woods ; ' son of Cú-ċoillín ' (hound of the little wood). Cf. Ṁac Conċoille above.

Ṁac conċollċoille—IV—Hazlewood, Hazlegrove, Hazleton, Hazelton ; ' son of Cú-ċollċoille ' (hound of the hazelwood).

Ṁac conċraṫa—IV—*M'Concroe, M'Encrogh, M'Ecroe*, MacEnchroe, MacEncroe, Crough, Crowe ; ' son of Conċraṫ ' (a rare Irish personal name) ; the name of an old Thomond family, still well known in Clare, Tipperary and Limerick.

Ṁac conċruaċan—IV—*M'Encroghan, M'Necroghan*,

M'Icrowghan, Croughan, Croghan, Crohan, Croan ; ' son of Cú-Cpuacán ' (hound of Croghan, in Roscommon, Ir. ' Cpuacu,' gen. ' Cpuacán ') ; an old Roscommon surname.

Mac conoui♭—IV—MacAnuff, MacAniff, MacEniff, MacKniff, MacNuff, MacNeffe, MacNiff, MacKiniff, MacEndoo, MacIndoo, MacAdoo, MacAdo, MacCaddoo, MacCaddo, Conniff, Conniffe, Conneffe, Cunniffe, Quinniff, Caddow, &c. ; ' son of Cú-ouʋ ' (the black hound) ; a Connacht surname.

Mac conꝺoꞃmaoile—IV—*M'Enormoyele*, Normoyle, Normile ; ' son of Cú ꝼoꞃmaoile ' (hound of Formoyle, a place in Co. Clare) ; the name of a Clare family who are probably a branch of the MacNamaras (v. Mac Conmapa) ; now common in Co. Limerick ; in the spoken language Mac Conoꞃmaoile.

Mac conꝼꞃaoic—IV—Conefry ; ' son of Cú-ꝼꞃaoic ' (hound of ꝼꞃaoc, a place-name).

Mac conᵹail, Mac conᵹaile—IV—*M'Congall*, Mac-Congail, MacConigly ; ' son of Conᵹal ' ; usually written Maᵹ Conᵹail, q.v. ; a Tirconnell surname, the same as Mac Conᵹaile below.

Mac conᵹaile—IV—MacIneely, MacNeely, MacNeela, MacNella, MacNealy, Coneely, Conneely, Conneally, Conneely, Conneelly, Connelly, Cunneely, Kennelly, (Connolly), &c. ; ' son of Conᵹal ' (high-valour, an old Irish personal name) ; an old surname in West Connacht ; still common in Galway and Mayo, but it is difficult, if not impossible, to distinguish its angl. forms from those of Mac Conᵹaola, q.v.

Mac conᵹalaiᵹ—IV—*M'Conalaye*, *M'Connally*, *M'Connolly*, Connolly ; ' son of Conᵹalac ' (deriv. of Conᵹal, high-valour) ; a rare surname, formerly in use in Sligo and Leitrim. In Co. Monaghan, it appears to have been sometimes used as an alias for Ó Conᵹalaiᵹ, q.v.

Mac conᵹamna—IV—*M'Kengawny*, *M'Engawney*, *M'Negowny*, (Gaffney, Caulfield) ; ' son of Cú-ᵹamna ' (calf-hound) ; the name of a branch of the Ui Fiachrach Aidhne, in the south of Co. Galway. It is still common in Longford and all the adjoining counties, also in Cork and Mayo, but now always disguised under the angl. forms of Gaffney and Caulfield.

mac conᵹaola—IV—MacCunneela, MacNeela, Mac Nella, &c.; 'son of Cú-ᵹaola' (hound of ᵹaola, a place-name in Co. Galway); the name of a family of Ui Fiachrach, in the south of Co. Galway. Its angl. forms can hardly be now distinguished from those of mac conᵹaile, q.v.

mac conleaᵹa, M'Kenlagh, M'Kinlea, MacKinlay, MacKinley, &c.; probably only a misspelling of mac an leaᵹa, q.v.

mac conleitreac—IV—(?) Letter, Letters; 'son of Cú-leitreac' (hound of leitir, a place-name); the name of an old family in Tirawley, Co. Mayo. They were seated at Ballykinletteragh, in the parish of Kilfian, but the name has long since disappeared from that district. It is not improbable, however, that it is the origin of Letters or Letter in other parts of Ireland.

mac conloca—IV—M'Anloghie, M'Inlocky, Kinlough, (?) Lough; 'son of Cú-loca' (hound of the lake). This surname seems to have originated in Co. Westmeath. It was always exceedingly rare.

mac conluacra—IV—M'Elvochra, Kiloughry, Kiloury; 'son of Cú-luacra' (hound of luacair, a place-name).

mac conluain—IV—M'Anleone, M'Anloyne, M'Collone, M'Colwan, Colvan, Colvin, Colavin, Cullivan, (Colvil, Colville, Collwell, Coldwell, Caldwell, &c.); a corruption of mac antuain; the name of a family of the Ui Fiachrach race, formerly seated in the parish of Dromard, Co. Sligo, where O'Donovan found the name under the angl. form of MacColwan. Before the end of the 16th century, it had passed into Co. Leitrim, and is still found in that county, and in the neighbouring county of Cavan, under strange angl. forms.

mac conⅿⱥⅽ—IV—*M'Conwicke, M'Conick,* Connick; 'son of Conⅿⱥⅽ' (an ancient Irish personal name, meaning 'son of the hound'); a branch of the O'Farrells in Co. Longford.

mac conⅿⱥoⅼ—IV—*M'Convale, M'Conwaile, M'Conwell,* MacConville, Conwell; 'son of Conⅿⱥoⱡ' (high-chief); a well-known Ulster surname; found chiefly in Antrim, Down and Armagh.

mac conmⱥрⱥ—IV—*M'Conmara,* MacNamara, Mac-Namarra, MacNamarrow; 'son of Cú-mⱥрⱥ' (hound of the sea). The MacNamaras who, next to the O'Briens, were the most powerful of the Dalcassian clans, derive their descent from Cⱥiрin, son of Cⱥр, the common ancestor of all the Oⱥⅼ ᵹCⱥiр. Their original territory was Ui Caisin, corresponding to the present deanery of Ogashin and comprising nine parishes in the east of Co. Clare; but in later times they ruled over a greatly enlarged territory which comprised the whole of Upper and Lower Tulla, and which, from their clan-name, was known as Cⱡⱥnn Ċuiⅼeⱥin. The MacNamaras were hereditary marshals of Thomond, and it was their privilege to inaugurate O'Brien. A branch of the family settled, sometime before the end of the 16th century, in Co. Down.

mac conmeⱥòⱥ, mac conmeⱥòⱥ—IV—*M'Conmea, M'Conmay, M'Convea, M'Convey, M'Convay, M'Conwaie, M'Nema,* MacConaway, MacConway, MacNama, Conmey, Convey, &c.; 'son of Cú-meⱥòⱥ,' (hound of meⱥò, a place-name); the name of a family who were anciently chiefs of muinnⱦeⱥр Lⱥoòⱥċⱥin, in Westmeath, but long dispersed.

mac conmiòe—IV—MacConamy, MacConomy, Mac-Namee, Conmee, Mee, Meath, &c.; 'son of Cú-miòe' (hound of Meath); the name of a family who were hereditary poets to the O'Neills of Tyrone; still common in Ulster

mac con nⱥ buⱥiⅼe—IV—MacNaboola; 'son of Cú nⱥ buⱥiⅼe' (hound of Boyle); a rare Roscommon surname.

mac connaċtaiʒ—VII—MacConnaughty, MacConnerty; 'son of the Connachtman' (Ir. 'Connaċtaċ ').

mac connaʒáin—IV—*M'Connigan*, *M'Konningham*, Cunningham, &c.; 'son of Connaʒán' (a dim. of Conn); a var. of mac Cuinneaʒáin, q.v.

mac connaiʋ—IV—*M'Conna*, *M'Conney*, *M'Cunny*, *M'Cony*, MacCona, Conney, and, by 'translation,' Woods; 'son of Connaʋ' (an old Irish personal name); a scattered surname. Its angl. forms are difficult to distinguish from those of mac Coinniʒ, q.v.; and MacCona may sometimes stand for Mac-Dona. Moore, in his 'Manx Names' (p. 25), gives Quinney as an angl. form of this surname, but the pronunciation in spoken Manx, as indicated by him, would rather point to mac Coinniʒ as the origin; and, as he shows (p. 28), mac Cainniʒ was an old Manx surname.

mac connla, mac connlaoʋa—IV—*M'Connley*, *M'Conley*, *M'Conly*, Conley, Conly; 'son of Connlaoʋ'; apparently an Offaly surname.

mac connṁaiʒ—IV—*M'Conough*, *M'Conowe*, Conway; 'son of Connṁaċ'; a rare surname in Clare and Offaly; apparently an alias for Ó Connṁaiʒ, q.v.

mac conorṁaoile, Normoyle, Normile. V. mac Conformaoile.

mac conraoi—IV—*M'Conrie*, *M'Conry*, Mac-an-Ree, Conree, Cunree, Conry, Conroy, and, by 'translation,' King; 'son of Cúraoi' (hound of the plain, or of battle); the name of a family, said to be of Dalcassian origin, who were anciently lords of Dealbna Thire-da-locha, in the barony of Moycullen, between Loch Corrib and Galway Bay, where they are still numerous. The name was also common in Kerry and Limerick; but both in Munster and Connacht it is now usually mistranslated King, owing to the erroneous belief that it is derived from ' ríʒ,' a king, and that the Irish form is mac an Ríoʒ, ' son of the king.'

mac conraṫa—IV—*M'Conraghe*, *M'Conraye*, Conrahy,

(Conroy) ; ' son of Cúṗaṫa ' (hound of prosperity) ; an old Offaly surname ; also Ó Conṗaṫa, q.v.

Mac Conriaḋa—IV—*M'Conryde*, MacConready, Mac-Aready, MacCready ; ' son of Cú-Riaḋa ' (Riada's hound).

Mac Conriain—IV—Cunreen, King ; ' son of Cú-Riain ' (Rian's hound) ; extremely rare ; sometimes ' translated ' King on the erroneous supposition that it is derived from ' ríġ,' a king. Cf. Mac Conṗaoi.

Mac Conruḃa—IV—*M'Conrowe*, *M'Enrowe*, *M'Erowe*, *M'ny Rowe*, MacEnroe, Enroe, Rowe, Roe ; ' son of Cú-Ruḃa ' (hound of Ruḃa, or Rowe, a place-name) ; a Breifney surname.

Mac Consaiḋín—V—*M'Considine*, Considine ; ' son of Constantine ' ; the name of a branch of the O'Briens in Co. Clare, descended from Domnall Mór Ó Briain, King of Munster.

Mac Consnáṁa—IV—*M'Conave*, *M'Kinnawe*, *M'En-awe*, MacAnawe, Kinnavy, Kineavy ; (Adams) ; Forde, Ford ; ' son of Cú-ṡnáṁa ' (the swimming-hound, expert swimmer) ; the name of a family in Co. Leitrim who were formerly chiefs of Muinter Kenny, in the present barony of Dromahaire. It was popularly supposed to be ' Mac an Áṫa,' son of the ford, and was accordingly ' translated ' Ford, Forde. I find it also angl. Adams, which shows that it must have been sometimes mistaken for Mac Áḋaiṁ, q.v.

Mac Conuisce—IV—*M'Enuske*, Uiske, Waters ; ' son of Cú-uirce ' (the water-hound) ; a Monaghan surname ; now also in use in Co. Mayo. It is popularly supposed to be ' Mac an Uirce,' son of the water, and is in consequence generally ' translated ' Waters.

Mac Conulaḋ—IV—*M'Anullo*, *M'Enully*, *M'Annoll*, *M'Cowla*, *M'Cowloe*, *M'Cowley*, MacAnulla, MacNully, MacAnaul, MacKinaul, (MacNall), MacCullow, Culloo ; ' son of Cú-Ulaḋ ' (hound of Ulidia, East Ulster) ; an East Ulster surname. The Cú of this surname is sometimes not inflected ; hence the old angl. forms

M'Cowla, M'Cowloe, and the modern MacCullow, Culloo, &c.

mac CORCÁin—IV—*M'Corkane*, *M'Corkan*, Corken ; ' son of Coṗcán ' (dim. of Coṗc) ; a rare Wicklow surname.

mac CORCRÁin—IV—*M'Corcrane*, *M'Corkrane*, Corcoran, Corkran, Corkeran, &c. ; ' son of Coṗcrán ' (dim. of ' coṗcair,' purple). The head of this family was chief of Clann Ruainne in Ely O'Carroll.

mac CORMACÁin—IV—MacCormiken, (MacCormack, MacCormick) ; ' son of Coṗmacán ' (dim. of Coṗmac) ; a rare Connacht surname. The angl. form is shortened in Co. Mayo to MacCormack and MacCormick.

mac CORMAIC—IV—MacCormac, MacCormack, MacCormick, Cormac, Cormick, Cormack ; ' son of Coṗmac ' (an ancient and very common Irish personal name) ; a common surname in all parts of Ireland.

mac CORRA, mac CORRAIḊ—IV—*M'Correy*, *M'Corr*, MacCorry, MacCurry, Corry, Curry, Corra, Corr ; ' son of Coṗraḋ ' (spear) ; a rare surname. In Co. Leitrim, it seems to have been a var. of mac Coṗraiḋín, q.v.

mac CORRAIḊÍN—IV—*M'Corrine*, *M'Curine*, Curreen, Currin, Curren ; ' son of Coṗraiḋín ' (a dim. of Coṗraḋ) ; the name of a family of the Ui Fiachrach race, formerly seated in the parish of Skreen, Co. Sligo, but, at the end of the 16th century, more numerous in Co. Leitrim ; written mac Coṗraoin by MacFirbis.

mac CORRḂUIḊE—IV—*M'Corboy*, *M'Corby*, Corboy, Corby ; ' son of Coṗṗḃuiḋe ' (yellow-crane) ; a rare surname in Leix and Tipperary.

mac COSCRACÁin—IV—*M'Cossrichan*, MacCuskern, Coskeran, Cuskern, (Cosgrave, Cosgrove) ; ' son of Coṗcṗacán ' (dim. of Coṗcṗac,' victorious) ; a Co. Down surname.

mac COSCRAIɢ—IV—*M'Cosegrave*, Cosgrave, Cosgrove ; ' son of Coṗcṗac ' (victorious) ; the name of a family who were anciently erenaghs of Clones. V. Ó Coṗcṗaiɢ.

Mac COSTAȝáiɴ, *M'Costegane, M'Costegan,* Costigan; a corruption of Mac Oiꞃτιcíɴ, q.v.

Mac CꞃáḃaȝáIn—IV—Crawford; 'son of Cꞃáḃaȝáɴ' (religious); a rare surname in Louth and Monaghan. I can find no early instance, and suspect that it is a substitution for Mac Cꞃáḃáɴ, q.v.

Mac CꞃáḃáIn—IV—*M'Craven, M'Cravin,* Craven, Cravin, Creaven; 'son of Cꞃáḃáɴ' (religious); an old surname in Louth and Monaghan; probably now replaced in some instances by Mac Cꞃáḃaȝáiɴ.

Mac CꞃaIτ—IV—MacCraith, MacCrea, MacGrath, &c., 'son of MacꞃaIτ' (an Irish personal name); a var. of Mac ꞃaIτ, owing to the attraction over of the c of Mac to the second part of the name. V. Mac ꞃaIτ and Maȝ ꞃaIτ.

Mac CꞃIaȝáIn—IV—*M'Crigan,* Cregan; 'son of ꞃIaȝáɴ'; a form of Mac ꞃIaȝáɴ (q.v.) due to the attraction over of the c of Mac to the second part of the surname; now always Ó CꞃIaȝáiɴ in the spoken language.

Mac CꞃíoḃáIn—IV—*M'Cridane, M'Credan,* Creedon, Creed; 'son of Cꞃíoḃáɴ'; an old surname in Cork, Limerick and Tipperary; now always Ó Cꞃíoḃáiɴ in the spoken language.

Mac CꞃIomṫaIɴɴ—IV—*M'Criffon, M'Criohin, M'Creohan,* MacCrohan; 'son of Cꞃíomṫaɴɴ' (fox); in the spoken language, now Mac CꞃIoτaɴ; the name of a branch of the O'Sullivans in Kerry. The MacCrohans once owned Letter Castle.

Mac CꞃíonáIɴ—IV—*M'Crenan,* Crennan; 'son of Cꞃíonáɴ.'

Mac CꞃíosTa—V—*M'Cristie,* Christy, Christie, &c.; 'son of Christy' (a pet form of Christian or Christopher).

Mac CꞃíosTaIl—V—*M'Christell, M'Christall,* MacChrystall; 'son of Christal' (a form of Christopher); a Co. Down surname.

Mac CꞃíosTóꞃa—V—Christopherson, Christopher; 'son of Christopher.'

ⱮⱭⱲ CRISⱦÍN—V—*M'Christeine,* *M'Christyne,* Mac-
Criskin, MacGriskin, Christian ; ' son of Christian.'

ⱮⱭⱲ CRÓNᵹⱭ⟆Le—IV—*M'Crongully, M'Cronilla,* Cronelly ; ' son of CⱃónᵹⱭ⟆.' V. Ó CⱃónᵹⱭ⟆Le.

ⱮⱭⱲ CRUⱢⱢ—IV—MacCrum, MacCrumb, MacRum ; ' son
of CⱃoⱢ ' (bent, crooked).

ⱮⱭⱲ CRUⱢⱦÍN—IV—*M'Crutten,* *M'Cruttan,* MacCurtin,
Curtin, (Curtis) ; ' son of CⱃuⱢⱦín ' (hunch-backed) ;
the name of a learned family of antiquaries in Thomond, whose patrimony was Carrowduff, in the parish
of Killaspuglonane, and Laghvally, in the parish of
Kilmacreehy, Co. Clare. A branch of the family
settled in East Limerick some time prior to 1600.
Andrew MacCurtin, who lived in the early part of
the 18th century, was one of the best Irish scholars
of his time.

ⱮⱭⱲ CUⱭCÁⱢN—IV—MacGoohan ; ' son of CuⱭCÁn ' (dim.
of cuⱭⱄ, a cuckoo) ; a rare Leitrim surname.

ⱮⱭⱲ CUⱭ⟆⟆ⱭCⱦⱭ — IV — *M'Gwolaghtie,* *M'Gwllaghty,*
(Goolden, Goulding, Golden) ; ' son of CuⱭ⟆⟆ⱭCⱦⱭ ' ; a
Sligo surname ; now changed to Ó ᵹuⱭ⟆⟆ⱭCⱦⱭ and
angl. Goolden, &c.

ⱮⱭⱲ CUⱭRⱦⱭ, ⱮⱭⱲ CUⱭⱢRⱦ—IV—*M'Cowrty, M'Cowart,*
M'Cuyrt, MacCourt, MacCort, MacCourtney, (Courtney) ; a Co. Louth surname ; not improbably a corruption of ⱮⱭⱲ ⱮuⱢⱃⱄeⱭⱃⱦⱭⱢᵹ, q.v.

ⱮⱭⱲ CUⱢ⟆ⱢⱢ—IV—*M'Cwlin, M'Cowlin,* MacCullen, Mac-
Quillen, Cullen, Quillen, and, by translation, Holly ;
' son of CuⱢⱦeⱭnn ' (holly) ; in use in Monaghan and
Louth.

ⱮⱭⱲ CUⱢ⟆⟆—IV—MacQuill, MacGuill ; ' son of Co⟆⟆ ' ;
very rare.

ⱮⱭⱲ CÚⱢ⟆RⱢⱭⱞⱭⱢᵹ—IV—*M'Coulray,* Culreavy, Colreavy
and, by translation, Gray, Grey ; ' son of CÚⱢⱃⱢⱭⱞⱭⱞⱠ '
(grey-poll), or more probably a corruption of ⱮⱭⱲ
ᵹⱢo⟆⟆ⱭⱃⱢⱭⱞⱭⱢᵹ, q.v. ; a midland surname.

ⱮⱭⱲ CUⱢⱢⱢÍN—IV—MacCumming, MacCummings, Cummin, Cuming, Cumming, Cummins, Cummings, Kimmins, &c. ; ' son of CuⱢⱢⱢín.' Also ⱮⱭⱲ CoⱢⱢⱢín, q.v.

Mac Cuinnuilis, Mac Cuinnuulis—IV—MacCandlis, Mac-
Candless, MacCanlis, MacAndless, &c.; 'son of
Cuinuuleaṙ' (an old Irish personal name). V. Ó
Cuinuuiṙ.

Mac Cuinn—IV—MacQuinn, MacQuin, MacGuinn,
Quinn, 'son of Conn' (sense, reason, also a freeman,
an ancient Irish personal name).

Mac Cuinneaġáin—IV—*M'Cunnegane*, *M'Quynegan*,
MacCunnigan, Cunnigan, Kinnegan, Cunagum, Cunningham; 'son of Cuinneaġán' (dim. of Conn); a
common surname in all parts of Ireland, but Ó Cuinneaġáin (q.v.) was nearly everywhere an alias.

Mac Cuinneáin—IV—*M'Cunayn*, *M'Kenane*, Cunnane,
etc.; 'son of Cuinneán' (dim. of Conn). V. Ó Cuinneáin.

Mac Cuirc—IV—*M'Kwirke*, MacQuirk, MacQuirke;
'son of Corc' (heart, an ancient Irish personal name);
also Maġ Cuirc, q.v.

Mac Cuirtín, MacCurtin, Curtin; a metathesized form
of Mac Cruitín, q.v.

Mac Cumascaiġ—IV—MacCumisky, MacCumesky, Mac-
Comiskey, Cumisky, Cumesky, Cumiskey, Comesky,
Comiskey, Commiskey, Cumisk, (Comerford, Cummer-
ford), &c.; 'son of Cumascac' (confuser). This
surname is almost peculiar to Cavan, Westmeath and
Longford.

Mac Curtáin—IV—*M'Curtaine*, *M'Curtayne*, MacCurtain, Curtayne, Courtayne, Curtain, Curtin, &c.;
'son of Artán' (dim. of Art); a Munster form of
Mac Cartáin, q.v. This surname was well established
in Cork before the end of the 16th century.

Mac Daḃóc, Mac Daḃóg, Mac Daḃuc, Mac
Daḃuic — V — *M'Davock*, *M'Davog*, *M'Dough*,
Doake, Doag, Doig; 'son of Davuc' (a dim. of
David).

Mac Daḃóc, Mac Daḃóg, Mac Daḃuc, Mac Daḃ-
uic—V—*M'Cawque*, *M'Cavoke*, *M'Cavog*, *M'Coag*,
M'Coke, MacAvock, MacCavock, MacCoog, MacCook,
Cooke; a var. of Mac Daḃóc, &c.; the name of a

branch of the Burkes in Co. Galway, and perhaps of
other families in different parts of Ireland.

Mᴀc Oᴀɩbᴇɩᴅ—V—*M'Daveyd*, *M'Deyt*, MacDavid, Mac-
Davitt, MacDaid, MacDevitt, MacDivitt, Davitt,
Devitt, Daid, Dade, &c. ; ' son of Davet ' (a dim. of
David) ; the name of a branch of the O'Dohertys of
Inishowen who derive their name and descent from
David O'Doherty who fell in battle in the year 1208 ;
numerous in N.W. Ulster where it is generally angl.
MacDaid and MacDevitt ; also in use in Co. Mayo,
angl. Davitt, but whether, or not, the descent of the
family is the same as that of Inishowen, I am unable
to say. The local pronunciation is Mᴀc Oᴀᴇɩᴅ.

Mᴀc Oᴀɩbᴇɩᴅ—V—*M'Caveat*, MacCavitt, MacKevitt,
MacCaet ; a var. of Mᴀc Oᴀɩbᴇɩᴅ, q.v. ; formerly a
Galway surname, now peculiar to S.E. Ulster and
Louth.

Mᴀc Oᴀɩbɩᴅ—V—*M'David*, *M'Davie*, *M'Davy*, *M'Dave*,
M'Day, *M'Da*, MacDavid, MacDavitt, Davy, Davey,
Day, Davies, Davis, Davidson, Davison, Dawson,
&c. ; ' son of David ' (a common name among the
early Anglo-Norman settlers in Ireland). There are
several distinct families of this name. Of these, two
are native Irish, namely, MacDavid of Thomond and
MacDavid of Wexford, the latter of the same stock
as the MacMurroughs ; and one Scottish, once
numerous and powerful in Badenoch. MacDavid was
also the title of the head of a branch of the Burkes
who, shortly after the Anglo-Norman invasion obtained possession of the district of Clann Connmhaigh,
the ancient patrimony of the O'Finaghtys, in Co.
Galway. The head of the MacDavids of Wexford
was known as Mᴀc Oᴀɩbɩᴅ Móꞃ, q.v.

Mᴀc Oᴀɩbɩᴅ—V—*M'Cavy*, MacCave, Cavey, Ceavey,
Cave ; a var. of Mᴀc Oᴀɩbɩᴅ, q.v. ; very rare.

Mᴀc Oᴀɩbɩᴅ Móꞃ, Mᴀc Oᴀɩbɩᴅ Móꞃ—V—*M'David
More*, *M'Davy More*, *M'Damore*, *M'Amore*, Davis ;
i.e., the great MacDavid ; the title of the head of
the family of Mᴀc Oᴀɩbɩᴅ in Co. Wexford, whose

patrimony lay in the north-east of that county. O'Donovan states, on the authority of the Book of Leinster, that this family is descended from Murchadh na nGaedheal, brother of Dermot MacMurrough. The name is now angl. Davis in Wexford.

Mac Dáil re Docair—IV—*M'Callredocker, M'Calradocker, M'Gallredocker*; 'son of Dáil re Docair' (an Irish designation); the name, in the 13th and 14th centuries, of followers of O'Donnell; in the 16th, peculiar to Roscommon; now either obsolete or changed into some other form, such as Ó Docraid, or Mac Giollavẟeascaiṁ, q.v.

Mac Dáire—IV—*M'Dary, M'Darey*; 'son of Dáire'; a famous patronymic in Irish literary history. It does not seem to have ever been a family name.

Mac Dara, Mac Daraċ, MacDara, Daragh, Darragh, Darrogh; Oak, Oakes, &c.; a shortened form of Mac Dubẟoaraċ, q.v.

Mac Diarmada—IV—*M'Dermody, M'Dermot, M'Dermonde, M'Derby*, MacDiarmod, MacDermott, MacDarby, Dermody, Darmody, Diarmid, Dermid, Dermond, Darby, &c.; 'son of Diarmaid' (an ancient and very common Irish personal name, angl. Dermot, Darby and Jeremiah). The most important family of this name are the MacDermotts of Moylurg. They were a branch of the Sil-Murray, long the ruling race in Connacht, of which, next to the O'Connors, they were the most powerful family. Their clan-name was Clann Maoilruanaiḋ, so called from Maolruanaiḋ, who was son of Tadhg O'Connor, King of Connacht, in the 11th century. They are, therefore, of the same stock as the O'Connors. From Diarmaid, who was the grandson of Maolruanaiḋ and died in 1159, they took the surname of Mac Diarmada, angl. MacDermott. About the middle of the 14th century, they divided into three distinct septs, each with a chief of its own, namely: MacDermott of Moylurg, who was overlord of all the MacDermotts, and had his fortress at the Rock of Lough Key, near Boyle;

MacDermottroe, or the Red MacDermott, who was chief of Tir-Thuthail, comprising the parish of Kilronan, and had his residence at Alderford ; and MacDermott Gall (or Gallda), the English or Anglicised MacDermott, who was chief of Artagh, comprising the parish of Tibohine. The two baronies of Boyle and Frenchpark now represent the patrimony of the MacDermotts. The MacDermotts played a conspicuous part in the history of Connacht. They retained their rank as lords of Moylurg down to the end of the 16th century ; and as successors to the O'Garas continued to hold considerable property at Coolavin, in Co. Sligo, down to recent times ; and The MacDermott is still known as Prince of Coolavin. V. Mac Diaṙmaḋa.

Mac Diaṙmaḋa — IV — *M'Kiermodie*, *M'Kearmode*, Kermode, &c. ; a var. of Mac Diaṙmaḋa, q.v. This is the usual form of the surname in the spoken Irish of Connacht, even when the radical ḋ is retained in the angl. form.

Mac Diaṙmaḋa Ġall, Mac Diaṙmaḋa Ġallḋa, MacDermott Gall ; the Anglicised MacDermott. V. Mac Diaṙmaḋa.

Mac Diaṙmaḋa Ruaḋ, *M'Dermody Roe*, MacDermottroe ; i.e., the Red MacDermott. V. Mac Diaṙmaḋa. It was in MacDermottroe's house at Alderford that Torlough O'Carolan, the last of the bards, died in 1737.

Mac Díomasaiġ — IV — MacGimpsey, MacJimpsey ; 'son of Díomasaċ' (proud) ; a rare Ulster surname.

Mac Domnaill—IV—*M'Donaill*, *M'Donall*, MacDonald, MacDonnell, MacDaniel, Donaldson, Donald, &c. ; 'son of Domnall' (world-mighty, an ancient and very common Irish personal name, angl. Donald and Daniel). There are three distinct families of this name : (1) The MacDonalds, or MacDonnells, of Scotland, who derive their name and descent from Domnall, or Donald, grandson of Somhairle thane of Argyle about the middle of the 12th century. They

were the most powerful and warlike of all the Highland clans, and as lords of the Isles played an important part in the history of Scotland. In the 14th
and 15th centuries, the MacDonalds came over in
large numbers to Ireland, where they became famous
as leaders of gallowglasses or heavy armed soldiers.
They formed a military clan under their own chiefs
who were often of high rank, and in reward for their
services obtained grants of land in different parts of
the country. In this way they seem to have formed
a permanent settlement in Leinster as early as the
middle of the 15th century, and acquired considerable
estates in Leix and the present Co. of Wicklow.
By the marriage John Mor, son of the Lord of the
Isles, with the heiress of MacEoin Bissett, about the
beginning of the 15th century, the Glinns of Antrim
came into their possession, but it was only about the
year 1520 that, in right of this marriage, they effected
a permanent settlement in that county. The Mac-
Donnells played a conspicuous part in the confederate
and Jacobite wars, and both in Ireland and Scotland,
were true to the last to the Stuart cause. The great
bulk of our Irish MacDonnells belong to this race.
(2) The MacDonnells of Clan-Kelly. They were chiefs
of Clan-Kelly in Co. Fermanagh, and even as late as
the end of the 16th century formed a distinct clan,
with a chief of the name. (3) The MacDonnells of
Thomond. This family, according to Dr. O'Brien
(Irish Dict. s.v. Ooṁnall, Conċobaɲ), is a branch of
that of O'Brien, being descended from Ooṁnall, who
was son of Murtagh Mor O'Brien, King of Ireland.
MacDonnell, or MacDonald, is now one of our most
numerous surnames. V. Mac Ooṁnaill.

Mac Ooṁnaill—IV—*M'Coenill*, *M'Conill*, *M'Gonell*,
MacConell, MacConnell, MacGonnell, &c. ; a var. of
Mac Ooṁnaill, q.v. This form of the surname is
common in the spoken language even when the angl.
form is MacDonnell, with the radical O retained.
In Co. Mayo it is sometimes pronounced Ó Coṁnaill.

Mac ⅅonncⱯꝺⱯ, Mac ⅅonncⱯıꝺ—IV—*M'Donoghue,*
M'Donnoghie, M'Donaghy, M'Donchie, M'Denis, Mac-
Donnagh, MacDonough, MacDonogh, MacDonagh,
MacDona, MacDunphy, Donoghue, Donohoe,
Donaghy, Donogh, Donagh, Dunphy, Duncan, Denni-
son, Denison, Dennis, &c.; 'son of ⅅonncⱯꝺ'
(brown warrior, or strong warrior, an ancient and
very common Irish personal name, angl. Donough,
Denis.) There are at least three distinct families
bearing this surname : (1) A branch of the
MacCarthys, who were chiefs of Duhallow, in Co.
Cork, and at one time very powerful. Their principal
seat was at Kanturk. (2) A branch of the MacDermotts of Moylurg, who were chiefs of Tirerrill and
Corran, in Co. Sligo, and resided at Ballymote. The
Book of Ballymote was compiled under their patronage.
An offshoot of this family settled in Co. Clare, and
thence spread into Co. Limerick. (3) A Scottish clan
in Perthshire, said to be a branch of the MacDonalds.
This family now angl. their name Duncan, and some
of them call themselves Robertson. V. Mac ⅅonncⱯꝺⱯ.

Mac ⅅonncⱯꝺⱯ, Mac ⅅonncⱯıꝺ—IV—*M'Conogho,*
M'Conough, M'Connagh, M'Conna, MacConachie, Mac-
Connachie, MacConnaghy, MacConaghy, MacCon-
naughey, MacConohy, MacCona, MacConkey, Mac-
Konkey, Conify, (Robertson) ; variants of Mac ⅅonncⱯꝺⱯ, Mac ⅅonncⱯıꝺ, q.v. ; common in the spoken
language even when the radical ꝺ is retained in the
angl. form.

Mac ⅅⱭRCⱯıꝺ—IV—MacArchy, MacDorcy ; a var. of
MⱭʒ ⅅoꝛcⱯıꝺ, q.v. O'Donovan gives the angl.
form as MacDorcy, Dorcey, which I am unable to
verify.

Mac ⅅuⱭRcⱭın—IV—MacGurgan, Gurkin, Durcan,
Durkan, Durkin, Zorkin ; 'son of ⅅuⱭꝛcⱭn'; the
name of a well-known North Connacht family who
were anciently lords of Cuil Neiridh, in Co. Sligo, and
are probably a branch of the O'Haras. This surname

is sometimes pronounced Ó Cuaṙcáin in the spoken language of Mayo.

Mac Ouḃoara, Mac Ouḃoaraċ—IV—*M'Dwdara*, MacAdarrah, MacAdarra, MacDara, Daragh, Darra, Darragh, Darrock, and, by translation, Oak, Oaks, Oakes ; ' son of Ouḃoaṙaċ ' (the black-man of the oak) ; also written Mac Ouiḃoaṙa, Mac Ouiḃoaṙaċ (q.v.), and shortened to Mac Oaṙa, Mac Oaṙaċ, q.v.

Mac Ouḃ§aill—IV—*M'Doole*, *M'Doell*, *M'Doile*, MacDool, MacDowall, MacDowell, MacDugal, Mac-Dougall, MacDugald, MacDougald, MacDole, Madole, Doole, Dowell, Dougall, Dugald, &c. ; ' son of Ouḃ-§aill ' (the black-stranger, a name given by the Irish to the Danes) ; the name of a Scoto-Irish family of the same stock as the MacDonalds, being descended from Soṁaiṗle, thane of Argyle (slain 1165), who was the common ancestor of both families. The Mac-Dugalds were lords of Lorne in Scotland. Some of them, like the MacDonalds, came over to Ireland, in the 14th and 15th centuries, as captains of gallow-glasses, and settled in Co. Roscommon and other parts of the west and north of Ireland. V. Mac Ouḃ§aill.

Mac Ouḃ§aill—IV—*M'Cowgall*, *M'Cougald*, *M'Co-wyle*, *M'Cooel*, *M'Cual*, *M'Coole*, *M'Cole*, *M'Coyle*, MacCool, MacCole, Coole, Cole, Coyle, Coiles, &c. ; a var. of Mac Ouḃ§aill, q.v. This is the usual form of the surname in the spoken language, even when the radical O is retained in the angl. form. Cf. Mac Oóṁnaill.

Mac Ouḃraoáin—IV—Doordan, Dordan ; ' son of Ouḃraoán ' (atom, pygmy) ; a rare Connacht surname. Maolṁaoóǵ, Mac Ouḃraoáin, abbot of Saul, Co. Down, died in the year 1156.

Mac Ouḃuioir—IV—MacDwyer ; ' son of Ouḃoaṙ ' (black Ooaṙ) ; usually, but less correctly, written Mac Ouiḃioir, q.v.

Mac Ouiḃ—IV—*M'Duffe*, MacDuff, Duff, and, by trans-lation, Black ; ' son of Ouḃ ' (an Irish personal name meaning ' black '). Besides the Irish families bearing this surname, there is a Scottish clan Mac Ouıb, of which the old Earls of Fife were the heads. V. Mac Ouıb.

Mac Ouıb—IV—*M'Cuffe*, Cuffe; a var. of Mac Ouıb, q.v. See also Maʒ Ouıb.

Mac Ouıbᴅara, Mac Ouıbᴅaraċ—IV—Mac-Adarragh, MacAdarra, &c. V. Mac Ouᴅᴅapa, Mac Ouᴅᴅapaċ.

Mac Ouıbeaṁna—IV—*M'Doyaoune*; 'son of Ouᴅ-eaṁna' (the black-man of Emania, near Armagh); the name of a family in Co. Down who, according to O'Dugan, were chiefs of Kinelawley. O'Donovan gives the angl. form as Devany, but the surname seems to be obsolete or changed into some other form.

Mac Ouıbᴘınn—IV—*M'Duffin*; 'son of Ouᴅᴘıonn' (black ᴘıonn). V. Maʒ Ouıbᴘınn.

Mac Ouıbıᴅıɼ, MacDwyer, MacDire; a var. of Mac Ouᴅuıᴅıɼ, q.v.

Mac Ouıbín—IV—*M'Kevine, M'Kevyn*, MacKevin, Mac-Evin, MacAvin; 'son of Ouıbín' (a dim. of ᴅuᴅ, black); a rare surname. In the 16th century, it was almost peculiar to Sligo and Donegal.

Mac Ouıbınse—IV—MacAvinchy; 'son of Ouᴅınɼe' (black-man of the island).

Mac Ouıbne—IV—*M'Duynie*, MacEvinie, MacEvinney, &c.; 'son of Ouıbne' (ill-going, an ancient Irish personal name, opposed to Suıbne); the name of a Breifney fam'y, one of whom was Bishop of Kilmore in the 15th century. Its angl. forms cannot easily be distinguished from those of Mac Aıbne, q.v. See also Maʒ Ouıbne, which is the more common spelling.

Mac Ouıbsíte—IV—*M'Duffyhe*, *M'Duffie*, MacAffie, MacAffee, MacAfee, MacHaffie, MacHaffy, MacFie, MacFee, Mahaffy; 'son of Ouᴅɼíte' (the black-man of peace); the name of a Scottish family who for many centuries held the island of Colonsay. They were a brave and warlike clan, and as followers of the Mac-Donalds of Islay and the Camerons of Lochiel, showed their prowess on many a field. They suffered severely at Culloden in 1745, when the whole clan was out for Prince Charlie. A branch of the family settled in Co. Antrim in the 16th century, and others probably came over at a later period.

Mᴀᴄ ᴅᴜɪɴɴ—IV—*M'Doyn, M'Dun*, MacDunn ; ' son of ᴅonn ' (lord, strong, brown, dark) ; a rare surname.

Mᴀᴄ ᴅᴜɪɴɴꞅʟᴇɪᴠᴇ—IV — *M'Donleive, M'Donleve, M'Donleavy*, Dunlief, Dunlop ; ' son of ᴅonnꞅʟᴇɪᴠᴇ ' (an Irish personal name, meaning ' ᴅonn of the mountain') ; now changed to Mᴀᴄ ᴅᴜɪɴɴꞅʟᴇɪᴠᴇ, Ó ᴅᴜɪɴɴꞅʟᴇɪᴠᴇ, q.v.

Mᴀᴄ ᴅᴜɪɴɴꞅʟᴇɪᴠᴇ—IV—*M'Anlevy, M'Enlievie, M'En-levie, M'Enleve, M'Inlewe, M'Inlowe, M'Colleve, M'Colley*, MacConloy, MacEleavy, MacAleavy, Mac-Alea, MacAlee, Macleavy, MacClew, MacCloy, Killevy, Killeavy, Levy, Leavy, &c. ; a var. of Mᴀᴄ ᴅᴜɪɴɴ-ꞅʟᴇɪᴠᴇ (q.v.), the initial ᴅ of the second part of the surname being now always aspirated. In Scotland, the final e is dropped, and it would appear from the early angl. forms that this also sometimes happened in Ireland. The MacDunlevys were an ancient and once powerful family in Co. Down. They derive their descent from ᴅonnꞅʟᴇɪᴠᴇ Ó ɴᴇoᴄᴀᴅᴀ, chieftain of Ulidia, who flourished in the 11th century. A remnant of the ancient inhabitants of Ulster, they maintained their independence, though in a greatly circumscribed territory, down to the coming of the English. Their patrimony, which was known as ᴜʟᴀᴅ (Latinised Ulidia), then comprised the present Co. Down and the southern portion of Co. Antrim. The invasion and conquest of Ulidia by John de Courcy, in the year 1177, was the turning point in the history of the clan. Marching his army to Downpatrick, he encountered MacDunlevy, defeated him in battle, though only after a brave resistance, and dispersed his clansmen. From this defeat they never recovered. Though they did not at once cease to exist as a distinct clan, their power was for ever broken, and branches of the family sought new homes in different parts of Ireland, and even in Scotland. In Tirconnell, some of them became famous as physicians to the O'Donnells. The surname has assumed a great variety of forms in Irish; and the corresponding angl. forms are very numerous. V. Ó Ꝺuinn-ꝼléiꝺe, Mac Ꝺuinnꝼléiꝺín; also Ultaċ, Ultaċán, Mac an Ultaiǥ, Ó hUltaċáin, and Mac an leaǥa.

Mac Ꝺuinnsléiꝺín—IV—*M'Inleavin, M'Inlene*, Mac-Lavin, MacLevin, Lavins, Levins, Levinson, Leveson, (Leviston, Levenston, Levinston, Levingston, Livingston, Livingstone, Livingstown); a dim. of Mac Ꝺuinnꝼléiꝺe, q.v. Cf. Ultaċ and Ultaċán.

Mac Ꝺúnaꝺaiǥ—IV—*M'Dowany, M'Downey, M'Doney* Dooney, Downey, Doney; 'son of Ꝺúnaꝺaċ' (deriv. of ꝺúnaꝺ, of the ꝺún or fort); the name of an old Galway family who are probably a branch of the O'Maddens. Also called Ó Ꝺúnaꝺaiǥ, q.v.

Mac Eaċaꝺa, Mac Eaċaiꝺ—IV—*M'Kaghoe, M'Caghie*, MacAghy, MacCahugh, MacCaghy, MacCaughey, MacCahy, Caughy, Cahy, (Hackett), and sometimes, by 'translation,' Steed, Steedman; 'son of Eaċaiꝺ'; var. of Mac Eoċaꝺa, Mac Eoċaiꝺ, Maǥ Eoċaiꝺ, q.v.

Mac Eaċáin—IV—*M'Keaghane*, MacCaughan, Mac-Cahan, MacCahon, Cahane; 'son of Eaċán' (a dim. of Eaċaiꝺ); an Ulster var. of Mac Eoċáin, q.v. See also Maǥ Eaċáin.

Mac Eaċmarcaiǥ — IV—*M'Cafferchie, M'Cafferkie*, MacCaffarky, MacCagherty, MacCaugherty, Mac-Cafferty, MacCaverty, MacCaharty, MacCaherty, (Mac-Carthy, MacCaffry), Cafferky, Cafferty; 'son of Eaċmarcaċ' (horse-rider); a Donegal surname, now also common in Mayo, but often disguised under the angl. form of MacCaffry. The local pronunciation is sometimes Ó Cearꝼarcaiǥ. The family is probably a branch of the O'Dohertys, among whom Eaċmarcaċ was a personal name.

Mac Eaċmíleaꝺa, Mac Eaċmíliꝺ—IV—*M'Agholy, M'Aughelie, M'Cafely*, MacCaughley, MacCaffaley, MacCaffely; 'son of Eaċmíleaꝺ' (horse-soldier); a rare East Ulster surname. The family is probably a branch of that of Maguinness, among whom Eacṁileaḋ was a favouite name.

Mac Eacṛáin—IV—*M'Eacherane, M'Ceagharan*, Mac-Cagheron, MacCaughern, MacCahern, &c.; 'son of Eacṗán'; a var. of Maᵹ Eacṗáin, q.v.

Mac Eaċtiᵹeirn — IV—*M'Acherin, M'Kagherne,* Caheerin, Keheerin; 'son of Eaċtiᵹeaṗna' (horse-lord); a rare and scattered surname. Also Mac Eiċtiᵹeiṗn, q.v.

Mac Eaḋḃáirḋ—V—*M'Edward*, [Edwards]; 'son of Edward'; an Anglo-Irish patronymic corresponding to the English surname Edwards.

Mac Eáin—V—*M'Eane, M'Keane, M'Cane*, MacKean, MacKane, MacKain, MacCain, &c.; 'son of John'; a var. of Mac Eóin, q.v. The Mac Eains were chiefs of Ardnamurchan in Scotland.

Mac Eamoinn, Mac Eamuinn—V—*M'Eamon, M'Edmond, M'Edmund*, MacAimon, MacEdmund, [Edmond, Edmonds, Edmundson, &c.]; 'son of Edmund'; an Anglo-Irish surname.

Mac Eanna—IV—*M'Enna, M'Eanny, M'Ena*, Mac-Keany, (MacKenna), 'son of Eanna'; a scattered surname, but found chiefly in Wexford and Carlow. Its angl. forms can hardly be distinguished from those of Mac Cionaoiṫ, q.v.

Mac Eanṛaic—V—*M'Henricke*, MacKendrick, Kenrick, Kendrick, Kinrock, Condrick, Conderick; 'son of Eanṛac' (a Teutonic personal name, the same as the English Henry); a var. of Mac Annṛaic, q.v.

Mac Eiḃir—IV—MacEver; 'son of Eiḃeaṗ'; extremely rare.

Mac Eiċṛí—IV—*M'Echrye, M'Keghrie*; 'son of Eiċṗí' (horse-king); an Ulster surname; always extremely rare, and probably now obsolete.

Mac Eiċtiᵹeirn—IV—MacEchern, Keheerin; a var. of Mac Eaċtiᵹeiṗn, q.v.

Mac Eiḋiᵹ—IV—MacKeady, Keady; a corruption of Ó Meiceiḋiᵹ, q.v.; a rare West Cork surname.

Mac Éimhir—IV—MacEver ; a var. of Mac Éibhir, q.v.

Mac Éinrí—V—*M'Enree, M'Henrie, M'Henry,* MacEnry, MacEndry, MacHenry, MacHenery, MacHendrie, MacHendry, MacKenery, MacKendry, Fitzhenry, Henry, Hendry, &c. ; 'son of Henry' ; (a very common name among the early Anglo-Norman settlers) ; the name of several distinct families in different parts of Ireland ; common in Ulster and in some parts of Connacht. The Fitzhenrys of Wexford are an Anglo-Norman family. Also Mac Annraoi and Mac Hannraoi, q.v.

Mac Eochadha—IV—*M'Eoghoe, M'Keoghoe,* MacKeogh, MacKeough, MacKeo, MacKough, Keoghoe, Keogh, Keough, &c. ; 'son of Eochaidh' (a very common Irish personal name in ancient times) ; the name (1) of a Leinster family, of the same stock as the O'Byrnes, at one time famous as poets ; (2) of a Co. Roscommon family, a branch of the O'Kellys of Ui Maine, who were chiefs of Moyfinn, in the barony of Athlone ; (3) of a Tipperary family who were anciently chiefs of Owney, but dispossessed many centuries ago by the O'Mulryans ; and (4) of a Roscommon family who were anciently chiefs of Moylurg, now the barony of Boyle, until dispossessed by the MacDermotts. V. Mac Eochaidh, Mag Eochaidh and Mac Eachadha, which are variants.

Mac Eochagáin — IV — *M'Keoghegane, M'Coghegan, M'Coogan,* Kehigan, MacCogan, Keogan, Coogan, Cooken, Cogan, &c. ; 'son of Eochagán' (a dim. of Eochaidh) ; a var. of Mag Eochagáin, q.v. ; rare and found only in Cavan and a few other parts of Ulster.

Mac Eochaidh—IV—*M'Oghie, M'Coghie, M'Cohy,* MacCoughy, Keoghy, Cuhy ; 'son of Eochaidh' ; a var. of Mac Eochadha and Mac Eachaidh, q.v.

Mac Eocháin—IV—*M'Keoghan,* Keoghane, Keohane, &c. This surname is now almost peculiar to West Cork, where it is pronounced Ó Ceocháin (with short eo). V. Mac Eacháin, which is the Ulster form ; also Mag Eocháin.

Mac eoġaiṅ—IV—MacOwen, MacEown, MacCone, Mac-
Kone, MacKeoan, MacKeown, MacEwan, Keown, Coen,
Cowan, Coyne, Owen, Owens, &c.; 'son of eoġaṅ' (an
old Irish personal name meaning 'well-born'); a Sligo
surname. Its angl. forms and those of Mac eóiṅ
(q.v.) are pronounced so nearly alike that it is impossible to distinguish them. V. Maġ eoġaiṅ.

Mac eóiṅ—V—MacEoin, MacKeon, MacKeone, Mac-
Keown, Keon, Keown, Johnson, &c.; 'son of John'
an Irish surname assumed by a branch of the Scottish
family of Bissett who settled, in the 13th century, in
the Glinns of Antrim. Its angl. forms cannot be
distinguished from those of Mac eoġaiṅ, q.v. See
also Maġ eoġaiṅ.

Mac eoṫaċ—IV—MacKeogh, Keogh; 'son of eoċaiḋ';
a var. of Mac eoċaḋa, q.v. See also Maġ eoṫaċ.

Mac ḟaċṅa—IV—Aughney; 'son of ḟaċṅa.'

Mac ḟaoiṫiġ—V—MacWhite, MacWhitty.

Mac ḟaoláiṅ—IV—M'Phillan, MacPhelan; 'son of
ḟaolán' (dim. of ḟaol, a wolf); extremely rare.

Mac ḟearaḋaiġ—IV—M'Farree, M'Farry, M'Ferry,
MacVarry, MacVerry; 'son of ḟearaḋaċ' (an old
Irish personal name meaning 'manly'); an Ulster
surname in use in Tyrone, Armagh and Down.

Mac ḟearaḋaiġ—IV—M'Karrye, M'Kerry, MacAree,
MacKaree, MacCarrie, MacKeary, MacHarry, Maharry,
and, by 'translation,' King; a var. of Mac ḟearaḋaiġ,
q.v. In the modern spoken language, this surname
is sometimes corrupted to Mac a' Ríoġ (son of the
king) and accordingly angl. King. V. Maġ ḟearaḋaiġ.

Mac ḟearċair—IV—M'Fearagher, Farquharson, Far-
quhar, Farquher, Farquer, Farghur, Farker, Forker,
&c.; 'son of ḟearċar' (very dear); the name of a
Scottish clan in Aberdeenshire, some of whom, doubtless, have come over to Ulster. V. Mac ḟearċair.

Mac ḟearċair—IV—M'Eragher, MacErchar, Mac-
Carragher, Caragher, Carragher, Caraher, Carraher,
Kerragher, Kerraher, &c.; a var. of Mac ḟearċair,

q.v.; in use in Ulster, but has always been very rare. The initial ꝼ is aspirated, even when pronounced in the angl. form.

Mac ꝼeaρᵹail—IV—*M'Farrell*, *M'Freill*, &c.; 'son of ꝼeaρᵹal.' V. Mac ꝼeaρᵹail.

Mac ꝼeaρᵹail—IV—*M'Karachill*, MacErrigle, Mac-Argle, Cargill, Carkill; 'son of ꝼeaρᵹal' (super-valour); also Maᵹ ꝼeaρᵹail, q.v.; a var. of Mac ꝼeaρᵹail, q.v.; an Antrim surname. For unaspirated ᵹ, cf. Mac Conᵹail.

Mac ꝼeaρᵹail—IV—*M'Carrell*, *M'Kerrell*, MacCarrell, MacKerrell, MacKerrall, MacCarroll, MacKarroll, Mackerel, Mackrell, &c.; a var. of Mac ꝼeaρᵹail, q.v. Its angl. forms are not always distinguishable from those of Mac Ceaρбaill, q.v. See also Maᵹ ꝼeaρᵹail.

Mac ꝼeaρᵹaile—IV—*M'Carrelly*, *M'Carley*, *M'Kearly*, *M'Errelly*, *M'Kyrrelly*, MacErrilly, MacKerlie, Car-rolly, Carley, Kerley, Kirley; a var. of Mac ꝼeaρᵹail, q.v.

Mac ꝼeaρᵹusa—IV—*M'Fargus*, *M'Faryse*, Farguson, Ferguson, Fergus, Vargus, &c.; 'son of ꝼeaρᵹur' (super-choice); the name of a Scottish family, some of whom settled in the north of Ireland in the early part of the 17th century.

Mac ꝼeaρᵹusa—IV—*M'Arrassie*, Hergusson, Fergu-son, &c.; a var. of Mac ꝼeaρᵹura, q.v.

Mac ꝼeiᵭlim—IV—*M'Phelim*, *M'Felim*, Phelim, Phelym, &c.; 'son of ꝼeiᵭlim' (short for ꝼeiᵭlimiᵭ); a var. of Mac ꝼeiᵭlimiᵭ, q.v.

Mac ꝼeiᵭlimiᵭ—IV—*M'Felemy*, *M'Phelimy*, Mac-Phelimy, MacPhellimy, &c.; 'son of ꝼeiᵭlimiᵭ' (an ancient Irish personal name, explained as meaning 'the ever good'); a rare surname.

Mac ꝼeóρais, Mac ꝼeóρuis—V—*M'Orish*, *M'Horishe*, *M'Keorish*, *M'Corishe*, *M'Keoris*, Korish, Corish, [Birmingham, Bermingham, &c.]; 'son of Piers' (a Norman form of Peter); the Irish name assumed by Anglo-Irish family of Bermingham, who are descended from an ancestor called Piers or Peter de Bermingham. V. ᵯac Ⴒⴈⴋⴐⴀⴈⴐ, ᵯac Ⴒⴈⴗⴀⴈⴐ and ᵯⴀⵝ Ⴒⴄⴍⴐⴀⴈⴐ, which are variants of the present surname.

ᵯac Ⴒⴈⴀⴆⴐⴀ, ᵯac Ⴒⴈⴀⴆⴐⴀⴆ—IV—*M'Keaghry, M'Keighera*, MacKeighry, MacKeefrey, MacKeary, Keaghery, Keahery, Keary, (Carey); 'son of Ⴒⴈⴀⴆⴐⴀ' (gen. Ⴒⴈⴀⴆⴐⴀⴆ, but the gen. ending is now generally, if not always, dropped); the name (1) of a family of Cinel Eoghain, who were anciently chiefs of Cinel Fearadhaigh, in the barony of Clogher, Co. Tyrone; (2) of a Galway family who were chiefs of Oga Beathra, in the S.W. of Co. Galway; and (3) of a family in Co. Meath. The first two families were well represented in the 16th century and are still extant, but the Meath family appears to be long extinct.

ᵯac Ⴒⴈⴀⴐⴀⴈⴑ—V—*M'Keriske*, Kerrison, Kearson, Kerris, Kerrish, Kierce, Kierse, Kearse, Kerisk, Kerrisk, [Healy]; 'son of Piers'; var. of ᵯac Ⴒⴈⴋⴐⴀⴈⴐ, q.v.; a rare and scattered surname. In East Kerry, it is corrupted to ᵯac Ⴚⴄⴈⴒⴈⴐⴂ and Ó Ⴚⴄⴈⴒⴈⴐⴂ, and very often angl. Healy, the family being probably descended from a person called Ferris O'Helie (Pierce Healy). Cf. ᵯac Ⴒⴄⴍⴐⴀⴈⴐ above.

ᵯac Ⴒⴈⴁⴈⴌ—V—*M'Fibbin*, MacKibbin, MacKibben, MacKibbon; 'son of Phipin' (a dim. of Philip).

ᵯac Ⴒⴈⴋⴈⴁ—V—MacKillip, MacKillop, MacKellop, MacKillops, Killips, Killops, Kellops, Philson, Philipson, Phillips; 'son of Philip'; a var. of ᵯac Ⴒⴈⴋⴈⴁ, q.v.

ᵯac Ⴒⴈⴋⴈⴁⴈⴌ—V—MacPhilpin, MacPhilbin, Philbin, &c.; a var. of ᵯac Ⴒⴈⴋⴈⴁⴈⴌ, q.v.; common in the spoken language of Co. Mayo.

ᵯac Ⴒⴈⴌⴂⴈⴌ—IV—*M'Kynine*, *M'Kennyne*, Kenning, Kennyon, Kenyon, Kennon, Keenan, &c.; 'son of Ⴒⴈⴌⴂⴈⴌ' (fair-offspring), a rare surname. Its angl. forms cannot easily be distinguished from those of ᵯac Ⴚⴍⴈⴌⴈⴌ, q.v. See also ᵯⴀⵝ Ⴒⴈⴌⴂⴈⴌ.

ᵯac Ⴒⴈⴌⴌ—IV—*M'Iyn*, MacKinn, MacKing; 'son of Ⴒⴈⴍⴌⴌ' (fair); a var. of ᵯⴀⵝ Ⴒⴈⴌⴌ, q.v.; in use in Derry and Mayo, but rare.

Mac ꝼinneaċṫa, Mac ꝼinneaċṫaiġ—IV—Kingarty, Kingerty; 'son of ꝼinneaċṫa' (white-snow); var. of Maġ ꝼinneaċṫa; extremely rare.

Mac ꝼíoḋḃuiḋe—IV—M'Eboy, M'Ebwy, M'Ewy, Mac-Evoy, MacAvoy, MacVoy, Evoy; a corruption of Mac ꝼíoḋḃaḋaiġ, 'son of ꝼíoḋḃaḋaċ' (i.e., of the wood, woodman); the name of a family in Leix, who were anciently chiefs of Tuath-Fiodhbhuidhe, which appears to have been situated in the barony of Stradbally.

Mac ꝼionġuine—IV—M'Kynnoun, MacKinnon; 'son of ꝼionġuine' (fair-child); the name of a celebrated clan in the west of Scotland. The final e is dropped in the spoken language. The pronunciation, as I heard it in Argyleshire, would be represented by Mac Cionúin.

Mac ꝼionnáin—IV—M'Kynnan, M'Kennan, Kinnan, Kennan; 'son of ꝼionnán' (dim. of ꝼionn, fair). This surname appears to have been in use in Tyrone, but its present angl. forms cannot be distinguished from those of Ó Cuinneáin and Ó Cianáin, q.v. See also Maġ ꝼionnáin, which is a variant.

Mac ꝼionnḃairr—IV—M'Inuyre, M'Kenor, Kenure; 'son of ꝼionnḃarr' (fair-head); a var. of Maġ ꝼionnḃairr, q.v.; very rare.

Mac ꝼionnġail—IV—M'Kenill; 'son of ꝼionnġal' (fair valour); now Maġ ꝼionnġail, q.v.

Mac ꝼionnlaoiċ—IV—MacKinley, MacKinlay; 'son of ꝼionnlaoċ' (fair-hero); the name of a Scottish clan; said to be a substitution for Mac ꝼionnloġa, q.v. The pronunciation in modern Scottish-Gaelic is Mac ꝼionnla (Mac Ciúlla). It does not appear to have been at any time an Irish surname, but is now sometimes erroneously substituted for Maġ ꝼionnġaile, q.v.

Mac ꝼionnloġa—IV—MacKinley, MacKinlay; 'son of ꝼionnluġ' (fair luġ); now written Mac ꝼionnlaoiċ, q.v.

Mac ꝼionnṁacáin—IV—Kinucane; 'son of ꝼionnṁacán (fair-son). Cf. Ó ꝼionnṁacáin.

Mac ꝼıꞃᵬıꜱıᵹ—IV—*M'Ferbishy, M'Firbisse, M'Firbis,* Forbish, Forbis, Forbes ; ' son of ꝼeaꞃᵬıꞃıᵹ ' (man of prosperity) ; the name of a celebrated family of historians and antiquaries in Connacht. They belonged to the Ui Fiachrach race, of which for many centuries they were the hereditary poets and chroniclers. Their original patrimony was Magh Broin, in Tirawley, but they afterwards settled at Rosserk, between Ballina and Killala, and finally at Lacken, in the parish of Kilglas, Co. Sligo, which continued to be the home of the family down to the year 1608, when they were dispossessed of their estates by James I. The castle of Lacken, now known as Castle Forbes, was built by Ciothruadh MacFirbis in the year 1560. Duald MacFirbis, the last and greatest scholar of the name, was foully murdered at Dunflin, Co. Sligo, in the year 1670, by an English soldier named Crofton. The MacFirbises were the compilers of the Book of Lecan and other important works on Irish history and antiquities. The surname is now generally angl. Forbes.

Mac ꝼıꞃꞁeıᵹınn—VII—*Machirleginn,* MacErlean, MacErlane, MacErlain, MacErleen ; a var. of Mac an ꝼıꞃꞁeıᵹınn, q.v. Dermit, Vicar of Drumcliffe, who flourished at the end of the 14th century, is surnamed in the Papal Register, Machinnirlegenn and Machirleginn.

Mac ꝼıᴄᴄeaꞁꞁaıᵹ—IV—MacFeeley, MacFeely ; ' son of ꝼıᴄᴄeaꞁꞁaᴄ ' (chess-player) ; very rare.

Mac ꝼꞁaıᴄᵬeaꞃᴄaıᵹ—IV—MacLaverty, MacClaverty, MacClafferty, MacCleverty ; ' son of ꝼꞁaıᴄᵬeaꞃᴄaᴄ ' (bright-lord) ; a rare Ulster surname.

Mac ꝼꞁaıᴄıṁ—IV—MacLave, Claffy, Claffey, Hand ; ' son of ꝼꞁaıᴄeaṁ ' (lord, ruler). V. Maᵹ ꝼꞁaıᴄıṁ.

Mac ꝼꞁannᴄaᵬa, Mac ꝼꞁannᴄaıᵬ—IV—*M'Clanachy, M'Clanaghy, M'Clanchy, M'Clanky, M'Clansy,* MacClancy, Clanchy, Clancy ; ' son of ꝼꞁannᴄaᵬ ' (ruddy-warrior) ; the name (I) of an ancient family in Co. Leitrim, who were chiefs of Dartry, now the barony of Rosclogher, and had their seats at Ros-

clogher and Dungarbry; and (2) of a Thomond
family, a branch of the MacNamaras, who were
hereditary brehons or judges to the O'Briens, and
resided at Knockfin and Cahermaclancy, in the
north-west of Co. Clare.

ḿac ꝑloinn—IV—*M'Flyn*, MacFlynn; 'son of ꝑlann'
(ruddy); a var. of ḿaᵹ ꝑloinn, q.v.

ḿac ꝑloinn—IV—MacLynn; a var. of ḿac ꝑloinn
and ḿaᵹ ꝑloinn, q.v.

ḿac ꝑualáin—IV—*M'Folaine*, Folan; 'son of ꝑaolan'
(dim. of ꝑaol, a wolf); a var. of ḿac ꝑaoláin, q.v.;
the name of an old family in Co. Galway. The initial
ꝑ is aspirated in the present spoken language. Cf.
the old angl. form O Folane for Ó ꝑaoláin.

ḿac ᵹabann—VII—MacGowan, Magowan, Gowen,
Smith; a var. of ḿac an ᵹobann, q.v.

ḿac ᵹaḋra—IV—*M'Gara*, MacGeary, Geary; 'son of
ᵹaoꝑa'; an old, but rare, Roscommon surname;
pronounced ḿac ᵹaoꝑa in Co. Galway where it still
survives.

ḿac ᵹaꝑraiḋ—V—*M'Gafferie*, MacGaffrey, MacCaffray, MacCaffrey, MacCaffery, Caffrey, Caffery, &c.;
'son of Godfrey'; also written ḿac ᵹoꝑraḋa, ḿac
Caꝑraiḋ, &c.; the name of a branch of the Maguires
of Fermanagh, now common in Ulster; to be distinguished from ḿac eaċṁarcaiᵹ (q.v.), which is
sometimes similarly anglicised.

ḿac ᵹairḃeiꞇ, ḿac ᵹairḃiꞇ—IV—*M'Garvie*, *M'Gar-
way*, MacGarvey, Garvey; 'son of ᵹaiꝑḃiꞇ'; an Ulster
surname, very common in Donegal.

ḿac ᵹaṁna—IV—*M'Gawna*, *M'Gawny*, *M'Gawne*, (Mac-
Gowan, Magowan, Magowen), Gaffney; 'son of
ᵹaṁain' (calf); a rare and scattered surname; now
generally assimilated to ḿac ᵹabann, q.v.

ḿac ᵹaoiꞇe—IV—*M'Giehie*, MacGeehee, (MacGee,
Magee), and, by translation, Wynne; probably a
shortened form of ḿac ᵹaoiꞇin, q.v.; now merged
in ḿaᵹ aoiḋ, q.v. It was a Donegal surname in the
16th century.

Mac Ʒαoιτίn—IV—MacGeehin, MacGeehan, Mageehan, Mageahan, MacGihen, MacGihan, MacGehan, MacGahan, Magahan, Megahan, MacGean, Magean, Gahan; 'son of Ʒαoιτίn' (probably a 'pet' form of Μαοιlʒαoιτε, chief of the wind); an Ulster surname. In the 16th century, it was almost peculiar to the counties of Down and Donegal.

Mac Ʒαrαcάin, v. Μαʒ Ʒαpαcάin.

Mac Ʒαrτlαn, MacGartlan. V. Ʒeαplαnn.

Mac Ʒeαlάin—IV—MacGellan; 'son of Ʒeαlάn' (dim. of Ʒeαl, bright, white); very rare.

Mac Ʒeαrαιlτ—V—M'Garilt, M'Gerald, FitzGerald, Fitzgerald; 'son of Gerald'; the Irish form of the Norman surname FitzGerald. The Fitzgeralds rank with the Burkes and Butlers as one of the most illustrious of the Anglo-Norman families in Ireland. They derive their name and descent from Gerald, Constable of Pembroke, whose wife was Nest, daughter of Rhys Ap Tewdwyr, King of South Wales. Gerald flourished in the early part of the 12th century. His son, Maurice Fitzgerald, was one of the companions of Strongbow, and from him are descended all the families of the name in Ireland. He received large grants of land which continued in the possession of his descendants down to recent times. Members of the family frequently filled the highest offices under the English Crown. The head of the Leinster branch of the family for centuries bore the title of Earl of Kildare, later Duke of Leinster, while the head of the Fitzgeralds of Munster was Earl of Desmond.

Mac Ʒeαrάin—IV—(?) MacGueran, Sharpe; 'son of Ʒeαpάn' (dim. of Ʒeαp, sharp).

Mac Ʒeαrʒάin—IV—M'Geregan, M'Gergaine, M'Gargan, MacGerrigan, MacGarrigan, Garrigan, Gargan; 'son of Ʒeαpʒάn' (dim. of Ʒeαpʒ, fierce); an old surname in Meath and Cavan; also Ó Ʒeαpʒάin, q.v.

Mac Ʒeαrόιο—V—M'Gerode, M'Garrott, MacGarrett; 'son of Gerald' (a Norman personal name); in use in Cork, but very rare.

Mac ᵹéıbeᴀɴɴᴀıᵹ—IV—MacGeaveny, MacKeaveny, MacKeaveney, Geaveny, Keaveny, Keaveney, Keveney; 'son of ᵹéıbeᴀɴɴᴀc' (fettered); originally a Fermanagh surname; found at the end of the 16th century in Sligo and Mayo; now common in Connacht, but very rare in Ulster.

Mac ᵹeıʀble—IV—M'Keribly, (Kirby); 'son of ᵹeıʀ-ble'; the name of an old Mayo family from whom the townland of Carrowkeribly, in the parish of Attymas, is so called. It is still extant in Co. Mayo, but always angl. Kirby.

Mac ᵹıb—V—Gibson; 'son of Gib,' short for Gilbert.

Mac ᵹıbne—IV—M'Gebenay, MacGibney; 'son of ᵹıbne' (grey-hound); an extremely rare surname. It survives in Co. Down.

Mac ᵹıleáın—IV—Magillane, MacGillan, MacGillen; 'son of ᵹıleáın' (dim. of ᵹeᴀl, bright); a var. of Mac ᵹeᴀláın, q.v.

Mac ᵹılbeıʀᴄ, Mac ᵹıllıbeıʀᴄ—V—M'Gillebert, M'Gilbert, Gilbertson, Gilberson, Gilbert; 'son of Gilbert.'

Mac ᵹıobúın—V—M'Gibbone, M'Gibowne, MacGibbon, MacGibben, MacKibbon, O'Kibbon, Gibbonson, Fitz Gibbon, Fitzgibbon, Gibbons, Gibbins, Gibbings, Gibbon; 'son of Gibbon' (a dim. of Gilbert); the name (1) of a branch of the Burkes of Connacht who were seated to the west of Croagh Patrick, in Co. Mayo; and (2) of a Co. Limerick family, usually said to be a branch of the Geraldines, but really descended from Gilbert de Clare who, at the beginning of the 14th century, possessed the manor of Mahoonagh and many other valuable estates in Co. Limerick. The head of this family was known as the White Knight.

Mac ᵹıollᴀ—IV—MacGill, Magill, Gill; a shortened form of some surname commencing with Mac ᵹıollᴀ.

Mac ᵹıollᴀ ᴀcᴀıꝺ—IV—Kilahy, Killackey. V. Mac ᵹıollᴀ ᴀıcce.

Mac ᵹıollᴀ ᴀꝺᴀṁnáın—IV—M'Eleownane, M'Eleownan, MacAlonan, MacLennan, MacLennon; 'son of ᵹ𝔦𝔬𝔩𝔩𝔞 𝔞𝔡𝔞𝔪𝔫á𝔦𝔫 ' (servant of Adamnan) ; a Co. Down surname ; also a Scottish surname, said to be the origin of Mac Lennan of Rosshire.

ᵹ𝔦𝔬𝔩𝔩𝔞 𝔞𝔦𝔫𝔡𝔯é𝔦𝔰—IV—MacLandrish, Gillanders, [Anderson] ; ' son of ᵹ𝔦𝔬𝔩𝔩𝔞 𝔞𝔦𝔫𝔡𝔯é𝔦𝔯 ' (servant of St. Andrew) ; a common surname in Rathlin Island, probably of Scottish origin.

𝔪𝔞𝔠 ᵹ𝔦𝔬𝔩𝔩𝔞 𝔞𝔦𝔱𝔠𝔢—IV—Kilahy, Killackey ; ' son of ᵹ𝔦𝔬𝔩𝔩𝔞 𝔞𝔦𝔱𝔠𝔢 ' (cf. ó 𝔪𝔞𝔬𝔩 𝔞𝔦𝔱𝔠𝔢).

𝔪𝔞𝔠 ᵹ𝔦𝔬𝔩𝔩𝔞 𝔞𝔫 𝔠𝔩𝔬𝔦ᵹ—IV—Bell ; most probably a ' translation ' of the English surname Bell.

𝔪𝔞𝔠 ᵹ𝔦𝔬𝔩𝔩𝔞 𝔞𝔯𝔯𝔞𝔦𝔱—IV — *M'Elearra,   M'Ellearay, M'Elearie, M'Elahray, M'Ellary, M'Calerie, M'Calery,* MacAlarry, MacAlary, MacClary, MacAleery, Mac- Eleary, MacCleary, MacCleery, MacLary, MacLeary, MacLeery, (?) Callery, (?) Calliry, Collery, (Cleary, Clarke) ; ' son of ᵹ𝔦𝔬𝔩𝔩𝔞 𝔞𝔯𝔯𝔞𝔦𝔱 ' (probably for ᵹ𝔦𝔬𝔩𝔩𝔞 𝔞𝔫 𝔯𝔞𝔦𝔱, the prosperous youth) ; the name of an old Sligo family, the head of which was sometimes chief of the barony of Leyny ; probably of the same stock as the O'Haras. A branch of the family settled with the O'Haras in Co. Antrim, sometime before the end of the 16th century. The name is now often in- correctly angl. Cleary and Clarke.

𝔪𝔞𝔠 ᵹ𝔦𝔬𝔩𝔩𝔞 𝔟á𝔫—IV—*M'Gilbane, M'Gillevane,* Mac- Gilvane, MacKilwane, MacIlwaine, McElvaine, Mac- Elwain, MacElwane, Macklewaine, Gillivan, Kilbane, and, by translation, White, Whyte ; ' son of ᵹ𝔦𝔬𝔩𝔩𝔞 𝔟á𝔫 ' (white, or fair youth) ; the name of a family of the Ui Fiachrach, in Co. Sligo, who formerly possessed the townland of Lisnarawer, in the parish of Dromard. O'Donovan found the family still in that neighbour- hood, but the name was always made White in English. It is also a Scottish surname, usually angl. MacIlvaine, but sometimes Whyte.

𝔪𝔞𝔠 ᵹ𝔦𝔬𝔩𝔩𝔞 𝔟𝔢𝔞𝔯𝔞𝔦ᵹ—IV—*M'Gilleverie,* Gilvarry,Gel- varry ; ' son of ᵹ𝔦𝔬𝔩𝔩𝔞 𝔟𝔢𝔞𝔯𝔞𝔦ᵹ ' (servant of 𝔟𝔢𝔞𝔯𝔞𝔠, or St. Barry) ; an old, but always very rare, Connacht surname. It still survives.

Mac ʒıoʟʟᴀ Bıʒ—IV—Kilbeg; 'son of ʒıoʟʟᴀ ʙeᴀʒ' (little fellow); a rare Galway surname.

Mac ʒıoʟʟᴀ ʙʀᴀ́ᴄᴀ—IV—MacGillivray; 'son of ʒıoʟʟᴀ ʙʀᴀ́ᴄᴀ'; (servant of doom, devotee of the Judgment); a Scottish surname.

Mac ʒıoʟʟᴀ ʙʀıʒᴅe—IV—*M'Gillebridy, M'Gillvrid, M'Killbridy, M'Elvride*, MacGillbride, MacKilbride, Macklebreed, MacBride, Gillbride, Kilbride, &c.; 'son of ʒıoʟʟᴀ ʙʀıʒᴅe' (servant of St. Brigid). This surname was formerly found in many parts of Ireland, notably in the North, where it is still common under the angl. form of MacBride, having been shortened in the spoken language to Mac 'ᴀ ʙʀıʒᴅe, for which cf. Mac ʒıoʟʟᴀ ʙuıᴅe below.

Mac ʒıoʟʟᴀʙuıᴅe—IV—*M'Gilleboy, M'Gilboy, M'Gillavoye, M'Gillewy*, MacGillowy, Magillowy, MacGilwee, MacGilvie, MacGilloway, MacGilway, MacKilvie, MacKelvey, MacIleboy, MacIlboy, MacIlbwee, MacIlwee, MacElwee, MacElvee, Mackilbouy, MacAboy, MacAvoy, MacEvoy, MacAvey, Gilboy, Gilvoy, Gilloway, Gilwee, Gilbey, Kilboy, Killby, Kilby, Kilvey, Ilwee, &c.; 'son of ʒıoʟʟᴀ ʙuıᴅe' (yellow lad). This surname originated in Co. Mayo, but in the 16th century it was common in Sligo, Leitrim and Donegal. Many of the name at present in Ireland are, no doubt, of Scottish origin. The popular form was often Mac 'ᴀ ʙuıᴅe; hence the angl. forms MacAvoy, &c.

Mac ʒıoʟʟᴀ ᴄᴀıʟʟín—IV—*M'Gillechallyn*, Kilcullen, Kilgallen, Kilgallon; 'son of ʒıoʟʟᴀ ᴄᴀıʟʟín' (servant of St. Caillin); a rare surname, scarcely found outside the counties of Sligo and Mayo.

Mac ʒıoʟʟᴀ ᴄᴀınnıʒ—IV—MacIlhaney, Gilheany, &c.; a var. of Mac ʒıoʟʟᴀ ᴄoınnıʒ, q.v.

Mac ʒıoʟʟᴀ ᴄᴀıs—IV—Kilcash; 'son of ʒıoʟʟᴀ ᴄᴀʀ' (curly youth); the name of an old Sligo family who formerly possessed the townland of Ballykilcash, in the barony of Tireragh. It still survives, but is exceedingly rare.

Mac ʒıoʟʟᴀ ᴄᴀoıᴄ—IV—*M'Kilchy, M'Ilky*, Kilkey;

' son of ᴣ1oᴌᴌᴀ cᴀoċ ' (the blind youth) ; a very rare surname.

mᴀc ᴣ1oᴌᴌᴀ Cᴀo1n, mᴀc ᴣ1oᴌᴌᴀ Cᴀo1ne—IV— *M'Gillekyne, M'Gillychyna, M'Gillechyny,* Kilcoyne, Coyne ; ' son of ᴣ1oᴌᴌᴀ cᴀo1n ' (the gentle youth) or ' son of ᴣ1oᴌᴌᴀ Cᴀo1ne ' (servant of St. Caoine, gentleness) ; apparently only different forms of the same surname which, in the 16th century, was found chiefly in Co. Leitrim and in the neighbourhood of Dublin. mᴀc ᴣ1oᴌᴌᴀ Cᴀo1ne was probably the original, and mᴀc ᴣ1oᴌᴌᴀ cᴀo1n an apocopated form. The same peculiarity, it will be noticed, attaches to Ó mᴀoᴌ-cᴀo1n and Ó mᴀoᴌ Cᴀo1ne, q.v.

mᴀc ᴣ1oᴌᴌᴀ CᴀRRᴀ1ᴣ—IV—*M'Gillecharry, M'Gillecarie,* MacGilharry, MacIlharry, MacElharry, MacHarry ; ' son of ᴣ1oᴌᴌᴀ cᴀppᴀċ ' (the scabbed, or bald youth) ; originally a Roscommon surname, but long since removed to Sligo.

mᴀc ᴣ1oᴌᴌᴀ Cᴀᴄᴀ1n—-IV—*M'Gillycattan,* MacIllhatton, MacIlhatton, MacElhatton, Maclehatton, MacClatton, MacHatton, Hatton ; ' son of ᴣ1oᴌᴌᴀ Cᴀᴄᴀ1n ' (servant of St. Catan) ; a well-known Ulster surname.

mᴀc ᴣ1oᴌᴌᴀ Cᴀᴄᴀ1R—IV—*M'Gillacahir, Macgillachair, M'Gillahare,* MacIlhar, MacIlhair, MacElhair, (?) MacGlare, Kilcar, Kilcarr, Carr ; ' son of ᴣ1oᴌᴌᴀ Cᴀᴄᴀ1p ' (servant of St. Cathair) ; a Donegal surname.

mᴀc ᴣ1oᴌᴌᴀ Ceᴀᴌᴌᴀ1ᴣ—IV—*M'Gillakelly, M'Killekelly,* MacKilkelly, Gilkelly, Kilkelly, Killkelly, Kilkelly, Kelly ; ' son of ᴣ1oᴌᴌᴀ Ceᴀᴌᴌᴀ1ᴣ ' (servant of St. Ceallach) ; the name of a family of the Ui Fiachrach Aidhne, in Co. Galway, who are of the same stock as the O'Clerys and derive their descent from Guaire the Hospitable, King of Connacht in the 7th century. Their chief resided at the castle of Cloghballymore, in the parish of Killeenavarra. A branch of the family settled in Mayo soon after the Anglo-Norman invasion.

mᴀc ᴣ1oᴌᴌᴀ Ce1Re—IV—*M'Gillykeyry, M'Gillicherie, M'Ilkerry,* Kilkeary, Keary ; ' son of ᴣ1oᴌᴌᴀ Ce1pe ' (servant of St. Ciar) ; once a common surname in many parts of Ireland, especially in Co. Cork. It has now almost disappeared, being probably disguised under the angl. forms of Keary, Carey and Carr. Mac Ꝼ́ioꞁꞁᴀ Ceᴀꞃᴀ, which, according to Father O'Growney, is the Irish for Carr in parts of Co. Galway, is probably a corruption of the present surname.

Mac Ꝼ́ioꞁꞁᴀ Ciᴀꞃᴀ́in—IV—*M'Gellecherane, M'Gillaghiran*, MacIlherron, MacKlern; 'son of Ꝼ́ioꞁꞁᴀ Ciᴀꞃᴀ́in' (servant of St. Kieran); a rare Midland surname.

Mac Ꝼ́ioꞁꞁᴀcꞁᴀoin—IV—*M'Gillecloyne, M'Gillacleyne, M'Killeclyne*, Kilcline, Cloyen, Cline, Clyne; 'son of Ꝼ́ioꞁꞁᴀ cꞁᴀon' (deceitful youth); an old surname in Roscommon and Longford.

Mac Ꝼ́ioꞁꞁᴀ Coiꞁꞁe—IV—*M'Gillechoile, M'Gillechill*, MacIlhoyle, MacElhoyle, MacElhill, (?) Hoyle, (?) Hoyles, (?) Woods; 'son of Ꝼ́ioꞁꞁᴀ Coiꞁꞁe' (a name given probably to one born on New Year's Day—not from coiꞁꞁ, a wood); a rare Ulster surname; perhaps sometimes erroneously 'translated' Woods, and sometimes shortened to Hoyle or Hoyles.

Mac Ꝼ́ioꞁꞁᴀ Coiꞁꞁín—IV—Kilcullen; a var. of Mac Ꝼ́ioꞁꞁᴀ Cᴀiꞁꞁín, q.v.

Mac Ꝼ́ioꞁꞁᴀ Cóimꞃeᴀꝟ—IV—*M'Killicomy, M'Gillcomy*, Comey; 'son of Ꝼ́ioꞁꞁᴀ Cóimꞃeᴀꝟ' (servant of the Lord); an old Cavan surname.

Mac Ꝼ́ioꞁꞁᴀ Coinniꞃ—IV—*M'Gillekennie, M'Gilleconnye, M'Gillacunye, M'Kilkennie*, MacElkenny, MacIlkenny, MacIlhenny, MacElhenny, MacElhinney, Ilhoney, MacElhoney, MacAloney, MacAlunny, MacAleney, MacAlinney, MacLehenny, Mac Lehinney, MacLhinney, MacLinney, MacLuney, Kilkenny, Ilhinney, Kenny, Heaney, &c.; 'son of Ꝼ́ioꞁꞁᴀ Coinniꞃ' (servant of St. Canice, or Kenny). This surname, in the 16th century, was found in Roscommon, Leitrim, Donegal and Down.

Mac Ꝼ́ioꞁꞁᴀ Coiꞃcꞁe—IV—*M'Gillecosgelie, M'Gilkuskley, M'Gilkuslie*, Cuskley, Cushley, Cuskelly, (Costello, Cosgrave, Cosgrove); 'son of Ꝼ́ioꞁꞁᴀ coiꞃcꞁe' (lad of the left leg) ; an old surname in Fermanagh, Monaghan and Offaly; sometimes, but less correctly, written ᵯᴀᴄ ᵹᴉoʟʟᴀ ᴄoᴉᴘᴄʟᴉᵹ.

ᵯᴀᴄ ᵹᴉoʟʟᴀ ᴄoʟᵯ, ᵯᴀᴄ ᵹᴉoʟʟᴀ ᴄoʟᴜᴉᵯ—IV—*M'Gillecolme, M'Gillacollom,* MacElholm; 'son of ᵹᴉoʟʟᴀ ᴄoʟᴜᴉᵯ' (servant of St. Columcille) ; a very rare and scattered surname.

ᵯᴀᴄ ᵹᴉoʟʟᴀ ᴄoᵯáᴉn—IV—*M'Gillecoman,* Kilcommons; 'son of ᵹᴉoʟʟᴀ ᴄoᵯáᴉn' (servant of St. Coman) ; a rare Connacht surname.

ᵯᴀᴄ ᵹᴉoʟʟᴀ ᴄoᵯ⁴ᴅᴀᴉn, v. ᵯᴀᴄ ᵹᴉoʟʟᴀ ᴄoᵯᵹᴀᴉn.

ᵯᴀᴄ ᵹᴉoʟʟᴀ ᴄoᵯᵹᴀᴉʟʟ—IV—*M'Gillachomhaill, M'Gillacoell, M'Gilleghole, M'Gillecole,* MacCole, MacCool, Glihool, Cole ; 'son of ᵹᴉoʟʟᴀ ᴄoᵯᵹᴀᴉʟʟ' (servant of St. Comgall) ; a Donegal surname.

ᵯᴀᴄ ᵹᴉoʟʟᴀ ᴄoᵯᵹᴀᴉn—IV—*M'Gillchoan,* MacIlhone, MacElhone, MacCowan, Cowan ; 'son of ᵹᴉoʟʟᴀ ᴄoᵯᵹᴀᴉn' (servant of St. Comgan) ; also ᵯᴀᴄ ᵹᴉoʟʟᴀ ᴄoᵯ⁴ᴅᴀᴉn ; a rare Ulster surname ; also a Scottish surname.

ᵯᴀᴄ ᵹᴉoʟʟᴀ ᴄoꞅᴄᴀᴉᴿ—IV—*M'Gillcosker, M'Gilcosker,* Cosker, Coscor, Cusker, Cuscor (Cosgrave) ; 'son of ᵹᴉoʟʟᴀ ᴄoᴘᴄᴀᴉn' (lad of victory, victorious youth).

ᵯᴀᴄ ᵹᴉoʟʟᴀ ᴄᴿᴉoꞅᴄ—IV—*M'Gillachrist, M'Gillacrist, M'Gillechreaste,* Gilchrist, Guilchrist, Gilcrist, Gilchrist, Gilchreest, Gilcriest, Gilcrest, Kilchrist, Kilchriest, Kilcreest, Kilgrist ; 'son of ᵹᴉoʟʟᴀ ᴄᴘᴉoꞅᴄ' (servant of Christ) ; a scattered surname, found chiefly in Leitrim, Longford, Westmeath and Carlow ; now also common in Ulster, where it is probably of Scottish origin.

ᵯᴀᴄ ᵹᴉoʟʟᴀ ᴄᴜᴅᴀ—IV—MacGillacuddy, MacGillecuddy, MacGillycuddy, MacIllicuddy, MacElcuddy, MacElhuddy ; 'son of ᵹᴉoʟʟᴀ ᵯoᴄᴜᴅᴀ' (servant of St. Mochuda, another name for St. Carthage of Lismore); the name of an old Kerry family, a branch of that of O'Sullivan More. The head of the family is known as MacGillycuddy of the Reeks.

ᵯᴀᴄ ᵹᴉoʟʟᴀ ᴄᴜᴉʟʟe—IV—Kilcooley, Cooley ; 'son of

ᵹioʟʟᴀ ṁocúiʟʟe' (servant of St. Mochuille) ; a rare Co. Clare surname.

ᵯᴀc ᵹioʟʟᴀ ᴅé—IV—*M'Gillegea, M'Gillegey, M'Gilgea,* Gildea, Kildea, Kilday, Gay ; 'son of ᵹioʟʟᴀ ᴅé' (servant of God) ; an old Donegal surname ; now also in Mayo.

ᵯᴀc ᵹioʟʟᴀ ᴅeᴀcᴀiᴦ—IV—*M'Gilledogher, M'Gill-dogher,* MacDacker, Harden, Hardy, Harman, Harmon; 'son of ᵹioʟʟᴀ ᴅeᴀcᴀiᴘ' (hard youth) ; probably a var. of ᵯᴀc ᴅáiʟ-ᴘe-ᴅocᴀiᴘ, q.v. In the 16th century, it was peculiar to Co. Roscommon.

ᵯᴀc ᵹioʟʟᴀ ᴅoṁnᴀiᵹ—IV—MacGilldowney, MacIl-downey, MacEldowney, MacDowney, Gildowney, Il-downey, Downey ; 'son of ᵹioʟʟᴀ ᴅoṁnᴀiᵹ' (servant of the Lord) ; a rare Ulster surname.

ᵯᴀc ᵹioʟʟᴀ ᴅoᴦcᴀ—IV—*M'Gilledoroughe,* (?) Mac-Ilderry, MacElderry, MacEldrew ; 'son of ᵹioʟʟᴀ ᴅoᴘcᴀ' (the dark youth, ᴅoᴘcᴀ, dark-complexioned).

ᵯᴀc ᵹioʟʟᴀ ᴅuḃᴛᴀiᵹ—IV—MacGilldowie, MacIl-dowie ; 'son of ᵹioʟʟᴀ ᴅuḃᴛᴀiᵹ' (servant of ᴅuḃᴛᴀc, the name of two Irish saints) ; an Ulster surname. I can find no early instance.

ᵯᴀc ᵹioʟʟᴀ ᴅuiḃ—IV—*M'Gilleduff, M'Gilleguffe, M'Gilduff, M'Kilduffe,* MacIlduff, MacElduff, Gilduff, Kilduff, Duff, Black ; 'son of ᵹioʟʟᴀ ᴅuḃ' (the black youth) ; the name (1) of a Cavan family, the head of which was formerly chief of the barony of Tully-garvey ; (2) of a family in Ui Maine, the head of which was chief of Caladh, in the barony of Kilconnell, Co. Galway ; and (3) of a family of the Ui Fiachrach race in Co. Sligo. The name was also common in other parts of Ireland and in Scotland.

ᵯᴀc ᵹioʟʟᴀ ᴅuinn—IV—*M'Gillydwine, M'Gillyedwn,* MacElgunn, MacElgun, Gilgunn, Kildunn, Kilgunn, Dunne, Gunn ; 'son of ᵹioʟʟᴀ ᴅonn' (the brown youth) ; an old, but rare, Sligo surname.

ᵯᴀc ᵹioʟʟᴀ eáin—IV—MacAlean, MacClean, Mac-Clane, MacLean, MacLaine, MacLane, &c. ; 'son of ᵹióʟʟᴀ eáin' (servant of St. John) ; the name of a numerous and powerful clan in the western Highlands of Scotland, whose patrimony from a remote period was the island of Mull. Some of this race settled in the 17th century in the North of Ireland.

Mac ʒiollA éAnáin, v. Mac ʒiollApáin.

Mac ʒiollA eARnA—IV—*M'Elearney*, MacAlearney, MacElerney, MacLerney; 'son of ʒiollA eApnA' (servant of Earna); an old, but rare Monaghan surname.

Mac ʒiollA eARnáin—IV—*M'Ellerinane*, MacAlernon, MacClearnon, MacClernon, MacClarnon, MacClernand, MacLernon, MacLarnon, MacLorinan, MacLarenon, MacLarinon; 'son of ʒiollA eApnáin' (servant of St. Ernan); the name of an old Co. Down family who, in the 12th century, were chiefs of Clann Ailebra. At the end of the 16th century, it was still common in that county, but was then also found in parts of Connacht; also a Scottish surname.

Mac ʒiollA eAspuiʒ—IV—*M'Gillaspick*, *M'Gillaspecke*, MacGillespie, Gillespie, Gillaspy, Gillespy, Galesby, Glaspy, Glashby, Clusby, Aspig, Bishop, &c.; 'son of ʒiollA eAppuiʒ' (the bishop's servant).

Mac ʒiollA eóin—IV—*M'Ellowen*, *Magloan*, Magloin, Maglone, Malone, MacAloon, MacAloone, MacClune, MacLoone, MacLune, Gilloon, Gloon, and, by 'translation' Monday, Munday; 'son of ʒiollA eóin' (servant of St. John); a scattered Ulster surname, found chiefly in Donegal and Tyrone. The popular pronunciation was often Mac ʒiollA lúin, which caused the last syllable to be mistaken for luain, Monday; hence the 'translated' forms Monday, Munday. V. Mac ʒiollA eáin.

Mac ʒiollA fAoláin—IV—*M'Gillallen*, MacClellan, MacLellan, MacClelland, MacLeland, Gilfillan, Gilfilland, Kilfillan, Gillilan, Gilliland, Gellan, Gelland, Cleeland, Clelland, Clellond, Leland, &c; 'son of ʒiollA fAoláin' (servant of St. Faolan); the name of a family of the Ui Fiachrach race in Co. Sligo; still extant at the beginning of the 17th century, but has apparently since died out. It is, however, at present common in Ulster where it is of late Scottish origin.

mac ʒıoʟʟa ꝼeaʀʒa—IV—MacIlhargy; 'son of ʒıoʟʟa ꝼeaʀʒa' (servant of St. Fearga); doubtless a Leitrim surname, but extremely rare.

mac ʒıoʟʟa ꝼınꝺéın—IV—*MacGillafyndean*, Mac-Alinden, MacAlingen, MacLinden, Glendon, Linden, Lindon; 'son of ʒıoʟʟa ꝼınꝺéın' (servant of St. Finnian); a var. of mac ʒıoʟʟa ꝼınnéın, q.v.

mac ʒıoʟʟa ꝼınn—IV—*M'Gilleffin*, MacGilpin, Gilpin; 'son of ʒıoʟʟa ꝼıonn' (the fair youth); the name of a family of the Ui Fiachrach who were formerly seated in the townland of Laragh, in the parish of Dromard, Co. Sligo.

mac ʒıoʟʟa ꝼınnéın—IV—*M'Gillinnion, M'Elinnan, M'Elynan, M'Linnen*, MacAlinion, MacAlinon, Mac-Aleenan, MacLennan, Gillinnion, (Leonard), &c.; 'son of ʒıoʟʟa ꝼınnéın' (servant of St. Finnian); a var. of mac ʒıoʟʟa ꝼınꝺéın, q.v. This family, which O'Donovan calls the most royal in Ireland, belongs by race to the Cinel Conaill, and is a branch of the ancient and once powerful family of O'Muldory, being descended from Giolla Finnein O'Muldory who flourished towards the end of the 11th century. Their patrimony was Muinntear Feodachain, on the borders of Fermanagh and Donegal, and their chief was sometimes styled 'Lord of Loch Erne.' The family is still numerous in the west of Co. Fermanagh, but the name is often angl. Leonard, which disguises its origin. This is also a Scottish surname, but the Scots write it Mac Gill'innein.

mac ʒıoʟʟa ꝼıonnáın—IV—*M'Gullyneane*, Gillinan (Leonard); 'son of ʒıoʟʟa ꝼıonnáın' (servant of St. Fionnan); very rare.

mac ʒıoʟʟa ꝼıonntáın—IV—MacAlindon, MacClinton, MacLindon, MacLinton, Linton, Lindon; 'son of ʒıoʟʟa ꝼıonntán' (servant of St. Fintan); a surname of Scottish origin, well known in Ulster.

mac ʒᵼoᴌᴌᴀ ꝼᴉoɴɴᴄóʒ—IV—MacClintock, MacClyntock, MacLintock (Lindsay) ; 'son of ʒᵼoᴌᴌᴀ ꝼᴉoɴɴᴄóʒ'; the name of a Scottish family who settled in Donegal towards the end of the 16th century.

mac ʒᵼoᴌᴌᴀʒáᴉɴ—IV—*M'Gillegane, M'Gillgan, M'Illegane*, MacGilligan, MacElgan, Gilligan, Gilgan ; 'son of ʒᵼoᴌᴌᴀʒáɴ' (dim. of ʒᵼoᴌᴌᴀ, youth, lad) ; an Ulster surname, peculiar to Antrim, Derry and Donegal.

mac ʒᵼoᴌᴌᴀ ʒᴀᴉꞃᴂ—IV—*M'Gilligariffe*, Kilgarriff, Kilgrew, Kilcrow, (?) Kilgore, (?) Kilcourse ; 'son of ʒᵼoᴌᴌᴀ ʒᴀꞃᴂ' (the rough lad) ; a rare Connacht surname.

mac ʒᵼoᴌᴌᴀ ʒᴀɴɴᴀᴉɴ—IV—Kilgannon ; 'son of ʒᵼoᴌᴌᴀ ʒᴀɴɴᴀᴉɴ' (servant of Gannan) ; a rare West Connacht surname.

mac ʒᵼoᴌᴌᴀ ʒeáᴉꞃꞃ—IV—*M'Gullygar*, Gilgar, Kilgar ; 'son of ʒᵼoᴌᴌᴀ ʒeáꞃꞃ' (short, low-sized youth).

mac ʒᵼoᴌᴌᴀ ʒeᴉmꞃᴂ—IV—*M'Gullyghirry*, MacAlivery, Winter, Winters ; 'son of ʒᵼoᴌᴌᴀ ʒeᴉmꞃᴂ' (winter lad ; ʒeᴉmꞃeᴀᴂ, winter).

mac ʒᵼoᴌᴌᴀ ʒéᴉꞃ—IV—*M'Kilger*, Kilker ; 'son of ʒᵼoᴌᴌᴀ ʒéᴀꞃ' (sharp lad) ; an old, but extremely rare, Mayo surname. Andrew Mac Gillegheir was Abbot of Cong in the 13th century.

mac ʒᵼoᴌᴌᴀ ʒᴌᴀᴉs—IV—*M'Gilleglas*, Green ; 'son of ʒᵼoᴌᴌᴀ ʒᴌᴀs' (grey lad ; ʒᴌᴀs, grey, green) ; a very rare Donegal surname, angl. Green, according to O'Donovan.

mac ʒᵼoᴌᴌᴀ ʒꞃᴉɴɴ—IV—Gilgrinn ; 'son of ʒᵼoᴌᴌᴀ ʒꞃᴉɴɴ' (bearded-lad, or humorous-lad) ; very rare.

mac ʒᵼoᴌᴌᴀ ʒuᴀᴌᴀ—IV—*M'Gillegowly M'Gilgowlye, M'Kellogulie*, Gillowly, Gillooly, Gilooly, Gilhooly, Killooley ; 'son of ʒᵼoᴌᴌᴀ ʒuᴀᴌᴀ' (glutton, Ir. ʒuᴀᴌᴀ, Lat. gula, gluttony) ; the name of a branch of the family of O'Mulvey in the east of Co. Leitrim, where it is still common. It has been corrupted to mac ʒᵼoᴌᴌᴀ ꞃúᴉᴌᴉʒ, q.v.

mac ʒᵼoᴌᴌᴀ ʒuᴉꞃm—IV—*M'Gilgrim*, MacIlgorm ; 'son

of ʒıoʟʟᴀ ʒoꞃm' (the blue youth); a rare North-east Ulster surname.

mᴀc ʒıoʟʟᴀ ıᴀꞅᴀċᴛᴀ—IV—*M'Gillesachta, M'Gillisachta, M'Gillysaghtie*, MacLysaght, Lysaght, Lysat; 'son of ʒıoʟʟᴀ ıᴀꞃᴀċᴛᴀ' (strange youth); a well-known Clare surname. The family is said to be a branch of the O'Briens, descended from Ꝺoṁnᴀʟʟ móꞃ Ó bꞃıᴀın, King of Munster (1163-1194).

mᴀc ʒıoʟʟᴀ íoꞅᴀ—IV—*M'Illiosa*, MacIleese, Mac-Aleese, MacAleece, MacAlish, MacLeese, MacLees, Maclise, MacLeesh, MacGleish, MacCleish, Gilleece, Gillis, &c.; 'son of ʒıoʟʟᴀ íoꞃᴀ' (servant of Jesus); an Ulster surname; also a Scottish surname.

mᴀc ʒıoʟʟᴀ ʟéıᴛ—IV—*M'Gillalea, M'Gilleley*, Killelea, Killyleigh; 'son of ʒıoʟʟᴀ ʟıᴀᴛ' (grey youth; ʟıᴀᴛ, grey); a scattered surname, but found chiefly in Co. Galway.

mᴀc ʒıoʟʟᴀ ʟuᴀıᴛꞃınn—IV—*M'Gillylworin, Mc-Gilliworyne*, Gilloran, Killoran; 'son of ʒıoʟʟᴀ ʟuᴀıᴛꞃınn' (servant of St. Luaithrenn); a rare Sligo surname.

mᴀc ʒıoʟʟᴀ ṁᴀıᴛ—IV—Goodman [Goodbody, Good-fellow]; 'son of ʒıoʟʟᴀ mᴀıᴛ' (the good youth); a rare Ulster surname. I can find no early instance.

mᴀc ʒıoʟʟᴀ ṁᴀoꝺóʒ—IV—MacElvogue; 'son of ʒıoʟʟᴀ ṁᴀoꝺóʒ' (servant of St. Mogue).

mᴀc ʒıoʟʟᴀ ṁᴀoıʟ—IV—*M'Gullemoyell, M'Gilleweele*, MacIlmoyle, MacIlmoil, MacElmoyle, Macklemoyle, MacElmeel, MacMeel; 'son of ʒıoʟʟᴀ mᴀoʟ' (the bald lad); an Ulster surname. It was also in use at one time in Co. Clare.

mᴀc ʒıoʟʟᴀ ṁáꞃᴛᴀın—IV—*M'Gillamartin, M'Gillavartin, M'Gilmartin*, Gilmartin, Guilmartin, Kilmartin, Martin; 'son of ʒıoʟʟᴀ ṁáꞃᴛᴀın' (servant of St. Martin); the name of an Ulster family who were anciently chiefs of Cinel Fearadhaigh. In the 16th century, it was common in Monaghan, Sligo and Roscommon, and was also found in many other parts of Ireland. It is, no doubt, in many instances now disguised under the angl. form of Martin.

Mac Ꝺᵻoᴸᴸᴀ ᵯᴇᴀɴᴀ—IV—MacElvenna, MacElvenny, MacElvany, MacIlvany, Gilvany; 'son of Ꝺᵻoᴸᴸᴀ ᵯᴇᴀɴᴀ' (servant of Meana); an Antrim surname.

Mac Ꝺᵻoᴸᴸᴀ ᵯᴇᴀʀɴóꝼ—IV—M'Gillavearnoge, Warnock; 'son of Ꝺᵻoᴸᴸᴀ ᵯᴇᴀᵽɴóꝼ' (servant of St. Mearnog); an old Co. Down surname, now shortened to Mac ᵯᴇᴀᵽɴóꝼ, q.v.; also in use in Scotland, where it is Englished Graham.

Mac Ꝺᵻoᴸᴸᴀ ᵯᵻċᵻᴸ—IV—M'Gillemichell, MacMichael, MacMeel, Michael, Mitchell; 'son of Ꝺᵻoᴸᴸᴀ ᵯᵻċᵻᴸ' (servant of St. Michael); the name of a family who were anciently chiefs of Cᴸᴀɴɴ Ċoɴꝼᴀᵻᴸᴇ, in Co. Fermanagh, but dispossessed by the Maguires in the 15th century. It is said to have been angl. Mitchell. Mac Ꝺᵻoᴸᴸᴀ ᵯᵻċᵻᴸ is also a Scottish surname.

Mac Ꝺᵻoᴸᴸᴀ ᵯíɴ—IV—M'Gillavyne, M'Gilvine, MacIlveen, MacElveen, MacKilveen; 'son of Ꝺᵻoᴸᴸᴀ ᵯíɴ' (gentle, tender youth); a Co. Down surname.

Mac Ꝺᵻoᴸᴸᴀ ᵯíʀ—IV—M'Gilver, M'Gilmer, Gilmer, Gilmor; 'son of Ꝺᵻoᴸᴸᴀ ᵯᴇᴀᵽ' (the merry, lively youth); the name of an old family of the Ui Fiachrach race in Co. Sligo, formerly seated in the townland of Finnure, in the barony of Tireragh.

Mac Ꝺᵻoᴸᴸᴀ ᵯoċᴜᴅᴀ, v. Mac Ꝺᵻoᴸᴸᴀ Ċᴜᴅᴀ.

Mac Ꝺᵻoᴸᴸᴀ ᵯᴜᵻʀᴇ—IV—M'Gilleworry, M'Gilmurry, M'Gilmore, MacIlmurray, MacElmurray, MacKilmurray, MacMurray, Kilmurry, Kilmary, Kilmore, Gilmore, Gilmour, Gilmor, Gilmer, Murry, Murray; 'son of Ꝺᵻoᴸᴸᴀ ᵯᴜᵻᵽᴇ' (servant of Mary); the name of a family in Co. Down who were chiefs of Ui Derca Cein, in the barony of Castlereagh. They are a branch of the family of O'Morna, formerly lords of Lecale, being descended from Ꝺᵻoᴸᴸᴀ ᵯᴜᵻᵽᴇ Ó ᵯoᵽɴᴀ, lord of Lecale, whose death is recorded in the Annals of the Four Masters at the year 1276. The name is also in use in Scotland, where it is angl. Morrison (i.e., Muire's son).

Mac Ʒiolla na naoṁ—IV—*M'Gillinaneave, M'Giller-
neve, M'Gillernae,* MacElnea, MacAneave, MacAnave,
and, by 'translation' Ford, Forde; 'son of Ʒiolla
na naoṁ' (servant of the saints); a West Connacht
surname; corrupted to Mac Ʒiollaṛnát, and erroneously translated Ford, Forde, from the resemblance of the final syllable to át, a ford.

Mac Ʒiolla na neaċ—IV—*M'Gillyneneagh,* Gilnagh;
'son of Ʒiolla na n-eaċ' (lad of the horses); the name
of a family of the Ui Fiachrach in Co. Sligo. It still
survives, but is extremely rare.

Mac Ʒiolla Páoraiʒ—IV—*M'Gillephadrick, M'Gilla-
patrick, M'Kilpatrick,* MacGilpatrick, MacIlpatrick,
MacIlfatrick, MacElfatrick, MacIlfederick, MacElfedrick, Gilpatrick, Kilpatrick, Kirkpatrick, Fitzpatrick; 'son of Ʒiolla Páoraiʒ' (servant of St.
Patrick). The principal family of this name are the
MacGillapatricks, or Fitzpatricks, of Ossory, who
took their name from Ʒiolla Páoraiʒ, son of Donn-
chadh, lord of Ossory, in the 10th century. In early
times they ruled over the entire of Co. Kilkenny and
part of the present Leix, but after the Anglo-Norman
invasion they were greatly encroached upon by the
Butlers and other English settlers in Kilkenny, and
their patrimony was limited to the barony of Upper
Ossory. Branches of the family settled in Clare,
Cavan, Leitrim, and other parts of Ireland. In 1541,
Brian Mac Giolla Patrick was created Baron of Upper
Ossory. There appears to have been also a Scottish
family of this name.

Mac Ʒiolla Peaoair—IV—*M'Gillepedire,* Gilfedder,
Kilfeder, Kilfedder, Gilfeather; 'son of Ʒiolla
Peaoaiṛ' (servant of St. Peter); a rare Sligo surname.

Mac Ʒiolla Póil—IV—*M'Gillaphoill, M'Gillfoile,
M'Killphoill,* MacGilfoyle, Gilfoyle, Guilfoyle, Kil-
foyle, (Powell); 'son of Ʒiolla Póil' (servant of St.
Paul); the name of an ancient family in Ely O'Carroll,
who were chiefs of Clann Choinlegan, near Shinrone, in
Offaly.

mac ȝiollaráin—IV—*Magillerane,* Gilleran, Gilrain, Gilrane, Killeran, Kilrain, Kilrane ; 'son of ȝiolla éanáin '(servant of St. Enan) ; a corruption of mac ȝiolla éanáin.

mac ȝiolla riabaiȝ—IV—*M'Gillereogh, M'Calreogh, M'Calreaghe, M'Callerie,* MacGillreavy, MacGilrea, MacElreavy, MacIlravy, MacElreath, MacElwreath, MacIlwraith, MacIlrea, MacAreavy, MacArevy, Gallery, Callery, Killery, Kilgray, Gray ; 'son of ȝiolla riabac ' (the grey youth, from riabac, grey, brindled) ; the name (1) of a family of the Ui Fiachrach, seated at Creaghaun, in the parish of Skreen, Co. Sligo ; and (2) of a Clare family who were servants of trust to the Earls of Thomond, and held the castle of Craigbrien, in the parish of Clondagad. The family is still in Thomond, but the surname is now always angl. Gallery. In the midlands, it was sometimes made Callery, and sometimes translated Gray. Kilgray is a half translation. mac ȝiolla riabaiȝ is also a Scottish surname. According to Dr. MacBain, it is angl. MacIlwraith, &c.

mac ȝiolla rónáin—IV—O *Kilronane,* Kilronan ; 'son of ȝiolla rónáin ' (servant of St. Ronan) ; the name of a bishop of Clogher, early in the 13th century. At the beginning of the 17th century, it appears as O Kilronane in Co. Cavan. It has always been very rare.

mac ȝiolla ruabáin—IV—*M'Gillaroyn,* MacElrone ; 'son of ȝiolla ruabán.' (servant of St. Ruadhan).

mac ȝiolla ruaib—IV—*M'Gillarowe, M'Gillaroe, M'Gillaroye, M'Killeroe, M'Killroy,* MacGillroy, MacGilroy, MacIlroy, MacElroy, MacAlroy, MacLeroy, Gilroy, Kilroy, Ilroy, Roy, and, by 'translation,' King ; 'son of ȝiolla ruab ' (red youth) ; the name of a Fermanagh family, the head of which resided at Ballymackilroy, in the parish of Aghalurchur, near Lough Erne. In the 16th century, it was common in Down, Cavan, Roscommon and Offaly. It is sometimes erroneously translated King.

Mac Ʒiolla Sámais — IV — MacClavish ; ' son of Ʒiolla ṫámaiṟ' (votary of pleasure) ; a rare Ulster surname, perhaps now obsolete.

Mac Ʒiolla Seaċlainn — IV — *M'Gillaghlin*, Mac-Glaughlin, MacClachlin, MacClafflin, Clafflin ; ' son of Ʒiolla Seaċlainn ' (servant of St. Secundinus) ; the name of an old Meath family who were lords of Southern Breagh until soon after the Anglo-Norman invasion, when they lost their power and were dispersed. The present angl. forms of Mac Ʒiolla Seaċlainn cannot be distinguished from those of Maʒ Loċlainn, Maʒ Laċlainn, q.v. ; but that the family is still extant is shown by the variant Mac Ʒiolla tSeaċlainn, q.v.

Mac Ʒiolla Seanáin, Mac Ʒiolla Sionáin — IV — *M'Gilsenane*, *M'Gylsinan*, MacGillshenan, Gilshenan, Gilshenon, Gelshinan, Gilsenan, Gunshinan, Gilson, (Nugent, Leonard) ; ' son of Ʒiolla Seanáin ' (servant of St. Senan) ; a common surname in Meath, Cavan and Tyrone, but now often disguised under the angl. forms of Nugent and Leonard, especially the former. Maʒ Uinnṟeanáin (q.v.) is a corruption. See also Mac Ʒiolla tSeanáin which is a variant.

Mac Ʒiolla Steaṟáin — IV — *M'Gilsteffan*, Stephens ; ' son of Ʒiolla Steaṟáin ' (servant of St. Stephen) ; a rare surname in Leix, &c.

Mac Ʒiolla Súiliʒ — IV — *M'Gillehowly*, Gilhooly, &c. ; a corruption of Mac Ʒiolla ʒuala, q.v. It is so written in the Annals of Loch Cé and by the Four Masters.

Mac Ʒiolla tSeaċlainn — IV — *M'Kintaghlin, M'Taghlin*, MacA'Taghlin, MacTaghlin, MacTaghlan, (Houston), &c. ; a var. of Mac Ʒiolla Seaċlainn, q.v. It was still a Meath surname in the 16th century ; now found in Donegal, where it is sometimes angl. Houston.

Mac Ʒiolla tSeanáin — IV — Giltenane, Giltinane, Giltenan, Shannon ; a var. of Mac Ʒiolla Seanáin, q.v. This form of the name is in use in Co. Clare, where it is corrupted to Ó Cilltṟeáin and often angl. Shannon.

mac ʒɪoʟʟᴀ ᴜɪᴅɪʀ—IV—*M'Elyre*, MacAleer, MacLear, MacLure, MacClure ; 'son of ʒɪoʟʟᴀ oᴅᴀʀ' (the pale youth ; oᴅᴀʀ, dun, pale) ; a rare Armagh surname. Eachdonn Mac Giolla uidhir was Primate of Armagh early in the 13th century. It is also a Scottish surname.

mac ʒɪʀʀ ᴀn ᴀᴅᴀsᴄᴀɪʀ, mac ʒɪʀʀ ᴀn ᴀʒᴀsᴄᴀɪʀ— VII—*MacGirrenagastyr, MacGirrenastyr, MacGirrnaystar*, Nestor ; 'son of the short-(man) of the halter'; now shortened to mac ᴀn ᴀᴅᴀʀᴄᴀɪʀ, q.v. ; the name of an old Thomond family who were followers of the O'Loghlens of Burren.

mac ʒʟᴀɪsín, mac ʒʟᴀsᴀ́ɪn—IV—MacGlashin, MacGlashan, Green ; 'son of ʒʟᴀɪʀín,' or 'ʒʟᴀʀᴀ́n' (dim. of ʒʟᴀʀ, grey, green) ; a West Ulster surname.

mac ʒʟeᴀᴅʀᴀ—IV—MacGladery, MacGladdery, MacGlathery, Gladdry ; 'son of ʒʟeᴀᴅʀᴀ'; an Ulster surname.

mac ʒʟúɪn—IV—*M'Clone, M'Cloane, M'Clowne, MacCloone*, Clune ; 'son of ʒʟún' (knee, probably a 'pet' form of ʒʟúnɪᴀʀᴀɪnn, iron-knee, or ʒʟúnᴄʀᴀᴅnᴀ, corn-crake knee); the name of an old Thomond family who were seated at Ballymacloon, in the parish of Quin, Co. Clare, where the name is still well known.

mac ʒoᴅᴀ, mac ʒoᴅᴀnn, v. mac ᴀn ʒoᴅᴀnn.

mac ʒoꝼʀᴀᴅᴀ, mac ʒoꝼʀᴀɪᴅ—V—*M'Goffrie*, MacCaffrey, &c. ; a var. of mac ʒᴀꝼʀᴀɪᴅ, q.v. See also mac ʒoᴄʀᴀɪᴅ.

mac ʒoɪʟʟ—IV—Giles, Gyles ; 'son of ʒoʟʟ'; a rare Galway surname.

mac ʒoɪsᴅeᴀʟᴅ, mac ʒoɪsᴅeᴀʟᴅᴀɪʒ, v. mac oɪʀᴅeᴀʟᴅ, mac oɪʀᴅeᴀʟᴅᴀɪʒ.

mac ʒoʀmᴀ́ɪn—IV—*M'Gormane, M'Cormaine*, MacGorman, Gorman, (O'Gorman) ; 'son of ʒoʀmᴀ́n' (dim. of ʒoʀm, blue) ; the name of a Leinster family who were formerly lords of Ui Bairche, in the barony of Slievemargy, in the south-east of the present Leix. Soon after the Anglo-Norman invasion, they were driven from this territory and settled, some in

Monaghan, others in the barony of Ibrickan, in West Clare, where they became very numerous. The head of the Clare branch of the family was marshal of O'Brien's forces. Even before the end of the 16th century, the name had spread into the neighbouring counties of Galway, Tipperary and Limerick. O'Gorman has been adopted in modern times, but incorrectly, as the angl. form by some of the name in Munster ; but MacGorman, the more correct form, is still retained in the North.

Mac ʒᴏʀmʒᴀɪʟ, Mac ʒᴏʀmʒᴀɪʟᴇ—IV—*M'Gormoyle, M'Cormally,* MacCormilla, Gormley ; 'son of ʒᴏʀmʒᴀɪʟ' (blue-valour) ; a rare surname ; perhaps a var. of Ó ʒᴏʀmʒᴀɪʟ, q.v.

Mac ʒᴏᴄʀᴀᴅᴀ, Mac ʒᴏᴄʀᴀɪᴅ—V—*M'Gorrie, M'Gorhae, M'Gorhy,* MacGorry, MacGurry, MacCorry, MacCurry, Godfrey, Gorry, Corry, Curry, (?) Curoe ; 'son of Godfrey' ; older Mac ʒᴏᴄᴘʀᴀᴅᴀ, Mac ʒᴏᴄᴘʀᴀɪᴅ ; a var. of Mac ʒᴏᴘᴘᴀᴅᴀ, Mac ʒᴏᴘᴘᴀɪᴅ and Mac ʒᴀᴘᴘᴀɪᴅ, q.v.

Mac ʒʀᴀɪɴɴᴇ—IV—Granny, Grant ; probably for Maʒ Ráɪʒne, q.v.

Mac ʒʀᴀɪᴄ v. Maʒ ʀᴀɪᴄ.

Mac ʒʀᴇᴀʒᴀɪʀ—V—MacGregor, Gregory ; 'son of Gregory' ; the name of a famous Scottish clan.

Mac ʒʀɪᴘɪɴ—V—*M'Griffine,* MacGriffin ; 'son of Griffin' (a personal name of Welsh origin, the same as the Lat. Rufinus).

Mac ʒʀɪᴏʒᴀɪʀ, v. Mac ʒʀᴇᴀʒᴀɪᴘ, of which it is a variant.

Mac ʒʀɪᴏʒᴀɪʀ—V—MacGreer, Greer, Grear, Grier, Grierson ; 'son of Gregory' ; a var. of Mac ʒʀᴇᴀʒᴀɪᴘ, q.v.

Mac ʒᴜᴀʒᴀɪɴ, Mac ʒᴜᴀɪᴄɪɴ, Mac ʒᴜᴀɪʒɪɴ—IV—MacGuigan, MacGuiggan, MacGuckian, MacQuiggan, MacGoogan, MacCookin, MacGuckin, MacWiggan, MacWiggin, Pigeon, Pidgeon ; a corrupt form of Mac ᴇᴏᴄᴀɪᴅɪɴ, q.v.

Mac ʒᴜᴀɪʀᴇ—IV—MacQuarrie ; 'son of ʒᴜᴀɪʀᴇ' ; a Scottish surname.

mac haiceív—V—*M'Hacket,   M'Hackett,*   Hackett; 'son of Hacket' (a Norman personal name); the name of a tiny family who were formerly seated at Island M'Hackett, Co. Galway. V. **haiceív.**

mac hanraoi, mac hannraoi—V—*M'Hanry,* Mac-Henry, MacHarry, Fitzhenry, Fitzharris, Feeharry, Henry, Harris, Harrison, &c.; 'son of Henry'; a var. of **mac Annraoi** and **mac Éinri**, q.v.

mac haol—V—*M'Caele, M'Keale, M'Heale, M'Howell,* MacHale, Hale, Hales, Howell, Howels, &c.; 'son of Howel' (a Welsh personal name); a surname of Welsh origin, in use in various parts of Ireland. In Co. Mayo, it is not infrequently heard, side by side with **mac héil** (q.v.), as the Irish for MacHale. The diphthong **ao** has, however, the Munster sound of **ae**, the final **l** being broad. The collective plural is also peculiar, viz., **Clann taol**, pronounced **Clann tael** (**l** broad).

mac héil—V—*M'Keale,* MacHale; 'son of Howel'; a var. of **mac haol**, q.v.; the name of a family, apparently of Welsh origin, who settled in Tirawley, in the 12th or 13th century; now always angl. Mac-Hale, and probably confused with the native name **mac Céile**, q.v.

mac hob—V—Hobson, Hopson, Hobbs; 'son of Hob' (a 'pet' form of Robert).

mac hoibicín, v. **mac Oibicín.**

mac hoirbín—V—Harbinson, Harbison, Harbeson, &c.; 'son of Harbin' (dim. of Herbert). V. **mac hoirpeabáiro.**

mac hoireabáiro,   mac   hoireabairo—V—*M'Harbard, M'Herbert,* [Fitzherbert, Herbertson, Herbison]; 'son of Herbert'; an Irish patronymic assumed by the family of Delamare in Co. Westmeath. V **hoirpeabáiro.**

mac hoiste—V—*M'Hostie,   M'Hoste,*   Hosty, &c.; 'son of Hodge' (a 'pet' name for Roger). V. **mac Oirte.**

mac hoisticín—V—Hodgkins, Hodgkinson, &c.; 'son

of Hodgkin' (dim. of Hodge, i.e., Roger). V. **Mac Oirticin.**

Mac huigín—V—*M'Hugin*, *M'Hugyn*, Hugginson, Higginson; 'son of Hugin' (a dim. of Hugh).

Mac hunfraið—V—MacHanfry, Machanfry, Humphries, Humphreys, &c.; 'son of Hunfrid.' V. **Unfraið.**

Mac Iagó—V—*M'Kiego*, *M'Kigo*, *M'Egoe*, Iago, Igo, Igoe; 'son of **Iagó**' (a Spanish form of James); an old Roscommon surname; locally supposed, according to O'Donovan, to be of Spanish origin. V. **Iagó.**

Mac Iagóg—V—*M'Kigog*, Igo, Igoe; 'son of **Iagóg**' (a dim. of **Iagó**); a var. of **Mac Iagó** (q.v.) in Co. Roscommon. It is still in use, but has now no distinct English equivalent.

Mac Iain—V—MacKean; 'son of John'; a var. of **Mac Eáin**, q.v.

Mac inneirge—VII—*M'Ineirie*, *M'Enerie*, *M'Keneyry*, MacKeniry, MacEniry, MacNeiry, MacKennery, MacKenery, MacEnery, MacEnry, Kiniry, &c.; 'son of **inneirge**' (the rising, early riser); the name of an ancient family in Co. Limerick, who for many centuries were chiefs of Corca Muicheat, now Corcomohide, an extensive district in the south of the county. The chief resided at Castletown MacEniry, where the ruins of his castle are still to be seen. Though greatly encroached upon by the Anglo-Norman settlers, the MacEnirys contrived to retain a considerable portion of their ancient patrimony down to the revolution of 1688.

Mac inNreactaig—IV—*M'Inrightighe*, *M'Enrichty*, *M'Kinraghty*, MacEnright, Inright, Enraght, Enright; 'son of **inNreactac**' (unlawful); a var. of **Mac Ionnractaig**, q.v.

Mac Iolracáin, Eagleton. I can find no early instance of this surname, and suspect that it is merely an attempt to find an Irish equivalent for the English surname Eagleton.

mac íomaiR, mac íomaiR—V—*M'Eiver*, *M'Kewer*, MacIvor, MacIver, MacKiver, MacKiever, MacKiver, MacKever, MacKevor, MacKeever, MacKeevor, Mac-Cure, MacIvers, Ivers, Eivers, Keevers, &c. ; ' son of Ivarr ' (an old Scandinavian personal name) ; a common surname in the North of Ireland, apparently of Scottish origin. See maʒ íomaiɲ which is the form in use in the West.

mac íomaiRe, Montgomery, Gomory, Ridge. This seems to be merely an attempt to represent the sound of the English surname Montgomery. Ridge is an attempted translation, on the erroneous supposition that the latter part of the surname is the Irish word ' íomaiɲe,' a ridge. In West Clare it is pronounced maʒompaċ.

mac íonṁain—IV—Love ; ' son of íonṁain ' (beloved).

mac íonnRaċaiʒ—IV—*M'Enraghtie*, *M'Kenraghta*, *M'Kenraght*, MacEnright, Enraght, Inright, Enright ; ' son of íonnɲaċtaċ ' (unlawful) ; a well-known Munster surname of Dalcassian origin. In the spoken language, it is pronounced 'a Ciúɲɲaċta.'

mac íosóc, mac íosóʒ—V—*M'Isock*, *M'Kysoke*, *M'Kyssock*, *M'Kysog*, MacKissock, MacCussack, Kissack, Cusack ; ' son of Isaac ' ; the name of an old Thomond family ; found also in Galway, Roscommon and Donegal. It was also an old surname in the Isle of Man, where it is still represented by Kissack.

mac íseóʒ—V—*M'Ishocke*, Cusack ; a var. of mac íoɼóʒ, q.v. ; still in use in Co. Galway.

mac laḃRaḃa—IV—*M'Lawry*, MacLavery, MacClory, Clowry ; ' son of laḃɲaiḃ ' (spokesman, advocate) ; a rare Ulster surname.

mac laḃRáin—IV—*M'Loyrane*, *M'Loran*, Cloran ; ' son of laḃɲán ' (a dim. of laḃɲaiḃ) ; an old Cavan surname ; always very rare.

mac laḃRainn—V—MacLaurin, MacLauren, Mac-Laren, [Lawrenson, Lawrinson, Laurison, Lawson], &c. ; ' son of Laurence ' ; a Scottish surname. V. laḃɲant.

Mac Laḃráis—V—*M'Laurence*, [Lawrenson, Lawrinson, Lawson, &c.]; 'son of Laurence.' V. Laḃṗár.

Mac Laclainn—V—MacLachlin, MacLachlan, Mac-Laughlin, MacClachlin, MacClaughlin, MacClafflin, Clafflin, &c. 'son of Loclainn' (a name of Norse origin); the Scottish and Ulster form of Mac Loc-lainn, q.v. The Scottish clan of this name was seated at Strathlachlan in Argyleshire. V. Mac Laḃmainn.

Mac Laḃmainn, Mac Laṡmainn—V—MacLamond, MacLimont, MacClamon, MacClymon, MacClimond, MacClimont, MacClemonts, MacClement, MacCly-monds, Clymonds, Climons, Lammon, Lamond, La-mont, Limond, Limont, &c.; 'son of Laṡmann' (a Norse personal name, meaning 'lawman' or 'lawyer'; found in Domesday Book as Laghemann and Lagman in the time of Edward the Confessor); the name of a Scoto-Irish family in Argyleshire. They are of the same stock as the MacSweenys and MacLachlins, all three families being descended, according to Mac-Firbis (p. 125), from three sons of Donnṡléiḃe Ó néill.

Mac Laiḃiṡ, v. Mac Laoiḋiṡ.

Mac Laitḃeartaiṡ—IV—*M'Laghertie*, MacLaverty, MacClafferty, MacCleverty; 'son of Flaitḃeaptac'; a var. of Mac Flaitḃeaptaiṡ, q.v. The omission of the initial F when aspirated is not uncommon.

Mac Laitiṁ—IV—*M'Glave*, MacLave, MacClave, Claffey, Claffy, and, by 'translation,' Hand; 'son of Flaiteaṁ'; a var. of Mac Flaitiṁ and Maṡ Laitiṁ, q.v. The surname was so pronounced as to be mis-taken for Mac Láiṁ; hence the erroneous translation Hand.

Mac Laoiḋiṡ—IV—MacLea, MacLee, Lea, Lee, Leigh; 'son of Laoiḋeac' (poetic); the name of an old family in Leix.

Mac Lataiṡ, Claffey, Clafry, &c.; a var. in the spoken language of Mac Latiṁ, q.v.

Mac Leannacáin—IV—*M'Clanaghan*, *M'Claneghan* MacLenaghan, MacLenahan, MacLeneghan, Mac-

Lenighan, MacLennon, MacClenaghan, MacClenahan, MacCleneghan, MacClenighan, MacClennon, Clenaghan, &c.; 'son of Leannacán' (dim. of Leannac, cloaked, mantled); an Ulster surname.

mac Leóiⅅ—V—MacLeod, MacCleod, MacCloud; 'son of Leóⅴ' (the Norse 'Ljotr,' ugly); the name of a well-known Scottish clan, once powerful in Lewis and Harris. Some of them settled in Ireland in the 16th century.

mac Liam—V—Wilson; 'son of Will' (a 'pet' form of William).

mac Loclainn—V—MacLochlin, MacLoghlin, MacLoughlin, Loughlin, &c., (Loftus); 'son of Loclainn' (a name of Norse origin); the name of the senior branch of the northern Ui Neill. Before the 13th century, they were the most powerful family in Ulster. They were seated in Inishowen, where the name is still common. A branch of this family settled in Mayo in the 17th century. It would appear that there was also a family of the name in Co. Leitrim, who were followers of the O'Rourkes. This surname is to be distinguished from Ó maoilfeaclainn (q.v.), which is now also angl. MacLoughlin. V. maz Loclainn.

mac Loineáin—IV—MacLennan, MacLennon, (Leonard); 'son of Lonán'; a rare Galway surname.

mac Loingseacáin—IV—M'Linchechane, Lynchehan; 'son of Loingreacán' (dim. of Loingreac); a rare Donegal surname; apparently an alias for mac Loingriz, q.v. See also Ó Loingreacáin.

mac Loingsiz—IV—M'Kilinsie, MacClinchy, Clinchy; 'son of Loingreac' (having, or belonging to, a fleet); a var. of maz Loingriz, q.v.; a Donegal surname.

mac Lúcáis—V—MacLucas, (?) MacCluggage, Clucas; 'son of Lucas' (an old form of Luke).

mac Luzaⅴa—IV—M'Lewe, M'Lowe, Lowe; 'son of Luzaiⅴ.'

mac tuinze—IV—MacLung, MacClung; 'son of Long' (?); a rare surname of Scottish origin.

Mac Luirg—IV—MacLurg, MacClurg; 'son of Lurg';
a rare surname of Scottish origin.

Mac Maoóc, Mac Maoóg—V—M'Vadocke, M'Vadog,
M'Vadick, M'Vadige, Vaddock, Wadock, Waddock,
Wadick, Waddick, Weadock, Weadick, Weddick,
Maddox; 'son of Madoc,' or 'Madog' (a Welsh personal name); the name of an old Wexford family,
said to be descended from Murcaó na nGaeóeal,
the brother of Diarmaid Mac Murrough; usually
angl. Maddox. V. Maoóc.

Mac Magnuis, Mac Magnusa—V—M'Manish,
M'Moenassa, MacManus, MacManis, Manus, Man-
asses; 'son of Magnur' (Lat. 'Magnus,' a name
adopted by the Northmen in honour of Charlemagne
—Carolus Magnus—and by them introduced into
Ireland, angl. Manus); the name (1) of a Roscommon
family, descended from Magnur, son of Turlough
Mor O'Connor, King of Ireland, who was slain in the
year 1181, formerly seated in Tirhoohil; and (2) of a
Fermanagh family, descended from Magnur, son of
Donn Maguire, chief of Fermanagh, who died in 1302.
The head of this family lived at Senadh Mic Maghnusa,
now Belle Isle, in Lough Erne. The name is often
pronounced Mac Maonuir, or Mac Maonura.

Mac Maicín—IV—M'Makine, M'Macken, MacMackin,
Mackin, Macken; 'son of Maicín' (youth, dim. of
mac, a son); a Donegal surname.

Mac Máige—V—Mackmawe, MacMay, Mawe, May, Mea
'son of May' (short for Maheu, i.e., Matthew); a var
of Mac Máigeóc, Mac Máigeóg, q.v.

Mac Máigeóc, Mac Máigeóg—V—MacMajoke
M'Maoge, M'Maogh-Condon, M'Mawige, M'Maug
Mackmawe-Condon, MacMay, Mawe, May, Mea
[Condon]; 'son of Mayoc' or 'Mayog' (dim. o
Maheu, the Norman-French form of Matthew); a
patronymic surname assumed by a branch of the
family of Condon in East Cork and Waterford. The
present angl. forms are derived from the shortened
form, Mac Máige, q.v.

Mac Máiʒiú—V—Mahew; 'son of Maheu' (or Matthew); the name of a Mayo family, probably an offshoot of the Barretts, among whom Maheu was a common name; extremely rare.

*Mac Maine—IV—*M'Many*, *M'Mane*, Mayne, Maynes; 'son of Maine.'

Mac Máirtín—V—*M'Martin*, [Fitzmartin], Martin, Marten, Martyn; 'son of Martin'; the name of a branch of the O'Neills of Tyrone.

Mac Maitís—V—*M'Mahishe*, *M'Mahise*, Mathias; 'son of Matthias.'

Mac Manainn—IV—*M'Mannan*, *M'Mannian*, Mac-Mannon, MacMannion; apparently a shortened form of Mac Manannáin, q.v.; a Donegal surname.

Mac Manannáin—IV—*M'Maynanan*; 'son of Manann-án' (the name of an ancient Irish sea-god); a rare Donegal surname; now obsolete, or shortened to Mac Manainn, q.v.

Mac Maoilʋúin—IV—*M'Molydon*, MacIldoon; 'son of Maolʋúin' (chief of the fort); a rare Ulster surname. V. Mac Maolʋúin.

Mac Maoilín—IV—*M'Myline*, MacMillin, MacMillen; 'son of Maoilín' (dim. of maol, bald); a var. of Mac Maoláin, q.v.

Mac Maoilíosa—IV—(?) *M'Myllis*, Malise, Mellis; 'son of Maol Íosa' (servant of Jesus). This surname, which was borne by an Archbishop of Armagh towards the close of the 13th century, is probably now obsolete in Ireland, but survives in Scotland, angl. Malise and Mellis.

Mac Maoilir—V—*M'Miler*, *M'Meyler*, *M'Moiler*, Mac-Moyler, Meyler; 'son of Meyler' (a Welsh personal name). V. Maoilir.

Mac Maoláin—IV—*M'Mowllane*, *M'Moylan*, Mac-Mullan, MacMullen, MacMullin, MacMullon, Mac-Millan, MacMillen, MacBlain, Mullin, Mullins, &c.; 'son of Maolán' (dim. of maol, bald). In the 12th century, Mac Maoláin was lord of Gaileang Breagh, in the north of the present Co. Dublin, but in later ages the name has been confined to North-East Ulster. There is also a Scottish mac maoláin.

mac maolcoluim—IV—Malcolmson, Malcomson, Malcolm; 'son of maolcoluim' (servant of St. Columcille); a surname of Scottish origin.

mac maolcraoibe—IV—*M'Elchrive*; 'son of maolcraoibe' (chief of craob, a place-name); a rare Ulster surname, now probably obsolete. V. Ó maolcraoibe.

mac maoldúin—IV—*M'Muldowne*; a var. of mac maoildúin, q.v.

mac maoltuile—IV—*M'Multully*. V. mac maoltuile.

mac maoltuile — IV — *M'Cultully*, *M'Cuntully*, *M'Cantully*, *M'Ethwille*, MacAtilla, Tully, and, by 'translation,' Flood; 'son of maoltuile' (devoted to the will, i.e., of God); older mac maoltuile, q.v.; the name of a medical family in Co. Roscommon, who were hereditary physicians to the O'Connors of Connacht. The name has been long corrupted to mac an tuile and mac tuile, erroneously supposed to signify 'son of the flood,' and accordingly angl. Flood. V. Ó maoltuile.

mac maonaig — IV — *M'Meeney*, MacWeeney, (?) Queeney; 'son of maonac' (wealthy, or dumb); the name of an ancient family of Moylurg, in Co. Roscommon.

mac maongail—IV—*M'Mounell*, *M'Monnell*, *M'Monnyll*, MacMonagle, MacMonegal, MacMonigal, MacMonigle, MacMunigal, Monagle; 'son of maongal' (wealth-valour); an old Donegal surname. For unaspirated g, cf. mac congail.

mac marcuis—V—*M'Marcus*, *M'Markus*, *M'Markes*, Marcus, Marks; 'son of Mark' (Lat. Marcus); the name of an Antrim family who are probably a branch of the MacDonalds.

mac mata—V—*M'Mahae*, *M'Maghie*, *M'Mah*, MacMagh, MacMath, MacMa; 'son of Matthew'; a rare Ulster surname. V. mac mata.

Mac Mata—V—Mathewson, Matheson ; a var. of Mac
Mata ; a Scottish surname.

Mac Matain—IV—*Macmaghan*, Matheson ; a Scottish-
Gaelic var. of Mac Matgamna, q.v.

Mac Matgamna—IV—*M'Mahowna,* *M'Maghowney,*
M'Maghone, *M'Machan,* MacMaghone, MacMaghon,
MacMaghen, MacMachon, MacMahon, MacMahan,
MacMann, Mahony, Mahon, (Matthews, Mathews) ;
' son of Matgamain ' (bear). There are two great
Irish families of this name, viz. : the MacMahons of
Thomond, and the MacMahons of Oriel. The Mac-
Mahons of Thomond are a branch of the O'Briens,
and derive their name and descent from Mahon, son
of Murtagh More O'Brien, King of Ireland (1094-
1119). Their patrimony was Corca Bhaiscinn, which
comprised the baronies of Moyarta and Clonderlaw
in the south-west of Co. Clare. The last chief of the
name was accidentally killed by his own son at Bear-
haven in the year 1602. To this family belonged the
celebrated Marshal MacMahon, Duke of Magenta and
President of the French Republic. The MacMahons
of Oriel were formerly one of the most powerful
families in Ulster. On the decline of the O'Carrolls
in the 13th century, they became lords of Oriel, a
rank which they retained down to the reign of Elizabeth ; and even as late as the Cromwellian wars, they
had considerable possessions and power in Co. Monaghan. The last chief of the family was Hugh Mac-
Mahon who was arrested for complicity in the plot
to seize Dublin Castle in 1641, sent to the Tower of
London, and, in 1644, beheaded at Tyburn. Besides
distinguished chiefs, this family produced many
eminent ecclesiastics, three of whom successively
filled the primatial see of Armagh in the first half of
the 18th century.

Mac Meadacain, Wade, Waide ; probably an attempted translation of the English surname Wade ;
in use in Mayo, but rare.

Mac Meanma—IV—*M'Mannamie,* MacManamy, Mac-

Menamy, MacMenemy, MacMinamy ; ' son of meᴀnmᴀ' (courage, high-spirits) ; a var. of mᴀc meᴀnmᴀn, q.v.

mᴀc meᴀnmᴀ—IV—MacVanamy ; a var. of mᴀc meᴀnmᴀ, q.v.

mᴀc meᴀnmᴀn—IV—MacManaman, MacManamon, MacMenamon, MacMenamen, MacMenemen, Mac-Menamin, MacMenimin, MacMeenamon, MacMenim, Menemin, Merriman, Merryman ; ' son of meᴀnmᴀ ' (courage, high-spirits) ; an old, and still common, surname in Tirconnell ; also in Thomond.

mᴀc meᴀʀᴀin—IV—M'Marran, M'Meraine, M'Meran, MacVerran, MacFerran ; ' son of meᴀpᴀn ' (dim. of meᴀp, active, lively) ; originally a Westmeath surname, but long since dispersed and now extremely rare.

mᴀc meᴀʀnóᵹ—IV—M'Varnocke, Warnock ; apparently short for mᴀc ᵹioʟʟᴀ meᴀpnóᵹ, q.v.

mᴀc meiᴅʀic, mᴀc meiʀic, mᴀc míᴅʀic—V—Mey-rick, Mayrick, Merrick ; ' son of Merick ' (the common Welsh personal name Meurug) ; the name of a family of Welsh origin who settled in the valley of Glenhest, to the west of Glen Nephin, Co. Mayo ; now more commonly meiᴅpic, meipic (q.v.) without mᴀc.

mᴀc mᴀᴅᴀcᴀin—IV—(?) MacMeechan, MacMeekan, MacMeekin, &c. ; ' son of miᴀᴅᴀcᴀn.'

mᴀc micil—V—MacMichall, MacMichael, MacMighael, MacMeel ; ' son of Michael ' ; not an old surname in Ireland, unless short for mᴀc ᵹioʟʟᴀ micil, which is not improbable.

mᴀc micilín—V—MacMichalin ; ' son of little Michael ' ; perhaps the same as mᴀc micil, q.v.

mᴀc míliᴅ—V—M'Meelye, M'Myle, M'Moylie, Miles, Myles, Moyles ; ' son of Milo ' (a Norman personal name). Cf. mᴀc ᴀn míliᴅ and míliᴅ.

mᴀc mílis—V—M'Myles, M'Myllis, Miles, Myles ; ' son of Miles ' (a Norman personal name). Cf. miʟip.

mᴀc míoʟcon—IV—M'Melchon, MacIlchon, MacConn ; ' son of mioʟcú ' (grey-hound) ; an old Fermanagh surname. The m of the second part of the surname is now aspirated, and sometimes altogether dropped ;

hence the present angl. forms, MacIlchon and Mac-
Conn.

Mac míoló‌ı‌‌ó—V—*M'Milode, M'Mylod, M'Moyloyde*;
'son of Milot' (a dim. of Milo) ; probably not a family
name. V. míoló‌ı‌‌ó.

Mac míolu‌ı‌‌c—V—*M'Meleke, M'Moylek, M'Mulleack*,
Malick, Mulick, Mullock, Mulleague ; 'son of Miluc'
(a dim. of Milo ; cf. míoló‌ı‌‌ó) ; a rare surname ; found
chiefly in Roscommon, Westmeath and Offaly.

Mac mo‌ʒ‌rá‌ı‌‌n, Mac mu‌ʒ‌ró‌ı‌‌n—IV—*M'Murrone*, Mac-
Murran, MacMurren, MacMouran, MacMorran, Mac-
Moran, MacMorin, MacMurrin ; 'son of mu‌ʒ‌ró‌n'
(slave-seal) ; the name of a Co. Leitrim family who
were erenaghs of Killanummery, and apparently also
of a family in Ui Maine, Co. Galway. Like Ó mu‌ʒ‌-
ró‌ı‌‌n (q.v.), Mac mu‌ʒ‌ró‌ı‌‌n was early corrupted to
Mac mo‌ʒ‌rá‌ı‌‌n.

Mac mu‌ı‌‌rce‌a‌rta‌ı‌‌ʒ—IV—*M'Murihertie, M'Mirirtie,
M'Moriertagh, M'Mortagh, M'Miertagh, M'Murtough,
M'Murthoe, M'Morte*, MacMurtrie, MacMurtery, Mac-
Murtry, MacMurdy, MacMordie, MacMutrie, Mac-
Mrearty, MacBrearty, MacBrairty, MacMearty, Mac-
Merty, Murtagh, Mortagh, Murtaugh, Murdough,
Murdoch, Murdock, Murdow, Murtha, Murta, Murdy,
Murt, (Mortimer) ; 'son of mu‌ı‌‌rce‌a‌rta‌c' (sea-director,
navigator) ; a very common Irish patronymic which,
in many instances, has undoubtedly become a family
name ; also the name of a Scottish family in Argyle-
shire, some of whom have settled in Ulster. V. Mac
mu‌ı‌‌rce‌a‌rta‌ı‌‌ʒ.

Mac mu‌ı‌‌rce‌a‌rta‌ı‌‌ʒ—IV—*M'Urarthie*, MacCurdy, Mac-
Kurdy, MacKirdy ; a var. of Mac mu‌ı‌‌rce‌a‌rta‌ı‌‌ʒ,
q.v. See also Mac Cu‌a‌rta.

Mac mu‌ı‌‌re‌a‌ó‌a‌ı‌‌ʒ—IV—*M'Murrey, M'Morrye*, Mac-
Murry, MacMorry, MacMorray, MacMurray, (Mac-
Morrow), Murry, Murray, (Morrow) ; 'son of mu‌ı‌‌re‌a‌ó-
a‌c' (belonging to the sea, a mariner ; also a lord) ;
an old Breifney surname, still common in the district,
but generally angl. MacMorrow.

Mac ṁuıreaḋaıʒ—IV—*M'Murrie*, *M'Murry*, Currie,
Curry ; a var. in Co. Antrim of Mac ṁuıpeaḋaıʒ,
q.v. ; dialectically Mac ṁuıpıċ. It is of Scottish
origin.

Mac ṁuırʒeaSa, Mac ṁuırʒıS—IV—*M'Morishey*,
M'Murrysse, MacMorris, Morrissey, Morris ; ' son of
ṁuıpʒeap ' (sea-choice, an ancient Irish personal
name) ; a rare surname ; to be distinguished from
Mac ṁuıpıp, q.v.

Mac ṁuırıS, Mac ṁuırıS—V—*M'Maurice*, *M'Morrice*,
M'Morish, MacMorris, Morrison, Fitzmaurice, Maurice,
Morris, &c. ; ' son of Maurice ' (a name introduced by
the Normans) ; the name (1) of a branch of the Geraldines in Kerry, who, as lords of Lixnaw, made a great
figure in the history of that county ; and (2) of a
branch of the Prendergasts in Co. Mayo.

Mac ṁuırıS ruaıḋ, Mac ṁuırıS ruaıḋ—V—
M'Morish roe, Morris-Roe, Morrisroe ; ' son of red
Maurice ' ; an old Roscommon surname. V. Mac
ṁuıpıp.

Mac ṁuırnıʒ—IV—*M'Murny*, *M'Morney*, *M'Mornie*,
Murney ; ' son of ṁuıpneaċ ' (a loveable person, or
member of a troop) ; extremely rare.

Mac ṁunna, Mac ṁunna—IV—MacMunn, MacPhun ;
' son of ṁunna ' (i.e., ṁo-ḟıonna, a ' pet ' form of
ḟıonnán) ; very rare.

Mac ṁurċaḋa—IV—*M'Murroghowe*, *M'Moroghoe*,
M'Murphewe, MacMurrough, MacMurrow, Morrowson, Murrough, Morrough, Morrogh, Murrow, Morrow,
Murphy ; ' son of ṁupċaḋ ' (sea-warrior, a very common Irish personal name) ; the name of three distinct
families in Ireland, viz. : Mac ṁupċaḋa of Leinster,
Mac ṁupċaḋa of Muinntear Birn in Ulster, and Mac
ṁupċaḋa of Clann Tomaltaigh in Connacht. The
MacMurroughs of Leinster derive their name and
descent from ṁupċaḋ, the grandfather of Dermot
MacMurrough, and were long the most powerful
family in Leinster, and one of the most powerful in
Ireland. From ḋoṁnall Caoṁánaċ, the son of

Dermot MacMurrough, they took the surname of
Caománac (q.v.), which is that by which they have
been known for centuries. The Ulster family of
Mac Murcaóa was seated in Tyrone, and at the end
of the 16th century was numerous in that county.
Murphy appears to be the angl. form, at least, in many
instances; O'Donovan gives it as MacMurray, which
I have failed to verify. The Connacht family of this
name was seated in Co. Roscommon.

Mac MURCAÓA CAOMÁNAC—IV—MacMurrough
Kavanagh; i.e., MacMurrough of St. Cavan's (v.
Caománac); the name of the head of the family of
MacMurrough, or Kavanagh, of Leinster. V. Mac
Murcaóa.

Mac MURCAIÓ—IV—*M'Murchie, M'Murphie*, Mac-
Murchy, Murchison, Murphy; a var. of Mac Murcaóa
of Ulster. V. Mac Murcaóa above.

Mac MURCÁIN—IV—*M'Moroghon, M'Morroghin*, Mac-
Moran, MacMorin, Murchan, Murkin, Morkin, &c.;
'son of Murcaóán' (dim. of Murcaó).

Mac MURGALÁIN—IV—MacMurlan, Murland, Murtland,
Morland, Mortland, Moreland, &c.; 'son of Murgal-
án' (dim. of Murgal, sea-valour); a rare Ulster
surname, apparently of Scottish origin.

Mac NAOIMÍN—IV—*M'Nyvine*, MacNiven, Nivin, Nevin,
Neven, Neavin, Nevins; 'son of Naoimín' (saintling,
dim. of naom, a saint); a South Leinster and also a
Scottish surname. To be distinguished from Mac
Cnáimín, q.v.

Mac NÁRAÓAIG—IV—MacNarry, MacNeary, Manary;
'son of Náraóac' (the noble one); a rare Ulster
surname.

Mac NAOIS, Mac NAOSA—IV—*M'Nyce, M'Nysse*, Mac-
Niece, MacNeece, MacNeese, MacNeice, MacNish,
Manice, Mannice, Meneese, Miniece, Minnis, Minnish,
Kinnish, Kennish, Mannix, &c.; 'son of Aongur'
(one-choice, an ancient Irish personal name); a
dialectical form of Mac Aonguir, Mac Aongura,
q.v.; in use in Ulster and the Isle of Man.

mac neaċτain—IV—*M'Neaghtane*, MacNaghten, Mac-
Naghton, MacNaughten, MacNaughton, MacCracken,
MacNaught, MacNeight, MacKneight, (MacKnight),
MacNight, MacNite, Mannight, Menaght, Menautt,
Minett, Minnitt, &c. ; ' son of neaċτan ' (the
pure one) ; a well-known Scottish surname from the
neighbourhood of Lochow. A branch of the family
settled in Co. Antrim, where it has flourished considerably. This family has produced many distinguished men.

mac neiꝺe—IV—MacNeigh, MacNeagh, MacNay, Mac-
Nea, MacNee ; ' son of nia ' (champion) ; a Connacht
family ; probably a branch of the O'Mulconrys.

mac neiġill—V—*M'Nigeyll*, *M'Nygel*, Neilson, Nielson,
Nelson ; ' son of Njall ' (a Norse form of the Ir. niall,
latinised Nigellus, and angl. Nigel).

mac neill—IV—MacNeill, MacNeile, MacNeal, &c. ;
' son of niall ' (champion) ; the name (1) of a Scottish
clan in Gigha and Barra, two islands off the coast of
Argyle, who were followers of the Lord of the Isles,
and to which belong probably the MacNeills of Antrim
and Derry ; and (2) of a branch of the Ui Fiachrach,
who were seated in Carra, Co. Mayo, where it is still
in use under the form of maġ Réill, q.v.

mac niaꝺ—IV—MacNea, MacNee, (?) Neeson ; ' son
of nia ' (champion) ; a var. of mac neiꝺe, q.v. ; also
a Scottish surname.

mac mallꝃuis, mac mallꝃusa—IV—*M'Nellus*, Mac-
Nelis, MacEneilis, MacEnealis, MacNeilage, Manelis,
Nealis, Nelis ; ' son of mallꝃur ' (champion-choice) ;
the name of a West Ulster family, some of whom have
settled in Mayo.

mac mic—V—Nixon ; ' son of Nick ' (short for Nicholas).

mac mocais—V—Nix, [Woulfe] ; ' son of Nicholas ; a
patronymic surname adopted by a branch of the
Woulfes in Limerick and Clare.

mac moclais—V—MacNicholas, Nixon, [Clausson,
Classon] ; ' son of Nicholas ' ; a Mayo surname.

mac mocóil, mac mocoil—V—*M'Nichoell*, *M'Nicholl*,

MacNicol, MacNickle, Nicolson, Nicholson, Nicholl.
&c. ; ' son of Nicol ' (a form of Nicholas).

Mac nuaὸaὸ, Mac nuaὸaτ—IV—*M'Gnoude*, Mac-
Nutt, Noud, Nowd, (Conway) ; ' son of nuaὸa ' (an
ancient Irish personal name, the name of a sea-divinity);
extremely rare.

Mac nuallάin—IV—Nolan ; 'son of nuallάn ' (dim.
of nuall, famous, noble) ; a common surname in Co.
Mayo, but I have failed to discover any early instance.

Mac óὸa—V—*M'Odo, M'Ode, M'Codo, M'Cody*, Cody,
Coady, [Archdeacon] ; ' son of Odo ' or ' Otho ' (a
Teutonic personal name, introduced by the Normans) ;
a patronymic surname assumed by the family of
Archdeacon, in Co. Kilkenny.

Mac oιbιcίn—V—Hobbikin, Hopkin, Hopkins, Hopkinson ; ' son of Hobkin ' (little Robert) ; a Mayo surname,
often pronounced ó Coιbιcίn.

Mac oιnseamάιn, Kingston. I find this surname in
use in West Cork, but I have not been able to discover
any early instance, Irish or English.

Mac oιsὸealb, Mac oιsὸealbaιʒ—IV—*M'Cosdal-
lowe, M'Costellowe, M'Costalighe*, Costelloe, Costello,
Costellow, Costily, Costley, &c. ; ' son of Oιrὸealb '
(Os-shaped, shaped like the god Os) ; a patronymic
surname assumed by the family of Nangle. It is
the earliest Anglo-Irish Mac-surname recorded in the
Annals (A.D. 1193). It is also written Mac ʒoιr-
ὸealb, Mac ʒoιrὸealbaιʒ and Mac Coιrὸealbaιʒ,
and has numerous variants in the spoken language.

Mac oιsίn—IV—MacCushen ; ' son of oιrίn ' (little deer,
dim. of or, a deer) ; an old Meath surname. V. maʒ
Oιrίn, which is probably the only form under which
it now survives.

Mac oιsτe—V—*M'Coisht, M'Coiste, M'Costy*, MacGusty,
Hosty, Hasty, &c. ; ' son of Hodge ' (a ' pet ' form of
Roger) ; the name of a Mayo family of Welsh origin,
so called from an ancestor named Hodge Merrick, who
was killed in 1272 ; also written Mac hoιrτe, q.v.

Mac oιsτιcίn, Mac oιsτιʒίn—V—*M'Costikine, M'Cos-*

tigine, *M'Costegine*, Costigan ; ' son of Hodgkin '
(dim. of Hodge, i.e., Roger) ; often corruptly,
in the spoken language, mᴀc Coꞃᴛᴀ𝔷áın and
Ó Coꞃᴛᴀ𝔷áın, q.v. ; a family of note in Ossory ;
apparently not of English descent, but a branch
of some one of the great Irish families of that
district.

mᴀc Oısᴛín—V—Costin, Costen ; ' son of Hodgin' (a dim.
of Hodge), or perhaps ' son of Oıꞃᴛín' (the Norse form
of Augustine ; cf. O hOıꞃᴛín) ; in the spoken language
Ó Coıꞃᴛín.

mᴀc Oıᴛıꞃ—V—*M'Cottyr*, *M'Cottir*, MacCotter, Mac-
Cottier, MacCottar, Cotter, Otterson ; ' son of Ottar '
(a Norse personal name) ; the name of an old and
respectable family, doubtless of Norse origin, seated at
Carrigtwohil, near the city of Cork ; also an Ulster
surname ; generally written mᴀc Coıᴛıꞃ, owing to
the attraction of the c of mᴀc over to the second part
of the surname.

mᴀc Oscᴀıꞃ—IV—*M'Cosquyr*, *M'Cowsker*, *M'Kuesker*,
MacOscar, MacUsker, MacCosker, MacCusker, Mac-
Kusker, MacKuscar, (Cosgrove, Cosgrave) ; ' son of
Oscar ' (a Teutonic personal name, found in Domes-
day Book in the time of Edward the Confessor, or it
may be from Oꞃcᴀꞃ, a combatant, champion) ; an
Ulster surname.

mᴀc Ospᴀıc—V—MacCosbey ; ' son of Oꞃpᴀc ' (the Norse
Ospakr).

*mᴀc Osꞃᴀıc—V—MacOstrich ; probably ' son of Osric '
(an Anglo-Saxon personal name).

mᴀc ṗáᴛꞃᴀıc—V—*M'Patrick*, MacPhatrick, Mac-
Fattrick, MacFettrick ; ' son of Patrick ' ; a surname
which came to us from Scotland.

mᴀc ṗáᴏꞃᴀıcín, mᴀc ṗáᴏꞃᴀıcín, mᴀc ṗáᴏꞃᴀı𝔷ín, mᴀc ṗáᴏꞃᴀı𝔷ín—V—*M'Pattrickine*,
M'Padrykine, *M'Padrigin*, Fitzpatrick, Patrician,
Parrican, Paragon ; ' son of ṗáᴏꞃᴀıcín ' (dim. of
ṗáᴏꞃᴀı𝔷 or Patrick) ; very rare.

mᴀc ṗáıᴏ—V—MacFate, MacFeat, Fade ; ' son of Pate '

(a Scottish and North English form of Pat, or Patrick). Cf. мас рáιⱱíп.

мас рáιⱱíп—V—*M'Paidin, M'Padine,* MacPaden, Mac-Padian, MacPadden, MacPaddan, MacPadgen, Pat-tinson, Patterson, Pattisson, Paddison, Padian, Patten, Payton ; ' son of Padin,' or ' Pattin ' (a dim. of Patrick). V. рáιⱱíп.

мас рáιⱱíп—V—*M'Phaddin, M'Faddine,* MacPhadden, MacFaden, MacFaddin, MacFadden, MacFeddan, Faddin, Vadin, (Fagin, Fagan, Patterson), Padden, Patten, (Cussane), &c. ; a var. of мас рáιⱱíп, q.v. ; a well-known surname in Ulster and in Mayo ; also a Scottish surname.

мас рáι̇ι—V—MacFall, MacFalls, MacVail, Vail ; ' son of Paul ' ; a dialectal var. of мас рóιι, q.v.

мас рarⱱaιáιп, мас рartaιáιп, мас рárta-ιáιп, мас рártaιáιп мас рártιáιп, мас рartιóιп, мас рarιáιп—V—*M'Parrhelan, M'Pharlane,* MacParlin, MacParland, MacPartlan, MacPartland, MacPartlin, MacPharland, MacFarlaine, MacFarlane, MacFarland, MacBartley, MacBarklie, Parlon, Partland, Bartley, &c. ; ' son of Bartholo-mew ' ; found chiefly in Tyrone, Armagh and Lei-trim ; also a Scottish surname.

мас реaⱱaιr—V—MacFeeters, Peterson, Petterson, Peters, Petters ; ' son of Peter.'

мас реáιrcíп—V—Parkinson, Parkins, Perkins ; ' son of Peterkin ' (dim. of Peter).

мас реaⱱruιs—V—MacFetrish, MacPhettridge, Mac-Fetridge, MacFettridge, MacFatridge, MacFattridge, Fettridge ; ' son of Petrus ' (the Latin form of Peter) ; the name of an Ulster family who are, not improbably, an offshoot of the O'Breslins.

мас реιce—V—*M'Peicke,* MacPeake, MacPake ; ' son of реιc ' (a var. of the Anglo-Saxon Pic) ; a rare West Ulster surname.

мас ріaraιc, мас ріaruιc—V—*M'Feyrick, M'Fer-rick,* Feerick ; ' son of Pieruc ' (dim. of Piers, or Peter) ; a rare Connacht surname.

Mac Piaṙais—V—*M'Piers*, *M'Peirs*, *M'Pierce*, Pierson, Peirson, Pearson, Pierce, Pearse, &c. ; 'son of Piers' (the Norman form of Peter). V. Piaṙaṙ.

Mac Piaṙais—V—*M'Fearis*, MacFeerish ; 'son of Piers'; a var. of Mac Piaṙaiṙ ; very rare.

Mac Pib—V—*M'Phibbe*, Phipson, Phipps, Phibbs ; 'son of Phib' (short for Philip).

Mac Pibín—V—*M'Fibbin*, Phippin, Phippen ; 'son of Phipin' (a dim. of Philip). Cf. Mac Fibín.

Mac Pilib—V—*M'Philip*, *M'Phillip*, MacPhillips, Phillips, Philips, Philipson, Philson, &c.; 'son of Philip'; a common surname in Ulster and Connacht. V. Mac Filib, which is a variant.

Mac Pilbín, Mac Pilibín—V—*M'Philibbene*, *M'Phillippine*, MacPhilpin, MacPhilbin, O'Filbin, Philipin, Phillipin, Philbin, Filbin, and, by 'translation,' Plover ; also written Mac Filibín, and often changed in the spoken language to Ó Filibín ; 'son of Philpin' (dim. of Philip) ; the name of a Mayo family who, according to O'Donovan, are a branch of the Burkes, but more probably are a branch of the Barretts. The head of the family resided at the Castle of Doon, near Westport.

Mac Póil, Mac Póil—V—*M'Poyle*, MacPaul, Mac-Phail, MacFall, MacFalls, MacVail, Vail, Paulson, Polson, Powlson, &c. ; 'son of Paul.'

Mac Póilín—V—MacPolin, MacPoland, Polin, Poland ; 'son of Paulin' (dim. of Paul) ; a rare Ulster surname.

Mac Raġailliġ—IV—*M'Reily*, *M'Crylly*, MacCrilly, Creilly, Crilly, Crelly, Creely ; 'son of Raġailleaċ,' or 'Raġallaċ.' Cf. Mac Raġallaiġ and Maġ Raġall-aiġ.

Mac Raġallaiġ—IV—*M'Craly*, *M'Crawley*, *M'Crawle*, *M'Crole*, Crawley ; 'son of Raġallaċ' ; a var. of Mac Raġailliġ and Maġ Raġallaiġ, q.v. See also Mac Roġallaiġ and Ó Cruaòlaoiċ.

Mac Raġnaill—V—*M'Rainell*, *M'Ranald*, *M'Randal*, MacRannall, MacRanald, MacRandell, MacCrindle, MacReynold, MacReynolds, Randalson, Rondalson,

Reynoldson, Rannals, Randals, Randles, Ranolds, Reynolds, &c.; 'son of Reginald' (v. Raġnaɪɫɫ); the name of a family of the same stock as the O'Farrell who were chiefs of Muinntear Eolais, in the south of Co. Leitrim; also a Scottish surname; often pronounced mac Ráġnaɪɫɫ and mac Raonaɪɫɫ.

mac Raɪ̇ɡɪɫɫɪ̇ɡ—IV—Crigley; a var. of mac Raġaɪɫɫɪ̇ɡ, q.v.

mac Raɪ̇ɡne—V—M'Reynie,   M'Creynie,   M'Kryny, Reyney, Ryney, Reinny, Rennie, Reany, Rainey, Raney, &c.; 'son of Rayny' or 'Rennie' (a pet form of Reginald or Reynold; v. mac Raġnaɪɫɫ and Raġ- naɪɫɫ).

mac Raɪ̇t — IV — M'Craythe,   M'Craye,   M'Cragh, M'Creagh, MacRay, MacRea, MacCraith, MacCray, MacCrea, MacWray, Rea, &c.; 'son of mac Raɪ̇t' (a common Irish personal name, meaning 'son of grace' or 'prosperity'). V. maġ Raɪ̇t, under which the chief families of the name are mentioned.

mac Raoɪs, mac Raosa—IV—M'Greece, MacCreesh, MacCreech; a corruption of mac Aonġuɪr, mac Aonġura, q.v.

mac Reaċtaɪn—IV—M'Kreaghane,   MacCracken;   a corruption of mac neaċtaɪn, q.v.   I have heard this form as the Gaelic for MacNaughten in Argyleshire. The family had settled in Co. Antrim before the end of the 16th century.

mac Reamoɪnn—V—M'Remon, MacRedmond, Redmond, &c.; 'son of Redmond' (a personal name introduced by the Normans); the name of a branch of the Burkes.

mac Reɪ̇órí—V—M'Reirie, M'Reyry; a dialectical var. of mac Ruaɪ̇órí, q.v.

mac Réɪɫɫ—IV—M'Crell, M'Krell, MacCrail; 'son of nɪaɫɫ'; a corruption of mac néɪɫɫ, q.v.

mac Rɪaɓaɪ̇ɡ—IV—M'Creve,   M'Krevie,   MacReavy, MacCreavy, MacCreevy, MacCrevey; 'son of Rɪaɓaċ' (greyish, brindled).

Mac Riada—IV—MacReedy, MacReady, MacCreedy, MacCready, &c. ; ' son of Riada.'

Mac Riagáin—IV—*M'Regan*, *M'Crigan*, Creegan, Cregan, Creggan, &c. ; ' son of Riagán.' V. Mac Criagáin and Ó Criagáin.

Mac Ricéid—V—Cricket, Ricketson, Rickets ; ' son of Ricket ' (a dim. of Rickard, or Richard).

Mac Riocáird, Mac Riocáird—V.—*M'Ricard*, *M'Richerd*, MacRichard, Crickard, Dickson, Dixon, [Sinclair], &c. ; ' son of Rickard ' or ' Richard '; a patronymic surname assumed by the Scottish family of Sinclair.

Mac Risteáird, Mac Risteáird—V—*M'Ristard*, *M'Risterd*, MacRichard, Richardson, Richards ; ' son of Richard.'

Mac Ritbeartaig—IV—*M'Criffortie*, *M'Creverty*, Mac-Crifferty ; ' son of Robartac ' ; the name of a Fermanagh family who were poets to the Maguires. Cf. Ó Raitbeartaig.

Mac Rob—V—MacRub, MacCrub, MacRubs, Robson, Robbs ; ' son of Rob ' (short for Robert).

Mac Robuic—V—*M'Robuck*, *M'Crobacke* ; ' son of Robuc ' (dim. of Robert) ; probably obsolete.

Mac Robartaig—IV—*M'Rortie*, MacRoarty ; ' son of Robartac ' ; the name of a Tirconnell family, the head of which lived at Ballymagroarty, near Donegal, and was keeper of the celebrated ' cathach ' of St. Columcille. V. Ó Robartaig.

Mac Rodaig—IV—*M'Ruddie*, Ruddy ; ' son of Rodac ' (strong) ; a rare Donegal surname.

Mac Rodáin—IV—*M'Rudane*, *M'Roddane*, *M'Crodane*, *M'Croddan*, MacCrudden, Crudden, Rodden, Roddon, Rudden, Ruddon, &c. ; ' son of Rodán ' (dim. of rod, strong) ; an Ulster surname.

Mac Rogallaig—IV—*M'Craly*, *M'Crawley*, *M'Crole*, Crowley, Croly, Crolly ; ' son of Rogallac ' (a var. of Ragallac, in use among the O'Mahonys of West Cork, and other families). This surname, which is a var. of Mac Rágallaig and Mag Rágallaig (q.v.), is

now corrupted in the spoken language, to Ó Cɲoʒaɩl-
aɩʒ, and written Ó Cɲuaóɩaoɩc, q.v.

Mac ROɩƀeáɩRƆ, Mac ROɩƀeáɩRƆ—V—*M'Robert,*
M'Robart, MacRoberts, MacCrobarts, Robertson,
Roberts ; ' son of Robert.'

Mac ROɩƀín—V—*M'Robyn, M'Roben,* MacRobin, Cribbin, Cribbon, Cribbins, Robinson, Robbinson, Robbins ; ' son of Robin ' (dim. of Robert).

Mac ROɩƀɩRƆ, v. Mac ROɩƀeáɩɲƆ.

Mac RUáɩÓ—IV—*M'Roe, M'Croy,* Roe, Rowe, Roy ;
' son of Ruaó ' (red).

Mac RUáɩÓRí—V—*M'Rury, M'Roory, M'Rowry,* Mac-
Roary, MacRory, MacArory, MacCrory, Rorison,
Rogerson, Rogers, Rodgers ; ' son of Ruaɩóɲɩ ' (the
Norse Hrothrekr, Domesday Book Roric, angl. Rory,
Roderick and Roger) ; the name (1) of a family who
were anciently chiefs of Tellach Ainbhith and Muinntear Birn, in Co. Tyrone, and erenaghs of Bally-
nascreen, in Co. Derry ; and (2) of a Scoto-Irish family
of the same stock as the MacDonnells, who came over
to Ireland as gallowglasses about the middle of the
14th century.

Mac RUáɩRC—V— *M'Rwrcke, M'Royrke* ; ' son of
Ruaɩɲc.' V. Maʒ Ruaɩɲc.

Mac RUáɩRCín, *Mac RUáRCáɩn—V—MacCrorken,
Croarkien ; ' son of Ruaɩɲcín ' or ' Ruaɩɲcán ' (dim.
of Ruaɩɲc).

Mac RUɩÓRí—V—*M'Rierie,* MacReery, MacCreery, Mac-
Creary ; a dialectical var. of Mac Ruaɩóɲɩ, q.v.

Mac SáMUeɩ—V—Samuelson, Samuels ; ' son of
Samuel.' Cairbre Mac Samuel, chief ollav of Ireland
in penmanship, died in 1162 (F. Masters).

Mac SánƆáɩR—V—Sanderson, Saunderson, Sanders,
Saunders ; ' son of Sander ' (short for Alexander).

Mac SáOʒáɩR—V—*M'Sawer,* Searson, Seares, Sears,
&c. ; ' son of Sigar ' (the Anglo-Saxon Saegaer ;
v. Saoʒaɲ).

Mac SCáɩĊʒɩl—IV—Scahill, Skahill, Schaill ; ' son of

Scaitᵹeal ' (flower-bright) ; an older form of Ó Scat-ᵹaıl, q.v.

Mac Scalaıᵹe—IV—*M'Scally*, *M'Skally*, *M'Skelly* Miskelly, Miscella, Miskella, Scally, Skally, Skelly ' son of Scalaıᵹe ' (crier) ; an old surname in the midlands. It appears to have been a var. of Ó Scalaıᵹe, q.v

Mac Sceacáın—IV—MacSkeaghan, MacSkean, Skehan and, by translation, Thornton ; ' son of Sceacán (peevish one, dim. of ꞃceac, a briar) ; a Monaghan surname. Cf. Ó Scéacáın.

Mac Scolóıᵹe—VII—*M'Scolloige*, *M'Skolog*, Mac Scollog, and, by translation, Farmer ; a var. of Mac an Scolóıᵹe, q.v.

Mac Seaꝼꞃaı́ᵹ—V—*M'Shaffrie*, *M'Shefferie*, *M'Geffrey*, MacShaffrey, MacSheffrey, MacShufrey, Shaffery Jefferson, Jeffreson, Jeffries, &c. ; ' son of Geoffrey. V. Seaꝼꞃaıd.

Mac Seaᵹáın, Mac Seáın—V—*M'Sheain*, *M'Sheane* *M'Shaine*, *M'Shaen*, MacShane, MacShan, MacCheyne Shane, Cheyne, Johnson, (Johnston, Johnstone) ' son of Jean,' the Norman-French form of John The MacShanes of Tyrone are a branch of the O'Neills

Mac Séamuıs—V—*M'Shemus*, *M'Sheames*, *M'James* Jameson, Jemison, &c. ; ' son of James.'

Mac Seanacáın—IV—*M'Shenaghan*, *M'Shincane*, Mac Shannon ; ' son of Seanacán ' (dim. of Seanac, froɱ ꞃean, old, wise) ; extremely rare.

Mac Seanáın—IV—MacShannon ; ' son of Seanán (dim. of ꞃean, old, wise) ; the name of a Meath family who were lords of Gaileanga until about the middle of the 12th century, when they disappeared from history

Mac Seanca, Mac Seancaıᵹe—VII—MacShanaghy Shanaghy, Shanahy, and, by ' translation,' Fox ; ' son of the historian,' or ' antiquary ' (Ir. ꞃeanca, ꞃeancaıᵹe) ; the name of a family originally from Co Sligo, but now found chiefly in Co. Leitrim. Fox an incorrect translation, being founded on the erroɲ eous supposition that the surname is derived froɱ ' ꞃıonnac,' a fox.

mac Seanlaoıc—VII—*M'Shanlie*, *M'Shanly*, Mac-
Shanley, Shanley; ' son of the old hero ' (Ir. Sean-
laoc) ; the name of an old family in Roscommon and
Leitrim.   Also maʒ Seanlaoıc, q.v.

mac Séarlaıs, mac Séarluıs—V—Charleson, Charles ; ' son of Charles.'

mac Searraıʒ—IV—*M'Sharrie*,   MacSharry,   Mac-
Sherry, Sharry, Sherry, and, by translation, Feley,
Foley ; ' son of Searpac ' (foal, flighty) ; an old Breifney surname ; found in the 16th century in Leitrim,
Cavan and Sligo, where it is still common ; now also
in Armagh and Donegal.   There was also a family of
the name in Co. Down which cannot now be traced
unless changed to Ó Searpaıʒ (q.v.), which is not
improbable.   Searpac signifies a foal, hence the
translated forms Feley (Filly) and Foley, the latter
common about the town of Sligo.

mac Séarta,   mac   Séartaıʊ—V—*M'Shearhie*,
M'Shearihy, *M'Shiary*, *M'Shera*, *M'Shire*, Shera,
Sheera, Shirra, [Hodnett, Fitzpatrick] ; ' son of Geoffrey ' ; a var. of mac Searpaıʊ, q.v. ; (1) a patronymic
surname taken by the Hodnetts of Co. Cork, from
whom Courtmacsherry is still called in Irish Cúıpt
mıc Séaptaıʊ ; and (2) a second surname assumed
by the Fitzpatricks of Ossory from one of their ancestors named Geoffrey Mac Giolla Phadraig.

mac Séartúın—V—*M'Sherhown*, *M'Sherone*, Shearhoon, (?) Syron, [Prendergast] ; ' son of *Geoffron '
(dim. of Geoffrey) ; a patronymic surname assumed
by a branch of the Prendergasts in Kerry.

mac Seınıcín—V—*M'Shinekine*, *M'Jenkine*, Jenkinson,
Jenkins, Jinkins, &c. ; ' son of Jenkin ' (i.e., little
Jean, or John).

mac Seınín—V—*M'Shenyn*, Jennens, Jennings ; ' son
of Jenin ' (dim. of Jean, the French form of John).
Cf. mac Seóının.

mac Seóın—V—*M'Shone*, *M'Jonne*, *M'John*, Johnson,
Joneson, Jones, &c. ; ' son of John.' (Cf. mac
Seáın, from the French Jean).

mac Seóınín—V—*M'Sheonin*, *M'Shonyne*, *M'Johnine*, *M'Jonine*, *M'Joning*, (Jennings), O'Keoneen, Keoneen ; ' son of Jonin ' (dim. of John) ; a patronymic surname assumed by a branch of the Burkes in Connacht from an ancestor named Seóınín, or little John Burke. The initial S of the second part of the surname is now always aspirated, and the pronunciation is often Ó Ceóınín ; hence the angl. forms O'Keoneen, Keoneen. The influence of the Norman-French Jenin (v. mac Seınín above) has, however, made Jennings almost universal as the angl. form.

mac Sıacaıs, mac Sıacuıs—V—*M'Sekays*, *M'Shekish*, Jackson ; ' son of Jaques ' (the Norman equivalent of James).

mac Sım—V—MacKim, Simson, Simpson, Sims, &c. ; ' son of Sim ' (a pet form of Simon) ; a Scottish surname.

mac Sımıʊ—V—MacKimmie, [Fraser] ; ' son of Simmie ' (a pet form of Simon) ; a patronymic designation of the Frasers of Lovat in Scotland.

mac Síoʊa—IV—*M'Shida*, MacSheedy, Sheedy ; ' son of Síoʊa ' (silk, silken) ; the name of a branch of the MacNamaras in Clare, Limerick and Tipperary.

mac Sıofraıʊ—V—MacShufrey ; a var. of mac Seafraıʊ, q.v.

mac Síoʒaır—V—Sigerson ; ' son of Sigarr ' (a Norse personal name). A family of Segersons was seated at Ballinskelligs, Co. Kerry, in the 18th century.

mac Síomóın, mac Síomoınn—V—*M'Shymon*, *M'Simon*, Fitzsimon, Fitzsimons, Fitzsimmons, Simons, Simmons, Symons, Simonds, Symonds, &c. ; ' son of Simon,' or ' son of Sigemund ' (a Teutonic personal name) ; these two names have been confused. The Fitzsimons are an old and respectable family of English origin in Dublin and Westmeath.

mac Síomóın, mac Síomoınn—V—MacKimmon, MacKeemon, MacKeeman ; var. of mac Síomóın, mac Síomoınn, q.v.

mac Sítıʒ—IV—*M'Shihy*, *M'Shiehie*, *M'Shee*, Mac-

Sheehy, Sheehy; 'son of Síteac' (peaceful); a branch of the MacDonnells of Scotland, descended from Síteac, great-grandson of Domnall, the ancestor from whom that family took its name. The Mac-Sheehys were famous as gallowglasses, and as such were employed in various parts of Ireland in the 14th and two succeeding centuries. The name is first mentioned in the Annals of the Four Masters at the year 1367, when they took part in a battle fought between two factions of the O'Connors, near Bally-sodare, Co. Sligo. In the year 1420, they came to Munster, and settled in Co. Limerick, as constables to the Earl of Desmond, where they built the castle of Lisnacolla (or Woodfort) in the parish of Clonagh, about four miles west of Rathkeale. The name is now almost peculiar to Munster.

Mac Sítig—IV—MacKeith, MacHeath; 'son of Síteac'; a Scottish var. of Mac Sítig, q.v.

Mac Sítric—V—MacKittrick, MacKitterick, Mac-Kettrick, MacKetterick, MacKirtrick, Munkittrick, Munkettrick, Kittrick, Kitterick, Setright; 'son of Sitreac' (the Norse Sigtryggr, a well-known name in the Irish Annals); a rare and scattered surname; also in use in Scotland.

Mac Siúrtáin—V—M'Shurtayne, M'Shurdan, M'Shordane, M'Jordaine, Jourdan, Jordan, Jurdan, &c.; 'son of Jordan' (v. Siúrdán); a patronymic surname assumed by the descendants of Jordan D'Exeter, an Anglo-Norman family who settled in Co. Mayo, but in 1571 were, according to Campion, 'very wild Irish.' The initial S of the second part of the surname is now always aspirated, and the pronunciation is often Ó Ciúrtáin.

Mac Sleimne—V—M'Sleyny, MacSliney, Sleyne, Sliney, Sliny; 'son of Stephen' (?); the name taken, according to O'Donovan, by the FitzStephens of Cork. A member of this family, Dr. John Baptist Sleyne, was Bishop of Cork and Cloyne from 1693 to 1712.

mac sluaġaḋaiġ—IV—MacSlowey, MacSloy; 'son of Sluaġaḋaċ' (one of a host, or hosting expedition).

mac soilliġ—IV—MacSolly, MacSoley, Solly; 'son of Soilleaċ (?)'; the name of a family who, in the 11th century, were erenaghs of Iniskeen, on the borders of Louth and Monaghan. It still survives, but is extremely rare.

mac solaiṁ—V—Soloman, Solomon, Solmons, &c.; 'son of Solomon.'

mac soṁairle—V—*M'Sorlie*, MacSorely, MacSorley, MacSurley; 'son of Soṁairle' (a personal name of Scandinavian origin); the name of a branch of the MacDonnells of Scotland; well known in the North of Ireland.

mac spealáin, mac spealláin—IV—*MacSpallane, MacSpollane*, (Spencer, Spenser); 'son of Spealán' (dim. of speal, a scythe); a Leinster surname, said to have been anglicised Spencer and Spenser. I have failed to trace it.

mac steafáin, mac steiṁin, mac stiaḃna, mac stiaṁna, mac stiḃin, mac stín, mac stiofáin, mac stiopáin—V—*M'Stephen, M'Stephin, M'Steyny, M'Stine*, MacSteen, Fitzstephen, Fitzstephens, Stephenson, Stevenson, Stevinson, Stenson, Steenson, Steinson, Stinson, Steveson, Stephens, Stevens, &c.; 'son of Stephen.'

mac suain—V—MacSwan, Swainson, Swanson; 'son of Swan' (v. Suain).

mac suiḃne—IV—MacSeveney, MacSwiney, MacSweeny, MacSweeney, MacSween, MacSwine, Swiney, Sweeney, &c.; 'son of Suiḃne' (well-going); the name of a great military family, formerly famous throughout Ireland as captains of gallowglasses. They derive their name and descent, according to MacFirbis, from Suiḃne, who was son of Donnṡléiḃe Ó Néill and lord of Knapdale in Argyle, about the beginning of the 13th century. The first of the name to come to Ireland was Murchadh, grandson of Suiḃne, who is mentioned in the Annals at the year

1267. Early in the next century, the MacSweeneys effected a permanent settlement in Tirconnell, where they became captains of gallowglasses to O'Donnell. They branched out into three great septs, viz. : Mac-Sweeny of Fanad who dwelt at Rathmullin Castle and had extensive possessions in the north-east of the barony of Kilmacrenan ; MacSweeney of Baghnagh, now the barony of Banagh, in the west of Co. Donegal ; and MacSweeney na dTuath, lord of Tuatha Toraighe, or the districts of Tory Island, sometimes incorrectly called MacSweeney of the Battleaxes. A branch of the MacSweeneys of Fanaid settled in Desmond as commanders of gallowglasses under the MacCarthys. They had several castles in the barony of Muskerry, and were celebrated for their hospitality. The Irish form of the surname is now sometimes Ó Suibne, q.v. ; in Scotland it is generally Mac Suibne (q.v.), but MacSween still survives as an angl. form.

Mac Suibne—IV—*M'Queyn, M'Quine*, MacQueen, Maqueen, &c. ; a var. of Mac Suibne, q.v. ; a Scottish surname.

*Mac Suigin—V—MacSwigin, MacSwiggin, MacSwiggan ; 'son of Swegen,' or 'Swen' (a common personal name in Domesday Book).

Mac Taidg—IV—MacTeigue, MacTigue, MacTeague, MacTague, Montague, Teige, Teigue, Teague, Tague, Tigue, Tighe ; 'son of Tadg' (poet, philosopher) ; a common surname in Ulster and North Connacht. A family of this name were anciently chiefs of Muinntear Siorthachain, in Co. Westmeath ; but there are, doubtless, many distinct families so called. V. Mac Taidg.

Mac Taidg—IV—*M'Heig, M'Keige*, MacAig, MacHaig, MacCaig, MacCaigue, MacKaige, MacKague, Mac-Kage, MacKaigue, MacKeag, MacKeague, Keag, Keague, &c. ; a var. of Mac Taidg, q.v. ; sometimes pronounced Mac Caog.

Mac Támais—V—MacTavish, Thompson ; 'son of Thomas' ; a var. of Mac Tómair, q.v. See also Mac Támair.

mac τámaιs—V—*M'Cawyshe, M'Cawys*, MacAvish, Mac-
Cavish, Cavish ; a var. of mac τámaιp, q.v. See also
mac τómaιp.

mac τιξeaρnaιξ—IV—MacTierney ; 'son of τιξeap-
nać' (lordly) ; very rare.

mac τιξeaρnáιn—IV—*M'Tiernane, M'Ternane,* Mac-
Tiernan, MacTernan, Tiernan, Ternan ; 'son of
τιξeaρnán' (dim. of τιξeaρna, a lord) ; a var. of mac
τιξeaρnáιn, q.v.

mac τιξeaρnáιn—IV—*M'Kiernane, M'Kernane,* Mac-
Kiernan, MacKernan, MacCarnon, MacHarnon, Kiernan, Kernan, Kernon, and, by translation, Lord ;
'son of τιξeaρnán' (dim. of ' τιξeaρna,' a lord) ; the
name (1) of a branch of the O'Connors in Co. Roscommon, who are descended from τιξeaρnán, grandson of Turlough Mor O'Connor, King of Ireland ;
(2) of a Breifney family, of the same stock as the
O'Rourkes, who were formerly chiefs of Tellach
Dhunchadha, now the barony of Tullyhunco, in the
west of Co. Cavan ; and (3) of a Fermanagh family,
of the same stock as the Maguires, who were formerly
chiefs of Clann Fearghaile. V. mac τιξeaρnáιn.

mac τoιmιlín,   mac   τoιmιlín—V—*M'Tomilin,*
M'Tomylin, Tomlinson, Tomlin, Tomlyn, Timlin,
Timblin, &c. ; 'son of Tomlin' (a double dim. of
Thomas) ; the name of a Welsh or Anglo-Norman
family long settled in Co. Mayo ; pronounced locally
Ó Cuιmlín and Ó τuιmlín, and incorrectly angl.
Timlin and Timblin.

mac τóιmιcín—V—Tomkinson, Tomkins, Tompkins ;
'son of Tomkin' (a dim. of Thomas).

mac τoιmín—V—*M'Tomeen, M'Tomyn, M'Tumyn,*
Timmin, Timmins, Timmons, Tymmins, Tymmons ;
'son of Tomin' (a dim. of Thomas) ; the name of a
branch of the Barretts of Tirawley.

mac τoιρδealbaιξ—IV—*M'Torrilogh, M'Turlogh,*
M'Terrelly, M'Tirlay, M'Terrens, Torley, Turley,
Terrence, Terry ; 'son of τoιρδealbać' (shaped like

the god Thor, the Scandinavian Jupiter ; an old Irish personal name, angl. Turlough and Terence). V. Mac Coipⱱealⱱaıᵹ.

Mac CoıⱤⱱeaℓⱱaıᵹ—IV—*M'Hurryly,* *M'Curyle,* *M'Kyrrelly,* MacCorley, MacKerley, MacKerlie, Mac-Gorley, Corley, Curley, Kerley, Kerly, Kirley ; a var. of Mac CoıⱤⱱeaℓⱱaıᵹ, q.v.

Mac Cóm—V—*M'Com, M'Come,* MacComb, MacCombs, MacCombes, Combes, Homes, Holmes ; ' son of Thome ' (a short form of Thomas). This surname probably came to us from Scotland, but it was in use in Sligo, Leitrim and Louth before the end of the 16th century. V. Mac CómaıⱤ.

Mac Cómuıc—V—*M'Tomock, M'Camacke,* MacComick ; ' son of Thomuc ' (a dim. of Thomas).

Mac Cómaıs, Mac Comáıs—V—*M'Thomas,* Thomson, Thompson, Thomas, &c. ; ' son of Thomas ' ; the first of these forms, which came to us from Scotland, reflects an older pronunciation of Thomas. In Co. Mayo, it is often made Ó CómaıⱤ.

Mac Cómáıs—V—MacComish, MacCombes, MacCombs, Comish, Combes, Homes, (Holmes) ; a var. of Mac CómaıⱤ and Mac CámaıⱤ, q.v. It is of Scottish origin.

Mac Comáıs—V—(Holmes) ; a var. of Mac CómaıⱤ, q.v. This surname is in use in Co. Cork.

Mac Comalⱦaıᵹ —IV— *M'Tomolty,* *M'Tumoltagh,* *M'Tymolty,* Tomilty, Tumalty, Tumilty, Tumelty, Tumiltey, Tumblety, (Timothy) ; ' son of Comalⱦaċ ' (formerly a common personal name, especially in Connacht). Cf. Ó Comalⱦaıᵹ.

Mac CoⱤcaⱱaıl—V—MacCorcadale, MacCorcodale, MacCorquodale, MacQuorcodale ; ' son of Thorketill ' (a Norse personal name).

Mac CoⱤcaıℓL—V—Thurkell, Thurkill, Thirkell, Thurkle, &c. ; ' son of Thorkell ' (a shortened form of Thorketill).

Mac CoⱤcaıℓL—V—MacCorkill, MacCorkell, MacCorrikle, MacCorkle, Corkhill ; a var. of Mac CoⱤcaıℓL, q.v. Mac Torcaill was a common surname among the Danes of Dublin, in the 12th century; but as a present-day surname, it seems to be of Scottish origin.

Mac Cᖇéinᖘ1ᖇ—IV—*M'Crenir*, *M'Kreaner*, MacCreanor, MacCranor, MacCrainor, Treanor, Trenor, Trayner, Trainor, Traynor, Tranor; 'son of Cᖇéanᖘeaᖇ' (an Irish personal name, meaning 'champion,' literally, 'strong-man'); a well-known Ulster surname.

Mac Cuaᖞail—IV—MacToole, Toole; 'son of Cuaᖞal' (people-mighty); in use in parts of Connacht, but very rare.

Mac Cuaᖞċaiᖇ—IV—MacTucker; 'son of Cuaᖞċaᖇ' (people-dear); very rare.

Mac Cuile—IV—Tully, Flood; a shortened form of Mac Maolᖞuile, q.v.

Mac Cuiᖇc—IV—MacTurk; 'son of Coᖇc' (boar).

Mac Cuᖇcaill, v. Mac Torcaill.

Mac Uaiᖌ—V—*M'Coode*, *M'Cowade*, *M'Quoid*, Mac-Quaid, MacQuaide, MacQuade, MacQuoid, MacWade, Quaid, Quaide, Quade, Quoid, &c.; 'son of Wat' (?) (a 'pet' form of Walter); a well-known Monaghan surname.

Mac Uailᖞᖇín,   Mac   Uailᖞᖇín—V—*M'Waldrin*, Waldron; a var. of Mac Ꮟailᖇín, Mac Ꮟailᖇín, q.v.

Mac Uaiᖞ—V—MacWatt, MacQuatt, Watson, Watts; 'son of Wat.' Cf. Mac Uaiᖌ.

Mac Uaiᖞéiᖇ—V—*M'Water*, MacWatters, MacQuatters, Waterson, Waters, Watters; 'son of Walter' (often pronounced 'Water').

Mac Uaiᖞín—V—*M'Watten*; a var. of Mac Ꮟaiᖞín, q.v.

Mac Ualᖌᖇáin—V—Waldron; a var. of Mac Ꮟalᖌ-ᖇáin and Mac Ualᖇonᖞa, q.v.

Mac Ualᖌaiᖇᵹ—IV—*M'Walrick*, *M'Collrick*, Coldrick; 'son of Ualᖌaᖇᵹ' (proud-fierce); a var. of Maᵹ Ualᖌaiᖇᵹ, q.v.

Mac Ualladáin—IV—*M'Coulaghan*,   *M'Wolleghan*, Coulahan, Coulihan, Colahan, Coolahan, &c.; 'son of Ualladán' (dim. of uallaċ, proud, haughty); the name of an ancient and respectable family in Offaly. They are of the same stock as the O'Maddens, and were at one time chiefs of Siol Anmchadha ; but for many centuries have been seated in the parish of Lusmagh, in Offaly, which originally formed part of Siol Anmchadha.

Mac Uaɫronᴛa—V—*M'Falronte, M'Valronte,* Waldron ; a var. of Mac Ḃaɫponᴛa, q.v.

Mac Uaɫᴛaır—V—MacWalter, MacQualter, Walters, Qualters, Walter, Qualter ; ' son of Walter.' V. Mac Uaıᴛéıp, which is a variant.

Mac Uıḋıɫín, Mac Uıꝺɫín, Mac Uıȝıɫín—V—*M'Uilin, M'Cuyllen, M'Cuilline, M'Quilline,* MacQuillin, MacQuillian, MacQuillan, MacQuillen, MacQuillon, &c., ' son of Hugelin ' (a double dim. of Hugh), or ' son of Hudelin ' (a double dim. of Hud, a ' pet ' form of Richard) ; the name of a family, said to be of Welsh origin, who settled, soon after the Anglo-Norman invasion, in the Route, in the north of Co. Antrim. Towards the close of the 16th century, the MacDonnells wrested from them the greater part of their territory and completely destroyed their power.

Mac Uıḋɫıꝺ—V—*M'Quylly, M'Willi,* MacQuilly, MacWillie ; a short form of Mac Uıꝺɫın, q.v.

Mac Uıɫcín—V—*M'Cwlkine,* MacQuilkin, MacQuilkan, MacQuilquane, MacWilkin, Kilken, Culkeen, Kulkeen, Culkin, Kulkin, Quilkin, Kilkisson, Kilkison, Wilkinson, Wilkison, Wilkins, Wilkin, &c. ; ' son of Wilkin ' (a dim. of William).

Mac Uıɫeaȝóıꝺ—V—*M'Killegode, M'Killigott, M'Eligott,* MacElligott ; ' son of Wilecot ' (i.e., little Ulick, a double dim. of William) ; the name of an old and respectable Kerry family. They are apparently of Anglo-Norman origin, notwithstanding the statement of Dr. O'Brien in his Irish Dictionary, that they are of the same stock as the MacCarthys. Ballymac-Elligott, near Tralee, was probably the first home of the family in Kerry, but at the beginning of the 17th century, they were seated in the parish of Galey, near

Listowel, where Thomas M'Kilgod, 'chief of his nation,' held considerable property which he forfeited on his attainder. The surname, in the spoken language, is shortened to Mac Cliogóiꝺ.

Mac uilliaṁ—V—*M'Eleam*, *M'Quillim*, MacWilliam, MacCullyam, MacWilliams, MacQuilliams, Williamson, Williams, Willison, Wilson, &c.; 'son of William.'

Mac uillimeiꝺ—V—*M'Ullemet*, *M'Collimet*, Killemeade, Killemet, Killimith, Kilmet, and, by 'translation,' Woods; 'son of Willemet' (Fr. Guillemet, a dim. of William); an old, but rare Westmeath surname; sometimes incorrectly 'translated' Woods because of the supposed identity of the latter portion of the surname with 'aꝺṁaꝺ,' wood.

Mac uiscín—IV—*M'Guyskine*, MacCuskin; 'son of Uiꝛcín' (probably a 'pet' form of Cú-uiꝛce, waterdog).

Mac úiscin—V—*M'Eustin*, MacQuiston, MacQuestion, MacQueston, MacWhiston, Whiston, Houstin, Houston, Hughston, Huston, &c.; 'son of Hutchin' (a dim. of Hugh); the name probably of a branch of the MacDonnells of Scotland.

Mac unꝼꝛaiꝺ—V—Humphreys, Humphries; 'son of Hunfrid.'

Maꝺóc, Maꝺóg—VIII—*Madocke*, *Madoge*, Maddock, Maddocks, Madox, Maddox, &c.; 'son of Madoc' or 'Madog' (a Welsh personal name); an old, but rare, surname in Kilkenny, Tipperary and Waterford.

Maᵹ áꝺaiṁ—V—Magaw, Megaw, MacGaw, &c.; a var. of Mac áꝺaim, q.v.

Maᵹ aiꝛeáctaiᵹ—IV—*M'Garraghtie*, MacGarrity, Magarrity, Megarrity, Magarty, Garity, Garrity, &c.; 'son of aiꝛeáctac' (member of a court or assembly, an old Irish personal name); an older form of Maᵹ Oiꝛeáctaiᵹ, q.v.

Maᵹ aṁalᵹaꝺa, Maᵹ aṁalᵹaiꝺ—IV—Magawley, MacGawley, MacGawlay, MacGaulay, Gawley; var. of Mac aṁalᵹaꝺa, Mac aṁalᵹaiꝺ, q.v.

Mag Annaiḋ—IV—*Maganye, Maganay*, Magan, MacGann; a var. of Mac Annaiḋ, q.v.; in use in Co. Roscommon. See also Mag Canna.

Mag Aoḋa, Mag Aoiḋ—IV—*M'Gay, M'Gey, M'Ghy*, Magee, MacGee, MacGhee, MacGhie, Ghee, Gee; var. of Mac Aoḋa and Mac Aoiḋ, q.v.; a very common surname in Ulster, where there are, doubtless, several families of distinct origin so called. A family of this name were chiefs of Muinntear Tlamain in Co. Westmeath, where they are still represented. Other families are mentioned under Mac Aoḋa.

Mag Aonġuis, Mag Aonġusa—IV—Maguiness, Maguinness, Magennis, Maginness, MacGuinnessy, MacGuinness, MacGenniss, Meginniss, &c.; 'son of Aonġus' (one-choice); var. of Mac Aonġuis, Mac Aonġusa; sometimes corrupted to Mag Naois and Mag Raois, q.v.; the name of an ancient and powerful family in Co. Down. They were originally dynasts of Clann Aoḋa, a subdivision of Ui Eathach Cobha, but in the course of the 12th century their power greatly increased, and they became chief lords of all Ui Eathach, now the baronies of Upper and Lower Iveagh. Many distinguished chiefs of the name are mentioned in the Irish annals. Towards the close of the 16th century, the name was found in many parts of Leinster and Connacht, and also in Co. Limerick, where the rare angl. form, MacGuinnessy, is now found.

Mag Aracáin, v. Mag Ġaracáin.

Mag Ascaill—V—MacGaskell; a var. of Mac Ascaill, q.v.

Mag Ḃrádaiġ—IV—*M'Gradie, M'Grade*, MacGrady, MacGrade; a var. of Mac Brádaiġ, q.v.

Mag Ḃradáin—IV—*M'Braddyn*, Graden, Groden; 'son of Bradán' (salmon). This surname, in the 16th century, was almost peculiar to Co. Down.

Mag Ḃraonáin—IV—*M'Grienan*, Greenan; 'son of Braonán' (dim. of Braon); a rare Sligo surname.

Mag Ḃruadair—V—*M'Broder*, Magroder, MacGrudder ; 'son of bruaoan' (a name of Norse origin) ; very rare.

Mag Cafraid, v. Mac Zaffaid.

Mag Cana, v. Mag Canna.

Mag Canann—IV—MacGannon, (Magann, MacGann); a var. of Mac Canann, q.v. ; in use in West Clare.

Mag Canna—IV—*M'Gana*, Magann, Magan, MacGann, MacGan, &c. ; a var. of Mac Canna, q.v. See also Mag Annaid, which is a more correct form.

Mag Carrgamna, v. Mac Carrgamna.

Mag Cineáit—IV—*M'Gennay*, MacKenna, Gennagh, Ginnaw, Ginna, Guinna, Kennagh, Gna, &c., (Ginnane). This well-known Munster surname is, undoubtedly, a corruption of Mac Cionaoit, q.v. It is popularly angl. Ginnaw, but in official documents MacKenna. Ginnane is the angl. form in parts of Clare.

Mag Coclám, v. Mac Coclám.

Mag Coilid, Mag Coilig—VII—Magilly, MacGilly, Cox, Coxe ; a var. of Mac an Coilig, q.v.

Mag Congail—IV—MacGonagle, MacGonigle, Mac-Gonegle, MacGonegal, MacGonigal, MacGonnigle, Mac-Gonnell, Gunnigle, Gunnell ; a var. of Mac Congail and Mac Congaile, q.v. ; a well-known Tirconnell surname. Donald MagCongail was Bishop of Raphoe from 1562 to 1589 ; he was one of the few Irish bishops who assisted at the Council of Trent.

Mag Corcráin, v. Mac Corcráin.

Mag Corraidín, Mag Corráin, Mag Corraoin—IV—MacGorrin, MacGurran, MacGorrian, MacGurrin, MacGurn, Gurrin, &c. ; 'son of Corrán' or 'Corraidín' (dim. of Corra) ; var. of Mac Corraidín and Mac Corráin, q.v.

Mag Crait—IV—MacGrath, MacGragh, Magrath, Ma-gragh, Megrath, Magraw, &c. ; 'son of Mac Rait.' This surname is frequently written Mac Craic (q.v.), but the most correct form is Mac Rait or Mag Rait (q.v.), under the latter of which the various families of the name are mentioned.

Mag Cuirc—IV—MacGuirk, MacGurk, MacGurke ; a

var. of ṁac Cuipc, q.v. ; a well-known Ulster surname.

ṁag ▽aḃuc, ṁag ▽aḃuic—V—MacGavick, MacGavock ; a var. of ṁac ▽aḃuic, q.v.

ṁag ▽onnagáin—IV—Gunnigan ; ' son of ▽onnagán ' ; extremely rare.

ṁag ▽orcaiḋ, ṁag ▽orcaiḋe—IV—*Magorchie, M'Gorche*, MacGourkey, MacGourty, MacGoorty, MacGorty ; a var. of ṁac ▽orcaiḋ, q.v. ; the name of a family in Connacht who were formerly chiefs of Cinel Luachain, comprising the parish of Oughteragh, in the east of Co. Leitrim. The last chief of the name died, according to the Four Masters, in the year 1403. This appears to be the only form under which the surname survives.

ṁag ▽uḃáin—IV—*Magwain, M'Gowane*, Maguane, MacGuane, MacGuone, (MacGowan, Magowan) ; ' son of ▽uḃán ' (dim. of ▽uḃ, black) ; the name of an ancient family in Tirconnell, who were chiefs of Tir-Enda, in the barony of Raphoe ; also found in Clare and Mayo. In the latter county it is always angl. Magowan or MacGowan, which greatly obscures its origin.

ṁag ▽uiḃ—IV—*Maguffe, M'Guffe, M'Guiff*, MacGuff, MacGiff ; ' son of ▽uḃ ' (black) ; a var. of ṁac ▽uiḃ, q.v. ; a scattered surname.

ṁag ▽uiḃp̃inn—IV—*M'Duffyn*, MacGuffin, MacGuffen, MacGiffen, MacGaffin ; ' son of ▽uḃp̃ionn ' (black p̃ionn) ; a rare Ulster surname.

*ṁag ▽uiḃín—IV—Giveen, Givin, Given, Givan ; a var. of ṁac ▽uiḃín, q.v.

ṁag ▽uiḃne—IV—*M'Gewnie, M'Giviny*, MacGivney, MacGivena ; a var. of ṁac ▽uiḃne, q.v.

ṁag ▽uineacair—IV—*M'Donoughor*, Ganagher ; ' son of ▽uineacap̃ ' ; extremely rare.

ṅag ▽uinneaḃáin—IV—Guinevan, Ginivan ; ' son of ▽uinneaḃán ' (an attenuated form of ▽onnaḃán).

ṅag eacaḋa—IV—MacGeagh, MacGagh, MacGaugh, &c. ; a var. of ṁac eacaḋa, q.v. V. ṁag eacaiḋ.

ṅag eacagáin—IV—MacGaffigan, Gahagan, Gavagan,

Gavigan, Gavacan, Gaffikan, Gaffikin, Gagan, &c.;
'son of eɑċɑᵹán' (dim. of eɑċɑiⱱ); a var. in Ulster
of mɑᵹ eoċɑᵹáin, q.v.

mɑᵹ eɑċɑiⱱ—IV—MacGahey, MacGahy, MacGaughey,
MacGaughy, MacGaggy, MacGaugie, Gahey, Gaffey,
Gaugy, (Hackett); an Ulster var. of mɑᵹ eoċɑⱱɑ, q.v.
See also mɑᵹ eɑċɑċ.

mɑᵹ eɑċáin—IV—M'Geaghan, MacGahan, Magahan,
Megahan, (Magan, Magann), Geghan, Gaughan, Gahan;
'son of eɑċán' (a dim. of eɑċɑiⱱ); a var. of mɑc
eɑċáin and mɑᵹ eoċáin, q.v. It appears to have
been sometimes used in the midlands as an alias for
mɑc eoċɑᵹáin, q.v.

mɑᵹ eɑċʀáin—IV—Mageaghrane, MacGaughran, Magaheran, Magahern, MacGahran, (?) MacGawran,
(?) MacGarran, Gaughran; 'son of eɑċʀán'; a var.
of mɑc eɑċʀáin, q.v. This surname, in the 16th
century, was found chiefly in Donegal, Armagh and
Monaghan.

mɑᵹ eɑnnɑ—IV—(?) MacGeany; a var. of mɑc eɑnnɑ,
q.v.

mɑᵹ eɑċɑċ—IV—M'Geaffe, MacGeagh, MacGagh, Mac-
Gaugh, Gaff; a var. of mɑᵹ eɑċɑiⱱ, &c.

mɑc eiⱱiʀ, mɑc eimiʀ—IV—MacGaver; a var. of
mɑc eiⱱiʀ, q.v.

mɑᵹ eiceɑᵹáin, mɑᵹ eiciᵹein—IV—Magettegane,
Magitegen, Magettigan, MacGettigan; 'son of eiciᵹein' or 'eiceɑᵹán.' The Magettigans seem to have
belonged originally to Cinel Eoghain, but have been
for centuries settled in Donegal.

mɑᵹ eiciᵹ—IV—Magetty, Getty; 'son of eiceɑċ' (?);
an old Derry surname.

mɑᵹ eoċɑⱱɑ—IV—M'Geoghoe, MacGeough, Mageogh,
Magough, MacGough, MacGoff, Gough, Goff; 'son
of eoċɑiⱱ' (rich in cattle); a var. of mɑc eoċɑⱱɑ
(q.v.), under which the different families of the name
are mentioned. See also mɑᵹ eɑċɑċ, mɑᵹ eɑċɑiⱱ.

mɑᵹ eoċɑᵹáin — IV — M'Geoghegaine, M'Goghagan,
Magoughegan, Magowghegan, M'Goigan, Mageoghegan,

MacGeoghegan, MacGoogan, MacGuigan, MacGuiggan,
Maguigan, Geoghegan, Gehagan, Gehegan, Geogan,
Geagan, Geghan, Gegan, Googan, Gogan, &c.;
'son of Eoċaġán' (a dim. of Eoċaiġ); the name
of an ancient and highly respectable family in Co.
Westmeath. They are a branch of the southern Ui
Neill, being descended from Fiacha, son of Niall of
the Nine Hostages, from whom they took their clan-
name of Cinel Fhiachach. The patrimony of Cinel
Fhiachach, in the 16th century, comprised the barony
of Moycashel, but was anciently much more extensive.
The Mageoghegans retained their rank as lords of
Moycashel down to the Cromwellian confiscations,
when they lost their estates. A branch of the family
was transplanted to Co. Galway, where the name is
still common. V. maġ Eaċaġáin, which is a variant.

maġ Eoċaiġ—IV—MacGoey, MacGoggy; a var. of maġ
Eoċaḋa, q.v.

maġ Eoċaiḋín—IV—M'Gokiane, MacGuickian, Mac-
Gughian, MacGuckian, MacGookin, MacGuckin,
Guckeane, Gucken, Guckian, Guigan, Guiken, &c.;
'son of Eoċaiḋín' (dim. of Eoċaiḋ); an Ulster surname.

maġ Eoċáin—IV—M'Geoghan, M'Gokiane, MacGoogan,
MacGuighan, MacGuigan, &c.; 'son of Eoċán' (a
dim. of Eoċaiḋ); a var. of maġ Eaċáin, q.v. Cf. maġ
Eoċaġáin.

maġ Eoġáin—IV—Mageown, MacGeown, Magowen, Mac-
Gowen, Magone, Gowen, Geon; a var. of mac Eoġain,
q.v.

maġ Eoṫaċ, v. maġ Eoċaḋa.

maġ Faċtna—IV—M'Gaghny, Magaffney, Gaughney,
Gaffney; 'son of Faċtna.'

maġ Fearaḋaiġ—IV—M'Garee, M'Garrye, Magearrye,
M'Gerrye, M'Girrie, MacGarry, Magarry, MacGeary,
MacGerry, MacGherry, Megarry, O'Garriga, Garahy,
Garrahy, Garrihy, Garry, Gerry, Gery, and, by 'trans-
lation,' O'Hare, Hare; 'son of Fearaḋaċ' (manly);
a var. of mac Fearaḋaiġ, q.v.; a not uncommon sur-

name, especially in East Connacht, Tyrone and Antrim ; in the spoken language, sometimes corrupted to Ó Ꞩ10ᵱᵱᵅᵻ⅄ᵫ, and erroneously translated O'Hare and Hare, as if from 'ᵹ1ᵱᵱᵼ1ᵅᵫ,' a hare; sometimes also to Ó ᵹᵉᵅᵱᵅᵹᵅ, angl. O'Garriga. Cf. ᵯᵅᶜ ᵱᵉᵅᵱᵅᵫᵅ1ᵹ.

ᵯᵅᵹ ᵱᵉᵅᵲᶜᵅ1ᵲ—IV—*M'Garragher*, Garragher ; a var. of ᵯᵅᶜ ᵱᵉᵅᵱᶜᵅ1ᵱ, q.v.

ᵯᵅᵹ ᵱᵉᵅᵲᵹᵅ1ᶫ—IV—MacGarrigal, MacGarrigle ; a var. of ᵯᵅᶜ ᵱᵉᵅᵱᵹᵅ1ᶫ, q.v.

ᵯᵅᵹ ᵱᵉᵅᵲᵹᵅ1ᶫ—IV—*M'Garrell, M'Garrile*, MacGarrell, MacCarroll, MacGirl, MacGorl ; a var. of ᵯᵅᶜ ᵱᵉᵅᵱᵹᵅ1ᶫ, q.v.

ᵯᵅᵹ ᵱᵉᵓᵲᵅ1ᶳ, ᵯᵅᵹ ᵱᵉᵓᵲᵫ1ᶳ—V—MacGorish, Mac-Gorisk, Magorisk, Gorish, [Bermingham, Birmingham] ; a var. of ᵯᵅᶜ ᵱᵉᵓᵱᵅ1ᵱ, q.v.

ᵯᵅᵹ ᵱ1ᵬ1ᵰ—V—MacGibbin, MacGibben, Gibbin, Gibben, Gibbins, Gibbings; 'son of Phippin' (dim. of Philip).

ᵯᵅᵹ ᵱ1ᵰᵰ—IV—Maginn, MacGinn, MacGin, MacGing, Megginn, Ginn ; a var. of ᵯᵅᶜ ᵱ1ᵰᵰ, q.v. This form of the surname was peculiar to Co. Down.

ᵯᵅᵹ ᵱ1ᵰᵰᵉᵅᶜᵗᵅ, ᵯᵅᵹ ᵱ1ᵰᵰᵉᵅᶜᵗᵅ1ᵹ, ᵯᵅᵹ ᵱ1ᵒᵰᵰ-ᵅᶜᵗᵅ, ᵯᵅᵹ ᵱ1ᵒᵰᵰᵅᶜᵗᵅ1ᵹ—IV—*M'Ginaghtie*, Maginnetty, MacGinnitty, MacGinety, MacGinity, MacGinty, Maginty, Ginnity, Ginaty, Ginity, Guin-naty, Ginty ; 'son of ᵱ1ᵒᵰᵰᵅᶜᵗᵅ' (fair-snow) ; a well-known Ulster surname. In the 16th century, it was almost peculiar to Armagh.

ᵯᵅᵹ ᵱ1ᵒᵰᵰᵅ1ᵰ—IV—*M'Gynnan*, *M'Gennan*, *M'Gean-ayne*, MacGannon, Ginnane, Gannon ; 'son of ᵱ1ᵒᵰᵰ-ᵅᵰ' (dim. of ᵱ1ᵒᵰᵰ, fair) ; the name of an ancient family, formerly of Erris, Co. Mayo, and still represented in that county.

ᵯᵅᵹ ᵱ1ᵒᵰᵰᵫᵅ1ᵲᵲ—IV—*M'Gynnowar*, *Magennure*, *Magennore*, *Magenor*, Geanor, Gainer, Gaynor ; 'son of ᵱ1ᵒᵰᵰᵫᵅᵱᵱ' (fair-head), now angl. Finbar. This family took its name from an ancestor called ᵱ1ᵒᵰᵰ-ᵫᵅᵱᵱ Ó ᵹᵉᵅᵱᵅᵫᵅ1ᵰ who flourished about the beginning of the 12th century. The head of the family was chief of Muinntear Gearadhain, in the north of

the present Co. Longford, down to the 17th century.
V. Ⅿⱥᵹ ꝼɪonnⴁⱥꞃꞃⱥ, which is a variant.

Ⅿⱥᵹ ꝼɪonnⴁⱥꞃꞃⱥ—IV—*M'Genura, M'Genury, Ma-genura*, Gaynor, &c. ; a var. of Ⅿⱥc ꝼɪonnⴁⱥɪꞃꞃ, q.v.

Ⅿⱥᵹ ꝼɪonnᵹⱥɪl—IV—*Magennill, M'Gennell, M'Gin-dale*, MacGennell, MacGindle, Ginnell, Gennell, Gennel ; 'son of ꝼɪonnᵹⱥl' (fair-valour) ; a var. of Ⅿⱥᵹ ꝼɪonnᵹⱥɪle, q.v.

Ⅿⱥᵹ ꝼɪonnᵹⱥɪle—IV—*M'Gennowlie, M'Gynnillye, M'Gennely*, Maginley, MacGinley, MacGinly, Ginnelly, Ginley ; 'son of ꝼɪonnᵹⱥl' (fair-valour) ; the name of a well-known Donegal family, some of whom settled in Westmeath and Longford. V. Ⅿⱥᵹ ꝼɪonnᵹⱥɪl.

Ⅿⱥᵹ ꝼlⱥɪcɪ́Ɱɪ́n—IV—*M'Glavyne*, Hand ; 'son of ꝼlⱥɪcɪ́Ɱɪ́n' (dim. of ꝼlⱥɪceⱥⱮ).

Ⅿⱥᵹ ꝼlⱥɪcɪⱮ—IV—*Maglaughy, M'Glaughye, Maglavey, M'Glaweye, M'Glawe*, MacGlave, Glaffey, Glavey, &c. ; 'son of ꝼlⱥɪceⱥⱮ' (ruler, lord). V. Ⅿⱥᵹ LⱥɪcɪⱮ.

Ⅿⱥᵹ ꝼlⱥnncⱥⴁⱥ, Ⅿⱥᵹ ꝼlⱥnncⱥɪⴁ—IV—*M'Glan-chie, M'Glannaghie*, Maglanchy, MacGlancy, Glancy ; a var. of Ⅿⱥc ꝼlⱥnncⱥⴁⱥ, q.v.

Ⅿⱥᵹ ꝼloɪnn—IV—*Maglen, Maglinne, McGlyn, Maglyne*, MacGlin, MacGlynn, Glinn, Glynn ; 'son of ꝼlⱥnn' (ruddy) ; a rather common surname in Connacht and Ulster. V. Ⅿⱥc ꝼloɪnn.

Ⅿⱥᵹ ꝼóᵹⱥꞃcⱥɪᵹ, Ⅿⱥᵹ ꝼuⱥᵹⱥꞃcⱥɪᵹ—IV—Gogarty, Gogerty, Googarty ; 'son of ꝼóᵹⱥꞃcⱥc' (proclaimed, banished) ; a rare North Leinster surname. Ruⱥɪⴁꞃɪ Ⅿⱥc ꝼóᵹⱥꞃcⱥɪᵹ, lord of South Breagh, died, according to the Four Masters, in 1027.

Ⅿⱥᵹ ᵹⱥꝼRⱥɪⴁ, v. Ⅿⱥc ᵹⱥꝼꞃⱥɪⴁ.

Ⅿⱥᵹ ᵹⱥoRⱥ, Geary.

Ⅿⱥᵹ ᵹⱥRⱥcáɪn—IV—*Magaraghan, M'Garaghan*, Mac-Garran, Garraghan, Garahan, Garron ; 'son of ⱥꞃⱥcán,' or 'ꞃⱥꞃⱥcán' ; written Ⅿⱥᵹ ⱥꞃⱥcáɪn in the Annals of Ulster ; a Fermanagh surname, formerly borne by an ecclesiastical family at Lisgool. Cf. Ó ꞃⱥꞃⱥcáɪn.

Mᴀɢ ʒᴀRᴀıᵼᴅ, MacGarry.

Mᴀɢ ʒᴀᵼᴀn—IV—MacGahan, Magahan, Gahan; a corruption of Mᴀc ʒᴀoıᵼín, q.v.

Mᴀɢ ʒeᴀRᴀᴄᴀıʒ, MacGarahy, Garahy, Garrihy; a corruption of Mᴀɢ ᵼeᴀᴘᴀᵼᴀıʒ, q.v.

Mᴀɢ ʒoRmᴀ́ın, v. Mᴀc ʒoᴘmᴀ́ın.

Mᴀɢ ʒRᴀ́nnᴀ, Granny, Grant; probably a corruption of Mᴀɢ Rᴀıʒne, q.v.

Mᴀɢ ʒRᴀ́ınne, Granny; doubtless a corruption of Mᴀɢ Rᴀıʒne, q.v.

Mᴀɢ ʒuᴀʒᴀ́ın, MacGoogan, MacGuigan, MacGuiggan, Maguigan, &c.; a corruption of Mᴀɢ eoᴄᴀʒᴀ́ın, q.v.

Mᴀɢ ʒuᴀlRᴀıc, Mᴀɢ ʒuᴀRlᴀıc, Magolrick, Magorlick, &c.; corruptions of Mᴀɢ uᴀıʒᴀıᴘʒ, q.v.

Mᴀɢ ʒuᴀRnᴀᴄᴀın—IV—M'Gorneghane, Magournahan, (Gordon); probably a corruption of Mᴀɢ Muıᴘneᴀᴄᴀ́ın, q.v.

Mᴀɢ íomᴀıR—V—M'Givor, MacGeevor, MacGeever, Mac-Gaver; a var. of Mᴀc íomᴀıᴘ, q.v.

Mᴀɢ lᴀᵼRᴀᵼᴀ—IV—M'Glawrie, MacGlory; a var. of Mᴀc lᴀᵼᴘᴀᵼᴀ, q.v.; a rare surname; found in different parts of Ulster, and also in Offaly.

Mᴀɢ lᴀᵼRᴀıᵼ—IV—(?) Maglamery; a var. of Mᴀɢ lᴀᵼᴘᴀᵼᴀ, q.v.

Mᴀɢ lᴀᵼRᴀıᵼín—IV—M'Glafferine, Maglowrine, M'Claverine; 'son of lᴀᵼᴘᴀıᵼín' (a dim. of lᴀᵼᴘᴀıᵼ); a rare Ulster surname; now probably obsolete, or re-placed by some variant, as Mᴀc lᴀᵼᴘᴀ́ın, q.v.

Mᴀɢ lᴀᵼRᴀınᵼ—V—Maglarent, M'Glarent; a var. of Mᴀc lᴀᵼᴘᴀınn, q.v.

Mᴀɢ lᴀᴄlᴀınn—V—M'Glaghlin, MacGlaughlin, Me-glaughlin; a var. of Mᴀc lᴀᴄlᴀınn, q.v.; not easily distinguishable from Mᴀc ʒıollᴀ Seᴀᴄlᴀınn, q.v.

Mᴀɢ lᴀ́ım, MacGlave, Hand; a contraction of Mᴀɢ lᴀıᵼım, q.v.

Mᴀɢ lᴀ́ımín, Hand; a contraction of Mᴀɢ lᴀıᵼımín, q.v.

Mᴀɢ lᴀıᵼım, Mᴀɢ lᴀᵼᴀıʒ—IV—Maglavey, Maglaghy, M'Glawe, MacGlave, Glaffey, Glavey, and, by 'trans-

lation,' Hand ; a var. of Ⅿⱷᵹ FʟⱭⁱᴄⁱⱦ and ⅯⱭc LⱭⁱᴄⁱⱦ,
q.v. ; in use in Longford, Leitrim and Sligo.

Ⅿⱷᵹ LⱭⁱᴄⁱⱦín—IV—*M'Glavyne*, Hand ; a var. of Ⅿⱷᵹ
FʟⱭⁱᴄⁱⱦín, q.v.

Ⅿⱷᵹ LeⱭnnáⁱn—IV—*Maglanan, M'Glanan, M'Glennan,
Maglinane*, Maglennon, Glenane, Glennon ; 'son of
LeⱭnnán' (dim. of ᴛeⱭnn, a cloak) ; a not uncommon
Leinster surname.

Ⅿⱷᵹ Léⁱⱱ, Maglade, MacGlade ; perhaps a form of ⅯⱭc
Leóⁱⱱ, q.v.

Ⅿⱷᵹ LоᴄlⱭⁱnn—V—MacGloughlin, MacGlaughlin ; a
var. of ⅯⱭc LоᴄlⱭⁱnn, q.v.

Ⅿⱷᵹ Lоⁱnᵹsⁱᵹ—IV—*Maglinchie, M'Glinche*, Mac-
Glinchy ; var. of ⅯⱭc Lоⁱnᵹгⁱᵹ, q.v. ; a Donegal surname.

Ⅿⱷᵹ ⱦuⁱꞦneⱭcáⁱn—IV—*M'Gornghane, M'Gornaghan*,
Magournahan, (Gordon) ; ' son of ⱦuⁱꞦneⱭcán ' (dim.
of muⁱꞦneⱭc, loveable, or one of a troop) ; pronounced
Ⅿⱷᵹ ᵹuⱭꞦnⱭcáⁱn in the spoken language of Co. Mayo.
Cf. ⅯóꞦⱱⱷⁱꞦneⱭc which is also angl. Gordon in the
same county. Apparently there is some connection.

Ⅿⱷᵹ neⱭcᴛⱭⁱn, v. ⅯⱭc neⱭcᴛⱭⁱn and Ⅿⱷᵹ ꞦeⱭcᴛⱭⁱn.

Ⅿⱷᵹ néⁱll, v. ⅯⱭc néⁱll and Ⅿⱷᵹ Ꞧéⁱll.

Ⅿⱷᵹ ⱮⱭllúⁱn, v. Ⅿⱷᵹ ꞦⁱⱭllúⁱn.

Ⅿⱷᵹ ⱮⱭllᵹuⁱs, Ⅿⱷᵹ ⱮⱭllᵹusⱭ ; var. of ⅯⱭc ⱮⱭll-
ᵹuⁱꞦ, ⅯⱭc ⱮⱭllᵹuꞦⱭ. V. Ⅿⱷᵹ ꞦⁱⱭllᵹuⁱꞦ, Ⅿⱷᵹ
ꞦⁱⱭllᵹuꞦⱭ.

Ⅿⱷᵹ nuⱭⱱⱭⱱ, Ⅿⱷᵹ nuⱭⱱⱭᴛ, Gonoude ; var. of ⅯⱭc
nuⱭⱱⱭⱱ, ⅯⱭc nuⱭⱱⱭᴛ, q.v.

Ⅿⱷᵹ ОⁱꞦeⱭcᴛⱭⁱᵹ—IV—MacGeraghty, Mageraghty,
MacGerety, MacGerrity, Geraghty, Geraty, Gerety,
Gerity, Gearty, Gerty, &c. ; ' son of ОⁱꞦeⱭcᴛⱭc '
(member of a court or assembly) ; a var. of Ⅿⱷᵹ
ⱭⁱꞦeⱭcᴛⱭⁱᵹ, q.v. ; the name of an ancient and respectable Connacht family, of the same stock as the
O'Connors. They were chiefs of Muinntear Roduibh
in Co. Roscommon until dispossessed about the middle
of the 16th century. Even as late as 1585, they
formed a distinct clan, with a recognised chief of the

name, who, however, was then seated in O'Kelly's country of Ui Maine. The name is still common in Connacht, and also in parts of Leinster, where branches of the family are long settled. The original surname was Ó Roṁuiḃ, but towards the end of the 12th century the descendants of Oineaċtaċ Ó Roṁuiḃ assumed the present surname. Maᵹ Oineaċtaiᵹ is often shortened in the spoken language to Maᵹ Oineaċt. Cf. Ó hOineaċt for Ó hOineaċtaiᵹ.

Maᵹ OISÍn—IV—MacGushion; 'son of Oinín'; an old Meath surname, now extremely rare.

MAᵹOMRAĊ, Montgomery, Gomery. V. Mac Iomaine.

Maᵹ OISCe, MacGusty; a var. of Mac Oince, q.v.

Maᵹ RAᵹALLAIᵹ—IV—*Magrawley, M'Grawlie, M'Graly,* Magreely, Greally, Grealy, Greely; a var. of Mac Raᵹailliᵹ and Mac Ráᵹallaiᵹ, q.v.; a not uncommon surname in Mayo and Galway, sometimes pronounced locally Maᵹ Raoᵹallaiᵹ and Maᵹ Roiᵹeallaiᵹ. Cf. Mac Roᵹallaiᵹ.

Maᵹ RAᵹNAILL, Maᵹ RÁᵹNAILL—V—*Magranaill, M'Gronnyll,* Magrannell, MacGranell, Grannell, Gronel, Reynolds, &c.; a var. of Mac Raᵹnaill, q.v.

Maᵹ RAᵹNAINN, MacGronan; a corruption of Maᵹ Raᵹnaill, q.v.

Maᵹ RAIᵹne, Maᵹ RÁIᵹne—V—*Magrina, Magriny, Magrany, Magreny, Magrene, Magrein,* Magrane, Mac-Grane, Magrean, MacGrean, Granny, &c.; 'son of Rayny,' a pet form of Raᵹnall, or Reginald.

Maᵹ RAIĊ—IV—Magrath, Magragh, MacGrath, Mac-Gragh, Megrath, Magraw, MacGraw, Megraw, MacGra, &c.; 'son of Mac Rait' (son of grace, or prosperity; a not uncommon Irish personal name); also written Mac Cnait, Maᵹ Cnait, Mac ᵹnait, Mac Rait, and Maᵹ Rata, q.v.; the name (1) of a Donegal family, the head of which was coarb of St. Daveog, or erenagh of Termon Daveog, now Tremon Magrath, at Lough Derg, and resided at the Castle of Termon Magrath at the northern extremity of Lough Erne, about half a mile west of Pettigo; (2) of a Thomond family who were hereditary poets and chroniclers to the O'Briens; (3) of a Scottish family in Kintail (v. Mac Raith), some of whom settled in the north of Ireland. The Magraths were also at one time an influential family in Co. Waterford; and there are, doubtless, many minor families of the name about which history is silent. The name is now very common all over Ireland.

Mag Raoghallaigh, v. Mag Raghallaigh.

Mag Raois, Mag Raosa—IV—*Magroice*, Magreece; a corruption of Mag Aonghuis, Mag Aonghusa, q.v. Cf. Mac Naois.

Mag Ratha—IV—*M'Graha, M'Grahy,* (?) *M'Grattie,* (?) MacGrotty; 'son of Mac Ratha' (the same as Mac Raith); a var. of Mag Raith, q.v.

Mag Reachtain—IV—(?) MacGrattan, Grattan; a corruption of Mac Neachtain. Cf. Mac Reachtain.

Mag Reannacháin—IV—*Magranchane, Magranachan, Magranechan,* MacGranahan, MacGrenehan; 'son of Reannachán' (dim. of reannach, sharp, spear-like); a Donegal surname.

Mag Réill—IV—MacGreal; a corruption of Mac Néill, q.v. Cf. Mac Réill.

Mag Riabhaigh—IV—*M'Grevye, M'Greave,* Magreevy, Magreavy, MacGreevy, MacGrievy, &c.; a var. of Mac Riabhaigh, q.v.; the name of a family who were anciently chiefs of Moylurg, in Co. Roscommon.

Mag Riada—IV—Gready. (Grady); a var. of Mac Riada, q.v.; in use in Galway and Mayo; often pronounced Ó Griada in the spoken language, and sometimes incorrectly angl. Grady.

Mag Riagáin—IV—MacGregan, Gregan; a var. of Mac Riagáin, q.v.

Mag Rialláin—IV—Magrillan, MacGrillan; 'son of Niallán' (dim. of Niall); a corruption of Mac Niall-áin.

Mag Raillghuis, Mag Riallghusa—IV—*Magriellassy, M'Grealis,* MacGrillish, Grealish, (Greely, Grealy, Greally, Griffin); corrupt for Mac Niallghuis, Mac ɴιαιιʒυρα, q.v. ; not uncommon in parts of Connacht.

ΟΙαʒ ΡΟΌ—V—Grubb ; a var. of Οαc Ροὺ, q.v.

ΟΙαʒ ΡΟΌαρϲαιʒ—IV—*Magourrtie*, Magroarty ; a var. of Οαc Ροὺαρϲαιʒ, q.v.

ΟΙαʒ ΡΟΌάιɴ—IV—Magrudden, Groden ; a var. of Οαc Ροὺάιɴ, q.v. ; an old Sligo surname, now extremely rare.

ΟΙαʒ Ροιϲίɴ—V—Gribbin, Gribben, Gribbon ; a var. of Οαc Ροιϲίɴ, q.v.

ΟΙαʒ Ρυαὺραιc—V—*Magrowricke, Magrorick*, M'Gro ricke ; 'son of Ρυαὺραc' (the Norse Hrothrekr) ; an older form of ΟΙαʒ Ρυαιρc, q.v. This form of the surname was still in use at the middle of the 17th century.

ΟΙαʒ Ρυαιὺρί—V—*Magrowry*, M'Grorye, Magrory, Mac-Grory, (Rogers, Rodgers, &c.) ; a var. of Οαc Ρυαιὺρί, q.v.

ΟΙαʒ Ρυαιρc—V—*M'Groirke*, M'Grorke, Grourke, Groarke ; 'son of Ρυαιρc' (older Ρυαὺραc, from Norse Hrothrekr, whence also Ρυαιὺρί ; cf. ϵιɴρί and ϵαɴραc) ; the name of an old Westmeath family, descended from Enna Fionn, son of Niall of the Nine Hostages. ΟΙαʒ Ρυαιρc was chief of Cinel Enda, a small territory near the Hill of Usnagh. The name is still extant in Co. Westmeath, but is more common in Co. Mayo. V. ΟΙαʒ Ρυαὺραιc, an older form of the name.

ΟΙαʒ Ρυιὺρί—V—Magrery, Greery ; a dialectical form of ΟΙαʒ Ρυαιὺρί, q.v.

ΟΙαʒ ϨαΟΙΡαὺάιɴ, ΟΙαʒ ϨαΟΙράιɴ—IV—Magoveran, Magovern, Magawran, Magauran, Magaurn, Magurn, MacGaveran, MacGovran, MacGovern, MacGowran, MacGouran, MacGauran, MacGaurn, Gooravan, Gore-van, Gorevin, &c. ; 'son of ϨαΟΙραὺάɴ' (dim. of ραΟΙραὺ, summer) ; the name of an old Breifney family, the head of which was chief of Tellach Eachach, now the barony of Tullyhaw, in the north-west of Co. Cavan ; still very numerous.

ΟΙαʒ Ϩϵαɴιαοιc—VII—*M'Ganleie*, Ganley, Ganly,

Gantley; 'son of the old hero' (Ir. 'ɼeᴀnᴌᴀoċ'); a var. of mᴀc Seᴀnᴌᴀoiċ, q.v. This family was seated in Corca Achlann, Co. Roscommon, and at Ballymacshanly, in Co. Leitrim.

mᴀᵹ ŚιꞄᴎꞀιc—V—MacGetrick, MacGetterick, &c.; a var. of mᴀc Śιꞇᴎιc, q.v.

mᴀᵹ ꞀοιꞄꞱeᴀᴌꞝᴀιᵹ—IV—M'Gorlighe, MacGorley, Gorley, Gourley; a var. of mᴀc ꞆοιɼꞱeᴀᴌꞝᴀιᵹ, q.v.

mᴀᵹ ꞄꞀÉιnꝒιꞄ—IV—MacGrenor; a var. of mᴀc ꞆɼéιnꝒιɼ, q.v.

mᴀᵹ uᴀᴌᵹᴀιꞄᵹ — IV — Magowlricke, Magollricke, M'Gworlick, Magolrick, Magorlick, MacGolrick, MacGoldrick, MacGouldrick, MacGorlick, Golrick, Goldrick, Goulrick, Gouldrick, Golderick, Godrick, (Goulding, Golding, Golden); 'son of uᴀᴌᵹᴀɼᵹ' (proudfierce, a favourite personal name among the O'Rourkes); the name of a branch of the O'Rourkes in Co. Leitrim and other parts of Connacht, in which province the name is very common, but generally angl. Golden, Goulding, Golding, which greatly obscures its origin. It is also a very common surname in Fermanagh and Donegal where, however, it probably represents a different family.

mᴀᵹ uιꞝιꞄ—IV—Maguier, M'Guier, M'Gwire, M'Guiver, Maguire, MacGuire, MacGiver; 'son of Oꞝᴀɼ' (pale, dun-coloured); the name of a great Fermanagh family, formerly one of the most powerful in Ulster. The name is first mentioned in the Annals at the year 956. Towards the end of the 13th century, the Maguires became chiefs of Fermanagh, a position which they held down to the reign of James I, when their country was included in the confiscation of Ulster. The family produced many valiant chiefs and learned ecclesiastics. The name is sometimes pronounced dialectically mᴀc ᵹuιꞝιɼ.

mᴀᵹ uιꞝꞄín—IV—Maguirin, M'Gwyrin, M'Guiverin, Magiverin, Magivern, Magiveran, MacGiverin, MacGiveran, MacGivern, Guerin; 'son of uιꞝɼín' (a dim. of Oꞝᴀɼ; v. mᴀᵹ uιꞝιɼ); an old Ulster surname.

Early in the 12th century, Eachmarcach Mac Uidhrin
was chief of Cinel Fearadhaigh, in the present Co.
Tyrone. In the 16th century, the name was peculiar
to Co. Down, and even at the present day is confined
to that county and the neighbouring counties of
Antrim and Armagh. For change of ʊ to ʊ, cf. ṁⱥᵹ
Uⁱⁱᵒⁱⱀ, angl. MacGiver.

ṁⱥᵹ Uⁱⱡⱡⱦⁱⁿ—V—*M'Gillkine*, Gilkinson, Gilkison, Gilkisson, Gilkeson, Gilkieson ; a var. of ṁⱥⱦ Uⁱⱡⱦⁱⁿ, q.v.

ṁⱥᵹ Uⁱⱡⱡⱦⱦ, ṁⱥᵹ Uⁱⱡⱦⱦ—*M'Gilleg*, MacGillick, MacGellick, Gillick ; ' son of Willuc,' or ' Ulick ' (a dim.
of William).

ṁⱥᵹ Uⁱⁿⁿⱥⱦⱥⁿⁿⱥⁱⁿ, ṁⱥᵹ Uⁱⁿⁿⱥⁱⱦⁿⁿⱥⁱⁿ, *M'Gwin-shenan*, *M'Gunchenan*, Gilsenan, Gunshinan, (Nugent,
Leonard) ; a corruption of ṁⱥⱦ ᵹⁱᵒⱡⱡⱥ Sⱦⱥⁿⱥⁱⁿ, q.v.

ṁⱥᵹûⁿ—VIII—*Mayon*, Maune, Mawne, and probably
Maume, Mawme ; ' son of Mayon ' (a Nor. dim.
of Matthew) ; an old Co. Limerick surname, still
in use, and probably sometimes represented by
Mawme.

ṁⱥⁱᵹⁱû—VIII—*Mayowe*, *Mao*, *Mawe*, Mahew, Mayhew,
Mayhow, Mayo, May ; ' son of Maheu ' (a Nor.
form of Matthew) ; very rare. Cf. ṁⱥⱦ ṁⱥⁱᵹⁱû.

ṁⱥⁱⁿᵹⁿêⁱʀ—VIII—*Magnel, Magnell*, Mangner, Magner,
Magnier, &c. ; probably ' son of Magnel ' (Nor. dim.
of Magnus). Castlemagner, Co. Cork, was formerly
known as Magnelstown, from William Magnel. The
family is an old one in Co. Cork ; now numerous also
in Co. Limerick.

ṁⱥⁱʀⱦⁱⁿ—VIII—*Martyne*, Martin, Marten, Martyn ;
' son of Martin.' There are many distinct families of
this name in Ireland, the most distinguished of which
were the Martyns of Galway.

ṁⱥⁱⱦⁱû—VIII—*Matheu*, Mathew, Matthew, Mathews,
Matthews ; ' son of Matthew.' There are several
scattered families of this name in Ireland. Of these
the most distinguished were the Mathews of Thomas-
town, Co. Tipperary, to which belonged the celebrated
Apostle of Temperance, Father Theobald Mathew.

mᴀ́ʟóⱱⱱ—VIII—*Malode, Mallot*, Mellot, Mylott, Mylotte ; probably a corruption of Ɱⁱoʟóⱱⱱ, q.v. ; at least, it has the same angl. forms. Malet was, however, an early Anglo-Norman surname in Ireland, and Malot, the corresponding dim. in -ot, might also have existed.

mᴀoⁱʟⁱⱼ—VIII—Meyler, Myler ; 'son of Meyler' (a Norman form of the Welsh Meilyr). The Four Masters, under the year 1205, mention a Maelir mac Maelir, who took forcible possession of Limerick, and give the gen. case of the name as Maoilir, the Irish spelling having been probably influenced by the Welsh word maeliwr, a trader, with which it was supposed to be identical. The Meylers were an old Wexford family. In Co. Waterford, the surname is pronounced Ɱⁱʟéⁱⱼ.

mᴀ́p—VIII—*Map*, Mape ; 'son of Mab' (sharpened to Map, a short form of Mabel) ; a rare Meath surname. In 1598, Map of Mapston and Mape of Maperath were two of the chief gentlemen of Meath.

mᴀⱼᴀsᴄᴀʟ—XII—Marshall ; Nor. 'le Marescal,' 'le Mareschal' (i.e., the marshal, the servant or official who had charge of the horses ; not the marshal in the sense of military title) ; a very common surname in early Anglo-Irish records.

mᴀⱼᴄus—VIII—*Markys*, Marks ; 'son of Marcus,' or Mark.

mᴀsûn—XII—*Masoun*, Mason ; Nor. 'le Macun' (i.e., the mason) ; an old surname in Ireland.

méᴀʟóⱱⱱ, *Melod*, Mellet, Mylott, Mylotte ; a var. in Co. Mayo of Ɱⁱoʟóⱱⱱ, q.v.

meᴀsᴀⁱᵹ, Massey ; a late English surname, probably of Norman origin, from Massy in Normandy.

meⁱⱱⱼⁱᴄ, meⁱⱼⁱᴄ—VIII—*Meuryk, Meryk*, Meyrick, Mayrick, Merrick ; 'son of Merick' (the Norman form of the Welsh Meurug). This family settled at an early period in Co. Mayo. Also Ɱᴀᴄ Meⁱⱱⱼⁱᴄ, Ɱᴀᴄ Meⁱⱼⁱᴄ, Ɱᴀᴄ Ɱⁱⱱⱼⁱᴄ, q.v.

mⁱᴄeᴀʟ—VIII—Michael, Michell, Mihell, &c. ; 'son of Michael.'

míȯeaċ—X—*Miache,* **Meagh,** *Miagh, Myagh,* Meade ; Ir. ' míȯeaċ' (i.e., the Meathman, native of, or in some way connected with, Meath). The Meades were merchant families who settled at an early period in Cork, Kinsale, Youghal and Kilmallóck. They were of Anglo-Norman origin and had, as the surname implies, previously settled in Meath. The anglicised form of the surname down to the end of the 16th century was always Meagh or Miagh. The modern form, Meade, seems to have been intended to represent 'Meath.' The Meades are still numerous in Cork and Limerick.

míléir, Myler, Meyler. V. maoilir.

mílíȯ—VIII—*Mile, Myle, Moyle,* Miles, Myles, Moyles ; 'son of Milo' (a Latin name introduced by the Normans, and later confused with Miles). V. mílir.

mílis—VIII—*Milys,* Miles, Myles, Moyles ; 'son of Miles' (the Latin 'miles,' a soldier, used in the Middle Ages as a title, and which became a personal name, probably by being confused with Milo). V. mílíȯ above.

miniȋéir, minȋéir—XII—*Myneter,* Miniter, Myniter ; Nor. 'le Myneter,' 'le Mineter' (i.e., the minter, maker of money) ; an old, but extremely rare, surname in Clare and Galway. It occurs frequently in the Black Book of Limerick.

míolóiȯ—VIII—*Mylode, Melod,* Mylott, Moylotte, Mellott, Mellet, Millet, Mylett, Mullet, &c. ; 'son of Milot' (dim. of Milo ; v. mílíȯ above) ; formerly a Tipperary surname, but now most common in Co. Mayo. In the latter county, méalóiȯ and málóiȯ (q.v.) are apparently variants and are similarly anglicised.

miséiȯ, Misset. V. ȯe míréiȯ.

mistéil—VIII—*Mesteil, Misdell,* Michell, Mitchell, &c., 'son of Michell' (a form of Michael). V. míċeal.

móicléir—XII—*Malclerk, Manclerk, Mauclerk, Mauclerc, Mauclere, Mowclere,* Mockler, Muckler ; Nor. 'Malclerk' (i.e., the unlearned clerk, bad scholar, opposed to Beauclerk). The family so called settled in Co. Tipperary, where John Mauclerk, in 1356, was a person of importance and the owner of extensive property.

móinbíol—XI—*Mandevill, Mandefill, Monfield, Mansfild, Maunsfield*, Mandeville, and in Co. Waterford Mansfield ; a var. of oe móinbíol, q.v. ; sometimes pronounced múinbíol. The assimilation to Mansfield is old in Waterford.

móinséil—XII—*Monshale, Monsheall, Mounsell, Mauncell*, Maunsell, Monsell, Mansell, and incorrectly Mansfield ; Nor. ' le Maunsel,' ' le Mansel ' (i.e., the farmer who cultivated a ' manse,' land sufficient to support a family, or received its revenues) ; the name of a family who settled early in Co. Kilkenny, and thence passed over into Tipperary and Cork.

moiréis, *Morresh*, Morris, and incorrectly Morrison and Morrissey. V. oe moipéir.

moirtéil—VIII—*Martel, Martell*, Mortell ; ' son of Martel ' (dim. of Martin) ; an old surname in Meath and Cork ; now also numerous in Co. Limerick.

mórboirneac—X—*Morvornagh, Morvernagh, Morvorny*, now always Gordon ; Ir.' mópboipneac,' i.e., belonging to mópboipeann, a place-name, meaning a rocky hill or district. This was formerly a Roscommon surname, but is now found chiefly in Co. Mayo, where it is not uncommon. It is as old at least as the 16th century. I can discover no satisfactory explanation of Gordon as its English equivalent.

morgán—VIII—*Morgane*, Morgan ; ' son of Morgan (a Welsh personal name). This surname, though fairly common in Ireland, is apparently not older than the 16th century.

mórtún, *Moretoun*, Moreton, Morton. V. oe móptún.

muilleóir—XII—Miller, Millar ; i.e., the miller.

muimneac—X—Moynagh, Moyna, Meenagh, Minnagh, &c. ; Ir. ' muimneac ' (i.e., the Munsterman) ; a descriptive epithet which supplanted the real surname. Cf. oéireac, Laigneac.

múinbíol, Mandeville, Mansfield. V. Móinbíol.
muiréis, Morris, &c. V. de Moiréir.

na bpaidir—XIII—Beades; Ir. 'na bpaidir' (i.e., of the prayers, or beads); a rare Roscommon name.
na bríghde, na bríde—XIII—*ny Brydy*, Bride; Ir. 'na Bríghde' (i.e., of the Bride River, from residence thereby); a rare East Cork surname.
noiréis, norais, nóras, Norrish, Norris, &c. V. de Noiréir.
nuaman—XII—Newman; Nor. 'le Neuman,' 'le Neweman' (i.e., the new man, newcomer, the newly settled stranger); an old surname in Cork and parts of the midlands.
núinnseann, Nugent. V. de Núinnseann.

ó ainmire, ó ainmireach, v. ó hAinmire, ó hAinmireach.
ó an cáinte—III—*O Encantie, On Conty*, Canty, County; 'des. of the satirist' (Ir. 'cáinteach'); the name of a bardic family in West Cork. Fearfeasa ó an Cáinte was a celebrated poet who flourished about the beginning of the 17th century, and took part in the 'Contention of the Bards.' V. ó Cáinte.
ó bachlaigh—III—*O Baghly*, Bockley, (Buckley); 'des. of the husbandman' (Ir. bachlach); a rare Mayo surname.
ó báire—I—*O Barre*, Barry; 'des. of Báire' (short for Bairrfhionn or Fionnbharr, fair-head); the name of a family of Corca Laoighdhe who anciently possessed the peninsula of Muinntear Bháire, or Muntervary, in West Cork; said to be still extant in Co. Cork, angl. Barry.
ó bairr—I—*O Barr*, Barr; 'son of Barr' (short for Bairrfhionn or Fionnbharr); a var. of ó Báire, q.v.; formerly in use in Carlow and Donegal, but rare.
ó baiscinn—I—Baskin, Buskin; 'des. of Bascaoin' (fair-hand); the name of a family who were seated in Corca Bhaiscinn in West Clare until dispossessed

by the MacMahons early in the 14th century ; now very rare.

Ó bAlbáin—III—*O Ballavane, O Ballevan,* Ballevan ; ' des. of the stammerer ' (Ir. bAlb, dim. bAlbán) ; originally a Connacht surname ; found at the beginning of the 17th century in Donegal and Tipperary ; now very rare and scattered.

Ó bAnAgáin—I—Banigan, Bannigan ; ' des. of bAnAgán ' (dim. of bán, white) ; a rare Donegal surname.

Ó bAnáin—I—*O Banane, O Bannan, O Bynnan,* Banane, Banan, Bannan, Bannon, Banim, &c., and, by translation, White ; ' des. of bAnán ' (a dim. of bán, white). There are several distinct families of this name, the best-known and most numerous being that of Ely O'Carroll, in the present Offaly. Other families of the name were seated in Mayo and Fermanagh.

Ó bAoъáin—I—' des. of bAoъán ' (simpleton, dim. of bAoъ) ; the name of a family formerly seated in the district of Badhna, in the east of Co. Roscommon ; now obsolete, or changed into the synonymous form Ó bAoiъín, q.v. O'Donovan erroneously supposed it to be the origin of the surname Boyton.

Ó bAoiъeAlláin—I—*O Boylane, O Boylan,* Boylan, Boyland ; des. of ' bAoiъeAllán ' (dim. of bAoiъeAll) ; the name of a well-known Ulster family who were anciently chiefs of Dartraighe, the present barony of Dartry, in the west of Co. Monaghan, and at one time of all Oriel.

Ó bAoiъill—I—O'Boyle, Boyle, &c. ; ' des. of bAoiъeAll ' (probably for bAoiъ-ъeAll, vain-pledge). The O'Boyles, who are one of the principal families of Cinel Conaill and of the same stock as the O'Donnells and O'Doghertys, were originally chiefs of the Three Tuaths in the north-west of Co. Donegal ; but when these territories passed into the possession of the MacSweeneys, O'Boyle became chief Tir-Ainmhireach in the west of the same county, which was thenceforward known as Cpíoъ bAoiъeAllAъ, or O'Boyle's country, now the barony of Boylagh. During the

wars in the reign of Elizabeth, the O'Boyles spread
into different parts of Ireland, and towards the close
of the 16th century were found in nearly every county.
The references to the name in the Annals of the Four
Masters and the Fiants of Elizabeth are very numerous.

Ó baoitín—I—Boyne; 'des. of baoitín' (simpleton,
dim. of baot, foolish); a very rare Connacht surname,
probably a substitute for the old Roscommon surname
Ó baoḋáin (q.v.), with which it is synonymous.

Ó baotġalaiġ—I—Bohill, (Bowes); 'son of baot-
ġalaċ' (foolhardy). The head of this family is
mentioned by O'Dugan as one of the chiefs of Clan
Fergus in Ulster. I have failed to discover any early
angl. form of the surname, and am by no means
certain that it is still extant. There was also a family
surnamed Ó baotġail or Ó baotġaile in the parish
of Skreen, Co. Sligo, but that too seems to have disappeared.

Ó bároáin—III—O Bardane, O Barden, Bardan,
Barden, Bardon; 'des. of the little bard' (Ir. báro,
dim. bároán); a rare surname; almost peculiar, in
the 16th century, to Wexford and Longford. The
O'Bardons of Longford seem to have been at one time
professional harpers.

Ó beacáin—I—O Beaghane, O Beghan, O Behan, Beaghan, Beahan, Behane, Behan, Beegan, Beane, Bean;
'des. of beacán' (dim. of beac, a bee, a name applied
to a child); the name of a literary family in Offaly
and Leix, now widely spread through Leinster and
Munster.

Ó beaġacáin—I—O Beggahan, O Begkehan, Begaddon;
'son of beaġacán' (dim. of beaġac, from beaġ
small); an old Carlow surname; very rare.

Ó beaġáin—I—O Begane, O Began, Begane, Biggane,
Beggan, and, by translation, Little, Littleton; 'des.
of beaġán' (dim. of beaġ, little); a rare and scattered
surname. In Co. Limerick, it is pronounced Ó biġeán
and sometimes Englished Littleton, a form also in use
in parts of Co. Clare.

Ó beaglaoic—III—*O Beagly, O Begely, O Biggely, O Begley*, Begley, Bagley, Bigly; 'des. of the little hero' (Ir. beaglaoc), but perhaps the original name was Ó beigfile,' des. of the little poet' (cf. the older angl. forms). In the 16th century, this surname was almost peculiar to Donegal and Cork. The O'Begleys of Cork seem to have come southwards with the Mac-Sweeneys, under whom they served as gallowglasses.

Ó beannacáin—I—*O Benachain, O Benachane, O Benahan*, Banahan; 'des. of beannacáin' (dim. of beannac, pointed, peaked, horned); the name of an old Sligo family who, according to O'Flaherty, are of Firbolgic descent.

Ó béara—?—*O Beara, O Berie, O Berry*, Bera, Beary, Berry; 'des. of béara (?)'; the name of an Offaly family of the same race as the O'Connors and O'Dempseys; also a Mayo surname.

Ó bearáin—I—*O' Barrane, O Barran*, Barron, Berrane (Barnes, Barrington); 'des. of beapán' (stripling, dim. of beap, a spear, spit, javelin); an old surname in Thomond and Tirconnell; also Ó biopáin, q.v.

Ó beargá—I—*O Barrie, O Barry*, Barrie, Barry; 'des. of beapga' (spear-like); the name of a Co. Limerick family who were anciently lords of Iveross, in the barony of Kenry. There need scarcely be a doubt that many of the Barrys of East Limerick are of this race, and not of Anglo-Norman origin. There was another family of the same name in Tirawley, Co. Mayo, but, according to O'Donovan, it is extinct. It is certainly not the surname which is angl. Berry in that county, the Irish of which is Ó béapa, q.v.

Ó bearnáin—II—Barnane, (Bernard); 'des. of beapnán' (dim. of beapn). MacFirbis mentions a Clann beapnáin among the descendants of Colla meann.

Ó béice—I—*O Beaky*, Beaky, Bakey; 'des. of béice' (clamour, weeping). Two persons of this name are mentioned in the Annals of the Four Masters as lords of Ó méit in the 11th century. O Huidhrin mentions another family of the name as lords of Bantry, Co.

Cork. The name is apparently long extinct in both places. 'O Beaky' was a Co. Wicklow surname at the beginning of the 17th century. O'Donovan gives Beck and Peck as the modern angl. forms of Ó béice, but this I have failed to verify.

Ó beig—I—*O Begg*, Begg, Beggs, Biggs, and, by translation, Little ; ' des. of beag ' (little).

Ó beigín—I—*O Beggin*, Beggan, Biggin, Biggins ; ' des. of beigín ' (dim. of beag, little) ; a var. of Ó beagáin and Ó bigín, q.v.

Ó beigleigínn—III—*O Begleyn*, Beglin, Beglan, (Begnall), &c. ; ' des. of the little scholar ' (Ir. beagléigínn) ; the name of a medical family in Longford, Leitrim and Sligo ; also Ó bigléigínn, q.v.

Ó beirgín—I—*O Bergin, O Bergen, O Bergan,* Bergin, Berigin, Berrigan, &c. ; a corrupt and shortened form of Ó háimeirgín, q.v.

Ó beirn—II—*O Beirn, O Berne,* O'Beirne, O'Bierne, Beirne, Berne, Beirne, Beirnes, &c. ; a var. of Ó birn, q.v.

Ó beollái̇n—I—*O Beollaine, O Beolane, O Bowlane, O Bolan,* Bolan, Boland, Bowland, &c. ; ' des. of beollán ' (Bjolan in Landnamabok) ; the name (1) of an ecclesiastical family in Co. Sligo, the heads of which were for many centuries erenaghs of the Columban church at Drumcliffe, and were noted for their hospitality ; (2) of a Co. Sligo family of the Ui Fiachrach race who were seated at Doonaltan, in the barony of Tireragh, where it is still numerous ; and (3) of a Dalcassian family, who are stated by Keating, but erroneously, to be descended from Mahon, son of Kennedy, and brother of Brian Boru, the real descent being from Mahon, son of Torlough (MacFirbis, Gen. p. 648).

Ó biaḋ, Beatagh, Beatty, &c. ; a Connemara surname, doubtless a corruption of biaḋtac, q.v.

Ó biasta—I—Beasty, Biesty ; ' son of biarta ' ; an old West Connacht surname, still well known in Mayo. The family derives its descent, according to MacFirbis, from Echean, King of Connacht in the time of St. Patrick.

Ó **bıȝeáın**—I—Biggane, Littleton ; a var. in Limerick and Clare of Ó **beaȝáın**, q.v.

Ó **bıȝıȝ**—I—Biggy ; ' son of **bıȝeać** ' (deriv. of **beaȝ**, small) ; a rare Mayo surname ; probably the modern equivalent of the old Mayo surname Ó **beacóa**, which was borne by a Bishop of Tirawley at the beginning of the 13th century.

Ó **bıȝín**—I—O *Beggin*, Biggin, Biggins ; ' des. of **bıȝín** ' (dim. of **beaȝ**, small) ; a var. of Ó **beaȝáın** and Ó **beıȝín**, q.v.

Ó **bıȝléıȝınn**—III—O *Biglean, O Bigleyn, O Biglene*, Beglin, Beglan, (Bignel, &c.) ; a var. of Ó **beıȝléıȝınn**, q.v. This seems to have been the more common form of the name.

Ó **bıoráın**—I—O *Birrain, O Birrane, O Byrran*, Birrane, Byrrane, Byrane, Byran, Brawn, (Byron, Byrne, Barnes, Burns) ; ' des. of **bıopáın** ' (stripling, dim. of **bıop**, a spear, spit) ; a var. in Tipperary and East Limerick of Ó **beapáın**, q.v.

Ó **bıoráınn**, Burns ; a rare Kerry surname, perhaps a var. of Ó **bıopáın**, q.v.

Ó **bıȝın**—I—O *Birgin, O Birgyn*, Bergin, &c. ; ' des. of **áıṁıpȝın** ' ; a var. of Ó **beıpȝın**, q.v.

Ó **bıpín**—I—Berreen ; a var. of Ó **bıopáın**, q.v. ; a rare Sligo surname.

Ó **bıpn**—II—O *Birn, O Birne, O Byrn*, O'Beirne, O'Bierne, O'Byrne, Birne, Beirne, Byrne, Birnes, Byrns, Byrnes, (Byron, Burns) ; ' des. of **bıopn** ' (the Norse personal name Bjorn) ; a var. of Ó **beıpn**, q.v. The present is the usual form of the name in the Annals ; Ó **beıpn** was apparently more common at a later period. There are two distinct families of the name in Connacht : (1) Ó **bıpn** of Siol-Muireadhaig. This family first came into prominence as stewards to the O'Connors, Kings of Connacht and sometimes of all Ireland. About the middle of the 13th century, they superseded the O'Monaghans as chiefs of Tir-Bhriuin, a

beautiful district in Co. Roscommon, a position which
they continued to hold for more than three hundred
years. In the year 1570, Teig Byrne, alias O Byrne,
was 'the chiefest of Tirowyne' (Tir-Bhriuin), and
several gentlemen of the name are mentioned in the
Fiants of Elizabeth. (2) Ó bıɼɼ of Ui Fiachrach.
This family enjoyed, at the beginning of the 15th
century, a considerable estate in Co. Mayo, a little to
the north of Ballinrobe, and there were respectable
families of the name in that county at the end of the
16th century. O'Donovan found the name, under
the angl. form of Byrne, in the very district anciently
occupied by the family. O'Beirne and O'Byrne were
in use in Lecale, Co. Down, at the beginning of the
17th century, but whether the Irish was Ó bıɼɼ, or
Ó bɼoın (q.v.), I am unable to say.

Ó blÁċmaıc—I—Blawick, Blowick, Blouk, (Blake) ;
'des. of blÁċmac' (blossom-son) ; an ancient and
beautiful Irish surname ; in use in Co. Mayo, but fast
becoming merged in the English surname Blake.

Ó blıċín, Bleheen ; a rare Galway surname ; a var. of Ó
maoılṁín or Ó maoılṁıċıl, q.v.

Ó blıᵹe—II—O Blie, O Blye, Bly, Bligh, Blighe ; 'des.
of blıᵹe' (the Norse personal name Bligr). Mac-
Firbis mentions two families of this name in Connacht,
one of Clann Bhriuin, descended from Echean who was
King of Connacht when St. Patrick came to Ireland ;
and the other of Ui Fiachrach, descended from Aonghus, grandson of Fiachra, from whom the Ui Fiachrach are named. This latter family were hereditary
proprietors of Dunfeeny in the barony of Tirawley,
Co. Mayo, about nine miles north-west of Killala.
The name is still in Mayo.

Ó boúꞃÁın—III—O Boherane, O Borhane, Boran ; 'des.
of the deaf-man' (Ir. boúꞃán, dim. of boúaꞃ, deaf) ;
a very rare surname ; in use at the beginning of the
17th century in Tyrone and Tipperary ; now peculiar
to the latter county and the adjoining parts of Co.
Limerick.

Ó boʒaiʒ—I—*Obuge*, Buggy; 'des. of boʒac' (deriv. of boʒ, soft, tender); a rare surname.

Ó boʒáin—I—*O Bogane*, Bogan, Boggan; 'des. of boʒán' (dim. of boʒ, soft, tender). This surname was peculiar to Wexford and Donegal.

Ó boinne—I—Byrne, (Burns); doubtless a shortened form of Ó Conboinne, an old Mayo surname, which O'Donovan found still extant under the angl. forms of Burns. V. Mac Conboinne.

Ó bolʒuibe—I—*O Bolgie, O Boulgye*, (Bolger, Bulger); an apocopated form of Ó bolʒuibin, q.v.

Ó bolʒuibin—I—*O Bolgier, O Bolger, O Bulger*, Bolger, Bulger, Boulger; 'des. of bolʒobán,' (i.e., bolʒ-obán, perhaps a nickname). The O'Bolgers were the great medical family of South Leinster. The name is still common in Wexford.

Ó bnacáin—I—*O Brahan*, Brahan; 'des. of bnacán' (pottage); an old Tipperary surname; now very rare, if not actually obsolete. It was in use fifty years ago.

Ó bnabacáin—I—*O Bradekin*, Bradican, (Brady); a var. in Co. Mayo of Ó bnabacáin, q.v.

Ó bnabacáin—I—*O Bradaghan*, (Bradagan, Bradican); 'des. of bnabacán' (dim. of bnabac, spirited); a var. of Ó bnabaʒáin, Ó bnabacáin, q.v.

Ó bnabaʒáin—I—*O Bradegane, O Bradagan, O Bradigan*, Bradagan, Braddigan, Brodigan, (Bradican); 'des. of bnabaʒán' (dim. of bnabac, spirited). This surname, in the 16th century, was almost peculiar to Co. Roscommon. V. Ó bnabacáin and Ó bnabacáin.

Ó bnabaiʒ—I—*O Brady*, Brady; 'des. of bnabac, (spirited); probably only a var. of Mac bnabaiʒ, q.v.; always very rare, but still extant.

Ó bnabáin—I—*O Bradane, O Bradan, O Bradden*, Bradan, Bradden, and, by 'translation,' Salmon, Sammon, Fisher; 'des. of bnabán' (dim. of bnabac, spirited; also a salmon); a rather scattered surname. In Co. Roscommon, it seems to have been an alias for Ó bnabaʒáin, q.v. Salmon, as an angl. form

of this surname, dates back to the year 1555 ; and
Salmon, of course, suggested Fisher.

Ó bRAOȝAIL, Ó bRAOȝAILe—I—*O Bradile*, Braddell ;
' des. of bʌAoȝʌl ' (spirit-valour) ; a rare Munster surname.

Ó bRAȝÁIn—I—*O Bragane, O Bragan*, Bragan ; ' des.
of bʌʌȝÁn.' Three bishops of this name are mentioned
in the Annals of the Four Masters.

Ó bRAnAȝÁIn—I—*O Branagan, O Branigan, O Brengan*,
Branagan, Branigan, Brannigan, Brennigan, Brangan,
Brankin ; ' des. of bʌʌnʌȝÁn ' (dim. of bʌʌn, a raven) ;
the name of a family of Cinel Eoghain in Derry. V.
Ó bʌʌnÁin.

Ó bRAnÁIn—I—*O Brannan, O Brennan, O Brynan*,
Brannan, Brannon, Brennan, Brinan, &c. ; ' des. of
bʌʌnÁn ' (dim. of bʌʌn, a raven) ; the name of an
ecclesiastical family in Ulster, who were erenaghs of
the church of Derry and of Derryvullan, Co. Fermanagh. They seem to have been also known by the
synonymous surname of Ó bʌʌnʌȝÁin q.v.

Ó bRAnOUIb—I—Braniff ; ' des. of bʌʌnoub ' (black
bʌʌn, black-raven, an old Irish personal name) ; a
rare surname.

Ó bRAnȝAIL, Ó bRAnȝAILe—I—*O Branyll*, Brannelly, Branley ; ' des. of bʌʌnȝʌl ' (raven-valour) ; a
very rare Connacht surname.

Ó bRAOIn—I—*O Brean, O Breen, O Bruen, O Browne*,
(O'Brien), Breen, Bruen, &c. ; ' des. of bʌʌon ' (sad-
ness, sorrow) ; the name of several distinct families,
of which the following are the most important : (1)
Ó bʌʌoin of Breaghmhaine. The head of this family,
which is descended from Maine, son of Niall of the
Nine Hostages, was lord of Breaghmhaine, now the
barony of Brawney, in Co. Westmeath, adjoining
Athlone and the Shannon. The family still flourishes
in this ancient territory, but the name has been incorrectly angl. O'Brien, which somewhat obscures
its origin. (2) Ó bʌʌoin of Luighne. The head of
this family was lord of Luighne, now the barony of

Lune, in the west of Co. Meath. This family disappeared from history at an early period, the last lord of Luighne mentioned in the Annals of the Four Masters having died in the year 1201. (3) Ó Ḃʀaoın of Loch Gealgosa. This family, which is mentioned by O'Dugan, was probably seated in the barony of Costello, Co. Mayo, but its subsequent history cannot be traced. (4) Ó Ḃʀaoın of Roscommon, the head of which was erenagh of the church of St. Coman. To this family belonged the celebrated annalist, Tighearnach Ó Braoin, one of the most learned men of his age. This family may now be represented by the Bruens in Co. Roscommon. O Bruen, O Bruyn, O Bruyen, &c., as angl. forms of Ó Ḃʀaoın in Leix and Carlow, in the 16th century, are a clear indication of the midland origin of the family of Bruen in these counties; while O Browne in Kerry is equally suggestive of the origin of the Breens in that county and in Limerick.

Ó Ḃʀaonáın—I—*O Brenane, O Brennan, O Brinane,* O'Brennan, Brennan, Brinane, Brinan, &c.; ' des. of Ḃʀaonán ' (dim. of Ḃʀaon); the name of several distinct families, viz.: (1) Ó Ḃʀaonáın of Ossory, the head of which was chief of Ui Duach, in the north of the present Co. Kilkenny, where the name is still very common; (2) Ó Ḃʀaonáın of Crevagh in Co. Westmeath, a numerous and powerful clan; (3) Ó Ḃʀaonáın of Siol Anmchadha, of the same race as the O'Maddens, seated in the barony of Longford, in the south-east of Co. Galway, where they were still numerous at the close of the 16th century; and (4) Ó Ḃʀaonáın of Dunkerron, who were followers of O'Sullivan More, and are still numerous in Kerry. It is almost impossible to distinguish the angl. forms of this surname from those of Ó Ḃʀanáın, q.v. The same angl. forms were to a great extent common to both; but, generally speaking, Ó Ḃʀanáın is the origin in Ulster, and Ó Ḃʀaonáın in the other provinces.

Ó Ḃʀeacáın—I—*O Breckan, O Brackan,* Bracken;

' des. of Ɗʀeacán ' (dim. of Ɗʀeac, speckled) ; the name of an old family in Offaly.

Ó Ƀʀeaȝaiȝ—III—*O Bray, O Brye*, Bray, Bree ; ' des. of the Bregian,' native of Bregia (Ir. Ɗʀeaȝać) ; written Ó Ɗʀeaȝóa by O Huidhrin ; the name of a family in the barony of Imokilly, Co. Cork.

Ó ɃʀeaɼaiL—I—*O Brassell*, O'Brazil, Brassill, Brazil, Brazel ; ' des. of Ɗʀeaɼaʟ ' (strife, war) ; a somewhat rare and scattered surname.

Ó ɃʀeaɼLáin, Ó ɃʀeiɼLeáin, Ó ɃʀeiɼLein—I—*O Breslane*, Breslane, Breslaun, Breslin, &c. ; ' des. of ƊʀeaɼLán ' (dim. of Ɗʀeaɼaʟ). The O'Breslins are a branch of the Cinel Enda, and were originally chiefs of Fanad, a district in the north-east of the barony of Kilmacrenan, in Co. Donegal. Some time in the second half of the 13th century they were driven from this territory, and settled in Fermanagh, where they became distinguished as brehons to the Maguires. They were also erenaghs of the church of Derryvullen, in the same county, in which office they succeeded Ó Ɗʀanáin. Ó ƊʀeaɼLáin was also the name of a family of the Ui Fiachrach, in Co. Sligo, who were chiefs of Kilanley, in the barony of Tireragh. The name is variously corrupted in the spoken language. V. Ó ƊʀeiɼLeáin, Ó ƊʀeiɼLein, Ó Ɗʀioɼláin, and Ó ƊʀiɼLeáin.

Ó ɃʀeóLLáin—I—*O Brollan*, Brolan, (Bolan, Boland) ; possibly the same as Ó ɃeóLLáin, q.v. MacFirbis gives the descent of this family from Ainmire, son of Cormac Caoch, son of Cairbre, son of Niall of the Nine Hostages. They belong, therefore, to Clann Chairbre of Co. Sligo, in whose territory the Uι ɃeóLLáin also were seated. This, together with the fact that the name is now almost universally angl. Bolan and Boland, would seem to point to the identity of the two names. Ó ɃʀeóLLáin is still in use in Co. Mayo, but is very rare, and there also is angl. Bolan and Boland.

Ó Ƀʀiain—I—O'Brian, O'Bryan, O'Bryen, O'Brien, Brien, &c. ; ' des. of Ɗʀian.' This family derives its name and descent from Brian Boru, King of Ireland, who was slain at Clontarf, in the year 1014. By his victories over the Danish invaders and their Irish allies, Brian raised his clan, the Ui Toirdealbhaigh, to a position of pre-eminence among the Dalcassians, and laid the foundation of the greatness of his posterity, who became not only the ruling family in Thomond, but one of the most powerful in Ireland. Some of them were kings of Munster, and some of all Ireland. Their possessions included the whole of Co. Clare and large portions of the counties of Limerick, Tipperary and Waterford. They divided into several branches, the principal of which were : the O'Briens of Ara, in the north of Co. Tipperary, whose chief was known as Mac I Bhriain Ara ; of Coonagh in the east of Co. Limerick ; of Pobelbrien, now the barony of that name in Co. Limerick, whose chief stronghold was Carrigogonnell, on the Shannon ; of Aherlow, in Co. Tipperary ; and of Cumaragh, in Co. Waterford, who had extensive possessions along the Cummeragh mountains comprising the valley between Dungarvan and the Suir. O'Brien is now one of the most common surnames in Ireland.

Ó bRIC—I—*O Brick*, Brick ; ' des. of bṅeac ' (speckled) ; the name of a Waterford family who were anciently lords of the Southern Decies, but sank at an early period under the power of the O'Phelans and disappeared from history. The family is said to be now extinct.

Ó bRíOSáIn—I—*O Brisan*, Briceson, Bryson ; a corruption, in Co. Donegal, of Ó muiṅġeaṙáin, q.v. It is by no means a late corruption ; O Brisan appears as the angl. form in the Patent Rolls of James I.

Ó bRíOSláIn, Ó bRISLeáIn—I—*O Brislane, O Brissleayn, O Brislan*, Brislane, Brislawn, Brislan, Brislin, Breslin, &c. ; a var. in the spoken language of Ó bṅeaṙláin, q.v.

Ó bROġaIb—I—*O Brogy*, Broggy ; ' des. of bṅoġaib ' (an ancient Irish personal name ; occurs in the Book of Armagh) ; a rare surname in Clare and Limerick.

Ó bRÓ5áin—I—*O Brogane, O Brogan,* Brogan ; ' des. of
bpó5án ' (dim. of bpó5, sorrowful) ; an old surname
in Mayo and Donegal ; still common in both counties.
The O'Brogans of Mayo anciently possessed estates
at Breachmaigh and Cnoc Spealain, in the barony of
Carra.

Ó bROileacáin—I—*O Brellighan, O Brilleghane, O
Brilehan,* (Bradley); an attenuated form of Ó bpoil-
cáin, q.v. ; apparently the more common form in
popular use.

Ó bROin—I—*O Birne,* O'Byrne, Byrne, Byrnes, (Burns,
Byron), &c. ; ' des. of bpan ' (raven). This family
derives its name and descent from bpan, son of
Maolmópóa, King of Leinster, whose death at Cologne
is recorded by the Four Masters under the year 1052.
The original patrimony of the family was Ui Faolain,
which comprised the northern half of the present Co.
Kildare ; but they were driven thence by the Anglo-
Normans soon after the invasion, and forced to take
refuge in the mountain fastnesses of Wicklow, where
they became very powerful and were long the terror
of the invaders of their ancestral homes. At the head
of the Wicklow clans, they maintained for a period of
three hundred years incessant warfare with the
foreigners, whom they defeated in many a fierce
engagement. Their country, which was called Cpíoc-
bpanac, comprised the entire of the barony of New-
castle and portions of those of Arklow and Ballina-
cor. This last belonged to the Gaval-Rannall, or
Ranelagh, a junior branch of the family, which in
time became very powerful and of which the celebrated
Fiach MacHugh O'Byrne was chief in the reign of
Elizabeth. The name is now very common in Leinster, and has spread into many other parts of Ireland.

Ó bROisneacáin, v. Ó bpopnacáin.

Ó bRÓiC, *O Brogh, O Broy,* Brophy, (Bray) ; a var. of
Ó bpóice, q.v. ; found in Iveleary, Co. Cork, where it
is sometimes angl. Bray.

Ó bRÓiCe—I—*O Broha, O Brohy, O Broghie,* Brofie,

Brophy; ' des. of b——————' ; written Ua bpoiʒte in the Annals of Ulster, A.D. 1165. The original patrimony of this family was Magh Sedna, in the barony of Galmoy, Co. Kilkenny; but they were driven thence into Upper Ossory, soon after the Anglo-Norman invasion, when their chief settled at Bally-brophy, in the present Leix. The family is still numerous in Ossory and the adjoining districts of Tipperary.

Ó bROLaċáin, v. Ó bpoicáin.

Ó bRÓLaiʒ—I—*O Broloe*, Broly, Brolly, Brawley; ' des. of bpólaċ ' ; the name of an old Derry family.

Ó bROLċáin—I—O'Brollaghan, O'Brallaghan, Broll-laghan, (Bradley); ' des. of bpoLaċán ' (dim. of bpó-Laċ) ; the name of a famous Ulster family, descended from Suibhne Meann, King of Ireland in the 7th century. They appear to have been seated originally in the barony of Clogher, Co. Tyrone, but removed thence at an early period and settled in the neighbour-hood of Derry, and in Tirconnell. The name is still well known in Ulster and in Co. Mayo, but is often absurdly angl. Bradley, which greatly obscures the origin of this historic family. A branch of the family seem to have also settled in Cork. Ó bpoiLeaċáin (q.v.) is a common variant in the spoken language of Mayo. For an account of the many distinguished bearers of this surname, see Healy's Ancient Schools and Scholars, pp. 352 et seqq.

Ó bROSNaċáin—I—*O Brosnaghane, O Brosneghan*, Brosnahan, Bresnihan, Brosnan, &c. ; ' des. of bpor-naċán ' (native of Brosna, in Kerry) ; the name of an old Kerry family, now also numerous in Co. Limerick.

Ó bRUaċáin—I—*O Broughan, O Broghan, O Brohan*, Broughan, Brohan, and, by ' translation,' Banks ; ' des. of bpuaċán ' (corpulent, or miser) ; originally a Connacht surname, but in the 16th century common in Westmeath, Kildare and Tipperary, and now also in Co. Clare. V. Ó bpuaċóʒ.

Ó bRUaċóʒ—I—Banks ; in use in Connacht, but apparently only a modern substitution for Ó bʀuaᴄáɩn (q.v.), with which it is synonymous.

Ó bʀuaᴅaɩʀ—II—*O Bruadar, O Brouder, O Broder, O Brother,* Brouder, Broder, Brooder, Bruder, Brother, Brauders, Brodders, Brothers, (Broderick), &c. ; ' des. of Bruadar ' (the Norse Broddr) ; the name of at least five distinct families in Ireland, viz. : (1) Ó bʀuaᴅaɩʀ of Ossory, the head of which was chief of Iverk in the south of Co. Kilkenny ; (2) Ó bʀuaᴅaɩʀ of Galway, a respectable family in the 16th century, and still numerous in that county ; (3) Ó bʀuaᴅaɩʀ of Carraic Brachaidhe in Inishowen, Co. Donegal, a family still in that district at the beginning of the 16th century ; (4) Ó bʀuaᴅaɩʀ of Ui Ceinnsealaigh, Co. Wexford ; and (5) Ó bʀuaᴅaɩʀ of Corca Laoighdhe, Co. Cork. To this last, which is of the same stock as the O'Driscolls, the O'Brouders of Co. Limerick almost certainly belong. (See full account of these families by Rev. John C. MacErlean, S.J., in his Introduction to the Poems of David O Bruadair, published by the Irish Texts Society.)

Ó bʀuaɩᴅeaᴅá—I—*O Briody,* Briody; des. of ' bʀuaɩᴅeaᴅ '; an old Cavan surname.

Ó bʀuᴈaᴅa—III—*O Browe, O Broe,* Broe, Browe, Brew ; ' des. of the bʀuᴈaɩᴅ ' (or farmer) ; an Ossory surname.

Ó bʀuɩc—I—*O Bruck, O Brick,* Brick, and, by ' translation,' Badger ; ' des. of bʀoc ' (badger) ; the name of a Dalcassian family, long settled in Kerry, and still well known in that county. The ' translated ' form, Badger, is found in Co. Galway.

Ó bʀúɩn, Bruin, Bruen ; v. Ó bʀaoɩn.

Ó buaᴄaʟʟa—I—*O Buoghelly, O Bowghilly,* O *Bohelly,* Boughla, Buhilly, Buckley ; ' des. of buaᴄaɩʟʟ ' (the boy, used as a personal name). This surname, in the 16th century, was peculiar to Cork, Tipperary and Offaly. It is now also common in Kerry, Kilkenny and Dublin. There are very few of the name in any other county.

Ó buaváčáin—I—*O Boughane, O Boughan, O Boghan,* Boughan, Bougan, Boohan, Bohane, Bohan, (?) Boyhan, (Bowen, Bohanan) ; ' des of buaváčán' (dim. of buaváč, victorious) ; a rather scattered surname. In the 16th century it was found chiefly in Cork, Kerry, Tipperary, Offaly and Kilkenny.

Ó buaváig—I—*O Boey, O Bowe, O Boye, O Bwoy, O Bowige,* Bowie, Bowe, Buie, Bwee, Bowes, Boyes, Boyce, O'Boyce, Bohig, Bogue, &c. ; ' des. of buaváč' (victorious) ; a very scattered surname, but most common in Donegal, Kilkenny and Cork. In the last-mentioned county, the final ᵹ is sounded ; hence the early angl. form Ó Bowige and the modern Bogue. The family is a branch of the Corca Laoighdhe, but was erroneously supposed to be a branch of the O'Sullivans, on account of the prevalence of the Christian name buaváč in that family ; and it is not improbable that some of them have adopted the name of O'Sullivan or Sullivan.

Ó buaváin—I—*O Bowdan, O Bodan,* Bodan, Bowden, Boden ; ' des. of buaván' (an ancient Irish personal name, older form buačán) ; an old Ossory surname.

Ó Caváin—I—*O Cadane,* Cadan, Cadden ; ' des. of Cavan' (an Irish personal name, Lat. Catanus) ; a rare Ulster surname ; possibly the same as Mac Caváin, q.v.

Ó Caváin—I—*O Coyne, O Kine,* Coyne, Kyne, Kine, and, by translation, Barnacle ; ' des. of Cavan' (wildgoose, barnacle) ; the name of an old family of Partry, who are still numerous in Connacht.

Ó Cavla—I—*O Keyle, O Kealy, O Quealy,* Kiely, Keily, Kealy, Keely, Keeley, (Kelly), Quealy, &c. ; ' des. of Cavla' (beautiful, comely, graceful) ; the name (1) of a Connacht family who were formerly chiefs of Connemara ; and (2) of a Thomond family who were chiefs of Tuath Luimnigh in the neighbourhood of the city of Limerick. Both families are still numerously represented in Connacht and Munster. To be distinguished from Ó Caollaiᵹe, q.v.

Ó Cáidín, Caden, Cadden; a corruption in the spoken language of Connacht of Mac Áidín, q.v.

Ó Caingne—I—*O Kangney*, Cangney, Cagney; 'des. of Caingean' (business, compact, dispute, etc.); a Munster surname. The family, which is a branch of the Corca Laoighdhe, was originally seated in the parish of Myros, in the barony of West Carbery, Co. Cork.

Ó Cainín—I—*O Canine, O Canin*, Caning, Canning; 'des. of Cainín'; a var. of Ó Coinín, q.v.; a rare midland surname.

Ó Cáince—III—*O Canty*, Canty, County; a short form of Ó an Cáince, q.v. Ó Canncaid is a common pronunciation of this surname in Kerry and Limerick, hence the angl. form County which is sometimes met with.

Ó Cairbre—I—*O Carbery, O Carbry*, Carbry, Carbery, Carberry; 'des. of Cairbre' (charioteer); the name of an old midland family who were anciently chiefs of Tuath Buadha, now Tuaith or Twy, in the barony of Clonlonan, Co. Westmeath.

Ó Caireallláin—I—*O Caralane, O Carlane*, Carellan, Carlan, Carland, Carlin, (Carleton); 'des. of Caireallán' (dim. of Caireall); the name of a branch of the Cinel Eoghain who were formerly chiefs of Clandermot, Co. Derry. William Carleton, the novelist, was of this family. V. Ó Coireallláin.

Ó Cairre, v. Ó Carra.

Ó Cairrín, v. Ó Carraidín.

Ó Cais—I—*O Case*, Cash; 'des. of Car' (bent, curly, &c.); very rare.

Ó Caisealláin—I—*O Cashellan*, Cushlane, Cashlan, Caslin; doubtless a corruption of Ó Caireadáin, angl. *O Cassidan*; a rare Ulster surname.

Ó Caiside—I—*O Cashedy, O Cassidy, O Kesedy*, Cassidy, Cassedy, Kessidy, &c.; 'des. of *Caiside*'; the name of a distinguished medical family in Fermanagh who were hereditary physicians to the Maguires. Branches of the family had settled in the midland counties before the end of the 16th century.

Ó Caisil, Ó Caisile—I—*O Cashell, O Cassell, O Cashuly,
O Cassely,* Cashel, Cassell, Cassilly, Casley, &c.;
doubtless corruptions of Ó Cairroe, q.v. Cf. Ó
Cairealáin above.

Ó Caisín—I—*O Cashine, O Cassin, O Kessan,* Casheen,
Cashin, Cashen, Cashion, Cashon, Cassian, Cassin,
Keshin; 'des. of Cairín' (dim. of cor, bent, curly);
apparently a var. in the south of Ireland of the
Ossory surname Mac Cairín, q.v.

Ó Caitniaó—I—*O Cahenney, O Cany,* Caheny, Canny;
'des of Caitnia' (battle-champion); the name of a
distinguished family of the Uí Fiachrach, in Co.
Mayo, who were lords of Erris, in the north-west of
that county, until dispossessed by the Barretts in
the 13th century. The family is still in Mayo.

Ó Calġaiġ—I—*O Colgy, O Calgie, O Kalligie,* Callagy,
Kellegy; 'des. of Calġać' (peevish); a scattered
surname, nowhere very common.

Ó Callaóa—I—Kelledy; 'des. of Callaro' (crafty);
extremely rare   The Four Masters under the year 1168
record the death of Maolpáoraiġ Ua Callaóa, coarb
of St. Cronan of Roscrea.

Ó Callanáin—I—*O Callanane, O Callinan,* Callanane,
Callanan, Callinan, Calnan, &c.; 'des. of Callanán';
the name of a distinguished medical family in South
Munster; also of a Galway family who were coarbs of
Kilcahill. The latter family is mentioned by Mac
Firbis.

Ó Callaráin—I—*O Calleran,* Colleran; perhaps a
corruption of Mac Allmuráin, q.v.; a rare Connacht
surname.

Ó Caltáin, Culhane; a metathesised form of Ó Cat-
láin, q.v.

Ó Camta—I—*O Comy,* Cowmey, Coumey, Coomey;
'des. of Camta' (bent, stooped); a Munster surname
extremely rare.

Ó Canáin—I—*O Cannane,* Cannan, Cannon, Canning,
&c.; 'des. of Canán' (an old Irish personal name,
probably dim. of Cano, a wolf-cub); the name of a

branch of the Ui Maine, in Co. Galway, of the same stock as the O'Maddens. V. Ó Conáin.

Ó canann—I—*O Cannan, O Cannon*, Cannan, Cannon, Canning, &c. ; ' des. of Cano ' (wolf-cub, whelp) ; an old Tirconnell surname ; probably a var. of Ó Canannáin, q.v.

Ó canannáin—I—*O Cananan, O Conanan, O Kannenan*, (?) Cannon ; ' des. of Canannán ' (dim. of Canann) ; the name of a family who were lords of Tirconnell from the beginning of the 10th to the middle of the 13th century, when they were supplanted by the O'Donnells and sank into obscurity. There were still a few scattered families of the name at the end of the 16th century.

Ó caocáin—I—*O Kieghane, O Keaghan, O Keahan*, Keahan, Keehan ; ' des. of Caocán ' (dim. of caoc, blind, Lat. caecus) ; a var. of Mac Caocáin, q.v.

Ó caováin, Kane, Kean, Keane ; a corruption in the spoken language of Co. Mayo of Mac Aováin, q.v.

Ó caozáin, Keegan ; a corruption in the spoken language of Connacht of Mac Aovazáin, q.v.

Ó caoilte, Ó caoiltiz—I—*O Cailte, O Kiltie, O Kiltagh*, O'Kielty, O'Kielt, Kielty, Kilty, Keelty, Quilty, Queelty, Keeltagh Kieltagh, and, by ' translation,' Small in parts of Ulster, and Woods in parts of Connacht ; ' des. of Caoilte ' (an ancient Irish personal name, probably meaning ' hardness ') ; a rather scattered surname ; found in Ulster, Munster and Connacht.

Ó caoim—I—*O Keeve*, O'Keeffe, Keeffe, &c. ; ' des. of Caoim ' (beautiful, noble, gentle, loveable). The O'Keeffes, who are of the royal race of Munster and of the same stock as the MacCarthys and O'Callaghans, derive their name and descent from Art Caom who was son of Fionghuine, King of Munster, and flourished in the 10th century. Donncaó Ó Caoim, the first to bear the surname, lived in the reign of Ceallachan of Cashel. The O'Keeffes were originally seated at Glanworth and possessed the district now called Roches' country, in the barony of Fermoy ; but they were driven thence shortly after the Anglo-Norman invasion, when they settled in a district in the north-west of the barony of Duhallow, to which they gave the name of Pobble O'Keeffe, and where they maintained themselves as a distinct clan down to the end of the 16th century.

Ó Caoiṁín—I—*O Kavine*, Kevin, Cavan ; ' des. of Caoiṁín ' (dim. of Caoṁ) ; extremely rare. V. Ó Caoṁáin.

Ó Caoinṁealḃáin—I—*O Guindelane, O Kennellan, O Kenolan, O Quinelane*, Kindellan, Kennellan, (Connellan), Kinlan, Kinlen, Kenlan, (Conlan), Quinlivan, Quinlan ; ' des. of Caoinṁealḃán ' (gracefully shaped) ; the name of a Meath family who were chiefs of Cinel Laoghaire, near Trim, until the Anglo-Norman invasion. They derive their name and descent from Caoinṁealḃán (died 925), the lineal descendant of Laoghaire, son of Niall of the Nine Hostages, who was King of Ireland in the time of St. Patrick. The name is still in Meath, but disguised under the angl. forms of Connellan and Conlon ; in other parts of Leinster it is angl. Kinlan, Kinlen, &c. ; and it is found in all the counties of Munster, but shortened to Ó Caoinleáin (q.v.), or metathesised to Ó Caoinlioḃáin, q.v.

Ó Caoinleáin—I—*O Kenlan, O Quinlan*, Quinlan, &c. V. Ó Caoinṁealḃáin.

Ó Caoinlioḃáin—I—*O Keynlewayn*, Quinlivan, &c. V. Ó Caoinṁealḃáin.

Ó Caoláin—I—*O Kealain, O Kayllan*, Keelan, Keelin ; ' des. of Caolán ' (dim. of caol, slender). It appears to have been a Meath surname.

Ó Caollaiḋe—I—*O Coely, O Kuelly, O Keally, O Kealy*, Kealy, Keely, (Kelly), Quealy, Queely, &c. ; ' des. of Caollaiḋe ' (an ancient Irish personal name) ; also written Ó Caollaiġe ; the name (1) of a Kilkenny family who were anciently chiefs of Ui Bearchon, in the present barony of Ida ; (2) of a Leix family who were chiefs of Crioch O mBuidhe, in the present barony of Ballyadams ; and (3) of a Tipperary family, anciently chiefs of Aolmhagh. The name appears to have been also in Ulster. It is now almost everywhere disguised under the angl. form of Kelly, for which it is the ordinary Irish in West Limerick and Kerry. In Waterford, it is angl. Queally. Cf. Ó Caóla.

Ó Caomáin—I—*O Keavane, O Kevane,* Kevane, Keevane, Keevan, Cavan, Kevans, (Cavanagh, Kavanagh, Cavendish) ; 'des. of Caomán' (dim. of Caom) ; the name of a branch of the Ui Fiachrach in Sligo and Mayo. They were at one time an important family, and it was their privilege to inaugurate O'Dowd in the chieftaincy of Ui Fiachrach. Some of them seem to have settled, before the end of the 16th century, in Westmeath, Offaly and Kilkenny ; and at the present day, the name is common in West Munster, but angl. Cavanagh and Kavanagh. It is sometimes absurdly made Cavendish in Mayo. There was also a family of the same name in Co. Tyrone, but it seems to be extinct.

Ó Caománaig—I—Cavanagh, Kavanagh, Keaveny, Kevany, (Kevane, Kevans) ; 'des. of Caománac' (der. of Caomán). This surname, which is common in the spoken language of Connacht and West Munster, appears everywhere side by side with Ó Caomáin (q.v.), of which it seems to be merely a modern variant. Ó Caománaig is also sometimes, but incorrectly, used for the surname Caománac q.v. I have failed to discover any early instance, Irish or English, of this surname.

Ó Caortannáin, Rountree ; probably only a 'translation' of the English surname Rowantree.

Ó Carra—I—*O Carra, O Carr, O Karr,* Carr, Karr, Kerr ; 'des. of Carra' (spear) ; a common Ulster surname, the same as that written Ó Cairpe in the Annals of Ulster and Four Masters. Also found in Co. Galway. V. Ó Corra.

Ó Carragáin—I—O'Carrigan, Carrigan, Carigan, Cargin. V. Ó Corragáin.

Ó CARRAIÓ—I—*O Carrie*, Carry; 'des. of Cappaó' (spear) ; a var. of Ó Cappa and Ó Coppaιó, q.v.

Ó CARRAIÓÍN—I—*O Carrine*, Caren, Carr ; 'des. of Cappaιóín' (dim. of Cappaó) ; a var. of Ó Coppaιóín, q.v. ; angl. Carr in Mayo and Galway.

Ó CARRÁIN—I—*O Carrane, O Carrain, O Carran*, Craan, Crain, Crane, Crean, Creane, (Crahan, Crehan, Creaghan, Carey) ; 'des. of Cappán' (dim. of cappa, a spear) ; a var. of Ó Coppáin, q.v.

Ó CARRξAṁNA, O'Growney, &c. ; a var. of Mac Cappξaṁna, q.v. ; so written by Keating.

Ó CARTA, Carr ; a var. in Co. Galway of Ó Cappa, q.v.

Ó CÁRTAIξ—I—*O Carhy, O Cartie*, O'Carthy, Carthy, Carty, &c. ; 'des. of Cáptac' (loving). There were families of this name in Tipperary, Clare and Roscommon. The last-named family ramified into Longford, Sligo and Donegal. Three of the name are mentioned by the Four Masters as chief poets of Connacht in the 11th and 12th centuries. The name is still common in many parts of Ireland. To be distinguished from Mac Cáptaiξ, q.v.

Ó CARTÁIN—I or IV—*O Cartaine, O Cartayne, O Cartan*, Cartan, Carton, Carten, Cartin, Curtan, Curtayne, Curtin, &c. ; 'des. of Captán,' if not a corruption of Mac Aptáin (q.v.), which seems probable. At the beginning of the 17th century, it was found chiefly in the midlands—Westmeath and Longford—but appears also at Castleisland, Co. Kerry, where it is now pronounced Ó Cuptáin, and angl. Curtin, &c., as it is also in West Limerick where it is now very common. V. Mac Caiptáin.

Ó CÁRTAIN—I—Cartan, Carten, (Carthy), &c. ; a rare West Connacht surname, the origin of which I cannot trace.

Ó CASAIÓE—I—*O Cassada*, Cassidy, &c. ; a var. of Ó Caιpιóe, q.v.

Ó CASAILE—I—Cassilly, Casley ; a var. of Ó Caιpιle, q.v.

Ó CASÁIN—I—*O Cossane, O Kessan, O Kissane*, Cussane, Kissane, (Cashman, Patterson) ; 'des. of Capán' (dim.

of caɼ, bent, curly, &c.) ; the name of a Galway family, formerly seated in Ui Maine, Co. Galway ; still represented in that county, but pronounced Ó Coɼáin, and angl. Cussane and Patterson. It is also a not uncommon surname in Kerry and Cork, where it is corrupted to Ó Cioɼáin, and angl. Kissane in the former county, and, very corruptly, Cashman in the latter.

Ó cɑċɑiʒ—I—*O Cahy*, Cahy ; ' des. of cɑċɑċ ' (war-like) ; a rare Offaly surname.

Ó cɑċɑil—I—*O Cahill*, Cahill ; ' des. of cɑċɑl' (battle-powerful). There are several distinct families of this name, of which the following are the most important : (1) Ó Cɑċɑil of Cinel Aodha, in the south-west of Co. Galway, of the same stock as the O'Shaughnessys ; (2) Ó Cɑċɑil of Crumthann, in the east of Co. Galway ; (3) Ó Cɑċɑil of Corca Thine, now angl. Corke-henny, in the parish of Templemore, Co. Tipperary, who gave its name to Ballycahill ; (4) Ó Cɑċɑil of Loch Lein, who were lords of the Eoghanacht of that district before the O'Donoghues ; and (5) Ó Cɑċɑil of Ui Flaithri, near Corofin, Co. Clare. These families were all well-represented at the end of the 16th century.

Ó cɑċáin—I—*O Caghane, O Cahaine, O Cahane, O Kahane, O Kaane*, O'Cahan, O'Caughan, O'Kane, O'Keane, Cahane, Cahan, Cane, Cain, Kane, Keane, &c. ; ' des. of Cɑċán' (a ' pet ' form of some name commencing with Cɑċ-) ; the name (1) of a branch of the Cinel Eoghain, who were lords of Keenaght and possessed the greater part of the present Co. Derry until their estates were confiscated at the time of the plantation of Ulster ; and (2) of a branch of the Ui Fiachrach in Co. Galway. A branch of the Derry family is said to have settled at an early period in Thomond. There are no doubt several distinct families of the name which is now a very common one all over Ireland.

Ó cɑċɑláin—I—*O Cahallane, O Cohallan*, Cahallane,

Cahillane, Cahalane, Cohalane, Cohalan, Callan, Culhane, Clahane, Clehane, &c.; 'des. of Caᴛaláɴ'
(dim. of Caᴛaɩ, battle-mighty); also written Ó Caᴛ-
ɩáɪɴ, q.v.; the name (1) of a Roscommon family who
were formerly chiefs of Clann Fogartaigh; (2) of a
Limerick family, formerly chiefs of Uaitne Cliach,
now the barony of Owneybeg, until dispossessed by
the O'Mulryans; (3) of an Ulster family, now represented by Callan in Monaghan and Louth; and,
doubtless, of other families in different parts of Ireland. All the above-mentioned families were well
represented in the 16th century; and the name was
then also in Offaly, Leix, Kildare, Cork and Kerry.

Ó CaᴛaoɪR—I—*O Cahir*, Cahir; 'des. of Caᴛaoɪ̨' (an
ancient Irish personal name); a rare Tipperary surname.

Ó CaᴛaRɴaɩʒ—I—O'Caharney, O'Caherney, Carney,
[Fox]; 'des. of Caᴛaɪ̨ɴaᴄ' (warlike); the name of
an old Meath family, descended from Maine, son of
Niall of the Nine Hostages. They were originally
chiefs of all Teffia, but their patrimony was afterwards narrowed down to Muinntear Tadhgain, now
the barony of Kilcoursey, in Offaly. They were
also known by the surname of Sɪoɴɴaᴄ (q.v.), from the
cognomen of their ancestor, Caᴛaɪ̨ɴaᴄ Sɪoɴɴaᴄ (the
fox), who was slain in the year 1084. The head of the
family was known by the title of aɴ Sɪoɴɴaᴄ, or The
Fox.

Ó Caᴛasaɩʒ—I—*O Cahessy*, O'Casey, Casey; 'des. of
Caᴛaɪ̨aᴄ' (vigilant, watchful); the name (1) of a
family in ancient Meath, who were lords of Saithne,
in the north of the present Co. Dublin, until dispossessed by Sir Hugh de Lacy soon after the Anglo-
Norman invasion; (2) of a Dalcassian family, seated
in the barony of Coshlea, Co. Limerick; (3) of a Cork
family who possessed a territory called Coillte Mai-
binacha, near Mitchelstown; (4) of a Tirawley family
who were erenaghs of Kilarduff, in the parish of Dunfeeny, Co. Mayo; (5) of a Roscommon family, formerly

erenaghs of Cloondara, in the parish of Tisrara ; and (6) of a Fermanagh family formerly erenaghs of Devinish. These families are all still well represented.

Ó Caṫḃaḋa—I—*O Caffoo, O Caffoe,* Coffey ; ' des. of Caṫḃaḋ ' (older Caṫḃoṫ, gen. Caṫḃoṫa, battle-tent, an ancient Irish personal name) ; a Tipperary surname. Cf. Áḃa Ua ʒCaṫḃaḋa, near Nenagh.

Ó Caṫḃuaḋaiʒ—I—*O Caphowagh, O Capphowe, O Caffowe, O Caffoye,* Coffey ; ' des. of Caṫḃuaḋaċ ' (battle-victorious) ; a West Munster surname ; very common in Kerry.

Ó Caṫláin—I—*O Callaine, O Collhane, O Callan,* Culhane, Callan, Callen, Callin, Cawlin, Clahane, Clehane, &c. ; ' des. of Caṫalán ' (dim. of Caṫal, battle-mighty); a shortened form of Ó Caṫaláin, q.v. Culhane is the usual angl. form in Co. Limerick, but the name is sometimes metathesised to Ó Cláṫáin, angl. Clahane and Clehane. Callan is more commonly the angl. form in the North.

Ó Caṫluain—I—*O Collone, O Cullone,* Calhoun, Colhoun, Colhoon, Culhoun, &c. ; ' des. of Caṫluan ' (battle-hound, battle-hero, or battle-joyful) ; originally a Breifney surname, now dispersed through Ulster. The Uí Caṫluain are mentioned in the Annals at the year 1145.

Ó Caṫmoʒa—I—*O Cowhow,* Coffey ; ' des. of Caṫmuʒ ' (battle-slave) ; a rare surname in south-west of Co. Galway ; to be distinguished from Ó Coḃṫaiʒ of the same county. The family is of the same stock as the O'Clerys and O'Heynes.

Ó Céaḋacáin, Ó Céaḋaʒáin—I—*O Kadegane, O Keadigan,* Cadigan, Cadogan ; ' des. of Céaḋacán,' or ' Céaḋaʒán ' (dim. of Céaḋaċ, possessing hundreds) ; an old West Cork surname.

Ó Céaḋaiʒ—I—*O Keddy,* Keady ; ' des. of Céaḋaċ ' (possessing hundreds ; a favourite personal name among the O'Moores and O'Farrells) ; the name of an old Co. Galway family, of the same stock as the O'Clerys and O'Heynes.

Ó ceaḷḷaċáın—I—O'Callaghan, O'Callahan, Callaghan, Callahan, Calligan, &c. ; ' des. of Ceaḷḷacán ' (dim. of Ceaḷḷaċ) ; the name of a well-known Munster family descended from Ceaḷḷaċán of Cashel, king of Munster, in the 10th century. The surname was not, however, taken from this Ceaḷḷaċán, but from a namesake of his four generations later. The O'Callaghans were originally chiefs of Cinel Aodha, now the barony of Kinalea, in the south of Co. Cork, but on being driven thence by Robert FitzStephen and Milo de Cogan, soon after the Anglo-Norman invasion, they settled on the banks of the Blackwater, to the west of Mallow, where they continued to enjoy considerable possessions, known as Pobul Ui Cheallachain, comprising the parishes of Kilshannig and Clonmeen, down to the time of the Cromwellian confiscations, when the head of the family was transplanted to Clare. There is also a Mayo family of the name, a branch of the Ui Fiachrach, who were anciently lords of Erris.

Ó ceaḷḷaıġ— I—O'Kelly, Kelly, Kelley ; ' des. of Ceaḷḷaċ ' (war, contention) ; the name of several distinct families, of which the following are the best known : (1) Ó Ceaḷḷaıġ of Ui Maine, a branch of the Oirghialla of Ulster. They were one of the most powerful families in Connacht, and as chiefs of Ui Maine ruled over an extensive territory in the counties of Galway and Roscommon, which they held down to the reign of Elizabeth. This family produced many distinguished chiefs, among them Caḋġ Móṙ Ó Ceaḷḷaıġ who fell at Clontarf in 1014. (2) Ó Ceaḷḷaıġ of Breagh, a branch of the southern Ui Neill, who were lords of Breagh, an extensive district embracing a large portion of Meath and the north of Co. Dublin, until after the Anglo-Norman invasion, when they were dispossessed and dispersed throughout Ireland. Conġaḷaċ Ó Ceaḷḷaıġ, the last lord of Breagh, died in 1292. (3) Ó Ceaḷḷaıġ of Cinel Eachach in the barony of Loughinsholin, Co. Derry, where they are still numerous ; (4) Ó Ceaᴌᴌaɪᵹ of Leighe, now Lea, (5) Ó Ceaᴌᴌaɪᵹ of Magh Druchtain, (6) Ó Ceaᴌᴌaɪᵹ of Gallen, all three in Leix ; (7) Ó Ceaᴌᴌaɪᵹ of Ui Teigh, in the north of the present Co. Wicklow ; (8) Ó Ceaᴌᴌ-aɪᵹ of Áᴘᴅ Ó ᵹCeaᴌᴌaɪᵹ, in the parish of Templeboy, Co. Sligo ; and (9) Ó Ceaᴌᴌaɪᵹ of Corca Laoighdhe, in the south-west of Co. Cork.

Ó ceanᵹᴌacáɪn, Tighe. This form is found in the spoken language of Mayo, but seems to be merely a 'translation' of the English or angl. surname Tighe.

Ó ceannᴅubáɪn—I—*O Cannovane, O Canavan, O Kennavain*, Cannavan, Canavan, Kinavan, and, by 'translation,' Whitehead ; 'des. of Ceannᴅubán' (dim. of Ceannᴅub, i.e., black-head) ; the name of a West Connacht family who, according to MacFirbis, were physicians to Muinntear Murchadha, the clan of which the O'Flahertys were chiefs. The name was also in Co. Cork and other parts of Ireland. Though really meaning black-head, it has been ' translated ' Whitehead, the termination having been mistaken for bán, white.

Ó ceannᴅuɪb—I—*O Canyve, O Kannife*, Canniff, Canniffe ; ' des. of Ceannᴅub ' (black-head) ; a rare Cork surname ; possibly an alias for Ó Ceannᴅubáɪn, q.v.

Ó cearáɪn—I—Kerrane, Kirrane, Kearon, Kearons, (Carr, Carey), &c. ; a corruption (or older form) of Ó Cɪaᴘáɪn, q.v. ; common in Mayo ; also Ó Cɪoᴘáɪn, q.v.

Ó cearbaɪᴌᴌ—I—*O Carrowill, O Carwell, O Carvill*, O'Carroll, Carroll, Carvill ; ' des. of Ceaᴘbaᴌᴌ ' (a very common Irish personal name). There are several distinct families so named, of which the following are the best known : (1) Ó Ceaᴘbaɪᴌᴌ of Eile, who derive their name and descent from Ceaᴘbaᴌᴌ, lord of Eile, who fought at Clontarf. The head of this family was originally lord of all Eile, which comprised the baronies of Clonlisk and Ballybritt, in the present Offaly, and Ikerrin and Eliogarty, in Co. Tipperary ;

but after the Anglo-Norman invasion, Ikerrin and Eliogarty became tributary to the Earl of Ormond, and only the portion of Eile subsequently called Ely O'Carroll, remained in possession of O'Carroll, who resided at Birr. This family is now very numerous. (2) Ó Ceaṅḃaill of Oriel. This family is of the same stock as the MacMahons and Maguires, and were chiefs of Oriel until about the period of the Anglo-Norman invasion, when they disappear from history. They are still numerous in Monaghan and Louth. (3) Ó Ceaṅḃaill of Loch Lein, anciently chiefs of the Eoghanacht of Loch Lein, the district about Killarney, until dispossessed by the O'Donoghues. (4) Ó Ceaṅ-ḃaill of Ossory who are descended from Ceaṅḃall, a celebrated chieftain of Ossory at the middle of the 9th century. (5) Ó Ceaṅḃaill of Tara, a branch of the southern Ui Neill. This family disappeared from history at an early period. (6) Ó Ceaṅḃaill of Calry, in Sligo and Leitrim. The MacBradys of Cavan are said, but erroneously, to be a branch of this family.

Ó ceaRḃÁın—I—*O Carvan, O Kervan,* Carvan, Carvin, Kervan, (Kirwan) ; ' des. of Ceaṅḃán ' (probably dim. of ceaṅḃ, a stag, Lat. cervus) ; a rare Leinster surname.

Ó ceaRḃaLLÁın—I—*O Carowlane, O Carolan,* Carolan, Carrolan, &c. ; ' des. of Ceaṅḃallán ' (dim. of Ceaṅ-ḃall) ; a well-known Ulster surname ; formerly common in Donegal, Tyrone, Monaghan and Cavan ; also in Meath. There are probably several distinct families of the name. To be distinguished from Ó CoiṅeaLLáın, q.v.

Ó ceaRmaoa—I—*O Carmody, O Kermody,* Carmody, Kermody ; ' des of Ceaṅmaiṽ ' (a very ancient Irish personal name) ; an old and still well-known Thomond surname.

Ó ceaRnacÁın—I—*O Kernaghan, O Kernan,* Carnahan, Kernaghan, Kernahan, Kernan, Kernon, &c. ; ' des. of Ceaṅnacán ' (dim. of Ceaṅnac, victorious) ; the name (1) of a Meath family who were anciently chiefs of Luighne, now the barony of Lune ; and (2) of a Tirconnell family who were chiefs of Tuath Bladhach, now angl. Doe, in the barony of Kilmacrenan.

Ó ceaᴚnaiᵹ—I—*O Carny*, O'Kearney, Carney, Kearney, &c. ; ' des. of Ceaᴘnac ' (victorious) ; the name (1) of a Dalcassian family who in later times attained to a high position at Cashel ; (2) of a family of Ui Fiachrach in Co. Mayo who formerly held extensive possessions in the parishes of Moynulla and Balla ; and (3) of an ecclesiastical family who were formerly erenaghs of Derry. The name cannot now always be distinguished from Ó Ceiceaᴘnaiᵹ, q.v.

Ó céaᴄᴘaᴅa—I—Keaty, (Keating) ; ' des. of Céaᴄᴘaiᴅ ' (sense) ; the name of a Dalcassian family who were anciently seated in the neighbourhood of the city of Limerick ; apparently also a Leinster surname.

Ó céile—I—*O Kely*, Kealy, Wisdom ; ' des. of Céile ' (servant, friend, companion) ; the name of an ecclesiastical family who were erenaghs of Tullow, Co. Carlow, and of another who were erenaghs of Slaine, Co. Meath. It is said to be now angl. by ' translation,' Wisdom in Co. Louth.

Ó céileaᴄáin—I—*O Kellechan*, *O Kellichan*, Kelaghan, Keleghan, Kellaghan, Keelaghan, Kelihan, (O'Callaghan, Callaghan), &c. ; ' des of Céileaᴄán ' (dim. of Céile) ; the name of an Armagh family who were anciently chiefs of Ui Breasail ; to be distinguished from Ó Ceallaᴄáin, q.v.

Ó céileaᴄaiᴚ—I—*O Keallaghir*, O'Kelliher, Kellegher, Kelleher, Kelliher, Keller, &c. ; ' des of Céileaᴄaᴘ ' (companion-dear, spouse-loving) ; the name of a wellknown family in Cork and Kerry. They are of Dalcassian origin, being descended from Donnchuan, brother of Brian Boru.

Ó céin—I—*O Keyne*, *O Kean*, Kean, Keane ; ' des. of Ciaɴ ' (an old Irish personal name) ; the name of a Waterford family who were anciently chiefs of a district bordering on the River Mahon. To this family belonged, according to O'Donovan, the two great tragedians, Edmund Keane and his son, Charles John

Keane. Ó Céin was also the name of a Derry family.
It is now very rare and its angl. forms cannot be distinguished from those of Ó Catáin, q.v.

Ó ceinnéroro, Ó ceinnéroiʒ, v. Ó Cinnéroro, Ó
Cinnéroiʒ.

Ó ceinnſeaʟaiʒ, v. Ó Cinnſeaʟaiʒ.

Ó céiriṅ—I—*O Kearin, O Kerine, O Kerrin*, Cairn,
Kearin, Kearn, Kereen, Kerin, Kerrin, Cairns, Kearns,
Kerins, Kerrins, Kerns, (Carey), &c. ; ' des. of Céiriṅ '
(dim. of ciaṅ, black) ; the name of a family who were
anciently lords of Ciarraighe Locha na n-airne, in the
barony of Costello, Co. Mayo, and doubtless of several
other families in different parts of Ireland. In the
16th century, it was very widespread, and is now
represented in every province. V. Ó Ciaṅáin, with
which it is synnoymous.

Ó ceiriſc, v. Mac Fiaṅaiſ.

Ó ceit—I—*O Kett*, Kett ; ' des. of Ceat ' ; a rare West
Clare surname. The family is probably descended
from Ceat, son of Flaithbheartach, lord of Corca
Modhruaidh, who flourished early in the 10th century.

Ó ceiteaRnaiʒ—I—*O Keherne, O Kerny, O Kerne*,
Keherny, Kerney, (Kearney, Kerns, Kearns) ; ' des.
of Ceiteaṅnac ' (foot-soldier, one of a ceiteaṅn,
or company of foot-soldiers) ; the name (1) of a family
in Co. Roscommon, also called Mac Ceiteaṅnaiʒ (q.v.),
who were chiefs of Ciarraighe, in the barony of Castlerea ; and (2) of a West Cork family. These are the
only families of which there is record, but there were,
doubtless, others, as the name in the 16th century was
rather widespread, being found in Tipperary, Kilkenny, Westmeath, Offaly, and Donegal, as well as
in Roscommon and Cork. Its angl. forms cannot
always be distinguished from those of Ó Ceaṅnaiʒ, q.v.

Ó ceocáin—IV—Keoghane, Keohane, &c. ; a corruption, in West Cork, of Mac Eocáin, q.v. The eo of
this surname, as I have heard it, is pronounced short.

Ó ceóiniṅ—IV—O'Keoneen, Keoneen, Jennings. V.
Mac Seóiniṅ.

Ó Ciaḃaiʒ—I—Keavy, Keevey ; ' des. of Ciaḃaċ ' (having long locks of hair) ; very rare.

Ó Ciaḃáin—I—*O Kivane*, Keevane, Keavan ; 'des. of Ciaḃán ' (dim. of Ciaḃaċ) ; the name of a family of Corca Laoighdhe, in West Cork. It can with difficulty be distinguished from Ó Caoṁáin, q.v.

Ó Cianaiʒ—I—O'Keeney, Keaney, Keany, Keeney, Keeny ; ' des. of *Cianaċ ' (der. of Cian) ; or perhaps more correctly Ó Caoinniʒ, ' des. of Caoinneaċ ' (a var. of Coinneaċ) ; in use in Galway and Donegal.

Ó Cianáin—I—*O Kinane, O Keynan*, O'Keenan, Keenan, Kinnan ; ' des of. Cianán ' (dim. of cian) ; the name of a literary family in Ulster, who were hereditary historians to the Maguires ; still numerous in that province.

Ó Ciaraʒáin—I—*O Kierregain, O Kerigane*, Kerigan, Kerrigan, Kergan, and, by 'translation,' Comber, Comer ; ' des. of Ciaraʒán ' (dim. of ciar, black) ; the name of a branch of the Ui Fiachrach, formerly seated at Baile Ui Chiaragain, now angl. Ballykerrigan, in the parish of Balla, Co. Mayo. Before the end of the 16th century, the name had ramified into Donegal and Tyrone. In the north of Co. Galway, it is often ' translated ' Comber and Comer, from its supposed connection with ' cíor,' a comb.

Ó Ciaráin—I—*O Kearane, O Kirrane*, O'Kieran, Kieran, Kearon, Kearn, Keern, Keirans, Kearons, Kerans, Kerons, Kearns, Kerns, Cairns, Comber, Comer, (Carey) ; ' des. of Ciarán ' (dim. of ciar, black) ; the name (1) of a Tirconnell family who were formerly lords of Fearmhaigh in Co. Donegal ; and (2) of a Cork family, originally seated in the barony of Imokilly. Ó Ciaráin is the same surname as Ó Céirín (q.v.), which is the more common form, and is also a var. in parts of Connacht of Ó Ciaraʒáin. For explanation of the angl. forms Comber and Comer, see under Ó Ciaraʒáin above.

Ó Ciarḃa—I—*O Kerby*, Kerby, Kirby ; a corruption, in Limerick and Kerry, of Ó Ciarṁaic, q.v.

Ó Ciarḋa—I—*O Kirry, O Kerry*, Keery, Keary, Karey,

Carey, &c. ; ' des. of Ciaróa ' (der. of ciar, black) ;
the name of a family of the southern Ui Neill who were
lords of Cairbre, the present barony of Carbury in
the north-west of Co. Kildare, until the period of the
Anglo-Norman invasion, when they disappear from
history. The name is, however, still common in
Kildare, Meath, Westmeath, and many parts of the
south of Ireland, but generally angl. Carey, which
makes it difficult to distinguish it from the many other
names similarly anglicised.

Ó CIARDUBÁIN—I—*O Kerevan, O Kerrywane*, O'Kirwan, Kierevan, Kiervan, Kirivan, Kerevan, Kerivan,
Kirvan, Kirwan, Kirwin, &c. ; ' des. of Ciardubán '
(dim. of ciardub, jet-black) ; the name of a family
who were anciently erenaghs of Louth, and apparently
of another family in Co. Clare. The Kirwans were
in later times an important family in the city of
Galway. Their claim to be of English origin is rightly
denied by O'Donovan, there being no such English
family name.

Ó CIARMACÁIN—I—*O Kerymokyn*, (Irwin, Irwine, Carey);
' des. of Ciarmacán ' (dim. of Ciarmac, black-son) ; a
rare Munster surname.

Ó CIARMAIC—I—*O Kervick, O Kerwick, O Kervy, O
Kerby*, Kerwick, Keerwick, Kerby, Kirby ; ' des. of
Ciarmac ' (black-son) ; the name of an ancient family
in East Limerick, who were chiefs of Eoghanacht
Aine, the district lying around Knockany, until after
the Anglo-Norman invasion, and are still numerous
not only in Limerick, but throughout Munster. It
would appear from the Annals of the Four Masters
(A.D. 1087) that there was another family of the same
name in Leinster, doubtless that now represented by
Kerwick in Co. Kilkenny. Ó Ciarmaic has long been
corrupted in the spoken language of Limerick and
Kerry to Ó Ciarba, q.v.

Ó CIBIL—I—*O Kiwilla*, Keville, Kiville ; apparently a
shortened form of Ó Cibleacáin, q.v. ; in use in Mayo
and Galway.

Ó cıbleаċáın—I—*O Kiveleghan*, Kevlihan, Kevlean, Keevlin ; 'des. of Cıbleаċán'; the name of a Westmeath family who were coarbs of St. Feichin at Fore ; now rare and scattered. V. Ó Cıbıl and Ó Cıblín, which appear to be shortened forms of this surname.

Ó cıblín—I—Keevlin, Kevlean, Keville, Kiville ; a var. in parts of Mayo of Ó Cıbıl (q.v.), and apparently the same as Ó Cıbleаċáın, q.v.

Ó cılleáın—I—*O Killane*, Killane, Killan, Killian, Killion ; 'des. of Cılleán' (dim. of Ceаllаċ) ; a var. in Clare and Galway of Ó Cıllín, q.v.

Ó cıllín—I—*O Killine, O Killen*, Killeen, Killen, Killian, Killion ; 'des. of Cıllín' (a 'pet' dim. of Ceаllаċ, war) ; the name of several distinct families in different parts of the country, as Clare, Galway, Mayo, Westmeath, Offaly, Kildare and Down, in all of which it is still extant.

Ó cıneáıċ, Kinna, Kenna, Kennah, &c. ; a var. in the spoken language of Ó Cıonаoıċ, q.v.

Ó cınᵹeаᵭ—I—*O Kinga, O King*, King ; 'des. of Cınᵹeаᵭ' (valiant). This surname belonged chiefly to Westmeath, Offaly, Galway and Clare. Also written Ó Cıonᵹа, q.v.

Ó cınnċnáṁа—I—Kinnavy, Kineavy ; 'des. of Ceаnnċnáṁа' (bone-head) ; the name of a branch of the Ui Fiachrach, who were anciently proprietors of a district in the barony of Carra, Co. Mayo, where the family is still extant. I have not been able to discover any early angl. form of the name.

Ó cınnᵭeаrᵹáın—I—*O Kinregane*, Kindregan, Kinregan ; 'des. of Ceаnnᵭeаrᵹán' (dim. of Ceаnnᵭeаrᵹ, red-head) ; a rare Thomond surname.

Ó cınnéıᵭe, ó cınnéıᵭıᵭ, ó cınnéıᵭıᵹ—I—*O Kinedy*, O'Kennedy, Kennedy ; 'des. of Cınnéıᵭıᵭ' (helmeted-head) ; the name of at least two families in Ireland : (1) Ó C. of Ormond, a branch of the ᵭál ᵹCаır, who derive their name and descent from Cınnéıᵭıᵹ, son of Donnchuan the brother of Brian

Boru. They were originally seated at Glenomra, co-extensive with the present parish of Killokennedy, in the east of Co. Clare, but on being driven thence at an early period by the O'Briens and MacNamaras, they settled in Tipperary, in the baronies of Upper and Lower Ormond, where they became very numerous and far more powerful than they had ever been in their ancient home in Thomond. From the 12th to the 16th century, they ranked as lords of Ormond, and were divided into three great branches, viz: Ó C. Fionn (the Fair), Ó C. Donn (the Brown), and Ó C. Ruadh (the Red). (2) Ó C. of Clann Cearnaigh, a branch of the Ui Maine, in Co. Galway. The name is now very common throughout Ireland.

Ó CINNḞAOLAIDH—I—*O Kenneally, O Kennelly,* O'Kinnealy, Kinnealy, Kinneally, Kennealy, Kennelly, &c.; 'des. of Ceannḟaoladh' (wolf-head, learned man); the name of a branch of the Ui Fidhgheinte, in Co, Limerick, who were seated in Ui Conaill Gabhra, now the baronies of Upper and Lower Connello, until dispossessed by the Fitzgeralds and other Anglo-Norman settlers soon after the invasion. The name is, however, still common in West Limerick and in Kerry. To be distinguished from Ó Coingeallaig, q.v.

Ó CINNSEALAIGH—I—*O Kynsillaghe,* Kinshela, Kinsella, Kinsley, &c.; 'des. of Cinnsealach'; the name of a Wexford family who are descended from Eanna Cinnsealach, son of Diarmaid MacMurchadha; usually Cinnsealach, without the Ó. Cf. Caomhánach.

Ó CINNSEAMÁIN, Kingston, Kingstone; a var. of Mac Oinseamáin, q.v.

Ó CIOḂLAĊÁIN—I—*O Kiveleghan,* Kevlihan, Coolihan; a var., in parts of Connacht, of Ó Ciḃleaċáin, q.v.

Ó CIOBÚIN—IV—O'Kibbon; a corruption of Mac Giobúin, q.v.

Ó CÍOCARÁIN—I—*O Kiereaghan,* Keighron, (Kerrigan); 'des. of Ciocarán' (hungry); the name of a branch of the Siol-Anmchadha in Co. Galway. It seems to have been sometimes metathesised to Ó Cíoraċáin, angl. *O Kiereaghan*, Kerrigan. It has always been very rare.

Ó Cionáiṫ, v. Ó Cionaoḋa.

Ó Cionaoḋa, Ó Cionaoiṫ—I—*O Kenaith*, *O Kenny*, *O Kenna*, Kinna, Kinney, Kenna, Kenny, &c.; 'des. of Cionaoḋ' (fire-sprung); the name of several distinct families in different parts of Ireland. It was common, in the 16th century, in all parts of Leinster and Munster, and in Galway, Roscommon and Tyrone.

Ó Cionᵹa—I or II—*O Kenga*, *O Kinga*, King; a var. of Ó Cinᵹeaḋ, q.v.

Ó Cioráin—I—*O Kirrane*, Kirrane, Kerrane, &c.; a corruption of Ó Ciaráin, q.v. See also Ó Ceapáin.

Ó Cíorḋuḃáin, v. Ó Ciarḋuḃáin.

Ó Ciosáin—I—*O Kissaine*, *O Kissane*, Kissane, (Cashman); a var., in Kerry and Cork, of Ó Caráin, q.v.

Ó Cirṁic—I—*O Kiervicke*, Keerivick, Kerwick; 'des. of Ciarṁac' (black-son); a var. of Ó Ciarṁaic, q.v.; very rare.

Ó Ciseáin—I—*O Kishane*, Keeshan; an attenuated form of Ó Cioráin, q.v.

Ó Claḃaiᵹ—I—*O Clabby*, Clabby; 'des. of Claḃaċ' (thick-lipped, wide-mouthed); the name of an old Roscommon family who were erenaghs of the church founded by St. Patrick at Oran, in the barony of Ballymoe, and noted for their hospitality.

Ó Claiṁín, Ó Claṁáin—I—*O Clavan*, Clavan, Claveen, Clavin, Swords, &c.; 'des. of Claiṁín' or 'Claṁán' (dim. of claṁ, a sick person, a leper); a not uncommon surname in Mayo, but generally angl. Swords, which is supposed to be a translation. Cf. claiḋeaṁ, a sword.

Ó Claonáin—I—*O Clenan*, Clinane, (Conlon); 'des. of Claonán' (dim. of claon, bent); a rare surname. It appears to have originated in Kildare, but I have found it as the Irish for Conlon in parts of Mayo.

Ó Claṫáin—I—Clahane, Clehane; a metathesised form of Ó Caṫláin, q.v.

Ó Cléireacáin, Ó Cléircín—I—*O Clearkane*, *O*

Clercan, Clerihan, Clerkan, Clerkin, Clarkins, Clarke, &c. ; ' des. of Cléipeacán,' or ' Cléipcín ' (dim. of Cléipeac, cleric, clerk) ; the name (1) of a family of Ui Fidhgheinte who were anciently lords of Ui Cairbre Aebhdha, in the east of Co. Limerick ; now represented by Clerihan in Co. Tipperary ; and (2) of a Meath family who were anciently lords of Coillte Fallamhain. This family probably removed to Monaghan and Cavan, where the name was common at the end of the 16th century.

Ó CLÉIRIₓ—I—O'Clery, O'Cleary, Clery, Cleary, Clarke, &c. ; ' des. of Cléipeac ' (cleric, clerk). This family derives its name and descent from an ancestor named Cléipeac who flourished about the middle of the 9th century, and was the seventh in descent from the celebrated Guaire the Hospitable, King of Connacht. They were at one time the ruling family of Aidhne, co-extensive with the diocese of Kilmacduagh, but early in the 11th century they lost their power, and towards the close of the 13th, were finally driven out of Aidhne and dispersed to different parts of Ireland. One branch of the family settled in Tirawley, Co. Mayo, another in Co. Cavan, and a third in the neighbourhood of Kilkenny. From the Tirawley branch sprang the O'Clerys of Tirconnell, who succeeded the O'Scingins as poets and chroniclers to the O'Donnells, and became celebrated in Irish literary history as the compilers of the Annals of the Four Masters and other valuable works on Irish history and antiquities. Besides the patrimony of the O'Scingins which they inherited by marriage, the O'Clerys obtained large grants of land from the O'Donnells. Their residence was at the castle of Kilbarron, near Ballyshannon. The family is now very numerous throughout Ireland, but the name is often disguised, especially in Ulster, under the translated form of Clarke.

Ó CLOCARTAIₓ—I—*O Cloghertie*, Clogherty, Cloherty, and, by ' translation,' Stone ; ' des. of Clocapcac ' ; a Galway surname.

Ó CLOCASAIᵹ—I—O'Cloghessy, O'Clohessy, Cloghessy, Clohessy ; ' des. of Cloċaṙaċ ' ; an old Thomond surname, still well known in Clare and Limerick. The O'Cloghessys, in the 16th and early 17th century, owned the townland of Ballynaglearach, in the parish of O'Gonnelloe, Co. Clare.

Ó CLOTACÁIN—I—O Cloghane, Clogan, (Callaghan) ; ' des. of Cloṫaċán ' (dim. of clotaċ, famous) ; the name of an old ecclesiastical family the head of which was ' steward of St. Patrick ' in Munster, now angl. Clogan in Co. Limerick. It appears to be the same as the name which is pronounced Ó Colaċáin in West Clare and angl. Callaghan.

Ó CLUAIN, O Clowne, Clune ; a shortened form of Ó Cluanaiᵹ, q.v.

Ó CLUANAIᵹ—I—O Clony, Cloney, Cluney, Clowney, Clowny, Cloony ; ' des. of Cluanaċ ' (deceitful) ; an old surname in South Leinster.

Ó CLUANÁIN—I—O Clonan, Clunan, Cloonan ; ' des. of Cluanán ' (dim. of Cluanaċ) ; a rare Galway surname.

Ó CLUASAIᵹ—I—O Closse, Close ; ' des. of Cluaṙaċ ' (having large ears) ; an old surname in Antrim and Tyrone.

Ó CLÚṁÁIN—I—O Clufwayne, O Clovane, O Clowan, Cluvane, Clovan, Cloven, (Coleman, Clifford) ; ' des of Clúṁán ' (dim. of clúṁaċ, hairy, from clúṁ, down, feathers, Lat. pluma) ; the name of a literary and bardic family in Co. Sligo who were poets and chroniclers to the O'Haras. Branches of the family settled early in South Leinster and West Munster, where the name is now common, but disguised under the angl. forms of Coleman and Clifford. The fact that these forms are also in use in the original territory is a proof that the families of the name in the south of Ireland are of the Sligo stock. Coleman, as an angl. form, seems to have arisen from confusion of the present surname with Ó Clomáin, a metathesised form current in the spoken language of Ó Colmáin.

Ó CNÁIṀÍN—I—O Knavin, Navin, Nevin, Bowen, (Neville) ; ' des. of Cnáiṁín' (dim. of cnáṁ, a bone, an old Irish personal name) ; the name of a Dalcassian family, descended from Coscrach, son of Lorcan, King of Munster. The name was common, at the end of the 16th century, in many places outside of Thomond. Bowen is intended as a translation (Ir. cnáṁ, a bone). Neville is used as an angl. form in parts of West Clare.

Ó Cnáiṁsiᵹe—I—*O Cnawsie, O Knawsie, O Crashie*, Kneafsey, Neaphsey, Neecy, Cramsie, Crampsey, &c., and, by ' translation,' Boner, Bonner, &c. ; ' des. of Cnáiṁreac' (a woman's name, corresponding to Cnáiṁín) ; a Donegal surname ; now also in Mayo, often corrupted to Ó Cráiṁriᵹe. It is one of our very few metronymic surnames.

Ó coḃċaiᵹ—I—*O Coffie, O Cohy*, Coffey, Cowhey, Cowey, Cowhig, &c. ; ' des. of Coḃċac' (victorious) ; the name of several distinct families in different parts of Ireland, viz.: (1) Ó C. of Corca Laoighdhe, an ancient and once powerful family in West Cork, of the same stock as the O'Driscolls. They were seated in the barony of Barryroe, where Dun Ui Chobhthaigh, angl. Dunocowhey, marks the site of their residence. The final ᵹ is often sounded in South Munster, hence the angl. form Cowhig. (2) Ó C. of Ui Maine, of the same stock as the O'Maddens, who possessed considerable property, down to the 17th century, in the barony of Clonmacnowen, Co. Galway, and had their residence at Tuaim Catraigh, angl. Tomcatry. (3) Ó C. of Umhall, anciently lords of Umhall, Co. Mayo. (4) Ó C. of Westmeath, a celebrated bardic family. (5) Ó C. of Derry, a family which produced many worthy ecclesiastics.

Ó coċláin—I—*O Coghlaine, O Coughlane*, Coghlan, Coughlan, Coughlin, Coghlin, Colin, &c. ; ' des. of Coċlán' (dim. of coċal, a cape or hood) ; an ancient and still common surname in Co. Cork ; to be distinguished from Ó Caċaláin, q.v.

Ó cooláca—I—*O Collitie*, Culloty, Cullity ; ' des. of

*Coᴅlaᴅ ' (sleep) ; a rare Kerry surname, pronounced Ó Collaca.

Ó coᴅlacáin—I—*O Colletane,* Colleton, Collotan, Culleton, Culliton, (Cullington) ; ' des. of Coᴅlacán ' (sleeper) ; an alias for mac Coᴅlacáin, q.v.

Ó cogaráin—I—*O Cogran,* Coghran, Caughran, (Cochrane, Cockrane) ; ' des. of Cogapán ' (possibly dim. of cogap, a confidant) ; an alias for mac Cogapáin, q.v.

Ó coiᴅᴅeanaig—I—Coveney, Keveny, (?) Keverney ; ' des. of Coiᴅᴅeanac ' (leader or member of a troop, Ir. coiᴅᴅean) ; the name of an Ossory family who were anciently chiefs of Magh Airbh, in the barony of Crannagh, Co. Kilkenny ; now very rare.

Ó coigealaig—I—*O Keagalagh, O Kegelagh, O Kegley,* Kegley ; ' des. of Coigealac ' (an untidy person) ; a var. of Ó Coiglig, q.v.

Ó coiglig—I—*O Cogly, O Cwigley, O Quigly, O Kegly,* O'Coigley, O'Quigley, Cogley, Kegley, Quigley, Twigley ; ' des. of Coigleac ' (der. of coigeal, a distaff, an untidy person, with unkempt hair) ; the name of a branch of the Ui Fiachrach who were anciently seated in the barony of Carra, Co. Mayo. In the 16th century, the name was common in Sligo, Donegal, Monaghan, Carlow, Wexford and Waterford.

Ó coileáin—I—*O Collaine, O Collan,* Collen, Collins ; ' des. of Coileán ' (whelp) ; the name of a family of the Ui Fidhgheinte in the present Co. Limerick, who are of the same stock as the O'Donovans and were originally lords of Ui Conaill Gabhra, now the baronies of Upper and Lower Connello. In the year 1178, they were expelled from this territory and the main body of the clan settled in West Cork. Those who remained continued to be lords of Claonghlas, a district in the south-west of the county, until towards the end of the 13th century, when they were dispossessed by the Fitzgeralds. The name is now very common in the original territory of the family and throughout

Munster, but is universally angl. Collins. V. Ó
Cuiteáin which is a variant.

Ó coilṁin—I—*O Culliggine*, Quiligan, Quilligan; an
attenuated form of Ó Colʒán, q.v.

Ó coiliʒ—I—*O Quilly, O Killie*, Cox, Woods; ' des of
Coileać' (cock); a rare surname in Donegal and
parts of Connacht.

Ó coiṁín—I—*O Comyn*, Comyn; ' des. of Coiṁín ' (dim.
of cáṁ, crooked); a var. of Ó Cuiṁín and Ó Comáin,
q.v.

Ó coineáin—I—*O Kenane*, Kennane; ' des. of Coineán '
(same as Coiṁín); a var. of Ó Cuineáin. q.v.

Ó coineóil—I—Conole, Connole; ' des of Coineóil ';
the name of a Sligo family who were anciently coarbs
of Drumcliffe; now represented by Conole and Connole in Co. Clare.

Ó coinʒeállaiʒ—I—*O Cangelly, O Connilla, O Ken-*
nelly, Kangley, Quinnelly, Kennelly, (Connelly), &c.;
' des. of Coinʒeállać ' (pledged, serving under con-
ditions); the name of a West Cork family who were retainers of the O'Donovans, from whom they held at one
time seven ploughlands in the parish of Drinagh, near
Drimoleague. The name was also in Ormond. Mac
Coinʒeállaiʒ was an alias in both places.

Ó coinʒill—I—*O Coniell, O Coinnill, O Kennell*, Quinnell; apparently a shortened form of Ó Coinʒeállaiʒ;
in use in Cork and Tipperary at the end of the 16th
century, but always very rare.

Ó coiṁín—I—*O Conyne, O Kenyn*, Conyeen, Cuneen,
Cunneen, Cunnien, &c., and, by ' translation,' Rabbit;
' des. of Coiṁín ' (probably a dim. of cáno, a whelp,
wolf, if not a var. of Conán); a rare surname; found
chiefly in the midlands.

Ó coinleisc, Ó coinlisc—I—*O Conliske, O Coynliske*,
Cunlisk, Quinlisk, Quinlish, (Grimes); the name of a
literary family in Connacht; now rare, and in West
Mayo strangely angl. Grimes. V. Ó Cuinoúir.

Ó coinne—I—*O Cunny, O Quiney*, Conney, Cunny,
Quinny, (Kenny, Quin), &c; ' des. of Coinne ' (a var.

of Coinneᴀċ) ; a not uncommon Ulster surname. The
family was originally seated in Ui Eachach, in Co.
Down, but seems to have afterwards removed to the
neighbourhood of Strabane.

Ó coinneᴀċáin—I—*O Kenaghan*, Kinaghan, Kinahan,
&c. ; ' des. of Coinneᴀċán ' (dim. of Conn) ; a var. of
Ó Cuinneᴀċáin, q.v.

Ó coirbín—I—*O Corbin*, O'Corrobeen, Coribeen, Corbin,
Kerbin, (Corbett, Kirby), &c. ; ' des. of Coirbín ' ;
var. of Ó Coṙbáin, q.v. ; in Connacht, often pronounced Ó Croibín, q.v.

Ó coireᴀlláin—I—*O Kerolan*, Curland, Kerlin, Kirlin,
Kirland ; ' des. of Coireᴀllán ' (dim. of Coireᴀll) ;
a var. of Ó Cairpeᴀlláin q.v.

Ó coirill—I—*O Kirle*, Kirrell ; ' des. of Coireᴀll '
(older Cairpeᴀll) ; very rare.

Ó coirín, Curreen, Currin, Creen, &c. ; a var. of Ó
Copparóin, q.v.

Ó coise—I—*O Coishe*, *O Cushie*, *O Coshe*, Quish ; the
name of an old Leix family ; now very rare and found
chiefly in Co. Tipperary, where it is angl. Quish.

Ó coistín—V—Costine, Costin, Costen ; a corruption
of Mᴀc Oirtín, q.v.

Ó coitil—II—Cottle ; ' des. of Ketill ' (a Norse personal
name ; cf. Mᴀc Coitil) ; the name of a branch of the
Ui Fiachrach in Co. Sligo, who resided at Baile Ui
Choitil, now angl. Cottlestown, in the parish of Castle-
conor. O'Donovan found it still in the district under
the angl. form of Cottle.

Ó colgán—I—*O Colgan*, *O Collogan*, *O Culligan*, Colgan,
Collogan, Culligan, Quilligan, &c. ; ' des. of Colgᴀ ' ;
more anciently Mᴀc Colgᴀn ; the name of an old
family in Offaly, of the same stock as the O'Connors,
O'Dempseys and O'Dunnes ; also common in Thomond.

Ó collᴀ—I—*O Collo*, *O Cully*, *O Colle*, Cully, Coll ; ' des.
of Collᴀ.'

Ó collᴀtᴀ, *O Collitie*, Culloty ; also written Ó Coolᴀtᴀ ;
a rare Kerry surname.

Ó colmáin—I—*O Colman, O Collomayne*, Colman, Coleman; 'des. of colmán' (dim. of colm, dove, a very common Irish personal name); the name of a family of the Ui Fiachrach, who were anciently seated in the townland of Grangemore, in the parish of Templeboy, Co. Sligo; and doubtless of several others in different parts of the country. It was most common, in the 16th century, in Cork, Tipperary, Waterford, Dublin, Wexford, Meath, Longford, Roscommon and Cavan. It is sometimes metathesised to Ó clomáin.

Ó colpa, Ó colpta—I—*O Colloupy*, Collopy; 'des. of colpta' (calf of the leg, an ancient Irish personal name); an old Limerick surname; very rare.

Ó coltair—I—O'Colter, Colter, Coalter, Coulter; 'des. of coltar'; seemingly a var. of Ó coltarpáin, q.v.

Ó coltaráin—I—*O Coultran*, O'Colter, Colter, &c.; 'des. of coltarán'; the name of an ancient family in Co. Down, from whom the parish of Ballycolter probably derives its name. It seems to have been shortened to Ó coltaip, q.v.

Ó comáin—I—*O Comane, O Comman, O Cowmane*, Coman, Commane, Cowman, Cummane, Commons, &c., and, by 'translation,' Hurley; 'des. of comán' (dim. of cam, bent, crooked); formerly a very common surname, and found in all the provinces, especially in Munster. The var. Ó cuimín (q.v.) seems to have been, in recent times, substituted for it in many instances. It is sometimes 'translated' Hurley. Cf. 'camán,' a hurly.

Ó comaltáin—I—*O Cowltayn*, Coul:on, Colton; 'des. of comaltán' (dim. of comalta, foster-brother); the name of a branch of the O'Clerys in South Galway; now very rare, if not actually obsolete.

Ó comdáin—I—*O Coain, O Coan, O Cowan*, Coan, Coen, Cowan, Cowen, (Coyne), &c.; 'des. of comgan' (cobirth); also written Ó comgain; the name of a branch of the Ui Fiachrach, anciently seated in the parish of Dunfeeny, Co. Sligo, but in the 16th century more numerous in Galway and Roscommon. The name is still well known in Connacht, usually angl. Coen.

Ó coṁṛaroe—I—*O Cowrie, O Cory*, O'Curry, Corey, Corry, Curry ; ' des. of Coṁṗaroe ' ; the name (1) of a Westmeath family who were anciently chiefs of Ui Mac Uais, now the barony of Moygoish ; (2) of a family of Corca Laoighdhe, in South-west Cork ; and (3) of a branch of the Dal gCais in Thomond, to which belonged the celebrated Eugene O'Curry.

Ó conaill—I—*O Conaill*, O'Connell, Connell ; ' des. of Conaill ' (high-powerful, an ancient personal name Welsh Cynvall, British Cunovalos, Celtic Kunovalos) ; the name of at least three distinct families in Ireland, viz. : (1) Ó Conaill of Derry, a branch of the Oirghialla, who were anciently lords of Ui Mac Carthainn, now the barony of Tirkeeran ; (2) Ó Conaill of Galway, a branch of the Ui Maine, who anciently possessed a territory in the south of Co. Galway, between the river Grian and the borders of Thomond ; and (3) Ó Conaill of Kerry, who were anciently chiefs of Magh O gCoinchin, in the east of that county, until dispossessed by the O'Donoghues about the middle of the 11th century. From the time of the Anglo-Norman invasion down to the 17th century, the O'Connells were followers of MacCarthy More and hereditary castellans of Ballycarbery, near Caherciveen. Maurice O'Connell, the head of the family in Cromwell's time, was transplanted to Brentir, near Lisdoonvarna, in Co. Clare. Several of this family became distinguished in the Irish Brigades in the service of France, among whom may be mentioned Count Daniel O'Connell, uncle of the Liberator, Daniel O'Connell, by whom this surname has been made for ever illustrious. O'Connell is now one of the most numerous of Irish surnames. O'Heerin writes the name of the Kerry family Ó Conġaile, but Ó Conaill is the form now universally in use in Munster.

Ó conáin—I—*O Conane, O Conan*, Conan, Cunnane ; ' des. of Conán ' (dim. of ' con,' high, or the ancient

Celtic personal name, Kunagnos) ; more commonly
Ó Cuineáin, q.v.

Ó conaing—I—*O Gunning,* Cunning, Gunning ; 'des.
of Conaing'; the name of a branch of the Dal gCais
who are descended from Donnchuan, brother of Brian
Boru. Before the Anglo-Norman invasion, they
were lords of Aos Greine, the present barony of Clanwilliam, Co. Limerick, and had their chief seat at
Caislean Ui Chonaing, now Castleconnell, but were
dispossessed, about the beginning of the 13th century,
by a branch of the Burkes. The name has now
entirely disappeared from Co. Limerick.

Ó conairce—I—Conarchy ; (?) 'des. of Cú-airce'
(hound of greed). Giolla Chriost Ó Conairce was
Bishop of Lismore and Papal Legate in Ireland about
the middle of the 12th century. The name is now
exceedingly rare.

Ó conaire—I—*O Connery, O Conrey,* Connery, Conry,
(Conroy), &c. ; 'des. of Conaire' (probably dog-
keeper, an ancient Irish personal name) ; an old
Munster surname, common throughout the province ;
to be distinguished from Ó Conraoi, q.v.

Ó conalláin—I—*O Connellane, O Conlan,* Connellan,
Conlan, &c. ; 'des. of Conallán' (dim. of Conall) ;
the name of a Roscommon family ; but in the 16th
century, it was found in all the provinces. Its angl.
forms cannot always be distinguished from those of
Ó Caoindealbáin, q.v.

Ó conallta—I—*O Conalty,* Conalty ; 'des. of Cú-
allaid' or 'Cú-allta' (wolf) ; a rare Ulster surname.

Ó conaráin—I—*O Conoran, O Coneran,* Conran, Conron, Condron, Condrin ; 'des. of Conarán'; an old
Offaly surname, now scattered through Leinster.

Ó conbáḡa—I—*O Conebaghe, O Conba,* Conba, Conbay,
(Conboy, Conaboy, Corbett) ; 'des. of Cú-báḡa'
(hound of battle) ; a rare surname. In the 16th
century, it was found chiefly in Offaly, Tipperary
and Cork ; now also in Connacht. In Co. Limerick it
is often disguised under the angl. form of Corbett.

Ó conbáin—I—*O Convane, O Convan,* Cunvane; 'des. of Cú-bán' (white-hound); very rare.

Ó conboirne—I—Burns; 'des. of Cú-boirne' (hound of Burren); apparently an alias for mac Conboirne, q.v.

Ó conburde—I—Conboy, Conaboy, Conwy, (Conway); 'des. of Cú-burde' (yellow-hound); the name (1) of a family of the Ui Fiachrach who were anciently seated at Dunneill, in the barony of Tireragh, Co. Sligo, and were still numerous in O'Donovan's time in the parish of Easky, in the same county; and (2) of a family of the Ui Maine, in Co. Galway. I have not been able to discover any early angl. form of the name in either district.

Ó conceanainn, Ó conceannainn—I—*O Concannen,* O'Concannon, Concannen, Concannon; 'des. of Cú-ceanainn' (fair-headed hound); the name of a well-known Galway family who were chiefs of Corca Mogha, angl. Corcamoe, in the north-east of that county. The head of the family resided at Kiltullagh, in the parish of Kilkerrin, or Corcamoe.

Ó concobair, Ó concubair—I—*O Conchor, O Connour,* O'Conor, O'Connor, Connor, Connors, &c.; 'des. of Concobar' (high-will or desire, an ancient Irish personal name); one of the most numerous and widespread of Irish family names. There are, at least, six distinct families so called, viz.: (1) Ó C. of Connacht who derive their name and descent from Concobar, King of Connacht in the latter part of the 10th century, and were long the ruling race in that province, and of whom two became kings of all Ireland. They were divided into three great branches, namely Ó Concobair Donn (the brown O'Connor), Ó Concobair Ruad (the red O'Connor), and Ó Concobair Sligeac (the O'Connor of Sligo). The present head of the family is known as The O'Conor Don. (2) Ó C. of Offaly who derive their descent from Ros Failghe, son of Cathaoir Mor, King of Ireland in the second century, and their surname from Concobar, son of Fionn, lord of Offaly, who died in the year 979. They were a powerful and warlike race, and for more than three hundred years successfully defended their territory against the English of the Pale. Their chief stronghold was Dangan, now Philipstown. They were dispossessed in the reign of Philip and Mary. (3) Ó C. of Kerry. Before the Anglo-Norman invasion, the head of this family was lord of that portion of Kerry lying between Tralee and the Shannon; but owing to the encroachments of the Fitzmaurices and other Anglo-Norman settlers this territory was narrowed down to the limits of the present barony of Iraghticonor (Oineacc Uí Concobaiṗ), which remained in the possession of the family until the close of the reign of Elizabeth, when it was confiscated and given to Trinity College. The chief stronghold of the O'Connors was Carrigafoyle, near Ballylongford. (4) Ó C. of Corcomroe. This family derives its name from Concobaṗ, son of Maelseachlainn, lord of Corcomroe, who was slain in the year 1002, and the head of the family was lord of the barony of Corcomroe, in West Clare, down to the close of the 16th century. (5) Ó C. of Keenaght. The head of this family was lord of Cianachta, now the barony of Keenaght, in Co. Derry, until dispossessed by the family of Ó Catáin, or O'Kane, shortly before the Anglo-Norman invasion. (6) Ó C. of Ui Breasail, a branch of the Oirghialla.

Ó Concobair ꝺonn—I—O'Conor Don; i.e., 'the brown O'Connor'; the designation of the head of a branch of the O'Connors of Connacht, in contradistinction to Ó Concobaiṗ Ruaꝺ and Ó Concobaiṗ Suigeac; now used as title of distinction.

Ó Conꝺubáin—I—O Condon, Condon; 'des. of Cú-ꝺubán'; the name of an Ulster family who were anciently erenaghs of Derryloran, in Co. Tyrone; now rare.

Ó Conꝺuiꝺ—I—Conniff, Conneff, Cunniffe, Quinniff, (Conliffe), &c.; 'des. of Cú-ꝺuḃ' (black-hound); a rare Connacht surname.

Ó conᵹaile—I— Conneely, Cunneely, (Connelly, Kennelly), &c. ; ' des. of Conᵹal ' (high-valour) ; the name (1) of a family of the Ui Fiachrach, who were anciently seated at Killarduff, in the parish of Dunfeeny, Co. Mayo ; (2) of an ecclesiastical family of Loch Erne who were connected with Devenish, Rossory and Lisgool ; and (3) of an ecclesiastical family at Clonmacnoise. The angl. forms of this surname cannot always be distinguished from those of mac Conᵹaile, mac Conᵹaola, and Ó Conᵹalaiᵹ, q.v. The last of these is sometimes substituted in the Annals for Ó Conᵹaile.

Ó conᵹalaiᵹ—I—*O Connally, O Connolly, O Conely,* Connolly, Connelly, &c. ; ' des. of Conᵹalac ' (valorous, der. of Conᵹal) ; the name (1) of a family of the southern Ui Neill who were seated in East Meath until dispossessed soon after the Anglo-Norman invasion, when they settled with the MacMahons in Co. Monaghan, where they became very numerous ; (2) of a Dalcassian family in Thomond who are said to be descended from Mahon, the brother of Brian Boru ; (3) of a branch of the Ui Maine in Co. Galway, of the same stock as the O'Maddens ; and (4) of a Roscommon family. The angl. forms of this surname cannot always be distinguished from those of Ó Conᵹaile, Ó Coinᵹeallaiᵹ, mac Conᵹaile, &c.

Ó conmeaᵈa—I—*O Convey, O Conwey,* Convey, (Conway) ; ' des. of Cú-meaᵈa ' (hound of Meadh, a placename) ; very rare.

Ó connacáin—I—*O Conoghane, O Cunnaghan,* Conaghan, (Cunningham) ; ' des. of Connacán ' (dim. of Conn) ; a var. of Ó Connaᵹáin, q.v.

Ó connactaiᵹ—I—*O Connaghty,* Connaghty, Conaghty, Conaty, Conotty ; ' des. of Connactac ' (Connachtman) ; the name of an old Breifney family, still well represented in Cavan. Flann Ó Connachtaigh was Bishop of Kilmore in the early part of the 13th century.

Ó connactáin—I—*O Connaghtane,* Connaghtane, Connaughton, Connorton, Connerton ; ' des. of Connacτán ' (dim. of Connaċτaċ) ; the name of a branch of the Ui Fiachrach, formerly seated in the townland of Cabragh, parish of Easkey, Co. Sligo, but at the end of the 16th century very scattered, being found in Roscommon, Donegal, Limerick and Kerry.

Ó connaჳáin—I—*O Connegaine, O Connigaine, O Conegan,* Connigan, (Conyngham, Cunningham) ; ' des. of Connaჳán ' (dim. of Conn) ; the name (1) of a family of Ui Fiachrach, formerly seated in the parish of Magh Gamhnach, now angl. Moygawnagh, Co. Sligo ; and (2) of a family of Ui Maine in Co. Galway, of the same stock as the O'Maddens. At the end of the 16th century this surname was common in Clare, Limerick, Kerry, Cork, Offaly, Kildare and Monaghan, as well as in Mayo and Galway, and is now nearly everywhere angl. Cunningham.

Ó connṁaċáin—I—*O Conawchane, O Connowghane, O Conoughan,* Kanavaghan, (Conway) ; ' des. of Connṁaċán,' (dim. of Connṁaċ) ; the name of a Sligo family who were followers of the O'Haras. At the beginning of the 17th century it was also found in West Ulster and in Offaly. It is now generally angl. Conway in Connacht.

Ó connṁaიჳ—I—*O Connowe, O Conway,* Conoo, Cunnoo, Conway ; ' des. of Connṁaċ ' ; the name of a Dalcassian family who were formerly ollaves of music in Thomond. At the end of the 16th century it was common throughout Munster and South Leinster, and was also found in Roscommon and Cavan. It is now generally angl. Conway.

Ó conna, Ó connaċ, *O Conorech, O Conra,* Conry ; ' des. of Conna ' ; very rare.

Ó connaoı—I—*O Conree, O Conrie,* Conroy ; ' des. of Cú-ნaoı ' (hound of the plain) ; the name of a branch of the Ui Maine in Co. Galway ; but in the 16th century very scattered.

Ó connaτa—I—*O Conrahy,* Conrahy, (Conroy) ; ' des. of Cú-ნaτa ' (hound of prosperity) ; also Ɱaც Connაτა ; written Ó Connსაτა by MacFirbis ; a Leix surname.

Ó connᴇ1ᴄe, v. Ó Conpaᴄa.

Ó coᴦᴅáin—I—*O Corbane, O Coribane*, Corbane, Corban, Corbin, (Corbett, Corbitt) ; ' des. of Coᴦᴅán ' (dim. of coᴦᴅ, a chariot, a pet form of some name commencing with Coᴦᴅ). This surname was formerly found in all the counties of Munster, and in Kilkenny, Carlow and Galway. It is now nearly always disguised under the angl. form of Corbett.

Ó coᴦcáin—I—*O Corkan*, Corken, Corkin, (Corcoran) ; ' des. of Coᴦcán ' (dim. of Coᴦc) ; a rare midland surname.

Ó coᴦcᴦa—I—*O Corkery*, Corkery, Corkerry ; ' des. of Coᴦcaiᴦ ' (purple) ; a Munster surname ; found chiefly in Cork, Kerry and Limerick.

Ó coᴦcᴦáin—I—*O Corcrane, O Corkerane, O Corkran,* Corcoran, Corkeran, Corkran, &c. ; ' des. of Coᴦcᴦán ' (dim. of Coᴦcaiᴦ, purple) ; the name of an ecclesiastical, literary and bardic family in many parts of Ireland. At the end of the 16th century it was largely represented in every province and, in the southern half of Ireland, almost in every county.

Ó coᴦmacáin—I—*O Cormacan, O Cormakane, O Gormacan*, Cormocan, Cormican, Gormican, (Cormack, Cormick, MacCormack, MacCormick) ; ' des. of Coᴦmacán ' (dim. of Coᴦmac) ; the name of at least four distinct families in different parts of Ireland, viz. : (1) Ó C. of Roscommon. This family appears to have been connected with the church of St. Coman. Fionn O Cormacain was one of the four hostages given by Cahal Crovderg O'Conor, King of Connacht, to King John, when the latter visited Ireland in 1210. (2) Ó C. of Thomond, a branch of the Dal gCais. These appear to have been an ecclesiastical family and erenaghs of the parish of Moynoe, in Co. Clare. Three of them were bishops of Killaloe in the 13th and 14th century. (3) Ó C. of Galway, a family formerly seated in the parish of Abbey-Gormican, in the barony of Longford, where they founded the abbey from which the parish derives its name. (4) Ó C. of Down, an ecclesiastical family who were erenaghs of Iniscourcey. The name appears to have been sometimes corrupted to Ó Ᵹoᴘmacáin, was often shortened to Ó Coᴘmaic (q.v.), and is now in many places disguised under the angl. form of MacCormack.

Ó CORMᴀıC—I—*O Cormack, O Cormick*, Cormac, Cormack, Cormick ; ' des. of Coᴘmac ' (son of Coᴘb, or son of a chariot, charioteer) ; the name (1) of a branch of the Oirghialla, seated in the barony of Tirkeeran, Co. Derry, until dispossessed by the O'Kanes ; (2) of a branch of the Corca Laoighdhe, in South-west Cork, where the name was common in the 16th century ; (3) of a Dalcassian family, probably the same as Ó Coᴘmacáın, q.v. ; and (4) of a Co. Down family, also probably the same as Ó Coᴘmacáın.

Ó CORRᴀ—I—*O Corry, O Corr*, Corra, Corry, Corr, Curry, and, by ' translation,' Weir ; ' des. of Coᴘᴘa ' (spear) ; a var. of Ó Cᴀᴘᴘᴀ (q.v.) ; a rather common Ulster surname. V. Ó Coᴘᴘaıᴅ, which is also a variant.

Ó CORRᴀᴅáın—I—*O Curridane, O Corridan*, Corridon, Cordan ; doubtless, a var. of Ó Coᴘᴘaᵹáın, q.v. ; apparently originally a Clare surname, but now found chiefly about Listowel, Co. Kerry.

Ó CORRᴀᵹáın—I—*O Corrigane, O Currigan*, Corrigan, Currigan, &c. ; ' des. of Coᴘᴘaᵹán ' (dim. of Coᴘᴘa) ; a rather widespread surname ; found in Ulster, Leinster and Connacht.

Ó CORRᴀıᴅ—I—*O Corrie, O Corry*, Corree, Corrie, Corry, Curry ; ' des. of Coᴘᴘaᴅ ' (spear) ; a var. of Ó Coᴘᴘa and Ó Cᴀᴘᴘaıᴅ, q.v.

Ó CORRᴀıᴅín—I—*O Corrin, O Corren, O Currine*, Curreen, Curren, Currin, (Curran), Creen, Crean ; ' des. of Coᴘᴘaıᴅín ' (dim. of Coᴘᴘaᴅ) ; a var. of Ó Coᴘᴘáın, q.v. ; also written Ó Cuıᴘín ; a common surname throughout Munster and South Leinster, but generally angl. Curran. Creen is a contracted form of Curreen,

Ó CORRáın—I—*O Corraine, O Currane, O Corhane*. O'Curran, Currain, Currane, Curran, Corran, Craan, Crain, Crane, Crahan, Creane, Crean, (Crehan, Creaghan,

Carey), &c. ; ' des. of Coppán ' (dim. of Coppaⱱ) ;
also written Ó Cuppáin ; a var. of Ó Cappáin, Ó Cap-
paiⱱín, Ó Coppaiⱱín, with which it was sometimes
used interchangeably ; a common Irish surname,
found in all the provinces.

Ó CORRⱱUIⱱE—I—*O Corbae*, Corboy, Corby, Curby ;
' des. of Coppⱱuiⱱe ' (yellow-crane) ; an old surname
in West Cork. The family belonged to Corca Laoighdhe.

Ó CORRⱱUIⱱ—I—*O Corduffe, O Curduffe*, Corduff ; ' des.
of Coppⱱuⱱ ' (black-crane) ; a rare West Ulster surname.

Ó CORⱮAIⱱ, Currid ; a Sligo surname. I cannot trace
its origin. The above is the local pronunciation as I
got it from an old Irish speaker at Grange.

Ó COSÁIn—I—*O Cossane*, Cussane, (Patterson) ; ' des. of
Capán ' (dim. of cap, bent, curly) ; a var. of Ó Capáin,
q.v.

Ó COSCAIR—I—*O Cosker, O Coskirr*, Coscor, Cosker,
Cusker, Cuskor, (Cosgrave, Cosgrove) ; a shortened
form of Ó Copcpaiⰼ, q.v.

Ó COSCRACÁIn—I—*O Coschrachan*, Coskeran, Cuskern,
(Cosgrave, Cosgrove) ; ' des. of Copcpacán ' (dim. of
Copcpac) ; a rare Ulster surname.

Ó COSCRAIⰼ—I—*O Coskry, O Cosgra*, Cosgry, Coskery,
Coskerry, Cuskery, Cosgriff, Cosgrive, Cosgreve, (Cosgreave, Cosgrave, Cosgrove) ; ' des. of Copcpac '
(victorious) ; the name (1) of a Wicklow family who
were lords of Feara Cualann, comprising the manor of
Powerscourt, until dispossessed soon after the Anglo-
Norman invasion by the O'Tooles and O'Byrnes ;
(2) of a Monaghan family who were anciently chiefs
of Feara Rois, in the neighbourhood of Carrickmacross ; and (3) of a Galway family who belonged to
the Ui Maine race, and are of the same stock as the
O'Maddens. The name is now generally angl. Cosgrave and Cosgrove.

Ó COSnACÁIn—I—*O Cosnechan*, Cusnahan, Cushanan ;
' des. of Copnacán ' (dim. of Copnac, or CopnaⱮac,
defender) ; very rare.

Ó COSⱵⱯⱢⱯⰟⱠ, Costigan; a corruption of Ⱄⰰⰹ OⱼⱤⱦⱠⱽⱠⱱ, q.v.

Ó ᴄⱤⱯⰂⱯⰟⱠ, Ó ᴄⱤⱯⰹⰂⱠⱱ—I—Cravane, Craven, Cravin, Creaven; ' des. of CⱤⱯⰂⱯⰂⱯⱱ ' (pious); the name of an old family of Ui Maine; still in use in Co. Galway.

Ó ᴄⱤⱯⰹⰂⰵⱯⱱ—I—O Kryane, O Kryan, Cryan; ' des. of CⱤⱯⰹⰂⰵⱯⱱ ' (dim. of cⱤⱯⰹⰂⰵ, a heart); a var. of Ó CⱤⱷⰹⰂⰵⱯⱱ, q.v.; a Roscommon surname.

Ó ᴄⱤⱯⰹⰟⱾⰹⰃⰵ—I—O Crashie, Cramsie, Crampsie, Crampsey, &c.; a corruption of Ó CⱱⱯⰹⰟⱤⰹⰃⰵ, q.v.

Ó ᴄⱤⱯOⰹⰂⰵ—I—O Crevy, Creevy, Creevey; ' des. of CⱤⱯOⰹⰂⰵⱯⱠ ' (branchy, curly, the dim., CⱤⱯOⰹⰂⰵⱯⱠⱯⱱ, occurs in the Annals, A.D. 760); a family of Cinel Eoghain, mentioned by MacFirbis.

Ó ᴄⱤⱯOⰂⱯⱱ—I—O Crevan, Creaven, Creavin; ' des. of CⱤⱯOⰂⱯⱱ ' (dim. of CⱤⱯOⰹⰂⰵⱯⱠ); a rare Sligo surname.

Ó ᴄⱤⰵⱯⱠⱯⱱ, Ó ᴄⱤⰵⱯⱠⱯⰟⱠ—I—O Creghan, Creaghan, Crehan, (Creaton), Crean; ' des. of CⱤⰵⱯⱠⱯⱱ ' (dim. of cⱤⰵⱯⱠ, or cⱤⱷⱯⱠ, blind); sometimes corrupted to Ó ⰃⱤⰵⱯⱠⱯⱱ; the name of a branch of the Ui Fiachrach who were formerly seated in Tirawley, Co. Mayo. V. Ó CⱤⱷⱷⱠⱯⱱ.

Ó ᴄⱤⰵⱯⱠⰟⱯOⰹⰎ, Craughwell; a rare Co. Galway surname, the origin of which I cannot trace. Croughwell is found in Cork.

Ó ᴄⱤⰹⱯⰃⱯⱱ—IV—Cregan; a corruption of Ⱄⰰⰹ ⱤⰹⱯⰃⱯⱱ, q.v.

Ó ᴄⱤⰹOⱠⱯⱱ, Ó ᴄⱤⰹOⱠⱯⰟⱠ—I—O Criaghan, O Creghan, Creghan, Creaghan, Creehan, Crehan, Creighan, (Creighton, Creaton), Creen, Crean; ' des. of CⱤⰹOⱠⱯⱱ ' (probably a var. of cⱤⰵⱯⱠⱯⱱ; also a small person); the name of an Oriel family who were lords of Ui Fiachrach of Ardsratha, now Ardstraw, Co. Tyrone. In the 16th century it was found in all the counties of Munster, and in Kilkenny, Carlow and Dublin. V. Ó CⱤⰵⱯⱠⱯⱱ.

Ó ᴄⱤⰹOⰂⱯⱱ—I—O Credane, Creedon, Creed; ' des. of CⱤⰹOⰂⱯⱱ '; also formerly Ⱄⰰⰹ CⱤⰹOⰂⱯⱱ; an old

Munster surname, still well known, especially in Cork, where the angl. form is often shortened to Creed.

Ó CRIONASÁIN—*O Crunegane, O Crinegine*, Crinigan, Crenegan ; ' des. of Cᵱonaᵹán ' (dim. of cᵱion, old, worn) ; a rare midland surname.

Ó CRÍONÁIN—I—Crennan, Crinion, Crinneen ; ' des. of Cᵱionán ' (dim. of cᵱion, old, worn out) ; a rare Leix surname.

Ó CROÓLAOIĊ, Ó CROᵹALLAIᵹ, v. Ó Cᵱuaólaoiċ.

Ó CROIBÍN—I—Cribbin, Cribbon, Cribbins ; a metathesised form of Ó Coiᵱbín, q.v.

Ó CROIÓEAᵹÁIN—I—*O Cridigan, O Crigane, O Crigan*, Creegan, Creigan, Cregan, Creggan ; ' des. of Cᵱoióeaᵹán ' (dim. of cᵱoióe, heart, a term of endearment) ; also written Ó Cᵱaióeaᵹáin and Ó Cᵱióeaᵹáin ; a var. of Ó Cᵱaióeáin and Ó Cᵱoióeáin, q.v. ; the name of a family of Cinel Eoghain who, in the 16th century, were seated in Donegal. Some of them later removed to Sligo where they became wealthy merchants and landed proprietors. MacFirbis (p. 140) gives the pedigree of the family.

Ó CROIÓEÁIN—I—*O Criane, O Creane, O Crean*, Crean, Creen, &c. ; ' des. of Cᵱoióeán ' (dim. of cᵱoióe, heart) ; a var. of Ó Cᵱaióeáin and Ó Cᵱoióeaᵹáin, q.v. ; the name of a family of Cinel Eoghain who settled at Sligo in the 16th century, where they became wealthy merchants, and later on acquired a considerable amount of landed property. The pedigree of the family is given by MacFirbis (p. 140).

Ó CROIMÍN—I—*O Cromine*, Cremeen, Cremen, Cremin ; ' des. of Cᵱoimín ' (dim. of cᵱom, bent). V. Ó Cᵱuimín.

Ó CRÓIN—*O Crone*, Crone ; ' des of Cᵱón ' (brown, swarthy) ; a rare and scattered surname ; formerly found in Donegal, Kilkenny and Galway.

Ó CRÓINÍN—I—*O Cronine, O Cronyn*, Cronin, Cronyn, Cronan ; ' des. of Cᵱóinín ' (dim. of cᵱón, brown, swarthy) ; the name of a family of Corca Laoighdhe, originally seated in the neighbourhood of Clonakilty, but now numerous throughout Cork, Kerry and Limerick.

*Ó CROmLAOIĊ, Crumley ; ' des. of the bent hero ' (Ir. Cʀomlaoċ).

Ó CROmRUISC—I—*O Cromruske, O Crumreske*, (?) Crumlish ; ' des. of Cʀompoʀc ' (squint-eye, perhaps a nickname) ; a Donegal surname, now probably represented by the angl. form Crumlish.

Ó CROmTA—I—*O Cromy*, Crummy ; ' des. of Cʀomta ' (bent) ; very rare.

Ó CRÓnAȜÁIn—I—*O Cronigane*, Cronekan, Croniken ; ' des. of Cʀónaȝán ' (dim. of Cʀón) ; a rare Munster surname, still extant in Waterford and Limerick.

Ó CRÓnÁIn—I—*O Kronane*, Cronan, Cronin ; ' des. of Cʀónán ' (dim. of Cʀón) ; a rare Leix surname. Cf. Ó Cʀóinín and Ó Cʀónaȝáin.

Ó CRÓnȜAIL—I—*O Cronegil, O Cronell*, Crangle ; ' des. of Cʀónȝal ' ; a var. of Ó Cʀónȝaile, q.v.

Ó CRÓnȜAILe—I—*O Cronowly, O Cronully*, Cronelly, Cranley ; ' des. of Cʀónȝal ' (compound of cʀón, brown, and ȝal, valour, an old Irish personal name) ; the name of an old Galway family who were coarbs of St. Grellan, patron of Ui Maine, and keepers of that saint's crozier, which was wont to be carried in battle by the king of Ui Maine. By the end of the 16th century, some of the family had crossed the Shannon into Offaly and Ormond.

Ó CROTAIȜ—I—*O Crotty*, Crotty ; ' des. of Cʀotaċ ' (hunch-backed) ; the name of a Waterford family, said to be a branch of the O'Briens of Thomond, who were formerly seated in the neighbourhood of Lismore and are now found in many parts of Munster.

Ó CRUAⱵLAOIĊ—I—*O Crowly, O Croley, O Croly*, O'Crowley, Crowley, Crawley, Croly, Crolly ; ' des. of CʀuaⱵlaoċ ' (hard-hero) ; the name of a branch of the MacDermotts in Co. Roscommon. MacFirbis, in his Genealogies (p. 228), gives the pedigree of this family, from which it appears that they derive their name and

descent from Ⴃιⲁⲣⲙⲁⲓⲇ, 'ⲁⲛ cⲣⲩⲁⲇⲗⲁⲟⲉ,' who was
fourth in descent from Ⴃιⲁⲣⲙⲁⲓⲇ, the eponymous
ancestor of the MacDermotts. This family is still
represented in Connacht. Ó Cⲣⲩⲁⲇⲗⲁⲟⲓⲉ is also used
as the surname of a family originally seated in West
Cork, but now numerous throughout Munster and
known in English as Crowley and Crawley. The
Irish pronunciation of the surname, as I have heard it
in different parts of that province, is Ó Cⲣⲟⲅⲁⲗⲗⲁⲓ⵷,
evidently a corruption of Ⴊⲁc Ꝛⲟⲅⲁⲗⲗⲁ⵷, q.v. The
family, which was once a strong one in West Cork, is
probably a branch of the O'Mahonys. Croly and
Crolly in the northern parts of Ireland are apparently
similar corruptions.

Ó cⲢⲩⲓⲙⵘⲛ—I—*O Crumyne*, Crimmeen, Cremeen, Cremin,
Cremen, Crimmins ; ' des. of Cⲣⲩⲓⲙⵘⲛ ' (dim. of cⲣⲟⲙ,
bent) ; the name of a well-known family in Cork,
Kerry and Limerick ; of West Cork origin, and said
to be a branch of the MacCarthys.

Ó cⲩⲁⲉⲁ́ⲛ—I—*O Coughane, O Cowghane, O Quoghane*,
(Gough) ; ' des. of Cⲩⲁⲉⲁ́ⲛ ' (dim. of cⲩⲁⲉ, a cuckoo) ;
the name of a family of Ui Fiachrach, formerly seated
in the barony of Carra, Co. Mayo, where O'Donovan
found it still extant under the angl. form of Gough.
At the end of the 16th century, it appears in Roscommon, Cavan and Cork, but I have failed to discover any modern angl. form of it in these counties.

Ó cⲩⲁⲅⲁ́ⲛ—I—*O Choogan, O Cowgan, O Cogan*, Coogan,
Cogan ; ' des of Cⲩⲁⲅⲁ́ⲛ ' ; the name of a family of the
Ui Maine in Co. Galway, of the same stock as the
O'Maddens. Before the end of the 16th century it
had ramified into Offaly, Kildare and Kilkenny. Ó
Cⲩⲁⲅⲁ́ⲛ was also the name of a Leitrim family who
were anciently chiefs of Cinel Duachain, but apparently
long extinct.

Ó cⲩⲁⲓⲛ—I—*O Cuayn, O Quane*, Quan, Quann, Quane,
Quaine, (Coyne, Quaid) ; ' des. of Cⲩⲁⲛ ' (probably a
' pet ' form of ⲇⲟⲛⲛⲉⲩⲁⲛ, lord of harbours ; hardly for
cⲩ́ⲁⲛ, dim. of cⲩ́, a hound) ; the name of a branch

of the Ui Fiachrach, anciently seated at Dun Ui Chobhthaigh, now angl. Doonycoy, in the parish of Templeboy, Co. Sligo. At the end of the 16th century it was very scattered, but found chiefly in Cork and Limerick, in the latter of which counties it is now angl. Quaine and Quaid.

Ó cuⱥnⱥ, Ó cuⱥnⱥċ—I—*O Cowna, O Cwony, O Coony,* Cooney; 'des. of Cuⱥnⱥ' (handsome, elegant); the name of a family who, according to O'Dugan, were chiefs of Clann Fergus in Ulster. At the end of the 16th century it was most common in Sligo and Cork.

Ó cuⱥnⱥċⱥin—I—*O Coonaghan,* Coonaghan, Coonahan, Coonihan, Counihan, (Cooney); 'des. of Cuⱥnⱥcⱥn' (dim. of Cuⱥnⱥ); a rare surname, now found chiefly in Kerry; angl. Cooney in some parts of Munster.

Ó cuⱥnⱥin—I—*O Cownan,* Coonan, (Conan); 'des. of Cuⱥnⱥn' (dim. of Cuⱥn); the name of a family formerly seated at Dunbeakin in the parish of Kilmacshalgan, Co. Sligo, but no longer found in that district. It is still extant, however, in parts of Leinster. Isaac O Cuanain was Bishop of Ely and Roscrea about the middle of the 12th century.

Ó cuⱥnⱥrcⱥiꝝ—I—Coonerty; des. of 'Cuⱥnⱥrcⱥċ' (having a pack of hounds; cf. Rⱥt Cuⱥnⱥrcⱥiꝝ); a rare surname. I cannot discover any early form, Irish or English.

Ó cuḃrⱥin—I—Cowran; 'des. of *Cuḃrⱥn'; a Breifney surname. It is mentioned in the Annals at the year 1145. O'Donovan gives the angl. forms as Cowran and Corran. But see Ó Cumrⱥin.

Ó cuiꝺiꝝciꝝ—I—*O Codihie, O Kuddyhy, O Cuddie,* Cuddihy, Cudihy, Cuddehy, Quiddihy, Cuddy, Cody, &c.; 'des. of Cuiꝺiꝝceⱥċ' (helper); an Ormond surname. Though apparently distinct, it is probably a mere substitution for Mⱥc Óꝺⱥ, q.v.

Ó cúile—I—Cooley; cf. Mⱥc ꝺioꞁꞁⱥ Cúile.

Ó cuiꞁeⱥꝫⱥin—I—Quiligan, Quilligan; an attenuated form of Ó Coꞁꝫⱥn, q.v.

Ó cuiꞁeⱥin—I—*O Cullaine, O Quillayne,* O'Cullane,

Cullane, Cullan, Cullen, Quillan, Quillen, Collins ;
'des. of Cuileán' (whelp) ; a var. of Ó Coileáin, q.v.
Besides the Uí Coileáin of Ui Conaill Gabhra, there
were distinct families of this name in Galway, Tyrone,
Tipperary and Cork, and perhaps also in Clare and
Sligo. The Galway family was a branch of the Ui
Maine ; that of the Cork of the Corca Laoighdhe, and
therefore distinct from the Uí Coileáin of Ui Conaill
Gabhra who settled in the same territory after they
were driven out of their native Ui Fidhgheinte. The
Uí Cuileáin of Tyrone were erenaghs of Clogher.

Ó cuileaṁain—I—*O Cullone, O Collone*, Culloon, Culhoun, Colhoon, Colhoun, Cullen ; ' des. of Cuileaṁan ' ;
the name of a South Leinster family to which belonged,
according to O'Curry, the late Cardinal Cullen.

Ó cuileannáin—I—*O Cullanayne, O Cullinan*, Cullinane, Cullinan, Quillinan, Culnane, Quilnan, (Callanane,
Callanan), &c. ; ' des. of Cuileannán ' (dim. of Cuileann) ; the name (1) of a Co. Louth family who were
anciently lords of Conaille ; and (2) of a family of
Corca Laoighdhe, formerly seated in the barony of
Barryroe, in South Cork. Dr. O'Brien, in his Irish
Dictionary, mentions another family of this name as
lords of Muscraighe-tri-maighe, now the barony of
Orrery, Co. Cork, but I have failed to trace it. There
was also a remarkable family of the name in Tir-
connell, to which belonged Dr. John O'Cullinan,
Bishop of Raphoe at the period of the Confederation.

Ó cuilín—I—*O Culline*, Cullin, Cullen, &c. ; a var., in
South Cork, of Ó Cuileáin, q.v.

Ó cuilinn—I—*O Cullin, O Quillin*, Cullen, Quillen, &c. ;
' des of Cuileann ' (holly).

Ó cuill—I—*O Cwill*, Quill, and, by ' translation,' Woods ;
' des. of Coll ' (hazel, also head) ; the name of a
celebrated literary and bardic family in Munster.
They are, according to MacFirbis (p. 622), of the same
stock as the O'Sullivans. The name is now found
chiefly in Cork and Kerry, but is sometimes disguised
under the angl. form of Woods, which is supposed to

be a translation, from its resemblance to 'coill,' a wood.

Ó cuimín—I—*O Cumyn*, Cumin, Cummin, Cummins, Cummings, &c. ; 'des. of Cuimín' (dim. of cam, bent, crooked) ; the name of several distinct families in different parts of Ireland. It is a var. of Ó Comáin (q.v.) for which, in many instances, it has been substituted. The Sligo family of the name is a branch of the Ui Fiachrach.

Ó cuindlis—I—Cundlish, Cunlish, Quinlish ; 'des. of Cuindleasr' (an ancient Irish personal name) ; the name of a literary family in Connacht, who had a share in compiling the Book of Lecan. It would seem that this name was changed into Ó Cointeirc, q.v. The same person is called Ó Cuindlir by Annalists of Loch Cé and Ó Cointeirc by the Four Masters. (See Annals, A.D. 1342.) The latter is the form now in use in Mayo.

o cuineáin—I—*O Kinane, O Kynnan*, Cunnane, Kinane, Kinnane, Guinane, Guinnane, Guinan, Quinane, Quenan, Queenane, &c. ; 'des. of Cuineán' (an attenuated form of Conán) ; a var. of Ó Coineáin, q.v. ; a common surname in many parts of Ireland. There is also a distinct surname Ó Cuinneáin, q.v.

Ó cuineóg—I—*O Conoge*, Kinnock ; 'des. of Conóg' (a var. of Conán) ; an exceedingly rare Thomond surname.

Ó cuinín—I—*O Quynnyne, O Kynnyne*, Cuneen, Cunion, Cunneen, Cunnien, Cunnion, Kinnian, and, by 'translation,' Rabbit ; a var. of Ó Coinín and Ó Cuineáin, q.v.

Ó cuinn—I—*O Quyn, O Quine, O Coyne*, O'Quin, Quin, Quinn, Queen, Coyne ; 'des. of Conn' (head, sense, reason, intelligence ; also a freeman) ; a very common surname in all parts of Ireland. There are several distinct families so called, of which the following are the best known :—(1) Ó Cuinn of Thomond, a branch of the Dal gCais, descended from Conn, lord of Muinntear Ifearnain, who flourished in the latter part of the 10th century. They were originally seated at

Inchiquin, and their territory which, from their clan-
name, was designated Muinntear Ifearnain, comprised
the country around Corofin, in Co. Clare. The Earl
of Dunraven is a member of this family. (2) Ó Cuinn
of Annaly, a branch of the Conmaicne and of the same
stock as the O'Farrells, who were chiefs of Muinntear
Giollagain, an extensive district in Co. Longford, until
towards the end of the 14th century when they were
supplanted by the O'Farrells. Quin is now a very
common surname in Co. Longford. (3) Ó Cuinn of
Antrim who were chiefs of Magh Lughadh and Siol
Cathasaigh. Conghalach O Cuinn of this family, ' a
tower of valour, hospitality, and renown of the North
of Ireland,' was slain by the English in the year 1218.
(4) Ó Cuinn of Magh Itha, in the barony of Raphoe,
now numerous in West Ulster. (5) Ó Cuinn of Clann
Cuain, a branch of the Ui Fiachrach, who were chiefs
of Clann Chuain, in the neighbourhood of Castlebar,
Co. Mayo. About the middle of the 12th century they
transferred their allegiance from the Ui Fiachrach to
the Siol Muireadhaigh and became tributary to Mac-
Dermott of Moylurg. Ó Cuinn is pronounced O'Coyne
in the south of Ireland ; hence the angl. form Coyne
which is sometimes used.

Ó cuinneacáin—I—*O Kineghan, O Kynaghan, O
Quenahan*, Cunnighan, Cunnahan, Cunihan, Kinaghan,
Kinahan, Kinnighan, Kinnan, (Keenan, Cunninghan)
&c. ; a var. of Ó Coinneacáin and Ó Cuinneagáin, q.v.

Ó cuinneagáin—I—*O Quinegane*, Cunnigan, Kinnegan,
Kinnighan, (Cunningham) ; ' des. of Cuinneagán '
(dim. of Conn) ; a common surname all over Ireland.
Mac Cuinneagáin (q.v.) was a variant. See also Ó
Connagáin.

Ó cuinneáin—I—*O Kinnane, O Kynnan*, Kinnane,
Guinnane, Quinane, &c. ; ' des. of Cuinneán ' (dim.
of Conn). This surname was in use in Tipperary,
Limerick, Clare, and perhaps other places, but it is
now impossible to distinguish it from Ó Cuineáin, q.v.

Ó cuirc—I—*O Cuirk, O Quirke*, Quirk, Quirke, Querk,

Kirk; 'des. of Coᵱc' (heart); the name of a family who were anciently chiefs of Muscraighe Breogain, also called Muscraighe Cuirc, in the present barony of Clanwilliam, Co. Tipperary; still common in Tipperary, and also in Cork and Kerry.

Ó Cuιrín—I—*O Curine, O Quyrrine*, Curreen, Creen, &c.; a var. of Ó Coᵱᵱaιóín, q.v.

Ó Cuιrnín, Ó Cúιrnín—I—*O Curnyne*, Corneen, Curneene, Curneen, Curnin, Courneen, (Courtney); 'des. of Cuᵱnín' (dim. of coᵱn, a horn, a drinking cup); the name of a literary family in Breifney who were poets and chroniclers to the O'Rourkes. The head of the family resided in Church Island, in Lough Gill.

Ó Cúlacáιn—I—*O Coullaghan, O Couloghan*, O'Colohan, Cuolohan, Coulihan, &c.; 'des. of Cúlacán' (dim. of cúlac, fat); the name of a family of the Ui Fiachrach who were formerly seated in the barony of Carra, Co. Mayo. At the end of the 16th century it was also found in Sligo, Tipperary and Limerick.

Ó Cumaráιn, Ó Cumráιn—I—Cameron; 'des. of *Cumᵱán'; apparently the same as Ó Cuᵬᵱáιn, q.v.; the name of an old Breifney family. It is, no doubt, the surname pronounced Cumaᵱán (without the Ó) and angl. Cameron, in Co. Mayo.

Ó Curnáιn, Ó Cúrnáιn—I—*O Kurnane*, Curnane, Cournane, (Courtney); 'des. of Cuᵱnán' (an ancient Irish personal name, the same as Cuᵱnín); a Kerry surname. It is a var. of the Breifney surname Ó Cuᵱnín, and there is reason for believing that the families are the same.

Ó Curráιn—I—*O Currane*, O'Curran, Currain, Currane, Curran, &c.; a corrupt spelling of Ó Coᵱᵱáιn, q.v.

Ó Curtáιn—I or IV—Curtayne, Curtin, &c.; a corrupt form of older Ó Caᵱtáιn, q.v.; common in the spoken language of West Limerick and Kerry.

Ó Dáᵬoιreann—I—*O Davoren, O Daverin, O Davern*, Davoran, Davoren, Davern; 'des. of Duᵬᵭáᵬoιᵱeann' (Black of the two Burrens); a shortened form of Ó Duιᵬᵭáᵬoιᵱeann; the name of a learned brehon family in Thomond. They belonged originally to Corcomroe, in north-west of Co. Clare, where for successive generations they maintained a great literary and legal school, of which the celebrated Irish antiquary, Duald MacFirbis, was at one time a pupil. The head of the family resided at Lisdoonvarna. The O'Davorans are also numerous in Co. Tipperary, where they seem to have settled before the end of the 16th century.

Ó Daġnáin—I—*O Dinan*, Dinan, Dynan; 'des. of Daġnán'; a not uncommon Munster surname.

Ó Daiġre—I—*O Dyry*, Derry, Deery; 'des. of Daiġre'; the name of an ecclesiastical family at Derry, of the church of which they were erenaghs.

Ó Dailḃre—I—*O Dallarie*, Dollery; 'des. of Dailḃre' (an ancient Irish personal name); a rare old surname in Co. Limerick, and also in Offaly. The Limerick family is almost extinct.

Ó Daimín—I—*O Davine, O Dovine*, O'Devine, Davine, Devine, Davin, Devin, Deven, Devon, Devins, (Davy, Davis); 'des. of Daimín' (dim. of Daṁ, bard, poet); the name of an Oriel family, of the same stock as the Maguires, who were chiefs of Tirkennedy, in the east of Co. Fermanagh. It is now generally angl. Devine in Ulster, and Davin in Munster and Connacht. In West Galway, where it is not uncommon, it is sometimes made Davy and Davis. It is to be distinguished from Ó Duiḃín, q.v.

Ó Dairḃre—I—*O Dwrrero, Derriroe*, Derow, Deroe, &c.; 'des. of Dairḃre' (an ancient Irish personal name); an old, but rare surname in Offaly.

Ó Dáire—I—*O Dawry, O Daire*, Adair; 'des. of Dáire' (an ancient Irish personal name).

Ó Daitġil, v. Ó Daċail.

Ó Dalaċáin—I—*O Dallaghan, O Dolaghan*, Dallaghan, Dolaghan, &c.; 'des. of Dalaċán' (dim. of Dálaċ); the name of an ancient family in Tirconnell who were chiefs of Tuath Bladhach, now angl. Doe, in the north of the barony of Kilmacrenan. In the 16th century, the name was found chiefly in the midlands, especially in Offaly, where the family was numerous and respectable. The castle of Liscloony, in the parish in Tisaran, the ruins of which are still to be seen, was built by Melaghlin O'Dalachain, in the year 1556. The angl. forms of this surname cannot always be distinguished from those of Ó Ⱶuⰱⱡaⱬáin or Ó Ⱶuiⰱⱡeaⱬáin, q.v.

Ó Ⱶaⱡaⱬaiⱃ—I—*O Dologher*, Dallagher, Dolaher, Dooler, Dowler; 'des. of Ⱶaⱡaⱬaⱃ'; always extremely rare.

Ó ⱵáⱡaiⰗ—I—O'Daly, Daly, Dawley, &c.; 'des. of Ⱶáⱡaⱬ' (holding assemblies, frequenting assemblies). The O'Dalys derive their descent from Maine, son of Niall of the Nine Hostages, and were originally chiefs of Corca Adain, or Corca Adhaimh, in the present county of Westmeath. In later times they became famous as a bardic family all over Ireland. "There is certainly no family," writes O'Donovan, "to which the bardic literature of Ireland is more deeply indebted than that of O'Daly." The first of the family to become famous for his learning was Cuchonnacht na scoile (C. of the school) who died at Clonard in 1139. He was the ancestor of all the bardic families of the name. "From his time forward," says O'Donovan, "poetry became a profession in the family, and Corca Adain sent forth poetic professors to various parts of Ireland." About the middle of the 13th century, a branch of the family, descended from Donough More O'Daly, a celebrated bard, settled at Finavarra, in Burren, Co. Clare, where they became poets to the O'Loghlens. To this branch belonged the Dalys of Galway, whose ancestor settled in Ui Maine in the latter part of the 15th century. Raghnall O Dalaigh, who settled in Desmond about the middle of the 12th century, and became chief ollave in poetry to MacCarthy, was doubtless the ancestor of the O'Dalys of Muinntear Bhaire and O'Keeffe's country. Another branch settled in Cavan, and became poets

to the O'Reillys ; while other branches were poets
to the O'Neills of Ulster and the O'Connors of Connacht. The name is now common all over Ireland.

Ó Ɗalaɼuaiɓ, Delaroe, Dollery ; evidently a corruption
of Ó Ɗailḃɼe, q.v.

Ó Ɗallá̇in—I—*O Dullane, O Dallan, O Dallon*, Dallon,
Delane, (Delany), &c. ; ' des. of Ɗallá̇n ' (dim. of
ɓall, blind) ; formerly a not uncommon surname
throughout the south of Ireland ; now also in use in
West Connacht, where it is incorrectly angl. Delany.
V. Ó Ɗuilleá̇in, which is a variant.

Ó Ɗaṁá̇in—I—*O Davan*, Davane, Devane ; ' des. of
Ɗaṁá̇n ' (dim. of ɓaṁ, a poet). Cf. Ó Ɗaiṁín ; a
rare Ulster surname. MacFirbis mentions a family
of the name among the Cinel Eoghain.

Ó Ɗaoɗa, v. Ó Ɗéaɓaiꞡ.

Ó Ɗaɼa, Ó Ɗaɼaċ—I—Daragh, Darragh, Darrah,
Darrock, Oak, Oakes, Oaks ; ' des. of Ɗuɓɗaɼaċ '
(Black of the Oak) ; short for Ó Ɗuɓɗaɼaċ. Cf. Ó
Ɗáɓoiɼeann.

Ó Ɗaꞇail—I—*O Dahill*, Dahill ; ' des. of Ɗaiꞇꞡeal '
(fair complexion) ; also written Ó Ɗaiꞇꞡil ; the name,
according to MacFirbis, of a family of the Siol Muireadhaigh, in Co. Roscommon ; now peculiar to Tipperary.

Ó Ɗaꞇlaoiċ—I—*O Dolly*, Dolly ; ' des. of Ɗaꞇlaoċ '
(bright or nimble hero) ; the name of a Galway family
who were anciently chiefs of Ui Briúin Ratha, to the
east and north-east of the town of Galway, where it
is still represented.

Ó Ɗeaɓꞇaiꞡ—I—*O Daffie*, Daffy ; ' des. of Ɗeaɓꞇaċ '
(quarrelsome) ; a rare West Clare surname.

Ó Ɗeaɓaiꞡ, v. Ó Ɗeaꞡaiɓ.

Ó Ɗéaɓaiꞡ—I—*O Deadie*, Deady ; ' des. of Ɗéaɓaċ '
(der. of ɓéaɓ, a tooth) ; a rare West Munster surname.
The pronunciation in Limerick and Kerry is Ó Ɗaoɓa,
which is apparently corrupt.

Ó Ɗeaꞡaiɓ—I—*O Daa, O Dawe, O Daye, O Deay*,
O'Dea, Dea, Day, Daw, Dee, Godwin, Goodwin, &c. ;
' des. of Ɗeaꞡaɓ ' ; the name (1) of a Dalcassian

family, still numerous in Thomond, who were chiefs of Ui Fearmaic, which comprised the greater part of the present barony of Inchiquin, Co. Clare, and had their principal strongholds at Tullyodea and Dyserttola ; and (2) of a Tipperary family who were anciently chiefs of Sliabh Ardacha, now angl. Slewardagh, in the east of that county.

Ó ⅮⅇⱯ⅁Ⱥⅈⅈ—III—*O Dyeane, O Deane, O Dane*, Deane, Dean, Deen, Dane ; ' des. of the dean ' (Ir. ⅮⅇⱯ⅂Ⱥⅈ or ⅮⅇⱯ⅁Ⱥⅈ) ; a scattered surname ; found at the end of the 16th century in many parts of the south of Ireland, and also in Donegal.

Ó ⅮⅇⱯⅯⱭⅈⅈ, v. Ó ⅮⅈⱭⅯⱭⅈⅈ.

Ó ⅮⅇⱯⱤⱭⅈⅈ—I—*O Dearain, O Derane*, Dearan, Derrane, Dirrane ; ' des. of ⅮⅇⱯⱤⱭⅈ ' (dim. of ⅮⅇⱯⱤ, great, large) ; a rare and scattered surname ; found chiefly in the 16th century, in Kildare, Leix and Galway. MacFirbis mentions a Muinntear Dearain among the Cinel Eoghain, in Ulster.

Ó ⅮⅇⱯⱤ⅁Ⱥⅈⅈ—I—*O Dargane, O Dergane, O Darigan*, Dargan, Dergan, Dorgan, Dorrigan ; ' des. of ⅮⅇⱯⱤ⅁Ⱥⅈ ' (dim. of ⅮⅇⱯⱤ⅁, red) ; an old surname in Westmeath, Offaly and Cork. In the last-named county, it is now angl. Dorgan, which is not very correct.

Ó ⅮⅇⱯⱤⅯⱭⅮⱭ—I—*O Darmodie*, Darmody ; ' des. of ⅮⅈⱭⱤⅯⱭⅮ ' ; a var. of Ó ⅮⅈⱭⱤⅯⱭⅮⱭ, q.v.

Ó ⅮⅇⱯⅾⅯⱯⅈ⅁Ⱥⅈ⅁—III—*O Dassuny, O Dasshowne, O Deason, O Desmonde*, Desmond ; ' des. of the Desmonian ' (Ir. ⅮⅇⱯⱤⅯⅯⱯⅈⱭȾ, native of Desmond or South Munster) ; a Cork surname.

Ó ⅮⅇⅈⱤⅮⱤⅇⱭ, Devereux, Devery, Derow, Deroe ; v. Ó ⅮⱭⅈⱤⅮⱤⅇ, of which it is apparently a corruption.

Ó ⅮⅇⅈⱤ⅁—I—*O Derig, O Derrick*, Derrig, Derrick, Durrig ; ' des. of ⅮⅇⱯⱤ⅁ ' (red) ; the name of a family of the Ui Fiachrach who were seated in the neighbourhood of Killala ; still extant in Mayo and Sligo.

Ó ⅮⅇⱰⱪⱭⅈⅈ—I—*O Dycane, O Decan*, Deacon ; ' des. of ⅮⅇⱰⱪȺⅈ ' (a personal name).

Ó ⅮⅇⱰⱤⱭⅮⱭⅈⅈ, Ó ⅮⅇⱰⱤⱭⅈⅮⅈⅈ, Ó ⅮⅇⱰⱤⱭⅈⅈ—I—*O*

Dorian, O Dowerine, O Doreane, O Dorrane, Adorian,
O'Doran, Dorian, Dorrian, Doran, Dorran, Durrian ;
' des. of Ʋeópaʋán ' or ' Ʋeópaiʋín ' (dim. of ʋeópaʋ,
an exile, stranger) ; the name (1) of a great brehon
family in Leinster, where it is still very common ; and
(2) a Co. Down surname. Ó Ʋeopáin is a shortened
form of Ó Ʋeópaʋáin ; Ó Ʋeópaiʋín was everywhere
a variant.

Ó Ʋiaȝaiʋ—I—*O Die,* O'Dea, Dea, Dee, Godwin, Goodwin ; var. of Ó Ʋeaȝaiʋ, q.v. The angl. form Godwin
was suggested by the similarity of the first syllable
to Ʋia, God.

Ó Ʋiamáin—I—*O'Diamain,* Diaman, Diamon, Diamond,
Dimond ; ' des. of Ʋiamán ' or ' Ʋéamán ' (more
correctly Ʋíomán, dim. of Ʋíoma, a personal name) ;
the name of an old ecclesiastical family in Ulster who
were erenaghs of Kilrea, in Co. Derry, and are still
numerous in Derry and Antrim.

Ó Ʋiarmaʋa—I—*O Diermoda, O Dermody, O Diermot,*
O'Dermott, Dermody, Darmody, Dermott, Darby,
&c. ; ' des. of Ʋiaṗmaiʋ ' (an ancient Irish personal
name signifying freeman) ; a scattered surname ; found
in all the provinces.

Ó Ʋíoċon—I—*O Deachan,* Deehan, Dehan, Deighan ;
' des. of Ʋíoċú ' (great-hound) ; a rare Ulster surname.

Ó Ʋíomáin, v. Ó Ʋiamáin.

Ó Ʋíomasaiȝ—I—*O Dymasa, O Demsy,* O'Dempsey,
Dempsey ; ' des. of Ʋíomasaċ ' (proud). The O'Dempseys, who are of the same stock as the O'Connors of
Offaly, derive their descent from Ros Failghe, eldest
son of Cathaoir Mor, King of Ireland in the second
century, and were long one of the most powerful
families in Leinster. Their territory was Clann
Mhaoilughra, an extensive district on both sides of the
river Barrow, and comprising the baronies of Port-
nahinch in Leix, and Upper Philipstown, in Offaly.
During the reign of Elizabeth, the O'Dempseys were
on friendly terms with the English, and their estates
for a time escaped confiscation ; Terence O'Dempsey

was knighted by Essex in 1599, and in 1631 created Baron of Philipstown and Viscount Clanmalier. They took, however, an honourable part in the Confederation of Kilkenny, and later on were staunch adherents to the cause of James II. For their loyalty on this occasion they suffered the loss of their estates.

Ó ᴅɪoʀáɪn—I—*O Derran*, Dirrane, Durrane ; a var. of Ó ᴅeaʀáɪn, q.v.

Ó ᴅíoʀmᴀ, Ó ᴅíoʀmᴀɪ5—I—*O Dierma, O Dermoe*, Diurmagh, O'Dermott, Dermott, &c. ; a shortened form of Ó ᴅuɪʙóɪoʀmᴀ, q.v.

Ó ᴅɪʀín—I—*O Derren*, Direen ; a var. of Ó ᴅɪoʀáɪn, q.v. ; a rare Kilkenny surname.

Ó ᴅíscín—I—*O Duskin*, Diskin ; ' des. of ᴅíʀcín ' (dim. of ᴅíoʀc, apparently not a personal name) ; the name of a family of the Ui Fiachrach who were formerly seated in the townland of Baile Ui Dhiscin, angl. Ballyeeskeen, in the parish of Templeboy, Co. Sligo ; now not uncommon in Co. Galway and other parts of Connacht.

Ó ᴅoʙᴀɪlein—I—*O Deublinge, O Devlin*, Develin, Devlin, &c. ; ' des. of ᴅoʙᴀɪlen ' ; the name (1) of a Sligo family who were anciently chiefs of Corca Firthri in that county, and are frequently mentioned in the Annals ; and (2) of a Tyrone family who were chiefs of Muintar Devlin, on the west side of Lough Neagh, and now very numerous throughout Ulster. Also written Ó ᴅoɪʙɪlein and Ó ᴅoɪʙɪlín, q.v.

Ó ᴅoʙᴀʀáɪn—I—Davoran, Davoren, Davern ; ' des. of ᴅoʙᴀʀán ' or ' ᴅoʙʀán ' (dim. of ᴅoʙᴀʀ, water, perhaps ' pet ' dim. of ᴅoʙᴀʀcú, water-dog, otter) ; a rare Connacht surname.

Ó ᴅocᴀʀᴛᴀɪ5—I—*O Doghartie*, O'Dogherty, O'Dougherty, O'Doherty, Dogherty, Dougherty, Doherty, &c. ; ' des. of ᴅocᴀʀᴛᴀc ' (hurtful, disobliging). The O'Dohertys, who are a branch of the Cinel Conaill and of the same stock as the O'Donnells, were originally chiefs of Cinel Enna and Ard Miodhair, now angl. Ardmire, in the barony of Raphoe, but about the beginning of the 15th century, they became lords of Inishowen and one of the most powerful families of Tirconnell, a position which they retained down to the reign of James I, when, after the rebellion of Sir Cahir O'Dogherty, their possessions were confiscated and granted to Sir Arthur Chichester. The O'Doghertys are now one of the most numerous of Irish families.

Ó DOĊRAIḊ, Ó DOĊRAIĠ—I—*O Dogrie, O Dockrey*, Dockeray, Dockery, Dockrey, Dockry; 'des. of Doċraḋ,' or 'Doċraċ' (unfortunate, hurtful, &c.); the name of a branch of the Siol Muireadhaigh in Co. Roscommon.

Ó DOĠAIR—I—*O Dowar, O Dower, O Dore*, Dower, Dore; 'des. of Doġar' (sad, sorrowful); a Munster surname, found chiefly in Co. Limerick.

Ó DOIḂILEIN, Ó DOIḂILÍN—I—*O Devline, O Devlin*, Develin, Devlin, &c.; a var. of Ó Doḃailein, q.v. Ó Doiḃilein is the usual form of the name in the Annals of Ulster.

Ó DOIĊEARTAIĠ—I—*O Dihirtie*, Deherty, Deharty, Doherty; an attenuated form of Ó Doċartaiġ, q.v.; found here and there in Munster.

Ó DOIĠRE—I—*O Dyry, O Deery*, Deery, Derry; a later form of Ó Daiġre, q.v.

Ó DOIṀÍN—I—*O Dovine, O Devine*, Devine, Devin, Deven, Devins, &c.; a var. of Ó Daiṁín, q.v.; so written in Annals of Loch Cé, A.D. 1278.

Ó DOINEANNAIĠ—I—Denanny, Dennany, Dennan; 'des. of Doineannaċ' (stormy, tempestuous); originally a midland surname. Ruithin O Doineannaigh, tanist of Teathbha, was slain, according to the Four Masters, in 1044. I cannot find any early angl. form.

Ó DOIRḂÍN—I—*O Durvin*, Derivin, Derwin; 'des. of Doirḃín' (dim. of doirḃ, peevish, quarrelsome).

Ó DOIREIḊ, Ó DOIRIḊ—I—*O'Derrie*, Derry; 'des. of Doireḋ'; the name of an ecclesiastical family in Donegal, who were erenaghs of Donoughmore, near Castlefin. O'Donovan seems to have regarded this as the same name as Ó Doiṡṙe, but, except that their angl. forms are the same, there is apparently no connection.

Ó Doirṙinne—I—*O Dorryny, O Dorreny, O Dorney,* Dorney, Darney; 'des. of Doiṙeann' (sullen, a woman's name). This is one of our very few Irish metronymic surnames.

Ó Doirṅín—I—*O Dornine,* Dornin, Durnin, Durnian, Dornan, &c.; a var. of Ó Duiṙnín, q.v.

Ó Doiṫe—I—*O Dohie,* O'Diff, (Duffy); an old Mayo surname, still common in that county and in Co. Galway, but always made Duffy in English. Baile Ui Dhoithe, angl. Ballyduffy, in the parish of Addergoole, Co. Mayo, marks the site of the ancient residence of the family.

Ó Domaġáin—I—Domigan, Domegan, Dumegan; 'des. of *Domaġán' (dim. of doma, want, scarcity). Cf. *O Domagh, O Duma,* for Ó Domaiġ; *O Demine, O Domyn* for *Ó Doiṁín.

Ó Doṁnaill—I—*O Donill, O Daniell,* O'Donnell, Donnell, Daniel; 'des. of Doṁnall' (world-mighty, an ancient and very common Irish personal name, now generally angl. Daniel); the name of several distinct families in Ireland, of which the following were the most important :—(1) Ó Doṁnaill of Tirconaill. This family is descended from Conall Gulban, son of Niall of the Nine Hostages, and for four centuries was one of the most powerful in Ireland. The original patrimony of this family was Cinel Luighdheach, a mountainous district between the Swilly and the Dobhar, but on the decline of the O'Muldorys and O'Canannains, some time after the Anglo-Norman invasion, they became the ruling family in Tirconnell. Previous to that event, only two of the immediate ancestors of the O'Donnells had been lords of Tirconnell, namely, Dalach, who died in 868 and from whom they derived their later clan-name of Clann Dalaigh, and his son, Eigheachan, who was the father of Domhnall from whom they took the surname of

Ó Domnaill, or O'Donnell. The family produced
many able chieftains who, during the four stormy
centuries that the O'Donnells held sway in Tirconnell,
not only defended their territory against foreign and
native foes, but made their power respected throughout the north and west of Ireland. The most celebrated of all the chieftains of Tirconnell was Red
Hugh O'Donnell, who so often led his clan to victory
in the closing years of the reign of Elizabeth. Many
of the O'Donnells were distinguished military commanders in the service of continental powers, and in
the last century, Leopold O'Donnell became prime
minister of Spain and Duke of Tetuan. The O'Donnells of Limerick and Tipperary are, according to
O'Donovan, descended from Shane Luirg, son of
Turlough O'Donnell of the Wine, lord of Tirconnell
at the beginning of the 15th century. (2) Ó Domnaill of Corcabaskin, in West Clare. This family
derives its descent from Domnall, son of Diarmaid,
lord of Corcabaskin, who was slain at the battle of
Clontarf in 1014. The O'Donnells continued to be
lords of Corcabaskin until dispossessed by the Mac-
Mahons early in the 14th century. They are, no
doubt, still numerous in Thomond. (3) Ó Domnaill
of Ui Maine, who were chiefs of Clann Flaitheamhail,
in the present Co. Galway. (4) Ó Domnaill of Carlow,
anciently lords of Ui Drona, now the barony of Idrone.
(5) Ó Domnaill of Cinel Binnigh, a sept of the Cinel
Eoghain. (6) Ó Domnaill of Ui Eathach, a sept of
the Oirghialla, who were seated in the present Co.
Armagh. The O'Donnells are now very numerous,
especially in Ulster and Munster.

Ó Domnalláin—I—*O Donellane, O Donnellan*, Donelan, Donnellan, Donlan, &c. ; ' des. of Domnallán'
(dim. of Domnall). The principal family of this
name is that of Ui Maine, in the present Co. Galway.
The head of this family, which is of the same stock as
the O'Kellys, was chief of Clann Bhreasail, a district
lying between Ballinasloe and Loughrea, and had his

residence at Ballydonnellan. This family produced some poets who are referred to in the Annals. Another family of the name, a branch of the Oirghialla, were anciently lords of Ui Tuirtre, comprising the modern baronies of Upper and Lower Toome, in Co. Antrim. There was also a Brehon family of the name in Offaly, and the name was not uncommon in that and the neighbouring districts of Leinster at the end of the 16th century. A family of the name is also mentioned as anciently chiefs of Teallach Ainbhith in Tyrone. Most of the Donnellans in Ireland at present belong to the Ui Maine family.

Ó 'Oonnabáin—I—O'Donovan, Donovan; 'des. of 'Oonn'oubán' (brown 'Oubán, or compound of 'oonn, brown, and 'oub, black, with dim. termination). The O'Donovans, who belong to the royal race of Munster, were originally chiefs of Ui Cairbre Aedhbha, a district lying along the banks of the River Maigue, in the present Co. Limerick. Their principal stronghold was at Bruree. About the year 1178, however, they were driven from Ui Cairbre and forced to take refuge in South-west Cork where, with the aid of their old allies, the O'Mahonys, they effected a settlement in O'Driscoll's country of Corca Laoighdhe, to which they gave their clan-name of Ui Cairbre, and where they retained considerable power and extensive possessions down to the close of the Jacobite wars. A branch of the family settled in Co. Wexford; and from another branch, settled in Kilkenny, the celebrated Irish antiquarian and scholar, Dr. John O'Donovan, was descended. There is also a family of O'Donovan in Tipperary, which, however, is not of this stock, but of that of the O'Mahers. See also Ó 'Oonnamáin.

Ó 'Oonnabáir—I—O Downever, O Donowre, O Donnor, Dooner, Dunner, Donor; 'des. of 'Oonnabar' (brown-eyebrow); also written Ó 'Oúnabra. This surname appears to have originated in Co. Roscommon. The Annals of the Four Masters at the year 1101 record the death of Ᵹⁱᴏᴌᴌᴀ ⁿᴀ ⁿᴀᴏ́ṁ Ó Ḋúⁿᴀḃⁱᴘᴀ, chief poet of Connacht. In the year 1297, Marian O Donnabhair was elected Bishop of Elphin, but died on his way to Rome, to uphold the validity of his election, which was contested. The surname had reached Tipperary before the end of the 16th century.

Ó ᴅᴏⁿⁿᴀċᴀ́ⁱⁿ—I—*O Donaghan, O Duneghan, O Dunchan*, Doonican, Dunican, Duncan ; ' des. of ᴅᴏⁿⁿᴀċᴀ́ⁿ' (dim. of ᴅᴏⁿⁿ, brown) ; apparently a var. of Ó ᴅᴏⁿⁿᴀᵹᴀ́ⁱⁿ, q.v. See also Ó ᴅᴜⁱⁿⁿᴇᴀċᴀ́ⁱⁿ.

Ó ᴅᴏⁿⁿᴀᵹᴀ́ⁱⁿ—I—*O Donegaine, O Dunegaine, O Donegan, O Dongane, O Dungan*, Donnegan, Dunnegan, Donegan, Dunigan, Dongan, Dungan, Duncan, &c. ; ' des. of ᴅᴏⁿⁿᴀᵹᴀ́ⁿ' (dim. of ᴅᴏⁿⁿ, brown); the name of several distinct families in Ireland. The O'Donegans of Tipperary and Limerick were in early times a very important family. They were chiefs of the extensive district of Ara, now the barony of Ara (or Duhara) in the north-west of Co. Tipperary, and of Ui Cuanach, now the barony of Coonagh in Co. Limerick. They are frequently mentioned in the Annals during the 11th and 12th century, but after the Anglo-Norman invasion they began to decline and soon disappeared from history. Their territory in later times was occupied by a branch of the O'Briens, the chief of which was styled Mac I Brien Ara. The O'Donegans of Cork were anciently chiefs of Muscraighe-tri-maighe, or Muskerry of the Three Plains, now the barony of Orrery in the neighbourhood of Rathluirc. Their patrimony was granted by King John to William de Barry, under the name of Muskerry-Donegan. There were, in early times, three distinct families of O'Donegans in Ulster, and the name is still extant in that province. The O'Donegans were numerous at the end of the 16th century in the midlands and in North Connacht ; and, though by no means common, the name is at the present day found in all the provinces.

Ó ᴅᴏⁿⁿᴀ́ⁱⁿ—I—*O Donayne, O Donnane*, Donnan ; ' des.

of Ɗonnán' (dim. of Ɗonn, brown); also written Ó Ʋúnáin, q.v.—

Ó Ɗonnamáin—I—O'Donovan, Donovan; 'des. of Ɗonnɒamán' (brown Ɒamán, or compound of ɒonn; brown, and ɒaṁ, a poet, with the dim. termination), the name of a family of Corca Laoighdhe, who were seated in Tuath O Feehily, in O'Driscoll's country, before the O'Donovans of Ui Cairbre settled in that district. "It is highly probable," says Dr. O'Donovan, "that a great number of the O'Donovans of the County of Cork are of this family." (Four Masters, p. 2483).

Ó Ɗonncaɒa, Ó Ɗonncaiɒ—I—*O Donochowe, O Donaghie, O Dunaghy*, O'Donoghue, O'Donohue, Donaghoe, Donoghue, Donohoe, Donaghy, Donagh, Dunphy, Dunfy, Dumphy, &c.; 'des. of Ɗonncaɒ' (brown-warrior, or strong-warrior, a very common Irish personal name). There are several distinct families of this name in Ireland, of which the following are the best known :—(1) Ó Ɗonncaɒa of Cashel, who are of the same stock as the MacCarthys and O'Callaghans, and derive their name and descent from Ɗonncaɒ, son of Ceallachan, King of Cashel. They were seated in Magh Feimhin, now the barony of Iffa and Offa, in the south-east of Co. Tipperary, and during the greater part of the 11th century were lords of Eoghanacht Caisil; but towards the close of that century, they were overshadowed by the growing power of the MacCarthys and disappeared from history. (2) Ó Ɗonncaɒa of Desmond, a branch of the Ui Eathach Mumhan and of the same stock as the O'Mahonys, who derive their descent from Eochaidh, son of Cas, son of Corc, King of Munster in the 5th century, and more immediately from Domhnall, the son of Dubhdabhoireann, King of Munster, who commanded, conjointly with Cian, ancestor of the O'Mahonys, the forces of Desmond at the battle of Clontarf. The descendants of Domhnall were at first surnamed Ó Ɗoṁnaill, but afterwards adopted the present surname of Ó Donncaḋa, which they took from Donncaḋ, his son. They were known by the clan-names of Cinel Laoghaire and Clann tSealbaigh. The original patrimony of the family lay in West Cork, but about the end of the 12th century or the beginning of the 13th, they were driven out by the MacCarthys and O'Mahonys, and settled in Kerry, where they became lords of all the country about Killarney, to which they gave the name of Eoghanacht Ui Dhonnchadha, angl. Onaght O'Donoghue. They divided at an early period into two great branches, namely Ó Donncaḋa of Loch Lein, the head of which was known as Ó Donncaḋa Móp, or O'Donoghue More, and resided at Ross Castle, and Ó Donncaḋa of Glenflesk, the head of which was designated Ó Donncaḋa an Ᵹleanna, or O'Donoghue of the Glen. The estates of O'Donoghue More were confiscated in the reign of Elizabeth, and ultimately passed into the possession of the ancestors of the Earl of Kenmare, but O'Donoghue of the Glen retained considerable property down to modern times. The head of this branch is now known as The O'Donoghue. (3) Ó Donncaḋa of Ossory who are of the same stock as the Fitzpatricks, and were anciently one of the ruling families of Ossory. Donncaḋ Ó Donncaḋa, the head of the family in the latter part of the 12th century, was the founder of Jerpoint Abbey. This family now anglicise the name Dunphy. (4) Ó Donncaḋa of Meath, who were chiefs of Teallach Modharain, which, according to O'Donovan, was probably in the barony of South Moyfenrath, but nothing is known of their history. (5) Ó Donncaḋa of Ui Maine, who are of the same stock as the O'Kellys, and were chiefs of Ui Cormaic, in the present Co. Galway. (6) Ó Donncaḋa of Tireragh, a branch of the Ui Fiachrach of the Moy. (7) Ó Donncaḋa of Teallach Dhonnchadha, who are still numerous in Co. Cavan. This surname, under various angl. forms, is now very common in all parts of Ireland.

Ó ᴅoɴɴcᴀᴄᴀɪ̵ʒ—I—Duncahy. V. Ó ᴅuɪɴɴcᴀᴄᴀɪ̵ʒ.

Ó ᴅoɴɴᴅᴀᵯ́ᴀ́ɪɴ, v. Ó ᴅoɴɴᴀᵯ́ᴀ́ɪɴ.

Ó ᴅoɴɴᴅuʙᴀ́ɪɴ, v. Ó ᴅoɴɴᴀʙᴀ́ɪɴ.

Ó ᴅoɴɴᴅuʙᴀʀᴄᴀɪ̵ʒ—I—*O Donnoartie, O Donorty, O Dunort*, Donarty, Donworth, Dunworth, Dunfort, Dunford, (Davenport) ; 'des. of ᴅoɴɴᴅuʙᴀʀᴄᴀᴄ, (brown ᴅuʙᴀʀᴄᴀᴄ) ; an old Munster surname, still well represented in the province. It appears to have originated in the neighbourhood of Clonmel.

Ó ᴅoɴɴʒᴀɪʟe—I—O'Donnelly, Donnelly, Donneely ; 'des. of ᴅoɴɴʒᴀʟ' (brown-valour) ; the name of a distinguished family of Cinel Eoghain in Ulster who derive their name and descent from ᴅoɴɴʒᴀʟ, the fourth in descent from ᴅoᵯ́ɴᴀʟʟ, King of Aileach and brother of ɴɪᴀʟʟ ʒʟúɴᴅuʙ, the eponymous ancestor of the O'Neills. The O'Donnellys were originally seated at Druim Lighean, now angl. Drumleen, a short distance to the north of Lifford, Co. Donegal, but were afterwards expelled by the Cinel Conaill, when they settled at Ballydonnelly, now Castlecaulfield, to the west of Dungannon. It was at Ballydonnelly that the celebrated Shane O'Neill was fostered by the O'Donnellys. O'Donnelly was hereditary marshal of O'Neill's forces ; and Donnell O'Donelly, who accompanied Hugh O'Neill to Kinsale as 'captain of one hundred men,' fought bravely until he and all his men were slain. Ballydonnelly was granted by James I to Sir Toby Caulfield, ancestor of the Earl of Charlemont. The family is now very numerous in Ulster. There were also families of the name in Sligo and Cork. The former were a branch of the Ui Fiachrach, and were seated at Dun Ui Chobhthaigh, now angl. Doonycoy, in the parish of Templeboy. The latter were a branch of the Corca Laoighdhe, and were seated near Dunmanway.

Ó ᴅoɴɴʒᴀʟᴀɪ̵ʒ—I—*O Donnowly*, O'Donnelly, Donnelly, &c. ; 'des. of ᴅoɴɴʒᴀʟᴀᴄ' (der. of ᴅoɴɴʒᴀʟ) ; the name (1) of a Tipperary family who were anciently chiefs of Muscraighe-Thire, now the barony of Lower

Ormond, but disappeared from history towards the
end of the 11th century ; and (2) of a Galway family,
a branch of the Siol Anmchadha, who were numerous
in that county at the beginning of the 17th century.
This surname is also written Ó Dúngalaig. Its angl.
forms cannot now be distinguished from those of Ó
Donngaile, q.v.

Ó Donngusa—I—*O Dangussa, O Danaisa, O Denisi,*
Dennis, Denis, Denison, Dennison, Denson ; ' des. of
Donngur ' (brown-choice) ; the name of an ecclesiastical family in Ulster ; also of a Munster family, chiefly
in Cork and Waterford.

Ó Dorraid—I—*O Durry,* Durry, (?) Dorr, (?) Durr ; ' des.
of Dorad ' (perhaps Doraid, strife ; cf. Ó maoldoraid).

Ó Dorbáin—I—Derivan, Derivin, ; a var. of ÓDoirbín,
q.v.

Ó Dorcaide—I—*O Doroghie, O Dorichie, O Dorchie,*
Dorcey, Darkey, Darcy, (D'Arcy) ; ' des. of Dorcaide ' (dark-man) ; the name (1) of a branch of the
Ui Fiachrach, who were chiefs of the extensive district
of Partry, to the west of Lough Mask, Co. Mayo ;
and (2) of a branch of the Ui Maine in Co. Galway.
Both families are still well represented. At the end of
the 16th century, the name was also found in nearly
every county in Munster, and in Kildare and Carlow.
It is now nearly everywhere angl. Darcy or D'Arcy,
which disguises the Irish origin of the family.

Ó Dorcáin—I—*O Dorchane,* Dorgan, Dorrigan, (?)
Doorigan ; ' des. of Dorcán ' (dim. of Dorcaide) ; a
rare surname in Cork and Kerry ; probably the same
as Ó Dorcaide, q.v.

Ó Dornáin—I—*O Dornane,* O'Dornan, Dornan, Durnan,
&c. ; ' des. of Dornán ' (dim. of dorn, a fist) ; a rare
surname ; found chiefly in Antrim and Down. V.
Ó Duirnín.

Ó Drae—III—*O Drea,* Drea, Drew, (Drewry, Drury) ;
' des. of the druid ' (Ir. drae) ; apparently the same
as the Thomond Ó Draoi, q.v. ; a rare surname in

Kerry and West Limerick. The family has been located for centuries in the parish of Duagh, near Listowel.

Ó ᴅʀᴀɢɴáɴ, Ó ᴅʀᴀɩɢɴᴇáɩɴ—I—*O Drinane, O Drenan*, Drinane, Drinan, Dreinan, Drennan, and, by translation, Thornton; 'des. of ᴅʀᴀɩɢɴᴇáɴ' (blackthorn); the name (1) of a branch of the Siol Anmchadha in Co. Galway; and (2) of a Clare family, who were formerly seated in the barony of Corcumroe. The name was also common in Cavan, Westmeath, Leix and Kilkenny.

Ó ᴅʀᴀᴏᴅᴀ—I—Drudy, Droody, Draddy; 'des. of ᴅ_____'; an old, but rare, Connacht surname. ɢɩᴏʟʟᴀ Cɩᴀᴘáɩɴ Ó ᴅʀᴀᴏᴅᴀ, erenagh of Cong, is mentioned by the Four Masters at the year 1128.

Ó ᴅʀᴀᴏɩ—III—*O Dree*, Drea, Drew, (Drewry, Drury); 'des. of the druid' (Ir. ᴅʀᴀᴏɩ); a rare Thomond surname; also Ó ᴅʀᴜᴀɩᴅ, q.v. Cf. Ó ᴅʀᴀᴇ.

*Ó ᴅʀᴀᴏɩʟᴇáɩɴ, Dreelan.

Ó ᴅʀᴇᴀᴅᴀ—I—*O Dready, O Dradye*, Draddy; 'des. of ᴅ_____'; a rare Cork surname. Sᴇᴀɴ Ó ᴅʀᴇᴀᴅᴀ was a Munster scribe at the beginning of the last century. V. Ó ɢʀᴇᴀᴅᴀ, of which it is possibly a variant.

Ó ᴅʀᴇáɩɴ—I—*O Dreane*, Adrien, Adrian, Drain, Draine; 'des. of ᴅʀᴇáɴ' (wren). The O'Dreains were anciently chiefs of Calraidhe in Co. Roscommon, and erenaghs of Ardcarne, near Boyle, but were dispossessed in the 13th or 14th century by the MacDermotts. They appear to have removed to Co. Antrim, which is the only place where the name was found in the 16th century.

Ó ᴅʀɩsᴄᴇóɩʟ—I—*O Driscole*, O'Driscoll, Driscoll, &c.; a corrupt form of Ó ʜᴇɩᴅɩʀsᴄᴇóɩʟ, q.v.

Ó ᴅʀɩsʟᴇáɩɴ—I—*O Drislane*, Drislane; 'des. of ᴅʀɩsʟᴇáɴ' (brier).

Ó ᴅʀᴏċᴛᴀɩɢ—I—*O Drughta, O Drought*, Drought; 'des. of ᴅʀᴏċᴛᴀċ' (from ᴅʀᴏċᴛ, a mill-wheel?). V. Ó ᴅʀᴏɩċɩᴅ.

Ó **ᴆᴿᴏᴉᴄᴉᴆ**—I—*O Drehitt*, Bridgeman ; probably a corruption of *Ó ᴆᴩᴏᴉᴄᴛᴉʒ, des. of ᴆᴩᴏᴉᴄᴛᴇᴀᴄ (bridgemaker or bridge-keeper) ; a rare Limerick surname. Cf. Ó ᴆᴩᴏᴄᴛᴀᴉʒ.

Ó **ᴆᴿᴏᴍᴀ**—I—*O Drommy*, Dromey, Drummy, Drum, Drumm, (Drummond) ; ' des. of ᴆᴩᴜᴉᴍ ' (back) ; the name of an ecclesiastical family who were erenaghs of the parish of Kinnawley, in the Counties of Fermanagh and Cavan, where they are still numerous. Some of them settled in Munster in the 16th century, Solomon O'Droma was one of the compilers of the Book of Ballymote.

Ó **ᴆᴿᴏᴍᴀᴉɴ**—I—Droman ; ' des. of ᴆᴩᴏᴍᴀɴ ' (dim. of ᴆᴩᴏᴍ, a back) ; a rare Waterford surname ; also Ó ᴆᴩᴜᴉᴍᴉɴ, q.v.

Ó **ᴆᴿᴏɴᴀ**—I—*O Drony*, Droney ; ' des. of ᴆᴩᴏɴᴀ '; a rare Clare surname.

Ó **ᴆᴿᴜᴀᴄᴀᴉɴ**—I—*O Drwoghane, O Droughane, O Droghane*, Droohan, Drohane, Drohan ; ' des. of ᴆᴩᴜᴀᴄᴀɴ '; a rare surname, found chiefly in Waterford and Cork. There was an ecclesiastical family of Ó ᴆᴩᴜᴄᴀᴉɴ at Armagh which may possibly be the same.

Ó **ᴆᴿᴜᴀᴉᴆ**—III—Drew, (Drewry, Drury) ; a var. of Ó ᴆᴩᴀᴏᴉ, q.v.

Ó **ᴆᴿᴜᴉᴍᴉɴ**—I—*O Dromen*, Drummin ; ' des. of ᴆᴩᴜᴉᴍᴉɴ ' (dim. of ᴆᴩᴜᴉᴍ, a back). Cf. Ó ᴆᴩᴏᴍᴀᴉɴ and Ó ᴆᴩᴏᴍᴀ.

Ó **ᴆᴜᴀᴄᴀᴉɴ**—I—*O Doughane*, Doughan, Doohane ; ' des. of ᴆᴜᴀᴄᴀɴ ' (dim. of ᴆᴜᴉ or ᴆᴜᴀᴄ) ; a Donegal surname ; to be distinguished from Ó ᴆᴜᴃᴄᴏɴ, which is often similarly anglicised.

Ó **ᴆᴜᴃᴀʒᴀᴉɴ**—I—*O Doogaine, O Dowgaine*, O'Doogan, Doogan, Doogan, Dougan, Dugan, Duggan, &c. ; ' des of ᴆᴜᴃᴀʒᴀɴ ' (dim. of ᴆᴜᴃ, black). There are several distinct families of this name, of which the following are the most important :—(1) Ó ᴆᴜᴃᴀʒᴀᴉɴ of Fermoy, who before the Anglo-Norman invasion were lords of the northern half of Feara Maighe, which comprised the modern baronies of Fermoy, Condons, and Clan-gibbon ; (2) Ó Ouḃaġáın of Ui Maine, a literary family, who were hereditary historians to the O'Kellys and compilers of the Book of Ui Maine, and had their residence at Ballydugan, near Loughrea ; (3) Ó Ouḃaġáın of Tirawley who are of the same stock as the MacFirbises, and were anciently seated in the parish of Kilmore-Moy, to the north-west of Ballina ; (4) Ó Ouḃaġáın of Corca Laoighdhe, in South-west Cork, where they are still numerous ; and (5) Ó Ouḃaġáın of Aidhne, in South-west Galway.

Ó Ouḃáın—I—*O Dovayne, O Dwane, O Duan, O Dowane, O Doane, O Downe,* Dewane, Devane, Divane, Divan, Dwane, Duane, Dwan, Duan, Dune, Doane, Dooan, Doon, Down, Downes, (Devine, Devany), &c., and by ' translation ' Kidney ; ' des. of Ouḃáın ' (a dim. of ouḃ, black) ; the name of several distinct families, viz. : (1) a Meath family, anciently lords of Cnodhbha, now angl. Knowth, in the parish of Monkstown, but dispossessed at an early period and dispersed through Leinster ; (2) a family of Corca Laoighdhe in South-west Cork, still numerous in that county, but sometimes calling themselves Kidney in English ; (3) a Connemara family, an old family in that district and still well represented, but the name is sometimes made Devany in English, as happens sometimes also in Mayo ; and (4) an old Limerick family who now sometimes anglicise the name Downes. At the end of the 16th century, Ó Ouḃáın was a common surname throughout the southern half of Ireland. Ó Ouıḃín, which is synonymous, is often used interchangeably with it, especially in Connacht.

Ó Ouḃánaıġ—I—*O Douvany, O Dowanie, O Devany,* Duany, Devany ; ' des. of Ouḃánaċ ' (der. of Ouḃáın) ; a rare suruame in Donegal and Sligo.

Ó Ouḃarтаıġ—I—*O Duarty, O Duhartie, O Dowhirty,* Duarty, Doorty, Dooherty, (Doherty) ; ' des. of Ouḃarтaċ ' (black Aптaċ, or compound of ouḃ, black, aпт, noble, bear, &c., and the adjectival suffix aċ) ; the name of a family of the Corca Laoighdhe, in south-

west Cork. The family, which has been long dispersed through Munster, is numerous in the counties
of Cork, Kerry, Limerick and Tipperary, but often
disguised as Dohertys.

Ó Ꝺuḃasa, v. Ó Ꝺuḃġuʀa.

Ó Ꝺuḃcaiʀ — I — *O Duchir, O Dougher,* Doughar,
Dougher, Dooher ; 'des. of Ꝺuḃcaʀ' (black-dear) ; a
rare and scattered surname. In the 16th century, it
was found in Donegal, Tipperary and Wexford.

Ó Ꝺuḃcon—I—*O Duchon, O Doghon, O Dughan, O
Dohon,* Doughan, Doohan ; 'des. of Ꝺuḃcú ' (black-
hound) ; the name of a family of the Corca Laoighdhe
in South-west Cork, but long peculiar to Tipperary
and Clare.

Ó Ꝺuḃconna—I—O'Dooghany, Dougheny, Dogheny,
Doheny, Deheny, Dahony, Dawney, &c. ; ' des. of
Ꝺuḃconna' (black Conna, a man's name) ; the name
of a family of the Corca Laoighdhe, in South-west
Cork ; now scattered through Munster.

Ó Ꝺuḃaḋoiʀeann—I—Davoran, Davoren, Davern ;
'des. of Ꝺuḃaḋoiʀeann ' (Black of the two Burrens) ;
now shortened to Ó Ꝺaḃoiʀeann, q.v.

Ó Ꝺuḃꝺa—I—*O Dowda, O Douda, O Dooda, O Dowdy,
O Duda, O Doddie,* O'Dowd, O'Doud, Dowda, Dowdie,
Doody, Duddy, Doud, Dowd, &c. ; ' des. of Ꝺuḃꝺa'
(black) ; the name (1) of a Connacht family, and (2)
of an Ulster family. The first of these derive their
descent from the celebrated King Dathi and were the
head family of the northern Ui Fiachrach. Before
the irruption of the English into Connacht in 1237,
they were the ruling family in all Lower Connacht,
including the greater part of the present counties of
Mayo and Sligo. And their power was great on sea
as well as on land. (See Annals, A.D. 1154.) In the
14th century they had in immediate succession three
able chieftains who drove the English out of their
territory, but they were never able to regain the
position of power and dignity which the family enjoyed before the English settlement in Connacht.

The O'Dowd lands were confiscated after the Cromwellian and Jacobite wars. Branches of the family had settled in Munster before the end of the 16th century, where they now anglicise the name Doody. The Ulster family, which is a branch of the Cinel Eoghain, is still numerous in Derry and other parts of that province.

Ó ᴅᴜʙᴅᴀᴄᴀ́ɪɴ, Ó ᴅᴜʙᴅᴀᴈᴀ́ɪɴ—I—*O Dowdegane, O Dwdigane*, Dowdican, Dudican; des. of 'ᴅᴜʙᴅᴀᴄᴀ́ɴ' or 'ᴅᴜʙᴅᴀᴈᴀ́ɴ' (dim. of ᴅᴜʙᴅᴀ); a rare Sligo surname. MacFirbis mentions a family of Ó ᴅᴜʙᴅᴀᴄᴀ́ɪɴ among the Cinel Eoghain.

Ó ᴅᴜʙᴅᴀ́ʟᴇɪᴅᴇ—I—Dudley; 'des. of ᴅᴜʙᴅᴀ́ʟᴇɪᴅᴇ' (Black of the two sides); a rare South Cork surname.

Ó ᴅᴜʙᴅᴜ́ɪɴ—I—*O Dughune, O Dwghune, O Dogowyn*, (?) Duggan; 'des. of ᴅᴜʙᴅᴜ́ɪɴ' (Black of the fort); an old Kerry surname, probably still extant, but disguised under the angl. form of Duggan.

Ó ᴅᴜʙᴈᴀɪʟᴇ—I—*O Dowilly*, (Doyle); 'des. of ᴅᴜʙᴈᴀʟ' (black-valour); an old surname in Co. Roscommon, where it is still extant under the angl. form of Doyle. It has always been extremely rare.

Ó ᴅᴜʙᴈᴀɪʟʟ—II—*O Dogaill, O Dowill, O Dowell, O Doole*, O'Doyle, Doyle, Dowell, Doole, &c.; 'des. of ᴅᴜʙᴈᴀʟʟ' (the black foreigner); a very common Irish surname, doubtless of Danish origin. It is found in all parts of Ireland, but is most frequent in the maritime counties of Leinster and Munster, and in the neighbourhood of the old Danish settlements.

Ó ᴅᴜʙᴈᴜsᴀ—I—*O Dwysy*, Doocey, Doocie, Doocy, Ducey; 'des. of ᴅᴜʙᴈᴜʀ' (black-choice); an old, but rare, Ormond surname.

Ó ᴅᴜʙʟᴀᴄᴀ́ɪɴ—I—*O Duelaghane*, Doolaghan, Dullaghan, Dolaghan, Dologhan; 'des. of ᴅᴜʙʟᴀᴄᴀ́ɴ'; also Ó ᴅᴜɪʙʟᴇᴀᴄᴀ́ɪɴ, q.v.

Ó ᴅᴜʙʟᴀᴅᴀɪᴈ—I—Doolady, Dooladdy; 'des. of ᴅᴜʙᴩʟᴀᴅᴀᴄ'; a rare Co. Leitrim surname. I cannot find any early angl. form.

Ó ᴅᴜʙʟᴀɪᴅᴇ, Ó ᴅᴜʙʟᴀɪᴈᴇ, v. Ó ᴅᴜʙʟᴀᴏɪᴄ.

Ó Ꝺυбⱡáιn—I—*O Doelane, O Dowlane, O Dolane,* O'Doolan, Doolan, Dolan, (Dowling, Delaney, Delany) ; ' des. of Ꝺυбⱡán ' (black defiance, challenge) ; a rather common surname in all parts of Ireland, but its angl. forms cannot always be distinguished from those of Ó Ꝺυбⱡαιnn and Ó Ꝺυnⱡαιƞᵹ, q.v. Felix O Dubhlain was Bishop of Ossory at the beginning of the 13th century.

Ó Ꝺυбⱡαιnn—I—*O Dowlan, O Dowlin, O Doolen,* O'Doolan, Doolan, Doolin, (Dowling), &c. ; ' des. of Ꝺυбⱡαnn ' (black Fⱡαnn) ; the name of a family of the Ui Maine, in Co. Galway. Its angl. forms cannot always be distinguished from those of Ó Ꝺυбⱡáιn and Ó Ꝺúnⱡαιƞᵹ, q.v.

Ó Ꝺυбⱡαċτα, Ó Ꝺυбⱡαċτnα—I—Doolaghty, Dooloughty ; ' des. of Ꝺυбⱡαċτnα' (black ⱡαċτnα, a man's name) ; a Clare surname.

Ó Ꝺυбⱡαοιċ—I—*O Dowlee, O Dowley, O Dooly,* Dowley, Dooley, Dooly ; ' des. of Ꝺυбⱡαοċ ' (black hero). There are three distinct families of this name, viz. : (1) Ó Ꝺυбⱡαοιċ of Feara Tulach who are of the race of Feidlimidh, son of Enna Ceinnsealach, and before the Anglo-Norman invasion were lords of Feara Tulach, now the barony of Fertullagh, in the south-east of Co. Westmeath. They were dispossessed soon after the invasion and their lands given to the Tyrrells. (2) Ó Ꝺυбⱡαοιċ of Clann Mhaonaigh, who, according to MacFirbis, are a branch of the O'Melaghlens of Meath, whence they were banished in the 11th century. They settled on the western side of Slieve Bloom, in Ely O'Carroll, where they are still very numerous. The head of the family had the privilege of inaugurating O'Carroll as king of Ely. MacFirbis writes the name of this family Ó Ꝺυιбⱡυιᵹe (Gen. p. 161). (3) Ó Ꝺυбⱡαοιċ of Siol Anmchadha who are of the same stock as the O'Maddens and were originally located in the south-east of the present Co. Galway.

Ó Ꝺυбⱡυαċрα—I—*O Dwlougherie,* Dilloughery, Deloughery, Delooghery, Delouhery, Delohery, Deloorey,

Delury, Deloury, Delacour, (Dilworth, Dillworth);
' des. of Ɗuḃluaċꞃa ' (Black of Luaċaiꞃ, a place-
name in West Munster) ; an old surname in Co. Cork.

Ó Ɗuḃꞃaic—I—*O Duvrick, O Durick, O Dowricke,*
Durack, Durick, Darrick ; ' des. of Ɗuḃꞃaṫa ' (Black
of prosperity) ; older form Ó Ɗuḃꞃaṫa ; the name of a
Dalcassian family who were anciently lords of Ui
Conghaile, now the parish of O'Connelloe, near Killaloe.
The family is almost extinct in Clare, but survives
in Tipperary and Offaly. Also Ó Ɗuiḃꞃic, q.v.

Ó Ɗuḃꞃosa, Ó Ɗuḃꞃuis—I—*O Durise,* Dooris,
Doorish, Doris ; ' des. of Ɗuḃꞃoꞃ ' (black Roꞃ);
formerly the name of a family in the neighbourhood
of Bruff in Co. Limerick, but it has long since disappeared from that part of the country. It occurs
in Fermanagh early in the 17th century. I find the
modern forms in Longford and Mayo.

Ó Ɗuḃꞃláine, Ó Ɗuḃꞃláinꞃe—I—*O Dowlaney, O*
Dulany, Delaney, Delany, Deleany, Laney, &c. ;
' des. of Ɗuḃꞃláine ' or ' Ɗuḃꞃláinꞃe ' (Black of the
Slaney) ; the name of a numerous family in Leix, who
were formerly chiefs of Coill Uachtarach, now Upper-
woods, at the foot of Slieve Bloom.

Ó Ɗuḃṫaiꞃ—I—*O Duffie, O Duhie, O Duhig, O Dowhie,*
O Dowey, O'Duffy, Duffy, Duhy, Duhig, Dowey,
Douey, Dooey, Doey, &c., and sometimes, by translation, Black ; ' des. of Ɗuḃṫaċ ' (black). This surname is found in all parts of Ireland, and, doubtless,
there are several distinct families so called. The
O'Duffys of Connacht are remarkable for the number
of eminent prelates they formerly gave to the church
in that province. The O'Duffys were also a family
of note in Monaghan. In Munster, the name is
generally anglicised Duhig, owing to the pronunciation of the final ꞃ. The family is, according to Keating,
of Dalcassian origin. In Ulster, where the name is
very common, especially in Monaghan and Donegal,
it is sometimes angl. Dowey and Dooey. V. Ó Ɗúiṫċe.

Ó Ɗuḃuiḋe—I—*O Dywoie, O Dyvoye,* Devoy, Deevey,

Deevy; 'des. of Oubobar' (Black Obar); also Ó Ouibibe, q.v.; an apocopated form of Ó Oubuibir, q.v.; cf. Ó Bolɲuibe for Ó Bolɲuibir; a Leix surname.

Ó Oubuibir—I—*O Duvire, O Duire,* O'Dwyer, Dwyer, Dwire, &c.; 'des. of Oubobar' (black Obar); also written Ó Ouibibir, q.v.; the name of a Tipperary family, of Leinster origin, who were chiefs of Coill na manach, now the barony of Kilnamanagh, in the west of that county. Philip O'Dwyer and Owen O'Dwyer were exempted from pardon for life and estate in the Cromwellian Act of 1652. Some of the name held high rank in the service of France, Austria and Russia. The name is now common in all the south of Ireland. Ó Ouibibir is also a Donegal name, but whether or not the family is a branch of that of Tipperary, I am unable to say.

Ó Oubuɲcuile—I—*O Dorhilly, O Durley, O Dowrley,* Dufferly, Doorley, Doorly; 'des. of Oubuɲcuile' (black Uɲcuile); the name of a family of Ui Maine in Co. Galway, who were seated near Loughrea. It is still common in Connacht.

Ó Ouib—I—*O Duff,* O'Diff, Duff, and, by translation, Black; 'des. of Oub' (Black); the name of an old family in Leix who were chiefs of Cinel Criomhthainn, in the present barony of East Maryborough; also apparently of a Connacht family.

Ó Ouibcinn, v. Ó Ouibɲinn.

Ó Ouibbíorma, Ó Ouibbíormaiɲ—I—*O Dughierma,* Dooyearma, Dyermott, Diarmod, Dermott, Dermond, (O'Dermott, MacDermott), &c.; 'des. of Oubbíorma(c)' (black-trooper); the name of a family of Cinel Eoghain who were anciently lords of Bredach, which comprised the eastern half of Inishowen, and are still numerous in Donegal; often shortened to Ó Oíorma, and angl. MacDermott.

Ó Ouibeamna—I—*O'Doveanna,* Devanny, Devany, &c.; 'des. of Oubeamna' (Black of Eamain, near Armagh); the name of an Ulster family who were anciently chiefs of Ui Breasail, in Co. Armagh. Its angl. forms cannot be distinguished from those of Ó Ouıbeannaıɠ, q.v.

Ó Ouıbeannaıɠ—I—*O Doveanna, O Devenie,* Devanny, Devaney, Devany, Devenny, Divenney, &c. ; ' des. of Ouƀeannaıɠ ' (perhaps Black of eanaċ, a place-name) ; the name of a Co. Down family, to which belonged the Bishop of Down and Connor, Cornelius, or Connor O'Devany, whose martyrdom at Dublin, in 1612, is so touchingly described by the Four Masters. Its angl. forms cannot be distinguished from those of Ó Ouıbeaṁna, q.v.

Ó Ouıƀƒınn—I—*O Duffin,* Duffin, Diffin ; ' des. of Ouƀƒıonn ' (black-ƒıonn) ; a rare surname ; found chiefly in Antrim, Cork and Waterford.

Ó Ouıbɠeaɔáın—I—Dugidan, Degidan, (Dixon) ; ' des. of Ouƀɠeaɔán ' ; a Clare surname.

Ó Ouıbɠeannáın—I—*O Duigenain,* Duigenan, Duig-nan, Dignan, Deignan, Duignam, Dignam, &c. ; ' des. of Ouƀɠeannán ' (dim. of Ouƀceann, black-head) ; the name of a distinguished literary family in Co. Roscommon, who were hereditary chroniclers to the Clann Mulrony and Conmaicne, that is, to the MacDermotts, O'Farrells, Magrannells, &c. Their chief residence was at Kilronan.

Ó Ouıbɠınn—I—*O Duygin, O Digin,* Digin, Diggin, Deegin, Digan, Deighan, Deegan, Duigan, (Dugan, Duggan, Duggen) ; ' des. of Ouƀceann ' (Black-head). There are three distinct families of this name, formerly seated respectively in Galway, Clare and Wexford. It was also common, at the beginning of the 17th century, in Offaly and Leix and also in Kerry. It is now sometimes disguised under the angl. form of Dugan, or Duggan.

Ó Ouıbɠıolla—I—Duffley, Diffily, Differly, Diffley, Deffely, Divilly, Devilly, Devily, Deely, Dealy, &c. ; ' des. of Ouƀɠıolla ' (black-lad) ; the name (1) of a family of the southern Ui Fiachrach, who were chiefs of Cinel Cinnghamhna, near Kinvara, in south-west of Co. Galway ; and (2) of a family of Siol Anmchadha, in the south-east of the same county.

Ó Ɗuıƃıɖe—I—*O Divie, O Devy*, Deevey, Deevy, Devoy ; a var. of Ó Ɗuƃuıɖe, q.v.

Ó Ɗuıƃıɖıʀ—I—*O Duire, O Diver, O Dyer*, O'Dwyer, O'Deere, Dwyer, Deere, Dyer, Diver, Divver, Dever, Devers ; a var. of Ó Ɗuƃuıɖıʀ, q.v.

Ó Ɗuıƃín—I—*O Dovine*, O'Devine, Devine, Deveen, Devon, (Devany, Devaney) ; 'des. of Ɗuıƃín' (dim. of ɗuƃ, black) ; a scattered surname ; often an alias for Ó Ɗuƃáın, q.v. It is not possible always to distinguish its angl. forms from those of Ó Ɗaıṁín, q.v.

Ó Ɗuıƃínnʀeáċᴄaıᵹ—I—*O Denrathay*, Dunroche, Denroche ; 'des. of Ɗuıƃínnʀeáċᴄaċ' (Black Innʀeáċ-aċ) ; a rare old Sligo surname.

Ó Ɗuıƃleaċáın—I—*O Duelaghane*, Delahan, Dillahan, (Dillon) ; an attenuated form of Ó Ɗuƃlaċáın, q.v.

Ó Ɗuıƃleaʀᵹa—I—Delargy, Delargey, De Largey ; 'des. of Ɗuƃleaʀᵹa' (Black of Leaʀᵹa, a place-name) ; an old Tirawley surname ; still survives in Galway and Antrim.

Ó Ɗuıƃluaċʀa, v. Ó Ɗuƃluaċʀa.

Ó Ɗuıƃne—I—*O Dynie*, Deeny, Deeney, Denny, &c. ; 'des. of Ɗuıƃne' (ill-going, opposed to Suıƃne).

Ó Ɗuıƃʀıc—I—*O Divrick, Diviricke*, (Devereux), Devery, &c. ; a var. of Ó Ɗuƃʀaıc, q.v.

Ó Ɗuılleáın—I—*O Dullaine, O Dyllane*, Dillane, (Dillon) ; an attenuated form of Ó Ɗallaın, q.v. ; common in Kerry, Limerick, Clare and Galway, but often disguised under the angl. form of Dillon.

Ó Ɗuıllín—I—*O Dulline, O Dilline*, Dilleen ; a var. of Ó Ɗuılleáın, q.v. ; very rare.

Ó Ɗuıneaċaıʀ—I—*O Dinagher, O Donogher*, Donogher, Danagher, Deneher, Donaher, Danaher, Daniher, Dannaher ; 'des. of Ɗuıneaċaʀ' (man-loving) ; the name of a family who were anciently lords of Crioch Cathbhaidh, in the neighbourhood of Nenagh, but were dispossessed soon after the Anglo-Norman invasion and dispersed through Munster, Leinster and Connacht ; now most numerous in Co. Limerick.

Ó ⒹⓤⓘⓝⓔⒶⒸⓄⒶ—I—*O Denaghie,* Dennahy, Dennehy, Dannahy, Danihy, Denehy, Denny, &c. ; ' des. of ⒹⓤⓘⓝⓔⒶⒸⒶⓄ ' (humane) ; a well-known Co. Cork surname.

Ó Ⓓⓤⓘⓝ——, v. Ó Ⓓⓤⓘⓝⓝ——, which is often pronounced, and sometimes written, Ó Ⓓⓤⓘⓝ——.

Ó Ⓓⓤⓘⓝⓘⓝ—I—*O Downine,* O *Downyne,* O *Dwnyn,* Dunion, Dunning, Downing, &c. ; ' des. of Ⓓⓤⓘⓝⓘⓝ ' (dim. of ⒹⓄⓝⓝ, brown) ; a var. of Ó Ⓓⓤⓘⓝⓝⓘⓝ, q.v.

Ó Ⓓⓤⓘⓝⓝ—I—*O Dunne,* O *Doyne,* Dunne, Dunn, Dun, Doyne, Dyne, &c. ; ' des. of ⒹⓄⓝⓝ ' (brown). There are two distinct families of this name : (1) Ó Ⓓⓤⓘⓝⓝ of Ui Riagain, a branch of the Ui Failghe, and one of the chief families of Leinster. The head of this family was lord of Ui Riagain, now angl. Iregan, which was co-extensive with the present barony of Tinnahinch, in Leix. (2) Ó Ⓓⓤⓘⓝⓝ of Tara. This family was dispossessed soon after the Anglo-Norman invasion. The name is now very common in Leinster and Munster.

Ó ⒹⓤⓘⓝⓝⒸⒶⒸⒶⒼ—I—Duncahy ; ' des. of ⒹⓄⓝⓝⒸⒶⒸⒶⒸ ' ; the name of a Sligo family who were anciently lords of Corann, now the barony of Corran ; now very rare, if not actually obsolete.

Ó ⒹⓤⓘⓝⓝⒸⓘⓝⓝ—I—*O Dingine,* O *Dongyn,* O *Dongen,* Dinkin, Dunkin, (Duncan) ; ' des. of ⒹⓄⓝⓝⒸⒺⒶⓝⓝ ' (Brown-head) ; an old Sligo surname ; rare and often disguised as Duncan. Some of the family migrated to Leinster.

Ó ⒹⓤⓘⓝⓝⒺⒶⒷⒶⒾⓝ—I—*O Dunivane,* Dingavan, Dennivan ; an attenuated form of Ó ⒹⓄⓝⓝⒶⒷⒶⒾⓝ, q.v.

Ó ⒹⓤⓘⓝⓝⒺⒶⒸⒶⒾⓝ—I—*O Duinaghan,* O *Dwynighan,* Dinahan, Dinihan, Denehan, Deenihan ; ' des. of ⒹⓤⓘⓝⓝⒺⒶⒸⒶⒾⓝ ' (dim. of ⒹⓄⓝⓝ, brown) ; an attenuated form of Ó ⒹⓄⓝⓝⒶⒸⒶⒾⓝ, q.v. ; a rare surname, found chiefly in Limerick and Kerry. The family, according to Dr. O'Brien, belonged originally to Uaithne, the present barony of Owney, in Limerick and Tipperary.

Ó Ꝺuιnneᴀ5ᴀιn—I—*O Dwinagane, O Dinegane,* Dinnegan, Denegan, Denigan ; an attenuated form of Ó Ꝺonnᴀ5ᴀιn, q.v.

Ó Ꝺuιnnín—I—*O Dunnyne, O Downine,* Dinneen, Dineen, Dunion, Dunning, Denning, Downing ; ' des. of Ꝺuιnnín' (dim. of Ꝺonn, brown) ; the name of a literary family of Corca Laoighdhe, in South-west Cork, who became hereditary historians to MacCarthy More ; also of a midland family. In Munster the name is generally angl. Dineen and Dinneen, but sometimes Downing, while it is made Dunning and Denning in Leinster.

Ó Ꝺuιnnsléιbe—I—*O Dunlevy, O Downlay,* Dunlevy, Dunleavy, Dunlavy, Dunleevy, Dunlea, Dullea, Delea, Delay, Delee ; ' des. of Ꝺonnsléιbe' (Brown of the mountain) ; the name of a branch of the family of Ó nEocᴀᴅᴀ of Ulidia, who were also known by the surname of Mᴀc Ꝺuιnnsléιbe and, from their place of origin, Ulᴄᴀc and Ulᴄᴀcᴀn. For history of family, see Mᴀc Ꝺuιnnsléιbe.

Ó Ꝺuιrnín—I—*O Durnyne,* O'Durnin, Durnin, Durnian, Durnion, Dornin, and, by ' translation,' Cuffe ; ' des. of Ꝺuιrnín' (dim. of Ꝺorn, a fist) ; an Ulster surname. In the 16th century it was found chiefly in Donegal, and Fermanagh. V. Ó Ꝺornᴀιn.

Ó Ꝺuιᴄᴄe—I—*O Dowghie, O Dowchy,* Dooey, Duffy ; a common corruption of Ó Ꝺubᴄᴀι5, q.v.

Ó Ꝺulᴄᴀoιnᴄι5, Ó Ꝺulᴄonᴄᴀ—I—*O Dulchenta, O Dulchienta, O Dologhintye, O Dullechonty, O Dullehonty, O Dulchante,* Dolohunty, Delahunty, Delahunt, Delhunty, Dellunty, Dulanty, Dullenty, Dulinty ; ' des. of Ꝺulᴄᴀoιnᴄeᴀc' (plaintive satirist) ; the name of an old family of Ely O'Carroll, in the present Offaly, who are of the same stock as the O'Carrolls. A branch of the family had settled in Kerry before the 17th century. Ó Ꝺulᴄonᴄᴀ is a corruption.

Ó Ꝺún——, v. Ó Ꝺonn——, which is often pronounced, and sometimes written, Ó Ꝺún——.

Ó Ꝺúnᴀbrᴀ, v. Ó Ꝺonnᴀbᴀιr.

Ó Ⅾúnacáin—I—*O Duneghan,* Doonican, Dunican ; a var. of Ó Ⅾonnacáin, q.v.

Ó Ⅾúnaⅾaιʒ—I—*O Downie, O Downy, O Duny, O Dony,* Dooney, Downey, Doney, Donney, Dunny, (Downing) ; ' des. of Ⅾúnaⅾac ' (belonging to a ⅾún, or fort) ; the name of, at least, three distinct families : (1) Ó Ⅾúnaⅾaιʒ of Siol Anmchadha, in Co. Galway, who are of the same stock as the O'Maddens ; (2) O Ⅾúnaⅾaιʒ of Corca Laoighdhe, in South-west Cork, who are of the same stock as the O'Driscolls ; and (3) Ó Ⅾúnaⅾaιʒ of Luachair, who were chiefs of Luachair, an extensive district on the borders of Cork, Kerry and Limerick. This family is still numerous in Kerry and Limerick, but in the former county, the name is sometimes incorrectly angl. Downing. The name was also found in Ulster and Leinster.

Ó Ⅾúnáin—I—*O Doonan,* Doonan, Donnan ; a var. of Ó Ⅾonnáin, q.v. ; a scattered surname, but now found chiefly in Leitrim and Roscommon. Ⅿaolⅿuιne Ó Ⅾúnáin was Bishop of Cashel in the early part of the 12th century.

Ó Ⅾúnʒaιle, v. Ó Ⅾonnʒaιle.

Ó Ⅾúnʒalaιʒ, v. Ó Ⅾonnʒalaιʒ.

Ó Ⅾúnʒuιs, v. Ó Ⅾonnʒura.

Ó Ⅾúnlaιnʒ, Ó Ⅾunlaιnʒ—I—*O Dowling, O Doolin,* Dowling, Dowlin, Dooling, Doolin, Doolen, Doolan, &c. ; ' des. of Ⅾunlanʒ ' (an ancient personal name, also written Ⅾúnlanʒ) ; the name (1) of a numerous family in Leinster, who were at one time lords of Leix ; and (2) of a family of Corca Laoighdhe, in South-west Cork, still numerous in Cork and Kerry. This surname is pronounced Ó Ⅾúllaing, and its angl. forms can hardly be distinguished from those of Ó Ⅾublaιnn, q.v.

Ó eaccιʒearna, Ó eaccιʒeιrn, Ó eιccιʒeιrn— I—*O Aghierny, O Aghierin,* Ahearne, Aherne, Ahearn, Aheran, Aheron, Ahern, &c. ; ' des. of eaccιʒeanna ' (horse-lord) ; the name of a Dalcassian family who were lords of Ui Cearnaigh, in the neighbourhood of

Six-mile-bridge, until about the year 1318, when they were driven out by the MacNamaras and dispersed through Munster. The name is now common in Limerick and Cork. Also Ó hEachtigheirn, q.v.

Ó FACHTNA—I—*O Faughny*, Faulkney, (Faulkner); 'des. of Fachtna' (just, an ancient personal name).

Ó FACHTNÁIN—I—Faughnan; 'des. of Fachtnán' (dim. of Fachtna).

Ó FÁGÁIN—I—*O Fagan*, Fagan, Fagin; a var. of Ó hÁgáin, q.v.; rare.

Ó FAGHARTAIGH—I—*O Fayerty*, Fagarty, Fagarthy, Whearty; 'des. of 'Fagharthach' (noisy); the name of a family of Ui Fiachrach who were anciently seated at Tulach Spealain, in the barony of Carra, Co. Mayo; now found chiefly in Leinster. It is the same as Ó Fathartaigh (q.v.) of Co. Galway, and by the aspiration of the initial F has in some places become Ó hAghartaigh, q.v.

Ó FAILBHE—I—*O Falvie, O Falvy, O Fallie*, O'Falvey, Falvey, Fealy, Fealey; 'des. of Failbhe' (lively); the name of an ancient family in Kerry, who before the Anglo-Norman invasion were lords of Corca Dhuibhne, the present barony of Corcaguiny; now rather rare; in parts of North Kerry sometimes pronounced Ó Fáile, angl. Fealy.

Ó FAIRCHEALLAIGH—I—*O Ferrally*, O'Farrelly, Farrelly, Farley, &c.; 'des. of Faircheallach' (super-war); the name of a distinguished ecclesiastical family who, until the suppression of the monastery, were coarbs of St. Mogue, or erenaghs of Drumlane, in Co. Cavan, and are now very numerous throughout the county. There was another family of the name in the neighbourhood of Duntryleague, in the east of Co. Limerick, but it has long since disappeared from that district and is probably extinct.

Ó FAITH—I—*O Fagh, O Faye*, Fay, Foy, Fahy, Fahey; a shortened form of Ó Fathaigh, q.v.; common in Connacht.

Ó ꝼaᴌᴌaṁaın—I—*O Fallowne, O Fallone, O Fallon*, Falloon, Faloon, Faloona, Fallon, &c.; ' des. of ꝼaᴌᴌaṁan' (ruler); also written Ó ꝿoᴌᴌaṁaın, and sometimes, by the aspiration of the initial ꝼ, changed to Ó ḣaᴌᴌaṁaın, q.v.; the name (1) of a Leinster family who were formerly lords of Crioch na gCeadach, which comprised the present parish of Castlejordan in Offaly; and (2) of a Connacht family who were lords of Clann Uadach, which comprised the parishes of Camma and Dysart, in the barony of Athlone. In 1585, O'Fallon had his residence at Milltown, in the parish of Dysart, where the ruins of his castle are still to be seen.

Ó ꝼaoḃaᵹáın—I—*O Fegane, O Fegan*, Feagan, Fegan, Fagan; a var. of Ó ḣaoḃaᵹáın, q.v.

Ó ꝼaoıᴌeáın—I—*O Foylane, O Fylane*, Whelan, Phelan, &c.; an attenuated form of Ó ꝼaoᴌáın, q.v.

Ó ꝼaoıᴌᴌeaᴄáın—I—*O Whyleghane, O Philaghane, O Feylaghan*, Wheleghan, Wheelahan, Whelahan, Whelehan, (Whelan, Phelan); 'des of ꝼaoıᴌᴌeaᴄán' (dim. of ꝼaoıᴌᴌeaᴄ, joyful; perhaps born in carnival time, the month of rejoicing, from middle of January to middle of February); an old Westmeath surname. Ó ḣaoıᴌᴌeaᴄáın (q.v.) is a Munster variant.

Ó ꝼaoᴌáın—I—*O Whealane, O Phelane, O Foelane, O Folane, O Fylane*, O'Phelan, Phelan, Whelan, Philan, Fylan, &c.; 'des. of ꝼaoᴌán' (dim of faol, a wolf); the name (1) of a numerous and once powerful Munster family, who before the Anglo-Norman invasion were lords of the Decies, in the present counties of Waterford and Tipperary; and (2) of a numerous Leinster family who were anciently seated at Magh Lacha, a plain in the barony of Kells, Co. Kilkenny. In the 16th century the name was found in nearly all the counties of Munster and Leinster, and also in Roscommon and Galway. It was often pronounced Ó ꝼuaᴌáın, and, by the aspiration of the initial ꝼ, changed to Ó ḣaoᴌáın and Ó ḣuaᴌáın, q.v.

Ó ꝼaoᴌᴄaıḃ—I—*O Fellaghy*, Falahy, Falahee, Falsey;

'des. of ꝼaoιċaᵭ' (wolf-warrior) ; a rare Thomond surname.

Ó ꝼaoιċaιꞃ—I—Fallaher ; 'des. of ꝼaoιċaꞃ' (wolf-dear) ; extremely rare.

Ó ꝼaꞃaċáιn—I—*O Farraghan, O Farrohan, O Farhan, O Farran, O Faran,* Farran, Farron, Farren, Faran, Forran, &c. ; probably for Ó naꞃaċáιn, 'des. of Aꞃaċán,' the initial ꝼ being intrusive ; a Donegal surname.

Ó ꝼaꞃannáιn—I—*O Farenane, O Ferrenan,* Farnan, Farnon, Farnand, (Farnham) ; 'des. of ꝼaꞃannán' (an ancient Irish personal name) ; also written Ó ꝼoꞃannáιn, q.v. ; the name of an ecclesiastical family in Ulster who were erenaghs of Ardstraw.

Ó ꝼaꞃꞃaιȝ, Farry, Forry ; a rare Mayo surname.

Ó ꝼaċaιȝ—I—*O Faughy, O Faghy, O Fahy, O Faye,* Faughy, Faghy, Fahey, Fahy, Fay, Foy, and, by 'translation,' Green ; also written Ó ꝼaċaᵭ ; 'des. of ꝼaċaᵭ' (older ꝼoċaᵭ, foundation) ; the name of a family of Ui Maine in Co. Galway, whose patrimony, which was known as Poblewinterfahy, lay in the barony of Loughrea, and a considerable portion of which remained in the possession of the family down to the Cromwellian confiscations. There is also an old and respectable family of the name in Co. Tipperary. The name, according to O'Donovan, was sometimes angl. Green from its resemblance to the Irish word 'ꝼaιċċe,' a green, or field.

Ó ꝼaċaꞃċaιȝ—I—*O Faherty,* Faherty, (Flaherty) ; written Ó ꝼaȝaꞃċaιȝ by MacFirbis, and Ó ꝼoȝaꞃċaιȝ by the Four Masters ; des of 'ꝼaċaꞃċaċ' or 'ꝼaȝaꞃċaċ,' or 'ꝼoȝaꞃċaċ' (all variants of the same name) ; the name of an old Galway family who were formerly chiefs of Dealbhna Cuile Fabhair, on the east side of Lough Corrib. It is still common in Co. Galway, but sometimes disguised under the angl. form of Flaherty; while by the aspiration of the initial ꝼ, it has become changed in Munster to Ó naċaꞃċaιȝ, q.v.

Ó ꝼéaᵭaȝáιn—I—*O Faddigane,* Fedigan ; 'des. of

ᵽéᴀᴅᴀᵹáɴ'; a rare Ulster surname. The family, according to MacFirbis, is a branch of the Oirghialla.

Ó ᵽeᴀʀáɪɴ—I—*O Feran, O Faran, O Ferran, O Farrane,* Feran, Feron, Ferran, Fearon, Fearen, Fearn, Fern, Farran, Farren, &c.; 'des. of ᵽeᴀᴘáɴ' (dim. of ᵽeᴀᴘ, a man, or 'pet' dim. of ᵽeᴀᴘᴀᴅᴀċ); the name of a branch of the Cinel Eoghain in Ulster.

Ó ᵽeᴀʀᴀᴅᴀɪᵹ—I—*O Farry,* O'Ferry, Farry, Ferry; 'des. of ᵽeᴀᴘᴀᴅᴀċ' (manly); a scattered surname, but found chiefly in East Ulster.

Ó ᵽeᴀʀċᴀɪʀ—I—*O Farragher,* Farragher, Faragher, Farraher, Faraher, Fraher; 'des. of ᵽeᴀᴘċᴀᴘ' (very dear); a Connacht surname. In Munster, where there are a few of the name, it is metathesised to Ó ᵽʀeᴀċᴀɪʀ, angl. Fraher; while the aspiration of the initial ᵽ gives rise to the further variants Ó ɦeᴀᴘċᴀɪʀ and Ó Reᴀċᴀɪʀ, q.v.

Ó ᵽeᴀʀᵹᴀɪʟ—I—*O Ferrall,* O'Farrell, Farrell, Ferrall, Farrahill, Frahill, Fraul; 'des. of ᵽeᴀᴘᵹᴀʟ' (super-valour); the name of several distinct families, of which the best known are the O'Farrells of Annaly, in the present Co. Longford, of which they were for many centuries the ruling race. The head of the family resided at the town of Longford, which was formerly known as Longphort Ui Fhearghail, or O'Farrell's fortress. In later times, the O'Farrells divided into two great branches, the heads of which were known respectively as O'Farrell Boy, the yellow O'Farrell, and O'Farrell Bane, the fair O'Farrell. The O'Farrells maintained their independence as a clan down to the year 1565, when Annaly was reduced to shire ground by the lord-deputy, Sir Henry Sidney. Though suffering severely from the plantation schemes of James I, the O'Farrells were able to take a prominent part in all the political and military movements of the 17th century, and many of them were afterwards distinguished officers in the Irish brigades in the service of France. This family is now very numerous. Other families of this name were seated in Wicklow

and Tyrone. The name is also written Ó ꝼeaꞃᵹaıle
and Ó ꝼıꞃᵹıl, q.v., and sometimes, by the aspiration
of the initial ꝼ, changed into Ó neaꞃᵹaıl, Ó neaꞃ-
ᵹaıle, q.v.

Ó ꝼeaꞃᵹaıle—I—*O Farrialla, O Ferralla,* Farrelly,
Frawley, Farrell, &c. ; ' des. of ꝼeaꞃᵹal ' ; a var. of
Ó ꝼeaꞃᵹaıl, q.v. ; sometimes metathesised to Ó ꝼꞃea-
ᵹaıle, angl. Frawley.

Ó ꝼeaꞃᵹuıs, Ó ꝼeaꞃᵹusa—I—*O Farguise, O Farris,
O Ferris, O Farrissa,* Fergus, Ferris, Farris, Farrissy,
&c. ; ' des. of ꝼeaꞃᵹuꞃ ' (super-choice) ; the name
(1) of a medical family in West Connacht who were
hereditary physicians to the O'Malleys ; and (2) of an
ecclesiastical family in Co. Leitrim who were coarbs
of St. Mogue, or erenaghs of Rossinver. At the end
of the 16th century, the name was very scattered.

Ó ꝼeaꞃnáın—I—*O Farnane, O Fernan,* Fernane, Fernan ; a shortened form of Ó nıꝼeaꞃnáın, q.v. By the
aspiration of the initial ꝼ, it often becomes Ó neaꞃ-
náın, q.v.

Ó ꝼéıc—I—*O Fey,* Fey, Fay, and, by ' translation,'
Hunt ; ' des. of ꝼıac ' (raven) ; a var. of Ó ꝼıaıc, q.v.

Ó ꝼéıcín—I—*O Feahine, O Fehin, O Fein,* Feehin, Fehen,
Feen, Feane, Fane ; ' des. of ꝼéıcín ' (dim. of ꝼıac, a
raven) ; a var. of Ó ꝼıacáın, q.v. ; originally a West
Connacht surname. The family is mentioned by Mac-
Firbis.

Ó ꝼéınneaᵭa, v. Ó ꝼıannaıᵭe.

Ó ꝼıaca, Ó ꝼıacac—I—*O Fiecha, O Fiaghy, O Fyhie,*
Fyfee, Fye, Fee, and, by ' translation,' Hunt and
Vingin ; ' des. of ꝼıaca ' ; a common surname in
Waterford and other parts of Munster, where it is
now angl. Hunt, by supposed translation. It was
also in use in Monaghan and Donegal, but seems to
have there been merged in the surname Ó ꝼıaıc, q.v.

Ó ꝼıacáın—I—*O Fighane, O Feehan, O Pheane,* Feighan,
Feehan, Fehane, Feghan, Fehan, Feane, Fane, (Fegan,
Fagan) ; ' des. of ꝼıacáın ' (dim. of ꝼıac, a raven) ;
same as Ó ꝼéıcín, q.v. ; a scattered surname.

Ó ꝼiacna, Ó ꝼiacnac—I—*O Fiaghny, O Fieghny,
O Feoghny,* Feighney, Feeheny, Feoghney, Feghany,
Faheney, (Fenton), and, by ' translation,' Hunt ; ' des.
of ꝼiacna ' (an ancient Irish personal name) ; the
name of a family of Sil-Murray in Co. Roscommon ;
now also in Cork, Limerick and Tipperary. It is
' translated ' Hunt, in parts of Sligo, and changed to
Fenton in parts of Munster.

Ó ꝼiacra, Ó ꝼiacrac—I—*O Fieghraie, O Fierhie,*
Feighry, Feighery, Feehery, Feerey, Feary, Hunt ;
' des. of ꝼiacra ' (an ancient Irish personal name) ; the
name of a family in Co. Tyrone, and of another in Co.
Wicklow. Both families have been long dispersed
and the name is now very rare. It is in some places
made Hunt, by supposed translation.

Ó ꝼiaic—I—*O Fee, O Fye,* Fye, Foy, Fey, Fay, Hunt ;
' des. of ꝼiac ' (raven) ; the same as Ó ꝼéic, q.v. ; the
name of an ecclesiastical family in Ulster who were
erenaghs of Derrybrusk, near Enniskillen ; also found
in Munster and Connacht.

Ó ꝼialáin—I—*O Fillan,* Fylan, Fyland, Philan, (Phelan) ;
' des. of ꝼialán ' (dim. of ꝼial, generous) ; the name of
a distinguished bardic family in the north of Ireland.
Its angl. forms can hardly be distinguished from those
of Ó ꝼaoláin, q.v.

Ó ꝼiangalaig, v, Ó ꝼionngalaig.

Ó ꝼiannacta—I—*O Fianaghta,* Feenaghty, Finnerty,
(Fenton) ; a common form of Ó ꝼionnacta, q.v. ; now
generally angl. Fenton in Munster.

Ó ꝼianna, Ó ꝼiannaide—I—*O Fynea, O Finnee,*
Feeney, Feeny, Finney, Finny ; ' des. of ꝼiannaide '
(soldier) ; a substitution for older Ó ꝼéinneada ; the
name of a family of the Ui Fiachrach who were formerly
seated at Finghid, now angl. Finned, in the parish of
Easkey, Co. Sligo, and are still numerous in Connacht.
To be distinguished from Ó ꝼione, q.v.

Ó ꝼioǵeallaig—I—*O Fielly, O Filla,* Feely, Feeley,
Field ; a var. of Ó ꝼitceallaig, q.v.

Ó ꝼione—I—*O Finny,* Finney, Feeny, Feeney ; ' des.

of *ꝼóne ' ; the name of a Galway family, still in use
in that county. The family is mentioned by Mac-
Firbis. Cf. Ó ꝼiannaióe.

Ó ꝼiliḃín—V—O'Filbin. V. mac ꝑiliḃín.

Ó ꝼíne, v. Ó ꝼóne.

Ó ꝼinġin—I—O Fynine, O Fenine, O Fynninge, O
Faninge, Finning, Fenning, (Fannin, Fanning) ; ' des.
of ꝼinġin ' (fair offspring) ; a South Leinster surname.

Ó ꝼinn—I—O Finn, O Finne, Finn, Fynn, Finne ; ' des.
of ꝼionn ' (fair) ; the name (1) of a Breifney family
who were chiefs of Calraighe of Lough Gill, now the
parish of Calry, near the town of Sligo ; (2) of a Monaghan family who were lords of Feara Rois, in the
neighbourhood of Carrickmacross ; and (3) of a Galway
family who were formerly erenaghs of Kilcolgan.
All these families are still well represented in their
native districts ; and the name is also found in various
other parts of Ireland.

Ó ꝼínne, v. Ó ꝼóne.

Ó ꝼinneaċta(iġ), v. Ó ꝼionnaċta.

Ó ꝼinntiġeaRn—I—O Finaran, Finneran ; ' des. of
ꝼinntiġeaṗna ' (fair lord) ; the name of a family who
were originally chiefs of Ui Mealla in Leinster, but are
now most numerous in Co. Galway.

Ó ꝼíoḋaḃaiR—I—O Feover, O Feure, O Feore, Feore ;
' des. of ꝼíoḋaḃaṗ ' (bushy-eyebrows) ; a var. of Ó
ꝼíoḋaḃṗa, q.v. The present form is found chiefly
in the neighbourhood of Kilmallock, in Co. Limerick.

Ó ꝼíoḋaḃRa—I—O Fiorie, O Fuery, O Fury, Fury,
Furey, (?) Fleury ; ' des. of ꝼíoḋaḃṗa ' (bushy-eyebrows, from ꝼioḋ, a wood, and ṗaḃṗa, an eyebrow) ;
also Ó ꝼíoḋaḃaiṗ, q.v. ; the name of an old Westmeath family who, not improbably, are a branch of
the O'Melaghlens. Two of them were bishops, or
abbots, of Clonmacnoise in the latter part of the 12th
century ; and in the next century, Donat O Fiodhabhra,
after filling the see of Clogher for nine years, was
translated to the primatial see of Armagh. He died
in England in 1237, as he was returning from Rome,

"with great honour and spiritual glory from the Pope." Before the end of the 16th century the name had spread into Roscommon, Sligo and Cork. It is now most frequently met with in Co. Galway. In Munster the present form is Ó ꝼıoꝺꝺꝼꝺꝺꝺıꝼ, angl. Feore.

Ó ꝼıoɴꝺ̇ᴄꝺ(ıᵹ), v. Ó ꝼıoɴɴꝺ̇ᴄꝺ.

Ó ꝼıoɴꝺ́ıɴ, v. Ó ꝼıoɴɴꝺ́ıɴ.

*Ó ꝼıoɴᵹꝺꝛꝺꝺıʟ, Finnerell.

Ó ꝼıoɴɴꝺꝺ̇ꝺ́ıɴ—I—*O Finoghane* Fenihan, Fanahan; probably only a var. of Ó ꝼıoɴɴꝺᵹꝺ́ıɴ, q.v.; extremely rare.

Ó ꝼıoɴɴꝺ̇ᴄꝺ, Ó ꝼıoɴɴꝺ̇ᴄꝺıᵹ—I—*O Fynaghta, O Fenaghtie, O Finatie,* Finnaghty, Finaghty, Feenaghty, Fenaghty, Fenaughty, (?) Feenaghy, (?) Fanaghey, Finnerty, Finerty, Fannerty, (Fenton); 'des. of ꝼıoɴɴꝺ̇ᴄꝺ' (fair-snow); also written Ó ꝼıoɴꝺ̇ᴄꝺ, Ó ꝼıɴɴᴇꝺ̇ᴄꝺ, Ó ꝼıꝺɴꝺ̇ᴄꝺ, Ó ꝼıoɴɴꝺ̇ᴄꝺıᵹ, &c., and, by the aspiration of the initial ꝼ, Ó ɴıoɴɴꝺ̇ᴄꝺ, q.v.; the name of a Connacht family who are a branch of the Siol Muireadhaigh, or Sil-Murry, and of the same stock as the O'Connors of that province. They seem to have formed two clans, known as Clann Chonnmhaigh and Clann Mhurchadha, seated respectively on the west and east side of the Suck, in the counties of Galway and Roscommon. Ó ꝼıoɴɴꝺ̇ᴄꝺ of Clann Chonnmhaigh, or Clanconoo, had his castle at Dunamon, in Co. Roscommon, and as the representative of the senior branch of the Sil-Murry had the privilege of drinking the first cup at every royal banquet. The family is frequently mentioned in the Annals, but soon after the Anglo-Norman invasion, they were supplanted by a branch of the Burkes, the head of which was known as MacDavid. There was another family of the same name, a branch of the Ui Maine, anciently settled in south-east of Co. Galway. The name is not uncommon in Munster, but is often disguised under the angl. form of Fenton.

Ó ꝼıoɴɴꝺᵹꝺ́ıɴ—I—*O Finegane, O Fenegane,* Finnigan,

Finnegan, Finigan, Finegan, Fanagan; 'des. of
ꝼıoɴɴᴀᴣᴀɴ' (dim. of ꝼıoɴɴ, fair); the name (1) of a
family of Ui Fiachrach, in Co. Mayo, and (2) of a
Breifney family. At the end of the 16th century
there were O'Finegans in all the provinces.

Ó ꝼıoɴɴᴀ́ıɴ—I—*O Finane, O Fenane, O Fanane,*
O'Finan, Finan, Finnan, Fannon, (Fannin, Fanning);
'des. of ꝼıoɴɴᴀ́ɴ' (dim. of ꝼıoɴɴ, fair); also written
Ó ꝼıoɴᴀ́ıɴ; the name of a Mayo family who were
chiefs of Coolcarney, a district which embraced the
parishes of Kilgarvan and Attymas, but now long
dispersed; also, according to MacFirbis, of a family of
Cinel Eoghain in Ulster.

Ó ꝼıoɴɴᴀʟʟᴀ́ıɴ—I—*O Fynnolane, O Fennelane,* Fenelon, Fenlon, Fendlon; 'des. of ꝼıoɴɴᴀʟʟᴀ́ɴ'; the name
of a Leinster family who before the Anglo-Norman
invasion were lords of Dealbhna Mor, now the barony
of Delvin, in the east of Co. Westmeath. They were
dispossessed by Hugh de Lacy, who granted their
lands to Gilbert Nugent.

Ó ꝼıoɴɴᴣᴀıʟ, Ó ꝼıoɴɴᴣᴀıʟe—I—*O Fynnull, O Fennell,* Finnell, Fennell; 'des. of ꝼıoɴɴᴣᴀʟ' (fair-valour).

Ó ꝼıoɴɴᴣᴀʟᴀıᴣ—I—*O Fynnola, O Fenellie,* Finnelly,
Fennelly, Finley, Fenley, Finlay, Findley, &c.; 'des.
of ꝼıoɴɴᴣᴀʟᴀċ' (fair-valorous, der. of ꝼıoɴɴᴣᴀʟ);
also written Ó ꝼıᴀɴᴣᴀʟᴀıᴣ, and, by the aspiration of
the initial ꝼ, changed to Ó ɴıoɴɴᴣᴀʟᴀıᴣ, q.v.; the
name of an Ormond family, doubtless descended from
ꝼıoɴɴᴣᴀʟᴀċ, son of ᴅoɴɴċᴜᴀɴ, one of the leaders of
Brian Boru's hosts at Clontarf.

Ó ꝼıoɴɴᴣᴜsᴀ—I—*O Finisey,* Finnessy, Fennessy; 'des.
of ꝼıoɴɴᴣᴜꝼ' (fair choice); an old, but rare, Munster surname.

Ó ꝼıoɴɴṁᴀċᴀ́ıɴ—I—Finnucane, Finucane; 'des. of
ꝼıoɴɴṁᴀċᴀ́ɴ' (fair little son); a rare, but well-known,
Munster surname. I cannot find any early angl.
form.

Ó ꝼıRᴣıʟ—I—*O Ferrill, O Phirell,* O'Freel, Freel, Friel,
Freal, &c.; 'des. of ꝼeᴀꝼᴣᴀʟ' (super-valour); a var.

of Ó ᚠeaᚱᚷaıl, q.v. ; the name of a family of Cinel Conaill who derive their descent from Eoghan, brother of St. Columcille, and were hereditary erenaghs of Kilmacrenan, in Co. Donegal. The name is still common in that county, but pronounced Ó ᚠᚱıᚷıl, q.v. O'Freel had the privilege of inaugurating O'Donnell as chieftain of Tirconnell.

Ó ᚠıᚱᚷıle, v. Ó ᚠᚱıᚷıle and Ó ᚠᚱıᚄıle.

Ó ᚠıᚄᚄeallaıᚷ—I—*O Fihillie, O Fihily, O Fielly*, Fihelly, Fihily, Fehily, Fehely, Feehely, Feehily, Feely, (Field, Fielding), &c. ; 'des. of ᚠıᚄᚄeallaᚄ' (chess-player) ; the name of a family of Corca Laoighdhe, in South-west Cork, where they were chiefs of Tuath O Fithcheallaigh, an extensive district in the neighbourhood of Baltimore. To this family belonged the celebrated Maurice de Portu, Archbishop of Tuam from 1506 to 1513, who on account of his great learning and other accomplishments was called 'Flos Mundi.' Field as an angl. form of this surname dates back to the middle of the 16th century ; Fielding is a modern development.

Ó ᚠıᚄᚄıll—I—*O Fihel*, Fehill, (Field) ; a shortened form of Ó ᚠıᚄᚄeallaıᚷ, q.v. This form is still in use in Limerick, where the family has been long settled.

Ó ᚠlaınn—I—*O Flayne, O Floyng*, Flang, Flyng, Flynn ; 'des. of ᚠlann' (red) ; usually written Ó ᚠloınn, q.v.

Ó ᚠlaıᚄᚁeaᚱᚄaıᚷ—I—*O Flagherty*, O'Flaherty, Flagherty, Flaherty, Flaverty ; 'des. of ᚠlaıᚄᚁeaᚱᚄaᚄ' (bright ruler) ; the name of a Connacht family who were originally chiefs of Muinntear Mhurchadha, now angl. Muntermorroghoe, a district on the east side of Lough Corrib, in the barony of Clare, Co. Galway, but on being expelled from there by the English, in the 13th century, settled on the other side of Lough Corrib, where they obtained extensive possessions in the barony of Moycullen, and were styled lords of Iar-Connacht. There is also a family of the name, but of an entirely different stock, in Thomond. In Ulster, owing to the aspiration of the initial ꝼ, the name has been changed to Ó Lᴀɪꞇḃeᴀꞃꞇ-ᴀɪᵹ, q.v.

Ó ꝼLᴀɪꞇeᴀṁáɪn—I—*O Flaghavane, O Flakevane, O Flavane*, Flahavan, Flahevan, Flahavin, Flavahan, Flavin ; ' des. of ꝼLᴀɪꞇeᴀṁán ' (dim. of ꝼLᴀɪꞇeᴀṁ, lord, ruler) ; an old Munster surname ; often found as Ó ꝼLᴀꞇᴀṁáɪn and Ó ꝼLᴀɪꞇɪṁín, q.v.

Ó ꝼLᴀɪꞇꝼɪLeᴀḃ, v. Ó ꝼLᴀɪꞇɪLe and Ó ꝼLᴀɪꞇɪꞃe.

Ó ꝼLᴀɪꞇᵹeᴀꞱᴀ—I—*O Flahysse, O Flayshe* ; ' des. of ꝼLᴀɪꞇᵹeᴀꞃ ' (dominion-choice) ; an old Wexford surname ; now changed, by the aspiration of the initial ꝼ, into Ó Lᴀɪꞇᵹeᴀꞃᴀ, q.v.

Ó ꝼLᴀɪꞇɪLe—I—*O Flatilly*, Flatley, Flattley ; ' des of ꝼLᴀɪꞇꝼɪLe ' (prince-poet) ; older form Ó ꝼLᴀɪꞇꝼɪLeᴀḃ ; the name of a branch of the Ui Fiachrach in Mayo and Sligo, where it is still well known. V. Ó ꝼLᴀɪꞇɪꞃe.

Ó ꝼLᴀɪꞇɪṁ—I—*O Flahiff, O Flahie*, Flahive, Flahy ; ' des. of ꝼLᴀɪꞇeᴀṁ ' (lord, ruler) ; a scattered surname. In the 16th century, it was found in Galway, Clare, Tipperary, Kilkenny and Wexford. It is now often changed, by the aspiration of the initial ꝼ, to Ó Lᴀɪꞇɪṁ, q.v. Also Ó ꝼLᴀꞇᴀɪᵹ, q.v.

Ó ꝼLᴀɪꞇɪṁín—I—Flahavin, Flavin ; a var. of Ó ꝼLᴀɪꞇeᴀṁáɪn, q.v

Ó ꝼLᴀɪꞇɪꞃe—I—*O Flattery*, Flattery ; ' des. of ꝼLᴀɪꞇꝼɪLe ' (prince-poet) ; a corruption of Ó ꝼLᴀɪꞇꝼɪLeᴀḃ ; the name of a family of Dealbhna Eathra, in the barony of Garrycastle, in the present Offaly, where it is still in use. The corruption of this name to its present form had taken place before the end of the 16th century. Cf. Ó ꝼLᴀɪꞇɪLe.

Ó ꝼLᴀnnᴀḃꞃᴀ—I—*O Flanura, O Flanory*, Flannery ; ' des. of ꝼLᴀnnᴀḃꞃᴀ ' (red-eyebrows) ; the name (1) of a family of the Ui Fidhgheinte, in the present Co. Limerick, but long dispersed through Munster ; and (2) of a family of Ui Fiachrach who were formerly seated in the neighbourhood of Killala, but are now dispersed through Connacht.

Ó ꝼlannacáin—I—*O Flanaghan*, Flanaghan ; ' des. of ꝼlannacán ' (dim. of ꝼlann, red) ; probably only a var. of Ó ꝼlannaᵹáin, q.v. ; extremely rare

Ó ꝼlannaᵹáin—I—*O Flannagaine*, O'Flanagan, Flanagan, Flanigan, &c. ; ' des. of ꝼlannaᵹán ' (dim. of ꝼlann, red) ; the name of at least five distinct families in different parts of Ireland, viz. : (1) of Fermanagh, a branch of the Oirghialla, who were chiefs of Tuathratha, now angl. Toorah, an extensive district in the barony of Magheraboy, in the north-west of Co. Fermanagh, and are still numerous in Ulster ; (2) of Roscommon, a branch of the Sil-Murry and of the same stock as the O'Connors, who were hereditary stewards to the kings of Connacht and chiefs of Clann Chathail, a district which embraced several parishes in the neighbourhood of Elphin ; (3) of Westmeath who were anciently lords of Comair and sometimes of all Teffia ; (4) of Ely O'Carroll in the present Offaly, who are of the same stock as the O'Carrolls, and were chiefs of Cinel Arga, a district nearly, if not exactly, co-extensive with the present barony of Ballybrit ; and (5) of Waterford, who were formerly chiefs of Uachtartire, now the barony of Upperthird, in the north-west of Co. Waterford, but were dispossessed by the Powers soon after the Anglo-Norman invasion.

Ó ꝼlanncaóa, Ó ꝼlanncaíó—I—*O Flanchy, O Flanahee*, Flanahy ; ' des. of ꝼlanncaó ' (red-warrior) ; a rare Thomond surname.

Ó ꝼlannᵹail—I—*O Flanhill, O Flanill*, (?) Flavell ; ' des. of ꝼlannᵹal ' (red-valour) ; a var. of Ó ꝼlannᵹaile, q.v.

Ó ꝼlannᵹaile—I—*O Flannylla*, O'Flannelly, Flannelly, (Flannery) ; ' des. of ꝼlannᵹal ' (red-valour) ; the name of a family of the Ui Fiachrach who were originally seated at Loch Glinne, in the parish of Crossmolina, Co. Mayo, but, on being driven thence by the English, settled at Finghid, now Finned, in the parish of Easkey, Co. Sligo. It is still common

in both counties, but often disguised under the angl.
form of Flannery.

Ó ꝼlataiᵹ—I—*O Flaghie, O Flahie,* Flahy ; a common
corruption, in the spoken language, of Ó ꝼlaitim,
q.v. ; sometimes, by the aspiration of the initial ꝼ,
changed to Ó lataiᵹ, q.v.

Ó ꝼlatamáin—I—*O Flaghavane,* Flahavan, Flahevan,
Flahavin ; a var. of Ó ꝼlaiteamáin, q.v.

Ó ꝼloinn—I—*O Floine, O Floinge,* O'Flynn, Flynn,
Flinn, &c. ; ' des. of ꝼlann ' (red) ; the name of several
distinct families in different parts of Ireland, of which
the following are the best known : (1) Ó ꝼloinn of
Siol Maolruain, a Roscommon family who were chiefs
of Siol Maolruain, a district which embraced the
parish of Kiltulagh and part of that of Kilkeevin, in
the west of Co. Roscommon. Another family of the
name were erenaghs of the church of St. Dachonna,
at Eas Ui Fhloinn, a short distance to the west of the
town of Boyle. (2) Ó ꝼloinn of Tirawley who were
seated in Magh hEleog, in the parish of Crossmolina ;
a branch of the family were hereditary erenaghs of
the church and monastery of St. Tighearnan at Errew,
on Lough Conn. (3) Ó ꝼloinn of Ardagh, a branch
of the Corca Laoighdhe, who were anciently chiefs
of Ui Baghamhna, now the barony of Ibawn, in the
south of Co. Cork. The head of the family resided
at Ardagh Castle between Skibbereen and Baltimore.
(4) Ó ꝼloinn of Muskerry, who were lords of an extensive district called Muscraidhe Ui Fhloinn, angl.
Muskerrylinn, lying between Blarney and Ballyvourney, in the barony of Muskerry, Co. Cork. The
O'Flynns continued to be lords of Muskerrylin until
about the beginning of the 14th century, when they
were dispossessed by the MacCarthys of Blarney.
(5) Ó ꝼloinn of Ui Tuirtre, an account of which is
given under Ó loinn, a form the name has assumed
as a result of the aspiration of the initial ꝼ. All these
families are still well represented in their native
districts.

Ó ꝼoꝊlaꝊa, v. Ó ꝼoꜩlaꝊa.

Ó ꝼóꜩaʀτaiꜩ—I—*O Fogartie, O Fogerty,* Fogerty, Fogarty ; ' des. of ꝼóꜩaʀτaċ' (proclaimed, banished, exiled) ; the name of a family of Dalcassian origin, according to O'Heerin, who were chiefs of Eile Ui Fhogartaigh, now the barony of Elyogarty, in Co. Tipperary ; sometimes changed, by the aspiration of the initial ꝼ, into Ó hÓꜩaʀτaiꜩ, q.v. ; in West Kerry Ó ꝼóꜩaʀτa.

Ó ꝼoꜩlaꝊa—I—*O Folowe,* O'Foley, Foley ; ' des. of ꝼoꜩlaiꝊ' (plunderer) ; originally a Waterford surname, but now common throughout Munster and South Leinster. ϻaelíoʀa Ó ꝼoꜩlaꝊa was Archbishop of Cashel early in the 12th century.

Ó ꝼoiʀτċeiʀn—I—*O Fortyerne, O Fortyn,* Fortin, Fortune ; ' des. of ꝼoiʀτċeiʀn' (an old Irish personal name, meaning ' over-lord,' doubtless the same as the British Vortigern) ; originally a Carlow surname, but now more numerous in Co. Wexford.

Ó ꝼollaϻáin, v. Ó ꝼallaϻáin.

Ó ꝼoʀannáin—I—*O Forenan, O Ferrenan, O Fornan.* V. Ó ꝼaʀannáin.

Ó ꝼʀaoċáin—I—*O Freaghan,* (French) ; ' des. of ꝼʀaoċán' (dim. of ꝼʀaoċ, prowess, fury) ; a rare Connacht surname. O'Donovan gives the angl. form as French, but I cannot verify it. It is found in the form Ó ꝼʀaoiċín, angl. Frehen, in the neighbourhood of Shrule.

Ó ꝼʀaoiċín—I—Frehen. V. Ó ꝼʀaoċáin.

Ó ꝼʀeaċaiʀ—I—Fraher ; a metathesised form of Ó ꝼeaʀċaiʀ, q.v.

Ó ꝼʀeaꜩaile—I—Frawley ; a metathesised form of Ó ꝼeaʀꜩaile, q.v.

Ó ꝼʀeaτail—I—Frahill, Fraul ; a metathesised form of Ó ꝼeaʀꜩail, q.v.

Ó ꝼʀiꜩil—I—*O Friell, O Freele, O Freall,* O'Freel, Friel, Freel, Freal ; a metathesised form of Ó ꝼiʀꜩil, q.v.

Ó ꝼʀiꜩile—I—*O Frealie,* Freely ; a metathesised form of Ó ꝼiʀꜩile ; a var. of Ó ꝼiʀꜩil, q.v.

534

Ó ꝼᴚιτιl—I—Frehill, Freehill ; a metathesised form of Ó ꝼιᴚṡιl, q.v.

Ó ꝼᴚιτιle—I—Frehilly, Freehily ; a metathesised form of Ó ꝼιᴚṡιle, q.v. ; a var. of Ó ꝼιᴚṡιle, q.v.

Ó ꝼuᴀᴅᴀ—I—*O Foodie, O Foedy*, O'Foody, Foody, Foudy, Foddy, Swift, Speed ; ' des. of ꝼuᴀᴅᴀ,' or ' uᴀᴅᴀ ' ; also written Ó ɴuᴀᴅᴀ, q.v. ; the name of a family of the Ui Fiachrach, formerly seated in the barony of Carra, Co. Mayo, but long dispersed. Swift and Speed are supposed translations.

Ó ꝼuᴀᴅᴀċáιɴ—I—Fodaghan, Swift ; ' des. of ꝼuᴀᴅᴀċ-áɴ ' (dim. of ꝼuᴀᴅᴀ) ; a rare Ulster surname ; synonymous with Ó ꝼuᴀᴅᴀ, q.v. Swift is a supposed translation.

Ó ꝼuᴀllᴀċáιɴ—I—*O Foulohan, O Whologhane*, Whoolahan, Whoolehan, Wholihane, &c. ; ' des. of uᴀllᴀċ-áɴ ' (dim. of uᴀllᴀċ, proud) ; a var. of Ó ɴuᴀllᴀċáιɴ, q.v. The initial ꝼ is intrusive.

Ó ꝼuᴀllᴀιṡ—I—*O Fowly*, Whooley, Wholey, Wholy ; ' des. of uᴀllᴀċ ' (proud) ; a var. of Ó ɴuᴀllᴀιṡ, q.v. The initial ꝼ is intrusive, as in the case of Ó ꝼuᴀllᴀċ-áιɴ above.

Ó ꝼuᴀᴚáιɴ, v. Ó ꝼuᴀᴚτáιɴ.

Ó ꝼuᴀᴚṡuιs—I—*O Fworishe* ; ' des. of ꝼuᴀᴚṡuᴩ ' (cold-choice) ; a Connacht surname, of which Ó ꝼuᴀᴩuιᴩce (q.v.) is probably a corruption. By the aspiration of the initial ꝼ it has become Ó ɴuᴀᴩṡuιᴩ, q.v.

Ó ꝼuᴀᴚᴚáιɴ, Ó ꝼuᴀᴚτáιɴ—I—*O Fuarayne, O Fowrane, O Forhane, O Fourhan, O Forehan, O Fordhane, O Forane*, Fourhane, Forehane, Forehan, Forhan, Foran, (Ford, Forde) ; ' des. of ꝼuᴀᴩᴩáɴ ' or ' ꝼuᴀᴩτáɴ ' (dim. of ꝼuᴀᴩ, cold) ; the name of an old Munster family, still numerous in Waterford, Cork, Kerry and Limerick, but often, especially in Cork, disguised as Ford or Forde.

Ó ꝼuᴀᴚuιsce—I—*O Fworiske*, Whoriskey, Whorriskey, Waters, Watters ; an old surname in Sligo and Donegal ; perhaps a corruption of Ó ꝼuᴀᴩṡuιᴩ, q.v. By the aspiration of the initial ꝼ, it becomes Ó ɴuᴀᴩuιᴩce, q.v. Waters is a ' translation.'

Ó ꝼuacaᵹ—I—Foohy, Fouhy, Fuohy, Fowhey; 'des. of ꝼuacac'; a rare Co. Cork surname.

Ó ꝼuacṁaráin—I—*O Whoheran*, (?) Forhan; 'des. of ꝼuacṁapán' (dim. of ꝼuacṁap, hateful); also written Ó nUacṁapáin; the name of a family of the Ui Fiachrach who were anciently seated in the parish of Ballintobber, Co. Mayo. In the 16th century, it was found in Westmeath, but was very rare, and is probably now obsolete.

Ó ꝼuilleacáin, v. Ó ꝼaoilleacáin.

Ó ᵹaḃáin—I—*O Gavan*, Gavan, Gaven, Gavin; 'des. of ᵹaḃaḃán' (dim. of ᵹaḃaḃ, want, need, danger); the name of at least two distinct families, the one of Munster, the other of Connacht, origin. The Munster family is a branch of the Corca Laoighdhe, in South-west Cork. Also Ó ᵹaiḃín, q.v.

Ó ᵹaḃann, v. Ó ᵹoḃann.

Ó ᵹaḃalaᵹ—I—*O Guly*, *O Gowle*, Gooley, Forke; 'des. of ᵹaḃalac' (forked, peaked); the name of an old Westmeath family who, according to MacFirbis, are descended from Brian, son of Maine, son of Niall of the Nine Hostages; now very rare, and changed, by translation, in some places to Forke. Cf. Ó ᵹaḃláin.

Ó ᵹaḃláin—I—*O Gowlane*, Goolden, Golden, Golding, Goulding, Forkan, Forkin; 'des. of ᵹaḃlán' (dim. of ᵹaḃal, a fork); a rare Donegal surname; now also current in Mayo and North Galway, where it is angl. Forkan and Forkin. Cf. Ó ᵹaḃalaᵹ.

Ó ᵹaḃráin—I—*O Gawran*, Gowran; 'des. of ᵹaḃpán' (dim. of ᵹaḃap, a horse, a goat); the name of a branch of the Ui Maine in Co. Galway; now very rare, if not obsolete. Ó ᵹaḃpáin, angl. MacGovern, which is common in the spoken language of Co. Mayo, is probably not the same, but merely a corruption of Maᵹ Saṁpáin, q.v.

Ó ᵹacáin—I—Gaughan, Gahan; a common contraction, in Co. Mayo, of Ó ᵹaiḃceacáin, q.v.

Ó ᵹaḃáin, v. Ó ᵹoḃáin.

Ó ᵹaḃra—I—*O Garry*, *O Garey*, *O Geary*, *O Geirie*, O

Gwyre, O'Gara, Gara, Garry, Geary, Guiry; ' des. of
ᵹᴀᴅᵲᴀ ' (an old Irish personal name, perhaps from
ᵹᴀᴅᴀᵲ, a dog, mastiff) ; the name of a Connacht
family, of the same stock as the O'Haras. Both
families were supposed to be descended from Lugh,
son of Cormac Gaileng, and had from him the common
clan-name of Luighne, which, in accordance with
Irish custom, was afterwards applied as a designation
of the clan-lands. These embraced not only the
modern baronies of Leyney and Corran, in Co. Sligo,
but also the barony of Gallen, in Co. Mayo, and Sliabh
Lugha, which formed about the northern half of the
present barony of Costello in the same county. When
the two families separated, about the end of the tenth
century, they divided this territory between them,
the O'Haras taking the northern, or Sligo, portion,
and the O'Garas the southern, in Co. Mayo. The
O'Garas were then styled lords of Sliabh Lugha, but
after the English invasion of Connacht they were
driven out of this territory by the Jordans, Costellos,
and other English families, and forced to seek a new
settlement. This they acquired in the district
anciently known as Greagraidhe, and now as the
barony of Coolavin, in Co. Sligo, from which in later
times they were known as lords of Coolavin. There,
at the north-eastern extremity of Lough Gara, they
built their castle of Moygara, in which the head of the
family resided. From the 10th to the 18th century,
the O'Garas held a prominent place in Lower Connacht.
About the middle of latter century, two members of
the family successively filled the archiepiscopal see
of Tuam. It is to the patronage of Fergal O'Gara
that we are indebted for the invaluable Annals of
the Four Masters. Branches of the family had
settled in Munster before the end of the 16th century,
and the name still flourishes in Cork, Kerry and
Limerick, under the angl. forms of Geary and Guiry.

Ó ᵹáıbín—I—*O Gawine*, *O Gawin*, *O Gawen*, Gavin,
Gaven ; a var. of Ó ᵹábáın, q.v.

Ó ʒᴀɪḃneᴀ́ɪn, Guinane, Guinan.

Ó ʒᴀ́ɪḃceᴀċᴀ́ɪn—I—Gavaghan, Gavahan, Gavagan, Gavacan, Gavigan, Gaffikan, Gaughan, Gahan; 'des. of ʒᴀ́ɪḃceᴀċᴀ́ɪn' (dim. of ʒᴀ́ɪḃceᴀċ, plaintive, querimonious); the name of a branch of the Ui Fiachrach who were anciently chiefs of Calraighe Muighe hEleog, a district nearly co-extensive with the parish of Crossmolina, in Co. Mayo; now pronounced Ó ʒᴀ́ċᴀɪn, and very common in Mayo and Sligo.

Ó ʒᴀɪlɪneᴀċ, Gallinagh; a rare Donegal surname.

Ó ʒᴀɪllɪ́n—I—O Gallin, Gallin, Gallen; 'des. of ʒᴀɪllɪ́n' (dim. of ʒᴀll, a cock); a rare Ulster surname; mentioned by MacFirbis among the families of Cinel Eoghain. Cf. Ó ʒᴀlᴀ́ɪn.

Ó ʒᴀɪʀḃḟéɪċ, Ó ʒᴀɪʀḃḟɪᴀɪċ—I—O Garyveigh, O Garrevey, Garveagh, Garvey; a Kerry surname, probably not distinct from, but merely a corruption of, Ó ʒᴀɪʀḃɪc, q.v.

Ó ʒᴀɪʀḃɪ́n—I—O Garvyne, O Garven, Garvin, Garavin, Garwin, Garven, (?) Girvin, Girvan, (Garvey); 'des. of ʒᴀɪʀḃɪ́n' (dim. of ʒᴀʀḃ, rough); a var. of Ó ʒᴀʀḃᴀ́ɪn, q.v. In Co. Mayo, where this surname is very common, it is always angl. Garvey, which would seem to indicate that the original form in that county was Ó ʒᴀɪʀḃɪċɪ́n, a dim. of Ó ʒᴀɪʀḃɪc, q.v.

Ó ʒᴀɪʀḃeɪc, Ó ʒᴀɪʀḃɪc—I—O Garvie, O Garvey, Garvey; 'des. of ʒᴀɪʀḃɪc' (rough peace); the name (1) of an ancient family in Co. Down, of the same stock as the Maguinnesses, who were chiefs of Ui Eathach Cobha, the present barony of Iveagh; (2) of an Oriel family who were anciently chiefs of Ui Breasail, in the present barony of Oneilland East, Co. Armagh, but dispossessed at an early period by the MacCanns; and (3) of a branch of the Ui Ceinnsealaigh who were anciently chiefs of Ui Feilmeadha Thuaidh, in the present barony of Rathvilly, Co. Carlow. The name is now well represented in all parts of Ireland. V. Ó ʒᴀɪʀḃḟéɪċ and Ó ʒᴀɪʀḃɪ́n.

Ó ʒᴀɪʀmleᴀʒᴀɪḋ, v. Ó ʒoɪʀmleᴀʒᴀɪḋ.

Ó ʒⱥᴌáɪn, Ó ʒⱥᴌᴌáɪn—I—*O Gallane, O Gallon*, Gallen, Gallon, Gollan ; ' des. of ʒⱥᴌᴌán ' (dim. of ʒⱥᴌᴌ, a cock), or ' ʒⱥᴌán ' (dim. of ʒⱥᴌ, valour) ; the name of a Breifney family who were anciently chiefs of Clann Dunghalaigh ; still in Co. Leitrim, angl. Gallon ; also in Donegal.

Ó ʒⱥᴌᴌċoḃⱥɪʀ—I—*O Galleghure*, O'Gallagher, Gallagher, Gallaher, Gallogher, Gollagher, &c. ; ' des. of ʒⱥᴌᴌċoḃⱥp ' (foreign help) ; the name of a numerous and once powerful family in Tirconnell, who derive their descent from Maolchobha, King of Ireland in the 7th century. As marshalls of O'Donnell's forces, the O'Gallaghers took a prominent part in all the military movements of Cinel Conaill during the 14th and subsequent centuries. Many of them were distinguished as Bishops of Raphoe and Derry. The name was sometimes shortened to Ó ʒⱥᴌᴌċú, q.v.

Ó ʒⱥᴌᴌċú—I—*O Gallchoe, O Galloghoe*, Gallahue ; an apocopated form of Ó ʒⱥᴌᴌċoḃⱥɪp, q.v. ; formerly common in all parts of Ireland.

Ó ʒⱥᴌᴌċuḃⱥɪʀ, v. Ó ʒⱥᴌᴌċoḃⱥɪp.

Ó ʒⱥṁnⱥ—I—*O Gawny, O Gawney*, Gooney, Gaffney, (Caulfield) ; ' des. of ʒⱥṁⱥɪn ' (calf) ; formerly common in Ormond, South Leinster, and North Connacht ; now generally angl. Gaffney, but sometimes disguised as Caulfield.

Ó ʒⱥṁnáɪn—I—*O Gawnaine, O Gownane*, Goonane, Goonan, (Guning, Gunning, Caulfield) ; ' des. of ʒⱥṁnán ' (dim. of ʒⱥṁⱥɪn, a calf) ; the name, according to MacFirbis, of a family of Clann Mhuirthuile in Connacht ; now very scattered. It is angl. Goonan in the neighbourhood of Limerick, Guning in Clare, and Caulfield in Galway and West Mayo. Cf. Ó ʒⱥṁnⱥ.

Ó ʒⱥṁnⱥɪʀe—I—*O Gownro, O Goonerie*, Goonery, Goonry ; ' des. of ʒⱥṁnⱥɪpe ' (calf-keeper) ; a rare Westmeath surname.

Ó ʒánⱥɪʀᴅ, Gaynard, Gaynor.

Ó Ȝᴀoɪᴄín—I—*O Gighine, O Gihine, O Gehin, O Gahan*, Guiheen, Gweehin, Guihen, Guighan, Guihan, Geehan, Gihan, Gihon, Gahan, and, by translation, Wynne, Wyndham; 'des. of Ȝᴀoɪᴄín' (dim. of Ȝᴀoᴄ, wind, a 'pet' form probably of Mᴀoɪȝᴀoɪᴄe, chief of the wind); the name (1) of a Leinster family who were formerly chiefs of Siol Elaigh, now the barony of Shillelagh, in the south-west of Co. Wicklow, and are still numerous in the neighbouring county of Wexford, where the name is angl. Gahan; and (2) of a Connacht family who are numerous in that province, but sometimes disguised as Wynnes and Wyndhams.

Ó Ȝᴀᴚʙáɪn—I—*O Garvane, O Garvan*, Garvan, Garavin, Garvin, Garven, Garwin, (?) Girvan; 'des. of Ȝᴀᴚʙán' (dim. of Ȝᴀᴚʙ, rough); the name of a family of the southern Ui Neill, formerly seated in Meath, but now found chiefly in Sligo and Cork. V. Ó Ȝᴀɪᴚʙín which is a variant.

Ó Ȝᴀᴄʟᴀoíᴄ—I—Gately, Keatley, Keitley, Keightly; 'des. of Ȝᴀᴄʟᴀoᴄ'; a Connacht surname.

Ó Ȝeᴀʟᴀȝáɪn—I—*O Gallegane, O Galgan*, Galligan, White; 'des. of Ȝeᴀʟᴀȝán' (dim. of Ȝeᴀʟ, bright, white); originally a Sligo surname, but long dispersed through the south of Ireland.

Ó Ȝeᴀʟáɪn—I—*O Gealane, O Geallane*, Gellan, Gellen, Gelland; 'des. of Ȝeᴀʟán' (dim. of Ȝeᴀʟ, bright, white); an old surname in Sligo and Offaly perhaps the same as Ó Ȝeᴀʟᴀȝáɪn, q.v.

Ó Ȝeᴀʟʙáɪn—I—*O Gealwaine, O Gallivain, O Galvane*, Gallivan, Galvan, Galven, Galvin; 'des. of Ȝeᴀʟʙán' (bright-white); the name of a Dalcassian family, now numerous in Munster, especially in Kerry; also found in Co. Roscommon.

Ó Ȝeᴀᴚᴀȝᴀ, O'Garriga; a corruption in the spoken language of Connacht of Mᴀȝ ꝼeᴀᴚᴀᴆᴀɪȝ, q.v.

Ó Ȝéᴀᴚáɪn—I—*O Gerane, O Gieran*, Geran, Gearon, Guerin, Gearn, Gearns, Sharpe; 'des. of Ȝéᴀᴚán' (dim. of Ȝéᴀᴚ, sharp); the name of a family of the Ui Fiachrach, originally seated in the barony of Erris,

Co. Mayo, but long dispersed ; also the original name of the family of Ⅿⱥᵹ ⰌⁱonnⱦⱥⁱⱤⱤ, or Gaynor.

Ó ᵹeⱥⱤᵹⱥⁱn—I—*O Gargan*, Gargan, Garagan, Garrigan ; ' des. of ᵹeⱥⱤᵹⱥn ' (dim. of ᵹeⱥⱤᵹ, fierce) ; a Meath surname ; more frequently Ⅿⱥᴄ ᵹeⱥⱤᵹⱥⁱn, q.v.

Ó ᵹeⁱⱒeⱥnnⱥⁱᵹ, Ó ᵹeⁱⱒeⱥnnⱥⁱᵹ—I—*O Geveney*, *O Giany*, *O Geany*, Geaveny, Keaveny, Kevany, Geaney, Geany, Guiney, Guiny ; ' des. of ᵹeⁱⱒeⱥnnⱥᴄ,' or ' ᵹeⁱⱒeⱥnnⱥᴄ ' (fettered, prisoner) ; the name of a family of Ui Maine in Co. Galway ; still common in Connacht ; also in Munster, where it is sometimes shortened to Ó ᵹeⁱⱒⁱnn, q.v.

Ó ᵹeⁱⱒⁱnn—I—*O Gaine*, *O Geyne*, *O Geane*, Gaine, Geane ; short for Ó ᵹeⁱⱒeⱥnnⱥⁱᵹ, or Ó ᵹeⁱⱒeⱥnnⱥⁱᵹ ; in use in Kerry.

Ó ᵹⁱⱥⱡⱡⱥⁱn—I—Geelan, Gealon ; ' des. of ᵹⁱⱥⱡⱡⱥn ' (dim. of ᵹⁱⱥⱡⱡ, hostage) ; the name of a Ui Maine family in Co. Galway.

Ó ᵹⁱⱒeⱥⱡⱡⱥⁱn—I—*O Gibbellayne*, *O Gibbelan*, Gibulawn, Giblin, (Gibson, Gibsey, Gipsey) ; ' des. of ᵹⁱⱒeⱥⱡⱡⱥn ' ; the name of a distinguished ecclesiastical family in Connacht, where it is still well known, though sometimes disguised under the angl. forms of Gibson and Gipsey.

Ó ᵹⁱⱒne—I—*O Gibney*, *O Gibny*, Gibney, Giboney ; ' des. of ᵹⁱⱒne ' (hound) ; a well-known surname in Meath and Cavan.

Ó ᵹⁱⱡⁱn—I—Gilleen, Gillen, Gellen, Gillon ; ' des. of ᵹⁱⱡⁱn ' (dim. of ᵹeⱥⱡ, bright, white) ; the name of two distinct families in Connacht, one in Tirawley and the other in Partry. Both families have been long dispersed, but the name is still extant in Connacht and in other parts of Ireland.

Ó ᵹⁱnⁱⰂe, Guinee, Guinea, Guiney. V. Ó ᵹuⁱnⁱⰂe.

Ó ᵹⁱoⱒⱥⱡⱡⱥⁱn, v. Ó ᵹⁱⱒeⱥⱡⱡⱥⁱn.

Ó ᵹⁱoⱡⱡⱥⱒuⁱⰂe—I—*O Gillavoye*, *O Gilboy*, O'Gilvie, O'Gilbie, Ogilby, Gilbey, Gillbee, Gilboy, Gilvoy, &c. ; ' des. of ᵹⁱoⱡⱡⱥⱒuⁱⰂe ' (yellow lad) ; a Donegal surname. Cf. Ⅿⱥᴄ ᵹⁱoⱡⱡⱥⱒuⁱⰂe.

Ó ᵹioᴸᴸaᵹáin—I—*O Gillegane*, *O Gilgan*, Gilligan, Gillgan, Gilgan ; des. of ᵹioᴸᴸaᵹán ' (dim. of ᵹioᴸᴸa, servant, youth) ; a var. of Ó ᵹioᴸᴸáin, q.v. ; a scattered surname ; formerly most common in Westmeath, Thomond, Galway, Roscommon and Sligo ; perhaps sometimes substituted for Ó ᵹeaᴸaᵹáin, q.v.

Ó ᵹioᴸᴸáin—I—*O Gillane*, *O Gillain*, Gillane, Gillan, Gilland, Gillon, Gillen ; ' des. of ᵹioᴸᴸán ' (dim. of ᵹioᴸᴸa, servant, youth) ; the name of a family of Cinel Eoghain ; given by MacFirbis as an alias for Ó ᵹioᴸᴸaᵹáin, q.v.

Ó ᵹioᴸᴸaráin, Gilleran, Gilrain, Gilrane, Killeran, Kilrain, Kilrane ; a corruption of Mac ᵹioᴸᴸa Éanáin, q.v.

Ó ᵹioᴸᴸaᴿnáᴄ, v. Mac ᵹioᴸᴸa na naoṁ.

Ó ᵹionnáin—IV—*O Ganon*, Gannon ; a corruption of Maᵹ Ⴒionnáin, q.v.

Ó ᵹioᴿᴿaiᵭe—IV—O'Hare, Hare, Haire ; a corruption of Maᵹ Ⴒeaᴙaᵭaiᵹ, q.v. ; supposed to be derived from 'ᵹiᴙᴘⴼiaᵭ,' a hare ; hence the angl. forms, O'Hare, &c.

Ó ᵹᴸacáin—I—*O Glackane*, Glackan, Glakan ; ' des. of ᵹᴸacán ' (dim. of ᵹᴸac, a hand) ; a rare surname, found chiefly in Donegal and Sligo.

Ó ᵹᴸáiṁín—I—*O Glavine*, Glavin ; ' des. of ᵹᴸáiṁín ' (glutton) ; the name of a family of the Ui Fiachrach, formerly seated in Tirawley, Co. Mayo, but now found chiefly in Cork, Kerry and Waterford.

Ó ᵹᴸaisín—I—*O Glassyn*, *O Glissine*, Glasheen ; ' des. of ᵹᴸaiᴙín ' (dim. of ᵹᴸaᴙ, grey) ; the name of a family who were anciently seated in the barony of Imokilly, Co. Cork, but long dispersed through Munster ; now very rare.

Ó ᵹᴸaisne—I—*O'Glassnie*, (Giles, Gyles) ; ' des. of ᵹᴸaiᴙne ' ; a rare Louth surname.

Ó ᵹᴸasáin—I—*O Glassane*, *O Glessaine*, *O Gleasan*, Glessane, Glissane, Glissawn, Gleason, Gleeson ; ' des. of ᵹᴸaᴙán ' (dim. of ᵹᴸaᴙ, grey) ; a common surname in all the south of Ireland, especially in Cork, Limerick,

Tipperary and Kilkenny; now generally pronounced
Ó Ӡuapáin.

Ó Ӡleaora—I—Gladdery, Gladdry; 'des. of Ӡleaopa';
an old surname in Ui Maine, Co. Galway; still in use
in Connacht, but extremely rare.

Ó Ӡuasáin, v. Ó Ӡuapáin.

Ó Ӡlóiairn—I—(?) Glorney; the name of a family
formerly seated at Callan, Co. Kilkenny. O'Donovan
says it was angl. Glory.

Ó Ӡním—I—O Gneiffe, O Gnyw, Agnew; 'des. of Ӡníom'
(action); the name of a literary and bardic family in
Ulster, who were hereditary poets to the O'Neills of
Clanaboy.

Ó Ӡoba—III—O Gowe, Gow, Smith; 'des. of the smith';
a var. of Ó Ӡobann, q.v.

Ó Ӡobáin—I—O Gobbane, O Gobban, O Gubben, Gobin;
'des. of Ӡobán,' (dim. of Ӡob, a mouth, snout); a
rare Ulster surname; in the 16th century, found
chiefly in Tyrone and Donegal; perhaps the origin of
Gubbins in Co. Limerick.

Ó Ӡobann—III—O Gowen, O Gowin, O Goen, O Goine,
O'Gowan, Gowan, Goan, Gowen, Gowing, Going,
Smith, Smyth; 'des. of the smith' (Ir. 'Ӡoba');
the name of an old Cavan family who, in the latter
part of the 16th century, were one of the most
numerous in O'Reilly's country, and were also found
in Monaghan, Down, Louth, Meath and Westmeath;
still very common in all these counties, but nearly
always disguised as Smith or Smyth. To be distinguished from Mac an Ӡobann, which is often
similarly anglicised.

Ó Ӡodáin—I—Goddan, (Godwin, Goodwin); 'des. of
Ӡodán' (dim. of Ӡod, stammerer); also Ó Ӡadáin;
the name of a Mayo family, originally seated in the
parish of Moygawnagh, in the barony of Tirawley,
but long dispersed. The angl. forms are given on
the authority of O'Donovan. I have, however,
failed to verify them, and have found the name only
in the form of Ó Ӡoroín, q.v.

Ó ᵹoɪbín—I—*O Gubben*, Gubbins; 'des. of ᵹoɪbín' (dim. of ᵹob, a mouth or snout); a var. of Ó ᵹobáɪn, q.v.

Ó ᵹoɪʊín—I—Godwin, Goodwin; 'des. of ᵹoɪʊín' (dim. of ᵹoʊ, stammerer). This surname, which appears to be a var. of Ó ᵹoʊáɪn (q.v.), is still in use in parts of Co. Mayo, angl. Godwin and Goodwin.

Ó ᵹoɪʟʟɪʊe—I—Golden, Golding, Goulding. V. Ó ᵹoɪʟʟín.

Ó ᵹoɪʟʟín—I—*O Gullin, O Gullyn*; 'des. of ᵹoɪʟʟín' (dim. of ᵹoʟʟ, one-eyed, or of ᵹaʟʟ, a cock); apparently a var. of Ó ᵹaɪʟʟín, q.v.; formerly in use in Cork and Kerry, and, doubtless, the original form of the surname now pronounced Ó ᵹoɪʟʟɪʊe, and angl. Golden and Golding in these counties.

Ó ᵹoɪʀmᵹɪaʟʟa, Ó ᵹoɪʀmᵹɪaʟʟaɪᵹ, Ó ᵹoɪʀm-ᵹɪoʟʟa—I—Gormilly, Gormley; 'des. of ᵹoɪʀm-ᵹɪaʟʟa' (blue-hostage); or 'ᵹoɪʀmᵹɪoʟʟa' (blue servant or youth); the name of a Mayo family who were formerly lords of Partry, in the west of the barony of Carra; possibly a substitution for Ó ᵹoɪʀm-ᵹaɪʟ(e), q.v.

Ó ᵹoɪʀmʟeaᵹaɪᵹ, Ó ᵹoɪʀmſʟeaᵹaɪᵹ—I—*O Gormeley, O Gorumley, O Grimeley*, Gormilly, O'Gorm-ley, Gormley, Gormilly, Grumley, Grimley, Bloomer; 'des. of ᵹoɪʀmſʟeaᵹać' (blue-spearman); the name of a distinguished Ulster family who were chiefs of Cinel Moen, a sub-clan of Cinel Eoghain, and originally seated in the barony of Raphoe, Co. Donegal. In the 13th century, they were expelled by the Cinel Conaill, whereupon they settled on the other side of Lough Foyle, between Strabane and Derry. They retained considerable property down to the plantation of Ulster in 1608. The name is now very common in Ulster.

Ó ᵹoʟʟáɪn—I—Gullan, Gulan; 'des. of ᵹoʟʟán' (dim. of ᵹoʟʟ, one-eyed).

Ó ᵹoʀmaᵹáɪn—I—*O Gormegaine*, Gormagan; (1) 'des. of ᵹoʀmaᵹán' (dim. of ᵹoʀm, blue), and (2) a corrup-tion of Ó Coʀmacáɪn.

544

Ó ȝoRmáin—I—*O Gormane*, O'Gorman, Gorman ; ' des. of ȝoᵱmán ' (dim. of ȝoᵱm, blue) ; a rare and scattered surname ; to be distinguished from mᴀc ȝoᵱmáin, which is often angl. O'Gorman, as well as Gorman.

Ó ȝoRmȝᴀil, ó ȝoRmȝᴀile—I—*O Gormowle, O Gormoill, O Gormaly, O Gormooly*, Gormaly, Gormilly, Gormley, (Gorman, Grimes) ; ' des. of ȝoᵱmȝᴀl ' (blue-valour) ; the name (1) of a Mayo family who were anciently lords of the barony of Carra ; and (2) of a Roscommon family who were formerly erenaghs of Elphin. It is still common in Connacht, and has spread into Leinster, but is often disguised under the angl. forms of Gorman and Grimes. ó ȝoᵱmᵱúil and ó ȝoᵱmᵱúiliȝ represent the local pronunciation in Connacht, and the name is so written in the Annals of Loch Cé.

Ó ȝoRmóȝ—I—*O Gormoge*, (Gorman) ; ' des. of ȝoᵱmóȝ ' (dim. of ȝoᵱm, blue) ; the name of a Mayo family who were anciently lords of the barony of Carra. O'Donovan found it still extant in that district, but angl. Gorman. It appears to have been an alias for ó ȝoᵱmȝᴀil, q.v.

Ó ȝoRmȘúil, ó ȝoRmȘúiliȝ, v. ó ȝoᵱmȝᴀil, ó ȝoᵱmȝᴀile.

Ó ȝoÈRᴀiÒ—IV—*O Gogherie, O Goherye*, Geoghery, Gohary, Godfrey ; ' des. of ȝoÈᵱᴀiÈ ' (God-peace, angl. Godfrey, a name introduced by the Danes and early adopted by the Irish) ; a not uncommon surname in East Limerick and Tipperary. The family, which is old in that district, is probably of Danish descent.

Ó ȝRᴀÒᴀ—I—*O Grada*, O'Grady, Grady, (Brady) ; ' des. of ȝᴅÒᴀ ' (noble, illustrious) ; the name of a distinguished Dalcassian family who were originally seated in the parish of Killonasoolagh, near the river Fergus, in the south of Co. Clare. After the year 1318, they removed to the neighbourhood of Tomgraney, where they obtained from the O'Briens an extensive tract of land, embracing several parishes in the counties of Clare and Galway. In 1543, Donogh

O'Grady, ' Captain of his nation,' was knighted by Henry VIII, and granted by letters patent the lands of his clan. Thenceforward the heads of the O'Grady family were steadily on the side of the English interest. The surname about this time, in some unaccountable way, got anglicised O'Brady and Brady. Hugh Brady, the first Protestant bishop of Meath, was a son of Sir Donogh O'Grady, and the ancestor of the Bradys of Raheen, Co. Clare. Another son, John O'Grady, alias Brady, who settled in Co. Limerick, was the ancestor of the O'Gradys of Kilballyowen. The name is now common in Munster and Connacht. To be distinguished from Ó Ʒʀeᴀᴅᴀ, q.v.

Ó Ʒʀáɪɴɴe—I—*O Graine, O Granie,* Greany, Greaney; ' des. of Ʒʀáɪɴɴe ' (a woman's name) ; a rather common surname in Kerry and Galway. It is one of our few Irish metronymics.

Ó Ʒʀáʟᴀɪʒ, Ó Ʒʀáʟʟᴀɪʒ, Greally, Grealy, Greely ; a corruption, in the spoken language of Mayo, of ᴍᴀʒ Rᴀʒᴀʟʟᴀɪʒ, q.v. Also Ó Ʒᴀoʟᴀɪʒ or Ó Ʒʀᴀoʟʟᴀɪʒ.

Ó Ʒʀᴀᴍɴᴀ—IV—O'Growney. V. ᴍᴀc Cᴀʀʀʒᴀᴍɴᴀ.

Ó Ʒʀeᴀcáɪɴ—I—*O Greghane, O Greaghan, O Grahin, O Gryhen, O Gryhme, O Grame,* Greaghan, Greahan, Grehan, Gregan, Greyhan, Grayhan, Greaham, Greham, Graham, Greame, Graeme, Grame, Greames, Grimes; ' des. of Cʀéᴀcáɴ ' (dim. of cʀéᴀc, blind) ; a var. of Ó Cʀéᴀcáɪɴ (q.v.) owing to the softening of the initial c to Ʒ. It is undoubtedly the name which has been corrupted to Ó Ʒʀeɪòm (q.v.) in Munster.

Ó Ʒʀeᴀᴅᴀ—I—*O Greadie, O Graddy,* O'Gready, Gready, Graddy, (O'Grady, Grady) ; ' des. of Ʒʀeɪc ' (gen. Ʒʀeᴀᴅᴀ, a champion) ; an old Munster surname.

Ó Ʒʀeɪòm—I—*O Gryhme, O Grame,* Grimes, Graeme, Graham ; undoubtedly a Munster corruption of Ó Ʒʀéᴀcáɪɴ, q.v.

Ó Ʒʀɪᴀბáɪɴ, v. Ó Ʒʀíoბcáɪɴ.

Ó Ʒʀɪᴀᴅᴀ—IV—Grady ; a corruption in Connacht of ᴍᴀʒ Rɪᴀᴅᴀ, q.v.

Ó Ʒʀɪᴀʟʟuɪs, Grealish, (Greally, Grealy, Greely, Griffin) ;

a corruption, in the spoken language of Galway and Mayo, of Ɱᴀᵹ ꞑɩᴀꞁꞁᵹuɩꞃ, q.v.

Ó ᵹꞃɩᴀꞑᴀɩꞃ—I—*O Greenane, O Grienan, O Greynan, O Grenan*, Greenan, Grennan, Grannon; ' des. of ᵹꞃᴀꞑᴀꞃ ' (dim. of ᵹꞃᴀꞑᴀċ, sunny, pleasant) ; a scattered surname.

Ó ᵹꞃɩᵬíꞃ—I—*O Gribbine, O Gribin*, Gribbin, Gribben, Gribbon ; ' des. of ᵹꞃɩᵬíꞃ ' ; a Donegal surname.

Ó ᵹꞃíᵬċíꞃ, Ó ᵹꞃíꝼíꞃ—II—*O Griffine*, Guffin ; ' des. of ᵹꞃíᵬċíꞃ ' or ' Grifin ' ; a Munster surname ; perhaps a var. of Ó ᵹꞃíoᵬċᴀ, q.v.

Ó ᵹꞃíoᵬċᴀ—I—*O Greefa, O Griffy, O Grighie*, Griffey, Griffy, Greehy, (Griffith, Griffiths, Griffin) ; ' des. of ᵹꞃíoᵬċᴀ ' (griffin-like, fierce warrior) ; the name of a Dalcassian family who were chiefs of Cinel Cuallachta, in the south-east of the barony of Inchiquin, and had their castle at Ballygriffy ; common in Thomond, but usually angl. Griffin.

Ó ᵹꞃíoᵬċᴀɩꞃ—I—*O Greffane, O Grevan*, Griffin, Greaven, Greven, (Griffith, Griffiths, Greaves, Grieves) ; ' des. of ᵹꞃíoᵬċᴀɩꞃ ' (dim. of ᵹꞃíoᵬċᴀ) ; a Connacht surname, found chiefly in Galway and Mayo.

Ó ᵹꞃíoċᴀ, Greehy ; a corruption of Ó ᵹꞃíoᵬċᴀ, q.v.

Ó ᵹꞃuᴀᵹᴀɩꞃ, Ó ᵹꞃúᵹᴀɩꞃ—I—*O Growgane, O Grogaine*, Groogan, Grogan, Groggan ; ' des. of ᵹꞃu(ᴀ)ᵹᴀꞃ ' (dim. of ᵹꞃuᴀᵹ, hair of the head, or of ᵹꞃúᵹ, fierceness, anger); the name of a Roscommon family who were erenaghs of Elphin ; now found in all parts of Ireland.

Ó ᵹuᴀɩꞃᴇ—I—Goorey, Gorey ; ' des. of ᵹuᴀɩꞃᴇ ' (noble) ; the name of a family who were anciently lords of Ui Cuilinn, in Leinster ; now very rare.

Ó ᵹuᴀɩꞃɩⱮ, Gorham ; a Galway surname ; probably a substitution for ᴅᴇ ᵹúꞃᴀⱮ, q.v.

Ó ᵹuᴀꞁꞁᴀċċᴀ—IV—Goolden, Golden, Goulding ; a corruption in Co. Mayo of Ɱᴀc Cuᴀꞁꞁᴀċċᴀ, q.v.

Ó ᵹuɩᵬíꞃ—I—*O Gubben*, Gobin, Gubbins ; a var. of Ó ᵹoɩᵬíꞃ, q.v.

Ó ᵹuɩꞃꞁᴅᴇ—I—*O Guinye*, Guinee, Guinea, Guiney ; ' des. of *ᵹuɩꞃꞁᴅᴇ ' ; a common surname in Kerry and North

Cork. Its angl. forms cannot always be distinguished from those of Ó ʒeıƀeᴀnnᴀıʒ, of which it is possibly a corruption.

Ó ʒusáın—I—Gossan, Gosson, Gasson, Gaussen; 'des. of ʒuʀán' (strength, force, action, anger); the name, according to MacFirbis, of a family of Sil-Murry, in Connacht. The death of Ruᴀıỗʃı Uᴀ ʒuʀáın is recorded in the Annals of the Four Masters at the year 992.

Ó hᴀƀᴀʀᴄᴀıʒ—I—*O Havorta, O Haverta*, Haverty; 'des. of Áƀᴀʀᴄᴀċ,' or more probably of 'ʃᴀʒᴀʀᴄᴀċ'; v. Ó hᴀʒᴀʀᴄᴀıʒ and cf. Ó hOʒᴀʀᴄᴀıʒ; a rare Galway surname.

Ó hᴀỗʟᴀıʒ—I—Addley, Addly; 'des. of ᴀ————'; a rare surname in parts of Mayo and Galway. The Annals of Ulster at the year 947 record the death of 'Anmere Ua Adlai,' coarb of St. Ciaran of Clonmacnoise.

Ó hᴀỗmᴀıʟʟ—I—*O Hammell*, O'Hamill, Hamill, Hamell, Hammill, Hammell; 'des. of Áỗmᴀıʟ' (quick, ready, active); also written Ó hÁʒmᴀıʟʟ; the name of a branch of the Cinel Eoghain, still numerous in Ulster.

Ó hᴀỗnᴀıỗ, Ó hᴀỗnᴀıʒ—I—*O Heynee, O Hyneye*, Hyney, Hiney; 'des. of ᴀỗnᴀỗ' (old age; wise); also Ó hᴀıỗne and Ó heıỗnıʒ; the name (1) of a Galway family who were anciently chiefs of Gno-beg, in the present barony of Moycullen; and (2) of a West Cork family. In the 16th century, it was very scattered and is now extremely rare.

Ó hᴀʒáın—I—*O Hagane*, O'Hagan, Hagan, Haggan, &c.; 'des. of Óʒán' (dim. of óʒ, young); a northern var. of Ó hOʒáın, q.v.; the name (1) of a distinguished family of Cinel Eoghain, who were chiefs of Cinel Fearghusa and were seated at Tullaghoge, in Co. Tyrone, where it was O'Hagan's privilege to inaugurate O'Neill; and (2) of another family of the same race who were chiefs of Cinel Tighearnaigh, in Ulster.

Ó hᴀʒᴀıʀᴄ—I—*O Haggart*, Heggert; short for Ó hÁʒᴀʀᴄ- ᴀıʒ, q.v.

Ó háʒaʀⱦaiʒ— I —*O Hagirtie*, Agarty, Hagarty, Hagerty, Hegarty, Hegerty, Heggerty, &c. ; ' des. of ꝼáʒaʀⱦać ' (same as ꝼóʒaʀⱦać) ; a var. of Ó hOʒaʀⱦaiʒ, q.v. Cf. Ó háʒáin for Ó hOʒáin.

Ó haʒaʀⱦaiʒ—I—*O Haerty*, Hearty, (Hegarty) ; ' des. of ꝼaʒaʀⱦać ' (same as ꝼáʒaʀⱦać) ; a var. of Ó ꝼaʒaʀⱦaiʒ (q.v.), owing to the aspiration of the initial ꝼ. Cf. Ó hOʒaʀⱦaiʒ.

Ó háʒmaill, v. Ó háⱱmaill.

Ó haiⱱiʀ—I—*O Haghir, O Hagher, O Hahir*, O'Hehir, O'Haire, O'Hare, Hegher, Hehir, Aher, Hair, Hare, Herr, &c. ; ' des. of aiⱦeaʀ ' (sharp, bitter, angry) ; also written Ó haiⱦⱦiʀ, Ó hOiⱦiʀ, &c. ; the name of a Thomond family who, at the end of the 11th century, were lords of Magh Adhair, between Ennis and Tulla, but afterwards settled in Ui Cormaic, on the west side of the Fergus, between Ennis and Slieve Callan. Though long settled in Thomond, the family was not of Dalcassian origin, but a branch of the Ui Fidhgheinte, in the present Co. Limerick. The name is still common in Clare and Limerick.

Ó haiⱱeiⱦ, Ó haiⱱiⱱe, v. Ó haiⱱiⱦ.

Ó haiⱱín—I—*O Hidiene, O Hidden*, Hadian, Haden, Hayden, Haydin, &c. ; ' des. of aiⱱiⱦín ' (dim. of aiⱱiⱦ) ; a var. of Ó heiⱱín, q.v.

Ó haiⱱiⱦ—I—*O Hidia*, Haidee, Haidy ; ' des. of aiⱱiⱦ ' (humility) ; also written Ó haiⱱeiⱦ, Ó háiⱱiⱱe, &c. ; the name (1) of an Ulidian family who were lords of Ui Eathach, now the barony of Iveagh, Co. Down, from about the middle of the 10th to the middle of the 12th century, when they were superseded by the Maguinnesses ; and (2) of a Connacht family, mentioned by MacFirbis. The name, which is now extremely rare, is current about Shrule, Co. Mayo, in the modernised forms of Ó heiⱱiⱱ and Ó heaⱱeaⱱa, q.v.

Ó haiⱱne, v. Ó háⱱnaiʒ.

Ó hailⱱeaʀⱦaiʒ—I—*O Helvertie, O Helfertie*, Halverty, Halferty, Hilferty ; ' des. of ailⱱeaʀⱦać ' (noble-bright) ; an old, but rare, Donegal surname.

Ó ḣáilce—II—*O Hallihey, O Hally,* Hally, Halley;
'des. of áilce' (a personal name of Danish origin,
meaning 'English'); the name of a family, probably
of Danish origin, who were seated in the neighbourhood of Templemore, Co. Tipperary. In the 16th
century, there were merchant families of the name
in Cashel and Kilmallock. It is still common in
Tipperary and parts of Limerick.

Ó ḣáilǵeánáin—I—*O Hallinaine,* O'Hallinan, Hallinan, Hallanan, Halnan; 'des. of áilǵeánán' (dim.
of áilǵeán, noble offspring); an old Munster surname,
found chiefly in Cork and Limerick; also apparently
a Connacht surname, now not uncommon in West
Mayo. macḃeataṁ Ó ḣáilǵeánáin was Bishop of
Cork at the beginning of the 12th century.

Ó ḣáilǵeása—I—*O Hallyse, O Hallishy,* Hallissy,
Hallissey, Hallessy; 'des. of áilǵear' (desire, request,
importunity); a Munster surname; found chiefly in
West Cork and South Kerry.

Ó ḣáilín—I—*O Hallyne,* Hallin, Hallion, Allin, Allen;
'des of áilín' (dim. of áil, noble, rock, a 'pet'
form of some name commencing with áil-); also
written Ó ḣáillín; a rare surname; found chiefly in
Ormond and Offaly.

Ó ḣáille—I—*O Hally,* Hally; 'des. of áille,' or 'áinte'
(handsome, beautiful; also a hero or warrior); the
name of a Thomond family who were seated at baile
uí áille, now angl. Ballyally, near Bunratty, in Co.
Clare. V. Ó ḣáinliǵe.

Ó ḣáilleácáin—I—*O Halleghane, O Hallaghan,* Hallaghan, Hallihane, Hallahan, Hallihan; 'des. of
áilleácán' (dim. of áille, handsome, beautiful);
also Ó ḣállacáin; the name of an old Cork family.

Ó ḣáilleaǵáin—I—*O Hallegane, O Hallagan,* Halligan,
Hilligan; 'des. of áilleaǵán' (dim. of áille, handsome, beautiful); also Ó ḣállaǵáin; an old Ulster
surname; now common also in Mayo and Roscommon.

Ó ḣáilṁic—I—*O Halwick, O Halvie,* (?) Halvey, Hanwick ; ' des. of ᴀᴉᴛᵐᴀc ' (noble-son) ; the name of a family of Ui Fiachrach in Connacht, now possibly represented by the Mayo surname Hanwick. For the angl. form ' Halvey,' cf. Kirby for Ó Cíᴘᵐᴉc.

Ó ᴑᴀᴉʟᴘíᴨ—I—*O Halpin, O Halpeny, O Halfpenny*, Halpin, Halpeny, Halfpenny ; ' des. of ᴀᴉʟᴘíᴨ ' (dim. of ᴀʟᴘ, a lump, a stout person). This surname appears to have originated in Co. Monaghan, but for centuries it has been found also in Co. Limerick. The angl. forms O Halpeny, Halpeny, &c., represent an older form, Ó ᴑᴀᴉʟᴘeᴨe.

Ó ᴑᴀᴉᵐeᴉʀᵹᴉᴨ, Ó ᴑᴀᴉᵐᴉʀᵹᴉᴨ—I—*O Havergan, O Hemergin*, Mergin, Bergin, Bergen, Bergan, Berrigan, &c. ; ' des. of ᴀᴉᵐᴉᴘᵹᴉᴨ ' (wondrous birth) ; the name of an Offaly family who were formerly chiefs of the barony of Geashill ; still common in Leinster, but long corrupted to Ó ᴍeᴉᴘᵹᴉᴨ and Ó ᴠeᴉᴘᵹᴉᴨ, q.v.

Ó ᴑᴀᴉᴨᴠeᴉᴛ, Ó ᴑᴀᴉᴨᴠᴉᴛ—I—*O Hanfy*, Hanvy, Hanvey, Hanify, Hanafy, Hannify, Hanway, &c. ; ' des. of ᴀᴉᴨᴠᴉoᴛ ' (storm) ; also written Ó ᴑᴀᴉᴨᴘeᴉᴛ, Ó ᴑᴀᴉᴨᴘᴉᴅ, Ó ᴑᴀᴉᴨᴘᴉᴛ, &c. ; the name (1) of a distinguished Oriel family who were chiefs of Ui Seaghain, some- times of Ui Meith, and sometimes of all Oriel ; (2) of a Meath family who were chiefs of Fearabile, now the barony of Farbil, in Co. Westmeath, until dispossessed by Sir Hugh de Lacy soon after the Anglo-Norman invasion ; (3) of an Ulidian family who were chiefs of Ui Eathach Cobha, now the barony of Iveagh, Co. Down ; and (4) of a branch of the Corca Laoighdhe, in South-west Cork. The name is now comparatively rare, having been corrupted or changed into other forms. See Ó ᴑᴀᴉᴨᴠᴛeᴀᴉᴨ, Ó ᴑᴀᴨᴀᴉᴛe, &c.

Ó ᴑᴀᴉᴨᴠᴛeᴀᴉᴨ, Ó ᴑᴀᴉᴨᴠᴛíᴨ—I—*O Hanavane, O Hene- faine*, *O Hannefean*, Hanefan, Hanifan, Hanafin, Hanifin, &c. ; ' des. of ᴀᴉᴨᴠᴛeᴀᴨ ' or ' ᴀᴉᴨᴠᴛíᴨ ' (dim. of ᴀᴉᴨᴠᴉoᴛ) ; also written Ó ᴑᴀᴉᴨᴘeᴀᴉᴨ, Ó ᴑᴀᴉᴨᴘᴉᴨ, &c. ; a well-known surname in Cork and Kerry, where, not improbably, it represents the old surname Ó ᴑᴀᴉᴨᴠᴉᴛ, of Corca Laoighdhe. See Ó

ɴₐɪɴbɪċ above (4). MacFirbis mentions a family of
the name in Roscommon.

Ó hₐɪɴċíɴ—I—*O Hanhine, O Hanhin*, Hanneen, Hannin,
Hannen, (Hannan, Hannon) ; ' des. of *ₐɪɴċíɴ '
(perhaps for ₐɪɴġeɪɴ, unborn) ; the name of a family
of Siol Anmchadha, in south-east of Co. Galway.
It was common at the end of the 16th century in many
parts of Connacht and Munster. See also Ó hₐɪɴɴíɴ.
MacFirbis mentions Ó hₐɪɴġeɪɴ as a Connacht surname.

Ó hₐɪɴꝼeɪċ, Ó hₐɪɴꝼɪʊ, Ó hₐɪɴꝼɪċ, v. Ó hₐɪɴbeɪċ,
Ó hₐɪɴbɪċ.

Ó hₐɪɴꝼeáɪɴ, Ó hₐɪɴꝼíɴ, Ó hₐɪɴꝼeáɪɴ, Ó hₐɪɴꝼíɴ, v. Ó hₐɪɴbċeáɪɴ, Ó hₐɪɴbċíɴ.

Ó háɪɴle, Ó hₐɪɴlɪġe, Ó háɪɴlɪġe—I—*O Hanlee, O
Hanley, O Henly*, Hanley, Handly, Hanly, Henly ;
' des. of áɪɴle ' (beauty, also a hero or warrior) ; the
name of a Connacht family who were chiefs of Cinel
Dobhtha, also called in later times Tuaohanly and
Doohy Hanly, a district in Co. Roscommon, extending along the Shannon and comprising the parishes
of Kilglass, Termonbarry, Cloontuskert, and the
eastern half of the parish of Lisonuffy. The O'Hanlys
continued to hold this territory, as tributaries to
O'Conor Don, down to the 17th century. In the year
1568-9, Gillyerneuf O Haly was nominated by Queen
Elizabeth to be captain of the country of Towohaly
in succession to his father, and in 1582, Fergananym
O Hanly, gentleman, was granted the office of seneschal of Tohahohanly. The name is now common in
many parts of the South of Ireland. Ó háɪlle of
Thomond is doubtless the same name.

Ó hₐɪɴṁɪɾe, Ó hₐɪɴṁɪɾeáċ—I—*O Hanvirre, O Han-
neraghe*, Hanberry, Hanbury, (Ansberry, Ansboro) ;
' des. of ₐɪɴṁɪɾe ' (compound of ₐɪɴ-, a negative
or intensive particle, and mɪɾe, madness, levity) ;
an old Connacht surname, corruptly Ó hₐɪɴmɴeáċ.
It still survives in Co. Galway under the English form
of Ansboro, Hanbury, &c. mₐelɪɾₐ Ó hₐɪɴṁɪɾe

was Archbishop of Cashel in the early part of the 12th
century.

Ó háinnín—I—*O Hanine, O Haneene,* Hannin, Hanneen,
Hannen, (Hannan, Hannon) ; ' des. of ᴀinnín ' ;
perhaps the same as Ó háinčín, q.v. mᴀeᴛóᵽíᵹᴅe
Uᴀ háinnín, ' noble martyr of Ireland,' died in the
year 1133.

Ó háinᴄe—I—*O Hanhie, O Henhie,* Hanify, &c. ; also
Ó hánᴀiᴄe ; a corruption of Ó háinóiᴄ, q.v.

Ó háiReᴀᴄᴛᴀiᵹ—I—*O Harrati, Harrity,* (Harty, Harrington) ; ' des. of ᴀiᵽeᴀᴄᴛᴀᴄ ' (holding assemblies, belonging to an assembly) ; a var. of Ó hOiᵽeᴀᴄᴛᴀiᵹ, q.v.

Ó háiRᵹeᴀóáin, v. Ó háᵽᵹᴀᴅáin.

Ó háiRḿeᴀóᴀiᵹ—I—*O Harvey,* Harvey, Hervy ; ' des.
of ᴀiᵽḿeᴀóᴀᴄ ' (having a herd of cattle) ; the name
of a family of the Ui Fiachrach, in Connacht ; now
very rare and scattered.

Ó háiRᴄ—I—*O Hairt,* O'Hart, O'Harte, Hart, Harte ;
' des. of ᴀᵽᴄ ' (bear, stone, noble) ; the name of a
Meath family originally seated in the neighbourhood
of Tara, but dispossessed soon after the Anglo-Norman
invasion, when they settled in the barony of Carbury,
in Co. Sligo. The name is still very common in
Connacht.

Ó háiRᴄnéᴀóᴀ—I—*O Hartnedy, O Harniady, O Harnett,* Harnedy, Hartnett, Harnett ; ' des. of *ᴀᵽᴄ-
néᴀóᴀ ' (battle-bear, battle-stone); the name of an old
West Munster family who are still numerous in Cork,
Kerry and Limerick.

Ó háiRᴄRí—I—Hartry, Hartery ; ' des. of ᴀiᵽᴄᵽí ' ; a
rare and scattered surname. The Four Masters, at
the year 1123, record the death of mᴀeᴛíᵽᴀ Ó háiᵽᴄᵽí,
steward of Connacht.

Ó háiseᴀóᴀ—I—*O Hassia, O Hassey, O Hassett,* Hassey
Hassett ; ' des. of ᴀiᵽió ' (strife, discord) ; the name of
an old Thomond family of the same stock as the Mac-
Namaras, being a branch of Clann Chuilean. The
name is still well known in the neighbourhood of the
city of Limerick and in other parts of Munster.

553

Ó háiccir, v. O háiċip.

Ó háiceása—I—*O Hahassie, O Hahesy,* O'Hahasy,
Hahasy, Hahessy, Ahessy; 'des. of áiċeap' (pain,
distress); the name of a family of Siol Anmchadha,
in the south-east of Co. Galway. At the end of the
16th century, it was found chiefly in Tipperary and
Waterford. It is now very rare.

Ó háiceió, Ó háicióe, v. Ó háióiċ.

Ó hallaċáin—I—*O Hallaghan,* Hallaghan, Hallahan,
Hallihan; a var. of Ó háilleaċáin, q.v.; the name of
an old family in Co. Cork.

Ó hallaióe—I—Halley, Hally; doubtless for Ó heal-
aióe, q.v.

Ó hallazáin—I—*O Hallagan,* Halligan; a var. of Ó
háilleazáin, q.v. This is the usual form in Connacht.

Ó hallamáin—I—Hallan, Allan, Allen; a var. of Ó
pallamain (q.v.), owing to the aspiration of the initial
p.

Ó hallmuráin—I—*O Halowrane, O Halloraine,* O'Halloran, O'Hallaran, O'Halleran, O'Halleron, Halloran,
Holloran, &c.; 'des. of Allmupán' (stranger from
beyond the sea); the name (1) of a Galway family
who were anciently chiefs of Clann Fearghaile, an
extensive district in the neighbourhood of the present
city of Galway; and (2) of a Thomond family, of the
same stock as the MacNamaras, who, before the year
1641, were seated in the parish of Ogonnelloe, in the
east of Co. Clare. The name is still very common in
both counties.

Ó hamráin—I—*O Heveran,* Haveron, Haveren, Havern,
Havron, Haffron, Heffron, &c.; 'des. of Amrán'
(dim. of amra, eminent, noble, prosperous); the name
of a Co. Down family who were anciently chiefs of
Dal Fiatach; still extant in East Ulster.

Ó hamailltín, Hamilton; in use in West Clare.

Ó hanaice—I—*O Hanhie,* Hanify, Hannify; a corruption of Ó háinóiċ, q.v.

Ó h-an Cáince—III—*O Hencainteyhe,* Canty; a var. of
Ó Cáince, q.v.

Ó hᵃɴᵷʟⁱuⁱɴɴ—I—*O Hanglin*, Anglin, Anglim ; ' des. of
ᴀɴᵷʟoɴɴ ' (hero, champion) ; an old Cork surname,
almost peculiar to that county ; sometimes corrupted
to Ó hᴀɴᵷʟuⁱm and angl. Anglim. The Four Masters,
under the year 1490, record the death of ꝼⁱoɴɴ Uᴀ
hᴀɴᵷʟuⁱɴɴ, chief tympanist of Ireland.

Ó hᴀɴʟuᴀⁱɴ—I—*O Hanlowne, O Hanlone, O Handlon*,
O'Hanlon, Hanlon, Handlon, Hanlan, &c. ; ' des. of
ᴀɴʟuᴀɴ ' (great hero or champion) ; the name of a
distinguished Oriel family who were chiefs of Ui
Niallain, now the barony of Oneilland in Co. Armagh,
and once of Oirthear, now the barony of Orier, in the
east of the same county. The O'Hanlons were a
powerful clan, and many valiant chiefs of the name
are mentioned in the Irish annals. In 1587, Sir Oghie
O'Hanlon, the then chief, surrendered his lands to
the crown and had them regranted by letters
patent in tail male, and the chieftaincy was
abolished. O'Hanlon was hereditary royal standard
bearer north of the Boyne, as O'Molloy was to the
south ; and, owing to his loyalty to the English
connection, seems to have retained possession
of most of the clan-lands down to the period of the
Cromwellian confiscations. The name is still numerous
in Armagh, and has spread to many other parts of
Ireland ; often written Ó hᴀɴɴʟuᴀⁱɴ, and sometimes
pronounced Ó hᴀɴɴʟáⁱɴ.

Ó hᴀɴɴᴀᴄáⁱɴ—I—*O Hanaghane, O Hanihane*, Hanihan,
Hannahan, Yanahan, (Hannan) ; probably a var. of
Ó hᴀɴɴᴀᵷáⁱɴ, q.v.

Ó hᴀɴɴᴀᵷáⁱɴ—I—*O Hannegan, O Hanigan*, Hannigan,
Hanigan ; ' des. of ᴀɴɴᴀᵷáɴ ' (dim. of ᴀɴɴᴀᵇ, delay) ;
an old Limerick surname, where it was probably a variant of Ó hᴀɴɴáⁱɴ, q.v.

*Ó hᴀɴɴᴀⁱᵇ, Hanna ; ' des. of ᴀɴɴᴀᵇ.'

Ó hᴀɴɴáⁱɴ—I—*O Hannaine, O Hanain*, Hannan, Hannon,
Hanan, Hanon, &c.; ' des. of ᴀɴɴáɴ' (dim. of ᴀɴɴᴀᵇ, delay); the name of an old family in Co. Limerick, where it
is still common. But see Ó hᴀⁱɴᴄíɴ and Ó hᴀⁱɴɴíɴ.

Ó hannluain, v. Ó hanluain.

Ó hannraċáin—I—*O Hawreghane*, *O Howreghan*,
O'Hourihane, Hourihane, Hourahan, Hourihan, Hourican ; a corruption of Ó hanpaváin, q.v. This form
of the surname is peculiar to Co. Cork.

Ó hannragáin—I—*O Howrigane*, *O Hourigan*, Hourigan ; a corruption of Ó hanpaváin, q.v. But see
Ó hoópagáin.

Ó hannraic—II—*O Hanrick*, *O Henricke*, Hanrick,
Handrick, &c. ; ' des. of annpac' (from Norse
Heimerkr) ; also Ó heanpaic, q.v. ; a rare and scattered
surname, probably of Norse origin.

Ó hannráin—I—*O Hawrane*, *O Howrane*, Haran, Haren,
Horan ; a corruption of Ó hanpaváin, q.v. Cf. Ó
happaċáin.

Ó hanraċáin—I—*O Hanraghane*, O'Hanrahan, Hanrahan, Handrahan ; a corruption of Ó hanpaváin, q.v.
This form of the surname is very common in Thomond.

Ó hanraċταιg—I—*O Hanraghty*, *O Hanratty*, Hanratty ; ' des. of anpaċτać' (unrighteous, unlawful) ;
also written Ó hionpaċταιg, and Ó hinpeaċταιg, q.v. ;
the name of an Oriel family who were chiefs of Ui
Meith Macha, now the barony of Monaghan, in Co.
Monaghan ; still common in Monaghan, Armagh and
Louth.

Ó hanraváin—I—O'Hanrahan, O'Hourihane, *O Har-*
raghan, *O Horoghane*, *O Hourigan*, *O Harragan*, *O*
Horigane, *O Horgane*, *O Hawrane*, *O Howrane*,
Hanrahan, Hourihane, Hourigan, Horrigan, Haran,
Horan, Horgan, &c. ; ' des. of anpaváin,' (dim. of
anpav, warrior, champion) ; variously corrupted in
different parts of Ireland to Ó hanpaċáin, Ó hannpaċáin, Ó hannpagáin, Ó happaċáin, Ó happagáin,
Ó hapgáin, Ó hannpáin, Ó hionpáin, &c. ; the name
(1) of a Dalcassian family in Thomond, where it is
still very common (v. Ó hanpaċáin) ; (2) of a West
Cork family who were anciently erenaghs of Ross (v.
Ó hannpaċáin) ; (3) of a Leix family who were anciently chiefs of Ui Creamhthainn, a district lying

around the rock of Dunamase, in the present Leix (v. Ó hⱭⱤⱤaᵹáin and Ó hⱭⱤᵹáin) ; and (4) of a Meath family who were formerly chiefs of Corca Raoidhe, now the barony of Corcaree, in Co. West-meath (v. Ó hⁱonⱤáin and Ó hⁱonnⱤáin). Ó hⱭnn-Ⱡaᵹáin (q.v.) appears to be a Tipperary form of this surname. The different forms are now very widely scattered.

Ó hⱭOⱱⱭ—I—*O Heaa, O Hay, O Hewe, O Hugh,* O'Hea, Hay, Hays, Hayes, Hews, Hughes, &c. ; ' des. of ⱭOⱱ ' (fire) ; the name of several distinct families in different parts of Ireland, of which the following are the best known : (1) a Tyrone family, formerly lords of Ui Fiachrach of Ardstraw ; (2) a Tirconnell family, chiefs of Eas Ruadh, in the neighbourhood of Bally-shannon ; (3) an Oriel family, chiefs of Fearnmaighe, now the barony of Farney, in Co. Monaghan ; (4) a Meath family, lords of Odhbha, in the neighbourhood of Navan ; (5) a Meath family, chiefs of East Tir Teathbha ; (6) a Wexford family, chiefs of Ui Deagh-aidh, a district nearly co-extensive with the barony of Gorey ; (7) a Cork family, lords of Muscraighe-Luachra, in the north-west of Co. Cork ; (8) a Cork family, sub-chiefs of Tuath O Donnghaile, in the south-west of Co. Cork, where they are still numerous ; (9) a Dalcassian family in Thomond; (10) a family of Ui Maine in Co. Galway ; (11) a family of Ui Fiachrach in Co. Mayo, formerly seated at Ard O nAodha, in the parish of Templemurray ; (12) another family of the same race, seated in the parish of Ballintobber ; and (13) a family of Ui Fiachrach, seated at Tonrego, in the parish of Dromard, Co. Sligo. This surname, which is numerically one of the strongest in Ireland, is generally angl. Hughes in the North and Hayes in the South. The O' is almost universally rejected, being retained only by the family of Ó hⱭOⱱⱭ of Corca Laoighdhe (8), who anglicise the name O'Hea.

Ó hⱭOⱱaᵹáin—I—*O Hegane, O Higane, O Heagan, O Heegan, O Heaken, O Hoogan, O Huggain,* O'Hegan,

Hegan, Heagan, Hagan, Hogan, Egan, Eagan, Eakin, Hegans, Hagans, Higgans, Huggins, &c. ; ' des. of Aoḃaʒán ' (dim. of Aoḃ) ; the name (1) of an Oriel family who, in the 10th and 11th centuries, were lords of Dartraighe, in Co. Monaghan, and of Ui Niallain, in Co. Armagh, and to which belonged Ivor O'Hegan, the tutor of St. Malachy and founder of the church of SS. Peter and Paul at Armagh ; and (2) of a family of Ely-O'Carroll, in the present Offaly. This surname, owing to the different dialectical pronunciations of the syllable ' Aoḃ,' is variously anglicised in different parts of Ireland. In Ulster, it frequently became Ó ꝼaoḃaʒáin (q.v.), angl. Fegan.

Ó ꞃAoileáin—I—Hylan, Hyland, &c. ; a var. of Ó ꞃAoláin, q.v.

Ó ꞃAoilleacáin—I—*O Hillichain, O Heleghane, O Helighane, O Hylegane*, Hellican, Helehan, Helihan, (O'Higgins, Higgins, Hedigan) ; a var. of Ó ꝼaoilleacáin, through the loss of the initial ꝼ. It is strangely angl. Higgins in the neighbourhood of Dungarvan and Hedigan about Kilkee.

Ó ꞃAoláin—I—*O Healane, O Heyllane, O Helane, O Hilane, O Hillane, O Hylane, O Heolane, O Hoolane, O Holane, O Hollan, O Holland*, Heelan, Helen, Hillane, Hillan, Holian, Heyland, Hiland, Hylan, Hyland, Holland, (Whelan), &c. ; ' des. of ꝼaolán ' (dim. of ꝼaol, a wolf) ; a var. of Ó ꝼaoláin (q.v.) through the aspiration of the initial ꝼ ; a common surname, in the 16th century, in Offaly and Leix, whence it spread into other parts of Ireland. Owing to the different dialectical pronunciations of ' Ao,' it is variously anglicised in the different provinces. In Munster, it is generally angl. Heelan ; Hyland is the usual form in Leinster ; Holland in Ulster. In Connacht, it is sometimes corrupted to Ó ꞃioláin, Ó ꞃoláin, Ó ꞃoileáin, and Ó ꞃóileáin, angl. Hillane, Hyland, Holland, &c., but the origin is clearly shown by the fact that these forms are nearly always also angl. Whelan. Cf. Ó ꞃAoḃaʒáin.

Ó hAonАСÁın, v. Ó hEАnАСÁın.

Ó hАonȝuıs—I—*O Henees, O Hennis*, Ennes, Ennis;
‘des. of Аonȝuʀ’; a var. of Ó hАonȝuʀА, q.v.

Ó hАonȝusА—I—*O Heanesey, O Hennesy, O Hensey*,
Hennessy, Hensy, Hinsy, Henchy, Hinchy; ‘des.
of Аonȝuʀ’ (one-choice); the name (1) of an Offaly
family who were lords of Clann Cholgan, a district co-
extensive with the barony of Lower Philipstown;
(2) of a Meath family who were lords of Ui Mac Uais,
in the barony of Moyfenrath; (3) of a Bregian family
who were chiefs of Gailenga Beaga, in Meath and the
north of the present Co. Dublin; and (4) of a Dalcassian family in Thomond. The name is now common throughout Munster and Leinster.

Ó hАorȶАıȝ, Hearty; a var. in the spoken language of
Ó hАȝАʀȶАıȝ, q.v.

Ó hАrАСÁın, v. Ó ʀАрАСÁın.

Ó hАrАȝÁın, v. Ó hАʀʀАȝÁın.

Ó hАrАılȶ—II—*O Harold*, Harold, Harrold; ‘des. of
Harold’ (Norse Haraldr); a Limerick surname,
apparently of Norse origin.

Ó hАrȝАѷÁın—I—*O Hargedaine, O Hardagane, O
Hargedan*, Hargaden, Hargadon, (Hardiman, Harman,
Harmon); ‘des. of АʀȝАѷÁn’ or ‘АıʀȝeАѷÁn’ (dim.
of АıʀȝeАѷ, silver, hence white, shining); also Ó
hАıʀȝeАѷÁın; a Connacht surname; now often, but
incorrectly, angl. Hardiman, Harman, &c.

Ó hАrȝÁın—I—*O Horgaine, O Horgane, O Horgan, O
Hargan*, Hargan, Horgan, Organ; a contracted form
of Ó hАʀʀАȝÁın, q.v. This form of the surname is
most frequent in Cork and Kerry.

Ó hАrrАСÁın—I—*O Harraghan, O Horoghane, O Horo-
han, O Horran*, Horahan, Harran, Haran, Horan, &c.;
a corruption of Ó hАnʀАѷÁın, q.v.; common in
Leix and Tipperary.

Ó hАrrАСȶÁın—I—*O Haraghtane, O Harreghtane, O
Harrighton, O Herraghton*, Harroughton, Haroughton,
(Harrington, Errington, Irrington), &c.; ‘des. of
АʀʀАСȶÁn’ (dim. of АʀʀАСȶА, tall, mighty, brave,

heroic) ; the name of a family of Ui Maine in Co. Galway. In the 16th century, it was scattered through all North Munster. To be distinguished from Ó ꞂꞲᴏꞂᵹᴀꞃᴏᴀɪʟ and Ó Ꞃᴏɪꞃᴇᴀᴄᴄᴀɪᵹ, which are also angl. Harrington.

Ó ꞂᴀꞆꞆᴀᵹᴀ́ɪꞀ—I—*O Harragan, O Horrogan, O Horigane,* Harrigan, Herrigan, Horrigan, Horrogan, Horagan, Horgan, &c. ; a corruption of Ó Ꞃᴀɴꞃᴀᴠᴀ́ɪꞀ, q.v. This form of the surname originated in Leix.

Ó Ꞃᴀ́Ꞇᴛᴀ, Ó Ꞃᴀ́Ꞇᴛᴀɪᵹ—I—*O Harta,* Harty ; a corrupt form of Ó Ꞃᴀᵹᴀꞃᴛᴀɪᵹ and Ó Ꞃᴀᴄᴀꞃᴛᴀɪᵹ, q.v.

Ó Ꞃᴀꞃᴛᴀᵹᴀ́ɪꞀ—I—*O Hartigan,* Hartigan, Hartican ; ' des. of Ꞇꞃᴛᴀᵹᴀ́ɴ ' (dim. of Ꞇꞃᴛ) ; the name of a Dalcassian family in Thomond, still well known in Clare and Limerick. Ꞇúɴʟᴀɪɴᵹ Ó Ꞃᴀꞃᴛᴀᵹᴀ́ɪɴ was one of the heroes of Clontarf.

Ó Ꞃᴀꞃᴛᴀ́ɪꞀ—I—*O Hartane, O Hartan,* Hartan, Harton, Harten, Hartin, Horton ; ' des. of Ꞇꞃᴛᴀ́ɴ ' (dim. of Ꞇꞃᴛ) ; a scattered surname, but found chiefly in Derry and Donegal. Cf. Ó Ꞃᴀꞃᴛᴀᵹᴀ́ɪɴ.

Ó Ꞃᴀꞃᴛᵹᴀɪʟᴇ—I—Hartley ; ' des. of Ꞇꞃᴛᵹᴀʟ ' (noble valour) ; the name of a South Leinster family who, before the Anglo-Norman invasion, were chiefs of a district near the town of Wexford.

Ó ꞂᴀᴄᴀɪꞆɴᴇ—I—*O Haherny, O Harney,* Harney, Hartney ; ' des. of Ꞇᴄᴀɪꞃɴᴇ ' (fatherly, paternal) ; a rare and scattered surname.

Ó Ꞃᴀᴄᴀꞃᴛᴀɪᵹ—I—*O Haherty, O Harty,* Harty ; ' des. of Ꞅᴀᴄᴀꞃᴛᴀᴄ ' (same as Ꞅᴀᵹᴀꞃᴛᴀᴄ) ; a var. of Ó Ꞅᴀᴄᴀꞃᴛᴀɪᵹ (q.v.), owing to the aspiration of the initial Ꞅ ; shortened in the spoken language to Ó Ꞃᴀ́ꞃᴛᴀɪᵹ and Ó Ꞃᴀ́ꞃᴛᴀ ; the name, according to Mageoghegan, of an Offaly family. At the end of the 16th century, it was common in Tipperary, Limerick, Cork and Kerry.

Ó Ꞃᴇᴀᴄᴀᴄ—I—*O Heagh, O Hagh,* Haugh, Hawe, Hawes ; ' des. of ᴇᴀᴄᴀɪᴠ ' ; a var. of Ó Ꞃᴇᴏᴄᴀᴠᴀ, q.v.

Ó Ꞃᴇᴀᴄᴀᴠᴀ, Ó Ꞃᴇᴀᴄᴀɪᴠ—I—*O Haghie, O Haghy,* Haghey, Haughey, Haffy, Hahee, Hawey, Hoey ;

'des. of eacaiυ' (a var. of eocaiυ) ; an Ulster surname. V. Ó ɴeocaυa.

Ó ɴeacaiυín—I—*O Haughine, O Heaghean,* Haughean, Haughian, (Hawkins) ; 'des. of eacaiυín' (dim. of eacaiυ) ; a var. of Ó ɴeacáin, q.v.

Ó ɴeacáin—I—*O Heaghane, O Haghaine, O Haghan,* Haughan, Haghan, Haghen, (Hawkins, Haughton) ; 'des. of eacán' (dim. of eacaiυ) ; more anciently Ó ɴeacaυáin and Ó ɴeocaʒáin ; the name of an Ulidian family, still well known in Down and Tyrone.

Ó ɴeacυubáin—I—Aghoon, Whitesteed ; 'des. of eacυubán' (black-steed) ; a rare Mayo surname. Whitesteed is supposed to be a translation ; Blacksteed would be more correct.

Ó ɴeacráin—I—Haughran, Haran ; 'des. of eacrán.' Cf. maʒ eacráin.

Ó ɴeactair—II—*O Haghtir,* Hoctor, Hocter ; 'des. of Hector' ; an old Tipperary surname ; still extant in that county.

Ó ɴeactiʒearɴa—I—*O Haghierny,* Aherne, &c. ; now usually Ó ɴeactiʒeirɴ, q.v.

Ó ɴeactiʒeirɴ—I—*O Haghierin, O Hagherne, O Haherne, O Hearne,* Ahearn, Aherin, Aherne, Ahern, Hearne, Hearn, &c. ; 'des. of eactiʒearɴ' (horselord) ; also written Ó eactiʒeirɴ, Ó ɴeactiʒearɴa, Ó ɴeictiʒeirɴ, &c. ; a common surname in Cork and Limerick, where it is generally angl. Aherne, and in Waterford, where it is made Hearne. For history of family, see Ó eactiʒeirɴ.

Ó ɴeaυamáin—I—*O Hedevan,* Heduvan, Hedivan ; 'des. of eaυamán' ; a rare Westmeath surname.

Ó ɴeaυra, v. ɴeaʒra.

Ó ɴeaυromáin—I—*O Hederiman,* Hederman, Hedderman ; 'des. of eaυtromán' (light, fickle) ; an old Limerick surname, still well known in that county.

Ó ɴeafa—I—*O Heafa,* Heaphy, &c. V. Ó ɴeamtaiʒ.

Ó ɴeaʒra—I—O'Hara, O'Harra, Hara ; 'des. of eaʒra' ; also written Ó ɴeaυra. The O'Haras, who are of the same stock as the O'Garas (v. Ó ʒaυra), derive their name and descent from Eaṡṗa, lord of Luighne, who died in the year 926, and were for many centuries lords of Luighne, now the barony of Leyney, in Co. Sligo. Since the 14th century, they were divided into two branches, the heads of which were known respectively as Ó neaṡṗa ḃuiḋe and Ó neaṡṗa Riaḃaċ, i.e., the yellow O'Hara and the speckled or brindled O'Hara. A branch of the family settled early in the Route, Co. Antrim, where they rose to importance and are still well known. The O'Haras of Leyney were all dispossessed at the Cromwellian period, except one family which threw in its lot with the Cromwellians.

Ó neaṡṙáin—I—*O Harane, O Haran*, Haran, Haren, Harran, Harren, &c.; ' des. of Eaṡṙán ' (dim. of Eaṡṙa); an old Galway surname.

Ó nealáḃaiṡ, Ó nealaiḋe, v. Ó néaluiṡṫe and Ó néiliḋe.

Ó néaluiṡṫe—I—*O Healihie, O Heally, O Healy, O Hely*, Healy, Heally, Hely, Hayles; ' des. of Ealaḃaċ ' (scientific, ingenious); often pronounced Ó neáluiṡṫe, but, without doubt, originally Ó nealaḃaiṡ; the name of an ancient family who, according to Dr. O'Brien, were proprietors of Donoghmore, in the barony of Muskerry, Co. Cork, and are still numerous in that county. See also Ó néiliḋe.

Ó néaṁaċáin, Hevaghan. V. Ó néiṁeaċáin.

Ó néaṁaiṡ—I—*O Hevie*, Heavy, Heavey, Havy, Havey, &c.; a var. of Ó néiṁiṡ, q.v. See also Ó néaṁṫaiṡ.

Ó néaṁáin—I—*O Heavane, O Hevane*, Evans, &c.; a var. of Ó néiṁin, q.v.

Ó néaṁṫaiṡ—I—*O Heafegh, O Heafa*, Heaphy, Heify; the same as Ó néaṁaiṡ and Ó néiṁiṡ, q.v.; a Munster surname, most frequent in Cork and Waterford.

Ó neanaċáin—I—*O Heneghane*, Heanaghan, Henaghan, Heneghan, Henehan, Henihan, Henekan, Heenan, Bird; a var., in Co. Mayo, of Ó néineaċáin, q.v. It is sometimes angl. Bird, on the erroneous supposition

that it is derived from ' ᴇᴀɴ,' a bird. No doubt, it
also stands for older Ó ɴᴀoɴᴀᴄáɴ.

Ó ɴᴇᴀɴᴀᴠᴀ—I—Heanue, Heaney, Heany; also Ó
ɴᴇɪɴᴇᴀᴠᴀ; a Galway surname, the origin of which
I cannot trace. It is possibly the same as Ó ɴᴇᴀɴɴᴀ,
or Ó ꝼᴇɪɴɴᴇᴀᴠᴀ, q.v.

Ó ɴᴇᴀɴᴀᵹáɪɴ—I—*O Heanagane, O Henegane, O Heni-
gane,* Hennigan, Henekan, Bird; a var. of Ó ɴᴇᴀɴ-
ᴀᴄáɪɴ, q.v.

Ó ɴᴇᴀɴᴀɪᵹ, Heaney, Heany.

Ó ɴᴇᴀɴáɪɴ—I—*O Henane, O Hennaine,* Henan, Heenan,
Hennan, Heanen, &c.; a var., probably, of Ó ɴᴇɪᴠ-
ɴᴇáɪɴ, q.v.

Ó ɴᴇᴀɴɴᴀ—I—*O Heany, O Heney,* Heaɴy, Heaney,
Heeny, Heney, &c., Bird; ' des. of ᴇᴀɴɴᴀ ' (Enda);
also written Ó ɴᴇɪɴɴᴇ; the name (1) of a family of Uí
Fiachrach who were formerly proprietors of Imleach-
loisce, in Co. Mayo: (2) of an Eoghanacht family in
the present Co. Limerick; and (3) of a Dalcassian
family in Thomond. This last-named family produced several distinguished ecclesiastics, two of whom,
Donald (1098) and Matthew (1206), filled the see of
Cashel, and one, Connor, that of Killaloe. Connor
died while returning from the Fourth General Council
of Lateran. This surname is to be distinguished from
Ó ɴᴇɪɴɪᵹ, q.v.

Ó ɴᴇᴀɴɴʀᴀɪᴄ, Ó ɴᴇᴀɴʀᴀɪᴄ—II—*O Henrick,* Henrick,
Hanrick, Hendrick, Handrick; a var. of Ó ɴᴀɴɴ-
ʀᴀɪᴄ, q.v.

Ó ɴᴇᴀʀᴀáɪɴ—I—*O Harrane, O Haran, O Heron,* O'Harran,
O'Haran, O'Hern, Haran, Harran, Heran, Herran,
Heron, Herron, Hearn, Herne; ' des. of ᴇᴀʀᴀᴠáɴ '
(dim. of ᴇᴀʀᴀᴠ, fear, dread); older Ó ɴᴇᴀʀᴀᴠáɪɴ; the
name of an Oriel family who were lords of Uí Breasail
Macha, in the barony of Oneilland, Co. Armagh; still
common in the north of Ireland.

Ó ɴᴇᴀʀᴀɪʀíɴ, Ó ɴᴇᴀʀᴀʀáɪɴ—I—*O Harreryne, O
Hererane,* Herrerin, Herreran; ' des. of ᴇᴀʀᴀɪʀíɴ,' or
' ᴇᴀʀᴀʀáɴ ' (dim. of ᴇᴀʀᴀʀ); a rare and scattered

surname. It still survives in parts of Ulster and Louth. Ó neaṗaiṗ, angl. O Herrere, also once existed. In the Annals of Ulster, at the year 1205, it is recorded that Maelḃṙiġte Ua neṗaṗan of Derry was chosen to be successor of St. Brendan, that is, very probably, made Bishop of Clonfert.

Ó neaRca—I—*O Herke*, Herky ; a var. of Ó neiṗc, q.v. ; very rare.

Ó neaRcaṫa, Ó neaRcaiṫ—I—*O Harroughow, O Harrochoe, O Horrochoe, O Horchoy, O Hurkoy, O Hurowe*, Haraghy, Hiraghy, Harrihy, Harkey, Horohoe, Horahoe, Harroe, Hurroe, (Hore, Hoare, Harris, Harrison) ; 'des. of eaṗcaiṫ' (noble warrior) ; an old Connacht surname, now variously anglicised, and in Mayo disguised as Harris and Harrison. It was not uncommon in Tipperary in the 16th and 17th centuries, but I have not been able to trace any modern angl. form in that county.

Ó neaRcáin—I—*O Harkane, O Harkan*, Harkan, Harkin, Harkins ; 'des. of eaṗcán' (dim. of eaṗc, red, speckled) ; a common surname in Donegal and Derry. See also Ó noṗcáin.

Ó neaRcaiR—I—Harragher, Harraher ; a var. of Ó feaṗcaiṗ (q.v.), owing to the aspiration of the initial f ; very rare.

Ó neaRġail—I—*O Herrall, O Herrell*, Harrell, Harrel, Herald, &c. ; a var. of Ó feaṗġail (q.v.), owing to the aspiration of the initial f.

Ó neaRġaile—I—*O Harrily, O Harely*, Harrily, Harley, Herley, Herly ; a var. of Ó feaṗṗġaile, q.v. Cf. Ó neaṗġail.

Ó neaRnáin—I—*O Hernane, O Harnan, O Hortenan*, Hernon, Harnon, Hartnane, Hertnan, Hertnon, (Heffernan) ; (1) 'des. of eaṗnán' (dim. of eaṗna, knowing, experienced) ; and (2) a short form in Munster of Ó nifeaṗnáin, q.v.

Ó neicċiġeiRn, v. Ó neaċċiġeiṗn.

Ó neiṫeaṫa, v. Ó neiṫiṫ.

Ó neiṫeaġáin—I—*O Hettigane, O Hedeghan*, Hedegan,

Hedigan, Haddigan; 'des. of Eıoeaʒán'; more anciently Ó neıceaʒán and Mac eıoeaʒáın; the name of an ecclesiastical family at Elphin, Co. Roscommon. William O Hetigan was Bishop of Elphin about the middle of the 15th century. The name is now more commonly Ó neıoeáın, q.v. Ó neıceaʒáın was also the name of a family of Cinel Eoghain in Ulster, but in that province it is generally changed to Maʒ Eıceaʒáın, q.v. MacFirbis also mentions a midland family of the same name.

Ó neıoeáın, Ó néıoeáın—I—O Hedayne, O Hedane, O Heyden, Heden, Headen, Haden, Hayden, Haydon, &c. ; 'des. of eıoeaóán' (dim. of eıoeaó) ; a var. of Ó neıoín and Ó neıoeaʒáın, q.v. In Roscommon it probably represents the older Ó neıoeaʒáın or Ó neıceaʒáın, q.v.

Ó néıoıó—I—O Hidia, Haidy, Haidee ; 'des. of Eıoeaó' ; also Ó néıoeaóa ; a modern form of Ó náıoıc, or Ó náıoıóe, q.v. ; current in the neighbourhood of Shrule, where it has been long established.

Ó neıoín, Ó néıoín—I—O Hedine, O Headyne, O Heden, O Headen, O Hedian, O Heyden, Heden, Headen, Hadian, Haydin, Hayden, Haydon, &c. ; 'des of eıoıóín' (dim. of eıoeaó) ; a var. of Ó neıoeáın, q.v. ; formerly a common surname, especially in Roscommon, Tipperary and South Leinster. See also Ó náıoín, and cf. Ó néıoıó and Ó neıoeaʒáın.

Ó neıoín—I—O Heine, O Heyne, O Hine, O Hyne, Heines, Hynes, Hyndes, &c. ; 'des. of eıoean' (ivy) ; the name of a Galway family who derive their descent from the celebrated Guaire Aidhne, King of Connacht in the 7th century, and for the space of six hundred years were the chief family of Ui Fiachrach Aidhne and lords of Aidhne, a district co-extensive with the diocese of Kilmacduagh. Maoıpuanaıó Ó neıoín, lord of Aidhne, who fell at Clontarf, in 1014, was the first person to bear the surname. There was also a family of the name formerly of considerable importance seated in the neighbourhood of Caherconlish, Co. Limerick, but it is now almost extinct. The name is however still common in Galway and the adjoining parts of Co. Clare.

Ó ḟéroṁn—I—*O Heane, O Haine, O Hayne,* Haines, Haynes, Hynes ; a var. of Ó ﻲéróṁn, q.v. ; rare and scattered.

Ó ḟéróiRsceóil—I—*O Hederscoll, O Hidirscoll,* O'Driscoll, Driscoll ; ' des. of éroiṁrceóil ' (interpreter); now shortened to Ó Oṁrceóil, q.v. ; the name of an ancient West Cork family who were chiefs of Corca Laoighdhe, a district which originally embraced the whole of the south-west of Co. Cork, namely, the baronies of Carbery, Beare and Bantry, but shortly after the Anglo-Norman invasion was narrowed down, through the encroachments of the O'Donovans, O'Mahonys and O'Sullivans, to a strip of sea-coast around the bay of Baltimore. The O'Driscolls, however, possessed considerable power and had several strong castles even as late as the beginning of the 17th century. They took an active part in the wars in Munster in the reign of Elizabeth. After the defeat of Kinsale, their property was confiscated and given to Lord Castlehaven.

Ó ﻲéróneaċáin, v. Ó ﻲéineaċáin.

Ó ﻲéróneáin—I—*O Hinane, O Hynane,* Hinan, Hynan ; ' des. of éróneán ' (dim. of éróean, ivy) ; a scattered surname. See also Ó ﻲéanáin.

Ó ﻲéróṁnᵹ—I—*O Hynye,* Hyney, Hiney ; ' des. of éróneaċ ' ; a var. of Ó ﻲáónaiᵹ, q.v.

Ó ﻲéiᵹceaRtaiᵹ, Ó ﻲéiᵹeaRtaiᵹ—I—*O Heagertie, O Hegertie, O Hagirtie,* O'Hegarty, Hegarty, Hegerty, Hagarty, Higerty, &c., (Hoverty) ; ' des. of éiᵹceaṁrtaċ ' (unjust) ; the name of a family of Cinel Eoghain, in Tyrone, Derry and Donegal. A branch of the family settled in Cork, where the name is now common. Cf. Ó ﻲáᵹaṁrtaiᵹ.

Ó ﻲéiᵹniᵹ, Ó ﻲéiᵹniᵹ—I—*O Hicknie, O Hignie,* Hegney, Heagney, Haigney ; ' des. of éiᵹneaċ ' ; the name of an Oriel family who in the 11th and 12th centuries

were lords of Fermanagh and sometimes of all Oriel ;
(2) of another family of the same race who were chiefs
of Clann Chearnaigh, apparently in the east of the
present Co. Armagh ; and (3) of a Mayo family who
were anciently chiefs of Clann Laoghaire, in Tirawley.
The name is now almost universally changed to Ó
ⁿéiʒniʒ, or Ó ⁿéiniʒ, q.v.

Ó ⁿeilʒeaʃáin—I—Ellison.

Ó ⁿéiliⱱe, Ó ⁿéiliʒe—I—*O Healie, O Healy, O Hely*,
Healy, Hely, &c. ; ' des. of of eaʟaⱱać ' (scientific,
ingenious) ; sometimes pronounced Ó ⁿeaʟaiⱱe (or
Ó ⁿeaʟaⱱaiʒ) and Ó ⁿéiliⱱe ; the name of a Sligo
family who formerly possessed the Curlews, Ballina-
fad, and the district lying around the western shore
of Lough Arrow, and had their chief residence at
ⱱaiʟe Uí Éiliⱱe, angl. Ballyhely, in the present
demesne of Hollybrooke. The O'Helys ranked among
the gentry of Co. Sligo down to the Cromwellian period.
The late Most Rev. John Healy, Archbishop of Tuam,
was a scion of this ancient family. In the 16th
century the name was very widely spread in Connacht
and Leinster ; and Ó ⁿéiliⱱe, it may be remarked,
is quite common in Munster. See Ó ⁿéaʟuiʒte.

Ó ⁿéiⱥeacáin—I—Hevaghan ; ' des. of éimeacán '
(dim. of éimeać, swift) ; the name (1) of a family of
Ui Fiachrach in Co. Mayo ; and (2) of a family of Cinel
Fhiachach, in Co. Westmeath. It is now extremely
rare, having been, most probably, changed to Ó
ⁿéiⱥiʒ, q.v.

Ó ⁿéiⱥiʒ—I—*O Hevie*, Hevey, Heavy, Heavey, &c. ;
' des of éimeać '(swift) ; probably short for Ó ⁿéiⱥeacáin, q.v. See also Ó ⁿéaⱥaiʒ and Ó ⁿéaⱥtaiʒ,
which are variants.

Ó ⁿéiⱥín—I—*O Hevine*, Evins, Evens, Evans ; ' des. of
éiⱥín ' (dim. of eiⱥ, swift, active) ; also Ó ⁿéaⱥáin,
q.v. ; an old surname in Ormond and Thomond ; still
represented in Munster.

Ó ⁿéiⱥⱥín—I—Heverine, Heveran, Heveron, Hefferin,
&c. ; ' des. of éiⱥⱥín ' (dim. of éiⱥeaⱱ) ; the name of

a family of Cinel Eoghain, still extant in Mayo. O'Donovan erroneously supposed it to be a corruption of Ó ⁿUᴀᴄṁᴀᴩáɪɴ. It is, however, mentioned by MacFirbis.

Ó ɦᴇɪɴᴇᴀᴄáɪɴ—I—*O Henechan, O Heneghane*, Heanaghan, Henaghan, Henehan, Henihan, Henekan, (Heenan), Bird; 'des. of ᴇɪᴅɴᴇᴀᴄáɴ'; the name of a family of Ui Fiachrach in Co. Mayo, who were formerly proprietors of a large estate in the parishes of Manulla and Balla; still common in that county, sometimes pronounced Ó ɦᴇᴀɴᴀᴄáɪɴ, and angl. Bird, being erroneously supposed to be derived from 'ᴇᴀɴ,' a bird.

Ó ɦᴇɪɴᴇᴀᴅᴀ, v. Ó ɦᴇᴀɴᴀᴅᴀ.

Ó ɦᴇɪɴɪɠ—I—*O Heany, O Heney*, Heany, Heaney, Heeny, &c., Bird; a modernised form of Ó ɦᴇɪɠɴɪɠ, q.v.; often angl. Bird, owing to the erroneous notion that it is derived from 'ᴇᴀɴ,' a bird.

Ó ɦᴇɪɴíɴ—I—*O Heanyne, O Henyne*, Heanen, &c.; a var. of Ó ɦᴇᴀɴáɪɴ, q.v.

Ó ɦᴇɪɴɴᴇ, v. Ó ɦᴇᴀɴɴᴀ.

Ó ɦᴇɪʀ—I—*O Haer*, O'Hare, Hare, Haire; a popular form of Ó ɦíʀ, q.v.

Ó ɦᴇɪʀᴄ—I—*O Herke, O Herrick*, Erke, Herrick, Herricks, Harricks; 'des. of ᴇᴀᴩᴄ' (red, speckled); the name (1) of an Oriel family who were chiefs of Ui Fiachrach Finn, and seated along the river Derg, in the north-west of Co. Tyrone; and (2) of a Tipperary family. The name seems to have disappeared from Ulster, having, most probably, been changed to Ó ɦᴇᴀᴩᴄáɪɴ (q.v.), but is still represented in Munster.

Ó ɦᴇɪʀᴇᴀṁóɪɴ—I—*O Hervan*, Ervine, Erwin, Irvine, Irwin; 'des. of ᴇɪᴩᴇᴀṁóɴ'; a rare South of Ireland surname. ᴀᴇᴅ Ó ɦᴇɪᴩᴇᴀṁóɪɴ was Bishop of Kildare at the end of the 11th century.

Ó ɦᴇɪѕʟᴇᴀɴáɪɴ—I—*O Hislenane*, (Heslin); 'des. of ᴇɪᴩʟᴇᴀɴáɴ'; a Breifney surname, now shortened to Ó ɦᴇɪᴩʟɪɴ, q.v.

Ó ɦᴇɪѕʟɪɴ—I—*O Hisclan*, Heslin; a shortened form of Ó ɦᴇɪᴩʟᴇᴀɴáɪɴ, q.v.

Ó neoċaċ—I—Hough ; ' des. of eoċaıʊ ' (possessing cattle) ; a var. of Ó neaċaċ and Ó neoċaʊa, q.v.

Ó neoċaʊa—I—*O Hoa*, Howe, Howes, &c. ; ' des. of eoċaıʊ ' ; also Ó neoċaċ, Ó neoċaıʊ, q.v. ; a var. of Ó neaċaʊa, q.v. ; the name (1) of an Ulster family who, in the 11th and 12th centuries, were kings of Ulidia, but lost their dignity soon after the Anglo-Norman invasion ; still common in Down and Antrim ; and (2) of a Meath family who were chiefs of Cinel Aonghusa, and are still numerous in Leinster.

Ó neoċaɰáın—I—*O Hoghegane*, Houghegan, (Hogan) ; ' des. of eoċaɰán ' (dim of eoċaıʊ) ; an old Ulidian surname, afterwards changed to Ó neaċáın, q.v. ; now found only in Co. Galway, where it is sometimes disguised under the angl. form of Hogan.

Ó neoċaıʊ—I—*O Hohy, O Hoye, O Huky*, Houghy, Hughey, Howie, Howey, Howay, Hoey, Huey, Hoye, Hoy, &c. ; ' des. of eoċaıʊ ' a var of Ó neoċaʊa, q.v. See also Ó neaċaıʊ.

Ó neoċaıʊín—I—*O Houghine, O Hughian* ; a var. of Ó neaċaʊín, q.v.

Ó neoʊasa, Ó neoʊusa—I—*O Hoasy, O Hosey, O Hossy*, Hosey, Hussey, (Oswell, Oswald) ; ' des. of eoʊar ' ; also written Ó neoɰara, q.v. ; the name of a family of Cinel Eoghain, in Ulster, who were chiefs of Cinel Tighearnaigh, but afterwards migrated to Fermanagh, where they became bards to the Maguires. The family produced several distinguished literary men, among them Eochaidh O hEodhasa and Bonaventure O hEodhasa who flourished at the beginning of the 17th century. The name is now very rare in Ulster, having, according to O'Donovan, been changed to Oswell, which apparently has been more recently further changed to Oswald. Before the end of the 16th century, it had spread to Leinster and Munster, but its angl. forms in these provinces cannot now be distinguished from the Anglo-Irish surname, Hussey.

Ó neoɰaın—I—*O Hoane, O Howen, O Hoyne*, Howen, Hone, Hoyne, Owen, Owens, Hoynes, Hoins, (Hynes) ;

'des. of eoʒan' (well-born); the name (1) of a Dalcassian family in Clare, who, according to Keating, are
of the same stock as the O'Neills of Thomond; and (2)
of an ecclesiastical family at Lough Erne, in the diocese
of Clogher; now very common in Ulster, angl. Owens,
and known in every part of Ireland.

Ó neoʒanáin—I—O'Honan, Honan; 'des. of eoʒanán,
(dim. of eoʒan); a Thomond surname.

Ó neoʒasa—I—O Hogasa, Hosey, Hussey; a var. of Ó
neoðara, q.v.

Ó neóluis, Ó neólusa—I—Olus; 'des. of eolur'
(knowledge); the name of a Leitrim family who were
anciently chiefs of Muinntear Eoluis, in that county.
They afterwards changed their name to Mac Raʒnaill,
q.v. O'Donovan, however, writes: "This family
name is still in use and anglicised Olus." It must be
extremely rare.

Ó niarflaṫa, Ó niarlaiṫe, Ó niarlaṫa—I—O
Hierlehy, O Herlehey, O Hurlihie, O'Herlihy, Herlihy,
Herley, (Hurley); 'des. of iarflait' (under-lord);
the name of an ecclesiastical family who were hereditary erenaghs of St. Gobnait's church at Bally-
vourny, Co. Cork; still common in Cork and Kerry, but
sometimes disguised under the angl. form of Hurley.

Ó niarnáin—I—O Hiernan, O Hernane, Hearnon,
Hernon; 'des. of iarnán'; the same as Ó nearnáin,
q.v.; the name (1) of a family of Ui Fiachrach, in Co.
Mayo, and (2) of a family of Corca Laoighdhe, in
south-west Cork.

Ó niceaða, Ó niciðe—III—O Hickee, O'Hickey,
Hickey, Hickie; 'des. of iceað' (healer); the name of
a medical family of Dalcassian origin who were hereditary physicians to the O'Briens and other families
in Thomond. They were seated at Ballyhickey, in
the parish of Clooney, Co. Clare. The name is now
common all through Munster.

Ó nifearnáin—I—O Hiffernane, O Hiffernan, O Hif-
feran, Hiffernan, Heffernan, Heffernon, Hefferan, &c.;
'des. of ifearnán'; the name of an ancient family,

who were chiefs of Uaithne-Cliach, now the barony
of Owneybeg, in the east of Co. Limerick, until dispossessed by the O'Mulryans in the 14th century;
still very common in Limerick and Tipperary, and
known all over Munster; sometimes shortened to
Ó feaṗnáin and Ó ṅeaṗnáin, q.v.

Ó ṅinneaċtaiġ—I—Hinnerty, Hennerty, Hingerty. V.
Ó ṅionnaċtaiġ.

Ó ṅinneiṙġe—I—*O Hinnerie*, *O Hennerey*, *O Henry*,
Henery, Henry, Hendry; ' des. of ınneiṙġe ' (the
rising, early riser); the name of a family of Cinel
Eoghain, who were chiefs of Cuileanntrach, in Co.
Tyrone. Cıan Ó ṅinneiṙġe was one of the chiefs who
fell at the battle of Down in 1250. The name is very
common in Ulster.

Ó ṅinnṙeaċtaiġ, v. Ó ṅanṗaċtaiġ.

Ó ṅinnṙeáin, v. Ó ṅionnṗáin.

Ó ṅinṙeaċtaiġ, v. Ó ṅanṗaċtaiġ.

Ó ṅioláin—I—*O Hillane*, Hillane, Hillan, (Hyland,
Holland, Whelan); a var. of Ó ṅaoláin, q.v., in the
spoken language of Connacht. See also Ó ṅoláin.

Ó ṅiolṙaċáin, Eagleton, Eggleton. V. Mac Ioṫṗaċáin.

Ó ṅiomaiṙ, Ó ṅíomaiṙ—II—*O Hyver*, *O Heiver*, *O
Hewer*, *O Hiur*, *O Houre*, *O Hoare*, *O Hawrde*, O'Hure,
Heever, Hever, Hoare, Howard, Ivors, Ivers, Eivers,
&c.; ' des. of ıomaṙ ' or ' íomaṙ ' (the Norse personal
name Ivarr); the name (1) of a Sligo family of the
Ui Fiachrach race who were formerly seated at Leacan,
now angl. Lackan, on the east side of Killala Bay;
and (2) of a Thomond family, now numerous in Clare
and Limerick, but generally known in English as
Howards.

Ó ṅiomna, Ellmore.

Ó ṅionġaṙoail—I—*O Hingerdell*, *O Hungerdell*, *O
Higerdell*, (Harrington); ' des. of ıonġaṙoaıl '; now
pronounced Ó ṅúṗoaıl; the name of well-known and
numerous family in West Cork and South Kerry;
also formerly common in Tipperary; now always
angl. Harrington.

Ó hIonṁáine—I—Nooney ; ' des. of Ionṁáine ' (love).
Cf. Ó hIonṁáineáin.

Ó hIonṁáineáin—I—*O Hununane, O Hinownan*,
Nunan, Noonan ; ' des. of Ionṁáineán ' (dim. of
Ionṁáin, beloved) ; now shortened to Ó Ñuanáin ;
the name of an ecclesiastical family who were erenaghs
of the church of St. Beretchert at Tullylease, in the
north-west of Co. Cork, and are now numerous in
Cork, Limerick, Tipperary and Clare. The Four
Masters at the year 1230 record the death of
Oonnḟléiḃe Ua hIonṁáineáin a holy monk of Boyle.

Ó hIonnácṫaiʒ—I—*O Hanortye*, Hinnerty, Hennerty,
Hannerty, Hanaty ; also Ó hInneácṫaiʒ, q.v. ; a var.
of Ó ḟionnácṫaiʒ, through the aspiration of the
initial ḟ.

Ó hIonnʒáil, Ó hIonnʒáile—I—*O Hannyle, O
Henyll*, Hannell, Hennelly ; var. of Ó ḟionnʒáil, Ó
ḟionnʒáile (q.v.) owing to the aspiration of the
initial ḟ.

Ó hIonnraḋáin, Ó hIonnráin, Ó hIonráin—I—
O Heneran, Henrion ; a var. of Ó hÁnraḋáin, q.v.
This form of the surname was peculiar to Westmeath.

Ó hIoruaiḋ—I—*O Hiery, O Heyry*, Heary, Heery ;
' des. of Ioruaḋ ' ; a rare Leinster surname.

Ó hIr—I—*O Hier, O Hire, O Heere*, O'Hear, O'Hare,
O'Haire, Hear, Heare, Hare, Hair, Haire ; ' des. of
Ír ' ; the name of an Oriel family, akin to that of Ó
hÁnLuain (q.v.), who were chiefs of Oirtheara, now
the baronies of Orier in the east of Co. Armagh ; to
be distinguished from Ó hOiċir (q.v.) of Thomond,
which is similarly anglicised. See also Ó hÉir.

Ó hIrʒil—I—*O Hirill, O Hirell*, Hirill, Hirl ; a var. of
Ó ḟirʒil, owing to the aspiration of the initial ḟ. Cf.
Ó hEarʒail.

Ó hIrʒile—I—*O Hirrely, O Hirley*, Hirrely, Hirley,
Herley ; a var. of Ó ḟirʒile, or Ó ḟirʒil (q.v.), through
the aspiration of the initial ḟ ; very rare.

Ó hIcċeallaiʒ—I—*O Hihilly, O Hilay*, Hilly, Hillee ;
a var. of Ó ḟicċeallaiʒ (q.v.), owing to the aspiration

of the initial ꝼ; extremely rare and found only in Kerry, where it has been in use since the 16th century. The family was located in the neighbourhood of Tralee.

Ó hÓURA, O'Hora.

Ó hÓURAȝÁIn—I—*O Hourigaine, O Hourigan*, Hourigan; 'des. of Oȯꝼaȝán' (dim. of oȯaꝼ, pale, dark-grey); apparently the name of a family of Corca Laoighdhe, in south-west of Co. Cork, but it cannot now be distinguished in pronunciation from Ó hAnnꝼaȝáin (q.v.), which is most probably the origin in Tipperary and Limerick.

Ó hÓURÁIn—I—*O Howrane, O Horane*, Horan; 'des. of Oȯꝼán' (dim. of oȯaꝼ, pale, dark-grey); not now distinguishable in pronunciation from Ó hAnnꝼáin and Ó hUȝꝼóin, q.v.

Ó hÓȝÁIn—I—*O Hogaine, O Hogane, O Hogan*, Hogan; 'des. of Óȝán' (dim. of óȝ, young); the name (1) of a Dalcassian family who derive their descent from Coscrach, uncle of Brian Boru, and were seated at Ardcrony, about four miles to the north of Nenagh, in Co. Tipperary; and (2) of a family of Corca Laoighdhe, in the south-west of Co. Cork; now very common in Munster, especially in Tipperary, Limerick, Clare and Cork. See Ó hÁȝáin, which is the Ulster form of this surname.

Ó hÓȝAIRT—I—Hogart; short for Ó hÓȝaꝼtaiȝ, q.v. Cf. Ó hÁȝaiꝼt.

Ó hOȝÁIRT—I—Howard; short for Ó hOȝaꝼtaiȝ, q.v.

Ó hÓȝARTAIȝ—I—*O Hogertie*, Hogarty, Hogerty, (Hegarty); a var. of Ó ꝼóȝaꝼtaiȝ (q.v.), owing to the aspiration of the initial ꝼ.

Ó hOȝARTAIȝ—I—*O Hoghertie*, Hoverty, (Hegarty); a var. of Ó hÓȝaꝼtaiȝ, q.v. Cf. Ó hÁȝaꝼtaiȝ.

Ó hOȝLAȮA—I—*O Holowe*, Holey; a var. of Ó ꝼoȝlaȯa (q.v.), owing to the aspiration of the initial ꝼ; very rare.

Ó hOȝRÁIn, v. Ó hUȝꝼóin.

Ó hOIBICÍn, v. hOIBICÍn.

Ó hoıċıR—I—*O Hegher*, O'Hehir, O'Hare, Hegher, Hehir, Haier, Herr, &c. ; a var. of Ó háıċıp, q.v.

Ó hoıleáın—I—*O Hilane, O Helane, O Hellan*, Hyland, (Whelan) ; a corruption of Ó háoláın, q.v.

Ó hóıleáın—I—*O Heolane, O Holane*, Holian, (O'Lyons) ; a corruption of Ó háoláın, q.v.

Ó hoıReaċtaıʒ—I—*O Heraghty, O Heyrity, O Heraght*, Hearaghty, Heraghty, Heraty, (Harty), Erraught, Erought, (Geraghty, Harrington, O'Connor) ; ' des. of Oıpeaċtaċ' (holding or frequenting assemblies) ; the name of several distinct families, formerly located in Galway, Westmeath and Donegal ; now most frequent in Donegal and Mayo ; often disguised under the angl. forms of Harty, Geraghty, Harrington, and even O'Connor. Nearly all the members of this family in the neighbourhood of Abbeyfeale have, for a peculiar local reason, now adopted the surname of O'Connor.

Ó hoısce, v. Ó hUıpce.

Ó hoıscín, v. Ó hUıpcín.

Ó hoıseáın—I—*O Hishane*, Hishon ; ' des. of Oıpeán' (dim. of op, a deer) ; a var. of Ó hOıpín, q.v. ; an old Tipperary surname.

Ó hoısín—I—*O Hussine, O Hushin*, Hussian, Hessian, Hession, Hishon ; ' des. of Oıpín' (dim. of op, a deer) ; an old surname in Connacht, where it is still common. Two members of this family filled the see of Tuam in the 11th and 12th centuries. Ó hOıpín seems to have been also an alias in Munster for Ó hOıpeáın, q.v.

Ó hoıstín—II—*O Hustyne, O Hustin*, Histon, Hestin, Hestion, Hasting, Hastings, Hestings ; ' des of Oıptín' (a Norse personal name) ; the name of a Connacht family who were followers of MacDermott of Moylurg ; still common in Connacht, especially in Mayo. Some of the family had settled before the end of the 16th century in Limerick and Kerry, where their descendants are still to be met with. The name is now also common in Clare.

Ó hoıstıR, Hester ; a Connacht surname, not uncommon in Roscommon and Mayo. I cannot trace its origin.

Ó noláin—I—*O Holane, O Hollan, O Holland*, Holland, (Hyland, Whelan) ; a corruption of Ó nAoláin, q.v.

Ó nonċon—I—*O Honechan*, Unehan, Ounihan, (Donegan) ; ' des. of Onċú ' (a leopard, warrior) ; the name of a Leinster family who, prior to the Anglo-Norman invasion, were seated in the north of Ui Feilme, in the neighbourhood of the town of Tullow, in Co. Carlow ; now very rare.

Ó nÓRA, O'Hora.

Ó noRcáin—I—*O Hurkan*, Horkan, Harkon, Horkin, Harkin, Harkins, Arkins ; ' des. of Oncán ' (dim. of onc, a pig) ; a common surname in Mayo and Clare ; but, not improbably, it is a corruption of Ó neancáin, q.v.

Ó nosáin—I—*O Hassane, O Hassan*, Hassan, Hasson, Hassin ; ' des. of Onán ' (dim. of on, a deer) ; the name of an old family in Derry and Tyrone.

Ó nuADA—I—Huddy ; ' des. of uADA.'

Ó nuADAiġ, O'Huadhaigh.

Ó nuAiniḋe, Ó nuAiċne—I—*O Honie, O Howny*, Hooney, (?) Houghney, Green ; ' des. of uAiċne ' (green) ; written Ó nuAiniḋe by Keating and Ó nuAiċniġ by the Four Masters ; the name (1) of a Cork family who were followers of O Laoghaire of Corca Laoighdhe ; and (2) of a Thomond family who, however, have long since changed it to Ó nuAiċnín, q.v.

Ó nuAiċnín—I—*O Hownyn, O Hunnyn*, Houneen, Huneen, Honeen, Oonin, Green, Greene ; ' des. of uAiċnín ' (dim. of uAiċne, green) ; written Ó nuAiniḋe by Keating ; the name of a Dalcassian family in Thomond ; now very often anglicised Greene, by translation.

Ó nuALLACáin—I—*O Huolighane, O Holeghane, O Holohan*, O'Houlihan, Houlihan, Hoolihan, Holohan, (Holland, Nolan), &c. ; ' des. of uALLACán ' (dim. of uALLAċ, proud) ; the name of several distinct families, the best known being those of Offaly and Thomond. The name was also very common in West Cork, where it is now often angl. Holland; also common in Mayo and Roscommon, where it is angl. Nolan. See Ó Nuallacáin.

Ó hUALLAIᵹ—I—*O Howley, O Howlig,* Howley; 'des. of uallac' (proud); apparently a var. of Ó hUallacáin, q.v. See also Ó fuallaiᵹ.

Ó hUAṁNACáIN—I—*O Honaghane, O Hownighan,* Honahan; 'des. of uaṁnacán' (dim. of uaṁnac, **fearful**, dreadful).

Ó hUARᵹUIS—I—(*O Fworishe*), Horish; 'des. of uarᵹur' (cold-choice); corruptly Ó hUaruirce, q.v.; the name of an Ulster family who were anciently lords of Ui Meith; now scattered through West Ulster and North Connacht, where, owing to local corruptions, it is variously anglicised. See Ó fuarᵹuir, Ó fuaruirce, Ó Cuaruir, Ó Cuaruirc, Ó hUirce, &c.

Ó hUARUISCE—I—*O Horiske,* Hourisky, Horisky, Waters, Watters, Coldwell, Caldwell, &c.; a corruption of Ó hUarᵹuir, q.v.; popularly supposed to be derived from 'fuar,' cold, and 'uirce,' water, and so 'translated' Waters, Coldwell, &c.

Ó hUBáIN—I—*O Hubane, O Howbane,* Huban, Hooban, Hoban; 'des. of úbán'; a Mayo surname. Mac-Firbis names 'Clann Ubain' in Connacht among the branches of Cinel Eoghain of Ulster.

Ó hUᵹRóIN—I—*O Hurrone, O Hurrane, O Horan,* Horan; 'des. of uᵹrón'; now corrupted to Ó hOᵹráin; the name (1) of a branch of the Ui Maine who were seated in the parish of Clonrush, in the south of Co. Galway, where they were very numerous and possessed considerable property down to the Cromwellian confiscations; and (2) of an ecclesiastical family who were coarbs of St. Mochua at Balla, Co. Mayo. Eóin Ó hUᵹróin, a member of this family, was appointed Bishop of Elphin, in 1245, but died the next year. The name, both in Galway and in Mayo, has long been corrupted to Ó hOᵹráin, and in the 16th century was generally angl. O Horane, or O Horan. Cf. Ó Muᵹróin, now Ó Moᵹráin.

Ó hui'o—I—O'Hood, Hood ; ' des. of *u'o ' ; the name of
an Ulster family who were bards to the O'Neills of
Clanaboy. The Annals of Ulster, at the year 1485,
record the slaying of bian Ua huiv, "an honoured
poet." Séamur Ó huiv, another distinguished poet
of this family, flourished in the latter part of the 17th
century. The name is still extant in Antrim and
Derry.

Ó huivir—I—Hoar, Hoare, Hore ; ' des. of Ovar '
(dark-grey) ; a rare Cork surname.

Ó huivrín—I—O Heerine, O Herine, O Heverine, O
Heveren, O Hevren, Hearon, Heron, Hearn, Herne,
Heveran, Heveron, Hefferan, Heffron, &c. ; ' des. of
Uivrín ' (dim. of ovar, pale, dark-grey) ; the name
of an Offaly family, still extant in Leinster and Munster, but its angl. forms can hardly be now distinguished from those of several other surnames, as :
Ó heACzigeiin, Ó hifeainain, Ó heimpín, Ó hain-
iáin, and Ó heaiáin, q.v. To this family, no doubt,
belonged the learned historian, Giolla na Naomh O
hUidhrin, who completed the celebrated poem on
the families of Ireland which had been commenced
by John O Dubhagain.

Ó huige, Ó huigín, Ó huiginn—I—O Higgin, O
Higgen, O'Higgins, Higgins, Higgens ; ' des. of uige '
(knowledge, skill, ingenuity) ; the name of a branch
of the southern Ui Neill, in the present Co. Westmeath, and one of the most distinguished literary
families in Ireland. The Four Masters mention no
fewer than eleven poets and professors of poetry of
the name. A branch of the family settled in Co.
Sligo, where they acquired large estates in the parishes
of Achonry and Kilmacteige which they retained
down to the Cromwellian confiscations. The name
is now common in most parts of Ireland. Ó huige
is still in use in East Cork. Ó huiginn probably represents an older form *Ó huigeann, angl. O'Higgan,
O'Higan ; while Ó huigín is a dialectical variant.

Ó huircuile, v. Ó huicuile.

Ó huisce—I—*O Hiskie, O Hesky,* Hiskey, Waters, Watters ; a Connacht surname ; sometimes pronounced Ó hOirce ; doubtless a corruption of Ó hUargtuir, q.v. See also Ó hUirín.

Ó huiscín—I—Heskin, Hoskins, Waters, Watters ; a Galway surname ; generally pronounced Ó hOircín ; probably of same origin as Ó hUirce, q.v.

Ó huiseáin, v. Ó hOireáin.

Ó huisín, v. Ó hOirín.

Ó hultacáin—I—*O Holteghan,* Hultaghan, Hultahan, Haltigan, (Nolan) ; ' des. of Ultacán ' (dim. of ' Ultac,' the Ultonian) ; a rare Fermanagh surname ; often disguised under the angl. form of Nolan.

Ó húrdail—I—Harrington ; a phonetic rendering of Ó nIongardail, q.v.

Ó hurmoltaig—I—Hamilton ; ' des. of Urmoltac ' or ' Turmoltac '; a rare surname in South-west Cork.

Ó hurnaide, *O Hurney,* Hurney ; ' des. of *Urnaide* '; a rare Galway surname. I cannot trace its origin.

Ó hurtuile—I—*O Hurrilly,* O'Hurley, Hurley ; ' des. of Urtuile ' ; also written Ó hUrtaile, and sometimes pronounced Ó hUirtuile ; the name of a Dalcassian family in Thomond, akin to those of O'Moloney and O'Kearney ; now dispersed throughout Munster. An important branch of the family settled at Knocklong, in the east of Co. Limerick, where the remains of their castle is still a conspicuous object on the Hill of Knocklong, and commands a magnificent view of the Galtee mountains and the plain of Co. Limerick.

Oileabard, Oileabard—VIII—Elfred, Elwood, Ellwood ; ' des. of Ailward ' (v. Aigleart) ; a rare Connacht surname.

Oilibéar—VIII—Oliver ; ' des. of Oliver.'

Oistín—VIII—*Austyn,* Austin, Austen ; ' son of Augustine,' formerly popular in England as Austin.

Ó labrada—I—*O Lowrowe, O Lawry,* Lowroo, Lowery, Lowry, Lavery ; ' des. of Labraid ' (speaker, spokesman) ; the name of an ancient family in Co. Down, where it is still common. The different branches of the family are distinguished by epithets attached to the name, as Ó Laḃraḋa ḃán, Ó Laḃraḋa Ruaḋ, and Ó Laḃraḋa Tréan, q.v. The Uí Laḃraḋa of Kilkenny and Galway are most probably migrants from Ulster.

Ó LAḂRAḊA Ḃán—I—Baun-Lavery; i.e. 'White O'Lavery.' V. Ó Laḃraḋa.

Ó LAḂRAḊA RUAḊ—I—Roe-Lavery; i.e. 'Red-O'Lavery.' V. Ó Laḃraḋa.

Ó LAḂRAḊA TRÉAN—I—Trin-Lavery, Tryn-Lavery, Trim-lavery, Armstrong; i.e., 'Strong O'Lavery'; sometimes angl. Armstrong, on the erroneous supposition that it is derived from 'tréan,' strong, and 'lám,' a hand (or arm).

Ó LAḂRAIḊ, Lowry, Lowery, Lavery; a var. of Ó Laḃraḋa, q.v.

Ó LACÁIN—I—O Laughane, O Laghan, Lahan, Duck; evidently the same as Ó Lócáin and Ó Leocáin, q.v. Duck is a 'translation.'

Ó LACLAINN—II—O Laghlen, O Laughlen, Lachlin, Laghlin, Laghlen, Laughlin; a var. of Ó Loclainn, q.v.

Ó LACTNA—I—O Laghna, Loughney; 'des. of Lactna' (grey, dun); the name of a family of the Uí Fiachrach, who were chiefs of the Two Bacs and of Glen Nephin, in the barony of Tirawley, Co. Mayo; now very rare, having been almost universally replaced by the diminutive form Ó Lactnáin, q.v.

Ó LACTNÁIN—I—O Laghnane, O Loghnane, O Loughnane, O Loughton, Laughnan, Loughnane, Loughnan, Loughrane, Loughran, Lawton, (Loughlan, Loughlin, O'Loughlin, MacLoughlin, Loftus); 'des. of Lactnán' (dim. of Lactna, grey); the name of several distinct families in different parts of Ireland, as:—(1) Ó Lactnáin of Mayo, also called Ó Lactna (q.v.), who were chiefs of the district called the Two Bacs, now the parish of Bacs, and of Glen Nephin, in the barony of Tirawley, and are still numerous in Connacht, but often disguise their name under the angl. form of Loftus. This family gave bishops to various sees in Connacht in the 13th and 14th centuries. (2) Ó

Laċtnáin of Teffia, a midland family who were an-
ciently chiefs of Teathbha, in the present counties of
Longford and Westmeath. (3) Ó Laċtnáin of Oriel,
who were anciently chiefs of Mughdorn Breagh, which
O'Donovan places in the north of Meath, where it
adjoins the county of Monaghan. (4) Ó Laċtnáin of
Ui Maine, who were followers of O'Kelly. (5) Ó
Laċtnáin of Cinel Eoghain ; and (6) Ó Laċtnáin of
Siol Muireadhaigh, both mentioned by MacFirbis.
In the 16th century, it was also found in Co. Down,
Kilkenny, Tipperary and Cork. It is often corrupted
to Ó Loċláin, angl. Loughlin and MacLoughlin, and
to Ó Loċráin, angl. Loughrane, Loughran. Lawton
is now the angl. form in Co. Cork.

Ó LAĊTRÁIN, O'Loughran, Loughrane, Loughran, &c. ;
a corruption of Ó Laċtnáin, q.v.

Ó LAIOEÁIN—I—Ladden, V. Ó Loroeáin.

Ó LAIOEANÁIN, Ó LAIÓ5EANÁIN, Ó LAIÓ5neÁIN
—I—*O Laynan, O Loynen, O Leynen, O Lynan, O
Leynam,* Lynan, Lynam, Lynham, Lyneham, Lineham, &c. ; ' des. of Laróʒneán ' (snow-birth) ; the
name of an ecclestiasical family in Leinster, who
were erenaghs of Ferns and of St. Mullins, Co. Carlow.
Many distinguished ecclesiastics of the name in various
parts of Ireland, but probably of this family, are
mentioned in the Annals. The name, which is still
common in Leinster, is now generally angl. Lynam.
The Irish form was also variously written Ó Laró-
neáin, Ó Laiʒeanáin, and Ó Laiʒneáin.

Ó LAIOIʒ, v. Ó Loroiʒ.

Ó LAIOIʒ, v. Ó Laoroiʒ,

Ó LAIOIN, v. Ó Laiʒin.

Ó LAIÓneÁIN, Ó LAIʒEANÁIN, v. Ó Laróʒneáin.

Ó LAIʒIÓ, v. Ó Laoroiʒ.

Ó LAIʒIN—I—*O Loyne, O Layne, O Leyne, O Lyne, O
Lyen, O Lane, O Leane, O Lien, O Lyan,* O'Leyne,
O'Lane, O'Lyons, Layne, Leyne, Lyne, Lane, Leane,
Lean, Leen, Lyons, &c. ; ' des. of Laiʒean ' (lance,
spear) ; the name (1) of an ancient family in Co.

Galway, who retained considerable property in the barony of Kilconnell down to the end of the 17th century; (2) of a Kildare family, formerly seated at Cill, now angl. Kill, near Naas; and (3) of an old Kerry family. The name is now very common all over Ireland. It appears to have been sometimes pronounced Ó Laoiġin. In Kerry at the present day it is generally pronounced Ó Leiġin, and sometimes Ó Liġin.

Ó Laiġneáin, v. Ó Laióġneáin.

Ó Laiġniġ—I—*O Leighnagh, O Leiny,* Leeney, Lyons; 'des. of Laiġneac' (Leinsterman); a very rare surname. For pronunciation, cf. Ó Laiġin.

Ó Láimín—I—*O Lavine, O Lavin, O Laven,* Lavin, Laven, Lavan, Hand; doubtless, a corruption of Ó Flaitimín, q.v.; the name of a family who were originally followers of MacDermottroe in Co. Roscommon; still common in that county, and also in Co. Mayo. It is supposed to be derived from 'lám,' a hand, hence the angl. form Hand. Also Ó Lámáin, q.v.

Ó Lainn—I—Laing, Layng, Lang; a var. of Ó Flainn, q.v. Cf. Ó Loinn.

Ó Lairġneáin, v. Ó Loirġneáin.

Ó Laiste, v. Ó Loirte.

Ó Laitbeartaiġ—I—*O Laffertie, O Laghertie, O Laherty,* O'Lafferty, O'Laverty, Lafferty, Laverty, Laherty; 'des. of Flaitbeartac'; a var. of Ó Flaitbeartaiġ, owing to the aspiration of the initial F; the name of a distinguished family of the Cinel Eoghain in Ulster, where it is still common, especially in Tyrone, Derry, Antrim and Donegal.

Ó Laiteasa, Ó Laitġeasa—I—*O Lahissa, O Lassy, O Lassie, O Lasy, O Lacy,* Lacy, Lacey, Leacy, (De Lacy); 'des. of Flaitear,' or 'Flaitġear'; older forms Ó Flaiteara and Ó Flaitġeara, q.v.; the name of an old Wexford family, still numerous in that county. To be distinguished from the Norman de Lacy (v. de Léir).

Ó Laitím—I—*O Lahiff, O Laffie, O Lahy*, Lahive, Lahiff, Lahiffe, Laffey, Laffy, Lahy, Lahey, &c. ; a var. of Ó Flaitím, q.v. ; also corruptly Ó Lataig, q.v.

Ó Laitimín—I—Lavin ; a var. of Ó Flaitimín, q.v. ; in use in Co. Kerry. It is doubtless the correct original of Ó Láimín, q.v.

Ó Lamáin—I—*O Lawan*, Lavan ; a var., doubtless, of Ó Flatamáin, q.v. ; rare.

Ó Laoċúa—I—*O Leaghy, O Leahy*, Leahy, Leehy, &c. ; ' des. of Laoċúa ' (heroic) ; an old Munster surname ; now very common in Cork, Kerry, Limerick and Tipperary ; to be distinguished from Ó Lataig, which is sometimes similarly anglicised.

Ó Laoúóg, v. Ó Laoġóg.

Ó Laoġaire—I—O'Leary, Leary, &c. ; ' des. of Laoġaire ' (calf-keeper) ; the name of a family of Corca Laoighdhe, who were originally chiefs of the country lying around Rosscarberry, in West Cork, but removed from there about the time of the Anglo-Norman invasion and settled in the parish of Inchigeelagh, where they became lords, under the Mac-Carthys, of the country between Macroom and Inchigeelagh. The head of the family resided at Carrignacurra, about a mile to the east of the village of Inchigeelagh. In 1642, Connor O'Leary of Carrignacurra, Auliff O'Leary of Cunnowley, and fourteen others of the name were attainted. The O'Learys are now very numerous throughout Munster.

Ó Laoġóg—I—*O Lioge*, Leeogue, Leogue, League, Luogue, Loogue, Logue, (Leech, Molloy, Mulloy) ; ' des. of Laoġóg ' (dim. of Laoġ, a calf) ; the name of an old Galway family who were chiefs of Caladh, which is supposed to have been co-extensive with the barony of Kilconnell, but now long dispersed. The name is now found in Longford, Westmeath, Mayo and Donegal, as well as in Galway, where it is sometimes angl. Leech. In Donegal, it may be merely a corruption of Ó Maolmaoúóg, q.v. In

that county, and also in Mayo, it is angl. Molloy.
Ó Laoġacáin appears to have been an alias in Galway.

Ó Laoıḃıġ—I—*O Loye, O Lye, O Leye, O Lie,* O'Lee,
Lee ; ' des. of Laoıḃeac ' (poetic) ; the name of a
West Connacht family, who, according to MacFirbis,
were chiefs of Ui Briuin Eola. They were also
erenaghs of Annadown, and some of them were distinguished as ecclesiastics ; but they are best known
as a medical family, having been for many centuries
hereditary physicians to the O'Flahertys. As early
as the 15th century, a learned member of the family
produced a most complete course of medicine, written
in Latin and Irish. The family is now widely dispersed.

Ó Laoıġıll—I—*O Leagail,* Lyle ; ' des. of Laoıġeall.'
This is probably the surname which is written Ó
Luccaıl in the Annals of Loch Ce.

Ó Laomḋa—I—*O Lemagh, O Leamy,* Leamy ; ' des. of
Laomḋa ' (bent, bowed). Keating writes it Ó Léıme.

Ó Lapáın—I—*O Lapane, O Lappan,* Lapin, Lappin,
Laphin, (De Lapp, Delap) ; ' des. of Lapán ' (dim. of
Lapa, a paw, or fist) ; the name of an Ulster family
who were anciently chiefs of Cinel Enda, in Co. Donegal, and erenaghs of Derry, but afterwards removed
to Co. Armagh. The name is still common in Ulster.
In Co. Mayo, it is sometimes made Delap in English.

OLÁRD, Ellard. V. Aıḋleaıpc.

Ó Laċaıġ—I—*O Lahy,* Lahy, Lahey, Laffy, Laffey,
(Leahy) ; a var. of Ó Flaċaıġ and Ó Laıṫıṁ, q.v.

Ó Léanacáın—I—*O Lenaghan, O Leneghan,* Lenaghan,
Leneghan, Lenahan, Lenehan, Lenihan, Lennihan,
&c. ; ' des. of Léanacán ' (dim. of Leannac or Léanac,
mantled, cloaked) ; the name of a Roscommon family;
still numerous, but dispersed through Connacht ;
sometimes pronounced Ó Lıonacáın.

Ó Leanḋáın—I—Lenden, Linden, Lindin, Lindon ; a
var. of Ó Leannáın, q.v. Also Ó Lıonḋáın, q.v.

Ó Leannáın—I—*O Lennane, O Lennan,* Linnane, Lan-

nan, Lannen, Lannon, Lennon, (Leonard) ; 'des. of
leannán' (dim. of leann, a cloak or mantle) ; the
name of at least three distinct families, seated respectively in the counties of Fermanagh, Mayo and
Galway. The O'Leannains of Fermanagh were an
ecclesiastical family and erenaghs of Lisgoole, near
Enniskillen. Those of Mayo are a branch of the Ui
Fiachrach and were seated in the neighbourhood of
Killala, while the Galway family were followers of
O'Kelly of Ui Maine. All these families are still well
represented, but the name is very often disguised
under the angl. form of Leonard. The pronunciation
is sometimes Ó lionnáin, sometimes Ó lionoáin.

Ó leARgusa—I—*O Larryse*, Larrissy, Laracy ; ' des. of
leangur ' (sea-choice) ; the name of a family of Ui
Fiachrach, who were formerly seated in the barony of
Carra, Co. Mayo, but are long dispersed.

Ó leatáin—I—*O Lahan, O Laane*, Laine, Lane ; probably a corruption of Ó liatáin, q.v. ; in use in the
neighbourhood of Shrule, but very rare.

Ó leatlobaiR—I—*O Lalour, O Lawler*, O'Lalor, Lalor,
Lawlor, Lawler ; ' des. of leatlobar ' (half-leper) ; the
name of an Ulidian family, descended from leatlobar, King of Ulidia, who died in the year 871. The
Ui leatlobair are mentioned in the Annals in the
early part of the 10th century as kings of Dalradia
and Ulidia, but after that period they disappear from
history. Another family of the name, kinsmen of
the O'Moores, were one of the ' seven septs of Leix.'
They were seated at Dysart Enos, near the Rock of
Dunamase, from which they were driven by the
English family of Pigott in the reign of Elizabeth,
and dispersed through Leinster. A remnant of them
was transplanted, together with the O'Moores, to
Kerry, in the early part of the 17th century, and their
descendants are now numerous and respectable in
that county. There was also a family of the name
in Co. Monaghan.

Ó leioin, Ó leigin, v. Ó laigin.

Ó Léime, *O Lemagh, O Leamy,* Leamy. V. Ó Laomḋa.

Ó Leoċáin—I—*O Loughane, O Lochan,* Loghan, Loughan,
Duck ; also variously written Ó Laċáin, Ó Lóċáin, Ó
Loċċáin, Ó Lógáin, Ó Leogáin, &c. ; the name of a
famous family in ancient Meath, who were chiefs of
Gailenga Móra and Luighne, now the baronies of
Morgallion and Lune, in Co. Meath, but were dis-
possessed, apparently about the time of the Anglo-
Norman invasion, and dispersed through Leinster,
Ulster and Connacht. The name, according to
O'Donovan, was ridiculously translated Duck, on the
erroneous supposition that it was derived from ' laċa,'
a duck.

Ó Leogáin—I—*O Lagane, O Lagan, O Logan,* Logan,
Lagan ; a var. of Ó Leoċáin, q.v.

Ó Liaṫáin—I—*O Lyhane, O Leaghan,* O'Lehane, Lyhane,
Leehane, Lehane, Leyhane, Lihane, Lyhan, Leehan,
Leeane, &c., (O'Lyons, Lyons) ; ' des. of Liaṫán ' (dim.
of liaṫ, grey) ; the name of two distinct families,
one seated in Cork, and the other in Sligo. The
Uí Liaṫáin of Cork were, according to O'Donovan,
one of the families into which the great old Cork
clan of Uí Liathain divided after the establishment
of surnames. The surname is not to be confounded
with the clan-name, which included several families
with distinct surnames. The surname Ó Liaṫáin is
still common in Co. Cork, but is very often angl.
Lyons. The Sligo family belonged to the Uí Fiachrach
race, and was formerly seated in the parish of Dromard. The name has now disappeared from Co.
Sligo, having, as it would seem, removed to Donegal,
where it still survives, angl. Lyons.

Ó Liḋeaḋa—I—*O Lyddie, O Lyddy, O Leddy,* Liddy,
Leddy ; ' des. of Liḋeaḋ ' ; the name of a Dalcassian
family, formerly seated in the east of Co. Clare. A
branch of this family has been long settled in Co.
Antrim.

Ó Lioḋáin, v. Ó Loḋáin.

Ó Líonaċáin, v. Ó Léanaċáin.

Ó Liondáin—I—*O Lyndane*, Lindon, Linden, &c. ; a
var. of Ó Leannáin, q.v.

Ó Lionnáin, v. Ó Leannáin.

*Ó Liseáin—I—*O Lishane, O Lyshane*, Leeson ; perhaps
a corruption of Ó Glasáin, q.v. Cf. *O Glishane* for
Ó Glaiseáin.

Ó Lóчáin—I—*O Loghane, O Loughane*, Loghan, Loughan,
Lohan, Chaff ; ' des. of Lóчán '; a var. of Ó Leóчáin, q.v. ;
in use in Co. Galway, angl. Chaff by ' translation.'

Ó Loчláin—I—*O Loughlane*, O'Loughlan, O'Loughlin,
Loughlan, Loughlin, (Loftus) ; a corruption of Ó
Laчtnáin, q.v. To be distinguished from Ó Loч-
lainn, q.v.

Ó Loчlainn—II—*O Loghlan, O Laghlan*, O'Loughlan,
O'Loughlin, O'Loghlen, Loghlin, Loughlan, Loughlen,
Loughlin, Laughlin, &c. ; ' des. of Loчlainn '; the
name (1) of a leading family of Cinel Eoghain, more
commonly called Mac Loчlainn, q.v. ; and (2) of an
ancient and distinguished family in Co. Clare, who
took their name from Loчlainn, lord of Corcomroe,
in the 10th century. The O'Loghlins and O'Connors
originally formed one clan, and ruled over a district
co-extensive with the diocese of Kilfenora. This
district, which was called Corcomroe from the clan-
name of its inhabitants, the Corca Modhruaidh, was
afterwards divided into two nearly equal parts between the two families, O'Loghlen ruling over East
Corcomroe, which was also called Burren, and
O'Connor over West Corcomroe. The O'Loghlens
were a powerful family, and retained their rank as
lords of Burren down to the reign of Elizabeth.
They are still numerous and respectable in Thomond.

Ó Lógáin—I—*O Logan*, Logan ; a var. of Ó Leóчáin, q.v.

Ó Lodáin, Ó Loideáin—I—*O Ludan, O Lydan, O
Leadon*, Ludden, Liddane, Leddan, Lydden, Lyden,
Lydon, Leyden, &c. ; ' des. of Lodán,' or ' Loideán ';
a common surname in many parts of Connacht, and
also in Co. Clare. Ó Loчáin and Ó Laiteáin were
probably older forms. See also Ó Luideáin.

Ó Loioiu—I—*O Loddie*, Luddy ; older form Ó Laioiu ;
' des. of Laioeau ' (mighty) ; the name of an old
West Cork family, who were followers of O'Leary.
It still survives in Co. Cork and in South Tipperary,
but is very rare.

Ó Loinṡeaċáin—I—*O Lynseghane*, Lynchahaun,
Lynchahan, Lynchehan, (Lynch) ; ' des. of Loin-
ṡeaċán ' (dim. of Loinṡeaċ) ; the name (1) of a family
of the Cinel Eoghain in Ulster, who are descended
from Loinṡeaċ, King of Ireland, and were seated in
the present county of Donegal ; also called Mac
Loinṡeaċáin and Ó Loinṡriṡ, q.v. ; and (2) of a
family of the Ui Fiachrach, formerly seated in Co.
Sligo. It is now almost always angl. Lynch.

Ó Loinṡriṡ—I—*O Lynchy, O Lynche, O Lensie*, Linchey,
Linchy, Lynchy, Lynch, Lindsy, (Lindsay) ; ' des. of
Loinṡeaċ ' (der. of Loinṡear, a fleet, i.e., having,
or belonging to, a fleet or navy) ; the name of several
distinct families in different parts of Ireland, as :
(1) Ó Loinṡriṡ of Dalradia, once a very important
family. In the 11th century, they were chiefs of
Dalradia, in the present counties of Antrim and
Down, and are frequently mentioned in the Annals.
They were dispossessed at the time of the Anglo-
Norman invasion of Ulster, but are still numerous
in Antrim and Down. (2) Ó Loinṡriṡ of Owney, also
a family of note in early times. Before the Anglo-
Norman invasion, they were chiefs of Uaithne-thire, now
the barony of Owney in Tipperary, but were afterwards
dispossessed by the O'Mulryans. (3) Ó Loinṡriṡ of
Breifney, a strong clan, who were chiefs of Cinel
Bacaid, and are still numerous in Co. Cavan. (4) Ó
Loinṡriṡ of Thomond. a Dalcassian family, still
numerous in Clare and Limerick. (5) Ó Loinṡriṡ of
Cork, a branch of the Corca Laoighe, who were
originally seated in West Cork. (6) Ó Loinṡriṡ of
Sligo, a branch of the Ui Fiachrach. (7) Ó Loinṡriṡ of
Meath. Ó Loinṡriṡ is often a shortened form of Ó
Loinṡeaċáin (q.v.), especially in Donegal, Mayo,

and Cork. In Co. Galway, it is sometimes metathe-
cised to Ó Loinrcig, q.v. Lynch is now one of the
commonest of Irish surnames, and, as might be expected, is found in every part of Ireland.

Ó Loinn—I—*O Linne, O Linge, O Lynt,* O'Lynn, Lynn,
Linn, Lind, (Lindsay) ; ' des. of Flann ' (ruddy) ; a
var., owing to the aspiration of the initial f, of Ó
Floinn, q.v.; the name of a famous Ulster family who,
from about the middle of the 11th until towards the
latter part of the 14th century, were chiefs of Ui
Tuirtre, a district comprised in the baronies of Upper
and Lower Toome, in Co. Antrim, and are frequently
mentioned in the Annals. In the year 1177, they
defeated John de Courcy when he advanced into
their territory, and for two centuries longer they
continued to maintain their independence. After
the year 1368 they disappear from history. The
name, according to O'Donovan, is sometimes angl.
Lindsay.

Ó Loinscig—I—Linskey, Lynskey ; a metathesised
form, in Co. Galway, of Ó Loingrig, q.v.

Ó Loirgneáin—I—*O'Largan,* Lerkinan, Learhinan,
Lerhinan, Largan, (Lardner). This surname is at
present in use in Clare and Galway, angl. Lerkinan
and Lerhinan in the former county, and Lardner
in the latter. It is clearly to be identified with
Ó Lairgnen, the name of a family who, in early times,
were chiefs of Oriel. O'Dugan writes :—

> " To lordship entitled by right,
> Is Ó Lairgnen full king of Oriel."

The family seems to have long since disappeared
from Oriel, and is now, so far as I know, represented
only in Clare and Galway, and even there by only a
few scattered families.

Ó Loiste—I—*O Lastie,* (Leslie, Lesley) ; also Ó Lairte ;
a rare Donegal surname, now always angl. Leslie or
Lesley.

Ó Lomáin—I—*O Loman, O Lymon,* Loman, Lomand,
Lomond, Lemon, Lemmon ; ' des. of Lomán ' (dim. of

ʟom, bare, lean) ; the name (1) of an Ulidian family,
once a clan of note, but now scarcely known ; and (2)
of a branch of the Ui Maine in Co. Galway. This
family, though now almost extinct, must have been
once powerful, for we learn from the Annals of the
Four Masters, at the year 949, that Ó ʟomáın of
Gaela (in Co. Galway) in that year defeated the people
of Ormond. In the 16th century, the name was
most common in Co. Wicklow. It is now everywhere
very rare.

Ó ʟomᴀsnᴀ—I—*O Lomasny*, O'Lomasney, Lomosney ;
' des. of ʟomᴀrnᴀ ' (bare rib) ; the name of an old
Munster family which apparently originated in S.
Tipperary, where bᴀıʟe uı ʟomᴀrnᴀ, now angl. Bally-
nomasna, in the parish of Tubrid, marks its ancient
home ; now very rare and scattered, but found chiefly
in South Cork. There are a few families of the name
in West Limerick.

Ó ʟonᴀᴢáın—I—*O Lonagan, O Lonegan, O Lanegane,
O Lannegan*, Lanigan, Lannigan, &c. ; probably ' des.
of ʟonᴀᴢán ' (dim. of ʟon, a blackbird ; cf. ʟonán),
but the origin is not quite clear. O'Donovan thought
it might be a corruption of Ó ʟonᴢᴀcáın ; and Ó
ꝼʟᴀnnᴀᴢáın is not an unlikely origin. Also Ó ʟuın-
eᴀᴢáın, q.v.

Ó ʟonáın—I—*O Lonane, O Lonan, O Lonnan, O Lannan,
O Lennane*, Lenane, Lanon, Lannan, Lannon, Lannen,
Lannin, Lennon, (Leonard) ; ' des. of ʟonán ' (dim. of
ʟon, a blackbird) ; the name (1) of a Cork family who
were originally settled in the neighbourhood of Ross-
carbery, where they were followers of the O'Learys ;
and (2) of a Wicklow family who were anciently
erenaghs of Kilranelagh ; also, not improbably, (3)
of an Ossory family. In Co. Cork, it appears to have
been generally pronounced Ó ʟıonáın, and is very
often angl. Leonard.

Ó ʟonᴢᴀcáın, v. Ó ʟuınᴢeᴀcáın.

Ó ʟonᴢᴀıᴢ—I—*O Longy, O Longe*, Long ; ' des. of
ʟonᴢᴀc ' (der. of ʟonᴢ, a ship, a camp) ; the name of

an old family who are still numerous in Cork, Kerry and Limerick.

Ó Longáin—I—*O Longane, O Langane, O Longan, O Langan,* Longan, Langan, Langin, (Long) ; ' des. of Longán ' (dim. of long, long, tall) ; the name (1) of an Ulster family who were anciently chiefs of West Ui Breasail, in Co. Armagh, and are now very numerous in Mayo ; and (2) of an ecclesiastical family who were erenaghs of Ardpatrick, in Co. Limerick, and Patrician stewards of Munster. After the destruction of the monastery of Ardpatrick, the family dispersed through Limerick, Kerry and Cork. In the last century, the O'Longans of Cork were a distinguished family of scribes and poets. V. Ó Luingeáin.

Ó Longargáin, Ó Lonnargáin, Ó Lonnragáin —I—*O Lonergane, O Lonregan, O Londregan, O Lorrigane,* Lonnergan, Lonergan, Londregan, Londrigan, Landregan, Ladrigan, Lorrigan, &c. ; ' des. of Longargán ' (dim. of lonngarg, strong-fierce) ; the name of a Dalcassian family who were seated in the east of Thomond until after the year 1318, when they were driven out by the O'Briens and Mac-Namaras, and settled in Co. Tipperary. This family produced several distinguished ecclesiastics. Three of them are mentioned by Ware as Archbishops of Cashel in the 12th and 13th century, two as Bishops of Killaloe, and one as Bishop of Cloyne. The name is now very common in Tipperary, Kilkenny and Waterford

Ó Lorcáin—I—*O Lurkaine, O Lorkan,* Lorkan, Lorkin, Larkin, Larken, Larkins, &c. ; ' des. of Lorcán ' (dim. of lorc, fierce) ; the name of several distinct families in different parts of Ireland, of whom the following were in early times the most distinguished : (1) Ó Lorcáin of Leinster. This family, which is of the royal race of Leinster, was seated in the barony of Forth, in the south-east of Co. Wexford, until dispossessed soon after the Anglo-Norman invasion, and is still numerous in Leinster. (2) Ó Lorcáin of

Oriel, an important family in early times, and still numerous in Co. Armagh. The head of this family is described at different times as lord of Ui Niallain, Lord of Farney, and lord of West Ui Breasail. (3) Ó Lopcáin of Ui Maine, a Galway family of the same stock as the O'Maddens, still numerous and respectable in that county. (4) Ó Lopcáin of Meath, the head of which was anciently lord of Caille Follamain. (5) Ó Lopcáin of Tipperary, an ecclesiastical family, the head of which was anciently erenagh of Lorrha. All these families are still well represented. MacFirbis mentions another family of the name, a branch of the Cinel Eoghain, in Co. Donegal.

Ó LÓRTÁIN—?—*O Lordane*, Lordan ; ' des. of *Lópráin ' ; the name of an old Cork family, still represented in that county. I cannot trace its origin.

Ó LOTCÁIN, v. Ó Leocáin and Ó Lócáin.

Ó LUACAIR, Ó LUACRA—I—*O Logher, O Lucry*, Loughry, Loughrey, Lockery, Rush ; ' des. of Luacán ' (white, pure) ; a corruption, according to O'Donovan, of the old Sligo surname Ó Luacáin ; the name of a branch of the Ui Fiachrach, formerly seated at Rosslee, in the parish of Easkey. It is now common in Co. Mayo, where it is usually ' translated ' Rush, from an erroneous belief that it is derived from luacaip, rushes.

Ó LUAIN—I—*O Loaine, O Loane*, O'Loan, O'Lone, Loane, Lamb, Lambe ; ' des. of Luan' (warrior, champion) ; the name (1) of a Limerick family who were anciently lords of Deisbeg, now the barony of Smallcounty, in the east of Co. Limerick, but have been long dispersed through Limerick, Cork and Kerry ; and (2) of a Monaghan family, now dispersed through Ulster. It is angl. O'Loan, Loane in the north of Ireland, but generally Lambe, by ' translation,' in the south.

Ó LUANAIġ—I—*O Lowny*, O'Looney, Looney, Loony, Lowney ; ' des. of Luanac ' (der. of luan, warrior, champion) ; a Munster surname, found chiefly in Cork and Clare.

Ó Luⱥnáin—I—*O Loonane, O Lonan*, Lambe ; ' des.
of Luⱥnán ' (dim. of Luⱥn, warrior, champion) ; a
rare Donegal surname. Cf. Ó Luⱥin.

Ó Luⱥsⱥⱥ—IV—*O Lwosie*, Lucey, Lucy ; undoubtedly
a corruption of Mⱥc Cluⱥrⱥⱥ ; a well-known Co.
Cork surname.

Ó Lúbⱥⱥ—I—*O Luby, O Looby*, Luby, Looby ; ' des. of
Lúbⱥc ' (crooked, deceitful) ; a rare and scattered
surname, now most numerous in Tipperary.

Ó Luⱥⱥireⱥin, Ó Luⱥráin—I—*O Lucherin, O Logh-
rane*, O'Loughran, Lougheran, Loughren, Laugheran,
Lochrane, Loughrane, Loughran, O'Loran, Loran ;
' des. of Luⱥⱥipeⱥn ' (dim. of Luⱥⱥip, bright, glittering) ;
the name of a celebrated ecclesiastical family in East
Ulster, and especially in the diocese of Armagh.

Ó Luioeáin, v. Ó Loioeáin.

Ó Luimbrⱥc—I—*O Lymbricke*, Limerick ; ' des. of
Lombreⱥc ' (bare-speckled) ; a rare Co. Down surname.

Ó Luineⱥⱥáin—I—*O Lenagan*, Lenagan, Lenegan,
Lenigan, Lanigan, Lynegan, &c. ; an attenuated
form of Ó Lonⱥⱥáin, q.v.

Ó Luinⱥeⱥⱥáin—I—*O Lunyghan*, Lunican, Lonican,
Linighan, Linahan, Linehan, Lenihan, &c. ; ' des. of
Lonⱥⱥⱥán ' (dim. of Lonⱥⱥⱥ) ; an attenuated form
of Ó Lonⱥⱥⱥáin, and apparently a substitution for
the old East Limerick or Tipperary surname Mⱥc
Lonⱥⱥⱥáin ; common in Cork, Limerick and Kerry.

Ó Luinⱥeáin—I—*O Lungane, O Liengan*, Lingane,
Linnane, Linane, Lenane, Lynane, (Leonard) ; an
attenuated form of Ó Lonⱥáin, q.v. ; now very often
disguised under the angl. form of Leonard, especially
in Co. Limerick.

Ó Luinⱥⱥ—I—*O Lonney, O Loney, O Loony*, Luny,
Lunny, Lunney, Lonney, Loney, Loony, Looney ;
' des. of Luineⱥc ' ; the name of a family of Cinel
Moen in Ulster. They were seated orginally in the
barony of Raphoe, but were afterwards driven across
the Foyle by the O'Donnells, when they settled in

Co. Tyrone, in a district to which they gave the name of Muinter Loony. The name is now very common in Co. Fermanagh.

Ó Luinín—I—*O Luinyn*, *O Lonine*, *O Lonin*, Lunneen, Lineen, Linneen, Linnen, Lennon, (Leonard, Linnegar, Lynegar) ; ' des. of Luinín' (dim. of Lon, a blackbird) ; the name of a distinguished Co. Fermanagh family who were erenaghs of Derryvullen, and for many centuries poets, historians, musicians, and physicians to the Maguires. Their chief residence was at Áṙo Uí Luinín, in the parish of Derryvullan. There were also old families of the name in Carlow and Waterford, where they still flourish. Ó Luinín is very often angl. Leonard, and, according to O'Donovan, it was also strangely angl. Linnegar and Lynegar in Co. Fermanagh.

Ó Macáin—I—*O Mackane*, Macken, Mackin ; ' des. of Macán' (dim. of Mac, a son, youth) ; a var. of Ó Maicín, q.v.

Ó Macáin—I—*O Maghane*, *O Mauchan*, *O Mahan*, Maghan, Maughan, Mahon, Mann, (Vaughan) ; a var. of Ó Mocáin, q.v.

Ó Macasa—II—*O Mackessy*, Macassy, Mackessy, Mac-Kessy, MacAssie, Maxey ; ' des. of Macur' (a form of Maṡnur) ; the name of a family of Ui Fidhgheinte who were anciently lords of Corca Oiche in the modern barony of Glenquin, in the west of Co. Limerick, but dispossessed soon after the Anglo-Norman invasion by a branch of the Fitzgeralds and disperesd through Munster and Leinster.

Ó Macḃa—I—*O Makie*, *O Macky*, Mackey ; ' des. of Macḃa' (virile, manly) ; an old Ormond surname, still common in Tipperary, Limerick and Cork ; to be distinguished from Mac Aoiḃ (q.v.) which is sometimes similarly anglicised.

Ó Maccíre—I—*O Macketyre*, Wolfe ; ' des. of Maccíre' (wolf) ; the name of a branch of the Ui Liathain in East Cork. Uaṁnacán Ua Maccíre was Bishop of

Cloyne at the end of the 11th century. The name is said to be still in East Cork, but now very rare.

Ó mᴀ́ᴅᴀʒᴀ́ɪɴ—I—*O Madagane, O Madigane*, Madigan, Maddigan ; the same as Ó mᴀᴅᴀ́ɪɴ or Ó mᴀᴅᴀɪᴅɪ́ɴ, q.v. ; an offshoot of the family of O'Madden of Co. Galway who settled in the 16th century in Clare and Limerick, where they are still numerous.

Ó mᴀᴅᴀɪ́ᴅ—I—*O Maddy*, Maddy ; ' des. of mᴀᴅᴀᴅ ' (dog) ; a var. of Ó mᴀᴅᴀ́ɪɴ, q.v., and an offshoot of the Galway family of that name ; very rare.

Ó mᴀᴅᴀɪᴅɪ́ɴ—I—*O Maddine, O Madden*, Madden ; ' des. of mᴀᴅᴀɪᴅɪ́ɴ ' (dim. of ' mᴀᴅᴀᴅ,' a dog) ; a var. of Ó mᴀᴅᴀ́ɪɴ, q.v. This seems to have been always the popular form of the name, and is at the present day almost universal in the spoken language of Connacht.

Ó mᴀᴅᴀ́ɪɴ—I—*O Maddane, O Madden*, Madden ; ' des. of mᴀᴅᴀᴅᴀ́ɴ ' (dim. of mᴀᴅᴀᴅ, a dog) ; older form Ó mᴀᴅᴀᴅᴀ́ɪɴ, now generally Ó mᴀᴅᴀɪᴅɪ́ɴ, q.v., with variants Ó mᴀᴅᴀɪᴅ and Ó mᴀᴅᴀʒᴀ́ɪɴ, q.v. ; the name of a distinguished branch of the Ui Maine in Co. Galway, who derive their descent from mᴀᴅᴀᴅᴀ́ɴ (slain in 1008), who was son of Gadhra Mór, chief of Ui Maine from 1014 to 1027, and are of the same stock as the O'Kellys, with whom they originally formed one clan—the Ui Maine. About the middle of the 11th century, Siol nAnmchadha, a sub-division of the Ui Maine, became independent, and from that period down to the middle of the 17th century the chieftaincy of Siol nAnmchadha continued in almost unbroken succession in the family of O'Madden. The clan-lands, which in accordance with Irish usage were named from the clan, comprised the barony of Longford, in the south-east of Co. Galway, and the parish of Lusnagh, on the other side of the Shannon, in the present Offaly. Many distinguished chiefs of the name are mentioned in the Irish annals. In 1612, Donal O'Madden, ' captain of his nation,' settled his manor and castle of Longford and all his other estates in Co. Galway on his son and heir, Anmchadh, or Ambrose, O'Madden, in tail male. Ambrose died in 1637, and was succeeded by his son, John O'Madden. John's property was confiscated after the Cromwellian wars, but was in part restored in 1677 by grant under the Act of Settlement. Five of the name were attainted in 1691. The O'Maddens of Co. Antrim (formerly called O Maddegane) are probably a distinct family. On the other hand, there is reason to believe that the Anglo-Irish family of Madden, formerly of Baggotrath, near Dublin, is a branch of the O'Maddens of Siol nAnmchadha.

Ó maele, v. Ó máille.

Ó maicín—I—*O Mackine*, Mackin, Macken; 'des of maicín' (dim. of mac, a son, youth); also Ó macáin, q.v.; a scattered surname, now found chiefly in Mayo, Monaghan and Louth. Comár Ó maicín was Bishop of Achonry in the 13th century, (1251-1265).

Ó maroín, O'Madden, Madden. V. Ó maoaroín.

Ó máille—I—*O Mailie, O Mallie, O Mally, O Maely*, O'Malley, O'Meally, O'Mealy, Malley, Meally, Mealley, Melly, Melia, &c.; 'des. of máille' (perhaps Old Celtic Maglios, chief); the name (1) of a Connacht family who were chiefs of the two Umhalls, now the baronies of Burrishoole and Murresk, in the west of Co. Mayo, and were particularly celebrated as naval commanders, being called the Manannans, or sea-gods, of the western ocean, and having a considerable fleet always under their command; and (2) of a Thomond family who were chiefs of Tuath Luimnigh, a district in the neighbourhood of the city of Limerick. Ó máille is often strangely anglicised Melia in Connacht, which may be explained on the supposition that Ó maele was formerly a popular variant. Ó maele was in use in the 10th century in Conmaicne.

Ó maincín—I—*O Manihin*, Manihin, Manihan, Manahan, Mannix; 'des. of maincín' (dim. of manač, a monk); a var. of Ó mancáin, q.v.; the name of a family of Corca Laoighdhe, in South-West Cork; now scattered through Munster, especially Cork, Kerry and Limerick, and generally angl. Mannix.

Ó máine—I—*O Many*, Many, (Meany) ; ' des. of máine ' ; the name of a Dalcassian family in Thomond ; now very rare, and its angl. forms can hardly be distinguished from those of Ó maonaíg, q.v.

Ó mainnín—I—*O Mannine, O Mannin, O Manynge,* Mannin, Mannion, Manion, Manning, Mangin, (Mangan) ; ' des. of mainnín ' (perhaps the same as maincín) ; the name of a Galway family who were formerly chiefs of Sodhan, a district nearly co-extensive with the barony of Tiaquin. Ó mainnín, King of Sodhan, is mentioned in the Chronicon Scotorum as early as the year 1135, and the O Mainnins continued to form a distinct clan down to the time of James I. The chief resided at Menlough Castle, in the parish of Killascobe. In 1617, Hugh O'Mannin surrendered his estates to the king and received them back by letters patent. The whole property was confiscated after the Cromwellian wars, but a small portion of it was restored under the Act of Settlement in 1676. The name is still common in Galway and Roscommon, and has spread into other parts of Ireland. It is sometimes pronounced Ó maingín and so incorrectly angl. Mangin and Mangan.

Ó máirtín—II—*O Martin, O Marten,* Martin ; ' des. of Martin.'

Ó manacáin, Ó mancáin—I—*O Managhane, O Manahan, O Monaghan,* Monaghan, Monahan, Manahan, etc., Monk, Monks ; ' des. of manacán ' (dim. of manac, a monk) ; the name of a Connacht family who derive their descent from Manacán, a famous warrior mentioned by the Four Masters at the year 866, and were chiefs of Ui Briuin na Sionna, in the barony of Ballintober, Co. Roscommon, until the year 1249, when they were ousted by the O Beirnes. The name at the end of the 16th century was very scattered. It is sometimes pronounced Ó mionacáin and Ó muineacáin, q.v.

Ó mАПАČАIR—I—*O Monegher*, Monaher; 'des. of mАПАČАp' (monk-dear); a rare surname in Offaly, where it has been in use for more than three hundred years. It is scarcely found outside that county.

Ó mАПАζÁIП—I—*O Monegan*, Monegan, (Mangan); 'des. of mАПАζÁП' (dim. of mАПАČ, a monk); probably only a var. of Ó mАПАČÁIП, q.v.

Ó mАПАППÁIП—I—*O Manynane, O Mananan*, Marrinan, Murnane, &c.; 'des. of mАПАППÁП' (the name of an ancient Irish sea-god); an old Thomond surname; now found chiefly in East Limerick, Tipperary, Cork, and parts of Leinster, but long corrupted to Ó mАpАПnÁIП, Ó mАpnÁIП, Ó mupnÁIП, and Ó mАПАpÁIП, q.v.

Ó mАПАRÁIП—I—*O Mannerane*, Mannering, Manron; a corruption of Ó mАПАnnÁIП, q.v.

Ó mАПČÁIП—I—*O Manchan, O Monghan*, Monaghan, Monahan, Manahan, Manghan, (Mangan); a var. of Ó mАПАČÁIП, q.v.

Ó mАППТÁIП—I—*O Mantane, O Mentane*, Montane, Montang, Montangue, Mountain, Menton, Mintin; 'des. of mАППТÁП' (dim. of mАППТАČ, toothless); an old surname in Ossory and Cork.

Ó mАПÓζ—I—*O Monoge*, Manogue, (Mannix); 'des. of mАПÓζ' (dim. of mАПАČ, a monk); more frequently Ó muiпeÓζ, q.v.

Ó mАОILАОᴅА, Ó mАОILАОIᴅ—I—*O Mylee, O Miley*, Millea, Mullee, Miley, Melay, (Malley, Mulloy, Molloy); a var. of Ó mАОLАОᴅА, q.v. In Connacht, where it is not uncommon, it is sometimes angl. Mullee, but generally Mulloy.

Ó mАОILᴅeАПnАČТА—I—Mulvanerty, Blessing; 'des. of mАОLᴅeАПnАČТА' (votary of the blessing); a rare surname. Blessing is a 'translation.'

Ó mАОILᴅeАПÓIП—I—*O Mulvanone, O Mulvanon*, Mulvennon; 'des. of mАОLᴅeАПÓIП' (servant of St. Benignus); a rare Meath surname.

Ó mАОILᴅeАRАIζ—I—*O Mulverie*, Mulberry; 'des. of mАОLᴅeАpАIζ' (servant of St. Barry); a rare Ulster surname.

Ó maoilbreanainn, Ó maoilbréanainn—I—
O Mulrenan, O Mulreanan, O'Mulrennin, Mulrenan,
Mulrenin, Mulrennan, Mulrennin, Mulreany, Renan ;
' des. of maoilbpeanainn ' (servant of St. Brendan) ;
the name (1) of a family of Siol Muireadhaigh who
were chiefs of Clann Choncobhair, or Clan Connor, in
the present Co. Roscommon, and were seated in the
parish of Baslick, near Ballintobber ; and (2) of a
family of Ui Eachach Muaidhe in Tirawley, Co. Mayo.
It has in some places been corrupted to Ó maoil-
bpeanaill and Ó maoilbpéana.

Ó maoilbreannoáin, Mulbrandon ; a var. in West
Clare of Ó maoilbpeanainn, q.v.

Ó maoilbrígoe—I—*O Mulbridy, O Mulridy,* Mulbreedy, Mulbride, Mullbride, Millbride, Mulready,
Murready, Reid ; ' des. of maoilbpígoe ' (servant of
St. Brigid) ; the name of a family of Ui Maine who
were chiefs of Magh Finn, or Bredach, in the barony
of Athlone, Co. Roscommon, but were dispossessed
many centuries ago by the MacKeoghs and dispersed
through the neighbouring districts of Connacht and
Leinster. St. Brigid was patroness of the family,
and Bredach was dedicated to her.

Ó maoilcéire—I—*O Mulchery, O Mulkery, O Mulcheir,
O Mulkere,* Mulkerry, Mulcair, Mulhare, Wilhere,
Wilhair ; ' des of maoilcéipe ' (servant of St. Ciar).
This surname probably originated in Co. Galway
where it was most common in the 16th century. It
was current at the same period in Clare, Limerick,
Tipperary and Donegal. For Wilhair, the angl.
form in the last-named county, cf. Vaughan for
Maughan.

Ó maoilciaráin—I—*O Mulchieraine, O Mulkerane,*
Mulkieran, Mulkearn, Mulkern, Mulkerrin, Mulheeran,
Mulheran, Mulherrin, Mulherron, Mulhern, Mulkearns,
Mulkerns, &c. ; ' des. of maoilciapáin ' (servant of
St. Ciaran) ; the name of an ecclesiastical family who
were erenaghs of Eaglais beg, at Clonmacnoise, and
of Ardcarne, in Co. Roscommon. A branch of the

family seems to have settled in Donegal sometime before the end of the 16th century. The name at that period was most frequent in Westmeath, Roscommon and Donegal.

Ó mᴀoιlᴅeιᴚʒ—I—*O Molderge*, Mulderg, Mulderrig, Reid, (Reddington, Ruthledge) ; ' des. of mᴀoιᴅeᴀᴘʒ' (the red chief), or very probably a corruption of the old surname Ó mᴀoιlʒιᴘιc, q.v. ; an old surname in Donegal, whence it has spread into Mayo, where it is strangely angl. Reddington and Ruthledge. Reid (for Red) is a translation.

Ó mᴀoιleᴀċáιn—I—Melican, Millican, Milliken, Millikin, &c. ; a var. of Ó mᴀoιleᴀʒáιn, q.v.

Ó mᴀoιleᴀċáιn—I *O Mulleghan*, (Mulligan), Diamond, Diamon ; an attenuated form of Ó mᴀolᴀċáιn, q.v. In Co. Galway, it is strangely angl. Diamond and Diamon, being erroneously supposed to be derived from ' muιlleᴀċ,' a diamond (in cards).

Ó mᴀoιleᴀċlᴀιnn—I—*O Melaghlin*, (MacLaughlin, MacLoughlin, &c., O'Loughlin, &c.) ; a var. of Ó mᴀoιlᵽeᴀċlᴀιnn, q.v.

Ó mᴀoιleᴀʒáιn—I—*O Moylegane*, *O Milligane*, *O Mellegan*, Milligan, Milligen, Millican, Melican, (Mulligan), &c. ; an attenuated form of Ó mᴀolᴀʒáιn, q.v.

Ó mᴀoιleáιn—I—*O Moylane*, *O Melane*, Moylan, Millane, Millan, Miland, Moylin, Mullen, &c. ; an attenuated form of Ó mᴀoláιn, q.v.

Ó mᴀoιleᴀnᴀιʒ—I—*O Mullany*, Mullany, Mullaney ; ' des. of mᴀoιᵽeᴀnᴀιʒ,' (servant of St. Seanach) ; a common surname in Connacht, especially in Roscommon (where in 1540 the family was seated in the neighbourhood of Loch Cé), Mayo and Sligo ; also found in Cork and Antrim.

Ó mᴀoιleᴀᴚcᴀ—I—*O Moylearky*, *O Mullarkie*, Melarkey, Mullarkey, Malarky ; ' des. of mᴀoιeᴀᴘcᴀ' (servant of St. Earc) ; formerly a Tirconnell surname ; now more common in Connacht.

Ó mᴀoιleᴀᴚnᴀ—I—(MacLarney) ; ' des. of mᴀoιeᴀᴘnᴀ' ; very rare.

Ó mᴀoιléιoιᵹ—I—*O Mulledy, O Mulleadie, O Maledy, O Meledy,* Mulleady, Melledy, Meleady, Meledy, Melody, Malady; 'des. of mᴀoιéιoιᵹ' (armoured chief). This surname, in the 16th century, was peculiar to the midlands, especially Westmeath and Offaly, where the family was highly respectable. There appears to have been also a family of the name in early times in Corcumroe, Co. Clare.

Ó mᴀoιléιṁín—I—*O Mulleven, O Mullivine,* Mullavin, Mallavin, M'Lavin; 'des. of mᴀoιéιṁín' (servant of St. Evin); very rare.

Ó mᴀoιleóιn—I—*O Mullone, O Melone, O Malone,* Malone; 'des. of mᴀoιeóιn' (servant of St. John); the name of a distinguished ecclesiastical family at Clonmacnoise, of which several O'Malones were abbots and bishops. In the 17th century, they rose to power and influence as landed proprietors, and after 1691 seem to have thrown in their lot with the English. Anthony Malone was a celebrated figure in Irish public life about the middle of the 18th century. His nephew, Richard Malone, was in 1785 created Baron Sunderlin; while another nephew, Edmond Malone, was the celebrated Shakesperian commentator.

Ó mᴀoιlᶠιnn—I—*O Molling, O Mullinn,* Mullin, Mullins; 'des. of mᴀoιᶠιonn' (fair chief); a rare South Leinster surname. The Four Masters at the year 1041 record the death of mᴀoιᵇᶈíᵹoe ua mᴀoιᶠιno, Bishop of Glendalough.

Ó mᴀoιlᵹειrιc, Ó mᴀoιlᵹιrιc—I—*O Mulgherick, O Mulhericke, O Mullerick,* Mullerick, Millerick; 'des. of mᴀoιᵹιᶈιc' (servant of St. Cyriacus); an old Tirconnell surname, formerly not uncommon, but now probably often corrupted to Ó mᴀoιᵈeιᶈᵹ, q.v. mᴀeιᶈᴀ Ó mᴀoιᵹιᶈιc, chief poet and ard-ollav of Ireland, is mentioned in the annals at the year 1088.

Ó mᴀoιlín—I—*O Moyline, O Mulline, O Myline,* Moylin, Mulleen, Mullin, &c.; 'des. of mᴀoιlín' (dim. of mᴀol, bald); a var. of Ó mᴀoιleáιn and Ó mᴀoláιn, q.v.

Ó Maoilíosa—I—Mellowes ; ' des. of Maolíosa '
(servant of Jesus) ; apparently modern.

Ó Maoilṁeaḋa—I—*O Moylevagh, O Molvay*, Mulvagh,
Mulvey ; ' des. of Maolṁeaḋa ' (probably chief of
Meadh, a place-name) ; the name of an old Thomond
family who were chiefs of Cinel mBaoith, and seated
in the neighbourhood of Milltown-Malbay.

Ó Maoilṁeana—I—*O Mowlvenna, O Mulvany*, Mulvany, Mulvanny, Mulvenna, Mulvenny, Melvenny ;
' des. of Maolṁeana ' (probably follower of Meana) ; the
name of an Ulster family who were ollavs to O'Kane.

Ó Maoilmiaḋaiġ—I—*O Mulmee*, Mulvey ; ' des. of
Maolmiaḋaċ ' (honourable chief) ; the name of a
family of the same stock as the MacRannals and
O'Farrells, who were chiefs of Muinnтeap Ceapḃall-
áin, in Magh Nisi, a district on the east side of
the Shannon, in the barony and county of Leitrim,
and sometimes of all Muinnтeap Eolaip. The family,
which was a distinguished one, is frequently mentioned
in the Irish annals, and is still well represented in Co.
Leitrim.

Ó Maoilṁiċil, Ó Maoilṁiċíl—I—*O Mulmichell, O
Mulvihill, O Mulveill*, Mulvihill, Melville, Mitchell,
Michael, &c. ; ' des. of Maolṁiċil ' (servant of St.
Michael) ; the name of a family of Síol Muipeaḋaiġ,
or Sil-Murray, in Co. Roscommon, who derive their
descent from Maolṁiċil, chief of Síol Muipeaḋaiġ,
who fought at the battle of Cill Ua nDaighre, near
Dublin, in 866. They were at one time chiefs of
Corca Sheachlainn, a district in the east of Co. Roscommon, but appear to have lost their rank at an early
period. The name was, however, common in that
county at the end of the 16th century, and branches
of the family had about the same time settled in
Tipperary, Limerick, Cork and Kerry, where they
still flourish.

Ó Maoilṁín—I—*O Mullivine*, Mullveen, Mulveen,
Mulvin, Molvin, Melvin ; ' des. of Maolṁín ' (polished
chief). Cf. Mac Ġiollaṁín.

Ó mᴀoɪlpeᴀᴅᴀɪʀ—I—*O Mulfadder*, Mullpeters ; 'des. of mᴀoɪpeᴀᴅᴀɪp' (servant of St. Peter) ; the name of a family of Corca Laoighdhe, in South-West Cork ; found in Leix at the close of the 16th century ; has always been exceedingly rare. Father O'Growney found Mullpeters in the United States of America.

Ó mᴀoɪlʀéᴀnᴀ—I—*O Mulriany*, *O Mulreany*, Mulreany ; a corruption of Ó mᴀoɪlɓpéᴀnᴀɪnn, q.v. All the evidence is in favour of this view.

Ó mᴀoɪlʀɪᴀɓᴀɪʒ—I—*O Mulreigh*, Mulreavy, Milreavy, &c. ; ' des. of mᴀoɪpɪᴀɓᴀċ' (grey or swarthy chief).

Ó mᴀoɪlʀɪᴀʒᴀɪn, Ó mᴀoɪlʀɪᴀɪn—I—*O Mulrigan*, *O Mulryan*, *O Mulrean*, Mulryan, Mulroyan, Mulryne, Mulrine, Mulrain, O'Ryan, Ryan ; ' des of mᴀoɪpɪᴀɪn' (follower of ʀɪᴀʒᴀn or ʀɪᴀn) ; the name of a family of Leinster origin who settled in the 13th or 14th century in Uaithne-tire and Uaithne-cliach, now the baronies of Owney, in Co. Tipperary, and Owneybeg, in the east of Co. Limerick, where they became very numerous and powerful. In 1610, William Ryan surrendered to the king all his landed property and all his rights of or in the barony of Owney O Mulrian, and received them back by letters patent. The family property was, however, lost in the confiscations of the 17th century. There are many very respectable families of the name in Tipperary and Limerick, and the name itself is very common in these counties. It is to be distinguished from Ó ʀɪᴀɪn, q.v.

Ó mᴀoɪlseᴀċlᴀɪnn—I—*O Mulshaghlen*, *O Melaghlin*, (MacLaughlin, MacLoughlin, &c., O Loughlan, O Loughlin) ; ' des. of mᴀoɪpeᴀċlᴀɪnn' (servant of St. Secundinus) ; the name of a once celebrated Meath family, of the race of Niall of the Nine Hostages, who derive their descent from Maelsheachlainn, or Malachy II, King of Ireland, who was dethroned by Brian Boru and died in the year 1022. The clan-name of the O Melaghlins and their co-relatives was Clann Cholmain. Before the Anglo-Norman invasion they were kings of Meath, but after that period their power greatly declined. Meath was granted to Hugh de Lacy, and for many centuries the O Melaghlens were confined to the barony of Clonlonan in Westmeath. They were, however, one of the five Irish families who had the privilege of using English laws. In the reign of James I they were again stripped of a considerable portion of what remained of their ancient patrimony ; and so completely had this ancient and once powerful family been ruined by the confiscations of the 17th century that in the attainders of 1691 there appears but one person of the name, Maolseachlin O Melaghlin, of Lough Mask, Co. Mayo. The name is now everywhere disguised under the angl. forms of MacLaughlin, MacLoughlin, &c.

Ó mᴀoılsᴄéıᵹe—I—*O Mulstegia, O Molstaygh, O Mulstey, O Mustey*, Mustay, M'Stay, MacStay ; ' des. of mᴀoırᴄéıᵹe ' ; the name of an ecclesiastical family in the diocese of Dromore, Co. Down ; now very rare.

Ó mᴀoılsıonóᵹ—I—Mulshinogue ; ' des. of mᴀoırıonóᵹ.'

Ó mᴀoɫᴀċᴀ́ın—I—*O Molaghan, O Molleghan*, Molohan, Mallaghan, (Mulligan) ; ' des. of mᴀoɫᴀċᴀ́n ' (from mᴀoɫ, bald) ; a rare surname. In Connacht it is generally angl. Mulligan. Ó mᴀoıɫeᴀċᴀ́ın, q.v., is an attenuated form.

Ó mᴀoɫᴀᵹᴀ́ın—I—*O Mollegane, O Mullegan, O Mulghan*, Mullagan, Mulligan, Mulgan, (Molyneux), Baldwin, &c. ; ' des of mᴀoɫᴀᵹᴀ́n ' (dim. of mᴀoɫ, bald) ; the name of a Tirconnell family who were chiefs of Tir MacCarthainn, in the east of the barony of Boylagh, but seem to have been dispossessed and dispersed at an early period. At the end of the 16th century, the name, while most frequent in Ulster, was not uncommon in the other provinces. It is said to have been anglicised Molyneux and Baldwin in Donegal, the latter form being intended as a translation, i.e., Bald one. Ó mᴀoıɫeᴀᵹᴀ́ın and Ó mᴀoıɫeᴀċᴀ́ın (q.v.) are attenuated forms.

Ó mAolÁin—I—*O Mollane, O Melane, O Moylane,* O'Mullane, O'Mullan, Mullane, Mulhane, Melane, Millane, Millan, Mullan, Mullen, Mullon, Mollan, Moylan, Mullins, &c. ; ' des. of mAolÁn ' (dim. of mAol, bald). This surname, which is one of the commonest in Ireland, is found in almost every part of the country, but under a great variety of angl. forms. There are, no doubt, several distinct families so called, but apparently the only dynastic family of the name was that of O'Kane's country, in Co. Derry. Ó mAoileÁin (q.v.) is a variant.

Ó mAolAinbte, v. Ó mAolAnpArò.

Ó mAolAit—I—(Mulloy) ; a shortened form of Ó mAolAitce, q.v.

Ó mAolAitce—I—Mullahy, (Mulloy) ; ' des. of mAol- Aitce ' or ' mAolAitgein ' (votary of regeneration) ; the name of a family of Ui Eachach Muaidhe, in Co. Mayo, where, though very rare, it still survives. It is sometimes shortened to Ó mAolAit and angl. Mulloy. The family was also called Ó mAolAitgein, q.v.

Ó mAolAitgein—I—(Mullahy, Mulloy) ; ' des. of mAolAitgein ' (votary of regeneration) ; an alias for Ó mAolAitce (q.v.), which is probably a corruption of it. The Four Masters, at the year 1099, mention an erenagh of 'Oún of this name.

Ó mAolAlArò—I—*O Mullaly, O Mullally,* Mullally, Mullaly, Lally ; ' des. of mAolAlAò ' (speckled chief) ; the name of a branch of the Ui Maine in Co. Galway. They are of the same descent as the O'Neachtains, and both families originally formed one clan, called Ui Fiachrach Finn from their ancestor, Fiachra Fionn, grandson of Maine Mór, the common ancestor of all the Ui Maine. The clan lands comprised the fertile plain of Maonmhagh, lying around Loughrea, but about the time of the Anglo-Norman invasion the O'Mullallys were dispossessed by the Burkes and forced to retire to the parish of Tuam, where they settled at Tulach na dála, angl. Tullaghnadaly, or Tolendal, four miles to the north of the town of Tuam.

In the wars of the 17th century, they adhered to the
Stuart cause. James Lally of Tullindaly sat as
representative of Tuam in King James's Parliament
of 1689. He was attainted in 1691 together with his
brother, Gerald, whereupon they both retired to
France. Gerald married a noble French lady, and
their son and grandson, the Counts Lally de Tollendal,
made the name celebrated in Europe.

Ó mαolαnpαιᵐ—I—Mullanphy, Melanphy; 'des. of
mαolαnpαιᵐ' (chief of the storm).

Ó mαol αn ṁuαιᵐ—I— (Molyneux); 'des. of mαol αn
ṁuαιᵐ' (follower of the noble); probably a distorted
form of Ó mαolṁuαιᵐ, q.v.; in use in North Kerry,
pronounced Ó mullαnuα and angl. Molyneux.

Ó mαolαoᵐα—I—O Mollaye, O Mullae, O Mulley, O
Mullye, O Mellawa, O Miley, O Moloy, O'Mealue,
(O Malley), Mallew, Melay, Millea, Miley, Mullee,
(Mulloy, Molloy, Malley); 'des. of mαolαoᵐα'
(servant of St. Aedh); the name of a family of Cinel
Aonghusa, a sept of the Cinel Eoghain, in Ulster,
Ó mαolαoᵐα was one of the hostages given by Aodh
O Neill to Roderick O'Connor, King of Ireland, in
1167. At the end of the 16th century, the name was
very scattered. In the North it seems to have been
generally anglicised by assimilation to Malley, but in
Connacht, where, under the form of Ó mαoιlαoᵐα
(q.v.), it is not uncommon, it is generally angl. Mulloy,
sometimes Mullee. See also Ó mαolαoᵐóg and Ó
mαolṁαoᵐóg.

Ó mαolαoᵐóg—I—O Mologe, O Molouge Loague,
Logue, (Mulloy, Molloy); a var. of Ó mαolαoᵐα and
Ó mαolṁαoᵐóg, q.v.; a Donegal surname; also in
use in Co. Mayo, angl. Mulloy and Molloy.

Ó mαolαoιᵐ—I—Mullee, Mulloy. V. Ó mαoιlαoιᵐ
and Ó mαolαoᵐα.

Ó mαolαᵐαᵐᵐαιᵹ—I—Mulhartagh; a var. of Ó mαol-
pαᵐαᵐᵐαιᵹ, q.v.

Ó mαolᵐáιn—I—O Mullowane, Mulvane; 'des. of
mαolᵐán' (white chief).

Ó mAoLbloȝAIn—I—*O Mollowne*, Mullowne, Malone ; 'des. of mAoLbloȝAIn' ; the name of an old Tipperary family who were seated in Muscraighe Treitherne, in the present barony of Clanwilliam. The family is still extant, but cannot always be distinguished from that of Ó mAoiLeóin, q.v.

Ó mAoLcAIsIL—I—*O Mulcashell*, Mulcashel, (Mountcashel), Cashel ; 'des of mAoLcAIrIL' (chief of Cashel) ; the name of a Thomond family who were seated originally at Ballymulcashel, near Six-mile-Bridge, Co. Clare. CopmAcÁn Ó mAoLcAIrIL was Bishop of Killaloe in the early part of the 11th century. The name is now very rare. In the neighbourhood of Kilmallock, the angl. form was changed about eighty years ago by the local registrar to Mountcashel, and so it remains to the present day.

Ó mAoLcALLAnn—I—*O Mulchallan, O Maghallon, O Mohallan,* Mulhallen, Mulhollan, Mulholn, Mulholland, Maholland, Holland, &c. ; 'des. of mAoLcALLAnn' (chief of the kalends) ; the name of three distinct families in Ireland : (1) of a branch of the Ui Fidhgheinte, who were chiefs of Caonraidhe, now the barony of Kenry, in the north of Co. Limerick ; (2) of a Meath family who were chiefs of Dealbhna beg, now the barony of Demifore ; and (3) of an ecclesiastical family in Ulster who from at least the beginning of the 12th down to the end of the 18th century were keepers of the Bell of St. Patrick, known as the Bell of the Testament, though it would appear from the Irish annals that the family of O'Meallain was at one time associated with them in the guardianship. This is apparently the only family of the name now extant. They were seated in the barony of Loghinsholin, in the present county of Derry. A branch of the family seems to have settled early in Co. Antrim. The name is common in Ulster, but is sometimes confused with Ó mAoLcoLuim, q.v.

Ó mAoLcAoin—I—*O Mulchine, O Mulkyne, O Mulqueen, O Mulquin,* Mulkeen, Mulqueen, Mulquin ;

'des. of ᵐᵃᴏⱡᴄᴀᴏⁱⁿ' (gentle chief) ; the name of a
bardic family in Thomond. The Four Masters, under
the year 1096, record the death of Ua Maelcain, ollav
of the Dál gCais. The name is still well known in
Thomond, and is also current in parts of Connacht.
Ó ᵐᴀᴏⱡᴄᴀᴏⁱⁿᵉ (q.v.) is a variant.

Ó ᵐᴀᴏⱡᴄᴀᴏⁱⁿᵉ—I—*O Mulqueeny, O Mulkeiny*, Mulqueeny, Mulqueen ; ' des. of ᵐᴀᴏⱡᴄᴀᴏⁱⁿᵉ ' (servant of
St. Caoine). This has been for centuries an alias for
Ó ᵐᴀᴏⱡᴄᴀᴏⁱⁿ in the spoken language of Thomond.
Thus, among the besiegers of Ballyally castle in 1641
was O'Mulqueen of Ballymulqueeny. It would appear
from the Annals of the Four Masters, A.D. 1096, that
Ó ᵐᴀᴏⱡᴄᴀᴏⁱⁿ is the original and correct form of the
name. Cf. ᵐᴀᴄ ᵹⁱᴏⱡⱡᴀᴄᴀᴏⁱⁿ and ᵐᴀᴄ ᵹⁱᴏⱡⱡᴀ-
ᴄᴀᴏⁱⁿᵉ.

Ó ᵐᴀᴏⱡᴄᴀᴛᴀ, Ó ᵐᴀᴏⱡᴄᴀᴛᴀⁱᵹ—I—*O Mulcaha, O
Mulcahy*, Mulcahy ; ' des. of ᵐᴀᴏⱡᴄᴀᴛᴀ' (battle-chief), or
' ᵐᴀᴏⱡᴄᴀᴛᴀᴄ' (warlike chief), or 'ᵐᴀᴏⱡᴄᴀᴛᴀⁱᵹ' (follower
of ᴄᴀᴛᴀᴄ, warlike) ; a well-known Munster surname.
It seems to have originated in South Tipperary, but
is now common also in Waterford, Cork and Limerick.

Ó ᵐᴀᴏⱡᴄᴀᴛᴀⁱⱡ—I—*O Mulcahill, O Molchaill*, Mulhall ;
' des. of ᵐᴀᴏⱡᴄᴀᴛᴀⁱⱡ ' (servant of St. Cathal) ; the
name of an old family in Offaly and Leix ; still
numerous in the latter county and other parts of
Leinster.

Ó ᵐᴀᴏⱡᴄᴀᴛáⁱⁿ—I—*O Mulchathayn, O Mulcayhan*, Mulhatton ; ' des. of ᵐᴀᴏⱡᴄᴀᴛáⁱⁿ ' (servant of St. Catan) ;
very rare.

Ó ᵐᴀᴏⱡᴄⱡᴀᴏⁱⁿ—I—Mulkeen, Mucleen ; ' des. of ᵐᴀᴏⱡ-
ᴄⱡᴀᴏⁿ ' (deceitful chief) ; a rare Connacht surname.

Ó ᵐᴀᴏⱡᴄⱡᵘⁱᴄᵉ—I—*O Molklyhy, O Mulclohy, O Mulclahy, O Mulcloy, O Mucklie, Mulclahy*, (Mulcahy),
Muckley, Stone ; ' des. of ᵐᴀᴏⱡᴄⱡᵘⁱᴄᵉ ' (gamester) ;
the name of a Sligo family who were chiefs of Cairbre,
now the barony of Carbury, in the north of that
county, until dispossessed by the O'Dowds in the
14th century. In the 16th century, the name was

very scattered, but found chiefly in Donegal, West-meath, Offaly and Cork. In the census of 1659, it appears as Mulclahy in Co. Limerick. It is now nearly everywhere angl. Stone owing to an erroneous idea that the latter part of the name is ' cloice,' gen. of ' cloc,' a stone, while really the gen. of ' cluice,' a game. In Limerick it has been turned into the more common surname, Mulcahy, while in Co. Cork it has become Muckley. The old form of the name is preserved in Inishmulclohy, also called Coney Island, in Sligo Bay.

Ó maolcolm, ó maolcoluim—I—*O Molcalm, O Molchalum*, Malcolm, Mulholm, Mulhollum, Maholm, Mahollum ; ' des of maolcolm' or ' maolcoluim' (servant of St. Columcille) ; an Antrim surname. The Four Masters, under the year 1061, record the death of muirpeaʒac ua maolcoluim, erenagh of Derry.

Ó maolcomaʒ—I—*O Mollchomy*, Mulumy, Molumby ; ' des. of maol comaʒ' ; the name of an ancient family of Corca Laoighdhe, in South-West Cork.

Ó maolconaire—I—*O Mulchonery, O Mulconry*, Mul-conry, Conry, (Conroy) ; ' des. of maolconaire' (follower of Conaire) ; the name of a celebrated literary family who were poets and chroniclers to the Kings of Connacht and other families of Siol Muire-adhaigh. They were seated at Clonahee, near Strokes-town, in Co. Roscommon, where they had consider-able property in right of their profession. Many distinguished poets and historians of the name are mentioned in the Irish annals. A learned branch of this family, to which frequent reference is made in Irish literary history, settled at Ardkyle, in the parish of Feenagh, Co. Clare. John O'Mulconry, a member of this family, who flourished during the first half of the 17th century, was a profound Irish scholar and ' chief teacher in history of all the men of Erin in his own time.' The O'Mulconrys also produced some eminent ecclesiastics among whom may be mentioned Florence O'Mulconry, Archbishop of Tuam and

founder of the Irish Franciscan convent of Louvain.
The name is now unfortunately too often disguised by
being anglicised Conry and Conroy.

Ó Maolcraoive—I—*O Mulcrieve, O Mulchrewe, O
Mulcrey*, Mulcreevy, Mulgrievy, Mulgrave, Mulgrew,
Mulgroo, Rice; 'des. of Maolcraoive' (chief of
Craov, a place-name); the name of an Oriel family
who were originally located westward of the Upper
Bann, but afterwards settled in Clannaboy, where
they were followers of the O'Neills. At the beginning
of the 17th century they occupied the west side of
Knockbreda, near Belfast, in Co. Down, but the name
was even then scattered through Tyrone, Armagh
and Antrim. It is still common throughout East
Ulster, but generally angl. Rice.

Ó Maolcróin—I—Mulchrone, Mulcrone, Mulcroan,
Mulcroon; 'des of Maolcrón' (swarthy chief); the
name of an old family of Ui Maine; now found chiefly
in Mayo, but rare even there.

Ó Maolcróine—I—Mulcrowney; 'des of Maolcróine' (servant of St. Croine); a rare surname. Cf.
Kilcroney for Cill Cróine, Co. Wicklow.

Ó Maolvomnaig—I—*O Muldowny*, Muldowney, Muldooney, Downey, Dawney; more frequently Ó Maolvomnaig, q.v.

Ó Maolvomnaig—I—*O Malowny, O Mollowny, O
Mullowny*, Malowny, Molowny, Mullowney, Moloney,
Molony, &c.; 'des. of Maolvomnaig' (devoted to
Sunday, or to the Church); the name of a Dalcassian
family who were chiefs of a district in the
barony of Tulla, Co. Clare; now very numerous
throughout Munster. Ó Maolvomnaig (q.v.) is
the same surname, but the family is apparently
different.

Ó Maolvoraiv—I—Muldarry, Mulderry, Meelderry;
'des. of Maolvoraiv' (contentious chief); the name
of a branch of the Cinel Conaill who in the 10th, 11th
and 12th centuries were chiefs of Tirconnell; still
extant, but very rare.

Ó maolduib—I—Maliffe ; ' des. of maoldub ' (black chief) ; the name of a family of Ui Maine ; very rare.

Ó maolduin—I—*O Muldoon*, Muldoon, Muldon, Meldon ; ' des. of maolduin ' (chief of the fort) ; the name of several distinct families, as : (1) of an Oriel family who until the end of the 14th century were chiefs of Feara Luirg, now the barony of Lurg, in the north of Co. Fermanagh, and are still numerous in that county ; (2) of a branch of the Ui Fiachrach in Co. Sligo ; and (3) of a Thomond family.

Ó maolfábail, Ó maolfábail—I—*O Mowlfoull*, *O Mulfall*, *O Maylawell*, Mulfaal, Mulavill, (Melville), Lawell, Lavelle, (MacFaal, MacFall, MacPaul, Paul) ; ' des. of maolfábail ' (fond of travel) ; the name (1) of a family of Cinel Eoghain who were chiefs of Carraig Brachaidh, angl. Carrickabraghy, in the north-west of the barony of Inishowen, Co. Donegal ; and (2) of a West Connacht family. It is generally angl. Mulfall, or MacFaal, in Ulster, but Lavelle in Connacht, where it is now most numerous.

Ó maolfactna—I—*Mullaghny*, *Meloughna*, Mulloughney, Mologhney, Mollowney, (Mollony, Moloney) ; ' des. of maolfactna ' (servant of St. Fachtna) ; an old Tipperary surname, now generally assimilated to Moloney.

Ó maolfatartaig—I—Mulhartagh ; ' des. of maolfatartaig ' (follower of fatartac) ; the name of a family of Cinel Eoghain in Ulster ; now very rare.

Ó maolfogmair, Ó maolfogmair—I—*O Mulfover*, *O Mullover*, (Milford, Palmer) ; ' des. of maolfogmair ' (chief of harvest) ; the name of a distinguished ecclesiastical family who were erenaghs of the church of Killala, and supplied several bishops to that see. O Donovan found the name still in the district, but angl. Milford. According to MacFirbis, the family of mac céile (q.v.) is a branch of that of Ó maolfogmair.

Ó maolgaoite—I—*O Mulgehy*, *O Mulgey*, Mulgeehy, (Magee), Wynne ; ' des. of maolgaoite ' (chief of the

wind) ; the name of a Tirconnell family who were
seated originally in the parish of Clondavaddock, Co.
Donegal ; now more common in Connacht, where,
however, it is generally disguised under the angl.
forms of Magee and Wynne (for Wind).

Ó mᴀoⱡ𝔤uᴀⱡᴀ—I—*O Mulloly*, Mulooly, Mulhooly ;
' des. of mᴀoⱡ𝔤uᴀⱡᴀ ' (glutton).

Ó mᴀoⱡ̇mᴀ𝔤nᴀ—I—*O Mulvanny*, Mulvany, Mulvanny ;
' des. of mᴀoⱡ̇mᴀ𝔤nᴀ '; the name of a Tirconnell
family who were chiefs of Magh Seiridh, in the north
of the barony of Tirhugh, Co. Donegal.

Ó mᴀoⱡ̇mᴀoᴅ̇ó𝔤—I—*O Mulmoge, O Mulvoge*, Mullavogue, (Mulloy, Molloy) ; ' des. of mᴀoⱡ̇mᴀoᴅ̇ó𝔤 '
(servant of St. mᴀoᴅ̇ó𝔤, or Mogue) ; a var. of Ó
mᴀoⱡᴀoᴅ̇ó𝔤, q.v. ; a Donegal surname ; now generally
disguised under the angl. form of Mulloy or Molloy.

Ó mᴀoⱡ̇mᴀ́Ɽⱦᴀın—I—*O Molmartine*, Martin ; ' des.
of mᴀoⱡ̇mᴀ́Ɽⱦᴀın ' (servant of St. Martin).

Ó mᴀoⱡ̇moċóıⱤ, Ó mᴀoⱡ̇moċóıⱤ𝔤e, Ó mᴀoⱡ̇-
moıċeıⱤ𝔤e—I—*O Mulmochore, O Mullmochory, O
Molvochory, O Mullucherie*, Early, Earley, Eardley ;
' des. of mᴀoⱡ̇moċeıⱤ𝔤e ' (chief of early rising, or fond
of early rising). Ó mᴀoⱡ̇moıċeıⱤ𝔤e was the original
form ; in the spoken language it became Ó mᴀoⱡ̇-
moċóıⱤ𝔤e, or Ó mᴀoⱡ̇moċóıⱤ, now generally shortened
to Ó moċóıⱤ𝔤e and Ó moċóıⱤ, q.v. ; the name of an
ecclesiastical family in the diocese of Kilmore, the
head of which was coarb of Drumreilly, in Co. Leitrim,
and of Drumlane, in Co. Cavan. MacFirbis mentions
a family of this name among the Siol Muireadhaigh
in Co. Roscommon. Before the end of the 16th
century, the name had spread into Sligo and Donegal.
It is now everywhere angl. Early, Earley or Eardley.

Ó mᴀoⱡ̇mónᴀ—I—Mulmona, Moss ; ' des. of mᴀoⱡ̇-
mónᴀ ' (chief of the bog) ; a rare Ulster surname.
Moss is a ' translation,'

Ó mᴀoⱡ̇muᴀıᴅ—I—*O Molmoy, O Mulmoy*, Milmo, Milmoe ; a var. of Ó mᴀoⱡ̇muᴀıᴅ, q.v. ; a rare Sligo
surname.

Ó maoLṁuaıṫ—I—*O Molwye, O Meloy, O Molloye, O Mulloye,* O'Molloy, Meloy, Molloy, Mulloy, &c. ; ' des. of maoLmuaṫ ' (noble chief) ; the name (1) of a distinguished family of the southern Ui Neill, in Meath. They are of the same descent as the Mageoghegans, and both families originally formed one clan, called Cinel Fiachach from their common ancestor, Fiacha, son of Niall of the Nine Hostages. In the 10th or 11th century, Cinel Fiachach and its territory was divided between the two families, Mageoghegan retaining the northern portion under the original clan-name, Cinel Fiachach, and O'Molloy becoming lord of the southern portion, under the name of Feara Ceall. This territory, which comprised the modern baronies of Fircall, Ballycowan and Ballyboy in Offaly, remained in the possession of the O'Molloys down to the beginning of the 17th century. The O'Molloys were hereditary bearers of the British standard in Ireland. (2) MacFirbis mentions another family of the name, a branch of the Siol Muireadhaigh, in Co. Roscommon. They belonged to the sept known as Clann Taidhg na h-oidhche and are now, according to O'Donovan, represented by the Molloys of Oakpark, near Boyle. Ó maoLmuaıṫ (q.v.) is a Sligo variant. See also Ó maoL an ṁuaıṫ.

Ó maoLṁuıRe—I—*O Moylery,* Mullery, Mulry, (Miles, Myles) ; ' des. of maoLṁuıṗe ' (servant of Mary) ; the name of a family of Cinel Eoghain who were at one time chiefs of Cinel Fearadhaigh, in Ulster ; now rare. In Co. Mayo it is angl. Myles.

Ó maoLṗáoRaıᵹ—I—*O Mulfadricke, O Mulpatrick,* (?) Fitzpatrick ; ' des. of maoLṗáoṗaıᵹ ' (servant of St. Patrick) ; once a common surname, especially in Cavan and Cork. In the year 1602, Conor O Molpatrick, ' chief of his name,' was included in a list of pardons for Co. Cavan. Though the name has disappeared, the family was too numerous to have died out, and the probability is that, like the Mac Gillapatricks of Ossory, they have anglicised it to Fitzpatrick.

Ó MAOLRUAIÓ—I—*O Melrewe*, Mulroe, Mulroy, Mulry, Mulrow, Melroy, Milroy, (Munroe, Monroe) ; ' des. of mAoLруиаÓ ' (red chief) ; the name of a family of Ui Fiachrach who were originally seated in the parish of Ardagh, in Tirawley, Co. Mayo. It is still common in Mayo and Galway, but sometimes angl. Monroe.

Ó MAOLRUAIn—I—*O Molrone, O Mulrowne*, Mulroon, Meldron ; short for Ó mAoLруаnаÓ, q.v.

Ó MAOLRUAnAIÓ—I—*O Mulruony, O Mulrony, O Moronie*, Mulrooney, Mulrony, Murroney, Morooney, Moroney, &c. ; ' des. of mAoLруаnаÓ ' (follower of RuаnаÓ) ; the name (1) of a Fermanagh family who antecedently to the Maguires were lords of that county ; (2) of a Galway family who were chiefs of Crumhthan, angl. Cruffan, a district comprising the barony of Killyan and part of the adjoining barony of Ballimoe ; (3) of a Dalcassian family who are still numerous in Clare, Limerick and Tipperary, where however, the name is corrupted to Ó muруаnаÓ and anglicised Moroney, &c. ; and (4) of a Roscommon family who afterwards adopted the surname of mAc ÓiаrmаÓА, or MacDermott.

Ó MAOLCuILe—I—*O Multilly, O Multully*, Tully, Flood ; ' des. of mAoLcuiLe ' (devoted to the will, i.e., of God ; erroneously supposed to mean chief of the flood) ; also mAc mAoLcuiLe and mAc mAoLcuiLe ; the name of a medical family in Connacht and other parts of Ireland. They were hereditary physicians to the O'Connors of Connacht, the O'Reillys of Breifney, &c. The name was not uncommon in Ossory, where, as early as the year 1571, it was angl. Fludd.

Ó MAOnAIᵹ—I—*O Moeny, O Mooney*, (?) *O Moyney, O Money*, Meany, Meeny, Mooney, Moany, Money ; ' des. of mAonаc ' (wealthy) ; the name (1) of a Roscommon family who were anciently chiefs of Clann Murthuile ; (2) of a family of the Ui Fiachrach who were seated on the southern shore of Sligo Bay, in the barony of Tireragh ; and (3) of a branch of the Siol nAnmchadha, in the south-east of Co. Galway. At the end of the 16th century, the name was found in all parts of Ireland.

Ó mαonáin—I—*O Monane*, Moonan, Moynan, Monan ; ' des. of mαonán ' (dim. of mαon, dumb).

Ó mαongαιle—I—*O Monhily, O Monnilly*, Munnelly, Monnelly, Monley, Manley; ' des. of mαongαι ' (gift-valour) ; found chiefly in Donegal and North Connacht.

Ó mαotαgáin—I—*O Mehegane*, Meehegan, Mehegan, Mehigan ; ' des. of mαotαgán ' (dim. of mαot, soft, tender) ; an old Cork surname ; also found in Kilkenny. Cf. Ó mαotáin.

Ó mαotáin—I—*O Meawhan*, Meehan ; ' des. of mαotán ' (dim. of mαot, soft) ; a rare surname, still in use in the neighbourhood of Shrule, Co. Mayo. Cf. Ó mαotαgáin.

Ó mαrcαcáin—I—*O Markaghaine, O Marcahan*, Markahan, Markan, (Markham), Ryder ; ' des. of mαrcαcán ' (dim. of mαrcαc, a rider) ; the name of an offshoot of Cinel Guaire, in south-west of Co. Galway. The family has been long settled in Thomond, where the name is now generally angl. Markham. Ryder, which is in use in some places, is a translation.

Ó mαrcαιg—I—Markey, Ryder ; ' des. of mαrcαc ' (rider) ; a Monaghan surname. Cf. Ó mαrcαcáin.

Ó mαrαnnáin, Ó mαrnáin—I—*O Marynayne, O Marrinan, O Marnane*, Marrinan, Marinane, Marnane, Marnan, Mornan, (Warren) ; a corruption of Ó mαnαnnáin, q.v. ; also Ó mωrnáin, q.v. It is angl. Warren in the neighbourhood of Kenmare.

Ó mártαιn—II—*O Marten, O Martin*, Martin, Marten ; ' des. of Martin.' The Four Masters, under the year 1216, record the death of Giollaarnain Ua Martain, chief ollav of law in Ireland. In 1431, Bishop O'Martain of Clogher died.

Ó mαtgαṁnα—I—*O Mahowny, O Mahown*, O'Mahony, Mahony, Mahon, Maughan, (MacMahon) ; ' des. of mαtgαṁαιn ' (bear) ; the name of a well-known Cork family who derive their descent from mαtgαṁαιn (slain in 1014), whose father, Cian, son of Maolmuadh, commanded the forces of Desmond at the battle of Clontarf, and were chiefs of Cinel mBeice, now known as the barony of Kinelmeaky, an extensive district along the River Bandon, in Co. Cork, and at a later period became masters of the district called Fonn Iartharach, that is, the western land, which comprised several parishes in the south-west of Co. Cork, and had previously belonged to Corca Laoighdhe. Another family of the name was very powerful during the 11th and 12th centuries in Ulidia, and is still extant in Co. Down and other parts of East Ulster, but disguised as Mahons and MacMahons.

Ó meaċair—I—O'Meagher, *O Magher*, *O Maher*, Meagher, Magher, Maher ; ' des. of meaċaṗ ' (hospitable) ; the name of a Tipperary family, of the same stock as the O'Carrolls of Ely-O'Carroll, who were lords of Ui Cairin, now the barony of Ikerrin, in the north of that county. O'Meachair resided at Druim Saileach, where now stands the castle of Moydrum, about five miles south of Roscrea. Shortly after the Anglo-Norman invasion, Ikerrin was added to Ormond, but O'Meachair was left in possession, as tributary, however, to the Earl of Ormond. The O'Meachairs have flourished exceedingly, and are now numerous and respectable, not only in their original territory at the foot of the Devil's Bit, but throughout the counties of Tipperary, Kilkenny and Carlow.

Ó meaḋra—I—*O Mary*, O'Meara, O'Mara, Meara, Mara ; ' des. of meaḋaiṗ ' (mirth) ; the name of a Dalcassian family who were chiefs of a district called Rosarguid, in the barony of Upper Ormond, Co. Tipperary. O'Meara had his seat at Toomyvara (Cuaim Uí meaḋṗa). The family retained considerable property down to the revolution of 1690.

Ó meallaiġ—I—*O Meallie, O Mellie, O Mella*, Melly, (Malley) ; ' des. of meallaċ ' (from ' meall,' pleasant) ; the name of an old West Connacht family. Three bishops of the name filled the see of Annadown in the 13th and 14th centuries.

Ó meaʟʟáın—I—*O Meallane, O Mellane, O Mallane*, O'Mellon, Mellan, Mellon, Mallan, Mallen, (Mullen), &c. 'des. of meaʟʟáın' (dim. of 'meaʟʟ,' pleasant); the name of an ecclesiastical family in Ulster—a branch of the Cinel Eoghain—who were hereditary keepers of the Bell of St. Patrick, known as the Bell of the Testament, and were seated in the parish of Donaghmore, near Dungannon, Co. Tyrone. The name is still common in Ulster, especially in Tyrone, Armagh and Antrim.

Ó meáʀᴀ, v. Ó meaᴏ́ʀᴀ.

Ó meaʀᴀᴏ́ᴀıᵹ—I—*O Marie, O Merye, O Merehey*, Mariga, Maree, Marry, Merry; 'des. of meaʀᴀᴏ́ᴀᴄ' (lively); the name of an ancient family who were chiefs of Ui Fathaidh, now the barony of Iffa and Offa West, Co. Tipperary. O'Donovan gives the angl. form as O'Meara or O'Mara, which is incorrect, the pronunciation being that represented by O'Merye and O'Merehey. It is undoubtedly the original form of the Waterford surname Merry, and synonymous with that now pronounced Ó meaᴏ́ʀᴀ (q.v.) in Waterford and East Cork. Dr. O'Brien, in his Irish Dictionary, and Dr. MacDermott, in his notes to Connellan's edition of the Annals of the Four Masters, both confound the families of Ó meaᴏ́ʀᴀ of Rosarguid and Ó meaʀᴀᴏ́ᴀıᵹ of Ui Fathaidh, although their respective territories were separated by nearly the whole length of Tipperary.

Ó meaʀáın—I—*O Mearan, O Meran*, Meran, Mearn, Marren, Marron; 'des. of meaʀáın' (dim. of 'meaʀ,' lively); a scattered surname, now most frequent in Co. Monaghan, where it is angl. Marron.

Ó meaʀᴏ́ᴀ—I—*O Merga, O Mergey, O Merye*, Mariga, Maree, Marry, Merry; 'des. of meaʀᴏ́ᴀ' (lively); a variant of Ó meaʀᴀᴏ́ᴀıᵹ, q.v.; a rare and scattered surname. For pronunciation of ending -ᴏ́ᴀ, cf. cʀᴏ́ᴏ́ᴀ, pronounced cʀᴏ́ᵹᴀ.

Ó meaʀʟᴀıᵹ—I—*O Marlie*, Marley; perhaps a corruption of Ó muʀᵹᴀıʟe, q.v.; in use in Mayo.

Ó meiÓiR—I—*O Myre, O Mire,* Myres, Myers, Meyers, &c.;
' des. of meiÓip ' (mirth ; cf. Ó meaÓpa) ; a Thomond
surname.

Ó meiRʒín—I—*O Mergyne, O Mergin, O Merigan,*
Mergin, Merrigan ; a corruption of Ó háimeipʒin, q.v.

Ó méiRleacáin—I—Merlehan ; ' des. of méipleacán ' ;
a Westmeath surname. It must have been always
exceedingly rare. The Four Masters, under the year
1001, record the killing of Meirleacan, son of Conn,
King of Gaileng, by Maelsechlainn. He was possibly
the ancestor from whom the family took its name.

(Ó) méiRnín, Mernin ; a Waterford surname. I cannot
trace its origin.

Ó meiscill—I—*O Meskill, O Miskill,* Meskell, Miskell,
Mescall, Mescel, (Maxwell) ; ' des. of meipceall.'

Ó miaÓacáin—I—*O Mighane, O Meaghane, O Meighane,
O Mehane, O Myhane, O Meghan,* O'Meehan, O'Meehon,
Meeghan, Meighan, Meghan, Myhane, Myhan, Mehan,
Meehan, &c. ; ' des. of miaÓacán ' (dim. of ' miaÓac,'
honourable) ; a common surname in nearly every part
of Ireland. There are, no doubt, several distinct
families so called. Ó míoÓcáin is a frequent, but
incorrect, spelling of the name. See also Ó miaÓ-
aʒáin.

Ó miaÓaʒáin—I—*O Miagan, O Megan,* Meegan ; no
doubt, the same as Ó miaÓacáin, q.v. ; found in
Donegal and Monaghan.

Ó miaÓaiʒ—I—*O Miey, O Mey,* Mee, Mea, May ; ' des.
of miaÓac ' (honourable) ; an old Westmeath surname,
still found in the midlands, but now more frequently
in Roscommon and the southern parts of Mayo. It
was an Ó miaÓaiʒ that terminated the career of Sir
Hugh de Lacy, ' the profaner and destroyer of many
churches,' by cutting off his head with a blow of an
axe at the castle of Durrow in 1186.

Ó mianáin—I—*O Minane, O Meanan,* Meenan ; ' des.
of mianán ' (dim. of mian, will, desire) ; the name of
an old Tirconnell family ; still common in Donegal
and Tyrone.

Ó micτíre—I—Wolfe. V. Ó mαcτίρe.

Ó miṁir, Ó mír—I—*O Meere*, Meere, Miers, Mears, Meares, &c.; probably the same as Ó meiṁiṗ, q.v.; found in Clare and Galway.

Ó mionαċáin—I—Minahane, Minahan, (Moynihan, Monahan); a var. in the spoken language of Ó mαnαċ-áin, q.v. To be distinguished from Ó muiṁneαċ-áin which has sometimes the same angl. forms.

Ó miríin—I—*O Mirren, O Merren*, Mirreen; ' des. of miṗín' (dim. of meαṗ, lively); the same as Ó meαṗáin, q.v.

Ó miτṁín—I—*O Myhiden, O Meehin*, O'Meehin, Meehin, Meehen, Meehan; ' des. of miτṁín' or ' miτʒein' (born in June); the name (1) of an ecclesiastical family of Ui Maine who were coarbs of Clontuskert, near Ballinasloe; and (2) of an ecclesiastical family in Co. Leitrim who were coarbs of St. Molaise at Ballaghmeehin, in the parish of Rossinver. About the middle of the last century, the termon lands of Ballaghmeehin were still farmed by a Mr. Meehin, a member of this ancient family. The angl. forms of this surname are apt to be confounded with those of Ó miαṁαċáin, which is an entirely different surname and much more widespread.

Ó moċαiṁein—I—MacKean; ' des. of moċαiṁein'; the name of an Oriel family who were anciently lords of Cṗioċ muʒṁoṗn, now the barony of Cremorne in Co. Monaghan; very rare.

Ó moċáin—I—*O Mochane, O Moghane, O Muoghane, O Moughan, O Moone*, Moghan, Mohan, Moughan, Moohan, Moan, Moen, Mowen, Moon, Mahon, Maughan, *Voghane*, Vaughan; ' des. of moċán' (a 'pet' form of some name commencing with moċ-, early); also Ó mαċáin, q.v.; the name (1) of a family of Cinel Ianna, in the diocese of Kilmacduagh, who are still numerous in Co. Galway, where they generally anglicise the name Mahon; (v. Ó mαċáin); and (2) of an ecclesiastical family—a branch of the Ui Fiachrach—in Co. Sligo, who were erenaghs of Killaraght, in the

barony of Coolavin, and keepers of the cross of St.
Attracta. They were great patrons of learning.
Many of them were distinguished ecclesiastics. Gregory
O Mochain was Archbishop of Tuam in the early part
of the 14th century. Ó Moċáin is now a fairly
common surname all through the South of Ireland,
as well as in Connacht. In Munster, it is generally
angl. Vaughan, a form evidently derived from the
gen. case Uí Moċáin. Cf. the old angl. form Voghane.

Ó MOĊÓIR, Ó MOĊÓIRȜe—I—*O Mucory*, Early, Earley,
Eardley; short forms of Ó Maoṫmoċóirȝe, q.v.;
very common in the spoken language.

Ó MOĊTA—I—*O Moght, O Mought*, Moughty; 'des. of
Moċta' (from 'moċt,' great); very rare.

Ó MOȜRÁIN—I—*O Mourane, O Mouran*, O'Moran,
Moran; 'des. of Muȝrón' (slave-seal); a corruption
of Ó Muȝróin, q.v.

Ó MÓIRÍN—I—*O Morine, O Moren*, *Moreen*, Morin,
Moren, (Moran); 'des. of Móirín' (dim. of mór,
great); a var. of Ó Móráin, q.v.

Ó MOITÍÐe—?—*O Mohedie*, Mahedy, Mahady; a rare
Connacht surname. I cannot trace its origin.

Ó MONȜAÐÁIN—I—*O Mongevaine*, Mongavan, Mungavan, Mungavin; 'des of Monȝḃán' (white hair);
an old Clare surname.

Ó MONȜAIȜ—I—Mongey, Mungay, Mungey; 'des. of
Monȝaċ' (hairy); a Mayo surname. Ó Monȝaċáin,
its diminutive, occurs in the Four Masters, A.D. 1168.

Ó MONȜÁIN—I—*O Mongane*, Mongan, Mangan, Mangin,
Mongon, (Mannion, Manning), &c.; 'des. of Monȝán'
(dim. of monȝaċ, hairy); the name of at least three
distinct families, seated respectively in Cork, Mayo
and Fermanagh. In the 16th century, it was not
uncommon in Galway, Clare, Kerry, Tipperary,
Kildare and Wexford. It is now generally angl.
Mangan, but Mongan, which is nearer the original, is
still preserved in Mayo and other parts of Ireland.
Ó Muinȝeáin (q.v.) is an attenuated form.

Ó MÓRÁIN—I—*O Moraine, O Morane, O Moran*, Moran;

'des. of **móɼán**' (dim. of **móɼ**, great) ; the name of a branch of the Ui Fiachrach, in the present counties of Mayo and Sligo, who ruled over an extensive district on both sides of the river Moy, and were a highly respectable family. The chief resided at Ardnaree, near Ballina. This surname is to be distinguished from **Ó muɡɼóın** (q.v.), which is also angl. Moran. O'Moran was a common surname in the 16th century in all parts of Connacht and Leinster, and also in Ormond and Thomond.

Ó móɼbɑ—I—*O Mora, O Morey,* O'More, O'Moore, Morey, More, Moore ; 'des. of **móɼbɑ**' (majestic) ; the name of a distinguished Leinster family who were chiefs of Leix. Their chief fortress was at Dunamase, near Maryborough, the ruins of which still remain. The O'Mores make a remarkable figure in Irish history, having with conspicuous bravery defied for several centuries all the power of the English invaders to conquer their territory. Rory O'More, a celebrated chieftain in the reigns of Mary and Elizabeth, defeated them in many engagements ; and his son, Owney O'More, was a famous commander in the wars against Elizabeth. Perhaps no Irish family suffered greater cruelties at the hands of the English. In 1609, the remnant of the clan was transplanted to Kerry, where they were settled in the neighbourhood of Tarbert. Many of them, however, returned to their native territory, and the family is now well represented in Leinster.

Ó moɼɼuɑnɑıb—I—*O Moronie,* Murroney, Morooney, Moroney ; a corruption of **Ó mɑoıɼuɑnɑıb**, q.v. ; common in Clare, Limerick and Tipperary.

Ó moċɑıɼ—I—*O Mogher, O Moher,* Moher, (Moore) ; 'des. of **moċɑɼ**' (dark) ; an old Cork surname ; still extant, but extremely rare ; sometimes attenuated to **Ó muıċıɼ**.

Ó moċlɑ, Ó moċlɑıɡ—I—*O Mohele,* Mohilly, Moakley ; 'des. of **moċlɑċ**' (shaggy) ; the name of a family of Corca Laoighdhe who were seated near Dromaleague in South-West Cork.

Ó moτlaċáin—I—*O Mohilaghane, O Moholane,* (?) Mullane ; ' des. of moτlaċán ' (dim. of moτlaċ, shaggy) ; formerly a very common Munster surname. It was too common to have died out, and must be disguised under some strange angl. form, perhaps Mullane.

Ó muaoaiż, Moody.

Ó muanáin—I—*O Monane,* Moonan ; a northern pronunciation of Ó maonáin, q.v.

Ó mużróin—I—*O Morone,* O'Moran, Moran ; ' des. of mużrón ' (slave-seal) ; the name (1) of one of the chief families of Clann Chathail, a branch of the Siol Muireadhaigh, in the present Co. Roscommon ; and (2) of a branch of the Ui Maine, in Co. Galway, who were chiefs of Cruffon, an extensive district comprising the barony of Killyan and part of that of Ballymoe. The name has been long changed to Ó możráin (q.v.) and is now angl. Moran.

Ó muiże, Moy.

Ó muiτir, v. Ó moτair.

Ó muimneaċáin—I—*O Moyneghane, O Myneghane,* Mynahan, Minahan, Moynahan, Moynihan, Moynan, &c., Munster ; ' des. of muimneaċán ' (Munsterman) ; the name (1) of a family of the Ui Fiachrach in Erris, Co. Mayo, in which county it is still extant, but sometimes translated Munster ; and (2) a very common surname in Kerry and West Cork, where it is almost universally angl. Moynihan. V. Ó muimniż.

Ó muimniż—I—*O Moyney, O Moynig,* Moyney, Mooney; ' des. of muimneaċ ' (Munsterman) ; the name of a family of Corca Laoighdhe, in South-West Cork. It is not improbable that it has been changed in most instances to the dim. Ó muimneaċáin (q.v.) now so common in West Cork and Kerry.

Ó muineaċáin—I—Menehan, Menahan, Meenehan, (Monahan), &c., Thornton ; an attenuated form of Ó manaċáin, q.v. It is popularly supposed to be connected with ' muineaċ,' thorny, and is consequently in some places ' translated ' Thornton.

Ó muineóg—I—*O Monoge*, Manogue, Minogue, Minnock, Mannix ; ' des. of muineóg ' (dim. of manac, a monk); an attenuated form of Ó manóg, q.v. ; a common surname in Clare and Offaly. Cléiṗcen Ó muineóg was Bishop of Leighlin in the 11th century.

Ó muinġeáin—I—*O Muynghan*, Mingane, Meenhan, Meenin,(Mangan); an attenuated form of Ó monġáin,q.v.

Ó muirceartaiġ—I—*O Morierty, O Murtagh*, Moriarty, Murtagh, Murtaugh ; ' des. of muirceartac ' (sea-director, expert navigator) ; the name (1) of a Kerry family who were anciently chiefs of Aos Aisde, a district lying probably along the river Mang ; and (2) of a Meath family still numerous in that county and in Monaghan, where it is angl. Murtagh. In Munster it is always angl. Moriarty.

Ó muireaḃaiġ—I—*O Murrey, O Murry, O Murrihy*, Murry, Murray, Murrihy ; ' des. of muireaḃac ' (seaman, mariner, also a lord) ; the name of several distinct families in different parts of Ireland. Of these, the Uí muireaḃaiġ, or O'Murrys, of Mayo, Roscommon, Westmeath and Cork were dynastic families who anciently ruled over extensive districts, but they have all been long dispossessed and dispersed. There were also many distinguished ecclesiastics of the name. Ó muiriġċe is a common pronunciation. Cf. O Murrihy above.

Ó muireaġáin—I—*O Murrigane, O Moregane, O Morgan*, Murrigan, Murricane, Merrigan, Maragan, Morgan ; ' des. of muireaġán ' (dim. of some name commencing with muir-) ; the name of one of the chief families of Teffia, in the present counties of Westmeath and Longford, and sometimes lords of all that district. About the beginning of the 12th century, they disappeared from history, and apparently dispersed to different parts of Ireland. In the 16th century, the name was most numerous in Down and Armagh. It is still common in many parts of Ireland.

Ó muireáin—I—*O Murrane, O Murran*, Murrane, Murran, Murrin, Murren, Morrin, (Moran) ; ' des. of

Muiɼeán ' (dim. of some name commencing with
Muiɼ-) ; possibly a var. of Ó Muiɼeaȝáin, q.v. ; the
name of a family of Ui Fiachrach, in the west of Co.
Mayo ; also common in many other parts of Ireland.

Ó muiʀȝeasa—I—*O Murrissa, O Morisa, O Morrissy*,
Morissy, Morrissey, Morrissy, &c., (Morris, Morrison) ;
' des. of Muiɼȝeaɼ ' (sea-choice) ; the name of a branch
of the Ui Fiachrach who were formerly chiefs of a
district on the southern shore of Sligo Bay, in the
barony of Tireragh. It is highly probable that there
were several other distinct families so called, as the
name, both in the present form and as Ó Muiɼȝiɼ, is
common in most parts of Ireland.

Ó muiʀȝeasáin—I—*O Murghesan, O Morrisane, O
Morrison, O Brisane*, Morrison, Briceson, Bryson,
(Price) ; ' des. of Muiɼȝeaɼán ' (dim. of Muiɼȝeaɼ) ;
an old Donegal surname ; pronounced Ó Bɼioɼáin
and angl. Briceson and Bryson. In Co. Mayo, the
pronunciation is Ó Pɼioɼáin, angl. Price.

Ó muiʀȝis—I—*O Morish, O Morris, O Morice*, Morris,
Morice, &c. ; ' des. of Muiɼȝeaɼ ' (sea-choice) ; a var.
of Ó Muiɼȝeaɼa, q.v.

Ó muiʀín—I—*O Morrine, O Murrin, O Murren*, Murrin,
Murren, Morrin, (Moran) ; ' des. of Muiɼín ' (dim. of
some name commencing with Muiɼ-) ; a var. of
Muiɼeáin, q.v.

Ó muiʀiȝte—I—*O Murrihey*, Murrihy, Murry, Murray,
common in the spoken language for Ó Muiɼeaȯaiȝ, q.v.

Ó muiʀneacáin—I—*O Murnyghan*, Murnaghan ; ' des.
of Muiɼneacán ' (dim. of muiɼneac, loveable) ; a rare
Ulster surname.

Ó muʀcaȯa—I—*O Morchowe, O Moroghoe, O Morphy*,
O'Muracha, O'Murphy, Murchoe, Murphy, Morphy ;
' des. of Muɼcaȯ ' (sea-warrior) ; the name (1) of a
family of Cinel Eoghain, who were chiefs of Siol
Aodha, in the present Co. Tyrone ; (2) of a family of
the Ui Fiachrach who were chiefs of a district on the
southern shore of Sligo Bay, now comprised in the
parishes of Skreen and Templeboy, but were dis-

possessed and dispersed in the 13th century ; (3) of a branch of the Ui Ceinnsealaigh, in Co. Wexford, who were chiefs of Ui Feilme, which comprised the barony of Ballaghkeen, in the east of that county, and formed a distinct clan down to the early part of the 17th century. This family is now very numerous throughout Leinster. It is not improbable that, in addition to those mentioned, there are several other families of the name in Ireland.

Ó muRcáin—I—*O Murchan, O Morghane, O Moraghan,* Morahan, Morohan, Murchan, Morkan, Morkin, Murkin, (Morgan), Morran, Morrin, (Moran) ; ' des. of mu-ncaoán ' (dim. of muncaoó, sea-warrior) ; the name (1) of an Offaly family who were formerly chiefs of Magh Aoife, in the barony of East Offaly, and are still numerous in Kildare and Offaly, but often disguised as Morrins and Morans ; and (2) of a family of Ui Maine in Connacht. The name is not uncommon in Co. Leitrim.

Ó muRgail—I—*O Moryle,* Morell ; ' des. of mungal' (sea-valour) ; a var. of Ó mungaile, q.v. ; very rare.

Ó muRgaile—I—*O Morchaile, O Moryly, O Morely, O Marlie,* Morrolly, Marrilly, Morley, Marley ; ' des. of mungal ' (sea-valour) ; a scattered surname ; found chiefly in Donegal and Mayo. See Ó muncuile.

Ó muRnáin—I—Murnane, Murnain, Murnan, Mornan, (Warren) ; a corruption of Ó manannáin, q.v. In recent years the angl. form has been absurdly changed to Warren in the neighbourhood of Kenmare.

Ó muRcuile—I—*O Murhilly, O Morhelly, O Murrilly, O Murley,* Murhilla, Murley, Morrolly, Morley, (Hurley) ; ' des. of muncuile ' (sea-tide) ; probably the same as Ó mungaile, q.v. ; a very common surname in Co. Cork where, however, it is now generally disguised under the angl. form of Hurley.

Ó naoióeanáin—I—*O Nenane, O Nynane,* Nynane, Neenan, Neenin, (Nunan, Noonan) ; ' des. of naoióeanán ' (dim. of naoióean, an infant) ; a rare Munster

surname ; sometimes disguised under the angl. form
of Nunan or Noonan.

Ó nᴀ́ʀᴀᴅᴀıᵹ—I—*O Narie, O Nary*, Nary, Neary, Nery ;
' des. of nᴀ́ᴘᴀᴅᴀċ ' (good, noble) ; a common surname
in Connacht and parts of Leinster.

Ó nᴀ́ċᴀn—II—*O Nahane, O Nahan, O Nane*, Nawn ;
' des. of Nathan ' ; also written Ó nᴀ́ᴀn ; the name of
an old ecclesiastical family in Tirconnell. Ċomᴀ́ʀ
Ó nᴀ́ᴀn was Bishop of Raphoe from 1299 to 1306 ;
and the Four Masters, under the year 1336, record
the death of Ċᴘıonóıċ Ó nᴀ́ᴀn, chief ollave of many
sciences, and of civil and canon law. Some of the
family at a later period removed to Cork. The name
is still extant, but exceedingly rare.

Ó neᴀċᴛᴀın—I—*O Naghtan, O Neaghten*, O'Naughton,
Naghten, Naghton, Naughtan, Naughten, Naughton,
Nocton, Natton, (Norton), &c. ; ' des. of neᴀċᴛᴀn '
(bright, pure) ; the name (1) of a Dalcassian family,
of the same stock as the O'Quinns and O'Hartigans,
still numerous in Thomond ; and (2) of a branch of
the Ui Maine in Galway and Roscommon. This
family derives its descent from Fiachra Fionn, grandson of Maine Mór, the eponymous ancestor of the Ui
Maine, and was closely akin to that of Ó mᴀoʟᴀʟᴀıᴅ
(q.v.), both families forming originally one clan under
the common designation of Ui Fiachrach Finn. The
O'Neachtains were chiefs of Maonmhagh, the plain
lying around Loughrea, until about the time of the
Anglo-Norman invasion, when they removed to the
Feadha, or Fews, of Athlone, where they formed a
distinct clan down to the reign of Elizabeth.

Ó néıᴅe, v. Ó nıᴀᴅ.

Ó neıᵹıʟʟ—I—*O Nehill, O Nihill, O Nyhill*, O'Nial,
Nehill, Nihill, Nyhill ; ' des. of Nigel ' (a Norse form
of nıᴀʟʟ) ; the name of an old Thomond family, still
well known about Limerick. The family is said,
but perhaps erroneously, to be a branch of the O'Neills
of Thomond ; it is more probably of Norse descent.
The name, however, is really the same as Ó néıʟʟ.

Ó néill—I—O'Neill, O'Neal, Neill, Neale, &c. ; ' des. of ℿɪᴀʟʟ' (champion) ; the name of several distinct families in different parts of Ireland, of which the following are the chief :—(1) Ó néill of Ulster. This family, which is one of the most illustrious in Ireland, derives its name and descent from ℿɪᴀʟʟ Ʒʟúnᴅᴜʙ, King of Ireland, who fell fighting against the Danes, near Dublin, in 919. His grandson, ᴅoṁnᴀʟʟ Ó néill, who is mentioned in the Annals at the year 943, was the first person to bear the surname of Ó néill. The O'Neills were the head family of the Cinel Eoghain, the most celebrated of all the Irish clans, whose territory, known as Tir Eoghain, from Eoghan, son of Niall of the Nine Hostages, ancestor of the clan, comprised the present counties of Tyrone and Derry, together with a large portion of Donegal. As chiefs of Tir Eoghain and Kings of Ulster, they make a most distinguished figure in Irish history from the 11th to the 17th century. In the reign of Henry VIII, Conn Ó néill, the then head of the clan, was created Earl of Tyrone. Shane the Proud and Hugh, Earl of Tyrone, in the reign of Elizabeth, and Sir Phelim and Owen Roe, at the period of the Confederation, were the last celebrated bearers of the name. Several of the O'Neills have been distinguished in the service of continental powers. A powerful branch of this family, known as Clann Aodha Bhuidhe, settled in the 14th century in Antrim and Down. (2) Ó néill of Thomond. The head of this family, which is of Dalcassian origin and descended, according to Keating, from Aodh Caomh, King of Cashel (A.D. 571-601), was chief of Clann Dealbhaoith, in the present barony of Bunratty, in the south of Co. Clare. The O'Nihills and Creaghs are, according to local tradition, branches of this family. (3) Ó néill of Leinster, an ancient family in Carlow and Wicklow. The patrimony of this family was Magh-dá-chon, now angl. Moyacomb, a parish in the barony of Rathvilly, Co. Carlow, and extending into the barony of Shillelagh, in Co. Wicklow, also called Farren O'Neill. Ó néiʟʟ of Magh-dá-chon is mentioned in the Annals of the Four Masters, A D 1088, as having fallen in a battle fought near Dublin, between the men of Munster and Leinster. (4) Ó néiʟʟ of Deisi. This family was seated in the south of the present Co. Tipperary.

Ó neoċaʟʟaiʒ—?—Nohally, Nohilly, Noakley. This surname is in use in the neighbourhood of Shrule, but I have failed to trace its origin.

Ó miaʋ—I—*O Nee, O Nea, O Ney,* O'Knee, Nee, Knee, (Needham, Neville) ; ' des. of miа ' (champion) ; the name of an ancient Kerry family who were originally seated in the neighbourhood of Tralee, but in later times were erenaghs of Knockpatrick, near Foynes, in Co. Limerick. The name is now most common in West Galway, where it is sometimes angl. Needham. In Kerry and Limerick, where it is now very rare, it is always angl. Neville.

Ó miaʋóʒ—I—(Newcombe) ; probably a var. of Ó miaʋ, q.v. ; in use in Co. Mayo. I can find no early instance.

Ó maʟʟaʒáin—I—*O Neligane,* Neligan, Nelligan ; ' des. of miaʟʟaʒán ' (dim. of miaʟʟ) ; a rare surname ; found chiefly in Cork and Kerry.

Ó maʟʟáin—I—*O Nillane, O Neilane, O Nelane, O Neylane,* Nilan, Nelan, Neilan, Nealon, Neylan, Neylon, Nilon, Niland, Neiland, Neyland, Neelan, Neeland, Neelands, &c. ; ' des. of miaʟʟán ' (dim. of miaʟʟ) ; a Thomond surname ; now also common in Connacht.

Ó maċáin—I—Neehan, Nyhane ; a Co. Cork surname ; probably a var. of Ó miaʋ, q.v. Cf. Ó miaʋóʒ. I can find no early instance.

Ó nuaʋan—I—*O Nowan, O Nowne,* Noone, (Noonan), Lambe ; ' des. of nuaʋa ' (the name of an ancient sea divinity) ; the name of a Sligo family of the race of Cairbre, son of Niall of the Nine Hostages. This family anciently possessed the district of Callraighe Laithimh, nearly co-extensive with the present parish of Calry, near the town of Sligo. The name is still veɪy common in Connacht. In the spoken language, as I have heard it, the final n is slender.

Ó nuaóat—I—*O Noude*, Noud, Nowd, Knowd ; ' des. of nuaóa ' ; the same as Ó nuaóan, q.v. ; a rare Donegal surname.

Ó nuallacáin—I—*O Nolloghaine*, (Nolan) ; ' des. of uallacán ' (dim. of uallac, proud). The form of this surname is peculiar, being really the gen. plural of Ó hUallacáin, q.v. With names of women it is quite regular, e.g., Óɲígɪo Ní Uallacáin.

Ó nuallán—I—*O Nowlane, O Nolane, O Noland*, O'Nowlan, O'Nolan, Nowlan, Nolan, Noland, &c. ; ' des. of nuallán ' (dim. of nuall, noble, famous) ; the name (1) of a numerous and respectable family in Leinster, the head of which was chief of Fothart Feadha, now the barony of Forth, in Co. Carlow, and had the privilege of inaugurating MacMurrough as King of Leinster ; and (2) of a family of Corca Laoighdhe, in south west Cork.

Ó nuanáin—I—*O Nownan, O Nonan*, Noonane, Noonan, Nunan, Newnan, (Noone) ; a corruption of Ó hIon-ṁaɪneáin, q.v. In Connacht, it may possibly be a dim. of Ó nuaóan, q.v.

Ó nútáin, Newton ; in use in the spoken language of Co. Cork.

Ó páɪoín—V—Payton ; a corruption in Co. Roscommon of Mac páɪoín, q.v.

Ó peatáin—II—*O Petane, O Pettane, O Pattane, O Patten*, Peton, Paton, Patten, Patton, Payton, Peyton ; ' des. of peatán ' (dim. of Patrick) ; the name of an old Ulster family, mentioned by MacFirbis among the families of Cinel Eoghain. They belonged to Cinel Moain, a subdivision of Cinel Eoghain, and were apparently seated in the barony of Raphoe, in the present Co. Donegal. The name occurs as early as the year 1178, when the Four Masters record the slaying of Muircheartach O Peatain in revenge for the death of Randal O Cathain. It is now common in

Mayo and North Galway, as well as in Donegal, but the pronunciation is Ó Ριοτáιη or Ó Ριτεáιη.

Ó Ριοτáιη, Ó Ριτεáιη, v. Ó Ρεατáιη.

Ó Ρρéιτ—XIII—*O Praye*, O'Pray, O'Prey, Prey, Pray; doubtless a corruption of ᴀ' Ρρéιτ, i.e., of the cattle-spoil; a rare Co. Down surname.

Ó Ρριοςáιη—I—Price; a corruption of Ó Μυιρξεαρáιη, q.v.; current in Co. Mayo. Cf. Ó Ϸρίοράιη.

Ó Ρροιηητιξε—XIII—*O Prenty*, *O Prontye*, Prunty, Brunty; doubtless a corruption of ηᴀ Ρροιηητιξε, i.e., of the refectory, or dining-room. Cf. Ó Ρρéιτ; a rare Ulster surname.

Ó Ραϸᴀρτᴀιξ—I—*O Roverty*, O'Rafferty, Rafferty, Raverty, Ravery; a var. of Ó Ροϸᴀρτᴀιξ, q.v.; now generally changed to Ó Ραιτϸεᴀρτᴀιξ, q.v.

Ó Ραξᴀιll—I—*O Raghell*, *O Reile*, *O Ryle*, *O Reale*, *O Raile*, O'Rahill, Rahill, Reihill, Ryle, Ryall, Rall, Rail, Riall, Real, Reel, &c.; a shortened form of Ó Ραξᴀllᴀιξ, q.v.; sometimes also pronounced Ó Ρáξᴀιll, Ó Ραιξιll, Ó Ρáιξιll, Ó Ραοξᴀιll, Ó Ρειξιll, &c.

Ó Ρáξᴀιll, v. Ó Ραξᴀιll.

Ó Ραξᴀιllιξ, Ó Ραξᴀllᴀιξ—I—*O Reyly*, *O Riellie*, *O Realy*, *O Reely*, O'Reilly, O'Reiley, O'Rielly, O'Realley, Reilly, Rielly, Really, Realy, Reely, Riley, &c.; 'des. of Ραξᴀllᴀᴄ'; also pronounced Ó Ρáξᴀllᴀιξ, Ó Ραιξιllιξ, Ó Ραοξᴀllᴀιξ, &c., and sometimes shortened to Ó Ραξᴀιll, &c., q.v. The O'Reillys, who are the same stock as the O'Rourkes, were chiefs of Breifney-O'Reilly, which originally comprised the greater part of the present Co. Cavan. In the course of the 13th and 14th centuries they became very powerful and extended their dominion over the whole Co. Cavan and parts of Meath and Westmeath; and they were sometimes chiefs of all Breifney. They maintained their independence as a clan down to the time of James I, and continued in possession of considerable property until the Cromwellian confiscations. Many of the O'Reillys attained to high ecclesiastical rank, no fewer than five of the name having been Primates of Armagh. The name is now one of the most common in Ireland, but owing to its numerous dialectical variations is variously anglicised in different parts of the country.

Ó Rágallaig—I—*O Rhawley, O Raly*, Rawley, Rally, (Raleigh, Rawleigh) ; a var. of Ó Ragallaig, q.v.

Ó Raigill, Ó Ráigill, v. Ó Ragaill.

Ó Raigill—I—Reckle ; a var. of Ó Raigill, q.v.

Ó Raigillig, v. Ó Ragallaig.

Ó Raigillig—I—*O Reigly*, Rigley ; a var. of Ó Ragallaig, q.v. For radical ʒ, cf. Ó Raigne ; also Mac Raigillig, angl. Crigley.

Ó Raigne, Ó Ráigne—II—*O Raine, O Ryney*, Ryney, Reyney, Reany, Rainey, Raney, &c. ; ' des. of Rayny ' (a pet form of Reginald or Reynold) ; pronounced Ó Ráigne in Co. Mayo. See Ó Raigne, wjhch is a variant.

Ó Raigne—II—*O Regne, O Regnie, O Rigney*, Rigney ; a var. of Ó Raigne, q.v. ; current in Donegal and Offaly. The O'Rigneys of the latter county were followers of Mac Cocláin, in the barony of Garrycastle, where the name is still common.

Ó Raitbeartaig—I—O'Rafferty, Rafferty, Raverty, Ravery ; a corruption of Ó Rabartaig or Ó Robartaig, q.v. The angl. form Ravery is due to the aspiration of the t of the final syllable.

Ó Raitile—I—*O Rathyly, O Rahillie*, O'Rahilly, Rahilly, (O'Reilly, Reilly) ; ' des. of *Raitile* ' ; the name of a family of Cinel Eoghain in Ulster, descended, according to MacFirbis, from Echean, son of Eoghan, son of Niall of the Nine Hostages ; but for several centuries it has been almost peculiar to Munster, where it is found chiefly in Cork, Kerry and Limerick. To this family belonged the greatest of our modern Irish poets, Egan O'Rahilly, whose poems have been published by the Irish Texts Society.

*Ó Raitne, Raheny, Ranny ; perhaps a var. of Ó Raigne, q.v. ; very rare.

Ó Raoġaill—I—*O Reale*, Real, Reel, Riall. V. Ó Raġaill.

Ó Raoġallaiġ—I—*O Realy*, *O Reely*, O'Realley, Really, Realy, Reely, &c. V. Ó Raġallaiġ.

Ó Reaḃaċáin, v. Ó Roḃaċáin.

Ó Reaċair—I—Raher; a var. of Ó Freaċair, or Ó Fearċair (q.v.), owing to the aspiration of the initial f.

Ó Reaċtaḃair—I—*O Raghtore*, *O Raghter*, Rafter, Wrafter, Raftiss; a var. of Ó Reaċtaḃra, q.v. The peculiar Kilkenny pronunciation of slender r is seen in the angl. form Raftiss.

Ó Reaċtaḃra—I—*O Raghtoury*, Raftery; 'des. of Reaċtaḃra' (reaċt, law, decree, and aḃra, fringe, border); also Ó Reaċtaḃair, q.v.; sometimes written Ó Reaċtaire, and so pronounced in Co. Mayo.

Ó Reaċtaġáin—I—*O Raghtagan*, Raghtigan, Ractigan, Ratican, Ratigan, Rattigan, Rhategan, Rhatigan, &c.; ' des. of Reaċtaġán' (dim. of reaċt, law, decree); the name of an ecclesiastical family in Co. Roscommon, who were coarbs of St. Finnen, in the parish of Clooncraff, near Elphin.

Ó Reaċtaire—I—Raftery. V. Ó Reaċtaḃra.

Ó Reaċtnín—I—*O Rachnane*, Raghneen, Rochneen, Roughneen, (Rochford); a rare Mayo surname. The older form was probably Ó Reaċtnáin.

Ó Réada—I—*O Readie*, Reidy, Ready, Readdy; a var. in the spoken language of Ó Riada, q.v.

Ó Réaġáin—I—*O Regaine*, O'Regan, Regan; a common var. in the spoken language of Ó Riaġáin, q.v.

Ó Reannaċáin—I—O'Renahan, Ranaghan, Reneghan, Renihan, Rinaghan, Rinahan, Rinihan, Ranahan, Renehan, Renahan, Ronaghan, &c., Ferns, Ferrons ' des. of Reannaċán' (dim of reannaċ, spear-like); Cf. Maġ Reannaċáin.

Ó Reiḋrí—II—*O Reyrye*; a var. in the spoken language of Ó Ruaiḋrí, q.v.

Ó Réiġín—I—*O Reggine*, *O Regin*, O'Regan, Regan; a var. of Ó Riaġáin, q.v.

Ó Reiġill, v. Ó Raġaill.

Ó Riaḃaiġ—I—*O Revoay, O Reogh, O Reogh, O Ria, O Ree*, Reavey, Ravy, Reigh, Rea, Ray ; ' des. of Riaḃac ' (brindled).

Ó Riaḋa—I—*O Ryada, O Ryedy, O Readie*, Reidy, Ready, Readdy ; ' des. of Riaḋa ' (tamed, trained) ; the name of a Dalcassian family, now numerous in Clare and Kerry ; sometimes pronounced Ó Réaḋa.

Ó Riaġáin—I—*O Riegaine, O Regane*, O'Regan, Regan ; ' des. of Riaġán ' ; the name of two distinct families, one seated in ancient Meath, and the other in Thomond. The O'Regans of Meath were a branch of the southern Ui Neill and one of the four tribes of Tara. Before the Anglo-Norman invasion, they were lords of South Breagh in Meath and the north of the present Co. Dublin, and appparently a powerful family. They took a leading part in the wars against the Danes. The annalists, under the year 1029, record a notable triumph of Maṫġaṁain Ó Riaġáin, King of Breagh, over the foreigners, when he made prisoner Amhlaoibh, son of Sitric, King of Dublin, and only released him on payment of an enormous ransom, including the celebrated sword of Carlus. The O'Regans were dispossessed soon after the Anglo-Norman invasion and dispersed through Ireland. The O'Regans cf Thomond are a Dalcassian family said to be descended from Riaġán, son of Donncuan, the brother of Brian Boru. The O'Regans are now numerous all over Ireland. The name is often pronounced Ó Réaġáin.

Ó Riaġain, Ó Riain—I—*O Rian*, O'Ryan, Ryan ; ' des. of Riaġan,' or ' Rian ' ; the name of a Carlow family who were lords of Uí Dróna, the present barony of Idrone, and are now numerous through Leinster ; to be distinguished from Ó Maoilriain of Munster and Ó Ruaiḋín of Connacht, which are both now incorrectly angl. O'Ryan or Ryan.

Ó Riṁeaḋa—I—*O Rive, O Rives*, Reeves ; ' des. of Riṁeaḋ ' (calculator) ; the name of an ancient family of the Ards of Co. Down ; always very rare, and now found chiefly in Co. Limerick. The Four Masters, under the year 1004, record the death of Maeltpigve Ua Rimeava, Abbot of Iona.

Ó Rinn—I—*O Rinne, O Ring,* Rinn, Rynn, Ring, Reen, Wrynn, Wren, Wrenn; 'des. of Reann' (spear); the name (1) of an old Cork family, a branch of the Ui Macaille, from whom the barony of Imokilly got its name; and (2) of a Roscommon family, still represented in that county.

Ó Ríogbarváin, Ó Ríorváin—I—*O Riverdan, O Riourdane, O Reerdan,* O'Riordan, Riordan, Reardan, Reardon, &c.; 'des. of Ríogbarváin' (royal-bard); written Ó Ríogbpaváin by Keating; the name of a family originally of Ely-O'Corroll, in the present Offaly, and probably a branch of the family of O'Carroll of that district, deriving its name and descent from Ríogbarváin, son of Cúcoirne (Ó Ceanbaill), lord of Ely, who fell at the battle of Sliabh gCrot, in the Glen of Aherlow, in the year 1058. In 1576, Gaven O Rewrdane was a freeholder in Ely-O'Carroll and one of Sir William O'Carroll's most important followers. The name appears about the same time in Leix and Kilkenny, but the bulk of the family had long before removed to Cork and Limerick. In 1597, Maurice O'Riordan of Croome was attainted and his lands granted to George Sherlocke. The O'Riordans are now very numerous in Cork, Limerick and Kerry.

Ó Robacáin—I—*O Rachaine, O Rawghan, O Rowghane, O Roaghan,* Roughan, Roohan, Ruhan, Rohan, Rowan; 'des. of Robacán' (crafty); also written Ó Reabacán; the name of an ecclesiastical family, anciently attached to the monasteries of Swords, Co. Dublin, and Lismore, Co. Waterford. In the 16th and 17th centuries, it was not uncommon in Co. Clare, where members of the family appear to have been stewards to the O'Gradys. In 1641, Donogh oge O'Roughan and Charles O'Roughan were proprietors of the townland of Sunnagh, in the parish of Inchicroman. The name is now rare and scattered, and its angl. forms cannot always be distinguished from those of Ó Ruaḋacáin, q.v.

Ó ROḊARTAIṠ—I—*O Roverty, O Rowarty,* Roarty; 'des. of Roḃaṛtaċ'; also written Ó Raḃaṛtaiṡ (q.v.), and generally corrupted to Ó Raitḃeaṛtaiṡ, q.v.; the name of at least two distinct families, anciently located respectively in Tirconnell and Sligo. The former family were coarbs of St. Columcille on Tory Island, off the north coast of Donegal; the latter, who are of Ui Fiachrach race, were seated in the parish of Skreen, in the barony of Tireragh, where they had extensive possessions. They are named by MacFirbis among "the pillars of Skrin and the props of the Kings of Ui Fiachrach." They were dispossessed by the Scottish settlers in the early part of the 17th century. There was also a Meath family of the name, but it was probably a branch of that of Tirconnell.

Ó ROḊAĊÁIN—I—*O Rodeghan,* Rodaughan, Rudihan, Rudican, Redahan, Redehan, (Redington, Reddington); 'des. of Roḋaċán' (dim. of Roḋaċ); the name of an ecclesiastical family in Co. Leitrim, who were coarbs of St. Caillin at Fenagh; still common in Connacht, but often shortened to Ó Roḋaiṡ, and sometimes disguised under the angl. form of Redington or Reddington.

Ó ROḊAIṠ—I—*O Roddy, O Ruddy, O Reddie,* Roddy, Ruddy, Reddy, &c.; 'des. of Roḋaċ' (der. of roḋ, strong); the name of a branch of the Ui Maine in Co. Galway; also a var. of Ó Roḋaċáin (q.v.) in Co. Leitrim.

Ó ROḊÁIN—I—*O Rodane, O Ruddane, O Rudden,* Rodan, Roden, Rodin, Rodden, Rudden, Ruddon, Reddan, Reddin; 'des. of Roḋán' (dim. of roḋ, strong); an old surname in Donegal, Monaghan and Clare. The O'Rodains of the last-named county were stewards to the O'Briens and MacNamaras, and held considerable property in the neighbourhood of Six-mile-bridge down to the Cromwellian confiscations.

Ó Roṡallaiġ—I—*O Rwollea, Rolley*, Rowley, Rawley, (Raleigh) ; ' des. of Roṡallaċ ' ; a var. of Ó Raṡallaiġ, q.v. Cf. Mac Roṡallaiġ.

Ó Roiḋeaċáin—I—Redahan, Redehan, (Redington), &c. ; an attenuated form of Ó Roḋaċáin, q.v. ; common in Mayo and Galway.

Ó Roiḋiṡ—I—*O Reddie*, Reddy ; an attenuated form of Ó Roḋaiṡ, q.v.

Ó Roileaċáin—I—*O Rellakan, O Relligan*, Relehan, Relihan ; probably ' des. of Roṡallaċán ' (dim. of Roṡallaċ), and an attenuated form of Ó Roṡallaċáin. ' Munter Raulaghan ' appears as a family name in Inishowen at the beginning of the 17th century, and about the same time O Rellakan, or O Relligan, was in use in Co. Antrim. The name is now peculiar to Co. Kerry, whither, apparently, the family migrated from Co. Antrim.

Ó Roiċleáin—I—(?) *O Rylan*, Roland, Rowland, Rowley ; an attenuated form of Ó Roċláin, q.v.

Ó Rónáin—I—*O Ronane, O Ronayne*, Ronane, Ronayne, Ronan ; ' des. of Rónán ' (dim. of rón, a seal) ; the name of several distinct families in different parts of Ireland, as (1) Ó Rónáin of Longford, who were chiefs of Cairbre Gabhra, in the barony of Granard, until about the period of the Anglo-Norman invasion, when they were dispossessed by the O'Farrells and dispersed through Ireland ; (2) Ó Rónáin of Mayo, a branch of the Ui Fiachrach ; (3) Ó Rónáin of Dublin, anciently erenaghs of Clondalkin ; and (4) Ó Rónáin of Cork, where the name is now most common.

Ó Rosna—I—Rossney ; ' des. of Rorna ' ; the name of an old family of Corca Laoighdhe, in South-West Cork ; still extant in West Kerry, but extremely rare.

Ó Roċláin—I—*Roolane*, Roland, Rowland, (Rowley) ; perhaps originally Ó Roṡalláin, a var. of Ó Roṡallaċáin (v. Ó Roileaċáin above) ; the angl. form Rowley would go to show that Ó Roṡallaiġ (q.v.) was a variant ; the name of a Connacht family, formerly chiefs of Coolcarney, in the barony of Gallen, Co.

Mayo ; still common in Mayo and Sligo, pronounced Ó Roiċleáin, q.v.

Ó Ruaḋaċáin—I—Roughan, Roohan, Rohan, Rowan, (Rogan), &c. ; ' des. of Ruaḋaċán ' (dim. of ruaḋ, red) ; a var. of Ó Ruaḋagáin, q.v. ; common in West Ulster and Connacht. Its angl. forms cannot always be distinguished from those of Ó Roḃaċáin, q.v.

Ó Ruaḋagáin—I—O Rogane, Rogan ; ' des. of Ruaḋagán ' (a dim. of ruaḋ, red) ; also written Ó Ruaḋaċáin, q.v. ; the name of an Oriel family who were chiefs of Ui Eathach, or Tuath Eathach, a district embracing the present barony of Armagh ; common in Ulster and Connacht.

Ó Ruaḋáin—I—O Ruane, O Rowane, O Roan, Ruane, Rouane, Roane, Ruan, Roan, Roon, Rowan, Rewan, Royan, (Ryan) ; ' des. of Ruaḋán ' (dim. of ruaḋ, red) ; also Ó Ruaiḋín ; the name (1) of an old Mayo family of the Ui Fiachrach, who possessed a district lying between Newbrook and Killeen, to the north of Ballinrobe ; and (2) of an old Galway family of the Ui Maine race. No fewer than seven of the name were bishops of various sees in Connacht, in the 12th and 13th centuries. The name is still very common in that province, generally angl. Ruane, but sometimes disguised as Ryan.

Ó Ruaḋraic—II—O Roreke, O Rorike, Roragh, Rorke, Rourke, &c. ; ' des. of Ruaḋrac ' (the Norse Hrothrekr) an older form of Ó Ruairc, q.v. ; the name of a family who were anciently proprietors of Lia Con, in the barony of Tireragh, Co. Sligo, and of another, the head of which was erenagh of Termon Feichin ; now almost completely absorbed in the modern form Ó Ruairc, q.v.

Ó Ruaiḋ—I—O Rowe, O Rewe, Rowe, Roe, (Ormond) ; ' des. of Ruaḋ ' (red) ; an old surname on the confines of Cork and Waterford ; now angl. Ormond in the latter county, owing to its similarity in sound to Urṁuṁa, the Irish name of Ormond, or East Munster.

Ó Ruaiḋín—I—O Ruyne, O Royn, O Roen, Rouine,

Royan, Rowen, (Ruane, O'Ryan, Ryan) ; ' des. of
Ruaiḋín ' (dim. of ruaḋ, red) ; the same as Ó Ruaḋáin,
q.v., both forms being used by the same family, and
equally common in Connacht. Some of the name
have been long settled in Leinster.

Ó RUAIḊRÍ—II—*O Roury, O Rorie,* Rory, (Rogers,
Rodgers) ; ' des. of Ruaiḋrí ' (Norse Hrothrekr) ; the
name originally of a Meath family, but long dispersed
and now very rare. In Munster, it is pronounced
Ó Reiḋrí, q.v.

Ó RUAIRC—II—*O Ruairc, O Rowarke,* O'Rourke,
O'Roarke, O'Rorke, Rourke, Roarke, Rorke, &c. ;
' des. of Ruairc ' (older Ruaḋrac, from Norse Hrothrekr) ; the name of several distinct families in different
parts of Ireland. The O'Rourkes of Breifney, one
of the most celebrated families in Irish history, were
chiefs of the great clan of Ui Briuin Breifne, whose
territory comprised the present counties of Leitrim
and Cavan. Three of them, in the 10th and 11th
centuries, were kings of Connacht. As lords of
Breifney, they sometimes ruled over a district extending from Kells in Meath to Drumcliff in Sligo ;
but after the 12th century, their power gradually
declined. O'Reilly became lord of East Breifney,
the present Co. Cavan, and O'Rourke's lordship was
confined to West Breifney, the present Co. Leitrim,
which was known as Breifney-O'Rourke. The
O'Rourkes took a leading part in the Elizabethan
wars, in which they suffered severely, but retained
considerable property down to the Cromwellian
confiscations. Many of them attained to high distinction in the military service of continental powers,
especially of Poland and Russia. A branch of the Ui
Maine, in Co. Galway, also bore this name, but was
never very numerous and, if it survives, cannot now
be distinguished from Ó Ruairc of Breifney. The
same applies to the other families of the name, some
of whom are mentioned above under the form of Ó
Ruaḋrac.

Ó Ruanaḋa, Ó Ruanaiḋ—I—*O Rownoe, O Roney,*
Roonoo, Rowney, Rooney, Roney, &c.; 'des. of
Ruanaiḋ' (hero); a common surname, at the end of
the 16th century, in Ulster, Leinster and Connacht.
The annalists, however, have but comparatively few
notices of the family. Ceallaċ Ó Ruanaḋa, chief
poet of Ireland, died in 1079; Eóin Ó Ruanaḋa, who
was chief poet to Magennis, died in 1376. Ó Ruanaiḋín (q.v.) is a variant.

Ó Ruanaiḋín—I—*O Roynian, O Runynge,* Runian,
Ruineen, Rooneen, (Rooney); 'des. of Ruanaiḋín'
(dim. of Ruanaiḋ); a var. of Ó Ruanaḋa, q.v.; common
in Sligo and other parts of Connacht; also Ó Ruanaḋáin, Ó Ruanáin, q.v.

Ó Ruanaḋáin, Ó Ruanáin—I—*O Roynian,* Roynane,
Roonane, Roonan, Ronane, Ronan; 'des. of Ruan-
aḋán' (dim. of Ruanaiḋ); a var. of Ó Ruanaiḋín
and Ó Ruanaḋa, q.v.; very rare.

Ó Ruḋġusa—I—(?) Roughasy; des. of Ruḋġur.

Ó Ruibín—?—Ribbon; a rare Connacht surname;
perhaps for Mac Roibín, q.v. Cf. Ó Piliḃín for
Mac Piliḃín.

Ó Ruis—I—*O Rushe,* Rush; perhaps for Ó Rora; a rare
Leinster surname.

Ó Saḃáin—I—*O Sawane, O Sawan,* Savin, (Savage);
'des. of Saḃán' (dim. of raḃ, strong, firm; also a cub,
whelp); an old Munster surname, found chiefly in
Cork, Kerry and Tipperary; now almost always
disguised under the angl. form of Savage.

Ó Samraiḋ—I—*O Sawrie, O Sawra,* Summers, Sommers,
Somers; 'des. of Samraḋ' (summer); an old South
Leinster surname, still well represented in Carlow
and Wexford; also now in Waterford, Limerick and
Kerry.

Ó Saoraiḋe, Ó Saortaiġ, Ó Saotraiḋe—II—
O Seyry, O Serie, Seerey, Seery, Freeman, Earner;
a substitute for the old Westmeath and Tirconnell
surname Ó Síoġraḋa, or Ó Síoġraiḋ, q.v. It is

sometimes angl. Freeman, on the erroneous supposition that it is derived from 'ᵱᴀoᵱᴀ1ᴅe,' a freeman. In Mayo and Galway, where it is pronounced Ó Sᴀoᵱᴈᴀ1ᵹ, or Ó Sᴀoᵱᴈuᵱᴅe, as if from 'ᵱᴀoᴈᵱuᴉᴅe,' a labourer (earner), the angl. form is Earner.

Ósbuᴩ—VIII—*Osbert*, (Osborne) ; ' son of Osbert' (a common Anglo-Saxon personal name) ; found in parts of Munster, incorrectly re-anglicised Osborne.

Ó scᴀᴌᴀ1ᵹe—I—*O Skallie, O Skelly*, Scally, Skally, Skelly ; ' des of Scᴀᴌᴀ1ᵹe ' (crier) ; also Mᴀc Scᴀᴌᴀ1ᵹe, q.v. ; a surname seemingly of midland origin.

Ó scᴀnnᴀ1ᴌ—I—*O Scandall, O Scannill*, O'Scannell, Scannell ; ' des. of Scᴀnnᴀᴌ ' (scandal) ; the name of a family of the race of Cairbre, son of Niall of the Nine Hostages, who were originally seated in the barony of Carbury, to the north of the town of Sligo. Mᴀo1ᵱᴀoᵱᴀ1ᵹ Ó Scᴀnnᴀ1ᴌ, Bishop of Raphoe, was translated to the primatial See of Armagh in 1261. The name, in the north-west of Ireland, has long been changed to the dim. form Ó Scᴀnnᴌᴀ1n, q.v. Ó Scᴀnnᴀ1ᴌ is now found chiefly in Cork and Kerry, whither the family must have migrated from Sligo or Donegal, some time before the end of the 16th century.

Ó scᴀnnᴌᴀ1n—I—*O Scanlaine, O Scanlan, O Scanlon, O Scandlon*, Scanlan, Scanlon, Scandlon, &c. ; ' des. of Scᴀnnᴌᴀn ' (dim. of Scᴀnnᴀᴌ) ; the name of several distinct families in different parts of Ireland, as : (1) of Sligo, who are the present-day representatives of the ancient family of Ó Scᴀnnᴀ1ᴌ of Carbury (see above) ; (2) of Galway, a branch of the southern Ui Fiachrach and of the same stock as the O'Shaughnessys and O'Heynes ; (3) of Cork, who were formerly erenaghs of Cloyne ; and (4) of Fermanagh, who were erenaghs of Devenish. At the end of the 16th century, the name was found in all the counties of Munster, being specially common in Cork, Limerick and Kerry. It is now common in Munster and Connacht, but is only rarely met with in the other provinces.

Ó scatsaıl—I—*O Scahill*, Scahill, Skahill, Schaill ;
' des. of scaıtseal ' (flower-fair) ; more anciently
mac scaıtsıl, q.v. ; the name of a Galway family
who were chiefs of Corca Mogha, now angl. Corcamoe,
which comprised the parish of Kilkerrin, until dispossessed by the O'Concannons soon after the Anglo-
Norman invasion. It is now always pronounced Ó
scatail in Galway and Mayo.

Ó scéacáın—I—*O Skeghan*, Skehan, Skeahan, Skeane ;
' des. of scéacán ' (dim. of ṗceac, a brier) ; an old
Tipperary surname. Cf. mac sceacáın.

Ó sceallaın—I—*O Scalain*, *O Skallen*, Scallan, Scullane,
Scullion ; ' des. of sceallán ' (kernel) ; an old surname
in Fermanagh and in South Leinster ; now very
scattered. In Connacht, it is pronounced Ó scol-
laın, q.v.

Ó scıngín—I—*O Skynegine*, *O Skingin*, *O Skynın*,
Skinnion, Delahide, Delahoyde ; ' des. of scıngín '
(probably dim. of ṗcıng, some article of dress) ; the
name of an ecclesiastical and literary family who were
originally erenaghs of Ardcarne, near Boyle, Co.
Roscommon, but afterwards migrated to Tirconnell,
where they became chroniclers to the O'Donnells.
Matthew O Scingin, who died in the year 1289, was
chief historian of Ireland in his time. The O Scingins
of Tirconnell became extinct towards the end of the
14th century and were succeeded by the O'Clerys,
whose ancestor married the heiress of the last ollav
of the name. The family has, however, survived in
other parts of Ireland ; but it would appear that some
members of it in Co. Cavan now call themselves
Delahide, or Delahoyde, doubtless on the erroneous
supposition that ' Skin-' of the one name is to be
equated with ' -hide ' of the other.

Ó scoıreaú, v. Ó scuıṗe.

Ó scolaıúe, Ó scolaıse—I—*O Scollee*, *O Scully*,
Scully ; ' des. of scolaıúe ' or ' scolaıse ' (crier) ; the
name of a Westmeath family who were chiefs of
West Delvin until dispersed early in the 12th century,

when they became erenaghs of the church of St.
Ruadhan at Lorrha, in Co. Tipperary. At the end
of the 16th century it was most numerous in Cork,
Dublin, Carlow, Offaly and Tipperary. It is apparently the same name as Ó Scalaiġe, q.v.

Ó scollám—I—Scullane, Scullion, Skoolin, (Scally,
Skally, Scully) ; a var. in Connacht of Ó Sceallám,
q.v. Cf. Ó Spolám for Ó Speálám. It is often incorrectly angl. Scally and Scully.

Ó scuire, Ó scuiriú, Ó scurra—I—O' Scurry,
Scurry ; ' des. of S————— '; the name, according
to MacFirbis, of a family of Cinel Eoghain in Ulster.
It was also borne by a family in Ui Maine in Co.
Galway, but is now little known, if at all extant.
MacFirbis writes it Ó Scuipe and Ó Scapa. It was
written Ó Scoipeaú in the title-page of a book pub-
lished by James Scurry at Waterford in 1820.

Ó seacnais—I—O Shaghnishe. O Shaghnes, Shaughness,
Shaughnessy, &c. ; a shortened form of Ó Seacnaraiġ,
q.v. ; rather common in the spoken language of
Connacht. I have heard it pronounced Ó Seacnair
(initial S aspirated) in West Limerick.

Ó seacnasaiġ—I—O'Shaughnessy, O'Shoughnessy,
O'Shannessy, O'Shanesy, Shaughnessy, Shannessy,
&c. ; ' des. of Seacnarac ' ; the name of a branch of
the Ui Fiachrach Aidhne, in Co. Galway. On the
decline of the kindred family of O'Cahill in the 13th
century, the O'Shaughnessys became chiefs of Cinel
Aodha, angl. Kinelea, the district lying around the
town of Gort ; but they are only rarely mentioned in
the Irish annals before the reign of Henry VIII. In
1533, Dermot O'Shaughnessy, the then ' chief of his
nation,' was knighted, and ten years later he surrendered all the clan-lands to the crown in order to
receive them back by letters-patent. During the next
two centuries the O'Shaughnessys were one of the most
celebrated families in Ireland. Sir Dermot O'Shaughnessy, the fourth in descent from Sir Dermot of the
time of Henry VIII, joined the Confederation of

Kilkenny and lost his estates in the Cromwellian confiscations, but received back 2,000 acres at the Restoration. This was again forfeited in 1697, and Colonel William O'Shaughnessy, the last chief of the name in the direct line, died in exile in France in 1744. O'Donovan was of opinion that the O'Shaughnessys of Co. Limerick are descended from Lieut.-Colonel William O'Shaughnessy, the uncle of Sir Dermot of the Cromwellian and Restoration period ; but this is unlikely, as the O'Shaughnessys were settled at Dromard, near Rathkeale, before the year 1600.

Ó SéaÓacáin—I—*O Sheahan, O Shaghan,* Sheahan, Shahan, Shean, Shane ; a common var. of Ó SíoÓ-acáin, q.v.

Ó SéaᵹÓa—I—O'Shea, O'Shee, Shea, Shee, &c. ; ' des. of SéaᵹÓa ' (stately, majestic, courteous ; also learned, scientific, ingenious) ; the name of a family of Corca Dhuibhne in West Kerry who until about the period of the Anglo-Norman invasion were lords of Ui Rathach, now the barony of Iveragh. A branch of the family settled, about the beginning of the 15th century, in the city of Kilkenny, where they became wealthy and highly respectable. The name was also borne by a branch of the Ui Fiachrach in the barony of Tirawley, Co. Mayo, but this family, if still extant, is very little known. The O'Sheas are now very numerous, especially in Kerry.

Ó Sealbaiᵹ—I—*O Shallowe, O Shallie, O Shelly, O Shielly,* Shalvey, Shallow, Shalloe, Shally, Shelloe, Shellew, Shelly, Shealy, Sheily, &c. ; ' des. of Sealb-ac ' (possessor, proprietor) ; the name of a branch of the Corca Laoighdhe in South-West Cork, whose seat was probably at baile Uí Sealbaiᵹ, about a mile to the east of Dunmanway. The Four Masters, under the year 1140, record the death of Ðomnall Ua Sealbaiᵹ, erenagh of Cork, ' pillar of the glory and splendour of Munster.' About the same period, four of the name were bishops of Cork, and one of Lismore. There was probably a distinct family of the name in the north of Ireland. At the end of the 16th century it was found in Cork, Waterford, Tipperary, Kilkenny and Donegal.

Ó Seanacáin—I—*O Sheanaghaine, O Shanahan*, Shanaghan, Shanahan, Shanihan, Shanan, Shannon, &c.; 'des. of Seanacán' (dim. of Seanac, old, wise); the name of a Dalcassian family who were chiefs of Ui Ronghaile, in the east of Thomond, until the year 1318, when they were expelled by Torlough O'Brien and the MacNamaras. They settled at first in Co. Waterford, but have long been scattered through Munster. See also Ó Sionacáin which is a Westmeath form of the name.

*Ó Seanacair—I -Shanagher; ' des. of *Seanacar.'

Ó Seanaig—I—*O Shanna, O Shanny*, Shannagh, Shanny; ' des. of Seanac' (der. of rean, old, wise); a rare surname in Co. Clare.

Ó Seanáin—I—*O Shenane, O Shanan, O Shennan*, O'Shannon, Shanan, Shanon, Shannon;; 'des. of Seanán' (dim. of rean, old, wise); a scattered surname.

Ó Seancáin—I—*O Shenchane, O Shenchan*, Shanahan, &c.; a var. of Ó Seanacáin, q.v.

Ó Searbáin—I—*O Sharvan*, Sharvin, Sherwin; ' des. of Searbán' (dim. of rearb, bitter); a rare surname which seemingly originated in Co. Roscommon.

Ó Searcaig—I—*O Sharkie, O Sherkie*, Sharkey; ' des. of Searcac' (loving); a surname which apparently originated in Tyrone, but is now common in many parts of Ulster and Connacht.

Ó Searcóid—I—*O Sherkott*, Sharket, Sharkett; ' des. of Searcoid' (lover); the name of a Roscommon family. ' Sean buide Ó Seitgoid, chief priest of Trinity Island, was drowned in Loch Cé, on Easter Sunday, 1578.' The name was never very common, but is still represented in Co. Roscommon.

Ó Searraig—I—*O Sharie*, Sharry, Sherry; ' des. of Searrac' (a foal, hence flighty); the name of an Ulster family who, according to MacFirbis, are of the race of Eoghan, son of Niall of the Nine Hostages;

also of a family the head of which was anciently chief of Dal mBuinne, in the present Co. Antrim ; still well represented in Ulster and in some of the adjoining counties of Leinster.

Ó seꜱꜱnáin—I—*O Sesnane, O Shesnan,* Shasnan, (Sexton) ; ' des. of Seꜱrnán ' or ' Seꜱrcnán ' ; the name of a Dalcassian family in Thomond. At the end of the 16th century it was found in different parts of Munster and also in Longford, Cavan and Monaghan. The angl. form ' Sexten ' appears as early as the year 1533 in the city of Limerick, where a respectable branch of the family had settled.

Ó seꜱꜱtꜱ—I—*O Siastie, O Cestie,* Cheasty ; ' des. of Seꜱrtꜱ ' ; a rare Munster surname. It apparently originated in Kerry, where Cuꜱt Ó Siortꜱ, angl. Tuosist, preserves the memory of the family.

Ó seibleáin, Ó seiblín—I—*O Syvelane, O Shevline,* Shevlin, Shovlin, Shovelin ; ' des. of Siblian ' (quick) ; older Ó Siblen, Ó Sibliain ; the name of a family who were anciently lords of Ui Failghe, or Offaly ; also of a branch of the Ui Eachach Muaidhe in Co. Mayo ; now found chiefly in Ulster.

Ó seigin—I—*O Sheine, O Sheyne, O Shyne,* Shine ; ' des. of Seigin ' (wild ox) ; an old Munster surname, still common in that province.

Ó seireꜱꜱáin—I—*O Sheridane, O Sheridan,* Sheridan, Sherridan, &c. ; a common form in the spoken language of Ó Sirroeáin, q.v.

Ó seiteacáin—I—*O Sheheghane,* Hyde ; ' des. of Seiteacán ' ; a rare surname in Co. Cork. Hyde is supposed to be a translation.

Ó siaꜱail, Ó siaꜱail—I—*O Siegall, O Shiell, O Sheale, O Sheill, O Shill,* O'Shiel, Sheil, Shiels, Sheils, Shields, Sheilds, Sheils, Shiles, Sheals, &c. ; ' des. of Siaꜱail ' or ' Siaꜱail ' (cf. riaꜱail, sloth) ; the name of a family of the race of Maine, son of Niall of the Nine Hostages, who became celebrated as physicians and surgeons in many parts of Ireland, as in Delvin-MacCoghlan, Oriel, Inishowen, &c. Owen O'Sheil, known as the 'Eagle of Doctors,' was physician to the armies of the Confederate Catholics of Ireland from 1642 to 1650.

Ó SIbleáin, Ó Siblláin, v. Ó Seibleáin.

Ó Sídeacáin, v. Ó Síobacáin.

Ó Sindile—XI—Singleton. V. ve Singealtún.

Ó SIOCFRAbA, Ó SIOCRAbA,—II—*O Shighrowe*, Shughrue, Shegrue, Sugrue, Segrue, Sugrew ; ' des. of Siocfraib ' (the Norse Sigefrith, victory-peace) ; an old Kerry surname. The family is said to be a branch of the O'Sullivans.

Ó SíobA—I—*O Shydie*, Sheedy, Silk ; ' des. of Síoba ' (silk) ; a rare and scattered surname. In Co. Galway, it is ' translated ' Silk.

Ó Síobacáin—I—*O Shieghane, O Shehane*, O'Sheehan, O'Sheahan, Sheehan, Sheahan, Sheean, Sheen, Shean, &c. ; ' des. of Síobacáin ' (dim. of ríobac, peaceful) ; the name (I) of a Dalcassian family, now very numerous throughout Munster, especially in Cork, Kerry and Limerick ; and (2) of an old Galway family who were followers of O'Kelly of Ui Maine and are still numerous in that county. Ó Sídeacáin and Ó Séabacáin (q.v.) are variants. The name is latterly sometimes written Ó Síotcáin.

Ó SíogRAbA, Ó SíogRAib—II—*O Shrue, O Shirie, O Shyry* ; ' des. of Síograib ' (the Norse Sigefrith) ; the same as Ó Siocfraba, q.v. ; formerly in use in the midlands and Tirconnell ; now changed to Ó Saoparbe or Ó Saocpuirbe, q.v.

Ó Sionacáin—I—*O Shinnaghan*, Shinnahan, Fox ; ' des, of Seanacán ' ; a var, of Ó Seanacáin, q.v. ; the name of a Westmeath or Cavan family ; sometimes incorrectly angl. Fox, as if from ' rionnac,' a fox.

Ó Sionaig—I—*O Sheny, O Sunny*, Shinny, Shunny, Shinnick, Shinwick, Fox, &c. ; ' des. of Seanac ' (wise, old) ; a var. of Ó Seanaig, q.v. But see Ó Sionnaig

Ó Sionáin—I—*O Sinan, Shinane, Shynane*, Shinnan, Sheenan, Synan ; ' des. of Seanán ' (dim. of rean,

old, wise); a var. of Ó Seanáin, q.v. The Synans
were once an important family in Cork and Limerick.

Ó Sionouile—XI—Singleton. V. ve Singealtún.

Ó Sionnaig—I—*O Sheny, O Sunny*, Shunny, Shinagh,
Shinnick, Shinnock, Shinwick, Fox; 'des. of Sion-
nac' (fox); probably not distinct from Ó Sionaig,
q.v.; the name of a family of Corca Laoighdhe in
South-West Cork; also of a Sligo family; now often
translated Fox.

Ó Sioraoáin—I—Shirdan, Shurdan, Sheridan, &c.;
a var. of Ó Siproeáin, q.v.

Ó Sioráin—I—*O Shearane, O Sherane*, Sheeran; ' des.
of *Siopán'; also Ó Sipín. q.v.

Ó Siosnáin—I—*O Sisnane*, (Sexton); a var. of Ó
Seapnáin, q.v.

Ó Siosta, v. Ó Seapta.

Ó Sioccáin, v. Ó Sioóacáin.

Ó Sirioeáin—I—*O Shiridane, O Sheridane*, Sheridan,
Sherridan, &c.; ' des. of Siproeáin'; the name of an
ecclesiastical family who were erenaghs of Granard,
in Co. Longford, but appear to have afterwards removed to Co. Cavan, where at the end of the 16th
century they were followers of O'Reilly and are still
numerous. The family rose to eminence in the 17th
and 18th century by the ability and learning of some
of its members. Thomas Sheridan who was Secretary
of State under James II, Sir Thomas Sheridan, tutor
to Prince Charles Edward, and the Right Hon. Richard
Brinsley Sheridan, orator, statesman, and dramatist,
belonged to this family. MacFirbis mentions a
family of the name among the Siol-Muireadhaigh in
Connacht.

Ó Sirín—I—*O Shirine, O Sherin*, Sherin, Sheeren,
Sheeran, Shirran; ' des. of *Sipín'; a var. of Ó Siop-
áin, q.v.

Ó Sicig—I—*O Shihie, O Shehy*, Sheehy; ' des. of Siteac'
(peaceful); doubtless, the same as Mac Sicig (q.v.),
by substitution of Ó for Mac; found here and there
in Munster.

Ó SLaTaRRa, Ó SLaTRa—I—*O Slattra*, *O Slattery*, Slattery ; ' des. of SLaTpa ' (bold, strong) ; the name of a Dalcassian family, formerly seated at Bally-slattery, in the east of Co. Clare, but now dispersed through Munster.

Ó SLéibín—I—*O Slevine*, *O Slevan*, Slevin, Sleavin, Sleevin, Slevan, Slavin, (?) Slamon ; ' des. of SLéibín ' (dim. of pliab, a mountain, a ' pet ' dim. of Oonn-fléibe) ; the name of a branch of the Cinel Eoghain in Ulster. Ziolla Comžaill Ó SLéibín, chief bard of Ulster, was the messenger chosen by King Malachy to rally the forces of the North in defence of Tara against Brian Boru.

Ó SLuažaóais—I—*O Slowey*, Slowey, Sloey, Sloy, (Molloy, Mulloy) ; ' des. of SLuažaóaċ ' (belonging to a host, fit for hosting) ; the name of a family which apparently belonged originally to Roscommon, but is now dispersed through Connacht and Ulster. The Four Masters, under the year 1015, record the death of maoipáopaiž Ua SLuažaóaiž, sage of Ireland ; and in 1190, Ziolla Óeapaiž Ó SLuažaóaiž was slain by Turlough O'Connor. The name is strangely angl. Molloy, Mulloy, in parts of Ulster.

Ó SLuažaóáin, Ó SLuažaióín, Ó SLuažáin, Ó SLuaižín—I—*A Sloan*, Sloane, Sloan, Slown, Slone, Sloyan, Sloyne ; ' des. of SLuažaóán,' or ' SLuažaióín ' (dim. of SLuažaóaċ) ; probably a var. of Ó SLuaž-aóaiž, q.v. ; a not uncommon surname in Co. Mayo, where it is angl. Sloyan and Sloyne. The Sloanes of Antrim and Down are of Scottish origin, but the Gaelic form of the surname is the same. Sir Hans Sloan, the founder of the British Museum, was of this family.

Ó Smealáin, Ó SmoLáin—I—Smallen, Smollan, Smollen, Smullen ; a corruption of Ó Spealáin, q.v. It is apparently a modern corruption, as I can find no corresponding early angl. forms.

Ó Sniaóaiž—I—Snee ; ' des. of Sniaóaċ ' ; an old Connacht surname, still extant in Sligo and Mayo.

Clement Ó Sniaḋaiġ was Bishop of Achonry early in the 13th century.

Ó soċlaċáin—I—*O Soghlaghane*, Soghlahan ; ' des. of Soċlaċán ' (dim. of Soċlaċ, renowned) ; a rare Connacht surname, borne by a family who were formerly erenaghs of Cong.

Ó soċlaiġ—I—Soughly, Suckley ; ' des. of Soċlaċ' (famed, renowned). Cf. Ó Soċlaċáin above.

Ó somaċáin—I—*O Somaghan*, *O Summaghan*, O'Summachan, O'Summahan, Somahan, Sumahean, &c., (Sommers, Summers, Somers, Summerly, Somerville, Summerville, &c.) ; ' des. of Somaċán ' (a soft, innocent person) ; the name of an old Sligo family who were formerly numerous and respectable in the parish of Ballysummaghan ; now generally angl. Somers.

Ó soraċáin—I—*O Soroghan*, Soraghan Soroghan, Sorahan, Soran ; ' des. of Soṙaċán ' (perhaps dim. of ṙoṙċa, bright, luminous, opposed to ḋoṙċa) ; an Ulster surname.

Ó spealáin—I—*O Spallane*, *O Spillane*, *O Spollane*, Spalane, Spellane, Spillane, Spollane, Spollan, Splane, Splaine, Smallen, Smollan, Smullen, (Spelman, Spellman), &c. ; ' des. of Spealán ' (dim. of ṙpeal, a scythe) ; the name (1) of a family, said to be of Dalcassian origin, who were anciently chiefs of Ui Luighdheach, or Ileagh, in the present barony of Eliogarty, Co. Tipperary, but long since dispersed through Munster and Leinster ; and (2) of a family of Ui Fiachrach who were formerly proprietors of Coillin Aodha, now Culleen, in the parish of Kilglas, Co. Sligo, and are still numerous in Connacht, but generally call themselves Spelman in English. The name is usually pronounced Ó Spoláin in Munster and Connacht, but sometimes also Ó Smoláin in the latter province ; and the angl. forms, Smollan, Smullen, &c., show that it was also sometimes so pronounced in Leinster.

Ó spealġusa, ó spilġeasa—I—Spelessy, Spellissy

Spillessy, Spilacy ; ' des. of Speaᴌᵹuɿ ' (scythe-choice) a rare Thomond surname. I can find no early instance.

Ó Spιoᴌáιn, Ó Spoᴌáιn—I—*O Spillane, O Spollane,* Spillane, Spollane, Spollan, &c. ; variants of Ó Speaᴌáιn, q.v.

Ó Sʀaιᴄeáιn, Ó Sʀuιᴄeáιn, Ó Sʀuᴄáιn—I—*O Srahane, O Shrihane, O Sreighan, O Shrean, O Streffan,* Shryhane, Sruffaun, Strohane, Strahan, Straghan, Strachan, Strain, Bywater, (Ryan) ; ' des. of Sɿuᴄán,' or ' Sɿuιᴄeán ' (dim. of ɿɿuᴄ, an elder, a sage, a man of letters) ; the name of an old Tirconnell family, the head of which was chief of Clann Snedhgile, a sept of the Cinel Conaill, seated in Glenswilly, to the west of Letterkenny, and also erenagh of Conwall in the same district. Some of the family had come southward before the end of the 16th century, probably as followers of the MacSweenys, and settled in Co. Cork, where the name is still extant, but often ' translated ' Bywater, as if from ' ɿɿuᴄán,' a streamlet. In Co. Mayo, it is sometimes strangely angl. Ryan.

*Ó Sʀιanáιn—I—Sreenan. Cf. Cell Srianáin in Hogan's Onomasticon.

Ó Sᴄeaɿáιn—II—*O Stephane,* Stephens ; ' des. of Stephen ' ; a rare Leix surname.

Ó Sᴄóιʀín, Storan ; a rare Co. Limerick surname, the origin of which I have failed to trace. The Four Masters, at the year 1098, record the death of maoιᴌɿa ua Sᴄuιɿ, scribe and philosopher of Munster.

Ó Suaιʀᴅ, Ó Suaιʀᴄ—II—*O Sworde, O Swerte,* Sword, Seward, Swords ; ' des. of Suaɿᴄ ' (probably the Norse Sigeweard, Siward) ; the name of an old family in Offaly. The Four Masters record the death of eιᴄne, daughter of ua Suaιɿᴄ, abbess of Kildare, in 1016.

Ó Suιᵬne—IV—*O Swynie, O Swenie,* O'Sevnagh, Sweeny, &c. ; a var. of mac Suιᵬne (q.v.), by substitution of Ó for mac ; very rare.

Ó Súιᴌeaᵬáιn—I—O'Sullivan, Sullivan, Sullevan, Soolivan, &c. ; ' des. of Súιᴌeaᵬán ' (i.e., Súιᴌ-ᴅuᵬ-án, black-eyed) ; also but less correctly written Ó

649

Súilleaḃáin; the name of a well-known Munster family of the same stock as the MacCarthys and O'Callaghans. The original patrimony of the O'Sullivans lay along the River Suir, in the present Co. Tipperary, and their principal seat was at Knockgraffon, about two miles to the north of Cahir. In the year 1192 they were forced by the progress of the Anglo-Norman invasion to exchange the fertile plains of Tipperary for the mountains of Cork and Kerry. In their new home on the shores of the bays of Kenmare and Bantry they, however, acquired extensive possessions and became one of the most powerful families in Munster and one of the most numerous in all Ireland. They divided into several branches, the heads of which were known respectively as O'Sullivan More, who possessed the barony of Dunkerron and had his castle at Dunkerron, near Kenmare; O'Sullivan Beare, who owned the territory of Beare, now the baronies of Beare and Bantry; O'Sullivan Maol; Mac Finghin Dubh, &c. Notwithstanding the confiscation of their estates in the 17th century, the O'Sullivans are still a respectable family, and the name is everywhere famous. "It has been honoured abroad," writes O'Callaghan, "in Spain, Belgium and Germany, with the titles of Count and Baron. It contributed its proportion of officers to the national regiments of Clare, Dillon, Bulkelely, &c., in France. It was one of note in the service of Naples. It has also attained high military, administrative, and diplomatic positions in the service of the United States of America, and the United Kingdoms of Great Britain and Ireland." (Irish Brigades.)

Ó Súilleacáin—I—*O Suleghane, O Soolechan, O Solloghan, O Sullaghan,* Sullahan, Sullehan, (Sullivan); 'des. of Súilleacán,' (dim. of Súileac, quick-eyed); formerly in use in Longford, Cavan and Louth, but now nearly everywhere incorrectly angl. Sullivan.

Ó Súiliġ—I—*O Swally, O Sewell,* Sewell, Suel, &c.; 'des. of Súileac' (quick-eyed).

Ó Súilleabáin, v. Ó Súileabáin.

Ó Caúgáin—I—*O Tagan*, Tagan, Teigan, Teegan, Tegan ; ' des. of Caúgán ' (dim. of Caúg) ; a rare and scattered surname ; found chiefly in Leinster.

Ó Caiclig, v. Ó Caiclig.

Ó Caiúg—I—*O Teige*, Teige, Teigue, Tague, Teague, Tigue, Tighe, Tyghe, Tye, Tee ; ' des. of Caúg ' (poet) ; the name (1) of a Leinster family who were anciently chiefs of Ui Mail, now angl. Imail, in Co. Wicklow, but were dispersed soon after the Anglo-Norman invasion ; (2) of an Ulster family who were anciently chiefs of Fir Li, in the present Co. Derry ; (3) of a Connacht family, of the same stock as the O'Connors, who were chiefs of the household of the Kings of Connacht, and are still numerous in Roscommon and Mayo ; and probably (4) of a Thomond family, to which belonged Caúg Ó Caiúg, Bishop of Killaloe, in the 11th century.

Ó Cailcig—I—*O Talty*, Talty, Taulty ; probably a metathesised form of Ó Caiclig, or Ó Caiclig, q.v. ; a Co. Clare surname.

Ó Caiclig—I—*O Talheighe*, Tally, Tully, Tilly ; ' des. of Caicleac ' (quiet, peaceful) ; also Ó Caiclig ; the name (1) of a Tyrone family who were chiefs of Ui Laoghaire ; and (2) of an ecclesiastical family in Fermanagh.

Ó Calcair—I—*O Tolcher*, Toler ; ' des. of Calcan ' (stubborn, obstinate) ; a rare midland surname.

Ó Calcaráin—I—Tolleran ; ' des. of Calcanán ' (dim. of Calcan) ; the name of a Mayo family who were anciently chiefs of Conmaicne Cuile, now the barony of Kilmaine. O'Donovan found a few families of the name still in the barony.

Ó Canaiveáin—I—Tannian, Tannion ; ' des. of Canaiveán ' (dim. of canaiv, thin, slender) ; a rare Connacht surname. In 1406, Turlough oge O'Connor, King of Connacht, was slain by Diarmaiv Ó Canaiveán.

Ó Caráin, v. Ó Copáin.

Ó ᴄᴀRᴘᴀ, Ó ᴄᴀRᴘᴀɪᴅ, Ó ᴄᴀRᴘᴀɪᴈ—I—*O Tarpy*, Tarpey, Torpy; ' des. of ᴄᴀᴘᴘᴀċ ' (stout, sturdy); the name (1) of a family of Ui Fiachrach who possessed a townland in the parish of Skreen, Co. Sligo, which from them was called Fearann Ui Tharpaigh, now angl. Faranyharpy; long dispersed through Connacht; and (2) of a family of Corca Laoighdhe in South-West Cork, where they were followers of the O'Learys. There are a few households of the name still in Munster; also written Ó ᴄóᴘᴘᴀ, Ó ᴄóᴘᴘᴀɪᴈ.

Ó ᴄᴀRSnáɪn, Tarsnane.

Ó ᴄéᴀċáɪn—I—*O Taughan, O Tauhan*, Teaghan, Teahan, Teehan, Tehane, Tehan; probably a contraction of Ó ᴄᴇɪᴄᴇᴀċáɪn (' des. of ᴄᴇɪᴄᴇᴀċán,' fugitive, runaway); the name of a Roscommon family. Ó ᴄéᴀċáɪn is an old surname in Kerry, where it is still well represented.

Ó ᴄᴇᴀnᴈᴀnᴀ—I—*O Tagney*, Tangney, Tagney; ' des. of ᴄ————— '; the name of an old Kerry family; peculiar to that county.

Ó ᴄᴇɪᴍɪn—I—*O Tine, O Tyne*, Tyne, Tynne; ' des. of ᴄᴇɪᴍᴇᴀn ' (dark, grey); a rare Co. Clare surname.

Ó ᴄᴇɪᴍneáɪn—I—*O Teynane, O Tyvnane, O Tinan, O Tynnan*, Tynan, Tinan, Tynnan, Tivnane, Tivnan, Tevnane, Tevnan, (?) Tivane, Teevan; ' des. of ᴄᴇɪᴍneán ' (dim. of ᴄᴇɪᴍᴇᴀn, dark, grey); (1) an Ossory surname, now common in Leinster and Munster; and (2) a Sligo surname, still extant in Connacht, angl. Tivnane, Tevnane, &c., but rare.

Ó ᴄᴇɪᴍnín—I—*O Tynine*, Tinin, Tinan, Tynan; ' des. of ᴄᴇɪᴍnín ' (dim. of ᴄᴇɪᴍᴇᴀn, dark, grey); a var. of Ó ᴄᴇɪᴍneáɪn, q.v.; very rare.

Ó ᴄᴇɪᴄᴇᴀċáɪn, v. Ó ᴄéᴀċáɪn.

Ó ᴄɪᴈᴇᴀRnᴀɪᴈ—I—*O Tierny, O Tearney*, O'Tierney, Tierney, Terney, (Tiernan), Lord; ' des. of ᴄɪᴈᴇᴀᴘnᴀċ ' (lordly); the name (1) of a branch of the Cinel Eoghain who were anciently chiefs of Fearnmaigh, in the present Co. Donegal; (2) of a branch of the Ui Fiachrach who were formerly lords of Ceara, now the barony of Carra, in Co. Mayo, and are still numerous in that county ; and (3) of a Westmeath family of the southern Ui Neill race. At the end of the 16th century, the name was common also in Clare and Tipperary. The Mayo family is often called Ó Tigeaɲnáin (q.v.) in Irish and Tiernan in English ; and MacFirbis also gives Ó Tigeaɲnáin as an alias for Ó Tigeaɲnaig of Westmeath.

Ó Tigeaʀnáin—I—*O Ternane, O Tiernan*, Tiernan, Ternan, (Tierney) ; ' des. of Tigeaɲnán ' (dim. of Tigeaɲnac, lordly) ; an alias, in Mayo and Westmeath, for Ó Tigeaɲnaig, q.v. ; but there are probably distinct families of the name, none however numerous, in other parts of Ireland. Of the Mayo family, O'Donovan writes : " They are a stout race of men and very proud of their descent, of which, however, they know nothing, except that their ancestors, a long time ago, had estates in Carra, and were strong men and courageous fighters. They look upon themselves as superior to their neighbours of the same rank, and always use a style of dress, particularly the great coat, by which they are at once distinguished from others of the same neighbourhood. This gave rise to an Irish saying in Carra : ' Iɼ geall le móɲgáil Muintiɲe Tigeaɲnáin é '—' It is like the ostentation of the O'Tiernans ' " (Hy Fiachrach, p. 186 n.).

Ó Tiobʀaiṫe—I—Tubridy, Tubrit ; ' des. of Tiobɲaiṫe ' (cf. tiobɲaiṫ, a well) ; a Clare surname.

Ó Tiomáin—I—*O Teman, O Tyman*, Timmin, Timmins, Tymmons, Tymmins ; ' des. of Tiomán ' (dim. of tiom, soft, tender, timid) ; a rare Fermanagh and West Ulster surname ; also found in South Leinster.

Ó Tiománaig—I—*O Tymonie*, Timony, Tymmany ; ' des. of Tiománac ' ; a rare West Ulster surname ; perhaps a var. of Ó Tiomáin, q.v.

Ó Tnútail, Ó Tnútṫail—I—*O Knowell*, Newell, Newill, Newells, Knowels, Knowles ; ' des. of Tnútṫail ' (envy-valour) ; originally a midland surname, now scattered.

Ó Togṫa—I—*O Toffey*, Towey, Tuffy ; ' des. of Togṫa '

(chosen or elected); the name of a family of Ui Fiachrach, who were formerly chiefs of Bredagh, a district in the west of the barony of Tirawley, embracing the parish of Moygawnagh and part of the adjoining parish of Kilfian; still common in Mayo and Roscommon; generally angl. Towey, but sometimes Tuffy.

Ó Coimín, v. Mac Coimín.

Ó Comáin, v. Ó Cuamáin.

Ó Comaltaiġ—I—*O Tomelty*, Tomilty, Tumelty, Tumilty, Tumblety, &c.; ' des. of Comaltaċ ' (large, bulky); a rare South Leinster surname.

Ó Comnair—II—*O Toner*, Toner; 'des. of Comṗaṙ' (a Norse personal name); older form Ó Comṗaiṙ; the name of a family of Cinel Eoghain who were seated near Lough Swilly, in Co. Donegal, where they built the church which was called from them Cill Ó ᴅComṗaiṙ, now angl. Killodonnell; still common in Ulster. Ó Comnṙa (q.v.) is a variant.

Ó Comnṙa—II—*O Thonery*, Tonra, Tonry; a var. of Ó Comnaiṙ, q.v.; found in Mayo and Sligo, but rare. John O Thonery was Bishop of Ossory in the reign of Queen Mary.

Ó Comṙair, v. Ó Comnaiṙ.

Ó Connaiġ—I—*O Tonney*, Tunny; 'des. of Connaċ' (glittering); a rare Sligo surname. The family, according to MacFirbis, is a branch of the Cinel Conaill.

Ó Coráin—I—*O Tarrane, O Tarran, O Turran*, Toran, Torran, Thoran, Thorn, Tarrant, Torrans, Torrens, Torrins, Torrance, Torrence, (Thornton), &c.; 'des. of Corán' (dim. of cor, a lord); also written Ó Caráin; originally a Derry surname apparently; now rare and scattered.

Ó Cormaᴅa, Ó Cormaiġ—II—*O Tormo*, Tormey, Tarmey; 'des. of Thormodr' (a common Norse personal name); a midland and South Ulster surname.

Ó Córna—I—*O Torno*, Torney, Turney; 'des. of Córna'; extremely rare. Mainircir Ó ᴅCórna. now angl. Abbey O'Dorney, in Co. Kerry, is named from the family.

Ó TÓRpᴀ, Ó TÓRpᴀιʒ, v. Ó Tᴀppᴀ.

Ó TRᴀιʒTιʒ—I—*O Trighie, O Trye*, Trahey, Trehy, Troy ; an older form of Ó Tpoιʒτιʒ, q.v.

Ó TREᴀbᴀιR—I—*O Trevir, O Trover*, Trevor, Trower, Trevors, (Travors, Travers) ; 'des. of Tpeᴀbᴀp' (prudent, wise, skilful) ; the name of an ecclesiastical family in Co. Leitrim, of the same stock as the Mac-Clancys, who were erenaghs of Killarga ; still common in Leitrim ; now also in parts of Ulster.

Ó TRÉᴀṁᴀιn, Troy ; a rare West Clare surname.

Ó TREᴀSᴀιʒ—I—*O Trassy, O Tressy, O Trasey*, Trassy, Tressy, Tracy, Tracey, Treacy ; 'des. of Tpeᴀpᴀċ' (fighter) ; the name (1) of a Leinster family who were anciently lords of Ui Bairrche, a district embracing the barony of Slievemargy, in Leix, but are long dispersed through Leinster and Munster ; and (2) of a Connacht family, of the same stock as the O'Maddens, who were seated in the south-east of Co. Galway, but are long dispersed. The name is now common in many parts of Ireland. The dim. Ó Tpeᴀpᴀċᴀιn appears to have been in use in the midlands, but is probably obsolete ; at least, it has no distinct angl. form.

Ó TREObᴀιn—I—*O Tredane*, Trodden, Troddyn ; 'des. of Tpeobᴀn' ; originally a Louth surname ; now very rare.

Ó TROιʒTιʒ—I—*O Trohie, O Trehie*, Trehy, (Troy), Foote ; 'des. of Tpoιʒτeᴀċ' (a foot-soldier) ; also Ó Tpᴀιʒτιʒ, q.v. This surname originated in North-West Clare, in or near Corcomroe, where the O'Trehys were a family of some note in the early history of the district. They have, however, been long dispersed, and for centuries have been settled in Offaly, North Tipperary, Limerick and Cork. The name is now generally angl. Troy.

Ó TUᴀιT—I—*O Toye*, Toy, Toye ; a rare Mayo surname ; possibly an abbreviated form of Ó Tuᴀτᴀιʒ, q.v.

Ó TUᴀLTᴀιn—I—Toulhan ; a metathesised form of Ó Tuᴀτᴀλᴀιn, q.v.

Ó τuαmα—I—O'Twomey, O'Toomey, Twomey, Toomey, Twoomey, Tuomy, Towmey, &c. ; ' des. of τuαim ' ; the name of a Dalcassian family, still common in Munster, especially in Co. Cork. Seáη Ó τuαmα was the most distinguished of the Maigue poets.

Ó τuαmáιη—I—*O Tumane*, *O Tomane*, *O Toman*, Tooman, Tumman, Tummon, Toman, (?) Tumpane, (?) Toompane ; ' des. of τuαmáη ' (dim. of τuαim) ; originally a Tyrone surname ; now very rare, and family long dispersed.

Ó τuαRuιs,   Ó τuαRuιsc—I—Turish,   Toorish, Tourisk, (?) Tidins, Waters, Watters ; probably a corruption of Ó ηuαηξuιη, q.v. ; a Donegal surname.

Ó τuαταιξ—I—*O Twohy*, *O Towie*, Twohy, Twoohy, Tuohy, Touhy, Toohy, Tuhy, Tooey, Towey ; ' des. of τuαταc ' (rustic ; also a lord) ; the name of a branch of the Ui Maine who were originally seated at Aughrim, in Co. Galway. At the end of the 16th century, it was not uncommon in many parts of Munster, especially in Co. Cork, and also in Offaly and Donegal. In Co. Cork, the final ξ is sometimes pronounced.

Ó τuαταιξ—I—*O Towhig*, Tuohig, Twohig, Touhig, Towhig, Toohig ; a var. of Ó τuαταιξ (q.v.) in Co. Cork, where the final ξ is sometimes not aspirated. Cf. Ó Cobταιξ and Ó Ôubταιξ.

Ó τuαταιξ—I—*O Thuoty*, Tutty ; a var. of Ó τuαταιξ, q.v. ; very rare.

Ó τuαταιl—I—*O Toughill*, *O Touhill*, *O Twohill*, *O Tuale*, *O Towell*, O'Toole, Toughill, Tuohill, Twohill, Toohill, Tohall, Tohill, Towell, Toole, Toal, Toale, &c. ; ' des. of τuαταl ' (people-mighty) ; also written Ó τuατξαιl and Ó τuατξαιle ; the name of at least two distinct families in Ireland, viz. : (1) Ó τuαταιl of Leinster, and (2) Ó τuαταιl of Ulster. The O'Tooles of Leinster, who are one of the most illustrious families of that province, derive their name and descent from τuαταl, son of Ughaire, King of Leinster, who died in the year 956. Their clan-name was Ui

Muireadhaigh. This afterwards became the designation of their territory, which originally comprised
the southern half of the present Co. Kildare. Driven
thence soon after the Anglo-Norman invasion by
Walter de Riddlesford, they settled in the mountain
fastnesses of Wicklow, first in Ui Mail and afterwards
in Feara Cualann, where in alliance with their kinsmen, the O'Byrnes, they carried on incessant warfare
with the English for a period of four hundred years,
and preserved their independence as a clan down to
the close of the reign of Elizabeth. In the reign of
James I, the whole of ' Fercuolen ' was confiscated
and granted to Sir Richard Wingfield. The O'Tooles,
however, retained considerable property down to the
Cromwellian and Williamite confiscations. A branch
of the family settled at an early period in West Connacht, and are still numerous in Mayo and Galway.
The Ulster family of the name is, according to Mac-
Firbis, a branch of the Cinel Eoghain.

Ó τυατаιᴸ—I—*O Thuathayll*, Tuthill, Tothill, Tuttell,
Tuttle, &c. ; a var. of Ó τυατаιᴸ, q.v. Cf. Ó τυατаιᵹ
for Ó τυατаιᵹ. I give this form on the authority of
O'Mahony (Keating's History), but I have not been
able to verify it. Tuthill is apparently an English
surname.

Ó τυατаᴸáın—I—*O Twohillane, O Towlane, O Toolane,
O Tolane*, Toulhan, Toolan, Toland, Tolan, Tolin,
Toolis, Thulis ; ' des. of τυατаᴸán ' (dim. of τυατаᴸ,
people-mighty) ; the name of an Ulster family who
were originally seated in Inishowen, Co. Donegal. A
branch of the family migrated, in the 17th century,
with the O'Donnells to Co. Mayo where they still
flourish, but strangely anglicise their name Toolis
and Thulis.

Ó τυατсаιʀ—I—*O Tougher, O Togher,*Tougher, Taugher,
Togher, Tooher, Toher, Tooker, Tucker ; ' des. of
τυατсаn ' (people-dear) ; the name of at least two
distinct families, the one seated originally in Ely-
O'Carroll, but now dispersed through the neighbouring

counties; the other in West Ulster, whence the name passed into Mayo, where it is now not uncommon.

Ó Tuatġail, v. Ó Tuatail.

Ó Tuatġaile—I—(?) Tooley; an Ulster var. of Ó Tuatail, q.v.; so written by MacFirbis.

Ó Tuile, v. Mac Maoltuile.

Ó Tuine—I—O Teny, O'Thina, Tunny, Tunney, Flood; probably a corruption of Mac Maoltuile. Cf. Ó Tuile.

Pádraig—VIII—Patryk, Patrick; 'son of Patrick' (a once popular Christian name in the north of England). The surname came into Ireland about the time of the Anglo-Norman invasion, but has always been rare and confined to a few places in Leinster.

Pagán—VIII—Payen, Poyn, Paine, Payne, Poyne, Pyne, &c.; 'son of Pagan' (Lat. 'Paganus,' a great Norman name). The surname came into Ireland at the time of the Anglo-Norman invasion.

Pagán—VIII—Fyan, Fyans, Foynes; a var. of Pagán, q.v. A family of this name settled early at Fyanston in Co. Meath. The name occurs several times in the list of mayors of Limerick in the 13th and 14th centuries. Cf. Fagán.

Páidín—VIII—Padyn, Padin, Paden, Padden, Pattin, Patten, Patton, &c.; 'son of Padin,' or 'Pattin' (dim. of Patrick). It will come as a surprise to most people to learn that our Páidín is of English origin. Yet, like Patrick, it was once very common in the north of England. 'Padin Urs' is one of the earliest entries in the Dublin Roll of Names (A.D. 1216), and 'Padyn' is a surname in the English Hundred Rolls.

Pailís—XI—Palys, Pallys, Pallice, Palles, Pallas; i.e., 'at the "palis" or stake-fenced enclosure,' from residence (Fr. 'palis,' a stake. Cf. Ir. 'pailír,' which enters into the composition of several place-names, as Pallaskenry, Pallasgreen, &c.); an old surname in Dublin, Louth and Cavan. In 1582, Patrick Palles of Dundalk obtained a grant of pardon from Queen

Elizabeth. In 1642, William Pallys of Dublin ;and Andrew Pallys of Collatrath, Co. Cavan, were attainted ; as were, in 1691, Andrew Pallace of Cloneanat, Co. Cavan, and Christopher Pallas of Dublin.

 pᴀɪⁿíⁿ—VIII—*Pannyn, Phanyn, Phannyne*, Panneen, Fannin, Fanning, &c. ; ' son of Panin ' (dim. of Pagan) ; more usually ꝓᴀɪⁿíⁿ, q.v. Panneen is still a Co. Limerick surname.

pᴀɪꞃcéɪꞃ—XII—Parker ; Nor. ' le Parkere,' i.e., the parker, custodian of a park. Also pᴀꞃcᴀꞃ.

pᴀmᴀꞃ—XII—Palmer ; Nor. ' le Palmer,' ' le Paumer,' i.e., the palmer, palm-bearing pilgrim from the Holy Land ; an old surname in Ireland.

pᴀoꞁ—VI—Powell ; Welsh ' Ap Howel,' i.e., son of Howel.

pᴀoꞃ Poer, Power. V. ᴅe pᴀoꞃ.

pᴀꞃcᴀꞃ, Parker ; a late form of pᴀɪꞃcéɪꞃ, q.v.

pᴀꞃⁿᴀɪꞁ, Parnell. V. peᴀɪꞃⁿéɪꞁ,

pᴀcúⁿ—VIII—*Patun*, Paton, Patton, Patten ; ' son of Paton ' (a Norman dim. of Patrick). Cf. pᴀɪᴅíⁿ.

peᴀcóc, peᴀcóᵹ—XII—*Pecoc, Pecok*, Peacock, Peacocke ; Mid. Eng. ' pecoc,' ' pecok,' i.e., the peacock, applied to a vain, proud person. The surname, though rare, is old in Ireland.

peᴀᵹum, Pegum.

peᴀɪꞃⁿéɪꞁ—VIII—*Peronel, Pernel*, Parnell ; ' son of Petronel,' double dim. of Peter.

peᴀꞃᴀɪꞁ—VIII—*Parale, Paral*, Parill, Parle ; probably ' son of Peverel ' (a Norman personal name, Lat. ' Piperellus ' and ' Peverellus ' in early Anglo-Norman documents) ; an old Wexford surname.

peᴀꞃóɪᴅ—VIII—Parrott, Perrott ; ' son of Perrot,' Nor. dim. of Pierre or Peter.

peɪcíᴅ, peɪcíᴅ—XII—Petit, Petite, Pettitt, Petty, and by translation, Little ; Nor. ' le Petit,' ' le Petite,' i.e., the little, small of stature. The Petits settled early in Meath and Westmeath where they obtained large grants of land from de Lacy. They were feudal barons of Dunboyne and of Mullingar.

Ṗιaṙaṡ—VIII—Pierce, Pierse, Pearse, &c.; 'son of Piers' (an Anglo-Norman form of Petrus, Latin for Peter, very common among the early Anglo-Norman settlers in Ireland). There are, no doubt, several distinct families so called in different parts of the country. The Pierses of Kerry are stated to be a branch of the Fitzmaurices of Lixnaw.

Ṗιaṙóιꝺ, Perrott; a var. of Ṗeaṙóιꝺ, q.v.

Ṗíc—VIII—Pike, Pyke; 'son of Pic' (an Anglo-Saxon and Norse personal name, found in Domesday Book). 'Robert Pic' occurs in the Dublin Roll of Names, A.D. 1216. Cf. Ṁac Ṗéιce.

Ṗιℓιn, Pillin, Pillon.

Ṗιocóιꝺ, Ṗιoᵹóιꝺ—VIII—*Picot*, Pickett, Pigott, Piggott; 'son of Picot' (dim. of Pic). 'Picot' occurs in Domesday Book as the name of a tenant-in-chief in Hampshire, and 'John Picot' is an early entry in the Dublin Roll of Names, A.D. 1216.

Ṗιoṁḃróc, Pembroke. V. ꝺe Ṗιonḃróc.

Ṗιonꝺaṙ—XII—Pindar, Pinder, Pender, &c.; Nor. 'le Pinder,' i.e., the pinder or pindar, keeper of a pound. But probably in the great majority of instances Pinder, Pender, &c., are shortened forms of Prendergast. V. Ṗιonꝺaṙᵹáṙ.

Ṗιonꝺaṙᵹáṡ, Ṗιonꝺaṙᵹṙáṡ, Pendergast, Pindergast, Prendergast; a corruption of ꝺe Ṗṙιonꝺaṙᵹṙáṙ, q.v.

Ṗιoḃaιṙe, Ṗιoḃaṙ, Ṗιoḃaṙc, *Pippart, Pipard, Pippard*, Piper, Pyper, Pipper, Pepper, Peppard, &c. This surname came into Ireland about the time of the Anglo-Norman invasion. I can find no satisfactory explanation of its origin.

Ṗιoṙóιꝺ, Perrott, &c.; a var. of Ṗeaṙóιꝺ, q.v.

Ṗιoꞇún, *Phitton*, Fitton, Fetton; a var. of Ḟιoꞇún, q.v.

Ṗℓéaṁonn, Ṗℓéιṁeann—XII—*Flamang*, Flemon, Fleming, &c.; Nor. 'le Fleming,' Lat. 'Flandrensis,' i.e., the Fleming, native of Flanders. Towards the end of the 11th century, an irruption of the sea compelled many Flemings to seek shelter in England. They were at first allowed to settle on the Scottish borderlands, but later on were removed by Henry I to the south coast of Wales, where they were granted a fertile district which had been wrested from the Welsh. From there they came to Ireland at the time of the Anglo-Norman invasion. Richard le Fleming obtained from Hugh de Lacy a grant of the barony of Slane and other estates in Co. Meath, which remained in the family down to the Cromwellian and Williamite confiscations. The name is now common in many parts of Ireland.

ploin̄ɣcéiⱅ, pluincéiⱅ, pluin̄ɣcéiⱅ—XII— *Blounket, Plonket*, Plunket, Plunkett ; Nor. ' Blanchet ' (dim. of Fr. ' blanc,' i.e., white, pale, from the complexion). The Plunkets must have come into Ireland about the time of the Anglo-Norman invasion. They settled in the north of Co. Dublin, and became in course of time one of the most distinguished families of the Pale. In 1403, Sir Christopher Plunket became lord of Killen, in Co. Meath ; and in 1628, Lucas Plunkett, tenth lord of Killen, was created Earl of Fingall. Branches of this family were also Barons of Dunsanny and Earls of Louth. Unlike most of the great Anglo-Irish families, the Plunketts contrived to retain the greater part of their estates in the Cromwellian and Williamite confiscations.

póil, Powell, Powel ; perhaps a shortened form of mac póil or mac ɣiolla póil, q.v. ; in use in Co. Galway.

póiléiⱅ—VIII—Paulett, Powlett, Pollett ; ' son of Paulet ' (dim. of Paul).

póilín—VIII—*Pawlin, Paulyn, Poleyn*, Polin, Pollen, and probably Poland ; ' son of Paulin ' (dim. of Paul). Paulin is a personal name in Domesday Book. Cf. mac póilín.

póirⱅéiⱅ—XII—Porter ; Nor. ' le Porter ' (from Fr. ' portier,' Mid. Eng. ' portere '), i.e., the doorkeeper ; an old Anglo-Norman surname in Dublin, Meath, Wexford, Waterford, &c. V. póⱅⱅúⱅ.

póirⱅin̄ɣéil—XI—*Portingale, Portingall*, Portabello. V. ⱅe póⱅⱅⱅin̄ɣéil.

Polárɒ—VIII or XII—Pollard; 'son of Polard' (dim. of Paul), or Mid-Eng. 'polard,' 'pollard,' i.e., the pollard, one who had his hair cropped short.

Polóc—VIII—Pollock, Pollick, &c.; 'son of Poloc,' dim. of Paul.

Ponns—VIII—*Ponz, Poyns, Poynz, Poyntz, Pounce* Pointz, Punch; 'son of Ponce' (Lat. Poncius, a not uncommon Norman personal name); an old, but rare, surname in Ireland; now found chiefly in Cork and Limerick, where the modern form is Púinre, q.v. Poynston was the old name of the present Punchestown in Co. Kildare.

Portuil—XI—Purtell, Purtill, Purtle; Nor. 'de Port-hull,' i.e. of Porthill; the name of an old family in Tipperary and Limerick.

Pórtúr—XII—Porter; Nor. 'le Portour,' from Fr. 'porteur,' i.e., the porter, carrier. V. Póirtéir.

Potar—XII—*Poter*, Potter; Nor. 'le Poter,' i.e., the potter, maker or seller of earthenware pots. This surname came into Ireland about the time of the Anglo-Norman invasion. 'Philys Poter' and 'John le Poter' occur in the Dublin Roll of Names, A.D. 1216.

Praiʒeas, Price; a late form of Prír, q.v.

Preastún, Preston. V. ɒe Preartún.

Prioɒáil, Pryall, Priall, Priel, Pryle; a Co. Mayo surname, of which I cannot discover the origin.

Prionnsa, Prionnsac, French; in use in Co. Roscommon; probably only a modern rendering into Irish of the surname French. V. ɒe Fréinr.

Priostún, Preston. V. ɒe Preartún.

Prís—VI—*Preece*, Pryse, Price, &c.; Welsh 'Ap-Rhys,' i.e., son of Rhys (a Welsh personal name). This is, no doubt, the origin in the great majority of instances, but such forms as 'le Pryce' and 'de la Prise' in early Anglo-Irish records show that it is not always so. Price is an old surname in Ireland.

Proinnɒíol, *Pronevill*, Prendeville, Prindeville, &c., and in East Cork, strangely Bransfield. V. ɒe Proinn-ɒíol.

Próinséis—XII—*Fronces*, Francey, Francis ; Nor. ' le
Fraunceys,' i.e., the Frenchman ; an early Norman
surname, but never very common.

Pruiséil, Purcell ; a metathesised form of Puinréil, q.v.

Prút—XII—*Prut, Prute*, Proud, Prout ; Nor. ' le Prut,'
' le Proute,' ' le Proud,' i.e., the proud (Old Eng.
' prut,' Mid. Eng. ' prout,' proute '). This surname
had come into Ireland before the middle of the 13th
century. The family settled in Kilkenny and Tipperary, in the latter of which counties, at least, it is
still extant.

Púinse, *Ponchye, Pounche, Pounce*, Punch ; a later
form of Ponnr, q.v.

Puirséil—XII—*Porcell, Purshell*, Purcell, Purcill,
Pursell ; Nor. ' porcel,' dim. of Old French ' porc,'
Lat. ' porcus,' i.e., the little pig, a nickname. This
surname is of record in Ireland since about the middle
of the 13th century ; at the beginning of the 14th
it was already common in Munster. The Purcells
were one of the most influential of the Anglo-Norman
families of Ormond (Kilkenny and Tipperary), where
they had many castles and manors. The head of
the family had the title of Baron of Loughmoe, near
Thurles, where the ruins of Loughmoe Castle are still
to be seen. There was also an important family of
the name at Ballyculhane, in Co. Limerick, and
another at Crumlin, Co. Dublin.

Rádulb—VIII—*Raulf, Rauf*, Rafe, Ralph ; ' son of
Radulf ' or ' Radulph,' a very common Anglo-Norman
personal name. As a surname it is inextricably confused with Rodulb, q.v.

Ragad, Ragat—XII—*Ragid, Raggid, Raggad*, Raggett;
Nor. ' le Raggide,' ' le Ragidde,' ' le Ragged,' i.e., the
ragged, the shaggy ; the name of an old family in Co.
Kilkenny, from whom Ballyragget was so called ;
now very rare.

Ragait, Wright ; a phonetic rendering of the English
surname Wright.

Raȝnall—VIII—*Reynald*, *Ranell*, *Reynell*, *Reynold*, Randall, Randell, Reynalds, Reynolds, Renolds, Ranolds, Rannals, &c. ; 'son of Reginald' (older Reginwald, Raginwald, a common Teutonic personal name) ; the name of an old Co. Dublin family, of record since the end of the 13th century. Charles Reynolds of Dublin, and John Reynolds of Blundelstown, Co. Dublin, were attainted in 1691.

Raȝnárd—VIII—Raynard, Reynard, Renard, Rynard, &c., 'son of Reynard,' (older Raginhard, Regenheard, &c.), a Teutonic personal name.

Raȝnóᵹ—VIII—*Reynaud*, *Reynott*, Reynolds, &c. ; 'son of Reynaud ' (a Fr. form of Reginald) ; a var. of Raȝnall, q.v.

Ráileiȝ, Rawleigh, Raleigh, Rawley, &c. V. ᵹe Ráiléiȝ.

Raincín—VIII—Rankin, Renkin, Renken ; 'son of Rankin,' dim. of Randolf.

Raistric—XI—Rastrick, Restrick ; 'of Rastrick ' in Yorkshire ; Rastric in Domesday Book ; the name of a Wexford family.

Rálaiȝ, Raleigh, &c. V. Ráiléiȝ.

Ramsaiȝ, *Ramesey*, Ramsey, Ramsay, V. ᵹe Ramᵹaiȝ.

Ranᵹal—VIII—*Randulf*, *Randolf*, Randell, Randall ; 'son of Randulf,' a very common Anglo-Norman personal name. It was Latinised, Rannulfus, Ranulfus, Ranulphus, as well as Randulfus, showing that the older pronunciation in England was Rannulf. The dropping of the final *f*, which was usual in names ending in -ulf, caused it to be confused with Rannall, the English form of Reginald (v. Raȝnall above). Randulph and Randal as Christian names are for this reason used as equivalents, especially among the MacDonalds, of Raȝnall which is really Reginald.

Réamonn—VIII—*Remund*, *Reymund*, Raymond, Redmond, &c. ; 'son of Remund ' (Fr. ' Raimond,' Frankish ' Raginmund '; not from Anglo-Saxon ' Raedmund,' as I think can be proved) ; the name of an old Wexford family. In 1598, Redmond of the

Hooke was one of the principal gentlemen of Co. Wexford, as was, in 1608, Redmond of the Hall. Several gentlemen of the name were attainted in 1691.

Réᵒᴅ—XII—Read, Reade, Reede, Reid, &c.; Nor. ' le Rede,' i.e., the red, from the complexion of the face or hair. This surname came into Ireland about the time of the Anglo-Norman invasion. It is sometimes incorrectly translated ᵹioᴛcᴀċ, q.v.

Riᴀbᴀċ—IX—Reagh, Reigh, Rea, &c.; Ir. ' ᴩiᴀbᴀċ,' i.e., grey, brindled; an epithet which supplanted the real surname.

Riᴀᴩ—VIII—Rafe, Ralph; ' son of Ralph '; a rare Mayo surname.

Riᴅeᴀᴌ, *Ridel, Rydel, Ridall*, Riddell, Riddle. V. ᴅe Rioᴅᴀᴌ.

Riobᴀ́Rᴅ—VIII—Robert, Roberts; ' son of Robert.'

Riocᴀ́Rᴅ, Riocᴀ́Rᴅ—VIII—Rickard; ' son of Rickard,' or Richard.

Rioᴅᴀᴌ, *Ridall, Rudel, Ruddel*, Ruddell, Ruddle; an old Co. Limerick surname; probably the same as Riddell. ' Ridall ' appears as a Co. Limerick surname in the Patent Rolls of James I. V. ᴅe Rioᴅᴀᴌ.

Ris—VIII—*Rys, Reys, Ryse*, Rice, Roice, Royce, Ryce; ' son of Rhys ' (a Welsh personal name). The Rices, who are of Welsh descent, settled in Ireland in the 14th or 15th century, especially at Limerick and Dingle, where they were wealthy merchants. Walter Ryce was mayor of Limerick in 1520. The Rices of Dingle came much into prominence in the 16th and 17th centuries.

Robusᴛún, Robusún, *Robuston*, Robertson, Robinson. This surname, which is as old at least as the 16th century, seems to be merely a phonetic rendering of the English surname Robertson.

Roᴅᴌᴀnn—VIII—*Roulant*, Rowland; ' son of Roland,' a personal name of Teutonic origin introduced by the Normans.

Roᴅmonn—VIII—Rodmont, Rodmund, Redmon, Red-

mont ; ' son of Rodmund,' the Teutonic personal name
Hrothmund. ' Rodmund ' occurs in Domesday Book.

Roóulb—VIII—Rolfe, Rolph ; ' son of Rodolf,' or
' Rudolph,' the Teutonic Hrothwulf ; confused with
Ráóulb, q.v.

Roibeál—VIII—*Revel*, *Revell*, Reville ; ' son of Rabel '
or Revel, an old personal name in England, of uncertain origin. Ravelin, its diminutive, occurs in
Domesday Book and Searle, and is evidently the origin
of the Irish name Raibilín, angl. Revelyn, borne by
the Savages of Co. Down. Reville is an old, but rare,
Wexford surname.

Roibeárd—VIII—Robert, Roberts ; ' son of Robert.'

Róisteác—XIV—Rostig, Roche, Roache. V. ve
Róirte.

Rós, *Roos*, Rose. V. ve Rúr.

Rósaiteár—XI—*Rowcester*, *Rawceter*, Rossiter, &c. ;
' of Rocester,' a parish in Staffordshire ; the name of
an old family in Co. Wexford. Rawceter of Rath-
macknee was one of the principal gentlemen of Co.
Wexford in 1598. The name is still common in the
county.

Rostárd, *Rostard*, Rochford ; a form in Co. Limerick
of ve Rorforc, q.v. It was evidently sometimes
mistaken for Richard, as in the Patent Rolls of Henry
VIII., where we find ' Rochford or Richards of Limerick.' Also Rortún, q.v.

Rostún, Rochford ; an Irish form in Co. Limerick of
Rochford. V. Rortárd and ve Rorforc.

Ruáb—IX—Rowe, Roe ; Ir. ' ruáb,' i.e., red, red-haired ;
an epithet which took the place of the real surname.
Roe is often merely the final syllable of such surnames
as MacEnroe, &c. Rowe is also an English surname.

Rucstón, Ruckston, Ruxton.

Ruiséil—XII—*Rushell*, *Rosel*, *Rossell*, Russell ; Nor.
' russel,' i.e., red-haired, dim. of ' rous.' This surname came into Ireland at the time of the Anglo-
Norman invasion and soon became very widespread,
being specially common in Dublin, Meath, West-

meath, Limerick, Cork, Waterford, Louth and Down. The Russells of Co. Down came over with Sir John de Courcy. They held extensive property down to the confiscations of the 17th century. The late Lord Russell of Killowen, Lord Chief Justice of England, belonged to this ancient and illustrious family.

ꞃuιꞇɫeιs, ꞃuιꞇɫιs—XI—*Rutlech*, Rutlege, Rutledge, Ruthledge, Routhledge, &c. ; ' of Rutledge,' some spot in England.

ꞃúꞇ—VIII—*Route*, Ruth, Routh, Roth, Rothe ; ' son of Rot,' Norse Hrutr, red-haired. Rot occurs in Domesday Book. Robert Rot de Kilkudbricht was a member of the Dublin Guild-Merchant, A.D. 1226. In later times, the name was chiefly associated with Kilkenny, of which city the Rothes were one of the chief families. The most illustrious bearer of the name was Dr. David Rothe, Bishop of Ossory, at the time of the Confederation of Kilkenny.

sɑbɑιsꞇe, Savage ; a var. in Kilkenny and Waterford of Sɑbɑoιꞃ, q.v.

sɑbɑoιs, sɑbɑoιs—XII—*Sauvage*, Savage ; Nor. ' le Salvage,' ' le Sauvage,' i.e., the savage, one of wild, fierce character ; the name of an old Anglo-Norman family planted in 1177 by Sir John de Courcy in the Ardes of Co. Down. The Savages are frequently mentioned in the Irish Annals. They possessed considerable property down to the revolution of 1689. Savage is also an old surname in Kilkenny and Waterford ; v. Sɑbɑιꞃꞇe.

sɑʒɑs—XII—*Says*, *Seys*, *Seise*, Size, Seix, Sex ; Welsh ' Sais,' i.e., the Saxon, Englishman, stranger ; a descriptive surname given by the Welsh to some family of English origin who afterwards settled in Offaly, Leix and Ormond. It is now very rare.

sɑιɫeɑsꞇɑꞃ, St. Leger, St. Ledger, Ledger, Lister, Lyster, &c.; a later form of Sɑιɫιʒéιꞃ, q.v. It was sometimes re-anglicised Lister and Lyster even as early as the 16th century.

Sₐᵢₗᵢⁿₑᵢᵣ, Saᵢₗᵢⁿₑᵢᵣ, Saᵢₗᵢⁿᵹₑᵢᵣ, Sallinger, Sellinger, St. Leger, Ledger, &c. V. ᴅe SaᵢₗᵢᵹéᵢⱤ.

Saᵢⁿséᵢₗ, Sarsfield; a var. of SáᵢⱤᵣéᵢₗ, q.v.; in use in
Co. Mayo.

Sáᵢᵣᵹeaⁿᴛ—XII—*Serjeaunt*, Sergeant, Sargeant, Sargent, &c.; Nor. ' le Sergant,' i.e., the sergeant, officer
(of the law, &c.); an early Anglo-Irish surname.

Sáᵢᵣséᵢₗ, Sarseil, Sarsfield. V. ᴅe SáᵢⱤᵣéᵢₗ.

Sáᵢséᵢₗ, Sausheil, Sarsfield; a corruption of SáᵢⱤᵣéᵢₗ,
q.v.; in use in Co. Mayo.

Sáₗ, *Saale, Sawle*, Sall, Saul. V. ᴅe Sáₗ.

Samsūⁿ—VIII—*Samsun*, Samson, Sampson; ' son of
Samson ' (a Biblical name in use among the Anglo-
Saxons and Normans); the name of an Anglo-Norman
family who came to Ireland about the time of the
invasion and settled at Naas, in Co. Kildare, and at
Callan, in Co. Kilkenny. Since the Cromwellian period,
it has been found chiefly in the parish of Galbally, Co.
Limerick, but is an old surname in East Limerick.

Saⁿᴅaᵢᵣ, Saⁿᴅaᵣ—VIII—*Sandre, Saunder*, Sanders,
Saunders; ' son of Sander ' (short for Alexander); an
old Anglo-Irish surname in Dublin, Meath, and other
parts of Leinster.

Saⁿᴅáₗ, Sandall, Sandell. V. ᴅe Saⁿᴅáₗ.

Saoᴅaₗ—VIII—*Sawald, Sewall*, Sewell, Suel, &c.;
' son of Saeweald,' an Anglo-Saxon personal name.

Saoᴅaᵣᴅ—VIII—*Saoward*, Seaward, Seward; ' son of
Saeweard,' an Anglo-Saxon personal name, but it can
hardly be distinguished from Sigeweard (Siweard,
Siward).

Saoᵹaᵣ—VIII—Sayer, Sear, Sayers, Sears; ' son of
Saegaer,' a common Anglo-Saxon personal name,
frequent in early Anglo-Irish records.

Saomaᵣ—VIII—*Seamer*, Semore, Seymore, Semour,
Seymour, &c.; ' son of Saemaer,' an Anglo-Saxon
personal name, hardly distinguishable from Sigemaer.

Scamᴛūⁿ, Sceaᵢmᵢᴛíⁿ—XI—Scamaton, Scampton;
i.e., ' of Scampton,' a parish in Lincolnshire; a rare
Co. Cork surname.

sceᴀꞃᴀᴄ, Skerrett. V. Scιṗéιꞁꞁo.

sceιṁeᴀʟᴄúꞁꞁ—XI—Skivington, Skeffington, Skiffington, &c. ; i.e., ' of Skeffington,' a parish in Leicestershire.

scιꞁoιꞁꞁꞁꞁ—VIII—*Skydy*, *Skiddie*, Skiddy ; ' son of Skithi '
(a Norse personal name, probably the same as ' skyti,'
an archer) ; an old Cork surname of Danish origin.
The Skiddys formed a clan after the Irish fashion,
with a ' chief of the name.' No fewer than thirty-
four Skiddys figure on the roll of mayors of Cork.

scιʟʟιꞁꞁꞁ, scιʟʟιꞁꞁꞁ—VIII—Skilling, Skillen ; ' son of
Scilling ' (a Norse personal name, the same as the
English ' shilling ' ; cf. ꞃeóιꞁꞁʟιꞁꞁꞁ). Mac Scelling was
the name of a naval commander from the Hebrides,
mentioned by the Four Masters at the year 1154.

scιꞁꞁéιꞁꞁ—XII—Skinner ; Nor. ' le Skynnere,' i.e., the
skinner, dealer in skins ; an old, but rare, surname
in Ireland.

scιꞁꞁéιꞁꞁo, *Skirret*, Skerrett. This surname, according to
Hardiman (History of Galway, p. 19), was originally
Huscared, which was shortened to Scared. The
Skerrets were an old and respectable Galway family.
Richard Scared, or Skeret, was provost of Galway
in 1378.

scoꞃuʟ, Scuffil, Scholefield. V. ꞁꞁe Scoꞃuʟ.

scoʟᴀꞁꞁo—XII—*Skolard*, Scolard, Scollard ; Eng. ' the
Scholar,' i.e., one belonging to a school, a learned
man ; an old, but rare, Kerry surname. In the year
1601, Maurice Skolard of Castleisland was the recipient
of a pardon from Queen Elizabeth.

scoꞃʟóꞁꞁ—XII—*Scorloge*, *Scorloke*, *Scurlok*, Scurlock,
Shirlock, Shearlock, Sherlock ; Ang.-Sax. ' Scortlog,'
i.e., short lock, one with shorn locks. This family,
which, to judge from the name, is of Anglo-Saxon
origin, had settled in Ireland before the beginning
of the 13th century, and soon after became very
widespread, being found in Dublin, Meath, Louth,
Wexford, Waterford, Tipperary, &c.

scoᴄ—XII—*Scot*, Scott ; Eng. ' the Scot,' i.e., the Scotchman, an immigrant from Scotland; an old surname in Ireland, but rare until the plantation of Ulster. Alḃanaċ (q.v.) was the corresponding Irish surname.

Sdonḋún, Sdonnḋún, Sdundon. V. Sconḋún.

Seac—VIII—*Jakes, Jak*, Jack, Jacke, and incorrectly Jackman; 'son of Jaques' (a French name, from Latin Jacobus, same as the English James); an early Anglo-Norman surname. The family seems to have settled in Kilkenny and Tipperary.

Seaḋaċ, Seaȝaċ, Shaw.

Seafraiḋ—VIII—Jaffrey, Jeffrey, &c.; 'son of Geoffrey,' a Norman personal name, the same as Godfrey.

Seamḃar, Seamḃars, Seamḃraċ—XI—*Chamber*, Chambers, Chamberlain; Fr. 'de la Chambre,' Lat. 'de Camera,' i.e., of the chamber, the chamberlain.

Seamróȝ—XI—Shamrock, Hamrogue; doubtless 'of Sambrook,' or 'Shambrook,' a parish in Shropshire. There is some connection between this surname and hampóc, q.v.

Séamus—VIII—James; 'son of James.'

Searlóȝ, Shearlock, Sherlock; a var. of Scoplóȝ, q.v.

Séarlus—VIII—*Sharles*, Charles; 'son of Charles.'

Searman—XII—*Shereman*, Sharman, Sherman, Shearman; Nor. 'le Sherman,' i.e., the shearman, cutter of cloth. This family had settled in Dublin before the middle of the 13th century.

Seartáin, *Shortaun*, Shorten; doubtless, a corruption of Seaptal or Soiptéil, q.v. Richard Shortaun of Limerick, Co. Wexford, was attainted in 1642. This form of the name is now peculiar to Co. Cork.

Seartal, Shortall; a var. of Soiptéil, q.v.

Seinicín—VIII—Jenkin, Jenkins, Jinkins, &c.; 'son of Jenkin,' dim. of John.

Seóȝ, Seóȝaċ, *Sheo, Joye*, Joy, Joyce. V. Seóiȝ.

Seoȝas—VIII—*Sheos, Josse, Joce*, Joyce; 'son of Joce,' or 'Josse' (a Breton personal name). This surname, which appears to be distinct from Seóiȝ (q.v.), was peculiar to Kilkenny and Cork. In Ireland, it dates back at least to the 13th century.

seóiʒ—VIII or XII—*Sheoye, Shoye, Joie, Joye,* Joy, Joyce; 'son of Joy' (probably a Norman personal name—Joie, Joye—corresponding to the Latin Letitia; but possibly merely a descriptive epithet bestowed on one of a joyous disposition). As a surname, it is of record in Ireland since the end of the 12th century, when the family seems to have come hither from Wales, and by the 16th century had become very widespread. The Joyces of Galway, according to Hardiman (Hist. of Galway, pp. 14-15), came from Wales in the reign of Edward I. They acquired considerable tracts of territory in the mountainous district of Iar-Connacht, called from them Duthaigh Seoghach, or the Joyce Country, now forming the barony of Ross, in Co. Galway, where they are still very numerous. They were, according to Hardiman, a race of men remarkable for their extraordinary stature. The surname is now almost everywhere anglicised Joyce. Joy, the correct rendering, is almost peculiar to Kerry. Cf. Seóʒaṛ above.

seóiʒeaċ, seóiʒeaċ—XIV—Joy, Joyce. V. Seóiʒ.

seóiṛse—VIII—George; 'son of George.'

seóns—*Johns,* Jones; 'son of John'; a phonetic rendering of the English surname Jones.

seoṛṫús—XII—*Shortus, Shorthose,* Shortis, Shortice; Ang-Sax. 'Sceorthosa,' i.e., of the short hose; not an old surname in Ireland.

seósaċ—XIV—Joyce. V. Seoʒaṛ.

siacus—VIII—Jacques; 'son of Jacques.' V. Seac.

síḃeaṛ—XII—*Chiver, Chevere,* Chivers, Chevers, Cheevers; Nor. 'le Chivere,' 'le Chevere,' i.e., the goat (Fr. chevre), a nickname; the name of a Norman family who came to Ireland about the time of the invasion and settled in Dublin, Louth, Meath, Kildare and Wexford. They were highly respectable, but lost their property in the Cromwellian and Williamite confiscations. A branch of the family was transplanted to Connacht by Cromwell.

sıᵹín—VIII—*Sigin, Siggin,* Siggins ; 'son of Sigewine,' an Anglo-Saxon personal name.

sımıcín—VIII—*Symikine,* Simkin, Simpkin, Simkins Simpkins ; 'son of Simkin' (dim. of Simon).

sınncléır, Sinclair, &c. V. ꝺe Sıncléıp.

sımıcín—VIII—Shinkwin ; 'son of Jenkin' (dim. of Fr. Jean, or John). V. Seınıcín.

sıomcóc, sıomcóᵹ—VIII—*Symcok, Symcock,* Simcox ; 'son of Simcock' (dim. of Simon).

sıonnᴀċ—X—Shinnagh, Shinnock, &c., and by translation Fox, Foxe ; Ir. 'Sıonnᴀċ,' i.e., the fox ; an epithet or nickname which supplanted the real surname, especially in the case of the family of Ó Cᴀċᴀpnᴀıᵹ (q.v.), anciently chiefs of Teffia.

sıonóıꝺ—VIII—*Signot, Synod, Synote, Synot,* Sinott, Synott, Sinnott, Synnott ; 'son of Sigenoth' (an Anglo-Saxon personal name) ; the name of an English family who came to Ireland at the time of the invasion and settled in Wexford, where they have ever since been both numerous and influential. In the reign of Elizabeth, the Sinnotts were great 'loyalists,' and were rewarded with grants of the confiscated lands of the MacMurroughs. David Sinnott was governor of Wexford when that town was besieged by Cromwell. The Sinnotts lost their estates in the Cromwellian and Williamite confiscations. There were also ancient families of the name in Dublin and Tipperary.

sıonúıꝛ, Shinnor, Shinnors, and in parts of Connacht incorrectly Sinnott, Synnott ; also Soınıúıp, q.v. V. ꝺe Sıonúıp.

sıosᴀl—XI—Chisholm ; Nor. 'de Cheseholme,' i.e., of Chisholm in Roxburgh ; a Scottish surname.

sıseᴀl—VIII—*Seysel, Seycel,* Chisel, Chissell, (Chisholm) ; evidently 'son of Cecil.'

sıúınéıꝛ—XII—Joyner ; i.e., 'the joiner,' or carpenter.

sıúıꞇ—XI—*Shute,* Chute ; i.e., 'of Chute,' a parish in Wiltshire ; not a very old surname in Ireland.

sıúꝛꝺᴀn, sıúꝛꞇᴀn—VIII—*Jurdane, Jordane,* Jurdan,

Jordan, &c.; 'son of Jordan' (a personal name, derived from the river Jordan, which became popular in crusading times throughout Western Europe, and nowhere more than in England, owing to flasks of Jordan water being brought home to be used for baptismal purposes). The Jordans were an Anglo-Norman family who settled early in Dublin, Meath, Limerick, &c. Jordan of Hilton was one of the chief gentlemen of Dublin at the end of the 16th century, and at the same period three of the name were mayors of Limerick. This surname is to be distinguished from Mac Siúrtáin, q.v.

Slócúm—XI—*Sloocume*, Slocum, Slocombe, &c.; i.e., 'of Slocombe,' a place-name in the south-west of England; apparently not a very old surname in Ireland.

Smeart—XII—*Smert*, Smart, Smartt; Anglo-Saxon 'Smeart,' i.e., quick, sharp; an old, but very rare, surname in Ireland.

Smroic—XI—*Smedick*, Smithwick; i.e., 'of Smethwick' in Staffordshire, written Smedewich in Domesday Book and still pronounced locally Smethick; a rare, and apparently not very old, surname in Ireland.

Smroig, Smroige—XI—*Smethy*, Smiddy, Smithwick; very probably 'at the smithy,' from residence thereby, but possibly 'of Smethwick,' as above (v. Smroic), to which the angl. form Smithwick would seem to point; a rare Co. Cork surname.

Smist—XII or XI—*Smeche, Smyche, Smytche, Smythes*, Smeeth, Smiddy, Smithwick; Mid. Eng. 'Smeche,' apparently for 'Smethe,' i.e., smooth, polished, suave, but Smirt has evidently been regarded as in some way connected with Smroige (q.v.), and so the origin may be 'at the smithies.' It is a not uncommon surname in the neighbourhood of Youghal.

Smisteać—XIV—Smithwick. V. Smirt.

Soinniúir, *Synur*, Shinnor, Shinnors, and, in parts of Connacht, incorrectly Sinnott, Synnott. Also Sionúir, q.v.

soircéil—XII—*Scorthals*, *Schorthals*, *Sertell*, *Sertill*,
Shorthall, Shortall, Shortell, Shortle, Surtill ; Ang.-
Sax. 'Scort-hals,' i.e., short-neck, a nickname or
descriptive name ; Langhals also once existed. This
family, which, to judge from the name, is of Anglo-
Saxon origin, probably came to Ireland early in the
reign of Edward I. They settled in Co. Kilkenny
where they became very influential. Their chief seat
was at Ballylorcan, but they had many other castles
in the barony of Iverk.

spáineac—X—*Spainagh*, Spain ; Ir. 'Spáineac,' i.e.,
the Spaniard, a descriptive name given to an Irishman
who returned from Spain, and which supplanted the
real surname.

spéiring, Spearing, Spearin.

sprac—VIII—*Sprot*, Spratt ; 'son of Sprot' (an Anglo-
Saxon personal name). This surname can boast of
considerable antiquity in Ireland.

scac—XI—*Stak*, *Stake*, Stack ; Mid. Eng. 'Stak,'
'Stake,' i.e., probably, 'at the stack' (steep rock or
hill), or 'at the stock' (stump of a tree), from residence
thereby. The Stacks are an old family in North
Kerry, where they have been settled, at least, since
the latter part of the 13th century. In the year 1450,
Maurice Stak was appointed Bishop of Adfert ; and
thirty years later, John Stak was bishop of the same
see. By the end of the 16th century, the Stacks had
become very numerous in North Kerry. They were
then thoroughly Irish. Garrett Roe Stack was one
of the principal leaders in the wars against Queen
Elizabeth.

scaforc, Stafford. V. ve Scaforc.

scancaro—XI—*Stanckard*, Stancard, Stanford ; doubtless, Nor. 'de Stanford,' i.e., of Stanford, a parish in
Kent ; an old surname in Co. Mayo.

scarcaio—VIII—*Starky*, *Starkye*, Starkie, Starkey ;
'son of Starkie' (a 'pet' form of one of the many
Anglo-Saxon names beginning with Starc-, as Starc-
beorht, Starcfrith, Starchere, Starcwulf). Instances

of this surname occur in Irish records since the end of
the 13th century.

Sτíḃin—VIII—*Stevyn, Stevene,* Steven, Steen, Steene,
Stevens, Stephens ; ' son of Stephen ' ; an old Anglo-
Irish surname.

Sτíoḃarᵹ, Sτíoḃarτ, Sτιúḃarᵹ—XII—*Stiward,*
Steward, Stewart, Stuart ; Nor. ' le Stiward,' i.e., the
steward. The royal Stuarts of Scotland derived their
name from the office of Lord High Steward which was
hereditary in the family for two centuries before
they came to the throne. Prior to the plantation
of Ulster, there are few traces of any families of the
name in Ireland, nearly all our Stewarts being the
descendants of late immigrants from Scotland.

Sτóc, *Stoke,* Stokes, Stoakes. V. ᵹe Sτóc.

Sτóiḃín—XI—*Stobyn,* Stubbin, Stubbins ; Nor. ' de
St. Obyn,' i.e., of St. Aubin in Brittany ; an old, but
rare, surname in Ireland. Cf. τóiḃín.

Sτonᵹún, Sτonnᵹún, Sτúnᵹún, Staunton, Stundon, Sdundun. V. ᵹe Sτonnᵹún.

Sτráinse—XII—L'Estrange,   Strange ;   Nor.   ' le
Estrange,' ' le Straunge,' i.e., the foreigner, the
stranger, the new-comer ; an old surname in Ireland.

Sτraoιτ, Sτraoιτs—XI—*Strete, Streate, Streete,
Stretys, Streytis, Streache, Streech, Stretch, Strytch,*
Stritch ; Nor. ' de la Strete,' Old. Eng. ' atte Strete '
i.e., at the street or paved (Roman) road, from
residence thereby. (The old forms Streache, Stretch,
&c., stand for Streets, monosyllabic surnames of
local origin often adding *s* after the manner of patronymics, as Williams, Jones, &c.) Stritch was the name
of an old and respectable merchant family in Limerick,
of which city Nicholas Stritch was mayor in 1427.
Among the twenty exempted from pardon by Ireton
when he took possession of Limerick in 1651, was
Alderman Thomas Stritch. There are very few of
this old name now in Limerick.

Sτronᵹ, Sτronnᵹ—XII—Strong, Stronge, Strange ;
Old. Eng. ' Strang,' Mid. Eng. ' Stronge,' ' Strange,'

i.e., strong, powerful, a descriptive surname. There were old and respectable families of this name in the cities of Kilkenny and Waterford.

sꞇuꝺaꞃꞇ—XII—Studdert.

suan—VIII—*Suan, Swane,* Swaine, Swayne, &c.; 'son of Swan' (a common Anglo-Saxon personal name). This surname appears in Anglo-Irish records soon after the invasion, but never became common in Ireland.

suaꞇman—VIII—*Swetman, Sweteman,* Sweetman; 'son of Swetman' (a not uncommon Anglo-Saxon personal name). This family, which, to judge from the name, is of Anglo-Saxon origin, came to Ireland some time before the middle of the 13th century and settled in Co. Kilkenny, where they were highly respectable

suillinꞣéiꞃ, Sellinger, St. Ledger, &c.; a var. of Saillinꞣéiꞃ, q.v.

suinꞣean—XI—Singen, Singin, St. John; Nor. 'de St. Jehan,' 'de St. Jean,' i.e., of St. John's, a common French place-name; an early Norman surname in Ireland. The family settled in Wexford, Kilkenny and Tipperary. Thomas de St. John was sheriff of Tipperary in 1296.

suipéil—XI—Suppell, Supple; Nor. 'de la Chapell,' Lat. 'de Capella,' i.e., of the chapel, from residence thereby; an old surname in Co. Limerick, where it is of record since the last quarter of the 13th century, and of which the Supples were, in the latter part of the 16th century, one of the chief families. They lost their property after the Desmond wars. The ruins of their castle are still to be seen at Kilmocua, near Croom.

suisꞇe—XI—*Souche,* Suche, Zouche; Nor. 'de la Zouch,' i.e., of the zouch (an old French word, meaning the stock of a tree), from residence thereby; an old, but extremely rare, surname in Limerick and Kerry.

suiꞇséiꞃ—XII—Switzer; i.e., 'the Swiss,' immigrant from Switzerland.

SúCAR—XII—Soutar, Souter, Sutter, Sutor, &c.; Nor. 'le Suter,' 'le Souter,' i.e., the shoemaker. The following interesting reference to a member of this family occurs in the Fiants of Elizabeth :—A.D. 1601 —Pardon to Nich. Suter, shoemaker.—F. E. 6517.

CáilliúiR—XII—*Taillur, Taillour*, Taylour, Taylor, &c.; Nor. 'le Tailleur,' i.e., the cutter, the tailor; an old Norman surname in Dublin, where the family settled about the time of the invasion. The majority of our Taylors are, however, the descendants of more recent immigrants.

CAlanc—XI—Tallan, Tallen, Tallant, Tallent; i.e., 'of Talland' in Cornwall; a rare surname in Limerick and Waterford.

CAlbóiv—VIII—*Talebot, Talbote*, Talbot; 'son of Talebot' (a Norman personal name). The Talbots came over to England with William the Conqueror. Richard Talebot is mentioned in Domesday Book. His descendant and namesake, Richard Talbot, accompanied Henry II to Ireland and was granted the lordship of Malahide, Co. Dublin, which has continued in his descendants to the present day. The Talbots have at different times filled many of the highest offices of Church and State in Ireland.

CAlún—VIII—*Talun, Talown, Tallone*, Tallon; 'son of Talon' (a Norman personal name). The Tallons were a Norman family who settled early in Dublin and other parts of the Pale.

CAnncáRo—VIII—Tankard, Tancard; 'son of Tancred' (a Norman personal name, Teutonic Tancrad, Ang.-Sax. Thancred, early corrupted to Tancard and Tankard); an old, but now extremely rare, surname in Ireland. In 1598 Tankard or Tancaid of Castletown was one of the chief gentlemen of Meath. The name was in use at the same period in Co. Cork.

CAnúiR—XII—Tanner; Nor. 'le Tanur,' 'le Tanour,' 'le Tanner,' i.e., the tanner; an old, but rare, surname in Ireland.

ᴄᴀᴏɪʟɪɴᵹ—VIII—*Theling, Teling, Teelin,* Teeling; apparently Ang.-Sax. ' Taeling,' i.e., son of Tael; the name of an old family in Co. Meath, where, at the end of the 16th century, the Teelings ranked among the gentry.

ᴄᴀʀᴀɴᴄ—XI—Tarrant; i.e., ' of Tarrant ' in Dorsetshire and other parts of England; a rare Co. Cork surname, apparently of late origin; also ᴄᴏᴘᴀɴᴄᴀ, q.v.

ᴄᴀᴄ—VIII—*Ta, Tath, Taath, Taaf,* Taff, Taaffe; ' son of David '; cf. modern Irish ᴅᴀᴄ and Welsh Taffy; the name of a distinguished family of Welsh origin who settled at an early period in Co. Louth. Towards the end of the 13th century, flourished Sir Nicholas Taaffe, Justice of the Common Pleas, whose son, John Taaffe, became Archbishop of Armagh. In the reign of Elizabeth, Sir William Taaffe did good service against Hugh O'Neill and subsequently against the Spaniards at Kinsale, for which he was rewarded by James I with large grants of confiscated lands in Co. Sligo. In 1628, his son, John Taaffe, was created Baron of Ballymote and Viscount Corren; and in 1661, Theobald, son of this John Taaffe, was made Earl of Carlingford. The Taaffes were most zealous supporters of the Stuarts, in whose cause they sacrificed everything. Nicholas, the second Earl of Carlingford, fell at the Boyne, and the family honours devolved on his brother Francis, the celebrated Count Taaffe of the German Empire.

ᴄɪɴᴄʟᴇɪʀ—XII—Tinckler, Tinkler; Eng. ' the tinkler,' i.e., the hawker, or other tradesman who made his approach known by a tinkling noise.

ᴄɪʀɪᴀʟ—VIII—*Torel, Turrill, Tyrel, Tirrell,* Tyrrell; ' son of Tyrel ' or ' Thurold ' (corrupt for Ang.-Sax. Thurwald, Norse Thorvaldr). This family, which is of Norman origin, came to England with William the Conqueror. At the time of the Anglo-Norman invasion, Hugh Tyrrell received from Hugh de Lacy the lordship of Castleknock; and his descendants were styled Barons of Castleknock until the line became extinct in 1385. In Co. Westmeath, the Tyrrells possessed the barony of Fertullagh down to the 17th century. Captain Richard Tyrrell was a celebrated commander in the Elizabethan wars in Ireland. Also τριαὶ.

τιú, *Tywe*, *Tue*, Tew. V. de τe τιú.

τιυιτ, Tuite. V. τe τιúιτ.

τóc—VIII—Toke, Tooke, Tuke; ' son of Toke,' a personal name of Norse origin, common in Domesday, where it is variously written Toc, Toke, Toka, &c.

τóιбíη—XI—*Tobine*, Tobyn, Tobin; Nor. ' de St. Aubyn,' ' de St. Obyn,' Lat. ' de Sancto Albino,' i.e., of St. Aubin, a town in Brittany, famous as the scene of a battle between the French and Bretons, aided by the English, in 1488. The Tobins settled early in Tipperary and Kilkenny, whence they spread into the neighbouring counties of Waterford, Cork and Limerick. The head of the family was styled Baron of Comsey, in Co. Tipperary.

τóιmιcíη—VIII—*Tomekin*, Tomkin, Tomkins; ' son of Tomkin ' (dim. of Thomas).

τοιmíη—VIII—*Tomine*, *Tomen*, Timmin, Timmins, Timmons, &c. ; ' son of Tomin ' (dim. of Thomas) ; an old surname in Carlow, Kildare and Wexford.

τοιριỏ, Terry. V. τυιριỏ.

τóm—VIII—*Tome*, Thom ; ' son of Thome ' (a short form of Thomas).

τοmάs—VIII—Thomas ; ' son of Thomas,' one of the commonest names in use among the Anglo-Norman settlers in Ireland.

τóη—VIII—*Toan*, Tone ; ' son of Tona ' (an Anglo-Saxon personal name, found in Domesday Book as the name of holders of land even in the time of Edward the Confessor). As a surname, it appears in Anglo-Irish records as early as the beginning of the 14th century, but has always been very rare, and is now hardly known except through Theobald Wolfe Tone.

τοράητα, Tarrant, and incorrectly Thornton ; a var. of τάραητ, q.v.

ᴄoᴚbóιᴅ—VIII—*Turbot*, Turbett, Turbit ; 'son of Turbot' (dim. of Turbert, or Torbert, Anglo-Saxon Thurbeorht, Norse Thorbiartr) ; an old, but always extremely rare, surname in Ireland.

ᴄoᴚnóιᴚ—XII—*Tornour*, *Tournor*, Turnour, Turnor, Turner ; Nor. ' le Turner,' i.e., the turner, lathe-worker, once a familiar occupation. Turnor is an old surname in Dublin, Wexford, and parts of Munster. ' Abrid le Turnur ' occurs in the Dublin Roll of Names soon after the Anglo-Norman invasion, and in 1226, William and Osbeit Turnur were members of the Dublin Guild-Merchant ; while somewhat later in the same century, Clement le Turnur was one of the Free Citizens of Dublin. The most important family of the name in the 16th century was that of Wexford, where, in 1598, Turnor of Ballyasshin was one of the principal gentlemen.

ᴄóᴚnuιl—XI—Thornhill ; i.e., ' of Thornhill,' in York-shire ; ' Tornil ' in Domesday Book.

ᴄoᴚsᴄán—VIII—*Trostane*, *Trustane*, and incorrectly Tristan and Tristram ; ' son of Thurstan ' (an Anglo-Saxon personal name, corresponding to Norse Thors-tein ; hardly from Welsh ' trystan ' the old Angl. forms being against this derivation) ; a rare Ros-common surname..

ᴄᴚáιbeaᴚs, Travers, Travors, Trevors. V. ᴅe ᴄᴚáιbeaᴚ.

ᴄᴚéanlámaċ, Armstrong ; doubtless a translation of the English Armstrong.

ᴄᴚeannᴄ, ᴄᴚeanᴄ, *Traunte*, Trant. V. ᴅe ᴄᴚeanᴄ.

ᴄᴚeó, *Treo*, *Troe*, *Troye*, Troy. V. ᴅe ᴄᴚeó.

ᴄᴚιal, *Tryal*, Tyrrell ; a syncopated form of ᴄιᴘιal, q.v.

ᴄᴚιnnse, ᴄᴚínse—XI—Trench ; i.e., ' at the trench,' or cutting ; not a very old surname in Ireland.

ᴄᴚιú—XII—*Trewe*, Trew ; Mid. Eng. ' Trewe,' i.e., the true, faithful, loyal man ; an old, but rare, surname in Kildare, &c.

ᴄᴚιúman—XII—*Treweman*, *Treuman*, Trueman ; Mid. Eng. ' Treweman,' i.e., the true man, same as ᴄᴚιú above ; an old, but rare, surname in Co. Down.

Cuinléig, Townley. V. ᴅe Cuinléig.

Cuirrᴅ—VIII—*Thirry, Tyrry, Tirry*, Terry; 'son of Tyrry' (a Norman form of the Anglo-Saxon personal name Thuri, short for Thured or Thored, common in Domesday Book). Tyrry occurs as a Christian name in the Black Book of Limerick. As a surname, it is of record in Ireland since the last decade of the 13th century, being then established at Kilkenny and Cork. In the latter city, the Tyrrys or Terrys, became one of the most influential families, and upwards of twenty of the name figure in the list of mayors.

Cunᴅar—XII—*Tunder*, Thunder; Nor. 'le Thunder,' i.e., the vintner, or the cask-maker; an old Dublin surname.

Cúnluiᴅ, Townley. V. ᴅe Cuinléig.

Curaoin, *Turien, Toran*, Torran, Torrans, Torrens, Torry, Terry, &c.; possibly for 'de Torigni,' i.e., of Torigny, a town in France.

uacan—XII—*Vachan, Vaghan*, Vaughan; Welsh 'vychan,' i.e., little, small of stature; the name of a Welsh family, some of whom settled, prior to the 16th century, in Dublin, Wexford, and perhaps other parts of Leinster. The great majority of our Vaughans are, however, of native origin.

uaᴅa—VIII—Wade, Waide, &c.; 'son of Wada' (a common Anglo-Saxon personal name). Thomas Wade was one of the free citizens of Dublin, 1225-1250.

*uaᴅlóc—XI—*Wodeloc, Woodloge*, Woodlock; i.e., 'at the woodlock,' or enclosure in or by a wood, from residence thereby. This surname came into Ireland about the time of the Anglo-Norman invasion. It appears to have been most numerous in Tipperary.

úgán—XII—*Ugan, Owgan, Wogane*, Ougan, Oogan, Ogan, Wogan, Vogan; Welsh 'gwgan,' from 'gwg,' a frown, a scowl. The Wogans settled soon after the Anglo-Norman invasion in Co. Kildare, where their chief seat was at Rathcoffey. The family produced several distinguished men.

uaioín—VIII—*Wadin*, Wadden, Wadding; 'son of Wadin' (a dim. of the Anglo-Saxon Wada or of the Norman Walter, the latter by far the more probable; 'Wadin White' occurs in Grace's Annals, A.D. 1316). The Waddings settled early in Wexford and Waterford. In Wexford their chief seat was at Ballycogly. The Waterford family produced several distinguished ecclesiastics, among them the illustrious Franciscan, Father Luke Wadding.

uaisléiʒ—XI—*Wesleie*, Wesley, Wellesley; Nor. 'de Welleslegh,' i.e., of Wellesley, corruptly Wesley, a spot in Somerset, a short distance from Wells. This family came to Ireland at the time of the Anglo-Norman invasion and settled in Kildare and Meath. They assumed the Irish patronymic surname of mac Uaʃʄponca, q.v. To the Meath branch belonged the Duke of Wellington.

uaicne—IX—*Woney*, Green; Ir. 'Uaicne,' i.e., green; a descriptive epithet which supplanted the real surname.

ualoʀán—VIII—*Walerand*, *Waleran*, Waldron; 'son of Walerand,' a Teutonic personal name, found in Domesday Book. V. mac Uaʃʄponca.

uasoún, uastún—XI—*Westoun*, Weston; Nor. 'de Westun,' i.e., of Weston, or the west-town, in England. 'Aluredus de Westun' occurs in the Dublin Roll of Names, A.D. 1216.

uicstéio—XI—Wixted; i.e., 'of Wickstead' in England; a Tipperary surname.

uioeas, Wise, Wyse. V. oe Uioeaʃ.

uilis, Willis, Wills; a phonetic rendering of the English surname Willis.

uileamóio, uilmic—VIII—Wilmot, Wilmott, Willmott, Willmit; 'son of Williamot' (dim. of William).

uinʒil—XI—Winkle, Windle, Wingfield; i.e., 'of Wincle' in Cheshire, or more probably merely a phonetic representation of the sound of the English name, Windle.

uinʒséil—XI—Wingfield; i.e., 'of Wingfield,' in England.

uinnseaoún—XI—*Unsedon, Winsedon, Wynchedon,* (Nugent) ; Nor. ' de Wynchester,' i.e., of Winchester, an ancient episcopal city in Hampshire. Members of the family of Nugent who came from this city and settled early in Cork were known in Irish by the surname **uinnreaoún**, which was intended to represent Winchester. These Nugents formed a clan after the Irish fashion. The chief lived at Aghavarten Castle, near Carrigaline. The original surname, Nugent, has been retained in English. Cf. **núinnreann**.

uinseann—VIII—Vincent ; ' son of Vincent.'

uiséir—XII—*Usshere,* Ussher, Usher ; Nor. ' le Ussher,' i.e., the doorkeeper. This surname is of considerable antiquity in Ireland.

ulf—VIII—*Ulfe, Wulf,* Woulfe, Wolfe ; ' son of Ulf,' or ' Wolf ' (a common personal name among all the Teutonic races). As a surname, it came into Ireland about the time of the Anglo-Norman invasion, and as such is found in the early Dublin rolls ; but it cannot now be distinguished from **oe bulb** (q.v.), which was the form in use in Kildare and Limerick.

ultac—X—Ultagh, (Dunleavy, Dunlevy) ; Ir. ' **ultac**,' i.e., the Ultonian ; a descriptive name given to members of the family of Ó **ouinnfléibe** (q.v.) from their place of origin, and which in some instances supplanted the real surname.

ultacán—X—(Dunleavy, Dunlevy) ; Ir. ' **ultacán**,' a dim. of **ultac** (q.v.), and similarly applied.

unfraio—VIII—Humfrey, Humphrey, Humphries, &c. ; ' son of Hunfrid ' (a Teutonic personal name, in English corruptly Humphrey).

uptún—XI—Upton ; i.e., ' of Upton ' (Ang.-Sax. **uptún**, the upper village or farmstead), a common place-name in England.

APPENDIX

CLAN-NAMES

Besides personal names, our Irish ancestors had from an early period, and even from pre-historic times, a complete system of fixed clan-names by which each family-group and its subdivisions had its own distinct name. These clan-names are of great importance in tracing the early history of families. Though long obsolete as people-names, they still survive in many instances as baronial and parochial designations, in the same way as Norfolk and Suffolk, which were originally people-names—north-folk and south-folk —became the names of two English counties. They were generally formed by prefixing certain words to the genitive case of the names of distinguished ancestors, sometimes gods and goddesses, or by the addition of terminations, and in many respects resemble the family names of a later period. Some, however, and probably the very oldest, appear to be plural names, like the names of the Celtic tribes of Gaul in Caesar's time ; while others are formed by prefixing certain words to place-names.

Of words prefixed to the names of ancestors to form clan-names, we have the following :

Cineal (Cinel, Cenel, angl. Kinel), kindred, race, descendants, as Cineal Eoghain, race of Eoghan, Cineal Conaill, race of Conall ;

Clann, children, race, descendants, as Clann Cholmain, race of Colman ;

Corca, race, progeny, as Corca Bhaiscinn, race of Baiscinn, Corca Dhuibhne, race of Duibhne ;

Dal, tribe, progeny, as Dál gCais, race of Cas, whence "Dalcassian" ;

Muintear, family, people, as Muintear Mhaolmordha, family of Maolmordha, Muintear Mhurchadha, family of Murchadh ;

Siol, seed, progeny, as Síol nAnmchadha, seed of Anmchadh, Síol Muireadhaigh, seed of Muireadhach ;

Sliocht, progeny, as Sliocht Aodha Sláine, progeny of Aodh Sláine ;

Teallach, family, household, as Teallach Dhunchadha, household of Dunchadh ;

Ui, grandsons, descendants, as Uí Breasail, descendants of Breasal, Uí Liatháin, descendants of Liatháin, Uí Néill, descendants of Niall.

Of terminations used to form clan-names, we have the following :

-acht, as in Cianacht, race of Cian, Eoghanacht, race of Eoghan ;
-na, as in Dealbhna, race of Dealbhaoth ;
-ne, as in Conmhaicne, race of Conmhac ;
-raighe, as in Caonraighe, Calraighe, Muscraighe, &c.

Of words prefixed to place-names, we have the following :

Aes, people, as Aes Aisde, Aes Gréine, Aes-trí-máighe ;
Feara, Fir, men, as Feara Luirg, men of Lurg, Fir Teathbha, men of Teffia ;
Pobul, people, as Pobul Uí Chaoimh, O'Keeffe's people, Pobul Uí Cheallacháin, O'Callaghan's people ;
Tuath, people, clan, state, as Tuath Luimnigh, people of Luimneach.

Some, if not all, of these ancient clan-names were capable of being turned into personal surnames by prefixing Moccu, later Mac U, to the genitive case of the eponym. Thus St. Molua, who belonged to Corca Oiche, is in the Annals of Ulster twice called Lugaid Mac U Ochae, that is, Lughaidh, son of the descendants of Ochae (Fochae, the ancestor of the Corca Oiche). Hence probably such modern forms as mac uí caoiṁ, mac uí Ḃrıaın, for persons surnamed O'Keeffe and O'Brien respectively (see page 22).

These ancient clan-names in many instances differ little, if at all, in form from modern family names. Muintear and Clann which occur so frequently in clan-names are also used to form the collective plural of family names, as muınⱦeaⱪ Loınsⱪıs, the O'Lynches, clann ⱦṠíⱦıs, the MacSheehys, or Sheehys. (See p. 25.) Similarly Uí, of frequent occurrence in clan-names, is also the plural of ua of family names. Hence very often the same form, or nearly the same, is a clan-name and a family name, but the meaning in each case is entirely different. muınⱦeaⱪ ⱦⱪeaⱪnáın, for instance, as a family name denotes the O'Heffernans of Owney, but as a clan-name the O'Quins of Thomond. Irish writers have been frequently led into error by this similarity or identity in form of names of widely different meaning.

Only such clan-names as are mentioned in the preceding notes are here explained, and they are taken in their original sense of people-names.

CIANACHT (Keenaght), race of Cian, son of Oilioll Olum, King of Munster in the 3rd century ; the families of Ó Ceaⱪḃaıll, Ó meaⱦáıⱪ and Ó Ríoⱬḃaⱪⱦáın of Eile, Ó Caⱦaⱪaıⱬ of Breagh, Ó Concoḃaıⱪ of Glen Geimhin, and Ó heaⱬⱪa and Ó Ⱬaḃⱪa of Luighne in Connacht.

CINEAL AODHA (Kinelea), (1) race of Aodh, the sixth in descent from Dahy, King of Ireland ; the name of a branch of Ui Fiachrach Aidhne (q.v.), seated in the barony of Kiltartan, Co. Galway, of which Ó Caⱦaıl and Ó Seaⱦnaⱪaıⱬ were

chiefs ; and (2) race of Aodh Dubh, father of Failbhe Flann,
King of Munster in the 7th century ; clan-name of the
O'Callaghans whose ancient territory is now represented
by the barony of Kinelea, Co. Cork.

CINEAL AONGHUSA, (1) race of Aonghus, son of Eoghan, son of
Niall of the Nine Hostages ; a branch of Cineal Eoghain
(q.v.) ; and (2) a branch of Clann Bhreasail (q.v.), in Co.
Armagh, of which the MacCanns were the chief family.

CINEAL BACAID, race of Bacad ; clan-name of the family of Ó
Loingrig of Breifney.

CINEAL mBAOITH, race of Baoth, a branch of the Dal gCais (q.v.)
descended from Aonghus Ceannathrach, son of Cas.

CINEAL mBEICE, race of Beice, grandson of Feidlimidh, King of
Desmond in the 6th century ; the clan-name of the
O'Mahonys, whose territory lay around the town of Bandon.

CINEAL mBINNIGH, race of Binneach, son of Eoghan, son of
Niall of the Nine Hostages ; a branch of Cineal Eoghain, q.v.

CINEAL CAIRBRE, race of Cairbre, son of Niall of the Nine
Hostages, who were seated in the barony of Carbury, in the
north of Co. Sligo.

CINEAL CINNGAMHNA, race of Seachnasach, surnamed Ceann-
gamhna, son of Eoghan Aidhne, who was grandson of the
celebrated King Dahy ; the name of a branch of Ui Fiachrach
Aidhne, q.v.

CINEAL CONAILL race of Conall Gulban, son of Niall of the Nine
Hostages, who were seated in Tirconaill and included the
families of Ó Canannáin, Ó Maoldoraid, Ó Domnaill, Ó
Dochartaig, Ó Baoigill, Ó Gallcóbair, &c.

CINEAL CRIOMHTHAINN, race of Criomhthann ; the clan-
name of the O'Duffs of Leix.

CINEAL CUALLACHTA, race of Cuallachta (or Collachtach) ; a
branch of the Dal gCais (q.v.) descended from Aonghus
Ceannathrach, son of Cas, and seated in the barony of
Inchiquin, Co. Clare. Ó Gríobta was the chief family.

CINEAL EACHACH, race of Eochaidh, son of Eoghan, son of
Niall of the Nine Hostages ; a branch of Cineal Eoghain
(q.v.), seated in the present barony of Loughinsolin, Co.
Derry, of which the O'Kellys were chiefs.

CINEAL ENDA, (1) race of Enda, son of Niall of the Nine Hostages,
a branch of the southern Ui Neill (q.v.), seated near the Hill
of Uisneach, in Westmeath ; and (2) race of Enda, son of
Conall Gulban ; a branch of Cineal Conaill (q.v.) seated in
the present barony of Raphoe.

CINEAL EOGHAIN, race of Eoghan, son of Niall of the Nine
Hostages, whose territory originally comprised the present
counties of Tyrone and Derry and the baronies of Raphoe
and Inishowen in Donegal. The O'Neills were for many
centuries the chief family.

CINEAL FAGHARTAIGH, race of Faghartach, the clan-name of the MacArtans, or MacCartans, and their correlatives in the present barony of Kinelarty, Co. Down.

CINEAL FEARADHAIGH, race of Fearadhach, son of Muireadhach, son of Eoghan, son of Niall of the Nine Hostages ; a branch of Cineal Eoghain (q.v.) whose territory embraced the barony of Clogher and other portions of Co. Tyrone.

CINEAL FIACHACH, race of Fiacha, son of Niall of the Nine Hostages, a branch of the southern Ui Neill (q.v.) whose territory extended from Birr to the Hill of Uisneach in Westmeath, and of which the chief families were the Mageoghegans and O'Molloys.

CINEAL GUAIRE, race of Guaire Aidhne, the celebrated King of Connacht in the 7th century ; the name of a branch of Ui Fiachrach Aidhne, q.v.

CINEAL IANNA, race of Ianna, a branch of Cineal Guaire, q.v.

CINEAL LAOGHAIRE, (1) race of Laoghaire, son of Niall of the Nine Hostages, seated in the baronies of Upper and Lower Navan, Co. Meath ; and (2) race of Laoghaire, the fourth in descent from Corc, king of Munster, the clan-name of the O'Donoghues of Desmond and their correlatives.

CINEAL LUACHAIN, race of Luachan, son of Onchu ; a branch of the Conmaicne Rein (q.v.) in the present Co. Leitrim, of which ᵹ Ɔoᵽ́ϲᴀɩᴃᴇ was chief.

CINEAL LUIGHDHEACH, race of Lughaidh, son of Seadna, who was grandson of Conall Gulban ; a branch of Cineal Conaill (q.v.) of which the O'Donnells were the chief family.

CINEAL MOAIN, race of Moan (or Moen), son of Muireadhach, son of Eoghan, son of Niall of the Nine Hostages ; a branch of Cineal Eoghain (q.v.), originally seated in the barony of Raphoe, but afterwards in the barony of Strabane.

CINEAL TIGHEARNAIGH, race of Tighearnach, son of Muireadhach, son of Eoghan, son of Niall of the Nine Hostages ; a branch of Cineal Eoghain, q.v.

CLANN AODHA, race of Aodh, clan-name of the Maguinnesses of Co. Down.

CLANN AODHA BHUIDHE, race of yellow Aodh, clan-name of a branch of the O'Neills in Antrim and Down.

CLANN BHREASAIL, (1) race of Breasal ; also Ui Breasail, q.v.; the clan-name of the MacCanns and their correlatives in Co. Armagh ; and (2) race of Breasal, the clan-name of a branch of the Ui Maine (q.v.) seated between Loughrea and Ballinasloe, of which O'Donnellan was chief.

CLANN CHAIRBRE, v. Cineal Cairbre.

CLANN CHATHAIL, race of Cathal, son of Muireadhach Muilleathan, King of Connacht ; a branch of Siol Muireadhaigh, q.v.

CLANN CHEALLAIGH, race of Ceallach, a branch of the

Oirghialla (q.v.) in the south-east of Fermanagh, of which MacDonnell was chief.

CLANN CHEARNAIGH, race of Cearnach, (1) a branch of Maine, q.v. ; and (2) a branch of the Oirghialla (q.v.) of which Ó heiʒniʒ was chief.

CLANN CHOINLEAGAIN, race of Coinleagan ; clan-name of the family of mac ʒiolla póil.

CLANN CHOLGAN, race of Colga, son of Maolduin, of the line of Rossa Failgheach, son of Cathaoir Mor ; an Offaly clan (v. Ui Failghe) of which the chief families were those of Ó hAonʒuſa and Ó huallacáin.

CLANN CHOLMAIN, race of Colman Mor, son of Diarmaid, son of Fearghus Cirrbel, son of Conall Cremhthainne, son of Niall of the Nine Hostages ; the chief clan of the southern Ui Neill (q.v.) ; the clan-name of the O'Melaghlens and their correlatives in Meath.

CLANN CHONCHOBHAIR, race of Conchobhar ; a branch of Siol Muireadhaigh (q.v.) ; the clan-name of the O'Mulrennans and their correlatives in Co. Roscommon.

CLANN CHONGHAILE, race of Conghal, a branch of the Oirghialla (q.v.), in Co. Fermanagh, of which mac ʒiolla míɕil was chief.

CLANN CHONNMHAIGH, son of Connmhach, son of Muireadhach Muilleathan, King of Connacht ; a branch of Siol Muireadhaigh (q.v.), of which the O'Finnaghtys were the chief family.

CLANN CHUAIN, race of Cuan, a branch of the Ui Fiachrach (q.v.) who were seated in the neighbourhood of Castlebar.

CLANN CHUILEAIN, race of Cuilean, a branch of the Dal gCais (q.v.) ; one of the clan-names of the MacNamaras and their correlatives in Thomond.

CLANN DALAIGH, race of Dalach, the eighth in descent from Conall Gulban ; a branch of Cineal Conaill (q.v.) ; the clan-name of the O'Donnells of Tirconnell.

CLANN DOMHNAILL, race of Domhnall, the clan-name of the O'Lavertys.

CLANN DUIBHSHIONNAIGH, race of Dubhsionnach, a branch of the Oirghialla, q.v.

CLANN FEARGHAILE, race of Fearghal ; the clan-name (1) of the O'Hallorans of Galway, and (2) of the MacKiernans of Fermanagh.

CLANN LAOGHAIRE, race of Laoghaire, son of Eochaidh Breac, son of Dahy, King of Ireland ; a branch of the Ui Fiachrach, q.v.

CLANN MHAOLRUANAIDH, race of Maolruanaidh (O'Connor), son of Tadhg an eich ghil, King of Connacht, A.D. 1014-1036 ; a branch of Siol Muireadhaigh (q.v.), of which the MacDermotts of Moylurg and the MacDonaghs of Tirerrill were the chief families.

CLANN MHAOLUGHRA, race of Maolughra, a branch of the Ui
Failghe (q.v.) ; the clan-name of the O'Dempseys and their
correlatives in Offaly.

CLANN MHAONAIGH, race of Maonach, the clan-name of the
O'Dooleys of Ely O'Carroll.

CLANN MHURCHADHA, race of Murchadh, the clan-name of a
branch of the O'Finnaghtys who were seated on the east
side of the Suck, in Co. Roscommon.

CLANN NEILL, race of Niall of the Nine Hostages ; v. Ui Neill.

CLANN tSEALBHAIGH, race of Sealbhach, one of the clan-
names of the O'Donoghues of Desmond and their correlatives.

CLANN TOMALTAIGH, race of Tomaltach, clan-name of the
MacMurroughs of the Magh Aoi, in Co. Roscommon.

CONMHAICNE, race of Conmhac, son of Fergus MacRoigh ; alias
Conmhaicne Rein ; the clan-name of the O'Farrells, Magran-
nals, and their correlatives, whose territory was co-extensive
with the Diocese of Ardagh.

CONMHAICNE CUILE, race of Conmhac, son of Ferghus Mac-
Roigh, seated in the barony of Kilmaine, Co. Mayo.

CORCA ACHLANN, alias Corca Seachlann, race of Seachlann, the
clan-name of the MacBrannains and their correlatives in the
east of Co. Roscommon.

CORCA ADHAIMH, alias Corca Adain, race of Adam, a branch
of the southern Ui Neill (q.v.) who were seated in the present
barony of Magheradernon, Co. Westmeath ; clan-name of
the O'Dalys.

CORCA BHAISCINN, race of Cairbre Baschaoin, seated in the
south-west of Co. Clare.

CORCA DHUIBNE, race of Duibhne, the name of a great clan in
West Kerry, whose territory is now represented by Corcaguiny, Iveragh and Magunihy, and of which the chief
families were O'Falvey, O'Shea and O'Connell.

CORCA LAOIGHDHE, race of Lughaidh Laidhe, grandfather of
Lughaidh MacCon, monarch of Ireland in the 3rd century ;
the name of a great clan in the south-west of Co. Cork,
whose territory was co-extensive with the Diocese of Ross,
and of which the O'Driscolls and O'Learys were the chief
families.

CORCA MODHRUADH, race of Modruadh, son of Fergus Mac-
Roigh ; the name of a great clan in the north-west of Co.
Clare, whose territory was co-extensive with the Diocese of
Kilfenora, and of which the chief families were the O'Connors
and O'Loghlens.

CORCA MUICHET, race of Muichet, said to have been son of
Brian, son of Eochaidh Muighmheadhoin, King of Ireland,
who possessed an extensive district in the south of Co.
Limerick, of which in later times MacEniry was chief.

CORCA OICHE, race of Ochae (or Fochae) Beg ; a celebrated Munster clan, whose territory comprised a great portion of the south-west of Co. Limerick, and of which Ó mᴀcᴀᴘᴀ was chief.

CORCA RAOIDHE, race of Fiacha Raoidhe, son of Feidlimidh Reachtmhar, seated in the barony of Corcaree, Co. Westmeath.

DLAL ARAIDHE, race of Fiacha Araidhe, a great Ulster clan whose territory stretched from Newry to Slemmish, and of which the O'Lynches and O'Lawlors were the chief families.

DAL mBUINNE, race of Buinne, alias Muinntear Bhranain, an Antrim clan whose territory was co-extensive with the parish of Kiltulagh, and of which Ó Seᴀᴘᴘᴀɪ̇ʒ was chief.

DAL gCAIS, race of Cas, the sixth in descent from Cormac Cas, son of Oilioll Olum, King of Munster in the 3rd century ; the name of the great clan of Thomond, or North Munster, which embraced several distinguished families and of which the O'Briens were the chiefs.

DAL bhFIATACH, race of Fiatach Fionn, king of Ulidia, a warlike clan seated in the present Co. Down, of which, in the 12th century, MacDunlevy was chief.

DEALBHNA, race of Lughaidh Dealbhaodh, said to have been son of Cas, the ancestor of the Dal gCais, q.v. ; divided into several branches seated in Meath and Connacht, as D. Mhor, now represented by the barony of Delvin, in Westmeath ; D. Bheag, now the barony ot Demifore, in Co. Meath ; D. Eathra, or MacCoghlan's country, in the barony of Garrycastle ; D. Cuile Fabhair and D. Tire-da-Locha, in Connacht.

EOGHANACHT, race of Eoghan Mor, son of Oilioll Olum, King of Munster in the 3rd century, which was sub-divided into E. Chaisil, E. Locha Lein, E. Aine, &c., and to which belonged the chief families of South Munster.

EOGHANACHT CHAISIL, a branch of the Eoghanacht, (q.v.) seated in the barony of Middlethird, Co. Tipperary.

EOGHANACHT AINE, a branch of the Eoghanacht (q.v.), seated at Knockany, in Co. Limerick, of which Ó Cɪᴀᴘᴍᴀɪc was chief.

FEARA BILE, men of Bile, in Westmeath, the clan-name of the O'Hanveys.

FEARA CEALL, men of churches, one of the clan-names of the O'Molloys, in the present Offaly.

FEARA CUALANN, men of Cuala, a clan whose territory included a great portion of the present counties of Dublin and Wicklow.

FEARA LUIRG, men of Lurg, the clan-name of the O'Muldoons and their correlatives who were seated in the barony of Lurg, in Co. Monaghan.

FEARA MAIGHE, men of the plain, the clan-name of the

O'Dugans whose territory is represented by the present barony of Fermoy.

FEARA ROIS, men of Ros, whose territory lay in the neighbourhood of the present Carrickmacross.

FEARA TULACH, men of the hills, the clan-name of the O'Dooleys, whose territory is now represented by the barony of Fertullagh, in Co. Westmeath.

FIR LI, men of Li, a famous Ulster clan descended from Colla Uais, monarch of Ireland in the 4th century, and originally seated on the west side of the Bann, until expelled by Ó Cátáin some time before the Anglo-Norman invasion.

FIR TEATHBHA, men of Teathbha, or Teffia, the clan-name of the descendants of Maine, son of Niall of the Nine Hostages, who were one of the chief clans of the southern Ui Neill, and whose territory embraced a great portion of Westmeath and also the barony of Kilcoursey in the present Offaly.

LUIGHNE, race of Lugh, the clan-name of the O'Haras and O'Garas in Co. Sligo.

MUINTEAR BHIRN, family of Biorn, the clan-name of the MacRorys and their correlatives in the present Co. Tyrone.

MUINTEAR CHEARBHALLAIN, family of Cearbhallan, a branch of Muintear Eoluis (q.v.) of which O'Mulvey was chief.

MUINTEAR CHIONAOITH, family of Cionaoth, the clan-name of the MacAnavas and their correlatives in the barony of Dromahare, Co. Leitrim.

MUINTEAR EOLUIS, family of Eolus, a branch of Conmhaicne Rein in Co. Leitrim ; the clan-name of the MacRannals and their correlatives.

MUINTEAR GHEARADHAIN, family of Gearadhan, the clan-name of the Gaynors in the north of Co. Longford.

MUINTEAR GHIOLLAGAIN, family of Giollagan, the clan-name of the O'Quinns in Co. Longford.

MUINTEAR IFEARNAIN, family of Ifearnan, a branch of the Dal gCais (q.v.), the clan-name of the O'Quins of Thomond who derive their descent from Ifearnan, son of Corc, the 15th in descent from Cormac Cas, the ancestor of the Dal gCais.

MUINTEAR LAOGHACHAIN, family of Laoghachan, the 13th in descent from Maine, son of Niall of the Nine Hostages, a branch of Fir Teathbha q.v.

MUINTEAR MHAOILSIONNA, family of Maolsionna, the 13th in descent from Maine, son of Niall of the Nine Hostages, a branch of Fir Teathbha of which mac Cappsamna was chief.

MUINTEAR MHAOLMORDHA, family of Maolmordha, the 14th in descent from Duach Galach, son of Brion, son of Eochaidh Muighmheadhoin, King of Ireland ; a branch of the Ui Briuin, q.v. ; the clan-name of the O'Reillys in Co. Cavan.

MUINTEAR MHURCHADHA, family of Murchadh, the 10th in descent from Duach Teangumha and 14th from Duach

Galach, son of Brion, son of Eochaidh Muighmheadhoin, King of Ireland ; the clan-name of the O'Flahertys in Connacht.

MUINTEAR RODHUIBH, family of Rodhubh, the clan-name of the Mageraghtys in Co. Roscommon.

MUINTEAR tSLAMAIN, family of Slaman, a branch of Fir Teathbha, q.v.

MUINTEAR TADHGAIN, family of Tadhgan, the eighth in descent from Brian, son of Maine, son of Niall of the Nine Hostages ; a branch of Fir Teathbha, q.v. ; the clan-name of the Foxes of Kilcoursey.

OIRGHIALLA (whence Oriel), the name of a great Ulster clan descended from the three Collas, who conquered the ancient Ultonians and wrested from them the greater part of Ulster ; but in later times their territory was confined to Louth, Armagh, Monaghan and Fermanagh.

SIOL ANMCHADHA, seed of Anmchadh, a branch of the Ui Maine (q.v.), descended from Anmchadh, the eighth in descent from Maine Mor, ancestor of the Ui Maine.

SIOL MAOLRUAIN, seed of Maolruanaidh, the seventh in descent from Duach Galach, son of Brion, son of Eochoidh Muighmheadhoin, King of Ireland ; a branch of the Ui Briuin, in Co. Roscommon, of which the O'Flynns were the chief family.

SIOL MUIREADHAIGH (Silmurray), seed of Muireadhach Muilleathan, King of Connacht, who died in the year 701 ; the clan-name of the O'Connors and their correlatives in Connacht, including the MacDermotts, MacDonoughs, O'Beirnes, O'Flanagans, Mageraghtys and O'Finnaghtys.

TEALLACH DHUNCHADHA, household of Dunchadh, son of Maonach, the eighth in descent from Duach Galach, son of Brion, son of Eochaidh Muighmheadhoin, King of Ireland ; a branch of the Ui Briuin, q.v. ; the clan-name of the MacKernans ; now represented by the barony of Tullyhunco, in the west of Co. Cavan.

TEALLACH EACHACH, household of Eochaidh, son of Maonach (v. Teallach Dhunchadha) ; a branch of the Ui Briuin, q.v. ; the clan-name of the Magurans ; now represented by the barony of Tullyhaw, in the north-west of Co. Cavan.

UI BAIRRCHE, dess. of Daire Barrach, son of Cathaoir Mor, King of Ireland in the 2nd century ; the clan-name of the O'Tracys and MacGormans in the barony of Slievemargy in Leix.

UI BLOID, dess. of Blod, son of Cas, a branch of the Dal gCais (q.v.), including the families of O'Kennedy, O'Shanahan, O'Durack and O'Ahern, whose territory lay in the east of Co. Clare, where the name is still preserved in the deanery of Omulled.

UI BREASAIL(MACHA), alias Clann Bhreasail (q.v.), dess. of Breasal, son of Eochaidh, son of Feidlimidh, son of Fiachra Casan, son of Colla-da-chrioch; a branch of the Oirghialla(q.v.) who were seated in the barony of Oneilland East, Co. Armagh.

UI BRIUIN, dess. of Brion, King of Connacht, son of Eochaidh Muighmheadhoin, King of Ireland, of whom there were different branches in Connacht and Breifney, as :

UI BRIUIN BREIFNE, a branch of the Ui Briuin seated in Breifney, of which the O'Rourkes and O'Reillys were the chief families.

UI BRIUIN EOLA, a branch of the Ui Briuin seated in West Connacht, of which the O'Lees were chiefs.

UI BRIUIN NA SIONNA, a branch of the Ui Briuin seated in Co. Roscommon, of which Ó manaċáın was chief.

UI BRIUIN RATHA, a branch of the Ui Briuin in West Connacht, of which Ó ᴅaċlaoiċ was chief.

UI CAIRBRE AEDHBHA, dess. of Cairbre Aedhbha, grandson of Fiacha Fidhgheinte, a branch of the Ui Fidhgheinte (q.v.), seated along the Maigue in Co. Limerick, of which Ó ᴅoꞃnaᴠáın was chief.

UI CAISIN, dess. of Caisin, son of Cas, the name of a branch of the Dal gCais of which mac Conmaꞃa was chief.

UI CEARNAIGH, dess. of Cearnach, a branch of the Dal gCais of which the Ahernes were chiefs.

UI CEINNSEALAIGH, dess. of Eanna Ceinnsealach, son of Cathaoir Mor, King of Ireland, whose territory was co-extensive with the Diocese of Ferns.

UI CONAILL GABHRA, dess. of Conall, the fourth in descent from Fiacha Fidhgheinte, a branch of the Ui Fidhgheinte (q.v.), of which the chief families were the O'Collins and O'Kinnealys, and whose territory comprised the baronies of Upper and Lower Connello, Shanid and Glenquin, in Co. Limerick.

UI CORMAIC, dess. of Cormac, the clan-name of the O'Hehirs in Thomond.

UI DRONA, dess. of Drona, the fourth in descent from Cathaoir Mor, King of Leinster and monarch of Ireland in the 2nd century ; the clan-name of the O'Ryans in the barony of Idrone, Co. Carlow.

UI DUACH, dess. of Dui, the clan-name of the O'Brennans of Ossory.

UI EACHACH, dess. of Eochaidh, grandson of Fiacha Casan, son of Colla-da-chrioch, a branch of the Oirghialla (q.v.) who were seated in the present barony of Armagh and of which Ó ᴅoṁnaıll and Ó Ꞃuaᴠaᵹáın were chiefs.

UI EACHACH, alias UI EACHACH COBHA, alias UI EACHACH ULADH, dess. of Eochaidh, the name of a branch of Clann Rudhraighe who were seated in, and gave its name to, the barony of Iveagh, in Co. Down.

UI EACHACH MUAIDHE, i.e., Ui Eachach of the Moy, a branch of the Ui Fiachrach (q.v.), descended from Eochaidh Breac, son of Dahy, King of Ireland.

UI EACHACH MUMHAN, i.e., Ui Eachach of Munster, dess. of Eochaidh, son of Cas, son of Corc, King of Munster, the clanname of the O'Mahonys and O'Donoghues of Desmond.

UI FAILGHE, dess. of Rossa Failgheach, eldest son of Cathoir Mor King of Ireland in the 2nd century, of whom the chief families were the O'Connors, O'Dempseys and O'Dunnes.

UI FAOLAIN, dess. of Faolan of the race of Cathaoir Mor, King of Ireland; the clan-name of the O'Byrnes and MacKeoghs who, prior to the Anglo-Norman invasion, were seated in the north of the present Co. Kildare.

UI FEARMAIC, dess. of Fearmac, of the race of Aonghus Ceannathrach, son of Cas ; a branch of the Dal gCais (q.v.), of which the O'Deas were the chief family.

UI FEILMEADHA, dess. of Feidlimidh, son of Eanna Ceinnsealach, King of Leinster in the 4th century, of whom there were two clans in Leinster, viz : Ui F. Teas and Ui F. Tuaidh, q.v.

UI FEILMEADHA TEAS, i.e., the southern Ui Feilmeadha (q.v.), seated in the present barony of Ballaghkeen, in the east of Co. Wexford, of whom Ó mu̇ṗċaḋa was chief.

UI FEILMEADHA TUAIDH, i.e., the northern Ui Feilmeadha (q.v.), who were seated in the present barony of Rathvilly Co. Carlow.

UI FIACHRACH, dess. of Fiachra, son of Eochaidh Muighmheadhoin, King of Ireland in the 4th century. Fiachra was a brother of Niall of the Nine Hostages and father of the celebrated King Dahy, the last pagan monarch of Ireland. The Ui Fiachrach were divided into two great branches, viz : Ui Fiachrach Muaidhe and Ui Fiachrach Aidhne, q.v.

UI FIACHRACH AIDHNE, or southern Ui Fiachrach, a branch of the Ui Fiachrach (q.v.), seated in the district of Aidhne, in the south of the present Co. Galway, co-extensive with the Diocese of Kilmacduagh. The Ui Fiachrach Aidhne derived their descent from Eoghan Aidhne, grandson of the celebrated King Dahy.

UI FIACHRACH ARDA SRATHA, i.e., Ui F. of Ardstraw, also called Ui F. Finn, dess. of Fiachra, son of Erc, son of Colla Uais ; a branch of the Oirghialla, q.v.

UI FIACHRACH FINN, dess. of Fiachra Fionn, son of Breasal, son of Maine Mor, a branch of the Ui Maine (q.v.) ; the clanname of the O'Naughtons and O'Mullalys of Connacht.

UI FIACHRACH MUAIDHE, i.e., Ui F. of the Moy, also called the northern Ui Fiachrach, a branch of the Ui Fiachrach (q.v.), descended from Fiachra, son of King Dahy, and seated in the present counties of Mayo and Sligo.

UI FIDHGHEINTE, dess. of Fiacha Fidhgheinte who was grandson of Oilioll Flanbeg, King of Munster, and flourished in the
4th century ; the name of a great clan whose territory was
co-extensive with the Diocese of Limerick and of which
Ó Ʋonnaɓáın was chief.

UI LIATHAIN, dess. of Eochaidh Liathanach, son of Oilioll Flanbeg,
King of Munster, whose territory was co-extensive with the
present barony of Barrymore, Co. Cork.

UI MAINE, dess. of Maine Mor, the fourth in descent from Colla-
da-chrioch, one of the ancestors of the Oirghialla (q.v.) ;
the name of a great Connacht clan, whose territory comprised part of the present counties of Galway, Roscommon,
Clare and Offaly, and of which O'Kelly was chief.

UI MEITH(MACHA), alias Ui Meith Tire, dess. of Muireadhach
Meith, son of Imchadh, son of Colla-da-chrioch ; a branch
of the Oirghialla (q.v.), seated in the barony and county of
Monaghan.

UI MUIREADHAIGH, dess. of Muireadhach, of the line of Cathaoir
Mor, monarch of Ireland ; clan-name of the O'Tooles, whose
territory, prior to the Anglo-Norman invasion, comprised
the southern half of the present Co. Kildare.

UI NEILL, dess. of Niall of the Nine Hostages, King of Ireland,
A.D. 379-406. They were divided into two great branches
called the northern and southern Ui Neill. The chief clans
of the northern Ui Neill, whose territory lay in the present
counties of Tyrone, Derry, Donegal and the north of Co.
Sligo, were Cineal Eoghain, Cineal Conaill and Cineal Cairbre ;
while those of the southern Ui Neill, whose territory was co-
extensive with the Diocese of Meath, were Clann Cholmain,
Cineal Fiachach and Fir Teathbha.

UI NIALLAIN, dess. of Niallan, son of Fiacha, son of Feidlimidh,
son of Fiachra Casan, son of Colla-da-chrioch ; a branch of
the Oirghialla (q.v.), whose territory is now represented by
the baronies of Oneilland in Co. Armagh.

UI RIAGAIN, dess. of Riagan, the tenth in descent from Rossa
Failgheach, son of Cathaoir Mor, King of Ireland ; a branch
of the Ui Failghe of which the O'Dunnes were the chief
family.

UI RONGHAILE, dess. of Ronghal, a branch of the Dal gCais
(q.v.) of which the O'Shanahans were the chief family.

UI TOIRDEALBHAIGH, dess. of Toirdealbhach (father of St.
Flannan), king of Thomond ; the clan-name of the O'Briens
and their correlatives in the east of Co. Clare.

UI TUIRTRE, dess. of Fiacha Tort, grandson of Colla Uais, a branch
of the Oirghialla (q.v.) seated to the east of the Bann and
Lough Neagh, in Co. Antrim.